BREWER'S DICTIONARY OF

IRISH PHRASE & FABLE

BREWER'S DICTIONARY OF

IRISH PHRASE
& FABLE

Sean McMahon and Jo O'Donoghue

Foreword by Maeve Binchy

WEIDENFELD & NICOLSON

Weidenfeld & Nicolson
Wellington House
125 Strand
London
WC2R 0BB

First published 2004

British Library Cataloguing-in-Publication Data
A catalogue entry for this book is available from the British Library

ISBN 0 304 36334 0

Typeset in Sabon by
Gem Graphics, Trenance, Cornwall
Printed in Finland by WS Bookwell

CONTENTS

FOREWORD

This book is going to be another Wonderful Distraction on the shelf beside my desk. Naturally I will call it a serious work of reference, something I will badly need when checking a fact or finding the origin of something. But in truth of course I will use it as a great escape, a series of magic doors opening up to more unexpected information, to thousands of fabulous facts that I don't really NEED to know but feel a much, much better person for having discovered.

There are sheer gold nuggets of information in this collection, most of them you will discover by accident when you are looking for something else. As when I looked up Colles' Fracture because that was what my poor broken arm was called. I knew Colles was an Irish surgeon but I didn't know he was called Abraham and was born in 1773 and I certainly didn't know, until I moved along the same page, all about *The Collegians* which was a novel about a murder in 1819, which later became a play, *The Colleen Bawn*, and later still the opera *The Lily of Killarney*; nor that the place Michael Collins was born was called Sam's Cross. This is what happens when you take up a book like this, your eye strays and the time passes and you become ludicrously well informed.

The *Brewer's* tradition has been an honourable one over the years and I am so proud to see a whole volume dedicated entirely to the Irish and the way we have adapted what has been called from time to time the Hated Tongue of the Oppressor entirely to our own taste. Irish people LOVE words and phrases and where they came from and what they mean and what they might have meant once. No amount of exposure to international television can empty the Irish vocabulary of its rich descriptive phrases, its inventive way of putting things or its convoluted way of saying something so that it will not offend even though it might not make anything clear. In Ireland we have many, many faults but we love the sound and feel of words, and regard a story full of interesting facts and well-turned phrases a story worth hearing. And for all that we think ourselves as completely in control of the language, we love a new word. I had never heard the word *Billyboshpeen* before. It apparently means a pounding in the head, a headache. Since I read it I have used no other word to describe this kind of ailment. And of course I now also know when Bono was born, and Terry Wogan.

I wish this lovely treasury of words, history, myth and culture great, great success. You may not hear from me again for some while, because I'll be too busy reading it.

Maeve Binchy
JULY 2004

INTRODUCTION

Brewer's Dictionary of Phrase and Fable has been in existence since 1870, ever since Ebenezer Cobham Brewer (1810–97), of sainted memory, devised and compiled that Aladdin's cave of treasures. Ever since then it has settled arguments, proved essential to compilers of quizzes and crosswords, sent browsers happily to sleep, saved the sanity of distracted parents beset by inquisitorial children and been the pursuit of the trivial. Its 1300 odd (at times extremely odd) pages have been compendious and comprehensive, its field the rich store of literature, myth, history, geography and romance, and its entries succinct and irresistibly cross-referenced. It has served as the essential desk reference book of gentle person and scholar (terms happily not mutually exclusive) and contributed, as Dr Johnson said of his friend and former pupil, David Garrick, to the gaiety of nations.

Among these nations is Ireland, and Brewer and his worthy successors have been generous in their inclusion of things green. One may find in its pages Cúchulainn, the legendary 'Hound of Ulster', St Patrick with his Trinitarian shamrock and his contribution to the union flag, the Molly Maguires (but not Molly Malone who drove her wheelbarrow through streets broad and narrow), the IRA, the IRB, Irish stew and rather a lot about the potato. Yet it seemed to some not necessarily chauvinist denizens of the Emerald Isle (see p. 390 of the 16th Edition) that an *Irish Brewer* (no not *that* one!) might honourably stake a claim to existence. It was the desire to provide a fuller account of Ireland that encouraged us, the compilers, to undertake *Brewer's Dictionary of Irish Phrase and Fable*. The result you hold in your hands. The close on 900 pages cover as many as possible of the printable aspects of Ireland and Irish life from the time of the island's earliest inhabitants to its relatively peaceful and prosperous condition in these early years of the 21st century.

The first Irish hunter-gatherers have been traced to Mount Sandel, near Coleraine in Co. Derry, and are thought to have built their circular dwellings around 7000 BC. In the intervening years, heading now for ten millennia, the languages of Ireland have been, naturally, Irish in its Old, Middle and Modern forms; Latin, the international language of scholars and churchmen, enabling us to read what was written 2000 years ago throughout western Europe; and English, now the vernacular of most of the country, brought, let us say, by the not always welcome strangers, the *Gaill*, as the natives called them. All these means of communication are part of the complicated tapestry of Irish history and as such are a necessary part of the *Irish Brewer*. The latter contains therefore many examples of (usually modern) Irish, lots of Latin, some standard English and a fair sampling of two associated sub-linguistic forms – Hiberno-English and Ulster-Scots. As delvers into the book will learn, such terms as 'asthore', 'mavourneen', 'macushla' come straight from the Irish, hiding in a kind of lexical halfway-house. When an Irish tenor sings of Kathleen Mavourneen or hears the voice of Macushla calling him, he is consciously or unconsciously rehearsing the terms of endearment from the older language. The *Irish Brewer* gives a full account of these and other not-so-endearing terms – *dulamú, lúdramán, táthaire, óinseach*, to mention but a few – in their Hiberno-English or original Irish language forms and with their literal meanings.

With the Irish language and a predominantly oral culture survived the belief of Irish people in the older myths. Cúchulainn and his battle at the Ford, Deirdre and the sons of Usna, Fionnuala and the other Children of Lir, the Red Branch Knights, the Fianna band of warriors (led by the paladin Fionn Mac Cumhail, his gifted son Oisin and his warrior son Oscar) were part of the oral culture of the country. Folk memory had established a series of invasions so they had to be incorporated into the history. Mythology provided an explanation for the mysteries of life as experienced by a literally unlettered but far from primitive people. Meteorology, topography, the changing seasons, darkness and light, crop growth and failure, reproduction in humans and animals all needed to be accounted for. Immortal longings, wish-fulfilment, courage, magnanimity and a sense of greater predecessors demanded some kind of objective correlative. And mythology supplied it. It is appropriate, then, that the *Irish Brewer* give a detailed coverage of the deep imagination of the Irish people.

As for the Latin, it was for many centuries an instinctive second language, a *lingua franca* that united Europe in its darkest age, made rather less gloomy by this persistence of a record of civilization. So if you wish to understand what exactly '*peregrinatio pro Christo*' means and what its relevance to the history of Europe is precisely, the truth can be found under the letter 'p'. '*Tabula tantum*' the witty response by the Irish scholar John Scottus Eriugena to the gibes of Charles the Bald is not only explained but set in context. The possible location of the last resting-place of the three Great Saints of Ireland is glossed under *In burgo Duno tumulo* (and free of extra charge a freer translation is pro-vided). The Irish took their saints very seriously, although only three, Malachy, Laurence O'Toole and Oliver Plunkett were papally canon-ized, and at times such giant figures as the three buried in Downpatrick were endowed in the people's imaginations with powers more appropriate to demi-gods.

There were also the twelve apostles of Ireland, including Brendan the Navigator, Ronan who drove poor Sweeney mad, Aidan of Lindisfarne, Adamnán of Iona, Columban and Gall of Switzerland and Italy, Fursa whose visions of Hell frightened even Dante, Fiachra who eventually gave his name to French taxi-cabs and may have had a cure for syphilis. The Irish understood that their monasteries had preserved the ancient classics of antiquity from destruction at the hands of the Asiatic hordes who all but smothered the flame of Western civilization. The European connections of the *peregrini* who founded these monasteries are fully listed, these men whose work and personalities led to their native place being called the 'Island of Saints and Scholars', as well as accounts of the Venerable Bede of Durham, Cathal of Taranto, Colmán of Lindisfarne, Donatus of Fiesole, Kilian of Würzburg and Virgil of Salzburg.

On we go through history with accounts of the Culdees, the stern reformers of Irish monasteries, the Anglo-Normans who stayed to become Old English behind the safety of the Pale, the Tudor conquest and the bleak 17th century that saw the Ulster plantation, Cromwell, Séamas an Chaca and King Billy, and the Popery Laws. The rich mix of the past continues: Dean Swift, the Volunteers, Grattan of the Parliament, the Rising of 1798, the Act of Union, the Liberator, Young Ireland, the Great Famine, the Uncrowned King, and, entering the last century, Pearse, Carson, the Easter Rising, the Long Hoor, his adversary the Big Fellow, Partition, the IRA and the Armed Struggle, two Bloody Sundays, the Loyalist Red Hand Commandos, the Armalite and the Ballot Box, the Jellybabies, the Peace Process – these latter part of the catalogue of misery that was the recent Northern Ireland Troubles.

History can be a nightmare but life goes on. Ireland's writers: Goldsmith, Sheridan, Mangan, Lady Gregory, John Synge, James Joyce, O'Casey and her Nobel laureates Yeats, Shaw, Beckett and Heaney, are as significant a part of the tapestry as her bombers and gunmen. So too are her entertainers, singers like Josef Locke (born Joe McLaughlin) Enya, Dana, Bono, U2, the dancing feet of Michael Flatley, the prodigious sporting talents of Roy Keane and Brian O'Driscoll. These brighter sparks lift the gloom that sometimes threatens to darken forever the green island. The Roman dramatist Terence (c.190–159 BC) once said: '*Humani nil a me alienum puto*' ('I count nothing human foreign to me'). In the same way nothing Irish is alien to this dictionary, good or bad, honourable or shameful. Whether it be the Irish besieged and outnumbered and fighting off the police at the Eureka Stockade in Australia in 1854, supplying America's first cardinal, grubbing a living in the Five Points in Manhattan (a slum that terrified even Charles Dickens), tatie-howking in Scotland or building the Jubilee tube line in London, they are all part of the Irishness of the globe and as such deserve their place. They are included, warts and all. Nor are the messier aspects of contemporary Irish life neglected: the murderers, the clerical scandals, the corrupt politicians, the recent tribunals, the Celtic Tiger which changed a cheerful, if poor people, into something lesser and greater.

The *Irish Brewer* is offered as a record of people, places, events, aspirations. Ireland's comedians, sportsmen, musicians, writers, actors, soldiers, statesmen, have forced their way into the world's eye. One of the best-known Irish phrases is *Céad Míle Fáilte* ('a hundred thousand welcomes'); that is the implicit message of this book. We should like to take this opportunity of thanking Art Byrne, Frank D'Arcy, Richard Doherty, Ken Thatcher, our patient, good-humoured copyeditor Ian Crofton and our publisher Richard Milbank of Weidenfeld & Nicolson, who was the originator of the *Irish Brewer*, a very present help in trouble and himself no mean authority on things Irish.

Guide to the use of the Dictionary

Entries are arranged in strict alphabetical order on a letter-by-letter basis. Thus, for example, **G-men** appears after **Glendalough**, and **Ball of malt** after **Ballocks of Henry the Eighth**.

The dictionary includes numerous examples of Irish usage, in Irish and Hiberno-English as well as in English. Headwords for 'pure' Irish-language words and phrases (such as *Áiféiseach*, *Bailc* and *Balbh*) appear in italic type, even in cases where the Irish word is also used, orthographically unchanged, in Hiberno-English. Hiberno-English words and phrases (such as **Bawn**, **Fooster** and **Pishogues**) that are derived from, but orthographically different from, their Irish-language source words, appear in roman type. Names in Irish that denote familiar Irish organizations or institutions (such as **Áras an Uachtaráin**, **Bord na Móna** and **Dáil**) also appear in roman type.

To help readers find their way around the dictionary, and to draw their attention to articles that are either directly or tangentially related, a large number of cross-references have been included. These are indicated by the use of SMALL CAPITALS.

Abbreviations used in the Dictionary

AD	anno Domini (year of Our Lord)		*fl.*	*floruit* (flourished)
b.	born		i.e.	*id est* (that is)
BC	before Christ		No.	number
c.	circa (about)		Rev.	Reverend
d.	died		Vol.	volume
e.g.	*exempli gratia* (for example)			

THE DICTIONARY

Aachen (French *Aix-la-Chapelle*). A city in North Rhine-Westphalia, Germany, where many of the Holy Roman Emperors were crowned up to the 16th century. As CHARLE-MAGNE's capital in the late 8th and early 9th century it became the centre of the so-called Carolingian Renaissance and a cultural magnet for scholars from all over Europe, including Ireland. The *Gesta Karoli Magni* ('The Deeds of Charles the Great'), by Nokter Babulus, the 9th-century writer known as the Monk of St Gall, describes the arrival in Aachen of Irish scholars offering wisdom: '*Si quis sapientiae cupidus est, veniat ad nos et accipiat eam!*' (Latin, 'If anyone wants wisdom, let him come to us and get it!'). The scholars in question were almost certainly CLEMENT SCOTTUS and DUNGAL. When asked by Charlemagne what fee they would charge for tuition they answered: 'Suitable places, ready students and food and clothing without which our *peregrinationes* ('journeyings') are impossible.'

Aback. An adverb and preposition signifying 'behind', 'to the rear', as in 'The load was a bit heavy aback.' The word was until recently in common use in Ulster.

Abbán. A 5th-century saint, said to be a contemporary of St PATRICK and a nephew of St IBAR. A member of one of the four chief families of Leinster, he founded the monasteries of Killabban in Co. Laois and Moyarney, near New Ross, in Co. Wexford. His feast day is 16 March.

Abbeylara Shooting, the. The fatal shooting, by two members of the Garda Emergency Response Unit (an armed squad of specially trained gardai, *see* GARDA SÍOCHÁNA), of a young man named John Carthy on 20 April 2000. Carthy had emerged from his house in Abbeylara, Co. Longford after a 25-hour siege that followed a domestic dispute. He was armed with a shotgun and refused to put down his weapon, whereupon he was shot four times from behind, the fourth shot piercing his heart. Public concern focused on the conduct of the siege and the fact that Carthy was shot so many times from behind; this concern was not allayed by a subsequent internal Garda inquiry. The Barr Tribunal of investigation into the events at Abbeylara was established in 2002.

Abbey Theatre. A theatre in Dublin established as the home of the Irish National Theatre Society largely through the efforts of W.B. YEATS and Lady GREGORY. It opened on 27 December 1904 with Yeats's *On Baile's Strand* and Lady Gregory's *Spreading the News* in a building in Abbey Street acquired thanks to the generosity of Annie Horniman (*see*

MISS HORNIMAN), a Quaker heiress. It was the main focus of the IRISH LITERARY REVIVAL and its company presented the plays of J.M. SYNGE (notably The PLAYBOY OF THE WESTERN WORLD) and those of Sean O'Casey (including The PLOUGH AND THE STARS). The small government grant begun in 1925 made it the first subsidized theatre in the English-speaking world, and it continues to be regarded as the country's national theatre, maintaining a repertoire of mainly Irish plays, though classical and world theatre are also represented. The original building (see OULD SHABBEY) was destroyed by fire in 1951 and the company used the much larger Queen's Theatre in Pearse Street before returning to the original site with a greatly improved new theatre in 1966. See also SODOM AND BEGORRAH.

Abbotstown Stadium. See BERTIE BOWL.

ABC. The red scorch left on a person's shins when they have sat barelegged too close to the fire. The derivation of the term is uncertain, but may come from the ABC bread company, the image being that of the person's legs being 'toasted' like a slice of bread. The usage dates from the 1920s.

> Maybe, if people saw yourself when yer potterin'
> about the house, it's the ashes bes on yer toes,
> an' the ABC on yer shins with toastin' them in
> the fire.
>
> PEADAR O'DONNELL (1893–1986): Islanders (1927)

Abduction Club. A loose association of young Anglo-Irish bloods in existence towards the end of the 18th century. The members of the club found it financially advantageous betimes to circumvent the tedious formalities of courtship and betrothal by direct action. They bound themselves by oath to assist one another in the carrying off of likely prospects, as Justice John Edward Walsh (1816–69) put it in his book Ireland Sixty Years Ago (1847):

> They had emissaries and confederates in every
> house, who communicated informations of
> particulars – the extent of the girl's fortune, the
> state and circumstances of the family, with details

of their domestic arrangements and movements. When a girl was thus pointed out, the members drew lots, but more generally tossed for her, and immediate measures were taken to secure her for the fortunate man by all the rest.

Peter Somerville-Large in Irish Eccentrics (1975) tells of the case of Mary Pyke, who though homely was heiress to a large fortune. In 1797 the club assisted an adventurer called Sir Henry Hayes in carrying her off and forcing her to go through a form of marriage in the presence of a man in clerical robes. The resolute Miss Pyke, however, pulled off her ring and threw it in the fire. She was eventually returned to her family unharmed. This form of DIY matchmaking tended, like so much else that was characteristic of 18th-century Ireland, to die out after the Act of UNION. The club's activities became the theme of a film, The Abduction Club, shot in Ireland in 2001.

Abercorn Restaurant. A restaurant in central Belfast that was the scene of a Provisional IRA bombing in the early days of the TROUBLES. On Saturday 4 March 1972 at 4.30 p.m. a bomb exploded without warning, killing 2 people (both women) and injuring 130 others.

Abortion referendums. Referendums on this most emotive of issues for a country with as strongly Roman Catholic a heritage as Ireland were held in 1983, 1992 and 2002. They came about as a result of open conflict between a liberalizing minority and radical-right pro-life pressure groups, the latter supported by the Catholic Church. Most citizens, even compliant or conservative Catholics, would have been satisfied with the existing statutory prohibition on abortion.

In the 1983 referendum Irish voters approved a constitutional change by a two-to-one majority after a bitter and divisive debate. This enshrined in the constitution an acknowledgement of 'the right to life of the unborn and, with due regard to the equal right to life of the mother, guarantees in its laws to respect, and, as far as practicable, by its law to defend and vindicate that right.' But as some lawyers had predicted, the X CASE in 1991 and the C CASE in 1997 showed that the amendment did not offer the expected absolute protection to the unborn.

The second abortion referendum, held in 1992, tried to close the loophole that allowed women to have a termination if there was a real risk of their committing suicide, but this proposal was rejected. The third abortion referendum, which was held on 6 March 2002, also aimed to 'row back' the Supreme Court ruling and to make abortion a criminal offence, punishable by a 12-year prison sentence. It was defeated by the narrowest of margins, perhaps because on this occasion some members of the pro-life movement (see DANA²) advocated a 'no' vote, considering the provisions not to be strong enough, while the more pragmatic Catholic Church advocated a 'yes' vote. By the 2000s it was estimated that every year almost 7000 Irish women were having abortions in the UK.

See also CADDEN, MAMIE.

Absentee landlords. Widely regarded as responsible for the neglect of their estates and for the miserable living conditions of their tenants, absentee landlords were reviled figures in 18th- and 19th-century Ireland. Their turpitude was usually regarded as being compounded by equally unprincipled AGENTS. William ALLINGHAM memorably summed up the iniquities of landlordism in his verse-novel *Laurence Bloomfield in Ireland* (1864):

> Joining Sir Ulick's at the river's bend
> Lord Crashton's acres east and west extend ...
> Great owner here, in England greater still.
> As poor folk say, 'The world's divided ill.'
> On every pleasure men can buy with gold
> He surfeited, and now diseased and old,
> He lives abroad; a firm in Molesworth Street
> Doing what their attorneyship thinks meet.

In fact not more than half of landowners in Ireland in the 19th century were absentees, while a half of these in turn were landholders elsewhere in Ireland and inevitably absent from one property when visiting another. Bad

management and ill-treatment of tenants depended as much on personality as upon absenteeism. Many rapacious landlords lived on their property and many absentees using responsible agents proved quite enlightened. Though absenteeism was an appropriate target for such radical movements as the LAND LEAGUE, there were other, equally great evils in the system. The general view was summed up in *A Tour in Ireland*, written by 'An Englishman' in 1816:

> The very finest and most expensive estates belong to great men living in another country, whose families, from generation to generation, never put their foot on the island, and know nothing about it, only that their support in the greatest style of grandeur is annually drawn from thence; and this is all that too many of them care about. The management of these estates is generally left to venal and improper agents, who, living at a distance from the estate, never visit it save for the purpose of receiving rents, setting lands, and pocketing fees.

Abstentionism. The policy followed by Republican and Nationalist candidates standing for election to the DÁIL, STORMONT or the UK Parliament of refusing to take up seats they have won as an indication of their rejection of the constitutional legality of these institutions. SINN FÉIN announced in 1917 that, if elected, candidates would not take their seats at Westminster. The first to follow this policy was George Noble, Count Plunkett (1851–1948), the father of Joseph Mary PLUNKETT, one of the signatories of the proclamation of the Irish Republic, who defeated a HOME RULE candidate in a by-election in Roscommon on 3 February 1917. In the postwar general election of 1918 Sinn Féin won 73 seats, and the clear endorsement by the electorate of the abstentionist policy resulted in the setting up of the Dáil and led to the ANGLO-IRISH WAR of 1919–21.

Abstentionism was continued by Ulster Nationalist politicians refusing to take their seats in the Northern Ireland Parliament at STORMONT, indicating their rejection of the whole principle of PARTITION. It remained the policy in some constituencies but by the 1940s many Nationalist politicians were attending Stormont – a frustrating experience since they were never in a position actually to influence policy. The policy had its finale in 1965 when Eddie McATEER responded to the talks between Terence O'NEILL and Sean LEMASS by becoming leader of Her Majesty's loyal opposition.

Abstentionism was also Republican policy in the North for many years, a view that gradually changed after the election of Bobby SANDS during his hunger strike in 1981. Though neither Gerry ADAMS nor Martin McGUINNESS took the seats they had won in the UK general election of 1997, they and other members of Sinn Féin eventually decided to join the Northern Ireland Assembly set up by the GOOD FRIDAY AGREEMENT. Similarly Caoimhín Ó Caoláin, elected to the Dáil for Sinn Féin in 1997, has taken an active part in parliamentary business in the South. The general election of May 2002 resulted in the election (and the taking of seats) of five Sinn Féin TDs (Dáil members) including Ó Caoláin.
See also ARMALITE AND THE BALLOT BOX, THE.

Aby. An Ulster preposition meaning 'in comparison to' as in 'He's small aby his brother.' The phrase is still used in rural areas.

Acallam na Senórach (Old Irish, *Colloquy of the Ancients*). A long 12th-century monastic text that seeks to construct a bridge between the pagan Celtic and the Christian ways of life. It exists in various manuscripts, including the *BOOK OF LISMORE*. In the text, St PATRICK, while on his mission to Christianize Ireland, meets the surviving members of the FIANNA, including OISÍN and the other great warrior, CAOILTE, who are very old. Caoilte travels throughout Ireland with Patrick, telling him about the Fianna's way of life and introducing him to the lore (DINNSENCHAS) of the hills, forests and rivers of the beloved homeland that they, as roaming hunters, know intimately. When Patrick asks what kind of man Fionn himself was, Caoilte answers, lyrically:

Were but the brown leaf which the wood sheds from it gold – were but the white billows silver – Fionn would have given it all away.

Caoilte also explains the code by which the Fianna lived:

Glaine inár gcroí, neart inár ngéag, beart de réir ár mbriathar.

(Honesty in our hearts, strength in our limbs and deeds to honour our promises.)

Patrick on several occasions expresses his approval of the stories he is hearing by saying: 'May victory and blessing attend you.'

ACC. The Agricultural Credit Corporation, the first of the Irish state-sponsored organizations (SEMI-STATES), established in 1927 in order to revitalize Irish agriculture, which had suffered from chronic under-capitalization. It was not until the progressive 1960s, however, that the ACC began to advance large loans to ambitious and expansionist farmers.

Acceptable level (of violence). A phrase used by Reginald Maudling, UK home secretary, on 15 December 1971. Speaking about the escalating violence in Northern Ireland, Maudling commented:

I don't think one can speak of defeating the IRA, of eliminating them completely, but it is the design of the security forces to reduce their level of violence to something like an acceptable level.

The phrase was the first admission by the British government that the violence could only be contained, not eradicated. The concept of an 'acceptable level of violence' amounted to a policy, its implicit toleration of death and destruction extending even to outrages in Britain. *See also* BLOODY AWFUL COUNTRY.

Accordion or **accordeon.** An instrument associated with traditional Irish music since the second half of the 19th century (it was patented in 1829). It is often referred to as 'the box', and in Irish as *bosca ceoil*. To play an accordion one depresses buttons (in a button accordion) or keys (in a piano accordion) while the bellows are opened and closed. Despite some initial snobbery among purists about its suitability for traditional music, it has always been a popular choice for CÉILÍ and SET DANCES, being portable and having good volume, and has more recently become the instrument of choice of virtuoso soloists like Sharon SHANNON. Button accordions especially are apt to be colloquially called melodeons, since they are basically the same instrument, but the name may be applied to all types of accordion.

A chara (Irish vocative, 'friend'). The Irish equivalent of the word 'Dear' at the beginning of letters in Irish and frequently also in English. It is pronounced 'ahara'. Thus *A Risteáird, A Chara* means 'Dear Richard'.
See also MEAS.

Achill (Irish, 'place of the cliffs'). The largest of the Irish islands, lying off Co. Mayo; it has an area of 148 sq km (57 sq miles) with a population (1996) of 976. It is pronounced 'ah-kill'. Achill has fine beaches and cliff scenery and has been connected to the mainland by a bridge across Achill Sound between Blacksod Bay and Clew Bay since 1888. Near Doogort on its north coast are the remains of the notorious MISSIONARY SETTLEMENT of the Rev. Edward Nangle.

Achill Disaster. A tragic incident in which a hooker carrying 100 migrant workers capsized in Clew Bay in June 1894, resulting in the drowning of 24 young men. The boat was sailing across the bay from Daly's Point on the island to Westport on the mainland. Those lost were mostly in their teens, and for many it was the first time they had left the island. The tragedy came about when the islanders, excited at catching sight of the steamer in which they were scheduled to travel to Glasgow, rushed to one side of the boat to take a closer look, thereby causing the hooker to overturn. Many more lives would have been lost but for the prompt action of the crew of the steamer.

ACNI. The Arts Council of Northern Ireland. It came into being at the start of 1963. Hitherto CEMA (Council for the Encouragement of Music and the Arts), which had been estab-lished in February 1943, was the chief arts sponsor. Inspired by the Arts Council operating in Great Britain since 1946, ACNI's main concern was to provide for Northern Ireland 'art exhibitions of first class work and dramatic and musical performances of the highest standard by professional and semi-professional artists', and to promote the arts generally in an effort to increase awareness and appreciation. ACNI is part of the responsibility of the Department of Education for Northern Ireland (DENI).

Acquitted by a Limerick jury. A verdict not necessarily indicating total innocence on the part of the defendant. It was the characteristic remark of the Limerick county court judge Richard Adams (*fl.*1880–90) to a prisoner in the dock, as reported in *The Old Munster Circuit* (1939) by Maurice Healy (1887–1943):

> You have now been acquitted by a Limerick Jury, and you may leave the dock without any further stain on your character.

Act the buck, to. A somewhat dated phrase meaning to indulge in macho or anti-social behaviour (especially on the part of young men). It is difficult to date it precisely but it would seem to derive from the 18th-century bucks – raffish members of the ascendancy like Thomas 'Buck' Whaley, a notorious member of the HELLFIRE CLUB, with time on their hands to commit pranks and misdemeanours.

Act the lapwing, to. To mislead someone deliberately. The phrase is still current, and comes from the bird's habit of luring dangerous intruders away from its nest and crying loudest when safely afar:

> Far from her nest the lapwing cries away.
> > WILLIAM SHAKESPEARE: *The Comedy of Errors*, IV.ii (1594).

The lapwing also has the capacity of moving quickly close to the ground without drawing attention to itself:

> For look where Beatrice like a lapwing runs
> Close to the ground, to hear our conference.
> > WILLIAM SHAKESPEARE: *Much Ado about Nothing*, III.i (1598)

The bird has thus become proverbial for clever manoeuvring:

> This manoeuvre of keeping in reserve an old or second set of apparatus for the purpose of acting the lapwing and misleading the gauger, was afterwards practised with success.
>
> WILLIAM CARLETON (1794–1869): 'Bob Pentland' in *Traits and Stories of the Irish Peasantry* (1830)

Act the maggot, to. To behave in a deliberately silly or unpleasant manner. The expression is of Irish provenance and has been in use since the 1950s.

Acushla machree (Irish vocative, *A chuisle mo chroí*, 'O pulse of my heart'). A HIBERNO-ENGLISH endearment.

> Dear Erin, how sweetly thy green bosom
> rises!
> An emerald set in the ring of the sea.
> Each blade of thy meadows my faithful heart
> prizes,
> Thou queen of the west! The world's cushla ma
> chree.
>
> JOHN PHILPOT CURRAN (1750–1817): 'Cushla Ma Chree' (*c*.1785)

Adale. A HIBERNO-ENGLISH intensifier that negates the sense of the preceding verb. Thus, 'I did adale' would mean 'I most certainly did not'. The word is a corruption of 'a deal' and is heard most commonly in Munster.

Adamnán. *See* VITA SANCTI COLUMBAE.

Adams, Gerry (Gerard) (b.1948). The president of SINN FÉIN from 1983 and, with Martin McGUINNESS, a significant member of the Republican hierarchy. He was born in Belfast on 6 October 1948, the first child of Gerry Adams, a Republican who was married that year after having spent five years in prison for IRA activity. Educated at St Mary's Christian Brothers School in Divis Street, the younger Adams then worked as a bartender and was engaged in Republican activities from 1968.

Interned in 1971, Adams gradually emerged as one of the shapers of the movement, attending talks in Britain in 1972 with William WHITELAW, having been released for the pur-

pose. He was Sinn Féin MP for West Belfast (1983–92) and again from 1997, though like McGuinness he did not take his seat under the party's policy of ABSTENTIONISM. In the 1980s Adams's perceived links with the Provisional IRA and unwillingness to condemn Republican terrorist activity (including such notorious attacks as the 1984 BRIGHTON BOMBING and the Remembrance Day bombing of Enniskillen in 1987) led to his widespread demonization outside Irish Republican circles. The British prime minister Margaret Thatcher – seeking, as she put it, 'to starve the terrorist … of the OXYGEN OF PUBLICITY' – imposed a media ban on Adams (he could be filmed, but his voice had to be overdubbed by an actor), a ban only lifted in 1994.

However, Adams's paramilitary links made him an important figure in the clandestine – and later public – negotiations for a peace settlement that began in the late 1980s. His intermittent meetings with John HUME between 1988 and 1994 were a contributory factor in the Provisional IRA ceasefire of August 1994. A second ceasefire announced by the ARMY COUNCIL in July 1997 may be taken as evidence of his wary search for peace and of his urging upon more traditional Republicans the virtues of the political process. The GOOD FRIDAY AGREEMENT and any positive progress made in the peace process since, including the vexed question of DECOMMISSIONING, owes an incalculable debt to him (literally incalculable, because of the secrecy surrounding all IRA dealings).

A recent book, *The Secret History of the IRA* (2002), by Ed Moloney, suggests that Adams was an IRA commander in the 1970s and may have been implicated in the killings of some of the DISAPPEARED. Equally Moloney suggests that he should have shared the 1998 Nobel Peace Prize with Hume and David TRIMBLE since his work for peace had begun early and is continuing. Though Adams speaks with the occluded rhetoric that is characteristic of the Republican movement, there is no reason to doubt the sincerity of the words with which he concludes his autobiography *Before the Dawn* (1996):

> The Nobel laureate Seamus Heaney put it well:
> Once in a lifetime the longed for tidal wave of
> justice can rise up and hope and history rhyme.
>> Let us ignore the naysayers and begrudgers.
>> Let us confound the sceptics and the cynics.
>> Let us make hope and history rhyme.

Adare Robbery. A robbery carried out by members of the Provisional IRA in Adare, Co. Limerick, on 7 June 1996 in which Detective Sergeant Jerry McCabe of the GARDA SÍOCHÁNA was shot dead. The 54-year-old garda was shot three times and his companion garda, Ben O'Sullivan, seriously wounded with a Kalashnikov. At first the IRA categorically denied that any of its members were involved but when Jeremiah Sweeney, Michael O'Neill, Kevin Walsh and John Quinn from Co. Limerick, together with Pearse McCauley of Strabane, were arrested, they engaged in a number of unconvincing rationalizations. At their trial for manslaughter McCauley and Walsh were given 14 years, Sweeney 12, O'Neill 11 and Quinn 6. At the time of the GOOD FRIDAY AGREEMENT and since, it was made clear that these men would not be eligible for the early release that was agreed for other political prisoners.

A dhaoine uaisle. The Irish-language equivalent of 'ladies and gentlemen' (literally 'noble people'). The phrase is used ceremonially at the start of speeches on political, social and cultural occasions, often by people with only a few words of Irish (*see* CÚPLA FOCAL). In the interests of symmetry, *Go raibh míle maith agaibh go léir* ('Thank you all very much') will then close the speech. The use of decorative phrases such as this is evidence of the widespread practice of paying lip-service to the Irish language.

Adhnuall. A hound belonging to the epic hero FIONN MAC CUMHAIL, the leader of the FIANNA. The word is pronounced 'ah-nooal'. In one of the tales associated with the band of warriors he is stolen by ARTHUR OF BRITAIN. The Fianna

give chase and recover the hound, after which the Briton swears allegiance to Fionn. Unlike BRAN[1] and SCEOLAN, the other hounds of Fionn, Adhnuall was never human. Having strayed during a battle, he makes a triple circuit of Ireland. When he returns to the battlefield he comes upon the grave of three Fianna warriors, and there he howls thrice and dies of grief.

Æ. The pseudonym of [William] George Russell (1867–1935), poet, editor and social reformer. The pseudonym derived from the first letters of the word *æon*, which came to him in a daydream he had at the age of 18 while on holiday at home in Lurgan, Co. Armagh. He was reassured shortly afterwards to discover that it was an actual word, from the Greek *αιων* 'eternity', which in Gnostic belief had a triple connotation: eternity, the power of the deity and the name of the earliest beings created by God. As such it was entirely appropriate to one, who in spite of a busy life as editor of the *Irish Homestead* (1905–23) and the *Irish Statesman* (1923–30), and active promoter of the IAOS, found time to paint and write about the dream visions he experienced as an adept in theosophy.

A close friend of YEATS and a significant contributor to the IRISH LITERARY REVIVAL, Æ published many aspirant poets in his journals, including Padraic COLUM (1881–1972) and Eva GORE-BOOTH (1870–1926). Yeats and JOYCE were also contributors. After the death of his wife Violet North, a fellow adept, in 1932, much at odds with de Valera's Ireland, he went to live in Bournemouth, dying there in 1935.

> We would no Irish sign efface,
> But yet our lips would gladlier hail
> The first born of the Coming Race
> Than the last splendour of the Gael.
>> 'On Behalf of Some Irishmen Not Followers of
>> Tradition', in *Sinn Féin*, 14 November 1908

Áedán. In Irish mythology, the warrior who slays Mael Fhothartaig, the son of the Leinster king Ronán, on Ronán's own instructions because of a false accusation of attempted rape by Ronán's second wife. Áedán does the deed by spearing Mael Fhothartaig to his chair as he sits at a feast, but is himself later killed in revenge by Mael Fhothartaig's sons. Ronán dies of grief on hearing the truth and the erring wife takes poison.

Aedes. An old expression for a week reckoned as eight days, as in 'Tomorra come aedes.' The word seems to have been a sound conflation of 'eight days'.

Aedh. In Irish mythology, one of three sons of the sea god LIR, who, with their sister FION- NUALA, are changed into swans by their step- mother AOIFE[1].

AEIOU. The suggestion by Stephen DEDALUS in Joyce's ULYSSES (1922) that one of those who helped finance Joyce's flight to Paris on 9 October 1904 was George Russell, who used the pseudonym Æ. Besides, the wordplay was irresistible:

> I that sinned and prayed and fasted.
> A child Conmee saved from pandies.
> I,I and I.I
> A.E.I.O.U.

AE prisoner. A special category of high-risk Irish paramilitary prisoners in British jails. Category A, the highest security rating, is reserved for inmates perceived as most likely to try to escape. The E tacked on to the A category – to denote that they are Irish paramilitaries – makes them a unique special category group and as such they are isolated from other prisoners.

Aer Arann. An airline that began as an operator of flights from Galway to the the small air- fields of the ARAN ISLANDS in 1970. It was bought by Pádraig Ó Céidigh in 1994 and com- peted successfully for regional routes such as Dublin–Donegal and Dublin–Kerry. Since being rebranded as Aer Arann Express in 1999 the airline's business has expanded greatly and it now operates nearly 300 scheduled services a week, with routes to England and Scotland as well as within Ireland.

Aer Lingus. The government-owned Irish na- tional airline, which provides scheduled ser- vices throughout Europe and to North America. The name is formed from *aer*, the Irish word for 'air', and *loingeas*, a corruption of the Irish word for 'fleet'. The company was incorporated in 1936, originally under the name of Irish Sea Airways, and the first flight of the new airline was from Dublin to Bristol. Aer Lingus jets, mainly Boeings and Airbuses, are named after Irish saints, and since the 1990s have been staffed by cabin crew in a distinctive Paul Costello-designed green/blue uniform.

Aer Rianta. The government-owned Irish airports authority. It was incorporated in 1937 and derives its income from landing fees, duty- free shops and rents paid by banks and busi- nesses in the airport complexes. The name is formed from *aer*, the Irish word for 'air', and *rianta*, Irish for 'ready' or 'prepared'. As air traffic increased enormously in the ten years before the end of the millennium, this business has proved to be a lucrative one.

Áes. The word in Old Irish for 'people' or 'folk'. It is found in *Áes Síthe*, the 'people of the mounds', a phrase from Irish mythology denoting the old gods of Ireland (downgraded in later folklore to fairies), and in ÁES DÁNA.

Áes Dána (Irish, 'people of the gift'). The skilled men of early Irish society, whose hereditary or demonstrated skills in law, medicine, history, music, masonry, carpentry, metalwork – but primarily in poetic composition – granted them social status. One of the old manuscripts lists the professionals practising at the court of the king of TARA as carpenter, smith, fighter, harper, warrior, poet and historian, sorcerer, physician, cupbearer and brazier. Of all the recognized groups only the poets (FILID) were granted hereditary status, maintained until two unproductive generations had passed. The term AOSDÁNA was adopted by the Irish Arts Council (*see* CHOMHAIRLE EALAÍON, AN) for its arts pension scheme.

Áes Síthe. *See* ÁES.

Aff. The Ulster dialect equivalent of the preposition and adverb 'off'. Thus 'I wont tell ye again to get aff ye and get intil bed!' would translate into standard English as 'I won't tell you again to take off your clothes and get to bed!'

Affane, Battle of. An engagement fought in February 1565 in the region of the River Affane, a tributary of the Blackwater in Co. Waterford, between the rival Anglo-Irish houses of ORMOND and DESMOND. Gerald Fitzgerald, Earl of Desmond, tried to levy traditional dues in the region known as the DÉISE, but Black Tom Butler, Earl of Ormond, defeated him with a much larger force. As the wounded Desmond was being carried from the field on the shoulders of some of Ormond's men one of them jibed, 'Where is now the great Earl of Desmond?' The Earl is said to have replied, 'Where but in his proper place, on the neck of the Butlers!'

Affane cherry. The first cherry to be grown in THESE ISLANDS, having been brought from the Canaries by Sir Walter RALEIGH and successfully domesticated in the fertile basin of the River Affane.

Affane House. The site of Affane Castle, the birthplace near Cappoquin, Co. Waterford, of Valentine GREATRAKES, 'the Stroaker', who affected to cure diseases by manipulation.

After doing something, to be. A common usage in HIBERNO-ENGLISH, particularly in Munster, denoting that a person has just carried out a specified activity. It derives from a literal translation of the Irish *Tá mé tar éis rud a dhéanamh* ('I am after doing something'), as in 'Are you after making sure that the gate is closed?'

Agenbite of inwit. The diagnosis by Stephen DEDALUS of the cause of Hamlet's mental torpor, as announced in the National Library episode in Joyce's ULYSSES. The typically Dedalian term is an archaism meaning 'self-attack of conscience' and is associated with the medieval condition *acedia* or accidie, which was regarded as an extreme form of the deadly sin of sloth. Joyce revived the term from the title of a medieval moral treatise, *Ayenbite of Inwyt*, which was translated in 1340 by Dan Michel of Northgate. The word *ayenbite* is a Middle English translation (literally meaning 'again-bite') of Medieval Latin *remorsum*, the source of the English 'remorse', and *inwyt* a similar translation of the Latin *conscientia*, the source of the modern English 'conscience':

> How now, sirrah, that pound he lent you when you were hungry?
> Marry I wanted it.
> Take thou this noble.
> Go to! You spent most of it in Georgina Johnson's bed, clergyman's daughter.
> Agenbite of inwit.

Agents. The local representatives of landlords in Ireland, responsible for the running of their estates. As such they were often the bearers of the brunt of the tenantry's resentment and violence in times of land agitation. Their low reputation in Irish folk memory is probably due to the excesses of a relatively few dishonest and ruthless men, and by their association with the execrated landlord class whose lifestyle in too many cases was in glaring contrast to the subsistence level of the lives of many of their tenants. The generalized sense of historic dispossession by alien colonists made it impossible for any agent's clients to view him dispassionately, and many hard-working and conscientious agents shared unjustly in the general condemnation.
See also ABSENTEE LANDLORDS.

Age of chivalry is gone, the. The most famous of many fine phrases in the rhetoric of Edmund BURKE, whose reputation as a benevolent but firm supporter of conservatism is partly based upon his condemnation of the revolution in France. It occurs in his *Reflections on the Revolution in France* (1790):

> The age of chivalry is gone. – That of sophisters, economists, and calculators, has succeeded; and the glory of Europe is extinguished for ever.

The statement of his firmest belief is to be found

in the same work: 'Those who attempt to level never equalize.'

Aggro Corner. *See* ROSSVILLE FLATS.

Agley. An Ulster word meaning 'awry'. Ulster speech has absorbed a number of native Scots words partly owing to Scotland's geographical proximity but also, more specifically, as a result of the influx of Scottish settlers in the Jacobean plantations of Ireland in the 17th century. For centuries the North Channel was a kind of inland sea, and it is no surprise to find that the Gaelic of Scotland developed from ERSE and that Ulster speech has strong elements of Ayrshire Scots dialect. The latter is famously exemplified in Robert Burns's (1759–96) poem 'To a Mouse' (1786):

> The best laid schemes o' mice an' men
> Gang aft a-gley
> An' lea'e us nought but grief an' pain,
> For promised joy!

The word has kept its meaning, as in, 'Things have all gone agley with him since he broke his ankle.'

Agra (Irish vocative *a ghrá*, 'love'). A HIBERNO-ENGLISH term of endearment, used mainly by an older person to someone significantly younger.

Agricultural Credit Corporation. *See* ACC.

Agus araile. The Irish term for 'etcetera'; *agus* is Irish for 'and', while *araile* literally means 'one another' or 'others'.

Ahasky (Irish vocative *a thaisce*, 'treasure'). A HIBERNO-ENGLISH term of endearment, used rather like AGRA, with the same suggestion of age difference. Grannies were still using it as late as the 1940s. The root Irish word is also found in An TAISCE.

Ahern, Bertie (b.1951). FIANNA FÁIL politician and taoiseach since June 1997. He was first elected TD in 1977 and has represented the constituency of Dublin Central since 1981. Ahern, a northside Dubliner possessing the common touch, managed to remain largely un-

tarnished by the scandals that beset his party in the 1990s, leading to him being dubbed the TEFLON TAOISEACH. He is popularly referred to simply as Bertie, as in BERTIE BOWL and BERTIESPEAK.
See also BERTIEAHERN.COM.

Ah-ha-dee. A HIBERNO-ENGLISH phrase used in Munster to denote delight in someone else's comeuppance. The phrase is of uncertain derivation, and is spoken with the stress on the second syllable. Its use is not confined, as perhaps it should be, to children.

Aidan (diminutive of the personal name Aodh, 'fire') (d.651). An Irish-born saint who is most strongly associated with the monastery of LINDISFARNE. The date of his birth is unknown, but he was educated at SENAN's monastery on Scattery Island in the estuary of the Shannon, offshore from Kilrush, Co. Clare, and was a monk of IONA in 635. From there he accepted the invitation of Oswald (*c.*605–42), king of Northumbria, to Christianize the northeastern kingdom. Though Aidan knew little English, Oswald was able to interpret for him, having learned Irish during his exile in Iona (616–33). As BEDE records in his *Historia Ecclesiastica Gentis Anglorum* ('Ecclesiastical History of the English People') (731):

> It was a pleasing sight to see the king himself interpreting God's word to his thanes and chief men, for he had learned the Irish tongue during his long exile.

Aidan established himself on Lindisfarne (Holy Island) off the Northumbrian coast near Bamburgh, site of the royal palace. For more than a decade and a half he founded churches, oratories and monasteries, including MELROSE. His patron Oswald, who was afterwards venerated as a saint of the English church, was slain by the heathen Penda of Mercia (*c.*577–655), but Oswald's successor, his cousin Oswine, continued the support of Aidan. The kingdom became Christian and Celtic in its rituals until the Synod of WHITBY. When in 651 Oswin (also venerated as a saint and martyr) was murdered by his cousin Oswy (d.670), Aidan seemed to lose heart and died a fortnight later. His feast day is 31 August, and his symbol is the stag, from the legend that he once made invisible a hart pursued by hunters.

Aidín. In Irish mythology, the wife of OSCAR, himself the grandson of FIONN MAC CUMHAIL. She dies of grief at her husband's death in the battle of Gabhra, near Dublin, and is buried in Beann Eadair (the modern Hill of Howth on North Dublin bay) by her father-in-law OISÍN. He marks the place with a cromlech inscribed in OGAM. 'Aideen's Grave' is a poem on the subject of the princess and the 'cromlech vast' by Samuel FERGUSON (1810–86).

Áiféiseach. An Irish word for 'exaggerated', used in HIBERNO-ENGLISH to mean 'absurd' or 'ridiculous', 'That dress is *áiféiseach* on you!'

Aiken, Frank (1898–1983). IRA leader and Republican politician. He commanded an IRA division in his native county of Armagh during the WAR OF INDEPENDENCE and took the anti-TREATY side in the CIVIL WAR. On 27 April 1923, Aiken, who had replaced Liam Lynch (*see* REAL CHIEF, THE) as IRA chief of staff, ordered 'the suspension of all offensive operations' from noon on the last day of that month.

A founder member of FIANNA FÁIL, Aiken was a member of all the governments formed by that party from 1932, holding the posts of minister of defence (1932–9), minister for co-ordination of defensive measures during the EMERGENCY (1939–45), and minister of external (i.e. foreign) affairs (1951–4; 1957–69). He was TÁNAISTE (i.e. deputy premier) from 1965 to 1968. One of the last of the founder members of Fianna Fáil to hold high office, Frank Aiken fittingly retired from public life in protest at the advancement of Charles HAUGHEY.

Ail, to. A HIBERNO-ENGLISH verb meaning to be sick or, by extension, to have reason to complain. The transitive verb phrase 'What ails you?' ('What's wrong with you?') is the most common use of the expression, but it may also be said that someone is 'ailing'.

Ailbe or **Ailbhe.** A pre-Patrician Irish bishop, who was consecrated in Rome early in the 5th century. He was the founder of the diocese of Emly, 14 miles west of Cashel, and it was there that he met St PATRICK and acknowledged him as his religious superior. As with many religious figures of the period (*see* ISLAND OF SAINTS AND SCHOLARS), the written records feature more that is hagiographical and miraculous than that which is plausibly factual. Ailbe is believed, as the child of a maidservant, to have been exposed at birth and then reared by wolves. He encouraged St ENDA to found the earliest Irish monastic settlement on Inis Mór in the Aran Islands (*c.*484) and is said to have baptized David of Wales.

Aileach (Irish, 'rocky place'). An Ulster fortress, built, according to the legend, by the TUATHA DÉ DANAAN on a 245-m (800-ft) mound about 6 km (4 miles) west of Derry. It was the place where the sister goddesses BANBA, FODLA and ÉIRE divided the land of Ireland between them. It was one of several Irish places marked on the map compiled by the Egyptian geographer PTOLEMY in the 2nd century AD, when it was the residence of the kings of Ulster. From the 5th century it was the seat of the UÍ NÉILL, its commanding position giving clear views of Lough Foyle and Lough Swilly to the northeast and northwest, and central Tír Conaill to the west.

Aileach was sacked in 1101 by the forces of Muirchertach Ó Brien, king of Munster, in revenge for the destruction of KINCORA by Domnal Mac Lochlainn, king of Aileach, three years earlier. Legend says that Ó Brien's men carried away the stones so that it could not be rebuilt. In spite of this, sufficient material remained for it to be reconstructed in 1870. The present site, known as the *GRIANÁN* of Aileach, consists of a CASHEL with walls about 4m (13 ft) thick, 6.6 m (18 ft) high and of interior diameter 23 m (77 ft). Persistent folk belief has it that the warriors of ancient Ireland lie asleep near the site waiting for the summons to set their country free:

'Tis told in tales of wonder how Aileach's palace
    under
Kings in countless number lie still as carven
    stone;
And steeds with them in hiding are reined for
    warriors' riding
To the last of Erin's battles from the cave of Inish
    Owen.
    ALICE MILLIGAN (1866–1953): 'The Horsemen of
    Aileach', in *We Sang for Ireland* (1950)

Ailill. The name of several characters in Irish
mythology, most notably Ailill Mac Máta, the
king of Connacht and pliable consort of MEDB,
who nags him to invade Ulster and secure
the BROWN BULL OF CUAILNGE. He is killed at
his wife's instigation by CONALL CEARNACH,
cousin and foster brother to CÚCHULAINN.

Aims-Ace. Double ace, the lowest possible score
in throwing dice, known more graphically in
America as 'snake-eyes'. The phrase was formerly used in Ireland to denote a piece of bad
luck, or, more commonly, a 'near thing':

    One of the Crokes made a woeful swipe at him one
    time with his caman and I declare to God he was
    within an aims-ace of getting it on the side of the
    temple.
    JAMES JOYCE: *A Portrait of the Artist as a Young Man*
    (1916)

Áine. A Celtic goddess of the sun and of love,
associated in folklore with *Cnoc Áine* (Knock-
ainey, 'Aine's Hill'), Co. Limerick. The name
is pronounced 'enya'. The cairn on top of the
163-m (537-ft) hill, 2.5 km (1.5 miles) west
of Hospital, marks the site of a folk practice
in which men made clockwise circuits (*see*
DEISEAL) while carrying blazing wisps of hay on
top of poles on St John's Eve (*see* MIDSUMMER'S
DAY). The men carrying the wisps then visited
local fields and herds to bring good yields. It
was also the site of AONACH Áine, a harvest
fair. In the older mythology Áine, associated
incorrectly with ANÚ, mother of the gods, is
noted for her affairs with humans and is raped
by Aillil Olom, a king of Munster. She cuts off
his ear and afterwards uses magic to kill him.

Ainlé. One of two brothers of NAOISE, the lover
of DEIRDRE, and son of USNA. He flees with the
lovers to the safety of ALBA and returns with
them under the false promise of safety. He
dies with his brothers at the hostel of the RED
BRANCH KNIGHTS.

Ainnis. A HIBERNO-ENGLISH adjective still in use,
especially in Munster, meaning 'awkward'. Its
meaning has expanded to denote 'inadequate',
'pitiful' or 'hopeless'. An 'ainniseoir' is someone
who exhibits these qualities.

Airey, Josie (1932–2002). A working woman
who brought about significant legal reform.
Josey Airey was born Josie Lynch in Cork city.
She married at 21 but by 1972 the marriage had
broken down. In the absence of free legal aid for
civil cases, Airey could not afford the several
thousand pounds she would need to win a high
court separation (without the cooperation
of her husband) *a mensa et toro*, which was
all that Ireland offered by way of solution to
marital breakdown at the time. Airey took her
case to the European Commission of Human
Rights in Strasbourg and, after several years of
representations and legal argument, in 1979
the Irish government was found in breach
of Articles Six and Eight of the European
Convention on Human Rights, and was obliged
to introduce free legal aid for family cases.

Airgialla or **Oirghialla.** The Celtic kingdom
comprising the modern counties of Armagh,
Monaghan, Tyrone and large areas of Fermanagh and Derry. Its name was anglicized
as Oriel, and the word in Irish probably means
'hostage-givers'. The territory diminished as
the UÍ NÉILL pushed south, and by the 13th
century the term was applied to that section of
Monaghan ruled by the MacMahons.

Airneán (also *airneál*, especially in Ulster
Irish). An Irish word for the night-visiting of
neighbours' houses in country areas for social
evenings. Though in particular districts one
house would gain a special reputation as a *teach
airneál* (Irish *teach*, 'house') because of the
ability of the host or his friends as storytellers

(*see* SEANCHAÍ), singers or dancers, other houses had their turn. Physical considerations also applied: a good fire, a space for dancing (*see* MIND THE DRESSER!) and sufficient economic surplus to supply a minimal supper for the guests were all desirable. It was largely through the existence of institutions such as this that the wealth of Irish *BÉALOIDEAS* was preserved (*see also* BOTHÁNTAÍOCHT; CÉILÍD-HING; RAMBLING HOUSE). Informality was the rule:

> We told her that during the winter months we would have airneals every night.
> 'What is an airneal?' said Jane.
> I said it was a gathering of all the people in the townland into one house for dancing, singing and storytelling.
> 'How could you pay for dances and you so poor?'
> I told her we did not have to pay; that the dance would be in Charlie's house tonight, my father's house the next, and in different houses every other night.
> 'Oh yes,' she said, 'but who pays the fiddler?'
> I told her that there was no fiddler, that it was all lilting.
> PATRICK GALLAGHER ('Paddy the Cope') (1873–1964): *My Story* (1939)

Airt. A non-specific point of the compass, used commonly in Ulster to indicate such things as wind direction and preserved in the phrase 'all arts and parts'. Thus: 'It's a bad airt for dry weather.' 'When the wind's in that airt it's hard to keep the fire in.' The word is also used in Scotland.

Airy. An adjective indicating 'light-hearted', but also with the darker meaning of 'eerie' or 'strange'. *Aerach*, its source word in Irish, has connotations of foolishness or giddiness. Its use in William ALLINGHAM's well-known poem 'The Fairies' (1850) suggests both the spooky and the meteorological:

> Up the airy mountain,
> Down the rushy glen,
> We daren't go a-hunting
> For fear of little men.

Airy fit. A term in folklore used to signify a fit of depression, thought to be caused by a spell cast by the fairies (*see* SIDHE). To be 'airy', that is under the influence of the fairies, was to be unsound of mind.
See also MIDSUMMER'S DAY.

Aisling (Irish, 'vision'). A type of Gaelic poem written in the 18th century and based upon the illusory belief that the return of the Stuart kings would mean the re-establishment of the Bardic order (*see* BARDIC POETRY). In an *aisling*, the poet tells of a vision of a *spéirbhean* (Irish, 'sky maiden') who personifies Ireland and bewails her sorry state. The poet asks her name and she announces that she is Ireland, bereft of her spouse. The poem usually ends with the prophecy that a rightful Stuart monarch will take the throne:

> *D'fhreagair an bhríd Aoibhill, nár dhorcha snua:*
> *'Fachain na dtrí coinnle do lasadh ar gach cuan*
> *In ainm an rí dhíoghras bheas againn go luath*
> *Igceannas na dtrí róchta, 's dá gcosnamh go buan.'*
> (The maid Aoibhill with her shadowed face answered: 'They had reason to light three candles above each harbour in the name of the true king who will be with us soon, to rule and protect the triple realm for ever'.)
> AOGÁN Ó RATHAILLE (*c.*1675–1729): 'An Aisling' (1720)

AK-47. A Russian-designed assault rifle used by both Republican and Loyalist paramilitaries in Northern Ireland. Increasingly straightforward to acquire after the collapse of the Soviet empire in Eastern Europe in the late 1980s, the AK-47 replaced the ARMALITE, hitherto the iconic weapon of choice of the Provisional IRA. Almost all the IRA's AK-47s were smuggled from LIBYA, where they had been purchased.

The AK-47 is more commonly known as the Kalashnikov, from its designer Mikhail Timofeyevich Kalashnikov (b.1919), who rose to the rank of major-general of the Red Army and was a deputy of the Supreme Soviet. 'AK' stands for *Avtomat Kalashnikov* ('automatic Kalashnikov'), and '47' for the year in which the weapon was adopted by Soviet forces.

(Kalashnikov announced in 2002 that it was a pity that his name should be associated with a rifle; he would have preferred to have invented something useful like a lawnmower.) The AK-47 continued to be manufactured in many communist countries and was the standard infantry weapon in their armies for some four decades. It has been widely used by national, guerrilla and other terrorist groups as well as the IRA.

Alanna (Irish *a leanbh*, 'child'). A HIBERNO-ENGLISH endearment, still common in parts of Ireland and frequently to be met in verse and song. 'Alanna' has also become a popular girl's name, seeming to have lost its previous slight connotation of stage-Irishness (*see* STAGE-IRISH).

Alba. An Irish name for Scotland, which – ironically – means the Land of the Irish (*see* SCOTIA). It is still used in Scots Gaelic, while the modern Irish word is *Albain*. Alba figures in many Irish myths, sometimes in the alternative forms Albu and Albain, notably as the place of safety for DEIRDRE and the SONS OF USNA and as the venue for CÚCHULAINN's early martial training. The name has a visible connection with Alban, Albany and Albion, all taken as ancient Celtic names for the whole island of Britain, and later applied exclusively to Scotland.

Alcock and Brown. The pair of aviators who first flew the Atlantic non-stop, landing near Clifden, Co. Galway. Sir John William Alcock (1892–1919) and Sir Arthur Whitten Brown (1886–1948) – both were knighted after the flight – took off from St John's, Newfoundland, on 14 June 1919 in a Vickers-Vimy biplane and crash-landed 16 hours 27 minutes later in Derrygimlagh bog. Alcock, who piloted the plane, died soon afterwards in a flying accident in France; Brown, the navigator, shared the £10,000 award given by the *Daily Mail*. They are commemorated by a monument unveiled in 1959, the 40th anniversary, at Derrygimlagh and by a more imposing sculpture in the shape of a tailplane at Dublin airport.

Alcuin (*c.*737–804). The chief cultural advisor of CHARLEMAGNE. Also known by his Anglo-Saxon name Ealhwine, Alcuin was born in York and educated at the cloister school there, becoming master in 778. His teachers were Irish monks; he mentions in his writings a certain Colchu, who may have been abbot of CLONMACNOISE, and Irish scholars were to be his colleagues in later life.

Alcuin met Charlemagne at Parma in 781 on his return from a pilgrimage to Rome and accepted his invitation to come to the court at AACHEN. At first he supervised the education of the extensive royal family but soon made the court a centre of intellectual and artistic activity – the so-called Carolingian Renaissance. He was responsible for bringing to the palace school such Irish scholars as DUNGAL, CLEMENT SCOTTUS, Joseph and Albinus. Other Irish scholars, including DICUIL, Thomas and Cruinnmaol, also played their parts in the brief flowering of culture.

In 796 Alcuin became abbot of Tours, making it the premier school in the empire. While there he developed the Carolingian minuscule calligraphy, which he had learned at York from the Irish and which was to become the standard cursive script until the invention of printing. He kept in constant touch with his patron by letter until his death. His self-composed epitaph reads:

> *Alchuine nomen erat, sophiam mihi semper amanti, pro quo funde preces mente, legens titulum.*
>
> (Alcuin was my name, ever a lover of wisdom. You who read this inscription, pray for my soul.)

Aldershot Bomb. A device placed by an active-service unit of the Official IRA (*see* STICKIES, THE[1]) in the headquarters of the Parachute Regiment in Aldershot, England, on 22 February 1972. The bombing was assumed to be a revenge killing for the events of BLOODY SUNDAY 1972 in which members of the regiment had shot and killed an eventual total of 14 Nationalists. As such it misfired: the bomb's seven victims comprised five canteen women, a Catholic padre and a gardener. Adverse reaction to the operation was a contributory factor in the Official IRA's ceasefire, effective from 29 May that year.

Alexander, Cecil Frances (1818–95). Poet and hymnist. Known universally as CFA, the initials she used for her various hymnaries, she was born Humphreys in Eccles Street in Dublin, spent her girlhood in Wicklow and moved to Strabane, Co. Tyrone, in 1833 when her father became land steward to the Duke of Abercorn. In 1851 she married the Rev. William Alexander (1824–1911) and eventually went to live in Derry when he was ordained Bishop of Derry and Raphoe.

CFA wrote a great deal of verse, most of it sacred, though she devised a ballad 'The Legend of Stumpie's Brae' (1850) about a legless ghost (based upon a local tale from Donegal) that has the true Border starkness, and also a verse epic, *The Siege of Derry* (1891). Her three best-known hymns, 'All Things Bright and Beautiful', 'Once in Royal David's City' and 'There Is a Green Hill Far Away', which are commemorated by stained-glass windows in the baptistery of St Columb's Cathedral, Derry, were first published in *Hymns for Little Children* in 1848. She died in Derry on 12 October 1895. Her husband later became Archbishop of Armagh and Primate of All Ireland, and was, unlike his wife, a confirmed opponent of HOME RULE. He died in Torquay.

> Ye think ye've laid me snugly here
> And none shall know my station;
> But I'll hant ye far and I'll hant ye near
> Father and son, wi' terror and fear,
>   To the nineteenth generation.
>   'The Legend of Stumpie's Brae'

Alexander, William. *See* ALEXANDER, CECIL FRANCES.

Alexander of Tunis and Errigal (1891–1969). The title assumed by Field-Marshal Harold Rupert Alexander on his elevation to the peerage (Errigal is a fine and famous mountain in Co. Donegal). He was born in Caledon, Co. Tyrone, on 10 December 1891 and spent most of his childhood on the family estates there. Educated at Harrow and Sandhurst, he was commissioned in the Irish Guards in 1911. He proved a brave and charismatic officer: wounded twice and awarded the MC and DSO in the First World War, as commander-in-chief in the Mediterranean theatre he played a significant part in the Allied victories in North Africa (1942–3) and Italy (1943–5). Alexander served as governor-general of Canada (1946–52) and was minister of defence (1952–4) in Winston Churchill's last government. He received the Order of Merit in 1959 and died on 16 June 1969.

Allaballa. An Ulster street game in which the leader tosses a ball over his or her head and then must try to guess who has picked it up. At the period when the game was popular (1900–50), the clothes of the children who played the game were likely to have been quite skimpy and it was relatively easy for the leader to identify the person with the ball. The leader had to forfeit the role if the ball was caught without a bounce or if the holder was not correctly guessed. The game was played to the chant:

> Allaballa, Allaballa, who's got the ball?
> I haven't got it in my pocket.
> Allaballa, Allaballa, who's got the ball?

All acclivity and declivity. The description, expressed with uncharacteristic asperity, by the 44-year-old Thomas MOORE of the mountainous topography of Co. Kerry. Moore noted in his *Journal* for 6 August 1823:

> All acclivity and declivity, without the intervention of a single horizontal; the mountains all rocks, and the men all savages.

All for Hecuba. The title of the theatrical autobiography (1947) of Micheál Mac Liammóir (*see* BOYS, THE[2]), co-founder with Hilton Edwards of the GATE THEATRE. The title comes from *Hamlet* (II.ii):

> Is it not monstrous that this player here,

But in a fiction, in a dream of passion,
Could force his soul so to his own conceit
That from her working all his visage wann'd,
Tears in his eyes, distraction in's aspect,
A broken voice, and his whole form suiting
With forms to his conceit? and all for nothing!
For Hecuba!
What's Hecuba to him or he to Hecuba
That he should weep for her?

Mac Liammóir took the extremes of emotion that the Player King showed in conveying the story of the death of Hecuba at the destruction of Troy as an example of the actor's professional dedication. This dedication seemed to him all the more poignant in the realization that the actor's art is so ephemeral, as he wrote in an article 'Hamlet in Elsinore' in *The Bell* (October 1952):

> We are born at the rise of the curtain and we die at its fall, and every night in the presence of our patrons we write our new creation, and every night it is blotted out forever.

Allgood, Molly (1887–1952). Actress and fiancée of J.M. SYNGE. She was born on 12 January 1887 and joined the ABBEY THEATRE company after a period as a dressmaker in 1905. She used the stage name Máire O'Neill to prevent confusion with her elder sister Sarah ALLGOOD. Synge fell in love with her almost immediately and they became engaged, though their relationship was often stormy. She proved an ideal Pegeen Mike (a part specifically written for her) in his controversial drama The PLAY-BOY OF THE WESTERN WORLD, which opened on 26 January 1907. Synge died on 24 March 1909 and there was an almost unbearable poignancy about her performance as the doomed heroine in his DEIRDRE OF THE SORROWS, which was staged in 1910.

In June 1911 Molly Allgood married George Herbert Mair, the drama critic of the *Manchester Guardian*, and worked with the Liverpool Rep until his death in 1926. Returning to Ireland, she began appearing at the Abbey again and married the actor Arthur Sinclair. They appeared in many Abbey plays, especially revivals of Sean O'Casey, and had successful American tours. In her later years she appeared in a number of low-budget films, made mainly in Britain, taking the same kind of 'Oirish' parts as her sister Sarah (*see* STAGE-IRISH). She died on 2 November 1952. Among Synge's poems was one without a title and not included in *Poems and Translations* (1911) but clearly written to Molly:

> Is it a month since I and you
> In the starlight of Glen Dubh
> Stretched beneath a hazel bough
> Kissed from ear and throat to brow
> ...
> And the wet and withered leaves
> Blew about your cap and sleeves,
> Till the moon sank tired through the ledge
> Of the wet and wintry hedge
> And we took the starry lane
> Back to Dublin town again.

Allgood, Sarah (1883–1950). Actress at the ABBEY THEATRE, and sister of the actress Molly ALLGOOD. Born in Dublin on 31 October 1883, she was associated with the Abbey from its beginnings, playing Mrs Fallon in Lady Gregory's *Spreading the News* on the theatre's opening night, 27 December 1904. She became a professional actress the following year, appearing in Yeats's *Cathleen ni Houlihan* and Synge's *Riders to the Sea*. Her most memorable performance was as Juno BOYLE in O'Casey's *Juno and the Paycock*, which opened on 3 March 1924, and she was a splendid Bessie Burgess in *The Plough and the Stars* when the Abbey took the play to London. After many tours in America she settled in Hollywood in 1940 for the last ten years of her life, playing subsidiary parts such as servants and barmaids in many films. Even these became scarce, and she died in comparative poverty on 13 September 1950. Before going to America she appeared in Alfred Hitchcock's first talkie *Blackmail* (1929), and as Juno in his film version of the play in 1930.

All graduats and gentlemen. *See* MARSH'S LIBRARY.

All Hallows Priory. An Augustinian priory ('All Hallows' means 'All Saints') situated in HOGGEN GREEN in the centre of Dublin. It was built by Dermot MACMURROUGH, king of Leinster, in 1166 in thanksgiving for surviving a serious illness. It also attracted the goodwill of the Anglo-Normans who ruled Dublin after 1170. It was dissolved on 16 September 1538 as part of the DISSOLUTION OF THE MONASTERIES of the early Reformation, and Trinity College was built on the site in 1593–4. The modern All Hallows in Drumcondra, Dublin, one of Ireland's first missionary seminaries, was founded by Father John Hand in 1842. Its first graduates ministered to the emigrants who left Ireland during the GREAT FAMINE.

Alliance Party. A Northern Ireland political party founded in April 1970, hoping for cross-community backing. Its main support is the urban middle class, and its political base has tended to be eastern Ulster. A number of members of the Northern Ireland Labour Party joined its ranks, thereby effectively undermining the older grouping. The hope of establishing a strong centre alliance was not realized, even with the introduction of proportional representation, returns showing about a 13% response in local elections and 10% in Assembly elections. Its leader since 2001 has been David Ford, and it held all six Alliance seats in the election in November 2003.

Allingham, William (1824–89). Poet and diarist. Born a Protestant in Ballyshannon, Co. Donegal, on 19 March 1824, he worked as a customs officer in different posts around Ireland until he settled in England in 1863. His early poems were published anonymously and sold as halfpenny broadsheets. *Poems* (1850) contains most of his best work, including the much-anthologized 'The Fairies' and 'Four Ducks on a Pond'.

With characteristic modesty and perhaps some slight insincerity Allingham dismissed his verse-novel *Laurence Bloomfield in Ireland* (1864) as dealing with 'Paddies, priests, and pigs'. His entry for 22 October 1863 in his diary (published in 1907) reads:

A story in 5000 lines,
Where Homer's epic fervour shines,
Philosophy like Plato's.
Alas, I sing of Paddies, Priests,
And Pigs, those unromantic beasts
Policemen and Potatoes!

Bloomfield had the honour of being quoted in Parliament by Gladstone a month after its publication and it is still an invaluable source for 19th-century life in Ireland.

Allingham's diary – edited by his wife, the artist Helen Paterson (1848–1926) – is a fascinating document, beginning with an autobiographical sketch of the author's first 22 years and giving remarkable portraits of Thomas Carlyle (1795–1881) and Alfred, Lord Tennyson (1809–92) (*see* GINTLEMAN WHO BROUGHT SO MUCH MONEY, THE) in old age.

On 14 September 1888 he was thrown from his horse and died, as he believed, from an illness generated by his injuries, on 18 November 1889 at his home in Hampstead. His ashes were buried in accordance with his wishes in the churchyard of St Anne, appropriately situated on Mullagnashee (*Mullach na Sí*, 'the fairy height') in Ballyshannon. *See also* KELTS AND ULTONIANS.

'All in the April Evening'. *See* TYNAN, KATHARINE.

All-Ireland. A term usually referring to the All-Ireland final of the Gaelic Athletic Association (*see* GAA) hurling and football championships. When these championships were initiated in 1887 (the first All-Ireland hurling final was held in Birr in 1888), it was normally the club that won that county championship that went on to represent the county. By the beginning of the 1920s, however, county teams consisted of the best players from all the county's clubs. In the years after independence the attendance at All-Ireland finals in CROKE PARK in Dublin grew steadily, so that by the late 1940s the average attendance at a football final was over 75,000 people. In 1944, because of a shortage of fuel, there was only one train to bring Kerry supporters to Dublin for the final with Roscommon, but there was still an attendance of 80,000. The 1961 football final between Down and Offaly was watched by a record 90,556 people. Kerry has won more football All-Irelands than any other county, 32, and Cork has won 28 hurling finals. No county has won more than four All-Irelands in a row in either sport. In 1971 an All-Ireland club competition was introduced. The term 'All-Ireland' also refers to the All-Ireland FLEADH CHEOIL.

See also ARTANE BOYS' BAND; SAM MAGUIRE CUP; POLO GROUND FINAL, THE; THUNDER AND LIGHTNING HURLING FINAL.

'All Kinds of Everything'. The title of a song with which DANA² won the 1970 EUROVISION Song Contest.

Allow. An Ulster verb meaning 'insist' or 'claim', as thus: 'She allowed that she had seen the doctor going into MacMullan's at the skrake.'

All Souls Day. The feast of All Souls, known more baldly in Irish as *Lá Fhéile na Marbh* ('feast of the dead'), celebrated on 2 November, the day after the feast of All Saints. In Catholic practice it is the day of prayer for the souls in Purgatory, with indulgences obtainable for visits to churches and graveyards. In Ireland the calendrical closeness of SAMHAIN – the Celtic feast of the dead and the arrival of winter, at which time of year the OTHERWORLD is traditionally deemed to be in closest proximity – gave an extra resonance to the atmosphere of the day. In the older liturgy, All Souls Day was, along with Christmas Day, the only occasion when priests had leave to say three masses.

All Souls Night. The best known play – first performed in September 1948 – of the Ulster dramatist and novelist Joseph TOMELTY. It deals with poverty and thrift in a fishing family on Strangford Lough in Co. Down. Katherine Quinn has by miserliness amassed a substantial sum of money, but she will not even touch the interest on it. Her husband John and son

Michael are forced to carry on their perilous trade with inferior equipment and a dangerously small boat, and she refuses to provide the cash for a deposit on a better vessel. At the Feast of the Dead – as the locals call it – Michael's older brother Stephen is prayed for, and Michael, heading out on a hazardous job of salvage, is drowned. His ghost returns in Act III speaking an effectively dramatic poetic language:

> *Michael:* Close to the warted perch. The blistered
> weed clipped my fingers, curled its heavy weave
> about my arms, circled in a neck around my neck,
> pocking its tartled tails into my eyes, until the
> swirling tide poured death into me.

It becomes clear that Stephen too was driven to his death by his mother's avarice:

> *Stephen:* I'd still be alive if she hadn't forced me
> out.
> *Michael:* To be sure. I would be too, if greed had
> thawed in her heart. She killed us both.

The play ends on a bleak note of acceptance as the kindly but weak father (played at the first production by the author) observes: 'Folk are kinder in death than they are in life.'

All Stars. The annual All-Star Award Scheme was introduced by the GAA in 1971 as a means to recognize the skills and achievements of hurling and football players during that year's championship games. All-Star teams are chosen by sports journalists after the championships are completed.

All the bars. A phrase meaning the full gossipy facts as known, as in 'Tell us all the bars about yer woman and the sailor.' The usage is prevalent in northwest Ulster. The word 'bar' (in the singular) is used for a choice item of scandal, 'I've a great bar for ye!' The usage may have its remote origin in the Irish idiom *An bhfuil aon bharr nuachta agat?* ('Have you any special news?'), where the word *barr* literally means 'extra'.

Ally Daly. A standard of excellence based upon the quality of the dairy products of Alice Daly (*fl.*early 19th century). The expression appears most famously in Joyce's *A PORTRAIT OF THE ARTIST AS A YOUNG MAN*. It reached a wider audience in Hugh Leonard's play *STEPHEN D*.

> Stephen looked at the plump turkey which had lain, trussed and skewered, on the kitchen table. He knew his father had paid a guinea for it in Dunn's of D'Olier Street and that the man had prodded it often at the breastbone to show how good it was, and he remembered the man's voice when he had said:
> —Take that one, sir. That's the real Ally Daly.
> JAMES JOYCE (1882–1941): *A Portrait of the Artist as a Young Man* (1916)

Alone it Stands. A play (1999) by John Breen taking its title from a line of 'THERE IS AN ISLE', the anthem of Limerick rugby club Thomond, and telling the story of Munster's unexpected and glorious 12–nil win over the All-Blacks at Thomond Park on 31 October 1978. In the play 6 actors play a total of 62 characters, including players, trainers, spectators, a dog and the Bunratty Medieval Singers. In real life Christy Cantillon, who scored a try, and Tony Ward, who converted it, were the heroes.

Altan. A traditional Irish music group, founded by the Belfast flute player Frankie Kennedy (1955–94) and his wife, the fiddler and singer Máiréad Ní Mhaonaigh (b.1959). The name is that of a romantically mysterious lake north-east of Errigal, a mountain in west Donegal not far from Máiréad's birthplace in Gweedore. Though the band has been taken on by the mainstream company Virgin Records they still draw a lot of material and inspiration from the local tradition. Máiréad's father Francie Mooney was a strong influence on their repertoire. A noted performer and composer in his own right, he maintained and nurtured the fiddle and vocal tradition of the area.

Aluminium. The nickname inflicted upon the millennium of the founding of the city of Dublin, celebrated in 1988 on somewhat dubious historical grounds, by its unimpressed citizens. Its chief sculptural celebration, entitled *Anna Livia Plurabelle*, was similarly mocked as the FLOOZIE IN THE JACUZZI.

Amadán. The Irish word for 'fool'. It has such currency as to be found often in HIBERNO-ENGLISH texts as 'amadaun' and 'ommad-hawn'. It is, however, less likely to be heard in Ulster, which has its own rich vocabulary of foolishness.

Amás. A common HIBERNO-ENGLISH expression of surprise or incredulity in the south of Ireland. Used variously, as in 'You're not going amás!' or 'Amás he didn't do that.' Also, intensively, 'Amás to God!' It is a corruption of the Irish *am baist*, literally 'by my baptism', which also had currency in Hiberno-English.

Am baist. *See* AMÁS.

Amergin. The chief poet of the MILESIANS, son of Milesius and first druid of the conquered Ireland. Three poems are ascribed to him in the *BOOK OF INVASIONS*, all addressed to Ireland. One of the poems, known as 'The Mystery', suggests a total identification between poet and subject:

> I am the wind which breathes upon the sea,
> I am the wave of the ocean,
> …
> I am the God who created in the head the fire.
> Who is it who throws light into the meeting on the mountain?
> Who announces the ages of the moon?
> Who teaches the place where couches the sun?
> (If not I).
> Translated by Douglas Hyde

It is Amergin who advises that the Milesians should make a second attempt to invade Ireland after their first inconclusive incursion by going out to sea again beyond the ninth wave (regarded as a magical boundary). He also decrees that his brother EREMON should be the first Milesian king of Ireland and adjudicates as to which of the claimant goddesses' names – those of BANBA, FODLA and ÉIRE – should be given to the conquered country.

American Association for the Recognition of the Irish Republic (AARIR). A support organization established by Éamon DE VALERA in America in November 1920 after his break with John DEVOY and CLAN NA GAEL in order to provide, in de Valera's words, 'a coordinated and unified movement to supply the channels by which the popular sentiment in the country [USA] in favour of justice might express itself.' The AARIR was active in support of the IRA during the WAR OF INDEPENDENCE, but, like the IRA, split over the TREATY and by 1926 had effectively ceased to exist.

American bronze. A breed of turkey very common in rural Ireland until the 1950s, at which time bronze and black turkeys were replaced by white breeds. White turkeys were held to be easier to fatten and to give more meat for weight, but they were also believed by some to be inferior in flavour to the bronze and black.

American Note. A note sent to Éamon DE VALERA in February 1944 by David Gray, the American ambassador to Éire, demanding that the taoiseach expel the German embassy staff. The reason given for the demand was the fear that details of the D-Day landings might be transmitted by Axis agents. Sir John Maffey (1877–1969), the popular British ambassador, attached his name to the note with some reluctance since Britain knew well that the transmitting equipment had already been removed by G2, the Irish Army Intelligence Unit, and that espionage levels in Ireland were minimal. There was mutual antipathy between Gray and the taoiseach, and there may have been an element of mischief in the ambassador's action. It was regarded by the Irish authorities as another stage in the campaign of attrition over Éire's neutrality that had continued since Pearl Harbor. Robert Fisk, in *In Time of War* (1983), his study of Anglo-Irish diplomatic relations during the Second World War, quotes Gray as predicting '… that his demand would be met with a negative reply, and the Éire government would then be on record as having refused a request which had the object of safeguarding the lives of American soldiers, sailors and airmen at a vital moment of the war'. The matter was resolved by Hubert Will, chief of the OSS (Office of Strategic Services) counter-espionage branch in Europe. He came to Dublin and put 16 questions to Colonel Dan Bryan, head of G2. His answers were deemed satisfactory and the Americans did not again question Irish counter-espionage measures.

American wake. A party held in the house of a young man or woman who was leaving for America the next day, customary from the mid-19th century until the Second World War. Despite the sadness of the occasion and the heartbreak of the family, these were usually occasions of great CRAIC: singing, dancing, storytelling and drinking. The next morning, the emigrant would leave the house early and be driven in a horse trap to the nearest station to catch the train for Cobh (Queenstown) from where the American liners sailed. These farewell parties were called wakes because until the late 20th century, when air travel became an option, nobody who remained at home expected ever to see the emigrant again. There was a saying that the best American wakes were in Ireland and the best Irish wakes were in America.

American Wild Geese. A description applicable to a number of Catholic Irish nationals or people of Irish descent who played a small but significant part in the history of the USA. The WILD GEESE left Ireland during the 17th and 18th centuries because of defeat at home and POPERY LAWS that made life untenable. They were mainly soldiers, but later their numbers included clerics and lay students who sought the education denied them at home, and displaced Irish merchants who settled in French and Spanish ports. Enrolment in the armies of France and Spain meant service for some in the New World. The governor of Spanish Louisiana in 1769 was Alexander O'Reilly, born in Co. Meath in 1722, and the Hispanic force that captured Pensacola, Florida, from the British during the American War of Independence contained a section known as Hibernia, because its personnel was Irish. The French armies which occupied Canada and penetrated south to Ohio to fight in the Seven Years War (1756–63) had their quota of Irish soldiers, and with them came some Irish priests who acted as army chaplains. European trade links with the West Indies burgeoned during the 18th century, and involved a share of Irish merchants. Though the numbers of Irish officials, clerics and academics were not great, there was undoubtedly a sprinkling of green, and when the next century saw the great surge of Irish immigration the migrants did not come to a land totally alien.

Amharc Éireann. A weekly Irish-language newsreel launched by GAEL LINN in 1959 and shown in cinemas throughout the country until the establishment of RTÉ television in 1962 made it redundant. The newsreels were produced by Colm Ó Laoghaire and distributed countrywide by the Rank organization, so they reached a considerable audience.

Amhráin mhóra. *See* SEAN-NÓS.

'Amhrán na bhFiann'. The title in Irish of 'A SOLDIER'S SONG', the Irish national anthem, which is usually sung in Irish. It is pronounced 'ouran na vee-an':

Sinne fianna fáil,
Atá faoi gheall ag Éirinn;
Buíon dár slua
Thar toinn do ráinig chughainn.
Faoi mhóid bheith saor,
Sean-tír ár muintir feasta
Ní fhágfar faoin tíoráin ná faoin tráill.
Anocht a théim sa bhearna baoill
Le gean ar Ghaeil chun bháis nó saoil;
Le gunnaí scréach, faoi lámhach na bpiléar
Seo libh canaíg' amhrán na bhfiann.
(Soldiers are we,
Whose lives are pledged to Ireland;
Some have come
From a land beyond the wave,
Sworn to be free.
No more our ancient sireland
Shall shelter the despot or the slave.
Tonight we man the 'bearna baoill'
In Erin's cause, come woe or weal;
'Mid cannons roar or rifles' peal
We'll chant a soldier's song.)

Amnesty Association. An association founded by John 'Amnesty' Nolan in 1868 to campaign for the release of Fenian prisoners who had been sentenced to long periods of penal servitude in British prisons after the FENIAN CAMPAIGN OF 1867. Isaac BUTT was its first president in Ireland, and the association in turn supported his Home Government Association, founded in 1870. By 1872 the Amnesty Association had accomplished its goal of the release of leading Fenians such as John DEVOY and Jeremiah O'DONOVAN ROSSA.

The Amnesty Association was revived in the 1890s to campaign for the release of the latter-day Fenians imprisoned for their part in the 'dynamite' campaign of the 1880s, who were also treated with conspicuous severity in prison. The Amnesty Association of Great Britain was formed by combining various amnesty branches in August 1894, and campaigned until the last imprisoned Fenian dynamiter, Thomas J. CLARKE, was released in 1898. Maud GONNE played a leading part in this campaign.

Amongst Women. The title of a novel (1990) by John McGAHERN, taken from the Marian prayer the 'Hail Mary', the central prayer of the ROSARY. It tells the story of Michael Moran, a violent and repressive ex-IRA man who cannot adjust to life in the new Ireland, which, he feels, betrays everything he fought for in the War of Independence:

What did we get for it? A country, if you'd believe them. Some of our own johnnies in top jobs instead of a few Englishmen. More than half of my own family work in England. What was it all for? The whole thing was a cod.

Rose, Moran's second wife, and his daughters by his first wife, Sheila and Mona, who gather in Moran's house for his final illness, are the 'women' of the title. They are deeply attached to the patriarch, despite his dogmatism and narrow piety, represented by his use of the family rosary as an instrument of repression. The novel was much admired, although for Irish readers who lived through the grim 1950s it held a mirror up to a life with which they were only too familiar. The novel was successfully adapted for television, starring Tony Doyle (*see* BALLYKISSANGEL) as Moran.

Amra Choluim Cille (Old Irish, 'Praise of Colum Cille'). The earliest surviving poem in the Irish language, written soon after the death of COLUM CILLE (St Columba) in 593. It is attributed to the semi-mythical poet DALLÁN FORGAILL (*fl*.600), who paid alliterative tribute to the great champion of the FILID. The excerpt below comes from the ANNALS OF THE FOUR MASTERS in John O'DONOVAN's translation:

> Like the cure of the physician without light, like the separation of the marrow from the bone,
> Like the song of the harp without the *céis* [bass string], are we after being deprived of our noble.

Anacreon Moore. The nickname bestowed by the *Morning Post* on Tom MOORE because of his first published book, *Odes of Anacreon* (1800), bowdlerized versions of the amorous poetry of the Ionian poet (*c*.572–*c*.488 BC).

> The women tell me every day
> That all my bloom has past away
> …
> But this I know, and this I feel,
> As onward towards the tomb I steal,
> That still as death approaches nearer
> The joys of life are sweeter, dearer,
> And had I but an hour to live
> That little hour to bliss I'd give.
> 'Ode IX'

Moore's later work, including *The Poetical Works of the Late Thomas Little Esq.* (1801), confirmed his racy reputation and gave Lord Byron some cause to label him:

> 'Tis Little! The young Catullus of his day
> As sweet, but as immoral in his lay.
> *English Bards and Scotch Reviewers* (1809)

This reputation stuck with Moore, even after he had achieved establishment respectability. When his oriental verse romance *Lalla Rookh* was published on 27 May 1817 it was greeted with the following anonymous squib:

> Lalla Rookh
> Is a naughty book

> By Tommy Moore,
> Who has written four;
> Each warmer
> Than the former,
> So the most recent
> Is the least decent.

Anaisy. A HIBERNO-ENGLISH version of the word 'uneasy', but having the extra connotation 'unconcerned' or 'disinterested'. In these latter senses it becomes paradoxically the equivalent of its antonym 'easy', as in 'I'm totally anaisy whether your father hears us or not.' The original meaning can be found in the following:

> One, two, three, balance like me.
> You're quite a fairy but you have your faults,
> For your right foot is lazy, your left foot is crazy
> But don't be anaisy: I'll teach you to waltz.
> ANONYMOUS: 'Teaching McFadden to Waltz' (late 19th century)

Anam Cara (Irish, 'soul friend'). An immensely successful and influential book (1997) by Clare-born Hegelian philosopher and former priest John O'Donohue. The book draws on the kind of spirituality current in the era of the Celtic Tiger, often pre-Christian but with a New Age slant. O'Donohue attributes to the 'Celtic' belief-system the wisdom that accepts Eros; that values light and darkness equally; that is in tune with the rhythm of the day, the year and the life of man and woman; that believes in the 'primordial innocence' of the body; that uses the circle and the spiral as a 'negative capability' (*see* NEWGRANGE); that is connected to the land in a numinous way; and that knows that the eternal world is close to the natural world. He sees the language of the Celts as one of 'lyrical and reverential observation' rather than a discursive one. *Anam Cara* was a bestseller in America as well as in Ireland, its popularity helped by the persona of its iconoclastic and charismatic author:

> The Celtic tradition offers us a sense of the freshness of spirit and the world of spirit. And also a sense of the passion of the diversities within the spiritual world, a diversity of spiritual presences. And also a kind of belonging, an embrace; that you

are embraced in the great circle of belonging, in some way united with everything that is, and that you won't fall out of that.

JOHN O'DONOHUE: press interview, 1999

Anam 'on diabhal. An expression of incredulity or displeasure (for instance on hearing surprising news). In Munster HIBERNO-ENGLISH it is likely to be in the form 'Th'anam 'on diabhal' (pronounced 'thonom on deel') or 'Hanam 'on diabhal' (pronounced 'honom on deel'). The phrase literally means 'Your soul to the devil!' (Irish *D'anam don diabhal*). It is an example of a curse that has lost its original meaning, to be used instead as a general-purpose exclamation. The variant forms 'Croí 'on diabhal' ('your heart to the devil') and 'D'anam 'on diúcs', in which 'diúcs' is a euphemistic form of 'diabhal', are also used.

Anatomies of death. The description by the English poet Edmund SPENSER in *A VIEW OF THE PRESENT STATE OF IRELAND* of the survivors of the suppression of the second DESMOND REBELLION (1579–83) and the famine that followed:

> Out of every corner of the woods and glens they came, creeping forth upon their hands, for their legs could not bear them; they looked like anatomies of death, they spake like ghosts coming out of their graves; they did eat the dead carrions, happy where they could find them, yea, and one another soon after, insomuch as the very carcasses they spared not to scrape out of their graves; and if they found a plot of water-cresses or shamrocks, there they flocked as if to a feast for the time, yet not able long to continue therewithal, that in a short space there were none almost left; and a most populous and plentiful country suddenly left void of man and beast; yet sure in all that war, there perished not many by the sword, but all by the extremity of famine.

Ancient Order of Catholic Orangemen. A nickname for the Ancient Order of Hibernians (*see* AOH).

Ancient Order of Hibernians. See AOH.

AnCO. An acronym for An Chomhairle Oiliúna (literally 'the training council'), the Industrial Training Authority established under the Industrial Training Act 1967, to provide training for industries and trades. AnCO performed valuable work in promoting training initiatives and providing accreditation, especially among early school-leavers. In January 1988, AnCO was subsumed into FÁS, an acronym for Foras Áiseanna Saothair (literally 'the institute for facilities for work'), which was established in January 1988, under the Labour Services Act 1987, to provide a wide range of services to the labour market in Ireland.

Andersonstown. A strongly Nationalist area of west BELFAST, popularly known as Andytown, and deriving its Lowland Scots name from the ULSTER PLANTATION settlement. Set in the townland of Ballydownfine, it was described in the 1832 survey as 'a village consisting of eleven families'. By the mid-20th century it was a middle-class suburb, but postwar urban housing and electoral zoning tended to make it working-class, and it became an area of confrontation and actual conflict at the height of the Troubles. It is close to another volatile district, Ballymurphy, and both were under intense security surveillance from permanent British Army observation posts on the Black Mountain that overlooks them.

Andrews, Eamonn (1922–87). Broadcaster. He was born in Dublin on 19 December 1922 and educated at Synge Street Christian Brothers school. He worked as an insurance clerk, won the Irish middleweight boxing title as an amateur, and began to do sports broadcasting in 1946. He moved to London in 1950 and became a successful BBC television presenter, known particularly for the light-entertainment shows *What's My Line* and *This Is Your Life*. Andrews maintained strong professional and business links with Ireland, including his own recording studios and an interest in the GAIETY Theatre, and advised the Irish government prior to the establishment of RTÉ television in 1961. He died in London on 5 November 1987.

Andrews, C.S. (Todd) (1909–85). Revolutionary and public servant. He was born in Terenure in Dublin, where his parents had a shop (according to his own account being nicknamed 'Todd' after a character in the *Magnet*) and took part in the 1916 Rising. After taking the ANTI-TREATYITES' side in the CIVIL WAR he was interned. Afterwards he returned to live in Dublin, took a degree at University College Dublin and became an accountant. He worked for the Tourist Board and for BORD NA MÓNA, but it is for his role in closing down the WEST CLARE RAILWAY and especially the Harcourt Street line in Dublin (recently rebuilt for the LUAS system) in the early 1960s while chairman of CIÉ that he is best remembered. He published two memoirs, *Dublin Made Me* (1979), which covers the period up to 1916, and *Man of No Property* (1982), which deals with his student and working life up to the 1950s. The title of the latter derives from Wolfe TONE's remark that if the propertied would not help him, then those who had nothing to lose would do so.

Andytown. *See* ANDERSONSTOWN.

Angela's Ashes. The now almost proverbial title of a Pulitzer prize-winning memoir (1996) by Frank McCourt (b.1933). McCourt was born in Brooklyn to a Limerick-born mother, Angela Sheehan, and a father from Co. Antrim. In 1935 the American Depression sent them home to Limerick, their passages paid for by their maternal grandmother, but the family fell into even worse poverty and deprivation, losing, separately, their twin baby boys to illness the first year after their homecoming. Thereafter there is little relief: the mother is improvident, the father drinks, and when work becomes available to him in England during the Second World War, he fails to send money home and effectively disappears from the family's life:

> When I look back on my childhood I wonder how I survived at all. It was, of course, a miserable childhood. The happy childhood is hardly worth your while. Worse than the ordinary miserable childhood is the miserable Irish childhood,

and worse yet is the miserable Irish Catholic childhood.

> People everywhere brag and whimper about the woes of their early years, but nothing can compare with the Irish version: the poverty; the shiftless loquacious alcoholic father; the pious defeated mother moaning by the fire; pompous priests; bullying schoolmasters; the English and the terrible things they did to us for eight hundred long years.
> Above all – we were wet.

When this story ends, McCourt, aged 19, is about to emigrate to America. In real life he put himself through college, overcame a drink problem and became a teacher.

Angela's Ashes sold in its millions the world over, although some commentators found it sentimental, manipulative and derivative. A film, directed by Alan Parker and starring Emily Watson, Robert Carlyle and a constantly raining Limerick city, followed in 1999. The book has drawn tourists to McCourt's city, safe in the knowledge that the tenements of the 1930s no longer exist, and there is an *Angela's Ashes* walking trail. But for many patriotic Limerick citizens the book is an unmerited and unpardonable insult and books of rebuttal by local authors such as *Ashes* by Gerard Hannan (1999) and Criostóir O'Floinn's THERE IS AN ISLE (1997) have also achieved respectable sales. The sequel, *'Tis* (1999), telling the more mundane story of McCourt's years in America, was a more modest success.

Angel of the Miners. *See* JONES, MOTHER.

Angels of Monasterevin. The nickname of the 700 Irishmen who, with the support of the Catholic Church, went to Spain to fight for Franco's Nationalists in the SPANISH CIVIL WAR (1936–9). They were led by General Eoin O'DUFFY, head of the quasi-fascist BLUESHIRT movement in Ireland, and in Spain became part of the XV Bandera Irlandesa del Terico of the Spanish Foreign Legion. They returned to Ireland in 1937 having seen little action.

Angelus, the. A universal Catholic devotion celebrating the incarnation of Christ and using in its first three verses the words of the Archangel Gabriel as recorded in the first chapter of Luke, especially verses 28 and 38. The name Angelus derives from the Latin of the first verse: '*Angelus Domini nuntiavit Mariae*' ('the angel of the Lord declared unto Mary'). The Angelus is especially popular in Ireland where it is marked on national radio and television. It used to be said at 6 a.m., noon and 6 p.m., with the Angelus bell ringing a total of 18 times in three sets of 3 followed by a set of 9 – one triad for each Hail Mary and the 9 for the finishing collect. Nowadays, to the relief of many, the first bell is not heard until 8 a.m.

Anglo-Celt. An Australian term denoting an individual or group of mixed Irish-English origin or loyalties. It is also the name of a local newspaper for counties Cavan and Monaghan, published in Cavan town.

Anglo-Irish. A term that may be applied to anything resulting from the merging of Irish and English (or British). HIBERNO-ENGLISH, or Irish-English as it is now officially known, is sometimes called Anglo-Irish. Anglo-Irish literature is the accepted academic term for the body of literature written by Irish people (or at least people born and resident in Ireland) in English, and the name under which university departments worldwide and their staff apply themselves to its study.

The term Anglo-Irish was also applied, often pejoratively, to descendants of English settlers before independence, or to those who were perceived, after independence, as never having been truly assimilated in Ireland or having given their allegiance to the Irish state. It is true that many Protestants of British descent left Ireland in the 1920s, finding little to like in the Free State. The term may still occasionally be heard, used jocosely and shortened now to 'Anglo': 'Did you hear his accent? He's very Anglo. What do you expect from him?'
See also ASCENDANCY, THE.

Anglo-Irish Agreement. The entente signed by the prime minister Margaret Thatcher and the taoiseach Garret FitzGerald on 15 November 1985, which provided for the frequent consultation between the Irish and British governments on matters concerning Northern Ireland. A joint ministerial conference of British and Irish ministers was set up with a permanent secretariat at Maryfield in STORMONT. The agreement was the most significant political development in Northern Ireland since the setting up of the state. In essence it permitted the Irish government to act as brokers for the Nationalist population, and, while it emphasized that the status of Northern Ireland could be changed only by the consent of a majority, it recognized the right of Dublin's voice to be heard.
See also OUT! OUT! OUT!

Anglo-Irish Chronicles. A term for a number of writings produced mainly as justifications by English commentators after the assumption of the title 'King of Ireland' by Henry VIII (1541). Though written as if based upon personal observation they tended to be rehashings of prejudices and misconceptions about Ireland since the days of GIRALDUS CAMBRENSIS. Typical of such works were *A VIEW OF THE PRESENT STATE OF IRELAND* (1596) by Edmund SPENSER, *A Discovery of the True Causes Why Ireland Was Never Entirely Subdued* (1612) by Sir John Davies (1569–1626) and *A New Description of Ireland* (1617) by Barnabe Rich (1540–1617).

> So as I may positively conclude in the same words, which I have used in the Title of this Discourse; That untill the beginning of his Maiesties Raigne, Ireland was never entirely subdued, and brought under the Obedience of the Crown of England.
>
> SIR JOHN DAVIES: *A Discovery of the True Causes Why Ireland Was Never Entirely Subdued* (1612).

Anglo-Irish Treaty (1921). *See* TREATY, THE.

Anglo-Irish War. A term synonymous with the WAR OF INDEPENDENCE and the TAN WAR, used to describe the armed conflict between Britain and its Irish colony (1919–21), fought on the Irish side by the IRISH VOLUNTEERS (later the

Irish Republican Army or IRA). The fighting ended with the TRUCE of 9 July 1921, and the TREATY of 6 December 1921 provided for dominion status (a measure of independence) for the Irish FREE STATE within the British Commonwealth.

The first incident of the war is widely accepted as having been the attack on the Royal Irish Constabulary at SOLOHEADBEG, Co. Tipperary, led by by Seán Treacy (*see* 'TIPPERARY SO FAR AWAY') and Dan BREEN, on 21 January 1919, perhaps because that was the day of the first sitting of the first DÁIL, although there had been an earlier incident, an attack on the RIC barracks in Gortatlea, near Tralee in Co. Kerry, in which two Volunteers had been killed. Initially the RIC bore the brunt of the war, as much activity centred on the raiding of local barracks in order to secure arms; when members began to resign in large numbers, the force was supplemented in the summer of 1920 by much more formidable adversaries for the IRA, the Auxiliaries (*see* AUXIES) and the BLACK AND TANS. Up to 50,000 British soldiers were also deployed.

It was essentially a guerrilla war: IRA battalions of dozens or scores of men would wait, for weeks or even months, for an opportunity to ambush a patrol, railway station or barracks, the survivors fading back into remote areas where they would remain 'on the run' until the next action (*see* FLYING COLUMN). It was also a propaganda war: the IRA depended on the assistance of the people, more and more of whom supported them after the Auxies and Tans carried out murderous reprisals on the civilian population, especially in the second half of 1920 (*see* BALBRIGGAN, SACK OF). It was also at this time that the HUNGER STRIKE entered the lexicon of Republicanism, with the death of Terence MacSwiney after 74 days without food, on 25 October 1920.

The guerrilla leaders – among the best known were Tom BARRY, Frank AIKEN, Liam Lynch (*see* REAL CHIEF, THE), Ernie O'MALLEY and Seán McEoin (*see* BLACKSMITH OF BALLINALEE, THE) – were only minimally controlled by the minister for defence (Cathal BRUGHA) of the Dáil to which they had sworn allegiance, and it was Michael COLLINS who, as director of intelligence and propagandist extraordinary, exerted the most influence on the IRA countrywide; he was also a member of the still-powerful Irish Republican Brotherhood (IRB). Collins and his SQUAD waged a different kind of war against British Intelligence in Dublin (*see* BLOODY SUNDAY 1920). The areas that saw most action – this depended entirely on the strength of the local flying column and the quality of leadership available – were counties Cork, Kerry, Tipperary, Longford and Clare. The most celebrated action of the whole war (from the Republican point of view) was the KILMICHAEL AMBUSH of 28 November 1920.

In traditional Nationalist history the Anglo-Irish War was seen as a David-and-Goliath struggle and the IRA leaders as heroes all; the recent Northern TROUBLES and REVISIONIST historians have caused many Irish people to re-evaluate the conflict, especially the tragic role of the RIC and the use of terror and intimidation by Irish freedom fighters as well as by Tans and Auxies.

Anglo-Normans. The most significant of the invaders of Ireland. They were descendants of the Norman conquerors of England and between *c*.1170 and *c*.1270 established an incomplete but long-lasting settlement in Gaelic Ireland. Henry II, the grandson of the conquering William, had already considered the island to the west as a possible site for expansion and had sought and obtained papal sanction as early as 1155, the second year of his reign (*see* LAUDABILITER). When Dermot MAC-MURROUGH came to the court in 1167 seeking help to recover his kingdom of Leinster, Henry agreed to allow some of his opportunistic and wilder nobles, especially the so-called 'Marcher' lords from the Welsh borders, to invade Ireland in Dermot's name (*see* STRONGBOW).

In 1171 the king arrived to reassert control over his barons, and a formal system of colonization was established. Large tracts of the

country were taken, and something of the feudal organization of the manor system introduced, thereby changing the nature of those parts of the country occupied by the Anglo-Normans. Many modern Irish towns grew out of the manors, and the immigrants actively encouraged to come to Ireland formed an English colony, which, though its fortunes varied over the centuries, maintained a link with the homeland. This link with England has proved the most significant fact of Irish life until modern times. Nevertheless, by the 16th century many of the Anglo-Norman families or OLD ENGLISH in Ireland had become thoroughly Gaelicized.
See also PALE, THE.

Angus Óg. *See* AONGHUS ÓG.

An Lár. *See* LÁR, AN.

Annaghdown Tragedy. On 3 September 1822, 11 men and 8 women drowned on Lough Corrib, on their way from Annaghdown to a fair in Galway, when a rowing boat sank after one of its cargo of sheep holed a plank with its hoof. Thirteen people survived, helped by a regiment of British soldiers. A poem by Antaine Ó Raifteirí (BLIND RAFTERY) called 'Eanach Dhúin' ('Annaghdown') commemorates the tragedy:

> *Má fhaighimse sláinte beidh caint is tráchtadh*
> *Ar an méid a báthadh as Eanach Dhúin.*
> (As long as I have health I'll be relating the story
> Of all the people who were drowned in
> Annaghdown.)

Annaghmakerrig. The name of a house 3 km (2 miles) southeast of Newbliss, Co. Monaghan, once the home of Sir Tyrone Guthrie, the theatre director, and now a centre for artists, writers and musicians. The beautiful, peaceful setting with its lake and woods has proved an ideal retreat for pondering, painting and working, and the communal evening meal at which attendance is not compulsory has proved a stimulus for more than good talk. The centre was opened by Brian FRIEL in 1988 and is maintained jointly by the Arts Council of Northern Ireland (ACNI) and An CHOMHAIRLE EALAÍON.

Guthrie was born in Tunbridge Wells on 2 July 1900, the son of a doctor and grandson, on his mother's side, of the barnstorming actor Tyrone Power. Fascinated by acting but precluded from the usual parts by his great height (1.98 m / 6 ft 6 in), he became first a radio producer and then in 1933 a hair-raisingly innovative director at the Old Vic where he worked, with intermissions, until 1946, laying the foundations for Britain's National Theatre and moulding the careers of such names as Laurence Olivier, Ralph Richardson, John Gielgud, Alec Guinness, Charles Laughton and Flora Robson. There was no gap in a busy career and no geographical bounds to his work. From Helsinki to Belfast, Sydney to Tel Aviv, Guthrie produced works of classical theatre sometimes shocking – as when in 1937 Alec Guinness as Hamlet used a cigarette lighter in an Elsinore where the courtiers wore 1930s evening dress – but always accessible. He opened a theatre in a tent in Stratford, Ontario, in 1953, and in a custom-built structure in Minneapolis in 1963. He married his cousin Judith Bretherton in 1931 and she shared his somewhat nomadic life.

When his mother died in 1956 Guthrie made Annaghmakerrig his home and, concerned at the high rate of emigration, established a jam factory in Newbliss in an attempt to stem it. He died on 15 May 1971. By the terms of his will the house reverted to the state at Judith's death on 25 July 1972 and in time the Annaghmakerrig Centre came into being.

Annala Ríoghachta Éireann. *See* ANNALS OF THE FOUR MASTERS.

Anna Liffey. The personification of the River LIFFEY. The name is an anglicized version of *Abhainn na Life* (Irish, 'the river Liffey'), and in the Latinate form 'Anna Livia' was current long before Joyce rhapsodized it in *FINNEGANS WAKE*:

> O
> Tell me all about

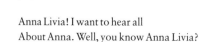

Anna Livia! I want to hear all
About Anna. Well, you know Anna Livia?
Yes, of course, we all know Anna Livia. Tell me all.

See also FLOOZIE IN THE JACUZZI.

Annals. The records of facts and dates of Irish history assigned, as the name implies, to particular years. They are a rich source of early Irish history, especially that of Gaelic Ireland, and were regularly gleaned from the introduction of Christianity up to the mid-17th century. Until the reform of the monasteries in the 12th and 13th centuries they were essentially monastic compilations and thereafter came into the care of learned secular families such as the Ó Maoilchonaires and the Ó Cléirighs. The annals were originally marginal notes in chronological tables used in the calculation of the date of Easter and the other movable feasts, and they later became part of the monastic work in the scriptoria. The principal annals are listed separately in their own entries.

Annals of Ballitore, The. An account by Mary Leadbetter (1758–1826) of life in the small Quaker village of Ballitore in Co. Kildare, where Abraham Shackleton (1697–1771) ran a famous school, attended by Edmund BURKE. The book includes a description of the local consequences of the REBELLION OF 1798.

Annals of Clonmacnoise. A record of events from earliest known times to the year 1408, containing material assembled at CLONMAC-NOISE monastery, also the source of parts of the ANNALS OF CONNACHT. An account of the career of the notorious GORMFLAITH, daughter of Flann Sinna, is also to be found in the annals. The *Annals of Clonmacnoise* survive in an English translation made in 1627 by Conall Mac Geoghan of Lismoyny, Co. Westmeath.

Annals of Connacht. A record of the events of the period 1224–1544, surviving in a manuscript written by members of the Ó Duibhgeannáin family of Kilronan, Co. Roscommon. As the name implies it is a significant source of CONNACHT history.

Annals of Inishfallen. The main source of the history of early medieval MUNSTER, recording events up to 1326. The monastery of Inishfallen was situated on the shores of the lower lake of Killarney and was the final resting place (before its transfer to the Bodleian Library in Oxford) of this work of many hands, which was begun in Emly, Co. Tipperary.

Annals of Loch Cé. A 16th-century compilation surviving in two manuscripts, the first written on a island in Lough Key in Co. Roscommon in 1588–9, containing material for the years 1014–1316 and 1462–1577, the second beginning with 1568 and taking the chronicle up to 1590. With the ANNALS OF CONNACHT they are the main source of early Connacht history.

Annals of the Four Masters. The best known of the Irish annals, properly known as *Annála Ríoghachta Éireann* ('Annals of the Kingdom of Ireland'), compiled by a Franciscan brother, Micheál Ó Cléirigh (1575–1643), and three lay scholars, his cousin Cúchoigríche Ó Cléirigh (d.1664), Fearfeasa Ó Maoilchonaire and Cúchoigríche Ó Duibhgeannain at the friary at Bundrowse, Co. Donegal, between 1632 and 1636. These were the 'four masters' of the popular title, though extra scribal help was from time to time obtained from Micheál's brother Conaire, and from Muiris, the brother of Fearfeasa Ó Maoilchonaire.

The book contains an invaluable Irish view of some of the country's darkest hours. It synthesizes the information of all the other books of annals and succeeds in removing the slur, promulgated by the ANGLO-IRISH CHRONICLES, that Ireland was a barbarous country. There is also a sense of the coming darkness that colonization had begun to signify for the Gaelic world. The standard translation is that of John O'DONOVAN. It begins:

The Age of the World, to this year of the Deluge
Forty days before the Deluge CESAIR came to
Ireland with fifty girls and three men …

The death of Colum Cille (Columba) – assigned to the wrong year – is described thus:

The Age of Christ 592. The twenty-fifth of Aedh [the HIGH KING]. Colum Cille, son of Feidhlimidh, apostle of ALBA … died in his own church in Hy in Alba, after the thirty-fifth year of his pilgrimage, on Sunday night precisely, the 9th of June.

Annals of Ulster. A manuscript incorporating material preserved in monasteries in Iona, Armagh and Derry. It is the prime source for the early medieval history of the UÍ NÉILL, and is preserved in Trinity College Dublin. It is also known as *Annála Senait*, as it was begun on the island of Senait (now Bellisle) in Upper Lough Erne, Co. Fermanagh, by Cathal MacManus Maguire (d.1498) and completed after his death. The chief scribe was Ruaidhri Ó Luinín, and it was he who made the copy that is in the Bodleian Library in Oxford.

Annegray. The site in the foothills of the Vosges Mountains near the border of Burgundy, eastern France, where St COLUMBAN established his first European monastery in 593. It was located in the Merovingian kingdom of Austrasia, which incorporated the basins of the Rhine, Moselle and Meuse rivers and had its capital at Metz. The king, Gunthram, welcomed the saint but was surprised when he chose so remote and inhospitable a place for his foundation. It had been the site of a temple to Diana and the monks used the ruins as the basis for their chapel. Columban himself preferred to live in a cave, where he often subsisted on bilberries. So popular did the foundation become that it was soon necessary to establish another house at LUXEUIL, 13 km (8 miles) to the west.

Anne Lovett Case. On 31 January 1984, a 15-year-old local girl, Anne Lovett, died after giving birth alone to a baby son in the grounds of a grotto to Our Lady near the Catholic church in Granard, Co. Longford. The baby died also. Anne Lovett's tragedy was a chastening experience for the Irish people, in the context of the for-and-against certainties surrounding the ABORTION REFERENDUMS of the previous year.

Annie. The nickname for a type of explosive

used regularly by paramilitaries during the TROUBLES. It is composed of ammonium *nitrate* (hence the nickname) and nitrobenzine mixed with diesel oil. It usually requires a separate booster charge of gelignite or SEMTEX for detonation.

Annoyed, to be. An expression used in its negative form in parts of Ulster to indicate a lack of interest in or enthusiasm for a particular item or activity, as in 'I'm not annoyed about going for a walk today' (i.e. 'I'm not keen on going for a walk today') or 'I'm not annoyed about Sinéad O'Connor' (i.e. 'I'm not keen on Sinéad O'Connor's music').

Annuities. *See* LAND ANNUITIES.

'Anois teacht an earraigh' (Irish, 'now with the coming of spring'). The opening line of one of the most famous poems in Irish, 'Contae Mhaigh Eo', or 'Cill Aodáin' as it is popularly called, by the poet Antaine Ó Raifteirí (?1784–?1835; *see* BLIND RAFTERY), known by heart by almost every Irish schoolgoer. A version of the poem was sung in SEAN-NÓS style by the great Seosamh Ó HÉANAIGH.

> *Anois teacht an earraigh beidh an lá ag dul chun síneadh*
> *Is tar éis na Féile Bríde ardoidh mé mo sheol*
> *Ó chuir mé i mo cheann é ní stopfaidh mé choíche*
> *Go seasfaidh me thíos i lár Contae Mhuigheo.*
> (With the coming of spring the days will lengthen,
> And after the feast of St Brigid I'll raise my sail.
> Once I take the notion there will be no stopping me,
> Until I find myself in the middle of County Mayo.)

'Another Life'. A weekly *Irish Times* column by journalist and naturalist Michael Viney (b.1933) begun in 1977 when Viney and his wife Ethna, also a writer, exchanged their jobs in Dublin for self-sufficiency on a smallholding in Thallabawn, near Louisburgh in Co. Mayo. Viney's blend of personal anecdote, illustrated by sketches, and acute observation of nature and the seasons has proved enduringly popular with readers.

An Phoblacht (Irish, 'the republic'). The official newspaper of the Provisional IRA. Established as a weekly in 1970, its readership is confined almost entirely to the faithful and those whose business it is to analyse all documents concerned with Republicans and Republicanism.

An Post. *See* POST, AN.

Ansbacher deposits. A tax-evasion scheme devised and operated for Ireland's richest people by Charles HAUGHEY's accountant, Des Traynor, from the 1970s until the mid-1990s. While the clients' money was nominally invested offshore (and untaxable) in a Cayman Islands company called Ansbacher Cayman, they had access to their money through the Guinness and Mahon private bank. Here their accounts were coded: accounts S8 and S9 belonged to Haughey. The Moriarty Tribunal (*see* TRIBUNALS) found that there was £38 million in the Ansbacher deposits in 1989.

Anseo (Irish, 'here!'). The answer given at roll call in schools where some little Irish is used:

> *Anseo*, meaning here, here and now,
> All present and correct,
> Was the first word of Irish I spoke.
>
> PAUL MULDOON (b.1951): 'Anseo', in *Why Brownlee Left* (1980)

Antient Concert Rooms. A concert hall in Brunswick (now Pearse) Street, Dublin, opened in 1848. It was the home of the IRISH ACADEMY OF MUSIC and the venue of concerts featuring Jenny Lind, Anton Rubinstein and Joachim. It was known for the excellence of its acoustics and features in Joyce's story 'A Mother'. It was also the venue for the first productions of the IRISH LITERARY THEATRE: Yeats's *The Countess Cathleen* (8 May 1899) and *The Heather Field* by Edward MARTYN (9 May 1899):

> Therefore she was not surprised when one day Mr Holohan came to her and proposed that her daughter should be the accompanist at a series of four grand concerts which his Society was going to give in the Antient Concert Rooms.
>
> JAMES JOYCE (1882–1941): 'A Mother', in *Dubliners* (1914)

In the 20th century it became a cinema, called in turn the Palace, the Embassy and the Academy, and it is intended to develop the site for an office block after demolition.

Antietam Creek. A battle of the American Civil War fought near Sharpsburg, Maryland, over the two days 17–18 September 1862. The first day was the bloodiest of the war with 22,719 casualties. The Irish Brigade, made up largely of Irish infantry regiments from New York, including the FIGHTING 69TH, lost 540 men.

Antiphonary of Bangor. The name given in the 18th century to the 7th-century Latin hymnary and prayer book that originated at the monastery of St COMGALL at BANGOR in present-day Co. Down. It was discovered at BOBBIO, a monastery founded by St COLUMBAN, and is now in a library in Milan. It was clearly a working book to be used by the monks in their community prayers and services. Three of the hymns were in praise of Irish saints, PATRICK, Comgall and Camelack, a saint of whom nothing else is known. Two other poems are written in praise of Bangor, one naming its first 14 abbots. One modern scholar has suggested that one of the hymns was written by Columban himself, and the Communion hymn '*Sancti Venite*' (Latin, 'Come, holy ones') may still be heard 13 centuries after its composition. If the BOOK OF KELLS is the glory of Iona, the *Antiphonary* similarly celebrates Bangor.

Anti-Treatyites. The general term for those who opposed the Anglo-Irish TREATY of December 1921. This opposition led to the outbreak of the CIVIL WAR.
See also CUMANN NA NGAEDHEAL; IRREGULARS.

Antrim (Irish *Aontruim*, 'single ridge'). A county of Ulster set in the northeast corner of Ireland with a population of 642,000 (1981) and an area of 2830 sq km (1092 sq miles). The county was named after the town of Antrim (population 23,500), the original name of which in Irish was *Aontreibh* (pronounced 'ain trev'), 'single house': this referred to an early monastery, now marked by a round tower known to locals as the 'steeple'. (The later name

Aontruim describes the long unbroken Antrim plateau.) The county is bounded by the North Channel on the east and north, and by Lough Neagh to the south. The Bann river forms its western boundary with Co. Derry. Antrim is noted for Bushmills distillery (*see* BLACK BUSH), the remarkable basaltic GIANT'S CAUSEWAY and the NINE GLENS.

Antrim, Battle of. A battle (7 June 1798) during the REBELLION OF 1798 in which a force of United Irishmen (mostly Presbyterians) under the command of Henry Joy MCCRACKEN were defeated by British troops. McCracken was later executed in Belfast.

Antrim Coast Road. A scenic route, with re-markable views of Argyll and the Isles, that follows each indentation of the east coast of Co. ANTRIM. The road was begun in 1834 by a Scots engineer named William Bald to a design by Sir Charles Lanyon (1813–89), the architect of Queen's University Belfast (QUB) and Crumlin Road jail. Until that time the famous NINE GLENS had tended to be isolated, rather inaccessible communities. The project began as a famine-relief scheme, and it gave access to the sea to each of the glens. Only in two places was it necessary to tunnel through a headland. It is now a popular tourist attraction stretching 100 km (60 miles) from Larne to Portrush, where it forms part of the CAUSEWAY COAST.

Anú. The Celtic mother figure, cognate with DANA[1].

Anúna. *See* RIVERDANCE.

Any time is Urney time. *See* URNEY TIME.

Aobh. The mother of Fionnuala, Aedh, Fiachra and Conn, known collectively as the Children of LIR (*see* FIONNUALA).

AOH. The familiar form of the name of the Ancient Order of Hibernians, an Irish-American fraternal society, founded in America in 1836 to succour newly arrived immigrants and maintain links within the Irish commu-nity. Originally known as the Friendly Sons of Erin, it was usually non-violent, though it may

have shared members with more radical groups like CLAN NA GAEL, especially during the period of FENIAN activity. Its members defended Old St Patrick's Cathedral in New York from attacks by the KNOW-NOTHING PARTY in 1850.

The AOH began to gather members in Ire-land and Great Britain after 1900, when the Belfast Nationalist leader Joseph Devlin (*see* WEE JOE) made it a highly successful political machine, its membership peaking at 60,000 in 1909. Regarded as insufficiently radical by SINN FÉIN and merely as a Catholic version of the ORANGE ORDER by non-members, it was the main rallying point for northern Nationalists after the setting up of Northern Ireland in 1921. Indeed with its green collarettes and banners, and the marching bands parading on 15 August (the Catholic Feast of the Assumption), it seemed closely to ape Orange practice, leading to the gibing nickname the Ancient Order of Catholic Orangemen. Since the beginning of the Ulster TROUBLES its numbers have severely contracted and it functions now as a business network with a mainly charitable agenda. In America it continues as a sentimental emigrant organization.

Aoibheall. The queen before whose court the protagonist of Brian Merriman's *CÚIRT AN MHEÁ-OÍCHE* (*The Midnight Court*) is brought to answer charges of celibacy and neglect of love:

> 'Twas Munster's friend and Craglee's queen,
> Aeval, of heart and spirit clean,
> Who has been picked to try and see
> If she can find a remedy.
>> Part I; translated by David Marcus (b.1924)

Aoibheall (which is a version of the Irish word *aoibheann*, 'beautiful') was the *bean sidhe* ('banshee/fairy woman') or titulary goddess of the DAL CAIS dynasty of counties Clare and Limerick who had her residence at Craglea, where the action of the poem takes place. Two placenames, Tobereevul (*Tobar Aoibhill*, 'well of Aoibheall') and Craganeevul ('crag of Aoib-heall') bear her name. Folklore relates that as BRIAN BORU knelt in his tent and prayed for the victory of the Dalcassians in the Battle of CLONTARF, he rejected entreaties to ride to safety: 'for Aibhill of Crag Liath came to me last night, and she told me that I should be killed today.'

Aoife[1]. The younger sister of AOBH. Aoife became the archetypal wicked stepmother of the children of LIR and turned them into swans (*see* FIONNUALA). When BODB DEARG, her foster-father, discovered her crime he turned her into a demon of the air.

Aoife[2]. The sister of CÚCHULAINN's martial arts instructor SCÁTHACH. Both were princesses of the Land of Shadows (the OTHERWORLD) and deadly enemies. Hearing of a combat to the death between the sisters, Cúchulainn entered the Land of Shadows, against Scáthach's advice, and was challenged in her place. In the fight Aoife shattered his sword and was about to kill him when he distracted her attention by shouting that her horse and chariot had fallen. (In his wily way he had previously discovered from Scáthach that these were the things Aoife held dearest.) He seized her and offered to spare her life if she made peace with her sister. Cúchulainn and Aoife briefly became lovers and she bore him a son called CONLAF, though the father did not know of his existence. Years later, when he engaged in combat with a young stranger, he discovered that the warrior he had killed was his only son.

Aonach (Irish *óenach*). An assembly of the people of a TUATH for political purposes and also for athletics contests, horse racing and commerce. In Old Irish law there is mention of kings making publicly binding announcements of wars, treaties and tributes at *óenig* (plural of *óenach*). On the site of the *óenach* there were pedlars, foodsellers and performers such as singers and storytellers. The modern Irish word for 'fair' is also *aonach*.

Aonach Tailteann (Irish *Óenach Tailten*). The most famous of the *óenig* (*see* AONACH), an annual week-long assembly for the purpose of athletic and racing contests held in Teltown,

Co. Meath, in the kingdom of TARA. In legend, the Tailteann Games, as they became known, were established by one of the Tuatha dé Danann kings, LUGH, in about the 19th century BC, and are thought to have been named after a Celtic goddess. They opened on 1 August, LUGHNASA, the feast of Lugh (*Lú-násadh* means 'Lugh's fair') and it is believed that the custom survived until the Anglo-Norman invasion of the 12th century.

A modern version of the Tailteann Games had been bruited as early as the 1880s, and in 1924 the Free State government and the GAA held games in CROKE PARK (2–17 August). The event – which included shooting, cycling and motorcycle races as well as Gaelic games – was repeated in 1928 and 1932. They are now held annually as school events.

See also RÁS TAILTEANN.

Aondacht na Gaeilge. *See* GAELIC UNION.

Aonghus Óg (also **Angus** or **Oenghus**). The name of several characters in Irish mythology, but primarily the Celtic god of love. *Óg* signifies 'young', and he is seen as a benevolent deity, anxious to right the wrongs perpetrated by evil adversaries. He is the marriage-broker for ÉTAIN and MIDIR and regularly comes to the aid of his foster-son DIARMAID UA DUIBHNE and his lover GRÁINNE in their flight from FIONN MAC CUMHAIL. His residence is at BRUGH NA BÓINNE beside the River Boyne and it was to this palace he took his own lover Cáer, the swan maiden, when he had successfully identified her from among 150 other swans at SAMHAIN, the one day in the year when she was to be found.

Aosdána. A group of artists in receipt of pensions from the Irish government. The scheme was set up in 1983 and is administered by the Arts Council of Ireland (*see* CHOMHAIRLE EALAÍON, AN). Its 200 members are entitled to an annual tax-free *cnuas* ('subsidy'); the sum in 1998 was £8500. The term derives from the old Irish social class ÁES DÁNA (literally 'men of art'). The five most highly regarded members are each elected as a SAOI ('wise person').

Apology. The unreliable and ghosted six-volume autobiography of 'Blue-eyed Bellamy', the actress George Anne Bellamy, chief rival at Drury Lane to Peg WOFFINGTON and Mrs Cibber (1714–66). She was born in north Co. Dublin, *c.*1727, the illegitimate child of Lord Tirawley and a Miss Seal, who opportunely married a sea captain called Bellamy before the birth. Tirawley acknowledged her and was, according to his daughter, inadvertently responsible for her curious combination of forenames: apparently he wished her to be called Georgiana but the minister presiding at the baptism misheard and christened her George Anne. Though such a combination of names was not a drawback at a period in theatre when 'breeches parts' were the rage, Bellamy in fact did better in romantic roles because of her good looks. She was a memorable Juliet to Garrick's Romeo in 1744, thus setting up enmity between her and Woffington for more than just thespian reasons, both being rivals for Garrick's affections. Her off-stage life was scandalous even by the standards of the time, with bigamy added to the usual misdemeanours. As she grew older and lost her beauty she found it hard to find work; a season in SMOCK ALLEY in 1780 proved disastrous and the publication of *Apology* in 1785 merely postponed the penury in which she died in London on 10 February 1788.

Apostle of Temperance, the. The popular title of Father Theobald Mathew (1790–1856), who did much to prevent alcohol addiction in Ireland. Born near Cashel, Co. Tipperary, he was ordained for the Capuchin Order in 1814 and worked among the poor of Cork for 25 years. Approached by some interdenominational philanthropists to lead a temperance society, on 10 April 1838 he signed a pledge of total abstinence with the words, 'Here goes in the name of God!'

So successful was the Irish Total Abstinence Society with its temperance clubs and libraries that between 1838 and 1844 the government revenue from liquor duty fell from £1.4 to £0.8 million, and there was also a remarkable reduction in the level of crime. In 1844 the total registered membership was 5,500,000.

Father Mathew was awarded a civil list pension of £300 a year in 1847. He retired in 1851 and lived with his brother in Cobh (Queenstown), suffering from premature senility for some years before his death. He is commemorated by statues in Dublin's O'Connell Street and in Cork (*see* STATUE, THE).

Apprentice Boys. A Protestant political society founded in 1814, analogous to the ORANGE ORDER and named after the 13 London apprentices who symbolically shut the gates of Derry against the Jacobite troops of Lord Antrim in December 1688. The brotherhood, which has members in Ulster, Britain and Canada, holds marches each year on 18 December and 12 August to celebrate the shutting of the gates and the relief of the city that marked the end of the siege. New members must be initiated within the circle of Derry Walls and, unlike the pattern of the Orange Order to which many belong, their collarettes and other insignia are coloured 'Derry crimson' in memory of the bloody flag that flew during the siege. As Charlotte Elizabeth Tonna (1790–1846), the siege's laureate, puts it in her poem 'No Surrender' (1825):

> And Derry's sons alike defy
> Pope, traitor or pretender;
> And peal to heaven their 'prentice cry
> Their patriot 'No surrender'.

The violence that followed the celebration on 12 August 1969 marked a serious escalation of the Northern Ireland TROUBLES.

See also COMBER LETTER, THE; LUNDY; MAIDEN CITY; DERRY, SIEGE OF; TWELFTH OF AUGUST.

'Aqua Vitae'. A paean of praise for Irish WHISKEY written by Richard Stanihurst (1547–1618) in his Irish chapters, *De Rebus in Hibernis Gestis* (Latin, 'concerning Ireland's past'), of Raphael Holinshed's *Chronicles* (1577). He begins with a statement of need:

> The soile of Ireland is very low and waterish,
> including diverse little islands, invironed with lakes

and marrish. Highest hills have standing pooles in their tops. Inhabitants, especially new come, are subject to distillations, rheumes and fleures. For remedie whereof they use an ordinary drinke of Aqua Vitae, being so qualified in the making, that it drieth more and also inflameth lesse than other hot confections doo.

Among many other cordial effects, the spirit

... sloweth age, it strengeneth youth, it helpeth digestion, it cutteth flegme, it abandoneth melancolie, it relishes the heart, it lighteneth the mind, it quickeneth the spirits, it cureth the hydropsie, it healeth the stangurie, it pounceth the stone, it expelleth grauell, it puffeth way all ventositie, it keepeth and preserueth the head from whirling, the eies from dazeling, the toong from lisping, the mouthe from maffling, the teeth from chattering, and the throte from ratling; it keepeth the weasen from stifling, the stomach from wambling, and the heart from swelling, the belly from wirtching, the guts from rumbling, the hands from shivering and the sinewes from shrinking, the veins from crumpling, the bones from aking & the marrow from soaking.

The conclusion is entirely proper: '... trulie it is a sovereigne liquor, if it be orderlie taken.'

Aran Islands. An archipelago of three rocky islands, Inishmore (*Inis Mór*, 'big island'), Inishmaan (*Inis Meáin*, 'middle island') and Inisheer (*Inis Oírr*, 'east island') running in descending order of size roughly southeast in the outer waters of Galway Bay. Their bare ridges of limestone seem incapable of sustaining life, yet they have been inhabited since prehistoric times.

In mythology the Aran Islands were held to be the place of retreat of the FIRBOLGS after their defeat at the Battle of MAGH TUIREADH (Moytura). The first Irish monastery was founded on Inishmore by St ENDA in the 5th century, and the islands continued to play a significant part in Christianity throughout the succeeding centuries. It was to Aran, as the group is collectively called, that W.B. Yeats sent J.M. SYNGE to find his true literary voice. The account of his five summer visits (1898–1902), during which he found the language

that suited his dramatic purposes, is given in *The ARAN ISLANDS* (1907). The film *Man of Aran* (1934), by the 'father of the documentary', the American Robert J. Flaherty (1884–1951), provided an unforgettable picture of the life of the islanders with their frail but buoyant tarred CURRACHS and their handmade fields. Now with a regular boat and air service, the islands are a leading Irish holiday destination.

Aran Islands, The. The main prose and first completed work of John Millington SYNGE (1907) describing in fascinating detail his life on the islands during five summers (1898–1902). Most of the total of 18 weeks was spent on Inishmaan, where Irish was the norm and where, though he was friendly with the inhabitants, he knew he remained an outsider. Synge played his fiddle at the islanders' dances and became enamoured of a local girl, but the chief purpose of his sojourns was to find an appropriate language for the plays he was about to write. *RIDERS TO THE SEA* (1904) was set on Inishmaan, and it was there that he heard the tale from his mentor Pat Dirane that was to give him the plot of *IN THE SHADOW OF THE GLEN* (1903).

Aran knitwear. An Aran jumper is traditionally knitted of homespun undyed wool, with panels of several different kinds of stitches. Because the wool of the jumpers contained so much oil, keeping the water out and the heat in, they were very well suited to fishing and other maritime pursuits of the Aran islanders. The stitches include: blackberry or Trinity stitch, in which three stitches become one and one becomes three, symbolizing the Holy Trinity; the tree of life, symbolizing a long life; moss or diamonds, representing wealth; honeycomb, a tribute to the bees; and various cables and knots deriving from seafaring. Families had their own patterns or combinations of stitches, and it was said that if a fisherman was lost at sea his body could be recognized, even after a long interval, by the jumper he wore. In J.M. Synge's *RIDERS TO THE SEA* (1904) a young girl identifies the body of her fisherman brother by the stitches in the stockings he is wearing, stockings she herself had knitted. Aran stitches have formed the basis of high-fashion garments by Irish designers, and Aran jumpers, perennially popular with tourists, are in vogue as a high-street fashion from time to time.

Áras an Uachtaráin (Irish, 'the abode of the president'). The official residence of the president of the Republic of Ireland, in PHOENIX PARK, Dublin. At its core is a small lodge built in 1751, which was purchased for the lord lieutenant in 1782 and enlarged to become his official residence. It was altered and further enlarged several times during the 19th century. The ornate plaster ceiling in the reception room showing Jupiter and the Four Elements was successfully transferred from MESPIL HOUSE in 1952. The attack of the INVINCIBLES took place in the driveway on 6 May 1882. It ceased to be the viceregal lodge with the appointment of Tim Healy as governor-general in 1922, when it became known as the governor-general's residence (or, more informally, as Uncle Tim's Cabin). It remained the governor-general's residence during the periods of office of Healy's successors James McNeill (1869–1938), who served 1928–32, and Dónal Ua Buachalla (1866–1963), who held the post 1932–8, largely as a figurehead, while Fianna Fáil diminished the significance of the office. The building assumed its Irish title with the appointment of Douglas Hyde (*see* CRAOIBHÍN AOIBHINN) as Ireland's first president in 1938.

Arbuckle, James. *See* HIBERNICUS.

Arch. A traditional feature of the celebrations of the ORANGE ORDER, APPRENTICE BOYS, ROYAL BLACK INSTITUTION and, to a lesser extent, the AOH. The arches are decorated with the same symbols as the BANNERS that are carried on the marches. In earlier times they were decorated with flowers, and streets, even those not on the route of the march, would vie with each other to make their arch the most elaborate and striking. Now they are to be found outside local halls, at points along the route

and at the entrance to the FIELD. The predominant colours of the pictures and decorations are orange, red, black and royal purple (with green for the AOH).

> I once helped to sell minerals and sandwiches from a roadside stall near the Field, which was being run for some sort of charity. That meant leaving Belfast at 3 a.m., pushing a handcart full of food and drink, and returning near midnight when nothing remained of the day's celebrations but the loyal arches across the streets and a lot of orange peel in the gutters.
>
> JOHN HEWITT (1907–87) as 'Campbell Barton': 'An Arch Purple Past', in *The Bell* (May 1943)

Ardagh Chalice. An 8th-century chalice regarded as one of the most beautiful of all the artefacts surviving from the golden age of Irish religious art. It can be seen in the NATIONAL MUSEUM OF IRELAND in Dublin. The chalice and a brooch were found in a RING FORT in Ardagh, Co. Limerick, in 1868 by a local man named Quin. Bishop Butler of Limerick bought it from the finder and presented it to the ROYAL IRISH ACADEMY in 1878. Along with the Cross of CONG and the TARA BROOCH it is one of the most recognizable of the national treasures and is sometimes used to represent the country itself. The prestigious SAM MAGUIRE CUP is a copy of the Ardagh Chalice.

Ardán. One of the sons of Usna who is killed with his brother NAOISE at EMAIN MACHA.

Ardchomhairle (Irish, 'supreme council'). The name, pronounced 'ard core-ly', for the executive council of some Irish political parties, including SINN FÉIN.

Ardee. The Co. Louth town now taken as the site of CÚCHULAINN's last battle. The Irish name Baile Átha Fhirdhia ('town of Ferdia's ford') recalls the myth of the Battle of the FORD. Ardee served as the headquarters of JAMES II while he was in Ireland.

Ardens sed virens (Latin, 'burning yet flourishing'). The motto of the PRESBYTERIAN church in Ireland, recalling the burning bush which though aflame was not destroyed, an obvious symbol of suffering and endurance. The burning bush features in Moses' encounter on 'Horeb, the mountain of God':

> And the angel of the Lord appeared unto him in a flame of fire out of the midst of a bush: and he looked, and, behold, the bush burned with fire, and the bush was not consumed.
>
> Exodus 3:2

The symbol was first used by French HUGUE-NOTS in the 16th century and adopted as a seal by the Church of Scotland. The words of the motto, dating from *c*.1842, are attributed to the Rev. William Gibson (1808–67) of the Rosemary Street church of the First Presbyterian Church in central Belfast.

Ardfert. One of the monastic foundations of St BRENDAN THE VOYAGER, near Tralee, Co. Kerry. The village now contains an important group of religious buildings, including a partially restored 12th-century cathedral, a graveyard, the ruins of an early Romanesque church that the cathedral replaced, and the ruins of Temple na Griffin, named after the griffins sculpted inside it. Nearby are the ruins of a Franciscan friary founded by the local Norman leaders, the Fitzmaurices, and built between the 13th and the 15th centuries.

Ard fheis (Irish, 'high festival'). A term (pronounced 'ord-esh') that is now applied to the annual conference of certain political parties, namely FIANNA FÁIL, FINE GAEL and SINN FÉIN. These are now televised and increasingly stage-managed events, although not always without incident. The most famous such incident of recent decades was Patrick HILLERY's robust defence of Jack Lynch and attack on Lynch's enemies in the Fianna Fáil *ard fheis* of January 1971, the first since the ARMS CRISIS of 1970: as Hillery was speaking, Kevin BOLAND's supporters heckled him. In exasperation he shouted, 'You can have Kevin Boland but you can't have Fianna Fáil.' The passion of this crucial moment was captured by the television cameras.

Ardilaun, 1st Lord. *See* GUINNESS.

Ard Macha. *See* ARMAGH.

Ardmore. A seaside town in Co. Waterford, with early Christian remains, including a cathedral and ROUND TOWER. The earliest foundation here was by St Declan, who, it is claimed, was Bishop of Munster before the arrival of St PATRICK. The round tower, also probably 12th century and one of the best preserved in Ireland, is 29 m (95 ft) high. Ardmore had its own bishop from 1170, and the cathedral was built at the end of that century. In 1642, 154 Confederate soldiers (*see* CONFEDERATE WAR) took refuge in the church and tower; they surrendered to the English but 117 were hanged there and then. Near the church is a small oratory, which has traditionally been regarded as the burial place of St Declan.

Ardnacrusha. A hydroelectric plant constructed on the River SHANNON in 1925–9, and still generating electricity. The project was masterminded by an engineer, Thomas McLoughlin, and the facility, controversially, was constructed by the German firm Siemens. The scheme came under the authority of minister for industry and commerce Patrick MCGILLIGAN (1889–1979), and was given state aid of £10,000 under the Electricity (Supply) Act of 1927, somewhat unjustifiably earning the nickname 'Mr McGilligan's White Elephant'. Every Irish child until the 1980s was able to chant the names of the four Irish hydroelectric generating stations: Ardnacrusha on the Shannon, Iniscarra on the Lee, Kathleen Falls on the Erne, and Poulaphooka on the Liffey.

Ardoyne. An economically deprived area of north Belfast, the scene of the burning of Catholic houses in 1969 by Loyalists. It is close to the Protestant areas of Woodvale and Ligoniel and became a defensive NO-GO AREA until these were dismantled in 1972. It has remained a strongly Nationalist and Republican enclave and the area has been the scene of frequent confrontations. Most recently the children attending the Holy Cross primary school, whose route lay through the Protestant Glenbryn housing estate, had to run a gauntlet of jeers, stones and missiles of all kinds.

Ard rí. *See* HIGH KING.

'Are ye right there, Michael?' The title and chorus line of a comic song by Percy FRENCH about an eventful day on the route of the WEST CLARE RAILWAY from Ennis to Kilkee. The words refer to an egregious engine driver, Michael Talty. According to the conceit of the song, a passenger on the tardy and temperamental train might 'hear a guard sing this refrain':

Are ye right there, Michael, are ye right?
Have ye got the parcel there for Mrs White?
If ye haven't, oh begorrah, say it's comin' down
  tomorrow,
And it might now, Michael, so it might.

Argenta. A wooden ship of American manufacture that was used as a holding centre for interned Nationalists in Northern Ireland in the 1920s. Dawson Bates, the flinty Unionist minister of home affairs, used the excuse of the killing of William Twaddell on 20 May 1922 to arrest 300 men and intern them without trial, using his SPECIAL POWERS ACT. The ship, originally berthed in the centre of Belfast Lough, was moved into Larne Lough, and the old Larne workhouse was used for overspill. The *Argenta* was regarded as cheaper and more secure than any of the land centres, but conditions were appalling, resulting in cases of pneumonia and tuberculosis.

The sense that the Nationalists of Belfast had been deprived of their only defence at a time when the UVF, many of them in B-SPECIAL uniforms, were engaged in an anti-Catholic pogrom, greatly increased tensions. During that summer sectarian troubles were responsible for the deaths of 257 Catholics and 157 Protestants. By 1926 all the *Argenta*'s inmates (in all 600 men had been 'lifted') had been released or transferred, and the ship was scuttled.

Argue and Phibbs. The authentic if scarcely credible name of a firm of solicitors in Teeling Street, Sligo.

Arianism. The 4th-century heresy that denied that Christ was co-equal with God the Father. It took its name from Arius of Alexandria

(*c.*250–336) and reappeared in the early years of the 19th century, causing a serious schism in Irish PRESBYTERIANISM.

Arigna. A small but celebrated coal mine on the borders of counties Roscommon and Leitrim. Until it closed in 1990, some 300 men – grandfathers, fathers and sons – were employed to mine a thin seam of coal under the rock, which was used to fuel the power station at nearby Lough Allen on the River Shannon.

Aristocratic Home Rule. A term invented by the Irish historian Edmund Curtis (1881–1943) to describe the politics of Ireland during the 15th-century WARS OF THE ROSES, when the English of Ireland considered the possibility of independence from the crown. A declaration made at the Irish Parliament at Drogheda in 1460 insisted that, 'the land of Ireland is and at all times had been corporate of itself.' The lordship of Ireland in that period was notably complex, but Curtis was probably correct in his postulation that some kind of 'home rule' sentiment existed. It was quickly discouraged on the accession of Henry VII (1457–1509) in 1485, and any hope of separation disappeared with the assumption by Henry VIII (1491–1547) of the kingship of Ireland in 1541.
See also FIT TO RULE ALL IRELAND.

Arkle (1957–70). A celebrated steeplechaser born on a Co. Dublin farm and named by his owner, the Duchess of Westminster, after a mountain on her estate in Sutherland in the far northwest of Scotland. He was ridden by Irish jockey Pat Taaffe (1930–92). Dubbed 'Lord of Cheltenham' because he won that course's Gold Cup on three successive occasions, Arkle was an Irish sporting idol. A full-time secretary was employed to answer his fan mail, which was addressed simply to 'Arkle, Ireland'. He won 22 of his 26 steeplechases between 1962 and 1966 (the televised clashes between him and English steeplechaser Mill House were legendary), but finished second in his final race, the George VI Gold Cup on St Stephen's Day 1966 and was discovered to have injured the pedal bone of his foot. He was retired at 9 and put down in 1970 at the age of 13, crippled by arthritis. His memory is celebrated by the Arkle Chase at Cheltenham's March meeting. *See also* SHERGAR; STEEPLECHASING.

Ark of the Covenant. Between 1899 and 1902 the Hill of TARA became the focus of a series of clashes between cultural Nationalists – notably Maud GONNE and Arthur GRIFFITH – and members of the British-Israel Movement, an association founded in the UK by a retired Anglo-Indian judge, Edward Wheeler Bird. The British-Israel Association of Ireland was established in Dublin on 17 March 1897. Members believed that the Anglo-Saxon race was descended from the lost tribes of Israel and that it was the members' duty to retrieve the Ark of the Covenant, which had been buried on the Hill of Tara, according to them the new or 'resuscitated' Jerusalem. The local landlord, Gustavus Villiers Briscoe, turned a blind eye to the excavations of the British Israelites.

For cultural nationalists Tara was symbolic of a native high kingship (*see* HIGH KING); it was described by Douglas Hyde, George Moore and W.B. Yeats, in a letter to the London *Times*, as 'probably the most consecrated spot in Ireland'. Maud Gonne and Griffith visited the Hill of Tara on Christmas Day 1900 to survey the extent of the damage done by the excavation, and Gonne wrote in a subsequent article in *The United Irishman*:

> I seemed to see shuddering, misty forms gazing curiously at us. Weird processions wound round the raths where the palaces had stood. Some tossed white arms as they moved in rhythmic circles.

The case became a cause célèbre; the press in Ireland joined with professional archaeologists and the cultural Nationalists to oppose the excavations of the British Israelites. In the end the latter were obliged to desist.

Arlo. A topographical transference of the name of the Glen of Aherlow to the summit of Galtymore in Co. Tipperary by Edmund SPENSER in his *Two Cantos of Mutabilitie* (1594):

> That was, to weet, upon the highest heights
> Of Arlo-hill (who knows not Arlo-hill?)
> That is the highest head in all men's sight.

As P.W. Joyce notes in his book *The Wonders of Ireland* (1911), '... the name Arlo was applied to the hill only by Spenser himself, who borrowed it from the adjacent valley.'

Armagh (Irish *Ard Macha*, 'MACHA's height'). The name of Ulster's smallest county (1250 sq km / 484 sq miles) and of its county town, the ecclesiastical capital of Ireland. The county is known as the 'orchard of Ireland', apples reputedly having been cultivated there since 3000 BC, and there is a tradition that St PATRICK himself planted an apple tree near the city. The name came from one of several Machas in Celtic mythology, probably Macha Mong Ruadh ('Macha of the Red Locks'). She is said to have founded the city *c.*370 BC, and her name is also to be found in EMAIN MACHA, a hill-fort 3 km (2 miles) west of the city (*see* NAVAN FORT). Its importance as a political and ritual centre made it the most appropriate site for the principal Patrician church, and Patrick himself became Archbishop of Armagh. Thereafter Armagh became one of the most important centres of religion and learning in Ireland, and it is now the primatial see for both the Catholic and Anglican churches:

> Armagh: where two cathedrals sit upon opposing hills like the horns of a dilemma.
>
> SAM HANNA BELL: *In Praise of Ulster* (radio broadcast 1960)

See also BOOK OF ARMAGH.

Armagh Outrages. A concerted campaign of Protestant attacks on Catholic households, mainly in Armagh but also in Tyrone and Monaghan, in the aftermath of the Battle of the DIAMOND (1795) and the foundation of the ORANGE ORDER. The attacks continued into 1796 and resulted in 7000 Catholics fleeing to areas of north Connacht, where some were willing participants in the RACES OF CASTLEBAR in 1798. The governor of Armagh, Lord Gosford, at a meeting of local magistrates on 28 December 1795, condemned the attacks:

The only crime which the wretched objects of this ruthless affray are charged with, is a crime of easy proof; it is simply a profession of the Roman Catholic faith ...

It was clear, however, that many of his listeners and a majority of local landowners actively encouraged this manifestation of Protestant supremacy.

Armalite. The generic name for the US M-16 automatic assault rifle, firing a 0.223-calibre round. It is a light (3.2 kg/7 lb) rustless automatic with armour-piercing bullets and accuracy up to 365 m (400 yds). It was the standard IRA rifle until it was replaced by the AK-47, by which time it had become a legend and had generated such graffiti as:

> God made the Catholics
> And the Armalite made them equal.

Armalite and the ballot box, the. The strategy of SINN FÉIN from 1981 until the IRA ceasefire of 1997. It was first articulated by Danny Morrison (b.1953), the party's director of publicity, at the party's annual conference (ARD FHEIS) in the Mansion House in Dublin on 31 October 1981. Earlier that year the hunger-striker Bobby SANDS had won a Westminster seat in the constituency of Fermanagh–South Tyrone, and the leadership believed that it was possible to pursue an electoral strategy at the same time as the ARMED STRUGGLE. The phrase was not prepared and polished beforehand by Morrison, as is popularly believed, but was a last-minute inspiration. It quickly came to be misquoted. What Morrison actually said was:

> Who here really believes that we can win the war through the ballot box? But will anyone here object if, with a ballot paper in one hand and the Armalite in the other, we take power in Ireland?

Armed struggle. The policy of the Provisional IRA and other Republican paramilitaries in the recent TROUBLES to set Ulster (and Ireland) free from British dominance. The phrase had an almost Biblical strength and its more hard-line adherents would countenance no political involvement other than the essentially dis-

missive policy of ABSTENTIONISM. The policy was replaced in the 1980s by the two-pronged approach of the ARMALITE AND THE BALLOT BOX, itself abandoned with the Provisional IRA's 1997 ceasefire.

Armour of Ballymoney. The name by which the liberal Presbyterian clergyman and HOME RULE advocate James Brown Armour (1841–1928) was popularly known. He was born in Lisboy, Ballymoney, Co. Antrim, on 20 January 1841 and after graduation from the Queen's Colleges of Belfast and Cork was called in 1869 to be minister of Second Ballymoney where he served until his retirement in 1925. He also lectured in classics at Magee College, Derry (1885–1908), to supplement his income. Politically he followed the strong north Antrim liberal tradition and by 1893 began to support Home Rule, arguing for self-government with full protection for the Presbyterian Church. He made these views public at a special meeting of the GENERAL ASSEMBLY on 15 March 1893. His speech was interrupted by jeering and shouting and his amendment was defeated by a large majority. He was ostracized by the Presbyterian Church in general, but his congregation remained faithful.

Armour continued to assert liberal views about TENANT RIGHT, Catholic education and the CHURCH OF IRELAND's political monopoly. Between 1912 and 1922 Armour, now old and unwell, deplored the Ulster Unionist arming, the Nationalist desertion of Home Rule for Republicanism and the PARTITION of Ireland. He died of pneumonia on 25 January 1928 and was mourned by independent Presbyterians and Catholics. Joe Devlin (WEE JOE) declared, 'A great light has gone out in Ulster,' but only a few Presbyterians accepted then (or accept now) his view expressed at the assembly in May Street Church, Belfast, in March 1893 that Unionism:

> ... sold its people into bondage, and through a senseless fear of Romanism sacrificed the power and progress of true Presbyterianism for generations.

Arms and the Man. A play by George Bernard Shaw (GBS), designated by him as 'pleasant' and subtitled 'an anti-romantic comedy', first staged on 21 April 1894 at the Avenue Theatre, London, with financial backing from MISS HORNIMAN. It satirizes both love and war, taking its apt title from the opening words of the *Aeneid* (29–19 BC) of Virgil (70–19 BC):

> *Arma virumque cano.*
>
> (I sing of arms and the man.)

It is set during the Serbo-Bulgarian War of 1885–6 and the anti-hero is Bluntschli, the Swiss mercenary soldier who carries chocolate creams rather than bullets in his cartridge case. He is contrasted with the inexperienced but warlike Bulgarian Sergius. Raina, Sergius's fiancée, finds Bluntschli in her bedroom, and after a lot of Shavian dialogue, allows him to escape, later choosing him over Sergius. It was obvious material for a musical comedy and was reconstituted as *The Chocolate Soldier* (original title *Der tapfere Soldat*) by Oskar Straus (1870–1954) in 1908. The most famous song, 'My Hero', which preserved some of Shaw's irony, is still sung unwittingly as a straightforward love song.

Arms Crisis. On 6 May 1970 two Fianna Fáil government ministers, Charles HAUGHEY and Neil Blaney (1922–95), were dismissed by the taoiseach Jack LYNCH for allegedly conspiring with others to use public funds to import guns for the IRA in order to defend Catholic communities in Belfast after the start of the Northern TROUBLES. This was the most serious constitutional crisis since the early years of the state and reflected a split in the Fianna Fáil party – mirroring divided opinion among the general public – about the proper approach to take in supporting the Nationalist minority in Northern Ireland, at that time under threat from Loyalists and a partisan police force. Subsequent controversy has centred on how much Lynch and his minister for defence, James Gibbons, knew at the time and whether the sacked ministers genuinely believed they were acting with the sanction of the government.

Later that year Haughey and Blaney were charged, along with Captain James Kelly (1929–2003), an intelligence officer in the Irish army, John Kelly, a Northern Republican, and Albert Luykx, a Belgian businessman, with conspiring to import arms. These trials were known as the Arms Trials. All the defendants were acquitted of conspiracy, in the case of Haughey and Blaney after a second trial, as the prosecution case collapsed.

Jack Lynch came through the Arms Crisis with solid party and overwhelming public support (*see* ARD FHEIS). Blaney and Kevin Boland (1917–2001), a minister who resigned in sympathy with him and Haughey, left Fianna Fáil, Boland to establish a new Republican party, Aontacht Éireann, that achieved little electoral impact. Blaney was re-elected to the Dáil as an independent until the end of his life, while Haughey began the slow process of rehabilitation that saw him elected taoiseach in succession to Lynch in December 1979.

Arms Trials. *See* ARMS CRISIS.

Army Comrades Association. *See* BLUESHIRTS.

Army Convention. The ultimate authority for the IRA, one of its roles being to make nominations to the ARMY COUNCIL. It was at the 1969 convention that the seeds of the split that generated the Provisional Army Council occurred. The convention voted to end ABSTENTIONISM, but a number of objectors withdrew and announced that there would be an IRA that supported abstentionism. A convention held soon after created the Provisional Army Council and the organization known since as the Provisional IRA continued the ARMED STRUGGLE. The convention remains as a kind of endorsing body for important decisions made by the IRA Army Council, such as the decision to end the ceasefire in 1995 and the acceptance of the GOOD FRIDAY AGREEMENT of 1998.

Army Council. The supreme executive body of the IRA, taking advisement from the delegates to the ARMY CONVENTION. Decisions about such matters as announcing and ending ceasefires, or decommissioning, have no authority unless they are made by the council.

Army Mutiny. On 6 March 1924 supporters of OLD IRA veterans within the national army, then 60,000 strong, presented a memorandum to the Free State government demanding an end to the projected demobilization of almost half the army and a restatement by the government of its commitment to the achievement of a republic. The mutineers also resented the continuing influence in the army of the IRB, which, they claimed, defence minister Richard MULCAHY encouraged. By October 1924 Mulcahy, who was scapegoated, and the minister for commerce, Joseph McGrath, who sympathized with the soldiers, had resigned, along with some high-ranking central staff. The crisis was firmly handled by minister for justice Kevin O'HIGGINS in the absence of W.T. COSGRAVE, the president of the executive. O'Higgins was determined that the army should be subject to the civil authority: 'Those who take the pay and wear the uniform of the state … must be non-political servants of the state.' O'Higgins's influence in government increased as a result of the mutiny.

Aroon (Irish vocative *a rún*, 'love, secret'). A HIBERNO-ENGLISH term of endearment, popular in song and poetry:

When like the early rose
Aileen aroon!
Beauty in childhood blows
Aileen aroon!
    GERALD GRIFFIN (1803–1840): 'Aileen Aroon' (1829)

Around the world for sport. A light-hearted description of apparently unnecessary circum-ambulation, as in, 'I searched every shop in town for it and I got it in Murphy's next door. Talk about around the world for sport!'

Arrah (Irish *ara, arú*, 'ah, really!'). A conversational response suggesting impatience, mild disbelief, or self-deprecation. It is still common in HIBERNO-ENGLISH speech: 'Do you believe him?' 'Arrah! Not at all, Sure, he's always blackguarding!' According to DINNEEN'S DIC-

TIONARY, 'It is often preceded by *a dhia* (Irish, 'God!') and the whole contracted to *dheara* (YERRA).'

Arrah-na-Pogue. A play by Dion BOUCICAULT, subtitled 'The Wicklow Wedding', first staged in Dublin in 1864 and the following year at the Princess's Theatre, London. In this latter production stage machinery enabled the author – as usual playing the resourceful, if comic, Irish lead (in this case Shaun the Post) – to indulge in the 'sensation' scene that was his trademark. The elaborate stage directions in Act III give some idea of the excitement:

Shaun is seen clinging to the face of the wall; he climbs the ivy. The tower sinks as he climbs; the guardroom windows lighted within are seen descending … As Shaun climbs past the window, the ivy above his head gives way, and a large mass falls, carrying him with it; the leaves and matted branches cover him. His descent is checked by some roots of the ivy, which hold fast.

The play is set after the REBELLION OF 1798 and features as heroine the eponymous Arrah Meelish (played by Boucicault's wife Agnes). The version of the name in the title itself is almost meaningless since it literally signifies 'Arrah of the Kiss' (Irish *póg*, 'kiss', *see* ARRAH). This picturesque nickname comes from an earlier incident when, during a kiss in a prison cell, she was able to push into the mouth of her foster-brother, Lord Beamish MacCoul, a document containing plans for his escape. The play is of its time, with great pace, intrusive songs, last-minute reprieves and a happy ending (however, the excellent court-martial scene in Act II was copied in some detail by George Bernard Shaw for *The Devil's Disciple* (1897)). *Arrah-na-Pogue* somewhat oversimplifies Irish history, and although Boucicault was all for conciliation the mood is strongly Nationalist. The London run coincided with the height of FENIAN activity, and it was decided to cut the singing of 'The WEARING OF THE GREEN' from Act I because of popular feeling.
See also COLLEEN BAWN, THE; SHAUGHRAUN, THE.

Arran's Cuirassiers. One of many nicknames of the 4th (Royal Irish) Dragoon Guards, so called because they were formerly known as the Earl of Arran's Horse. They were also known for obvious reasons as the 'Mounted Micks', and were amalgamated with the 7th Dragoon Guards (to form the 4th/7th Dragoon Guards) in 1922.
See also BLUE HORSE, THE; BUTTERMILKS, THE.

Arse, to do in one's. A popular expression used to connote incredulous denial: 'I did in my ['me' in Dublin] arse.' Other expressions involving arses and incredulity include 'in our arse' and simply 'me arse': 'We will in our arse have our own gentry,' says the farmer to the promoter of Home Rule in Breandán Ó Heithir's *A Begrudger's Guide to Irish Politics* (1986), while 'Happy Christmas your arse / I pray God it's our last' sings Kirsty MacColl (1959–2000) in Shane McGowan's popular duet, 'Fairy Tale of New York' (1987). There is also, of course, the immortal POGUE MAHONE ('kiss my arse').

Arse about face. A mildly coarse expression signifying 'out of proper sequence', 'in the wrong direction', 'preposterous'. It is also heard across the Irish Sea.

Arse over tip. A mildly coarse expression literally signifying 'head over heels', thus any (unintended) somersault. It is used in all metaphorical senses as well, and is also heard in Britain.

Art. The son of CONN OF THE HUNDRED BATTLES and father of CORMAC MAC ART. He falls foul of his stepmother BÉCUMA, a goddess from TÍR TAIRNIGIRI ('the Land of Promise'), and has a GEIS imposed upon him when she defeats him with supernatural aid at FIDCHELL. He has to rescue the maiden Delbchaem from her monstrous parents and win her hand. On the way he faces giant toads, rivers of ice and poisoned chalices before he reaches the palisade behind which the maiden is imprisoned. The pales are topped by the heads of previous suitors, but Art succeeds in beheading the parents and carrying Delbchaem off. The evil Bécuma is banished by Conn.

Artane. A notorious INDUSTRIAL SCHOOL run by the CHRISTIAN BROTHERS in the suburb of Artane on the north side of Dublin city. It and about 30 other industrial schools were funded by the government and run by religious orders to cater for the needs of children who were orphaned or neglected or whose mothers were unmarried; they also catered for a small percentage of juvenile offenders. In 1950 there were more than 6000 children in these institutions, and when the Artane industrial school closed in 1969 there was still a total of 2000 children in its care.

Artane had a fearsome reputation for severe discipline (*see* LEATHER), and it later emerged that there was widespread physical and sexual abuse of children who lived there. Books and television documentaries have exposed industrial schools such as Artane and LETTERFRACK and orphanages such as Goldenbridge (run by the Sisters of Mercy) as places of misery, loneliness, hunger and suffering for children. Some of the orders involved have taken steps to apologize to victims and to offer counselling and compensation, but it now seems that successive governments and Irish society as a whole are also guilty of turning a blind eye to what was going on for so many years.

Artane Boys' Band. A brass and reed band originally comprising pupils of ARTANE industrial school and strongly associated with championship matches in CROKE PARK, where the band plays the county anthems at the half-time interval of the ALL-IRELAND. Founded in 1872, it first played at a GAA match on 14 June 1886, before the stadium in Croke Park existed. In 1988 the CHRISTIAN BROTHERS retired from day-to-day management of the band, and it was opened to girls.

Arthur of Britain. The 'once and future king' of Geoffrey of Monmouth (d.1155) and Sir Thomas Malory (d.1471) intrudes only minimally into Irish mythology, being rather associated with stories from the Brythonic (i.e. Cornish and Welsh) tradition. He is said to have stolen the three hounds of FIONN MAC CUMHAIL and to have sworn allegiance to him when the FIANNA arrived to recover them. It was inevitable in the minds of the myth-makers that the semi-legendary British hero-king should have met the lieutenant of the semi-legendary high king, CORMAC MAC ART.

Article. A colloquialism used in certain circumstances to denote a person. The noun is used in affection or a mock-derogatory manner, often of children or young people. 'Well you're a right article!' might indicate the frustration of a parent with a teenager.

Article 44. An article of the CONSTITUTION OF 1937, the first part of which recognized the special position of the Catholic Church as the church of the majority of the population of the state while granting equal rights to other religious denominations. Its 'special position' was removed after a constitutional referendum in 1972 and the article now reads:

> The State acknowledges that the homage of public worship is due to Almighty God. It shall hold His Name in reverence, and shall respect and honour religion.

Articles 2 and 3. The CONSTITUTION OF 1937 affirmed the unity of Ireland, Article 2 asserting that:

> The national territory consists of the whole island of Ireland, its islands and the territorial seas.

However Article 3 recognized *de facto* the existence of NORTHERN IRELAND:

> Pending the re-integration of the national territory, and without prejudice to the right of Parliament and Government established by this Constitution to exercise jurisdiction over the whole of that territory, the laws enacted by that Parliament shall have the like area and extent of application as the laws of Ireland and the like extra-territorial effect.

Article 2, which was a political holy cow, appeared to displease Unionists and was seen by many in the South as a barrier to reconciliation, while Article 3 displeased some in the South because it effectively recognized the Northern state. When Articles 2 and 3 were removed from the constitution after a referendum in 1998, Unionists reacted by claiming that they had never mattered to them anyway.

Arts Council, the. *See* CHOMHAIRLE EALAÍON, AN.

Arts Council of Northern Ireland. *See* ACNI.

Asachán. A word used in the HIBERNO-ENGLISH of Munster to mean 'insult', 'inconvenience', 'misfortune'. It is a morphic corruption of the Irish *acasán*, 'insult'. The sympathetic remark, 'That's an awful asachán' might be addressed to someone whose car has been crashed into.

Ascendancy, the. An emotive and ambiguous term applied to the Anglican Protestant upper classes who for nearly two centuries from the end of the WILLIAMITE WAR in 1690 owned most of the land of Ireland, maintained a BIG HOUSE hegemony and controlled the administrative, legal, economic and social aspects of Irish life. Known also loosely as the ANGLO-IRISH, they tended to be regarded as English by the Irish and Irish by the English. It is reckoned that fewer than 5000 families had a monopoly of political power because of the disenfranchisement of Catholics and Presbyterians.

Their relationship with those they might designate as English 'cousins' was complex and ambivalent, and they were often regarded by the English upper classes as the worst kind of backwoodsmen. The poet Louis MacNeice summed up 20th-century attitudes to them, writing that they possessed, 'nothing but an insidious bonhomie, an obsolete bravado, and a way with horses'. Their heyday was the 18th century, when the bucks of the Ascendancy acquired a reputation for hard riding, drinking, gambling, duelling and general hellraising (*see* ABDUCTION CLUB), combined with an utterly cavalier attitude towards the Catholic peasantry and the ideals of Irish nationhood. However, their defenders insist that not all members of the Ascendancy were sectarian or unpatriotic, and they point to the glories of Georgian Dublin as evidence of an exclusivist but real urban culture.

The Ascendancy's ownership of land was severely affected by the cataclysm of the GREAT FAMINE and gradually dismantled by the LAND ACTS of the late 19th century. The members of the perceived Ascendancy were by then marginalized, and the scattered survivors are now wisely regarded as a cherished part of Ireland's moral and aesthetic wealth.

See also ABSENTEE LANDLORDS.

Aschled. One of many versions of the name of the city of Dublin. It was clearly an attempt to render the sound of the last two words of the name in Irish: BAILE ÁTH(A) CLIATH.

Asgard. The boat used for the HOWTH GUN-RUNNING. It was a 28-ton white yacht owned by Erskine CHILDERS, given to him as a wedding present by his father-in-law, and it conveyed 900 rifles, the larger part of the consignment bought by him and Darrell Figgis in Hamburg in May 1914. Childers's crew consisted of Mary Spring Rice, a British soldier and two Donegal fishermen, and the voyage was made through the worst Irish Sea storm in 30 years. Owing to his excellent seamanship Childers was able to sail the heavily overloaded yacht into Howth harbour on Sunday 26 July just as 1000 volunteers mobilized by Bulmer HOBSON arrived at the jetty to receive them. The boat was preserved and is now on display in KILMAINHAM JAIL in Dublin.

Ashe, Thomas (1885–1917). Revolutionary. He was born and raised in Kinard, Co. Kerry, and educated locally and at De La Salle College, Waterford. A primary schoolteacher by profession, Ashe became a member of the GAELIC LEAGUE, the GAA and the IRB, and commanded the Fingal Battalion of the IRISH VOLUNTEERS.

In the EASTER RISING of 1916, he showed himself to be among the few effective leaders, controlling part of north Co. Dublin and demolishing a railway bridge on the Belfast–Dublin line. His battalion is remembered for capturing the Rice House Barracks in Ashbourne, Co. Meath, after a long battle, leaving 11 Royal Irish Constabulary (RIF) officers dead and more than 20 wounded as opposed to 2 dead on the Volunteer side.

Ashe was sentenced to death on 11 May 1916, but his sentence was commuted to penal servitude for life and he was sent to Lewes jail along with Eámon DE VALERA. It was during his time there that he wrote the long poem, 'Let Me Carry Your Cross for Ireland, Lord!', an example of the sacrificial imagery used both by and about the insurgents of 1916:

> Let me carry your cross for Ireland, Lord,
> The hour of her trial draws near,
> And the pangs and the pains of the sacrifice
> May be borne by comrades dear.
> But, Lord, take me from the offering throng,
> There are many far less prepared,
> Though anxious and all as they are to die
> That Ireland may be spared.
> …
> For the empty homes of her golden plains;
> For the hopes of her future, too!
> Let me carry your cross for Ireland, Lord!
> For the cause of Roisin Dubh.

In June 1917, Ashe was released along with the other prisoners and internees, but was arrested in late August and charged with having made a seditious speech in Ballinalee, Co. Longford (where he was courting Granard woman Maud Kiernan, sister of Kitty Kiernan, who later became engaged to Michael COLLINS). Ashe was tried and sentenced to two years' imprisonment. With other Republicans in MOUNTJOY JAIL he began a hunger strike on 20 September in pursuit of a demand for prisoner-of-war status. The strikers were forcibly fed and on the fourth day of force-feeding, Ashe collapsed and was taken to the Mater Hospital, where he died on 25 September of heart and lung failure. As he lay dying he said to the lord mayor of Dublin, Laurence O'Neill, 'If I die, I die in a good cause.' It is estimated that 30,000 people attended his funeral in Dublin on 30 September, at which a volley was fired and Michael Collins gave the oration:

> That volley which we have just heard is the only speech which it is proper to make over the grave of a dead Fenian.

Addressing the coroner's jury, Tim HEALY said, 'They have added another blood-spot to the Irish cavalry.' Ashe's example was hugely influential: the hunger strike became a potent propaganda weapon during the War of Independence, the Civil War and the more recent Northern Troubles (see SANDS, BOBBY).

Ashypet (also **ashypot**). A term of mild disapproval aimed at someone hogging the fire. The Irish equivalent is the phrase *peata an ghríosaigh* ('pet of the ashes'), which is a literal translation of the English, and would serve as a Gaelic version of Cinderella.
See also GREESHY.

As I roved out. An exclamatory phrase expressing incredulity or scorn. A tall story might merit the reaction 'That's all as I roved out!' The origin of the phrase is the classic opening line of ballads of derring-do or amorous exploits (or disasters), such as 'As I roved out one fine May morning / ... / Who should I spy but my own true lover ...'. *As I Roved Out* was the title of a traditional music series broadcast by BBC Northern Ireland from 1951 to 1960, featuring singers and musicians whose work was assembled by collectors such as Séamus ENNIS and Seán O'BOYLE. The collector and singer David Hammond (b.1928) was a producer on this programme. The programme's title and signature tune came from the song of that name performed by Sarah MAKEM.

As I Was Going Down Sackville Street. The first volume of impressionistic non-sequential reminiscences of Oliver St John GOGARTY about his life in Dublin in the first three decades of the 20th century. Published in 1937, it contains sketches of such worthies as Æ, Arthur GRIFFITH, James JOYCE, Horace PLUNKETT and Jack B. YEATS, and describes the burning of his house by the IRA during the Civil War:

> Why should they burn my house? Because I am not an Irishman? Because I do not flatter fools? If the only Irishman who is to be allowed to live in Ireland must be a bog-trotter, then I am not an Irishman.

Its mood is darkened by the perceived occlu-

sion of the rich life of Ireland under DE VALERA's first Fianna Fáil government, though the Corinthian wit and aesthetic zest for life still shine through. It was typical of Gogarty to persist in referring to Dublin's main thoroughfare as Sackville Street, even though it had been renamed O'CONNELL STREET in 1924. The book was the subject of a successful libel case brought by Henry Morris Sinclair, an antique dealer. The trauma of the proceedings was a contributory factor in the author's self-imposed exile in England and America.
See also ENDYMION.

Askeaton Affair, the. An affray at Askeaton, Co. Limerick, in August 1821 between a number of WHITEBOYS who had surrounded the house of a tithe proctor and a force of policemen under the command of Major Richard Going, who was a well-known ORANGE ORDER activist. A number of Whiteboys were killed and the others, taken prisoner, were forced by Going to bury the dead in quicklime. It was believed that not all of those so dealt with were actually dead. Going was removed from his post and was later killed by a band of Rockites, another contemporary group of agrarian protesters, led by the typically named 'Captain Rock'.

As old as Atty Hayes's goat. A simile for age still common in Cork city. The original goat lived *c.*1780 and was the property of Sir Henry Brown Hayes, a local landlord.

Assembly's College. The popular name for the chief PRESBYTERIAN college in Ireland, built in College Green, Belfast, in 1853, from plans by Sir Charles Lanyon (1813–89), who designed the adjoining Queen's College, the forerunner of QUB. The need for a separate theological college for divinity aspirants was hotly debated by the GENERAL ASSEMBLY, with a majority opting for a confessional approach to the teaching of theology, philosophy, Greek and Hebrew. The college was seen as a counter to the perceived ARIANISM of the curriculum of the Belfast Academical Institution. The question was one of several that exercised Presbyterianism in the mid-century.

Assisted passage. A scheme by which the passages of much-needed Irish emigrants to Australia were paid for, at first by the British government (beginning in 1831). Later the colonies developed their own assisted-passage schemes. Assisted passage tended to favour the slightly more prosperous because the applicants were assessed on grounds of respectability and employability.

Ass's roar, within an. An expression used in HIBERNO-ENGLISH to convey nearness: 'That house is within an ass's roar of the church.' *See also* HEN'S KICK.

Asthore. A general HIBERNO-ENGLISH term of endearment, from Irish *a stór*, 'store, treasure', hence 'darling'.

Astronomy. Irish scientists of the late 18th and early 19th centuries were at the forefront of astronomical research. Dunsink Observatory in Co. Dublin was established by Trinity College Dublin in 1783; Armagh Observatory was established by the Church of Ireland primate, Archbishop Richard Robinson, in 1790; at Daramona, Co. Westmeath, William Edward Wilson (1851–1908) established an observatory in 1871, where he determined the heat of the sun and made photographic studies of nebulae and clusters. The most famous observatory was at Birr Castle (*see* LEVIATHAN OF PARSONSTOWN, THE). In 1885 Agnes Mary Clerke (1842–1907) published the *Popular History of Astronomy During the Nineteenth Century*. *See also* TYNDALL, JOHN.

ASU. The abbreviation for 'active service unit', applied to a (usually Provisional) IRA group on a military operation involving explosives or weapons. The language is deliberately militaristic as a reminder that the movement sees itself as engaging in a just war to achieve legitimate aims.

Atallatall. An intensifier of 'at all', often used mischievously, to indicate incredulity or in a self-parodying STAGE-IRISH way: 'Do you mean he didn't come atallatall?' There is an old joke about double yellow lines on a street in Ireland meaning that one cannot park there atallatall.

Athair Peadar, an t- (Irish, 'Father Peter') (1839–1920). Novelist and translator. He was born in Clondrohid in Co. Cork and educated in Maynooth, serving as a priest in the diocese of Cloyne for the rest of his life. His surname was Ó Laoghaire but he was always known by the familiar title. He began writing in Irish in the 1890s, after the foundation of the Gaelic League, using '*caint na ndaoine*', the living language still spoken in GAELTACHT areas, rather than any more literary form of Irish. He produced a large body of work, original novels such as *SÉADNA* and *Niamh*, translations into Irish of devotional and religious works, and versions in modern Irish of older texts. His detractors criticize him for narrow-mindedness, which took the form of bowdlerizing texts, and for glorifying Irish peasant culture at the expense of everything else. He was made a canon in 1906 and died on 21 March 1920. His autobiography, *Mo Sgéal Féin* (*My Own Story*) (1915), was a classic for decades, and includes powerful descriptions of the famine in his part of Cork:

> You saw them there every morning after the night out, stretched in rows, some moving and some very still, with no stir from them. Later people came and lifted those who no longer moved and heaved them into carts and carried them up to a place near Carrigstyra, where a big pit was open for them, and thrust them into the pit.
>
> Next day a neighbour came to the hut. He saw the two of them dead and his wife's feet clasped in Paddy's bosom as though he were trying to warm them. It would seem that he felt the death agony come on to Kate and her legs grow cold, so he put them inside his own shirt to take the chill from them.

Athenry. A town in east Co. Galway that, for strategic reasons – it lies halfway between Loughrea and Galway and commands a ford over the River Clareen – became an outpost of the Anglo-Norman conquest in the 13th century. Where Richard de Burgo (Burke) built a castle in Loughrea (1236), his main vassal, Myler de Bermingham, built a keep with towers and bawn (*see* BAWN³) in Athenry, which became known as 'Bermingham's Court', and endowed a monastery for French-speaking Dominicans. These early frontiersmen envisaged that Athenry would grow into a great city, but the abbey and the castle (now converted into a heritage centre) are all that gave concrete representation to their dream. In 1316 Athenry was the scene of a major battle between the Anglo-Norman family of de Burgo and the O'Connors, Gaelic chieftains of CONNACHT under Felim O'Connor. The Irish were defeated with great loss of life and lost for ever their supremacy in the province.

See also 'FIELDS OF ATHENRY, THE'.

Athens of Ireland, the. A somewhat presumptuous description of CORK at the beginning of the 19th century because of the presence in that city of such bright literary lights as Thomas Crofton CROKER, William Maginn (*see* O'DOHERTY, SIR MORGAN), Francis Sylvester Mahony (FATHER PROUT) and Richard Milliken (1767–1815), the satirist who wrote the burlesque 'The GROVES OF BLARNEY'.

See also ATHENS OF THE NORTH, THE.

Athens of the North, the. A name given, perhaps slightly tongue-in-cheek, to BELFAST in the second half of the 18th century and beginning of the 19th century because of the founding of such institutions as the Belfast Reading Society (1788) (which became the Belfast Library and Society for Promoting Knowledge), the Belfast Academical Institution (1814) and the Belfast Natural History and Philosophical Society (1821). The name was originally applied to Edinburgh because of the classical buildings on Calton Hill, but it was seized by the buoyant Belfast merchants as of right.

Charles Monteith, the publisher, who was a student at INST (which grew from the Academical Institution), recalls once asking a teacher if Belfast *was* actually called the

'Athens of the North'. The teacher responded: 'I cannot pronounce on that, young Monteith, but I am certain that Athens was never known as the "Belfast of the South"!'

Turn back in thought to when a little town
at Long Bridge end, this city wore the name
of Northern Athens with no irony
staining that title for along its streets,
High Street, Ann Street, round the Linen Hall,
men walked, of many skills and sciences,
scholars, orators, philosophers,
physicians, poets of no meagre fame.
JOHN HEWITT (1907–87): '*Pro Tanto Quid Retribuamus*' (Latin, 'What return shall we make for so much?', the city's motto) (1954)

A thiarcais. An exclamation, used mainly in Kerry HIBERNO-ENGLISH, of astonishment or dismay. The derivation is obscure but the expression may be a euphemism for *a Thiarna* (Irish, 'Lord God').

Athlone. A large town on the River Shannon, Co. Westmeath, in Ireland's central plain, near Lough Ree. A Victorian folly 5 km (3 miles) from the town is said to mark the centre of the country. A stone castle was constructed at Athlone in 1210 by John de Grey, Bishop of Norwich, Irish justice to England's King JOHN. Athlone is one of the notable success stories of the CELTIC TIGER, attracting multinational industries and a greatly increased and youthful workforce.

The strategically crucial bridge over the River Shannon at Athlone, made famous by Aubrey DE VERE's 'A Ballad of Athlone', is the gateway to CONNACHT. The first great bridge at Athlone was built by Sir Henry Sidney in 1566. De Vere's ballad tells of an incident during the second siege of Athlone by Dutch general GINKEL in June 1691 (the previous year its governor, Richard Grace, had successfully held the town against the Williamite General Douglas). In this incident, 12 heroic Irishmen, of whom 10 were killed, destroyed the bridge in an attempt to thwart the besiegers:

St Ruth in his stirrups stood up and cried,
'I have seen no deed like that in France!'

With a toss of his head Sarsfield replied,
‘They had luck, the dogs, ’twas a merry chance!’
O many a year, upon Shannon’s side,
They sang upon moor and they sang upon heath,
Of the twain that breasted that raging tide,
And the ten that shook bloody hands with Death!

Despite this valour, on 30 June 1691 Williamite troops waded shoulder-deep across the Shannon to take the town. It was a major defeat for the Jacobites, and ten days later they made their last stand 30 km (19 miles) southwest of Athlone at AUGHRIM, Co. Galway. Custume army barracks in the town is called after one of the heroes of the day, a Sergeant Custume. ‘The Bridge of Athlone’ is also a CÉILÍ dance.

Atmospheric Road, the. The name of an early railway service, propelled by compressed air, that plied the 2.8 km (1.75 miles) of track between Kingstown (DÚN LAOGHAIRE) and Dalkey. It was an extension of Ireland’s very first line that ran from Dublin to Kingstown. This had been engineered by William DARGAN and opened on 17 December 1834. The Atmospheric was initiated on 29 March 1844, and though closely studied by the scientists of the day proved neither popular nor economical. In 1854 the company began using conventional steam locomotives.

Atomy. An Ulster expression for a person of little significance physically and otherwise. It is a form of the word ‘anatomy’, which was used as the equivalent of skeleton. Its entry into Ulster speech must have come with the PLANTATION since it is a 16th-century usage, mentioned only once in Shakespeare, when Mistress Quickly refers to the Beadle as ‘Thou atomy, thou!’ in *Henry IV Part 2* (1597), V. iv, having earlier called him a ‘starved bloodhound’.
See also ANATOMIES OF DEATH.

At oneself, to be. An Ulster phrase meaning to be in a state of comfort, harmony or health, often used in the negative: ‘I’m not at myself today.’
See also LOSE THE RUN OF ONESELF, TO.

At Slieve Gullion’s Foot. A classic work of folklore (1941) about his native place by Michael J.

Murphy (1913–96), who was born in Liverpool but reared in Co. Armagh. The publication attracted the attention of James DELARGY, and Murphy collected folklore for the IRISH FOLKLORE COMMISSION in Dublin until 1983. He published many other books, including *Tyrone Folk Quest* (1973), and also wrote stories, poems and plays.

At Swim-Two-Birds. The first and most characteristic novel (1939) of Flann O’BRIEN (pseudonym of Brian O’Nolan). Clearly influenced by JOYCE, its modernist structure allows the narrator – a student at University College Dublin (O’Brien’s old college) who is engaged in writing a book about a writer who finds himself at the mercy of his characters (some of them the stereotypes of popular fiction) – to lead a humdrum life in his uncle’s house while turbulence reigns within his head. The writer in the narrator’s book is called Dermot Trellis (named after a dividing fence in the O’Nolans’ back garden in Blackrock, Co. Dublin, which the author and his brothers had continually to repair), and he draws upon the rich mythology of Ireland, used mock-heroically, to help people his book. FIONN MAC CUMHAIL figures largely (as Finn Mac Cool, the received English version of his name) as does SUIBHNE GEILT. It was this ‘Mad Sweeney’ legend that supplied the odd title, a literal translation of the place-name *Snámh Dá Én* (‘swim two birds’), where Sweeney rested on one of his furious journeys. Scholars suggest that it was on the right bank of the Shannon opposite Clonmacnoise.

The narrator’s often deliberately mundane account of his undergraduate life is something of a *roman-à-clef*, but the book as a whole is both an exploration of Irish culture and a commentary on the nature of fiction. The novel, which always had a cult following in Ireland, is now an internationally appreciated text about texts. The first sentence gives something of the comic temper and texture of the book:

> Having placed in my mouth sufficient bread for three minutes chewing, I withdrew my powers of sensual perception and retired into the privacy of

my mind, my eyes and face assuming a vacant and preoccupied expression.

Jamie O'Neill adapted O'Brien's title for his novel *At Swim, Two Boys* (2001), a story of comradely love at the time of the Easter Rising. *See also* SWIM-TWO-BIRDS.

Attercap. A term of dismissive abuse for a malicious person, as in, 'That poisonous wee attercap; I wouldn't trust him as far as I'd throw him!' The word originally meant 'spider'.

Attracta (also **Athrachta**). A 5th-century saint contemporary with St PATRICK. According to legend she left home to escape a marriage arranged by her father Talan and was received by the saint into the religious life. As he blessed her, a veil fell from heaven and she reluctantly accepted it. She founded a convent near Lough Gara in Co. Roscommon and set up a hostel for travellers, which later became a hospital. Killaraght, near Boyle, Co. Roscommon, is a memorial to her name. Her feast day is 11 August.

Auchinleck, Sir Claude John Eyre (1884–1981). British army general. He was born in Co. Tyrone in 1884 but was taken to India as a small child. His nickname 'the Auk' came from the shortening of his surname and the convenience of the existence of a short-winged, heavy-bodied seabird of that name. He joined the Indian Army in 1903 and fought in Mesopotamia in the First World War. After service in Norway, where he commanded the unsuccessful raid on Narvik (1940), he was commander-in-chief (CIC) India, then CIC Middle East. His most significant military achievement was the creation of the 8th Army that eventually stopped Rommel at El Alamein (October 1942), though he was made the scapegoat for the earlier tactical retreat from Cyrenaica and replaced by General Alexander (*see* ALEXANDER OF TUNIS AND ERRIGAL). He returned to India and, with the rank of field marshal (1946), was made supreme commander of all armed forces in India and Pakistan – 'lord of war' as the natives called him. He left after independence in 1947 and became an honorary colonel of the SKINS.

Aughinish. An alumina plant located near Askeaton in Co. Limerick, about 30 km (20 miles) from Limerick city, with its own port on the Shannon estuary. Aughinish processes alumina, the raw material of aluminium, from bauxite imported from Africa and Brazil. In the mid-1990s local farmers alleged that emissions from Aughinish caused health problems among cattle, but the plant was exonerated by the Environmental Protection Agency.

Aughrim, Battle of. The decisive battle (12 July 1691) of the WILLIAMITE WAR, in which Catholic Ireland and its JACOBITE allies were defeated. The Jacobite leader, Charles Chalmont, Marquis de St Ruth, made a stand on Aughrim Hill in east Co. Galway, but his forces were out-manoeuvred by Williamite cavalry and he himself was decapitated by a cannon ball. The Jacobites suffered the enormous loss (for the time) of 7000–10,000 men, many of them killed while fleeing. A lament played by the CHIEFTAINS, 'After Aughrim's Great Disaster', emphasizes the seriousness of the lost battle for Irish hopes, as does the slow air collected by James Goodman from among musicians of the Dingle peninsula, '*Ag fágaint Eachdhroim*' ('Leaving Aughrim'). Brendan BEHAN in 'The Confirmation Suit' writes of the jacket of his suit, a jacket (or 'coat') not at all to his boyish taste: 'But the coat itself, that was where Aughrim was lost.'
See also LUTTRELL, HENRY; SARSFIELD, PATRICK.

Augustinian Canons. The religious order introduced into Ireland in the 12th century by St MALACHY as part of his reform of the Irish church. Their observances, which incorporated many Cistercian practices, were in notable contrast to the traditions of the older Irish monasticism.

Auld. *See* OULD BIDDY etc.

Australian Rules. A style of football played in Australia, and the closest form of football to Gaelic FOOTBALL: in both games the ball can be caught and carried as well as kicked. An international series between Australia and an Irish national football team, using what are called COMPROMISE RULES, was held for the first time in 1984, the Irish team captained by Jack O'Shea (*see* JACKO). Such Compromise (or International) Rules games are the only occasion on which Gaelic footballers can be capped for their country.

Auxies. A nickname for members of the Auxiliary Division of the RIC (Royal Irish Constabulary) recruited from demobilized British army officers from July 1920 to counter escalation in the ANGLO-IRISH WAR of 1919–21. Winston CHURCHILL is credited with the idea of recruiting a force of 8000 ex-soldiers to reinforce the RIC, although the numbers never were greater than 2000. Known as 'cadets' and wearing a distinctive blue uniform, the Auxies had a total strength of 1900 by November 1921, and though nominally under RIC command they often worked independently, especially in areas outside Dublin.

Three of their more notorious operations were the Sack of BALBRIGGAN (20 September 1920), BLOODY SUNDAY 1920 (21 November 1920) and, in a joint operation with the BLACK AND TANS (with whom they are often confused), the burning of Cork on 11 December 1920 as a reprisal for an IRA ambush in the city in which an Auxie cadet, Spencer R. Chapman, was killed. The Auxies achieved an even more fearsome reputation than the Black and Tans for drunkenness, cruelty and 'unauthorized' reprisals. Their commander, Brigadier General Frank Crozier, found their behaviour so unacceptable that he resigned in protest in February 1921. A total of 31 cadets were killed in the war, 17 of them in the KILMICHAEL AMBUSH (28 November 1920). Stood down in 1922, many Auxies joined the police force in Palestine (then a British mandate).

Avick (Irish vocative *a mhic*, 'my son', 'my boy'). A common and friendly HIBERNO-ENGLISH greeting, not necessarily indicating blood relationship:

> Och, Father O'Flynn, you've a wonderful way wid
> you,
> All ould sinners are wishful to pray wid you,

> All the young childer are wild for to play with you,
> You're such a way wid you, Father avick.
> A[RTHUR] P[ERCIVAL] GRAVES (1846–1931): 'Father
> O'Flynn' (1875)

Avondale. The birthplace near Rathdrum, Co. Wicklow, of Charles Stewart PARNELL. The estate is now owned by Coillte (the government-established forestry service) and the house is in use as an agricultural school. *See also* BLACKBIRD OF AVONDALE, THE.

A-waitin'-on. An expression, found usually in Ulster, to indicate that someone is close to death, as in, 'Mary's father is a-waitin'-on. They say he won't last the night.'

A-wantin'. A cry used by children to indicate a parental summons as in, 'Jimmy, you're a-wantin' for your tea!'

Away! An expression of incredulity, heard in the northernmost parts of Ireland, and also in Scotland.

Away on a hack. A colloquialism meaning 'fortunate', 'successful'. A new job, house, partner, or winning the LOTTO might be reasons for an individual to be considered 'away on a hack'. 'Hack' is an abbreviation of 'hackney', a horse-drawn vehicle for hire, and also means 'saddle horse'; the expression may derive from either.

Away with the fairies. A phrase indicating a ridiculous action or an absurd, absentminded person: 'That girl has no sense: she's away with the fairies.' The phrase is now used lightly, but once signified mental instability. *See also* AIRY; AIRY FIT; SIDHE.

Awniduff (Irish *Abhainn Dubh*, 'black river'). The Irish name for the two rivers Blackwater, in Tyrone/Monaghan/Armagh and in Kerry/Cork/Waterford. The form *Abhainn Mhór* ('big river') was also used of each, with some justice since the Ulster river is 80 km (50 miles) long and the Munster one more than twice that:

> Swift Awniduff which of the Englishman
> Is cal' de Blackwater.
> EDMUND SPENSER (*c.*1552–1599): *The Faerie Queen*
> (1590–6) IV. xi. 41

B

BA. The abbreviation used by Republicans for the British army as an alternative to 'the Brits'.

Baby Power. The nickname for a small bottle of WHISKEY manufactured by John Power & Co., containing a 'glass' or measure, and favoured by women and the poor.

BÁC. An acronym used as an abbreviation for the somewhat unwieldy BAILE ÁTH(A) CLIATH, the Irish name for Dublin, in correspondence or addresses written in Irish.

Bacach (Irish *bacach*, 'lame', 'crippled'). A general mild (and not very politically correct) HIBERNO-ENGLISH term of abuse: 'You dirty bacach you.'
See also BOCKETY.

Bachelor's Walk. The scene of a bloody confrontation in Dublin on 26 July 1914 – thereafter known as Bloody Sunday – between civilians and a detachment of the King's Own Scottish Borderers supplemented by the DMP (Dublin Metropolitan Police). The security forces, on their way back to barracks having failed to impound 1500 rifles brought in at Howth by the IRISH VOLUNTEERS (*see* HOWTH GUN-RUNNING), opened fire on a hostile crowd that had gathered along the Liffey quay. The officer who ordered the confrontation was unaware that the rifles were loaded and there was no clear signal to fire. Four people were killed and 37 wounded in the shooting. Jack B. YEATS's painting of 1915, *Bachelor's Walk, In Memoriam*, commemorates an incident that he had noted in his diary: 'a flower girl placing her own offering on the scene of a killing'.

The military response at Bachelor's Walk was in sharp contrast to the British government's reaction to arms importation on a much larger scale (35,000 rifles and 2 million rounds) by Protestant gun-runners in Ulster the previous April (*see* LARNE GUN-RUNNING), when no action was taken, and enrolment in the IRISH VOLUNTEERS increased significantly as a result.

Backend. For Irish migrant workers, the time of year when autumn had not yet turned to winter but the main work in Atlantic seaboard smallholdings was done and the men were free to travel abroad for seasonal work. In the postwar years the main work available was tunnelling for hydroelectric schemes in Scotland, though a large contingent of mainly Mayo labourers worked on the construction of the Jubilee Line in London in the 1970s.
See also TATIE-HOWKERS; TUNNEL TIGERS.

Back Lane Parliament. The disparaging nickname applied by its detractors to the CATHOLIC CONVENTION, which met in TAILORS' HALL, situated in Back Lane in the LIBERTIES of Dublin on 3–8 December 1792. Its petition for the removal of penal disabilities from Catholics was in fact rejected. Sir Boyle ROCHE, no social ornament himself, described the members, one of whom, Edward Byrne, was one of the richest men in Ireland, as 'turbulent shopkeepers and shoplifters'.

Back of God speed. A place so remote that even the force of the blessing 'God speed' will not extend as far as it. The phrase dates from the 19th century and is not now in general use.

Backstone. A projection at the back of a fire-place on which it was possible to keep a kettle singing or a meal warm:

> There on the crickets' singing stone
> She stirs the bogwood fire
> And hums in sad sweet undertone
> The song of heart's desire.
>
> JOSEPH CAMPBELL (1879–1944): 'My Lagan
> Love' in *Songs of Uladh* (1904)

Bacon, Francis (1909–92). Painter. He was born on 28 October 1909 in Baggot Street, Dublin, to English parents. His mother, Winifred Margaret Supple, was a Yorkshire heiress, his father an army captain who kept horses in Co. Kildare. After a dispute with his father at the age of 16 he went to live with his grandmother at her home near Abbeyleix, Co. Laois; shortly afterwards he moved to London, where he ran gambling parties during the Second World War. By the 1960s he was hailed as Britain's most important postwar artist. His later work, with its themes of loneliness and despair, now commands very high prices. Bacon died in Spain on 28 April 1992. In 1998 the Hugh Lane Gallery in Dublin received from his heir a gift of the studio Bacon had used for the last 30 years of his life, together with its contents. These were re-mounted in the gallery and can be visited there.

Bad cess! A casual imprecation expressing annoyance or displeasure and meaning 'Bad luck!' 'Cess' was a form of government taxation, and later a local-government exaction resembling modern-day rates. The original force of the curse has been lost with use, although the imprecation is still heard in the HIBERNO-ENGLISH of rural areas. 'Bad cess to

them [politicians] for reducing the old-age pension.'

Bad drop. *See* LOW DROP.

Badly off. A HIBERNO-ENGLISH comment or remonstration of considerable subtlety and force. A parent might say 'You're badly off!' to a teenager requesting permission to go, say, to one dance too many with friends, meaning that the young person is anything but badly off for entertainment. As a comment on behaviour, to say someone is 'badly off' can convey surprise, disapproval or downright condemnation of an action perceived as unwise, thoughtless or immoral.

Bad scan! *See* BAD SCRAN!

Bad scran! A HIBERNO-ENGLISH imprecation meaning 'Bad luck!' 'Scran' is thought to mean food unfit for human consumption and its derivation is unclear. 'Bad scan!' is a corruption of 'Bad scran!' 'Bad scran to him anyway for letting the cow out of the byre.'

Bagenal, Henry (d.1598). English administrator and military commander. He succeeded his father Nicholas Bagenal (1508–91) as marshal and, based in the important outpost of Newry, Co. Armagh, in 1591 was appointed chief commissioner, with the job of imposing English rule in Ulster. The Battle of CLONTIBRET (1595) was Bagenal's first open engagement with his sworn enemy Hugh O'NEILL, Earl of Tyrone. O'Neill attacked Bagenal's troops on their way back to their base in Newry from a relief mission to Monaghan fort and caused heavy English losses, of horses and weapons as well as men. Estimates of English casualties ranged from 140 by the English to more than 700 by the Irish. Bagenal was killed early in the Battle of the YELLOW FORD in August 1598, when his force of more than 4000 men was catastrophically defeated by O'Neill in the major battle of the NINE YEARS' WAR.

Bagenal, Mabel (*c*.1571–96). The sister of Marshal Henry BAGENAL, who eloped with Hugh O'NEILL, Earl of Tyrone, in 1591, when she was about 20 and he was twice that age.

She was O'Neill's third wife (he had divorced the first, and the second had died), and they were married by the Protestant Bishop of Meath. This elopement and O'Neill's subsequent treatment of Mabel (he continued to have numerous other mistresses) earned him the implacable hostility of Henry Bagenal. Mabel Bagenal was described by Victorian historian Richard Bagwell (1840–1918) as the 'Helen [of Troy] of the Elizabethan wars'. Disillusioned by his infidelities, she left O'Neill after a short time, and returned to her brother's home in Newry, where she died in 1596.

Baginbun. *See* CREEKE OF BAGGANBUN, THE.

Bailc. An Irish word for 'downpour' taken directly into HIBERNO-ENGLISH and indicating a sudden squall of rain, as in such phrases as 'I was doing rightly and nearly home when a *bailc* soaked me to the skin.'

Baile Áth(a) Cliath. The Irish name for Dublin, pronounced 'Blaw Klee', the *Áth Cliath* component meaning 'a ford with hurdles' (*Baile*, 'town', occurs frequently in Irish placenames). This crossing place of the tidal River LIFFEY, which is thought to have been upstream of the contemporary Father Mathew or Church Street Bridge, would, it is estimated, have been passable at spring tides for about 10 hours out of 24. The hurdles refer to a mat of woven saplings, which may have been secured into the bed of the river at the ford. *Áth Cliath* was known in 770 and the name may be much older. The ANNALS OF THE FOUR MASTERS relate the discovery of 'five principal roads to Teamhair [Tara]' on the night of the birth of CONN OF THE HUNDRED BATTLES in about AD 100. One of these, Slighe Midluachra, ran south from Ulster, crossing Dublin Bay and the Liffey by this ford 'of the hurdles'.
See also BÁC; DUBLIN.

Bailegangaire. A play (1985) by Tom MURPHY that starred Siobhán MCKENNA in the central role of Mammo in the original DRUID THEATRE production. It tells the tragic-comic story of three women – Mammo, her granddaughter Mary, and Dolly, who is pregnant but does not know who the father is – and of a laughing competition and its consequences. (*Bailegangaire* means 'town without laughter'). Mammo dominates the action from a bed centre-stage, an archetypal figure combining elements of King Lear and the Hag of Beara (*see* CAILLEACH BÉARA).

Baileys®. The original Irish cream liqueur, a mixture of cream and whiskey, which first appeared in 1974. The name, Irish but not so Irish that foreigners, particularly Asians, cannot pronounce it, derives from the name of a restaurant that somebody in the company happened to see. By 2000 it had become one of the top-selling spirits in the world and had given rise to 160 imitators. Baileys®, a brand both ambitious and sensitive to the marketplace, originally targeted the not-so-young female drinker, but recent advertising campaigns have attempted to broaden its appeal among men (with Baileys on the rocks) and among younger women (with pub scenes asserting that the liqueur is seriously sexy).

Bailiff, the. A figure of hate among the Irish peasantry, as evidenced by the following lines from 'The Devil and the Bailiff' by Cathal McGarvey. This ballad was collected in Northern Ireland by Sean O'Boyle and Peter Kennedy in 1952. The tune is a traditional jig, and the ballad is also known as 'The Devil and Bailiff McGlynn'. Nothing at all is known about its author:

> Well one of these lads was the devil,
> The other was Bailiff McGlynn,
> And one was as nice as the other,
> For both were as ugly as sin.
> ...
> As they walked on a lassie espied them,
> And in to her mother she fled,
> 'It's the bailiff!' says she to her mother,
> Who clasped her two hands as she said,
> 'May the devil take that ugly bailiff!'
> Says the devil 'Bedad, that I'll do –
> It was straight from the heart that came surely,
> So Bailiff McGlynn I'll take you!'

Baily Lighthouse. A lighthouse in Baily, near Howth Head in Co. Dublin. A warning beacon is said to have been lit on Howth Head, at the northern end of Dublin Bay, since the 9th century. The celebrated Baily Lighthouse came into operation in its current location in 1816; it was then called 'the new lighthouse'. It was the last Irish lighthouse to be automated, in 1997.

> ... look, across
> dark waves where bell-buoys dimly toss
> the Baily winks beyond Howth Head
> and sleep calls from the silent bed;
> while the moon drags her kindred stones
> among the rocks and strict bones
> of the drowned ...
>
> DEREK MAHON: 'Beyond Howth Head', from *Collected Poems* (1999)

Báinín. A type of homespun woollen cloth, usually white. The word is sometimes anglicized as 'bawneen'. Hence the description of the Connemara migrant worker: *fear an bháinín bháin* ('the man wearing a white flannel jacket'). Originally used for homemade peasant over-shirts, *báinín* became an haute-couture material in Irish fashion houses after the Second World War.
See also CONNOLLY, SYBIL.

'Baint an Fhéir'. *See* CÉILÍ DANCES.

Baithín. An Ulster saint, first cousin of COLUM CILLE (Columba), with whom he shares the same feast day. Baithín went with Colum Cille to IONA and succeeded him as second abbot of the monastery there. According to tradition Baithín died on 9 June 598, the first anniversary of his patron's death.

Bake¹. A crude Ulsterism for the human mouth, being the local pronunciation of 'beak': 'If ye don't shut yer gob ah'll hit ye up the bake!'

Bake². A Cork slang word for 'disappointment', 'disaster': 'That concert was a bake!'

Balbh. An Irish word for 'dumb' used in HIBERNO-ENGLISH to indicate a fuzzy, unharmonious or echoing sound: 'That radio sounds very *balbh*.'

Balbriggan, Sack of. A notorious incident that took place on 20 September 1920, during the ANGLO-IRISH WAR, following the killing near Balbriggan, Co. Dublin, of Head Constable Peter Burke. Burke and his brother had stopped for refreshment at a pub when both were shot. Burke had been a popular instructor at the Phoenix Park RIC depot, with special charge of the Auxiliary Division. As an act of reprisal for the shooting a party of AUXIES from the depot at Gormanston, 5 km (3 miles) northwest of Balbriggan, set fire to houses and shops in Balbriggan and bayoneted two local men to death in an orgy of drunken looting. Women and children of the town had to seek refuge in barns and hayricks in the surrounding countryside.

The SINN FÉIN version of the story is that the Burkes were accompanied by Auxie cadets when they arrived after hours at the pub. When they were refused entry the local RIC were called, but they left on seeing a superior officer. Later two Sinn Féin 'police' arrived; Burke, it is claimed, drew his gun and the Sinn Féin men fired 'in self-defence'.

Balcaire. An Irish word for a strong, stout person, more likely in HIBERNO-ENGLISH to be used of a man.

Balcombe Street Siege, the. A stand-off that occurred in December 1974 when a London IRA active service unit (comprising Eddie Butler, Harry Duggan, Joe O'Connell and Hugh O'Doherty) was cornered in the first-floor flat of an elderly couple in Balcombe Street in the Marylebone district of London after a car chase and running gun battle. The British used hostage-bargaining techniques to ensure a surrender without injuries. The men involved were sentenced to life imprisonment in 1977, transferred to Portlaoise Prison in 1997 as part of the GOOD FRIDAY AGREEMENT, and soon released.

Bale, John. *See* BILIOUS BALE.

Balfe, Michael. *See* SIGNOR BALFO.

Balfour, Arthur (1848–1930). Conservative chief secretary for Ireland 1887–91. Born in East Lothian, he was educated at Eton and Cambridge. He adopted a repressive approach towards Irish land agitation and the PLAN OF CAMPAIGN, enacting coercive legislation (the Criminal Law and Procedure Act) in 1887, which remained in force until the early stages of the WAR OF INDEPENDENCE. He was nicknamed 'Bloody Balfour' for his association with the MITCHELSTOWN MASSACRE of 1887, when police fired on a crowd. But it was he who established the CONGESTED DISTRICTS BOARD, one of the main initiatives of the policy of 'Constructive Unionism' (*see* KILLING HOME RULE WITH KINDNESS; COERCION), in 1891, and in the same year he passed a Land Purchase Act (*see* LAND ACTS). Balfour served as British prime minister (1902–5), and later, as foreign secretary (1916–19), he issued the famous Balfour Declaration on the creation of a Jewish state in Palestine. His brother, Gerald Balfour (1853–1945), also served as chief secretary for Ireland (1895–1900).
See also SMILE LIKE MOONLIGHT ON A GRAVE-STONE.

Ball. A word used in HIBERNO-ENGLISH to indicate a big strong man, as in 'a fine ball of a man'.

Ballad groups. The rise of ballad groups was an Irish musical phenomenon of the 1960s, influenced by the rediscovery and popularity of folk music in the UK, USA and elsewhere and by a new self-confidence among young musicians. Among the best-known of such groups were The CLANCY BROTHERS, The DUBLINERS and The WOLF TONES. Patriotic ballads were a stock-in-trade of some of these groups, beards and chunky jerseys the uniform, and guitars, banjos and tin whistles the most popular instruments. Solo performers such as Danny Doyle and Johnny McEvoy continued to perform, either at home or in America, for decades after ballad groups in general had fallen from favour. 'Singing pubs' also provided a stage for ballad groups for many years, enticing a mainly tourist audience with posters promising an authentic ballad experience.

Ballast Board, the. *See* DUBLIN PORT AND DOCKS BOARD.

Balliboe (Irish *baile bó*, 'place of pasturage'). An Irish unit of land reckoned not by area but by productivity. It was taken to be one-sixteenth part of a BALLYBETAGH, also a unit of yield rather than acreage. Misinterpretation of the basis of these units was to have a particular significance at the time of the ULSTER PLANTA-TION, resulting in the allocation of much larger areas of land than had been intended. The English surveyors' arbitrary decision that the balliboe averaged 60 acres meant that the larger unit was approximately the 1000 acres that they intended as the standard plantation unit.

Ballinasloe Horse Fair and Festival. A horse fair and major tourist event held in October in Ballinasloe, east Co. Galway. The fair was held from the 1730s until it went into decline in the early years of the 20th century. It was revived in the 1950s as part of a local festival initiative. Up to 60,000 people now attend the fair each year.

Ballingeary. *See* MUSKERRY GAELTACHT, THE.

Ballinglass Evictions. On 13 March 1846 the entire population of the village of Ballinglass in Co. Galway was evicted by the landlord, Mrs Gerard, who wanted to devote her whole estate to grazing, which was more profitable and less troublesome. The evictions were widely condemned, but the decision was allowed to stand. In a statement to the House of Lords on 30 March 1846, Lord Londonderry, who had investigated the evictions, said:

> Seventy-six families, comprising 300 individuals, had not only been turned out of their houses but had even – the unfortunate wretches – been mercilessly driven to the ditches to which they had betaken themselves for shelter ... these unfortunate people had their rents actually ready.

Ballinspittle. *See* MOVING STATUES.

Ballitore. *See* ANNALS OF BALLITORE, THE.

Ballocks of Henry the Eighth, the. *See* MAGAIRLE ANNRAOI RÍ.

Ball of malt. An unspecified measure of whiskey, but usually taken to be a glass:

> Jody, old bootlegger, old friend of mine, old friend of Al Capone, serve me a drink to sober me up.
>
> Austin, said Jody, what will it be?
>
> A ball of malt and Madame Butterfly.
>
> That's my friend, Austin, she said, he always says that for a joke.
>
> BENEDICT KIELY (b.1919): title story from *A Ball of Malt and Madame Butterfly* (1973)

'Ballroom of Romance, The'. The title of a short story (1972) by William TREVOR, which was afterwards made into a successful teleplay in 1983. It touches on an Irish phenomenon of the 1950s and 1960s when huge barnlike structures with comically inappropriate names – such as that in Trevor's title – became the venues for SHOWBANDS. The dancehall may have been 'miles from anywhere, a lone building by the roadside with treeless boglands all around and a gravel expanse in front of it', but it was, along with the church, the main source of social intercourse in rural communities. These halls were 'dry', carefully supervised (often by the priest) and were beginning to replace the older social pattern of 'wakes and weddin's'.

The main narrative strand in Trevor's story, set in 1953, is a glimpse of the life of 36-year-old Bridie, who has to do all the work of the farm since her father lost a leg through gangrene. She has been twice disappointed in love and will probably in the end agree to marry the loutish Bowser Egan:

> She would wait now and in time Bowser Egan would seek her out because his mother would have died. Her father would probably have died by then. She would marry Bowser Egan because it would be lonesome being by herself in the farmhouse.

The weekly dance, with all its inadequacies, does offer the faint hope expressed in the hall's name, and it is marvellously depicted by Trevor, as is the backdrop of the Ireland of the time,

with its late marriages, high emigration, inert economy and *cafard* (blinding boredom). In 'The Ballroom of Romance' the author has devised a representative icon for the period as appropriate and significant as the POOR OLD WOMAN was for earlier generations.

Ballybetagh (Irish *baile biataigh*, 'food-providing land'). An Irish division of land, which, like the BALLIBOE, assumed a special significance at the time of the ULSTER PLANTATION. It was taken by the English survey to be the equivalent of the 1000 acres that was to be the standard plantation unit, but was in fact equal to 16 balliboes and therefore a variable unit based upon productivity rather than area. The divergence was all the greater in that much of Ulster's land was unworked. The actual ballybetagh corresponded with the old Gaelic sept (clan) division, and the re-allocation meant that the old boundaries were seen to be retained but with foreign masters.

Ballycastle. A town in Co. Antrim, the site of the OULD LAMMAS FAIR. Nearby is the magnificent FAIR HEAD.

Ballydehob. A village in west Cork, picturesquely situated on Roaring Water Bay, between Schull and Skibbereen, in an area that has attracted many BLOW-INS, The name has become proverbial for a picturesque Ireland with its roots in mythology.

Ballyeagh Strand. A beach by the mouth of the River Cashen in Co. Kerry, just south of Ballybunion, some 15 km (9 miles) northwest of Listowel. It was the scene of the most spectacular of a series of FACTION FIGHTS that took place in the south of Ireland in the early decades of the 19th century. On 24 June 1834, the day of the Ballyeagh Races, around 2500 people, some from the Cooleen faction and some from the Lawlor-Blacks Mulvihills, engaged in a bloody encounter on Ballyeagh Strand. Reports of casualties have, however, been greatly exaggerated (there were rumours of as many as 200 dead): a police report of early July 1834 said 15 bodies had been recovered, and recorded two people still missing. Most of the deaths were caused by drowning in the River Cashen.

Ballygobackwards. The rural town as viewed from Dublin, the name combining Bally- (Irish *baile*, 'town') with the gibe in English. There is an irony in the fact that many who use the term originated in such little towns themselves:

> They don't pension off Ballygobackwards stationmasters. We just drop dead. I've been on this job, man and boy, for the last forty years, and my father before, and his father. My father was ninety when he died and finished up doing the job in a bathchair. And his father was a hundred – what they call a centurion.
>
> HARRY O'DONOVAN (1896–1973): 'The Lost Railway', sketch for Jimmy O'Dea (*see* MULLIGAN, BIDDY) in *Stop Press* (1949)

See also BALLYSLAPADASHAMUCKERY.

Ballygowan. A leading Irish bottled water, produced since 1984. The brand was founded by Geoff Read and the water bottled by Richard Nash and Co. of Newcastle West, Co. Limerick. The Ballygowan natural mineral water source is a well near the town of Newcastle West, originally called St David's Well by the Knights Templar who discovered it in the 12th century. The drinking of water in pubs is a relatively recent phenomenon in Ireland, prompting old-stagers to lament: 'I never thought I'd see the day people would be buying water in pubs.'

Ballygullion. A fictional Ulster town that was the location of many humorous short stories by Lynn DOYLE. It was based upon DOWNPATRICK, the author's birthplace, a district of which was known as the 'Gullion' (Irish *goilín*, 'creek', 'gullet'), the name indicating a muddy, not to say sewery, stream. The first book, *Ballygullion* (1908), set the pattern, with the omniscient Mr Pat Murphy making life exciting and miserable by turns for the staid small-town solicitor Mr Anthony. The facts of the sectarian nature of Ulster life are treated with gentle satire, with the icons of both sides mildly mocked. Selections from the six collections, including *Lobster Salad* (1922), *Dear Ducks* (1925), *Me and Mr Murphy* (1930), appeared in *The Ballygullion Bus* (1957) with illustrations by William CONOR.

Ballyhoo. Originally a fairground barker's spiel, now usually associated with hyped publicity, especially in the USA. Some etymologists have suggested that the Irish word *bailiú* ('collection'), may be a source, the barker calling *bailiú* in order to extract money from the punters before allowing them into his booth to view the 'attraction'. Ballyhoo is also the name of a village in Co. Wexford.

Ballyhooly. A village near Fermoy, Co. Cork, notorious for its FACTION FIGHTING and hence giving its name to any form of rough treatment or unfriendly reception:

> Father Carroll has neglected to visit his relatives, the Kearneys, for a long time, so that he knows he's in the black books with Mrs Kearney, and expects Ballyhooly from her the first time he meets her.
>
> CHARLES KICKHAM (1828–82): *Knocknagow; or the Homes of Tipperary* (1879)

Ballyjamesduff. A town in Co. Cavan, immortalized by Percy FRENCH in his haunting song, written in 1912:

> The Garden of Eden has vanished they say,
> But I know the lie of it still,
> Just turn to the left at the bridge of Finea
> And stop when halfway to Cootehill.
> 'Tis there I will find it I know sure enough
> When fortune has come to my call,
> Oh the grass it is green around Ballyjamesduff
> And the blue sky is over it all,
> And tones that are tender and tones that are gruff
> Are whispering over the sea,
> Come back, Paddy Reilly, to Ballyjamesduff,
> Come back, Paddy Reilly, to me.

Paddy Reilly was a real person who had emigrated from the town.

'Ballykay'. *See* BALLYKISSANGEL.

Ballykissangel. A popular BBC TV light drama series, broadcast, although with changes in personnel, in six series (1996–2001). It was based on the doings of a fictional Co. Wicklow village, and was filmed on location in the village of Avoca, Co. Wicklow, and in Ardmore Studios near Bray in the same county. Initially Dervla Kirwan starred as publican Assumpta Fitzgerald, Stephen Tompkinson as Peter Clifford (the young English priest serving in the parish who falls in love with her), Tony Doyle (d.28 January 2001) as unscrupulous businessman Brian Quigley, and Niall Tóibín as Father Mac. Known to its fans as 'Ballykay', its popularity was also helped by the off-screen romance between Kirwan and Tompkinson.

Ballyknocken granite. A granite quarried near Blessington, Co. Wicklow. It was used in the construction of RUSSBOROUGH HOUSE and for façades, sills and piers in Edwardian Dublin.

Ballymagash. The fictional Irish small town created by Newry-born Frank Hall (1921–95) for the RTÉ TV programme *Hall's Pictorial Weekly*, of which 250 episodes were broadcast between autumn 1971 and spring 1980. The cast included Eamonn Morrissey and Frank Kelly, and the characters Councillor Parnell Mooney and Father Romulus Todd (who said of Queen Elizabeth I: 'She was the virgin queen but she was no more a virgin than I am!') are thought to have been based on real people from Hall's own area. Frank Hall had earlier presented *Newsbeat*, a magazine programme about provincial Ireland, in which actors read out the utterances of county councillors or county managers. He spotted the potential for satire in this and created his own satirical show. 'Ballymagashery', as its brand of humour became known, was a mixture of knockabout and pointed satire, described as 'subversive in a folksy way' by Frank Kelly. The programme lampooned finance minister Richie Ryan as 'minister for hardship' and anointed Jack LYNCH 'the REAL TAOISEACH'. The country's chaotic telephone service was a frequent object of derision. In 1978 Hall was appointed Ireland's film censor.

Ballymagraw Gazette, The. The title of a series

of variety programmes broadcast by BBC Northern Ireland in 1936. Set in a fictitious east Ulster village, it had a revue-style format, with material by Ruddick Millar and music by Dudley Hare. Because of the nature of the 'Most Contrary Region' (as Rex Cathcart described Northern Ireland in his book of that title in 1984), no hint of sectarian difference disturbed the tranquil rural scene.
See also MCCOOEYS, THE.

Ballymena (Irish *An Baile Meánach*, 'the middle townland'). A market town in central Co. Antrim with a population of 27,800 (1991). It is associated with another Antrim town, Ballymoney, in the children's chant:

> The people of County Antrim are bally mean about bally money.

Ballymena had until recently the reputation of being the heartland of Co. Antrim Protestantism, with strict Sabbath observance.

Ballymurphy. *See* MURPH, THE.

Ballyrag, to. An expression originating in 18th-century Ireland meaning 'to chide' or 'to rebuke'. Its slight air of STAGE-IRISHness has tended to soften its effect, and it is now used as the equivalent of 'tease'.

Ballyseedy Massacre. The reprisal killing of eight Republican prisoners by Free State forces under Commandant Ned Breslin on 7 March 1923, during the Irish CIVIL WAR. Nine prisoners, selected by Colonel David Neligan, were taken from Ballymullen Barracks in Tralee to Ballyseedy 5 km (3 miles) away, where a mine had been placed in a pile of stones. The prisoners were tied together and the mine was detonated; soldiers then shot those who remained alive. One man, Stephen FULLER, was blown clear and lived to tell the tale, appearing for the first time on television on Robert Kee's *Ireland: a Television History* in 1980, to the astonishment of many Irish people who had never realized the extent of Civil War brutality. The Free State army issued a statement that the prisoners had been killed while clearing a mine laid by the Republicans. The remains of the men were put into nine coffins and brought for burial to Tralee.

See also COUNTESS BRIDGE KILLINGS; KNOCKNA-GOSHEL AMBUSH; *TRAGEDIES OF KERRY*.

Ballyslapadashamuckery. An imaginary rural Irish town invented by the Dublin comedian Jack Cruise for his sketches in twice-yearly shows at the Olympia Theatre, Dublin, in the 1960s and 1970s. He also invented an apparently gormless character to feature in them. Though the humour depended upon an urban mixture of disdain and wariness towards rural Ireland, the sketches were not unkind. They were also written with the consciousness that many of the audience still were or had recently been inhabitants of a town like the invented one.

See also BALLYGOBACKWARDS.

Ballyvourney. *See* MUSKERRY GAELTACHT, THE.

Balm out. A Cork slang expression meaning to stretch out in exhaustion.

Balor of the Evil Eye. A Celtic death god, one of the dreaded FOMORIANS. Balor's eye gained its power from an accidental splash of a druidic draught of wisdom, the result being that anyone who looks upon it will die; and when its deadly power is needed in battle, it takes four men to lift the lid. In order to prevent the fulfilment of the prophecy that he will be slain by his own grandson, Balor shuts up his only daughter ETHLINN in a glass tower on TORY ISLAND. CIAN, the son of the DIAN CECHT, seduces her, and their son LUGH eventually kills Balor at one of the battles of MAGH TUIREADH (Moytura).

Baltic Exchange, the. The commodity and freight-chartering market in St Mary Axe in the City of London that was the scene of an IRA van bomb explosion involving 45 kg (100 lb) of SEMTEX on Friday 10 April 1992. Three people were killed in the blast, 91 injured and many millions of pounds worth of damage done to other City institutions as well. The British government paid £700 million compensation. The explosion took place on the day when the UK general election results showed the return of a fourth consecutive Tory government with a majority of 20 for John Major, and the atrocity was regarded as a grisly comment.

Baltinglass, Battle of. The name by which a cause célèbre of 1950 was known in the Irish media. The dispute was caused by the actions of a PARISH-PUMP POLITICIAN, James Everett (1890–1967), Labour TD for Wicklow. Everett was appointed minister for posts and telegraphs in the INTERPARTY GOVERNMENT that took office in 1948. In 1950, ignoring the rights of the incumbent family, the Cookes, he appointed one of his own supporters, Michael Farrell, as postmaster of the sub-post office in the village of Baltinglass, Co. Wicklow. The Cooke family protested, and many politicians were appalled by such naked JOBBERY. But after Labour's coalition partners, CLANN NA POBLACHTA, whose election plank included opposition to corruption, failed to demand justice from Everett, it was the people of Baltinglass themselves who took up cudgels in the Battle of Baltinglass. They arranged a boycott of the general store that Michael Farrell also owned in the village and the following year, 1951, Farrell resigned his position as postmaster. An anonymous contemporary ballad described the battle:

> There were Bren-guns and Sten-guns and whippet
>   tanks galore
> As the battle raged up and down from pub to
>   gen'ral store.

Baluba. A word indicating a person of extreme nastiness, in general use in Ireland since the 1960s. On 8 November 1960 nine Irish soldiers serving with the UN in Katanga, Congo, were killed in an ambush by members of the Baluba people. Since then certain unsavoury parts of cities may be referred to as Balubaland.

Bambrick, Joe (James) (1905–83). A prodigious professional soccer player and goalscorer known as 'Joe, Head, Heel or Toe' because of his abilities with any of the means referred to in this nickname. Born in Belfast, he played for the east Belfast team Glentoran and LINFIELD, and then joined in turn Chelsea and Walsall. He scored a double hat-trick in an international against Wales at Celtic Park, Belfast, in 1930, having scored 94 goals in the 1929–30 season with Linfield. Capped 11 times between 1929 and 1938, he is reckoned to have scored 1000 goals between 1925 and 1940.

Ban, the. From its inception in 1884 the GAA (Gaelic Athletics Association), as a defensive measure, banned its members not just from playing any 'foreign game', like soccer, hockey or rugby, but from attending any such game. So zealous was the organization in applying the ban that in 1939 it removed as patron of the association the president of Ireland, Douglas HYDE, because he had attended a rugby match.

The ban on foreign games was finally and belatedly dropped in 1971, and from then on, given the contemporary eruption of the Northern Troubles, the term 'ban' was reserved for a restriction that had always existed: that no member of UK forces in Northern Ireland (including the RUC) could participate in any GAA game. During this period in Northern Ireland, disputes frequently flared between the British army and the GAA: pitches were commandeered for military purposes in south Armagh, and players were harassed on their way to training. As a Nationalist organization, mainly composed of young men, the GAA drew the suspicions of the security forces, and in 1979 the GAA congress endorsed a motion 'unequivocally to support the struggle for national liberation'. With the advent of the peace process, pressure has mounted on the GAA, from both within and without, to relax the ban to allow members of the new PSNI to participate, as a large Catholic membership was envisaged for the revamped police force.

Banagher. The name of a town in Co. Offaly and a reservoir valley in Co. Derry, both of which are claimed to be the source of the expression: 'That beats Banagher and Banagher beats the band', which expresses surprise at something unusual. Anthony TROLLOPE lived in the Offaly town on his first appointment as a Post Office official in 1841, and it was there that he began his first two novels, *The Macdermots of Ballycloran* (1847) and *The Kellys and the O'Kellys* (1848). He used a variety of the expression in the second of these: 'Conspiracy! av that don't bang Banagher!' The expression is more likely to have originated with the town of Banagher, which was a notorious rotten borough: when a member of Parliament spoke of a family borough where every voter was a man employed by the owner, it was not unusual to reply, 'Well, that beats Banagher.' The expression assumed with time a personification in the version: 'That beats Banagher and he beat the divil.'

Banba. A TUATHA DÉ DANANN goddess, who, like her sisters, ÉIRE and FODLA, vies to have Ireland named in her honour. They are part of the fifth wave of colonists, descendants of the mother goddess DANA[1], and have to acquiesce in the conquest of the MILESIANS. She loses out to Éire when AMERGIN makes his decision, but is compensated by the regular use of her name in poetry.

Banbh. The Irish term for 'sucking pig', anglicized as 'bonham':

> … shying clods against the visage of the stars till he'd put the fear of death into the banbhs and the screeching sows.
>
> J.M. SYNGE (1871–1909): *The Playboy of the Western World* (1907)

Banbh is also the word used in Irish for the ace of hearts.

Banbridge. *See* TOWN WITH THE HOLE IN THE MIDDLE, THE.

Bandit Country. A name given to the southern part of Co. Armagh, by the then Labour secretary of state for Northern Ireland, Merlyn Rees, in November 1975. Rees used the name after the shooting by the IRA of three British soldiers at Drummuckavall, near Crossmaglen:

> There has never been a cease-fire in South Armagh for a variety of reasons – the nature of the countryside and the nature of the people. It is an unusual area – there is little support for the security forces in South Armagh. The government

is not trying to buy off terrorism by the release of detainees as the number of terrorists arrested and charged shows. The release of detainees has nothing to do with the violence of the bandit country of South Armagh There is wholesale gangsterism there.

The term was resented by Nationalists, who saw it as typical of British efforts to portray as the actions of thugs and outlaws what they regarded as blows for Irish freedom. Some Republicans, however, revelled in it as a 'badge of honour' and as triumphant proof of the effectiveness of the IRA's military strategy in the area. South Armagh is bordered on three sides by the Irish Republic and its largely Catholic population is historically sympathetic to the Republican cause. From the outset of the troubles it was dominated by the Provisional IRA, who operated here with greater freedom of action than in any other part of Northern Ireland. Attacks by the local brigade of the IRA included the sectarian massacre at KINGSMILLS, near Newry, in January 1976, of 12 Protestants (itself a revenge attack for the slaughter of 3 Catholics by Loyalists), the ambush and murder of 18 British soldiers at Narrow Water, near WARRENPOINT, in August 1979, and the assassination of Captain Robert NAIRAC, a maverick Grenadier Guards officer, whose body has never been found. A bestselling book, *Bandit Country*, by Toby Harnden (1999) exploited the cliché of South Armagh's lawlessness.

Bandle (Irish *banlámh*, 'cubit'). A measure of 52.5 cm (21 in), a dated term used in HIBERNO-ENGLISH for homespun cloth in particular.

Bandon. A market town in Co. Cork, on the river of the same name, situated 30 km (20 miles) southwest of Cork city. It was established in 1608 by Richard BOYLE, Earl of Cork. Through marriage the town passed to the Dukes of Devonshire, who were responsible for the construction of most of the public buildings. In the summer of 1921, in a famous incident in the Anglo-Irish War, the home of Lord Bandon, Castle Bernard, was burnt down and its owner kidnapped by the IRA under the leadership of Tom BARRY. Lord Bandon was released a few days later.

See also BIG HOUSE; EVEN THE PIGS ARE PROTESTANTS.

'Band Played On, The'. A popular Irish-American song, written in 1895. The words were by John F. Palmer, an American actor, and the music by Charles B. Ward, whose stage performances made it popular. The sheet-music sales eventually reached a million copies, and its continuing popularity has given the title an almost proverbial resonance:

> Casey would waltz with a strawberry blonde and
> the band played on.
> He'd glide 'cross the floor with the girl he ador'd
> and the band played on.
> But his brain was so loaded it nearly exploded
> The poor girl would shake with alarm.
> He married the girl with the strawberry curls
> And the band played on.

Bang Bang. A Dublin character who has featured in many memoirs, so called because he had a habit of pointing a key at people he met and shouting 'Bang Bang!' He would also engage in mock gun battles with children. His real name was Tommy Dudley (1905–81).

Bangharda (Irish, 'policewoman'). The word used for a woman garda when females were first recruited for the GARDA SÍOCHÁNA on 9 July 1959. The first woman to be gazetted was Mary Margaret Browne from Castlerea, Co. Roscommon, and in April 2000 Catherine Clancy from Portnoo, Co. Donegal, was appointed the first female chief superintendent. Since 1991 the term *bangharda* has been discontinued and the general term 'garda' applied to all officers.

Bangor. A commuter town 20 km (12 miles) northeast of Belfast on the south bank of Belfast Lough. A popular seaside resort and centre for yachting, it was the site of the leading 6th-century Ulster monastery founded by St COMGALL in 555 and ruled by him for 50 years. Among its most famous alumni were

COLUMBAN, GALL, MAELRUBHA and MALACHY. Its greatest treasure is the ANTIPHONARY OF BANGOR, which travelled with Columban to Bobbio and so escaped destruction when the abbey was sacked by the Vikings in 824 and regularly thereafter.

Bang-up. An overcoat of frieze (a heavy woollen material) with a high collar and long cape common in the early 19th century:

> A green coat cut round in jockey fashion, and over it a white bang-up.
>> CHARLES LEVER (1806–72): *Jack Hinton the Guardsmen* (1843)

Banim, John (1798–1842) and **Banim, Michael** (1796–1874). Two novelist brothers, born in Kilkenny. Together they wrote a series of novels (in attempted imitation of those of Sir Walter Scott) that aimed to present the Irish in an acceptable light to the British. It was John who, after the severe trauma of a tragic love affair, suggested writing the O'Hara tales: 24 books followed, of which 13 were written by Michael. Though overly sentimental and with Irish locutions embarrassingly rendered (*see* HIBERNO-ENGLISH), they gave an honest picture of post-Union Ireland, with its tithe and repeal struggles and its violent secret-society culture, and thus showed the way for better writers. Of most significance are the contemporary tales, for example *Crohoore of the Billhook* (1825) and *The Mayor of Windgap* (1835), both by Michael, and *The Nowlans* (1826) by John, who also wrote the historical novel *The Boyne Water* (1826). In *The Croppy* (1828), Michael, by now a prosperous Kilkenny merchant and briefly mayor of the city, tended to play down the violence and question the wisdom of the UNITED IRISHMEN. John, who died prematurely of the spinal tuberculosis that blighted his life, is also the author of the well-known poem SOGGARTH AROON.
See also ROTHE HOUSE.

Banjax. A Dublin slang term, still in vogue, meaning 'break', 'ruin', 'destroy'. The word is more often used in its adjectival form: 'That drill is banjaxed,' or (heard frequently in the recessionary 1980s), 'The whole country is banjaxed.' Gay BYRNE attracted the criticism of politicians and many members of the public for broadcasting this comment on his popular morning radio show. The word is of obscure derivation, possibly a composite of 'banged' and 'bashed'.

Banjo. A four-stringed instrument that is played by plucking. Its origins are thought to be African, and banjos were associated with American 'minstrel' shows. Percy FRENCH played a banjo to accompany his songs in the 1880s. The banjo came to Irish traditional music from Irish-America and became popular among BALLAD GROUPS in the 1960s, its greatest exponent being Barney McKenna of The DUBLINERS.

Bank. To cover the embers (*see* GRÍOSACH; GREESHY) of the fire with ashes in such a way that the fire could be revived in the morning. In some houses a prayer was said as the fire, the symbol of the life of the house, was banked:

> With the powers that were granted to Patrick I bank this fire.
> May the angels keep it in, no enemy scatter it.
> May God be the roof of our house for all within and all without,
> Christ's sword on the door till tomorrow's light.

In traditional rural society in Ireland until the 1960s, no other means of ignition existed except the hearth. If the fire went out seed would have to be fetched from a neighbour's house to relight it.

Bank Buildings. *See* INTERNATIONAL DATE LINE.

'Banks, The'. The abbreviation by which the Cork anthem 'On the Banks of My Own Lovely Lee' is known to citizens of the second city and their detractors. The definite article in the title is often rendered as 'de' in a supposed attempt at a Cork accent. A persistent air of mystery surrounds the song since nothing is known of its composer, except his name (Jonathan C. Hanrahan) and the fact that the song was written for a local pantomime. The MARDYKE was a fashionable promenade:

How oft do my thoughts in their fancy take flight,
To the home of my childhood away,
To the days when each patriot vision seem'd bright
Ere I dream'd that those joys could decay.
When my heart was as light as the wild winds that
    blow,
Down the Mardyke by each elm tree,
Where I sported and played 'neath each green leafy
    shade
On the banks of my own lovely Lee.

Bann. The name of two rivers (conveniently referred to as one) in Ulster, the Upper Bann which flows for 60 km (40 miles) from the MOURNE MOUNTAINS into Lough Neagh, and the Lower Bann, which runs also for 60 km (40 miles) from the lough's northwest corner and flows into the Sea of MOYLE between Coleraine and Castlerock on the north coast. To Edmund SPENSER the river was 'the fishy fruitfull Ban' (*The Faerie Queen* IV xi 41), and since it was the border between counties Antrim and Derry in the north, there was a sense that, with the lough, it formed a natural division between east and west Ulster. When in the 1950s and 1960s it was observed that government industrial investment and development seemed to be concentrated in the east, the term 'west of the Bann' assumed a political significance, as an index of STORMONT's deliberate deprivation of the Nationalist west.

Bannalanna (Irish *bean a' leanna*, 'alewoman'). The woman who served liquor in a SHEBEEN; the term dates from the 19th century and earlier.

> *Chuaigh mé 'steach i dteach aréir*
> *'s d'iarras deoch ar bhean a' leanna …*
> (I went into a house last night
> And asked the alewoman for a drink …)
> ANON: 'Níl Sé 'na Lá'

Banner. An important part of the regalia of procession. Banners came into general use at the beginning of the 19th century when trade guilds and other societies began to appear in public at demonstrations and galas, and were particularly appropriate in the ORANGE ORDER tradition of the WALK. Each LOL (Loyal Orange Lodge) tended to have its own highly decorated banner, behind which they marched to rallies, and which also acted as an identifier at the FIELD. Orange banners usually depict scenes from the Williamite War, though many also have biblical imagery, especially those of the ROYAL BLACK INSTITUTION. The AOH and the IRISH NATIONAL FORESTERS also employ banners in their processions, the predominant colour being green, with representations of such paladins as St PATRICK and Robert EMMET as the main motif.

> The Orangemen have their dramatic traditions and when I speak of traditions I don't mean fictions, for many of them have contributed to the tumultuous history of Ireland, They are painted on their banners: The Closing of the Gates of Derry by the Apprentice Boys, The Death of Schomberg, The Mountjoy Breaking the Boom that Barred the Foyle …
> SAM HANNA BELL (1909–90): 'To Chap the Lambeg' in *Erin's Orange Lily* (1956)

Banner County, the. The nickname of Co. Clare, deriving from the visual support given to the parliamentary candidature of Daniel O'CONNELL at an 1828 election rally of monster proportions. This and other county nicknames are now used mainly as fillers in media commentaries for the GAA football and hurling ALL-IRELAND championships.

Bannock. A flat cake popular in Ulster, usually made of oatmeal and baked on a griddle. The word is of Scots origin.

Bann Valley Exodus. The move by 200 Presbyterians from the villages of Macosquin and Aghadowey, Co. Derry, in 1718 to the territory north of the Merrimac River in what is now New Hampshire, USA. Led by the Rev. James McGregor of Aghadowey and the Rev. William Boyd (d.1772) of Macosquin, they settled at Nutfield, which they renamed Londonderry in honour of Ulster Protestantism's 'finest hour'. They brought with them their skills in linen manufacture, founding the colony's first mill. McGregor's last sermon concluded with these Mosaic words:

Brethren, let us depart, for God has appointed a new country for us to dwell in. It is called New England. Let us be free of these Pharaohs, these rackers of rent and screwers of tithes, and let us go into the land of Canaan.

Banshee (Irish *bean sí*, 'fairy woman'). A female spirit who wailed in sympathy near the houses of certain families when death was expected. She was usually seen to comb her long grey hair. In some parts of Ireland she was known as *bean chaointe* (Irish, 'weeping woman').

> O'er the wild heath I roam,
> On the night wind I come;
> And beauty shall pale at the voice of my wail!
> Hush! Hark to my tiding of gloom and sorrow!
> Go weep tears of blood, for – Och! *D'éag an corra*.
>
> J. L. FORREST: 'The Banshee's Song' (1907) (Irish
> *D'éag an corra*, 'the dear one died')

Bantry Band, the. The political machine controlled by Tim HEALY, who came from Bantry.

Bantry Bay. A long (34km/21miles) and beautiful sea lough in Co. Cork, the inspiration for one of Ireland's favourite parlour pieces, and the site of two visits by French fleets, in 1689 in support of JAMES II, and in 1796 abortively to aid an insurrection by the UNITED IRISHMEN. On 1 May 1689 the French landed a number of troops and after an indecisive engagement in the bay with an English force returned home. On the later occasion the French force consisted of 43 ships and 15,000 men, led by Lazare Hoche (1769–97), with Wolfe TONE on board the *Indomptable*. The fleet was scattered by December storms and command disagreements, and returned home to Brest – to Tone's terrible frustration, as he recorded in his diary for 21 December: '… we were near enough to toss a biscuit ashore'.

A century later the bay became the inspiration of James Lynam Molloy's (1837–1909) best-known Irish ballad, 'Bantry Bay' (1879):

> As I'm sitting all alone in the gloaming,
> It might have been but yesterday,
> That we watched the fisher sails all homing,
> Till the little herring fleet at anchor lay.
> Then the fisher girls with baskets swinging,

> Came running down the old stone way;
> Every lassie to her sailor lad was singing,
> A welcome back to Bantry Bay.

See also WHIDDY ISLAND DISASTER.

Banville, John (b.1945). Novelist. He was born in Wexford on 8 December 1945 and educated at St Peter's College. He worked as a journalist with the *Irish Press* from 1980, and was literary editor of *The Irish Times* (1988–98). His first book, *Long Lankin* (1970), is a collection of linked stories with a novella that incorporates most of the characters, the effect being a kind of literary tarot pack. *Nightspawn* (1971) is a deliberately confusing novel about Greece in 1967, the year of the Colonels' takeover. *Birchwood* (1973) is Irish Gothic set in a BIG HOUSE at an uncertain date and including a spontaneous combustion. Banville's next four novels are a consideration of the imaginative lives of such scientists as Copernicus, Kepler and Newton. *The* BOOK OF EVIDENCE (1989), *Ghosts* (1993) and *Athena* (1995) deal with the moral life of a confessed murderer, Freddie Montgomery, who, having 'explained' his action in the first book, finds himself on an island full of noises; in these books Banville explores the meaning and nature of fiction as he creates his cerebral, often cold characters. Recent novels include *The Untouchable* (1997), *Eclipse* (2000) and *Shroud* (2002).

Bap, to lose the. An expression, most often heard in Ulster, meaning to lose one's temper or self control. A bap is a light breakfast roll very popular in Scotland and Ulster, which, from its shape, is taken to be like the human face.

Barbados. The most easterly of the West Indies, an independent island state since 1966. A former British colony, it was uninhabited at the time it was appropriated as a British possession in 1627. Barbados was intended as a tobacco island, and its first inhabitants were indentured servants. As such it seemed a suitable destination for many Irish deportees sent by Oliver CROMWELL after his conquest of Ireland (1649–50) (*see* TRANSPORTATION). An estimated 12,000 men, women and boys were sent to it and other West Indian islands:

> It hath pleased God to bless our endeavour at Drogheda ... I believe we put to the sword the whole number of the defendants. I do not think thirty of the whole number escaped with their lives; those that did are safe in custody for Barbadoes ...
>
> OLIVER CROMWELL (1599–1658): 'Dispatch to the Speaker of the House of Commons' (1649)

Barber, Mary. *See* SAPPHIRA.

Barcelona. A silk scarf, formerly smuggled from Spain:

> His clothes spick and span new without e'er a speck;
> A neat Barcelona tied round his neat neck.
>
> EDWARD LYSAGHT (1763–1810): 'The Sprig of Shillelah' (*c*.1800)

Bardicks (Irish *bardóg*, 'pannier'). A word signifying by metonymy 'possessions or baggage':

> So sez I, 'I'll not stan' it no longer,
> Ye can take me or lave me, an min'
> Here's the cowlt can take me in the seddle
> With you an' yir bardhix behin'.
>
> W.F. MARSHALL (1888–1959): 'The Runaway' (1929) in *Ballads and Verses from Tyrone* (1929)

Bardic order. *See* BARDIC POETRY.

Bardic poetry. The classical writings of members of the bardic order of Ireland and Gaelic Scotland. The bardic tradition goes back to pre-Christian Celtic Gaul, and classical Gaelic poetry continued to be composed until the middle of the 17th century. The words *file* and *bard* were used interchangeably in early times for 'poet', but gradually the FILID, the class of professional poets, came to be regarded as the keepers of ancient lore, while the bards (a term of some disparagement in the ANGLO-IRISH CHRONICLES) were professional versifiers whose main occupation was the composition of praise poems for their aristocratic patrons, elegies, epithalamiums and, should the occasion arise, metric incitements to battle. The distinctions were eventually reconciled, and over the centuries bardic schools were established in which a highly stylized and excessively

rigid form of verse known as the *dán díreach* ('straight poetry') was learned by apprentices with a dedication and a commitment that was almost monastic. The bardic order fell with the collapse of the Gaelic aristocracy in the 16th and 17th centuries, but ironically the poetic flame burned brightest with its termination as the poets expressed agony and confusion as their world fragmented.

See also AISLING.

Bard of Bansha, the. The name by which Tipperary poet Darby Ryan (1777–1855) was known. He was born in the Glen of Aherlow and attended a local HEDGE SCHOOL. Because he showed an early talent for literature he was allowed access to the library in the local BIG HOUSE, Bansha Castle. A local priest arranged for him to study for the priesthood in Rome, but he was never ordained. He wrote a great deal of poetry in Irish and English but is remembered for '*Aréir Cois Taoibhe na hAtharlaigh*' ('last night by the side of the Aherlow River') and especially for the satirical 'The PEELER AND THE GOAT'. In 1997 the local community erected a memorial stone over his grave in Bansha.

Bard of Thomond, the. The self-awarded title of Michael Hogan, who was born in Thomondgate, Co. Limerick, in 1832 and produced much McGonagallesque verse for *The* NATION and other periodicals. His best-known poem, compared vainly with Burns's 'Tam o'Shanter' by some partisans, is 'Drunken Thady and the Bishop's Lady' (1860):

> At half-past one the town was silent,
> Except a row raised in the Island,
> Where Thady – foe to sober thinking –
> With comrade boys sat gaily drinking!
> A table with a pack of cards
> Stood in the midst of four blackguards ...

He worked for Limerick Corporation and died in 1899.

Bard of Wexford, the. *See* WEXFORD BARD, THE.

Barge. An Ulster-Scots word, functioning as both verb and noun, equivalent to the English 'scold'. Drunken Irish husbands have from time to time found it necessary to plead with Arctic wives, 'Don't barge me, dear!'

Barlow, Jane (1857–1917). Poet and novelist. She was born in Clontarf, Co. Dublin, the daughter of the Rev. James Barlow, later vice-provost of Trinity College Dublin. Though by no means a strident Nationalist, she had a sense of an independent Ireland and showed great resentment of British imperialism. Her best-known collection of poetry is *Bogland Studies* (1892), but it was in her prose, especially in *Irish Idylls* (1892), that she showed her empathy with Connacht peasants. *Irish Idylls* went into eight editions and was the main spur to her honorary D.Litt. from Trinity. She died in Bray, Co. Wicklow, on 17 April 1917.

> No need to hush the children for her sake
> Or fear their play …
> She will not wake, mavrone, she will not wake,
> 'Tis the long sleep, the deep long sleep she'll take
> Betide what may.
> 'Out of Hearing'

Barmbrack or **barnbrack** (Irish *bairín breac*, 'speckled loaf'). A large bun made with sugar, dried fruit and spices, generally popular but particularly associated with Hallowe'en cele-brations, when significant tokens such as rings, buttons and coins are inserted at the preparation stage. The slice with the token indicates the recipient's future, a ring meaning marriage and a button blessed singleness:

> 'Twas Thesie cut the barnbrack and found the ring inside;
> Before next Hallows' E'en has dawned herself will be a bride.
> WINIFRED LETTS : 'Hallows' E'en', in *Songs of Leinster* (1913)

Barmbracks are now produced commercially, some of them still containing the afore-mentioned tokens.

Barnacle, Nora (1884–1951). Mistress, wife and widow of James JOYCE. She was born in Galway and after leaving school at 13 worked as doorkeeper at the Presentation Convent. At the age of 20 she ran away from home after a

beating from a maternal uncle/guardian for walking out with a Protestant. She worked as a chambermaid in Finn's Hotel in Leinster Street off Nassau Street beside Trinity College in Dublin. When Joyce's ebullient father heard the name of his eldest child's mistress he said, 'Well. At least she'll stick to him!' The name is in fact simply a clumsy English version of the fairly common Connacht name Ó Cadhain or Coyne (the Irish word *cadhan* means 'barnacle goose'). She and Joyce met on 16 June 1904, the day since sanctified as Bloomsday (*see* ULYSSES), and on 8 October they left together for Pola in Croatia (then part of Austria-Hungary), where Joyce taught English in a Berlitz school. She lived up to her surname, sticking by her Jim through much poverty, homesickness, worry and changes of address. She was bright, witty, terse in her comments but not especially inter-ested in literature. She once said, 'Jim should have stuck to singing instead of writing.' They married in 1931 (*see* GREENE, GRETTA) and she survived him by ten years, dying of uremic poisoning on 10 April 1951. She is buried near him in Fluntern Cemetery in Zürich (the space beside him being taken). The presumptuous Swiss priest who described her at the graveside as, '*eine grosse Sünderin*' ('a great sinner') could hardly have been wider of the mark.

Barnardo's Homes. The charitable institutions founded by the Dublin philanthropist, Thomas John Barnardo. He was born on 4 July 1845, the son of a furrier, and at the age of 17 was converted to Christianity. He decided that if he were to be a successful missionary a medical degree would prove useful, and it was as a student in London that he realised his true voca-tion. Seeing the condition of homeless children in Stepney, he set up the East End Mission in 1867. His first home for boys was opened in 1870, and a girls' village followed in 1874. Though often in financial difficulties, he lived up to his own rule that 'No destitute children should be turned away.' By the time of his death on 19 September 1905 he knew that he had taken 250,000 waifs off the streets. There are now over a hundred Dr Barnardo's Homes (the 'doctor' being an honorary title, since he had never found time to complete his medical training).

Barnbrack. *See* BARMBRACK.

Barnewall, Sir Patrick (d.1622). Brother-in-law of Hugh O'NEILL and a leading spokesman for OLD ENGLISH Catholics in Ireland during the lord deputyship of Arthur CHICHESTER (1605–15). This was at a time of persecution of Catholics under the so-called 'Mandates' policy. Mandates were letters sent to chosen individuals – the first 16 were wealthy Dublin merchants, including a number of aldermen – in the name of the king, ordering them to attend Protestant worship under pain of punishment. If they did not obey the mandate, they were summoned to appear before the Court of Castle Chamber in Dublin Castle. The first such hearing was scheduled for 22 November 1605, and Chichester had withheld news of the Gunpowder Plot of earlier that month to achieve maximum effect during the proceedings. The accused were heavily fined (£100 in place of the normal recusancy fine of one shilling) and imprisoned until such time as they conformed. Barnewall appealed to Robert Cecil, Earl of Salisbury and English secretary of state, on behalf of Old English Catholics, claiming that, 'by this unlawful course of proceeding ... even now are laid down the foundations of some future rebellion.' He was imprisoned in Dublin and later moved to the Tower of London, but he continued his campaign from prison and returned to Ireland in triumph when the policy was suspended.

Barney. A HIBERNO-ENGLISH word with two distinct meanings: firstly 'row' or 'fight', from the reputation of the Irish abroad, the forename being commonly used as a diminutive of Brian (*see also* PADDY[1]); and secondly 'head', as in the phrase: 'Don't bother your barney about them.'

Barnies. *See* BARONIAL CONSTABULARY.

Barn of Scullabogue. *See* SCULLABOGUE, BARN OF.

Baronial Constabulary. The Irish police force until a centrally controlled Irish Constabulary (later the Royal Irish Constabulary; *see* RIC) was established in 1822. The responsibility for law enforcement in Ireland lay for the most part with local grand juries who recruited constables on the basis of BARONIES. These 'Barnies' were exclusively Protestant and ineffective, being part-time, poorly paid, unarmed, badly managed and corrupt.

Baronies. The name for administrative units of British jurisdiction. There were 273 in all, and they are thought to have originally coincided with the territories of Gaelic chieftains. They were used for the purposes of taxation and law enforcement (*see* BARONIAL CONSTABULARY) until the local government reforms of the 19th century, particularly the Local Government Act of 1898. The 1901 census was the last to be taken on the basis of baronies.

Barracks. The word commonly used in Ireland for 'police station', a relic of the paramilitary nature of the Royal Irish Constabulary (RIC) at its foundation. These symbols of British rule housed members of the RIC in towns and villages all over Ireland, often in fine stone houses. Although an armed force, the RIC, comprising mainly Catholics from rural Ireland, achieved a high degree of acceptance in the peaceful conditions at the end of the 19th century and the beginning of the 20th.

Many of the early actions of the ANGLO-IRISH WAR of 1919–21 consisted of IRA attacks on RIC stations in order to seize arms, with frequent fatalities. Soon barracks were sandbagged and fortified to withstand attack, but many, particularly those in isolated rural areas, proved impossible to defend, and were closed during the course of 1920 and 1921. Many RIC barracks were converted into GARDA SÍOCHÁNA barracks after the establishment of the Irish Free State. The word continued to be used in both parts of Ireland after the force's disbandment, applied equally to Royal Ulster Constabulary (RUC) and to Garda Síochána stations.

Barrett, Dick. One of four Republican prisoners executed by a Free State firing squad in MOUNT-JOY JAIL on 8 December 1922.
See also O'CONNOR, RORY.

Barrett, Eaton Stannard. *See* POLYBUS.

Barrington, Sir Jonah. *See* HALF-MOUNTED GEN-TLEMEN; *PERSONAL SKETCHES*.

Barrow. A river that rises in the Slieve Bloom mountains and flows 190 km (118 miles) south to meet the River NORE just north of New Ross and the River SUIR at Waterford (*see* THREE SISTERS, THE). It still lives up to its Spenserian description:

> … the goodly Barow, which doth hoord
> Great heapes of Salmons in his deepe bosome.
>> EDMUND SPENSER: *The Faerie Queen* (1590),
>> IV. xi. 43.

Barr Tribunal. *See* ABBEYLARA SHOOTING, THE.

Barry, James (*c.*1799–1865). A noted army surgeon. Barry was in reality the Cork-born younger daughter of Mary Ann Bulkeley, who emigrated to London at the turn of the 19th century. So precociously brilliant was 'James' Barry that 'he' graduated in medicine from Edinburgh University at the age of about 17, appearing to observers to be a small, effeminate boy. Barry then enlisted in the British army's medical corps and was posted to Cape Town, where she distinguished herself as a skilful and humane doctor, performing one of the first Caesarean sections. Before she retired she had reached the rank of inspector-general of British Hospitals. She died of dysentery in London in 1865 and the truth, that she was a woman not a man, did not emerge until the woman who had come to lay her out saw her naked body.

Barry, John. *See* FATHER OF THE AMERICAN NAVY.

Barry, Kevin. *See* 'MOUNTJOY JAIL ONE MONDAY MORNING, IN'.

Barry, Michael Joseph. *See* BRUTUS.

Barry, Sebastian. *See* STEWARD OF CHRISTEN-DOM, THE.

Barry, Spranger. *See* HARMONIOUS BARRY.

Barry, Tom (1897–1980). The IRA leader in west Cork in the Anglo-Irish War of 1919–21.
See also BANDON; BIG HOUSE; 'BOYS OF KIL-MICHAEL, THE'; *GUERRILLA DAYS IN IRELAND*; KILMICHAEL AMBUSH.

Barrytown. *See* DOYLE, RODDY.

Basin, the. *See* BLESSINGTON BASIN.

Bastable. A cast-iron pot with a snug-fitting lid used for baking bread. It was suspended over the open fire of turf or coal, and hot embers were placed on the lid as well to secure balanced heating (*see* GREESHY). The name comes from Barnstaple in Devon, once famous for pottery and metal ware.
See also CAKE.

Bastable cake. A loaf of bread baked in a BASTABLE oven.

Bastins. *See* BEESTINGS.

Bastoon (Irish *bastún*, 'poltroon'). A HIBERNO-ENGLISH term still in use, meaning 'bounder' or 'blockhead'. It is usually applied to males only.

Bat. A word meaning a hard blow with the hand. Its use is most common in Ulster: 'I hit him a right bat up the BAKE[1].'

Bata scóir. *See* TALLYSTICKS.

Bate. A Cork slang word for a thick slice of bread: 'Go home to your mother and she'll give you a bate of bread.'

Bates, Dawson. *See* SPECIAL POWERS ACT.

Batter. To perform a SEAN-NÓS dance, a type of step-dance found in parts of Connemara, also called a *battráil* in Irish, a borrowing from the English term. Traditionally only men danced the heavy 'battering' dances, women confining themselves to reels and the lighter jigs.

Batter, to be on the. A current slang phrase, especially common in Dublin, meaning to be on a drinking binge, often a prolonged one. *See also* SKITE.

Battle of … *See under* the main part of the name, e.g. BOYNE, BATTLE OF THE.

Baukie. An Ulster word for 'louse'.

Baukie bird. An Ulster and Scots dialect word for a 'bat' (i.e. the flying mammal).

Bawn¹ (Irish *bán,* 'white' or 'fair-haired'). A HIBERNO-ENGLISH term of endearment, as in 'girl bawn' or 'boy bawn'. A small child might be addressed as 'Boyeen bán' by adding the diminutive suffix 'een' (Irish *ín*). A 'white-haired boy' is someone who can do no wrong. *The Whiteheaded Boy,* the title of Lennox Robinson's 1916 play, is a variant. The term is still in use in rural areas if Ireland and among older people.
See also COLLEEN BAWN, THE.

Bawn² (Irish *bán,* 'lea-ground', 'pasture'). A HIBERNO-ENGLISH word for an untilled field.

Bawn³ (Irish *babhún,* 'walled enclosure'). The term applied to the fortified part of an individual settlement during the early days of the ULSTER PLANTATION. Undertakers (i.e. those who were prepared to take an active part in the plantation) of more than 1000 acres (400 ha) were expected to build a defendable forecourt against attack from the original dispossessed landholders. The term is preserved in such place-names as Bawnboy (Irish *An Bábhún Buí,* 'the yellow bawn') in Co. Cavan. The term 'bawn' was also used for any fortified enclosure attached to a tower house or castle, much favoured by the Anglo-Normans in medieval Ireland.

Bawneen. *See* BÁINÍN.

Bawnoge (Irish *bánóg,* 'green patch'). A HIBERNO-ENGLISH word for the flat green patch to be found outside a cattle byre, and hence also an area used as an open-air dance floor.

Bax, Sir Arnold. *See* O'BYRNE, DERMOT.

Bazzer. A Cork slang term for 'haircut'.

Béal bán (Irish, 'white mouth'). An Irish expression adopted unchanged into HIBERNO-ENGLISH to indicate flattery or soft words, and synonymous with the more common PLÁMÁS.

Béal bocht, an (Irish, 'the poor mouth'). An uncomplimentary phrase mocking those pretending to be poor: 'She's aye puttin' on the poor mouth.'

An Béal Bocht is also the title of a comic novel in Irish (1941) by Myles na Gopaleen (aka Brian O'Nolan, aka Flann O'BRIEN; *see* CRUIS-KEEN LAWN), satirizing the gloom and doom of books written about the GAELTACHT areas of the Atlantic seaboard, notably *An t*-OILEÁNACH by Tomás Ó Críomhtháin and CAISLEÁIN ÓIR by Séamus Ó Grianna:

> *Tharraing an máistir an maide ina ghlaic athuair*
> *agus níor stop sé go raibh fuil an mhacaoimh seo*
> *go líonmhar aige a dórtadh, an an mhacaoimh*
> *féin gan aon mhothú anois ann acht a mhalairt go*
> *fírinneach, é sínte 'na chuachán fola ar an urlár.*
> *Agus le linn an bhuailte scread an mháistir arís*
> 　　'Yer nam is Jams O'Donnell.'
> *Mar sin go dtí go raibh gach créatúr sa scoil*
> *buailte aige agus Jams O'Donnell tabartha mar*
> *ainm ar gach duine acu. Ní raibh aon cloigeann óg*
> *sa dúiche gan scoilteadh an lá sin.*
>
> (The master again shook the oar that was in his grasp and continued until he was shedding blood extensively, the child stretched motionless on the floor, a bloody heap. During the beating the master screamed again,
> 　　'Yer nam is Jams O'Donnell.'
> He continued in this fashion until he had flattened every child in the school and each had been re-named Jams O'Donnell. That day not a single young skull remained unsplit in the district.)
> 　　MYLES NA GOPALEEN: *An Béal Bocht* (1941)

An English translation by Patrick C. Power appeared in 1964, under the title *The Poor Mouth.*

Béal na mBláth (Irish, 'the mouth of the flowers'). A gully on the road between Bandon and Macroom in west Cork, where Michael COLLINS was shot on 22 August 1922. As

Collins's convoy drove back to Cork city it was ambushed at 7.30 p.m. by a party of Republicans who had been waiting all day. At the end of the engagement, Collins, who had insisted on stopping and giving fight when others of his entourage wanted to 'drive like hell', was shot in the head. His colleague Emmet Dalton whispered an act of contrition in his ear, but he was probably already dead. The question of who killed Michael Collins was in the past a subject of controversy, with Republicans refusing to believe that he was killed by his former comrades not far from his own home near CLONAKILTY: some tried to prove that the British or the Free State side had had him killed because he wanted to seek accommodation with ANTI-TREATYITES as well as pursuing the military side of the CIVIL WAR. These theories have been disproved by recent research. It is indisputable that Collins's death exacerbated the bitterness of the internecine conflict and robbed the infant state of an able statesman.

Béaloideas (Irish *béal*, 'mouth', and *oideas,* 'teaching' or 'education'). The Irish word for folklore and tradition, what is passed on by word of mouth. *Béaloideas* was also the name of the journal established in 1927 by the Folklore of Ireland Society, which later became the IRISH FOLKLORE COMMISSION.

Bealtaine or **Beltaine** (anglicized as **Beltane**). May Day, the beginning of the Celtic summer – *Lá Bealtaine, an chéad lá geal den tsamrad* ('May day, the first bright day of summer'). At Bealtaine, as at its winter counterpoint SAM-HAIN, the door between the perceived cosmos and the OTHERWORLD was thought to be partially open. A significant part of the ritual occurred at dawn, when farmers drove cattle through the embers of the previous night's bonfires so that the animals would not succumb to the powers of the Otherworld. The second element in the word is close to *teine*, the Irish word for 'fire', while the first is clearly connected with Bel, a universal Celtic god of death, usually appearing in Irish mythology as Bilé. For Yeats's play *The Countess Cathleen*,

the first production of the IRISH LITERARY THEATRE, his friend Lionel Johnston (1867–1902) wrote a verse prologue, later published in the literary magazine *BEALTAINE*, which began:

> The May fire once on every dreaming hill
> All the fair land with burning bloom would fill;
> All the fair land, at visionary light
> Gave loving glory to the Lord of Light.

In later folk practice May Day was believed to be on one of the two days of the year when the SIDHE were abroad, moving in *Sí Gaoithe* ('the fairy wind') from winter to summer quarters. As they passed they were liable to carry with them a child or a young bride (*see* CHANGE-LING), a belief that gave rise to the fact that, contrary to usual custom, beggars were not welcomed on May Day, lest they should be supernatural beings in disguise. It was customary well into the 20th century to decorate houses with ragwort to deter the Sidhe. May Day was also the best day to work PISHOGUES (charms and spells).

See also IMBOLG; LUGHNASA.

Bealtaine. A literary magazine edited by W.B. YEATS, with contributions by Lady GREGORY, George MOORE and Edward MARTYN. It was first published in May 1899 to publicize the formation of the IRISH LITERARY THEATRE. In it Yeats announced the theatre's policy, really a further elaboration of the STATEMENT OF INTENT of 1897:

> The Irish Literary Theatre … will produce,
> somewhere about the old festival of Beltaine, at
> the beginning of every spring, a play founded
> upon an Irish subject. The plays will differ from
> those produced by associations of men of letters
> in London and Paris, because times have changed,
> and because the intellect of Ireland is romantic and
> spiritual rather than scientific and analytical, but
> they will have as little of a commercial ambition.

Bean a' tí. Irish for 'woman of the house'; the phrase connotes the hostess in a guesthouse or lodgings for students doing Irish courses, especially but not exclusively in the GAEL-TACHT. The concept is well known to students at IRISH COLLEGE, where the *bean a' tí* is *in loco parentis* for the period of their stay in the Gaeltacht. In HIBERNO-ENGLISH in is rendered as 'vanithee'.

'Bean Dubh an Ghleanna'. *See* MUSKERRY GAELTACHT, THE.

Beany and Barney. The names of two 1980s cartoon characters, dressed as minstrels and performing song-and-dance routines in television advertisements, as part of the campaign by Dublin company Batchelors to promote its canned beans.

Bear and Ragged Staff. The name of an inn in Celbridge, Co. Kildare, run by Richard Guinness, the father of the first Arthur GUINNESS, founder of the brewing business. Even before the foundation of the business, the inn was already famous for its home-made dark beer.

Beara Peninsula. A peninsula straddling counties Cork and Kerry in the far southwest of Ireland, having its entrances on the Kerry side at Kenmare and on the Cork side at Glengarriff. The Caha Mountains make up some of the county border. An area of unsurpassed natural beauty, combining coast and upland areas, Beara has been called the last unspoiled peninsula in Ireland, having escaped thus far the grosser kind of tourist development. The area south of Kenmare belonged to the Petty-Fitzmaurice family, ennobled as Marquesses of Lansdowne (*see* KENMARE); their gardening skills are evident in the beautiful gardens of Derreen, in Lauragh. The Healy Pass, which links Lauragh and Adrigole, on the south side of the peninsula, is named after Tim HEALY. Just outside the town of Castletownbere, a busy fishing port facing Beare Island, are the ruins of the castle of Dunboy, the stronghold of O'SULLIVAN BEARE. When it fell to Sir George CAREW in 1602, Carew hanged the defenders. After this, O'Sullivan Beare and his family and retainers set out on the LONG MARCH.

Beart. An Irish word borrowed by HIBERNO-ENGLISH and meaning 'bundle', 'parcel': 'That's a heavy *beart* you're carrying.'

Beaten docket. An Ulster metaphor for a state of collapse or inadequacy, from the value of a bookmaker's betting slip for a losing horse. It is also the name of a pub in Amelia Street, Belfast, close to a large bookie's office.

Beat the lard out of, to. A slang expression meaning 'to thrash severely', lard replacing other, less pleasant, substances that appear in similar phrases.

Beat the wee wheel, to. An Ulster expression of pleased surprise:

'A lobster,' the mother said, almost as excited as himself.

'Aye,' he said, nodding eagerly. 'I caught him in the hole behind the black rock. I gave him to Neil Jack. He gave me sevenpence.' He opened his fist and exposed a sixpence and a penny.

'Well, glory be to God,' the mother exclaimed, 'if that doesn't beat the wee wheel. Away with ye an' get the egg from Peggy. Ye'll have threepence halfpenny left after the sugar.'

PEADAR O'DONNELL (1893–1988): *Islanders* (1927)

Beatty, Alfred Chester (1875–1968). Art collector and philanthropist. He was born in New York and educated at Princeton, but two of his grandparents were Irish. He made his fortune as a mining engineer, having devised a new method of extracting copper from ore, and had business interests in Europe, Africa and South America. He began his priceless collection of oriental artefacts and manuscripts in Egypt in 1913, and in 1953 moved to Dublin, where he built a special library in Shrewsbury Road in Ballsbridge to house his treasures. He left the entire collection in trust to the Irish nation, and in recognition of his generosity he was made a freeman of Dublin and the first honorary citizen of the state. He died in Monte Carlo on 20 January 1968 and was given a state funeral in Glasnevin Cemetery. The Chester Beatty Library is now located in Dublin CASTLE.

Beaufort, Francis (1774–1857). Sailor and

mathematician. He was born in Navan, Co. Meath, the son of a rector, and enlisted in the British navy as a boy in 1787, serving in the Napoleonic wars and rising to the rank of rear admiral. He was wounded in Malaga in 1800, and while recuperating at home he helped his brother-in-law, Richard Lovell EDGEWORTH, to construct a telegraph line from Dublin to Galway. In 1805 he devised what has come to be known as the Beaufort Scale of wind velocity; this was adopted internationally in 1874. He was hydrogopher to the British navy 1829–55 and was honoured for his achievements. He died in London on 17 December 1857.

Beaux' Stratagem, The. The last and best comedy (1707) of George FARQUHAR, and the only one that did well financially in his lifetime. Even then it came too late: he died of tuberculosis as it was being played. *The Beaux' Stratagem* marks the beginning of the end of the run of licentious Restoration plays, since decency and morality triumph. Aimwell, one of the beaux on the make, confesses his originally venal intentions to his victim, the heiress Dorinda, and Farquhar's delineation of the unhappily married Mrs Sullen is meant to be regarded sympathetically. The play ends with Aimwell, restored to fortune in his own right, about to marry honourably his erstwhile victim, and his friend Archer rescuing Mrs Sullen from her brutal husband. One of the other characters in the play is the proverbial Lady Bountiful (*see* MY LADY BOUNTIFUL). The villainous Foigard (in reality an Irish priest called MacShane), though originally conceived as was typical in plays of the period as a Catholic Irish stereotype, is in fact rather more complex than this, and, because of the author's background, more genuinely Irish than the norm:

> The gallows! Upon my shoul I hate that same gallows, for it is a diseash dat is fatal to our family.
>
> IV.ii

Beckett, Mary (b.1926). Novelist and short-story writer. Beckett was born in Belfast and worked as a teacher until 1956, moving to Dublin on her marriage. Her early stories were printed in *Threshold*, *Irish Writing* and *The BELL*, but it was not until 1980 that a selection of them was published as *A Belfast Woman*. This was followed by an award-winning novel about the Troubles in Belfast, *Give Them Stones* (1987), and *A Literary Woman* (1990). Beckett's work is characterized by unwavering realism and honesty, leavened by touches of dark humour. She has also written beautifully crafted stories for children.

> There is hope for all of us. Well, anyway, if you don't die you live through it, day in, day out.
>
> MARY BECKETT: 'A Belfast Woman', in *A Belfast Woman* (1980)

Beckett, Samuel (1906–89). Playwright and novelist. Beckett was born in Dublin on either 13 May 1906 (the date on his birth certificate) or on his own preferred nativity, 13 April, Good Friday, and educated at Portora Royal School in Enniskillen and at Trinity College Dublin (TCD). He taught French at Campbell College, Belfast, and English in Paris, where he became a kind of amanuensis to James JOYCE. He lectured for some time in TCD and after a period of depression and much travel finally settled in Paris in 1937. He elected to remain in France during the German occupation, working with the French Resistance and earning the Croix de Guerre. In 1951 he published the novel *Molloy*, a comic depiction of life's hopelessness and the myth of reality, which was applauded by the Parisian literary elite and was followed by two further novels, also both originally written in French, *Malone Dies* (1951) and *The Unnamable* (1953), to form a trilogy with the same preoccupations.

Much more popular was Beckett's play WAITING FOR GODOT (written 1949, first performed as *En attendant Godot* in 1952), which caused equal amounts of approval and dismay. (Its English language première was at the PIKE THEATRE in 1953.) Other plays, notably *Endgame* (1957), *Krapp's Last Tape* (1958) and *Happy Days* (1961) used disease, physical disability and various forms of restraint to convey aridity and ultimate dissolution; for example, *Happy Days* required one of the two characters to remain largely silent while the other, his wife Winnie, talks incessantly while buried up to her waist in sand (up to her neck in Act II).

Beckett's later work grew ever more terse, but was still written in well-wrought prose and with a remarkable number of Irish allusions. He also wrote a number of short plays, often directed by himself and featuring such actors as Jack McGowran (1918–73) and Billy White-law (b.1932). The bleak austerity in Beckett's work was matched by a personal reticence; he did not attend the ceremony for the award of the Nobel prize for literature in 1969 and resolutely refused to be photographed, filmed or interviewed, none of this detracting from his reputation as a modern master. He died in Paris on 22 December 1989.

Bécuma. The name of a goddess from TÍR TAIRNGIRI ('the Land of Promise'). She is banished into the world of mortals after she has an affair with Gaiar, the son of the sea-god MANANNÁN MAC LIR. There she marries CONN OF THE HUNDRED BATTLES, but is again banished because of her jealousy of and lust for Conn's son ART.

Bedad. A euphemism for 'By God!'. Like BEGORRAH, it was once a natural part of HIBERNO-ENGLISH vocabulary but its use now is artificial and STAGE-IRISH:

Bedad he revives! See how he raises!
An' Timothy, jumping from the bed,
Cries, while he lathered around like blazes:
'Bad luck to yer sowls! D'ye think I'm dead?'
ANONYMOUS (19th century): 'Tim Finnegan's Wake'

Bede (673–735). The saint known as 'venerable', who was born near Monkwearmouth in Co. Durham in 673. He lived in the monastery of Wearmouth with its founder, St Benedict Biscop (*c.*628–*c.*690), from the age of 7 and went with him to his new foundation at Jarrow in 684. His whole life was spent in Northumbria devoting all his energies, as he put it, 'to the study of the Scriptures, observing

monastic discipline and singing my daily services in church; study, teaching and writing have always been my delight.' Though most of his writings are in Latin, he was the first known writer of English prose. His *Historia Ecclesiastica Gentis Anglorum* (*Ecclesiastical History of the English People*) (731) is the prime source for early English history and of the lives of the Irish saints in England. It was in the *Historia* that he recorded the famous analogy about the life of man:

> *… quale cum te residente ad caenum, cum ducibus et ministris tuis tempore brumali … adveniens unus passerum domum citisse pervolaverit; qui per unum ostium ingrediens, mox per aliud…*
> (… as if at wintertime when you sit feasting with your dukes and earls … a single sparrow might fly swiftly into the hall, coming in by one door and immediately flying out by another …)
> II. xiii

Bede died in 735 and was canonized in 1899 by Pope Leo XIII.

Bedell, William. *See* BEDELL'S BIBLE.

Bedell's Bible. The translation of the Old Testament into Irish that was urged by William Bedell at a conference of the Church of Ireland in 1624. The work, intended to supplement the existing translation of the New Testament (1603) by William DANIEL, was completed in 1640. Bedell was born in Black Notley, Essex, in 1571, and after education at Emmanuel College, Cambridge, took holy orders. He served as British embassy chaplain in Venice and was appointed provost of Trinity College Dublin in 1627. While there he insisted that native-born divinity students learn Irish, the better to minister to their flocks and carry on the work of converting Catholics. Bedell set a good example by learning Irish himself, finding it 'learned and exact', and conducting college prayers in the language. In 1629 he was appointed Bishop of Kilmore and Bishop of Ardagh (he later resigned the latter see because of his objection to pluralism). In 1631 he published *Aibigtir* (Irish, 'rudiments'), an Irish catechism with excerpts from the Bible.

The main work of Old Testament translation was carried on in his own house with assistance from Muircheartach Ó Cionga (d.1639) and Séamus de Nógla. The completed Bible was published in 1685, 43 years after Bedell's death on 7 February 1642 from typhus, contracted during imprisonment for harbouring Confederate fugitives during the REBELLION OF 1641. 'Bedell's Bible' was still being used by Catholics up to the 1970s, and parts of the original manuscript are preserved in MARSH'S LIBRARY.

Beef to the heels. *See* MULLINGAR HEIFER.

Beef Tribunal. The first of the major tribunals of the 1990s. The Beef Tribunal sat from May 1991 until July 1994, under Justice Liam Hamilton, to investigate allegations of corruption, abuse of grants and tax evasion against Larry Goodman's Anglo-Irish Beef Processors. Although some of the allegations were proven to be true, no action was taken against the principals.

Beehive huts. The name for small hive-shaped stone huts, a large number of which have survived on the DINGLE PENINSULA in Co. Kerry and also on SCEILIG MHICHÍL off the south Kerry coast. These were the early Christian monastic cells of a treeless countryside, although it is believed that some were built more recently and used for agricultural purposes.

Beel. A verb, common in Ulster, meaning 'fester' or 'suppurate': 'He cut his finger on a rusty tin and it beeled.'

Beelie (Irish *píle*, 'huge person or thing'). A HIBERNO-ENGLISH term for a large, apparently useless cat.

Beere, Thekla (1901–91). Public administrator. She was secretary (civil service head) of the Department of Transport and Power (1959–66), the first time a woman had reached such a senior position in the Irish civil service. She was also a founder-member of An ÓIGE and served on the board of several private and public bodies.

Bees. Bees were considered part of the family in rural Ireland, and it was believed that they should be told what was going on. For instance, on the morning of a child's first day at school the father would knock on the hive and say: 'Michael is gone to school today, bees.' News of a death in the family was also told to the bees, and in some places a crape (black mourning band) was hung on the hive. It was considered lucky for a fisherman to see a hive before going to sea as it symbolized a plentiful catch.

Beestings. The first milk from a calving cow, yellow in colour, and highly prized as a delicacy and health tonic. The form 'bastins' is used in Ulster.

Beeswisp. A tangled mass, often used as a simile, probably from the rough appearance of a wild bee's nest: 'Your desk drawer's like a beeswisp.' The form 'peaswisp' is also used. The word 'wisp' signifies a twist of hay, sheep's wool, etc.

Beetle. A heavy wooden club used for mashing potatoes and other vegetables. It was also used for pounding washing and as the Irish equivalent of the rolling pin in stories of battered husbands. The word comes from Old English *bietl*, from *beatan*, 'to beat'.

Begob. A HIBERNO-ENGLISH exclamatory euphemism for 'by God!'
See also BEDAD; BEGORRAH.

Begorrah. An exclamatory euphemism for 'by God!', once heartfelt, but now regarded as STAGE-IRISH:

> It's a great day for the Irish; it's a great day for a fair!
> Be gosh, there's not a cop to stop a raiding;
> Begorra all the cops are out parading …
> ROGER EDENS: 'It's a Great Day for the Irish' (1940)

As Terry Eagleton has observed: 'If you hear anyone saying "Begorrah" during your stay in Ireland, you can be sure he's an undercover agent for the Irish Tourist Board pandering to your false expectations.'

Begrudger. A word meaning a person who is jealous of, or hostile to, the success or achievement of others. Begrudgery is said to be endemic in the post-colonial Irish psyche, prevailing with poverty and hypocrisy. In the era of tribunals, an accusation of begrudgery is still levelled, on occasion, at those who question the source of wealth of politicians and businessmen. Breandán ó HEITHIR's entertaining *The Begrudger's Guide to Irish Politics* (1986) is a sustained exploration of the theme of political begrudgery or cynicism, written by a journalist steeped in Irish politics.

Behan, Brendan (1923–64). Playwright. Behan was born in Dublin on 9 February 1923 and educated by the CHRISTIAN BROTHERS and by his own extremely well-read and heritage-saturated family. He left school at 14 to join Fianna Éireann, the cadet branch of the IRA, while learning the trade of painting from his father, who had been interned during the CIVIL WAR. He was arrested in 1939 for IRA activity in England and spent three formative years at borstal in Suffolk. He returned to Dublin and in 1942 was sentenced to 14 years imprisonment for attempting to kill a detective. On his release 5 years later he resumed his trade, while determined to become a writer. One of his earliest pieces, 'I Become a Borstal Boy', appeared in *The BELL* in June 1942 and Behan was strongly encouraged to write by Sean O'FAOLAIN.

The years in prison yielded Behan's best prose work *Borstal Boy* (1958) and his finest play *The QUARE FELLOW* (1954), which had already been offered to the ABBEY THEATRE as *Casadh Súgáin Eile* (*The Twisting of Another Rope*) – a curtsy to Douglas HYDE's *CASADH AN TSÚGÁIN* (*The Twisting of the Rope*) – but had its first performance at the PIKE THEATRE. After the success of *The Quare Fellow* in London (and some controversial television appearances), Behan became public property. Until then his reputation had been based on dark wit, alcoholic intake and an appreciative readership for his pieces in *The IRISH PRESS* (published as *Hold Your Hour and Have An-other* in 1964). His next play, written in Irish as *An Giall* (1958), was heavily adapted by Joan Littlewood as

The Hostage, a revue-type show in which the original was almost lost. Nevertheless, it increased his worldwide reputation.

The years of success were accompanied by alcoholism and neglected diabetes, and although Behan made many attempts to dry out he died prematurely on 20 March 1964. His funeral was the largest seen in Dublin since that of Michael Collins. The tape-recorded books of his later years, including *Brendan Behan's Island* (1962) and *Confessions of an Irish Rebel* (1965), were edited by Rae Jeffs, an indulgent editor seconded from his publisher Hutchinson.

Behan, Dominic (1929–89). Playwright and songwriter. He was born in Dublin, the brother of Brendan BEHAN, and like Brendan followed his father's trade of house painter. After emigrating to England, he worked as a scriptwriter for the BBC, mainly for the Third Programme. A play on the subject of Republicanism, *Posterity Be Damned*, was produced in the Dublin's GAIETY Theatre in 1959, and he wrote a television documentary *My Brother Brendan* (1965) and a dramatization of the story of the Behan family entitled *Teems of Times* (1979). Among his best-known songs are 'Liverpool Lou' and 'The PATRIOT GAME', both in waltz time and popular among BALLAD GROUPS in the 1960s. He died at his home in Glasgow on 3 August 1989.

Behind the door. An adjectival phrase, usually in the negative and meaning not lacking or not unready, as in: 'She wasn't behind the door when they were giving out brains' or 'He wasn't behind the door when it came to making money.'

'Beidh an lá 'dul 'un síneadh' (Irish, 'there will be a stretch to the day'). A sign of the coming of spring in the poem *'Cill Aodáin'* (Irish, 'Killeadan') associated with Antaine Ó Raifteirí (*c*.1784–*c*.1835), the wandering Connacht poet (BLIND RAFTERY of the Yeats poems):

Anois teacht an earraigh beidh an lá 'dul 'un síneadh,
'S tar éis na Féil' Bríde ardóidh mé mo sheol.

(Now with the coming of spring there'll be a stretch
  to the day
And after the feast of Brigid, I'll hoist my sail.)

Beit Collection. *See* RUSSBOROUGH HOUSE.

Bejaysus. A Dublin expletive, a version of 'By
Jesus!'

Belfast. The second city in Ireland (population
approximately 290,000), capital of NORTHERN
IRELAND, and since the mid-19th century a byword for sectarian conflict. The Irish name *Béal
Feirste* means 'the mouth of (or approach to) the
ford', referring to a sandbank where the River
Lagan reaches Belfast Lough. (There is a small
tributary river, the Farset, also named from the
sandbank.)

The settlement grew out of a castle built in
1177 by John de Courcy (the Anglo-Norman
who settled eastern Ulster) and was developed
by Arthur CHICHESTER from 1603 as the centre
of the ULSTER PLANTATION. The important
linen industry came with the HUGUENOTS at the
end of the 17th century, and after the Act of
UNION Belfast developed as an industrial city
– at the expense of the too-Nationalist DUBLIN –
with shipbuilding and heavy engineering, as
well as linen manufacture, as its chief industries.

An early reputation for liberalism that led to
the foundation there of the UNITED IRISHMEN
in 1791, was lost largely owing to the city's
prosperity after the Union and the charismatic
preaching of such politico-religious leaders as
Henry COOKE. From the 1860s Belfast was the
centre of unrelenting Unionist opposition to
any form of HOME RULE, the scene of a massive
show of strength at the signing of the ULSTER
COVENANT in 1912 and the seat of the Northern
Ireland Parliament from 1921 (*see* PROTESTANT
PARLIAMENT FOR A PROTESTANT PEOPLE; STOR-
MONT). A centre of recurring rioting, the
city and its sectarian working-class ghettos
suffered greatly during the late 20th-century
TROUBLES, and the fear and suspicion engendered have not perceptibly lessened in spite
of the GOOD FRIDAY AGREEMENT of 10 April
1998. Despite all the city has suffered, its

social, intellectual and artistic life has steadily
reinvigorated itself in recent years.

Belfast Academical Institution. *See* INST.

Belfast Agreement. Another name for the
GOOD FRIDAY AGREEMENT.

Belfast Blitz. The German air raids on Belfast
in April and May 1941, which dispelled the
illusion that Northern Ireland was immune
from air attack. On 15 April, a week after the
first raid in which 13 people had been killed,
German bombers dropped a hundred tons of
bombs, damaging 56,000 houses, killing 745
people and injuring 1500. (Two parachute-
mines fell in Derry that same night, killing
15 and wrecking two houses.) In a gesture of
solidarity Éamon de Valera dispatched 13 fire
engines from Dublin and east coast towns, but
the STORMONT war cabinet was more concerned to protect Edward CARSON's statue in
front of the parliament building than to devise
adequate air-raid shelters for the slum-dwellers
whose 'sub-human behaviour' they deplored
so much. The Luftwaffe returned on 4 May,
killing a further 150 people, by which time a
nightly exodus into the safety of the Antrim
countryside (or in the case of Derry into Co.
Donegal) had become the rule.

Belfast Boycott. A measure ordered by the
Dáil in 1920 in an attempt to stop the attacks
on Northern Irish Catholics (in the so-
called 'Belfast pogrom') and the exclusion of
Catholics from factories and shipyards, and
to demonstrate the economic consequences
of PARTITION. Business with northern banks
and insurance companies was affected, and
the importation of goods was effectively
prohibited, with embargoes placed on some
Protestant businesses in border counties. The
boycott lasted for several years, but had the
opposite result to that intended, with the new
state of Northern Ireland discovering, with
British support, a workable independence.

Belfast Celtic. The name of a Nationalist-
supported Belfast soccer team, arch-rivals of
the Unionist LINFIELD. The behaviour of sup-

porters in expressing this rivalry is replicated in that of the present-day Glasgow teams Celtic and Rangers, and to a lesser extent that of Hibernian and Heart of Midlothian in Edinburgh. The grounds of Belfast Celtic and Linfield were within view of each other: Celtic Park on Donegall Road near the Nationalist FALLS ROAD, and Windsor Park across the BOG MEADOWS. Belfast Celtic was founded in 1891 and enjoyed a distinguished history, but eventually grew tired of the risk and the inevitability of the fans' confrontations. A climax was reached at a match in Windsor Park on 26 December 1948, when a mob of Linfield supporters rushed on to the pitch and Jimmie Jones, a Celtic player, sustained a broken leg in the ensuing mêlée. The team withdrew from competitive football at the end of the 1949 season, leaving a considerable gap in the sporting life of Ulster.

'Belfast Child'. A folk-influenced song by the Scottish rock group Simple Minds, released in 1989 and based on a traditional Irish air entitled 'She Moved through the Fair'. The creative prompting for the song was the Troubles in Northern Ireland and, in particular, the deaths in ENNISKILLEN in 1987 of 11 people in the Remembrance Day bomb attack by the IRA. The song's wistful refrain, bracketing an apocalyptic middle section, looks forward to a peaceful time beyond the Troubles: 'One day we'll return here, when the Belfast Child sings again.' The song is the second longest, after the Beatles' 'Hey Jude', to reach number one in the UK singles charts.

Belfast confetti. The city slang for hand missiles, cartridge cases and other debris associated with riot or confrontation. Earlier it referred to the bolts and rivets thrown by shipyard workers, often at Catholics, especially during the expulsions in 1920:

Suddenly as the riot squad moved in, it was raining exclamation marks,
Nuts, bolts, nails, car-keys. A fount of broken type.
And
    the explosion

Itself – an asterisk on the map …
CIARAN CARSON (1948): 'Belfast Confetti', in *Belfast Confetti* (1989)

Belfast cradle. The position of the arms adopted by British soldiers when carrying rifles on urban patrol during Northern Ireland's Troubles. The system was used elsewhere by other forces in the light of the Belfast experience.

Belfast Harp Festival. A significant event in the preservation of the residual musical tradition of Ireland, when ten harpers (six of whom were blind) assembled in Belfast in July 1792 to be judged on prowess and possession of original material. The event was organized by members of the BELFAST SOCIETY FOR PROMOTING KNOWLEDGE, including Dr James McDonnell, Robert Bradshaw, Robert Simms and Henry Joy MCCRACKEN. Present at the festival, which was held in the Assembly Room of the Belfast Exchange, was Edward BUNTING, the Armagh-born organist of St Anne's Cathedral, and friend of the McCrackens. He had been employed to record the music, which the members realized was in serious danger of being lost. He published, in all, three collections of *Ancient Irish Music*, in 1796, 1809 and 1840. The first of these supplied Tom MOORE with many of the melodies for his Irish airs.

Belfast Natural History and Philosophical Society. A development of the BELFAST SOCIETY FOR PROMOTING KNOWLEDGE that led to the foundation of Ireland's first museum. The driving force was Dr James Lawson Drummond (1783–1853), professor of anatomy at INST, and it was at his house that the inaugural meeting was held in 1821. The society acquired property close to Inst in College Square and in 1831 opened the museum, which had been financed by public subscription. A vigorous policy of acquisition and research, and a soberly attractive façade, made it a building of significance in a city not over-endowed with elegance. As the Old Museum building it still serves as an arts centre in present-day Belfast.

Belfast News-Letter. One of Belfast's two morning papers, founded in 1737, making it Ulster's first and Ireland's oldest news-sheet. It was begun by a printer, Francis Joy (*c*.1697–1790), and was originally a PATRIOT journal. After 1795, under a new owner, it became more conservative, and for the last two centuries has been a Protestant/Unionist paper.

Belfast Quasimodo. The description by T.P. (TAY-PAY) O'Connor, 'Father' of the House of Commons, of Joe Biggar (1828–90), the physically unattractive but passionate Nationalist and supreme parliamentary obstructionist. O'Connor's exact characterization ran: 'The Belfast Quasimodo to the Irish Esmeralda'. (Quasimodo and Esmeralda are characters in Victor Hugo's novel *Notre-Dame de Paris* (1831), and were, respectively, a grotesquely ugly hunchback and a beautiful gypsy girl with whom he falls in love and whom he tries to protect.)

Joseph Gillis Biggar was born in Belfast in 1828, the son of a prosperous butcher, taking over the running of the firm in 1861. He became interested in the HOME RULE movement, was elected MP for Cavan in 1874 and represented the constituency until his death in 1890. Biggar was a member of the IRB until he was expelled for continuing to hold his Commons seat. The policy of 'obstructionism' that he developed with PARNELL kept the IRISH QUESTION in the forefront of public life – and caused many changes in the rules of UK parliamentary procedure. (He once 'named' the Prince of Wales as a 'stranger' and had him removed from the Commons.) Though born a Presbyterian, he became a Catholic in 1877, partly, it was said, to annoy his staid sister. He died in London on 19 February 1890.

Belfast Regiment, the. The informal name for the old 35th Foot, raised in Belfast in 1701. It later became the 1st Battalion Royal Sussex Regiment, and subsequently the 3rd Battalion, the Queen's Regiment.

Belfast Society for Promoting Knowledge. A society founded on 11 September 1792 out of the Belfast Reading Society (1788), which had laid the foundations of the LINEN HALL LIBRARY. The urge for self-improvement had gathered strength in the closing decades of the 18th century among the self-conscious and prosperous citizens of the growing industrial town, and the new name was a signal that the earlier enthusiasm should have a more formal structure. Its purpose was best stated in a revision of the rules on 1 January 1795: 'The object of this society is the collection of an extensive Library, Philosophical Apparatus, and such productions of Nature and Art as tend to improve the mind and excite a spirit of general enquiry.'

Bell, John Stewart. *See* BELL'S INEQUALITIES.

Bell, Sam Hanna (1909–90). Writer and radio producer. In the years 1945–69 he redefined local radio to initiate a kind of golden age of broadcasting in Northern Ireland, perhaps most notably with his series *Within Our Province*. Bell was born in Glasgow of Scots–Irish parents on 23 October 1909, but, on the death of his journalist father in 1918, was brought 'home' with his two younger brothers to his mother's house in Co. Down. The family moved to Belfast in 1921 and the next 19 years were spent in a bewildering series of occupations, including that of nightwatchman. With the coming of the Second World War he became a senior welfare officer with the ARP (Air Raid Precautions), and when peace was declared joined BBC Northern Ireland, having been encouraged by Louis MACNEICE, who had read some of his scripts. Bell eventually became senior features producer.

Bell wrote many radio features and plays that reflected the hitherto unheard voice of Ulster, and did much to collect the vanishing folklore and traditional music of the province. In addition to *Within Our Province*, such series as *Country Bard*, *Fairy Faith*, *Loughs Remembered* and *Music on the Hearth*, along with many individual dramatized features exploring Ulster's colourful past, showed the province its own face. Compared with the dumbed-down offerings of today, they suggest a glory that is departed.

Yet Bell's more important work was as a writer of historical fiction in which he portrayed, as no other writer, the psyche of the Ulster working-class Protestant, both rural and urban. *December Bride* (1951), his first and best-known novel (later successfully filmed in 1990), is set near Strangford Lough, the scene of his adolescence, and delineates a notorious *ménage à trois*; *The Hollow Ball* (1961) is set in the poverty-stricken Belfast of the 1930s; *A Man Flourishing* (1973) is concerned with the growth of Belfast from radical village to conservative industrial city; and *Across the Narrow Sea* (1987) is a romance, after the manner of Sir Walter Scott, about the 17th-century ULSTER PLANTATION. His collection of short stories, *Summer Loanen* (*see* LOANEN), appeared in 1943. Other work includes *Erin's Orange Lily* (1956), a breezy account of Ulster folkways, and the authoritative *The Theatre in Ulster* (1972). He died on 9 February 1990.

Bell, The. A monthly cultural journal founded by Peadar O'DONNELL (1893–1986) and Sean O'FAOLAIN (1900–91), who was its first editor. It ran from October 1940 until December 1954, with some breaks towards the end. The title of the journal, which gave rise to all kinds of campanological jokes, had at the beginning no especial significance, as O'Faolain wrote in his first editorial: 'Any other equally spare and hard and simple word would have done: any word with a minimum of associations.' The early work of many famous Irish writers was published in its pages: Brendan BEHAN, Sam Hanna BELL, Austin CLARKE, Brian FRIEL, Patrick KAVANAGH, Mary LAVIN and Micheál Mac Liammóir (*see* BOYS, THE[2]) all contributed, and its challenges to the contradictions of a smug, isolationist and publicly pious Ireland prepared the ground for the growth of a more liberal country. It was never intended to be elitist: in its first number O'Faolain urged his readers to contribute:

> You know a turn of the road, an old gateway somewhere, a well-field, a street corner, a wood, a handful of quiet life, a triangle of sea and rock,

something that means Ireland to you. It means the whole world …These are the things that come at night to tear at an exile's heart. That is Life. You possess a precious store of it. If you will share it with all of us you will make this bell peal out a living message.

Bellamy, George Anne. *See* APOLOGY.

Belleek. A kind of Parian porcelain (a fine marble-like porcelain which gets its name from the Aegean island of Paros) called after a village (Irish *Béal Leice*, 'flagstone mouth' or 'flagstone ford') on the River Erne in Co. Fermanagh. Until recently the image of Belleek was that of a product for (mainly American) tourists: delicate pieces bearing shamrocks or other Irish symbols. Improved design has greatly widened its appeal.

The industry was established in 1858 by local landowner John Caldwell Bloomfield, who had inherited the Castlecaldwell estate from his father in 1849 and was anxious to provide employment. Bloomfield was a keen amateur mineralogist, and a geological survey of his land located kaolin and other raw materials necessary for the manufacture of pottery. The power of the River Erne was harnessed to grind the elements into slip, the raw material of pottery, and Bloomfield, along with his partners, Robert Armstrong and David McBirney, enticed 14 skilled potters from Stoke-on-Trent to teach the skill. The arrival of the railway service to Belleek, importing coal for the kilns and exporting the finished product, was another great advantage.

Belleek is now associated only with Parian porcelain, but until 1920 ordinary domestic pottery was its main product. In recent years the success of Belleek porcelain has led the parent company to acquire related enterprises such as Galway Crystal and Aynsley China (Stoke-on-Trent). The Belleek Group today employs over 600 people with a yearly turnover of €40 million.

Bell's Inequalities. A series of mathematical propositions devised by John Stewart Bell that are essential in quantum physics. Bell was born in Belfast of working-class parents on 28 July 1928 and worked as a laboratory assistant at Queen's University (QUB) in 1944–5 before becoming an undergraduate. After graduation he conducted research in Geneva into acceleration physics and was appointed FRS in 1972. His assertion that 'prediction of certain hidden variable theories was bounded by inequalities' led ultimately to the proof 'that the world we live in is truly quantum mechanical' (*Chambers Biographical Dictionary*, 1997). He died suddenly of a cerebral haemorrhage in Geneva on 1 October 1990.

'Bells of Shandon, The'. A poem (1835) by Francis Sylvester Mahony, which, though written as a squib, gained a lasting reputation as a sentimental song for Irish exiles. The bells are those of St Anne's parish church, Shandon (1772–6), in the centre of Cork city, and Mahony, who was an ordained Catholic priest and wrote under the pseudonym FATHER PROUT, contributed the piece to *Fraser's Magazine*. The rhyming of 'Moscow' with 'kiosko!' indicates how lightly the author regarded this verse, quite appropriate for the son of the owner of the Blarney Woollen Mills (*see* BLARNEY STONE). Mahony is buried in the vaults of the church where one may still hear:

> The bells of Shandon
> That sound so grand on
> The pleasant waters
>   Of the River Lee.

According to Hilton Edwards (*see* BOYS, THE²) visiting actors were accustomed to chorus in reply to the too-often quoted quatrain:

> But the bells of St Nicholas
> Sound so ridiculous
> On the dirty waters
> Of Sullivan's Quay!

Belt of the crozier. A phrase used to signify interference by the Catholic hierarchy in public policy or administration, which was especially common in the first 50 years of the Irish state. *See also* BISHOP AND THE NIGHTIE, THE; HOUSE DANCES; MCQUAID, JOHN CHARLES; MOTHER AND CHILD SCHEME.

Ben Bulben (Irish *Binn Ghulbáin*, 'Gulban's peak'). A mountain (524m/1730 ft) in Co. Sligo, rich in the lore of myth and early Irish history. Its geological configuration, like the hulk of an upturned ship, makes it a natural division between north and west. It was the scene of the death of DIARMAID UA DUIBHNE and the site of the Battle of CÚL DREIMHNE, the legendary cause of COLUM CILLE's exile from Ireland. W.B. YEATS is buried in the churchyard of Drumcliff at the mountain's foot, as his poetic epitaph confirms:

> Under bare Ben Bulben's head
> In Drumcliff churchyard Yeats is laid.
>   'Under Ben Bulben' (1938)

Benburb, Battle of. The major battle of the CONFEDERATE WAR, fought between the Irish, led by Owen Rua O'NEILL and the Scottish army of General Robert Munroe in Benburb, Co. Tyrone on 5 June 1646. It was one of the relatively few pitched battles fought on Irish soil and a decisive win for O'Neill, with between 2000 and 3000 casualties among Munroe's troops. It is said by historians that, like his uncle Hugh O'NEILL after the Battle of the YELLOW FORD, Owen Rua O'Neill failed to follow up his advantage after the battle.

Ben Dunne Kidnapping. The seizure by the IRA in November 1981 of the senior member of the family that owns Dunne's Stores, one of Ireland's largest and richest businesses. He was taken at Killeen, on the Louth–Armagh border near Newry, and held for six days. On his release it was assumed that a large ransom had been paid, though this was denied by the Dunne family.

Bennett, Louie (1870–1956). Feminist, socialist, trade unionist, Republican and pacifist. Bennett was born in Dublin to a prosperous merchant family and had early literary aspirations, publishing two novels (1902, 1908). She and her friend Helen Chenevix were instrumental in founding the Irish WOMEN'S SUFFRAGE Federation in 1911, and with Hanna

SHEEHY-SKEFFINGTON she edited *The IRISH CITIZEN*, the organization's newspaper, for many years. As a trade unionist she established the Irish Women's Reform Movement in 1911 and organized the IRISH WOMEN WORKERS' UNION (IWWU) with Helen Chenevix, Delia LARKIN and Helena MOLONY; it was registered in 1918. She was the first woman to be nominated for election to the House of Commons – for the Labour Party in the 1918 general election – although her party withdrew its candidates in favour of SINN FÉIN. In 1932 Bennett became the first woman president of the Irish Trade Union Conference (now ICTU), but she maintained that women should be organized separately from men and remained general secretary of the IWWU until 1955, a year before her death. One of the IWWU's greatest achievements was the right to two weeks' paid holidays for all workers, achieved as a result of the laundry workers' strike in 1945.

Benweed. The common Ulster word for ragwort (Irish *buachalán buí*), a plant formerly used to decorate lintels on May Day (*see* BEALTAINE).

Beresford, John (1766–1843). Public administrator. Beresford was born in Dublin and was called to the Bar, but did not practise. He was MP for Waterford from 1761 to 1805, and a member of the WIDE STREET COMMISSIONERS. He was made commissioner of revenue in 1770, then first commissioner of revenue in 1780 and remained in this powerful position of patronage until 1802, except for a brief period at the time of the FITZWILLIAM EPISODE in early 1795. It was Beresford who, despite public opposition, retained James GANDON to design the CUSTOM HOUSE, and in 1791 he laid the foundation stone of Carlisle (now O'Connell) Bridge. The residential crescent of Beresford Place, near the Custom House, which was also designed by James Gandon, was named after him.

During the 1780s Beresford became informally known as William Pitt's chief adviser on Irish affairs, and he was appointed a British privy councillor in 1786. A member of a powerful triumvirate (the THREE JACKS) that effectively ruled Ireland under different lord lieutenants (the others being the chancellor of the exchequer, John FOSTER, and the lord chancellor, John FITZGIBBON), Beresford was considered so powerful that he was nicknamed 'king of Ireland'. He was a member of the 'secret committee' set up in 1797 to report to the government on the effects of its policy in the lead-up to the expected rebellion. His home was Abbeville, near Kinsealy in north Co. Dublin (a mansion later occupied by Charles Haughey), but he moved to another residence in Co. Derry when he retired in 1802, and died there in 1805.

Beresford's son John Claudius succeeded his father in public service as an MP and member of the Wide Street Commissioners, and had a reputation for severity in the suppression of the REBELLION OF 1798: he called it 'unmanly to deny torture as it was notoriously practised', and was a particular enthusiast for the triangle, a frame used for whipping. He speculated extensively, and not always successfully, in land and property.

In 1826 a coordinated campaign among tenants by the CATHOLIC ASSOCIATION saw John Beresford's cousin, the local landlord Lord George Beresford, defeated in a landmark election in Co. Waterford by Henry Villiers Stuart, who favoured CATHOLIC EMANCIPATION.

Beresk. A comic distortion of the word 'berserk', meaning uncontrollably angry. 'Berserk' derives from old Norse *berserker*, perhaps denoting a warrior wearing a bearskin who fought with a bear's fierceness.

Bergin, Osborn (Osborn Ó hAimhirgín) (1872–1950). Poet, editor and Irish-language scholar. Bergin was born in Cork city and educated at what was then Queen's College in Cork (where he joined the Gaelic League and lectured for a time) and in Germany. He was appointed first professor of Early and Medieval Irish at University College Dublin in 1909 and held that position until 1940, when he became, briefly, director of the School of Celtic Studies in the Dublin Institute for Advanced Studies. Thereafter he devoted himself to scholarship, particularly Celtic philology. His scholarly work included writings on bardic poetry and an edition of parts of Seathrún CÉITINN's *Foras Feasa ar Éirinn*, but he is also remembered for the much-anthologized poem '*Maidin i mBéarra*', which was published in a collection of the same name (1908) and may be sung to the air of 'Danny Boy'. Bergin died in Dublin on 6 October 1950.

Berkeley, George (frequently referred to as **Bishop Berkeley**) (1685–1752). Cleric and philosopher. Berkeley was born in Castle Dysart, Co. Kilkenny, on 12 March 1685, and educated at Trinity College Dublin, where he remained as a tutor and fellow until 1713. It was in these years that his main works of idealistic philosophy, *Essay towards a New Theory of Vision* (1709), *A Treatise concerning the Principles of Human Knowledge* (1710) and *Three Dialogues between Hylas and Philonous* (1713), were written. In these he developed his proposition that *esse est percipi*, 'to be is to be perceived', viz. that the elements of the material world are 'ideas' with no existence unless perceived by a human mind, and that existence has its source in a supreme being known to theologians as God.

In 1724 Berkeley was appointed to the valuable deanery of Derry and actually paid the place a visit in May of that year, praising '... the agreeable situation, the town standing on a peninsula in the midst of a fine spreading lake ...'. With the money received from letting the tithe lands of the deanery, he began an unsuccessful attempt to set up a college in Bermuda, but, after waiting three years (1728–31) in Rhode Island, USA, for a government grant that never materialized, returned home to become Bishop of Cloyne in Co. Cork in 1734. A conscientious resident pastor, Berkeley continued his philosophical speculations, wrote about the need for religious toleration and praised the medicinal virtues of tar

water, which he had seen used against smallpox in America. And it was of America that he wrote, just before his death in 1752, 'Westward the course of empire takes its way.'
See also QUERIST, THE.

Berlioz, Madame. *See* SMITHSON, HARRIET.

Bertie. *See* AHERN, BERTIE.

Bertieahern.com. A (very mildly) pornographic internet site (www.bertieahern.com) registered by what are known as cybersquatters in Taoiseach Bertie AHERN's name in April 2000. On 12 April Ahern spoke in the Dáil about this site and the alleged attempts of the perpetrators to get him to buy it back for a large sum. Another such site was www.thetaoiseach.com. Both sites are now defunct.

Bertie Bowl. The proposed 80,000-seater national sports stadium in Abbotstown in north Co. Dublin, promoted personally by Taoiseach Bertie AHERN. The one billion euro project was dogged by uncertainty and political controversy from the outset, although Ahern, a keen soccer supporter, was not alone in deploring the Republic's lack of a first-class sporting arena. The Irish government finally announced, in September 2002, that no public money would be spent on the stadium. In January 2004 it was announced that LANSDOWNE ROAD was to be redeveloped as a national rugby and soccer stadium, to be completed by 2008.
See also NELSON'S PILLAR.

Bertiespeak. The journalistic shorthand for the kind of public speech favoured by Taoiseach Bertie AHERN, likely to be inarticulate, ambiguous and all things to all people. Ahern is, however, regarded as a fine negotiator and conciliator.

Besom (also **bisom**). A word (also used in Britain) meaning a home-made broom fashioned of heather or twigs bound to a wooden handle. The term is applied metonymically, in Ireland, Scotland and the north of England, to its usual wielder, largely in an uncomplimentary fashion, probably because of the vigour of its action:

But the women, those shapers of opinion and prejudice, would hear nothing in Sarah's favour, and the men for peace's sake agreed she was a shameless bisom and worth the watching.

SAM HANNA BELL (1909–90): *December Bride* (1950)

Bessie Bell and Mary Gray. The names of two hills in the Baronscourt estate of the Duke of Abercorn in Co. Tyrone, west and east of the main Derry–Omagh road. They were possibly named by an early Duke of Abercorn after the heroines of a Scottish ballad mentioned by Sir Walter Scott in *Minstrelsy of the Scottish Border* (1802–3), although a persistent local story has it that the hills were called after nannies employed in the ducal household. Scott laments in a long footnote in Book I that only two stanzas of the ballad survive, though the story of the young women was still told in the region. They were close friends and wooed by the same young gallant. When plague struck the district the girls, with sound instincts, built themselves a safe retreat away from the source of infection:

Bessie Bell and Mary Gray,
They were twa bonnie lasses;
They bigged a bower on yon burn-brae
And theckit it ower wi' rashes.

Unfortunately they allowed their wooer, who had already caught the disease, to visit their bower, and soon all three died.

Best, George (b. 1946). Footballer. Best was born in Belfast on 22 May 1946 to a working-class Presbyterian family of Scottish origin. A scout recognized his talent when he was still a teenager and he joined Manchester United, then under the charismatic management of Matt Busby, in 1961. Best first began to attract attention in the 1964–5 season, the football press lionizing him after a game with Chelsea. Over the next seven years he played in hundreds of league and cup games, becoming in the process a celebrity known as much for his boyish good looks, his drinking and his philandering as for his considerable athletic and goalscoring skills. His professional football career effectively ended when he left Manchester United in 1973, and despite many attempts at a comeback, his drinking always got in the way. Since then his personal and business life has followed a pattern of (often alcohol-related) setback followed by rehabilitation followed again by setback. He may still be seen on chat shows or at celebrity events. His autobiography is the aptly titled *The Good, the Bad and the Bubbly* (1990); in it Best remarks, perhaps a shade wistfully:

Pelé called me the greatest footballer in the world. That is the ultimate salute to my life.

Best, Ranger William. A 19-year-old British soldier who was killed on leave home to Derry by an Official IRA unit (*see* STICKIES, THE[1]) on 20 May 1972 and his body left on William Street. The subsequent public revulsion was the chief reason for the Official IRA's declaration of an indefinite ceasefire on 29 May.

Best thing since Leather-Arse died, the. A vulgar but popular term of approbation. Neither the cause of death nor the identity of the fundamentally tough character is known.

Betelgeuse. *See* WHIDDY ISLAND DISASTER.

Be to. A verb indicating necessity, equivalent to 'has to' or 'must':

He was lookin' would I call him,
Och, me heart was woe –
Sure it's lost I am without him
But he be to go.

ELIZABETH SHANE (Gertrude Hine; 1877–1951): 'Wee Hughie' (1920)

Better hang at home than die like a dog in Ireland. *See* YELLOW FORD, BATTLE OF THE.

Betty, William Henry. *See* YOUNG ROSCIUS.

Between the jigs and the reels. A phrase used to indicate the culmination or outcome of an activity, synonymous with 'finally' or 'as a result of everything that happened': 'Between the jigs and the reels I missed the plane.'

Between the two Christmases. The period between 25 December, BIG CHRISTMAS, and 6 January, Small or WOMEN'S CHRISTMAS. In the mild southwest there was a saying that snow would not stay on the ground 'unless it fell between the two Christmases'. Because this was a period of leisure in rural Ireland, in the past it was popular for MATCHMAKING.

Bewitches. An example of typically compressed Dublin speech, as in the jokey response to the command: 'Put the word "bewitches" in a sentence.' 'Bewitches in a mina!' (i.e. 'I will be with you in a minute.')

Beyond the beyond(s). A phrase meaning 'incredible', or 'excessive'. 'That's going beyond the beyonds' might be said in frustration or weary resignation.

B from a bull's foot. A distinction, which if not made, indicates stupidity. The phrase derives partly from alliteration and partly from a supposed resemblance between the letter and the animal's footprint: 'He wouldn't know B from a bull's foot.'

Bianconi, Carlo. See BIANS.

Bians. The fast horse-drawn 'cars' that before the age of the railways provided the most efficient transport service in Ireland. They were named after Carlo Bianconi (1786–1875), a Lombard Italian, who had been a travelling print-salesman and recognized the need for a better means of transport in Ireland. He founded the service in 1815 and over the next 25 years developed a system that worked daily over a provincial network of 5000 km (3000 miles) of road. He began with a service on the 13-km (8-mile) route between Clonmel and Cahir in Co. Tipperary, having found a buyer's market in high-class horses after the Napoleonic Wars. A pious Catholic, Bianconi became an Irish citizen (with his name reduced colloquially to a more manageable 'Brian Cooney') and a strong supporter of Daniel O'CONNELL, and when in 1865 he decided to retire he sold the network (now extending over 6400 km/ 4000 miles) to his drivers and agents on liberal terms, having earned the sobriquet 'King of the Roads'.

At the British Association meeting in Cork in 1843, Mr Bianconi was called upon to read a paper, from which it appeared that his establishment numbered 100 vehicles, including mail coaches and different-sized cars, capable of carrying from 4 to 20 passengers each, and travelling eight or nine miles an hour, at an average fare of one penny farthing, and performing daily 3800 miles, passing through 140 stations for change of horses, consuming 3000 to 4000 tons of hay and from 30,000 to 40,000 barrels of oats annually. He also added: 'This establishment does not travel on Sundays, for the following reasons: First, the Irish being a religious people, will not travel on business on Sundays; and secondly, experience teaches me that I can work a horse eight miles per day, six days in the week, much better than I can six miles for seven days.'

Irish Tourist's Handbook (1843)

See also JAUNTING CAR; STAGE COACHES.

Bickerstaffe, Isaac. *See* LOVE IN A VILLAGE.

Bicylic. An Ulster mispronunciation of the word 'bicycle', once innocent but now exclusively comical.

See also BISCAKE.

Biddy boys or **Biddies.** A party of young people performing and collecting money house-to-house on St Bridget's Eve (31 January), called 'biddies' after the saint (Biddy, short for Brigid, is a girl's name). Anonymity was essential (to add a bit of drama and mystery to the enterprise), so women dressed as men and vice versa. Some biddies ('or mummers', as they are sometimes described) used straw as part of their disguise, or sheets with tinsel belts, or masks or lace curtains to cover their faces. They carried a *brídeog*, an effigy of the saint, consisting of a straw body on a brush with a turnip for the head. With the money, a half-tierce (half barrel) of porter was bought and a 'biddy ball' was held before Lent. The custom survived in rural Ireland until the mid-20th century, declining, like so much else, after the advent of the motor car and television. It is thought that some of the customs associated with ST BRIGID'S DAY or IMBOLG are far older than Christianity.

Biddy Byrne. *See* BYRNE, BIDDY.

Biddy Moriarty. *See* MORIARTY, BIDDY.

Biddy Mulligan. *See* MULLIGAN, BIDDY.

Bidet Mulligan. The mocking name for the fountain celebrating the millennium of the founding of DUBLIN (1988) and punning on the popular song 'Biddy MULLIGAN, the PRIDE OF THE COOMBE'.
See also ALUMINIUM; FLOOZIE IN THE JACUZZI.

BIFFO. The acronymic sobriquet of Brian Cowen (b.1960), Fianna Fáil TD and able holder of various ministerial posts, including minister for foreign affairs (1997 to date). Cowen, a solicitor from Clara, Co. Offaly, achieved ministerial office early and his personality and debating style, blustering rather than aggressive, earned him the nickname BIFFO, to wit, '*Big Ignorant Fucker From Offaly*'.

Big Aggie's Man. A mysterious entity evidenced by graffiti that appeared first on walls near the ISLAND in Belfast in the 1930s, and then on every possible surface throughout the province of Ulster. Like the word QUIZ in Dublin 150 years earlier, the elusive spouse was soon ubiquitous and his doings were on everybody's lips. Even in the new millennium he still makes the odd mural and conversational appearance:

> He brooded over the deliberations in Stormont, raised hell in the City Hall, brought in 100–1 winners, refereed football matches with a warm-hearted partiality, partnered ten thousand lonely spinsters, was identified, amid delighted chuckles, on the fringe of Society weddings, and had a finger in every accident, cantrip and stroke of luck that could befall a Belfast working-class family.
>
> SAM HANNA BELL (1909–90): 'I Work Down the Island', in *Erin's Orange Lily* (1956)

Big Beggarman, the. Thomas Carlyle's nickname for Daniel O'CONNELL:

> Both [Sir Charles] DUFFY and him [John MITCHEL] I have always regarded as specimens of the best kind of Irish youth seduced, like thousands of them, in their early day, into courses that were at once mad and ridiculous, and which nearly ruined

the life of both, by the Big Beggarman who had £15,000 a year, and *pro pudore* [for shame], the favour of English ministers instead of the pillory from them, for professing blarney with such and still worse results.

> *Journal* (1846)

Big Chapel, The. *See* KILROY, THOMAS.

Big Christmas (Irish, *Nollaig Mhór*). Christmas Day, although Big Christmas begins on the night of 24 December, which is always called 'Christmas night' in rural Ireland. It was the custom on that night for the men to visit each other's houses for BOTHÁNTAÍOCHT or CÉILÍDHING. It is 'big' in relation to Little or WOMEN'S CHRISTMAS.
See also BETWEEN THE TWO CHRISTMASES.

Big-endians. A party in the empire of Lilliput in Swift's GULLIVER'S TRAVELS (1726), who made it a matter of conscience to break their eggs at the big end. They were looked on as heretics by the orthodox party who broke theirs at the little end. The Big-endians represent the Catholics and the Little-endians the Protestants:

> It is computed, that eleven thousand persons have, at certain times, suffered death, rather than submit to break their eggs at the smaller end. Many hundred large volumes have been published upon this controversy: but the books of the Big-endians have been long forbidden, and the whole party rendered incapable by law of holding employments.

Big fella. *See* THANKS A MILLION, BIG FELLA.

Big Fellow, the. A nickname given by his peers to Republican leader and statesman Michael COLLINS (1890–1922), both because of his physical stature and his tendency towards arrogance and stubbornness. It is the title of an admiring biographical study (1937) of Collins by Frank O'CONNOR.
See also LONG FELLOW, THE.

Big Four, the. The nickname by which Dan BREEN, Sean Hogan, Seamus Robinson and Seán Treacy, the participants in the SOLOHEAD-BEG ambush, became later known in IRA circles.

Biggar, Joe. *See* BELFAST QUASIMODO.

Bigger, Francis J[oseph] (1863–1926). Antiquarian. Bigger was born in Belfast in 1863, educated at INST and qualified as a solicitor in 1888. He became interested in the revival of Irish and made his large Belfast house, Ardrigh, a centre for the movement. Keenly interested in all things Irish, including the Ulster dialect, he restored at his own expense many mouldering relics of a more glorious past, and established the Glens of Antrim FEIS CHEOIL with Roger CASEMENT and Robert LYND. He died in Belfast on 9 December 1926, and left his 3000-volume personal library to Belfast Central Library. His grave at Mallusk north of the city was blown up by Loyalists in the 1970s.
See also IN BURGO DUNO TUMULO.

Big house. The generic term for the homes of the ASCENDANCY, not all of them castles or mansions but likely to exceed greatly in size the cottages of their Irish tenants, most of whom entered them only as servants of the house or the estate. In certain areas big houses were burnt during the 1920–1 period of the ANGLO-IRISH WAR as reprisals or as a result of generations-old malice, an activity not sanctioned by the IRA leadership in Dublin. Tom BARRY, IRA leader in West Cork, justified this 'war on property':

> It was Percival started it [Major Percival of the Essex Regiment]; they started burning up the houses in the martial law area, small farmers' houses, labourers' cottages. Well the only way you can fight terror is with terror, that's the only thing that an imperialist nation will understand. We sent a message to them that for every house of ours they burned we'd burn two of the big houses, and Loyalist mansions. That wasn't a policy laid down from Dublin … The last places I burned were the workhouse and the Earl of Bandon's castle … The 'twin evils of the Conquest' someone called them: one was for the lords of the Conquest and the other was the house of the dispossessed.
>
> Personal testimony in K. GRIFFITH AND T. O'GRADY: *Curious Journey: An Oral History of Ireland's Unfinished Revolution* (1981)

Among the surviving big houses that have been turned into tourist attractions are WESTPORT HOUSE and POWERSCOURT. Others, such as MUCKROSS HOUSE, have come into the ownership of the state or of local authorities.

Big Ignorant Fucker From Offaly. *See* BIFFO.

Big Jim. *See* LARKIN, JAMES.

Big Wind, the. The great storm that caused huge damage especially in the north, west and midlands of Ireland on the night of Sunday, 6 January 1839, and which has lived in folk memory since. Ninety people died, about a third of them at sea. When the old-age pension scheme was introduced in 1909 memories of the storm were among the tests to prove that people were over the qualifying age of 70.

Bilingualism. The gradual whittling down of the great national aspiration of an Irish-speaking Ireland led to a more realistic contemporary desire for some measure of bilingualism (Irish *dátheangachas*). Cultural activities became increasingly bilingual – TG4, for instance, now subtitles all its Irish-language programmes. Nor is it expected that children in GAELTACHT areas should be educated to understand and speak only Irish. But the great language debate that has always simmered below the surface and has erupted periodically since the foundation of the Irish state has encouraged, in a small minority, fanaticism, a conviction of the superiority of Irish over English. For an increasingly small and diehard minority, bilingualism is a betrayal of a core value.
See also REVIVAL, THE.

Bilious Bale. The name given by Catholics to John Bale, the Reformation Bishop of Ossory, because of his Protestant zeal. He was born in Dunwich in Suffolk in 1495 and trained as a Carmelite friar. Converting to Protestantism in 1530, he was the author of a number of anti-Catholic dramas, which he and his troupe of strolling players performed. His play *King John* (*c*.1540), about that notable anti-papist adversary of Pope Innocent III, is taken to be the first historical drama in English. Bale was appointed to Ossory by Edward VI in 1552, but so annoyed his unwilling flock that they burned his house and killed his servants. He fled Ireland on the accession of the Catholic Mary Tudor in 1553 and was made prebendary of Canterbury in 1558 when Elizabeth I became queen.

Billy, King. *See* KING BILLY.

Billyboshpeen. A word of uncertain origin still used in HIBERNO-ENGLISH to mean a pounding in the head or a headache.

Billy Boys. The identifying mark of the more raucous and extreme members of the ORANGE ORDER and similar organizations as they chant:

> We are, we are, we are the Billy Boys,
> Up to our necks in Fenians' blood.

The reference is to William III, known to all Ulster folk as KING BILLY. In the 1930s Glasgow had a notorious Protestant gang called the Billy Boys.

Billy in the Bowl. The nickname of an 18th-century Dublin beggar who, born without legs, moved about by the use of his arms, with his lower body set in a wooden bowl covered with metal. He was described as attractive, with 'fine dark eyes, aquiline nose, well-formed mouth, dark curling locks, with a body and arms of Herculean power'. He escaped from the institution in which he had been placed because of complaints about his intemperate behaviour and managed to stay free for two years, until he was arrested again for attacking two women. He was imprisoned in Green Street jail for life at hard labour, but his journey to the prison in a wheelbarrow was more like a royal progress than a journey of shame.

BIM. The acronym for Bord Iascaigh Mhara, the sea fisheries board established in 1952.

Binchy, Maeve (b.1940). Novelist and journalist. She was born in Dublin and educated at University College Dublin. She spent some years teaching before joining the staff of *The Irish Times* in 1969, where her droll, honest articles made her very popular. Her first books were collections of well-written, engaging stories set in London and middle-class Dublin, but it was with *Light a Penny Candle* (1982), about the friendship between two girls, Aislinn and Elizabeth, from strikingly different backgrounds in the arctic Ireland of the 1940s and 1950s, that she made her name. She has written many bestselling novels since, including *Firefly Summer* (1987), *Silver Wedding* (1988), *Circle of Friends* (1990), which was made into a successful film, *The Glass Lake* (1994), *Evening Class* (1996), *Tara Road* (1998) and *Quentins* (2002), all noted for their readability, humour and excellent character sketching.

Bindings. The marriage agreement pertaining to a made match (*see* MATCHMAKING), relevant in rural Ireland until the mid-20th century. The dowry was paid down to a solicitor in case of any dispute. If relevant, a proviso was inserted that the old couple, who would remain in the house with the bridal couple, would get their requirements of food and fuel, and a seat in the horse car to Sunday Mass.

Bin lids. The bush telegraph of West Belfast and other Nationalist/Republican areas during the early years of the TROUBLES. The lids, then made of galvanized metal, were battered against the pavements, usually by women or children, to warn of the imminence of an army or police raid.

Bird never flew on one wing, a. A phrase used in pubs and other drinking places, highlighting or assenting to the necessity for a second drink: 'Ah, you'll have another pint. Sure a bird never flew on one wing.'

Birl. A verb (originally Scots) meaning 'rotate'. Children used to talk about 'birling a hoop', but the word has still a colloquial metaphorical use, as in: 'Let's give it a birl and see what happens.'

Birmingham, George A. (pen name of Canon James Owen Hannay) (1865–1950). Novelist and playwright. Born in Belfast on 16 July 1865, Hannay was educated at Haileybury and Trinity College Dublin. He was ordained in 1889 and served as rector in Westport, Co. Mayo, from 1892 till 1913. He became an army chaplain in 1916, vicar of Mells, Somerset, in 1924 and, after his wife's death in 1933, served in a quiet London parish. His prolific writing began as a means of supplementing his meagre stipend, and from *The Seething Pot* (1905) to *Two Scamps* (1950) he wrote 60 novels out of a total of 80 published works. Many of these are frothy but very entertaining, and the ones set in Ireland give a genial but accurate account of the author's native country.

In spite of a Unionist background, Birmingham was a Nationalist, and counted among his friends Horace PLUNKETT, Arthur GRIFFITH, Standish James O'GRADY and Douglas HYDE. When his mildly satirical play *General John Regan* (1913) was staged by a touring company in Westport in 1914 there was a riot, and Birmingham had the unsettling experience of seeing himself burnt in effigy in his beloved home town by Catholics he took to be his friends. This naivety (or determined satiric purpose) was shown again in the dedication of his novel *Up the Rebels* (1919) to 'any friends I have left in Ireland'. (The novel, written two years after the EASTER RISING, was a humorous account of a bloodless Irish insurrection.)

Birmingham's understanding of the Ulster Protestant temper was precise, as *The Northern Iron* (1907), his novel about the UNITED IRISHMEN and the 1798 Rebellion, clearly showed. *The Red Hand of Ulster* (1912), a dark comedy about the UVF, was partially prophetic about inevitable PARTITION. Like many another liberal, wounded by the intransigence of the IRISH QUESTION, he found life in England, especially in neo-Trollopean close quarters, more congenial than at home. He died on 2 February 1950, writing until the end.

Birmingham Six, the. The six Irishmen who were arrested following the bombing of two crowded pubs in Birmingham on 21 November 1974, killing 21 and wounding more then 150. Billy Power, Gerry Hunter, Hugh Callaghan, John Walker, Paddy Joe Hill and Dick McIlkenny – all Irishmen living in England – were tried in 1975, convicted on 21 murder counts and sentenced to life imprisonment. They spent nearly 17 years in British prisons before the last of several appeals concluded that they had been wrongly convicted; this was after protracted agitation led by the British labour MP Chris Mullin and the Bishop of Derry, Edward Daly. They were released on 15 March 1991.

See also ERROR OF JUDGEMENT; GUILDFORD FOUR, THE; WINCHESTER THREE, THE.

Birr. A small town (pronounced 'burr') with some fine Georgian buildings in west Co. Offaly. It was developed by the Parsons family, the Earls of Rosse, and known as Parsonstown until the foundation of the Free State in 1922, although the seat of the family, granted to Sir Lawrence Parsons in 1620, was always known as Birr Castle. Birr is apocryphally and onomatopoeically believed to have the lowest winter temperatures in Ireland.

The 3rd Earl of Rosse was a world-famous astronomer, his wife Mary a pioneering photographer. The Parsons are said to have responded humanely to the Great Famine of the 1840s – Birr Castle's moat was constructed as a famine relief project in 1847–8. The Parsons children were educated at home until they reached the age for university (usually Trinity College Dublin), which may have contributed to the inventive genius exhibited by several of the family. Sir Charles Parsons (1854–1931), youngest son of the 3rd Earl, developed, among other things, the steam-turbine engine, and in 1894 established the Marine Steam Turbine Company. His experimental vessel *Turbinia* persuaded the Royal Navy of his invention's merits, and from 1897 the Navy commissioned his turbine engine for destroyers and battleships; it was later adopted by Cunard liners such as the *TITANIC* and *LUSITANIA*.

Birr Castle's 130-acre demesne and gardens, which were developed by generations of Parsons from the 17th to the 20th century and contain many introductions from Nepal, Tibet and

China, are open to the public. (The 7th Earl of Rosse and his family still live in the castle.) The 3rd Earl's great telescope, the LEVIATHAN OF PARSONSTOWN, may be seen in operation, and there is also a science museum, mainly concerned with astronomy and photography.

Birrell, Augustine (1850–1933). Liberal chief secretary for Ireland (1907–16). Birrell was born in Liverpool and educated at Cambridge. A cultured man, barrister and wit, he felt at home in Dublin and cultivated the Liberal–Nationalist alliance initiated by PARNELL and GLADSTONE. The two legislative successes of his career in Ireland were the Irish Universities Act (1908), establishing the NATIONAL UNIVERSITY of Ireland, and the Land Purchase Act of 1909, which granted further concessions to tenants (*see* LAND ACTS). He greatly underestimated the strength of Nationalist feeling in Ireland, however, and was on holiday in England when the EASTER RISING of 1916 broke out. He resigned his position immediately after the Rising and left public life in 1918.

Biscake. A mispronunciation of the word 'biscuit' by false analogy, originally genuine but now largely used jocosely.
See also BICYLIC.

Bishop and the Nightie, the. A clash between the Catholic hierarchy and the forces of modernization that arose from an episode of *The LATE LATE SHOW* on 12 February 1966. The compère Gay BYRNE held a spoof couples' quiz in which a wife, Eileen Fox, was asked questions about her husband, Patrick, while Patrick, out of earshot, was asked questions about Eileen. Neither party could remember what colour nightie the woman wore on her wedding night and she jokingly offered 'None.' The Bishop of Clonfert, Thomas Ryan, was outraged, and had his secretary, Father O'Callaghan, protest to RTÉ and telephone the *Sunday Press* newspaper with a statement. He planned to deliver a sermon the next morning (the show was then broadcast on Saturday nights) condemning the show. The episcopal ire made front-page

Sunday news, and among the bodies that joined with the bishop in denouncing the broadcasting of such lewdness were Loughrea Town Commissioners, Mayo GAA County Board and Meath Vocational Educational Committee. It was soon clear, however, that *The Late Late Show* and Gay Byrne were the winners in the war for liberalization against the forces of reaction. Although the Catholic Church remained a dominant force in Irish life for many years, more and more people began to ignore its more egregious attempts at interference, particularly in the area of personal morality.
See also ABORTION REFERENDUMS; IRISH SOLUTION TO A PARTICULARLY IRISH PROBLEM, AN; TREVASKIS, BRIAN.

Bishop Brendan. The Catholic Bishop of Ferns (Co. Wexford), Brendan Comiskey, who resigned his see in March 2002 after persistent criticisms of his management of cases of clerical paedophilia in his diocese, especially the cases of Fathers Jim Grennan and Sean Fortune. Comiskey, who was born in Clontibret, Co. Monaghan, in 1935, was an able administrator, a media-friendly ecumenist and a possessor of the common touch, as testified by the name by which he was known by many people countrywide. In 1995 he caused consternation in the Catholic hierarchy by suggesting that it was time for the church to reconsider the issue of priestly celibacy, but shortly afterwards took leave from his duties to seek treatment for alcoholism in the United States. In his resignation statement in 2002 he said, 'I can only assure you that I did my best. Clearly, this was not good enough. I found Father Fortune virtually impossible to deal with.'

Bishopsgate. The scene of a low-tech IRA lorry bomb in London on 24 April 1993. It killed one person, injured a further 45 and caused damage estimated at £800 million to London's financial district. Despite this the negotiations between prime minister John Major and taoiseach Albert REYNOLDS continued, and the DOWNING STREET DECLARATION was signed on 15 December.

Bisom. *See* BESOM.

Blácam, Aodh de. *See* DE BLÁCAM, AODH.

Black. A word used as an intensifier: 'black frost' (but not in this sense 'black ice'), 'black Protestant' (even to the extent of: 'Orange? He's as black as yer boot'), 'black Republican', etc. 'The tide is black out' is used to describe absolute low tide.

Black and Tans. The name (originally of a pack of hounds from Scarteen, Co. Limerick) given to non-Irish recruits who supplemented the beleaguered RIC (Royal Irish Constabulary) during what came to be known in Ireland as the TAN WAR but is known to historians as the WAR OF INDEPENDENCE or the ANGLO-IRISH WAR. When they were first recruited in January 1920 there was a shortage of full police uniforms, and for a short period they wore a mixed uniform of khaki army trousers with standard dark-green police tunics. The name stuck. The Black and Tans soon achieved a notorious reputation for ferocity and reprisal (though often confused with the AUXIES), and the sobriquet became the general hate name for all the police forces opposed to the IRA. The Black and Tans were disbanded with the rest of the RIC in 1923.

Black babies. African children, represented appealingly on collection boxes in schools, for the benefit of whom Irish children donated pennies to Catholic missionaries. A mother might exhort her child to make a sacrifice of not eating sweets for Lent and channel the money saved into the collection box: 'Give them up for the black babies.' With the advent in the 1970s of a more enlightened, humanitarian attitude to what came to be called 'development', black babies disappeared.

'Blackbird, The'. The name of one of the most famous of the 19th-century 'long' solo dances choreographed by DANCING MASTERS. It is still a popular competition dance. The fiddler Denis Murphy (*see* DENIS THE WEAVER) was proud to be able to simultaneously play on the fiddle and dance 'The Blackbird'.

'Blackbird of Avondale, The'. The affectionate name given to Charles Stewart PARNELL in the ballad of the same name (AVONDALE being Parnell's birthplace):

Near to Rathdrum in the County Wicklow
This brave defender of Granuaile
First tuned his notes on old Ireland's freedom,
In the lovely woodlands of Avondale.
(GRANUAILE was one of the many personifications of Ireland.)

Black Bush. A liqueur whiskey made at the Old Bushmills distillery, Co. Antrim (founded 1602). Its currency and popularity have given rise to coarse pubic allusions.

Black Death, the. An epidemic of bubonic plague that swept through Europe from the east during the years 1347–51, killing about 25 million people in all, a quarter of the entire population of the continent. In August 1348 the plague made its appearance in the coastal areas around Dublin, and during that year alone it was claimed that 14,000 people had died of the disease in the city. It spread more rapidly in towns, particularly affecting fishermen and sailors in ports and harbours; in 1351 it was reported that almost all the citizens of Cork had died of the disease. Estimates of fatalities in Ireland range from one-third to a half of the total population. The Black Death had very serious recessionary effects on the economy and on agriculture. In all, there are thought to have been six major epidemics of the plague in Ireland from the 11th to the 17th century; the country appears to have escaped infection by the Great Plague that affected London in 1664–5, partly because steps were taken to quarantine travellers from England.

Black Diaries, the. The alleged homosexual diaries of Roger CASEMENT, so called because they were said to have been written in parallel with the 'White Diaries' during his humanitarian travels in Africa and South America. While the former consist of short entries – fewer than 150 words per day – detailing sexual activities with young men, some of whom paid for sex, the latter comprise long, detailed reports about the exploitation and abuse of native peoples. Some of Casement's Black (1903 and 1910) and White Diaries were published in New York in 1959 in *The Black Diaries: An Account of Roger Casement's Life and Times, with a Collection of His Published Writings.* Anglo-Irish TREATY negotiators Eamonn Duggan and Michael COLLINS saw the Black Diaries in 1921; Collins appeared to verify the authenticity of the handwriting, while Duggan was disgusted by the 'details of sex perversion', and by the diarist's description of 'the personal appearance and beauty of native boys, with special reference to a certain portion of their anatomy'. Republicans long held that the Black Diaries were forged by MI5 to blacken Casement's reputation after his execution, in order to prevent him becoming a martyr among the generally conservative Irish. Most historians now accept that the Black Diaries were indeed written by Casement, although there are still some experts who reject them as forgeries.

Blacker, William. *See* OLIVER'S ADVICE.

Black '47. The worst year of the GREAT FAMINE, following the second failure of the potato crop in the autumn of 1846. Misery was aggravated by the decision of the Liberal prime minister, Lord John Russell, that all relief schemes for the 'potatophagi' (as the London *Times* referred to the lesser Hibernian breeds), would have to be financed by local rates, with all the attendant likelihood of inefficiency, local difficulties and corruption. By January 1847 the numbers on relief works had risen to 570,000; they reached 750,000 by March. The winter was unusually severe, and the devout head of the Treasury, Charles TREVELYAN, decided that to save the exchequer money the meaningless public works (*see* BÓTHAR NA MINE BUÍ) should be paid on piecework rather than at a flat rate. This decision meant in practice that all but the strongest could not earn enough to feed themselves, let alone their large families. People were literally dropping dead, but Trevelyan and his fellow cabinet members, bound as they were by devotion to *laissez-faire* and certain that the

hand of God was clearly to be seen in this great mercy, were unwilling to act. When it became clear that the tiny farmsteads of the COTTIERS were being neglected and that no peat had been cut nor seed set, the sensible suggestion was made that, instead of building roads across bogs, or surrounding estates with superfluous walls, the public works for which the starving were being paid should consist of work on their own holdings. Trevelyan was horrified at the idea of paying people to work their own land. It was then that he made the statement for which he is best remembered, showing as it did his misconception of the lives and conditions of the Irish peasant: '… a fortnight's planting, a week or ten days' digging and fourteen days of turf-cutting suffice for his existence. During the rest of the year he is at leisure to follow his own inclinations.'

> No; the blood is dead within our veins – we care not now for life;
> Let us die hid in the ditches, far from children and from wife!
> We cannot stay and listen to their raving famished cries –
> Bread! Bread! Bread! and none to still their agonies.
> SPERANZA (Jane Francesca Wilde) (1821–96): 'The Famine Year' (1847)

Blackguarding. A word originally meaning 'vilifying', but now used rather with the sense of not very serious 'teasing' or 'misleading', as in, 'Sure I was only blackguarding when I said that she was kissing Murphy.' It is pronounced 'blaggarding', as in 'blackguard'.

Blackham, Hugh. *See* DE BLÁCAM, AODH.

Black Irish. A description applied especially in the USA to the expatriate Irish, suggesting a different persona from the jolly, bibulous, all-singing, all-dancing protective guise that they donned away from home. This alternative persona was characterized by silence, brooding and possible danger, but with the same recourse to liquor.

The term 'Black Irish' is also applied to the descendants of Irish migrants and indentured servants who colonized the small island of

Montserrat in the Lesser Antilles in the 17th century. (It had been discovered by Columbus in 1493 and called after the mountain in Spain.) The island's tourist industry sells it as a uniquely Irish Caribbean location, and encourages the myth that the Irish inhabitants were kind to their slaves (imported in the 1660s). In fact they behaved towards them exactly as did the English and Scots, displaying brutal attitudes to Africans and to Amerindians from neighbouring islands. The island became a British possession in 1783, with the usual penal disadvantages applied to any Catholic inhabitants. Montserrat has been internally self-governing as a British dependent territory since 1960.

Black List Section H. An autobiographical novel (1971) by Francis Stuart in which H, the protagonist, lives out Stuart's own life, including his internment after the CIVIL WAR, his marriage to Iseult GONNE, his time in Germany during and after the Second World War and his meeting with the woman who became his second wife. Stuart was born in Australia in 1902, but was brought home to Ireland after his father's suicide. While in Germany as a university teacher he was one of several 'neutrals' paid by the Nazis to broadcast during the war. This led to a period of internment and great deprivation, during which his recurring theme of redemption through suffering, in line with his idiosyncratic Catholicism, was forged. It led to such novels as *The Pillar of Cloud* (1948), *Redemption* (1949) and *The Flowering Cross* (1950), the middle one set in the publicly religious Ireland of the immediately postwar years, and to his last novel, *A Compendium of Lovers* (1990), in which Thérèse Martin (St Theresa) did not after all enter a convent to become the Little Flower but married the narrator Joel Samuel. Most of his later work – especially the five experimental novels *Memorial* (1973), *A Hole in the Head* (1977), *The High Consistory* (1981), *Faillandia* (1985) and *A Compendium of Lovers* – deals with love, sex, the state of Ireland (and the world) and the purpose of religion. Stuart, who died on

2 February 2000, delighted in a sober way in his uncategorizability, but he remains one of Ireland's most original and, in its old sense, crankiest writers.

Black Militia. An armed force that, according to a firmly believed piece of Irish folklore, would one day be murderously unleashed upon Irish Catholics. It was identified with the ORANGE ORDER, especially in the early years of the Order's existence.

Black North, the. The province of Ulster regarded by the South as Protestant. The term may have originated with the Black Preceptory (*see* ROYAL BLACK INSTITUTION) but is more likely to have been associated with the word's negative aura. The coinage is ascribed to the writer Aodh DE BLÁCAM and is the title of his book (1938).

Black Oath, the. The name given to the Oath of Abjuration imposed by Lord Deputy Thomas WENTWORTH – urged on by Scots Royalists in Ireland – on Presbyterian Scottish settlers (nearly all resident in Ulster) in 1639. The oath was administered with a military presence to all Presbyterians over the age of 16, and required them to disown the Scottish National Covenant (February 1638), which rejected the Anglican church in favour of Presbyterianism and by implication supported Parliament against Charles I. Most accepted the abjuration, but many fled back to Scotland rather than be untrue to the Kirk, and the REBELLION OF 1641 helped to re-establish the faith of many Ulster Presbyterians.

Black Pig's Dyke. An incomplete Iron Age earthwork (also known as the 'Worm Ditch') in south Ulster, dating from *c*.500–50 BC. It is thought that it was built as a protection against cattle raiders from Leinster, and the name is used symbolically as a mark of Ulster separateness from the rest of Ireland; this separateness is emphasized by a broad band of DRUMLINS and lakes that stretches west right across the province as far as Donegal Bay. The earthwork's name comes from a folktale of a magician transmogrified into a pig who roots up the earth as he runs westwards. *See also* DORSEY.

Black rabbit. An expression from the days when the MISSION was the most important event in the Catholic parish year. One of the most significant elements in the fortnight was the personal interview, by one of the mission priests, of defaulters in the hope of persuading them to return to the sacraments. These were known in some parishes as black rabbits, probably by colour transference from their benign hunters.

Black Santa. The name applied to a number of deans of St Anne's Anglican Cathedral, Belfast, who spend the week before Christmas outside the main doors dressed in canonical cloaks soliciting alms. The first Black Santa was Dean Sammy Crooks who in 1976 decided to use the festive season to beg alms, especially for children's charities. It was the local media who gave him his nickname. Succeeding deans Jack Shearer and Houston McKelvey have continued the practice, which has cross-community support. The voluminous cloak and hood is often a necessary protection against winter weather: as Dr McKelvey put it, 'The experience is breathtaking both physically and spiritually.'

Blacksmith of Ballinalee, the. The sobriquet of Seán MacEoin (1894–1973), an active and successful commandant in his home county of Longford in the ANGLO-IRISH WAR. The name derived from his trade and from his successful ambush of the BLACK AND TANS in Ballinalee on 3 November 1920 (or from a subsequent engagement in February 1921). In March 1921 MacEoin was captured and sentenced to death despite several attempts by Michael COLLINS to free him, but he was released under the terms of the TRUCE. He took the pro-TREATY side in the CIVIL WAR and led the western command of the Free State army, after taking over Longford barracks from the British army. He subsequently had a long career as a TD for CUMANN NA NGAEDHEAL and later FINE GAEL (1929–65). Always known as General MacEoin, he served as minister for justice and minister for defence in the INTERPARTY GOVERNMENTS of 1948–51 and 1954–57 and was twice, in 1945 and 1959, an unsuccessful candidate for the presidency.

Blacksmiths. *See* GABHA.

Blacksmith's money. The name given to crude coinage minted in 1649 by Royalists in Kilkenny.

Black stuff. A somewhat dated colloquialism, formerly used, particularly in Dublin, for stout, especially GUINNESS.

Black Tom. The nickname of Thomas Butler, 10th Earl of Ormond (1532–1614) and lord high treasurer of Ireland, from his ungracious ways and black looks. He was a loyalist and sworn enemy of the 15th Earl of DESMOND.

Black Tom Tyrant. *See* WENTWORTH, THOMAS.

Blackwater. *See* AWNIDUFF.

Blade. An Ulster word for a free-spirited, non-conforming young person, usually female.

Bla-flum. An Ulster word meaning deliberately misleading nonsensical chat.

Bláithín (Irish, 'little flower'). The name given affectionately by the BLASKET islanders to Robin Flower (1881–1946), the English-born Celtic scholar, translator and poet who was a frequent visitor to the Blaskets. He was deputy keeper of manuscripts at the British Museum 1929–1944. *The Western Isle* (1944) is a classic account of Flower's experiences on Great Blasket.

Blanchflower, Danny. *See* INTELLECT OF THE GAME, THE.

Blaney, Neil (1922–95). Politician. Blaney was born on 29 October 1922 in Rossnakill, Co. Donegal. Educated locally and at St Eunan's College, Letterkenny, he won the by-election caused by the death of his father, a Fianna Fáil TD, in 1948. He held a number of ministerial posts: posts and telegraphs (1957), local government (1958–66) and agriculture and fisheries (1966–70). With the coming of the TROUBLES his instinctive Republicanism caused him to offer uncompromising support for Nationalists in Ulster and he was arrested in April 1970 for alleged involvement in the illegal importation of arms (*see* ARMS CRISIS). Though the charges were dismissed, he and Charles HAUGHEY were removed from office by the taoiseach, Jack LYNCH, for allegedly not subscribing fully to the government's policy on Northern Ireland. Blaney was expelled from the Fianna Fáil parliamentary party in November 1970, but as leader of Independent Fianna Fáil continued his political career until 1994, when illness prevented his contesting of the election. With an unbroken parliamentary record of 47 years service he was the longest-serving TD when he retired. He died on 8 November 1995, still the most forthright Republican voice in the Dáil.

Blanket Protest. The refusal of the Republican prisoners in Long Kesh (*see* MAZE, THE) to wear prison clothing. The protest began in 1980 when, at the urging of prime minister Margaret Thatcher, Humphrey Atkins, the secretary of state for Northern Ireland (1979–81), withdrew special status in an effort to criminalize IRA activities. The right to wear ordinary clothes in prison was a special privilege, won by the hunger-striker Billy McKee in 1971. Refused that right, the prisoners wrapped themselves in prison blankets; such prisoners were said to be 'on the blanket'. Some prisoners went on to hold a DIRTY PROTEST. The question of SPECIAL CATEGORY led to the H-BLOCK HUNGER STRIKES of 1980 and 1981.

Blarge. A strong and usually clumsy action, often applied to a kick at football: 'He hit the ball such a blarge that it nearly put the goalkeeper into the back of the net.' *See also* BLEENGE.

Blarney Stone. A stone set on the inside wall of the tower of Blarney Castle (8 km/5 miles from Cork) that is supposed to endow anyone who kisses it with 'sweet persuasive wheedling eloquence' (J.S. Coyne: *Cork Historical and Archaelogical Journal*, Vol. 18, 1912):

> She sighs and she blushes, and looks half afraid,
> Yet loses no word that her lover can say.
> What is it she hears but the Blarney.
> Oh a perilous thing is the Blarney!
>> SAMUEL CARTER HALL (1800–89): 'The Blarney' (1843)

Blarney Castle was once the home of the MacCarthys, and its reputation for PLÁMÁS ('cajolery') is said to have originated with Cormac MacCarthy, who in 1602 temporized so endlessly (and so volubly) with Sir George CAREW, Elizabeth I's Lord of Munster, that he was permitted to keep his lands and avoid SURRENDER AND REGRANT (the Tudor government's mechanism for recasting the Gaelic system of clan chieftainship into an English mould of earldom and baronetcy). Elizabeth is supposed to have remarked: 'This is all blarney; what he says he never means.'

In 1825 FATHER PROUT, the son of the owner of the Blarney Woollen mills, added some verses to 'The GROVES OF BLARNEY', confirming the stone's virtues:

> There is a stone there,
> That whoever kisses,
> Oh! he never misses
> To grow eloquent;
> 'Tis he may clamber
> To a lady's chamber,
> Or become a member
> Of parliament.
> A clever spouter
> He'll soon turn out, or
> An out-and-outer …

Kissing the stone is a must for tourists, although the position for the osculation, lying on one's back hanging over a big drop with legs anchored by willing helpers, may be off-putting for some.

Blas (Irish, 'flavour', 'taste'). A complimentary word applied to eloquence in the Irish language, as used in the following proverb which obviously emanates from the west:

Tá blas gan ceart ag an Muimhneach;
Tá ceart gan blas ag an Ultach;
Níl ceart ná blas ag an Laighneach;
Ach tá ceart agus blas ag an gConnachtach.
(The speech of the Munsterman is eloquent but inaccurate; the Ulsterman is accurate but pedestrian; the Leinsterman's Irish has neither flavour nor accuracy; but the Connachtman has both.)

The word also means the taste or flavour of food. A proverb in Irish claims, '*Bíonn blas ar an mbeagán*' ('A little has a good taste').

Blasket Islands. A group of five islands southwest of the Dingle Peninsula in Co. Kerry, traditionally reached by NAOMHÓG (coracle) from Dunquin. The largest, the Great Blasket (*An Blascaod Mór* in Irish, and known locally as *An tOileán Thiar*, 'the western island'), was inhabited until 1953, when all remaining inhabitants were moved to the mainland. The islandmen and women eked out a living from rocky ground and treacherous sea, but their cultural traditions and the Irish they spoke were very rich and ancient, and the island became a Mecca for folklorists, ethnographers and Irish-language enthusiasts. Native laureates included Tomás Ó Criomhthain (*see* OILEÁNACH, AN T-), Muiris Ó Súilleabháin (*see* FICHE BLIAN AG FÁS) and Peig Sayers (*see* PEIG).
See also BLÁITHÍN; HUNGRY FOR HOME: LEAVING THE BLASKETS.

Blast. A word meaning any sudden phenomenon, often pronounced 'blasht' in a mock-Connacht accent, as in, 'A blast of a cold kept me in bed.'

Blather (Irish *bladar*). A word common in HIBERNO-ENGLISH and meaning 'nonsense', 'guff', 'flattery': 'Will you stop that old blather and give me a straight answer!'
See also BLETHER.

Bláthmacc. An 8th-century religious poet who has left two long meditations on the Blessed Virgin. He was probably born in Co. Monaghan and is likely to have been part of the CULDEE movement.

Soer a ngein ro genair úait
Rot rath, a Máire, mórbúaid.
Críst macc Dé Athar di nim
É ron-ucais i mBeithil.
(A noble child was born from you;
You, Mary, received a great gift:
Christ the son of God the father of heaven
Was the one you bore in Bethlehem.)

Blathnát (also **Blanaid**, Irish for 'little flower'). A maiden in love with CÚCHULAINN. She is carried off by Cú Roí, Cúchulainn's patron, as his wife. Cúchulainn sets off to rescue her, but finds that Cú Roí's Munster fortress has no obvious entrance. The resourceful Blathnát pours milk into an inner stream, revealing the portal as the liquid seeps out, thus enabling Cúchulainn to attack and slay Cú Roí and rescue Blathnát. Among the prisoners is Cú Roí's bard Fercherdne, who is determined to avenge his master. As the victorious party is making its way along the cliffs of the Beara peninsula (shared by Cork and Kerry) Fercherdne seizes Blathnát and jumps with her into the sea.

Blayney's Bloodhounds. An alternative nickname for the Royal Irish Fusiliers (*see also* FAUGHS). It dates from the time when – as the 87th Foot and commanded by Andrew Thomas, 11th Lord Blayney – they were successful in capturing United Irish rebels in 1798.

Blaze of whins. An Ulster simile for rapidity, based upon the flammability of dead WHINS (gorse), often deliberately ignited on May Eve: 'He scooted off like a blaze of whins.'

Bleeding for St Martin. A ritual associated with the feast of St Martin, or Martinmas (10 November), but certainly dating from pagan times. In some rural areas, in living memory, the necks of cocks were cut and they were left to bleed to death. It was believed that a cloth dipped in the blood of an animal or bird killed on Martinmas cured aches and pains.

Bleenge. An Ulster word close in connotation to BLARGE, with a hint of some more grace: 'He made a bleenge at him and sent him flying.'

Blefuscu. The island whose similarly diminutive inhabitants were the mortal enemies of the people of LILLIPUT in Swift's GULLIVER'S TRAVELS. Blefuscu was intended to represent France, a country as vain and silly as Georgian England (with Ireland included). Wolfe TONE, who was greatly influenced by Swift, used the word as a code for Belfast in his diaries.

Blessings. It is said that there is always a blessing on the lips of an Irish person (*Bíonn beannacht i gcónaí i mbéal an Ghaeil*), something certainly true of an Irish person speaking Irish. A deceased person is never mentioned without the addition of, '*Go ndéana Dia grásta dó*' ('May God have mercy [literally 'grace'] on him'), while a worker earns the blessing, '*Bail ó Dhia ar an obair*' ('The blessing of God on the work'). The everyday salutation in Irish is, '*Dia dhuit*' ('God be with you') or, '*Dia's Muire dhuit*' ('God and Mary be with you'). One has only to listen to the Irish-language broadcasting services, especially to RAIDIÓ NA GAELTACHTA, which transmits directly from the GAELTACHT areas, to observe how frequently the speakers spontaneously invoke blessings. Little of this has transferred to HIBERNO-ENGLISH, with the exception of the parting salutation 'God bless' (as in GOODNIGHT, GOD BLESS AND SAFE HOME), which is no longer fashionable in the urban Ireland of today. Traditionalists, particularly in rural areas, still offer a blessing, 'God have mercy on him' or 'God be good to him', when referring to a deceased person.

Blessington Basin. A reservoir in Blessington Street, close to the north side of Dublin's city centre, which supplied water for the area until the Vartry Reservoir in Co. Wicklow was constructed. It is now a public amenity and home to waterbirds.

Blether (also **blather** and **bletherskite**). A word signifying both a person who talks incessantly and the often meaningless gabble generated. The word is also used in Scots, and is said to derive from Old Scandinavian *blathr*, 'nonsense'.

Bliain an áir (Irish, 'year of the slaughter'). The year 1741, when a famine killed 300,000 people. It was the result of extremely bad weather and poor harvests in 1739 and 1740, and was compounded by a failure of the potato crop and epidemics of typhoid and dysentery.

Bligh, Captain William (1754–1817). English mariner and surveyor. He sailed on Captain Cook's second voyage of exploration in the South Seas in 1772 but in the popular mind is most associated with the mutiny on his ship, the *Bounty*, in 1787. He was appointed governor of New South Wales in 1805. He was an excellent marine surveyor and hydrographer and his 1801 report on Dublin Bay suggested the strengthening of a section of the recently complete GREAT SOUTH WALL and the building of a North Wall from Ringsend to the Spit Buoy (*see* BULL WALL, THE).

Blind and ignorant town. The description by W.B. YEATS of the Dublin that would not provide the money for the new gallery to receive the LANE PICTURES. It is to be found in a poem with a deliberately ironic and extended title: 'To a Wealthy Man who promised a Second Subscription to the Dublin Municipal Gallery if it were proved the People wanted Pictures' (1913), in *Responsibilities* (1914). The 'wealthy man' was probably Arthur Edward Guinness, Lord Ardilaun (1840–1915), of the brewing dynasty:

> You gave but will not give again
> Until enough of Paudeen's pence
> By Biddy's halfpennies have lain
> To be 'some sort of evidence',
> Before you'll put your guineas down,
> That things it were pride to give
> Are what the blind and ignorant town
> Imagines best to make it thrive.

Blind Billy's Bargain. A phrase meaning no bargain at all, from the story of the attempt of Blind Billy, the early 19th-century Limerick hangman, to wrest money from the local high sheriff. Blind Billy refused to carry out his grisly duty without a fee of £50; in response the sheriff gave him the money, but refused to provide the usual escort without a fee of £50.

Blind Poetess of Donegal, the. The nickname of Frances Browne (1816–79), born in Stranorlar, Co. Donegal, on 16 January 1816, the 7th of 12 children of the local postmaster. She went blind in infancy after an attack of smallpox, but attended the village school (where one of her fellow-pupils was Isaac BUTT, founder of the Home Rule movement) and acquired her education through hearing the other children repeat their lessons. Discovering that she had a talent for writing, she became a prolific author, publishing poetry, novels and a remarkable collection of fairy-tales, *Granny's Wonderful Chair* (1856), which was republished a dozen times, most recently in 1995. She moved first to Edinburgh in 1847 and then to London in 1852 (helped by a gift of £100 from the Marquess of Lansdowne). She died in Notting Hill on 25 August 1879 of a heart complaint. Two years previously Frances Hodgson Burnett (1849–1924) had published a version of *Granny's Wonderful Chair* as *Stories from the Lost Fairy Book as Retold by the Child Who Read Them*, but the book as originally written by Browne was reissued in 1880. Like many expatriate writers she continually returned to Ireland in her imagination, and the exile's homecoming became the theme of many of her poems.

> Oh, thus let it be with the hearts of the isle,
> Efface the dark seal that oppression hath set;
> Give back the lost glory again to the soul,
> For the hills of my country remember it yet!
>
> 'The Last Friends', in *Pictures and Songs from Home* (1856)

Blind Raftery. The name by which W.B. Yeats referred to Antaine Ó Reachtarbha (also Reachtaire and Raifteirí), the itinerant blind musician and poet of Connacht. He was born near Kiltimagh, Co. Mayo, *c.*1784, the son of a weaver from Co. Sligo. Blind from the age of 9, he became an itinerant fiddler who entertained hospitable households and crowds at fairs with his own homespun verse. Ironi-

cally '*MISE RAIF-TEIRÍ AN FILE*', the poem by which he is best known, was not actually composed by him but put together from some of his sayings by a devotee. His patch was the area including Gort, Athenry and Loughrea as well as Mayo, and he responded in verse to local and national events. '*Cill Aodáin*' (*see* 'BEIDH AN LÁ' DUL 'UN SÍNEADH'), his hymn to spring, is one of the most quoted poems in modern Irish, while '*Eanach Dhúin*' (*see* ANNAGHDOWN TRAGEDY), his lament for the drowned in the Corrib tragedy in 1822, shows his vigour and fluency. Máire Ní Eidhin, Raftery's Beatrice, died shortly after he had written of a poem in her praise, creating for the poet a reputation for bringing bad luck. His poetry recaptures a lost age, not wholly mournful and full of a rough energy that was lost with the Great Famine and never totally recovered. His Irish is accessible and it is no surprise that he was adopted as a patron saint of both the Gaelic revival and the Literary Renaissance. He died *c.*1835 and was buried near Craughwell, Co. Galway, in a grave now marked by a commemorative stone placed there in 1900 by Lady Gregory and Douglas Hyde.

Blink. A HIBERNO-ENGLISH transitive verb meaning to curse by using the evil eye: 'I was doing grand until somebody blinked me.'

Blirt. A general term of abuse, usually applied to males:

> 'He's a crabbit ould blirt, too,' grumbled the servingman, referring to Andrew, as he and Pentland turned away.
>
> SAM HANNA BELL *December Bride* (1950)

Blitter. A verb meaning to fart continuously, especially after food:

> Whiskey makes you frisky
> An' stout makes you shout;
> But atin' well-cooked peas or beans
> Will make you blitter out.
>
> Quoted in LORETO TODD: *Words Apart* (1990)

Blood and bandages[1]. A bed of red and white roses, regarded by some as unlucky. Red and white roses are also considered unlucky in a hospital context.

Blood and bandages². A description of the Cork colours (red and white), used especially by supporters of the county's main Gaelic football rivals, Kerry.

Blood's Plot. A Protestant conspiracy of 1663 in which the eponymous Thomas Blood (c.1618–80), a former Parliamentary soldier, may have been an *agent provocateur*. The intention was to seize Dublin Castle, arrest the Duke of ORMOND and regain some of the lands that the Act of Settlement (1662) had restored to the original owners (a very small minority). The plot was discovered in March, and by June seven MPs had been arrested and Colonel Alexander Jephson, member for Trim, hanged. Blood escaped and survived to attempt to assassinate Ormond in London in 1670. Escaping again, he was arrested the following year attempting to steal the crown jewels from the White Tower. When he was pardoned by Charles II and given a grant of Irish lands worth £500 a year, the suspicions that he was a government spy seemed to have been confirmed. He died in his home in Westminster on 24 August 1680.

Bloody awful country. Reginald Maudling, UK home secretary, reportedly used this phrase on a flight back to London on 1 July 1970, after a visit to Northern Ireland in the early years of the Troubles: 'For God's sake, someone bring me a large Scotch. What a bloody awful country.' *See also* ACCEPTABLE LEVEL (OF VIOLENCE).

Bloody Balfour. *See* BALFOUR, ARTHUR; MITCHELSTOWN MASSACRE.

Bloody Friday. The name (echoing BLOODY SUNDAY) given to 21 July 1972 when, between 2.15 and 3.30 p.m., the Provisional IRA set off 26 explosions in Belfast in which 11 people, including 2 soldiers, were killed and 130 injured. Seven of the fatalities took place at the crowded Oxford Street bus station and the rest at a shopping centre on the Cavehill Road. It was the worst day of violence Belfast had seen and marked the point of absolute political isolation of the Provisionals.

Bloody O'Reilly. The nickname of Alexander O'Reilly (1722–1794), one of the WILD GEESE in the service of Spain, who earned the sobriquet in New Orleans, USA, in 1769 because of the ruthlessness of his quelling of the revolt against the Spanish governor of Louisiana. His own period as governor was regarded as liberal.

Bloody Sunday 1914. *See* BACHELOR'S WALK.

Bloody Sunday 1920. The name given to 21 November 1920, one of the bloodier days of the ANGLO-IRISH WAR. At precisely 9.00 a.m. that morning eight different assassination teams from the SQUAD shot and killed 11 members of the CAIRO GANG (members of British Intelligence) in eight different locations; these included private houses and hotels in Dublin. In retaliation, that afternoon AUXIES fired a machine gun indiscriminately into a crowd watching a Dublin–Tipperary Gaelic football match in CROKE PARK. In all, 12 spectators were killed, as well as a Tipperary player, and 60 wounded. That evening, the leaders of the IRA's Dublin Brigade, Peadar Clancy and Dick McKee (who had been arrested on Saturday night and were thus not involved in the killings), were killed in Dublin Castle by way of reprisal, along with Conor Clune, a non-combatant who had been arrested the night before for breaking the curfew, all three allegedly while trying to escape. The IRA claimed that the three men had been tortured and bayoneted to death. Michael Collins himself, although a wanted man, helped carry a coffin at the ensuing funerals in the pro-cathedral. These and the civilian deaths were as much a propaganda victory for the IRA as the killings of the G-MEN (exactly as Collins intended), intensifying the conflict with British forces. The KILMICHAEL AMBUSH occurred exactly a week later.

Bloody Sunday 1972. The incident on 30 January 1972 when 13 unarmed civilians demonstrating against INTERNMENT in Derry were shot by members of the British Parachute Regiment and, as was revealed in a Channel 4 documentary in January 1997, the Royal

Anglian Regiment. A 14th died later. Great anger and controversy followed; the British Embassy in Dublin was burned down and Bernadette DEVLIN struck Reginald Maudling in the House of Commons, announcing afterwards: 'I am just sorry I didn't go for his throat' (see MURDERING HYPOCRITE). Edward Heath, the British prime minister, announced an inquiry by Lord Widgery (1911–81), the lord chief justice, but by the time his WIDGERY REPORT – which many regarded as a whitewash of government and army – was issued in April, the STORMONT parliament had been suspended.

During the succeeding years many attempts were made to have a new inquiry and an apology, but it was not until 30 January 1998, the 26th anniversary of Bloody Sunday, that prime minister Tony Blair and the secretary of state for Northern Ireland, Mo Mowlam, announced the setting-up of a tribunal to be chaired by Lord Saville of Newdigate. It held its first meeting in the Guildhall in April of that year and is still (as at August 2004) in intermittent session. Bloody Sunday was later seen to have been the source of much IRA recruitment.

> We accuse the Commander of Land Forces of being accessory after the fact. We accuse the soldiers of firing indiscriminately into a fleeing crowd, of gloating over casualties … these men are trained criminals. They differ from terrorists only in the veneer of respectability that a uniform gives them.
>
> Statement signed by seven Derry priests (including Bishop Edward Daly) on 31 January 1972 and printed in *The Irish Times* on 1 February 1972

Bloomsday. A celebration of ULYSSES and James JOYCE, held annually in Dublin on 16 June, taking its name from Leopold Bloom, the main protagonist of Joyce's epic. It was instituted in 1954, the 50th anniversary of 16 June 1904, the day on which the action of the novel is set. It involves walks through the locations mentioned in the novel and pageants and recreations in some of the key places, like Sandycove Martello Tower, now the James Joyce Museum, where the action of the novel begins.

Blootered. One of a myriad Ulster synonyms for 'drunk' – in fact, 'very drunk indeed'. Its association with 'blooter', a coarse and clumsy man, is obvious: 'He was blootered outa his mind.' The word is also used in Scotland.

Blow. A current HIBERNO-ENGLISH verb meaning 'boast', whether or not with justification. Its use is largely confined to Ulster.

Blowhard. Methylated spirits mixed with a little cheap wine, favoured as a tipple by derelicts.

Blow-in. A term meaning someone living in an area who did not originate there: in rural Ireland this could be someone who moved from Dublin or another city or, more likely, a foreigner. Since the 1960s, scenic areas along the western seaboard have seen a big influx of Continental and English blow-ins, some of them wealthy, others on the poverty line and practising some kind of self-sufficiency. The phrase 'blow-in' may be used positively – and there are many Irish people who appreciate the diversity that has resulted from such cross-fertilization – but it is just as likely to have a disparaging connotation: for instance in the ongoing controversy about planning permission in rural and scenic areas, locals complain about blow-ins who try to stop other people from building houses while themselves being in the area only for a 'WET WEEK'. Given the fragility of the Irish language, the settlement of non-Irish-speaking blow-ins is a particularly sensitive issue in GAELTACHT areas on the western seaboard.
See also BALLYDEHOB; BUNGALOW BLIGHT; TAISCE, AN.

Blue Bangors (also **Bangor blues**). A name now used generically for traditional grey slates, but originally meaning thick and heavy slates weighing 4.5–6.8 kilos (10–15 lb) and ranging in size from 30 cm by 90 cm (1ft by 3 ft) to 90 cm by 120 cm (3ft by 4 ft). They were once seen on castles, churches, jails and most municipal buildings across Ireland. The name comes from a large slate quarry near Bangor, Gwynedd, in North Wales.

Blue Blouses. *See* BLUESHIRTS.

Blue flu. The nickname given by the media to industrial action by the GARDA SÍOCHÁNA in 1998. Because gardai are forbidden to strike by the 1928 Garda Síochána Act, members in-stead stayed at home in force on sick leave. The action was named 'blue flu' because of the colour of the garda uniform.

Blue Horse, the. A nickname for the 4th (Royal Irish) Dragoon Guards, from the blue facings of their uniform in the 18th century. They were also nicknamed ARRAN'S CUIRASSIERS and the BUTTERMILKS.

Blueland. The name given to a part of Munster (with the River Blackwater as its northern border) in an extensive Irish army exercise carried out in September 1942. Blueland was taken to be a small independent democratic state at risk of invasion from its totalitarian southern neighbour Redland. Greenland to the west and Brownland to the east stayed neutral.

Blues, the. See LINFIELD.

Blueshirts. The nickname given to the Army Comrades' Association formed in 1932 'in self-protection' against the IRA after DE VALERA's success in the Dáil elections of that year. The nickname – analogous with Mussolini's Blackshirts and Hitler's Brownshirts – refers to the blue shirts worn by its members (female supporters were known as 'Blue Blouses'). The idea of ANTI-TREATYITES – whom they regarded as dormant gunmen – taking their seats in the Dáil was intolerable to the Blueshirts. When de Valera's Fianna Fáil government was returned in 1932, the Association, consisting mainly of supporters of the TREATY and members of CUMANN NA NGAEDHEAL, assumed military trappings, wearing blue shirts and berets and using a quasi-fascist salute. The verbal extremism of the Association's most flamboyant leader, Eoin O'DUFFY, together with the violent clashes with Anti-Treatyites and the successful facing down of a Blueshirt show of strength in August 1933 by the government, all served to weaken the movement, although it had sufficient members in 1936 to form an IRISH BRIGADE² to fight on General Franco's side in the Spanish Civil War. Shortly afterwards Cumann na nGaedheal, the Centre Party and the National Guard (as the Army Comrades' Association was now called) combined to found FINE GAEL; O'Duffy was president of the new political party for a short time. Among those who briefly sympathized with the Blueshirt movement was the poet W.B. YEATS.

Blunt, Wilfred Scawen. See IN VINCULIS.

Blythe, Ernest (Earnán de Blaghd) (1889–1975). Politician, theatre administrator and Irish-language activist. Blythe, who was strongly associated with the ABBEY THEATRE and the RE-VIVAL of Irish, was born in Lisburn, Co. Antrim. He was a member of the GAELIC LEAGUE and the IRB, and a participant in the Easter Rising, the Anglo-Irish War and the Civil War. He was a CUMANN NA NGAEDHEAL minister in the Free State government until he lost his seat in 1933. He was responsible for making the Abbey Theatre the first government-granted theatre in the West, but his fanatical devotion to the revival of Irish hampered artistic development during his period of management (1941–67). Blythe also founded the government-funded Irish-language publishing company, An GÚM, and encouraged the Galway-based TAIBHD-HEARC theatre.

B-Men. See B-SPECIALS.

BMW. An acronymic abbreviation standing not as usual for the prestigious *Bayerische Motoren Werke* but for the considerably less prestigious Border, Midlands and Western region of Ireland. There is a palpable sense of irony in its use for one of Ireland's nondescript and rather unloved regions, somewhere between the Ulster border and the wilder, more romantic west.

Bó-aire (Irish, 'cattle freeman'). A prosperous client farmer in early Ireland. In return for land or stock from a local lord he would pay him an annual food-rent of a milch cow (the meaning of the word *bó*) and other stuffs including bread and bacon. Other requirements were a spell of labour at spring sowing and harvest, and the provision of a winter feast. The *bó-aire* could be a client of not more than three lords.

Boann. In Irish mythology, the mother of AON-GHUS ÓG by the DAGDA, who gains access to her by sending her husband Elcmar on an errand that makes the nine months seem like a single day. Boann is associated with the creation of the River Boyne in Leinster: she refuses to honour the GEIS associated with the WELL OF KNOWLEDGE and is drowned when the water pursues her, thus forming the river.

Boazia's 'Irelanda' (1599, 1609). Famous hand-coloured maps of Ireland by Baptista Boazia, an artist and cartographer for the Earl of ESSEX. The source of the maps is the surveying of Robert Lythe, an Elizabethan military engineer who served in Ireland from 1567 to 1571.

Bobbio. The town in Italy, about 80 km (50 miles) south of Milan, that was the site of COLUMBAN's last monastery. It was founded in 612, three years before the saint's death on 23 November 615. Bobbio, like many of Columban's other foundations, turned to the gentler Benedictine rule at an early stage in its history, until its suppression by Napoleon in 1803. It was once famous for its library, which held the *ANTIPHONARY OF BANGOR*, but its contents are now scattered among many European collections.

Bob's Own. *See* MICKS, THE.

Bockety. An adjective current in HIBERNO-ENGLISH, meaning 'broken', 'unstable', as in: 'That chair has a bockety leg.' The word is thought to derive from Irish BACACH, 'lame'.

Bodach (Irish, 'clown', 'churl'). An ignorant, headstrong person, usually male. '*Bodach an Chóta Lachtna*' ('The Clown in the Grey Coat') is a famous folktale.

Bodb Dearg (Irish, 'Bodb the Red'). The son of the DAGDA, said in some legends to have succeeded him as father of the gods and to have become by extension ruler of the TUATHA DÉ DANAAN. He is the deity most associated with Connacht and the father of SADB, who was the mother of OISÍN, the son of FIONN MAC CUMHAIL.

Bodenstown Churchyard. The burial place of Wolfe TONE, the so-called father of Irish Republicanism, near Sallins, Co. Kildare. As a site of Republican pilgrimage it has been appropriated since the 1970s by SINN FÉIN, and largely eschewed by the rest of the Irish people because of this association with physical force. On 'Bodenstown Sunday', the second-last Sunday in June, thousands of Republicans throng there, especially from Northern Ireland, and it has become the custom for the president of Sinn Féin to give a keynote address during the commemorations. On the wall behind the grave are inscribed the words of Padraic PEARSE, who described Bodenstown as 'the holiest spot in Ireland':

> Thinker and doer, dreamer of the immortal deed and doer of the immortal deed, we owe to this dead man more than we can repay him ... to his teaching we owe it that there is such a thing as Irish nationalism and to the memory of the deed he nerved his generation to do, to the memory of '98, we owe it that there is any manhood left in Ireland.

A poem written by Thomas DAVIS, 'Bodenstown Churchyard', may be sung to a melancholy air. It appeared for many years on ballad sheets without the poet's name:

> In Bodenstown churchyard there lies a green grave
> And wildly around it the winter winds rave.
> Small shelter is weaned from the cruel walls there
> When the storm clouds blow down on the plains of
>   Kildare.
> Once I stood on that sod that lies over Wolfe Tone
> And I thought how he perished in prison alone,
> His friends unavenged and his country unfreed,
> Oh pity, I thought, is the patriot's need.
> ...
> In Bodenstown churchyard there lies a green
>   grave
> And wildly around it let the winter winds rave;
> Far better it suits him the wind and the gloom
> Until Ireland a nation might build him a tomb.

Bodhaire Uí Laoghaire ort. A common Irish

imprecation, with the literal meaning 'deafness (or mental confusion) of O'Leary'.

Bodhrán. A percussion instrument, the only such manufactured especially for traditional Irish music. It takes its name from Irish *bodhrán*, 'deafener'. It is a large shallow one-sided drum, made by stretching goatskin over a wooden frame (it is said that the skin of a she-goat produces a stronger reverberation). It is normally played with a special stick with two heads, but can also be played with the open palm. It looks simple to play, but is far from easy to play well. The bodhrán is now used to accompany traditional music, but some purists still reject it as not being an *echt*-traditional instrument because it came into general use only in the 1960s. Before that it was used simply to make noise, for instance by WRENBOYS, BIDDY BOYS or other revellers, and a harassed mother might say, 'My head is in a *bodhrán*' (i.e. humming with noise). Good bodhráns, which are hand-made by specialists, are very much prized. It is likely that the bodhrán originated as a piece of farm equipment for holding or measuring corn.

Body snatchers. The name given to people who removed bodies – especially those of the poor – from their graves for anatomy schools in Ireland and Britain (*see* BURKE AND HARE).

Bog¹ (from Irish *bogach*, 'swamp', in turn from *bog*, 'soft'). A characteristic feature of the Irish landscape, especially in the Midlands and in the southwest and west. When the lakes left by the last Ice Age receded and dried up, the vegetation was absorbed into the earth and over time this damp earth, rich in organic matter, built up layers of peat or bog. Bogs naturally preserve matter, so items such as bog 'butter' (cheese) many centuries old, bones of a giant IRISH ELK and even human remains have been found in them in good condition. The bog is a fragile ecosystem with unique flora and fauna, and much Irish bogland has been destroyed by over-cutting of TURF (peat) for fuel, by the commercial extraction of moss peat for gardening (*see*

BORD NA MÓNA) and by over-grazing of upland bog by herds of subsidized sheep.
See also BOG DEAL.

Bog². A derogatory HIBERNO-ENGLISH prefix indicating contempt for perceived rusticity or lack of culture, as in 'bog-ignorant', 'bogman', 'bog-stupid' and 'BOGTROTTER'. The phrase 'from the bogs' is also used. There is a popular saying: 'You can take the man out of the bog, but you can't take the bog out of the man.'
See also MOUNTAINY.

Bog, the. The nickname given to PORTLAOISE prison, in the middle of the boggy Irish Midlands, by the more metropolitan residents of the JOY in Dublin.

Bogán. An Irish word, borrowed by HIBERNO-ENGLISH, meaning an egg laid with a soft membrane only. *Bog* is Irish for 'soft'.

Bog Commissioners. A body established in 1809 by act of Parliament 'to enquire into the nature and extent of the several bogs in Ireland, and the practicability of draining and cultivating them.' Between 1809 and 1814, 14 bogs were surveyed in 22 counties by 51 engineers, as well as surveyors and assistants. These included the Scottish engineers William Bald and Alexander NIMMO, Richard GRIFFITH and Richard Lovell EDGEWORTH. Nimmo worked mainly on the bogs of Co. Kerry and produced an elegant map of the IVERAGH PENINSULA in 1811. All in all 40 maps and accompanying reports were published.

Bog deal. Ancient pinewood preserved in boggy land. It is pronounced 'bogdale'. In the past, when dug up, bog deal was crucial for the rural economy, as fuel and for the making of furniture. It was difficult to work but very sturdy and durable. Bog deal has been used effectively for sculpting. Bog oak was also found in bogs.
See also CREACHAILL; THATCH.

Bog deal splinters. A primitive means of illumination in rural Ireland in the days before RURAL ELECTRIFICATION or even proper oil lamps.

Splinters, thin strips cut off a CREACHAILL of BOG DEAL, were lit from the fire, providing a spark of illumination at night.

Bogging. An Ulster adjective meaning 'very dirty', from the dark brown earth associated with turf bogs, as in: 'By the time he had changed the wheel his hauns were boggin'.' Relatedly, in the west of Scotland, if you are bogging, then you are extremely smelly.

Bogging, to go. To sink in wet, marshy ground, a HIBERNO-ENGLISH phrase deriving from the condition of boggy ground, in which an animal drawing turf, no matter how light and skilful (see KERRY BOG PONY), might sink to its knees. 'To go bogging' is also used metaphorically to describe a person losing his or her place or performing badly, particularly in an examination or a public performance: 'I knew the lines very well but I went bogging at the dress rehearsal.' Like many expressions deriving from rural Ireland, it began to lose its currency from the 1960s onwards.

Bogland Act. One of the early relief measures that represented the first dent in the POPERY LAWS in 18th-century Ireland. On 2 June 1772 a relieving Act, passed not without opposition, permitted Catholics to take out 61-year leases on up to 50 acres of reclaimable bogland.

Bogman. *See* BOGTROTTER.

Bog Meadows. A marshy area in Belfast drained by the River Blackstaff which flows into the Lagan. It lay to the southwest of the city and was a kind of *cordon sanitaire* between the Catholic FALLS ROAD and the Protestant area west of the Lisburn Road clustering round the Dublin railway track. Once the haunt of geese, wild duck and golden plover, it has disappeared under an extensive industrial estate.

> God ordained that even the Bog Meadows should end and had set a great hill at their limit which we called the Mickeys' Mountain ... The mountain was inaccessible because to reach it we had to cross territory held by the Mickeys. Being children of a staunch Protestant quarter, to go near the Catholic

idolators was more than we dared for fear of having one of our members cut off.
> ROBERT HARBINSON (b.1928): *No Surrender* (1960)

Bogside. The part of Derry (*see* STROKE CITY) to the west of the city walls where Catholics, not permitted to live within the walls, tended to settle. During the 19th century they were joined by country people, mainly from Donegal, especially during the years of the Great Famine, making the area almost exclusively Nationalist in politics. Sir Henry DOCWRA (d.1631), the first English governor of the city, wrote in *Narration* (c.1630):

> Derry ... a place in manner of an island ... the river called Loughfoyle encompassing it all on one side, and a bog most commonly wet, and not easily passable except in two or three places, dividing it from the main land.

Bogside, Battle of the. The serious rioting (12–14 August 1969) that led to the British army being deployed as peacekeepers on Derry streets and regarded as the beginning of the years of violence in Northern Ireland. Trouble had been anticipated, and one of the stories from the event is that a note left for a milkman read: 'No milk, but leave 200 bottles.' Rioting began around 5 o'clock on the Tuesday evening of the 12th after a particularly inflammatory march by APPRENTICE BOYS during their annual celebration of the relief of the city in 1689. The riots continued until about the same time on the Thursday, when a company of the Prince of Wales's Own Regiment took over security from the police. The main weapons thrown from behind the barricades in Rossville Street and William Street, the Aggro Corner of later years (*see* ROSSVILLE FLATS), were bricks and petrol bombs, while the police replied with CS gas and rubber bullets. The perceived need to defend the area arose from the behaviour of the RUC on earlier incursions, as after the BURNTOLLET AMBUSH on the morning of 5 January, when they had wreaked havoc in the Bogside, and at the time of the DEVENNY INCIDENT.
See also FREE DERRY; STAND IDLY BY, WE CAN-NOT.

Bogtrotter. A term of abuse, levelled originally against the Irish in Britain. Much more common nowadays is 'bogman', applied by Irish city dwellers to intrusive rustics, as in the cry, 'Back to the bog, ye bogman!' Large parts of Ireland, especially the Midlands, are covered with bog and Portlaoise prison was always referred to by the inmates of the JOY as 'the BOG'. Some have perversely taken the term as a badge of distinction, as in the case of the Munster writer Sigerson Clifford (1913–85), who published a book of verse entitled *Ballads of a Bogman* (1955).

Boke. An Ulster and Scots verb meaning 'retch' or even 'vomit', often used metaphorically: 'The way these politicians go on wud mick ye boke.'

Boland, Harry (1887–1922). Revolutionary. He was born in Dublin to a family steeped in Fenianism. His father, Jim, was a member of the IRB, and after his death in 1895 local IRB and GAA members contributed to a fund that enabled his widow to open a tobacconist's shop in Wexford Street, Dublin. Boland became a tailor – he was noted until the end of his life for his sharp suits and natty dressing – eventually opening his own tailoring business in Middle Abbey Street. As well as becoming a member of the IRB (in 1904) and of the GAELIC LEAGUE, he was keenly interested in the GAA and himself represented Dublin at hurling, although his involvement in clandestine political activities interfered with his training.

Boland took part in the EASTER RISING and was interned in England. After his release he returned to Dublin where he met Michael COLLINS and was active in SINN FÉIN. It was during a by-election campaign in Co. Longford in March 1918 that Boland and Collins met the Kiernan sisters in the family hotel, the Greville Arms in Granard. Both men fell in love with Kitty Kiernan. Boland was elected TD for Roscommon in the general election of December 1918 and in April 1919 DE VALERA sent him as a special representative to the US people and to the Irish-American organization

CLAN NA GAEL prior to his own visit to America in June of that year. Boland spent most of the next two years in America, finding on his final return in January 1922 that Collins and Kitty Kiernan had become officially engaged, although he had proposed to her many times in person and by letter and she had never actually refused him.

Boland opposed the TREATY 'because it denied the recognition and the sovereignty of the Irish nation' and because of the OATH OF ALLEGIANCE, although he tried his best to prevent an open conflict. During the CIVIL WAR he was on the run in Dublin, and several times evaded capture by Free State troops, many of them former comrades who knew his haunts. He was wounded in the abdomen in a raid on the Grand Hotel in Skerries, Co. Dublin, and died in St Vincent's Hospital a few days later, on 1 August 1922. In Neil Jordan's film, *Michael Collins* (1996), Boland, played by Irish-American actor Aidan Quinn, dies in the sewers like Harry Lime in *The Third Man*. *See also* IN GREAT HASTE.

Boland, John Pius (1870–1955). Athlete and Nationalist politician. He won two gold medals for tennis, singles and doubles, at the 1896 Olympic Games in Athens. This event, the first games of the new Olympiad, was a totally amateur affair, and some of the events had to be cancelled for want of competitors. It is said that Boland, an Oxford student and keen athlete, competed only because he happened to find himself a tourist in Athens at the time of the games and that he had to borrow tennis clothes (he played in ordinary leather shoes). He later qualified as a barrister and served as Nationalist MP for South Kerry and as chief whip of the party.

Boland, Kevin (1917–2001). Politician. A son of former revolutionary and Fianna Fáil politician Gerald Boland (1885–1973), he served in various Fianna Fáil administrations under Éamon de Valera, Seán Lemass and Jack Lynch (1957–1970). Boland was a notably successful director of elections for his party

on several occasions, capitalizing on the work done by his father in building up the grassroots constituency organization of Fianna Fáil. However, his career with Fianna Fáil ended with the ARMS CRISIS, after which he established a new party, Aontacht Éireann, which made little electoral impact.
See also CAMORRA, THE; SINGLE TRANSFERABLE VOTE.

Bold. A word used in HIBERNO-ENGLISH with none of the normal connotations of fearlessness or bravery. It means instead naughtiness or mischievousness in a child. In fact, the words 'naughty ' and 'mischievous' were unknown in the Hiberno-English vocabulary of the South until the modernization that has occurred since the 1970s.

Bolg an tSoláthair (Irish, literally 'the belly of provision', i.e. 'miscellany'). A single edition Irish-language magazine (1795), compiled by a Gaelic scholar, Patrick Lynch (1757–*c*.1820), and published in Belfast by the NORTHERN STAR, the newspaper of the Ulster UNITED IRISHMEN. It contained poems and songs (with translations by Charlotte BROOKE) and a grammar of the Irish language, which was reissued in 1837. Its publication marked the beginning of an interest in the Irish language in the then radical Belfast. The magazine helped to preserve a link to the material of Ireland's literary past (as opposed to the continuing vernacular existence of the Irish language in the GAELTACHT). Lynch was a widely learned schoolmaster from Quin, Co. Clare, and was proficient in Latin, Greek and Hebrew as well as English and Irish. He published *An Introduction to the Knowledge of the Irish Language*, another useful textbook, in 1815.

Bollix or **bollox.** A multi-purpose HIBERNO-ENGLISH version of 'bollocks' (testicles) used variously and creatively, especially in Dublin, as: an interjection ('Oh bollix!'); a noun conveying disparagement or criticism ('He's a right bollix, that fellow'); or a noun phrase signifying incredulity ('He did, in my bollix' or

'Lost, me bollix!'). One may also 'make a right bollix' of something, if one does not carry it out successfully.

Bomb Alley. A sequence of Dublin streets – South Great George's Street, Aungier Street, Wexford Street, Camden Street, Richmond Street, Lower Rathmines Road – that led effectively from the city centre to Portobello Barracks in Rathmines, which was held by the British army until 1922. During the ANGLO-IRISH WAR the route, with its many side streets, was a convenient place for attacking troop carriers. It was also known as the Dardanelles, after the First World War campaign in which many Dubliners had been killed in Turkey.

Bombay Street. The scene of serious civil violence in ARDOYNE, Belfast, when many Catholic houses were set on fire by Protestant rioters on the night of the 14–15 August 1969. Sectarian tensions had been increasing and there had been sporadic rioting during the summer, but the Battle of the BOGSIDE of 12–13 August in Derry and a sympathetic Nationalist response in Belfast caused boundary areas to explode. The British army, already on the streets of Derry, was mobilized on 16 August to separate rival bands of rioters, and soldiers were fêted by the harried Nationalists. The honeymoon did not last.

Bomber Liston (b.1957). The nickname of a Kerry GAA footballer, Eoin Liston, because of his strength and speed on the field of play. He was born in Ballybunion, near Listowel, on 17 October 1957 and played for his local club, Beale, as well as for the great Kerry football team of the 1970s and 1980s, winning six ALL-IRELAND medals (1978–9, 1981 and the three-in-a-row 1984–6). He won also two RAILWAY CUP medals with Munster and four ALL STARS awards, and played COMPROMISE RULES against Australia.

Bona fide. A licensing concession of the Defence of the Realm Act (*see* DORA) for *bona fide* or genuine travellers, allowing them to drink at any time in a pub more than 3 miles (5 km)

from their homes. The term (pronounced 'bona-feed' or 'bona-fide' to rhyme with 'side') came to be applied to anyone who exploited this loophole to drink outside Dublin – 'do the bona fide' – after the city's pubs were closed.

> ... what would the polis want spying on me, and not a decent house within four miles, the way every living Christian is a bona fide, saving one widow alone?
>
> J.M. SYNGE: *The Playboy of the Western World* (1907)

Bonar Law, Andrew. *See* LAW, ANDREW BONAR.

Bond, Oliver (1760–98). United Irishman. He was born in Ulster and became a woollen trader in Pill Lane in Dublin in 1782. A member of the Society of UNITED IRISHMEN since its foundation in 1791, he was a significant figure in the Dublin executive, and was imprisoned for seditious libel for five months in 1793. Information provided in 1797 by Thomas REYNOLDS, himself a high-ranking member of the society, led to the arrest of Bond and 14 others in March 1798. In July of that year Bond was tried for treason and sentenced to death, but died in Newgate prison on 6 September 1798, allegedly of apoplexy. John BERESFORD, chief commissioner of the revenue, wrote to Lord Auckland:

> We got rid of one enemy last night. Oliver Bond after playing ball all the evening died suddenly of apoplexy.

It was suspected, however, that he had been murdered by one of his jailers. He is buried in St Michan's in Church Street, Dublin. A local authority housing complex in Dublin's north inner city is named Oliver Bond House in his memory.

Bondi, County. A nickname given to a celebrated seaside residential area outside Sydney, Australia, because of the number of young Irish people on temporary visas living in the area in the late 1990s and early 21st century. The pub at Bondi Junction frequented by Irish people is called The Cock and Bull.

Bones. A percussion accompaniment to tradi-tional music consisting of two animal rib bones held loosely between the fingers and hitting off each other, in the same way as SPOONS. Like the BODHRÁN, bones made their real début in Irish traditional music in the 1960s when they were used, to considerable effect, by CEOLTÓIRÍ CHUALANN under the direction of Seán Ó RIADA.

'Bonnán Buí, An'. The title of a well-known poem by Cathal Buí Mac Giolla Gunna (1690–1755), born in Co. Cavan. He was, according to his own claim, destined for the priesthood, but took to the more profane pleasures of drink and women. He is famous for his rakehelly life, and for two excellent poems: '*Aithreachas Chathail Bhuí*' ('Repentance of Cathal Buí'), written, it is said, with a burnt stick on the wall of the hut in Carrickmacross in Co. Monaghan where he lay dying; and '*An Bonnán Buí*', finely translated by Thomas MACDONAGH as 'The Yellow Bittern'. This latter poem describes the finding of a dead bittern by a frozen lake and points out parallels with the life of the poet:

> *Dúirt mo stór liom ligean den ól*
> *nó nach mbeinnse beo ach seal beag gear;*
> *ach dúirt mé léi go dtug sí bréag*
> *is gurbh fhaide mo shaolsa an deoch úd a fháil ...*
> (My darling told me to drink no more
> Or my life would be o'er in a little short while;
> But I told her 'tis drink gives me health and strength
> And will lengthen my road by many a mile ...)

Bonner, 'Packy' (b.1960). Soccer player. He was born in Co. Donegal on 24 May 1960 and joined Glasgow Celtic as a teenager, playing nearly 500 league matches for the club. He was first capped for the Republic of Ireland in 1981, and won 80 caps in all as goalkeeper under Jack CHARLTON. He is remembered by sporting fans for a crucial penalty save against Romania during the World Cup finals of 1990, which famously put Ireland in the quarter-finals of that competition.

Bonnyclabber (Irish *bainne clábair*, 'sour thick milk'). A name for buttermilk, assumed to be a staple part of the Irish diet in the 16th and 17th centuries, both as a forerunner and accompaniment to the potato. It emigrated to the West Indies to appear in Creole as *banikleva*. The word *clábair*'s primary meaning is 'mud', an indication of its most desirable consistency:

> To enjoy his land or any part
> His bannin clabber and pottadoes
> Without these French and Dutch granadoes.
> RICHARD FLECKNOE (d.1678)

Bono. *See* U2.

Book¹. A class in primary school, the expression deriving from the prescribed textbook containing a year's study material. 'What book are you in now?' a schoolchild might be asked by an older person.

Book². A term applied to a number of manuscript collections, which contain what survives of early Irish literature. The chief examples are listed in the relevant entries below.

Book of Armagh (Latin *Liber Armachanus*). A Latin manuscript compiled 807–8, under the direction of Abbot Torbach of Armagh, by the scribe Ferdomhnach. It contains biographies of several saints and the text of the CONFESSIO of St PATRICK. A later interpolation names BRIAN BORU as *Imperator Scottorum* (Latin, 'emperor of the Scoti', i.e. Irish). The manuscript is now in Trinity College Dublin.

Book of Ballymote (Irish *Leabhar Bhaile an Mhóta*). A manuscript in Irish compiled in 1390 in Co. Sligo for Tomaltach Mac Donnchaidh, the Lord of Tirerril, by Maghnus Ó Duibhgeannáin and assistants. It passed into the possession of the O'Donnells of Tír Chonaill in 1522 in forced exchange for seven score dairy cows. It contains a useful key to the OGAM alphabet, a version of Virgil's *Aeneid*, the BOOK OF RIGHTS, the BOOK OF THE DUN COW and bardic tracts on grammar.

Book of Common Prayer. *See* COMMON PRAYER, BOOK OF.

Book of Evidence, The. The title of a novel (1989) by John BANVILLE, described as 'the first-

person testimony of Freddie Montgomery' and inspired by the real-life case of the murderer Malcolm MacArthur (*see* GUBU). It is one of Banville's finest and most accessible works.

Book of Invasions (Irish, *Lebor Gabála Érenn*, literally 'book of the taking of Ireland'). An anonymous medieval chronicle of legendary Ireland from the Creation until the 12th century. It is mainly concerned with the waves of incomers who colonized the country, including CESAIR, PARTHOLÓN, NEMED, the FIRBOLG, the TUATHA DÉ DANAAN and finally the MILESIANS (the historical Gaels).

Book of Kells. An illuminated Latin manuscript of the four gospels of the New Testament, based upon the Vulgate version of St Jerome (*c*.404). It is regarded as one of the glories of medieval art and clearly intended as a ceremonial book, perhaps of the abbey of IONA, where it may have had its origin. Some scholars think it may have been intended as a celebration of the bicentennial in 797 of the death of COLUM CILLE (Columba), the abbey's founder, and may have been taken to Kells, Co. Meath, in 807 when the Abbot Ceallach moved the Iona foundation and its treasures to the relative safety of this part of Ireland at the time of the VIKING raids. The book may have been completed there or at LINDISFARNE. It passed into the keeping of the Anglican diocese of Meath in the 17th century and was presented to Trinity College Dublin shortly after the Restoration of Charles II.

Book of Leinster. A 12th-century compilation made at GLENDALOUGH *c*.1150 under the auspices of Dermot MACMURROUGH. It contains parts of the TÁIN BÓ CUAILNGE (*The Cattle Raid of Cooley*), two recensions of DINNSHENCHAS, the BOOK OF INVASIONS, a plan of the seating arrangements in the banquet hall at TARA and other material, contained in 187 vellum folios, most of which are housed in Trinity College Dublin.

Book of Lismore (also known as the *Book of Mac Carthaigh Riabhach*). A compilation of 198 folios written in Irish, made on the orders of Finghin Mac Carthaigh Riabach and his wife Caitilín, and named after the Co. Waterford castle where it was discovered by workmen in 1814. It contains mainly religious material, such as hagiography, monastic rules and holy texts, but also lay material, including a translation of Marco Polo's account of his travels. The manuscript is now in the possession of the Duke of Devonshire at Chatsworth in Derbyshire, England.

Book of Rights (Irish *Lebor na Cert*). A compilation in Irish that contains a codex of rights and due service to Irish kings. Compiled originally in 450, it was revised by Cormac Mac Cuileannáin about 900.

Book of the Dun Cow (Irish *Lebor na hUidre*). An 11th-century manuscript collection in Irish. The fanciful title came from the belief that it was partly written on vellum from the skin of the cow that followed St CIARÁN to CLONMACNOISE. It contains an early version of the *TÁIN BÓ CUAILNGE* (*The Cattle Raid of Cooley*) and other early tales including the *Immram Brain* (*see* BRAN[2]). Its whereabouts were unknown for several centuries until 1837, when it came into the possession of a Dublin bookseller and was acquired by the ROYAL IRISH ACADEMY.

Books Ireland. A monthly periodical founded by Jeremy Addis in 1976 and published by him in Dublin. It provides comprehensive coverage of books of Irish interest in Irish and English and is valued for the independence of its reviews and its trenchant and sometimes provocative commentary on publishing and related areas.

Boolanthroor (Irish *buail an triúir*, 'the stroke of three persons'). A complicated system of flail threshing, using three men instead of two and very dependent upon timing.

'Boolavogue'. A ballad by P. J. MCCALL to commemorate the Wexford Rising of 1798 and especially the courage of the rebel leader Father John MURPHY. It was the burning of the Catholic chapel at Boolavogue, a village near Ferns, that sparked off the rebellion.

McCall's ballad was very popular in schools and in musical pubs, until the advent of the Northern TROUBLES in the late 1960s and the rise of historical REVISIONISM made it and many more of its kind unacceptable. Only groups like The WOLF TONES remained unrepentantly and unreconstructedly Republican.

> At Boolavogue, as the sun was setting,
> O'er the bright May meadows of Shelmalier,
> A rebel hand set the heather blazing
> And brought the neighbours from far and near,
> Then Father Murphy from old Kilcormack,
> Spurred up the rock with a warning cry
> 'Arm! Arm! he cried, 'for I've come to lead you
> For Ireland's freedom to fight or die.'

Boole, George. *See* BOOLEAN ALGEBRA.

Boolean Algebra. The application of the basic rules of algebra to logic, pioneered by George Boole, a largely self-taught mathematician. He was born in Lincoln in 1815, the son of a cobbler, and although without a degree was appointed professor of mathematics at Queen's College, Cork (later University College Cork) in 1849. His chief writings in his subject are to be found in *Mathematic Analysis of Logic* (1847) and *Laws of Thought* (1854). His work in symbolic logic greatly assisted the development of set theory and circuit theory and their application to computer design. He was the father of Ethel Voynich (1864–1960), whose book *The Gadfly*, about the Italian *Risorgimento*, was a bestseller. Boole died the year of Ethel's birth in Ballintemple in Cork city.

Booley (Irish *buaile*, 'milking place in summer pasture'). A temporary habitat in grassy uplands to which people drove their dairy cattle during summer months, living with them until returning to their farms in autumn. The word is also used as a verb, equivalent to 'transhume'.

Boomtown Rats. *See* GELDOF, BOB.

Border Campaign. The IRA's campaign in Northern Ireland (1956–62), known to its participants as Operation Harvest. It began on 11–12 December 1956 with IRA attacks on customs posts in the border counties of Tyrone, Fermanagh and Armagh, and continued with a diminishing scale of activity until it had petered out by the spring of 1962. The usual targets were electricity transformers, army bases and occasional 'Baedeker' objectives such as Derry Courthouse. The situation was complicated by the presence of a Republican splinter group known as *Saor Uladh* ('free Ulster'), which had attacked the RUC barracks in Roslea, Co. Fermanagh, on 26 November 1955.

The dramatic high point of the campaign was the death in action of Seán South (*see* 'SEÁN SOUTH FROM GARRYOWEN') and Fergal O'Hanlon (*see* 'PATRIOT GAME, THE') on 1 January 1957 during an attack on Brookeborough police station. South's funeral attracted tens of thousands of mourners, but the gesture was probably personal and sentimental because there was little support for the campaign in either north or south except among traditional hardline Republicans. The Northern Ireland government introduced internment and other measures under the SPECIAL POWERS ACT from 21 December 1956, mobilizing the B-SPECIALS for border patrols from Derry to Newry. The government in the Irish Republic was equally stringent. In the entire period six RUC men, eight IRA men, two civilians and two members of *Saor Uladh* were killed.

The comparative failure of Operation Harvest was regarded as a triumph for Brian Faulkner, the Northern Ireland minister of home affairs (1959–63), leading him to attempt the same measures in 1971 – with disastrous results. Many IRA members stood down at the ceasefire declared on 26 February 1962 became active again in 1970.

Border Fox, the. The name adopted by the IRA/INLA terrorist Dessie O'Hare (b.1956 in Keady, Co. Armagh) in statements to the press. It subsequently became his nickname. On 13 October 1987 O'Hare kidnapped Dublin dentist John O'Grady, it is believed in error. Before O'Grady was rescued on 5 November, O'Hare had cut the tops off his victim's two little fingers. In a ransom call O'Hare said; 'I'm going to chop off two of his fingers now … I'm going to chop them up in bits and pieces.' On 27 November 1987 he was arrested in a shoot-out in Urlingford, Co. Kilkenny, and sentenced to 40 years in prison. He was not released under the terms of the GOOD FRIDAY AGREEMENT of 1998 although his legal team have agitated for his release.

Bord Fáilte. The Irish tourist board (*see* FÁILTE; *IRELAND OF THE WELCOMES*; TOURISM).

Bord na Gaeilge (Irish, 'board of Irish'). A state agency established in 1978 with the aim of advancing the use of Irish as a spoken language. It had its headquarters in Merrion Square in Dublin and was involved in many educational, cultural and media initiatives. Bord na Gaeilge was superseded by Foras na Gaeilge, an all-Ireland body for the promotion of Irish, established under the terms of the GOOD FRIDAY AGREEMENT of 1998.

Bord na gCapall (Irish, 'horse board'). A state agency established in 1971 under the Horse Industry Act (1970) to promote the horse industry, to advise the minister for agriculture in relation to horse breeding, and to manage vocational training in related areas. Its remit extends to non-thoroughbred horses only. The breeding and sale of horses form a very important and lucrative industry in Ireland.

Bord na gCon (Irish, 'greyhound board'). A commercial SEMI-STATE body established under the Greyhound Industry Act (1958) with the brief of developing and regulating greyhound racing in Ireland. It owns eight tracks in the Republic and licenses nine others, operating a tote in all tracks, the profit from which goes to fund the company.

Bord na Móna (Irish, 'bog board'). The Irish Turf (Bog) Board, established in 1946 as a statutory body deriving from the Turf Development Board of 1933, with the minister for finance the sole shareholder (*see* SEMI-STATES). In 1999 it became a public limited company, solely owned by the state. Of the great raised bogs of the Irish Midlands 300,000 acres (120,000 ha) have been depleted by the activities of Bord na Móna, harvesting turf for fuel and moss peat for horticultural use (the latter now discouraged on ecological grounds). There are differing opinions about the future of these cutaway bogs, their ecology and their possible use for forestry.

See also BOG¹; TURF.

Boreen or **bohreen** (Irish *bóithrín*, dimunitive of *bóthar*, 'road'). A country lane:

> Bells are booming down the bohreens,
> White the mist along the grass.
> Now the Julias, Maeves and Maureens
> Move between the fields to Mass.
>
> JOHN BETJEMAN (1906–84): 'Ireland with Emily', in
> *New Bats in Old Belfries* (1945)

See also CASÁN; LOANEN.

Borey dancers. The aurora borealis or northern lights. The term is still used in parts of Ulster.

Borumborad, Dr Achmet. The alias of Patrick Joyce from Kilkenny. He appeared in Dublin *c*.1770, 'a refugee from Constantinople', and set up with government aid 'Hot and Cold Sea-Water Baths' in Dublin. Magnificent in Turkish dress and an immense black beard, he began each parliamentary session with a party for the MPs at which 'the singers were of the first order; the claret and champagne excellent'. On one such occasion Sir John Hamilton, a relatively sober member, rose to leave but was harried by the more serious guests, as Sir Jonah Barrington records in his PERSONAL SKETCHES (1827–32):

> The carousers were on the alert instantly; Sir John opened the door and rushed out; the ante-chamber was not lighted; some one or two and twenty staunch members clung to his skirts – when splash at once comes Sir John, not into the street, but into the great cold bath, the door of which he had opened in mistake! The other Parliament men were too close upon the baronet to stop short, like the horse of a Cossack; in they went by fours and fives; and one or two, who, on hearing the splashing of the water, threw themselves down on the brink to avoid popping in, operated directly as stumbling-blocks to those behind, who thus obtained their full share of a *bonne bouche* none of the parties had bargained for.

When the Doctor returned he found 'a full committee of Irish parliament-men either floating like so many corks upon the surface, or scrambling to get out like mice who had fallen into a bason'. The government grants eventually stopped and the baths were sold in 1784 to the WIDE STREET COMMISSIONERS. Borumborad himself shaved off his beard and donned occidental clothes to marry a Miss Hartigan, thus revealing himself as Irish Mr Joyce: 'The devil a Turk, any more than yourself, my sweet angel.'

Bosca ceoil. The Irish name (literally 'music box') for the ACCORDION, and also for the melodeon and concertina.

Boss, The. The title of a 1983 book by Joe Joyce and Peter Murtagh detailing some of the more colourful episodes of Charles HAUGHEY's period in government in 1982, the GUBU period. Haughey was called 'Boss' by his ministers and backbenchers, a fact used to advantage by the creators of SCRAP SATURDAY.

Boston Strong Boy, the. The poster title of John L. Sullivan, the last of the barefist pugilists, also known as 'Trip-Hammer Jack'. He was born in Roxbury, Massachusetts, USA, the son of an immigrant from Tralee, Co. Kerry. Apprenticed to a plumber, he lost his job when he broke his employer's nose during an argument, but he was soon earning a good living with his fists, knocking out his first professional opponent at the age of 19. He became famous with his defeat of the reigning champion Paddy Ryan in nine rounds on 7 February 1882 at Mississippi City. He was then aged 25. In addition to the purse he won a side bet of $5000. Ryan afterwards said, 'I thought a telegraph pole had been shoved against me endways.' In spite of a riotous and bibulous lifestyle over the next decade he earned a million dollars, knocking out at least 200 opponents. He was fêted as a celebrity on a European tour in 1886, wearing a $10,000 gold belt with his name set in diamonds. He met

Bertie, the Prince of Wales, and asked kindly after 'all the littles Waleses'. On 23 July 1889 in Richburg, Michigan, he took part in the last bareknuckle championship bout in the USA, against Jake Kilrain. The fight lasted two hours in heat greater than 100° F. Though much overweight, Sullivan went 75 rounds with Kilrain until the latter's seconds threw in the towel.

Sullivan's last fight, and only defeat, took place on 7 September 1892. He was deeply in debt, having had to sell the fabulous gold belt and become a vaudeville act. He could not afford to refuse the chance of another purse, and when he met his opponent GENTLEMAN JIM Corbett in New Orleans, he was the heavier by 96 kg to 81 kg (212 to 178 pounds). By now the Queensberry rules were in force and the combatants wore boxing gloves, fighting in rounds of three minutes (see CHALLENGE, A). By the application of his famous 'scientific' principles Corbett succeeded in avoiding any of Sullivan's trip-hammer blows and knocked him out in the 21st round. Sullivan in true style admitted: 'I fought once too often but I'm glad it was an American who licked me and that the championship stays in the country.' The last six years of his life were spent in comparative happiness with his second wife Kathleen Harkins on their farm in West Arlington, Maryland, from which he would emerge from time to time to lecture on the 'evils of John Barleycorn'. Sullivan never recovered from her death in 1917 and died a few months afterwards on 2 February 1918.

Botany Bay. A harbour near Sydney in New South Wales, Australia, that was the destination of the first transport ship to bring convicts from Ireland in 1791. Although the penal colony was subsequently developed not in Botany Bay but at nearby Sydney Cove, the term 'Botany Bay' became synonymous with the penal settlements of New South Wales to which Irish convicts were transported. About 45,000 Irish convicts, men and women, were transported to Australia in the period 1791–

1853, in more than two hundred consignments, sailing from Dublin or Cobh (Queenstown). A square in Trinity College Dublin is still named Botany Bay, allegedly because of the unruliness of some of its early-19th-century inmates.
See also TRANSPORTATION.

Bothán. An Irish word for hut or hovel, and by extension any run-down or decrepit building.

Bothántaíocht. The Munster name for the custom of informal evening visiting, for gossip, stories, music or perhaps dancing.
See also AIRNEÁN; CÉILÍDHING; RAMBLING HOUSE; SEANCHAÍ.

Bóthar na mine buí (Irish, 'Indian meal road'). A pointless 'public work' decreed as essential from June 1846 by the Whig government under Lord John Russell for the famine-stricken Irish (*see* GREAT FAMINE, THE). The winter of 1846–7 was particularly severe, especially on COTTIERS (the lowest level of tenant-at-will, operating entirely at subsistence level), who, once used to warm turf fires and full bellies from the normally bountiful potato, found themselves in near-rags and without food from morning to night. They were made to lay tracks through bogs that in fact led nowhere, raise unnecessary walls round landlord's estates (or in some places round nothing at all) and even build piers where no boats could land. Many places, especially in the sorely tried Irish-speaking western counties, can point to their own *bóthar na mine buí*.
See also BLACK '47.

Bothy Band. A successful and admired traditional music group that existed 1974–9 and that at various stages included Donal Lunny, Tommy Peoples, Matt MOLLOY, Paddy Keenan and Tríona Ní Dhomhnaill. The band played Scots Gaelic as well as Irish material, and its members were popular both as performing and as recording artists.

Bots, the. The popular name for the Botanic Gardens in Glasnevin, Dublin. They were founded by the Dublin Society (since 1821 the ROYAL DUBLIN SOCIETY) in 1795 with a grant of £300 from the Irish Parliament, and were taken over by the state in 1878. One of the conservatories is by Richard Turner, who made the glasshouses in the botanic gardens in Belfast and at Kew. The gardens are especially rich in conifers, orchids and herbaceous borders.

Bottle or **battle** (Irish *batáil*). A word for a bundle of straw, hay or bent grass for thatching. During haymaking several bottles would go to make a stook.

Bottom. A ball or spool of thread or wool:

> One of the tricks of girls on Hallow-eve to find out the destined husband is to go out to the limekiln at night with a ball of yarn; throw in the ball still holding the thread; re-wind the thread, till it is suddenly stopped; call out 'who howlds my bottom of yarn?' when she expects to hear the name of the young man she is to marry.
>
> PATRICK WESTON JOYCE (1827–1914): *English As We Speak It in Ireland* (1910)

Bouchalaun (Irish *buachalán* or *buachalán buí*, 'ragweed'). A name for ragwort used commonly in HIBERNO-ENGLISH. The word GEOSADAWN (Irish *geosadán*, 'thistle') was used interchangeably with 'bouchalaun' in some areas of Munster. Ragwort, which grows readily on poor soil, is poisonous to cattle and it was the sign of a neglectful or lazy farmer to have his fields full of geosadawns. Besides, it was illegal, and in the absence of more serious crimes the local garda would occasionally come by on his bicycle to instruct the errant farmer to weed his fields. With Ireland's entry into the Common Market in 1973, farming practices and laws appertaining to them changed out of all recognition.

Boucicault, Dion (*c*.1820–90). Playwright, best known for three Irish comic melodramas, *The* COLLEEN BAWN, ARRAH-NA-POGUE and *The* SHAUGHRAUN, and for his cultivation of theatrical SENSATION. Boucicault was born Dionysius Lardner Boursiquot, the illegitimate son of a scientist, Dr Dionysius Lardner, who later became his guardian. He was brought up in Dublin, and went to London University, but left it after a year to go on the stage as 'Lee

Moreton'. By 1841 he had written his first great success, *London Assurance*, and 150 more plays were to follow. *The Octoroon* (1859) was the first play to deal with the black population of the United States, and his 'sensation' drama *The Poor of New York* (1857), with its hair-raising rendering of a tenement fire, could with a simple titular adjustment play Liverpool, Dublin or Boston. He settled in New York, USA, and, having spent most of his acquired wealth, ended his days as a poorly paid acting coach, dying on 18 September 1890, insisting to the end, as he wrote in a letter to a Christchurch newspaper in 1885, his hatred of 'the clowning character, known as "the stage-Irishman", which it has been my vocation, as an artist and as a dramatist, to abolish' (*see* STAGE-IRISH).

Boulogne Expedition. The incursion into France in 1544 by 600 Irish kerns (*see* RUG-HEADED KERNS) with officers from the Pale as part of Henry VIII's army in his war with Francis I (1494–1547). They fought so valiantly and so ruthlessly that the French ambassador wondered if Henry had brought with him 'men or devils'.

Boundary Commission. A commission established in 1924, in accordance with Article 12 of the Anglo-Irish TREATY, whose brief was 'to determine in accordance with the wishes of the inhabitants, so far as may be compatible with economic and geographic conditions, the boundaries between Northern Ireland and the rest of Ireland'. For many who accepted the Treaty, including Michael Collins and Arthur Griffiths, the promise of this Commission allowed them to hope that so much of Northern Ireland would revert to the Free State that the remaining statelet would not be a viable economic unit. The Commission sat for most of 1925, under the chairmanship of Justice Richard Feetham, a South African; the Free State representative was Eoin MACNEILL, while J.R. Fisher represented Northern Ireland, nominated by London because the Northern Ireland government had refused to make an appointment.

On 7 November 1925 the findings of the Commission – namely that the border should remain as it was for 'economic and geographic reasons', except that south Armagh would go to the Free State and part of east Donegal to Northern Ireland – were controversially leaked by the *Morning Post*. Eoin MacNeill resigned, protesting that he could never have agreed with such findings. The affair was resolved for the time being when the three governments agreed, on 3 December 1925, that the border should remain as it was, thereby ratifying the state of Northern Ireland. The report of the Commission was not published until 1969.

Bound down to. A HIBERNO-ENGLISH phrase meaning 'to be apprenticed to'. There were three stages for a man to learn his craft or trade: apprentice, journeyman (when the young tradesman would travel the country to practise his trade and gain experience) and master, when he would be entrusted with apprentices to train. (There is no record of women tradespeople.)

Bountiful, My Lady. *See* MY LADY BOUNTIFUL.

Bourke, Ulick J. (1829–87). Irish-language activist. Bourke was born in Castlebar, Co. Mayo, in 1829, and ordained at Maynooth for the Tuam archdiocese in 1858. While still a student he published *College Irish Grammar* (1856) and was appointed professor of Irish, logic and humanities at his old school, St Jarlath's, becoming president in 1865. He became parish priest of Claremorris in 1878 and remained there till his death. He devised simple lessons in Irish, which were published in *The* NATION. He was first chairman of SPIL (the Society for the Preservation of the Irish Language) at its founding in 1876, and at the inevitable split went with David Comyn to found the GAELIC UNION in 1880 and to edit *Irisleabhar na Gaedhilge* (*The Gaelic Journal*). Both these societies were necessary forerunners of the GAELIC LEAGUE.

Bouzouki. A four-stringed, lute-like instrument of Greek origin adapted to Irish traditional music from the 1960s by musicians such as Johnny Moynihan, Alec Finn, Andy IRVINE and Donal LUNNY.

Bowen, Elizabeth (1899–1973). Novelist and short-story writer. She was born in Dublin into an Anglo-Irish family that had settled in Farahy, near Kildorrery in Co. Cork, in the 17th century. The family home there was called Bowen's Court. Elizabeth left school at 17, published her first book, *Encounters* (a collection of short stories), in 1923, and married Alan Cameron, an educationalist, the same year. Her novels are noted for their poetic sensitivity and their impressive understanding of adolescent girls. *The Last September* (1929) and *A World of Love* (1955) were set in Ireland: the first dealing with the emotional awakening of Lois Farquahar, niece of the Naylors of Danielstown House in Tipperary, during the Troubles of 1920; the second with the eventually relieved obsession of young Jane Danby with the dead Guy Montfort, the former owner of a 'big house'. Her finest novel, *The Heat of the Day* (1949), like the short-story collection *The Demon Lover* (1945), gives a remarkable picture of the wartime London in which she served as an air-raid warden. Bowen was a frequent visitor to Ireland during those years, on semi-official business for the Ministry of Information, with a brief to report on national attitudes to the war. Of her 90 stories the 10 set in Ireland, though small in number and written comparatively late, show her as a significant writer on Irish themes. She died in London and is buried near the front door of the church at Bowen's Court. The Bowen family house, which had been sold to a local man, was demolished.

Bowles, Mary. *See* 'PRIDE OF SWEET CLOGHEEN, THE'.

Bowl (in), to (also **boul**). A HIBERNO-ENGLISH verb meaning 'to pay a casual call on', 'to visit', similar in meaning to KNOCK². *See also* RAMBLING HOUSE.

Bowling. A game played only in Ireland. It is pronounced 'boweling'. Not to be confused with lawn bowls, this is a road game popular in counties Cork and Armagh, and parts of Limerick and Waterford. A 790-gm (28-ounce) iron ball, or 'bullet', is thrown from one point to another, about 5 km (3 miles) further on, and the player to cover the distance in the least number of throws is the winner. The bowlers have to keep the ball in play on the road or its verge and need to exercise considerable skill to spin the ball around corners. Betting by onlookers is popular.

Bowsie. A Dublin noun of uncertain derivation with a negative connotation and usually but not exclusively applied to men. The word is often used with adjectives like 'drunk' or as an exclamation on hearing of bad behaviour: 'The bowsie!'

Box, the. The popular name for the ACCORDION, melodeon or CONCERTINA. The word comes from 'squeezebox', denoting the push–pull method of playing all these instruments. The Irish for accordion and melodeon is *bosca ceoil*, 'music box'.

Box and dice. An expression used to indicate a total amount, as in 'I'll send you the whole jingbang, box and dice.'

Boxty (from the Irish *bacstaidh*). A potato dish common in the northern half of the country. Raw potatoes are grated finely and the water extracted, then shaped into a cylinder, cut into slices and fried or grilled. The idea originated at harvest-time – and became associated with SAMHAIN – when potatoes were dug that were too big to be boiled whole. Sometimes a mixture of raw and cooked potato was used; sometimes too the potato was shaped into a kind of dumpling and boiled before being sliced and eaten with butter. Boxty pancakes, in which grated raw potato was added to the flour to make a batter, were a Shrove Tuesday speciality in parts of the north of Ireland. Boxty was also made with the grated potatoes that were left after water was extracted to make starch. It is still available commercially in some areas, particularly in Ulster.

See also CHAMP; COLCANNON; POUNDIES; THUMP.

Boyce, John. *See* PEPPERGRASS, PAUL.

Boycott. To refuse to have any dealings with a person or group of people as a means of protest or coercion. The term dates from 1880, when such methods were used by the LAND LEAGUE against Captain Charles Cunningham Boycott (1832–97) as a means of coercing him to reduce rents. As land agent to Lord Erne in Co. Mayo, Boycott was treated, in the words of Charles Stewart PARNELL as a LEPER OF OLD. He responded by drafting in 150 Orangemen to help him save the harvest. The experiment proved ruinous, however, since he had to maintain 1000 soldiers to protect them.

Boyd, John (1912–2002). Playwright, editor and broadcaster. He was born in Belfast of working-class parents and educated at INST and Queen's University Belfast. Like Sam Hanna BELL and John HEWITT he became a committed socialist in the 1930s and in 1943 helped found the magazine LAGAN, which blazed its intellectual and aesthetic light amid the encircling sectarian and philistine gloom. He gave up teaching in 1947 to join BBC Northern Ireland as a talks producer. Like his colleague Bell he did his best to subvert the monolithic Unionism of the service, but he retired in 1972 with no great regret. He became literary adviser to the LYRIC PLAYERS THEATRE, edited its journal THRESHOLD and wrote a number of plays about the sectarian and intermittently violent nature of life in Northern Ireland. These included *The Flats* (1971), *The Farm* (1973) and *The Street* (1977). *Out of My Class* (1985) and *The Middle of My Journey* (1990) are volumes of autobiography.

Boyd, William. *See* BANN VALLEY EXODUS.

Boyle, Captain. The 'paycock' of Sean O'Casey's play *JUNO AND THE PAYCOCK*, whose maritime experience was rather limited. In the words of his wife Juno:

> Everybody callin' you 'Captain', an' you only wanst on the wather, in an ould collier from here to

Liverpool, when anybody, to listen or look at you, ud take you for a second Christo For Columbus.

This does not prevent imaginative reminiscence:

> Boyle: Ofen, an' ofen, when I was fixed to the wheel with a marlinspike, an' the wins blowin' fierce an' the waves lashin' an' lashin', till you'd think every minute was goin' to be your last, an' it blowed, an blowed – blew is the right word, Joxer, but blowed is what the *sailors use* ...
>
> Joxer: Aw, it's a darlin' word, a daarlin' word.
>
> Boyle: An', as it blowed an' blowed, I ofen looked up at the sky an' assed meself the question – what is the stars?

The part provided Barry Fitzgerald (William Shields; 1888–1961) with one of his greatest successes, the other being Fluther in *The PLOUGH AND THE STARS*. He went to America in 1930 and divided his time between Broadway and Hollywood, winning an Oscar as best supporting actor in the part of the old priest Father Fitzgibbon in the Bing Crosby film *Going My Way* (1944), and taking the part of the village matchmaker in *The QUIET MAN* (1952).

Boyle, Juno. The eponymous chief female character of Sean O'Casey's play *JUNO AND THE PAYCOCK*:

> Bentham: Juno! What an interesting name! It reminds one of Homer's glorious story of ancient gods and heroes.
>
> Boyle: Yis, doesn't it? You see, Juno was born and christened in June; I met her in June; we were married in June, an' Johnny was born in June, so wan day I says to her, 'You should ha' been called Juno,' and the name stuck to her ever since.

She is the strongest character in the play, an obvious tribute to O'Casey's mother, Susan Archer. It was a gift of a part for the actress Sarah ALLGOOD.

Boyle, Richard, 1st Earl of Cork (1566–1643). Colonist and entrepreneur. He was born in Faversham in Kent and educated in Canterbury and at Cambridge University, arriving in Dublin on 23 June 1588 with a small amount of money, a gold bracelet and a diamond ring.

His first wife, Joan Apsley, whom he married in 1595, brought him a large dowry. She died in 1599. Although known to be an unscrupulous adventurer – he acquired land in the aftermath of the MUNSTER PLANTATION by exploiting defects in titles – he was appointed clerk of the council of Munster by Elizabeth I in 1600 and knighted by Sir George CAREW, president of Munster, in 1603, becoming a privy councillor in 1606. It was he who founded the towns of BANDON and CLONAKILTY, bringing in English settlers and craftsmen, and increasing his own wealth through industry and exports. He was created Earl of Cork in 1620, lord justice in 1629 and lord high treasurer in 1631.

In 1602, at the insistence of George Carew, Boyle bought Sir Walter RALEIGH's estates (42,000 acres / 16,800 ha for the very low price of £1500) in counties Cork, Waterford, and Tipperary. These estates included 13 castles, which were garrisoned by retainers. He himself lived with his family in YOUGHAL, Co. Cork, a town he also helped to develop. The only impediment to Boyle's progress was Thomas WENTWORTH, who came to Ireland in 1633 as lord deputy and tried to deprive him of some of his privilege and income for having defrauded the crown at the beginning of his career: 'A most cursed man to all Ireland and to me in particular,' he wrote of Wentworth in his diary.

Boyle has been described as the 'first colonial millionaire', and managed even at the time of the upheaval of the English Civil War not to alienate either side; wealth interested him much more than politics. He had 15 children, all by his second wife; his surviving daughters made good marriages and his 14th child was the scientist and philosopher Robert BOYLE. Oliver CROMWELL is reputed to have said of Richard Boyle: 'If there had been an Earl of Cork in every province it would have been impossible for the Irish to have raised a rebellion.' 'The Great Earl of Cork', as he was known, is buried in Youghal.

Boyle, Robert (1627–91). Scientist and philosopher. Boyle was born on 25 January 1627 in Lismore Castle, Co. Waterford, one of 15 children of Richard BOYLE, 1st Earl of Cork, who had been granted extensive estates in the MUNSTER PLANTATION and who devoted himself to arranging dynastic marriages for almost all his children (although Robert never married). Educated at Eton and at home, Robert Boyle travelled on the Continent as a young man, and came into contact with the theories of Galileo. He settled on a family estate in Dorset, thereafter living in Oxford and in London.

With the help of other scientists Boyle created the first air pump and used it to develop what became known as BOYLE'S LAW, as well as carrying out many novel experiments in chemistry and physics. As a natural philosopher he strongly upheld the empirical or experimental rather than the purely speculative scholastic method of science, and his best-known book was *The Sceptical Chymist* (1661) in which he challenged medieval scholastic theories of scientific phenomena. He was, however, a deeply religious man and used much of his money to further the Anglican religion, including paying for the printing of BEDELL'S BIBLE in Irish. He died in London on 31 December 1691 and was described in an epitaph as 'Father of chemistry and uncle of the Earl of Cork'.

Boyle, William (1853–1922). Playwright born in Drumiskin, Co. Louth. His naturalistic plays, including *The Building Fund* (1905) and *The Mineral Workers* (1906), though popular and profitable, were not the kind of drama that Yeats wanted for the ABBEY THEATRE, nor did they suit the style of acting that he hoped to develop. Yeats thought *The Eloquent Dempsey* 'inexpressibly vulgar', but Boyle had, in fact begun a style and tradition that Lennox ROBINSON, George SHIELS and Padraic COLUM were to continue. He was usually at odds with Yeats and, finding *The PLAYBOY OF THE WESTERN WORLD* distasteful, had no contact with the Abbey Theatre for five years after its production in 1907. He died in London in 1922.
See also LANNA MACREE'S DOG.

Boyle Abbey. A well-preserved ruined abbey in the town of Boyle, Co. Roscommon, one of the most important in Connacht. A sister-house of the Cistercian monastery at MELLIFONT, Co. Louth, it was founded in 1161 by the local rulers, the MacDermott family. Because it was built between the Romanesque and Gothic periods, it contains features of both styles of architecture, for instance a row of rounded arches on one side of the nave facing a row of pointed arches on the other. Most Cistercian churches are very plain, but Boyle has elaborately carved columns at the western end of the abbey. It was not consecrated until 1220, and was then subject to attack as a result of the feuds between the warring MacDermott and O'Connor clans. The building was used as a military garrison during the 17th and 18th centuries, and occupied in 1659 by Cromwellian troops, who did extensive damage to the building.

Boyle Balderdash, Sir. *See* ROCHE, SIR BOYLE.

Boyle's Law. The scientific law devised by the Irish-born scientist Robert BOYLE, stating that the volume of a gas is inversely proportional to its pressure.

Boyne, Battle of the. A significant but not decisive battle in the WILLIAMITE WAR in Ireland that took place on 1 July 1690 (old style) at Oldtown on the River Boyne, 5 km (3 miles) from Drogheda. It was the last confrontation between two monarchs in THESE ISLANDS. William III (KING BILLY) stayed at the centre of the fighting, but JAMES II's uncharacteristic flight from the field caused mockery on both sides (*see* SÉAMAS AN CHACA). James's JACOBITES were out-manoeuvred, with only a small force under the Earl of TYRCONNELL in a position to face the main Williamite army. The Williamites were forced to retreat after some dashing Tyrconnell cavalry charges, but because of the long stand-off and the distancing of the main Jacobite army, losses were relatively few: 1000 of James's army of 25,000 and 500 of William's 36,000. The crucial battle in the war took place a year later at AUGHRIM.

Though little was made of the victory at the time, its commemoration became the ultimate Orange festival, celebrated each year on the TWELFTH OF JULY and secure in its place in the mantra: 'Derry, Aughrim, Enniskillen and the Boyne':

> Hurrah! hurrah! for liberty, for her the sword we drew,
>
> And dar'd the battle, while on high our Orange banners flew;
>
> Woe worth the hour – woe worth the state, when men shall cease to join
>
> With grateful hearts to celebrate the glories of the Boyne.
>
> WILLIAM BLACKER (1777–1855): 'The Battle of the Boyne – 1690' (1849)

Boyne Valley. The fertile plain of the River Boyne in counties Meath and Louth, which is rich in historical and archaeological remains: the Hill of TARA, the megalithic tombs of NEW-GRANGE, Knowth and Dowth, and the monasteries of MONASTERBOICE and MELLIFONT ABBEY, as well as lesser sites.
See also BRUGH NA BÓINNE.

Boys, the[1]. A way of referring to members of the IRA, especially in the days of the ANGLO-IRISH WAR (1919–21) when they were on the run. The phrase continued to be used with residual affection right up to the end of the BORDER CAMPAIGN (1962).
See also LADS, THE.

Boys, the[2]. The affectionate nickname given to Mícheál Mac Liammóir (1899–1978) and his partner Hilton Edwards (1903–1982). Born Alfred Willmore in London, Mac Liammóir was a boy actor by 1912 and learned his adult trade touring with his brother-in-law, the actor-manager Anew MacMaster (1894–1962). He met Edwards in 1927 and they became life partners. After launching An TAIBHDHEARC in 1928 they established in the same year the GATE THEATRE, which found a permanent home in Parnell Square in 1930, though the first productions were held in the PEACOCK, the ABBEY THEATRE's alternative auditorium. For many years the Boys provided theatre

complementary to the Abbey's repertoire, balancing, often on a shoestring, classical plays with modern Irish and international drama. The strikingly handsome Mac Liammóir not only played the leads but also painted the scenery and designed the costumes. Edwards directed, played character parts and used his flair for stage lighting to produce, with necessary economy, remarkable effects. Among the most famous of their productions was the *The OLD LADY SAYS NO!.*

Mac Liammóir wrote many plays, the best-known being *Where Stars Walk* (1940), based upon the myth of ÉTAIN and MIDIR, and *Ill Met by Moonlight* (1946); he also wrote several volumes of theatrical reminiscences including ALL FOR HECUBA (1946). His one-man show *The IMPORTANCE OF BEING OSCAR* (1963), which Edwards directed, gave him worldwide celebrity (and his partnership with Edwards financial security for the first time in their colourful lives). *The Boys* was also the title of Christopher Fitz Simon's biography of MacLiammóir and Edwards (1994).
See also SODOM AND BEGORRAH.

Boys-a-boys. An expression of surprise or disbelief. In Ulster the form 'boys-a-dear' is slightly more common.

Boys in Blue, the. A nickname for the GARDA SÍOCHÁNA because of the colour of their uniform: navy blue with a light-blue shirt.
See also BLUE FLU.

'Boys of Fair Hill, The'. A Cork squib in the tradition of FATHER PROUT but rather more vulgar, in mock-homage to the 'boys' of a northside locality, Fair Hill. It was written by Seán O'Callaghan:

> The smell on Patrick's Bridge is wicked,
> How does Father Mathew stick it?
> Here's up 'em all says the boys of Fair Hill ...

The reference is to the statue of Father Theobald Mathew, the APOSTLE OF TEMPERANCE, whose statue is by St Patrick's Bridge in Cork (*see* STATUE, THE).

'Boys of Kilmichael, The'. A popular ballad celebrating one of the most significant engagements of the Anglo-Irish War (1919–21), the KILMICHAEL AMBUSH of 28 November 1920. It is sung to the tune of 'Rosin the Beau'. For many years the author was thought to have been a local schoolteacher called Jeremiah O'Mahony, but a recent biography of Tom Barry authoritatively claims that the ballad was written by John F. Hourihane of Ballineen, Co. Cork, a member of the 3rd Cork Brigade, who later emigrated to Boston, USA, and whose brother Dan took part in the Kilmichael Ambush (Meda Ryan, *Tom Barry: Freedom Fighter*, 2003). The final verse quoted here was written in 1998 by Cork poet Patrick Galvin (b.1927) as a broadside against REVISIONIST historians and politicians:

[Chorus:]
Oh forget not the boys of Kilmichael,
Those brave boys both gallant and true,
They fought with Tom Barry's bold column
And conquered the red, white and blue.

Whilst we honour in song and in story
The memory of Pearse and McBride,
Whose names are illumined in glory
With martyrs that long since have died,
Oh forget not the boys of Kilmichael
Who feared not the ice and the foe,
Oh the day that they marched into battle
They laid all the Black and Tans low.

On the twenty-eighth day of November
The Tans left the town of Macroom,
They were seated in Crossley tenders
Which brought them right into their doom.
They were on the high road to Kilmichael
And never expecting to stall,
'Twas there that the boys of the column
They made a clear sweep of them all
...

There are some who will blush at the mention
Of Connolly, Pearse and McBride,
And history's new scribes in derision
The pages of valour deny,
But sure here's to the boys who cried, Freedom!
When Ireland was nailed to the mast,
And they fought with Tom Barry's bold column
To give us our freedom at last

Boys' Town. A pioneering settlement in Nebraska, USA, established for troubled, neglected, homeless boys by Father Edward J. Flanagan (1886–1948). Flanagan started off in 1917 with five boys in a rented house in Omaha. Flanagan was born in Ballymoe on the border of counties Galway and Roscommon in 1886. The 1938 film *Boys' Town*, starring Spencer Tracy, made his work famous all over the world. In 1946 Flanagan returned to Ireland, where he was shocked and saddened by what he saw of childcare institutions (*see* INDUSTRIAL SCHOOLS). He called them a 'disgrace to the nation', but his pleas for improvement fell on deaf ears. Sent to Germany by President Truman to advise on the plight of homeless and displaced children in the aftermath of the Second World War, he died in Berlin in 1948. In 2002 Ballymoe was twinned with Boys' Town, Nebraska.

There are no bad boys. There is only bad environment, bad training, bad example, bad thinking.
FATHER EDWARD J. FLANAGAN

Boyzone. The first successful Irish boy band, created by pop manager Louis Walsh. The line-up comprised lead singer Ronan Keating (b.1977), Stephen Gately (b.1976), Shane Lynch (b.1976), Keith Duffy (b.1974) and Mikey Graham (b.1972). Boyzone's pre-eminent appeal was to early teens and pre-teen girls. Ronan Keating succeeded in establishing a solo career after the demise of the band. *See also* WESTLIFE.

Brach. An Ulster word for a ring round the moon, taken as a sign of bad weather.

Brachán. The Irish word for 'porridge', extant even in plantation Ulster.

Braddy (Irish *bó bhradach*, 'thieving cow'). A term used in HIBERNO-ENGLISH for a cow that is not satisfied with her own field but must trespass on to the land of a neighbouring farmer.

Brady, Liam (b.1956). Soccer player, nicknamed

'Chippy'. He was born in Dublin on 13 February 1956. One of the best Irish soccer players of all time, he was a successful midfielder for Arsenal (1973–80), scoring 43 goals in 225 matches. For a period from 1980 he played in Italy, where he played for Juventus, Sampdoria and Internazionale, returning to English football before his retirement in 1990. He was first capped for the Republic of Ireland in 1974, and won 72 caps in all, scoring nine goals. He was manager of Celtic 1991–3, and in 1996 he returned to Arsenal as youth team coach.

Brady, Paul (b.1947). Musician and songwriter. He was born in Strabane, Co. Tyrone, and educated at St Columb's College in Derry and University College Dublin, during which time he played with rock and beat groups. In 1967 he joined the folk group The Johnstons, later playing with PLANXTY[2]. Since the 1970s he has at times mined the traditional vein, recording celebrated versions of the ballads 'Arthur McBride' and 'The Lakes of Ponchartrain', from the words of which the title of his successful 1978 album *Welcome Here Kind Stranger* was taken. He also toured with rock performers Dire Straits and Eric Clapton, and recorded rock albums such as *Hard Station* (1981). His songs have been recorded by artists as diverse as Carlos Santana and Tina Turner.

Brae. The Scots word for a hillside or grassy slope, still in general use in Ulster, where it can also mean a stony track:

> I was thinking on those flowers, all doomed to decay
> That bloom around ye bonny, bonny Sliabh Gallion braes.
> ANON. (19th cent.)

Bran[1]. One of two semi-human hounds of FIONN MAC CUMHAIL and also his nephew. Fionn's sister Tuireann is changed into a bitch by her husband's mistress and gives birth to the twin hounds, Bran and SCEOLAN. They follow him faithfully, but Fionn is forced to kill Bran by crushing him to death between his legs because he attacks SADB, the mother of his son OISÍN, when she is in the form of a fawn.

Bran[2]. The hero of the voyage tale IMMRAM *Brain*. It recounts how he and his companions meet the sea-god MANANNÁN MAC LIR and stay for an ecstatic year in the Land of Women (*see* TÍR NA MBAN). In human terms they have spent aeons there and are advised that should they ever set foot in Ireland again they would revert to their natural ages. In spite of this they set sail for home, but when one of their number leaps ashore he turns immediately to dust. Bran turns his ship and sails away into the unknown.

Branagh, Kenneth (b.1960). Actor and director. He was born in Belfast on 10 December 1960 and after studying at RADA became a highly successful actor and director of stage and screen. He played major Shakespearean roles with the Royal Shakespeare Company and directed film versions of *Much Ado about Nothing* (1993) and *Hamlet* (1996). He married the actress Emma Thompson in 1989, but the couple separated in 1995.

Brandt, Muriel (1909–81). Painter. She was born in Belfast, won a scholarship to the Royal College of Art in London and settled in Dublin after her marriage. She was well known as a portrait painter, and her paintings of Micheál Mac Liammóir, Hilton Edwards (*see* BOYS, THE[2]) and Christine Longford may be seen in the foyer of the Gate Theatre, Dublin. She died in Dublin on 10 June 1981.

Brasser. A Dublin slang term for a prostitute, presumably from the connection with brass and brazen, meaning forward or impudent.

Brass money. The copper alloy coinage issued by JAMES II in 1689 when he landed in Ireland. Its value diminished with the fortunes of the Jacobites, and it was one of the miseries that Protestants claimed that William III – KING BILLY – saved them from: 'popery, slavery, arbitrary power, brass money, and wooden shoes' (*see* ORANGE TOAST).

Brat. The cloak worn by Irish kings, lords and commoners in ancient times. The cloaks worn by the nobility were dyed crimson or purple, while lesser people wore black, yellow, grey or striped cloaks. In one of the heroic tales, CÚCHULAINN is said to have worn a voluminous cloak called a *fuan*, which had five folds running crossways. These cloaks were fastened by a brooch or pin at the shoulder. The TÁIN BÓ CUAILNGE (*The Cattle Raid of Cooley*) and other Irish sagas contain descriptions of warriors and maidens wearing vivid cloaks of all the colours of the rainbow. The number of colours worn by members of what was a very hierarchical society was laid down in the BREHON LAWS. These rules applied even to children's clothes.

Brattle. The usual Ulster word for a peal of thunder.

Brave Irishman, The. A play (1743) by Thomas Sheridan the Younger (the father of Richard Brinsley SHERIDAN), taken as the quintessence of 18th-century STAGE-IRISHness. The main character, Captain O'Blunder, with his shaky grasp of English mixed with residual expressions in Irish spoken in a stage BROGUE, together with his bluster, pugnacity, courage and lack of subtlety, set a pattern to be followed by Charles MACKLIN, John O'KEEFFE, and, with modifications, by Dion BOUCICAULT and even J.M.SYNGE, not to mention many early Hollywood movies. The English, with their perennial ambivalence about the Irish, were oddly comforted by such portrayals and the character became a popular and reassuring stereotype. O'Blunder is lured into a lunatic asylum to remove him as a rival for the heroine Lucy:

> *Dr Clyster:* Brother, you plainly perceive that the systole and diastole are obstructed.
>
> *O'Blunder:* My Piss-hole and Arse-hole – Fat the devil ails them? Eh! Sure de're mad …
>
> *Dr Galypot:* Pray sir, how do you rest?
>
> *O'Blunder:* In a good Feather-bed, my Jewel – and sometimes I take a nap in an Arm-chair.
>
> *Dr Clyster:* Do you sleep sound?
>
> *O'Blunder:* Faith I sleep and snore all night, and when I wake in the morning I find myself fast asleep.

Breaca. A 5th–6th-century saint, a votary of St

BRIGID. She went to Cornwall *c*.460, landing in St Ives Bay with a number of other religious sisters, and established a convent on the east bank of the River Hayle. Her feast day is 4 June.

Bread-and-cheese. The fresh new leaves of hawthorn eaten by Ulster children as a palliative against hunger.

Breadeen (Irish *bréidín*). Tweed. The word is still used by the Irish diaspora in Australia. Donegal is the home of Irish tweed manufacture, an age-old skill. As many as 60 operations are needed for the manufacture of a tweed jacket. Magee is the Donegal company most associated with tweed tailoring.

> They had slept on fresh rushes and bundles of woolen breadeen.
> DAVID MALOUF: *The Conversations at Curlew Creek* (1996)

Breasal. The king of Hy-Breasal or HY-BRASIL, the Irish Atlantis. He is known to the Celts as the 'high king of the world' and his land is deliberately submerged by MANANNÁN MAC LIR after a quarrel.

Breathnach, Breandán (1912–85). Musicologist. One of the 20th century's great collectors and promoters of traditional music and set dancing, Breathnach was born in Dublin. He worked as a civil servant in the Department of Agriculture, and did his collecting in his spare time, but was able to collect full-time when he was transferred to the Department of Education, moving 'from pigs to jigs' as he himself put it. In all he collected thousands of dance tunes, published in the three volumes of *Ceol Rince na hÉireann* (*The Dance Music of Ireland*; 1963–77). He was involved with the foundation of Na Píobairí Uilleann (an association for Uilleann pipers; he himself was a player) and the Folk Music Society of Ireland. He also established and edited the journal *Ceol* (*Music*), publishing eight volumes of 22 issues between 1963 and his death.

Breeders' Cup. A classic horse race held in Melbourne since the middle of the 19th century and only twice won by a trainer from outside Australia: both times by Irish trainer Dermot Weld, in 1993 with Vintage Crop and in 2002 with Media Puzzle.

Breen, Dan (1894–1969). IRA leader during the ANGLO-IRISH WAR (1919–21). He was born in Soloheadbeg, Co. Tipperary, the son of a small farmer. It was here at a quarry on 21 January 1919 that he led an attack on a pair of unarmed RIC constables, McDonnell and O'Connell, who were escorting a load of gelignite from Tipperary town to the quarry for blasting purposes. They were the first policemen to be shot since 1916. The ambush is regarded as the first action in the war and was universally condemned at the time (*see* SOLOHEADBEG). Breen had a number of narrow escapes from capture, being several times wounded, but survived to serve as Fianna Fáil TD for Tipperary South (1932–65). He published his memoirs of his guerrilla experiences in 1924, giving it the immodest title *My Fight for Irish Freedom*. *See also* FLYING COLUMN.

Breffni or **Breifne**. An area approximating to modern counties Cavan and Leitrim, until the 15th century dominated by the Irish O'Rourke chieftains, although with some incursions by the Anglo-Norman family of de Lacy. From the 15th century east Breffni (Cavan) was controlled by the O'Reillys, and west Breffni (Leitrim) by the O'Rourkes. Co. Cavan's main GAA stadium in Cavan town is called Breffni Park. *See also* MACMURROUGH, DERMOT.

Bregenz. A town, known as Brigantium to the Romans, in the Vorarlberg, Austria, on the east shore of the Bodensee (Lake Constance). It was at Bregenz that in 610 St COLUMBAN and St GALL parted company in some acrimony. Gall declared he was too ill to travel further. His illness, striking in such a beautiful place, may have been psychosomatic; certainly his flinty superior thought so, since he placed upon him the doom of never saying Mass while he, Columban, lived. The arrival of his abbatial staff five years later was the sign that the doom was lifted and that Columban was dead.

Brehon laws (Old Irish, *breithem*, 'judge'). An extremely complicated system of law in pre-Christian Ireland, based mainly upon compensation for crimes, and with variations in sentences depending upon relationships and class.

Bremen. The plane in which the Irish aviator Colonel James Fitzmaurice and two German colleagues, Baron Von Hünefeld and Hermann Köhl, made the first east–west crossing of the Atlantic, in 1928. Fitzmaurice was born in Dublin on 6 January 1898 and learned to fly in the Royal Flying Corps during the First World War. He joined the new Irish Air Corps and became commandant in 1927. ALCOCK AND BROWN had successfully landed at Clifden, Co. Galway, in 1919 on the first transatlantic flight from America, and Fitzmaurice had tried unsuccessfully to find sponsorship for the more difficult westward crossing. Von Hünefeld was manager of a German shipping line and saw the flight as a means of rehabilitating his country's reputation after the war. They took off from Baldonnel Airport, Co. Dublin, at dawn on 12 April and covered 3712 km (2320 miles) in 36.5 hours to land on a frozen lake on Greenly Island, off Newfoundland. Fitzmaurice retired from the Air Corps in 1929 and lived abroad for 22 years, returning to live in Dublin in 1951. He died in 1965.

Brenach. An Irish saint who settled in Wales sometime in the 5th century and set up his holy place at the foot of a mountain called *Carn-Englyi* ('mountain of angels') near Nefyn on the Lleyn peninsula in modern Gwynedd. The hill is so named because Brenach is said to have communed with angels at its top. His feast day is 7 April.

Brendan of Birr. A contemporary of BRENDAN THE VOYAGER and a friend of COLUM CILLE, whose body he saw in a vision being carried to heaven by angels. His foundation was at Birr, Co. Offaly, and his feast day is 29 November.

Brendan Smyth Affair. A crisis concerning a paedophile priest that brought down the Irish government in December 1994. Brendan

Smyth was born in west Belfast in 1927 and entered the novitiate of the Norbertine order in Kilnacrott, Co. Cavan, in 1945 (it is the order's only foundation in Ireland). From his early days in religious life it appears that he abused children in his home area of Belfast and wherever he was sent to minister after his ordination, including the USA. The response of his superiors was to move him on to another parish whenever complaints were made.

From 1990 the RUC in Belfast investigated claims against Smyth, and on 30 April 1993 delivered nine extradition orders to the office of the attorney-general in Dublin – Smyth at this time was living in Co. Cavan. In October 1994 a UTV investigative programme, *Suffer Little Children*, exposed Smyth's past and revealed that the extradition warrants received in Dublin had never been processed. It was this that brought down the Fianna Fáil–Labour government led by Albert REYNOLDS in December 1994, although neither Reynolds nor the attorney-general, Harry Whelehan, had known about the warrants.

Smyth subsequently served a prison sentence in Northern Ireland, and in July 1997 he stood trial in Dublin, also for sexual abuse of children. He died in August 1997 in the Curragh prison and was buried in secret at Kilnacrott Abbey. The Brendan Smyth Affair did enormous damage to the credibility of the Catholic Church in Ireland.

See also BISHOP BRENDAN; *FORBIDDEN FRUIT*; SINGING PRIEST, THE.

Brendan the Voyager (also **Brandan** or **Brendan the Navigator**). The saint whose name is associated with an 11th-century account of marvellous voyages, *Navigatio Brendani*, in which he is said to have reached America. He was born *c.*483 near Fenit, Co. Kerry, where Mount Brandon still celebrates his name, and became in turn a pupil of St ITA, St FINNIAN OF CLONARD, St ENDA, St JARLATH and St Gildas at Llancafarn, near Cardiff. He founded several monasteries, including Ardfert, near his birthplace, and the great house of Clonfert, which

was noted for the austerity of its rule. He died *c.*578 at Annaghdown on Lough Corrib, at the convent founded by his sister St Briga. It is difficult to separate the man from the legendary tale, according to which he and his monks fasted for forty days before setting out west. They called with Enda at Aran and landed on an island with sheep that was really the back of a whale. The 'land of plenty' that they finally reached has been identified variously as the Canary Islands and Florida. The saint undoubtedly *did* travel to Wales and Scotland, and may indeed have made the epic seven-year journey that the *Navigatio* romanticizes. He is venerated as the patron saint of sailors and his feast day is on 16 May.

See also BRENDAN VOYAGE, THE.

Brendan Voyage, The. A book (1978) by adventurer and author Tim Severin (b.1940), who recreated the legendary epic voyage of BRENDAN THE VOYAGER. He built a boat of tanned oxhides stitched together on a wooden frame, such as that described in the many medieval manuscripts that tell Brendan's story. In 1976 he and a small crew began a hazardous crossing of the Atlantic in the *Brendan* in order to demonstrate the feasibility of such a voyage. They arrived in Newfoundland in June 1977. The *Brendan* is now on display in a glass pyramid in CRAGGAUNOWEN. *The Brendan Voyage* (1980) is also the title of a suite of orchestral music by Shaun Davey (b.1948). In this and other compositions Davey added traditional instruments and voices to the traditional orchestra; especially notable has been his use of the uilleann piper Liam Ó Flynn.

'Brennan on the Moor'. The subject of a rousing ballad made popular by the CLANCY BROTHERS, Willie Brennan (d.1840) was a highwayman and folk hero. He was born in Co. Waterford but his base was the uplands around Kilworth in north Cork. He was finally arrested and hanged at Clonmel jail:

> 'Tis of a famous highwayman a story I will tell,
> His name was Willy Brennan and in Ireland he did dwell,

'Twas in Kilworth Mountain he commenced his
  wild career,
Where many a gallant gentleman before him shook
  in fear.
Chorus:
Brennan on the Moor [*bis*],
Bold, brave and undaunted was young Brennan on
  the moor.

Breslin, Commandant Ned. *See* BALLYSEEDY
MASSACRE.

Breslin, Patrick (1907–42). Irish intellectual
who became a victim of Stalinism. He was
born in London of Irish parents, but the family
returned to live in Dublin in 1920. He joined
the Communist Party of Ireland in 1922 and
became an activist in the youth section. In
1927 he was sent to Moscow, along with seven
other young people, to be educated at the International Lenin School. However, he refused to
conform ideologically and was expelled from
the ILS course. He found employment in the
school as a translator and produced many fine
verse translations of Russian and Spanish
poetry. In 1936, shortly after he had renounced
his Irish citizenship in favour of that of the
Soviet Union, he fell in love with an Irish linguist
and wished to return to Ireland to live with
her and their daughter. The Soviet authorities
refused him permission and neither the Irish
nor the British foreign offices were prepared
to give him a passport. In 1940 he was arrested
as a 'suspect foreigner' and sentenced to eight
years in a gulag. He died of tuberculosis in a
camp in Soviet central Asia in 1942.

Brethrenism. A religious sect of evangelical
Christians that was founded in Dublin *c.*1828
by J.N. Darby, once an Anglican priest, and his
associates A.N. Groves and Edward Cronin.
Its adherents are known outside of Ireland as
Plymouth Brethren because it was in that Devon
town that the English centre was set up and
there that it gathered its greatest following.
Brethren gather into self-governing units, worship in gospel halls, where the Sabbath breaking
of bread is central, and have no ordained clergy.
They live by strict moral principles and limit
the kinds of occupations that they may follow.
In 1849 they split into Open and Exclusive
Brethren. The sect's greatest strength is in
Ulster, the 1991 census showing a membership
there of 12,500.

Brew (Irish *brú*, 'brink'). A word cognate with
'brow', meaning 'edge', as in 'He sheltered from
the BAILC under the brew of the sandbank.'

Brian Boru (*c.*941–1014). The name by which
Brian Bóruma ('Brian of the Tribute') is known
in Ireland and beyond. The most charismatic
figure in pre-Norman Ireland, his reputation
has been obscured by the propagandist 12th-
century O'Brien tract *Cogad Gaedel re Gallaibh* ('the war of the Irish and the foreigners'),
which made him into a kind of saintly paladin. In fact he was a wily and ruthless politician and a clever tactician, who made effective
use of naval power in his successful campaign
to become *Imperator Scottorum* (Latin, 'emperor of the Scoti', i.e. Irish) – as he caused
himself to be described in the BOOK OF ARMAGH
in 1002.

Brian Boru came from the remote family
of the Dál gCais in east Clare and emerged as
its leader after the murder of his older brother
Mathgamhain in 976. Over the next 30 years
he gradually extended his power over all
of Munster, Leinster and the Viking city of
Dublin, assuming virtual hegemony over the
southern half of Ireland, and facing down his
occasional ally, the HIGH KING Máel Sechnaill.
By 1002 he was the undisputed ruler of all
Ireland, and four years later made a triumphal
circuit of the country, 'keeping the sea on his
left-hand'. The decade 1002–12 was relatively
stable, with an occasional rap on the knuckles
for uppity northern kings.

Romantic 19th-century writers tended to
glamorize his court as a kind of Irish Camelot,
with Brian as an Irish Arthur making good
the depredations of the Vikings, restoring the
church to its elevated position in society, and
advancing art and learning. No modern historian would agree to Brian's canonization, but
the icon of his death at the hands of Brodir

at the Battle of CLONTARF for long illustrated many Irish textbooks and adorned the walls of many parochial halls. Hagiography aside, Brian seems to have been a practising Christian and to have understood the need for a spiritual element in the stable society he was attempting to build. However, the ideal of a united and disciplined Ireland created out of the warring local kingships died with him at Clontarf, on 23 April 1014.
See also KINCORA.

Bricriu. In Irish mythology the chief trouble-maker at the court of CONCHOBHAR at EMAIN MACHA. He earns his nickname *Nemthenga* (Old Irish, 'poison-tongue') when he gives a feast for the men of Ulster and the men of Connacht. It is the tradition that the honour of carving the meat should go to the greatest hero present, and in a spirit of fun Briciu secretly persuades three of the warriors present, CÚCH-ULAINN, CONALL CEARNACH and Laoghaire Buadach, to claim the honour. The story is told in *Fled Bricenn* ('Bricriu's feast') in the ULSTER CYCLE, and it requires many tests and trials (including a willingness to be beheaded) before Cúchulainn's supremacy is established, as judged by both MEDB of Connacht and Cú Roí Mac Dáire of Munster. Bricriu is later asked to adjudicate between Donn Cuailnge (the BROWN BULL OF CUAILNGE) and Finnbhenach (the White Bull of Connacht) and is trampled to death by the fighting animals.
See also TÁIN BÓ CUAILNGE.

Brídeog. *See* BIDDY BOYS.

Bridges in Dublin. *See* LIFFEY.

Bright, Honor. *See* HONOR BRIGHT CASE.

Brighton Bombing. The explosion of an IRA bomb in the bathroom of room 629 of the Grand Hotel, Brighton, at 2.54 a.m. on 12 October 1984, during the Conservative party conference. The bomb had been placed about a month earlier and the explosion claimed a total of six lives. The intended targets were Margaret Thatcher and her government, but of the cabinet only Norman Tebbit (secretary of state for industry) was injured. The IRA were reported as having commented: 'We only have to be lucky once.'

Brigid or **Brigit** (Irish **Bríd**, pronounced 'breedge'). The name both of a Celtic goddess and of a Christian saint, with consequent confusions of traditions. In mythology she is a triune goddess of healing, metalwork and poetry, daughter of the DAGDA. Her festival was IMBOLG, the beginning of the Celtic spring. The saint was born, according to tradition, at Faughart, near Dundalk, Co. Louth *c*.450, but her sphere of influence was Kildare, where she founded a double abbey, the first Irish convent for women, where a perpetual flame was kept burning in her honour until the Reformation. The saint may have been a priestess of the goddess before her conversion and the fixing of her feast as 1 February compounded the confusion. One story associated with the saint is that while she sat by the bed of a dying pagan chieftain she plaited rushes into the form of a cross; when he asked about the significance of the cross she explained and he asked to be baptized. The elaborate rush crosses associated with her feast day (*Crasóg Bhríde*, 'Brigid's cross') are taken to spring from that story, but even they may be part of an older pagan rite.

Briquette, Pete. *See* PETE BRIQUETTE.

Bristol, Earl of. *See* HERVEY, FREDERICK AUG-USTUS.

British Isles. A geographer's collective description of the islands of Britain and Ireland, but one that is no longer acceptable in the latter country. Attempts to overcome the inconvenience of having nothing to replace the older term have included the cumbersome and inaccurate 'Hibernian Archipelago', but the phrase in most frequent use is the cute and unsatisfactory THESE ISLANDS.
See also MAINLAND, THE.

Brits out! An admonition that appeared on many walls in Republican areas of Northern Ireland in the early 1970s when the 'honeymoon' of the British army's deployment in 1969 was emphatically over.

Broderick, John (1927–89). Novelist. He was born in Athlone, the only son of a prosperous baker. Financial independence allowed him the freedom – a freedom that other Irish writers of the time could not usually attain – to write as he chose about the dark side of Irish sexuality and small-town life. He was bisexual, and there is in all his books an interest in the epicene and homoerotic, while his view of women, especially in his early novels, *The Pilgrimage* (1961), *The Fugitives* (1962) and *The Waking of Willie Ryan* (1965), tends towards the misogynistic. He eventually found Ireland too oppressive and spent the last years of his life in comfortable if lonely exile in Bath. However, he retained an interest in Irish affairs, especially in the changes of church attitudes and in the fortunes of the Irish in England, as *The Trial of Father Dillingham* (1975), *The Pride of Summer* (1976) and *London Irish* (1979) show. The Northern TROUBLES upset and fascinated him – *The Fugitives* dealt with IRA activity in the late 1950s – and themes of murder and madness, as in *The Rose Tree* (1985), began to appear in his later work. His last completed novel, his eleventh, was *The Flood* (1987), intended to be the first of a 'Bridgeford trilogy' and set somewhat nostalgically in the Athlone of the 1930s. It viewed the world with a more benign eye and the mood was of forgiveness and a sense of kinder times. He died before the trilogy could be completed; the second volume, the unfinished *The Irish Magdalen*, was published in 1991.

Brogue. The HIBERNO-ENGLISH term for an Irish accent. Several origins of the word have been suggested, associated with two Irish words: *bróg*, 'stout shoe' (*see* BROGUES), and *barróg*, 'speech impediment'. The first comes from the suggestion that the attempts to render English speech by Irish-speakers sounded as if they had shoes obstructing their tongues. The second is sufficiently close to the English word to suggest a back formation.

The word was first used on stage in George FARQUHAR's play *The Twin-rivals* (1702), in which the hero Hermes Wouldbe says of his valet Teague: 'Though this fellow travelled the world over he would never lose his brogue nor his stomach.' Other more fanciful suggestions include William Boyle's 'The Origin of the Brogue' in *A Kish of Brogues* (1899):

When St Patrick to taich that ould monarch a
  lesson
An' give such offenders his left-handed blessin'
Just stooped where he stood an' unloosened his
  brogue,
And flung it right in the mouth of the rogue,
Where it fastened an' stuck till his death like a leech
An' evermore flavoured the tone of his speech.
An' all his posterity still have it there
Whatever the title or the tongue they bear,
An' the only reward that the punishment brings
Is the knowledge they all are descended from kings.

Towards the end of his life Alfred, Lord Tennyson was anxious to write a poem using the brogue. He showed a draft of 'Molly Maghee' to his friend William ALLINGHAM, who asked him to strike out the 'h' and by no means approved of the idea. When the laureate insisted, Allingham gave him a mild lecture on the subject, as he records in his *Diary* (1907) for Friday, 6 November 1885:

I told him that Irish brogue has many *nuances*,
especially in sound; it differs in different parts
of the island; and there are vulgar and unvulgar
brogues; and the possessor of a vulgar brogue
is the subject of frequent imitation and ridicule
among his own countrymen. But a mild brogue in
the mouth of an educated person, and especially
of a pretty woman, is sweet and soothing, pleasant
and coaxing. Her way of speaking is very different
from the way an ignorant Connaught or Munster
peasant would *shpayke*. I could not bring myself to
use the vulgar brogue in verse, unless it were for a
broadly comic purpose.

See also STAGE-IRISH.

Brogues. Stout leather shoes (Irish *bróg*) stitched with a leather thong instead of the normal waxed thread. Broguemaking was considered to be different from shoemaking until the end of the 19th century; brogues were cheaper than other shoes, and thus popular among ordinary people. There was a tradition that the right and left shoe of a pair of brogues were identical, both shoes fitting either foot. Brogues were sold by their makers from a basket or 'kish' (Irish *cis*) at fairs and markets.

Broighter Hoard. A treasure cache of Iron Age gold ornaments, including the Broighter, TORC, two necklaces, a bowl and a delicate golden boat complete with oars. It was discovered in February 1896 by Tom Nicholl, a farm labourer, who was ploughing at Broighter, 4 km (2.5 miles) northwest of Limavady, Co. Derry, on land that had once been under the sea. This fact was central to lengthy legal proceedings between the trustees of the British Museum, who held the articles had been a votive offering to MANANNÁN MAC LIR (the Irish Neptune) and the crown, which claimed them as treasure trove, deposited with a view to recovery. Mr Justice Farwell was ultimately persuaded by the geologist's report that the land, 5m (16 ft) above sea level, had emerged in Neolithic times and was therefore dry land when the cache had been buried sometime between 300 and 100 BC. In June 1903 he ordered that the hoard should be handed over to the National Museum in Dublin, where it is still on display. Local tradition suggests that the pieces may have been part of the treasures of Broighter monastery, presented to the monks after the convention of DRUIMCEATT in AD 575, and that it was buried for safe keeping during the period of the Viking raids.

Broke. A west Ulster word meaning 'embarrassed': 'She was all broke when her mother joined [scolded] her.'

Bronach (Irish, 'sorrowful'). A 6th-century saint known as the Virgin of Glenshesk (*see* NINE GLENS, THE), but mainly associated with the churchyard of Kilbroney near Rostrevor, Co. Down. The place was supposed to be haunted by the ringing of an invisible bell, and after a storm in 1885 a bell with a worn clapper was discovered in the fork of a fallen oak. It was found to be of 6th-century design and is now revered as Bronach's Bell. She is the patron of seafarers, with a feast day on 2 April.

Brontë, Patrick. *See* PRUNTY, PATRICK.

Broo. *See* BUROO.

Brooke, Charlotte (1740–93). Irish-language collector and translator. She was born in Rantavan, Co. Cavan, the only one of the 22 children of Henry Brooke (*c.*1703–83) to survive him. (He had some reputation as a playwright, poet, novelist and pamphleteer, whose anti-Catholic writings, associated with his fear of possible support for the YOUNG PRETENDER, changed in time to pamphlets against the POPERY LAWS.) Charlotte Brooke was brought up in Co. Kildare, educated by her father and encouraged by him to study Irish. She devoted any time left over from acting as secretary and later nurse to her father to collecting and translating many kinds of Irish verse, including material from the ancient sagas. In 1789 she published *Reliques of Irish Poetry, Consisting of Heroic Poems, Odes, Elegies and Songs*, which includes her own paraphrases and original text, and is the first collection to include Irish songs. After her father's death unwise investments reduced her to near-poverty, but the publication of *Reliques* and her edition of her father's works somewhat restored her fortunes. Some of her translations were published in BOLG AN TSOLÁTHAIR (1795).

Brookeborough, Lord (1888–1973). Prime minister of Northern Ireland (1943–63). He was born Basil Brooke on 9 June 1888 at Colebrooke, Co. Fermanagh, the family seat since Tudor times, and was educated at Pau, southern France (where his grandparents lived in an English-speaking colony), Winchester and, following family tradition, Sandhurst. He served in the 10th Hussars in India, returning to sign the ULSTER COVENANT and help train the UVF. During the First World War he served for a time in the trenches, winning the Military Cross and Croix de Guerre before joining General Byng's staff as interpreter with Marshal Foch. After the war he returned to manage the family

estates, becoming county commandant of the B-SPECIALS and an ORANGE ORDER activist. He was a successful minister of agriculture (1933–41) in the STORMONT Parliament, though on appointment he notoriously sacked all Catholic workers on his estates, a quarter of the total. A competent minister of supply (1941–3), he replaced J.H. Andrews as prime minister in 1943 and held the post for 20 years, eventually persuading his followers to accept the new health and education reforms introduced by the 1945–51 Labour government in Westminster. He resigned from office in 1963 and from Parliament in 1967, having presided over a regime that was marked by a lack of official contact with Catholics or trade unions. He was made 1st Viscount Brookeborough in 1952 and died on 18 August 1973, an unrepentant and unyielding Unionist.
See also PROTESTANT PARLIAMENT FOR A PROTESTANT PEOPLE.

Brookeborough Raid. *See* BORDER CAMPAIGN.

Brosna. An Irish word, borrowed directly in HIBERNO-ENGLISH, for small sticks or twigs used for kindling, often collected in ditches or fields. *Brosna* is also the title of a celebrated collection (1964) by Irish-language poet Seán Ó RÍORDÁIN.

Brother, the. One of the creations of Myles na Gopaleen (Brian O'Nolan, or Flann O'BRIEN), part of the family of His Satanic Majesty, Sir Myles of Santry, who, like the DA, made his way with gnomic matter into O'Nolan's *Irish Times* column CRUISKEEN LAWN:

The brother has it all worked out.
  What?
  The war. How we can get through the war here in the Free State. I mean the rationing and brown bread and all that class of thing. The brother has a plan. Begob you'll be surprised when you hear it. A very high view was taken when it was explained in the digs the other night.
  What is the nature of this plan?
  It's like this. I'll tell you. We all go to bed for a week every month. Every single man, woman and

child in the country. Cripples, drunks, policemen, watchmen – everybody. Nobody is allowed to be up. No newspapers, 'buses, pictures or any class of amusement allowed at all. And no matter who you are you must be stuck inside in the bed there … The effect would be a savings of 25% in the consumption of essential commodities but everybody would have to get up after a week because the bakers would have to get up to bake more bread 'and if wan is up, all has to be up'.
  The Best of Myles (1968)

Brother Barnabas. An early avatar of Flann O'BRIEN (Brian O'Nolan). Brother Barnabas was the name used in the early 1930s for O'Nolan's contributions to the University College Dublin student magazine *Comhthrom na Féinne* (Irish, 'fair play'). The material (and the character) were an early run of CRUISKEEN LAWN, with the same mock claims to grandeur, the same multilingual puns, the same weary but gracious condescension towards his audience. In one of the later issues there is a clear anticipation of the revolt of created characters that was to be a feature of AT SWIM-TWO-BIRDS; a character called Carruthers McDaid in a novel being written by Barnabas refuses to rob a poor-box in a church:

'Sorry old chap,' he said, 'but I absolutely can't do it.'
  'What's this, Mac,' said I, 'getting squeamish in your old age?'
  'Not squeamish exactly,' he replied, 'but I bar poor-boxes …'
  The Best of Myles (1968)

Brotherhood, the. *See* FENIANS; IRB.

Broth of a boy. A description of a young man, once entirely laudatory, but now degenerated into an expression either pejorative or condescending:

A good manly brave boy: the essence of manhood, as broth is the essence of meat.
  PATRICK WESTON JOYCE (1827–1914): *English As We Speak It in Ireland* (1910)

Brougham's Lyceum. The Broadway theatre later to have a starry career as Wallack's. It was built by John Brougham at the corner of

Broadway and Broome Street, New York, and opened on 23 December 1850, but within two years the popular Irish actor had to relinquish it to J.J. Wallack (1820–88). Brougham was born in Dublin on 9 May 1814 and gave up medical studies at Trinity College Dublin to appear in July 1830 in TOM AND JERRY. In 1842 he and his wife went to America, where he specialized in the standard STAGE-IRISH parts: Sheridan's Sir Lucius O'Trigger, Charles Macklin's Sir Callaghan O'Brallaghan and Denis Brulgruddery. After the failure of the Lyceum, Brougham continued to act, and was tempted to try owner-management again, opening a new theatre on the site of the present Madison Square on 25 January 1869. It too failed within a few months. He went back to acting and writing, claiming that he was part-author of Dion BOUCICAULT's *London Assurance* (1841), in which he had starred as Dazzle. Of his many plays, burlesques and adaptations, none has survived in the repertoire. His last appearance was as Felix O'Reilly in Boucicault's play *Rescued* on 25 October 1879; he died in New York City the following year.

Brown, Christy. *See* MY LEFT FOOT.

Brown Bull of Cuailnge. The magnificent bull, known in old Irish as Donn Cuailnge, that is the object of the Cattle Raid of Cooley (*see* TÁIN BÓ CUAILNGE) and the cause of the war between Connacht and Ulster. It is owned by DAIRE and desired greatly by Queen MEDB of Connacht. The bull (who was once human) is finally stolen and taken to Queen Medb's territories, where he has a bloody fight with Finnbhenach, the White Bull of Connacht. The Connacht bull is bested and carried on Donn Cuailnge's horns through the two provinces and scattered piecemeal until Donn Cuailnge too dies.

Browne, Frances. *See* BLIND POETESS OF DONEGAL, THE.

Browne, Noël. (1915–97). Physician and pioneering politician. He was born in Waterford on 20 December 1915. The family moved a good deal, and he was educated in Athlone, Co. Westmeath, and Ballinrobe, Co. Mayo.

His parents both died of tuberculosis, his father in 1925 and his mother in 1927, and he went to London to live with an elder sister. He won a scholarship to Beaumont, a Jesuit public school, where he came in contact with a wealthy and generous Dublin family, the Chances, who recognized his potential and paid for him to study medicine at Trinity College Dublin. In 1940 he too contracted tuberculosis, but was treated in England, recovered to sit his final exams and graduated in 1942. He worked in sanatoria in England and what he saw of tuberculosis, as well as the deaths of his parents, convinced him that only political will could eradicate the scourge of the disease.

Browne was elected TD for CLANN NA POBLACHTA in 1948 and appointed minister for health in the INTERPARTY GOVERNMENT on his first day in the Dáil. He successfully implemented the previous government's white paper on tuberculosis, helped by the development of new drugs. He also introduced free testing for the disease, in the mass x-ray scheme. In 1950 he supported the implementation of the MOTHER AND CHILD SCHEME, which was opposed by the Catholic Church, and as a consequence he resigned as minister in 1951.

Browne maintained a presence in Irish politics until 1982, serving as TD for most of the period until 1978, initially in Fianna Fáil, then in the National Progressive Democratic Party, which he had founded with Jack McQuillan, also formerly of Clann na Poblachta. He joined the Labour Party in 1963 and became a Labour TD (1963–5 and 1969–73). He won a seat in the Seanad (Senate) in 1973 and was elected to the Dáil as an independent in 1977, retiring from politics in 1982. His career shows him to have been idealistic and deeply committed to the underprivileged; he was also stubborn, independent, wayward and lacking the pragmatism that would have made him a more effective politician. He was a greatly admired figure in Irish political life, even by those who did not share his views, and his autobiography *Against the Tide* (1986) was a bestseller. *See also* TUBERCULOSIS.

Brown paper bag. A phrase associated with the Irish political scandals of the 1990s and after, exposed in various TRIBUNALS, especially the Flood Tribunal. It refers to cash given to a national or local politician, in return for such things as planning favours by a builder or developer, the cash being passed across a table in a pub or other informal setting in a brown paper bag. There is, naturally, no paper trail for payments of this kind.

Brown rain. The colour of rain falling through the filthy thatch-and-sod roof of a primitive Irish cabin:

> *Lag in a dhroim 's na gabhla ag lúbadh*
> *Is clagarnach dhonn go trom ag tuirlint.*
> (Weak in its ridge and end-rafters bending
> And the patter of brown rain never ending.)
>   BRIAN MERRIMAN (?1745–1805): *Cúirt an Mheá-Oíche* ('The Midnight Court')

Broy Harriers. An armed auxiliary force of the GARDA SÍOCHÁNA established by Éamonn (Ned) Broy (1887–1972), who succeeded Eoin O'DUFFY as Garda commissioner in 1933. Broy, a civil servant, had been Michael Collins's 'eyes and ears' inside Dublin Castle during the Anglo-Irish War (1919–21). The Broy Harriers, who were recruited from among men who had been IRA Volunteers during the war, were established to counter the threat to public order posed by the BLUESHIRTS and were disbanded in 1935 when the Blueshirts lost support.

Bruen, James (1920–72). Golfer. He was born in Belfast, but his family moved to Cork, where he was educated and spent most of his working life as an insurance broker. As a youth he had an excellent record in competitions, winning the British boys' title in 1936. The only time he won the British amateur championship was in 1946, although he continued to compete in the event until 1960, and he was three times leading amateur in the Irish open (1937–9). Bruen perfected a stroke called the 'Bruen loop', for which he is still remembered by golfers.

Brugha, Cathal (1874–1922). Revolutionary. He was born Charles Burgess in Dublin on 18 July 1874 and educated at Belvedere College, later helping to set up a candle-manufacturing company, Lalor and Co. He became an enthusiastic cultural and political Nationalist, joining the GAELIC LEAGUE, the GAA and the IRISH VOLUNTEERS. In the EASTER RISING of 1916 he was second-in-command to Éamon CEANNT (Kent) in the South Dublin Union and was permanently lamed as a result of an injury he suffered in the fighting. A member of the first DÁIL in 1919, he was chief of staff of the IRA (1917–19) and minister for defence (1919–22). Brugha was a passionate and bitter opponent of the TREATY (and, on a personal level, of Michael Collins) and was a member of the FOUR COURTS garrison at the outbreak of the CIVIL WAR. After the fall of the Four Courts, Brugha and some other Republicans took up a position in the Hamman Hotel in O'Connell Street, and he was fatally wounded there by Free State troops. He died two days later, on 7 July 1922.

Brugh na Bóinne (Irish, 'dwelling place of the Boyne'). The palace in the BOYNE VALLEY identified with NEWGRANGE, home of AONGHUS ÓG. The name is also applied collectively to the three megalithic tombs of Newgrange, Knowth and Dowth, and the visitor centre appertaining to them.

Bruise (Irish *brúigh*, 'to press'). A common term in the HIBERNO-ENGLISH of Munster, meaning to mash potatoes.
See also CHAMP; POUNDIES; THUMP.

Brúitín. *See* COLCANNON.

Brus. A borrowing from Irish which in HIBERNO-ENGLISH means 'broken straw', 'fine fragments', 'dust'. The word is also used to connote small change: 'I have only *brus* in my purse.'
See also SMITHEREENS.

Bruscar (Irish, 'fragments'). The commonly used term for 'rubbish', in its original meaning close to BRUS. Every Irish classroom and street has a *bosca bruscar*.

Brutal. A contemporary colloquialism meaning 'very poor', 'disappointing', 'not worth going to see' (for instance of a dance band or spectacle).

Bruton, John (b.1947). Leader of FINE GAEL (1990–2001), and taoiseach (1994–7). He was born in Dublin on 18 May 1947 and educated at Clongowes and University College Dublin. Elected Fine Gael TD for Meath in the 1969 general election, he was at that time the youngest member of the Dáil. In the Fine Gael–Labour coalition of 1973–7 he served as a junior minister, first in education, then in industry and commerce. His expertise and interest in economics led to his promotion to minister for finance in Garret FITZGERALD's first coalition (1981–2), and it was his decision in his first budget of March 1982 to levy VAT on children's shoes that caused the revolt of Labour Party TDs and the collapse of the government. Disagreement on budgetary principles also undermined the short-lived coalition of 1986–7.

Bruton was an obvious contender for the leadership of his party when Garret FitzGerald resigned after the 1987 general election, but he was defeated by Alan Dukes. However he replaced Alan Dukes in 1990 after the party's candidate came a poor third in the presidential election. Fine Gael's customary coalition partner, Labour, chose to ally itself with Fianna Fáil after the 1992 elections, in which Fine Gael lost ten seats, but fortune finally favoured Bruton and his party when in December 1994, as a result of the BRENDAN SMYTH AFFAIR, Labour abandoned Fianna Fáil and agreed to form the government that became known as the RAINBOW COALITION. The longstanding problem (for Labour and especially for Dick SPRING) of having Bruton as minister for finance was solved by giving that ministry, for the first time, to a Labour TD, Ruairí Quinn, who succeeded Spring as leader of his party in 1997. With Bruton as taoiseach and the economy finally emerging into its CELTIC TIGER summer, the coalition governed until the general election of 1997.

Bruton was obliged by his Fine Gael background and constituency to take a hard line on SINN FÉIN – the first IRA truce lasted from August 1994 to February 1996, during the term of his government – and he was perceived by some of his countrymen as being excessively conciliatory towards Unionism. But his government and especially his minister for foreign affairs, Dick Spring, contributed greatly to the developing peace process that culminated in the GOOD FRIDAY AGREEMENT of 1998. John Bruton, who, although diligent and well-meaning, was perceived as uncharismatic and inflexible, was replaced as leader of Fine Gael by Michael Noonan in January 2001.

Brutus. The pen name of Michael Joseph Barry for his poetic contributions to *The NATION*, notably the stirring march tune 'Step Together'. He was born in Cork in 1817 and, although a barrister, was imprisoned in 1843 as a YOUNG IRELANDER. In later life he became more conservative, serving as a police magistrate, writing leaders for *The Times* of London and contributing to *Punch*. His humorous contributions to the Dublin University magazine were written under the pseudonym *Bouillon de Garçon* (BROTH OF A BOY). He died in 1889:

Step together – boldly tread,
Firm each foot, erect each head,
Fixed in front be every glance –
Forward, at the word 'advance'.
'Step Together' (1845)

B-Specials. The name by which members of the longest-lasting category of special constable in Northern Ireland were known and execrated. They were also sometimes referred to as B-Men. There were originally four categories, recruited in November 1920 to deal with unrest following the establishment of the Northern Ireland state: A-Specials were full-time, temporary constables; B-Specials were essentially a civilian, local, part-time militia; C-Specials were older and essentially an emergency reserve force; and a short-lived C1 force was a kind of territorial army. The B-Specials, a totally sectarian force, contained many ex-UVF members, and they were accused of the killing, sometimes in uniform, of Nationalists, notably five members of the McMahon family in Belfast on 29 March 1922. They continued to be used as back-up for the RUC after the other categories were stood down in 1926, being mobilized annually during the marching season, as Home Guard during the Second World War and on border patrols during the IRA BORDER CAMPAIGN of 1956–62. Their partial and undisciplined behaviour during the CIVIL RIGHTS agitation and the accusation that the Tynan (Co. Tyrone) corps were responsible for a civilian death in August 1969 led to their disbandment in the spring of 1970. They were replaced by the UDR, which many of them immediately joined, thereby creating the same kind of partial and Protestant force.

Bualadh bos (Irish, literally 'banging the palms of the hands'). The Irish term for applause, pronounced 'boola bus' and often used in HIBERNO-ENGLISH. '*Déan bualadh bos anois*' ('A big clap now please') is the request of many a *FEAR A TÍ* at a CÉILÍ, concert or school play.

Bucked, to be. A phrase meaning 'to be exhausted', 'played out'.

Buckled, to get. A slightly dated tongue-in-cheek phrase meaning to get married. 'To be buckled' is a Dublin slang term for intoxication.

Buck Mulligan. *See* MULLIGAN, BUCK.

'Buckshot' Forster (1819–1886). A nickname applied to William Edward Forster, the Liberal Quaker who did much relief work during the Great Famine, and who was later chief secretary for Ireland in Gladstone's 1880 administration. He had been responsible for the Education Act of 1870, which provided for universal elementary education but, unhappy in Ireland, his name was universally and somewhat unfairly associated with COERCION. The nickname arose from his defence, in the House of Commons on 23 August 1880, of the RIC's method of riot dispersal: 'It is more humane that buckshot be used' (as opposed to

the usual dangerous alternative, the ball cartridge). He resigned when Gladstone released Parnell in 1882 under the terms of the KILMAINHAM TREATY.

Buile Shuibhne. *See* SUIBHNE GEILT.

Bulling. In rural Ireland a cow in heat was described as 'bulling'. A strong farmer was once defined as one who 'killed his own pigs and bulled his own cows'.

Bullock, Shan F[adh] (1865–1935). Novelist. Bullock was born at Crom, Co. Fermanagh, son of the land steward of the Earl of Erne. He was educated in Westmeath and became a civil servant in London. His quasi-Gaelic Christian names he took from a character in William Carleton's *TRAITS AND STORIES OF THE IRISH PEASANTRY*, changing them from John William in a gesture of solidarity with Catholic neighbours in Fermanagh, whom he felt were socially and economically disadvantaged by the Orange Order. His Irish novels and stories, *By Thrasna River* (1895), *Dan the Dollar* (1902) and *The Loughsiders* (1924), are set on Lough Erne in Fermanagh and urge a nonsectarian community spirit among the hardworking small farmers of the area. They are characterized by precise observation of the two religious traditions and their emotional and economic interdependency, and by a nostalgia for the simple, goodly, industrious life remembered from a happy childhood. Bullock also collaborated with Emily LAWLESS in a novel of the French invasion of Connacht in 1798, *The Races of Castlebar* (1915).

Bullring, the. An open area in the centre of Wexford town, used as a bull-baiting arena from 1621 to 1770. The sporting event, introduced to the town by the butchers' guild, was held twice a year and the hides of the dead bulls presented to the mayor. According to tradition it was in the Bullring that Cromwell massacred much of the civilian population after he took the town in October 1649. During the 1798 Rising, the area became an armaments factory, with smiths manufacturing pikes and other weapons for the rebels. The Bullring was reconstructed in 1998 as a 1798 bicentenary project and holds a large statue of a Wexford pikeman.

Bull's Head Musical Society, the. *See* FISHAMBLE STREET.

Bull Wall, the. A stone sea wall, which when constructed was known as the Great North Wall, running from the shore at Clontarf on the northside of Dublin Bay, to the North Bull lighthouse. It can be walked for 1.6 km (1 mile) of its length. The idea of constructing a north wall to make Dublin Bay safer for shipping was first mooted by Captain William BLIGH in 1801, and a decision was taken in 1804 to proceed with a different version of it. However, funds – from the sale of the PIGEONHOUSE FORT to the British army – did not become available for the project until 1814. Construction began in 1819, to a design by Francis Giles, an English engineer, and was completed in 1824. *Bull* is another word for 'strand', and the strands on either side of the mouth of the Liffey were known as North Bull and South Bull.

'Bumpers, Squire Jones'. A popular drinking song written *c.*1735 by the Rt Hon. Baron Arthur Dawson (1696–1775) to the tune '*Pléaracha na Jones*' ('Jones's revelry') by Turlough CAROLAN. Dawson wrote the song in honour of his neighbour Squire Jones of Moneyglass, near Toomebridge, Co. Antrim; Dawson himself was a member of the founding family of Castledawson, Co. Derry:

> Come hither, I'll show ye how Phyllis and Chloe
> No more shall occasion such sighs and such groans.
> For no mortal's so stupid as not to quit cup
> When called by good claret and 'Bumpers, Squire Jones.'

Bunched, to be. A current colloquialism meaning 'to be exhausted'.

Bungalow blight. Architects, conservationists, and An TAISCE have for years deplored the construction of separate single-family bungalows in linear or 'strip development' style, along major and minor roads in rural Ireland.

The style of these houses has no connection with vernacular architecture and, according to planners and conservationists, this kind of housing weakens the structure of villages (particularly in counties with low populations, like Leitrim and Mayo), increases dependency on private transport, and stores up social problems for the future. Ireland is, however, a strongly individualistic society, and there is no doubt that many people, perhaps even a majority in rural areas, do not agree with what they think of as the begrudgery (*see* BEGRUDGER) of the expert commentators about what they term the 'suburbanization' of rural Ireland. The term 'bungalow bliss' is used ironically or derogatively of the same phenomenon. Much of the blame for the blight is blamed on a popular do-it-yourself manual, Ted McCarthy's *The Irish Bungalow Book* (1976), which offered off-the-peg plans for bungalows of various sizes and shapes without any reference to the needs of the users, the landscape or the other houses in the area.

Bunratty Castle. A castle situated near the Shannon estuary, Co. Clare. The present Bunratty Castle was built in the middle of the 15th century, although a stone castle is believed to have stood on the site for 200 years previously. It was acquired in a state of dereliction by Lord Gort in 1945; he began the restoration of the castle and bought early furniture and works of art for it. He left the castle and contents in trust to the state and it is now administered by Shannon Heritage. During the summer, banquets are held in the great hall, during which fetching young women play harps and sing, and revellers eat traditional fare and drink mead. The pageant is based on what are believed to have been the customs and menu at the time of the 6th Earl of Thomond, The O'Brien, around the middle of the 17th century. It has become a popular tourist attraction, mainly for American visitors who arrive at the nearby Shannon Airport.

Bunratty Folk Park. A folk park situated beside

Bunratty Castle in Co. Clare, containing reconstructions of elements of Irish rural life as it might have been lived around the year 1900: farmhouses of various types, whitewashed and thatched, a forge, a school, a pub, a village street and various outbuildings. Some of the buildings are occupied, and demonstrations are made of traditional crafts such as weaving and knitting: a BEAN A' TÍ in one of the farmhouses bakes soda bread in the BASTABLE that visitors may sample. There is a fine collection of farming equipment, the Talbot Collection, presented to the folk park by the Rev. M.J. Talbot in 1976. The folk park is a popular tourist attraction, emulated on a smaller scale by MUCKROSS HOUSE in Killarney, Co. Kerry, with its Muckross Traditional Farms.

Bunt. A Dublin colloquialism for a 'hoist' or a 'lift-up'. A child might say to his playmate, 'Gi's a bunt.'

Bunting, Edward (1773–1843). Musician and collector. He was born in Armagh and at the age of 11 was appointed sub-organist in St Anne's Cathedral in Belfast. For the next 30 years 'Atty' Bunting lodged with the McCracken family and was a firm friend of both Mary Ann and Henry Joy (*see* MCCRACKEN, HENRY JOY; MCCRACKEN, MARY ANNE), although he never showed any interest in their revolutionary politics. He was appointed musical scribe to the BELFAST HARP FESTIVAL of 1792 and thereafter was greatly interested in Irish traditional music, travelling the country collecting tunes. He published 66 of these in *A General Collection of the Ancient Irish Music* (1796) and further collections in 1809 and 1840. He has been accused of prettifying the old tunes that he garnered, but the fault may have been that of his publishers. A portly, sophisticated and rather lazy bachelor, he married a Miss Chapman in 1819 and moved to Dublin to become organist at St Stephen's, Mount Street (*see* PEPPERCANISTER). His many Belfast acquaintances continued to visit, advised by his oldest friends to bring 'sweetys, his greatest temptation, for he despises both money and

praise'. Bunting died in 1843 and is buried in MOUNT JEROME.

Burgh, Thomas. *See* CUSTOM HOUSE, THE; COLLINS BARRACKS.

Burgh Castle. A Norfolk fortress, once the Roman *Gariannonum*, and part of a chain of defences along the east coast of England. In the middle of the 7th century (*c.*640), when it was known as Cnobheresburg, the ruins were adapted by the Irish missionaries St FURSA, his blood brothers SS FOILLÁN and ULTAN, and his brothers in Christ, to the creating of an important Celtic monastery.

Burial Place of the Earls. The burial place of Hugh O'NEILL, Earl of Tyrone, in the Spanish church of San Pietro in Montorio in Via Garibaldi in Rome. His grave is marked by a simple slab beside one of the chapels at the end of the church. O'Neill and Roderick O'Donnell of Tyrconnell had arrived in Rome along with their families and followers on 30 April 1608 (*see* FLIGHT OF THE EARLS, THE). Pope Paul V made a residence available to them and they were accorded many honours. Hugh O'Neill's son and two sons of Roderick O'Donnell are also buried in San Pietro in Montorio.

Burke, Edmund (1729–97). Orator and political philosopher. He was born in Arran Quay, Dublin, on 12 January 1729, the son of a Protestant lawyer and a Catholic mother, Mary Nagle from Co. Cork, and spent some of his childhood among his mother's relatives. Educated at Abraham Shackleton's Quaker school in Ballitore, Co. Kildare, and at Trinity College Dublin, he moved to London as a young man and produced a number of works of serious but varied character, among them a philosophical treatise on aesthetics (1757) and an incomplete history of England. He undertook from 1758 the editing of the *Annual Register*, a record of the events of the time.

Opting for a career in politics, Burke spent a period back in Ireland in the 1760s and was later elected to Parliament in Westminster, which led to his production of a long series of pamphlets and speeches on contemporary crises and problems. Particularly notable were his *Thoughts on the Causes of the Present Discontents* (1770) and some outstanding speeches in favour of conciliating the American colonists, such as *On American Taxation* (1774) and *On Conciliation with America* (1775). Two other causes engaged his attention: the government of India and the state of his native land, particularly the disabilities of the Catholic community. These resulted in speeches such as those impeaching Warren Hastings (1778), and his *Letter to Sir Hercules Langrishe* (1792).

It was the issue of the French Revolution that provoked Burke's most widely read and controverted work, especially *Reflections on the Revolution in France* (1790) and *Appeal from the New to the Old Whigs* (1791). In these his ferocious opposition to the revolutionaries, his upholding of religion and his defence of the privileges of the different orders of society were clearly displayed. Even towards the very end, his power and pugnacity in riposte were evident. In his final years he was deeply engaged in trying to make the Irish administration adopt a more conciliatory policy towards the Irish Catholics, fearing what might happen if they did not. He died on his estate in Beaconsfield on 9 July 1797, and is hailed by some as the founder of modern British Conservatism.
See also AGE OF CHIVALRY IS GONE, THE.

Burke, Joe (b.1939). ACCORDION player. He also plays fiddle, pipes and flute. He was born near Loughrea, Co. Galway, where he returned to live after spending some time in the USA. Burke has recorded many solo albums and collaborated with a range of other musicians.

Burke and Hare. The suppliers of corpses to Dr Robert Knox (1791–1862), the principal of an extramural anatomy school in Edinburgh in the 1820s. As a popular rhyme of the period put it:

Burke's the murd'rer, Hare's the thief
And Knox the boy who buys the beef.

Before the Anatomy Act of 1832 it was illegal (and was held to be immoral) to anatomize cadavers, but Knox was prepared to pay good money for fresh material. The so-called Resurrectionists used to haunt graveyards and, unless the family of the deceased could afford to hire guards, the corpse of their dear departed was likely to end up on Knox's dissecting table. William Burke (1792–1929) from Urney, near Strabane, Co. Tyrone, and William Hare from Derry devised a system that cut out the labour of gravedigging. Burke lived in a lodging house kept by Hare (of whose previous life nothing, apart from his place of birth, is known.) When he got £10 for the corpse of an old Highlander from Knox he suggested to Burke that it was a neat way of making money without having to body-snatch. Aided by their 'wives', Burke and Hare disposed of 16 people by getting them drunk and asphyxiating them: Hare covered their mouths and noses while Burke drove all the air out of their lungs.

Burke and Hare were finally arrested after the painstaking work of a policeman called Ferguson. Hare turned King's evidence and Burke was hanged on 28 January 1829; with fitting irony his body was ordered to be delivered to the anatomists. Before he died Burke exonerated Knox from all complicity. Hare is thought to have gone south to work at a limekiln and to have been blinded by his fellow workers when they discovered who he was. He died old, blind and destitute, having worked a begging-pitch outside the British Museum.

Burkitt, Denis Parsons (1911–93). Physician and medical scientist. Born in Enniskillen, Co. Fermanagh, he qualified as a doctor at Trinity College Dublin. He was a devout Christian and he and his wife Olive, a nurse, decided to work in the developing world. He took up a surgical post in Uganda, where in 1957 he began research on the cancer that was to bear his name, Burkitt's lymphoma, a disease common among children in Africa. He travelled 16,000 km (10,000 miles) across Africa to establish the distribution and incidence of this lymphoma, and eventually discovered a cure for it. After his return to research in London, Burkitt became famous among the general public for his contribution to the nutrition debate: in 1971 he published an influential and ground-breaking paper linking bowel cancer with lack of dietary fibre and recommending a far higher fibre intake in the normal diet. Among his recommendations was 'piebald' mashed potatoes, with the skins retained for added fibre. Burkitt maintained an active professional life, writing and lecturing until the day he died.

Burkitt's lymphoma. *See* BURKITT, DENIS PAR-SONS.

Burntollet Ambush. The end of the radical PEOPLE'S DEMOCRACY protest on 4 January 1969 at Burntollet bridge, about 13 km (8 miles) from Derry. After a four-day march from Belfast, during which the mainly student protesters had been continually harassed by Loyalists, they were, it was later established, led by RUC officers into a well-organized and vicious ambush by a hostile crowd, containing members of the B-SPECIALS. The 'ambush' was followed early the next morning by a violent incursion into Derry's BOGSIDE by the RUC. *See also* FREE DERRY.

Buroo or **broo**. The Ulster and Scots word for both the employment exchange and the un-employment benefit. The word derives from 'bureau'. Being 'on the buroo' was the Ulster equivalent of 'on the dole', especially after the 1927 Employment Insurance Act. The Dublin version was 'on the Labra'. There was an in-evitable sense of resentment with the often petty officialdom associated with 'signing on':

> Last night on my bed as I lay a-dreaming
> I dreamt that I stood in the Labour Buroo.
> The Clerk, he came out and he says. 'I am sorry
> For keeping you standing so long in the queue.'
> He says, 'Take a seat for I'm sure you are tired.
> Just give me your form and I'll sign it for you,
> And if you feel hungry just call for the waiter.'
> I murmured, 'Good heavens, is this the Buroo!'
> 'The Buroo', in *Songs of Belfast* (1978), ed. David Hammond

Burren, the. An extensive area of karst scenery and limestone pavement in Co. Clare, the only such area on the Irish mainland, although it is also to be seen on the ARAN ISLANDS, especially Inis Mór. The Burren covers 130 sq km (50 sq miles) of north Co. Clare, and features caves (of which the Ailwee in Lisdoonvarna is the most celebrated), potholes and TURLOUGHS (seasonal lakes). It is also an area rich in archaeological remains, especially pre-Celtic stone forts and dolmens. There are about 70 ancient burial places, the most famous being the Poulnabrone dolmen, a portal dolmen dat-ing from *c*.4000 BC, about 1.8 m (6 ft) in height. One of Cromwell's surveyors apocryphally described the area as a savage land, yielding not enough water to drown a man, nor a tree to hang him, nor soil to bury him. Although there are no trees the area is of great interest to botanists, the limestone providing a habitat for many species of Alpine plants, especially in the month of May. Of 1400 species of plants native to Ireland about 1100 of them originated in the Burren; there is a comparable richness of butterfly and bird life. The Burren has become a destination for the discerning tourist.

Burton books. A name used for cheap reprints used by children in HEDGE SCHOOLS, after the name of the publishers. They were also known as 'sixpenny books'.

Busáras (Irish, literally 'abode of buses'). Dublin's central bus station in Store Street, near the north city centre. It was opened in October 1953 and is regarded as a classic of modernist Irish architecture. The architect Michael Scott (1905–89) was commissioned by de Valera in 1945 to design what were then envisaged as the CIÉ headquarters, but when the INTERPARTY GOVERNMENT led by John A. Costello came to power in 1948 it rejected the extravagant plan of the previous government and decided to turn the building into an employment exchange for women (christened 'bust station' by Myles na Gopaleen). Work on the building, which cost £1 million in total, was not completed until after Fianna Fáil returned to power in 1951. Civil servants of the Department of Social Welfare occupied part of it, and for many years there was a theatre, the Eblana, in the basement.

Busby Babes. The nickname given to the great Manchester United side of the 1950s built by manager Matt Busby. Dubliner Liam Whelan, who was then 22 years old, was one of eight Busby Babes killed in a plane crash at Munich airport on 6 February 1958.

Bush for every gap (Irish *sceach le h-aghaidh gach bearna*). A term used in HIBERNO-ENGLISH to describe a person who has an answer, an argument or a justification for everything: 'That child has a bush for every gap,' a frustrated mother might complain. In rural Ireland until the modernization of the 1960s and 1970s, most openings in fields would be secured by bushes and branches rather than gates, which were too expensive for farmers' budgets. So rare were gates that a particular field on a farm that had a gate might be designated 'the field of the gate'.

Bushmills. A town in Co. Antrim noted for its WHISKEY distillery, which was first licensed in 1608, and is thus taken to be the world's oldest licit source of whiskey. As well as a regular product known as 'Old Bushmills', the company markets a smoother, more mature blend known as BLACK BUSH, so named from its distinctive label. The name has recently been the source of coarse anatomical jokes.

But. A conjunction meaning 'though' or 'however', placed at the end of a sentence in HIBERNO-ENGLISH, particularly in the city of Dublin, where the final 't' is not pronounced: 'She didn't recognize me but' instead of 'She didn't recognize me, however.'

But as little (Irish *ach chomh beag*). A phrase used in the HIBERNO-ENGLISH of rural Ireland to mean 'either': 'He didn't hurt me, but as little.'

Butler, Eleanor, Countess of Desmond (1545–1638). Eleanor Butler, one of the Ormonds of Co. Kilkenny, married Gerald Fitzgerald, 14th Earl of DESMOND and traditional enemy of her own family, in 1565. The Fitzgeralds of Desmond resented Tudor attempts to interfere in their vast estates, which comprised most of the province of Munster, and two years after her marriage Gerald was arrested and imprisoned at the queen's pleasure in the Tower of London. During this time Eleanor managed his estate and travelled to England, where she petitioned the queen for his release and bore her husband an heir, James. Gerald was eventually released but his infant son was kept in custody. In 1579 Gerald Fitzgerald, incited by his brothers, rebelled against the crown (*see* DESMOND REBELLIONS). During the three brutal years that followed Eleanor stayed by her husband's side, protecting him from danger as they fled from the soldiers or tried to make a stand. In the eyes of the forces of William Pelham, the lord deputy, Eleanor seemed to have supernatural powers, spiriting her husband away on horseback as they were about to capture him. After a final defeat Gerald was captured by bounty hunters and beheaded near Tralee in 1583; all his estates were forfeit. In 1597 Eleanor married a Sligo lord, Donogh O'Connor, and spent the rest of her life in Sligo Castle. Her son died in the Tower in 1601, having had in his lifetime only a few months of freedom.

Butler's Catechism. A catechism devised in 1777 by James Butler, bishop of the Catholic diocese of Cashel and Emly (1774–91). Anglo-Irish by birth and educated in France, he set out in his catechism to impart basic religious instruction in question and answer form, along the lines of 'Who made the world? God made the world.' A later version, *A General Catechism for the Kingdom* (1802), commonly known as the 'Butler General', was a product of collaboration between the four Irish archbishops and the state, which approached church leaders to suggest that the duties of citizenship be emphasized in the aftermath of the 1798 Rebellion. This catechism was the cornerstone of Catholic religious instruction in Ireland until the 1960s, and because of Irish evangelization abroad, influenced religious instruction in Australia (where the Maynooth-Butler Catechism of 1882 was adopted as the national catechism in 1885) and New Zealand, America and parts of Africa.

Butlers of Ormond. *See* ORMOND.

Butt¹. A HIBERNO-ENGLISH term for a small, sturdy person. A person might be described, tautologically, as 'a low-sized butt of a man'. The term 'butty' is also used as an adjective or sobriquet.

Butt². A horse or donkey-cart with high sides, used, for instance, for bringing turf from the bog.

Butt³. A HIBERNO-ENGLISH term for the bottom of a room (i.e. the part furthest from the fire), for instance 'the butt of the kitchen'.

Butt, Isaac (1813–79). Founder of the HOME RULE movement. Born at Cloghan, Co. Donegal, on 6 September 1813, the son of an Anglican clergyman who ministered in Stranorlar in that county, Butt was educated at the Royal School, Raphoe, and at Trinity College Dublin, where he had an outstanding academic career. Between 1834 and 1838 he edited the DUBLIN UNIVERSITY MAGAZINE, which he had helped to found, but relinquished his chair of political economy in 1841 for the greater excitement and richer pickings of the Bar. He gained a forensic reputation almost as great as that of Daniel O'Connell, with whom he regularly engaged in public debate as the voice of conservatism and Protestant ascendancy. The GREAT FAMINE destroyed his faith in the Act of UNION, and he was defence counsel for Smith O'Brien after the abortive rising of 1848 (*see* WIDOW MCCORMICK'S CABBAGE PATCH). He was to defend the FENIANS with equal skill and similar loss of reputation two decades later.

Acquaintance with the aims and ideals of these militants was one of the chief causes for the arch-conservative becoming liberal. It led to a political career based upon the belief that the best solution of the perennial Irish Question lay in some federal association of Ireland and Britain instead of the unworkable Union. Butt's Home Government Association (1870) became the Home Rule League in 1873, and in the general election of 1874 he was returned as member for Limerick and head of a party that had won half the Irish seats in the House of Commons.

However, Butt's extreme constitutionalism and reluctance to embarrass the government led to impatience on the part of younger supporters like Joe Biggar (the BELFAST QUASI-MODO) and Charles Stewart PARNELL, whose policy of obstructionism he found ungentlemanly. He was effectively dismissed as leader of what was to become the IRISH PARTY in February 1879 and died on 5 May in Dundrum, Co. Dublin. He was buried in Stranorlar.

Buttermen. Men who collected the butter from farms and delivered it to the butter markets in the city or town (*see* CHURN).

Buttermilks, the. One of several nicknames for the 4th (Royal Irish) Dragoon Guards. The name is said to come from the fact that they spent much of the 18th century in Ireland and, while there, engaged in dairy farming. Their other nicknames included ARRAN'S CUIRASSIERS and the BLUE HORSE.

Butty. A word meaning a close male friend, almost the equivalent of the American 'buddy', though imported from the north of England:

> The foreman at Killesther – oh yis, yis. He's an oul' butty o' mine – oh, he's a darlin' man, a daarlin' man.
>
> SEAN O'CASEY (1882–1962): *Juno and the Paycock* (1924) Act I

'By Killarney's lakes and fells'. The opening line of a parlour song by Edmund Falconer (1814–79):

> By Killarney's lakes and fells,
> Emerald isles and winding bays,
> Mountain paths and woodland dells,
> Memory ever fondly strays.

Later on in the song, Killarney is described as 'heaven's reflex'.

Byrne, Alfie (1882–1956). Politician. Byrne represented Dublin over a long career (1914–55), first as a Westminster MP, then in the Dáil as an Independent TD (1923–8, 1931–55) and senator (1928–31). He was, most notably, lord mayor of Dublin (1930–9, 1954–5). The dapper, genial Byrne is said to have shaken the hand of every man, woman and child in the city.

Byrne, Biddy. A leading character in the RTÉ rural soap GLENROE. Played by the actress Mary McEvoy, she was sharp-tongued and often driven to distraction by her easy-going husband Miley (Mick Lally). She died in a car accident in the penultimate series.

Byrne, Charles (1761–83). Giant. At the age of 19 he was 2.44 m (8 ft) tall, and travelled about Ireland, England and Scotland exhibiting his great height. In London he inspired a pantomime entitled *The Giant's Causeway*. He died at Charing Cross, London, on 1 June 1783 and his skeleton is preserved in the College of Surgeons in Lincoln's Inn Fields.

Byrne, Donn (pseudonym of Brian Oswald Donn-Byrne or O'Beirne (1889–1928)). Novelist. He was born in New York but brought up in Co. Armagh and Co. Antrim. He learned Irish at University College Dublin and also attended the Sorbonne and Leipzig, returning to New York in 1911. He wrote many stories for popular magazines and an autobiography, *The Rock Whence I Was Hewn* (1929). Among many sentimental romantic novels about Ireland, the most popular are *Blind Raftery* (1924), *Hangman's House* (1924) and *Destiny Bay* (1928). Two novels stand out for their psychological conviction: *Brother Saul* (1925), a gripping account of the career of St Paul, and *The Power of the Dog* (1929), a sympathetic portrait of Lord Castlereagh, the architect of Pitt's Act of Union and Lord Liverpool's foreign secretary. Byrne lived in Dublin from 1922 to 1925 before moving to Co. Cork, where he died in a car accident in Courtmacsherry.

Byrne, Gabriel (b.1950). Actor. He was born in Dublin on 12 May 1950 and educated at University College Dublin. He began his acting career as Coriolanus with the Dublin Shakespeare Company in 1976 and played some minor roles in the Focus Theatre in Dublin. His television début was in the RTÉ drama series *Bracken* with Joe Lynch in 1978, and

his first film was Thaddeus O'Sullivan's *On a Paving Stone Mounted* (1978). During a prolific career, he has played a wide variety of screen roles, in films such as *The Usual Suspects* (1995) and *Smilla's Sense of Snow* (1997). A memoir, *Pictures in my Head*, was published in 1994.

Byrne, Gay (b.1934). Broadcaster. He was born in Donore Avenue, Rialto, Dublin, in what he calls a 'Guinness ghetto' – his father worked on the Guinness barges – on 5 August 1934. Unable to get a job in Guinness like other members of the family, and prevented from attending Trinity College Dublin by his father's early death from cancer in 1952, he worked for a time in insurance and the cinema business before finding work in continuity and newsreading with RTÉ radio. The LATE LATE SHOW, the most successful Irish television programme of all time, ran from 1964 to 1999, and the equally successful radio show, the *Gay Byrne Show*, was broadcast from 1972 to 1997. Byrne's autobiography, *The Time of My Life*, was published in 1989; an earlier volume of memoirs was called *To Whom It Concerns* (1972) in homage to the credit line of *The Late Late Show*.

See also BISHOP AND THE NIGHTIE, THE; FLYNN, PEE; FORBIDDEN FRUIT.

Byrne, Miles (1780–1862). United Irishman. He was born in Monaseed, Co. Wicklow, on 20 March 1780, joined the Society of UNITED IRISHMEN in 1797 and fought at VINEGAR HILL[1] in 1798. Like many of the Wexford rebel leaders, he came from Catholic gentry stock who retained a consciousness of having been dispossessed of their lands a century before:

> How often has my father shown me the lands which belonged to our ancestors now in the hands of the descendants of the sanguinary followers of Cromwell who preserved their plunder and robberies after the restoration of that scoundrel Charles II.
>
> MILES BYRNE: *Memoirs* (1863)

He escaped to the Wicklow Mountains after the rising and went to Dublin, where he worked in a timber yard. Robert EMMET sent him to

Paris to secure French assistance for another rising, but it never materialized. Byrne stayed in France and fought with distinction in the French army during the Napoleonic Wars. He retired from the army in 1835 and spent the rest of his life in Paris, where he died on 24 January 1862. His *Memoirs*, published in 1863, give valuable insight into the 1798 rising in Wexford, asserting that it was a United Irish rebellion rather than a DEFENDERS uprising, as was sometimes claimed.

Byrne, Seamus (1904–68). Playwright. He was born in Dublin and graduated in law from University College Dublin. He practised law in Leitrim for nine years until his arrest in 1940 for IRA involvement. Though given a two-year sentence, he was released nine months later after a three-week hunger strike. His play *Design for a Headstone*, about hunger-strikers in MOUNTJOY JAIL, was produced in the ABBEY THEATRE to the accompaniment of right-wing protests. He was drama critic for the *Catholic Standard* in the 1950s, and his play *Little City*, rejected by the Abbey because of its theme – abortion – was staged by the GATE THEATRE in 1964 as part of the Dublin Theatre Festival. He died in Dublin.

By the neck. A phrase meaning to drink a bottle of beer from the bottle without pouring it into a glass. 'By the neck' is an instruction to the barman. In urban Ireland in the final years of the 20th century, it became common for young people to drink beer 'by the neck', especially if swigging trendy, so-called designer beers. 'By the neck and off the shelf' means 'not poured, not chilled'.

By the new time. A phrase used in HIBERNO-ENGLISH to mean 'at a great rate' or 'without delay': 'She set up a new business and she's getting customers by the new time.' It may derive from the distinction between 'old' (winter) time and 'new' (summer) time, when an extra hour of daylight would allow for extra activity.

By the way. A HIBERNO-ENGLISH phrase meaning 'in pretence': 'He was by the way reading the paper when I was trying to talk to him.' It is the exact equivalent of MORYA.

C

CAB. The Criminal Assets Bureau, established in 1996 and given sweeping powers under the Proceeds of Crime Act of that year to enable the government to seize the (often considerable) ill-gotten gains of drug dealers and other criminals. It has a staff of more than 50, and, operating within the civil legal system, it can freeze assets, seize the property of criminals and liquidate it. It also serves tax and interest penalty summons on those who, although not convicted of crime, cannot explain where they acquired their wealth. CAB collected more that €23 million in tax and interest charges in 2001.

Cabbage Patch Rebellion. A derogatory nickname for the YOUNG IRELAND rising of 1848 (*see* WIDOW MCCORMICK'S CABBAGE PATCH).

Cábóg (Irish, 'clown', 'rustic'). An Irish word used pejoratively in HIBERNO-ENGLISH to mean an ignorant or loutish man. It is sometimes, tautologically, used with 'ignorant': 'Would you look at that ignorant *cábóg*!'

Caboose (Irish *cabús*). A HIBERNO-ENGLISH term, often synonymous with CLEVVY, for a nook or small cupboard in the house in which to squirrel a precious substance like tea, tobacco or money.

Cac or ***caca*** (Irish, 'excrement'). A word borrowed directly from Irish and used in HIBERNO-ENGLISH to mean something or somebody worthless, as well as the obvious excrement. It is sometimes anglicized as 'cack'.
See also SÉAMAS AN CHACA.

'Cad a dhéanfaimíd feasta gan adhmad?'. The opening line of '*Caoineadh Chill Cais*' ('Lament for Cill Cais'), a mournful but rousing ballad from the DÉISE region of Co. Waterford. It is known to many Anglophone Irish people, and often sung at sessions or weddings:

> *Cad a dhéanfaimíd feasta gan adhmad?*
> *Tá deireadh na gcoillte ar lár;*
> *níl trácht ar Chill Cais ná ar a teaghlach*
> *'s ní bainfear a cling go bráth ...*
> (What will we do for timber,
> Now that all the woods are gone?
> Cill Cais and its household have disappeared,
> And its bell will be used no more ...)
> ANON.

Cadden, Mamie (1891–1959). Abortionist. Mary Anne Cadden was born in Scranton, Pennysylvania, USA, the eldest child of Irish immigrants, but grew up in Co. Mayo after the family returned home. In 1926 she qualified as a midwife in Holles Street maternity hospital in Dublin and opened her own nursing home in Rathmines. She served two sentences with hard labour in Mountjoy jail (1939–40 and 1945–50): the first for 'child abandonment', abandoning an unwanted baby born in her nursing home; the latter for 'procuring a miscarriage', that is, carrying out an abortion. On her release she re-established her business in Hume Street, off St Stephen's Green in Dublin.

In 1956 the body of a Mrs Helen O'Reilly was found by a milkman early one morning on Hume Street. She was found to have been five months pregnant and to have died as a result of an embolism when air entered her uterus during the course of an attempted abortion. Mamie Cadden was found guilty of murder and was the last woman sentenced to death in Ireland. However, her sentence was commuted to life imprisonment and she began her sentence in Mountjoy in 1957. The following year she was declared insane and transferred to the Central Lunatic Asylum, where she died in custody in 1959. Although it was clearly not the case that Mamie Cadden intended to kill her clients, the death of Helen O'Reilly is routinely treated as having been wilful and features in collections of Irish murder stories.

Cadráil. A HIBERNO-ENGLISH verb still current, meaning to ramble on tediously or at excessive length (much the same meaning as the original Irish).

Caffler (Irish *cafaire*, 'cheeky fellow'). A Cork slang word for a cheeky young boy, a layabout or a no-good. In Frank O'Connor's short story 'First Confession', Jackie's sister, Nora, calls him a 'dirty little caffler' when he disgraces her in the church.

Caher. *See* RING FORT.

Cahir Castle. A massive 15th-century castle in Co. Tipperary, built on what was an island in the River Suir by the Butlers of ORMOND. It sits on the site of an earlier, 13th-century Butler castle. Its location and superb defensive structures made it virtually impregnable until it was battered by the artillery of the Earl of ESSEX in 1599. It surrendered to Cromwell in 1650 without a struggle. The castle comprises three sections, surrounded by a thick fortifying wall, with the main towers around the innermost section. Because it is in such a good state of preservation and because it is unique among Irish castles in having a fully functioning portcullis, it is a

popular location choice among film-makers: parts of John Boorman's *Excalibur* and of the more recent *Braveheart* were shot here.

Caid (Irish, 'football'). A term still used in Co. Kerry Irish for GAA football (heard, for instance, in match commentaries on RAIDIÓ NA GAELTACHTA). The nominative of the word is given by DINNEEN'S DICTIONARY as *cad*, the possessive form *caid* presumably deriving from the influence on the noun of the verbal noun *ag imirt* ('playing'). *Caid* was the name used in Kerry in pre-GAA days for lengthy and often brutal cross-country contests, in which the whole male population of a parish would turn out to play a neighbouring parish. Such games are documented from as far back as the 14th century. The word is thought to derive from the oxhide or horsehide ball containing an inflated animal bladder that was used for these games.

Caifirín. An Irish word for 'kerchief', 'shawl', used in HIBERNO-ENGLISH to mean a scarf or other informal headdress.

Caighdeán (Irish, 'standard'). The standardization of written Irish, in particular for the purposes of teaching and textbooks, because of the differences between the three main CANÚINTTÍ (dialects) of the Kerry, Connemara and Donegal GAELTACHTs.

In 1945 the publication of *Litriú na Gaeilge – Lámhleabhar an Chaighdeáin Oifigiúil* (*Irish Spelling – the Handbook of the Official Standard*) marked the first attempt at standardization. This was followed in 1958 by *Gramadach na Gaeilge agus Litriú na Gaeilge* (*The Grammar and Spelling of Irish*). Since Niall Ó Dónaill's *Foclóir Gaeilge–Béarla* (*Irish–English Dictionary*) was published in 1978, it has come to be used as the standard spelling resource. The *caighdeán* to be followed in the classroom and used for textbooks and other teaching materials is perceived as being based largely on Connemara Irish (Connemara is the biggest Gaeltacht). This development displeased many people, seeming for teachers in the Gaeltachts outside Connemara to devalue the *canúint* of the local Irish-speaking children; it has gained most currency in Dublin. Irish pupils have never been penalized in examinations for failing to use the *caighdeán*, and for many teachers it co-exists in the classroom with their own preferred kind of Irish.

A *caighdeán* is also seen to exist in traditional music, whereby adjudicators at the All-Ireland FLEADH CHEOIL favour a musician in competition because, for instance, he or she plays fiddle in the Coleman style (*see* COLEMAN, MICHAEL) rather than in the SLIABH LUACHRA style. (COMHALTAS CEOLTÓIRÍ ÉIREANN branches on the ground are dedicated to preserving regional styles when teaching young players.)

Cailleach. An Irish word for 'old woman', 'hag'; the term is reserved in HIBERNO-ENGLISH for a very old woman or witch-like creature.

Cailleach Béara (Irish, 'the hag of Beara'). In Irish folklore a mountain goddess associated with the BEARA PENINSULA on the border of Kerry and Cork, between the Kenmare River and BANTRY BAY. She outlives seven periods of fertility and seven husbands who die of old age; she thus becomes synonymous with extreme longevity.

> *Mise Éire – Sine mé ná an Chailleach Béara.*
> (I am Ireland: I am older than the Old Woman of Beare.)
> PADRAIC PEARSE (1879–1916): 'Mise Éire' (1915)

Cainneach. *See* CANICE.

Cainteoir dúchais. *See* NATIVE SPEAKER.

Caint na ndaoine (Irish, 'talk of the people'). The Irish revival at the end of the 19th and the beginning of the 20th century faced the problem of which kind of language to encourage for the writing of Irish, since so little Irish had been written in the previous hundred years. Those who won the battle favoured *caint na ndaoine,* insisting that the wellspring of Irish was the living language spoken in the GAELTACHTS and that this rather than a literary language should be used for writing. The disadvantages of this decision were that modern literary trends passed Ireland by for decades, and that it encouraged a narrow parochialism rather than a breadth of vision.

See also ATHAIR PEADAR, AN T-.

Cairbre. In Irish mythology, the son of CORMAC MAC ART who brings about the destruction of the FIANNA.

Cairbre Caithcheann (Irish, 'cat-head'). In Irish mythology, a king who had the ears of a cat. He reigned at the time of the MILESIANS over a land stricken with sterility.

Cairo Gang. The intelligence system organized by Sir Henry Wilson (1864–1922) during the ANGLO-IRISH WAR (1919–21) to counter that devised by Michael COLLINS. The gang was effectively destroyed on the morning of BLOODY SUNDAY (21 November 1920), by Collins's SQUAD, whose commander commented:

> There is no crime in detecting and destroying in war-time the spy and the informer. They have destroyed without trial. I have paid them back in their own coin.

The name came from the successful counter-intelligence operation mounted by Wilson's men during the Egyptian rebellion of 1919. Wilson himself was assassinated on 22 June 1922 by two IRA members who had been in the British army, by special order of Collins.

Caisearbhán. The Irish word for 'dandelion', used in HIBERNO-ENGLISH to refer not just to the weed, which was fed to pigs, but to a person considered sour or sulky.

Caisleáin Óir (Irish, 'golden castles'). The title of the best-known novel (1924) of Séamus Ó Grianna, who used his mother's Christian name, MÁIRE, as a pseudonym. An often bitter account of life in the ROSSES of Donegal, the novel describes the young love of Séimí Phádraig Dhuibh for Babaí Mháirtín, his parting to labour in Scotland, and the long years of exile before his return from the Yukon, a rich man. The last chapter describes his slow journey home and his meeting with the faithful Babaí, no longer young or beautiful. He leaves, unrecognized, with the words, ostensibly about the weather: '*Is é a tá … fuar, fuar*' ('It is indeed … bitterly cold'). Though the characters are one-dimensionally sentimental, the book gives a vivid picture of the life and culture of that part of the Donegal

GAELTACHT, with its English-speaking schools, GOMBEEN MEN, knitting as an underpaid cottage industry, and AIRNEÁN. The title, literally 'golden castles', means 'castles in the air', and refers to the wishful dreams of the two young lovers as they gaze upon the occasional spectacular sunset.

Cáit Ní Dhuibhir. A Jacobite personification of Ireland, deriving from the beautiful AISLING of that name. The poem is anonymous, belonging to the category known as *amhráin na ndaoine* ('songs of the people') and was first published in *BOLG AN TSOLÁTHAIR* in 1904.

> Tráithnóinín beag déanach 's mo thréada agam á
>   gcur ón síon,
> ar leataoibh chnoic im aonar, 's do ghléasta do bhí
>   mo phíob,
> bhí an ceol ba bhinne ab fhéidir ag éanlaith is gach
>   nóta fíor,
> 's do réir mar thuigeas féin iad, beidh Éire 'ge Cáit
>   ní Dhubhir.
> (Late one evening as I was sheltering my herd from
>   the weather,
> I was alone on the side of a hill with my pipe tuned.
> I heard the birds singing most sweetly, every note a
>   true one.
> And insofar as I could understand them, they were
>   saying that Ireland would revert to Cáit Ní
>   Dhuibhir.)

Cake. A round of soda bread, made with white, brown or yellow meal. This was traditionally baked in a BASTABLE or pot oven over the fire, with hot coals piled on the lid. 'Sweet cake' was the term used for a cake with fruit and eggs, or a shop-bought confection, to distinguish it from a 'cake of bread'. The word is also used metaphorically, as in 'That lad is going to make a cake of himself' (if he continues with a particular behaviour).

Calamity Water. A kind of rough POTEEN, as described by William ALLINGHAM in his *Diary* (1907) for 12–13 May 1863:

> The English rustic, getting drunk, bellows
> discordant song, tumbles down and snores, the
> Irishman quarrels and strikes. Perhaps the kind of
> drink has something to do with it. Pothouse beer

is bad, but raw public house whisky is a frightful potation. What a country is Ireland! her chief manufacture is *Calamity Water*, a name too of her own devisal.

See also DOUBLE; SINGLINGS.

Calidcheann (Old Irish, 'hard head'). The sword of CÚCHULAINN. It is pronounced 'kalid kin'.

Call. A word used in HIBERNO-ENGLISH to mean 'need' or 'right', often used in the negative, as in 'He had no call to insult me like that.'

Callanan, Jeremiah Joseph (1795–1829). Poet and pioneering translator of Irish verse. He was born in Ballinahassig, Co. Cork, and studied for the priesthood at Maynooth. He left in 1816 (before being ordained) and attended Trinity College Dublin for two years before poverty drove him to enlist in the British army. Bought out, he joined the staff of Dr Maggin's school (*see* O'DOHERTY, SIR MORGAN). He already had some reputation as a poet, mainly of English versions of Gaelic poems that he had collected, notably 'Droimeann Donn Dílis' and 'Príosún Cluain Meala' ('The Convict of Clonmel'), which is a lively and faithful version of the original:

> How hard is my fortune
> And vain my repining;
> The strong rope of fate
> For this young neck is twining!
> My strength is departed,
> My cheeks sunk and sallow,
> While I languish in chains
> In the gaol of Clonmala.

He attempted a Byronic sequence with *The Recluse of Inchidoney* (1830), but is now remembered mainly for 'The Outlaw of Loch Lene' and the lyric 'Gougane Barra'. He fell in love with Alicia Fisher, but they parted because she was a Methodist and refused to become a Catholic. He died of a throat infection aggravated by tuberculosis when working as a tutor to a Cork family living in Lisbon.

Call a set, to. The term used for the calling aloud of the different figures or movements of the SET DANCES by an experienced dancer, usually a teacher, at a CÉILÍ or other traditional dance.

Call My Brother Back. The first and best-loved novel (1939) of Michael MCLAVERTY. It is set partly in Rathlin Island and partly in Belfast at the time of the Anglo-Irish War (1919–21), the danger increased by added sectarian freelancers. The McNelis family have had to leave their home on the island after the death of their father and at the urging of Alec, the eldest son, and now live in a Belfast slum. The book is mediated through the child Colm, whose confusion and sadness the reader shares. Sent as a boarder to a college in Belfast by the local curate, he pines for his family and the life he knew, but his joy at regaining them is marred by the realization that Rathlin is lost to him forever. The family's grief becomes unbearable when Alec is shot as a Volunteer. McLaverty's pleasure in the bustle and life of what was in normal times a friendly city shines through his account of urban life.

Calmie Custure Me. Part of Ancient Pistol's response to his French prisoner's flattery:

> *Pistol:* Yield, cur.
> *French soldier:* Je pense que vous êtes le gentilhomme de bonne qualité.
> *Pistol:* Qualtitie calmie custure me. Art thou a gentleman? What is thy name? Discuss.
> WILLIAM SHAKESPEARE: *Henry V,* IV.iv

Dismissed by early editors as 'Pistolese French, of which the meaning is irrecoverable', the words are actually a garbled version of a refrain from an Irish song. The line (which is also the title of the song) should read: '*Cailín as cois tSiúire mé*' ('I am a girl from the banks of the (River) Suir'), and is pronounced 'colleen is cush tur-uh may.' The fact that Pistol used it as mock-French indicates its familiarity to Shakespeare's contemporaries, and argues for a considerable Irish presence in Elizabethan London.
See also CONCOLINEL.

Camán (Irish 'hurling stick', 'crooked stick'). The implement used to play the GAA games of HURLING and CAMOGIE.
See also CLASH OF THE ASH, THE.

Cameron, Charles. *See* HOUSEFLY CAMPAIGN, THE.

Cameron Commission. A three-person inquiry team under the chairmanship of Lord Cameron, the other members being Professor Sir John Biggart and J[ames] J[oseph] Campbell (1910–79) (*see* ULTACH). The inquiry was set up in January 1969 by Terence O'NEILL to inquire into the civil disturbances after 5 October 1968 in Derry. They reported in September 1969, when the rush of events had made their conclusions largely irrelevant and certainly redundant. They found that most of the complaints made by the CIVIL RIGHTS MOVEMENT were justified: the perpetuation of Unionist control by electoral manipulation, the discrimination in the Unionist councils (a majority) in jobs and housing, the 'hidebound' and 'complacent' attitude of the STORMONT government, the SPECIAL POWERS ACT, the continued existence of the B-SPECIALS, and the general 'second-class' citizenship of Catholics in Northern Ireland. They also criticized the 'ineptness' of the RUC, and ominously drew attention to the manipulation by Republicans of the Civil Rights Movement.

Camogie. The female equivalent of HURLING, although with no physical contact allowed. It was formally established in 1904 in order to provide women with a Gaelic sport of their own, and the first inter-county game was held in Jones's Road (later CROKE PARK) in 1912. Camogie has a separate governing body, Cumann Comagaíochta na nGael, but is closely associated with the GAA. Camogie teams are twelve-a-side, the same type of SLIOTAR and CAMÁN are used, and there is the same scoring system as in Gaelic hurling and football, involving both goals (three points) and points, although the game lasts for only 50 minutes. There is also an ALL-IRELAND championship in camogie, although it is not organized on a provincial basis, as not all counties participate. Despite some improvement in recent years, it is still felt by players and supporters of women's Gaelic games that they are very much the poor relation, as regards the GAA itself and especially as regards the media.

Camorra, the. The term used by Fine Gael leader

James DILLON to describe a gang of five – Neil BLANEY, Brian Lenihan, Donogh O'Malley, Kevin BOLAND and Charles HAUGHEY – during the Dáil debate on Jack LYNCH's nomination as taoiseach in December 1966: 'the camorra, who are now sharpening their knives and whirling their tomahawks'. (The camorra is a Neapolitan secret society similar to the mafia.)

Campbell, Joseph (Seosamh Mac Cathmaoil) (1879–1944). Poet and playwright. He was born in Belfast and educated at St Malachy's College. He left school at the age of 16 suffering from a debilitating condition resulting from scarlatina. His enforced idleness was put to good effect. By the time he was 20 he was not only running his father's construction business with the help of his younger brother John, but had also become extremely well-read in poetry and Irish history. He was naturally drawn to that burst of literary activity that might be regarded as the Ulster branch of the IRISH LITERARY REVIVAL. It was exemplified in the periodical *Uladh* (November 1904–September 1905), the four issues of which were rather like SAMHAIN and BEAL-TAINE but with a distinctive Ulster flavour. The most obvious evidence of Ulster-based literary activity was seen in the plays of the ULT (*see* DAMN YEATS, WE'LL WRITE OUR OWN PLAYS! and DUNGANNON CLUBS).

Campbell wrote a play, *The Little Cowherd of Slaigne* (1905), and set words to traditional airs that had been collected by the composer Herbert Hughes. These were published as *Songs of Uladh* (1904) under the name Seosamh Mac Cathmaoil, with decorations by his brother as Seaghan Mac Cathmaoil. Among the songs was the famous 'My Lagan Love' (*see below*), which has since become a standard concert piece and has been recorded even by popular musicians. Other collections of poetry followed: *The Rushlight* (1906), *The Gilly of Christ* (1907) and *The Mountainy Singer* (1908).

Campbell settled in Lackendarragh, Co. Wicklow, with his wife Agnes Maude in 1912. Always of strong Nationalist feelings, he was peripherally involved in the EASTER RISING and as a known Republican was interned for 18 months in the Curragh during the CIVIL WAR. He lived in the United States from 1925, having parted from his wife. He later returned to Ireland and lived a reclusive life on a small farm in Glencree in Co. Wicklow until his death.

> Where Lagan stream sings lullaby,
> There blows a lily fair.
> The twilight is in her eye,
> The night is on her hair.
> And like a lovesick leananshee,
> She hath my heart in thrall.
> Nor life I own, nor liberty,
> For love is lord of all.
>
> SEOSAMH Ó CATHMHAOIL: 'My Lagan Love', in *Songs of Uladh* (1904)

Campbell, Michael (1924–84). Novelist. He was born in Dublin and educated at Trinity College Dublin and King's Inns. He became the *Irish Times* London correspondent and was the author of several novels: *Peter Perry* (1956), about Dublin art circles, *Oh Mary, This London* (1961), *Across the Water* (1961) and *The Princess in England* (1964), about the Irish in Britain. His best-known work, *Lord Dismiss Us* (1967), deals with homosexuality in his old school, St Columba's, in Rathfarnham, Dublin. He became 4th Baron Glenavy on the death of his brother Patrick CAMPBELL in 1980.

Campbell, Patrick (1913–80). Humorist. He was born in Dublin, brother of the novelist Michael Campbell and son of the 2nd Baron Glenavy, acceding to the title in 1963 on the death of his father. He was educated at Oxford, the Sorbonne and in Germany. He served in the Irish Marine Service during the war and was on the staff of the *Irish Times* from 1944 till 1947 under R.M. SMYLLIE (NICHEVO), becoming its wittiest 'Quidnunc' and third-leader writer. He continued as a humorous columnist for the rest of his life, working for London papers such as the *Sunday Dispatch* and *Sunday Times*. A slight speech impediment he turned to advantage, finding copy in the disability and overcoming it sufficiently to become a much-loved personality on television. His articles were reprinted in 16 volumes, including *The P-p-penguin Patrick Campbell* (1965) and *A Short Trot with a Cultured Mind* (1952), a title that sums up his comic genius. He died in Cannes, his home in later life.

Canary Wharf. The site in London's Docklands of a massive bomb, detonated at 7.01 p.m. on 9 February 1996. Two men were killed, 100 were injured and damage worth more than £85 million sustained. It spelt the end of the Provisional IRA ceasefire, which had been established on 31 August 1994. The RUC immediately reintroduced security measures and began to wear flak jackets again on patrol. SINN FÉIN claimed surprise at the event, the political effect of which was generally negative: it reinforced the hardline stance of the Ulster Unionist Party and the Democratic Unionist Party on DECOMMISSIONING, and dismayed not only the Nationalist population but peace brokers such as US President Bill Clinton.

Candida Casa (Latin, 'white house'). The novitiate built of white stone *c.*400 at Whithorn, near Wigtown in Galloway, Scotland, by St Ninian, (d.*c.*432), a British bishop who was sent from Rome to preach the gospel to the Picts. It was the school of such Irish abbots as ENDA of Aran and FINNIAN OF MOVILLE, and played an important part in the development of Irish monasticism.

Canice (also **Cainneach** or **Kenneth**). A Pict born in the Roe valley of Co. Derry *c.*525 and educated by FINNIAN OF CLONARD and Cadoc of Llancarfan near Cardiff. He worked for many years among the islands of the west coast of Scotland and acted with COMGALL as guide and interpreter for COLUM CILLE (Columba) in his missions to the Picts. His name is preserved in several places, notably Inch Kenneth, a small island off Mull, and it is by that name that he is venerated in Scotland as a saint. He built a church on the site now known as St Andrews, in Fife. Returning to Ireland, he founded the monastery of Aghaboe in Co. Laois and was buried in its precincts *c.*599. He is the patron saint of the diocese of Ossory and has given his name to its capital, Kilkenny (Irish *Cill Chainnigh*, 'Canice's church'). His feast day is 11 October.

Cannawaun (Irish *ceannbhán*, literally 'white-headed'). A word used in HIBERNO-ENGLISH for bog cotton, the white-headed plant that blows in summertime in bogs and moors.

Canny. An Ulster (originally Scots) word, sometimes pronounced 'conny', meaning 'careful' or 'cunning'. On a frosty morning, a driver might declare the intention of 'taking it conny on the roads'.

Cant[1]. *See* SHELTA.

Cant[2]. An auction, deriving from the Irish word *ceant*. Canting was the system, common in the 18th and early 19th centuries, by which the lease to a rented farm was auctioned off to the highest bidder when it expired. The tenant had no right to maintain his tenancy unless he could match the highest bid.
See also THREE FS.

Canúint (Irish, 'speech', 'expression'). Any of the several dialects of Irish spoken in the GAELTACHTS, notably in Connemara, Donegal and west Kerry, but also including the lesser differences between Kerry and the other Munster Gaeltachts of the DÉISE and MUSKERRY. All Irish-speakers are mutually comprehensible, especially since the advent of RAIDIÓ NA GAELTACHTA made them more familiar with one another's speech (although the differences in pronunciation may still appear considerable to the non-Irish speaker).

CAO. An acronym for the Central Applications Office, based in Galway. Part of every Irish student's life, the CAO is a clearing-house for all third-level (post-secondary) applicants in the Republic of Ireland. The CAO application form has to be completed every year by 1 February. Broadsheet newspapers give much space to CAO applications, change-of-mind forms and, after the results of the Leaving Certificate appear in August, to the awarding of college places.

Caoilte (Irish, 'thin man'). The fleetest of the warriors of the FIANNA and their finest poet. A Christianization of the myth has him returning from the OTHERWORLD to relate to St Patrick the adventures of the brotherhood. In a late story he appears as a living torch to guide a king through a forest:

> The host is riding from Knocknarea
> And over the grave of Clooth-na-Bare;
> Caoilte tossing his burning hair,
> And Niamh calling, *Away, come way…*
>
> W[ILLIAM] B[UTLER] YEATS (1865–1939): 'The Hosting of the Sidhe' (1893), in *The Wind among the Reeds* (1899)

See also ACALLAM NA SENÓRACH.

Caoineadh. *See* KEEN.

'Caoineadh Airt Uí Laoghaire'. The most famous of all Irish KEENS, inspired by the violent death of Art Ó Laoghaire in 1773 but not written down from the oral tradition until the 19th century. In it, Art's wife Eibhlín Dubh (*see* NÍ CHONAILL, EIBHLÍN DUBH) laments in language that is formal, incantatory and traditional but also impassioned:

> *Mo ghrá go daingean tú!*
> *Lá dá bhfaca thú*
> *ag ceann tí an mhargaidh*
> *thug mo shúil aire dhuit*
> *thug mo chroí taitneamh dhuit*
> *d'éalaíos óm charaid leat*
> *I bhfad ó bhaile leat.*
> (My love for ever
> The day I caught sight of you
> at the gable of the market house
> my eye took you in
> my heart opened to you
> I ran away from my friends with you
> far from my home.)

It is one of the most beautiful love poems in modern Irish and has been much translated.

'Caoineadh Mhuire' (Irish, 'Mary's lament'). The most famous song of a traditional cycle of the Passion, which also includes 'Caoineadh na Páise' ('the Passion'), 'Caoineadh na dTrí Muire' ('Lament of the three Marys') and 'Caoineadh na Maighdine' ('Lament of the Virgin'). Although they are devotional songs, they draw heavily on the Irish custom of keening (*see* KEEN), which often expresses defiance and anger rather than resignation:

> *A Pheadair a aspail an bhfaca tú mo ghrá geal?*
> *Ochón agus ochón ó!*
> *Do chonaic ar ball é i lár a namhad*
> *Ochón agus ochón ó!*
> (Oh Peter, apostle, have you seen my bright love
> My grief, my grief
> I saw him a while ago in the middle of his enemies
> My grief, my grief!)

Nóirín NÍ RIAIN's album *Caoineadh na Maighdine* (1980) brings together many devotional songs of this type from all the Gaeltachts.

Caorán. An Irish word for 'clod' or 'fragment', used in HIBERNO-ENGLISH (particularly that of Munster) for a small, hard piece of dry turf, such as might be used for lighting a fire.

Captain Boyle. *See* BOYLE, CAPTAIN.

Captain Fantastic. The nickname given to Barnsley-born soccer player Mick McCarthy (b.1959), who captained the Republic of Ireland team managed by Jack CHARLTON with distinction in the World Cup campaigns of 1990 and 1994. *Captain Fantastic* was also the title he gave to his World Cup diary, published in 1990. McCarthy won 57 Irish caps in all. When he became manager of the Irish team after Charlton's retirement in 1996, Roy Keane (*see* KEANO) inherited McCarthy's heroic nickname. McCarthy resigned as manager in late 2002, a victim of fierce media and public criticism for, among other things, his handling of a major dispute with Keane during the World Cup finals of summer 2002.

Captain Mac. The nominally nautical editor of the children's column of the *IRISH PRESS*, which has a drawing of a handsome, not too old sea-dog at its top. Members of his club could obtain a metal badge with coupons cut from the paper and a small fee. Any members who successfully proposed six new members were sent an extra chevron that hung below the membership badge. The word *cinnire* printed on the chevron indicated that they were 'leaders'. The column's tone was rather serious, with plenty of reminders of national pride.

Captain Moonlight. A personification of agrarian outrage. For more than 80 years from the 1760s until the Great Famine, SECRET SOCIETIES with such names as WHITEBOYS, TERRY ALTS, CARDERS and MOLLY MAGUIRES inflicted intermittent assaults and property damage on tenant farmers and landlords at times of scarcity or agricultural change. Threats were issued in the name of a supposed leader with the rank of captain – for instance 'Captain Rock' led the Rockites in the 1820s. When PARNELL was threatened with arrest in 1881 he warned, 'Captain Moonlight will take my place.'

Captain Moonlite. The nickname of Andrew George Scott, a 19th-century Irish bushranger in Australia.

Caravats and Shanavests (Irish, *carabhaití*, 'cravats', 'nooses'; *sean-bheisteanna*, 'old waistcoats'). The names of two rival factions (*see* FACTION FIGHTING), whose feuding in the years 1806–11 caused much violence in the counties of Munster and south Leinster, with minor outbreaks in Queen's County (Laois) and Kildare. Originally regarded as an example of classical faction fighting, the feud is now seen as having a deeper sociological dimension. The Shanavests were small but prosperous farmers, while the Caravats were largely labourers, and the impetus to violence came from the Shanavests' determination to resist the challenge from below.

Carbery, Ethna (1866–1902). The pseudonym of Anna MacManus (*née* Johnson), a Nationalist poet, who was born in Ballymena, Co. Antrim. She contributed many poems to *The* NATION and *United Ireland*, and with Alice MILLIGAN founded in 1896 the Nationalist newspaper SHAN VAN VOCHT (originally the *Northern Patriot*). It was suppressed after three years because of Unionist complaint and the existence of a Nationalist journal, Arthur Griffith's *The* UNITED IRISHMAN. She married Seumas MACMANUS in 1901. Her poetry, mainly patriotic and including the famous ballad 'Roddy

McCorley' and 'The Passing of the Gael' (quoted by Joxer in JUNO AND THE PAYCOCK), was published in *The Four Winds of Ireland* (1902). Her prose was collected as *The Passionate Hearts* (1903), stories set in the west of Ireland, and *In the Celtic Past* (1904).

Carders. A rural protest movement of cottage weavers, also called Threshers or Shakers, who were active in Co. Mayo in the first decade of the 19th century. The name came from their threats to use their spiked carding combs on any who crossed them. Their activity – as with many similar groups – was directed against Anglican tithes and stipends paid to Catholic clergy, but there was also an instinctive opposition to the increased mechanization of the weavers' trade.

Cardinal points. The compass points applied to the human body. In Ireland from the most ancient times positions were based on the supposition that one was facing east. East was, therefore, front, west back, north left and south right. A patient, for example, might explain to a doctor that the pain was west in his throat.

Cards of the Gambler, The. A novel (1953) by Benedict KIELY that imaginatively mixes folklore with a realistic story. In it the elements of magic and cleverness, and the symbols and significant locations, are wonderfully and wittily matched: the gambler of the title is granted limited magical power, survives a descent into hell and discovers that heaven is rather like an airport.

> The gambler went off until he came to the gates of heaven. But the gates were closed against him and he wouldn't be allowed to enter. He sat outside on a rock and began to play patience. Peter of the Keys took pity on him.

Care. A noun used colloquially in Dublin to mean children or family in remarks directed to a parent: 'How's the care?'

Carew, Sir George (1555–1629). Elizabethan soldier and administrator. He served as president of Munster 1600–3, brutally suppressing the rebellion in that province (*see* NINE YEARS' WAR). In June 1602, after the Battle of KINSALE had put an end to the hopes of the Ulster chieftains, he stormed Dunboy Castle on the Beara Peninsula in Co. Cork, the event that precipitated the Long March (see O'SULLIVAN BEARE, DONALL). He enjoyed considerable prestige at the court of Queen Elizabeth because of his success in Munster, and was also involved in the planning of the ULSTER PLANTATION.

Carleton, William (1794–1869). Novelist. He was born to a family of Irish-speaking farmers at Prillisk in the Clogher Valley of Co. Tyrone. He was the youngest of 14 children and inherited from his mother a store of BÉALOIDEAS, which stood him in good stead in his vocation. His memories of youth were entirely idyllic and his account of poor 19th-century Irish peasantry is unmatched. His education was the rough and ready but remarkably extensive one of the hedge scholar (see HEDGE SCHOOLS), and in the largely autobiographical TRAITS AND STORIES OF THE IRISH PEASANTRY he shows acquaintance with experiences as diverse as LOUGH DERG pilgrimages, FACTION FIGHTING and RIBBONMEN. Though he lived for much of his life in Dublin, he still wrote of the people he knew, and such realistic novels as *Fardorougha the Miser* (1839), *The Black Prophet: A Tale of the Famine* (1847) and *The Tithe Proctor* (1849) show his genius at its best. In his *Anglo-Irish Essays* the critic John Eglinton (1868–1961) wrote:

> Carleton was the man sent by God in response to the general clamour for an Irish Walter Scott.

Carn (Irish, 'pile', 'mound'). A word often applied to a pile of stones on top of a mountain, and often anglicized to 'cairn'. A court cairn is a megalithic burial chamber topped by a mound of earth and stones.

Carn aoiligh (Irish, 'pile of manure'). A manure heap, such as stood in every Irish farmyard until the mechanization of agriculture from the 1960s onwards.

Carney, James (1914–89). Gaelic scholar, born in Portlaoise and educated at University College Dublin and Bonn. A professor at the Dublin Institute of Advanced Studies, he was an authority on Old and Middle Irish poetry. His published works include *The Problem of St Patrick* (1961) and *Early Irish Poetry* (1965).

Carolan, Turlough (1670–1738). Harper and composer. He was born in Nobber, Co. Meath, but as a small child moved to Co. Roscommon. He was blinded by smallpox at the age of 18, but learned to play the harp and became an itinerant player, welcomed into the houses of aristocracy and gentry. He set his own words to music, and as a composer was influenced by the style of Italian contemporaries like Arcangelo Corelli. His wake at Kilronan, near Keadue in Co. Roscommon, is said to have lasted for four days, with thousands of mourners from all over Ireland. One collection of Carolan's music was published during his lifetime and several others in the 18th and 19th centuries, when his reputation was high (Edward BUNTING included some of Carolan's tunes in his 1809 and 1840 collections). It is estimated that up to 200 of his pieces survive, many with words as well as music. Some of these were arranged by musicians such as Seán Ó RIADA and PLANXTY[2] and became enduringly popular in the traditional repertoire.
See also HARP.

Carrageen moss (Irish *carraigín*, 'little rock'). A kind of seaweed picked at low tide. It is harvested in the west of Ireland and sold in dried form. Because it contains a natural thickening agent, it may be used as a gelatine substitute, for instance in carrageen mould, a type of blancmange. When reconstituted in boiling water with honey and lemon juice it is an effective cure for coughing or 'chestiness'.

Carrantuohill. The highest mountain in Ireland, at 1041 m (3414 ft). It is in the MACGILLICUDDY REEKS of Co. Kerry, near Killarney. The challenging terrain and unpredictable weather of the area have caused regular deaths, even among experienced mountaineers.
See also KERRY MOUNTAIN RESCUE TEAM.

Carrickmacross lace. Carrickmacross in Co. Monaghan produced some of the finest lace in Europe in the early 19th century. Grey Porter, wife of the rector of Donaghmoyne, introduced the craft to local women. The nuns of the St Louis order in the town later helped to preserve lacemaking.

See also CLONES LACE.

Carried away. A term used in HIBERNO-ENGLISH to describe someone who had the appearance of a CHANGELING.

Carrowkeel. A site overlooking Lough Arrow, near Ballinafad, Co. Sligo, containing 14 Neolithic passage graves topped by stone cairns. These were built by Stone Age farmers and date from *c.*3000 BC.

Carrowmore. A megalithic cemetery and sacred ground situated just outside Sligo town and containing about 40 passage graves, some topped by cairns and dolmens. The oldest tomb dates from about 4200 BC, but it is thought that the burial place was used in turn by Bronze Age and Iron Age people. Artefacts recovered in excavation include items of personal adornment and tools.

Carruth, Michael (b.1967). Boxer. He was born in Dublin on 9 July 1967, one of triplets, and learned to box at the Drimnagh Club. He sensationally beat Cuban Juan Hernandez, the reigning world champion, to win a welterweight gold medal at the 1992 Barcelona Olympics, Ireland's first gold medal in boxing. He had many other competitive successes, both as an amateur and after he turned professional in 1993.

Carson, Edward (1854–1934). Lawyer and Unionist leader. He was born in Dublin on 9 February 1854, and after an undistinguished academic career at Trinity College Dublin was called to the Irish Bar in 1877. He was nicknamed 'COERCION Carson' because of his vigour as crown prosecutor during the PLAN OF CAMPAIGN. Elected Liberal-Unionist MP for Dublin University in 1892 he began to make a name for himself at the English Bar, to which he was called in 1893. His most public case was in the Oscar WILDE vs. Marquess of Queensbury libel action (1895) when his successful defence of his client, mainly by the unnerving and dram-

atic cross-questioning of Wilde himself (with whom he had been friends as an undergraduate), led to the plaintiff's being arraigned for homosexual acts.

Carson was knighted in 1900 and appointed English solicitor-general. Though he became very rich through his law practice his political preoccupation was a determination to preserve the UNION of Ireland with Britain. This meant alliance with Ulster Unionists with whom he had little affinity except in their united opposition to HOME RULE. He became leader of the Unionist Party in 1910 and provided the charismatic leadership that led to the foundation of the UVF (*see* CARSON'S ARMY). He was tireless in his platform appearances and gave the public impression that he was prepared to embark on a civil war (while being considerably more conciliatory in private):

> In the event of this proposed parliament being thrust upon us, we solemnly and mutually pledge ourselves not to recognize its authority … I don't care whether it is treason or not.
>
> Speech in Coleraine, Co. Derry, 21 September 1912.

The clearest evidence of his charisma was the signing of the ULSTER COVENANT, when, on 28 September 1912, 218,000 men pledged themselves 'to use all means to defeat the present conspiracy'. During the First World War Carson was in turn attorney-general, first lord of the Admiralty and a member of the war cabinet. The partitioning of Ireland in 1920 he regarded as a miserable second best, and he had little to do with the new regime in Northern Ireland except to represent Duncairn as MP at Westminster. He was created Lord Carson of Duncairn, served as lord of appeal (1921–9) and died at his home in Kent on 22 October 1935. He was given a naval funeral at St Anne's Cathedral, Belfast, where he is buried.

Carson remains a paradoxical figure, notoriously hypochondriacal, deeply Irish (he never lost his Dublin accent) and utterly convinced of the virtues of the Union. His last years were spent happily with his second, much younger wife, and their son, who was born in 1920. He is remembered in the anonymous squib:

Edward Carson had a cat
That sat upon the fender
And every time it caught a rat
It shouted 'No surrender!'

Carson's Army. The nickname of the first manifestation of the UVF, founded in January 1913 to counter the third HOME RULE bill. Edward CARSON was the charismatic figure, with a brilliant rhetorical style, but the real mobilization, during the years 1911–12, was the work of James CRAIG, later Lord Craigavon. He assembled a force of 90,000, mainly through Orange lodges, and drafted a number of willing retired British army officers to train and lead them. Their arms were eventually supplemented by the LARNE GUN-RUNNING; although the guns obtained were not entirely suitable, Carson, intending the existence of the force to be a tool in his implacable defence of the Union, had succeeded in a significant political coup. Many of the UVF joined Kitchener's New Army to form the 36th (Ulster) Division in the First World War, thus postponing the problem of resistance to Home Rule for the time being. About 5500 of them, many wearing Orange collarettes, were slaughtered at the Ancre, a tributary of the Somme, in July 1916 (*see* OBSERVE THE SONS OF ULSTER MARCHING TOWARDS THE SOMME). The UVF was revived again in July 1920 during the Anglo-Irish War, but was soon brought under the official aegis of the Ulster Special Constabulary (*see* B-SPECIALS).

> We will set up a government. I am told it will be illegal. Of course it will. Drilling is illegal. I was reading an act of parliament forbidding it. The Volunteers are illegal and the government know they are illegal, and the government dare not interfere with them. Don't be afraid of illegalities.
>
> From a speech by Carson at Newry, Co. Down, on 7 September 1917

Carton House. A handsome Palladian mansion situated just outside the town of Maynooth in Co. Kildare. It was designed by Richard CASTLE, who also designed the family's town house, LEINSTER HOUSE, for the 19th Earl of Kildare. The land at Carton had belonged since 1176 to the Fitzgerald family (Earls of Kildare from 1315). In 1747 James, 20th Earl of Kildare (from 1766 1st Duke of Leinster), married Lady Emily Lennox, who was responsible for the landscaping of the estate at Carton. One of their 23 children was Lord Edward FITZGERALD. In 1815 the 3rd Duke sold Leinster House to the ROYAL DUBLIN SOCIETY and enlarged Carton House. It remained in the possession of the Fitzgeralds until the 1920s, when the future 7th Duke, then the third in line of succession to the title, mortgaged his birthright to pay off a gambling debt of £67,500. It is now in private ownership.

Cary, [Arthur] Joyce [Lunel] (1888–1957). Novelist. He was born in Derry, a member of a family that had held land at Castle Cary near Moville in Inishowen since the reign of Elizabeth I. The family fortunes were then in decline, and Cary was reared in London where his father was a civil engineer. Holidays were spent in his grandmother's house in Inishowen and two of his novels, *Castle Corner* (1938) and *A House of Children* (1941), draw heavily upon these summer visits and paint a picture of life in a decaying BIG HOUSE, without Somerville and Ross gothicism, but as half-understood by an intelligent child. However, most of Cary's novels – notably *Aissa Saved* (1932), *Mr Johnson* (1939) and *The Horse's Mouth* (1944) – are set in either England or Nigeria, where he served as district officer from 1917 until 1920. After his return from Nigeria he lived in Oxford, until his death of motor neurone disease in 1957. He is now regarded as a major figure in 20th-century English literature.

Casadh an tSúgáin (Irish, 'the twisting of the rope'). A play by Douglas HYDE, based upon an idea by W.B. Yeats and translated into English by Lady Gregory. The Irish title is pronounced 'casoo an toogan'. It was one of the first plays written in Irish and was highly successful when it was staged in the GAIETY on 21 October 1901, with Hyde in the part of Ó hAnnracháin, the arrogant wandering poet from Connacht. At a country dance in Munster at the turn of the 19th century the poet insists on claiming the exclusive attention of Úna, the daughter of the house, who is betrothed to Séamus. Séamus resents the attention being paid to his girl but Máire, Úna's mother, is afraid to have Ó hAnnracháin ejected: *'Tá mallacht aige sin do scoiltfeadh na crainn, deir said.'* ('That man has a curse, they say, would split trees.') Eventually Ó hAnnracháin is tricked, by appealing to his vanity, into twisting a straw rope as he walks backwards out through the open door. Some of the love talk that so entrances Úna anticipates that of Christy Mahon to Pegeen in *The* PLAYBOY OF THE WESTERN WORLD, largely because it comes from the same folkloric source:

> *'Nois, a réalt na mban, taisbeán dóibh mar imíonn Iúnó imeasg na Déithe, nó Helen fá'r scriosadh an Traoi. Dar mo láimh, ódéag Déirdre, fá'r cuireadh Naoise mac Uisnigh chum báis, ní'l a hoidhre in Éirinn inniu acht tú féin.*
> (Now, O star of women, show me how Juno goes among the gods, or Helen for whom Troy was destroyed, forsooth since Deirdre dies for whom Naoise, son of Usnech, was put to death, her heir is not in Ireland today but youself.)

The original title of *The* QUARE FELLOW, Brendan Behan's play about the execution of a murderer, was *The Twisting of Another Rope*, a grisly tribute to the original.

Casán. The usual word in Ulster Irish for 'path' or 'lane', which passed into limited HIBERNO-ENGLISH use unchanged. It was the Donegal equivalent of the much more common BOREEN. *See also* LOANEN.

Casement, Roger (1864–1916). Colonial servant and revolutionary. He was born in Sandycove, Co. Dublin, on 1 September 1864 and educated at Ballymena Academy in Co. Antrim. He joined the British colonial service in Africa in 1892 and investigated the cruel treatment of African workers in the Belgian Congo, publishing his findings in a 1904 report. After he was promoted to consul-general at Rio de Janeiro he performed a similar service for the Peruvian rubber-plantation workers along the Putamayo River: that report was published in 1912, the year he returned from the colonial service. Although he

was knighted in 1911 for his services to the Empire he had grown to detest colonialism, believing that there was little will for reform among the imperial rulers of Africa and South America: 'They make me sick, these paltry English statesmen with their opportunistic souls and grocers' minds,' he commented.

In 1913 Casement returned to Ireland and was a founder member of the IRISH VOLUNTEERS, helping to raised money in America for the HOWTH GUN-RUNNING. He went to Germany in October 1914 with the aim of recruiting an Irish brigade among Irishmen who were being held as prisoners of war, but this was not a success. He did, however, prevail on the Germans to send 20,000 rifles to Ireland to arm the Volunteers and IRB members who were planning a rebellion for Easter 1916 (*see* EASTER RISING). The *Aud* arrived in Tralee Bay on 20 April 1916; Casement followed in a submarine. After a series of misunderstandings and breakdowns in communication, the *Aud* was captured but scuttled by its crew, and Casement himself was captured near Banna Strand, 10 km (6 miles) from Tralee – he suffered from malaria and stayed near the place he had come ashore because he was too weak to walk to Tralee. Although at first the RIC men who arrested him had no idea who he was, he was taken to London and tried for high treason, found guilty and hanged in Pentonville prison on 3 August 1916, despite campaigns for clemency in Ireland, Britain and the USA. It was during the summer of 1916 that the existence of his alleged BLACK DIARIES was revealed.

Casement's execution meant that he joined Pearse, Connolly and the rest of the rebels of 1916 in the pantheon of Irish martyrs. In February 1965 the return of his remains to Dublin for a state funeral in the Republican Plot in GLASNEVIN CEMETERY was the occasion of countrywide commemoration. Sir John LAVERY painted a thin and tragic-looking Casement in the dock in London, and it is to this painting that W.B. YEATS refers in his 'The Municipal Gallery Revisited' (1937): 'Casement upon trial, half hidden by the bars, / Guarded'. In two other poems in the same collection, 'Roger Casement' and 'The Ghost of Roger Casement', Yeats testifies to Casement's tragic appeal:

> Come speak your bit in public
> That some amends be made
> To this most gallant gentleman
> That is in quick-lime laid.

W.B. YEATS: 'Roger Casement', in *New Poems* (1938)

See also 'LONELY BANNA STRAND, THE'.

Case of Ireland's Being Bound by Acts of Parliament in England Stated, The. *See* MOLYNEUX, WILLIAM.

Casey, Bishop Éamonn. *See* FORBIDDEN FRUIT.

Casey, Elizabeth. *See* OWENS, BLACKBURNE E.

Casey, John Keegan. *See* LEO.

Cashel (Irish *caiseal*, '[ancient] stone fort'). A ráth (RING FORT) found especially in areas of shallow soil where unmortared stone rather than earth was used for the walls. It is frequently found as a placename element, including the town of Cashel, Co. Tipperary, which is dominated by the impressive ROCK OF CASHEL. The Archaelogical Survey of Donegal (1983) lists 209 cashels, including the Grianán of AILEACH.

Cashel, Rock of. *See* ROCK OF CASHEL.

Casino (Marino). *See* CHARLEMONT, JAMES CAULFEILD, 1ST EARL OF.

Cassells, Richard. *See* CASTLE, RICHARD.

Castle, Richard (also **Cassells**) (*c*.1695–1751). Architect of the Palladian movement. German by birth, he spent some years in London, moving to Ireland around 1728. He worked initially with Edward Lovett PEARCE on the Parliament building in COLLEGE GREEN, taking over Pearce's practice on his death in 1733 and achieving considerable success with Palladian country houses such as POWERSCOURT, RUSSBOROUGH HOUSE, STROKESTOWN PARK and WESTPORT HOUSE. He also designed Dublin buildings such as LEINSTER HOUSE (1745–51) and the ROTUNDA hospital.

Castle, the. The colloquial way of referring to Dublin Castle, which was begun in 1204 on the orders of King John and extensively furbished in 1684 after a fire. 'The Castle' was a metaphor for British rule in the Irish capital until its formal handing over to the Free State government in January 1922. John Morley (1838–1923), the radical politician, commented at a speech in Manchester on 12 May 1902, 'Dublin Castle [is] the best machine that has ever been invented for governing a country against its will.' Described as 'the worst castle in the worst situation in Christendom', it was the official residence of the lord deputy or lord lieutenant, and built to withstand any serious attack. Now its purpose is mainly diplomatic and decorative, though it is used for the new Irish pastime of holding tribunals. The Clock Tower holds the Chester BEATTY Library.

See also CASTLE CATHOLIC.

Castlebar. *See* RACES OF CASTLEBAR.

Castle Catholic. An Irish person whose political opinions and attitudes were perceived as running counter to the prevailing Nationalism of most co-religionists. The notion of the cultivation of a pro-British Catholic middle class first occurred to Sir Robert PEEL when he was chief secretary (1812–18) – and he achieved some success, as the writer Sean O'Faoláin records in his biography of Daniel O'Connell, *King of the Beggars* (1938):

> He began in Ireland a policy that many of his successors copied and developed – the formation of a class that became known … in mockery of their affected half-English accents, 'Cawstle Cawtholics'. These were the seduced Irish who turned their eyes – not unnaturally, Heaven knows, in so impoverished an island – on Dublin Castle and British rule as the only means and centre of preferment.

Castle Garden. The reception area for immigrants landing in New York, USA, from 1855 until the opening of ELLIS ISLAND in 1892. It processed the many thousands who left Ireland in the decades after the Great Famine:

When I landed at swate Castle Garden
I'd just came from the say.
In my pockets I had not a farthing
As I stepped out up the Broadway.
ANON.: 'Swate Castle Garden' (*c*.1860)

Castle Rackrent. The first and best novel (1800) by Maria EDGEWORTH (1767–1849), and a significant key to the understanding of Ireland in the period of the Act of Union and the decline and fall of the landlord class. The story is narrated by Thady Quirk, an old family retainer, who is a marvellously unreliable witness. His account of the rackety Rackrents, Sir Patrick the lavish sot, Sir Murtagh the litigious miser, Sir Kit the unuxorious gambler and Sir Condy the ineffectual politician, is deliberately comic but not entirely inapplicable to the unabsentee landlord classes of the time. Sir Walter Scott praised it as the first of the 'regional' novels, and its HIBERNO-ENGLISH register provided a language for the novelists and playwrights that followed.

Castlereagh, Viscount. The courtesy title (1796) of Robert Stewart (1776–1822), son of the Marquess of Londonderry and chief architect of the Act of UNION. He was born in Dublin on 18 June 1776 and educated at the Royal School, Armagh, and St John's College, Cambridge. He became chief secretary for Ireland in 1798, and the rising of that year convinced him that only Union with Britain would preserve the empire. His method of 'compensation' to secure the passing of the bill was not regarded as bribery in the culture of the time. When George III refused to grant CATHOLIC EMANCIPATION as promised he resigned along with the prime minister, William Pitt the Younger, but joined the government again as secretary for war in 1805. Though execrated in Britain for his repressive legislation against reform movements at home and for his work as foreign secretary (1812–22) in re-establishing the old monarchies of Europe, his early years in Ireland were reformist. He studied Irish and was willing to consider Catholic relief, but like many another liberal (including O'CONNELL) the extremes of the Terror

in France drove him to crush all movements he considered revolutionary. He committed suicide (*see* 'TIS ALL OVER) on 12 August 1822.

Posterity will ne'er survey
A nobler grave than this:
Here lie the bones of Castlereagh
Stop, traveller, and p*ss!
BYRON (1788–1824): 'Epitaph' (1822)

Castletown House. An 18th-century mansion in Co. Kildare, designed in 1718 in the Palladian style by the Italian architect Alessandro Galilei (1691–1737) for its owner William Connolly. The architectural work was continued from 1725 by Edward Lovett PEARCE.

Catacombs, the. The basement of a large Georgian house in Fitzwilliam Street in Dublin used as a sort of after-hours club by writers such as Brendan Behan, Anthony Cronin and John Ryan in the late 1940s and early 1950s. They drank in pubs such as McDaid's earlier in the evening.

Cat and Mouse Act. The nickname by which the Prisoners (Temporary Discharge for Health) Act 1913 was known. Originally used against Suffragettes, it was again found useful in dealing with hunger-striking Republicans during the ANGLO-IRISH WAR of 1919–21. The act allowed prisoners to be released after a short time on HUNGER STRIKE only to be rearrested as soon as they had regained their health.

Cat breac, the. The name given by BLASKET islanders to the Irish primer supplied by Protestant evangelists who settled on the Great Blasket and opened a school there as part of the SECOND REFORMATION. *Cat breac* means 'speckled cat'; there was a picture of a speckled cat on the cover or title page, with the accompanying Irish phrase.

Catch and kick. *See* FOOTBALL.

Catechism of Cliché. An intermittent and popular feature of Myles na Gopaleen's CRUISKEEN LAWN:

What physical features have all barristers in common?
Keeness of face and hawkiness of eye.

Their arguments are –
Trenchant
Their books?
Dusty tomes; but occasionally musty old legal
    tomes.
In what do they indulge?
Flights of oratory.
If they are women, what is their description?
They are Fair Portias.
    The Best of Myles (1968)

Cathair Chrobh Dhearg. *See* CITY, THE.

Cathal or **Cathaldus**. A 7th-century Munster saint who studied at the monastery of Lismore and eventually became abbot there. Returning from a pilgrimage (*c.*666) to the Holy Land he stopped at Taranto in southern Italy and was asked to fill the vacant see. He accepted and spent the rest of his life there as bishop, dying *c.*681. He is still venerated in the city, where a large statue of him guards the entrance to the harbour, and a freshwater stream in the bay is known as *l'annelle di san Cathaldo* ('the ring of Saint Cathaldus'); it marks the place where he is believed to have stilled a storm by throwing his ring into the water. He was the patron saint of the Italian army during the First World War, and his feast day is 10 May.

Cathbad. A druid, the grandfather of CÚCHU-LAINN, and father of CONCHOBHAR, whose mother is NESSA. Among his prophecies are details of the fate of DEIRDRE and the short but glorious career of his grandson.

'Cath Chéim an Fhia'. *See* NÍ LAOGHAIRE MÁIRE BHUÍ.

Cathleen Falls. The name of a hydroelectric generating station on the River Erne. It is situated in Northern Ireland, but only a few miles outside the town of Ballyshannon in Co. Donegal.

Cathleen Ní Houlihan (Irish *Caitlín Ní Uallacháin*). One of the names of Ireland personified as a woman, especially in 18th-century Irish poetry. It is the title of a typical Jacobite poem (*see* AISLING) by Liam Dall Ó hIfearnáin (?1720–1803). It was used eponymously by W.B. Yeats in his play for Maud Gonne, CATH-LEEN NÍ HOULIHAN.

See also CÁIT NÍ DHUIBHIR; POOR OLD WOMAN, THE; *RÓISÍN DUBH*.

Cathleen Ní Houlihan. A one-act play written by W.B. YEATS (with considerable help from Lady Gregory) for Maud GONNE. It is set in Killala in 1798 and deals with the clash between domestic and patriotic responsibilities. Michael Gillane leaves his bride unmarried to help an old woman recover her four green fields from a stranger, while news comes of the landing of the French. The play was presented in St Teresa's Hall, Clarendon Street, on 2 April 1902 with Maud Gonne in the part of the old woman by 'Mr W.G. Fay's Irish National Dramatic Company'. The effect was electrifying, since it could have been interpreted as an open incitement to revolution; at least so the besotted Yeats believed. In one of his very last poems 'The Man and the Echo' (1938) he wrote: 'Did that play of mine send out/Certain men the English shot?', suggesting somewhat presumptuously that it might have been a contributory factor in the EASTER RISING.

Peter: Did you see an old woman going down the
    path?
Patrick: I did not; but I saw a young girl, and she
    had the walk of a queen.

Catholic Association. An association formed in May 1824 to campaign for CATHOLIC EMANCI-PATION. It was distinguished from previous organizations of this kind (*see* CATHOLIC COM-MITTEE; CATHOLIC CONVENTION) by the participation of the masses, who supported the organization by paying a CATHOLIC RENT. It was the first genuine mass movement in Irish history. The association was suppressed in 1825, but reformed subsequently with a different rubric.
See also CATHOLIC RELIEF ACTS.

Catholic Church, special position of the. *See* ARTICLE 44.

Catholic Committee. A committee representing the interests of Catholics when Catholics were still discriminated against under the POPERY LAWS. It was founded in 1760 by Charles

O'CONOR, John Curry (*c*.1710–80), a Dublin doctor, and Thomas Wyse (*c*.1700–1770), a member of an aristocratic family from Waterford. The association became more radical in the 1790s, with some members of the leadership belonging to the UNITED IRISHMEN. It brought together the CATHOLIC CONVENTION in December 1792, winding itself up in 1793 in response to the passing of the CATHOLIC RELIEF ACTS.

Catholic Convention. An assembly organized by the CATHOLIC COMMITTEE with the purpose of agitating against the residual POPERY LAWS against Catholics. It was held in TAILORS' HALL in Dublin, on 3–8 December 1792. There were 231 delegates, with a strong presence of UNITED IRISHMEN, including Wolfe Tone. The convention put together a petition for Catholic relief, which they sent directly to the king. The CATHOLIC RELIEF ACT of 1793 was in direct response to the convening of the Catholic Convention, called the 'popish convention' by its Protestant opponents.

See also BACK LANE PARLIAMENT.

Catholic Emancipation. The repeal in April 1829 of the remaining measures of the POPERY LAWS in order to give Catholics equality with Protestants in public life, the law and the army. The most important provision was that a Catholic could take a seat in Parliament without having to swear the Oath of Supremacy, recognizing the monarch as head of the church. The granting of emancipation, at first strongly resisted by the Westminster Parliament and by King George III – although advocated by the prime minister William Pitt and Viscount CASTLEREAGH – was the result of unremitting constitutional pressure since the CATHOLIC ASSOCIATION was first founded in 1760. It was Daniel O'CONNELL's finest hour.

See also WELLINGTON, ARTHUR WELLESLEY, 1ST DUKE OF.

Catholic Relief Acts. A series of measures passed between 1774 and 1793 that removed most of the penal legislation against Irish Catholics (*see* POPERY LAWS). The main source of pressure to reform was the Westminster Parliament, which saw in the Catholic population a source of recruits for foreign wars, but the CATHOLIC COMMITTEE had gathered sufficient strength to have a limited political effect. Bishop HERVEY's Oath of Allegiance Act of 1774 had devised an acceptable formula for Catholics to express loyalty to George III without offence to their religion, and Gardiner's Relief Act of 1778 extended the leasehold term to 999 years or 'five lives'. Two acts of 1782 allowed the purchase of land and removed the restrictions imposed upon the Catholic clergy and the education rights of their flocks. By 1793 Britain was at war with Revolutionary France and the government felt that further relief for Catholics might at once provide them with manpower and stem the threat of Jacobinism. Acts in 1792 and 1793 allowed Catholics to practise law, attend Trinity College Dublin and hold most civil and military offices. Full equality, however, had to wait until CATHOLIC EMANCIPATION in 1829; it had been promised several times, especially during the passing of the Act of UNION (1801), but required considerable agitation finally to achieve it. The virulent Anglo-Irish opposition to these measures, rising to a crescendo in 1793, was one of the contributory causes of religious conflict in Ireland, resulting in the rise of the DEFENDERS and the foundation of the ORANGE ORDER.

Catholic rent. The subscription levied on members of the CATHOLIC ASSOCIATION, founded in 1824. In order to broaden the base of the movement, Daniel O'CONNELL suggested that all members should subscribe a minimum of one penny per month. He thereby created a mass movement with effective local organization. The substantial sum of £52,000 was raised in this way between 1824 and 1829.

Catholic University. The Irish hierarchy's response in 1854 to Sir Robert PEEL's godless QUEEN'S COLLEGES, with earnest approval by Pope Pius IX. The founding rector was John Henry NEWMAN and during its existence (until the opening of the Royal University in 1879) the faculty included Gerard Manley HOPKINS as lecturer in classics, Eugene O'CURRY as professor of archaeology and Irish history, and the poet Aubrey DE VERE as professor of English literature. Newman left in 1859, but the university struggled on in spite of being charterless and lacking state funding. It was taken over by the Jesuit Order in 1883 and it eventually formed the nucleus of University College Dublin.

Cats, the. The sobriquet of the county hurlers or camogie players of Co. Kilkenny, from the expression 'to fight like KILKENNY CATS'.

Cattle Raid of Cooley, The. See TÁIN BÓ CUAILNGE.

Caubeen (Irish *cáibín*). A HIBERNO-ENGLISH word for an old cap or hat. A caubeen may also be used to describe a formal, traditional cap: the headdress of the Royal Irish Regiment was described as a 'shamrock-green caubeen with deep-green hackle'. In the lively if sentimental anonymous ballad 'Way down in the County Kerry' the wife exhorts her husband:

> Put on your old knee britches and your coat of
> emerald green.
> Take off that hat me darlin' Pat and put on your old
> caubeen.
> For today's our golden wedding and I want you all
> to know,
> Just how we looked when we were wed fifty years
> ago.

Causeway Coast. A convenient invention by the Northern Ireland Tourist Board to describe the more than 110 km (70 miles) of striking scenery from Magilligan in Co. Derry to Larne in Co. Antrim. As the name indicates it includes the fabulous GIANT'S CAUSEWAY and also features the resorts of Portstewart, Portrush, Ballycastle, Cushendun and Cushendall. It also provides views of Rathlin Island and the coasts of Kintyre, Ayrshire and Galloway.

Cavan, Co. See POTHOLES.

Cavan Orphanage Fire. On the night of 23 February 1943 a fire broke out in the laundry of St Joseph's Orphanage in Cavan town, a certified INDUSTRIAL SCHOOL run by sisters of the enclosed order, the Poor Clares. Despite the rescue efforts of local people and an inadequate fire service, 36 children died in the fire. They were buried in eight coffins in one grave carrying neither names nor date. In his funeral oration on 25 February the Bishop of Kilmore, Dr Lyons, spoke of 'Dear little angels, now before God in heaven, they were taken away before the gold of their innocence had been tarnished by the soil of the world.' A government tribunal of inquiry with counsel representing various interests – the dead children had no representation – reported in September 1943, laying the blame for the tragedy mainly on inadequate fire safety and rescue services, but it was believed by witnesses and townspeople that all the children could have been moved in time from their dormitories had not the nuns wanted to avoid them being seen in their nightclothes. Brian O'Nolan (*see* O'BRIEN, FLANN), who was secretary to the tribunal of inquiry, composed the following limerick in a pub in Cavan:

> In Cavan there was a great fire;
> Joe McCarthy [tribunal chairman] came down to
> inquire.
> If the nuns were to blame
> It would be a shame
> So it had to be caused by a wire.

The Poor Clare orphanage closed in 1967.

Cavendish, Lord Frederick (1836–92). Liberal politician, appointed chief secretary for Ireland in May 1882 in succession to 'BUCKSHOT' FORSTER. On the evening of the day he arrived in Ireland, 6 May 1882, he and his Irish-born under-secretary, T.H. Burke, were murdered by a group of INVINCIBLES as they walked in the Phoenix Park (*see* PHOENIX PARK MURDERS).

Caveto, Filole (Latin, 'beware, son'). The notorious advice attributed to St COLUMBAN:

> *Caveto, filole,*
> *Feminarum species*
> *Per quas mors ingreditur,*
> *Non parva pernicies.*
> (Beware, my son, womankind, by whom death
> enters, a grievous peril!)

CBS. An acronym for 'CHRISTIAN BROTHERS school'. Among the best known in Ireland are Mount Sion in Waterford, the original Christian Brothers foundation, the NORTH MON in Cork and O'Connell's Schools and Synge Street in Dublin.

C Case. In 1997 the Supreme Court ruled that a young TRAVELLER girl in the care of a health board, who had been raped and was pregnant and suicidal, could be brought to England for an abortion.
See also ABORTION REFERENDUMS; X CASE.

Céad Míle Fáilte (Irish, 'a hundred thousand welcomes'). A universal Irish greeting (correctly pronounced 'kade meela fall-cha') preserved in HIBERNO-ENGLISH in its original Irish, giving rise to some odd attempts at pronunciation.

> Céad míle fáilte, here!
> Eivlin a rúin
> Céad míle fáilte, here!
> Eivlin a rúin.
> (A hundred thousand welcomes, dear,
> Nine hundred thousand welcomes here.
> O welcomes forever here!
> Eivlin a rúin.)
>> CEARBHALL Ó DÁLAIGH (*fl. c.*1597–1630): '*Eibhlín, a rún*' ('Eileen, love') (*c.*1601); this version by George Sigerson (1836–1925)

Ceallach or **Celsus**. A 12th-century Ulster saint who was a Benedictine monk at Glastonbury when he was ordained as the last hereditary Archbishop of Armagh. He began the work of reform of the whole Irish church and was instrumental in securing the archbishopric for MALACHY, then the reluctant Bishop of Connor. His last action as he lay dying in 1129 was to send Malachy his crozier. His feast day is 1 April.

Ceann comhairle. The name given to the chair of the DÁIL. The ceann comhairle was traditionally a member of the government party, but in recent years it has sometimes proved more useful in terms of voting strength for the party in power to appoint a senior member of the other party. The ceann comhairle has a casting vote in case of necessity. There is another office, that of leas-cheann comhairle, a deputy for the ceann comhairle.

Ceannt, Éamonn (Eamonn Kent, 1881–1916). Revolutionary. He was born in Ballymore, Co. Galway, and came to Dublin to work as a clerk for the Dublin Corporation. Like many of the revolutionaries of the period he joined in turn the GAELIC LEAGUE (1900), SINN FÉIN (1908) and the IRB (1913), to the last of which he was introduced by Seán MCDERMOTT. A talented player of UILLEANN PIPES, he was involved in the foundation of the DUBLIN PIPERS CLUB. He was also a founder-member of the IRISH VOLUNTEERS and took part in the HOWTH GUN-RUNNING. He was a signatory of the PROCLAMATION OF THE REPUBLIC and commanded the rebel forces in the South Dublin Union (later St James's Hospital) during the 1916 EASTER RISING. After the Rising he was court-martialled, and executed by firing squad on 7 May 1916.

Cearc ar gor. The Irish term, also used in HIBERNO-ENGLISH, for a hatching hen.

Cease fire and dump arms. The order that officially ended the CIVIL WAR, issued to Republicans by Frank AIKEN on 24 May 1923. In the previous weeks, since their unilateral ceasefire of 30 April – made possible by the death on 10 April of their diehard leader, Liam Lynch (*see* REAL CHIEF, THE) – the Republicans had failed to secure terms from the Free State government, insisting that they would not lay down their arms. At the time of the 'dump arms' order, Éamon de Valera made a statement acknowledging defeat and conceding victory to the Free State:

> Military victory must be allowed to rest for the moment with those who have destroyed the Republic.

Céide Fields. A heritage and interpretive centre near Newcastle on the coast of west Co. Mayo. The layout and boundaries of large Neolithic (2500 BC) fields – likely to have been used for animal husbandry and preserved underneath layers of peat – have been uncovered using long steel probes.

Céilí. An evening entertainment involving Irish dances – SET DANCES and what are called CÉILÍ DANCES or figure dances. The first céilí is held to have taken place in Bloomsbury Hall, London, on 30 October 1887, under the auspices of the London Gaelic League, members of which had visited Scottish céilí nights for inspiration. Traditional musicians – normally on fiddle or accordion – or CÉILÍ BANDS play for the dances, and the evening may also feature individual singers, performing SEAN-NÓS or ballad-type songs, and the performance of STEP DANCES by individual dancers. Sometimes, in order to give the dancers a rest, vigorous set dances are interspersed with old-time or céilí waltzes danced to Irish tunes. The organization COMHALTAS CEOLTÓIRÍ ÉIREANN holds weekend céilís in its headquarters in Monkstown, Co. Dublin.

Céilí band. A band involving a large group of musicians, perhaps seven or eight in number, who play for CÉILÍ dances on instruments such as accordions, fiddles, banjos and flutes, and with piano or double bass accompaniment. Among the most famous ensembles in the heyday of the céilí bands in the 1950s and 1960s were the GALLOWGLASS CÉILÍ BAND, the TULLA CÉILÍ BAND (Co. Clare) and the Kilfenora Céilí Band. COMHALTAS CEOLTÓIRÍ ÉIREANN encourages the tuition of young musicians to play in céilí bands.

Céilí dances. A term for figure dances, sometimes simply called 'Irish dances', which can be danced solo or in groups and which are normally shorter than SET DANCES. Céilí dances were originally promoted at the céilís organized by London's GAELIC LEAGUE at the end of the 19th century as being more *echt*-Celtic than sets. Among the simplest and most popular for céilís are 'The Walls of Limerick', 'The Siege of Ennis' (these choreographed by Bean Uí Chorráin, secretary of the Limerick branch of Conradh na Gaeilge), 'The Waves of Tory' and '*Baint an Fhéir*' ('The Haymaker's Jig'). Céilí dances, especially solo dances, have a formal, hands-by-the-side style, a style that RIVERDANCE exploited, while bor-

rowing heavily from the steps and movement of these dances.

Céilídhing. The phrase still used in Ulster to describe informal evening visiting, sometimes including a game of cards or another pastime: 'I went céilídhing [or 'on a céilidh'] to my aunt's house last night.' This word is similar in meaning to BOTHÁNTAÍOCHT in Munster and AIRNEÁN, and may be anglicized as 'kayleying' or some variant spelling.

> I just came over on my kailie to have a crack with you about old times.
> ROBERT BRATTON: (*fl.*1925–35): 'A Hal'eve Party', in *Round the Turf Fire* (1931)

Céitinn, Seathrún (Geoffrey Keating) (*c.*1580–*c.*1644). Historiographer and Irish-language poet. He was born at Burges near Cahir in Co. Tipperary, into a family of Anglo-Norman extraction and of sufficient prosperity to send him to ecclesiastical colleges at Bordeaux and Salamanca. He returned to Ireland in 1607, a doctor of divinity, to serve as a curate for the parish of Tubrid near his birthplace. His *Foras Feasa ar Éirinn* ('foundation of/for a knowledge of Ireland'), a groundwork for the history of Ireland written to counter the slanders of GIRALDUS CAMBRENSIS, Edmund SPENSER and other English writers (*see* ANGLO-IRISH CHRONICLES), was completed by about 1634.

Céitinn's poetic output was small but impressive. '*Óm Sceol ar Ardmhagh Fáil*' ('From my grief on Fál's high plain'; Fál in this instance is Ireland) is about the dispersal of the Gaelic aristocracy after the Battle of KINSALE and the FLIGHT OF THE EARLS, and '*Mo Beannacht Leat, A Scríbhinn*' ('My blessing with you, oh letter') is a nostalgic letter home from France. His famous poem '*A Bhean Lán de Stuaim*' ('Oh lady full of prudence') shows an acquaintance with sensuality unexpected in a priest, especially the author of *Trí Biorghaithe an Bháis* (*The Three Shafts of Death*), a theological tract.

Facts about Céitinn's life are obscure. There is a story that a sermon preached by him against a local squireen's mistress caused him to go into hiding, and another that he was murdered by Cromwellian soldiers in Clonmel in 1649. He is buried in his own parish of Tubrid, Co. Tipperary.

Céle Dé. *See* CULDEE.

'Celtic'. A contemporary marketing and media formulation for the purpose of the commercial exploitation of things Irish – music, art, jewellery, books. Much of what is regarded as *echt*-Celtic, such as the NEWGRANGE spirals, predate the Celts by thousands of years. It is based on the CELTIC TWILIGHT sense of Celtic uniqueness and the realization that there is an advantage to be gained, in a commercial sense, by appearing not to belong to the Anglo-Saxons, either racially or culturally. To give two contemporary examples: Author John O'Donohue specifically invokes Celtic spirituality in *ANAM CARA*, while ENYA, one of the world's most successful singers, purveys a kind of ethereal 'Celtic' mood music.

Celtic Revival. The revival of interest in the residual literature and culture of the Welsh, Scots, Cornish, Manx and Bretons that sprang out of the Romantic movement in literature. Translations from Welsh, Gaelic and Irish became very popular from the middle of the 19th century; these influenced such writers as Tennyson, Peacock and the Scot Fiona McLeod (the pseudonym of William Sharp, 1855–1905), and received critical respectability with Matthew Arnold's 'Lectures on Celtic Literature' at Oxford in 1865–6. In Ireland the IRISH LITERARY REVIVAL had the most obvious success, largely because it coincided with a number of factors: a strong interest in the revival of the Irish language as a vernacular; the rich talents of Douglas HYDE, Lady GREGORY and superlatively W.B. YEATS and J.M. SYNGE; and a sense of cultural nationalism that helped to fill a vacuum after the fall of PARNELL.

Celtic Tiger. A sobriquet given to Ireland during the period of rapid economic development and high growth rates achieved since the mid-1990s. The basis of this prosperity was the attraction offered to multinational companies, especially in the technology and international financial

services sectors, to set up operations in Ireland. This was done largely by offering extremely preferential rates of corporate tax. Only ten years previously Ireland had been in recession, with government borrowing out of control, and, ironically, it was the FIANNA FÁIL government of Charles Haughey from 1982 that began to preach and impose financial rectitude. Other reasons cited for the arrival of the Celtic Tiger are the existence of a young, well-educated and ambitious workforce, and the use of Ireland by American companies in particular as a stepping-stone into the lucrative European Union market. It is a far cry from the PROTECTIONISM that was in force until the 1960s; now Ireland is as open as any economy in Europe and will consequently be extremely vulnerable when the chill wind of recession blows again.

Celtic Twilight, the. One of the main elements of the IRISH LITERARY REVIVAL, positing a special poetic vision for the residual Celts (lost, it was implied, by the Anglo-Saxons). The term originated as the title of a book of folk and supernatural writings, mainly by W.B. YEATS, which was published in 1893. The stories were collected in Galway (with the help of Lady GREGORY) and Sligo. The book's title suggested a theme for much of the writings of the revival.

Celts. A people who began to dominate Europe about 1200 BC, and who first arrived in Ireland around the 1st century BC. At the time of the advent of Christianity in the 5th century AD, Celtic language, customs and religion were well established in Ireland, although it is not clear how they had established domination over the country. It is now generally agreed by historians that the Celts were culturally rather than racially different from other European peoples.

Censorship. A puritanical mindset existed from the foundation of the Free State until the end of the 1960s. This was reflected in the Censorship of Publications Act of 1926 and in the Censorship Board that began its duties in 1930. It was a corollary of the economic PROTECTIONISM from which Ireland suffered for most of the same period, and was heavily influenced by the Catholic Church. So zealous was the Censorship Board that it banned at least some of the works of almost all of the country's best contemporary writers – including John MCGAHERN, Brian MOORE, Edna O'BRIEN, Kate O'BRIEN, and even *The TAILOR AND ANSTY* – as well as works by the major authors of the outside world. The censorship legislation was gradually amended during the 1960s, and known liberals appointed to the board, so that gradually the climate of fear and repression eased.

See also BELT OF THE CROZIER; ROSE TATTOO AFFAIR, THE.

Centlivre, Susannah or **Centlivre** (?1667–1723). Playwright. She was probably born in Co. Tyrone, the daughter of a Cromwellian settler called Freeman. Details of her early life are obscure and romantic: apparently she co-habited, dressed as a boy, with one Anthony Hammond at Cambridge, having had two husbands killed in duels, and after some years as a strolling player finally settled down in marriage with the French royal chef Centlivre who tended both Queen Anne and George I as 'Yeoman of the Mouth'. By then she had overcome sexual prejudice to become a successful playwright. The best known of her 19 plays are her first, *The Perjur'd Husband* (1700), and *A Bold Stroke for a Wife* (1718), which contains the character 'the real SIMON PURE'. She was assailed in Pope's *Dunciad* because of the perceived anti-Catholic and anticlerical tone of her plays:

> So from the mid-most the nutation spreads
> Round, and more round, o'er all the sea of heads.
> At last Centlivre felt her voice to fail...
> *Dunciad*, Book II (1728)

Ceol. *See* BREATHNACH, BREANDÁN.

Ceol agus craic (Irish, 'music and CRAIC'). The phrase (*Beidh ceol agus craic ann*, 'There will be music and craic') is used to anticipate an evening or weekend of sessions in pubs, drinking, singing and perhaps dancing. Ceol and craic are particularly associated with the FLEADH CHEOIL weekend.

'Ceol an Ghrá' (Irish, 'the music of love'). The title of Ireland's only Irish-language entry in the Eurovision Song Contest, sung by Sandy Jones in Edinburgh in 1972. It was no accident that an Irish-language song was chosen a few months after Derry's BLOODY SUNDAY of that year and the burning of the British Embassy in Dublin.

Ceolawn (Irish *ceolán*). A word used in HIBERNO-ENGLISH to mean 'cry-baby', 'whinger'.

Ceoltóirí Chualann. A group of traditional musicians of the highest calibre brought together by Seán Ó RIADA to play the music he had written for the performance of Bryan MACMAHON's play, *The Honey Spike*, at the Abbey Theatre in Dublin in 1961. They included Paddy Moloney, Martin Fay, Seán Potts, and Michael Tubridy. Ó Riada's arrangements, influenced by jazz, had a profound effect on Irish musical tastes, especially after they were heard on *Fleadh Cheoil an Raidió* on Raidió Éireann. The group performed and recorded with Cork-born tenor Seán Ó Sé: a notable recording is of a 1969 live concert at the Gaiety in Dublin, called *Ó Riada sa Gaiety*. The final performance of the group was in Cork the same year. After Ó Riada's death, some of the members of Ceoltóirí Chualann formed The CHIEFTAINS.

Cesair. In Irish mythology, the daughter of the biblical Noah. She is denied entrance into the Ark, so builds her own ship. On board are 50 women and three men – her father Bith (a son of Noah), her husband FINTAN and the pilot LADRA. Uncertain of the time of the coming of the Deluge, they put to sea and sail for seven years. They finally reach Ireland, becoming the first settlers, though Ladra leaves to seek another kingdom. Abandoned by Fintan, Cesair dies of grief just before the Flood actually arrives.

Cet. In Irish mythology, a warrior from Connacht in the army of MEDB. He is active in the war related in the TÁIN BÓ CUAILNGE (*The Cattle Raid of Cooley*), driving the 'brain ball' into the forehead of CONCHOBHAR, causing his death seven years later. He had stolen the lethal device – which was made from the brains of Mac da

Thó (king of Leinster) mixed with lime – from its manufacturer, CONALL CEARNACH.

CFA. *See* ALEXANDER, CECIL FRANCES.

Chainies. *See* CHANEYS.

Chalk Sunday. The first Sunday of Lent. The clothes of those who had not done the right thing and got married during SHROVETIDE would be marked with chalk on this Sunday to indicate the disapproval of the community. Children or young people did the marking, and the victims appear to have taken the ritual in good part. In some areas of the country Chalk Sunday was, instead, the Sunday before Shrove Tuesday, so there was still time to cobble together a match before Lent. According to SEANCHAÍ Éamon Kelly, in Kerry 'there was no knowing the amount of people that'd get married at that time between Chalk Sunday and Shrove Tuesday.'

'Challenge, A'. A letter from John L. Sullivan, the BOSTON STRONG BOY, that appeared in all the sporting pages in the USA on 23 March 1882:

> There has been so much newspaper talk from parties who state that they are desirous of meeting me in the ring that I am disgusted. Nevertheless, I am willing to fight any man in this country, for five thousand dollars a side: or, any man in the old country for the same amount at two months from signing articles, – I to use gloves, and he, if he pleases to fight with the bare knuckles. I will not fight again with the bare knuckles, as I do not wish to put myself in a position amenable to the law. My money is always ready, so I want these fellows to put up or shut up.

Chalmont, Charles. *See* AUGHRIM, BATTLE OF.

Chaloner's Corner. A small graveyard in Trinity College Dublin named after the first provost, Dr Luke Chaloner, who was interred there in 1613.

Champ. A dish (rather like COLCANNON) made of mashed potatoes, milk, onions or scallions with a central reservoir of melting butter. The term is an Ulster one confined mainly to the counties west of the River Bann.

Chancer. A richly connotative word in HIBERNO-ENGLISH, often used half-admiringly, of someone who tries and does not mind failing: 'He's such a chancer, that fellow!' On a more serious level, it carries the meaning of confidence trickster or fraudster.

Chance your arm, to. To attempt or risk something, without necessarily being confident about the outcome: 'Yerra, chance your arm anyway, boy!' The phrase is said to derive from an apocryphal encounter in St Patrick's Cathedral, Dublin, in 1492 when the Earl of Kildare cut a hole 75 by 15 cm (30 in by 6) in the door plank and thrust the arm of friendship through the hole to where his enemy the Earl of Ormond might cut it off with a sword, thereby healing the breach.

Chaneys or **chainies.** Pieces of china. Chaneys, found in gardens and among rubble, were traditionally used by children for playing shop or house, sometimes called 'playing chaneys':

> There were rust-eaten tin cans lying neglected on the waster, and fragments of coloured delf that she could have gathered to play chaneys had she had the time.
>
> JAMES PLUNKETT: 'Janey Mary', in *The Trusting and the Maimed* (1955)

Changedale. *See* RUNDALE.

Changeling. The simulacrum of the stolen child left by the fairies in his or her place. In the folklore of rural Ireland it was believed that the fairies or SIDHE, in malevolent mood, occasionally stole a male baby or small child, leaving a fairy child, a changeling, FETCH or freak in its place. Yeats's poem 'The Stolen Child' has this theme: 'Away with us he's going.' Various stratagems were used to shield boy children, such as having them wear long curls and a dress in order to confuse the fairies. It was also believed possible for the Sidhe to steal an older person, leaving a corpse in his or her place. *See also* BEALTAINE; CLEARY, BRIDGET.

Charlemagne (Latin *Carolus Magnus*, 'Charles the Great') (742–814). Frankish ruler. Charlemagne became sole king of the Franks in 771, king of the Lombards in 774 and the first Holy

Roman Emperor in 800, crowned so on Christmas Day by Pope Leo III in gratitude for rescue of the pontiff from the rebellious Romans. He ruled most of western Europe, and was so noted as a law-giver, administrator, protector of the church and promoter of education that his court at AACHEN was the centre of an intellectual and artistic renaissance. He invited the greatest scholars of the day to take part in his work, the most notable being ALCUIN of York and the Irishmen CLEMENT SCOTTUS, DICUIL and DUNGAL. Charlemagne was such a colossus in all aspects of kingship that he and his paladins (palace officers) figured in later romances of chivalry, in which magical powers were ascribed to them. The legend of his readiness to lead the last battle with the Antichrist is shared by many other semi-mythical figures including ARTHUR OF BRITAIN and BRIAN BORU.

Charlemont, James Caulfeild, 1st Earl of (1728–99). Patriot leader. He was born in Dublin on 18 August 1728, the descendant of an Elizabethan soldier, Captain Toby Caulfeild, who was granted lands along the Ulster Blackwater in Tyrone and Armagh. He was made earl in recognition of his gallantry against the French invasion of Antrim in 1760. Although he preferred to live in fashionable London he elected to reside in Ireland as a patriotic duty. He severely overstretched his income in building (1761–3) Charlemont House (now the MUNICIPAL GALLERY OF MODERN ART) in Parnell Square, Dublin, and the exquisite Casino in his demesne at Marino in the northern suburbs. Though his interests were mainly aesthetic and scholarly – he was the virtual founder of the ROYAL IRISH ACADEMY – he found himself commander-in-chief of the VOLUNTEERS in 1780, earning the nickname 'the Volunteer Earl', and played a significant part in the securing of legislative independence for the Dublin Parliament. He was equally opposed to Catholic relief and Union with Britain, and though his attitude to emancipation softened considerably in his last years he remained strongly anti-Union, rejoicing in the parliamentary defeat of

the first attempt to pass the act in January 1799, declaring, 'We are yet a nation!' He died on 4 August 1799.

Charlesfort. An extensive coastal fortification just outside Kinsale in Co. Cork. Built to protect the interests of the crown on the southwest coast, it was designed by Sir William Robinson (c.1643–1712), who also designed the ROYAL HOSPITAL in Kilmainham, Dublin. In 1677 Captain James Walker, a Catholic military engineer who had earned valuable experience in the French army after the confiscation of his estates in the Cromwellian plantation, was appointed overseer of the construction of Charlesfort. Building began the following year. The fort remained a military barracks until the handover of power to the provisional government of the Free State in 1922.
See also WHITE LADY, THE.

Charles the Bald (823–877). The grandson of CHARLEMAGNE, who became Charles I of the Holy Roman Empire when his father, Louis the Pious (778–840), reverted to Merovingian type and divided his Frankish empire between his sons. Charles received the territory destined to become modern France. He had the same scholastic instincts as his grandfather and set up schools that attracted scholars from far and wide – especially from Ireland. John Scottus ERIUGENA was the doyen of the palace school at LAON in northern France.

Charlton, Jack (b.1935). Soccer player and manager. He was born in Northumberland and first capped for England in 1965, winning 35 caps between then and 1970 and participating in England's World Cup victory of 1966. He was manager of the Republic of Ireland soccer team during the glory days of the 1990 (Italy) and 1994 (USA) World Cup finals, in recognition of which he was awarded honorary citizenship of Ireland, one of only six individuals to be so honoured. During his time as manager there was a considerable growth in interest in soccer in Ireland and JACK'S ARMY, as the supporters came to be called, followed the national team around the world. During the period he was manager the Irish team played 93 matches, won 46, drew 30 and lost 17. The 1994 World Cup finals saw a lacklustre performance by Ireland, and when the team failed to qualify for the finals of the European Championship in 1996, Charlton handed the reins to his former captain, Mick McCarthy (*see* CAPTAIN FANTASTIC).

Charvet shirts. It was revealed by the MCCRACK-EN TRIBUNAL that two bills totalling £15,832 for Charvet shirts from Paris for Charles HAUGHEY had been paid for from the FIANNA FÁIL party leader's account.

Chas Mahal. The nickname (along with Taj Mahaughey) given to a government building in Merrion Street in Dublin which was lavishly refurbished by Taoiseach Charles HAUGHEY at a time of national economic stringency in 1990. The building was originally the Engineering Department of the National University of Ireland; it dates from 1910 and has a façade of fine Portland Stone. It is open to the public at weekends.

Chaw. *See* HARD CHAW.

Cheltenham Festival. A National Hunt festival (over hurdles) held every March at the Gloucestershire town of Cheltenham. About 50,000 Irish people attend each year, and it is rumoured that 10% of all the Guinness consumed annually in the UK is consumed in the three days of the festival.

See also ISTABRAQ; SWAN, CHARLIE.

Chester Beatty Library. *See* BEATTY, ALFRED CHESTER.

Chichester, Arthur (1563–1625). English soldier and viceroy of Ireland. He was born in Devon, England, and came to Ireland as a professional soldier with ESSEX in 1597 after a stormy early career (he had assaulted a tax official while at Oxford *c.*1583 and took part in the defeat of the Armada). Appointed constable of Carrickfergus Castle in 1599, he was notable for the ferocity of his scorched-earth policies against Hugh O'NEILL in 1601. He was made lord deputy in 1604, and with the defeat of Cahir

O'DOHERTY and the FLIGHT OF THE EARLS was free to help the ULSTER PLANTATION take root. He was granted lands around Belfast and created Lord Chichester of Belfast in 1613 with the territory of Inishowen added to his possessions, but was required to relinquish the deputyship in 1614 because he was not regarded as vigorous enough in his repression of Catholics. As a form of compensation he was made lord treasurer of Ireland, a post he retained for the rest of his life. Though determined to break the Gaelic clan system, he added the harp to the English arms on the Irish coinage. He is remembered by a city centre street in Belfast and by an elaborate tomb in the church of St Nicholas in Carrickfergus.

> I was the rector's son, born to the anglican order,
> Banned for ever from the candles of the Irish poor;
> The Chichesters knelt in marble at the end of a transept
> With ruffs about their necks, their portion sure.
> LOUIS MACNEICE (1907–63): 'Carrickfergus' (1937)

Chichester-Clarke, James (1923–2002). Unionist politician. After a career in the Irish Guards (1942–60), from which he retired with the rank of major, he was elected to STORMONT in 1960, becoming minister of agriculture in 1967. He was unwilling to support Terence O'NEILL's attempts at reform and resigned from the cabinet in April 1969. He became prime minister on 1 May after an internal election in which he defeated Brian FAULKNER by 17 votes to 16. The serious civil disorder following the August violence in Derry persuaded him that British troops were required to maintain peace. Essentially it meant that his cabinet no longer had control of internal security. He was forced to agree to the disbandment of the B-SPECIALS, and, unable to face the Loyalist backlash or contain the early activities of the IRA, he resigned on 20 March 1971. He was succeeded by Faulkner, and was later created a peer, as Lord Moyola.

Chick. A child. In HIBERNO-ENGLISH the noun is usually used in the negative: 'And not a chick nor a child for her to look after.'

Chief, the. A nickname used for Charles Stewart PARNELL by members of the Irish Party and his many supporters throughout Ireland, especially during the years of his greatest success (1881–1890) when, under the terms of the KILMAINHAM TREATY, he laid the foundations for the final settlement of the Land Question, thus ending the LAND WAR. The partnership with Gladstone (see GOM) lasted until the O'Shea scandal.

Chieftains, The. A traditional group established in 1963–4 to make a recording for Claddagh Records and featuring in its five-man line-up several members of CEOLTÓIRÍ CHUALANN, including Martin Fay, Seán Potts and Michael Tubridy. The group took its name from John Montague's 1964 short-story collection, *Death of a Chieftain* and a distinctive graphic was based on a lithograph by sculptor Edward Delaney (see TONEHENGE). The group, under the leadership of piper Paddy Moloney and with some changes in personnel, has since released scores of albums, often in collaboration with traditional artists from other countries, such as the Galician player of *gaitas* (bagpipes), Carlos Nuñez, and has achieved great international critical and commercial success.

Child. A HIBERNO-ENGLISH term for a female baby, as distinct from a boy. A query as to a baby's sex might be phrased, 'Is it a boy or a child?'

Childers, [Robert] Erskine (1870–1922). Novelist and patriot. He was born in Mayfair to an English father and an Irish mother, Anna Barton, from Glendalough in Co. Wicklow, but spent much of his youth in the home of his uncle, Charles Barton, in Glendalough, because of his father's premature death and his mother's illness with tuberculosis. After education at Haileybury and Trinity College, Cambridge, he became a committee clerk in the House of Commons. He fought in the Boer War, and in 1903 published his classic maritime thriller *The Riddle of the Sands*, set in the Baltic and dealing with German preparations for an invasion of England; it is regarded as the first modern espionage novel. He married an American, Molly Osgood, in 1904 and with her raised two sons. He used his yacht, the ASGARD, to bring in guns to Howth for the Irish Volunteers in 1914 (see HOWTH GUN-RUNNING). A convert to SINN FÉIN in 1919, he was principal secretary for the TREATY negotiations but, a loyal follower of de Valera, he took the Republican side in the CIVIL WAR, earning the enmity of Arthur Griffith in the debates on the Treaty, who snapped: 'I will not reply to any damned Englishman in this assembly.' He was executed by a Free State firing squad in Beggar's Bush Barracks in November 1922 for having in his possession a firearm, prohibited by law, when he was arrested in Co. Wicklow. Legend has it that this was a small pearl-handled revolver given to him by Michael Collins, but a government communiqué claimed that it was an automatic pistol. Winston Churchill called him 'a mischief-making, murderous renegade'. The heroic and courteous manner of his death – contemporary accounts describe him shaking hands in turn with all the members of the firing squad, who were overcome with emotion – have ensured him a permanent place in Republican hagiography. In his final letter to his wife he wrote about his death: 'It seems perfectly simple and inevitable, like lying down after a long day's work.'

Childers, Erskine [Hamilton] (1905–75). The son of [Robert] Erskine CHILDERS. He served as a FIANNA FÁIL minister (1951–73) and as TÁNAISTE (1968–73). He was appointed as the fourth president of Ireland in 1973, without an election, but died in office two years later.

Children of Lir. *See* FIONNUALA.

Children of Mary. The name given to members of the confraternity of the Blessed Virgin Mary, an association formally established in Rome in 1864. Membership was limited to women and girls, and recruitment traditionally took place among girls in their final years of secondary school. Members pledge to be faithful to Catholicism and to lead a virtuous life through devotion to the Blessed Virgin. The insignia of the Children of Mary is the MIRACULOUS MEDAL. Women who had been members of the Children of Mary had the privilege of being buried in a special blue-and-white habit. Like most of the outward manifestations of Catholicism, this confraternity has been in decline since the 1960s and it is not clear whether new members continue to be recruited.

Chime in the Slime. The Dublin nickname for a millennium clock installed in the River LIFFEY near O'Connell Bridge in 1996. Technical problems soon caused the clock to be removed and the project abandoned.
See also CRANK ON THE BANK; DISH WITH THE FISH; FLOOZIE IN THE JACUZZI; STILETTO IN THE GHETTO; TART WITH THE CART; URINATION ONCE AGAIN.

Chink in the floor. The source according to J.M. SYNGE of the inspiration and speech patterns that he found useful for his plays:

> When I was writing the 'Shadow of the Glen', some years ago, I got more aid than any learning could have given me from a chink in the floor of the old Wicklow house where I was staying, that let me hear what was being said by the servant girls in the kitchen.
>
> Preface to *The Playboy of the Western World* (21 January 1907)

Chipper. A Dublin colloquialism for 'chip shop'.

Chirpaun. A HIBERNO-ENGLISH term for a love child, from the Irish *tiarpán*, a sack or load carried on the back or hip:

> 'You're my daughter, I'm that chirpaun's grandfather.'
>
> TOM MACINTYRE: *The Gallant John-Joe* (2002)

Chisler/chiseller. A Dublin slang word for 'child', being a corruption of 'children'.

Choctaw Donation. The sum of $710 sent by the Choctaw Nation to alleviate the suffering of the people of Co. Mayo at the height of the GREAT FAMINE. They had got to hear of the deaths of 600 Irish people as they crossed the mountains in an attempt to reach the workhouse in Westport, Co. Mayo. The incident reminded them of their nation's own trek, the 'Trail of Tears', when, in 1830, 13,000 of the 20,000 forced from their

tribal grounds in Mississippi to a reservation in Oklahoma died on the journey. Chief Hollis Roberts, the head of the Choctaws, joined the memorial Mayo Famine Walk in 1990.

Chomhairle Ealaíon, An (Irish, 'the arts council'). The Arts Council, the Irish arts development body, established in 1951. The council itself is a voluntary body of 16 members, appointed by the minister for arts, sport and tourism (the funding department) for a term of five years. There is a substantial executive staff. The council has a strong commitment to promoting the arts in Irish, and supports creative artists through AOSDÁNA. It cooperates on many issues with local authorities, who are also empowered to fund the arts, and with ACNI. Sean O'FAOLAIN was chair of the council 1956–9.

Christ Church Cathedral. The cathedral in Dublin of the Church of Ireland diocese of Dublin and Glendalough. It was founded by the Viking king of Dublin, SITRIC SILKBEARD, in about 1028. Construction of a new cathedral was begun after the Anglo-Norman invasion at the end of the 12th century, and additions were made during the 14th and 16th centuries. The English Yorkist pretender Lambert SIMNEL was crowned king there in 1487. Like the neighbouring ST PATRICK'S CATHEDRAL it was extensively restored in the 1870s and now contains little of the original building.

Christian Brothers. A religious order with a mission to educate poor boys, founded by Edmund Ignatius RICE at the beginning of the 19th century. Until recent decades it played a key role in Catholic primary and secondary education in Ireland. As well as the order's mother house, Sion Hill in Waterford, among the most famous schools founded by Rice was O'Connell's School in Dublin's north inner city (1828). During the late 19th and early 20th century, scores of Christian Brothers schools were established in the UK, the USA, India, Australia and South Africa – all over the English-speaking world – and the badge of the Christian Brothers education is worn with pride by thousands of men who never set foot in Ireland.

In Ireland the Christian Brothers were regarded as diligent educators, but were also known to maintain a fearsome regime of discipline based on corporal punishment – the leather or the strap. 'Bet into him by the Christian Brothers' was a phrase used, sometimes half-admiringly, by parents. The 'Brothers' also inculcated traditional patriotic values, Gaelic games and the Irish language: the rosary beads, the SLIOTAR and the *fáinne* (*see* FÁINNE ÓIR) might be said to exemplify their ethos.

While there is no doubt that the majority of Christian Brothers were conscientious and moral teachers, the order has suffered from a serious decline in reputation over recent decades, particularly in relation to allegations of sexual abuse of boys in schools and in industrial schools like LETTERFRACK and ARTANE which were under their care. The order has had to take remedial action both for the sake of its public image and for the welfare of its ever-declining number of mostly ageing members.

Christmas, Little. *See* BETWEEN THE TWO CHRISTMASES; BIG CHRISTMAS; WOMEN'S CHRISTMAS.

Christmas box. A gift given by shopkeepers to their customers for Christmas. In rural areas shopkeepers would give regular customers a gift of several items of food or drink depending on how valuable their custom was. In the early years of the 20th century the box would normally include a CHRISTMAS CANDLE and a CHRISTMAS JUG.

Christmas candle. A large candle lit in the window or windows of all houses in rural Ireland on Christmas Eve and on certain nights during the Christmas period to welcome the Christ Child. It was a tradition that on Christmas Eve the candle was lit by the youngest person in the household. This custom survives, even in urban areas in Ireland, although more recently the candles have tended to be electric.

Christmas jug. A china jug filled with jam, which was often part of the CHRISTMAS BOX that shopkeepers gave to customers on Christmas Eve.

Christy Mahon. *See* MAHON, CHRISTY.

Chuckies. *See* TIOCFAIDH ÁR LÁ.

Church cess. The charge levied on all members of an Irish parish for the upkeep of Anglican churches (a *cess* is a local tax). In Ireland in the 1830s there were 850,000 members of the CHURCH OF IRELAND compared with nearly 7 million Catholics. This anomaly of large support from non-members led to the TITHE WAR and the eventual disestablishment of the Church of Ireland in 1869.

Churchill, Lord Randolph (1849–94). Conservative politician. His father, the 6th Duke of Marlborough, was viceroy in Dublin (1876–80) and Churchill's interest in the Irish Question dated from that time. Leader of a radical group within the Conservative Party, he was a brilliant demagogue, remembered mainly for encouragement of Ulster Unionist and Orange extremism with the phrase, 'ULSTER WILL FIGHT and Ulster will be right.'

Churchill, Winston (1874–1965). British statesman, the son of Lord Randolph CHURCHILL. He was secretary of state for war during the Anglo-Irish War of 1919–21 and advocated stern measures against the IRA, especially the hanging of those who killed police: 'It is monstrous,' he said at a meeting with the Irish chief secretary on 31 May 1920, 'that there we should have 200 murders and no one hung.' He finally got his way when Kevin Barry was hanged on 1 November 1920 (*see* 'MOUNTJOY JAIL ONE MONDAY MORNING, IN'), giving the IRA a major propaganda boost. Churchill was a member of the British team in the TREATY negotiations and came to respect the ability of Michael Collins, who faced him on the Irish side. The tone of his radio broadcast of 13 May 1945 (*see* CHURCHILL–DE VALERA RADIO EXCHANGES) was bitterly resented in Ireland.

Churchill–de Valera radio exchanges. A criticism of Éire's neutrality made by Winston Churchill in his broadcast victory speech on 13 May 1945 was answered by de Valera with judicious diplomacy three days later. Churchill had suggested that because of his insistence on neutrality, 'so much at variance with the temper and instinct of thousands of southern Irishmen who hastened to the battlefront to prove their ancient valour, the approaches which the southern Irish ports and airfields could so easily have guarded were closed by the hostile aircraft and U-boats.' The speech was seen by most Irish people as gratuitously offensive, especially in the use of such language as '… we left the de Valera government to frolic with the German and later with the Japanese representatives to their hearts' content'. The taoiseach's response on 16 May was quietly effective (*see* PHRASES MAKE HISTORY HERE):

> Mr Churchill is proud of Britain's stand alone, after France had fallen and before America entered the war. Could he not find it in his heart the generosity to acknowledge that there is a small nation that stood alone, not for one year only, but for several hundred years against aggression; that endured spoliations, famines, massacres in endless succession; that was clubbed many times into insensibility, but that each time, on returning consciousness, took up the fight anew; a small nation that could never be got to accept defeat and has never surrendered her soul?

Church of Ireland. The largest Protestant church in Ireland, with 368,467 (1991 census) members, three-quarters of whom live in Northern Ireland. It was the established church from 1537 to 1870 (*see* DISESTABLISHMENT OF THE CHURCH OF IRELAND) and still has full communion with the see of Canterbury, though the archbishop has no jurisdiction over Irish Anglicans. The Church of Ireland claims descent from the church founded by St Patrick and regards itself as a uniquely Irish institution. It has a diocesan structure not dissimilar to the Catholic Church and like the latter regards ARMAGH as the primatial see.

Churn. A verb used in HIBERNO-ENGLISH in relation to the making of butter. Butter was a source of income – often the only regular one – for many rural families, and the churning of butter was a crucial part of the week's work. There were many PISHOGUES or superstitions associated with the weekly making of butter, as there were times when the churn did not 'make'. Anyone passing by while the churn was being made was expected to pause, bless the work and lend a hand to show that there was no ill-will. The passer-by was said to 'put the size of his head in the churn' or 'put the sign of his hand on the churn', it being believed that this was the amount of profit he could take with him if he didn't give a hand. Nor could fire (even in the form of a lighted cigarette or pipe) be taken out of the house until the churn was made. Butter was transported to the nearest trading point – one of the most notable such was the Butter Market in Cork, near the church of St Anne's in Shandon. In many parts of the country can be seen the remains of 'butter roads', along which butter was transported in former times. Some of these are now in use as walking trails: for instance, the butter road between Killarney and Kenmare now forms part of the Kerry Way. Some families would not have enough butter regularly to fill the requisite barrel or firkin, so they would 'join in butter' with another family, combining their butter output in one firkin. The wives would all gather in one house once a week to wash and blend the butter and pack the firkins for dispatch to the market. It was said that families that were joined in butter never quarrelled.

Ciachán (Irish *ceochán*, 'hoarseness' or 'fuzziness'). A HIBERNO-ENGLISH term for 'hoarseness' or a 'frog in the throat'.

Cian. In Irish mythology, the son of DIAN CECHT and god of medicine. Dressed as a woman, he makes his way to Tory Island to recover his cow, the GLAS GAIBHLEANN, which had been stolen by BALOR OF THE EVIL EYE, the Irish cyclops. While there he manages to penetrate the crystal tower in which Balor had imprisoned his daughter ETHLINN and proceeds to seduce her. Their child is LUGH. Cian is eventually slain by the sons of Tuireann (whom he fathered on the triune goddess Brigid) in spite of turning himself into a hare.

Ciarán of Clonmacnoise. The founder of the greatest of all the monasteries/universities of early Christian Ireland. He was born in Connacht c.516 and educated by St FINNIAN OF CLONARD and St ENDA. According to legend he left home when still a young boy driving a fine dun cow before him for sustenance. (The BOOK OF THE DUN COW was traditionally written on vellum made from this animal's skin.) He was led by visions to CLONMACNOISE on the Shannon where he began his foundation c.547. He did not survive long there, perhaps as little as seven months, but he left behind a notably austere rule and a tradition of piety, learning and fine art. He died in 549. His feast day is 9 September.

Ciarán of Saighir. The first-born of the saints of Ireland, as he was known, was said to come from Clear Island, Co. Cork, and to have been sent back to Ireland by St PATRICK as his precursor after religious training in Tours and Rome. He became one of the TWELVE APOSTLES OF IRE-LAND, trained by St FINNIAN OF CLONARD. Ciarán founded the monastery of Saighir, near Birr in the diocese of Ossory, of which he was the first bishop and patron saint. His feast day is 5 March.

Ciaróg (Irish, 'beetle', 'cockroach'). There is an Irish proverb, the equivalent of 'Birds of a feather flock together': '*Aithníonn ciaróg ciaróg eile*' ('One beetle recognizes another').

CIÉ. Córas Iompair Éireann (literally 'transport system of Ireland'), which was instituted by the state on 1 January 1945, when the great Southern Railways company was amalgamated with the Dublin United Transport Company under the terms of the Transport Act of 1944. A state enterprise originally responsible for all countrywide and rural transport, CIÉ has suffered from chronic under-investment and was not in a position to capitalize on the prosperity and increased population of the 1990s.

'Cill Cais'. *See* 'CAD A DHÉANFAIMÍD FEASTA GAN ADHMAD?'; DÉISE, THE.

Ciotóg (Irish). A left-handed person; the adjective is *ciotach*. Colkitto (Colla Ciotach) Mac-

Donald and his regiment of Highlanders, who were billeted in the British army barracks at CHARLESFORT in Kinsale, were all killed in an attack in north Cork during the REBELLION OF 1798.

Cith or a foul. *See* CLIP O' THE REEL.

Citizen, the. The nickname of Michael Cusack and referred to as such in Joyce's ULYSSES. He was one of the founders of the GAA, having called the inaugural meeting at Hayes's Hotel, Thurles, Co. Tipperary, on 1 November 1884. He was born in Carron, Co. Clare, in 1847 and after holding several teaching posts in Newry, Blackrock and CLONGOWES WOOD established the Civil Service Academy, a cramming establishment, which continued to bring him in a substantial income. At the Thurles meeting he was elected president of the association and continued in the post until his death on 27 November 1906. The nickname arose from his pleasure in being called 'Citizen Cusack'.

Citizen Army. *See* IRISH CITIZEN ARMY.

City, the (Irish *Cathair Chrobh Dhearg*, 'the city of Red Crobh'; Crobh being a pagan god). A site of pagan and Christian worship at the foot of the Paps mountains (in Irish *Dhá Chích Danainn*, 'the two breasts of DANA¹') in Shrone, Co. Kerry. The monument, now partly destroyed, comprised a circular wall, 3m (10 ft) high and 1.8 m (6 ft) thick. Inside the walls there was also a large stone circle with traces of OGAM writing and a holy well. The site has been associated with human sacrifice, as witnessed by the names of nearby townlands, Gortdearg ('red field') and Gort na gCeann ('field of the heads'). The great Celtic feast of BEALTAINE – May Day – was observed in the City in living memory as a Catholic PATTERN day. People made rounds of the site (of varying degrees of complexity), reciting prayers of atonement and supplication, but other aspects of the pilgrimage – the merriment, dancing and drinking associated with the pattern day, and the leaving of money or pieces of cloth tied to bushes or trees in the City – suggest a ritual far older than Christianity.

City of the Broken Treaty. *See* LIMERICK, TREATY OF.

City of the Tribes. A description of medieval Galway because of the presence in the prosperous city of a mercantile oligarchy of Anglo-Norman or English extraction. The 'tribes' were the families of Athy, Blake, Bodkin, Browne, Darcy, Deane, Font, French, Joyce, Kirwan, Lynch, Martin, Morris and Skerret. The chief of these was the Lynch family, who provided 84 mayors for the city between 1485 and 1654, but all were rich, Catholic, loyal to the English crown and terrified of the wild Gaels without. An inscription dated 1549 read: 'This gate was erected to protect us from the ferocious O'Flaherties Good Lord deliver us.' The 'ferocious O'Flaherties' would themselves provide the city with mayors in 1951 and 1964.

Civic Guard. The English name for the GARDA SÍOCHÁNA, the official name for Ireland's police force since independence.

Civil Rights Movement. The campaign – reaching a climax in the winter and spring of 1968/9 – to abolish sectarian discrimination in Northern Ireland in jobs, housing and local elections; the movement also sought the abolition of the SPECIAL POWERS ACT and the B-SPECIALS. The Northern Ireland Civil Rights Association (NICRA), founded in Belfast in 1967, subsumed initially a number of other reform groupings including the Dungannon-based Campaign for Social Justice and PEOPLE'S DEMOCRACY, a radical student group, mainly associated with Queen's University Belfast, and led by Michael Farrell and Bernadette DEVLIN. NICRA's constituency was broad, including liberals, communists and middle-class Nationalists. Influenced by the spirit of the times, and especially by the success of Martin Luther King (1929–68) in the USA, it received practical help from the British National Council for Civil Liberties.

After several significant protests in the summer of 1968 it was decided to hold a march on 5 October in Derry – the Unionists' iconic MAIDEN CITY, her latter-day virginity preserved by Byzantine ward-rigging that deprived a large Catholic majority of civic power. The march was banned by William Craig, the hardline minister of home affairs, and the marchers were met with the traditional RUC and B-Special 'vigour' in the form of baton charges and water cannon. It was the kind of scene that had not been uncommon in Ireland for at least two centuries, but on this occasion the news cameras of the world were there to record this usually un-emphasized aspect of Ulster life. The serious rioting that followed in Derry that night was to be repeated many times.

In essence the Northern Ireland TROUBLES began then, but the civil rights that were reluctantly granted (including that required by the cry 'One man, one vote') were regarded as 'too little, too late'. Peaceful protest was replaced by the ARMED STRUGGLE, and the movement's honourable motives have subsequently tended to be obscured in the violence of the Troubles.

Civil War. The name given to the war that broke out between supporters and opponents of the Anglo-Irish TREATY of December 1921, that is between the FREE STATE government and the IRA. The war proper may be said to have begun on 28 June 1922 when a Republican garrison that had been holding the FOUR COURTS since 13 April was bombarded by Free State guns. It was not a war of pitched battles, but rather of small-scale guerrilla fighting. Although the casualties of the ten months of war were not very high (between 600 and 700), the period has remained in the memory of the people as a time of unparalleled bitterness and cruelty, as brother fought against brother. Among the remembered events are: the court martial and execution of Erskine CHILDERS in November 1922; the execution of Dick Barrett, Joe McKelvey, Liam MELLOWS and Rory O'CONNOR on 8 December 1922 in reprisal for the murder of the TD Seán Hales; and the BALLYSEEDY MASSACRE in Co. Kerry in March 1923. The civil war ended with the unconditional surrender of the Republicans under Frank AIKEN on 24 May (*see* CEASE FIRE AND DUMP ARMS) after the death of the most intransigent Republican leader, Liam Lynch (*see*

REAL CHIEF, THE) earlier that year. More than 10,000 anti-Treaty Republicans were arrested and interned, but most of them were released within the year.

See also COLLINS, MICHAEL; COUNTESS BRIDGE KILLINGS; DE VALERA, ÉAMON; IRREGULARS; KNOCKNAGOSHEL AMBUSH; O'HIGGINS, KEVIN; SEVENTY-SEVEN.

Clab. An Irish word for the 'mouth', used in HIBERNO-ENGLISH for an open mouth, as in impolite expressions such as 'Will you shut your clab!'

Clabber. A HIBERNO-ENGLISH word for 'mud' or 'general household dirt', from the Irish word *clábar* 'mud':

> The deil a man in this townlan'
> Wos claner raired nor me
> But I'm livin' in Drumlister
> In clabber to the knee.

> W.F. MARSHALL: 'Me an' Me Da', in *Ballads and Verses from Tyrone* (1929)

Claddagh, the. An ancient and once self-governing fishing village, now part of Galway (*see* CITY OF THE TRIBES). For many centuries the inhabitants of this Irish-speaking village arrogated to themselves exclusive fishing rights over the whole of Galway Bay. The name comes from the Gaelic word *cládach* ('shore') referring to the place where the fishermen beached their boats, but the days when the fishermen put to sea were governed by rules Byzantine in their complexity. James Hardiman (1782–1855) can hardly conceal his impatience with the innate recalcitrance of Claddagh dwellers in his *History of the Town and County of Galway* (1820):

> … though they sometimes exhibit a great shew of industry, they are still so wedded to the old customs that they invariably reject, with the most inveterate prejudice, any new improvement in their fishing apparatus, which is consequently now very little superior to that used centuries ago by their ancestors … When they do not themselves think it proper to fish, they invariably prevent any other from attempting it.

The Claddagh disappeared in urban redevelopment in the mid-1930s, and such glories as the festival of St John's Day (24 June) – when the whole village dressed in special costume to elect mayor, sheriff and other civic officers – are hardly even memories. What does survive is the ever-popular CLADDAGH RING.

Claddagh Records. An Irish record label founded in 1959 by Garech Browne and others. Its first recording was of UILLEANN piper Leo Rowsome. As well as issuing The CHIEFTAINS' eponymous first album (1965) and 12 others by that group, the company has promoted the work of a galaxy of traditional musicians and singers, such as SLIABH LUACHRA fiddlers Denis Murphy and Julia Clifford (*The Star above the Garter*), singer Dolly MacMahon and harper Derek Bell. There is also a Claddagh record shop in Dublin's TEMPLE BAR.

Claddagh Ring. A ring with a bezel of two hands grasping a crowned heart, associated with the fishing village of the CLADDAGH. The sentimental association of its motto: 'This is my heart which I give to you crowned with my love' has made the ring increasing popular as a wedding band. Also associated with the ring is the wish: 'Let love and friendship reign.' If the band is a gift of a loved one the ring is worn with the heart pointing inwards, but should that love vanish the ring, if worn, has the heart reversed.

Claideamh Soluis, An (Irish, 'the sword of light'). The bilingual journal of the GAELIC LEAGUE. It replaced *FÁINNE AN LAE*, and the title, pronounced 'clay-oo solish', came from the invincible sword of NUADA in Irish mythology. It was first issued on 18 March 1899, and under the editorship of Eoin MacNeill and Patrick Pearse became also the voice of the IRISH VOLUNTEERS. The famous article 'The North Began', MacNeill's call for the founding of an armed force like the UVF, appeared on 1 November 1913. The journal was suppressed in 1916, and resumed the name *Fáinne an Lae* 1918–30, with a hiatus during the Anglo-Irish War (1919–21), when it was known as *Misneach* (pronounced 'mish-nach' and meaning 'courage'). It reverted to the title *An Claideamh Soluis* for its final two years after 1930.

Claisceadal. An Irish-language choir singing in unison. Cóir Chúil Aodha (the choir of Coolea in the MUSKERRY GAELTACHT in west Cork) is the best known of its kind, performing at the local Mass but also in concert venues and on radio and television. It was established by Seán Ó RIADA in 1964 to perform his *Mass*, and subsequently led by his son Peadar.

Clancy, Liam. *See* CLANCY BROTHERS, THE.

Clancy, Peadar. *See* BLOODY SUNDAY 1920.

Clancy, Willie (1918–73). Musician, singer and dancer. He was born in Miltown Malbay, Co. Clare, and spent some years in Dublin and London before returning permanently to Co. Clare in 1957. He began to play the UILLEANN PIPES at the age of 20 and within a few years was a master of the instrument. The WILLIE CLANCY SUMMER SCHOOL in named in his honour.

Clancy Barracks. The former Islandbridge Cavalry Barracks in Dublin, which was handed over to the provisional government of the Free State in December 1922. It was renamed Clancy Barracks in 1942 in memory of Peadar Clancy (*see* BLOODY SUNDAY 1920).

Clancy Brothers, The. A ballad group comprising three brothers from Carrick-on-Suir, Co. Tipperary – Paddy (1923–90), Tom (1923–98) and Liam (b.1936) – and Armagh-born Tommy Makem (b.1932), who popularized ARAN jumpers and Irish folksongs ('The Shoals of Herring', 'The Irish Rover') in the late 1950s and 1960s. Liam Clancy was the lead vocalist and had the longest singing career, recording with Tommy Makem until the late 1980s. He moved to New York in 1956 and performed with the group in the folk clubs of Greenwich Village in New York. The Clancys' lucky break came with an appearance on the *Ed Sullivan Show*, which was seen by 50 million people. They subsequently achieved iconic status in the United States (Bob Dylan admired them), later becoming equally popular in Ireland and in Europe. Tommy Makem and Liam Clancy were the first to leave the group, in 1969. The Clancys

spawned many imitators, and were in any case overtaken by the *echt*-traditional revival of the 1970s, but for many people – practitioners and audiences alike – they provided an introduction to traditional Irish music.

Clannad. A traditional group formed in 1970, who achieved great success with their particular brand of Celtic traditional/folk music, which included traditional Donegal Irish-language material. The band included several members of the Ó Braonáin (Brennan) family of Gweedore, Co. Donegal, and the name (a coinage) is based on the Irish word *clann* ('family'). Their original theme song for the 1982 TV series *Harry's Game* reached the British charts, a first for an Irish-language song. Eithne Ní Bhraonáin (ENYA) left the group to pursue a solo career in 1982.

Clan Na Gael (imperfect Irish for 'the Irish race'). An Irish-American organization founded after the failure of the FENIAN CAMPAIGN OF 1867 with the intention of keeping alive the PHOENIX FLAME and preparing for a coming armed struggle. The chief personality was John DEVOY, and by the end of the 1870s there were 10,000 members and strong links with the IRB in Ireland. Both organizations kept themselves in a state of readiness, aware that 'England's difficulty was Ireland's opportunity'. Clan Na Gael was of use to PARNELL during the NEW DEPARTURE, but the resulting strengthening of constitutional Nationalism in a sense thwarted the movement's purpose. It was not until the resurgence of the IRB in the early 20th century and the founding of the IRISH VOLUNTEERS that Devoy and his organization were able to assist the armed struggle that they believed was the only means of securing their objectives.

Clann na Poblachta (Irish, 'family of the republic'). The name of the political party, popularly called 'the Clann', founded in July 1946 by Sean MACBRIDE, Jack McQuillan and Noel Hartnett. It was supported by some still-active IRA members, and saw itself as a radical, modernizing force in Irish political life. The party grew rapidly, winning several by-elections in 1947 and ten seats in the general election of 1948, to form the first INTERPARTY GOVERNMENT with FINE GAEL, the LABOUR PARTY and CLANN NA TALMHAN. Two Clann members became ministers: MacBride for foreign affairs and Noël BROWNE for health. The most important elements of the legislative progamme of that government were the passage of the Government of Ireland Act 1948, whereby Ireland was declared a republic (see REPUBLIC OF IRELAND), and the MOTHER AND CHILD SCHEME. After Browne resigned over the latter, a general election was called in 1951 and FIANNA FÁIL returned to power, while the Clann won only two seats. Although one Clann deputy, Jack Tully of Co. Cavan, remained in the Dáil until 1965 and the party was not dissolved until 1969, it was a spent force by 1951, and MacBride lost his Dáil seat in 1957.

Clann na Talmhan (Irish, 'family of the land'). A political party founded in Athenry, Co. Galway, by Michael Donnellan in 1938, with the aim of representing the interests of the small farmers of the west of Ireland. It gained its strongest support in those areas, winning 14 seats in the 1943 election and seven seats in 1948, forming an INTERPARTY GOVERNMENT with CLANN NA POBLACHTA, FINE GAEL and the LABOUR PARTY. After the collapse of that government in 1951 the party lost support, and it had disappeared by 1965.

Clare hearse. A nickname for the ten of clubs, a card of bad portent in fortune-telling. The origin of the name is obscure.

Claribel. The pen name of Charlotte Alington, who was born on 23 December 1830. Unusually for the period, she was encouraged by her husband Charles Barnard to continue her career as composer and lyricist. In the last ten years of her shortish life she wrote many popular pieces, and is credited with establishing the system of royalties for ballads. She is remembered now for one immortal song 'Come Back to Erin' (1866), which many still believe to be an Irish folk song. She died in Dover on 30 January 1869.

Then come back to Erin, Mavourneen,
  Mavourneen;
Come back, aroon, to the land of my birth.
Come with the shamrocks and springtime,
  Mavourneen,
And it's Killarney shall ring with our mirth.

Clarke, Austin [Augustine Joseph] (1896–1974). Poet and verse-playwright. Clarke was born in Dublin and educated at Belvedere and University College Dublin. He succeeded in 1917 to the lectureship at UCD left vacant by the execution of Thomas MACDONAGH, but a mental breakdown and an unhappy and shortlived marriage to the playwright Geraldine Cummins led to a retreat to London in 1922. He supported himself there as a book reviewer for 15 years, during which time he forged a poetic technique that reflected in English the assonantal strength of Gaelic prosody. All his writing is imbued with a sense of the Celtic past, as exemplified in the sagas, and the contrast between its perceived heroic sensuality and the Catholic piety of the Ireland in which he grew up mirrored his own sexual guilt. In all he published 18 books of poetry, from *The Vengeance of Fionn* (1917) to the *Collected Poems* (1974), the latter giving a map of his poetic progress, including the 17-year hiatus between *Night and Morning* (1938) and *Ancient Lights* (1955). The later poetry was notably satirical of his country and happily erotic, the Catholic Church's Laocoön-like coils shrugged off. During the 1930s Clarke wrote two of his three prose romances about medieval Ireland and founded the Lyric Theatre (arising out of his Dublin Verse-Speaking Society) for which he wrote 11 plays, published as *Collected Plays* (1963) and including *The Son of Learning* (1927) and the satirical *Black Fast* (1941). He wrote two books of autobiography, *Twice Round the Black Church* (1962) and *A Penny in the Clouds* (1968).

Clarke, Harry (1889–1931). Artist. He was born in Dublin on St Patrick's Day, 1889, the son of an English father whose business was the decoration of churches, and to whom he was apprenticed after education at Belvedere. In 1910 he began to study at the Metropolitan School of Art, and he visited France in 1914 on a scholarship. He worked as a book illustrator, but it is for his stained-glass church windows that he is best known, his first commission being University College Cork's Honan Chapel in 1917. His work can also be seen in the Presentation Convent chapel in Dingle (now An Díseart), St Joseph's Terenure in Dublin and Castlehaven, Co. Cork. In 1930 he set up his own studios in North Frederick Street in Dublin, but he had already spent a year in Switzerland to try to combat the tuberculosis that would kill him. He died in Coire, Switzerland, on 6 January 1931.

Clarke, Kathleen (1878–1972). Republican activist. She was born Kathleen Daly to a Republican family in Limerick city and worked in her own dressmaking business. In 1901, against family opposition, she married Thomas J. CLARKE, the last Fenian to be released after serving 15 years in Portland jail. He was 28 years her senior. The couple lived in New York until 1907 and had three sons, and after they returned to Dublin they were deeply involved in the IRB; Kathleen was one of the founders in 1913 of CUMANN NA MBAN, the women's division of the IRISH VOLUNTEERS. She lost her husband, her brother (the executed leader Edward Daly) and her unborn baby as a result of the Easter Rising. In the months after the Rising, she established the Irish Volunteers' Dependents' Fund to support the families of the dead and the imprisoned, and was elected to the executive of SINN FÉIN. During the Anglo-Irish War she worked in the DÁIL COURTS. She opposed the TREATY but joined FIANNA FÁIL on its foundation in 1926 and served as a senator 1927–36, although, like Hanna SHEEHY-SKEFFINGTON, she was deeply critical of the CONSTITUTION OF 1937. In 1939 she was elected the first woman lord mayor of Dublin. She resigned from Fianna Fáil because of de Valera's treatment of Republicans during the EMERGENCY and for the final years of her life she lived in Liverpool with her son.

Clarke, Sister Sarah. *See* JOAN OF ARC OF THE PRISONS.

Clarke, Thomas J. (1858–1916). Revolutionary. He was born on the Isle of Wight, where his father was serving in the British army, and grew up in South Africa. He emigrated to the USA in 1880, and there joined CLAN NA GAEL. With Thomas Gallagher he began a dynamiting campaign in England, and in 1883 was sentenced to life imprisonment for treason and felony. He was treated very harshly in prison, and was the last of the FENIAN prisoners to be released, in 1898 (*see* AMNESTY ASSOCIATION). He returned to America, continuing his involvement with Clan na Gael and working on its newspaper, the *Gaelic American*. In 1907 he and his wife (*see* CLARKE, KATHLEEN) returned to live in Dublin, where they ran a tobacconist's shop in Parnell Square that became a centre of Republican activity. Clarke became a member of the supreme council of the IRB and was one of the main driving forces behind the EASTER RISING of 1916. He was the first signatory of the PROCLAMATION OF THE REPUBLIC, and after the rising was court-martialled. He was executed on 3 May.

Clash. An Ulster word signifying 'tell tales', 'inform' as in: 'Away, ye clashbag; ye'll no clash on me!'

Clash of the ash, the. A phrase used to signify, romantically, the game of HURLING: hurleys are traditionally made from the wood of the ash tree. The tree is supposed to be 30 years old, and the wood taken from where the roots spread, so that the grain of the wood will not go with the length of the stick, making it liable to split.

Clatty. A near onomatopoeic and enthusiastic Ulster word meaning 'extremely dirty'. The word is no doubt cognate with Scots *clarty*, meaning the same. There is also a noun 'clat', meaning one possessing the quality of clattiness:

> An if me shirt's a clatty shirt
> The man to blame's me da.
>
> W.F. MARSHALL: 'Me an' me Da', in *Ballads and Verses of Tyrone* (1929)

Claudius Ptolemaeus. *See* PTOLEMY.

Claudy Bombing. A Provisional IRA operation on 31 July 1972, intended as a response to OPERATION MOTORMAN, in which three no-warning car bombs left in Claudy, a village in Co. Derry, killed 6 people and injured 34; 2 more died later from their injuries. The telephone box in the nearby town of Dungiven that was to have been used for a warning had been destroyed in an earlier IRA operation and no alternative was found. Calls for an inquiry into the incident were made in 2002 on the 30th anniversary of the incident because of the suggestion that a Catholic priest, a known IRA sympathizer, had driven one of the cars.

> And Christ, little Katherine Aiken is dead,
> and Mrs McLaughlin is pierced through the head.
> Meanwhile to Dungiven the killers have gone
> And they're finding it hard to get through on the
> phone.
>
> JAMES SIMMONS (1933–2001): 'Claudy', in *West Strand Visions* (1974)

Cleary, Bridget (*c*.1869–95). A woman burned as a witch by her husband, who believed she was a CHANGELING. Bridget Boland was born near Fethard in Co. Tipperary, and married a local cooper, Michael Cleary, in 1887. She was childless, and behaviour that he deemed strange led her husband to believe that she had been spirited away by the fairies and a changeling put in her place. After attempting to solve the problem using PISHOGUES (charms and spells) and folk remedies, Cleary finally poured paraffin over his wife and set her alight. Her father, aunt and cousins were witnesses to the murder but did not attempt to save the young woman. When the case came to court the jury was convinced that Michael Cleary genuinely believed that he could get his real wife back from the fairies once the 'changeling' was killed: he waited for her by a local RING FORT (long associated with the fairies) for three nights. He was found guilty of manslaughter.

Cleary, Michael. *See* SINGING PRIEST, THE.

Cleas na péiste (Irish, 'trick of the worm'). A folkloric cure for worms in calves in Co. Kerry, which involved putting nine knots on a string and hitting the calf on its back nine times, after each time untying one knot.

Cleburne, Patrick R[onayne] (1828–64). Confed-erate general. He was born on 16 March 1822 in Co. Cork and rose to the rank of corporal in the 41st Regiment of Foot in the British army. His family decided to emigrate to the USA in 1849 and in order to join them he had to buy himself out. They landed at New Orleans after 50 days at sea and for the next 11 years Cleburne kept a store, studied law and in 1860 joined the 1st Arkansas militia. By 1862 he was a brigadier general, the hero of Shiloh, the battle fought in Tennessee on 6–7 April, and which had the highest number of Confederate casualties of any battle in the American Civil War. In all 23,000 soldiers in both armies died in the encounter, which showed that the war was going to be 'modern' and bloody. Cleburne was far from unique as a man of Irish birth fighting on the side of the South, though the majority of fighting Irish-Americans were in the Federal army. Cleburne came out strongly against slavery, proposing emancipation in 1864, which prevented any further promotion. His force – noted for its dashing bravery and un-conventional tactics – was easily distinguishable by its standard of a blue flag with a white moon. Cleburne was killed on 30 November 1864 during a sortie in Tennessee; he was on foot, having had two horses shot from under him. Robert E. Lee, the Confederate commander-in-chief, described him as 'shining like a meteor in a clouded sky', while an anonymous poet in *The* NATION mourned him thus:

> There were hearts that bled
> When its course was spread
> And old Ireland felt your loss.

Cleever. A term used in counties Louth, Monaghan and Cavan for a person who deals in hens and other fowl. It derives from the Irish *cliabh* ('basket', used for carrying fowl).

Cleggan Bay Disaster. On the night of 27–8 October 1927, 45 fishermen from Inishkea, Lacken, Inishbofin and Cleggan were lost in a sudden and ferocious storm in Cleggan Bay off the Galway coast. In 1909 the CONGESTED DISTRICTS BOARD had supplied the fishermen of Cleggan with 'nobbies', boats of about

15 m (45 ft) in length. These allowed them to go further afield than in their traditional CURRACHS, but by 1919 catches were poor and many fishermen who had invested in vessels and gear were in debt. In the summer of 1927 the mackerel and herring had returned. It is believed that so many fishermen need not have died in the storm if they had not been so anxious to save their equipment.

Clement Scottus. An Irish *doctus* (scholar) who was part of the court of CHARLEMAGNE from 791 and succeeded ALCUIN as chief scholastic in 796. Tradition ascribes to him a perhaps unjustified reputation for arrogance. None of his writings have survived except *Ars Grammatica*, ('the art of grammar', 809–12), in which he lays stress upon the universal use of Greek in teaching. He died in Würzburg and is buried in the cathedral crypt.

Clevvy. A small shelf or set of shelves, particularly a shelf over the fire on which tobacco for the man of the house or snuff for the woman might be kept.
See also CABOOSE.

Clifden. (Irish *Clochán*, 'stepping-stones') An attractive market town and fishing port in Co. Galway, known as the capital of Connemara (*see* CONNEMARA PONY) and a major tourist centre. It was founded in about 1812 by a local entrepreneur, John D'Arcy of Killtullagh, whose derelict castle, built in 1815, may still be seen two miles to the west of the town. It was the site of the Clifden Marconi Wireless Station, the first transatlantic telegraphic base in Europe. A monument to ALCOCK AND BROWN, the aviators, was erected near the Derrygimlagh bog, the place where they crash-landed in 1919 after their flight from Newfoundland. To the east of the town is the range of mountains known as the Twelve Pins. The town, with its gourmet restaurants and fashionable shops, is a kind of index of a more modern Ireland, precisely attuned to visitors' expectations in a steadily growing tourist trade.

Clifford, Julia. *See* DENIS THE WEAVER; SLIABH LUACHRA.

Cliffs of Moher. A spectacular 8 km (5 miles) of sea cliffs on the west coast of Co. Clare. The cliffs, rising to 231m (700 ft), are 5 km (3 miles) northwest of Liscannor, Co. Clare.

Clift. A foolish person, wild rather than stupid, perhaps from the word 'cleft' suggesting some kind of cranial fissure, as in 'He's a kind of clift – not a complete eejit!'

Cline Maggie. *See* 'DRILL, YE TARRIERS DRILL'.

Clinic. A time and place for consultation offered by TDs (members of the Dáil), especially those of the rural PARISH-PUMP variety, where their constituents can make requests for representation on matters relating to social welfare and justice, and air their grievances.

Cliodna. A Celtic goddess of beauty who lives in TÍR TAIRNIGIRI ('the Land of Promise') and falls in love with a mortal, Ciabhán of the Curling Locks. They live happily on the shore at Glandore, Co. Cork, until at the bidding of her father Gebann, the chief druid of MANANNÁN MAC LIR, the sea-god sends a huge wave that carries her back home and leaves her lover grieving.

Cliotar. An Irish word for 'rattling noise', 'clatter', used in HIBERNO-ENGLISH for any unwelcome noise or fuss, for example what might be heard from a crowd of teenagers. The word also describes the noise associated with the banging of saucepans and other kitchen implements.

Clip o' the reel (also **kip of the reel**). An activity that would occasion disturbance and CRAIC: 'The same old clip o' the reel when the girls came home from the dance.' The phrase is often used with the synonymous 'cith or a foul', and like it probably originates in a mimicking of the sound of speedy activity.

Clismirt. An Irish word for 'struggle', used also in HIBERNO-ENGLISH to signify a 'conflict', or a 'wrangle'.

Clive, Kitty (1711–85). Comic actress and sketch writer. She was born Catherine Rafter, probably in Belfast, the daughter of a Jacobite lawyer from Kilkenny who moved to London to improve his prospects. She joined Colley Cibber's company in 1728 during his management of the Theatre Royal, Drury Lane, and by 1731 she had established herself as one of the leading comediennes of the day. That year she married George Clive, but the marriage lasted only a few months. They parted amicably, but in the style of the theatre programmes of the period she was thereafter known as Mrs Clive.

She had a magnificent singing voice, appearing in the first performance of Handel's *Samson* (1743). It was said that she was the only actress whom the great Garrick feared, although the two remained close friends. The cause of their friction was her insistence on trying tragedy and high comedy for which she was unfitted. Her Portia in 1741 opposite Charles MACKLIN's famous Shylock was a disaster: rather than being 'a Daniel come to judgement' she gave imitations of the leading lawyers and judges of the day. She retired from the stage in 1749, largely because of increasing girth, to live in a cottage – christened Clive's Den – in the grounds of Strawberry Hill, provided by Horace Walpole. Here she displayed her talent as a hostess; she was a friend of Dr Johnson, Handel, Goldsmith, Gay and Hogarth, who painted her portrait. She died there on 6 December 1785.

> He said, 'Clive, Sir, is a good thing to sit by; she always understands what you say.' And she said of him, 'I love to sit by Dr Johnson; he always entertains me.'
>
> JAMES BOSWELL (1740–95): *Life of Dr Johnson* (1791)

Clock. An Ulster-Scots word used universally for a 'beetle' (i.e. the insect), and also as a verb meaning 'brood' or, metaphorically, 'idle':

> I've fothered all the kettle, and there's nothin' afther that
> But clockin' roun' the ashes wi an oul Tom cat.
>
> W.F. MARSHALL (1888–1959): 'Sarah Ann', in *Ballads and Verses from Tyrone* (1929). ('Fothering the kettle' is dialect for 'foddering the cattle')

Clocking. A HIBERNO-ENGLISH word that is used to describe a hen sitting on her nest hatch-ing her eggs and making 'clucking' noises. *See also* CEARC AR GOR.

Cló Gaelach (Irish, 'Irish script'). The Gaelic script in which Irish was written prior to the mid-1960s, a skill that had to be mastered during their early schooldays by all pupils in Ireland: the letters a, b, d, f, g, r, s and t were formed differently. *Cló Rómhánach* ('Roman script') then replaced *Cló Gaelach* in schools and in all printed texts. DINNEEN'S DICTIONARY is still available in *Cló Gaelach* only.

Clogh Oughter Castle. A 12th-century Anglo-Norman fortress, on a man-made island in Lough Oughter, Co. Cavan. It was built by the De Lacys but fell into the hand of the O'Reillys after a De Lacy rebellion in 1224. It was the principal seat of the O'Reillys until Giolladh Iosa Rua O'Reilly moved to what is now the site of Cavan town in the 1300s. It remained in O'Reilly hands until the Plantation of Ulster, after which it became a royal castle, garrisoned by a small force of government troops. It was recaptured by the O'Reillys during the Ulster REBELLION OF 1641 and subsequently became an important garrison for Owen Rua O'NEILL during the CONFEDERATE WAR. Owen Rua died there on 9 November 1649. It was the last garrison in Ireland to surrender to Cromwellian forces, in April 1653.
See also KILLYKEEN FOREST PARK.

Clonakilty. A small town in west Cork, near the birthplace of Michael COLLINS. The phrase 'Clonakilty-God-Help-Us', expressing despair in the face of financial adversity, derives from the former location here of a large WORK-HOUSE.

Clonard. A village in Co. Westmeath. A monastery was founded here in 515 by St FINNIAN OF CLONARD (d.c.549), and became a notable centre of learning, famous throughout Europe in the Middle Ages (COLUM CILLE was one of Finnian's pupils). Despite frequent attacks by Vikings and Anglo-Normans, it survived until the Dissolution of the Monasteries under Henry VIII. Nothing now remains.

Clones Cyclone, the. The nickname of the popular boxing champion Barry McGuigan (b.1961). He was born in Clones, Co. Monaghan, on 28 February 1961. His father, singer Pat McGeegan (sic), was an amateur boxer and encouraged Barry in the sport. In 1976 he won the all-Ireland amateur bantamweight championship, going on to win a gold medal as bantamweight champion at the 1978 Commonwealth Games in Edmonton (representing Northern Ireland). McGuigan turned professional in 1981, under the guidance of a new manager, Barney Eastwood. His finest sporting hour was the WBA world feather-weight title match, held in London on 8 June 1985, in which he defeated defending champion Eusebio Pedroza in 15 rounds. But his reign as world champion was shortlived: in June 1986 he was defeated in the desert heat of Las Vegas by Steve Cruz. After he retired from boxing, McGuigan, always a popular chat-show guest, had a brief career as a chat-show presenter on Irish television.

Clones lace. A crochet lace, named after the small town in Co. Monaghan where it was developed. The town and surrounding area were badly affected by the Great Famine, and Cassandra Hand, wife of the local Church of Ireland minister, introduced lacemaking to Clones as a famine relief scheme in 1847. Lace-making became very popular among the women of Clones, and the town became the leading lace centre in the north of Ireland (Cork was the leading centre in the south). The women of each family had their own closely guarded motifs, and families acquired nicknames from the motifs that they used, such as the 'Rosie Maguires'. Cassandra Hand herself successfully managed the lace industry in Clones until her death in 1868, and had a school for females and infants built from her share of the proceeds. The CONGESTED DISTRICTS BOARD and the St Louis Sisters, who established a school in Clones, helped to maintain or revive the cottage industry of lacemaking, and in 1990 the Cassandra Hand Summer School was established to celebrate and preserve the craft. Lace-

making was a portable activity and women often crocheted while herding animals or in company: as one lace-maker remarked: 'You wouldn't go on your céilidh [see CÉILÍDHING] without your crochet.'

See also CARRICKMACROSS LACE.

Cloney, Thomas (1774–1850). Leader of the REBELLION OF 1798 in Wexford. He was born in Moneyhore, a hunting squire and member of a family of what he himself described as 'respectable middlemen' who farmed 300 acres (120 ha). He was one of the leaders of the rebels at NEW ROSS and in the unsuccessful attempt to capture Wexford town. He was imprisoned but escaped execution under an amnesty offered by Lord CORNWALLIS, claiming (in contradiction of the evidence of others) never to have been a UNITED IRISHMAN. His sentence was commuted to two years' exile, which he spent in England. In February 1803 he returned to Ireland, settling in Graiguenamanagh in Co. Kilkenny, where he was active in Nationalist politics and became a supporter of Daniel O'CONNELL; it was because of Cloney that O'Connell held a MONSTER MEETING in Graiguenamanagh. Cloney, who in 1832 published his *Personal Narrative* of the 1798 Rebellion in Wexford, was known until the end of his life as 'the old general of '98'.

Clongowes Wood. A Jesuit college near Naas, Co. Kildare, founded in 1814 and known as 'the Eton of Ireland'. It was there that James Joyce went as a little boy ('half-past six') on 1 September 1888:

> And his father had given him two five-shilling pieces for pocket money. And his father had told him if he wanted anything to write home to him and, whatever he did, never peach on a fellow.
>
> JAMES JOYCE (1882–1941):*A Portrait of the Artist as a Young Man* (1916)

Clonmacnoise. The foundation that was one of the most important and largest of the monastic centres in Ireland. It was built close to the geographical centre of Ireland on the east bank of the Shannon where the ESKER RIADA meets the river, and thus the junction of two important medieval routes. It was established in the 6th century by St CIARÁN OF CLONMACNOISE, who died less than a year after its foundation, and by the 8th century was ARMAGH's only rival for fine art and learning. Its reputation as a virtual university attracted both novices and lay students, from Britain as well as Ireland. Its wealth (and accessibility) made it a prime target for the marauding Vikings, and it was sacked 35 times between 834 and 1163, but was still of such substance that when the ANGLO-NORMANS raided it in 1179 they burned 105 houses. Its end as a religious centre came in 1552 when it was destroyed by occupying English forces dissolving yet another monastery. It is still rich in archaeological remains, including high crosses and a round tower.

> In a quiet water'd land, a land of roses,
>   Stands Saint Kieran's city fair;
> And the warriors of Erin in their famous
>   generations
>   Slumber there.
>
>   T[HOMAS] W[ILLIAM] ROLLESTON (1857–1920):
>   'The Dead at Clonmacnoise' (1909)

See also BOOK OF THE DUN COW; ANNALS OF CLONMACNOISE.

Clonmacnoise and West Offaly Railway. A narrow-gauge railway that provides a 9-km (5.5-mile) trip through the bogland of Offaly. It is now a tourist attraction operated by BORD NA MÓNA, but the train originally drew turf from the bog to supply the electricity generating station at Blackwater Bog near Shannonbridge.

Clontarf, Battle of (Irish *Cluain Tairbh*, 'bull meadow'). The last confrontation between BRIAN BORU on the one hand, and on the other the alliance of Leinstermen and Ostmen (Norse settlers in eastern Ireland), supplemented by Viking allies from the Orkneys and the Isle of Man. It was fought on Good Friday, 23 April 1014, on high ground near the River Tolka on the north shore of Dublin Bay. The battle was bloody and formed a significant part of the medieval Viking saga, *Burnt Njal*. The Munstermen were victorious though it cost them their leader and two of his sons, Murchad and

Turloch. Brian, now in his 70s, was slain by Brodir, a Viking fleeing from the battle, and in 19th- and 20th-century Nationalist imagery his death became an icon – with the old king pictured kneeling before a crucifix as the evil bearded 'Dane' is about to slaughter him – while the battle itself became a symbol of final Irish victory over the foreigner. Nationalist tradition and *Cogad Gaedel re Gallaibh* (*see* BRIAN BORU) inflated a complicated but not-uncharacteristic dynastic struggle into the mother of all Irish battles (although in this quasi-pious history the Byzantine story of Brian's wife, GORMFLAITH, was largely ignored). The battle did not annihilate the power of Leinster, but it did accelerate the Ostmen's instinct to settle down as merchants rather than mercenaries, and the hope of a unified country was crushed. The site of the battle had gained such an aura of past glories by the 19th century that it became the ideal location for the the last of Daniel O'CONNELL's MONSTER MEETINGS.

Clontibret, Battle of. The first official battle of the NINE YEARS' WAR (27 May 1595), between Hugh O'NEILL and his sworn enemy Henry BAGENAL, at Clontibret, Co. Monaghan. It was a resounding victory for O'Neill, who was proclaimed a traitor the following month, his rebellion now an open one.

Clootie. An Ulster-Scots word for the cleft of an animal's hoof, and by extension for Satan as the proverbial owner of cloven hooves:

> O Thou! Whatever title suit thee
> Auld Hornie, Satan, Nick or Clootie ...
>
>   ROBERT BURNS (1759–96): 'Address to the Deil', in
>   *Poems* (1786)

Cluricaune (Irish *clúrachán*, 'elf'; also *luch-arachán*). A sprite (in later Irish folklore) who lives in pantries or cellars, helping himself to the store. He was blamed by servants for any missing items. The word is still current in HIBERNO-ENGLISH as a term of abuse.

Clydagh Valley Flood. In August 1831 a flood 275 m (300 yds) wide and 5 m (16 ft) deep swept without warning through the valley of the River Clydagh, Co. Kerry. It took everything with it, including a baby in his cradle, which floated on the flood for 3 km (2 miles) before it overturned, drowning the baby.

Cnáimhseáil. An Irish verb used in HIBERNO-ENGLISH (sometimes in the form *knauvshaul*) and meaning 'grumble', 'complain'. A person might be described as 'a terrible *cnáimhseáiler*', and the verbal noun *cnáimhseáiling* is also used.

Coal Quay, the. A famous, picturesque and characterful quarter of Cork city. The street's proper name is Cornmarket Street, but it is called the Coal Quay (pronounced 'kay') because like many streets in central Cork it once gave on to the River Lee, and coal and other goods were formerly dispatched from it (silting and reclamation have moved the river further away). A traditional Saturday-morning market was held at the Coal Quay, where local women, some of them SHAWLIES, sold food but also second-hand clothes and household goods:

> On the Fourth of July eighteen hundred and six we
> set sail from the Coal Quay of Cork.
> We were sailing away with a cargo of bricks for the
> grand City Hall in New York.
> 'Twas a wonderful craft, she was rigged for and aft
> and oh, how the wild wind drove her.
> She stood several blasts, she had twenty-seven
> masts and they called her the *Irish Rover*.
> ANON.: 'The Irish Rover'

Cock¹. In the Irish house and farm, the cock was treated with great respect: because he was believed to have the power to dispel the power of the supernatural or OTHERWORLD with his first crow at dawn, he himself was thought to possess a share of that supernatural power. Cocks were also believed to have the power of prophecy. According to the place or the time they crowed (other than at dawn) a visitor would arrive or someone would die in the townland. They were never killed when they had outlived their usefulness, but instead let go in a wood. At that time people who went barefoot during the day used to wash their feet before going to bed at night: the custom was for the youngest male child to wash his feet first, but if there were no sons in the family, the man of the house would take the cock off his perch over the coop (cocks were too valuable to be allowed to sleep out of doors) and wash his feet first.

Cock². A Cork slang word for a male baby, used approvingly, as in: 'That's a fine cock you have there.'

Cockles. The phrase 'the cockles of your heart' has been accepted as Irish in origin by the OED (*Oxford Engish Dictionary*). Dymphna Lonergan, a PhD student at Flinders University in Australia, successfully established that it comes from the Irish word *cochall*, which means 'capsule', 'pod' or 'membrane of the heart'. *See also* DIDGERIDOO.

'Cockles and Mussels'. *See* 'MOLLY MALONE'.

Cockstride. A measure of the lengthening of days after the winter solstice, by the shadow of the sun on the floor.

Cod. A noun and verb formerly widely used to mean 'folly', 'deceit', 'pull the wool over someone's eyes', or it could denote the person doing these things: 'He's a right cod.' 'Only codding', may simply mean 'only joking'.

Coddle. A dish traditionally popular among Dublin working-class and tenement families. Potatoes, onions, sausages and rashers of bacon were all cooked together in one pot as a stew.

Code word. A means of distinguishing between authentic bomb warnings and hoaxes. Code words, updated regularly, were agreed by paramilitaries and the security forces during the Northern Ireland TROUBLES.

Codladh grifin. A HIBERNO-ENGLISH phrase borrowed from Irish and indicating numbness or pins-and-needles in the limbs. The Irish words *codladh* and *grífín* both mean 'sleep'.

Codology. Nonsense play-acting, behaviour perceived as childish or inappropriate. An exasperated mother might say to her child: 'Stop that old codology.' The word may derive from 'codswallop'.

Coemgen. *See* KEVIN.

Coercion. The general name given to successive

acts that involved the suspension of habeas corpus and the granting of greater powers to the police and judiciary, which were passed and enforced by British governments between 1880 and 1921, but especially during the LAND WAR of 1881–7. The popular concept of 'coercion' is strongly associated with the Coercion Act of July 1887 and with the chief secretary of the time, Arthur BALFOUR.

The first Coercion Bill of the Land War, known as the Protection of Person and Property (Ireland) Act, was introduced by Liberal chief secretary 'BUCKSHOT' FORSTER in early 1881 in response to the widespread agrarian disturbance that accompanied the foundation of the LAND LEAGUE. Invariably the stick of coercion was accompanied by a carrot – on this occasion the LAND ACT of 1881. The PHOENIX PARK MURDERS of May 1881 provoked a fresh Coercion Bill.

In January 1887 the Conservative government of Lord Salisbury decided that an even sterner Coercion Act was needed to deal with the PLAN OF CAMPAIGN, and this – opposed bitterly by the Irish MPs at Westminster – passed into law in July. It was intended to be 'perpetual', that is a permanent part of Irish law. The act greatly strengthened the administration's hand in dealing with boycotting, unlawful assembly, criminal conspiracy and incitement to violence, and also gave the courts leave to transfer a trial from one area to another, where it was believed a conviction could be achieved. Lord Salisbury's nephew, Arthur Balfour, ably applied the Coercion legislation, passing the same year the LAND ACT of 1887.

Coercion was again applied in 1901–2 as a result of the activities of the UNITED IRISH LEAGUE, but by this time it appeared that the British administration itself did not really believe in it, failing to arrest the League's leaders. As a counterbalance the chief secretary, George WYNDHAM, introduced a significant land act, the Wyndham Act, in 1903.

Coffin ship. A term deriving from the GREAT FAMINE of the 1840s when the demand for passage to America and Canada was so enormous that it was very difficult to enforce the Passenger Acts, and many thousands of people died during the voyages. All types of sailing ships, many of them cargo vessels that would otherwise have returned empty to America, were pressed into service and bunks hastily constructed, and ship owners made enormous profits from the transportation of people during the period. Conditions on board the ships were appalling and the journey to America could take as long as six weeks. Men and women were crowded together, sometimes as many as four to a berth 1.8 m (6 ft) square, and dysentery and cholera were rife. No one knows how many thousands of people died on these ships, but in 1847 alone there were 17,465 documented deaths from typhus or cholera. Most deaths were unreported, the body simply tossed overboard. Campaigns by humanitarians such as Vere FOSTER and Stephen de Vere, the landlord brother of poet Aubrey de Vere, gradually brought about some improved legislation. De Vere described a famine ship voyage to a House of Commons Select Committee in 1847:

> Hundreds of poor people, men, women and children, of all ages, from the drivelling idiot of ninety to the babe just born, huddled together without light, without air, wallowing in filth and breathing a fetid atmosphere … living without food or medicine, dying without the voice of spiritual consolation, and buried in the depths without the rites of the church.

Cog. To cheat, especially in the sense of cribbing, as in: 'He was caught coggin' and got nought in his exam.'

Cogar. An Irish word for 'whisper', 'conspire', used in HIBERNO-ENGLISH to request attention to a story or question, as in 'Listen!' 'Come here!' '*Cogar i leith*' is also used with similar but intensified meaning.

Cogar-mogar. A formulation synonymous with 'hugger-mugger'.

Coghlan, Eamonn (b.1952). Athlete. He was born in Drimnagh, Dublin. During the 1970s and 1980s he dominated Irish running but failed to win any medals at the 1976 Olympic Games, excelling instead at the indoor 1500 m or mile, especially in the USA, where his indoor prowess acquired him the nickname 'Chairman of the Boards'. In 1983 he became the first man to break the 3 minutes 50 seconds barrier for the indoor mile. That same year he became World 5000m champion at the unaugural World Athletics Championships in Helsinki.

Cohan, George M[ichael]. *See* 'YANKEE DOODLE DANDY'.

Coigley, James (1761–98). United Irishman. He was born in Co. Armagh and ordained a priest in Paris. On his return to Ireland he became active in the Society of UNITED IRISHMEN. He seems to have been an important go-between between them and the French Directory, although he denied any involvement when he was arrested with Arthur O'CONNOR at Margate on 28 February 1798 as he attempted to return to France. He was convicted on 22 May, perhaps incriminated by O'Connor, who was acquitted. Contemporary opinion felt that his execution on 7 June was exemplary and based upon inconclusive evidence:

> Quigley has been executed, and died like a hero. If ever I reach Ireland, and that we establish our liberty, I will be the first to propose a monument to his memory; his conduct at the hour of death clears everything.
>
> WOLFE TONE (1763–98): *Journal* (1826)

Cois. An Irish word for 'beside', used in HIBERNO-ENGLISH to mean the strip of bog-land beside the bank where turf was cut and on to which the wet sods would be thrown by the person wielding the SLEÁN. It is usually wet, marshy land.

Coláiste Íde ('college of St Ita'). A beautifully situated BIG HOUSE 3 km (2 miles) outside Dingle, Co. Kerry. Originally the seat of Lord Ventry, it became a preparatory college and later an all-Irish boarding school for girls. When it was threatened with closure in the 1990s, parents and Irish-language interests rallied to its defence. An SEABHAC, whose father worked for Lord Ventry, spent his early years on this estate.

Coláiste na Mumhan. *See* MUSKERRY GAELTACHT, THE.

Coláistí Samhraidh, Na. The summer schools established in the Munster (Ballingeary, Co. Cork, 1904), Connacht (Tourmakeady, Co. Mayo, 1905) and Ulster (Cloughaneely, Co. Donegal, 1906) GAELTACHTs, where teachers of Irish could have access to native speakers.

Colcannon. A dish of mashed potatoes, chopped kale or green cabbage, and onions or scallions. It is served with butter melted into a hole in the centre and taken with buttermilk. It was at one time so popular as to be celebrated in verse:

> Did you ever eat colcannon
> What 'twas made with yellow cream
> And the kale and praties blended
> Like a picture in a dream?
> Did you ever scoop a hole in top
> To hold the melting lake
> Of the clover-flavoured butter
> That your mother used to make?
>
> Author unknown, quoted in Bríd Mahon, *Land of Milk and Honey* (1991)

The dish is known in the Donegal Gaeltacht as *brúitín* (literally 'mashed matter').

Coleman, Michael (1891–1946). Fiddler. He was born in Killavil in south Co. Sligo, and it was there that he acquired his fiddling skills – there is a local style of playing known as the 'Sligo style'. He moved to the USA in 1914, and spent most of his life in New York. He began to record in 1921 and made a number of gramophone and radio recordings. Although all these recordings were made in the USA, they were sent home to Ireland and his style and repertoire became a major influence on other musicians. The area where he was born, which has always had many fine traditional musical practitioners of all types, is known as Coleman Country. There is a monument to Michael Coleman in Gurteen, Co. Sligo, near his birthplace, and a music heritage centre dedicated to his memory was completed in 1990.

Coleraine (Irish *Cúil Raithin*, 'ferny corner'). A town on the Lower BANN river, population (1991) 16,100. There was an early Patrician monastery here, and the town itself was a 17th-century Plantation settlement on land wrested from the O'Cahans. Coleraine was also the name of the county, but this was changed to Londonderry when the territory was granted to the HONOURABLE, THE IRISH SOCIETY.

Colgan, John (c.1590–1658). Hagiographer. He was born at Priestown near Cardonagh, Co. Donegal, and educated in Ireland and the Netherlands. Ordained as a secular priest in 1618, he joined the Franciscan order at St Anthony's College, LOUVAIN, on 26 April 1620. After teaching in various seminaries he was appointed master of novices at Louvain in 1634, and a year later took charge of the project to publish *Acta Sanctorum Hiberniae*, on the lives and works of the Irish saints. The *Acta* were to consist of nine volumes, which would include royal genealogies, lives of saints and martyrologies. The first three volumes, detailing the lives of saints with feast days January–March, were published in 1645, but lack of money from an Ireland under Cromwellian rule prevented the publication of other work already compiled. In 1647 Colgan published *Triadis Thaumaturga* ('the wonder-works of the three'), comprising lives of Patrick, Brigid and Colum Cille (Columba), but chronic ill-health diminished his output. He refused the position of commissary of the Irish colleges of Louvain, Vielun and Prague, and published only one more work, a life of Duns Scotus (1655), whom he claimed as Irish. He died on 15 January 1658. For most of his work Colgan was dependent on the Irish language expertise of Mícheál Ó Cléirigh, and it was Colgan who named Ó Cléirigh's great work *ANNALS OF THE FOUR MASTERS*.

Colkitto. *See* CIOTÓG.

Coll, Vincent. *See* MAD DOG COLL.

Collarette. The usual regalia of members of the ORANGE ORDER, the APPRENTICE BOYS and the ROYAL BLACK INSTITUTION on official occasions. Originally intended for indoor wear, the collarette has all but replaced the more cumbersome SASH on parades and rallies. Collarettes are marked with the member's LOL (Loyal Orange

Lodge) number or that of other lodges, and also bear mystic symbols. Plural membership was often indicated in the past by wearing the appropriate number of collarettes.

Colleen. An anglicized version of *cailín* (Irish, 'girl'). The word gained a sentimental popularity during the 19th century, and had a brief vogue as a forename in the USA. Now its use tends to be facetious.

> Thine is my ev'ry vow!
> For ever dear, as now!
> Queen of my heart be thou!
> My Colleen Rua.
>
> > DENNY LANE (1818–95): 'Kate of Araglen' (1844). (Irish *rua*, 'red-haired').

Colleen Bawn, The (Irish *cailín bán*, 'fair-haired girl'). The best-known play of Dion BOUCICAULT, which opened at Miss Laura Keene's Theatre, New York, on 27 March 1860. It was based on Gerald Griffin's novel *The COLLEGIANS* (1829), which in turn was inspired by an actual murder committed in Limerick ten years before. Boucicault transferred the action to Killarney, which gave him a glorious scenic background, and the first staging included real water for the lake where the heroine is nearly drowned. The plot describes how Danny Mann, the half-crazed hunchbacked manservant, tries to drown his mistress, Eily O'Connor, hearing that her husband Hardress Cregan has grown tired of her. She is saved by Myles-na-Coppaleen ('Myles of the ponies'), 'that poaching scoundrel – that horse-stealer' (played, of course, by Boucicault), and the grim conclusion of the novel is softened into an acceptable happy ending.

The melodrama was a hit from the beginning, and when it opened at the Adelphi Theatre in London a few months later it had the same success. Queen Victoria saw it three times in one fortnight and had portraits painted of Boucicault and his wife Agnes (who played Eily) for Windsor Castle. The play had a further avatar as an opera, *The LILY OF KILLARNEY* (1862) by Sir Julius Benedict (1804–85), although Boucicault had already filled his play with such intrusive favourites as 'CRUISKEEN LAWN',

'Limerick is Beautiful' and 'Brian O'Linn', and had taken care to build in dramatic music cues as in a movie soundtrack.

See also ARRAH-NA-POGUE; SHAUGHRAUN, THE.

Collège des Irlandais. The Irish College in Paris, *Collegium Clericorum Hibernorum* according to its own plaque. It is situated in a small side street, Rue des Irlandais, in the 5th arrondissement, near the Latin Quarter. The college was founded in 1578, one of 29 Irish clerical colleges throughout Catholic Europe at a time when the Reformation had ended the education of priests in Ireland. The current building and courtyard, occupying approximately 2.5 sq km (1 sq mile), was designed in 1769 by the court architect, François-Joseph Belange. Polish priests who had survived the Dachau concentration camp used it as a refuge after the Second World War on the invitation of the Irish hierarchy, and the Polish connection lasted until the 1990s (Pope John Paul II spent time there as Karol Wojtyla). After extensive restoration work, a 'Centre Culturel Irlandais', Ireland's first cultural centre abroad, was formally opened in the college in 2002.

College Green. The location of the seat of the Irish Parliament in Dublin until its abolition in 1801 by the Act of UNION, and synonymous with the Parliament itself. In 1602 George Carey was given a grant of land on HOGGEN GREEN to build a hospital, but by 1605 the building was being used for law courts, and was later used as a residence by Sir Arthur CHICHESTER, who was lord deputy from 1604 to 1615. The first Parliament that met in Ireland after the Restoration assembled in Chichester House in May 1661, and in 1673 the crown took a lease on the property for use as a Parliament house. By 1728 the building was in a state of decay, and the Commons appointed the architect Edward Lovett PEARCE (1699–1733) to design a new building, the foundation stone being laid in 1728. Parliament assembled there for the first time in 1731 and the work was completed in 1739 under the supervision of Arthur Dobbs, Pearce having died suddenly. In 1778 the peers decided to extend the building to provide extra

accommodation for the House of Lords, and this section, designed by James GANDON, was begun in 1785. In 1802 the Bank of Ireland purchased the building, which had been made redundant by the Union; it was adapted internally by Francis JOHNSTON, and opened for business in 1808. The House of Lords, restored by the bank, is now used as a venue for concerts. The outside of the building was cleaned and restored during the 1980s.

College Green is also the location of Trinity College (*see* TCD).

See also GOOSE PIE.

Collegians, The. A novel (1829) by Gerald GRIFFIN, based on events in Co. Limerick in 1819 when John Scanlon was tried for the murder of his mistress Ellen Hanley. The novel describes how Eily O'Connor is murdered by Danny Mann at the suggestion of his master, her husband Hardress Cregan. Mann and Cregan are finally brought to justice, the perpetrator hanged, the other transported. The title refers to Cregan and his friend Kyrle Daly, who had been his contemporary at Trinity College Dublin; Daly later marries the heiress Anne Chute, who had been the principal cause of Cregan's tiring of the beautiful but uneducated Eily. The novel was dramatized as *The* COLLEEN BAWN (1860) by Dion BOUCICAULT, who transferred the action to the more romantic Killarney. Sir Julius Benedict (1804–85) in turn made Boucicault's melodrama into an operetta, *The Lily of Killarney* (1862).

Colles' fracture. The name given to a fracture of the radius near the wrist, with backward displacement of the hand, after Abraham Colles (1773–1843), an Irish surgeon.

Colley, George. *See* LOW STANDARDS IN HIGH PLACES; WELL-HEELED ARTICULATE WOMEN.

Collins, Michael (1890–1922). Revolutionary and statesman. Collins was born on a small farm in Sam's Cross, outside Clonakilty, Co. Cork, on 18 October 1890 and educated locally. In 1906 he went to London to work as a clerk in the Post Office Savings Bank, later getting a job with a stockbroking firm, and became heavily involved with the Irish expatriate community and their associations: the GAA (he played hurling for a London club), the GAELIC LEAGUE (although he never became fluent in Irish) and the IRB. He returned to Ireland in January 1916 to escape conscription and fought in the GPO during the EASTER RISING as aide-de-camp to Joseph Mary PLUNKETT. After the rising he was imprisoned in Frongoch internment camp in Wales with hundreds of other Republicans, an important formative influence and a means of establishing a network of relationships that he would exploit to the full during the ANGLO-IRISH WAR that followed.

Collins was elected to the first Dáil of January 1919 and served as minister for home affairs, then, from April 1919, as minister for finance, promoting and administering the Dáil loan, which was raised from Irish people in order to finance the alternative administration. He became increasingly powerful in the IRA as director of intelligence and organization, becoming associated with the 'hard men' like Dan BREEN, Seán TREACY and Tom BARRY, who often carried out ambushes and other military activities without the sanction of headquarters, although Collins never fired a shot himself. For this and other reasons he gradually became estranged from DE VALERA, who resented his popularity and unsuccessfully tried to get rid of him by sending him to America in early 1921 (see LONG HOOR, THE). As the war escalated Collins deliberately provoked crown forces into brutality and reprisal, knowing that the Irish people would support their own terrorists rather than British terrorists. At the same time he waged his own terrorist campaign against British Intelligence in Dublin – the 'G' men of Dublin Castle (see CASTLE, THE) – using his hand-picked assassination SQUAD to deadly effect, especially on the morning of 21 November 1920 (see BLOODY SUNDAY 1920). Part of the appeal of Collins for future generations arises from the fact that he managed somehow to evade arrest while remaining in Dublin under the nose of the military during the course of the Anglo-Irish

War, relying on a network of safe houses run by women friends. He was a reluctant member of the Irish delegation at the TREATY negotiations of October–December 1921, signing the agreement because he believed that it would not be feasible for the IRA to return to war against the British (a truce had been in operation since July 1921), although believing that he had 'signed his death warrant'. Collins became commander-in-chief of the Free State army, responsible for the bombardment of his former comrades in the Republican garrison in the FOUR COURTS that marked the beginning of the CIVIL WAR on 28 June 1922. He was killed by a Republican ambush party at BÉAL NA MBLÁTH, not far from his home in Co. Cork, while on a tour of inspection on 22 August 1922. His body was brought by sea to Dublin, and a huge crowd attended his funeral.

Since the 1980s Michael Collins has attracted so much attention that it is easy to forget that until then he was an unsung hero, 'written out' of the official version of events purveyed by FIANNA FÁIL, the governing party for most of the period 1932–73. Neil Jordan's romantic portrayal of Collins in his film of 1996 as a man of action and a true friend and lover is now probably the accepted one throughout the world. There is no doubt that he was an administrator and guerrilla leader of great ability, charisma, determination and ruthlessness, but he was disliked and resented by many of his colleagues because of his arrogance and stubbornness. He was called the BIG FELLOW not just because of his height but because of his 'big' (conceited) head. For the Irish people he was both 'laughing boy' and a deadly enemy of the British, and it was because he died before he reached the age of 32 that he has been mythologized. Other revolutionary leaders grew old and grey, revealing themselves to be just as conservative as the British administrators they replaced; de Valera himself, Collins's *bête noire*, survived to hold on to power for much too long.

Collins Barracks. A military barracks in Dublin, recently converted into part of the NATIONAL MUSEUM OF IRELAND. They occupy a site with a frontage of nearly 300 m (328 yds) on the north quays of the River Liffey, not far from Phoenix Park. The Royal Barracks, as they were originally called, were designed by Thomas Burgh (1670–1730), the surveyor-general, and constructed between 1701 and 1709. They were said at the time to be the largest military barracks in Europe, the buildings grouped around three sides of each of four squares (subsequently modified). During the 19th century sanitary conditions at the barracks were distinctly substandard, and enteric fever was rife because of poor drainage and disposal of rubbish. In December 1921 Sir Neville MACREADY took the final salute of the British army from Albert (now Wolfe Tone) Quay near the barracks, which were then handed over to the National Army and immediately given the name of the commander-in-chief, Michael COLLINS. In 1997 Collins Barracks were formally opened as part of the National Museum, housing and displaying the Museum's holdings in the areas of military history and costume.

Collops. The calves of the legs, from the Irish *colpa*. Collop Monday was the day before Shrove Tuesday, for reasons that are now obscure.

Colmán of Kilmacduagh (*c*.550–*c*.632). A saint born in Kiltartan, Co. Galway, the son of the Irish chieftain Duac. He was educated by ENDA on Inishmore, the largest of the Aran Islands, then lived as a recluse in the Burren of Co. Clare until his meeting with King Guaire Aidhne of Connacht. The legend tells how the king's feast was whipped from before him on Easter Sunday, and when he and his train followed it they found Colmán, weak from his Lenten fast, happily tucking in. The king prevailed upon him to found a monastery in his territory, and as they walked about, Colmán's girdle fell to the ground. He took this to be a sign and founded a great abbey at Kilmacduagh near Gort. His feast day is 29 October.

Colmán of Lindisfarne (d.676). A saint born in Connacht who, after a spell as a monk on IONA, was chosen as the third bishop of LINDISFARNE

(Holy Island) in 661 on the death of FINAN. He was an unrepentant supporter of the Celtic Church against the 'Romans', storming out of the council hall of the Synod of WHITBY in 664 and taking his monks with him to Ireland. He set up a monastery on Inishbofin off the Galway coast, but, owing to a dissension between the English monks and the Irish, was forced to establish a separate house for the former on the mainland in Mayo under an English abbot called Gerald. The region was known for long after as *Muigheó na Sacsan* ('Mayo of the Saxons'). Church politics aside, Colmán was noted for his piety and the excellence of his rule at Lindisfarne. He died in 676 and his feast day is 18 February.

Colmán of Lismore (d.*c*.702). A saint who became abbot of LISMORE in Munster in 689. Under his care the abbey reached the height of its fame. His feast day is 23 January.

Colmán of Stockerau (d.1012). An Irish monk, the son of the HIGH KING Maolsheachlainn II, who in 1012 was seized, tortured and hanged by local ruffians at Stockerau near Vienna while on pilgrimage to the Holy Land. Holy Roman Emperor Henry II (973–1024), canonized as a saint in 1146, erected a tomb in Colmán's honour in MELK, a town about 64 km (40 miles) west of Vienna, after a number of miracles were attributed to his relics. The town became a regular port of call for Irish pilgrims and Colmán was made a patron of Austria. Many churches throughout Hungary and southern Germany, as well as Austria, were dedicated to the saint and Colmán remains a popular baptismal name. He is prayed to on 13 October, his feast day, by women in search of husbands.

Colmán of Terryglass (d.549). A saint, a prince of Leinster, and a fellow student of COLUM CILLE at CLONARD. He founded the monastery of Clonenagh at Mountrath in Co. Laois but preferred the solitude of Terryglass on the shore of the Shannon at Lough Derg. He died there of the plague in 549 and his feast day is 13 December.

Cologne. A large city in western Germany, site of the 'Irish' monastery of St Martin the Great, which flourished in the 11th and 12th centuries. It most famous *doctus* (scholar) was MARIANUS SCOTTUS (OF COLOGNE) (Mael Brígte from Moville on Strangford Lough).

Colombia Three, the. Three Irish Republicans, James Monaghan, Martin McCauley and Niall Connolly, travelling on false passports, who were arrested at Bogotá airport on 11 August 2001 on suspicion of training members of the Revolutionary Armed Forces of Colombia (FARC), a Marxist guerrilla group. In 2004 a court in Bogotá acquitted the three of training the guerrillas but found them guilty of passport offences. It was alleged that the suspects were mistreated in Colombian prisons notorious for violent strife.

Colouring. A term for milk used to 'colour' the tea. The word was sometimes corrupted to 'cuddling'.
See also STRIPPING.

Colum, Mary (1884–1957). Writer and critic. She was born Catherine Gunning Maguire in Collooney, Co. Sligo, on 13 June 1884. She taught for a period at ST ENDA'S SCHOOL in Rathfarnham, Dublin, and married Padraic COLUM in 1912, while she was still a student at University College Dublin. In 1914 she emigrated to America with him and, like him, taught literature at Columbia University in New York. In *Life and the Dream* (1947), her autobiography, the acquaintance of the Colums with all the writers of the IRISH LITERARY REVIVAL and later is memorialized. She also published a collection of essays on modern literature, *From These Roots* (1938), and, with Padraic Colum, a memoir of *Our Friend James Joyce* (1959). She died in New York on 22 October 1957.

Colum, Padraic (1881–1972). Poet and dramatist. He was born Patrick McCormac Colm on 8 December 1881, son of the master of Longford workhouse. The family moved to Sandycove, Co. Dublin, and Padraic worked for five years as a clerk before a scholarship from a wealthy American allowed him to study and write. He wrote a number of plays for the ABBEY THEATRE including *The Land* (1905) and *Thomas Mus-*

kerry (1910), about a workhouse master who ends up an inmate, establishing a tradition of realism in what had been intended as an epic or poetic theatre. He emigrated to America in 1914 and spent the rest of his life there. Remembered now mainly for such anthology favourites as 'The Drover', 'The Old Woman of the Roads', 'She Moved through the Fair' (which many still think a traditional folk song) and 'Cradle Song', Colum also wrote many books for children and a late novel, *The Flying Swans* (1957). He died in Enfield, Connecticut, on 11 January 1972 and is buried in Sutton, Co. Dublin.

> My eyelids red and heavy are,
> With bending o'er the smould'ring peat.
> I know the Aeneid now by heart,
> My Virgil read in cold and heat,
> In loneliness and hunger smart.
> 'A Poor Scholar of the Forties', in *Wild Earth* (1907)

Columba. *See* COLUM CILLE.

Columban (or in Latin **Columbanus**) (*c*.540–615). A saint sometimes referred to as 'the younger Columba' (COLUM CILLE being 'the older Columba'). He was born in south Leinster *c*.540. and educated by COMGALL of Bangor, having as an unusually handsome young man been driven to the monastic life by the attentions of *lascivae puellae* ('lewd girls'). He was noted for his austerity: the rules he devised for his foundations in Europe were eventually replaced by the more benign rule of St Benedict. At the age of 45 he obtained permission to preach the Gospel in the nominally Christian land of the Franks. He took with him 12 monks, the same number as Christ's apostles, including St GALL with whom he is said to have quarrelled, and after many travails established houses at ANNEGRAY, LUXEUIL and Fontaine in Austrasia (a kingdom incorporating the basins of the Rhine, Moselle and Meuse rivers, with its capital at Metz). In 612, still driven by the need to preach the Gospel and confound heretics (and perhaps to see Rome), he crossed the Alps into Italy and thence to BOBBIO, south of Milan. It was a harrowing journey for a man in his 70s, ancient by the standards of the time. He died in this last monastery on 23

November 615, now kept as a feast day in the universal Church.

Columban was witty, abrasive and, though eternally on the move, a voluminous writer of letters, sermons and scriptural commentaries. One typical pun-laden sentence occurs in a letter written in 610 to Pope Boniface IV (608–15). Columban feared that he, like Pope Vigilius (537–55) half a century earlier, might not stand up to heretical rulers:

> *Vigila itaque, quaeso, papa, vigila et iterum dico vigila, quia forte non bene vigilavit Vigilius.*
> (Be watchful, I urge you, Pope, be watchful and again I say be watchful, since perhaps he who was called Watchman did not watch well.)

It is in this letter, too, written near the end of his life, that he makes a rare mention of his home: *toti Iberi, ultimi habitatores mundi ...* ('all of us Irish, denizens of the world's edge ...').
See also CAVETO, FILOLE.

Columban Fathers. A missionary order, originally known as the Maynooth Mission to China, and founded in 1918 by two diocesan priests, John Blowick and Edward J. Galvin; the latter had belonged to the diocese of Cork and had worked in China for a number of years. Having received the blessing of Pope Benedict XV, the order took the Irish missionary St COLUMBAN as its patron and established a seminary in Dalgan, in the diocese of Galway, which transferred to Dalgan Park near Navan in Co. Meath in 1942. Dalgan Park is still the headquarters of the order. A sister order, the Missionary Sisters of St Columban, has worked with the priests on their missions in the Far East, notably in China, Japan, Korea, Burma and the Philippines. Father Galvin, who went with the first group of 16 Columban missionaries to China in 1920, was made first Bishop of Hanyang in 1946, but all the Columbans were expelled from China by the communist regime in 1952. They have continued to minister in other parts of Asia and also in South America.

Colum Cille or **Columba** (521–597). The saint known as Ireland's first exile. Colum Cille and twelve apostolic companions imposed upon

themselves the WHITE MARTYRDOM of alienation from their extended families and the dear land of their birth. He founded the important monastery of IONA in the Inner Hebrides and largely converted Pictish Scotland to Christianity. He was the first of those who went *perigrinatio pro Christo* ('wandering for Christ'), and his example was followed by many others, notably COLUMBAN, GALL and FURSA.

Born at Gartan in the heart of Tír Chonaill in modern Co. Donegal in 521, Colum Cille (or at least his name) is associated with foundations at Swords, Durrow and Derry (of which he is the patron). He visited Ireland only rarely, most notably for the convention of DRUIMCEATT, and returned immediately to his island monastery. After PATRICK he is the chief saint of the early Celtic church, and there is about him the same accretion of folklore. His exile, for example, was supposed to have been imposed by his confessor because of his involvement in the Battle of Cúl Dreimne (561) (*see* TO EVERY COW HER CALF) and the many stories about his saintly wrath are probably folk memories of his austere rule as abbot. He died according to tradition on Whit Sunday, 9 June 597, and his remains, also traditionally, are buried in Ireland. (*see* IN BURGO DUNO TUMULO). He is known to the Universal Church as St Columba (Latin 'dove'; Colum Cille itself means 'dove of the church'), and his feast day is on 9 June.

Comber Letter, the. A hoax letter written to a Protestant gentleman in Comber, Co. Down, in December 1688 purporting to warn of an impending massacre of Protestants in a repeat of the REBELLION OF 1641:

> ... Irish men through Ireland is sworn, that on the ninth day of this month, they are to fall on to kill and murder, man, wife, child ...

The Comber Letter was one of several similar fraudulent documents in circulation designed to increase opposition to the Catholic JAMES II. News of it and the arrival of Lord Antrim's REDSHANKS was the cause of the closing of the gates of Derry by the APPRENTICE BOYS and the eventual SIEGE OF DERRY.

Come-all-ye. A popular type of traditional song, usually anonymous, taking its name from the words 'Come all ye', often used in the first lines. A typical opening might be: 'Come all ye lads and lasses, and listen to me a while.' Some other common first lines/titles are: 'Come all ye airy bachelors, a warning take by me', 'Come all ye handsome comely maids', 'Come all you true-born Irishmen, wherever you may be.'

> Come all ye lads and lasses and hear my mournful tale;
> Ye tender hearts that weep for love to sigh you will not fail.
> 'Tis all about a young man and my song will tell you how
> He lately came a-courting of the Maid of the Sweet Brown Knowe.
> ANON.: 'The Maid of the Sweet Brown Knowe'
> (19th century, from Co. Derry)

The term is also used, inaccurately, to mean SEAN-NÓS singing.

Come here till I tell you. A common prelude to narrative or gossip (*see* COGAR).

Comely maidens. *See* DE VALERA, ÉAMON.

Comgall (*c.*516–601). The abbot of the great monastic school of BANGOR in Co. Down. He was a Pict born in Antrim *c.*516 and spent some time as a soldier. He was among the party that accompanied COLUM CILLE on his tour of the Pictish parts of northeast Scotland, probably as an interpreter. This visit won the goodwill of King Brude of Inverness and it is believed it resulted in the king's conversion to Christianity. On Comgall's return to Ulster he founded, in 555, the abbey at Bangor, doubly famous for its dedication to learning and the austerity of its rule. Among its alumni were COLUMBAN, GALL, MOLUAG, MAELRUBHA and MALACHY. The ANTIPHONARY OF BANGOR, the abbey's treasure, contains a long hymn in praise of its founder. Comgall died in Bangor in 601 and his feast day, as a patron of the diocese of Down and Connor, is 10 May.

Comhalta den IRA (Irish, 'member of the IRA'). A phrase used (not by Republican fellow-travellers) in mock-discretion or secretiveness in connection with the Northern Troubles.

Comhaltas Ceoltóirí Éireann or **CCÉ** (Irish, 'brotherhood of musicians of Ireland'). A largely voluntary organization for the promotion of traditional music, instruments and dance, known informally as simply 'Comhaltas' and often pronounced, erroneously, 'Ceoltas'. It was founded in 1952 (originally as Cumann Ceoltóirí Éireann, 'association of musicians of Ireland') and has its headquarters and a permanent staff in Monkstown, Co. Dublin. Comhaltas stated that its principal aim was 'to stimulate the interest of the public in the restoration of Irish music to its proper place in the cultural life of our nation'. It is grant-aided by government, and has a network of about 400 local branches in all 32 counties and among Irish emigrant communities abroad, usually called after the town or village of origin.

The main functions of the branches are to preserve tradition by transmitting it through the teaching of traditional instruments and to organize SESSIONS and CÉILÍS to showcase emerging musicians. Since 1952 Comhaltas has organized the All-Ireland FLEADH CHEOIL, although such is the modest profile and the voluntary ethos of the organization that even participants are not always aware of this, instead associating ownership of the *fleadh* with the town in which it is held. Musicians also take part in international concert tours under the auspices of Comhaltas.

The organization has in the past – to the unease of many members – occasionally adopted a political stance, for instance when in 1971 it cancelled the *fleadh* in protest against the introduction of INTERNMENT in Northern Ireland. But there is no doubt that Comhaltas is a hugely important force for good in the preservation and promotion of traditional Irish music, and many musicians of international reputation, including Sharon SHANNON and Martin HAYES, were youthful prize-winners in the Comhaltas *fleadh*.

Comiskey, Bishop Brendan. *See* BISHOP BRENDAN.

Commat. A lesson learned by heart, from 'commit to memory'. The usage came from the 19th-century practice in national schools and is now archaic: 'I have my writing work done but I still have my commat to do.'

Commissioners of Irish Lights. A commission established by an act of Parliament in 1867 to provide navigational aids for shipping around the Irish coast, mostly in the form of lighthouses.

Committee Room 15. The room in the Westminster House of Commons where on 1 December 1890 PARNELL was to face 'the rabble' – as he, with characteristic disdain, described his severely split IRISH PARTY after the undefended divorce action of O'Shea (*see* O'SHEA WHO MUST BE OBEYED). Already such old associates as John DILLON, William O'BRIEN and TAY-PAY felt that he must go, and the hitherto silent Catholic Church now indicated that it could not appear to be less righteous than the chapel supporters of Gladstone (*see* GOM). The bitterest moment occurred when John REDMOND, who twenty years later brought a reunited party closer to Home Rule by constitutional means than anyone else, referred to Gladstone as 'the master of the party', to which Tim HEALY riposted with characteristic savagery, 'Who is to be the mistress of the party?' Incensed, Parnell moved to strike him. At this, 45 members led by Justin McCarthy (1830–1912) left the room, leaving the Chief with just 27 still loyal followers.

Common. The word CAMÁN ('hurling stick') as heard by English visitors in Ireland *c.*1800:

> Among other amusements the game of 'shinny' [shinty], as it is called by some, and 'common' by others, is worthy of note. Common is derived from a Celtic word, 'com' [*cam*], which signified 'crooked', as it is played with a stick bent at its lower extremity something like a reaping-hook. The ball, which is struck to and fro, in which the whole amusement consists, is called 'nag' or in Irish 'brig'. It resembles the game called golf in Edinburgh. Christmas is the season in which it is most generally played. It prevails all through Ireland and in the Highlands of Scotland.
>
> *Statistical Account of County Down*

Common car. A horse- or donkey-cart used for farm work. Sprung cars and traps were also common, and used by the ladies or for the family to go to Mass. Carpenters made the common cars and all that went with them: wheels, butt, rail, guards and seat across.

Common Market. In 1973, after years of negotiations, Ireland (at the same time as the UK) joined what was then known as the Common Market. Jack LYNCH, who was taoiseach for all the years of preparation, deserves much credit for this achievement, and for the large majority of the Irish electorate (83%) who voted in favour of joining, in a referendum in May 1973. Membership of the Common Market, then formally known as the European Community and now the European Union (EU), was to have far-reaching consequences, both positive and negative, particularly for Irish agriculture. Membership also enabled Ireland to attract inward investment from North American companies that wished to use the country as a gateway to Europe. In areas of social policy and workers' rights (for instance the right of women in the civil service to work after marriage), membership brought largely positive benefits.

Common Prayer, Book of. The authoritative liturgical text for the Church of Ireland, standardized in 1560. An Irish translation from Cranmer's text was made by William Daniel (Uilliam Ó Domhnaill; *c.*1570–1628), later Protestant Archbishop of Tuam, who had already supervised the translation of the New Testament. *Leabhar na nUrnaightheadh gComhcoídchíond* was published in 1609, the year its main translator was made archbishop.

Company of old countrymen, the. The source, according to W.B. Yeats, of Douglas HYDE's fluency in Irish, which he bundled together in his account of their first meeting with Hyde's taste for snuff and poteen.
See also TORRENT OF DARK, MUDDIED STUFF.

Composition. *See* SIDNEY, SIR HENRY.

Compromise Rules. A set of rules for football that are a compromise between AUSTRALIAN RULES and GAA (Gaelic Athletic Association) FOOT-

BALL. In Australian football the ball is oval, like a rugby ball, and there are no goalkeepers. After a goal is scored the ball is brought back to the centre of the field and bounced to restart the game. The first Compromise Rules series was played between Ireland and Australia in CROKE PARK in 1984 as a three-match test (won by the high-scoring Australians); there were no goalkeepers and the game was played in alternate tests with an oval ball and a round ball. The GAA has since preferred the term 'International Rules' to describe such encounters.

Compulsory tillage. During the Second World War (*see* EMERGENCY, THE) the FIANNA FÁIL government passed a law making it compulsory for all farmers to till a quarter of their arable land in order to grow cereal; a quarter of this in turn had to be wheat. A tillage inspector would decide how much of a given farmer's land was arable, and failure to comply with the legislation resulted in fines. As much of the land was unsuitable for tillage and fertilizers were unavailable the quality of the grain produced in some areas was very poor and the policy was not a success.

Comstock Lode. A rich silver deposit found in June 1859 at Washoe, USA, in what was then the Nevada Territory, by two Irishmen, Peter O'Riley and Patrick McLaughlin. They sold it to a mining company for $300. The mines were named after a local shepherd. President Lincoln was later to say that the lode saved the credit of the Union during the Civil War. By 1898 most of the diggings had been exhausted.

Comyn, David. *See* GAELIC UNION.

Conacre. A system whereby small areas of land were rented for a fixed term for the cultivation of a single crop, usually potatoes. These pieces of land were rented from tenant farmers, often by the landless, such as tradesmen or agricultural labourers, at an annual rent of between £6 and £14 per Irish acre (in 1840). The sometimes excessive rents charged were a frequent cause of agrarian disorder in the pre-Famine period of the 19th century. The term is still in use for a short-term renting of land.

Conall Cearnach (Irish, 'Conall of the victories'). In Irish mythology, the chief warrior of the RED BRANCH KNIGHTS until the coming of his cousin and foster brother, CÚCHULAINN. He is one of the warriors sorely teased at BRICRIU's feast and the deviser of the deadly brain ball that CET used against CONCHOBHAR. He is killed in combat by an unknown warrior who is later revealed as CONLAÍ, Cúchulainn's son by AOIFE[2].

Conan Maol (Irish, 'Conan the bald'). The brother of GOLL MAC MORNA, who appears as a boastful and foul-mouthed clown in some of the stories of the FIANNA. As a brother of Goll, the old leader of the company and enemy of FIONN MAC CUMHAIL, he is naturally suspect, but he is as brave a warrior as the rest.

Concern. A humanitarian organization established in response to the Biafran War (1967–70) in Nigeria by Irish Holy Ghost Fathers who were working in the region at the time. Father Aengus Finucane, one of the founders, headed the organization until 1996. As well as raising and distributing relief funds, Concern has sent many hundreds of specialist volunteers to Africa.

Concertina. A hexagonal instrument played with buttons, called a 'squeeze-box' or simply 'box' because of its push-pull movement like the related ACCORDION. It is particularly popular in Co. Clare. Elizabeth Crotty (1885–1960) and Martin 'Junior' Crehan (1908–98) were among its finest exponents. Noel Hill (b.1958) is the most notable concertina player of his generation and has recorded extensively.

Conchobhar. In Irish mythology, a king of Ulster whose headquarters at EMAIN MACHA are defended by the RED BRANCH KNIGHTS. His mother is NESSA and his father is taken to be the giant Fachtna, who was then king, but he may have been the natural son of the druid CATHBAD. Nessa marries FERGUS MAC ROTH, who becomes the king on Fachtna's death, and obtains from him the boon of letting Conchobhar rule for a year. He proves so popular a leader that he is confirmed on the throne. He marries MEDB of Connacht, but she leaves him for AILILL. His tragic and treacherous love of DEIRDRE, who prefers death to marriage to anyone but NAOISE, is the theme of one of the great romances of Irish mythology. Conchobar dies seven years after the 'brain ball' from CET's slingshot lodged in his forehead during an ambush in a war with the men of Leinster; he had been warned that if he rode a horse or got in a rage he would die. A late version of his story has him born on the same day as Christ, and another tells of his death from rage on hearing of the Crucifixion:

> Out dropped the brain ball from his forehead;
> And King Conor macNessa fell dead.

Concolinel. A snatch of song sung in *Love's Labour's Lost* (III.i) by Moth, Armado's page. It may conceal the Irish words, '*Can cailín gheal*' (pronounced 'can coil-yeen yal' and meaning 'Sing bright maid'), and, if so, suggests the popularity of an Irish song in Shakespeare's London. *See also* CALMIE CUSTURE ME.

Conduct unbecoming. In 1985, Des O'Malley was expelled from Fianna Fáil for 'conduct unbecoming', having abstained on a vote on a Fine Gael–Labour bill to liberalize Charles Haughey's contraceptive bill of 1979 (*see* IRISH SOLUTION TO A PARTICULARLY IRISH PROBLEM, AN). 'I stand by the Republic,' declared O'Malley, arguing for a separation of church and state. O'Malley, a protégé of Jack LYNCH, had never supported Haughey and in the early 1980s had spearheaded various 'heaves' to remove him from the leadership of the party. In 1984 O'Malley had lost the Fianna Fáil whip for dissenting from Haughey's response to the findings of the New Ireland Forum. After his expulsion O'Malley, along with former Fianna Fáil TD Mary Harney, founded the Progressive Democrats (*see* PEE DEES).

Confederate Catholics. An alliance between Old Irish, OLD ENGLISH and some Catholic New English, also known as the Confederation of Kilkenny, that resulted from a meeting in Kilkenny on 7 June 1642. It was a consequence of the REBELLION OF 1641 in Ulster, and

Catholic fear of an English Parliament that had become increasingly Puritan-dominated. The Confederate assembly took as its motto '*Pro Deo, Rege et Patria, Hibernia Unanimis*' ('For God, king and country, Ireland united') and established a supreme council, consisting of lay and clerical members, which continued to meet in Kilkenny and which acted as a government, minting money and raising taxes. This confederation, although never cohesive, conducted the CONFEDERATE WAR of the 1640s.

Confederate War. A war (1642–53) that took its name from the Confederation of Kilkenny (*see* CONFEDERATE CATHOLICS). It developed from the REBELLION OF 1641, in which the OLD ENGLISH had joined, and is also known as the 'Eleven Years War', lasting as it did until 1653.

In 1642 the Confederation established four provincial armies, the Ulster army to be commanded by Owen Rua O'NEILL, and the Leinster army by the Old English Thomas Preston. The war was complicated by the increasing dominance of Parliament in England and by the English Civil War. The Royalist leader, the Duke of ORMOND, agreed a ceasefire with the Confederates in 1643 that allowed him to send troops to England to the king's aid; it was the breakdown of this ceasefire in 1646 that gave Owen Rua O'Neill the opportunity to win a major victory over General Munroe at the Battle of BENBURB.

After long months of plague, economic hardship, famine and military defeat at the hands of Lord Inchiquin (*see* MURROUGH OF THE BURNINGS) and Parliamentarian leader Michael Jones during 1647–9, the Confederate Catholics eventually agreed a second peace with Ormond in January 1649. But by this time it was too late for cooperation with the Royalists; Cromwell's army sailed into Ringsend, Dublin, in August and the lord protector's brutal campaign of reconquest began with the Siege of DROGHEDA the following month, and one by one the Confederate strongholds fell. The war ended with the CROMWELLIAN SETTLEMENT of 1653.

Confessio. The apologia of St Patrick (5th century), written in deliberately unornamental Latin. He calls himself *indoctus* ('unlearned'), but this is taken to be a mark of the blunt honesty and gravitas of the man. The work is partly autobiographical, partly spiritually self-critical, and is significantly defensive of his work and conduct against criticism and innuendo. It is the second of his extant writings; the first, the 1300-word *Epistola ad Milites Corotici*, is an admonition of the soldiers of the Romano-British prince, Coroticus, who had killed some of the saint's converts and enslaved others. The result was severe criticism from members of the church in Britain, and the suggestion that Patrick had acted *ultra vires*. The *Confessio* was his effective response. It and the *Epistola* are the oldest documents in Irish history.

> Ego, Patricius, peccator rusticissimus et minimus omnium fidelium et contemptibilissimus apud plurimos …
>
> (I am Patrick, a sinner, the least learned of men, least of all the faithful, most worthless in the eyes of many …)

Confraternity. The name by which a regular series of church devotions, usually held weekly, was known. The devotions consisted of ROS-ARY, sermon and Benediction of the Blessed Sacrament. In this context the word 'Confraternity' did not retain its literal meaning of 'brotherhood' or men only: there were separate nights for men's confraternity and women's confraternity and even, in some places, boys' and girls' confraternity. In towns and cities where there was an 'order church', the confraternity tradition was stronger; Limerick's Redemptorist confraternities were famous for their hellfire-and-brimstone sermons; Clonard Redemptorist monastery in west Belfast had a 'perpetual devotion', a sort of endless super-confraternity. The practice was yet another means used by the Catholic Church in Ireland to control its lay members: men and women were looked upon askance by their neighbours if they missed the Tuesday or Wednesday night devotion without good reason. Like other devotional practices, attendance at confraternities declined sharply from the 1960s.

Cong (Irish *conga*, 'isthmus'). A village on a strip of land between Lough Mask and Lough Corrib, Co. Mayo. It is the site of Ashford Castle, now a hotel, and known to fans of the John Ford/John Wayne cult film *The* QUIET MAN (1952) as the place where many of the scenes were shot. Cong was also the location of an Augustinian abbey built on an early Celtic site by Turloch Mór Ó Connor, the father of Rory Ó Connor (*see* LAST HIGH KING, THE), who is buried here. Turloch was also responsible for the manufacture of the Cross of Cong (now in the National Museum) said to hold a relic of the True Cross. Rory died there in 1198.

Congested Districts Board. A government agency set up in 1891 to encourage agriculture and industry in areas on the western seaboard, from Co. Donegal to Co. Cork, where, it was believed, acute poverty and dense population had stifled initiative. The board's sphere was later extended to perceived regions of need inland, and eventually covered about a third of the country. The board was established by Arthur BALFOUR when chief secretary and was initially successful, partly because of the large budget available (increased to £250,000 annually from 1909). Harbours were built, land purchased for low-rent tenure and experts on cottage industries and agriculture sent to advise the local population. It was seen as another example of 'Constructive Unionism', in its policy of KILLING HOME RULE WITH KINDNESS. Whatever social achievements may have resulted, that primary purpose was not attained.
See also CLEGGAN BAY DISASTER; CROMANE PIER.

Conlaí. In Irish mythology, the son of CÚCHU-LAINN and AOIFE[2]), who stays with his aunt SCÁTHACH in ALBA, where she teaches him the same martial skills as his father. He grows up to become a formidable warrior and comes to Ireland to seek adversaries. He is warned beforehand not to reveal his identity, and after killing CONALL CEARNACH finds himself matched with his father. EMER, Cúchulainn's wife, warns her husband that this new champion could well be his own son, but he refuses to heed her. Only when Conlaí lies dying does he reveal himself to his father, who is then overcome with grief.

Conleth (d.c.519). A saint who was an associate of BRIGID. He was spiritual director of her double abbey in Kildare, and abbot-bishop of the monastery. Before joining her he had been a hermit on the banks of the River Liffey. Tradition accords him with the reputation of being one of the chief artificers of Ireland, known for his metalwork and penmanship. His feast day is 4 May.

Conn. The name of one of the Children of Lir (*see* FIONNUALA).

Conn, Billy (William H. Conn) (1895–1973). Cartoonist and illustrator. Conn was born in Belfast and educated at what is now Friends' School, Lisburn, and from 1921 earned his living as a commercial artist. He was appointed staff artist of the *Belfast Telegraph* in 1946 and contributed cartoons to its sports weekly, *Ireland's Saturday Night*, especially his comic series 'The Doings of Larry O'Hooligan'. He was a regular contributor to the humorous monthly DUBLIN OPINION, with sentimental black and white drawings of a vanishing rural Ireland.

Connacht. An ancient kingdom and historic province of Ireland, named after the Connachta tribe, who once dominated the region (their name possibly derives from Old Irish *cond* 'head'). Traditionally, however, the province is said to be named after the legendary 2nd-century king, CONN OF THE HUNDRED BATTLES. Connacht (also anglicized as Connaught) comprises the western counties of Leitrim, Roscommon, Galway, Mayo and Sligo. The ancient kingdom, along with the four others (ULSTER, MEATH, LEINSTER and MUNSTER), emerged at the beginning of the Christian era. It came to be dominated by the O'Connors, whose power was later threatened by the Anglo-Norman de Burghs. In the 16th century Connacht was broken up by plantations and divided into shires.

Connaught Rangers Mutiny. *See* DEVIL'S OWN, THE.

Conn Cetcathach. *See* CONN OF THE HUNDRED BATTLES.

Connell, Jim. *See* 'RED FLAG, THE'.

Connemara pony. A type of pony indigenous to Connemara, Co. Galway. Connemara ponies can be up to 14.2 hands and are nowadays used mainly for jumping and as children's mounts. Like the KERRY BOG PONY, however, they were once industrious workers on farms, drawing seaweed, turf, hay and wood and pulling the family trap to Mass on Sunday. The Connemara Pony Society was set up in 1923 with the aim of maintaining or improving the bloodlines.

Conniption. A fit of anger or indignation, often used in the phrase: 'She nearly had a conniption.' The word may derive in part from 'convulsion'.

Conn of the Hundred Battles (*Conn Cetcathach*, in Irish). A mainly mythical character with some basis in historical fact as a 2nd-century king. In the myth his second wife BÉCUMA marries him only because of her lust for Conn's son ART. He is said to be the grandfather of the semi-historical CORMAC MAC ART, and in one tale he has a vision in which a woman representing sovereignty and the god LUGH lists his royal descendants. His byname indicates a martial career.

Connolly, James (1868–1916). Trade unionist and patriot. He was born in the impoverished Cowgate area of Edinburgh to Irish parents on 5 June 1868. He served for a time in the British army and in 1896 came to Dublin as a paid organizer for the Dublin Socialist Club, helping to found the socialist paper *Workers' Republic*, which was published 1898–9, and the *Irish Socialist Republican*, which had the aim of securing 'the national and economic freedom of the Irish people'. Between 1903 and 1910 Connolly and his family lived in the USA, where he was involved in the establishment of the union called the Industrial Workers of the World, known as the 'Wobblies'. But he was an outsider among Irish-Americans because of his socialism and among American socialists for his Catholic beliefs, and he considered the time he spent in America a failure.

On his return to Ireland Connolly worked as the Belfast organizer of the ITGWU and published the work for which he is best known, *Labour in Irish History* (1910). In 1912 he co-founded the Irish Labour Party. When James LARKIN, leader of the ITGWU in Dublin, was imprisoned during the 1913 LOCKOUT, Larkin stood in for him, and later when Larkin went to America, Connolly succeeded him as leader of the union. In November 1913 he established, with Captain Jack White, the IRISH CITIZEN ARMY, with the aim of defending workers against police harassment and attacks.

Connolly led the Citizen Army into the EASTER RISING in 1916 in support of the IRISH VOLUNTEERS, having reached agreement on this strategy earlier that year with the military council of the IRB. Connolly was one of the signatories of the PROCLAMATION OF THE REPUBLIC of 1916, which reflects his influence in its insistence on the rights of all the Irish people to the 'ownership of Ireland', and was appointed commander of the Dublin district during the Rising. Badly wounded in the leg, he stayed in command in the GPO until the surrender of the rebels. Like the other leaders of the Rising, after a court martial he was shot in Kilmainham Jail (12 May 1916); for his execution he had to be strapped to a chair because of his leg wound, and for this reason achieved a particularly heroic martyr status. There is a statue of Connolly facing LIBERTY HALL, the ITGWU headquarters in Dublin, but it is certain that the independent Irish state paid little attention to his socialist principles.
See also CONNOLLY STATION.

Connolly, John. *See* FIRST NEW YORK BISHOP, THE.

Connolly, Sybil (1921–98). Fashion designer. She was born in London of a Waterford father and a Welsh mother, and studied dress design. She moved to Dublin in 1939 and from 1957 based her fashion house in her home at 71 Merrion Square. In 1953 her international career was launched when she received favourable coverage in the American fashion magazine *Harper's Bazaar* – it then had an Irish-born editor, Carmel Snow (1887–1961) who was sympathetic to Connolly's 'hand-crafted' look. In the same year the cover of *Life* magazine on 10 August announced, 'Irish invade fashion world'. She turned Irish fabrics such as BÁINÍN into high fashion, her trademark material being pleated handkerchief linen. Her style was romantic and classic, and her clients included Jackie Kennedy and the actresses Merle Oberon and Elizabeth Taylor. She did not move with 1960s fashion, saying, 'I never liked the mini and I always remember what Dior said to me in Paris: "A woman should show her curves not her joints."' In the 1970s and 1980s Connolly also designed ceramics and crystal for Tiffanys and Bloomingdales in New York.

Connolly Station. The Dublin terminus for trains to the north and east of the country. Connolly Station (formerly Amiens Street Station, a name still used by many people) was built in 1846 as a terminus for the Dublin and Drogheda Railway, to a design by William Deane Butler. In 1876 it became the terminus for the Great Northern Railway Company. The name of the station was changed to Connolly on Easter Sunday 1966 in honour of James CONNOLLY, an executed leader of the 1916 Easter Rising.

Connorys, the. Three brothers – Patrick (d.1880), James (d.1857) and John (d.1851) – from the Sliabh gCua area of Co. Waterford who were outlaws and rebels in the early 19th century. As symbols of agrarian dissent they received great popular support among Waterford's poor tenant farmers. After a series of violent clashes with land agents and equally daring escapes from custody in various jails, in 1838 the brothers were finally sentenced to 14 years' transportation to New South Wales, Australia for jailbreaking. Patrick and James subsequently made good in Sydney. Three traditional songs celebrate their memory (one is sung by Nioclás TÓIBÍN):

*Is go bhfuil a fhios ag gach éinne nach rabhadar
ciontach riamh in aon chor,
Ach ag seasamh dá gceart féineach is gan é acu le
fail.*
(Everyone knows they never did anything
untoward,
But stood up for their rights when they were denied
them.)

Connradh na Gaeilge. *See* GAELIC LEAGUE.

Conor, William. *See* MAKE NS MEET.

Consanguinity. In rural Irish society consanguinity was a barrier to marriage. Even distant relatives – third or fourth cousins – were discouraged
from marrying each other. This was because, in
the days before motorized transport, most
young people were confined to a very limited
area when choosing a partner, and older people
worried about the danger of in-breeding.

Conscription Crisis. The event in 1918 now credited with creating most widespread support
for SINN FÉIN among the Irish public in the
aftermath of the EASTER RISING of 1916 was
the decision of the British government of David
LLOYD GEORGE to introduce conscription into
Ireland in April 1918. The Irish Parliamentary
Party withdrew from Parliament in protest,
but it was the more extreme Nationalists who
gained most support.

Constitution of 1937. The constitution drafted
by Éamon DE VALERA and his FIANNA FÁIL
government, accepted by referendum in July
1937 and in force from the end of that year. It
superseded the 1922 constitution of the FREE
STATE. De Valera's intention was that Ireland
should be a republic in all but name – formal
declaration of the republic did not come until
1949 – and Article 5 stated that Ireland was a
'sovereign, independent, democratic state'. Britain responded officially to the new constitution
by declaring that it did not affect Ireland's
membership of the Commonwealth.

Catholic social teaching, and especially the
views of the soon-to-be Archbishop of Dublin,
John Charles MCQUAID, strongly influenced de
Valera in his drafting of the Constitution. Its

controversial provisions included: ARTICLES
2 AND 3, relating to national sovereignty and
Northern Ireland; Article 41, which offended
feminists by recognizing, 'that by her life within the home, woman gives to the State a support without which the common good cannot
be achieved'; and ARTICLE 44, which acknowledged the special position of the Catholic
Church in Ireland.

There have been numerous amendments to
the Constitution by referendum, and among the
articles that have been repealed are Articles 2,
3 and 44 – all in an effort to reassure Northern
Unionists. The 26th Amendment, passed in November 2002, allowed for the ratification of the
Treaty of Nice (*see* NICE REFERENDUM). Despite
its limitations, the fact of having a written Constitution is generally seen by Irish people as a
very positive thing: it protects the rights of individuals and is often appealed to in relation to
infringement of civil liberties and equality issues;
the MCGEE CASE was a notable example.

Constructive Unionism. *See* KILLING HOME RULE
WITH KINDNESS.

Continuity IRA. A group that claims to have
existed since 1986 when SINN FÉIN voted to end
ABSTENTIONISM. It was originally known as the
Continuity Army Council, and in practice is co-
terminous with Republican Sinn Féin (RSF). Its
active period began in 1996 when it reasserted
its rejection of peace talks and ceasefires. It was
responsible for a bomb hoax in Derry in August
1997, and the following month caused serious
damage to the centre of Markethill, Co. Armagh.
A 227-kg (500-lb) bomb was defused in Derry
in October, as was a similar device in Banbridge
in January 1998. The RSF leaders were Ruairí
Ó Brádaigh (b.1932) and Dáithí Ó Conaill
(1937–89), but Ó Brádaigh has denied that the
Continuity IRA is the military wing of RSF. After
the REAL IRA bombing of Omagh in August
1998 (*see* OMAGH BOMB), only the Continuity
IRA refused to announce a ceasefire.

Contraception. *See* IRISH SOLUTION TO A PAR-
TICULARLY IRISH PROBLEM, AN; CONTRACEP-
TIVE TRAIN.

Contraceptive Train. A publicity stunt undertaken by members of Ireland's Women's Liberation Movement to highlight the country's antiquated family planning laws. On Saturday 22 May 1971 a group of women, some of them well-known journalists, left Dublin for Belfast by train (a popular Saturday shopping trip for Dubliners because of price differentials and the greater range of fashion stores in Belfast). They returned that evening carrying condoms and approached customs officials in Dublin's Connolly Station, challenging them to confiscate their banned merchandise. The customs officials wisely declined, but the image of the women and the condoms, captured by print and broadcast media, was an enduring one.

'Convergence of the Twain, The'. A poem by Thomas Hardy (1840–1928) on the loss of the Belfast-built TITANIC. It was written in 1912, the year of the catastrophe. It shows a typically Hardyesque fatalism, but it has a kind of chilling neatness:

> And as the smart ship grew
> In stature, grace and hue,
> In shadowy silent distance grew the Iceberg too.

Conversation lozenge. A kind of sweet with a written message impressed in red; the messages, once sentimental, are now likely to be at best facetious.

Convey. A noun deriving from the verb, 'to convey'. After a dance a young man might ask a girl whether he could, 'give her the convey', i.e. escort her home.

Cooke, Henry (1788–1868). Presbyterian leader. He was born in Grillagh, near Maghera, Co. Derry, on 11 May 1788 and educated at Glas-gow College and Trinity College Dublin. Or-dained in 1808, by 1829 he was minister at May Street church in Belfast, an imposing edifice specially built for him. He quickly gained fame as a preacher, as a stern upholder of theological orthodoxy, as the enemy of ARIANISM in INST and as Daniel O'CONNELL's main Ulster adversary. By constant agitation and apparently endless energy he obtained government recognition for a separate Presbyterian system of primary education and endowment for ASSEMBLY'S COLLEGE. Cooke's political activities tended to be more obvious than his religious ones, and it is interesting that his city-centre statue, known as the 'Black Man', was erected not by people of his own faith but by the ORANGE ORDER (originally largely Anglican), in mute token of his having purged mainstream Presbyterianism of its quondam liberalism. He died in Belfast on 13 December 1868.

Cookstown. A plantation town in Co. Tyrone, noted for its linear design and the longest main street in Ireland (2 km/1.25 miles). It was founded in 1609 by a planter called Allen Cook on land leased from the Archbishop of Armagh. The present town was laid out in 1750 by William Stewart. The oddity of its design has given rise to the external gibe that depends for its effect on the Ulster pronunciation of the word 'meaner':

> The longest main street in Ireland and the longer you go the meaner it gets.

Coole Park. The home of Sir William and Lady GREGORY, 3 km (2 miles) east of Gort, Co. Galway. Wantonly razed in 1941, it had been a powerhouse of literary activity, providing hospitality not only for W.B. YEATS, a regular visitor, but also for Synge, O'Casey, Shaw, Violet Martin, Æ and others, who were invited to carve their names on the trunk of an immense copper beech, which still stands. It was the inspiration of some of Yeats's finest poems, including 'The Wild Swans at Coole' and 'Coole Park, 1929', the final verse of which sums up its value and is prophetic of its end:

> Here, traveller, scholar, poet, take your stand
> When all those rooms and passages are gone,
> When nettles wave upon a shapeless mound
> And saplings root among the broken stone,
> And dedicate – eyes bent upon the ground,
> Back turned upon the brightness of the sun
> And all the sensuality of the shade –
> A moment's memory to that laurelled head.
>
> 'Coole Park, 1929', in *The Winding Stair and Other Poems* (1933)

Cooney, Brian. *See* BIANS.

'Coortin in the Kitchen'. A popular mid-19th-century ballad with an irresistible jig tune. It describes the betrayal by Miss Henrietta Bell of the narrator when their 'coortin' in Captain's Phibbs's kitchen is discovered:

> I said she did invite me, but she gave a flat denial;
> For assault she did indict me, and I was sent for trial.
> She swore I robbed the house in spite of all her screechin'
> So I six months went round the rack for coortin' in the kitchen.

Coote, Sir Eyre (1726–83). Anglo-Irish soldier. He was born in Ash Hill, Limerick, the son of a gentleman cleric. In 1754 he was an officer in the first contingent of British soldiers to land in India and was instrumental in persuading Robert Clive (1725–74) to risk attacking the Nawab of Bengal at Plassey in 1757. His defeat of French forces at Pondicherry in 1761 secured India for the British. He returned to the subcontinent in 1777 as commander-in-chief and removed the last threat from the native leaders to British dominance with the defeat of Haidar Ali at Porto Novo in 1781. He fell ill in 1782 and died a year later.

Cop on, to. A phrase very common in colloquial speech throughout Ireland, meaning to understand, to get the picture, also to behave appropriately, as in the exasperated cry: 'For heaven's sake, will you cop on!' Cop-on is also used as a noun: 'Has that fellow any cop-on?' The word 'cop' on its own is used with a similar meaning.

Coppin, William (1805–95). Shipwright and mariner. He was born in Kinsale, Co. Cork, and had his first salt-water baptism when as a boy he saved six customs men from drowning when their boat overturned on the Shannon. His interest in ship design showed itself in 1825 when he devised an ice-breaking boat that could handle the frozen rivers of New Brunswick. In 1835 he took over the shipyard in Derry and built ships that he captained on their maiden voyages between Derry and Liverpool and across the Atlantic. His moment of glory was the launch of the *Great Northern* in January 1843. She was the largest screw-driven vessel in the world at her launch and 20,000 people attended the function. Coppin, however, was unable to persuade the government to buy the ship, as he had hoped, and he was forced to take a loss on the deal. A sister ship, completed in 1846, was completely destroyed by fire just before the launch. The effect of these two disasters was to deflect him from shipbuilding, although he continued to run a salvage business and began an iron foundry in the city. His last ship was the triple-hulled iron *Tripod Express*, which was used on the Atlantic run in the 1880s.

> Hail! Captain Coppin, Neptune's brightest star,
> That shines with splendour and effulgence bright;
> Whose buoyant spirit like a jolly Tar,
> Will yet burst forth with more effective might;
> Give to mechanics full employment here,
> And pay them for their labour so severe.
> > R. TAGGART: 'Neptune's Brightest Star' (1839), quoted in Annesley Malley and Mary McLaughlin, *Captain Coppin: Neptune's Brightest Star* (1992)

Córas Iompair Éireann. *See* CIÉ.

Corbett, James John. *See* GENTLEMAN JIM.

Corbinian (670–730). A saint of Irish birth and education who made a pilgrimage to Rome after 14 years as a hermit. There he was ordained bishop by Pope Gregory II and given the task of assisting St Boniface (*c.*675–754) with the evangelizing of Germany. He established his see at Freising in Bavaria. His later years were made difficult by the local magnate Duke Grimoald, whose incestuous marriage Corbinian had denounced. His feast day is 8 September.

Core value. According to many within the party, single-party (majority) government was a core value of FIANNA FÁIL, despite which the party has found itself repeatedly in coalition since 1989.

Cork. The second-largest city in the Republic of Ireland, and the county town of Co. Cork. The name derives from Irish *corcaigh*, 'marsh'. It is centred on an island formed by two branches of the River Lee, before it enters the inlet known as Cork Harbour (in which the port of Cobh

(Queenstown) is situated). Until the 18th century the area occupied by the city was intersected by channels of water:

We have often heard Cork called the Venice of Ireland, but have never heard Venice called the Cork of Italy.

ANON.: quoted by John Betjeman in a letter to Michael Rose, 25 September 1955

Cork was also once known as the ATHENS OF IRELAND.

Originally Cork grew around the monastery and school founded on the edge of a marsh in the 7th century by St Finbarr. The settlement that grew up around the monastery was raided by the VIKINGS in the 9th century; however, the Vikings went on to settle peacefully and Cork developed as a thriving trading centre. The Normans took the place in 1172, and it subsequently became a royal borough. In 1690 Cork fell to William III after a devastating siege. In the following century it developed as an important Atlantic port, although its commerce declined in the 19th century.

During the ANGLO-IRISH WAR Cork suffered again: in 1920 its lord mayor, Tomás MAC-CURTAIN, was assassinated by the British, and his successor, Terence MACSWINEY, died on hunger strike in Brixton Prison; at the end of that year the BLACK AND TANS and the AUXIES burnt down the city centre, in reprisal for an IRA ambush. During the CIVIL WAR, it was held for a while by the Republicans. Since the 1950s Cork has attracted much inward investment.

See also BELLS OF SHANDON, THE.

Cork, Richard Boyle, 1st Earl of. See BOYLE, RICHARD, 1ST EARL OF CORK.

Corkery, Daniel (1878–1964). Man of letters. He was born in Cork and educated at St Patrick's Training College in Dublin and at the Crawford Municipal School of Art in Cork, where he discovered a talent for watercolour. A lifelong bachelor and crippled by poliomyelitis, he was a dedicated not to say obsessive enthusiast for the Irish language. He taught in Cork, eventually, not without controversy, holding the chair of English at University College (1931–47) in

place of his former and better-qualified pupil, Sean O'FAOLAIN. His academic work benefits from his dedication to the Irish language. *The Hidden Ireland* (1924) was followed by *Synge and Anglo-Irish Literature* (1931), which is rather more complimentary to Synge than one might have expected. Corkery's short-story collections *A Munster Twilight* (1916), *The Hounds of Banba* (1926) and *The Stormy Hills* (1929) are sited in the city and county of Cork, where people earn a living in factory and farm, their grey lives only briefly affected by the shocks of insurrection. He also wrote a bleak novel, *The Threshold of Quiet* (1917), and a number of plays, including *The Yellow Bittern* (1917), about the death of the happily dissolute poet Cathal Buí Mac Giolla Gunna (*see* 'BONNÁN BUÍ, AN').

Cormac Mac Art. A semi-historical HIGH KING who probably reigned in the 3rd century and about whom many myths accreted. In these he is a patron of the FIANNA and the father of GRÁINNE. He loses an eye while trying to defend his son Cellach, and, because now imperfect in body, can no longer rule as high king, and has to relinquish his throne to his son CAIRBRE. Depicted as a wise and ideal king, later stories have him coming to the truth of Christianity by his own reasoning and ordering that his body be buried at Rosnaree (near Slane, Co. Meath) rather than the traditional pagan site at NEWGRANGE. When the druids try to thwart this wish the River Boyne rises three times and eventually washes his bier to its proper resting place.

'Crom Cruach and his sub-gods twelve,'
Said Cormac, 'are but carven treene;
The axe that made them, haft or helve,
Had worthier of our worship been.'
...
At morn, on the grassy marge
Of Rosnaree, the corpse was found,
And shepherds at their early charge
Entomb'd it in the peaceful ground.

SAMUEL FERGUSON (1810–86): 'The Burial of King Cormac', in *Lays of the Western Gael* (1864)

Cormac's Chapel. An exquisite chapel in the

Irish Romanesque style on the ROCK OF CASHEL. Cormac's Chapel was begun in 1127 by the Bishop of Cashel, Cormac McCarthy, and consecrated in 1134. Many of the carvings and much of the painted decoration have now been lost. Honan Chapel in University College Cork is a copy of Cormac's Chapel.

Corno de Bassetto. The pseudonym used by George Bernard Shaw (*see* GBS) when music critic of the *Star* (1889–90). His ideal readership he saw as the polytechnic-educated who had little money and no evening suits but who had as much genuine appreciation of Mozart as more fashionable audiences. His 'hidden socialism' did not appeal to the editor TAY-PAY who effectively starved him out by refusing to increase his salary. To their mutual relief Corno de Bassetto of the *Star* became G.B.S. of the *World* after 16 May 1890.

Cornwallis, Charles, 1st Marquess (1738–1805). Lord lieutenant and commander-in-chief of the army during the REBELLION OF 1798. He had previously led British forces during the American Revolution (his surrender at Yorktown in 1781 brought hostilities to an end), and had been governor-general of India (1786–93). During the 1798 Rebellion he refused to sanction indiscriminate repression and violence by the militia and the yeomanry, and made clear his support for CATHOLIC EMANCIPATION, which he believed would be granted after the passing of the Act of UNION; along with CASTLEREAGH he is regarded in Nationalist historiography as the architect of the act. He resigned his position in February 1801 when it became clear that the opposition of George III rendered impossible the achievement of emancipation. In 1805 he again became governor-general of India, where he died.

Corpo, the. The popular diminutive of (Dublin) Corporation, used extensively in that city. Dublin Corporation changed its name to Dublin City Council in 2001, as did the corporations of all the other Irish cities.

Corpse on the Dissecting Table, the. The condi-tion of Ireland as descried by Sir Charles Gavan DUFFY when he left the country in 1855 for self-imposed exile in Australia. In his last editorial for *The NATION* he wrote:

> … there seems to be no more hope for the Irish
> cause than for the corpse on the dissecting table.

Corragiob. The Irish word for 'haunches'. It is borrowed in HIBERNO-ENGLISH in phrases such as, 'He was there sitting on his corragiob', meaning squatting or sitting on one's haunches.

Corrs, The. A successful family group from Dundalk, Co. Louth, combining pulchritude with instrumental and vocal skills. Their music, for which they have a considerable international audience, is pop, but influenced by traditional elements. Their bestselling albums are *Forgiven Not Forgotten* (1995), which sold more than 3 million copies, and *Talk On Corners* (1997), which sold 8 million. The members are Andrea (b.1974), the youngest but best known, Caroline (b.1973), Jim (b.1964) and Sharon (b.1970).

Cosgrave, Liam (b.1920). FINE GAEL politician. He was born in Dublin, the son of W.T. COSGRAVE, and educated at Synge Street Christian Brothers school and the Kings' Inns. He worked as a barrister, becoming a senior counsel in 1958. He was elected to the Dáil in 1943 and served in both INTERPARTY GOVERNMENTS (formed respectively in 1948 and 1954). In 1965 he became leader of Fine Gael in succession to James DILLON and was taoiseach of the national coalition government (with the LABOUR PARTY) from 1973 to 1977. He resigned as leader after the party's heavy defeat by Fianna Fáil in the general election of 1977.

Cosgrave, William T. (1880–1965). Statesman. He was born in James's Street in Dublin on 6 June 1880, and as a youth began to work in the grocery trade. In 1905 he was a delegate to the first SINN FÉIN conference and was elected a member of Dublin Corporation in 1909. He joined the IRISH VOLUNTEERS in 1913 and fought in the EASTER RISING of 1916. Sentenced to death after the Rising, he was instead interned in FRONGOCH until the amnesty of January

1917; he was elected MP for Carlow–Kilkenny in the general election of 1918 and sat in the first Dáil, holding the position of minister for local government in the alternative Sinn Féin administration of 1919–22, a period during which he was often on the run and imprisoned several times.

After the deaths of Arthur Griffith and Michael Collins in the summer of 1922 Cosgrave assumed their roles as chairman of the Provisional Government and president of the Dáil respectively, and in September of that year he became the first president of the executive council of the Free State. In 1923 he founded CUMANN NA NGAEDHEAL and became its first head; he led the government formed by that party until its election defeat by FIANNA FÁIL in 1932. Cosgrave succeeded Eoin O'DUFFY as leader of the newly-formed FINE GAEL in 1935 and led that party until his retirement in 1945, but never again served in government. He died in Dublin on 16 November 1965.

W.T. Cosgrave was essentially the safe pair of hands needed in Ireland after the CIVIL WAR, bringing a socially conservative stability to the governance of the country. His son, Liam COSGRAVE, also became leader of Fine Gael and was taoiseach (1973–7).

Costello, John A. (1891–1976). FINE GAEL politician. He was born in Dublin and educated at O'Connell's Christian Brothers school and University College Dublin. He was called to the Bar in 1914, and his first political appointment was as attorney-general to the CUMANN NA NGAEDHEAL government of 1926–32. He was elected to the Dáil in 1933 and was taoiseach of the INTERPARTY GOVERNMENT of 1948–51 because the then leader of Fine Gael, Richard MULCAHY, was unacceptable to the CLANN NA POBLACHTA coalition partners. On Easter Monday 1949 his government formally established the REPUBLIC OF IRELAND. Costello also became leader of the second interparty government in 1954, which fell in 1957 as a result of the BORDER CAMPAIGN. He retired to the backbenches in 1963.

Cosy. A taxi driver who rents the car and taxi plate from the owner for part of the time; if, for instance the owner works by day, the cosy will work by night. The term may derive from 'co-driver'.

Cosy homesteads. *See* DE VALERA, ÉAMON.

Cotamore or **costamore.** A HIBERNO-ENGLISH word for an overcoat, from the Irish *cóta mór*, 'big coat'.

Cottier. Generally a person who lived in a cabin or small hovel-like cottage and managed a subsistence living from the little piece of land he sharecropped. Technically the term meant a labourer who was not paid in money but in habitation (the cabin) and some few roods of land which gave him the potatoes and the bit of grazing for the cow. Much of his work would have been for the tenant farmer.
See also GREGORY CLAUSE, THE.

Coughlin, Charles. *See* SOCIAL JUSTICE.

Coulter, Phil (b.1942). Singer, composer and arranger of music. He was born in Derry and since the 1970s has had a successful career as a writer and arranger of hit pop songs – he arranged Dana's 1970 Eurovision winner 'All Kinds of Everything' (*see* DANA²) as well as ballads and traditional songs for groups such as The DUBLINERS and PLANXTY². From 1983 he has produced a very successful series of easy-listening solo albums, featuring well-known Irish airs and his own compositions, which he plays on the piano. He is a very popular entertainer both in the Republic and in the North.

Countess Bridge Killings. On 7 March 1923, the same day as the BALLYSEEDY MASSACRE in the final bitter stages of the CIVIL WAR in Kerry, five Republican prisoners were taken from jail in Killarney and brought to a railway bridge outside the town known as the Countess Bridge. They were ordered to move stones from a barricade across the road and then a mine was set off. The fatally injured men were finished off with grenades and shotguns. As at Ballyseedy, one man, Tadhg Coffey, survived and escaped.

Country markets. A locally based series of commercial outlets for the produce of the rural economy – poultry, vegetables and other garden produce, cakes and preserves. The country markets were founded to provide some small independence for farm women by the IRISH COUNTRYWOMEN'S ASSOCIATION in 1947, under the dynamic leadership of Muriel Gahan (d.1995). Country markets are now more popular than ever among discerning consumers. *See also* GRIANÁN.

County Bounds. A mountainous and remote but scenic area that forms the boundary between Cork and Kerry. The main road from Cork to Killarney is the 'County Bounds Road'.

Courts of poetry. During the 18th century, Gaelic poets, deprived by the collapse of the old order of their patrons and their formal schools of poetry, assembled in an informal way at what were called 'courts of poetry', in a private house or a pub, or even at a funeral. At these meetings, they recited poetry and generally had conversation, CRAIC – and much drink. Among the most famous courts were those of SLIABH LUACHRA, Croom in Co. Limerick (the MAIGUE POETS) and Blarney in Co. Cork. Galway's Cúirt literary festival, held in April–May every year, is a modern version of the poetry court.

Covanna. The horse with which George Henry Moore, the father of George MOORE, won the Chester Cup, winning him £10,000 and thus enabling him to protect his tenants from the ravages of the Great Famine.

Cove of Cork. The old name of Cobh (Queenstown), a town set 22 km (14 miles) from the city on Great Island in Cork Harbour. It was the main Irish port of call for transatlantic shipping and as such its chief emigration centre. Known as QUEENSTOWN from 1849 to 1922, it is the burial place of the Rev. Charles Wolfe (1791–1823), the author of 'The Burial of Sir John Moore' (1815), and of the many victims of the sinking of the LUSITANIA on 7 May 1915. Trollope often recalled a happy summer spent there in 1850 with his wife and young children.

Crabbid or **crabbit.** A common word of obscure derivation, also heard in Scotland, meaning 'bad-tempered', 'cantankerous', and used, for instance, to describe a demanding child or a colicky baby. It is also used, in a less derogatory way, to mean precociousness in a child.

Cracked. A word used in HIBERNO-ENGLISH to mean 'giddy', 'silly'. The word is sometimes used indulgently of those possessing the effervescence of youth.

Craggaunowen. An out-of-doors archaeological museum in an extensive rural setting, situated 29 km (18 miles) from Shannon Airport in Co. Clare. It consists of reproductions of Iron Age habitations such as a CRANNÓG, a RING FORT with souterrain and a FULACHT FIADH (cooking place). It was the brainchild of art historian and philanthropist John Hunt (1900–76), and opened to the public in 1975. Hunt bought the site from the LAND COMMISSION in 1965, and his reconstruction of the crannóg was inspired by the excavations at LOUGH GUR in Co. Limerick. When he died in 1976 he left Craggaunowen and the collection now housed in the HUNT MUSEUM in trust for the nation. Carraunowen is administered by Shannon Heritage. The name Craggaunowen derives from Irish *creagán* 'rocky outcrop' and *Owen* or *Eoghan*, (an Irish version of 'John'), the name of the builder of the original 16th-century tower house on the site.

Craic. A popular and useful word that does not derive from Irish. It is pronounced 'crack', and until the very recent past was also spelt 'crack'. The Irish media then decided, perhaps to give the word an Irish gloss in the interests of tourism or because of the association of the term 'crack' with crack cocaine, to promote the watered-down *faux*-Gaelic spelling. Craic at its most basic is any kind of fun, especially that associated with drinking and the pub, with traditional music SESSIONS and with CÉILÍs. You would have craic at a football match, but even more so in the pub afterwards if your team won. The word 'craic' is also used with the definite article, as in 'The craic was mighty,' or 'We were having the craic.' The opening line of Dominic Behan's song 'MCALPINE'S FUSILIERS' runs, 'The crack [sic] was good in Cricklewood / We wouldn't leave the Crown.' However, the word 'crack' is an old one, of Anglo-Saxon derivation; it had the meaning of friendly gossip in Restoration drama, and is still used in this context by some Irish people. If you meet someone and they ask you: 'What's the crack?' or 'Any crack?' they are not asking about the session you were at last night.

Craiftine. The harpist of LABRAID LOINSEACH. His skill in music lulls the parents of the Gaulish princess Moriath to sleep so that she and Labraid can make love. He uses the same means to render Labraid's enemies ineffective.

Craig, James, 1st Viscount Craigavon (1871–1940). Politician. Son of a millionaire distiller, he fought in the Boer War and returned to Ulster to play an active part in the opposition to the third HOME RULE Bill in 1910. He became Carson's chief lieutenant in the UVF, helping with the LARNE GUN-RUNNING in 1914 and accepting the leadership of the permanent Unionist government in Northern Ireland, the six counties of which he chose judiciously to maintain that hegemony. Though amiable with individual Nationalists, like 'WEE JOE' Devlin, he allowed such extreme colleagues as Dawson Bates (*see* SPECIAL POWERS ACT) to establish a regime in which Catholics were severely discriminated against. He died on 24 November 1940, having failed to counter the manifest injustices that eventually brought the STORMONT regime down.

Crane Bag, the. In Irish mythology, a bag made from the skin of a nymph called Aoife who is killed after she is turned into a crane by MANANNÁN MAC LIR, the father of her lover. It is a source of magical articles, empty at low tide and full only at the top of the tide. *The Crane Bag* was also the name of a cultural and political journal (1977–81) edited by Mark Hederman and Richard Kearney.

Crank on the Bank. A Dublin rhyming nickname for the memorial to Patrick KAVANAGH on the GRAND CANAL; Kavanagh had a reputation for being contrary and litigious.

See also CHIME IN THE SLIME; DISH WITH THE FISH; FLOOZIE IN THE JACUZZI; STILETTO IN THE GHETTO; TART WITH THE CART.

Crannóg (Irish *crann óg*, 'young tree', or, in this case, 'small wood'). A type of habitation built on an island, partly natural, partly man-made, in a lake (usually a small and sheltered one). The earliest examples date from the late Neolithic / early Bronze Age. Timber on a base of stones was the main building material, and a stone causeway linked some crannógs with the shore, although others could be reached only by boat. Evidence of crannógs is found mainly in a cluster across the northwest of Ireland and the DRUMLIN belt, and also in counties Meath, Offaly and Westmeath; the most famous crannóg of all is at Lagore, near Dunshaughlin in Co. Meath, and it dates from the early Iron Age. It is believed that there are up to 2000 crannógs in Ireland, most never excavated, and there may be hundreds more undetected in the 'lakeland' regions of Cavan and Leitrim. The 6th and 7th centuries AD were the main period for the building of crannógs, but they were in use until as late as the end of the 16th century, at which date the availability of gunpowder made it possible for them to be bombarded from the shore. Crannógs appeared on Elizabethan military maps during the NINE YEARS' WAR, one such map dated 1600 showing an attack on an Ulster crannóg. In 1604 one of the 'Articles for the Better Reformation of the Kingdom of Ireland' proposed:

> that none of the Irish do build any house on loughs but be enjoined to build castles or houses upon the firm land and those houses that now are built upon loughs be defaced.

Craoibhín Aoibhinn (Irish, 'pleasant little branch'). The pseudonym of Douglas HYDE (1860–1949), founder of the GAELIC LEAGUE and first president of Ireland.

Crawford, Julia. *See* KATHLEEN MAVOURNEEN.

Craw-sick. Hungover, under the weather from drinking; from *craw*, 'throat'.

Craythur. A word for spirits, especially WHISKEY or POTEEN, usually occurring in the phrase 'a drop of the craythur'. 'Craythur' derives from the distinctive Irish way of pronouncing 'creature'.

Crazy Crow. An 18th-century Dublin resurrectionist who plied his trade with limited success at St Andrew's graveyard, and after some prison terms decided to make a career as a one-man band. A contemporary caricature shows him with trumpet, flute and fiddle in his hands, a French horn round his neck, two tin-whistles in his belt and a cello-case strapped to his back. He was immortalized in verse:

> With looks ferocious and with beer replete
> See Crazy Crow beneath his minstrel weight;
> His voice as frightful as great Etna's roar
> Which spreads its horrors to the distant shore,
> Equally hideous with his well known face
> Murders each ear – till whiskey makes it cease.

> Quoted in Peter Somerville-Large, *Irish Eccentrics* (1975)

Creachaill. A crooked, gnarled piece of wood, especially of BOG DEAL.

Crean, Tom. *See* SOUTH POLE, THE.

Crease. A parting in the hair.

Creased. Beaten in a fight; totally exhausted.

Credit Union Movement. *See* O'HERLIHY, NORA.

Creeke of Bagganbun, the. The supposed place of the landing in Ireland in 1169 of a band of Anglo-Normans under Robert FitzStephen (d. after 1186), an event taken as the beginning of the Anglo-Norman invasion. It was given as such in 'A Plaine and Perfect Description of Ireland' in Holinshed's *Chronicles* (1587) by Richard Stanihurst:

> At the creeke of Bagganbun
> Ireland was lost and wun.

Baginbun Head is on the south coast of Wexford near the village of Fethard. Modern research has assigned the landing to Raymond le Gros's (d. after 1189) party the following May. He arrived with the vanguard of STRONGBOW's army, and routed a combined force of Irish and settled

Norse from Waterford. The chief citizens of the city had their limbs broken and were then thrown into the sea.

Creepie. A low three-legged stool, such as might be used by children at the fireside. The word comes from the Scots *creepie-stool*, 'stool of repentance', upon which minor sinners were obliged to sit in church (Robert Burns had to suffer this indignity after one of his early amorous adventures).

Crehan, Junior. *See* CONCERTINA.

Crios. The Irish word for 'belt'. A *crios* is also the name for the multi-coloured sash traditionally woven by hand on the ARAN ISLANDS and until recently worn by men over homespun trousers. *See also* LÉINE.

Cró. The Irish word for a hovel or hut used for housing animals. The diminutive *cróitín* is also used. *Cró* also means the eye of a needle.

Croagh Patrick. *See* REEK, THE; TÓCHAR PHÁDRAIC.

Croak Park. A punning name for GLASNEVIN CEMETERY, which is near CROKE PARK on the north side of Dublin.

Crochet. *See* CLONES LACE.

Croke, Thomas William (1824–1902). Archbishop of Cashel. He was born in Ballyclough in north Co. Cork in January 1823 and studied for the priesthood in Paris and in Rome, before being ordained in 1847. He served in the diocese of Cloyne in Co. Cork and for five years as Bishop of Auckland in New Zealand. In 1875 he was appointed Archbishop of Cashel and Emly, one of the most important ecclesiastical posts in Ireland. Croke was a robust and influential supporter of all the constitutional Nationalist movements and leaders of his time – O'CONNELL, YOUNG IRELAND, the LAND LEAGUE, PARNELL – but he gradually withdrew from political activity after the fall of Parnell. A promoter of the temperance movement and in the 1890s of the GAELIC LEAGUE, he was also a patron of the GAA, which was founded in his own diocese in 1884. The organization's flagship stadium in Dublin, CROKE PARK, is named in his honour. He died in Cashel on 22 July 1902.

Croke Park. The national stadium of the GAA (Gaelic Athletic Association) and venue for the ALL-IRELAND finals and other championship matches. Croke Park – nicknamed Croker by Dubliners – occupies a 15-acre (6-ha) site to the north of Dublin city centre, and is named after Dr Thomas CROKE, Archbishop of Cashel, a founder-patron of the GAA, which purchased the site in 1913. It is famous for stands such as the Hogan (named after the footballer killed on BLOODY SUNDAY 1920), the Cusack (named after one of the founders of the GAA) and especially the terrace at the railway end of the field, called HILL 16. A €250 million development project designed by Gilroy McMahon architects and heavily dependent on corporate sponsorship was completed in 2002 and gave the stadium a capacity of almost 80,000. Hill 16 is to be redesigned as the last remaining standing area. The complex also includes the GAA museum. In 2003 Croke Park was the chief venue for the Special Olympics, an international games for the physically and mentally disabled. *See also* CROAK PARK.

Croker. The Dublin nickname for CROKE PARK.

Croker, Thomas Crofton (1798–1854). Folklorist and antiquary. He was born in Cork city on 15 January 1798, educated locally and apprenticed to an accountant. From 1818 he held an Admiralty clerkship in London. As a boy he became interested in Munster folklore and collected many stories and songs. Though his work was flawed by a scanty knowledge of Irish, books such as *Fairy Legends and Traditions of the South of Ireland* (1825) (which was translated into French and German) and *Legends of Killarney* (1832) secured an amount of lore that might otherwise have been lost, and it is probably due to him that knowledge of such icons as the CLADDAGH RING and the BLARNEY STONE reached a wider public. Croker retired from the Admiralty in 1850 and died in London on 8 August 1854.

Cromane Pier. In May 1895 a huge meeting was held between the public and members of the CONGESTED DISTRICTS BOARD. Local interests agitated for a pier to develop deep-sea fishing in Castlemaine Harbour in Co. Kerry, but it never happened. A century later the development of Cromane Pier was an election promise in 1997 of the PARISH-PUMP POLITICIAN Jackie Healy-Rae.

Crom Cruach (Irish, perhaps 'the bent bloody one'). In myth, the gold idol with 'sub-gods twelve' to which first fruits and human sacrifices are offered until it is vanquished by St PATRICK. According to the story, it stands in Magh Schlecht ('the plain of adoration') in Co. Cavan. It bends over St Patrick in a threatening manner, but then sinks back, overcome by the sanctity of the apostle.

Crom Dubh (Irish, 'dark bent one'). An idol worshipped in pre-Christian times in Connacht and Munster and associated with FRAUGHAN SUNDAY, which until recently was known as *Domnach Chrom Dubh* ('Chrom Dubh Sunday').

Cromwell, Oliver (1600–58). One of the great hate-figures of Irish history, because of the massacres of the civilian population committed by his soldiers, and because of his open detestation of Catholicism, the religion of the majority of Irish people in the 17th century – as now. The CROMWELLIAN SETTLEMENT is credited with robbing the people of Ireland of their land.

Cromwell came to Ireland as lord lieutenant after the execution of Charles I (30 January 1649) in order to put an end to the CONFEDERATE WAR and establish the authority of the English Parliament, tasks facilitated by divisions among the Confederate leaders and by widespread famine and plague. On 13 August 1649 he left England with 32 ships and arrived in Ringsend in Dublin on 15 August, having been, according to one report, 'as sick at sea as any man I ever saw'. Coming so soon after the victory of the Parliamentarians under

Michael Jones at the Battle of RATHMINES, Cromwell's arrival was seen by his supporters as a triumph. He addressed the crowd, saying that, 'he did not doubt that as God had brought him thither in safety, so he would be able by Divine Providence to restore them all to their just liberties and properties'. His son-in-law, Henry Ireton, followed him to Dublin with a fleet of 42 vessels; in all nearly 15,000 soldiers were assembled in the city under Cromwell's command.

The army stayed in Dublin for two weeks, and on 31 August Cromwell left with 10,000 men on his way to Drogheda, which he took on 11 September 1639 (*see* DROGHEDA, SIEGE OF). After he captured Wexford the following month his New Model Army killed 2000 civilians in the marketplace (*see* BULLRING, THE). This pattern was repeated in many places during the nine months of his campaign in Ireland. Only in Clonmel (17 May 1650) did his army suffer serious casualties (1000–2000 men) because of a clever defensive measure devised by Hugh Dubh O'Neill. Cromwell initiated the practice of TRANSPORTATION, sending large numbers of clergy and other Catholics to Barbados. On 29 May 1650 he embarked at Youghal and sailed back to Bristol, keeping control of Ireland through his sons-in-law Ireton and Fleetwood, and later through his younger son Henry Cromwell. He ruled England as lord protector from 1653 until his death.

Cromwellian Settlement. A settlement that transferred ownership of vast areas of Irish land in Ulster, Munster and Leinster from Catholic land-owners to English adventurers (speculators who had invested in or financed the war), Cromwellian soldiers and Old-English Protestants. The 1652 Act for the Settlement of Ireland identified 'rebel' or treasonous landowners whose estates would be forfeit. Some of the more important were executed or transported, others lost some or all of their estates or were transplanted to Connacht (*see* HELL OR CONNACHT, TO). William Petty, who carried out the DOWN SURVEY, reckoned that 11 million of the total of 20 million acres (4.5 million out of 8 million ha) in Ireland had been confiscated and re-allocated. Many of the estates established in consequence were very large, soldiers having sold their title to officers and some adventurers buying out the title of several others. The settlement did not involve the arrival of English tenants, so that by the end of the 1650s many Catholics were back in their own lands as tenants of Cromwellian settlers, or had never left, merely exchanging one landlord for another. The significant thing was that most of the land was now owned by Protestants instead of Catholics, a situation that was to endure until the settlement of the land question at the end of the 19th and the beginning of the 20th century.

Cronán (d.617). A saint who was born in the O'Carroll territory of Éile in Munster and educated at CLONMACNOISE. His first habitation was on a promontory in Lough Cré, which proved difficult of access for the poor and others who wished to visit him. He set up another cell on the site of the modern town of Roscrea, Co. Tipperary, where the ruins of St Cronán's monastery may still be seen. The 7th-century *Book of Dimma*, a copy of the Gospels now in the library of Trinity College Dublin, which was written 'in forty days and forty nights without break' by the scribe Dimma, originated at St Cronán's monastery. Cronán's feast day is 28 April.

Cronebane. A copper coin, worth one halfpenny, issued in *c*.1790, and which has subsequently become the epitome of worthlessness, as in such expressions as, 'It's not worth a cronebane!' The coin takes its name from a copper mine in Co. Wicklow.

Cronin, Anthony (b.1928). Poet, critic and novelist. He was born in Wexford and educated at University College Dublin. He was a sub-editor of *The* BELL in its final days and then edited the liberal journal *Time and Tide*. In 1980 he became cultural adviser to Charles HAUGHEY, and is credited with having helped to establish AOSDÁNA. His most significant work of poetry is

RMS *Titanic* (1964), while his comic novels *The Life of Riley* (1964) and *Identity Papers* (1979) are mordant accounts of Dublin literary and pub life (in so far as they differ). *Dead as Door Nails* (1976) is probably the best account of the Dublin of Brendan Behan, Patrick Kavanagh and Flann O'BRIEN that is likely to be written, and *No Laughing Matter* (1989) is a full treatment of the career of O'Brien (Brian O'Nolan). His critical works include *Heritage Now* (1982) and a biography of Beckett, *Samuel Beckett: the Last Modernist* (1996).

Cronyism. The distribution of favours and jobs to supporters of the party in power.
See also BALTINGLASS, BATTLE OF; JOBBERY; PARISH-PUMP POLITICIAN.

Croppies Acre. An area near COLLINS BAR-RACKS (formerly the Royal Barracks) in Dublin, bounded by the River Liffey and Liffey Street. It was used as a mass grave for those executed after courts martial in the Royal Barracks, and takes its name from the nickname of the 1798 rebels, so many of whom are buried here (*see* CROPPY). The place was also known as 'Croppies Hole'. Robert EMMET wrote about Croppies Acre in a poem of ten verses called 'Arbour Hill':

> No rising column marks this spot,
> Where many a victim lies;
> But Oh! The blood which here has streamed
> To Heaven for justice cries.
> ...
> Unconsecrated is this ground,
> Unblessed by holy hands;
> No bell here tolls its solemn sound,
> No monument here stands.

In 1985 soldiers of the Irish army erected a memorial at the site, a large granite block marked with a cross and the date 1798.

Croppy. A term applied to the Wexford insurgents in the REBELLION OF 1798 because of their close-cut hair, following the practice of the Jacobins.

'Croppy Boy, The'. The title of several ballads, but most notably the poem written for *The Nation* by William McBurney (1844–92), who used the pseudonym Carroll Malone. It became

the quintessential ballad commemorating the REBELLION OF 1798, the CROPPY rising. In the ballad the boy makes his confession to a priest who tuns out to be a YEOMANRY captain 'in fiery glare':

> At Geneva barracks that young man died
> And at Passage they have his body laid.
> Good people who live in peace and joy,
> Breathe a prayer, shed a tear for the Croppy Boy.

Another (anonymous) song of the same name, with a tone less unctuous and more despairing begins:

> It was early early all in the spring;
> The bird did whistle and sweetly sing,
> Changing their notes from tree to tree
> And the song they sang was old Ireland free.

It ends:

> And as I stood on the scaffold,
> My own dear father was standing by,
> My own dear father did me deny
> And the name he gave me was the Croppy Boy.

It has a beautiful air and a feeling of authenticity, and is favoured by traditional singers.

Cross, Eric (1905–80). Biographer and short-story writer. He was born in Newry and trained as a chemical engineer. He is best known as the Boswell of Tim Buckley, the tailor of Gougane Barra, and his interrupting wife Ansty, recorded in *The TAILOR AND ANSTY* (1942), though the Tailor first appeared in print in *The BELL* in February 1941. *Silence Is Golden*, a collection of stories and essays, appeared in 1978.

Cross-belts. The nickname of the 8th King's (Royal Irish) Hussars. In 1710 they defeated a unit of Spanish cavalry at Almenera, during the War of the Spanish Succession (1702–13), stripped them of their sword belts and wore them in contravention of the regulation that permitted only horse or heavy cavalry regiments to carry their swords from a shoulder belt. This practice was regularized in 1769. They are now part of the Royal Hussars (Queen's Own and Royal Irish).

Crossroad dances. Dances held at the crossroads on summer evenings in rural Ireland until the

middle of the 20th century. The decline of cross-road dancing has also been attributed to the effects of the Second World War: footwear was rationed and dancing sets on the roadway caused great wear and tear on shoes.
See also HOUSE DANCES.

Crotty, Elizabeth. *See* CONCERTINA.

Crow Street Theatre. The 'other' theatre in 18th-century Dublin, SMOCK ALLEY's more persistent rival. It was founded in the street off Dame Street in 1758 by Spranger Barry (*see* HARMONIOUS BARRY) and Henry Woodward (1717–77). It became the Theatre Royal in 1759 when Barry became master of the revels, and could call upon the services of Charles MACKLIN. Though a splendid showman, Barry was no businessman, and the history of the playhouse was one of dazzle and dunning, in that the elaborate spectacles did not cover the expenses and they were followed by debt collectors. The story of the theatre was symbolically encapsulated on its opening night, when there was a riot in which several people were killed. When Smock Alley closed in 1786 it was the sole professional theatre in Dublin until 1819, when another THEATRE ROYAL was opened in Hawkins Street. It in turn was pulled down in 1830.

Crubeen (Irish *crúibín*). The word used in HIBERNO-ENGLISH for pig's trotter boiled and eaten from the hand. It was considered a delicacy, although cheap, and often eaten with a bottle of porter as a weekend treat.

Cruindmel. An Irish *doctus* (scholar) who lived in some part of the Frankish empire in the first half of the 9th century. His treatise on poetic scansion and metrication is useful because of the examples taken from classical and early Christian writings, including those of BEDE, Virgil, Horace, Aldhem and DONATUS.

Cruise O'Brien, Conor (b.1917). Writer and politician. He was born in Dublin to a liberal Nationalist family: his father, Francis Cruise O'Brien, was a journalist; his mother, Katherine Sheehy, was a daughter of the MP David Sheehy, the sister of Hanna SHEEHY-SKEFFINGTON and the

model for Miss Ivors in James Joyce's story 'The DEAD'. Educated at Trinity College Dublin (TCD) and precociously brilliant – his first book, *Maria Cross* (1952), a series of critical essays on Catholic novelists such as Graham Greene and François Mauriac published under the pseudonym Donat O'Donnell, is still both readable and useful – he went to work in the Department of Foreign Affairs and was seconded to the UN in 1961, at the time of the Katanga crisis in the Congo. His book *To Katanga and Back* (1962) tells the story of this turbulent period. In 1962, while still in Katanga, he was divorced from his first wife, Christine Forster, and married the Irish-language poet Máire MHAC AN TSAOI. After spending the years 1962–5 as chancellor of the University of Ghana and 1965–9 as Albert Schweitzer professor of humanities at New York University he returned to Ireland to contest the 1969 general election for the Labour Party, which campaigned with the optimistic but soon to be disproved slogan 'The Seventies Will Be Socialist'.

Having won a seat in Charles HAUGHEY's constituency of Dublin North-East, Cruise O'Brien served as minister for posts and telegraphs in the Fine Gael–Labour coalition of 1973–7, a sensitive position involving the management of public broadcasting at the time of the escalation of the Northern Ireland TROUBLES. His liberal credentials were questioned when he supported the continued implementation of SECTION 31. Himself an intellectual and polemicist who knew the value of propaganda, he developed a strong antipathy to PHYSICAL-FORCE REPUBLICANISM and those he deemed to be fellow-travellers, and his *States of Ireland* (1972) was a milestone in the growth of REVISIONIST or counter-Republican historiography. He lost his seat in the 1977 general election – less because of his anti-Republicanism, it was suggested, than because of the truly atrocious state of Ireland's telephone system at the time.

Thereafter Cruise O'Brien's influence on public life in Ireland was indirect; he held academic positions in various US universities and served as editor-in-chief of the London *Observer*

(1979–81), to which newspaper he contributed a lively, controversial and invariably anti-Nationalist column. In his late seventies he went even further and became a Unionist, winning a seat for Bob McCartney's UK Unionist Party in the 1996 elections to the NORTHERN IRELAND FORUM. He abhors the GOOD FRIDAY AGREEMENT and the current 'peace process', viewing current difficulties with undisguised satisfaction: 'I'm glad to see this bloody thing crash. It's been a horrible fraud,' (interview with Geoffrey Wheatcroft, in the *Guardian*, 12 July 2003). For most of his compatriots this is simply one position too far, although many still respect him for being fearless and disinterested. Cruise O'Brien's books include the seminal *Parnell and His Party* (1957), which was based on his PhD thesis at TCD, a magisterial study of Edmund Burke, *The Great Melody* (1996), and an autobiography, *My Life and Themes* (1998).

Cruise O'Brien's inevitable and only slightly disrespectful nickname 'the Cruiser', acquired after he entered political life, attracted equally inevitable puns, as when then Labour leader Dick Spring addressed the party conference on 8 April 1995. Referring to a remark on the Shannon–Erne Waterway, he added, 'Imagine that other Cruiser, so well known to us, never again predicting a bloodbath on this island.' *See also* GUBU.

Cruiser, the. The nickname of politician and writer Conor CRUISE O'BRIEN.

Cruiskeen Lawn (Irish *cruiscín lán*, 'full jug'). The title of a satirical column written in the *Irish Times* (1940–66) by Brian O'Nolan (*see* O'BRIEN, FLANN) using the pseudonym Myles na Gopaleen (sometimes Myles na gCopaleen). Both the title of the column and the pseudonym (meaning 'Myles of the ponies') come from Dion Boucicault's melodrama *The* COLLEEN BAWN (1860). Originally intended by the commissioning editor R.M. Smyllie (1894–1954) as an Irish-language feature, Cruiskeen Lawn gradually modulated into English and gained a huge following. Among the characters that

peopled the column were the BROTHER, Sir Myles na Gopaleen – His Satanic Majesty of Santry, the PLAIN PEOPLE OF IRELAND and 'the Man who Spoke Irish when it was neither Profitable nor Popular'. Also notable were the CATECHISM OF CLICHÉ and the many adventures of KEATS AND CHAPMAN. The title of the column came from a popular 18th-century MACARONIC VERSE:

Immortal and divine, Great Bacchus, God of wine,
Create me by adoption thy son,
In hopes that you'll comply that my glass will ne'er
    run dry,
Nor my smiling little Cruiskeen lawn, lawn, lawn,
Nor my smiling little Cruiskeen lawn.
Gra-ma-chree mo cruiskeen,
Slainte gal mavourneen,
Gra-ma-chree mo cruiskeen lawn, lawn, lawn
O my smiling little cruiskeen lawn.

> ('Gra-ma-chree mo cruiskeen', i.e. *Grá mo chroí, mo cruiscín*, 'love of my heart, my little jug' ; 'Slainte gal mavourneen', i.e. *Sláinte geal, mo mhuirnín*, 'good health, my darling'; 'Gra-ma-chree mo cruiskeen lawn, lawn, lawn', i.e. *Grá mo chroí, mo cruiscín lán, lán, lán*, 'love of my heart, my full little jug')

Cruitire. *See* HARP.

Cuailnge. The modern Cooley peninsula in Co. Louth, home of Donn Cuailnge, the BROWN BULL OF CUAILNGE, which was the subject of the epic *TÁIN BÓ CUAILNGE*.

Cuala Press, The (1908–78). The publishing company formed by Lily and Lolly YEATS, the sisters of the poet, as a separate venture from the Dun Emer Industries that they had established with Evelyn Gleeson. It took its name from an area of south Co. Dublin and part of Co. Wicklow in the ancient kingdom of Leinster. The Cuala Press was based in Churchtown, Dublin, and became the best-known literary press in Ireland, publishing 77 handsome volumes in all over the 80 years of its existence. Many of these were the work of their brother, but they also published other leading Irish writers of the day, including Elizabeth Bowen, Oliver St John Gogarty, Patrick Kavanagh and Lennox Robinson. George Yeats, wife of W.B., also worked in the press. Its last publication was in 1978 and its archive, along with the company's printing press, was donated to the library of Trinity College Dublin by the Yeats family in 1986.

Cuba Five, the. *See* O'DONOVAN ROSSA, JEREMIAH.

Cúchulainn (Irish, 'the hound of Culann'). The greatest of the epic heroes of Irish mythology, and the protagonist of many martial and amorous tales. Born with the name Setanta, Cúchulainn is the son of the god LUGH and DECHTIRÉ, who is spirited to the OTHERWORLD on the eve of her wedding to Sualitim Mac Roth. Setanta demonstrates his preternatural powers as a child, able to run fast enough to catch a ball that he has hit with his own hurley-stick – hence the abundance of Setanta golf courses in Ireland – and leap in the air like a salmon. His adult name results from his killing of the hound of the warrior Culann (who may have been MANANNÁN MAC LIR) and his agreeing to serve in the mastiff's place until a replacement could be found.

Cúchulainn loses his life in the struggle between his master CONCHOBHAR of Ulster and MEDB of Connacht, as recounted in *TÁIN BÓ CUAILNGE*. He is chief of Conchobhar's RED BRANCH KNIGHTS and uses to murderous effect his sword CALIDCHEANN and his secret weapon the GAE-BOLG. (He is taught the use of this by his Scottish druidic tutoress SCÁTHACH. It is in ALBA too that he captures AOIFE² who bears him a son, CONLAÍ, whom he afterwards kills. On his return to Ireland he marries EMER.) Most daunting of all among Cúchulainn's martial attributes is his battle-frenzy, recovery from which requires immersion in three tubs of ice-cold water and, on one occasion, a parade of naked women led out from EMAIN MACHA. He single-handedly slays all comers at the Battle of the FORD, including his best friend FERDIA, but dies eventually of hunger and loss of blood. His enemies find the courage to approach the rock to which he has bound himself only when they see the MÓRRÍGAN, the Celtic goddess of death, whose sexual advances he has rejected, perch on his shoulder in her customary guise of a crow.

Cugger-Mugger. Whispering, low-voice gossiping, from the Irish word *cogar*, 'whisper', with duplication rhyme word. The similarity to the word used by Claudius in *Hamlet* suggests a possible use-word in Tudor England:

> Thick and unwholesome in their thoughts and
> whispers
> For good Polonius' death – and we have done but
> greenly
> In hugger-mugger to inter him ...
> William Shakespeare: *Hamlet*, IV. v)

Cúig Cúige na hÉireann. *See* FIVE FIFTHS, THE.

Cúirt an Mheán-Oíche (*The Midnight Court*). A brilliant piece of comic literature in Irish (*c*.1780), in the form of a 1206-line poem. It is the work for which Brian MERRIMAN is known. Its Rabelaisian tone and parodic elements show an informed appreciation not only of the Irish poetry of Merriman's predecessors but of the formal European tourneys, the courts of love. The poet-narrator, who is a bachelor, is summoned in a dream to the court of Queen AOIBHEALL to account for his being unmarried when so many women are longing for love. The women who accompany her and who espouse the values of sensuality and fertility give long diatribes on celibacy and loveless (sexless) marriages. The narrator wakes up as he is being severely chastised by the women. The poem gives an excellent picture of rural Ireland in the late 18th century, and its feminism and denunciation of celibacy (including that of the clergy) make it seem contemporary. Although utilizing elements of the contemporary AISLING form, the work is predominantly comic and bawdy, and was in the past much censored by conservative educationalists. It has been translated by many different writers, notably Frank O'CONNOR.

Culchie. A country person, a term originally used derogatively to indicate rusticity. The noun is thought to have derived from a phonetic rendering of *Coillte Mach* (Kiltimagh in Co. Mayo), a small town in Ireland's western rural heartland very far from the home of Dublin's JACKEENS.

Because of the rise in the standard of living and in educational standards in Ireland from the 1960s onwards, the term now tends to be used jokingly or affectionately, if at all, and is sometimes adopted as a badge of honour by the culchies themselves.

Culdee (Old Irish *Céle Dé*, 'client of God'). A member of an ascetic movement that flourished in the 8th and 9th centuries, which had as its aim the reform of the Irish church. The chief personalities were monastic: MAELRUAIN (d.787), Fothad na Canóine (Fothad of the Canon) (*fl.* 800) and Oengus (*fl.*824), reviser of a famous *féilire* (an ecclesiastical calendar, with appropriate devotions). Máel Ruain founded the abbey of Tallaght (in modern Dublin), and surviving documents describe the rigorous life of prayer, mortification and charity that was led there. His insistence on total abstinence from alcohol was rejected by a fellow abbot from Finglas to the north, who said that his flock would still get to heaven in spite of drinking beer. SCEILIG MHICHÍL off the Kerry coast was a typically austere Culdee foundation. The coming of Viking depredation inhibited the natural development of Irish monasticism, and by the time the threat had passed few Culdee houses survived and a different system prevailed.

Cúl Dreimhne, Battle of. A battle (561) fought between the northern and southern UÍ NÉILL, the latter commanded by the HIGH KING Diarmait mac Cerbaill. The battle took place at the base of BEN BULBEN in Co. Sligo, an obvious natural division between Ulster and Connacht. The causes of the conflict are not clear, but there is a suggestion, probably reliable, that it was a late confrontation between the forces of Christianity and pagan druidism. The annalists ascribe the Ulster victory to the prayers of COLUM CILLE (Columba), and the historiographic vacuum was readily filled by a series of Columban legends, notably the supposed enmity between him and Diarmait (*see* TO EVERY COW HER CALF) and his self-imposed exile to IONA to recover for Christ a number of souls equal to those lost in the battle, stated as a convenient 3000.

Adamnán, the saint's biographer, gives the reason for his WHITE MARTYRDOM as his wish to be a pilgrim for Christ, and mentions the significant battle as a convenient means of dating the departure. It is likely that Colum Cille was present at the battle, drafted, perhaps, by his aristocratic kinsfolk as a kind of super army chaplain. Exile, though grievous, may have seemed preferable to endless involvement in politics.

Cullen, Paul (1803–78). Ireland's first cardinal. He was born in Prospect, Co. Kildare, on 29 April 1803 and educated at Shackleton Quaker School in Ballitore, Co. Kildare, Carlow College and the College of Propaganda, Rome, where he became professor of Greek and oriental languages. He was ordained in Rome in 1829 and became rector of the Irish College in 1836, acting as the agent for the Irish hierarchy and counterbalancing British influence with the Vatican. He was in Rome during the period of Garibaldi's occupation and his manifest horror of revolutionary movements, particularly YOUNG IRELAND and the FENIANS, dates from that experience.

After being out of Ireland for 30 years, Cullen was appointed Archbishop of Armagh (1849–52) and then Archbishop of Dublin (1852–78). He recreated out of an Ireland morally and economically laid waste by the GREAT FAMINE a country with strong, standardized and clerically controlled devotional practices that were to continue until the early 1980s. Although moderately Nationalist he had little time for any political movements that did not advance the interests of the church. He set himself against the 'godless' QUEEN'S COLLEGES, persuading Pope Gregory XVI to condemn them, and was the chief architect of the CATHOLIC UNIVERSITY (1854) with John Henry NEWMAN at its head, though relations between the two men were not always trouble-free.

Cullen made frequent visits to Rome, where he had the by now illiberal ear of Pope Pius IX, who made him cardinal in 1866. Strongly ULTRAMONTANIST, Cullen was one of the chief organizers of the First Vatican Council (1870), for which he is believed not only to have drafted the dogma of papal infallibility but to have energetically lobbied for its acceptance. He died in Dublin on 24 October 1878 and was buried in the grounds of Holy Cross College, the Dublin diocesan seminary that he founded in 1859.

Cullen's outwardly mild exterior concealed a strong will and led to the nickname given to him by the Fenians, 'the foxy Kalmuck' (referring to a member of a Mongolian tribe, because of the supposed oriental cast of the cardinal's features). He remains the archetypal right-wing, controlling cleric, utterly convinced of his rectitude.

Cumann na mBan (Irish, 'society of women'). The women's division of the IRISH VOLUNTEERS, founded at the same time as the men's organization in November 1913 and led by Countess Markievicz (see REBEL COUNTESS, THE) and Kathleen CLARKE. It supported the EASTER RISING of 1916, offering non-combatant support such as nursing and carrying of dispatches. One member, Margaretta Keogh, died in St Stephen's Green during Easter week, and it was another member, Elizabeth O'Farrell, a midwife, who delivered the surrender notice from the GPO to General Maxwell. During the Anglo-Irish War of 1919–21 Michael Collins made good use of some members in Dublin for intelligence-gathering. Most of the members rejected the TREATY and supported the Republicans during the Civil War. Led by Maud GONNE in the 1920s, Cumann na mBan continued to be associated with diehard Republicanism.

Cumann na nGaedheal (Irish, 'the society of Irish'). A political party founded by W.T. COSGRAVE on 8 April 1923 to unite supporters of the TREATY. It formed the government of the Free State until 1932. It had a natural constituency among former Irish Unionists, moderate Nationalists and Home-Rulers, and was very much an establishment party, supported by the *Irish Times* and other daily newspapers, and by strong farmers and the business and professional classes. The party was conservative

on social and economic issues and tough on Republicanism (see O'HIGGINS, KEVIN; PUBLIC SAFETY ACTS). Cumann na nGaedheal was subsumed into FINE GAEL in 1933.

Cummian Fada (592–662). A saint of the royal house of the Eoganacht (a Munster dynasty), who was born in Killarney. He was in charge of the monastic school at Clonfert, Co. Kerry, and later founded a house at Kilcummin (which preserves his name), near Killala, Co. Mayo. He was a noted defender of the 'Roman' systems later established at the Synod of WHITBY, and managed by writing and preaching to prepare the Irish church outside of Ulster to accept the Roman rules about the date of Easter, tonsure and other contentious issues. He died on 12 November 662, a date kept since as his feast day.

Cummian of Bobbio. An Irish saint, known only from an epitaph found in the monastery of BOBBIO. The memorial stone with his Latin name *Cummianus* was erected by a Duke Liut-prand of Lombardy, who reigned 712–44. According to the inscription, the saint served at Bobbio as bishop for the last 17 years of his life, and died in old age.

Cúpla focal (Irish, 'a few words'). An expression sometimes used in mock self-deprecation, indicating a real if limited knowledge of the Irish language. It is also used in an ironic sense to mean the lip-service paid to the Irish language by politicians and other public figures, who produce a *cúpla focal* on state occasions, but make no effort to learn or use the language they are in theory committed to promoting.

Curate. A jocose city term applied to a grocer's assistant or bartender, originating from ecclesiastical practice. Its use among medical students and journalists may have arisen out of a need for discretion in disapproving company. In the past, the word also had another meaning: according to P.W. Joyce (1827–1914) in *English as We Speak It in Ireland* (1910) it was 'a common little iron poker kept in use to spare the grand one'.

Curly Wee and Gussie Goose. The chief characters in a children's strip cartoon published daily in the *Irish Independent* until the end of the 1950s. Count Curly Wee was a rather aristocratic, paternalistic pig and Gussie Goose his more excitable amanuensis. The text, remarkably literate for such a strip, was in rhyming couplets, and the adventures of the animals in Fur-and-Feather Land were relished as much by adults as by its target audience. It could be said to have been the Irish equivalent of the British Rupert Bear.

Currach or **curragh.** A small coracle or rowing boat, traditionally used on the Atlantic coast from Clare to Donegal (the NAOMHÓG was a similar craft in Cork and Kerry). It was made by stretching canvas (originally cowhide) over a wooden frame and coating the canvas with pitch to make it watertight. It was rowed by up to six men using bladeless oars. Although light, the currach was strong and well adapted to fishing the local seas and bringing merchandise from the mainland to the islands.

Curragh. *See* CURRACH.

Curragh, the. An unbroken plain in Co. Kildare, 10 km (6 miles) long and 3 km (2 miles wide), lying immediately east of Kildare town. It is the centre of Ireland's horse-breeding industry, and its racecourse hosts several classics, including the Irish Derby. To the south lie the military barracks still in use by the Irish army; this complex includes the Curragh prison.

Although temporary canvas camps had existed previously in the Curragh of Kildare, the Crimean War (1853–6) led to the construction of the first permanent camp there. To meet the growing need for barrack accommodation, Gen. Sir John Burgoyne, inspector general of fortifications, suggested to the commanding Royal Engineer in Ireland on 24 January 1855 that a camp for 10,000 infantry 'would probably be required at the Curragh of Kildare'. Work on the site began on 18 March 1855, and on 9 July accommodation for 5000 men was ready for occupation. Accommodation consisted of 430 wooden huts for soldiers, 10 huts for staff sergeants and 10 huts for officers' stables. Water supply was crucial, as it was lack of water that had led to the camp being abandoned previously, so a deep well was bored for this purpose. Some of the stone buildings constructed at this time are still in use.

The Curragh was used as an internment camp (nicknamed Tintown) by the British during the ANGLO-IRISH WAR of 1919–21, and by the Free State during the CIVIL WAR of 1922–3. During the latter conflict, seven Republicans were executed by firing squad on one day in the Curragh, on 19 December 1922. They had been tried by a military court for possession of arms without authority and sentenced to death. It was the biggest single execution carried out in the Civil War. Republicans were interned in the Curragh during the EMERGENCY and in the 1950s at the time of the BORDER CAMPAIGN.

See also WRENS.

Curragh Incident. The mutiny of British officers based in the main army camp at the Curragh, Co. Kildare, in March 1914, shortly before the passing of the third HOME RULE bill and after the mobilization of CARSON'S ARMY. Major-General Sir Hubert Gough chaired a meeting of 56 officers who stated that they would offer their resignations rather than act against Ulster opponents of Home Rule, should such action be required of them. The War Office reacted mildly to news of this decision and the government decided to evade the issue, informing the officers that the incident was caused by a misunderstanding. Gough later claimed that he had been offered a guarantee that his officers would never be sent to enforce Home Rule in Ulster, saying that if it came to conflict he would prefer to fight for Ulster than against it. The incident gave a clear message to the Nationalist community in Ireland that there would be one law for Ulster and quite a different one for the rest of the country (*see*, for example, BACHELOR'S WALK).

Curran, John Philpot (1750–1817). Lawyer, patriot and orator, the father of Sarah CURRAN.

During his illustrious career at the Bar Curran ably defended many United Irishmen, including William DRENNAN, Napper TANDY, Oliver BOND and Wolfe TONE, but he refused to defend Robert EMMET on learning that his daughter was engaged to him. As MP for Kilbeggan (Co. Westmeath), he strongly opposed the Act of UNION.

> The condition upon which god hath given liberty to man is eternal vigilance.
>
> JOHN PHILPOT CURRAN: Speech, 10 July 1790

See also ACUSHLA MACHREE; MONKS OF THE SCREW.

Curran, Sarah (1782–1808). A young woman admired in Nationalist iconography as the beloved of Robert EMMET. She was born in Rathfarnham in Dublin, the youngest of nine children of the famous barrister John Philpot CURRAN. Her brother Richard introduced her to Robert Emmet, a fellow-student at Trinity College Dublin, and Emmet fell in love with her, finding her pretty, sensitive and feminine. Her father banned him from the Curran house, but she met him in secret and corresponded with him through Anne DEVLIN. When Emmet was arrested after his abortive rebellion in 1803, letters on his person led Major SIRR to Sarah Curran, who left her home, banished by her father and 'blotted' from his society and the 'place she once held in his affections'.

For two years Sarah lived with friends in Cork, and there on 24 November 1805 she married Captain Robert Henry Sturgeon, an officer in the British army who was to die in the Peninsular War in 1813. As an officer's wife she accompanied her husband on his postings, and it was on the voyage home from Tangier that a 'poor little *weak* child' was born on 26 December 1807. Sarah remained ill, probably from residual puerperal fever, and died on 3 May 1808. Her last letter written on 20 March to her Cork friend Anne Penrose describes 'a hectic fever that so debilitates me that I am now barely able to walk across the room'.

Sturgeon brought the body home to Ireland, hoping that her father might relent and allow her to be buried, as she had requested, beside her sister Gertrude in the orchard of the Priory, her old home at Rathfarnham, but he was adamant. She rests in the churchyard of Newmarket in Co. Cork. It was the indefatigable R.R. MADDEN, the historian of the UNITED IRISHMEN, who found its location and erected a tombstone over it. Curran was immortalized by one of Thomas Moore's 's most beautiful melodies, 'She is far from the land' (1811):

> She is far from the land
> Where her young hero sleeps,
> And lovers around her are sighing;
> But coldly she turns from their gaze and weeps
> For her heart in his grave is lying.

Cusack, Cyril (1910–93). Actor. He was born on 26 November 1910 in Natal in South Africa, the son of a policeman and an actress, Alice Violet Cole. After his parents separated, his mother brought him to Ireland and with her partner joined a touring company, the O'Brien and Ireland Players. Cyril made his first stage appearance at the age of 7. He was educated at Newbridge College and University College Dublin, but left without taking a degree and joined the ABBEY THEATRE in 1932, appearing in more than 60 productions and excelling in O'Casey and Shavian roles. He also worked for several seasons with the Royal Shakespeare Company in the 1960s, and became known as a character actor on screen. He published three collections of poetry. He has four talented actress daughters: Sinéad, Sorcha, Niamh and Catherine.

Cusack, Michael. *See* CITIZEN, THE.

Cusack Stand. *See* CROKE PARK.

Custom House, the. One of Dublin's finest 18th-century buildings. Dublin's original custom house was situated in the area of what is now Crane Lane in TEMPLE BAR, so called because the customs apparatus consisted of 'custome house, crane and wharfe', to be used, according to the lord deputy and his council in 1621, for 'the loading, landing, putting aboard or on shore, any goods, wares, merchandise, or commodities whatsoever, to be by sea exported or imported into or forth of the said Port of Dublin' – that is, to control all maritime trade. In 1705 a proposal was made to build what is known today as the 'Old Custom House' in the same area around Essex Street, and Thomas de Burgh designed a building three storeys high and with attic space. Although the Custom House was extended during the course of the century by acquiring neighbouring buildings, it was clear that the quay on which it stood was too small for the increasing port traffic, and that the building itself was deteriorating.

When proposals, spearheaded by John BERES-FORD (1738–1805), first commissioner of revenue, were made to relocate the Custom House, business interests vehemently opposed this, as they did the relocation of the FOUR COURTS to Inn's Quay at about the same period, and petitioned George III to this effect in 1774. Early in 1781 Beresford retained James GANDON to design and supervise the construction of the new Custom House further down-river, and himself laid the foundation stone on 8 August 'without any formality', according to a witness. The building was substantially completed in 1791. A series of sculpted heads created by Edward Smyth (1749–1812) was placed over the windows and door, representing the Atlantic Ocean and 13 Irish rivers, including a very feminine ANNA LIFFEY.

On 25 May 1921, at the suggestion of Éamon de Valera, about 120 members of the IRA attacked and set fire to the Custom House. Valuable records were destroyed, the dome collapsed and the building was gutted by fire. During the 1920s it was for the most part restored and the exterior, including the sculptures, was recently cleaned and restored. The building now houses the Department of the Environment.

Cut¹. A county or barony cess tax (*see* BAD CESS!).

Cut². A verb used in the context of a clerical student's deciding he has no vocation and leaving a seminary: 'I think your brother won't be long after me. He'll cut too.'

Cut³. General apppearance, shape, presentation. The word is sometimes used derogatively, as in, 'Look at the cut of him,' but may also be approving, as in, 'He's a fine cut of a man.'

Cute. An abbreviation of 'acute'. The word is frequently used to describe someone clever, devious, secretive, opportunistic or perhaps simply reserved. Some counties, for instance Kerry and Cork, are alleged to produce more cute people than others: these may be called 'country cute'. Cute people do not let their right hand know what their left is doing. People who are very cute are described as being 'so sharp they'd cut themselves' or 'so clever they'd meet themselves coming back'. Sometimes cuteness loses its effectiveness by being simply and recognizably no more than low cunning. *See also* CUTE HOOR.

Cute hoor. A phrase similar in meaning to CUTE, but meant more intensively and disparagingly. It is also used as an adjective, for instance in 'cute hoor politicians', usually rural politicians of the PARISH-PUMP variety. *See also* STROKE¹.

Cúthaileach. A word borrowed from Irish and meaning 'shy', 'modest', 'bashful'. There is a saying: 'Shy but willing like an ass eating thistles.'

Cuthbert. Saint and bishop of LINDISFARNE (who may have been Irish in spite of his English name). He is taken to have been born in Northumbria *c*.634 and appointed to Holy Island in 684 after serving at MELROSE under EATA. Like the young PATRICK he herded sheep, and according to BEDE was granted a vision in which he saw angels conveying AIDAN's body to heaven. He made it his life's work to try to heal the dissension caused by the decisions at the Synod of WHITBY. Like any Irish monk he had a recurring need for solitude to pray, and this solitude he found on the Farne Islands, about 5 km (3 miles) off the coast. There he built a monastic cell with no window, but there was a hole in the roof through which he could see heaven. When he died there in 687 the news of his death was signalled to the community at Lindisfarne by torchlight. He was buried in Lindisfarne, but after the Viking raids his remains were reinterred in Durham Cathedral for safety. His feast day is 20 March.

Cutty. A usually affectionate term for a young girl:

> She's a fine cutty that one – there's plenty of go in her.

BRAM STOKER (1847–1911): *The Snake's Pass* (1891)

Cypress. The evergreen shrub and tree *Cupressus*, usually associated with graveyards. It was often called palm in Ireland, and was at one time blessed in a garland with laurel leaves on Palm Sunday. It used to hang in Irish houses until replaced with the new spring's fresh garland. Nowadays the feast is celebrated with strips of real palm, usually fashioned into the form of a cross.

Da, the¹. A term of affection when referring to one's father, used particularly in Dublin.

Da, the². The father of Myles na Gopaleen in CRUISKEEN LAWN who is spoken of with proper awe and *pietas* whenever he appears in the column:

> Sir Myles na gCopaleen (the da) was 87 yesterday. The grand old man spent the day quietly at his country place. His breakfast tray (frugal in keeping with the times) was littered with messages of congratulations from notabilities of every rank and colour, including some of the notorious uncrowned heads of Europe. …
>
> The baronetcy, of course, is one of the oldest in the country. Sir Myles is reckoned to be the 57th of that ilk. Lady na Gopaleen is one of the Shaughrauns of Limerick, a very distinguished county family. Round after round of spontaneous applause have been won by her seat and hands at countless point-to-points. A lover of Scotch, she is reputed to be one of Europe's foremost bottle-women.
>
> *The Best of Myles* (1968)

Dab or **dab hand.** A widespread colloquialism, meaning an expert, someone skilled in a particular art or trade: 'She's a dab [or 'dab hand'] at baking.'

Daff. A schoolboy term for 'excrement'. In the plural, *daffs* means 'lavatories'.

Dagda, the. In Irish mythology, the head of the TUATHA DÉ DANAAN. He is the son of the earth goddess DANA¹ and the father of the Irish gods. He owns a magic harp that can produce the three types of music, *goltraí*, *geantraí* and *suantraí*, inducing sorrow, laughter and sleep respectively, the last helping him to subdue his chief adversaries, the FOMORIANS. In later versions of the tales he seems to degenerate into a buffoon, appearing as a fat blunderer at the second battle of MAGH TUIREADH (Moytura) but possessing a magic cauldron of limitless food and drink. The Irish Celts associated him with abundance and gross sexuality. He is supposed to have mated with the MÓRRIGÁN as she stood astride a river, and to have illicitly impregnated BOANN to produce AONGHUS ÓG. After the occlusion of the Tuatha Dé Danann he allots a portion of underground Ireland to each of the deities, reserving BRUGH NA BÓINNE to himself, although he is tricked out of ownership by his son Aonghus Óg.

Dagenham Yanks. The nickname given to workers in the Cork Ford factory, who in the 1930s were transferred to the company's main works in Dagenham, Essex.

Dáibh Scoil Mhúscraí (Irish, 'Muskerry bardic school'). An annual gathering for local poets to meet and recite their work. This modern bardic school had its first meeting in 1926. Donal Mullins's song 'An POC AR BUILE' was first heard at it.

Dáil (Irish, 'meeting', 'tryst', 'assembly'). The lower house of the Oireachtas (*see* OIREACH-TAS, AN T-[1]) in Ireland, in full *Dáil Éireann*, pronounced 'doyle erin'. A member of the house is called a *Teachta Dála* ('assembly deputy'), pronounced 'tochta dolla', and abbreviated to TD. The first Dáil was established in 1919 by the 73 SINN FÉIN members elected in 1918 who refused to take their seats at Westminster.
See also SEANAD.

Dailc. The Irish word for a strong, stout, low-sized person, used also in HIBERNO-ENGLISH.

Dáil Courts. The name given to courts of law established under the authority of the first DÁIL and based on the law as it stood on 2 January 1919, as part of the Republican alternative administration during the Anglo-Irish War. The decisions of the courts were enforced by special police, one appointed by the Dáil for each brigade area of the IRA. Attempts were made to suppress these courts, with the result that they went underground, to emerge again during the period of the TRUCE.

Daire. In Irish mythology, the owner of the BROWN BULL OF CUAILNGE, so desired by Queen MEDB of Connacht. At first she tries to obtain it peacefully but her emissaries, drunk at a feast, boast that they will take it anyway. At this Daire refuses to bargain, and the war begins. *See also* TÁIN BÓ CUAILNGE.

Daisypicker. A term, the equivalent of 'gooseberry' or 'gooseberry-picker', originating in the mid-19th century to signify a chaperone. The third party is imagined as saying, 'Don't mind me; I'm just picking daisies.'

Dal Cais. A dynasty that originated in Co. Limerick and that achieved hegemony in Munster from the 10th to the 12th centuries, adopting the surname Uí Briain, the name of their most famous king BRIAN BORU. They claimed, retrospectively, an ancient right to the kingdom of Cashel, and had this claim inserted into the ANNALS OF INISHFALLEN and other so-called historical works of the time. Their dominance declined during the reign of Murcheartach Ua Briain (d.1119). Members of the dynasty were formerly referred to by the latinized name Dalcassians.

Dalcassians. *See* DAL CAIS.

Dalk. In HIBERNO-ENGLISH, a punch or blow. The word is of uncertain derivation.

Dallamulóg. An Irish word for 'blindness', 'concealment', used in HIBERNO-ENGLISH for 'bluff' or 'deception'. To put a *dallamulóg* on somebody is to pull the wool over his eyes.

Dallán Forgaill. A semi-legendary 6th-century poet who is credited with authorship of AMRA CHOLUIM CILLE. As chief of the bardic poets he owned the debt that the FILID owed to COLUM CILLE, and celebrated the saint as their champion. He is supposed to have been assassinated because of his continuing lobbying on their behalf.

Dallapookeen (Irish *dalladh púicín*, 'blinding mask'). A blindfold.

Dál Riata (anglicized as **Dalriada**). The name of the Gaelic kingdom that in the late 6th and early 7th century comprised roughly the present-day counties of Argyll in Scotland and Antrim in Ulster. The overarching kingdom, which regarded the stormy North Channel as a kind of open-ended inner lake, contained in its territory the monastic island of IONA. Since its population on both sides was largely Irish, the foundation and abbots of Iona had considerable say in the political as well as the spiritual life of the kingdom. The public precedent for this was the involvement of COLUM CILLE (Columba) in the convention of DRUIMCEATT, where he helped to settle dynastic problems in the kingdom.

D'Alton, Louis (1900–51). Playwright and novelist. He was born in Dublin, the son of Charles A. D'Alton, a touring actor-manager. He worked as a civil servant before forming his own theatre company. His first success was *The Man in the Cloak* (1937), a play about the life of James Clarence MANGAN set against a cholera outbreak in the Dublin slums. He is best known for the comedies *They Got What They Wanted* (1947), filmed as *Talk of a Million* (1951), *The Devil a Saint Would Be* (1951), about Irish piety, and *This Other Eden* (1953), about the oppressive dullness of Irish life in the immediate postwar years. A darker imagination is at work in *Tomorrow Never Comes* (1939), about the moral disintegration of a murderer, and in *Lover's Meeting* (1941), about the dire consequences of a made marriage. An early novel, *Rags and Sticks* (1938), deals with the final years of a 'fit-up' company. D'Alton died in London.

> *Mangan:* I would teach men wisdom and am known for my folly. I ambitioned praise and admiration ... I excite ridicule, pity, contempt. I would sing great songs, but most often I can make nothing but trifles. I have had moments of genius in years of mediocrity.
>
> *The Man in the Cloak* (1937)

Daly, Edward (b.1933). The retired Roman Catholic Bishop of Derry. He was born in Belleek, Co. Fermanagh, on 5 December 1933 and educated at the PONTIFICAL IRISH COLLEGE in Rome. He was curate in St Eugene's Cathedral, Derry, in the years 1962–73, and as a young, vigorous man with a flair for showbiz was given the responsibility of providing entertainment for the city with bingo, Sunday-night concerts and yearly pantomimes, the proceeds going to parish funds. He became known to worldwide television as the 'priest with the hankie', because of his ministering to the dying on BLOODY SUNDAY 1972. The description, often to his exasperation, has stuck. After a period as religious adviser to RTÉ he was appointed to the see of Derry on 31 January 1974 and retired in 1994. His period as bishop was marked by much terror in his diocese, and he used every effort to search for justice and bring about a cessation of violence. He was at the forefront of the agitation to have the BIRMINGHAM SIX released. The following quotation is from his first book of autobiography, *Mister, Are You a Priest?* (2000),

in the chapter on Bloody Sunday called 'A Defining Moment':

> I took a handkerchief from my pocket and waved it for a few moments and then got up into a crouched position and I went to the boy. I knelt beside him. There was a substantial amount of blood oozing from his shirt; I think it was just inside the arm, on the right or left side, I cannot remember which. I put my handkerchief inside the shirt to try and staunch the bleeding ... I felt I should administer the last rites to the boy and I anointed him.

Daly, Ita (b.1944). Novelist and short-story writer. She was born in Drumshanbo, Co. Leitrim, moving to Dublin in 1957. She graduated from University College Dublin with an MA and taught for some years. She contributed stories to David MARCUS's 'New Irish Writing' page in the *Irish Press*, and married Marcus in 1972. Her stories, two of which won the Hennessy Award, were collected as *The Lady With the Red Shoes* (1980), and her novels *Ellen* (1986), *A Singular Attraction* (1987), *Dangerous Fictions* (1989) and *Unholy Ghosts* (1996) show her to be a subtle delineator, in apparently effortless prose, of thoughtful, not very successful women. *All Fall Down* (1992), something of a departure, shows a fine satirical talent. She has also written two books for children.

Daly, Joxer. The chief comic character of Sean O'Casey's play JUNO AND THE PAYCOCK. His special epithetical phrase 'a daarlin'...' was borrowed by the author from a fellow worker on the Great Northern Railway. He is essentially a parasite, but wonderfully resilient, well able in a chameleonlike way to adapt to changing situations, and full of wise saws and modern instances:

> ... if you gently touch a nettle it'll sting you for your pains; grasp it like a man of mettle, an' as soft as silk remains!

The realization of the part was in the hands of the greatest of all the ABBEY THEATRE actors, F.J. McCormick (stage name of Peter Judge;

1889–1947). who appeared in over 500 plays, and whose promising film career was ended by his unexpected death.

Damer, An (Damer Hall). An Irish-language theatre established in Dublin by GAEL LINN in 1955. Brendan Behan's *An Giall* (*The Hostage*) was first performed there in 1958.

Damer of Shronell. The proverbially mean Dublin banker Joseph Damer (1630–1720), who was born in Shronell, Co. Tipperary, and built Damer House, a Georgian building now being restored. 'As rich as Damer' became a proverb soon after his death, and he is recalled in this anonymous rhyme:

> There was old Paddy Murphy had money galore,
> And Damer of Shronell had twenty times more –
> They are now on their backs under nettles and
> stones.

His career was also the seed of Lady Gregory's play *Damer's Gold* (1913).

Damhnat. *See* DAVNET.

Damned Green Flag. A cry supposed to have been uttered by a Confederate general at the battle of ANTIETAM CREEK (17 September 1862) in the American Civil War: 'Here comes that damned green flag again!':

> And hosts will whisper listening guests
> The Southern foeman's wild refrain,
> When glared he o'er the green-plumed crests,
> And sprigs of green on Irish breasts –
> 'Here comes that damned Green Flag again!'
> And hearts will fire and pulses bound
> At thoughts of Antietam's day;
> When hemmed by fire and foeman round,
> The Irish stormed the vantage ground –
> And claimed the glory of the fray
> > JAMES J. BOURKE: *Thomas Francis Meagher* (n.d.)

See also FIGHTING 69TH.

Damn Yeats, we'll write our own plays! The cry uttered by the 19-year-old Bulmer HOBSON as he and his friend David Parkhill returned to Belfast on the Dublin train in the autumn of 1902 after an unsatisfactory meeting with W.B. YEATS about developing drama in Ulster.

The ULT (Ulster Literary Theatre) may be said to have had its inception at that moment.

Dana¹ or **Danu.** In Irish mythology, the Celtic mother goddess from whom the TUATHA DÉ DANAAN take their name. She is the mother of the DAGDA by Bilé, a god of death.

Dana² (b.1951). The showbiz name of Rosemary Scallon MEP. She was born Rosemary Brown in Derry on 30 August 1951 and educated at Thornhill College. In 1970, as a Derry ingénue in a simple *BÁINÍN* dress with a Celtic design, she was the first Irish winner of the Eurovision Song Contest with 'All Kinds of Everything'. She continued her career in entertainment, with successful singles and albums, and in pantomime as a very pretty Snow White.

During the 1990s Dana, always a vehement defender of Christian values in public life, entered politics as an independent candidate, running against Mary MCALEESE in the presidential election of 1997. Though unsuccessful, she was elected to the European Parliament for the Connacht–Ulster constituency in 1999, and took her seat as an independent with the Christian Democrat bloc. She was active in the 2002 ABORTION REFERENDUM campaign, controversially advocating a 'no' vote (against the recommendation of the Catholic hierarchy) because she considered the proposals to be too liberal.

Danaher, Kevin (Caoimhín Ó Danachair; 1913–2002). Folklorist. A pioneer of Irish ethnological studies and a military historian, Kevin Danaher was born in Athea, Co. Limerick. He studied archaeology at University College Dublin and served in the army during the Emergency. His work for the IRISH FOLKLORE COMMISSION included extensive research into rural life, vernacular architecture and folk traditions. As well as writing many enduring books on these subjects, including *In Ireland Long Ago* (1962) and *The Year in Ireland: Irish Calendar Customs* (1972), he devised BUNRATTY FOLK PARK in Co. Clare and was adviser to the trustees of MUCKROSS HOUSE in Killarney, Co. Kerry.

Dance costumes. Costumes worn for the performance of Irish figure or *CÉILÍ* dances, especially in competition. From the era of the late 19th-century CELTIC REVIVAL there has been the development of formal costumes for both female and male dancers: for girls an elaborate, pleated stiff-skirted dress in green, red, purple or black, heavily embroidered with Celtic motifs such as the TARA BROOCH; for young men, a plaid kilt with knee socks, shirt, BRAT (small ornamental cloak) and sash. Men now wear trousers rather than kilts, and RIVER-DANCE has influenced the material and shape of girls' costumes, as it has so much else. Little girls still compete in traditional festivals (*see* FEIS) in the most elaborate of costumes, often wearing wigs of long ringlets.

Dancing, down below for. *See* UP HERE YOU WANT IT, DOWN BELOW FOR DANCING.

Dancing at Lughnasa. The title of one of Brian FRIEL's most successful plays (1990). Its chief characters are the five unmarried Mundy sisters and their brother Jack, a retired and befuddled missionary priest, who live near Ballybay, Friel's Irish Everyvillage. The festival of LUGHNASA, dedicated to LUGH, the Celtic god of light, at which first fruits were celebrated by fire, feasting and dancing, is informally enacted in their country kitchen. Father Jack's memories of similar ceremonies in Uganda combine with modern (1936) ballroom steps and local folk memory to provide a marvellous dance sequence full of manic joy, courage and stoic acceptance before the family disintegrates:

> Dancing as if language had surrendered to movement – as if this ritual, this wordless ceremony, was now the way to speak, to whisper private and sacred things, to be in touch with some otherness ...

Dancing masters. Travelling dance teachers who imparted the skills of (Irish) dancing – reels, jigs and hornpipes, and also 'long dances'

of their own composition such as 'The Blackbird' – to individuals and families for remuneration. This type of 'step' dancing is still to be found in many parts of Ireland as a traditional art, not dependent on the CELTIC REVIVAL figure or CÉILÍ DANCES. The earliest extant reference to a dancing master dates from 1718. By the end of the 19th century, many of the dancing masters had been replaced by dancing mistresses, and the profession has since been dominated by women.
See also SEAN-NÓS.

Dancing on a plate. Solo dancing as taught by the DANCING MASTERS of the 18th and 19th century, which has survived as *SEAN-NÓS* dancing. Such solo dances were to be danced in a very small area (hence the 'plate'), such as the half-door of the house, which would be removed from its hinges and laid on the floor for the purpose (*see* RATTLE THE HASP). Custom also dictated that the feet should not be lifted high from the floor, and that the soles of the shoes should never be seen. A recent *sean-nós* prizewinner was said to be able to perform on a dart board.

Dander. A general Irish term for a short stroll: 'It's a grand evening for a wee dander.' The word is also a more general English-language colloquialism for 'anger', as in: 'He really got his dander up.'

Dandle. *See* DILDER.

Daniel, William (also **Daniell**) (*c.*1570–1628). Protestant Archbishop of Tuam, Co. Galway, known by the Irish form of his name Uilliam Ó Domhnaill. He was responsible for a vigorous idiomatic translation of the New Testament into Irish as *Tiomna Nuadh* (1603). It continued to be printed for use in Ireland and Scotland for many years, and was used by Catholics as well as Protestants. He also translated Cranmer's *Book of Common Prayer* (1609) as *Leabhar na nUrnaightheadh gComhcoidchiond*. He died in Tuam.

'Danny Boy'. *See* LONDONDERRY AIR.

Dargan, William (1799–1867). The engineer

known as the 'Father of the Irish Railways'. He was born in Carlow on 28 February 1799 and studied engineering under Thomas Telford (1757–1834), who built the Caledonian Canal and the Menai Bridge. His first railroad, opened on 17 December 1838, ran from Westland Row station in Dublin to Kingstown (Dún Laoghaire). The locomotive had a tall smokestack like George Stephenson's *Rocket* and the carriages looked like a line of coupled stage-coaches. Dargan also built a canal to link Lough Erne and Lough Neagh, and created out of the Lagan sandbanks the island in Belfast Lough where the shipyard was later situated (*see* DARGAN'S ISLAND). By 1853 his trains ran on 960 km (600 miles) of track linking Dublin to Belfast and Cork.

A typically optimistic Victorian, Dargan was so impressed by Prince Albert's Great Exhibition of 1851 that he decided to do the same for Dublin. He set up an exhibition of art and science in 1853, losing £20,000 on the promotion but creating thereby the nucleus of the NATIONAL GALLERY OF IRELAND. (He refused a baronetcy from the queen when she visited his house in Dundrum; she was not amused.) Later business projects were unsuccessful, and a serious fall from his horse and resultant neglect of his businesses brought financial difficulties. He died on 7 February 1867 and is commemorated by a statue outside the gallery with the single word 'Dargan' on its plinth. His gravestone in GLASNEVIN CEMETERY is similarly unadorned.

Dargan's Island. An earlier name for Queen's Island, Belfast, which had been artificially created from the sludge removed when the Victoria Channel was created. The cut ran from Garmoyle Pool right up to the High Street quays, and enabled large vessels to come up the River Lagan at any state of the tide. The name came from that of William DARGAN, the railway engineer, who had constructed the channel. It was opened on 10 July 1849 and formally named a month later when Victoria and Albert visited the city. Dargan's Island

was thereafter known by its later name but there was no indication then that it would become the site of one of the world's leading shipyards.

Dark, The. The second novel (1965) of John MCGAHERN, based partly on boyhood memories. The unnamed central character is the only child of a widower. Living in his home in the west Midlands, he has to face the stress of sexual frustration, the unhappiness of his father and the need to win a university scholarship. At the end the character finds sufficient maturity to make a gesture of reconciliation with his father and to decide not to accept the scholarship. The book, which describes in some detail the character's regular masturbation and features a homosexual priest, was banned.

Dark Druid, the (Irish *Fer Doireach*, literally 'dark man'). In Irish mythology, the black magician who changes SADB, the daughter of BODB DEARG, into the shape of a fawn.

Darkley Church. The scene, near Keady in Co. Armagh, of an unapproved attack by, it was believed, members of the INLA on Protestant churchgoers on Sunday 21 November 1983. Three people were killed at the entrance of Darkley Mountain Gospel Lodge Pentecostal Church and seven others – four men and three women – wounded inside by three men using the name Catholic Reaction Force. This cover name was chosen to indicate that the attack was in retaliation for PROTESTANT ACTION FORCE attacks on Catholics in the area over the previous two years.

Dark of turf. A term used in the HIBERNO-ENGLISH of Donegal to describe the amount of turf cut by a MEITHEAL in one day.

Dark Rosaleen. *See* RÓISÍN DUBH.

Dark stain on the national conscience. *See* FREE EDUCATION.

Darling. A Dublin adjective meaning 'fine', 'excellent', sometimes used hyperbolically or ironically.

Darling little queen, the. Daniel O'CONNELL'S

effusive praise for Queen Victoria after her refusal in 1839, despite Sir Robert PEEL's instructions, to dismiss two of her ladies-in-waiting in the 'Ladies of the Bedchamber' incident, thus allowing Lord Melbourne to form another Whig government. O'Connell and the queen had met in 1838 shortly after her accession and she, expecting the subhuman grotesque of the caricaturists, was quite taken with the tall, handsome, charming Kerryman. 'Why he's a gentleman!' she exclaimed later. The description came in a letter written to Dr Mac-Hale, Archbishop of Tuam, on 10 May 1839: 'Hurrah for the darling little queen … she has shown great firmness and excellent heart.'

Darling of Erin, the. A ballad description by Thomas Maguire (*fl.*1895) of Robert EMMET:

Bold Robert Emmet, the darling of Erin,
Bold Robert Emmet will die with a smile;
Farewell companions both loyal and daring,
I'll lay down my life for the Emerald Isle.

Darling of the Army, the. *See* SARSFIELD, PATRICK.

DART, the. An acronym, borrowed from Dallas, Texas, and other cities, for Dublin Area Rapid Transport, an electric commuter train that runs along Dublin Bay from Malahide south as far as Greystones in Co. Wicklow, utilizing for much of its length what was originally the Dublin–Kingstown (Dún Laoghaire) track. For many years it provided Dublin's commuters with the city's only reliable, punctual public transport. Because most of the areas served by the DART were salubrious suburbs ('Dort-land' in the local pronunciation) there emerged in the public mind a perception of a kind of DORT-speak, popular especially among young females.
See also LUAS; ROADWATCH.

Dauncey or **donsie.** A word signifying 'weak', 'sickly', as in: 'After the flu he was feeling a bit dauncey.'
See also DAWNY.

Davey, Shaun. *See* BRENDAN VOYAGE, THE.

Davies, Christian (1667–1739). Woman sol-

dier. She was born Kit Cavanagh in Dublin, the daughter of a prosperous brewer and innkeeper. She inherited the inn at 21, and married Richard Welsh, one of the servants, who disappeared in 1692. A year later he wrote saying he had been pressed into the army in Flanders. Kit dressed herself in man's attire and enlisted as Christopher Welsh, seeing action at Nijmegen (1702), Blenheim (1704) and other battles of the War of the Spanish Succession (1702–13). She eventually found Welsh in 1705 and accompanied him as his wife until he was killed at Malplaquet (1709). Her gender had been discovered when she was wounded at Ramillies (1706), but she was allowed to serve as a cook in the officers' mess, by then known as 'Mother Ross'. She next married a grenadier called Hugh Jones, who was killed a year later at St-Venant. Returning to England she was presented to Queen Anne, who granted her a pension of a shilling a day for life, a bounty that her next husband, a dissolute Dublin soldier called Davies, helped her spend. As appropriate for an old soldier she was admitted to Chelsea Royal Infirmary and was buried with full military honours in July 1739. A supposed autobiography, *The Life and Adventures of Mrs Christian Davies* (1740), is not regarded as genuine.

Davis, Francis (1810–85). Ulster poet. He was the son of a Presbyterian farmer from Hillsborough, Co. Antrim, but quarrelled with his family to the extent that he claimed that he came from Cork. He worked as a muslin weaver but soon began to contribute poems to *The* NATION as 'The Belfast Man'. He was employed as an assistant librarian in Queen's College, Belfast, the forerunner of QUB. His poetical work was collected as *Earlier and Later Leaves, an Autumn Gathering* (1878). He was buried in FRIAR'S BUSH graveyard in Stranmillis, Belfast, a Catholic cemetery.

I loved, I love thee, Kathleen, in my bosom's
　warmest core –
And Erin, injured Erin, oh! I loved thee even
　more.
　'Kathleen bán Adair', in *Poems and Songs* (1849)

Davis, Thomas (1814–45). Poet, journalist and patriot. He was born on 14 October 1814 in Mallow, Co. Cork, the posthumous son of an English army surgeon, but lived in Dublin for most of his short life. Educated at Trinity College Dublin, he was called to the Bar in 1838. While at Trinity he was the leader of a group of Protestant intellectuals who tried to interest their fellows in things Irish, reminding them in his inaugural speech as auditor of the Historical Society: 'Gentlemen, you have a country.'

> Gentlemen, you have a country ... I do not fear that any of you will be found among Ireland's foes ... Your country will, I fear, need all your devotion. She has no foreign friends. Beyond the limits of green Ireland there is none to aid her. She may gain by the feuds of the stranger; she cannot hope for his peaceful help, be he distant, be he near; her trust is in her sons.
>
> THOMAS DAVIS: Auditor's address to the Historical Association in Trinity College (1840)

With Charles Gavan DUFFY, and John Blake DILLON, Davis founded *The* NATION, the organ of their movement YOUNG IRELAND. From its first appearance on 15 October 1842 *The Nation* was tireless in its purpose of teaching nationhood to a demoralized people. Davis wrote a great deal of the paper's material on a wide variety of subjects. His style was sober and deliberately didactic, and the topics of his essays ranged from round towers to Ireland's economic resources. He was especially strong on the need for the preservation of Irish as a spoken language: 'To lose your native tongue and learn that of an alien is the worst badge of conquest ...' He was impatient with the national attitude of despondency, and sought to raise the spirits of the Irish people with stirring ballads that recalled Ireland's former glories, such as 'The West's Asleep', 'Clare's Dragoons', 'Fontenoy' and the poem forever associated with his name, 'A NATION ONCE AGAIN'.

Davis disagreed with Daniel O'CONNELL on educational policy, believing it should be non-denominational, an issue brought to a head by the QUEEN'S COLLEGES proposals; he also believed that O'Connell was too subservient both to the Catholic hierarchy and to the Whig Party. If he had not died of scarlatina on 16 September 1845, he might well have dissuaded Smith O'Brien from his inept rising in 1848 (*see* WIDOW MCCORMICK'S CABBAGE PATCH).

Davis escape chamber. A jocular term applied to a pub or shebeen that evaded the licensing laws and provided decompression for drinkers in sore need. The reference was to the submarine escape device invented by Sir Robert H. Davis (1870–1965).

Davitt, Michael (1846–1906). Founder of the LAND LEAGUE. He was born to a poor tenant family in Straide, Co. Mayo. When he was 4 the family was evicted from the Knox estate and their house burned. After spending some time in the local workhouse they emigrated to Lancashire, where, at the age of 8, Michael went to work in a local cotton mill. When he was 11 he lost his right arm in an accident at the mill.

In 1866 Davitt joined the FENIANS and was imprisoned with hard labour in Dartmoor on the charge of incitement to murder. After his release in 1877 he first went to the USA, where he met John DEVOY, then returned to Co. Mayo, becoming involved in agrarian agitation and helping to found the Land League of Mayo in 1879. His greatest achievement was to unite Fenianism and PARNELL's constitutional Nationalism in the form of the tactical agreement known as the NEW DEPARTURE, following which Parnell became president of the Land League. Like Parnell, Davitt was imprisoned in 1881 under the COERCION Acts, becoming familiar while in prison with the works of the socialist Henry George, who influenced his thinking towards land nationalization.

Differences with Parnell that originated at the time of the KILMAINHAM TREATY (1881) – 'the vital turning point of Mr Parnell's career and unfortunately he turned the wrong way' – led to an open breach in 1884; in Davitt's opinion Parnell cared only for the interests of the prosperous tenant farmers with big holdings. Davitt supported the Liberal–Nationalist alliance and was one of Parnell's most vociferous critics at the time of the split in the Irish Party in 1890. He served as an Irish Party MP (1892–3 and 1895–9) and with William O'BRIEN helped to found the UNITED IRISH LEAGUE in 1898, but his socialism marginalized him. He published many books, including *Leaves from a Prison Diary* (1885) and *Defence of the Land League* (1891). His 1904 will specified: 'Should I die in Ireland I would like to be buried at Straide, Co. Mayo, without any funeral demonstration.' He died in Dublin of acute septic poisoning after having had two teeth extracted, and was buried in accordance with his will.

Davnet or **Damhnat** (*fl.*6th century). A saint who founded a nunnery at Tydavnet ('Davnet's house') near Monaghan. Her staff, the *bachall Damhnait*, was used as a test for the truth of oaths and was believed to have the capacity to leave lying mouths permanently twisted; it is now in the National Museum of Ireland. The rendering of her name in English as Dympna has led to the confusion of Davnet with Dympna of Gheel in Flanders, patron of the mentally ill, who is also claimed as Irish in origin. Davnet's feast day is 13 June.

Daw. A person who is stupid or easily fooled, as in the disclaimer, 'I'm no daw!' It refers to the presumed stupidity of the jackdaw.

Dawn, The. A feature film (1936) set during the Anglo-Irish War of 1919–21 and regarded as an important milestone in Irish cinema. It was made by Tom Cooper, a garage and cinema owner from Killarney, Co. Kerry, who had been in command of a FLYING COLUMN during the war; he was assisted by local amateurs and used equipment supplied by the Kerry Electrical Company. The film's success was partly due to its high moral tone and partly due to its still sensitive subject. It told the story of a Brian Malone, a member of a 'respectable' family, which had failed to live down the reputation of having had one of its number accused of being an informer in FENIAN times. Brian is dismissed from the IRA because of this unjust reputation and joins the RIC (Royal Irish Constabulary) in a fit of temper. He eventually sees the light as the dawn of (partial) Irish freedom is descried.

Dawny, dawnie or **donny.** A word most commonly found in Dublin speech, meaning 'weak', both as a permanent physical state and to describe a sudden onset of faintness:

… the son of poor oul' Batty Owens, a weeshy, dawny, bit of a man that was never sober an' was always talkin' politics.

SEAN O'CASEY (1880–1964): *The Shadow of a Gunman* (1923)

Dawson, Arthur. *See* BUMPERS, SQUIRE JONES.

'Dead, The'. The final story (1907) of James JOYCE's *Dubliners* (1914), concerning a journalist, Gabriel Conroy, and his wife Gretta, who attend a post-Christmas party in Gabriel's aunt's house. For Gabriel the key moment is when another guest sings the beautiful traditional song 'The Lass of Aughrim' and Gabriel, to his chagrin, realises that Gretta is still mourning Michael Furey, a boy who loved her when she was young in Galway and who, she says, died of love for her. Gretta and her story are based on the romantic history of Joyce's own wife Nora. In the final paragraph, one of the most famous in all of Irish literature, Gabriel thinks of snow falling, unifying the country, bringing together past and present:

Yes, the newspapers were right; snow was general all over Ireland. It was falling on every part of the dark central plain, on the treeless hills, falling softly upon the Bog of Allen and, farther westward, softly falling into the dark mutinous Shannon waves. It was falling, too, upon every part of the lonely churchyard on the hill where Michael Furey lay buried. It lay thickly drifted on the crooked crosses and headstones, on the spears of the little gate, on the barren thorns. His soul swooned slowly as he heard the snow falling faintly through the universe and faintly falling, like the descent of their last end, upon all the living and the dead.

'The Dead' was successfully filmed by John Huston in 1987 (it was Huston's last film) starring the fine Irish actor Donal MCCANN as Gabriel.

Deadbell. A ringing in the ears, regarded in Ulster as a reminder to pray for the souls in Purgatory.

Deán (Irish, 'channel'). An Ulster word meaning a residual stream, often quite deep, in a strand at low tide. Pronounced 'jan', it is a popular source of sand eels.

Dean, the. The common appellation, also used by himself, of Jonathan Swift (1667–1745), who after being thwarted in political and ecclesiastical preferment settled to a gloomy acceptance of the minor post of Dean of St Patrick's Cathedral in Dublin in 1714, staying there till his death, 'a poisoned rat in a hole', as he wrote in a letter in 1729.

Swift was born on 30 November 1667 at 7 Hoey's Court between the two Dublin cathedrals, St Patrick's and Christ Church, that marked his fate and his ungratified ambition. He was educated at Kilkenny School and at Trinity College Dublin, where he was an unimressive student. He became secretary to Sir William Temple in 1689, and after various clerical appointments in Ireland acquiesced in the deanship. A friend of Joseph Addison and Sir Richard Steele (of the *Spectator*) and of Alexander Pope while he lived in England, Swift found Dublin society provincial and stifling. His loneliness was mitigated by two inconclusive and troubled relationships with two women, Esther Johnson ('Stella') and Esther Vanhomrigh ('Vanessa'). He wrote much verse ranging from extremes of scatology to Augustan austerity, but it was the prose satire GULLIVER'S TRAVELS (1726) that proved his greatest work.

Though Swift's attitude to Ireland and the Irish was barely tolerant, his sense of justice and outrage caused him to engage in a series of highly effective anti-government pamphlets, especially The DRAPIER'S LETTERS and A MODEST PROPOSAL. Though anonymous, their authorship was an open secret. The 'Englishman born in Ireland' had become 'a Hibernian patriot' because of English malpractice. His last years were darkened by Ménière's syndrome and dementia. He was buried beside Stella in St Patrick's, having written his own epitaph (*see SAEVA INDIGNATIO*).

> My female friends, whose tender hearts
> Have better learned to act their parts,
> Receive the news in doleful dumps,
> The Dean is dead, (*and what is trumps?*).
> 'Verses on the Death of Dr Swift' (1739)

See also VARINA.

Deane, Seamus (b.1940). Poet, critic and novelist. He was born in Derry and educated at St Columb's College (along with Seamus Heaney), Queen's University Belfast and Cambridge, where he took his PhD. He was professor of modern English and American literature at University College Dublin before moving to Notre Dame, Indiana, USA in August 1993 as Keough Professor of Irish Studies. His critical works, mainly about Irish literature, include *Celtic Revivals: Essays in Modern Irish Literature 1880–1980* (1985), *A Short History of Irish Literature* (1986), *The French Revolution and Enlightenment in England, 1789–1832* (1988) and *Strange Country: Modernity and Nationhood in Irish Writing since 1790* (1997). He was also general editor of the *Field Day Anthology of Irish Writing* (1991) (*see* FIELD DAY). His collections of poetry, *Gradual Wars* (1972), *Rumours* (1977) and *History Lessons* (1983), are passionately intellectual, concerned, among other things, with nationality, culture and the sectarian division in the North. *Selected Poems* appeared in 1988. *Reading in the Dark* (1996) is a searingly beautiful semiautobiographical novel of childhood and youth in a troubled Republican family in Derry in the 1940s and 1950s.

'De-anglicizing the Irish People, The Necessity for'. The title of the presidential address given by Douglas HYDE on 25 November 1892 to the National Literary Society in the Leinster

Hall in Molesworth Street, Dublin. The immediate effect was no greater than that of Thomas DAVIS's 'Gentlemen, you have a country!' address to the Historical Society in Trinity College Dublin in 1840, but it was to have nearly as dramatic a sequel. The text was later published as a pamphlet, and it became the spur that led Eoin MACNEILL and Hyde to found the GAELIC LEAGUE the following July:

> I should like to call attention to the illogical position of men who drop their own language to speak English, of men who translate their euphonious Irish names into English monosyllables, of men who read English books, and know nothing about Gaelic literature, nevertheless protesting as a matter of sentiment that they hate the country which at every hand's turn they rush to imitate ... It is a fact, and we must face it as a fact, that although they adopt English habits and copy England in every way, the great bulk of Irishmen and Irishwomen over the whole world are known to be filled with a dull, ever-abiding animosity against her, and – right or wrong – to grieve when she prospers, and joy when she is hurt ... In conclusion, I would earnestly appeal to every one, whether Unionist or Nationalist, who wishes to see the Irish nation produce its best – and surely whatever our politics are we all wish that – to set his face against this constant running to England for our books, literature, music, games, fashions and ideas. I appeal to every one whatever his politics – for this is no political matter – to do his best to help the Irish race to develop in future upon Irish lines.

De Barra, Leslie (1893–1984). Revolutionary and Red Cross official, the wife of IRA leader Tom BARRY. She was born Leslie Price in Dublin and trained as a teacher at St Mary's College Belfast. She was active in CUMANN NA MBAN, travelling throughout the country, and in this way met Tom Barry, whom she married in 1921. They set up home in Cork and she devoted the rest of her life to humanitarian works. She was chairperson of the Irish Red Cross from 1950 and also national president of Gorta (Irish, 'famine'), the freedom-from-hunger association. She died on 9 April 1984.

De Bhaldraithe Dictionary, the. A dictionary first published in 1959, properly entitled *English–Irish Dictionary*. It was edited by Tomás de Bhaldraithe (1916–96), scholar, lexicographer and editor in Irish, who became professor of modern Irish language and literature at University College Dublin in 1960. The dictionary made a lasting contribution to the modernization of vocabulary in the Irish language. De Bhaldraithe also collaborated with Niall Ó Donáill on the latter's *Foclóir Gaeilge-Béarla* (*Irish–English Dictionary*; 1977).

De Blácam, Aodh (1890–1951). Journalist and man of letters. He was born Hugh Blackham in London of Ulster parents, his father being an MP from Newry. He was taught Irish in London by Robert LYND and moved to Ireland with his artificially constructed Gaelic name in 1915 to begin a career of journalism. Arrested by the BLACK AND TANS for 'propagandist' writings in 1921, he continued to celebrate Ireland 'free and Gaelic'. His novel *Holy Romans* (1920) is semi-autobiographical and describes his journey to Nationalism and Catholicism. He worked for the *Irish Times*, edited the *Standard*, and, using the pseudonym 'Roddy the Rover', wrote for many years a very popular column in the *Irish Press*. His published work includes biographies of Wolfe TONE, St PATRICK and St COLUM CILLE, plus novels, plays and short stories. His *Gaelic Literature Surveyed* (1929) is still a significant work. *The Black North* (his own coinage) written in 1938 expresses an uncompromising view of the Unionist province. He was a member of the executive of FIANNA FÁIL until 1947, when he left to join CLANN NA POBLACHTA. He stood unsuccessfully for the Dáil in 1948 and died in January 1951.

> Aye, but Derry walls – Derry walls. What have we to say about that siege of Derry in 1689 which is commemorated every year with processions, drums and angry speeches? It was in the defence of Derry against the Jacobites that the slogan 'No Surrender' was first uttered.
> *The Black North* (1938)

De Blaghd, Earnán. *See* BLYTHE, ERNEST.

Dechtiré or **Dectera.** In Irish mythology, the daughter of the druid CATHBAD, granddaughter of AONGHUS ÓG and mother of CÚCHULAINN. She is carried away with 50 handmaidens by LUGH on the eve of her wedding to Suailtim Mac Roth and reappears three years later with a child called SETANTA, who is accepted by Suailtim as his son. The fact that the child who grows up to be Cúchulainn has not been born in Ulster enables him to withstand the curse of MACHA, which rendered the men of that province feeble during the war of the *TÁIN BÓ CUAILNGE*.

Decies. *See* DÉISE, THE.

Declaratory Act. A law passed by the British Parliament in 1720, more popularly known as the 6th of George I. It asserted the right of the British Parliament to pass legislation binding on Ireland. This act and POYNING'S LAW were traditionally seen as the great restraints on the independence of the Irish Parliament; the repeal of both was demanded by the PATRIOTS of the 18th century.
See also YELVERTON'S ACT.

De Clare. *See* STRONGBOW.

De Cogan, Miles. *See* LE GROS, RAYMOND; MAC-THORKIL, ASKULV; O'TOOLE, LAURENCE.

Decommissioning. The putting beyond use of paramilitary arms, considered an essential part of the implementation of the GOOD FRIDAY AGREEMENT. SINN FÉIN continue to claim that they cannot 'deliver' the IRA and all parties are conscious of the psychological significance of arms in the armed struggle. Equally the Unionists use the lack of substantial decommissioning as their reason for refusing to share power with Sinn Féin. *They* inevitably riposte that such elements of the agreement as 'demilitarization' and the full implementation of the PATTEN REPORT on the reform of the police service in Northern Ireland, also part of the agreement, have not been fully implemented. A few gestures of decommissioning confirmed by an international commission led by John de Chastelain, a Canadian general, have taken place, but not enough to satisfy either the British or Irish governments desperately seeking a formula to placate the Unionists outraged by the IRA's refusal to disarm. Though formally added as an afterthought in all discussion, the question of Loyalist decommissioning is not otherwise mentioned. The perceived or stated need for Republicans to defend their areas against possible Loyalist incursion provides them with a further tactical reason not to implement the desired decommissioning.

Dedalus, Stephen. The hero of Joyce's *A PORTRAIT OF THE ARTIST AS A YOUNG MAN* (1916), subsidiary hero of his *ULYSSES* (1922) and essentially a self-portrait of the author. The surname is that of the 'old father, old artificer' apostrophized at the end of *A Portrait*: 'Old father, old artificer, stand me now and ever in good stead.' In Greek myth it was Dedalus who devised the labyrinth in ancient Crete, and it was his decision to find a means of escape from Minos that led to the death of his son Icarus, who flew too near the sun on wings constructed by his father. The epigraph to *A Portrait* is from the story of Dedalus as told by Ovid in *Metamorphoses*, VIII, 18:

> *Et ignotas animum dimittit in artes.*
> (He engaged his genius in hitherto unimagined devices.)

DéDanann. A folk/traditional group named after the TUATHA DÉ DANAAN. It has achieved both critical and commercial success by virtue of its exceptionally fine instrumentalists (including leader fiddler Frankie Gavin, plus Andy Irvine, Alec Finn and Johnny Moynihan) and equally fine vocalists (including Dolores Keane, Maura O'Connell and Eleanor Shanley). Founded in 1974, the group recorded albums in many styles, including *Star Spangled Molly* (1978) and *Ballroom* (1987).

Deevy, Theresa (1894–1963). Playwright. She was born in Waterford and exchanged University College Dublin for University College Cork to be nearer home because of an attack of Ménière's disease, which left her totally deaf before graduation. She studied lip-reading in London and became so proficient that she could enjoy the theatre, which became her passion. Her plays are distinguished by the excellence of the dialogue. Her best-known works are *The King of Spain's Daughter* (1935) and *Katie Roche* (1936), which involve unlikely romantic heroines and their reconciliations in not-so-loveless marriages. The ABBEY THEATRE, where her plays were produced was, during her most fertile period, a pretty fustian place; in other decades there might have been greater encouragement for her to continue with theatrical work. As it was, her later work was done mainly for radio. She died at home in Waterford.

Defence of the Realm Act. *See* DORA.

Defenders, the. A Catholic SECRET SOCIETY established as a defence against the violence of the Protestant PEEP O' DAY BOYS in Co. Armagh in the late 1780s. Unlike such predecessors as the WHITEBOYS, the movement was highly politicized, and like the ORANGE ORDER used rituals copied from Freemasonry. Associated with the UNITED IRISHMEN, the society was dispersed following the defeat of the REBELLION OF 1798, but reappeared in 1811 as the RIBBONMEN.

Deffo. A casual Dublin abbreviation for 'definitely'.

De híde, Dubhglas. *See* HYDE, DOUGLAS.

Deirdre or **Deirdru.** The tragic heroine of the ULSTER CYCLE, the Helen of Irish mythology. She is the daughter of Felim Mac Dall, an Ulster chieftain, and destined, according to the prophecy of the druid CATHBAD, to be the most beautiful woman in all Ireland, who would marry a king but bring nothing but misery and destruction on the country. The warriors of CONCHOBHAR want to kill the child, but the king insists she be spared and raised to be his queen. She is placed in the nursing charge of LEBARCHAM, who becomes her confidante as she grows up. One winter day, as she watches an unkindness of ravens tearing at the carcass of a lamb, she vows to love a man whose hair would be like the raven's wing, whose skin would be as white as the unblemished snow and whose lips would be red as the blood from the lamb.

When from the platform of EMAIN MACHA Deirdre sees NAOISE, the eldest of the SONS OF USNA, she knows that her destiny is about to be fulfilled. She flees with Naoise and his brothers AINLÉ and ARDÁN to Glen Etive in ALBA (Scotland), where they live in great happiness before returning at Conchobhar's request to Ireland, under the safe conduct of FERGUS MACROTH. The brothers are treacherously killed and Deirdre keeps a year's silence as Conchobhar's wife until in anger he presents her to Eoghan MacDurthacht who had killed Naoise. As she is being driven to his house in a chariot with hands bound, she throws herself against a rock, dashing her brains out. She is buried beside her lover, and from their graves grow two interlinking pine trees.

Deirdre of the Sorrows. The last, unfinished play by J.M. SYNGE, based on the story of DEIRDRE and the SONS OF USNA, one of the greatest of tragic Irish love stories. Its sense of fatality mirrored Synge's own struggle for life, and the fact that it was written for his love Molly ALLGOOD, who had been so successful as Pegeen Mike in *The* PLAYBOY OF THE WESTERN WORLD. The play was staged at the ABBEY THEATRE on 13 January 1910, using the unfinished script with only a few alterations. Reactions were predictable, with the *Irish Times* enthusiastic and SINN FÉIN strongly critical, though in the circumstances no Irish reviewer had the heart or the courage to fault Allgood's performance. The most effective lines were given to her sister Sarah, who played Lavarcham, Deirdre's nurse:

> Deirdre is dead, and Naisi is dead; and if the oaks and the stars could die for sorrow, it's a dark sky and a naked earth we'd have this night in Emain.

Déise, the. The area of the small GAELTACHT of An Rinn (Ring, or Rinn Ó gCuanach), around the fishing village of Helvic in Co. Waterford, although the traditional area of the Déise (anglicized as Decies) formerly included all rural Waterford and parts of Co. Tipperary. The Déise has its own CANÚINT (dialect) and a unique style of SEAN-NÓS singing, as typified by the great Nioclás TÓIBÍN. For the layman, the ballad 'Cill Cais' (*see* 'CAD A DHÉANFAIMÍD FEASTA GAN ADHMAD?') is the song most associated with the region. Ring has a large IRISH COLLEGE, where children can spend a summer or even a school year. The word *déisí* is the Old Irish for 'tenants' or 'vassals' and became the name of a number of tribes in ancient Ireland.

Deiseal (from Irish *deis*, 'right hand'). A turning to the right, following the sun, clockwise. Proceeding in this direction was regarded as propitious. Proceeding in the opposite direction, widdershins, had a black-magic significance.

Delaney, Edward. *See* CHIEFTAINS, THE; TONE-HENGE.

Delaney, Ronnie (b.1935). Athlete. He was born in Arklow, Co. Wicklow, on 6 March 1935. He was the first Irish runner to win an Olympic gold, in the 1500 m at the Melbourne Olympics of 1956, achieving a world record for the distance at 3 minutes, 41.2 seconds and astounding Irish supporters listening to the radio commentary. He also won a European bronze, and had a very successful competitive career in the USA, becoming world university champion in 1961.

Delany, Mary Granville. *See* MRS DELANY'S COLLAGES.

Delargy, James Hamilton (Séamus Ó Duillearga) (1899–1980). Folklorist and founder of the IRISH FOLKLORE COMMISSION. He was born in Cushendall, Co. Antrim, and educated in Dublin. He became a lecturer in Irish at University College Dublin, and his interest in the oral tradition – particularly the stories of Seán Ó Conaill from Cill Riailig in south Kerry, which he later published as *Leabhar Sheáin Í Chonaill* (1948) – convinced him of the need to establish a means of recording stories and

traditions that would otherwise go to the grave with their tellers. Delargy, a charismatic and determined man, was appointed professor on the establishment of the Department of Irish Folklore at University College Dublin.

Delay. A term used in HIBERNO-ENGLISH for a limp or physical impediment: 'He has a delay in one leg.'

Delira and excira. A favourite catchphrase of approval used by Gay BYRNE on his morning radio show: the expression stands for 'delighted and excited', in exaggeration of the Dublin tendency to drop 't's and modify pronunciation.

Dem dat know. The response of a FIANNA FÁIL activist in Cork when asked about the difference between his party and FINE GAEL:

> Dem dat know don't need to ask and dem dat don't know don't need to know.

Democratic Left. *See* DE ROSSA, PROINSIAS; RAINBOW COALITION; WORKERS' PARTY.

Democratic Unionist Party. *See* DUP.

De Montmorency, Hervey de. *See* DUNBRODY; HOOK HEAD.

Denis the Weaver (Denis Murphy) (1910–74). Musician. A member of a family of talented fiddlers in the SLIABH LUACHRA area of Kerry/Cork, Denis Murphy was born in Gneeveguilla and learned fiddle from Pádraig O'KEEFFE. Although his talents were recognized early, because of the demise of HOUSE DANCES and the declining prestige of traditional music he was obliged to spend much of his life working in the USA. He returned permanently to Gneeveguilla in 1965 and thereafter played locally, as well as making some recordings, the best known a CLADDAGH RECORDS album called *The Star above the Garter*, a collaboration with his sister Julia Clifford. Like Johnny O'LEARY he played for set dancing in Dan Connell's pub in nearby Knocknagree and died suddenly one Sunday night after he had spent an evening playing for sets there. Denis the Weaver is famous for the skill and feeling of his slow airs as well as for his playing of the POLKA SET and KERRY SLIDES of his native place. As a party piece he demonstrated his expertise at dancing the set dance 'The Blackbird' while playing the tune on the fiddle.

Denny, The Hon. Arabella (1707–92). Philanthropist. She was born Arabella Fitzmaurice, daughter of Thomas Fitzmaurice, Lord of Kerry, and granddaughter of William Petty (*see* DOWN SURVEY; KENMARE), and was reared on the family estate in Co. Kerry. In 1727 she married Colonel Arthur Denny, MP for Kerry, and lived with him in Lixnaw Castle, Tralee, until his death in 1743. They had no children and after his death Arabella moved to Dublin and became involved in philanthropic works in the Dublin Foundling Hospital, where the poorest of the city's poor children were cared for. She was variously described as 'civil', 'sensible' and 'a model of amiability and independence', but it is clear that she knew exactly how to get her way. In 1767 she established in Leeson Street in Dublin the first MAGDALEN(E) HOME – called after the repentant prostitute of the New Testament, Mary Magdalen – to provide shelter and rehabilitation for young, fallen, Protestant women. Girls stayed in the home for up to two years, receiving religious instruction, praying and carrying out useful activities like sewing. In order to support this charity Arabella Denny exploited all her aristocratic connections (Queen Charlotte, wife of George III, was patron). When the Magdalene's chapel was opened in 1768 it became so popular by virtue of its distinguished congregation and equally distinguished preachers that anyone wishing to attend had to buy a ticket for a shilling. Arabella Denny remained involved with her Magdalene asylum until she was 79, and bequeathed money to it and to the Foundling Hospital.

Denvir's Penny Library. A series of books published in 1870 dealing with aspects of Irish history, biography, poetry and fiction. The series – properly the *Illustrated Irish Penny Library* – was the idea of John Denvir (1834–1916), an editor and author born in Bushmills, Co. Antrim, but who spent most of his life in England. His booklets, a successful enterprise in adult education, were extremely popular, written essentially for the Irish of the diaspora. His *The Irish in Britain* (1892), a demographic and cultural survey, is the standard work on the subject for this period. An autobiography, *The Life Story of an Old Rebel*, was published in 1910.

Deoch an dorais (Irish, 'drink at the door'). A drink offered to a parting guest, the equivalent of the English stirrup-cup. The expression, which is pronounced 'joch an doris', was made popular by the Scots entertainer, Sir Harry Lauder (1870–1950), with his song 'Just a Wee Deoch-an-Doruis' (1912).

> As they said goodbye after many a deoch a'dorais
> CANON PATRICK AUGUSTINE SHEEHAN (1852–1913): *Glenanaar* (1905)

De Paper. *See* PAPER, DE.

Derg, Lough. *See* LOUGH DERG.

Dergaboo. The term used in Co. Tyrone in the 19th century for a planned fight, from the war cry of the Clan O'Neill, *Lámh Dearg Abú!* (Irish, 'victory to the red hand'; *see* RED HAND OF ULSTER).

De Rossa, Proinsias (b.1940). Politician. He was born in Dublin on 15 May 1940 and educated at Kevin Street College of Technology. As a youthful Republican activist he was interned in the Curragh (1956–9) at the time of the BORDER CAMPAIGN. He worked in his family's fruit and vegetable business before being elected TD for the WORKERS' PARTY in 1982, succeeding Tomás Mac Giolla as leader of that party in 1988. Six of the party's seven deputies relinquished all ties with Republicanism to form the Democratic Left (DL) in 1992; henceforth fully constitutional, DL was the smallest party in the RAINBOW COALITION of 1994–7, influencing social and health policy – de Rossa himself served as minister for social welfare. He was a popular local representative and solid performer in the Dáil; elected MEP for Dublin in 1999, he no longer plays a role in national politics.

Derreen Gardens. Situated in Lauragh on the BEARA PENINSULA near Kenmare in Co. Kerry, these gardens were developed in the 19th century by successive Lord Lansdownes, who, after the manner of Victorian gentlemen gardeners and amateur botanists, introduced many new species from the Himalayas, especially ferns. In 1903 Edward VII and Queen Alexandra visited Derreen, as guests of the then Lord Lansdowne, the 5th Marquess (1845–1927), who was British foreign secretary at the time. A damp path lined with ferns, still to be seen, was named 'King's Oozy' in honour of the royal visit.

Derrick, John (also **Derricke**) (*fl.*1578). English engraver. He accompanied Sir Henry Sidney (1529–86) on his campaigns against Hugh O'NEILL and left in *Image of Ireland* (1581) a number of woodcuts regarded as authentic representations of the appearance of the 16th-century Irish. Derrick's text is undistinguished verse and his engravings are specifically anti-Irish and anti-Catholic, but they give a graphic idea of how Irish men and women dressed, how an Irish harpist played his tunes, and how 'wild' the Irish were.

Derry. *See* STROKE CITY.

Derry, Siege of. An iconic historical event, commemorated as lasting from 7 December 1688 (when the APPRENTICE BOYS closed New Gate against the Earl of Antrim's REDSHANKS) until 31 July 1689. However, the city's support of William III (KING BILLY) during the WILLIAMITE WAR was not overt until 18 April 1689, when JAMES II appeared before Bishop Gate. In a dispiriting downpour he was met with gunfire and cries of 'No surrender!' (subsequently a rallying cry of Northern Unionists). The city's population, normally 2000, was inflated by 30,000 Protestant refugees and 7000 soldiers. Accretion of myth lists 15,000 dead, mainly women and children, of disease and malnu-

trition, though the city gates were never actually closed. The defenders are said to have eaten rats, mice and dogs that had previously fed on unburied corpses. The besieging forces had no investing equipment and were beset with bad weather and a lack of coordination between the French, English and Irish contingents. Starving out the inhabitants failed when on 28 July, two ships, *Mountjoy* and *Phoenix*, broke through the boom that Rosen, the French commander, had stretched across the north end of Rosses Bay at the narrowest part of the Foyle estuary. On 1 August the besieging armies marched away, having conceded defeat. The siege lasted 105 days and became with justice one of the great elements of Unionist tradition. The 'Relief of Derry' is celebrated each TWELFTH OF AUGUST (the calendar having been changed in 1752) by the Apprentice Boys.

> Our drink was nothing but Water, which we paid very dear for, and cou'd not get without great danger; We mixt in it Ginger and Anniseeds, of which we had great plenty; Our necessity of Eating the Composition of Tallow and Starch, did not only Nourish and Support us, but was an infallible Cure of the Looseness ...
>
> REV. GEORGE WALKER (*c.*1646–91): *A True Account of the Siege of London-derry* (1689)

See also MAIDEN CITY.

Derry, the whole of. *See* WHOLE OF DERRY, THE.

Derrynaflan Hoard. A hoard of precious religious items, including the Derrynaflan Chalice, dating from the 8th or 9th century. They were found by Michael Webb and his teenage son, also Michael, at Derrynaflan, the site of the monastery of St RUADHAN of Lorra in Killenaule, Co. Tipperary, on 17 February 1980. As well as the chalice, the hoard consisted of a strainer, a paten (eucharistic dish) and a large bronze bowl.

Dervorgilla (d.1193). The wife of Tiernan O'Rourke, chieftain of BREFFNI, who was abducted in 1152 by Dermot MACMURROUGH, king of Leinster. In retaliation, O'Rourke attacked MacMurrough's territory and burned his castle in Ferns in Co. Wexford, precipitating Dermot's invitation to the Norman lords who invaded Ireland in 1169. Dervorgilla spent the rest of her life in the nun's convent attached to the Cistercian monastery of Mellifont, which she endowed.

Desmond. A historic territory (11th–17th centuries) in the southwest of Ireland, broadly in the modern counties of Kerry and Limerick. The name derives from Old Irish *Des-Muma*, 'south Munster'. Up to the later 12th century, the ruler of Desmond alternated with the ruler of THOMOND as king of Munster. The Anglo-Norman Fitzgeralds became Earls of Desmond in the 14th century. The 8th Earl, Thomas Fitzgerald (*c.*1426–68), was appointed lord deputy in 1463, but he was opposed by the gentry of the Pale and eventually executed for treason in Drogheda. The Desmonds were more Gaelicized and remote than the other two great earldoms, those of Kildare (*see* SILKEN THOMAS) and ORMOND and did not survive the period of the 16th century known as the TUDOR RECONQUEST (*see* DESMOND REBELLIONS).

Desmond Rebellions. The name given to two separate revolts by the Fitzgeralds of DESMOND. The first Desmond Rebellion (1569–73) was led by James Fitzmaurice Fitzgerald, and was suppressed by BLACK TOM, Earl of ORMOND and, ferociously, by Sir John PERROT, president of Munster from 1571, who is said to have executed 800 rebels in the space of two years. James Fitzmaurice, having sought help from France and Spain with limited success, was killed in 1579.

The new English governor, Malby, was so provocative that eventually the 14th Earl, Gerald Fitzgerald (1533–83), rebelled. During the second Desmond Rebellion (1579–83) the lord deputy, Lord Grey de Wilton, burnt and pillaged to the exent that a large proportion of the general population died from famine and disease (*see* ANATOMIES OF DEATH; SPENSER, EDMUND). The rebel earl, an outlaw whose lands had already been attainted, was killed by a bounty hunter in a hut in near Tralee. *See also* BUTLER, ELEANOR, COUNTESS OF DESMOND.

Despard, Charlotte (1844–1939). Philanthropist, feminist and Republican activist. She was born Charlotte French in Kent, England, to a landed family of Roscommon origin, and was orphaned and wealthy at the age of 21. In 1870 she married Maximilian Despard, and after his death in 1890 became involved in working with the poor of London, later in the suffrage movement and labour politics. Charlotte, who was described by her friend Maud GONNE as 'intensely Irish in feeling', bought a house in Dublin and supported the ITGWU during the 1913 LOCKOUT, and SINN FÉIN thereafter. Her brother John Denton FRENCH was appointed lord lieutenant of Ireland in May 1918. Initially Charlotte refrained from political activity in Ireland for his sake, but after Terence MacSwiney's death on hunger strike in October 1920 she moved permanently to Ireland and worked to highlight crimes of violence by the British army. With Maud Gonne and Hanna SHEEHY-SKEFFINGTON she formed the Women's Prisoners Defence League in 1922. In the 1920s she became a communist, visiting Russia with Hanna Sheehy-Skeffington in 1930. She spent the last years of her life in Belfast, having left her Dublin home to Maud Gonne, still campaigning for the poor but now virtually penniless. As an aristocratic English socialist, she was an object of suspicion to both Southern Catholics and Northern Protestants and was known to the Dublin working classes as 'Mrs Desperate'.

Dev. The most commonly used (neutral) nickname of Éamon DE VALERA throughout his long career as statesman. 'Up Dev!' was the rallying cry for the Fianna Fáil troops.

De Valera, Éamon (1882–1975). Revolutionary and statesman; taoiseach (1932–48, 1951–4, 1957–9) and president (1959–73). He was born in New York of an Irish mother and Spanish father, but reared in Co. Limerick. He studied mathematics at the Royal University and later taught in Dublin, although for most of his life he was a full-time politician. In Dublin he joined the GAELIC LEAGUE and the IRISH VOLUNTEERS, commanding the battalion in Boland's Mills during the EASTER RISING of 1916. He was sentenced to death but reprieved because of his American citizenship, and imprisoned until 1917.

On his release de Valera became president of both the Volunteers and SINN FÉIN and was elected MP for East Clare and president of the first DÁIL in 1919. During the long period he spent in America (June 1919–December 1920) – where he was attempting to raise money for the Republican cause and to heighten international awareness of the separatist struggle – he lost control of the situation in Ireland, finding the 'hard men' like Michael COLLINS dominant on his return. This may be one of the reasons why he did not form part of the TREATY delegation, sending in his place the very reluctant Collins. He vehemently opposed the Treaty, proposing instead a concept of his own called 'external association' and rejecting in particular the oath of allegiance that all members of the Dáil had to take. During the Treaty debates, not his finest hour, he made this egregious claim:

> Whenever I wanted to know what the Irish people wanted, I had only to examine my own heart and it told me straight away what the Irish people wanted.
>
> Speech in Dáil Éireann, 6 January 1922

It was only after the death of Liam Lynch (see REAL CHIEF, THE) that he was able to assert any control over the militant ANTI-TREATYITES and work to bring the CIVIL WAR to an end. He was jailed for a year (1923–4).

Because of Sinn Féin's policy of ABSTENTIONISM, de Valera was politically impotent until, in 1926, he and other veterans of the Civil War founded FIANNA FÁIL – the SLIGHTLY CONSTITUTIONAL PARTY, as described by Seán Lemass. The party's TDs entered the Dáil on 12 August 1927, finding the OATH OF ALLEGIANCE feasible after all:

> I am not prepared to take an oath. I am not going to take an oath. I am prepared to put my name down in this book in order to get permission to go into the Dáil, but it has no other significance.

The oath, he said, was an 'empty formula'. In his effort to regain political power de Valera turned Fianna Fáil into a formidable electoral machine, establishing the IRISH PRESS, which became a valuable propaganda tool.

Fianna Fáil duly came to power in 1932, and from then until 1959, when he retired as TAOISEACH, de Valera was in power for all but the short periods of the INTERPARTY GOVERNMENTS (1948–51 and 1954–7), so that Fianna Fáil did come to feel it was 'the natural party of government'. He used his former IRA comrades to defeat the BLUESHIRTS in the early 1930s (see BROY HARRIERS), but executed some of them during the EMERGENCY. Among his achievements was the CONSTITUTION OF 1937, which though flawed, strongly and constitutionally asserted the country's independence of Britain. Also notable was his success in keeping Ireland 'neutral on the allied side' during the Second World War, and his calm, statesmanlike response to Churchill's flights of fancy at the end of it (see CHURCHILL–DE VALERA RADIO EXCHANGES).

De Valera was, however, blinkered in many ways: he was fanatically devoted to the Irish language, but this devotion was marred by the element of compulsion and hypocrisy in the REVIVAL; he was too strongly influenced by Catholic teachings, and especially by Archbishop MCQUAID; and he persisted with a protectionist economic policy even though it had shown itself to be disastrous. He presided over the repressive atmosphere of the 1950s, doing nothing to improve it, and so hungry was he for power that he remained as president from 1959 until 1973, when he was 91 years old. In a much-quoted (and misquoted) radio broadcast on St Patrick's Day 1943, de Valera expounded his vision of:

> … a land whose countryside would be bright with cosy homesteads, whose fields and villages would be joyous with the sounds of industry,

with the romping of sturdy children, the contests of athletic youths and the laughter of comely maidens, whose firesides would be the forums for the wisdom of serene old age.

And, naturally, Irish-speaking, because:

> To part with it [the Irish language] would be to abandon a great part of ourselves, to lose the key of our past, to cut away the roots from the tree. With the language gone we could never aspire again to being more than half a nation.

It seemed to many people that what he wanted was a return to the peasant society of his youth, only with different political masters. Éamon de Valera died on 29 August 1975.

See also LONG FELLOW, THE; LONG HOOR, THE.

De Valera, Sinéad (1878–1975). Writer and wife of Éamon DE VALERA, in later life called 'Sinéad Bean de Valera' or simply 'Bean' (Irish, 'woman', 'wife of'). She was born Sinéad Flanagan in Balbriggan, Co. Dublin, on 3 June 1878. She trained as a teacher, taught in a national school and was involved in amateur dramatics. When she asked George Moore about whether she ought to make the stage her career, he is said to have replied: 'Height, five feet four; hair, red; name, Flanagan – no, my dear.' She met de Valera at a GAELIC LEAGUE class in Parnell Square where she was teacher, and they were married on 8 January 1910. They had five sons and two daughters, but she saw little of her husband in the years 1916–23. Michael Collins visited her and brought her money when de Valera was in America in 1920, but he was not pleased when Collins arranged for her to go to see him there, nor was he anxious to live with his family when he returned. From the 1930s on she published stories and versions of myths and legends, which were popular among Irish children. She died in Dublin on 7 January 1975.

De Valois, Ninette (1898–2001). Dancer and choreographer. She was born Edris Stannus in Baltyboys House in Blessington, Co. Wicklow, the daughter of an army officer and a celebrated glassmaker, Lillith Graydon-Smith. As a child she lived with her grandmother in Kent and attended ballet lessons, and in 1914 she was principal dancer in a pantomime at the Lyceum Theatre in London. The Russian impresario Sergei Diaghilev engaged her as a dancer in his company, Les Ballets Russes (1923–5) – by now she had adopted the glamorous stage name of Ninette de Valois – but it was as a choreographer with the Old Vic Theatre and Sadler's Wells Theatre, and later as director of Sadler's Wells Ballet, that she was best known. At the request of W.B. Yeats she choreographed a production for the ABBEY THEATRE School of Dance in 1928 featuring three dances, 'Venetian Suite', 'Rhythm' and 'The Curse of the Aspen Tree'. The production was a huge success, but by 1934 De Valois had left Ireland, lured by the continuing development of the Vic-Wells School of Ballet. In total she created 100 works, including 40 complete ballets. The Sadler's Wells Ballet moved into the Royal Opera House in 1946 and in 1955 it was granted a royal charter, its name changed to the Royal Ballet. De Valois retired from the directorship of the Royal Ballet in 1963 but continued as a governor. She also helped to establish ballet companies in Ireland and other countries, and attended performances until she was almost one hundred years old. She died in London in 2001, at the age of 102.

Devenish Island. A small island in Lower Lough Erne, 5 km (3 miles) northwest of Enniskillen, Co. Fermanagh, rich in early and medieval ecclesiastical remains. St MOLAISE OF DEVENISH founded a monastery there in the 6th century which, because of its accessibility to Viking longboats, suffered the fate of many such monastic sites in the 9th century, when Scandinavian visitors established a base in Lough Erne in 837. It was burned again in 1157 but remained an important religious centre until the 17th century. Among the remains are a 12th-century round tower and an elegant 15th-century high cross. The Soiscél Molaise (Middle Irish, 'Molaise's Gospel'), an early 11th-century book shrine now in the National Museum in Dublin, originated in Devenish.

Devenny Incident. A contributory factor in the sequence of events leading to the Battle of the BOGSIDE in Derry in 1969. On the night of Saturday 19 April 1969, during rioting that followed the banning of a Civil Rights march, eight uniformed RUC officers burst into the home of Samuel Devenny (1927–69) and severely batoned him and friends. Devenny's death three months later from a heart condition was attributed to the incident. Charges of murder were laid against the force and his funeral attracted a cortège of 20,000 mourners. Sir Arthur Young, appointed chief constable of the RUC by the home secretary James Callaghan in August, found that during his investigation of the incident in 1970 he was met with a 'conspiracy of silence' and no charges have ever been brought.

De Vere, Aubrey (1814–1902). Poet. He was the son of Sir Aubrey de Vere (1788–1846) of Curragh Chase, Co. Limerick, also a poet and a responsible landlord. He was educated at Trinity College Dublin and, through his father, became friendly with most of the mid-Victorian poetic establishment, including Tennyson. He assisted his elder brother Stephen in relief schemes during the Great Famine (*see* COFFIN SHIP), and afterwards wrote *English Misrule and Irish Misdeeds* (1848). He became a Catholic in 1851 and wrote much religious poetry. His main Irish work is *Inisfail* (1861), and he also produced a sanitized English translation of *Táin Bó Cuailgne* under the title *The Foray of Queen Maev*. His ballad 'The Death of Conor Mac Neasa' and the rousing 'A Ballad of ATHLONE' used to figure in school anthologies, while 'The Little Black Rose' still finds its place. He lectured in English literature to the students of Newman's Catholic University.
See also TORC WATERFALL.

Devereux, Walter and **Devereux, Robert.** *See* ESSEX, WALTER DEVEREUX, 1ST EARL OF; ESSEX, ROBERT DEVEREUX, 2ND EARL OF.

Devil a bit. A popular HIBERNO-ENGLISH means of indicating mild but total disagreement, usually pronounced 'divil a bit'. In answer to a query as to whether an incident might cause someone to lose her job, 'Divil a bit!' means 'Not at all!'

Devil and all, the. A HIBERNO-ENGLISH phrase signifying great achievement, often aspirational rather than actual: 'He's going to do the devil (divil) and all when he starts the new job.'

'Devil and Bailiff McGlynn, The'. *See* BAILIFF, THE.

Devil-Doubt. One of the stock characters in the parade of rhymers who took part in Christmas mumming. He was the last to arrive and after the parade of patriots or tyrants he brought the proceedings to a mock fearful climax. He had his own patter:

> Here comes I, Divil Doubt,
> The best wee divil that ever went out.
> Money I want and money I crave.
> If I don't get money
> I'll sweep ye all away to your grave.

Devil mend you! In HIBERNO-ENGLISH, an expression of disapproval or lack of sympathy, deployed, for instance, when a particular course of action has turned out badly.

Devilment. A common phrase in HIBERNO-ENGLISH that has lost its original stronger meaning and now connotes 'mischief', 'high spirits' or 'pranks'. It is usually said indulgently: 'That child is full of devilment.'

Devil's bedpost. *See* DIVIL'S BEDPOST.

Devil's dandruff. A name by which heroin is known among Dublin drug-users.

Devil's Half-Acre. The nickname devised by Michael COLLINS for Dublin CASTLE, the centre of British administration in Ireland.

Devil's Own, the. The nickname of the Connaught Rangers, who were said to have been 'the devil's own' at fighting. In 1920 the regiment's B and C company (some 300 soldiers in all) stationed in the Punjab, India took part in a mass refusal to obey orders (28 June–2 July). The 'mutiny' was inspired by accounts of the atrocities of the BLACK AND TANS at home in Ireland. One private, James Joseph Daly, from Tyrrellspass in Co. Westmeath, was shot (on 2 November 1920) and others received long prison sentences, though they were released in 1923. Daly's body was brought home for reinterment on 31 October 1970.

Devlin, Anne (1780–1851). Colleague and supporter of Robert EMMET. She was born of farming stock near Rathdrum, Co. Wicklow. Members of her family were active in the REBELLION OF 1798 and her father was imprisoned until 1801. The family then moved to Rathfarnham, now a suburb of Dublin, where Anne came into contact with Robert Emmet, who was planning another rebellion for July 1803. He rented a house nearby, which became the nerve centre of the uprising, and Anne Devlin became a courier, delivering Emmet's messages throughout Dublin (she was not, as was later thought, his domestic servant). When the rebellion began prematurely in July 1803, Anne Devlin was arrested, as were all of her extended family over the next few weeks. She was interrogated by Major SIRR but refused to reveal the name of Emmet's co-insurgents, even after Emmet himself was executed on 20 September. She was imprisoned for three years although never convicted of any crime, and her health was ruined by the time she was released in 1806. She worked as a maid until 1810, and later married and had two children. On 18 September 1851 she died in poverty.

Devlin, Bernadette (b.1947). Republican activist, also known since her marriage as Bernadette McAliskey. She was born in Cookstown, Co. Tyrone, on 23 April 1947 and studied at Queen's University Belfast, where she became involved with NICRA and PEOPLE'S DEMOCRACY. She was elected on the Unity platform to the Westminster Parliament as member for Mid-Ulster in April 1969, taking her seat on her 22nd birthday, and was sentenced to six month's imprisonment in 1970 for 'riotous behaviour' in Derry. She remained an active figure in the Republican movement, supporting the H-BLOCK HUNGER STRIKES of 1981 although she and her husband had been injured in a Loyalist gun attack on their home earlier that year. She has consistently opposed the peace process, believing it to be a sell-out for Republicans.

See also MURDERING HYPOCRITE.

Devlin, Joseph. *See* WEE JOE.

Devoy, John (1842–1928). Fenian. He was born in Kill, Co. Kildare, on 3 September 1842 and worked as a clerk in Dublin. For his part in the rebellion – trying to organize support for the FENIANS among members of the British army in Ireland – he was imprisoned in England (1866–71). Released on condition that he would not live in Ireland or England, he emigrated to America, where for the rest of his life he was pivotal in organizing Irish-American support for the national struggle.

In the USA Devoy joined CLAN NA GAEL and worked as a journalist in New York, setting up his own paper, the *Irish Nation*, in 1881 (it was suppressed in 1885) and a weekly, the *Gaelic American*, which he edited from 1903. He was instrumental in developing, with Michael DAVITT, the policy of supporting both PARNELL's constitutional Nationalism and the LAND LEAGUE in what was known as the NEW DEPARTURE, although this was rejected by the IRB and divided Clann na Gael.

Aware of the potential as a pressure group of the substantial Irish and Irish-American population in America, Devoy worked to mobilize voters to ensure the election of presidents, whether Republican or Democrat, who would be favourable to Irish aspirations. He raised money for Patrick Pearse's ST ENDA'S SCHOOL, and in the lead-up to the EASTER RISING of 1916 he negotiated with the Germans to acquire guns for the Rising and raised funds for the defence of Roger CASEMENT.

However, when in 1920 DE VALERA went on a fund-raising visit to America his relations with Devoy were strained and eventually broke down altogether in a struggle for power over Irish-America. Devoy accepted the Free State

and made a visit to Ireland in 1924 on the occasion of the Tailteann Games (*see* AONACH TAILTEANN). He died in relative poverty in Atlantic City, New Jersey, USA on 29 September 1928 and his remains were brought to Dublin for burial in GLASNEVIN CEMETERY. His autobiography, *Recollections of an Irish Rebel*, was published posthumously in 1929.
See also HOLLAND, JOHN PHILIP.

'Dhroimeann Donn Dílis, A'. *See* SILK OF THE KINE.

Dia. The Irish word for God, often used as a visitor's greeting on entering a house: *Dia sa teach!* (pronounced 'jee-ah sa chach', and meaning 'may God be in this house!') The expression *duine le Dia* ('a person with God') was used for a simpleton.

Diamond, Battle of the. A sectarian affray that took its name from a crossroads about 3 km (2 miles) from Loughgall, Co. Armagh, in which Protestants – largely from the faction known as the PEEP O' DAY BOYS – beat off an attack by Catholic DEFENDERS on 21 September 1795, killing 30 of them. The trouble – which was exacerbated by the sectarian activities of the YEOMANRY and the hints of a UNITED IRISHMEN rising – began when the Defenders fired Dan Winter's shop. The immediate sequel was the foundation of the ORANGE ORDER, the first neophyte being inaugurated at a well in Winter's garden.

Dian Cecht. The god of medicine in Irish mythology. He fashions a silver hand to replace the one lost by NUADA at the first battle of MAGH TUIREADH (Moytura), Nuada thereafter being known as Airgetlámh ('silver-handed'). However, the physical defect precludes Nuada's kingship until Dian Cecht's son MIACH, who is a more cunning artificer, provides Nuada with a hand of flesh and blood. As a consequence Miach is killed by his father, Dian Cecht, in a fit of envy.

Diarmaid Ua Duibhne (Irish 'Dermot of the love spot'). The Lancelot of the FIANNA. His nickname comes from a mole placed on his fore-head by a goddess of youth, making him irresistible to women, and he is seduced by GRÁINNE, the young wife of the Fianna leader FIONN MAC CUMHAIL. Though one of the foremost of Fionn's lieutenants, he cannot break the GEIS under which Gráinne has placed him, and together they evade the pursuit of Fionn and the Fianna for 16 years. In this the couple are aided by Diarmaid's foster father AONGHUS ÓG, the Celtic god of love. (Some of the places where they conceal themselves, as far apart as Donegal and Kerry, are still known as 'Dermot and Grania's Bed'.) Eventually Aonghus arranges a cessation of hostilities, and the couple settle down to a tranquil life and have four sons and a daughter.

Diarmaid is finally gored to death on a boar hunt with the Fianna near BEN BULBEN, and the boar that kills him is his transmogrified half-brother. As Diarmaid lies mortally wounded, Fionn refuses to bring him the water that in his hands will restore life. When OSCAR, Fionn's own grandson, threatens to kill the chief, Fionn appears to comply, but lets the water trickle through his fingers. Aonghus and the sorrowing Gráinne take Diarmaid's body to BRUGH NA BÓINNE.

The story is told in *Toraigheacht Dhiarmada agus Ghráinne* ('the pursuit of Dermot and Grania'), one of the greatest of the Fionn cycle of Celtic myths. The parallels with the Arthurian triangles of Arthur, Guinevere and Lancelot, and of Mark, Isolde and Tristan are striking.

Diarmait na nGall. *See* MACMURROUGH, DERMOT.

Diaspora. A Greek word originally used to describe the dispersion of the Jews after the Babylonian Captivity, and now for Jews living outside of Israel. In its Irish context it describes the large-scale emigration from the country, especially from the mid-1840s until the 1960s. It is reckoned that there are 70 million people throughout the world who have some claim to call themselves Irish. Most live in America, Australia and Britain, and they have retained a significant political and economic voice that still has some effect in what they call the 'old country':

> … the Irish diaspora is the outworking of two forms of colonialism, those of Mother England and Mother Church.
>
> TIM PAT COOGAN (b.1935): *Wherever Green is Worn* (2000)

Diceman, the. The nickname of Thom McGinty (1954–95), an actor who created street pageants, mostly in Grafton Street, Dublin. His most famous costume was in the form of a dice. He died of AIDS on 22 February 1995.

Dichul (also known by his Latin name **Diecola**) (d.*c.*625). A monk of BANGOR and a companion of COLUMBAN in his travels in Burgundy. He helped his master found LUXEUIL. When Columban was expelled by Queen Brunehaut of Austrasia for refusing to baptise the children of her son's concubines, Dichul was too old to travel but stayed as a recluse in the Vosges, founding the abbey of Lutra. His feast day is 18 January.

Dicuil (d.*c.*825). An Irish *doctus* (scholar) about whom little is known except what can be garnered from his writings. We discover that his teacher was Suibne (an Ulster name) and that in 767 he met a monk called Fidelis who had visited the Holy Land and was able to give him reasonably accurate information about Egypt and the Nile. Fidelis was almost certainly an abbot of IONA who died in 772. Dicuil went to the continent *c.*806, probably to escape Viking attacks, and became a teacher at the palace school of CHARLEMAGNE at AACHEN. He was known as an early geographer and astronomer, and presented his *magnum opus*, *Liber de Mensura Orbis Terrae* ('the book of measurement of the earth') shortly before his death. The detailed account of the Scottish Isles as far north as the Faroes suggests personal knowledge, and he was aware that Iceland's inshore waters were ice-free all year round. This information he had obtained from venturesome Irish monks, who also told him of the midnight sun. Scholars believe that he

was the anonymous poet who wrote a verse tribute to Charlemagne under the pseudonym *Hibernicus Exul* ('Irish exile').

Diddy (Irish *dide*, 'nipple'). A familiar or usually vulgar word for a woman's breast, normally used in the plural, as in 'She has a fine pair of diddies.'

Didgeridoo. The Australian aboriginal instrument, which, though thousands of years old, may have been named by Irish settlers, according to recent research. The name has no connection with any other Aboriginal word, but may come, according to Dymphna Lonergan, a PhD student at Flinders University in Australia, from the Irish word *dúdaire* ('crooner', 'hummer', 'long-necked person', 'hornblower') and *dubh* ('black') or *duth* ('native'). *See also* COCKLES.

Diet. A now somewhat dated term for 'board', 'daily meals' (as in board and lodgings).

Dig. A HIBERNO-ENGLISH word for mockery, criticism or a sharp reminder: 'I gave him a dig about the trouble his son was in.'

Diggle. A HIBERNO-ENGLISH euphemistic version of 'devil', often used as an exclamation, as in, 'She did, you diggle!'

Dig with the left foot, to. A Catholic euphemism or code for a Protestant in Ulster, which may be innocent or viciously sectarian, depending on circumstances. According to folklore the custom in the Protestant northeast of Ireland, unlike the rest of Ireland, was to dig with the left foot. 'Dig with the wrong foot' is also used. Contrariwise, in Scotland a 'left-footer', or someone who 'kicks with the left foot', is a Roman Catholic. However, the phrase 'right-footer' for a Protestant does not exist.

Dilder or **dandle.** To play with a baby by rocking on the knee or gently tossing it up and down in fun or pacification.

Dillon, Gerard (1916–71). Painter. He was born in Belfast and after finishing school at 14 was apprenticed to a house painter. He moved to London when he was 18 and began to paint pictures some years later. After living in Dublin and Belfast during the Second World War, he returned to live in London but began to exhibit regularly at the RHA and in commercial galleries in Dublin. In the popular mind he is most associated with Connemara, where he spent much time and of which he painted primitive landscapes and seascapes in oil. He re-turned to live in Dublin in 1968. As well as painting he designed sets for the ABBEY THEATRE and executed public commissions; he also wrote stories and made a record of folk songs. He died in Dublin on 14 June 1971.

Dillon, James (1902–86). Politician. He was born in Dublin on 26 September 1902, the fourth son of Nationalist politician John DIL-LON, and educated at University College Dublin and the King's Inns. He was called to the Bar in 1931 but worked in the family's business in Ballaghadereen, Co. Roscommon. He was first elected to the DÁIL as an independent TD, but became vice-president of FINE GAEL at its foundation in 1933. He represented the Monaghan constituency for that party and as an independent from 1937 until he retired in 1968.

Dillon was the only member of Dáil Éireann to attack publicly Ireland's neutrality in the Second World War – a position he maintained and reiterated in public until the end of his life – and he resigned from Fine Gael in February 1942 in protest at party policy. However, he was appointed minister for agriculture in the first INTERPARTY GOVERNMENT (1948–51) and rejoined Fine Gael before the 1951 election, serving in the same ministry in the second interparty government (1954–7). He succeeded W.T. Cosgrave as leader of the party in 1959, retiring to the back benches in 1965.

Dillon was an able, colourful politician and a fine orator with decided views, but the achievements of his career do not adequately reflect that ability, his misfortune being that his period at the head of his party coincided with the total dominance of FIANNA FÁIL. He died on 10 February 1986.

Dillon, John (1851–1927). Nationalist politician. He was born in Dublin, the son of John Blake Dillon, and educated at University College Dublin and the Royal College of Surgeons. As a student he was involved in HOME RULE politics, and in 1879 he became prominent as a militant land agitator, strongly promoting the policy of BOYCOTT. He was elected MP for Tipperary (1880–3) and Mayo East (1885–1918), despite the opposition of Parnell, and supported the PLAN OF CAMPAIGN. Dillon was imprisoned several times under the COERCION Acts and made several fundraising visits to the USA. He was in America in 1890 when the O'Shea affair became public (see O'SHEA WHO MUST BE OBEYED), and after some hesitation followed Justin McCarthy to the anti-Parnellite side. He replaced McCarthy as leader of that group in 1896, continuing his campaigns to help the small farmers of the west as well as his parliamentary career.

After the death of John Redmond in March 1918 Dillon was elected leader of the Irish Party, withdrawing the party from Westminster in protest at the Military Service Bill passed the following month (see CONSCRIPTION CRISIS). Dillon was one of those moderate Nationalists who were overtaken by events, and he fittingly lost his seat to a still imprisoned Éamon DE VALERA in December 1918 (de Valera also stood and won in East Clare). He retired from public life shortly afterwards. His son, James Dillon, was leader of FINE GAEL.

Dillon, John Blake (1816–66). Young Irelander. He was born in Ballaghaderreen, Co. Roscommon, and educated at Maynooth and Trinity College Dublin. With Thomas Davis and Charles Gavan Duffy he founded *The NATION* in 1842. He took part in the Rising of 1848 (see WIDOW MCCORMICK'S CABBAGE PATCH) and afterwards escaped to France, thence to the USA, where he practised law. An amnesty allowed him to return to Ireland in 1855, and he went on to serve as MP for Roscommon. He died of cholera in Killarney on 15 September 1866. John MITCHEL said of him that he was all wrong on almost every question but that he was nevertheless better than many people who were all right.

Dillon, Wentworth, 4th Earl of Roscommon (1633–85). Royalist poet and translator. He was born in Dublin and educated at the University of Caen. His estates were confiscated by the Commonwealth but restored at the time of the Restoration. His *Poetical Works* (1701) comprise many volumes, and some of his epigrams are still quoted. He was exercised by the relationship between poetry and nationality, and favoured freeing poetry from the demands of rhyme. He died in London and was buried in Westminster Abbey. He features in Samuel Johnson's *The Lives of the Poets* (1779–81).

Dillon's Regiment. A group of Irish soldiers in France led from 1690 by Arthur Dillon (1670–1733), one of the leading WILD GEESE. The regiment continued for a whole century under a succession of Dillon commanders, and became widely known in France and beyond.

Dinger or **dinging.** A term used in HIBERNO-ENGLISH and meaning 'first class', referring to a person or an object: 'She's a dinger of a pianist.' In Brendan Behan's 'The Confirmation Suit' the hero is 'dressed out in a dinging overcoat, belted, like a grown-up man's'. The word may derive from the American 'humdinger'.

Dingle Peninsula. The northernmost of the three Kerry peninsulas, with the busy market town of Dingle (Irish *Daingean uí Chúis*) as its main commercial centre. On the north and west side, separated from the rest of the peninsula by the scenic Conor Pass, is the GAELTACHT area of Corca Dhuibhne (Irish, 'race or people of Duibhne'), satirized as 'Corca Dorcha' by Myles na Gopaleen in An *BÉAL BOCHT*. Garraun Point at the peninsula's tip is the most westerly mainland point in Ireland, and thus in Europe. Tourism, including the language tourism associated with Irish colleges, is now the main industry in the area. The Great Blasket in the BLASKET ISLANDS can be reached from Dunquin.

See also DUNQUIN SCHOOL; KRUGER KAVANAGH; *RYAN'S DAUGHTER*.

Dingle Regatta. A major local and tourist event held annually in August. It earned nationwide fame in the 1990s when it was officially opened each year by Charles Haughey.

Dinneen, Patrick. *See* DINNEEN'S DICTIONARY.

Dinneen's Dictionary. An excellent Irish–English dictionary (*Foclóir Gaeilge agus Béarla*), first published in 1927. It was compiled by an eccentric Jesuit priest, Pádraig Ó Duinnín (Dinneen) (1860–1934).

Ó Duinnín was born on Christmas Day 1860 at Corrans, near Rathmore in the SLIABH LUACHRA area of east Kerry, one of ten children of poor tenant farmers. He was educated at the Royal University in Dublin and ordained a priest in 1894. In 1900 he left the Jesuit order, the better to devote himself to the study of Irish language and poetry and to the revival of the language. He published 15 books, including scholarly editions of the work of the Sliabh Luachra poets Aogán Ó RATHAILE and Eoghan Rua Ó Súilleabháin (see EOGHAN AN BHÉIL BHINN), as well as numerous articles, and was active in the GAELIC LEAGUE. He had a passionate belief in the central importance of the living language, and it is the richness of this language, particularly that of the Munster dialects, that is the basis of his great dictionary.

Pádraig Ó Duinnín's brother Joe Dinneen (1869–1928) was well known locally as 'The Bard of Sliabh Luachra', and wrote ballads about the HEADFORD AMBUSH and the MOVING BOG DISASTER. He died on 29 April 1928 after being struck by a train at Headford station.

Dinner in the middle of the day. According to the maverick PARISH PUMP POLITICIAN Jackie Healey-Rae, the PLAIN PEOPLE OF IRELAND (i.e. his own constituency) have their dinner in the middle of the day. This is in contrast with the aristocrats and parish priests of old – and perhaps also of the present day.

Dinnle or **dindle** or **dinnel.** Persistent noise, such as the rattling of windows.

Dinnsenchas. A collection of topographical lore assigning stories and name origins to Irish places. A typical example was the 12th-century compilation to be found in the BOOK OF LEINSTER.

Dint or **dunt.** A noun used in HIBERNO-ENGLISH to mean 'a blow', or, as a verb, 'to hit' or 'to strike'.

Dint of, with the. A phrase used in HIBERNO-ENGLISH to mean 'as a result or consequence of': 'I had a backache with the dint of digging the garden,' or 'I missed the turn with the dint of talking.'

Dip. A gravy made of flour and water with perhaps an onion for flavouring. It was used for family dinner on a Friday, the day of abstinence, when no meat was served, in the absence of a substitute such as fish or eggs. It was originally devised as a sauce in which to dip potatoes or bread. A table exhortation to children went: 'Dip in the dip and leave the herring to your father.'

Dirty Dick. *See* SEVENTY-SEVEN.

Dirty Protest. The campaign for the recovery of special status for paramilitary (mainly Republican) prisoners granted by William WHITELAW, secretary of state for Northern Ireland, in June 1972 after a hunger strike. It was phased out by Merlyn Rees, secretary of state for Northern Ireland (1974–6), from 1 March 1976 and stopped all together on the instructions of Margaret Thatcher through secretary of state Humphrey Atkins in 1980. The prisoners refused to cooperate with the removal of special status, declining to wear prison clothing (*see* BLANKET PROTEST). From March 1978 about 300 prisoners refused to wash or use the toilets, fouled their cells and smashed the furniture. This 'Dirty Protest' lasted until March 1981, to focus on the terminal hunger strike of Bobby Sands in the spring of 1981 (*see* H-BLOCK HUNGER STRIKES).

Dirty Shirts, the. A nickname of the Royal Munster Fusiliers, deriving from the time when, as the 101st Foot, they fought in their shirtsleeves at Delhi during the Indian Mutiny (1857–8). The regiment was one of the first to dye its white tunics with tea, producing the colour khaki. The received origin of the term is an Urdu word meaning 'dusty', but the Munsters always insisted, as an Irish-speaking regiment, that the resulting colour was rather like that of shit, for which the Irish word was *cac*.

Disappeared, the. A term first used during the period of military government (1976–83) in Argentina to describe those many dissidents – numbering between 6000 and 15,000 men and women – who opposed the government and who disappeared (or were 'disappeared') without trace. The term has also been applied to at least ten victims of the IRA who 'disappeared' during the Northern Ireland Troubles and who were buried in unknown places. Since the beginning of the peace process, a number of bodies have been discovered with IRA help, mainly across the border in Co. Louth, the most recent being that of Jean McConville, a mother of ten children who was abducted in 1972 when she was 37 because she had gone to the aid of a fatally wounded British soldier. She was shot in the back of the head and buried at Shelling Hill beach. Her body was discovered in August 2003. The IRA issued an apology on 24 October, which was rejected by some of the families. The Disappeared are also referred to as 'the Missing'.

Discovery. The means, created by an act of the Irish Parliament in 1709, by which a Protestant who filed a bill in chancery could 'discover' a property transaction proscribed under the PROPERTY LAWS and thereby become entitled to the Catholic interest in the transaction. A notorious example was the discovery brought in the late 18th century by the younger brother of Charles O'CONOR against him to claim his estate .

Disestablishment of the Church of Ireland. A

bill passed by Gladstone (the GOM) in 1869 that meant that the Church of Ireland, the Anglican church in Ireland, was no longer the country's established church, supported by contribution of all the people (*see* TITHE). The church was disendowed of its property, except for churches and graveyards, and compensated for the loss of revenue by a payment of £16 million. The land previously held by the church was divided among 6000 tenants. At the same time, the government ceased to support other religions: the MAYNOOTH grant and the *REGIUM DONUM* paid to Presbyterians were also abolished and the churches compensated. The position of the Church of Ireland, to which only about 12% of the population adhered, had been greatly resented by Catholics and Nationalists, and also by Ulster Presbyterians, and its disestablishment was a popular and important measure for the great majority of the population. The Disestablishment Bill became law on 26 July 1869, but was not effective until 1 January 1870.

Dish with the Fish. The slick appellation of the statue in Dublin to the city's most famous vendor, MOLLY MALONE; the nickname following the oral success of the FLOOZIE IN THE JACUZZI. The sculpture is also known as the Tart with the Cart.

Disremember. A verb deliberately contrived as a Dublin colloquialism and meaning to forget, whether accidentally or deliberately, or to fail to recall.

Dissolution of the Monasteries. The name given to the process of closing down the monasteries in Ireland, England and Wales during Henry VIII's Reformation. In 1534 the English Parliament passed the Act of Supremacy, declaring Henry VIII to be Supreme Head of the church in England. Between 1536 and 1538 the same Parliament passed laws suppressing or dissolving first the small and then the larger religious foundations. When the Irish Parliament met (May 1536–December 1537) under the lord deputy, Sir Leonard GREY, it too eventually passed a law (1537) ordering the dissolution of all Irish religious houses, and for this it became known as the REFORMATION PARLIAMENT.

The main beneficiaries of the dissolution of 42 monasteries and 51 friaries in the Pale and Ormond (the actual extent of the dissolution) were the OLD ENGLISH lords of these areas, who acquired some of the lands that were redistributed. Even greater beneficiaries were Sir Leonard Grey himself and other English officials, while the English Treasury gained less than £2000 in all.

The Dissolution of the Monasteries was not as great a social disaster as might initially appear, since municipal charities and philanthropists among the wealthy of the Pale and Leinster had by then largely taken over the functions of health care, education and relief of the poor. In Gaelic Ireland, where the king's writ did not run, monasteries and friaries were left untouched until later in the century.

Divarsion. A HIBERNO-ENGLISH pronunciation of the noun 'diversion', meaning CRAIC, entertainment. The adjective 'divarting' is also used.

Divil. The normal pronunciation of the word 'devil' in HIBERNO-ENGLISH to this day, as used in such expressions 'devil a bit', 'devil and all'.

Divil's bedpost. The four of clubs in a set of playing cards, regarded as the unluckiest card in the pack.

Divination. The practice of superstitious rituals to foretell the future, in particular to find out the name of the partner for whom one is destined. In traditional rural society, there were many ways for girls to divine the young men they would marry. At Hallowe'en a ring (a symbol of matrimony) and symbols of the single life, the poor life or the rich life were inserted in the BARMBRACK and COLCANNON while they were being prepared: the girl who got the slice or portion with the ring would be married within the year. When a girl washed her shift (undergarment) in the river and hung it to dry she hoped to see the face of the right young man reflected in the water. A girl might also hope to dream of the man she would marry: she would go to bed thirsty so that she would dream of a young man offering her water, or with her face washed but not dried so that in her sleep a young man might come and offer her a towel.

Divis Flats. A complex of high-rise flats built at the lower end of the FALLS ROAD in Republican West Belfast. At the height of the Troubles it housed at least 7000 people, and became known as PLANET OF THE IRPS. The towers were largely demolished by 1995.

Divorce. Until 1997 Ireland was one of the few countries in the West not to have legal provision for divorce, since, in 1925, the introduction of private divorce bills was banned. The CONSTITUTION OF 1937 contained a complete ban on divorce, but in 1996 Irish voters agreed in a referendum to remove the constitutional prohibition on divorce, and conservative divorce legislation was introduced in February 1997. After the establishment of the state of Northern Ireland, private divorce bills continued to be introduced in Parliament, until, in 1939, civil divorce was introduced.

DMP. The Dublin Metropolitan Police, a civic service created in 1836 on the model of Peel's London equivalent (1829). The members were unarmed, unlike the RIC (Royal Irish Constabulary), and the regulations governing them were on the whole more relaxed than those of the paramilitary force. The height regulations (at least 1.8 m/6 ft) and their tall silver-faced helmets gave officers of the DMP an impressive appearance. By 1901 they covered an area of 93 sq km (36 sq miles), divided among six divisions of uniformed men, with a seventh (G-division) of detectives (known as G-Men, before J. Edgar Hoover was born). The G-MEN, who had always played a significant role in investigating political crime, became the main non-military adversaries of Michael COLLINS in the ANGLO-IRISH WAR.

The force was reasonably popular with the Dublin citizens, and generated many ballads from its inception:

These wondrous men each day we view, sirs,
Drest from top to toe in blue, sirs,
Their lofty heads a glazed top hat on,
And in their hands a warlike baton;
A rattle two they have behind them,
To make a noise should it incline them,
In short as guardians of the peace then,
None can surpass the New Policemen.
ANON.: 'The New Policemen of Dublin' (*c*.1830)

Their darkest hour was the 1913 LOCKOUT when they brutally attacked gatherings of strikers. They strongly resisted a suggestion that they be amalgamated with the RIC in 1917, insisting that they were a city and civic force, unlike the RIC who were provincial and armed. They were eventually combined with the GARDA SÍOCHÁNA in 1925.

Dobbs, Arthur (1689–1765). Economist and colonial governor. He was born in Scotland of an Ulster family from Castle Dobbs, Co. Antrim. He was high sheriff of Co. Antrim in 1720 and surveyor-general of Ireland from 1733 and as such responsible for much new building in Dublin, including the Parliament House. A strong advocate of union with Britain, he also approved of her colonial expansion in North America and instigated two expeditions to find a northwest passage to the Pacific. (In tribute to his patronage a promontory in Hudson's Bay is called Cape Dobbs.) In 1745 he purchased land in North Carolina, USA, filling it with immigrants from his own estates, and in 1754 arrived to become governor of the state. In 1762, at the age of 73, he married Justina Davis, who was 15 years old. He intended to return to Ireland but died of a stroke three years later.

Dobbs, Margaret Emmeline (1873–1961). Irish-language activist. She was born in Dublin, but spent much of her life in Cushendmen where with Roger CASEMENT and Francis Bigger (*see IN BURGO DUNO TUMULO*) she initiated Feis na nGleann ('feis of the glens', a festival of Irish dance, music and song in the Antrim Glens) in 1904, and continued to serve on the committee until the end of her life. She gave financial and personal support to Irish colleges in Rathlin and Gortahork, and contributed to the defence fund for her close friend Roger Casement. Though her funeral was intended to be quiet and confined to family members, hundreds of people from the Glens came in tribute.

Dobharchú (Irish, 'water hound'). The legendary monster, half-dog, half-otter (pronounced 'dower koo'), which is said to have lived in the lake of Glenade (*Gleann Éid*, 'glen of jealousy') in northwest Co. Leitrim. It is represented in a tombstone carving in Conwell graveyard near Kinlough in that county. The stone commemorates a woman named Grace Connolly, allegedly killed by the monster that arose from the lake as she washed clothes at the lakeside in September 1722. Her husband, Terence McLoghlin, in turn killed the monster by stabbing it with his dagger as it lay on his wife's body. *Dobharchú* is in use as one of the Irish words for otter (also *madra uisce*, 'water dog').

Dochal (also **du'hill** or **duchall**). An Ulster word for a dunghill, probably by back-formation but perhaps also associated with the Irish word *doícheall*, 'inhospitable'. It is in common use as a term of personal abuse.

'Dóchas linn Naomh Pádraig'. The title and first line of a hymn to St Patrick that was sung by every schoolchild in previous decades:

Dóchas linn Naomh Pádraig
Aspal mór na hÉireann.
Ainm oirdhearc gléigeal,
Solas mór an tsaoil é.
Sé do chloí na draoithe,
Croíthe dúra gan aon mhaith.
D'isligh dream an díomais,
Tré neart Dé ár dtréan-fhlaith.
(Hail to St Patrick our hope,
The great apostle of Ireland.
Of the noble shining name,
The great light of the world.
He it was who defeated the druids,

With their hard evil hearts.
He humbled the proud,
Through the might of the great Lord God.)

Docken. The weed dock (*Rumex*) used as an antidote to nettle sting. The sting was vigorously rubbed with a dock leaf while the victim or nurse chanted, 'Docken in; nettle out!'

Docti (Latin, 'learned people'; singular *doctus*). A term applied to the educated Irishmen who in the Middle Ages made Ireland famously the ISLAND OF SAINTS AND SCHOLARS. The list of notable *docti* includes CLEMENT SCOTTUS, CRUINDMEL, DICUIL, DUNGAL, JOHN SCOTTUS ERIUGENA, MARIANUS SCOTTUS (OF COLOGNE), SEDULIUS SCOTTUS.

Document No. 2. A counter-proposal to the Anglo-Irish TREATY of 1921 presented by Éamon DE VALERA to a private session of the Dáil on 14 December 1921 as part of the Treaty debate. The main difference between it and the Treaty was the absence of both the OATH OF ALLEGIANCE and the proposed governor-general. Ireland would continue to be attached to Britain by 'external association', a form of words devised by de Valera himself and rejected by the British government before the treaty negotiations proper. De Valera withdrew the document before it could be discussed in public session in the Dáil.

Docwra, Sir Henry (d.1631). The founder of Derry. He was part of the English force sent against Hugh O'NEILL during the NINE YEARS' WAR; on 14 May 1600 he landed at Culmore with 4000 men, took the the tiny monastic settlement of Derry without opposition and began to fortify it. He made useful alliances with local Irish chieftains and made Cahir O'DOHERTY, the scion of INISHOWEN, his protégé. His harrying of O'Neill from the west, combined with Lord Deputy MOUNT-JOY's scorched-earth policy in Tyrone, finally defeated him. Docwra left Derry in 1606, having sold his interests to his deputy George Paulett. His *Narration of the Services Done by the Army Employed to Lough Foyle under* *the Leading of Me, Sir Henry Docwra, Knight* suggests that he and his men had been unrewarded for all their efforts on behalf of the crown. His description of the town's topography is graphic and precise:

> ... in form of a bow bent, whereof the bog is the string and the river the bow.

Dodds, E[ric] R[obertson] (1893–1979). Classicist and autobiographer. He was born on 25 July 1893 in Banbridge, Co. Down, and was educated at Campbell College and Balliol College, Oxford. He lectured in classics at Reading and Birmingham Universities, and was regius professor of Greek at Oxford. Rejecting the Unionism and Protestantism of his family, he became a vocal Irish Nationalist, and also had a continuing interest in psychic research. He was editor and friend of Stephen MACKENNA, the translator of the Greek philosopher Plotinus, and became the literary executor of his protégé Louis MACNEICE. His prizewinning autobiography *Missing Persons* (1979) contains vivid portraits of MacNeice and his friend W.H. Auden. He died on 8 April 1979.

Dog's abuse. A common term in HIBERNO-ENGLISH for a severe scolding or verbal abuse: 'She gave me dog's abuse for coming home late.'

Dogs in the street, the. *See* STREET.

Doheny and Nesbitt's. A pub in lower Baggot Street in Dublin known as the haunt of politicians, journalists and spin doctors. In the recession of the late 1980s some right-wing economists associated with the pub earned the nickname the 'Doheny and Nesbitt School of Economics'.

Doherty, Ken (b.1969). Snooker player. He was born in Ranelagh, Dublin, and educated at Westland Row Christian Brothers school. He became a professional snooker player in 1990. His greatest achievement was to defeat Stephen Hendry in the Embassy World Snooker Championship in 1997.

Dolan's ass. *See* LANNA MACREE'S DOG.

Dollion. A scrap of cloth: 'There she stood, with not a dollion on her.'

Dollop. A substantial serving of a liquid or semi-liquid substance, for instance a dollop of cream or milk. The word, which is of uncertain derivation, is common in HIBERNO-ENGLISH.

Dolly's Brae. The scene of a violent sectarian affray on 12 July 1849. Orangemen from Rathfriland went considerably out of their way to parade through the 'Brae', a Catholic district near Castlewellan, Co. Down, in the annual TWELFTH OF JULY celebration commemorating the Battle of the Boyne. They were subsequently entertained in Tollymore Park, the home of Robert Jocelyn, 3rd Earl of Roden (1788–1870), and escorted on their way home by troops. They insisted on marching back through the same district, and at Magheramayo they were confronted by a group of Catholics, including some armed RIBBONMEN. In the ensuing encounter, and in the burning of houses that followed, 30 Catholics were killed and many wounded. The affair led to the passing of the Party Processions Act of 1850, which was intended to outlaw provocative marches and meetings. Roden was censured and dismissed from the magistracy.

Dolly's Brae has remained an important part of Orange mythology and has been celebrated in several ballads, including one which ends with the line, 'We'll kick the Pope all over Dolly's Brae!'

> 'Twas on the 12th day of July in the year of '49
> Ten hundreds of our Orangemen together they did combine,
> In memory of King William, on that bright and glorious day,
> To walk all round Lord Roden's park, and right over Dolly's Brae.
> ...
> Come all ye blind-led papists, wherever that ye be,
> Never bow down to priest or Pope, for them they will disown,
> Never bow down to images, for God you must adore,

Come, join our Orange heroes, and cry Dolly's
    Brae no more.

Dolmen Press. A literary publishing house
founded in 1951 by Liam Miller (1924–87)
and associated with 8 Herbert Place in Dublin.
Among its notable successes were the works of
Thomas KINSELLA, including a fine edition of
Kinsella's translation of the *TÁIN BÓ CUAILNGE*,
with illustrations by Louis Brocquy, and *An
DUANAIRE 1600–1900* (1981). The company did
not survive the death of its founder.

Dolocher, the. A monstrous creature in the
form of a black pig that terrorized women
who walked in the centre of Dublin at night,
as described in the *Dublin Penny Journal* of
24 November 1832. So great was the fear of
the dolocher – whispered to be the spirit of
a man who committed suicide in the Black
Dog prison in the Cornmarket, near James's
Street – that groups of young men killed any
pigs they found abroad after dark, and were
perplexed to find no trace of the carcasses the
next morning. When eventually the dolocher
was apprehended, it turned out to be a man
who had been a warder in the Black Dog
prison and, knowing the story of the suicide,
had used it to his own material advantage: the
sale of a quantity of fresh pork from the pigs he
found dead around the city. The origin of the
word dolocher is unknown.

Donaghadee (Irish *Domnach Daoi*, 'Daoi's
church'). A town in Co. Down, noted in the
chorus of a popular song as being 6 miles (10
km) from Bangor, though suburban growth
has cut the distance to 4 miles. Until 1865 it
was linked to Portpatrick in Ayrshire as the
shortest crossing from Ireland to Scotland
(32 km/20 miles). The unsuitability of Portpatrick, because of its susceptibility to dangerous southwestern gales, was the reason
for the discontinuation of the service, which
was removed to Larne–Stranraer. In 1947
Tom Blower swam from Donaghadee to Portpatrick in 16 hours.

Toora loo, toora lay, oh it's six miles from Bangor
    to Donaghadee.

Donahue, Jack. An Irish bushranger (Australian outlaw). He was transported from Dublin
to Australia in 1825. With his gang he robbed settlers in the Bathurst area of New South
Wales for two years, until shot dead by police.
An anonymous ballad glorifies him:

This bold undaunted highwayman as you may
    understand
Was banished for his natural life from Erin's
    happy land,
Dublin, city of renown, where his first breath he
    drew,
'Twas there they christened him the brave and
    bold Jack Donahue.

See also KELLY, NED; WILD COLONIAL BOY, THE.

Donatus (*fl.*9th century). Bishop of FIESOLE, a
town north of Florence. He was returning
to France from a pilgrimage to Rome in 829
at a time when the see was vacant, and his
visit was regarded as heaven-sent. He ruled
as bishop until 876, and in that time wrote
much poetry, including a verse life of St
BRIGID and a description of his Irish homeland.

Donegal (Irish *Dún na nGall*, 'fort of the foreigners'). The name of the most northwesterly
county of Ireland, and also of one of its
towns. The main part of the county, excluding INISHOWEN (the territory of the O'Dohertys), is known in Irish as *Tír Chonaill*
('Conall's land'). Conall was a son of the
semi-mythical NIALL OF THE NINE HOSTAGES,
and the land was owned by the O'Donnells
up to the beginning of the 17th century. The
foreigners (*Gall*) of the name Donegal were
the VIKINGS, who found Donegal Bay a good
anchorage. The town of Donegal was the site
of a 15th-century Franciscan monastery and of
an O'Donnell castle. Donegal is known as 'the
Town of the Four Masters', after the scholars
who compiled the 17th-century ANNALS OF
THE FOUR MASTERS.

Donegall. The title taken by the Chichester
family, who by the end of the 18th century
were the largest landowners in Ireland. The
early acquisition of territories in Antrim and

Down by Sir Arthur CHICHESTER in the 17th century was consolidated by the 3rd Earl at the end of the WILLIAMITE WAR. During the 18th century the family were noted absentee landlords, and the indiscipline and extravagance of George Augustus, the 2nd Marquess (1769–1844), caused huge debts, which meant that the property had to be disposed of by the 3rd Marquess (1797–1883).

Donegal tweed. *See* BREADEEN.

Donegan, Patrick. *See* THUNDERING DISGRACE, A.

Doneraile. A village between Mallow and Mitchelstown in Co. Cork, part of the estate of the poet Edmund SPENSER. Tadhg Ó Duinnín, the last hereditary poet of the MacCarthys of Blarney, died as parish priest there in 1726, and Canon SHEEHAN, who was also parish priest at Doneraile (1895–1913), wrote his ten novels there. Near Doneraile was situated Bowen Court, ancestral home of the novelist Elizabeth BOWEN.
See also STEEPLECHASING.

Doneraile Conspiracy. An event connected with agrarian conflict in the early 19th century. Extensive WHITEBOY activity in the area around Doneraile near Mallow in north Cork prompted local landlords led by George Bond Law to collect money and offer a large reward for information leading to their conviction. On the basis of perjured 'bought' evidence 21 men were brought to trial in stages in Cork before a packed jury. On 22 October 1829 four of these were sentenced to death. That night the brother of another of the accused made a legendary night ride to Derrynane, Co. Kerry, to enlist the aid of Daniel O'CONNELL. O'Connell, after another long ride through the night, appeared in Cork court the next morning and in cross-questioning thoroughly discredited the witnesses for the prosecution. The jury failed to agree, and the rest of the accused were acquitted. The four who were sentenced to death had their sentences commuted to transportation to New South Wales.

This trial and the agrarian violence that lay behind it was the subject of Canon SHEEHAN's novel, *Glenanaar* (1905).

Done up to the veins of nicety. *See* VEINS OF NICETY, DONE UP TO THE.

Donnán (d.617). A disciple of COLUM CILLE, and founder of a monastery on EIGG *c*.600. At Easter 617 he and 50 other monks were massacred by 'sea-rovers'. These may have been Scandinavian and could have been a 'hit-squad' hired by local Picts to show their disapproval of the Irish. Tradition says that the culprit was a local chieftainess who wanted these holy men away from her islands. The monks were herded into the refectory and the building was set on fire. Donnán is venerated throughout western Scotland and he has given his name to the castled island of Eilean Donan in Loch Duich.

Donn Cuailnge. *See* BROWN BULL OF CUAILNGE.

Donnelly, Dan (1786–1820). Pugilist. He was born in Dublin and like his father became a carpenter. His greatest success was in 1815, when he defeated Cooper, the reigning English bare-knuckle champion, in 11 rounds; the venue, in the Curragh of Kildare, has since been called Donnelly's Hollow. Donnelly earned vast sums by the standards of the time – 100 guineas was his fee for one early fight – but he drank and spent the money just as quickly. He owned several public houses in Dublin, returning to fighting in England when he needed to boost his flagging fortunes. He died at home in Dublin, of a sudden chill, on 17 February 1820. Legend has it that he was buried in the common graveyard, Bully's Acre, in Dublin, that his body was snatched by medical students, and that a surgeon made a particular study of his arm, 'the longest arm in the history of pugilism'. A pub in Kilcullen, Co. Kildare, now claims to hold this arm, which is displayed in a glass case.

Donnybrook. A rowdy brawl – taking its name from DONNYBROOK FAIR.

Donnybrook Fair. A riotous fair held annually in what is now a suburb of Dublin city. Its charter was granted in 1204 and it reached its peak in the 18th century, when its primary purpose of selling goods was largely pushed aside to make way for a weeklong popular entertainment. It became synonymous with riot and public disorder tolerable, perhaps, in the rackety 1700s but ill-befitting Victorian Ireland. It was suppressed in 1855 and mourned as the lost 'Bartholomew' of Dublin. At least two poems entitled 'The Humours of Donnybrook Fair' celebrate it, the first of anonymous origin and dating from the late 18th century, the second written about 1820 by Charles O'Flaherty, a Dublin journalist:

'Tis there are dogs dancing, and wild beasts a-prancing,
With neat bits of painting in red, yellow and gold;
Toss-players and scramblers, and showmen and gamblers,
Pickpockets in plenty, both of young and of old.
There are brewers, and bakers, and jolly shoemakers,
With butchers, and porters, and men that cut hair;
There are mountebanks grinning, while others are sinning,
To keep up the humours of Donnybrook Fair.
ANON. (18th century)
When he came to the midst of the Fair
He was all in a paugh for fresh air,
For the Fair very soon
Was as full of the moon,
Such mobs upon mobs as were there,
Oh! rare.
So more luck to the sweet Donnybrook Fair.
CHARLES O'FLAHERTY (1794–1828)

Donsie. *See* DAUNCEY.

Doolin. A fishing village on the west coast of Co. Clare, from where boats leave for Inis Oírr, the smallest of the ARAN ISLANDS. It is famous for its traditional music, especially the SESSIONS in O'Connor's Pub on Fisher Street. The proprietor, Gus O'Connor (1926–2003), and his wife Doll were great supporters of musicians, notably the Russell brothers, Micho, Packie and Gussie. The RTÉ radio programme *Céilí House* was often recorded there.

Dooshie. A HIBERNO-ENGLISH word denoting someone exceptionally small and neat, especially a child or a woman.

Dooter. An Ulster word meaning to wander aimlessly, perhaps cognate with the English 'dodder'. Its use is not necessarily pejorative. Casual telephone calls often end with some such dismissive sentence as: 'Well. If you've no more crack I'll dooter on.'

DORA. The Defence of the Realm Act, which passed into law on 27 November 1914, was emergency legislation enabling the government to respond to threats to public security, for instance by substituting courts martial for jury trials. The executed leaders of the EASTER RISING of 1916 were court-martialled under this legislation. Other powers, such as the restricting of firearms and the right to carry out searches in designated areas, were particularly useful against the IRA during the Anglo-Irish War of 1919–21.
See also BONA FIDE.

Dorn (Irish, 'fist'). A HIBERNO-ENGLISH word (pronounced 'durn') for a fistful. It is still in common use: 'Give the child a dorn of sweets before you go.'

Dorsey or **Dursey.** A double line of earthworks in south Armagh, constructed about 100 BC, which takes its name from the Irish *doirse* ('doors'). It was traditionally held to be the gateway to Ulster, and the old coach road from Dublin to Armagh was taken to have run through the gaps.
See also BLACK PIG'S DYKE.

DORT. *See* DART, THE.

Dose. A useful and common pejorative term in HIBERNO-ENGLISH, meaning a 'tedious or gloomy' person: 'She stayed all morning to complain and she's a dose,' or a person who looks gloomy, tired or sick: 'You look a right dose today.' The word also means a bout of illness such as flu: 'I got a funny dose while I was on holidays.' In all its senses it is often used with the intensifier 'right'.

Dote. A common word in HIBERNO-ENGLISH, especially in Munster, meaning a pretty or appealing baby or child, or a cute object or building. The word is suggestive of the diminutive, but is often used in conjunction with the word 'little': 'She's a little dote.' The adjective or adverb 'dot(e)y' is also used: 'It's a dotey little house.' 'Dote' and 'dotey', which carry a connotation of intimacy, are more likely to be used by women. 'Dote' may also be used as a general vocative, for instance by a shop assistant as a replacement for 'dear' or 'love': 'Wait a minute there, dote, and I'll get you your change.' The word is presumed to derive from the fact that a dote is something that is doted on.

Double or **dooble.** The second run of POTEEN through the still to increase potency.
See also CALAMITY WATER; SINGLINGS; WRECK.

Downhill. The grand house and demesne conceived and built (1775–85) by the Earl Bishop, Frederick Augustus HERVEY, on a bare plateau above the sea on the north coast of Co. Derry. It was the earliest – and the most eccentrically sited – of the three palaces that Hervey built, the others being at Ballyscullion in the south of the county and at Ickworth in Suffolk. Though there were magnificent views from the cliff top (especially from the elegant folly known as the MUSSENDEN TEMPLE) the house was built with its back to the sea. (It was on the long strand below that the bishop's unfortunate clergy were required to take part in horse races.) The interior was magnificent, with a library and two-storey art gallery to house the many pieces that the acquisitive bishop brought back from his frequent continental tours (early Baedeker raids!). Much of the collection was lost in a fire in 1852 and the house was not restored until 1878. It was used as a military billet during the Second World War and is now derelict. Various interesting relics of the former grandeur still

survive, including the remains of a walled garden and the ornamental Lion Gate. The Bishop's Road, now a scenic route, was built to allow easier access to the demesne from Limavady.

Downing Street Declaration. An agreement between the Irish and British governments, formulated in 1993 and proclaimed on 15 December of that year. It owed a great deal to the affinity between Albert REYNOLDS and John Major (who had previously met as finance ministers) and was the first significant step forward on the tortuous road to peace in Northern Ireland.
See also ANGLO-IRISH AGREEMENT; GOOD FRIDAY AGREEMENT.

Downing Street Mortar Attack. An attack by the Provisional IRA on 7 February 1991 using a lorry containing primed mortars 230 m (250 yds) from Downing Street. One shell landed behind Number 10, blowing in the windows of the meeting room of the War Cabinet.

Downpatrick (Irish *Dún Pádraig*, '[St] Patrick's fort'). The county town of Down, population (1991) 8300, once known as Rathkeltair (*Ráth Cealtchair*, 'Cealtchar's ring fort') from the rath on the hill where the cathedral (now Protestant) for the Down diocese is built. It became the chief castle of the Anglo-Norman adventurer John de Courcy in 1177, and is the alleged triple burial site of Ireland's chief saints, PATRICK, BRIGID and COLUM CILLE.
See also IN BURGO DUNO TUMULO.

Down Survey. A survey made in 1654 of confiscated Irish land and set 'down' in maps and charts (hence its ambivalent title) by Dr William Petty (1623–87), physician-in-chief to the Cromwellian army. The maps, drawn by parishes, were the most accurate at that date, and Petty's *Hiberniae Dilineatio* (1685), on a scale of 12 Irish miles to the inch, was used as the standard until the ORDNANCE SURVEY.

'Down Went McGinty'. An unrespectable but very popular Irish-American bar-room song

(1889). Its composer was a performer called Joe Flynn, who flourished in burlesque in the 1880s and 1890s and is remembered chiefly for this one piece. It enshrined all the undesirable characteristics of the stage Irish-American (*see* STAGE-IRISH), and was so popular it spawned a flood of even worse 'McGinty' songs. It gave Preston Sturges (1898–1959) the title for his mordant film *The Great McGinty* (1940), about an Irish tramp who becomes governor of a state. The song tells of the punishment self-inflicted by McGinty to win a $5 bet that a younger colleague could not carry him to the top of 'a very high stone wall'. He lets go 'never thinking just how far he'd have to drop'. The downward spiral continues until he commits suicide when his wife, 'Bedaley Ann' runs off with their child:

> Down went McGinty to the bottom of the say
> And he must be very wet
> For they haven't found him yet;
> But they say his ghost comes round the docks
> Before the break of day …
> Dress'd in his best suit of clothes.

Dowth. *See* NEWGRANGE.

Doyle, Jack. *See* GORGEOUS GAEL, THE.

Doyle, James Warren. *See* JKL.

Doyle, Lynn (1873–1961). The pseudonym of the Ulster humorist, novelist and dramatist, Leslie Alexander Montgomery, who was born on 5 October 1873 in Downpatrick, Co. Down, the 'Ballygullion' of his many comic stories written between 1908 and 1951. These feature the omniscient narrator, a character that owes something to Flurry Knox of the Irish RM stories of SOMERVILLE AND ROSS. Montgomery's account of Ulster life and of the misadventures of 'wee Mr Anthony', a staid Protestant solicitor, touches gently on sectarian differences – one of his many books was called *Green Oranges* (1947) – but is too genial to go very deep. Montgomery became a clerk with the Northern Bank at the age of 16 and stayed with the firm until his retirement in 1934, having been manager of the branch

at Skerries, Co. Dublin, for 28 years: His pseudonym (originally Lynn C. Doyle, from the wood preservative) was considered necessary for a bank official in 1914 when his play *Love and Land* was put on by the ULT in the Grand Opera House in Belfast.

Doyle, Roddy (b.1958). Novelist and playwright. He was born in Dublin and educated at Sutton Christian Brothers school and University College Dublin. He taught in Kilbarrack (the 'Barrytown' of his comic and dark fiction), and this contact with young north Dublin undoubtedly contributed to the demotic accuracy of the dialogue in his novels and in the stark and violent four-part teleplay *Family* (1994). The novels of his Barrytown trilogy, *The Commitments* (1989), *The Snapper* (1990) and *The Van* (1991), a funny and scabrous account of contemporary working-class Dublin, were all successfully filmed. *PADDY CLARKE, HA, HA, HA* deals with a bright middle-class lad's response to parental separation, and *The Woman Who Walked into Doors* (1996) is a prose version of *Family*. A historical novel, *A Star Called Henry*, was published in 1999. Doyle has also written children's books and an engaging memoir of his parents, *Rory and Ita* (2002).

'Do you want your old lobby washed down, Con Shine?' The title and chorus of an anonymous comic ballad in waltz tempo that became a catchphrase when recorded by Brendan Shine in 1979 (it was a major hit in 1980). However, experts would say that the version by Cork singer Jimmy Crowley is more authentic, the song being said to originate in Cork.

> Do you want your old lobby washed down, Con Shine?
> Do you want your old lobby washed down?
> When I goes to court, I says here goes for sport,
> Do you want your old lobby washed down?

Dozen of work, a. An expression from the shirt-manufacturing industry in Derry; whole shirts or individual components of shirts were made up into bundles of 12 for costing purposes.

As they were carried from store to bench they could constitute a formidable weapon: 'If you don't get outa my way, I'll blind you wi' this dozen of work!'

Dracula. *See* UNDEAD, THE.

Draft Riots. The response to the introduction of conscription in 1863 during the American Civil War. All unmarried men under the age of 45 and married men between the ages of 20 to 35 were liable for service with the Union armies, but those who could afford it might be granted a waiver on the payment of $300. There was resistance to the draft throughout the northern states, but the most serious violence was in New York City. The rioters were mainly immigrant Irish workers who were too poor to pay the indemnity and came out on strike. Their work was taken over by blacks, who had drifted into the city after emancipation and were considerably poorer than the Irish. When violence broke out 11 of them were lynched and a black orphanage was set on fire. The trouble began on Monday 13 July when about 1000 workers, mostly Irish, marched to the draft office, calling at City Hall, crying 'rich man's war, poor man's fight'. The trouble escalated and there were lynchings, looting, arson and deaths. The violence lasted until the Thursday, in spite of a largely ineffectual personal intervention by Archbishop John Hughes. It was not until five regiments were withdrawn from Gettysburg and cannon and Gatling guns were turned on the rioters that order was restored. The death toll was put at 105, many of them Irish. The waiver clause was abolished by Congress in 1864, and anti-draft riots were never again allowed to get out of control.

Dragging down some noble stag. The remark recorded in *Conversations with Goethe* (1837) by Johann Peter Eckermann (1792–1854), concerning the Duke of WELLINGTON's earlier stand against CATHOLIC EMANCIPATION. The great German, who regarded the Iron Duke as the saviour of Europe because of Waterloo,

had only a tenuous grasp of Irish history: 'The Irish seem to me like a pack of hounds, always dragging down some noble stag.' W.B. Yeats used the phrase in *Autobiographies* (published 1955) to describe the hue and cry after the Parnell crisis.

Draperstown. A village in Co. Derry, situated on land granted to the Drapers Company of London in the early years of the 17th century in what was originally known as the Cross of Ballynascreen. Unlike the Salters Company who built Salterstown (later incorporated in Magherafelt), the company showed little interest for two centuries, but in 1818 they named the site and in 1830 built the village around a triangular green to a plan by the company's surveyor, W.J. Booth.

Drapier's Letters, The. The letters written (1722–5) by Jonathan Swift (*see* DEAN, THE), under the pen name 'M.B. Drapier', when Dean of St Patrick's, as part of a broad campaign against the patent granted to William Woods, a Wolverhampton manufacturer, to mint copper coins for Ireland. The patent, originally granted to the Duchess of Kendal, the mistress of George I, was withdrawn in 1725.

Dreary Steeples. The Irish question as envisioned by Winston Churchill (1874–1964) in a speech in the House of Commons in 1922:

> The whole map of Europe has been changed ... The modes of thought of men, the whole outlook on affairs, the grouping of parties, all have encountered violent and tremendous changes in the deluge of the world. But as the deluge subsides and the waters fall short, we see the dreary steeples of Fermanagh and Tyrone emerging once again. The integrity of their quarrel is one of the few institutions that has been unaltered in the cataclysm which has swept the world. That says a lot for the persistency with which Irishmen on the one side or the other are able to pursue their controversies.

Dreech. The Ulster equivalent of the Scots 'dreich' (with the same pronunciation), meaning 'dull', 'long drawn out', dreary'.

Dreich. *See* DREECH.

Drennan, William (1754–1820). United Irishman, physician and poet, remembered especially for 'The EMERALD ISLE'. Drennan was born in Belfast on 23 May 1754 and became a doctor, settling to a practice in Dublin in 1789. He joined the Society of UNITED IRISHMEN and wrote their original prospectus. Arrested in 1794 he was acquitted of treason, ably defended by John Philpot CURRAN, but played no further part in politics. He married a wealthy Englishwoman in 1800, moved to Belfast in 1807, began the *Belfast Monthly Magazine* (1808–15) and was one of the founders of INST. His liberal instincts – demonstrated in the 'The Wake of William Orr', his still anthologized ballad, about a Co. Antrim farmer (1766–97) who was hanged for administering the United Irish oath to two soldiers – did not necessarily extend to Catholics. He died in Belfast on 5 February 1820.

> Here our murdered brother lies
> Wake him not with women's cries;
> Mourn the way that manhood ought;
> Sit in silent trance of thought.
>> 'The Wake of William Orr', in *Fugitive Pieces in Verse and Prose* (1815)

See also YELVERTON'S ACT.

Dress Code. The 28th law passed in the Dublin Parliament by Henry VIII in 1536–7 and reissued in May 1550 during the reign of Edward VI, attempted to regulate not only hairstyles (*see* GLIB) but also clothing. The inhabitants were forbidden to

> … use or wear any shirt, smock, kerchief, bendel, neckerchief, mocket or linen cap, coloured or dyed with saffron, nor yet use nor wear in any their shirts or smocks above seven yards of cloth, to be measured according to the King's standard, and also that no woman use or wear any kyrtle or coat tucked up, or embroidered or garnished with silk, or couched or laid with usker, after the Irish fashion.
>> (A *bendel* was a scarf or fillet, a *mocket* a bib or kerchief, and an *usker* (Irish *uscar*) an ornament or jewel.)

See also IRISH MANTLE; SAFFRON.

'Drill, Ye Tarriers, Drill'. The most famous song of the literally loud-mouthed MAGGIE CLINE, who specialized in 'rough' bar-room songs. She was born of Irish parents on 1 January 1857 in Haverhill, Massachusetts, and in her heyday turned the scale at 104.5kg (230 lb). With her deep contralto she could be heard above the din of the bars and vaudeville theatres where she sang such 'male' songs as 'DOWN WENT MCGINTY' and 'Throw Him Down McCloskey'. Her audiences were often composed of the very people she sang about. 'Tarriers' were the Irish excavation workers, the transatlantic equivalents of the 'navvies' who dug Britain's canals. The song had also been sung (and spoken) by a Thomas Casey, who had been briefly a 'tarrier' himself, but both composer and lyricist remain anonymous. The last verse jokingly adumbrates the primitive working conditions and the resentment at 'foreign' infiltration. Big Jim Goff had been blown 'a mile in the air' with 'a premature blast':

> When payday next it came around
> Poor Jim's pay a dollar short, he found.
> 'What for?' says he; then came this reply
> 'You were docked for the time you were up in the sky.'
> (*Spoken*: More oatmeal in the bucket, McCue. What's that you're reading, Duffy? The *Staats Zeitung*?)
> *Chorus*:
> Then drill, ye tarriers, drill,
> Drill, ye tarriers, drill.
> Oh it's work all day without sugar in your tay
> When you work beyant on the railway,
> And drill, ye tarriers, drill!

Cline survived until 11 June 1934, dying in Fairhaven, New Jersey, USA at the age of 77.

Drink Lough Erne dry, to. A phrase meaning to have a great capacity for consumption of liquid, usually taken to mean alcohol. A phrase of similar meaning is 'to drink the cross off a donkey'.

Drink of water or **long drink of water, a.** A pejorative term suggesting a man too slender for his height, with a connotation of weakness and insipidity.

Drink taken, to have. A phrase often used comically or euphemistically to mean really drunk, and featuring in rural courts as a plea for mitigation: 'My client had drink taken, Your Honour.'

Dríodar. An Irish word for 'waste', 'dregs', commonly used in HIBERNO-ENGLISH to mean the dregs or residue of a liquid, or drops left in the bottom of a cup: 'There's nothing but old *dríodar* left. I'll make a fresh pot of tea.' *Dríodar an áil* means 'the runt of the litter'.

Driongán. An Irish word for something that is worthless or unwieldy, used in the HIBERNO-ENGLISH of Munster to mean old items of apparel, pieces of equipment without much value or general bits-and-pieces, as in, 'Wait here a minute until I put on my old *driongáns*.'

Drisheen. A Cork delicacy, traditionally sold in the ENGLISH MARKET. It is a type of smooth white pudding normally made from sheep's blood and oatmeal and packed in the intestine of the sheep.

Drogheda, Siege of. The first action in CROM-WELL's Irish campaign, remembered for its brutality. Cromwell's army turned north-wards the month after his arrival in Dublin and attacked the town of Drogheda with artillery on 9 September 1649. It was defended by a CONFEDERATE CATHOLIC garrison under Sir Arthur Aston – it had been won from the Parliamentarians the previous year – but fell to the Cromwellians on 11 September. In the aftermath of the siege it is estimated that about 3500 people were killed, 1000 of them civilians. The massacre was justified by Crom-well as a reprisal for the killing of Protestants during the REBELLION OF 1641 in Ulster, and *pour encourager les autres,* as he moved on other towns held by the Confederates, includ-ing Wexford (October 1649); *see* BULLRING, THE.

Drogheda weavers. A phrase (after the town in Co. Louth) used to describe a workman who has run short of some necessary material:

Idle for want of weft, like the Drogheda weavers.

Drogheda was known for the cloth called DRUG-GET, and was famous as a weaving town in the 19th century; however, at times there were more weavers than there was work to give them – hence the expression.

Droll. A word used in HIBERNO-ENGLISH with a greater variety of meanings than in standard English: it may mean 'funny' or 'humorous', but is likely to suggest a kind of low-key, ironic or indirect humour. The term is also used pejoratively to describe a person eccentric in appearance or manner, shy or reclusive: 'All that family are very droll; they never left the house when they were young.'

Drone, The. With THOMPSON IN TÍR NA NÓG (its regular playbill companion) the most suc-cessful of the plays generated by the Ulster Lit-erary Theatre (ULT), though it had its première in the ABBEY THEATRE in 1908. Written by Rutherford Mayne, it became so popular with amateurs that when an actor waiting for the curtain confessed to another that he was un-sure of his lines he was consoled with the words: 'Don't worry. If you need a prompt the audience will give it.'

A kitchen comedy, *The Drone* contains all the trusted ingredients: a rural setting, a ripe mixture of Ulster wit and exasperation, a threatened breach-of-promise suit, a pair of young lovers, and (quite literally) a *deus ex machina* in that the eponymous drone's inven-tion saves the day. The contrast between John Murray, the hardworking, kindly Co. Down farmer, and his feckless inventor brother Daniel, who lives free in his house, is a comedic hint of Mayne's recurring preoccupation with the clash between the practical and the aes-thetic more obvious in an earlier play, *The Turn of the Road.* This had opened in Belfast in 1906 and gave to Ulster theatre its flagship character, Robbie John. It is set in a farm kitchen of the period and deals with the strains imposed upon farm-kitchen mores by Robbie John's talent as a violinist and his duties as a farmer's son. His decision to stick by the fiddle causes his father to drive him away from home.

Rutherford Mayne was the pseudonym of Samuel John Waddell, the brother of the classical scholar, Helen WADDELL. He was born in Japan in 1878, the son of an Ulster academic and Presbyterian minister. Educated at INST and Queen's College, he became an engineer and was also a fine actor. He became chief inspector for the Irish LAND COMMISSION, but found time to write a dozen plays including *The Troth* (1908), *Red Turf* (1911), *Peter* (1930) and *Bridgehead* (1934). He died in 1967 at his home in Dalkey, Co. Dublin.

Drontheim. A long (6–8.5 m / 20–28 ft) double-ended open clinker-built fishing yawl that was once common about the north coast of Ireland and especially in Donegal. Also known locally as druntons, they were first imported from Norway, the name being a corruption of Trondheim, the port of origin.

Drop[1]. A word used in combination with a pejorative adjective to describe a genetic predisposition to an undesirable quality, as in 'LOW DROP' or 'bad drop'.

Drop[2] (Irish *braon*). A half-glass (half-measure) of whiskey. The word is also used euphemistically, as in, 'He takes a drop' (i.e. he's a heavy drinker). The DUBLINERS ballad group, known for their association with hard liquor, released a celebrated album called *A Drop of the Hard Stuff* (1967).

Dropeen. A word used commonly in HIBERNO-ENGLISH, meaning a small drop, formed by combining 'drop' with the diminutive suffix -een (Irish, *ín*).

Droppin' Well, The. The scene of an INLA atrocity in the village of Ballykelly, Co. Derry, on 6 December 1982. The pub disco was close to a large British base at Walworth and used regularly by British personnel and their families. The no-warning bomb claimed 17

lives: 11 soldiers and 6 civilians, mostly from the village. It was the worst incident of the TROUBLES to occur in Co. Derry. The INLA insisted that their general warning about pubs serving members of the occupying forces was sufficient, but the incident was generally condemned.

Drostan (d.*c.*610). A monk of IONA who became abbot of the monastery of Deer, in Aberdeenshire, Scotland, thought to have been the last foundation of COLUM CILLE. It survived until the 13th century, when it became Cistercian. The saint has a holy well at Aberdour on the Firth of Forth, and is a patron of the Scottish church. His feast day is 11 July.

Drown the shamrock, to. To celebrate St Patrick's Day by drinking a great deal. The phrase seems more Oirish than Irish, but it is certainly the case that the national feast day has always been a great day for drinking, offering as it does a respite during the penitential season of Lent.

Drugget. A type of cloth woven of woollen and flaxen thread; perhaps from the name of the town of Drogheda where the material was made.

Druids. The historical, quasi-religious class, both of men and women, who were the educated elite of Celtic society. Their knowledge of philosophy, history, medicine, law and natural science made them respected and even feared. *Draoi*, the modern Irish word for druid, is cognate with *draíocht* ('magic'). In myth they appear as wizards. It is clear that druids had considerable power both over individuals and over the regulation of society, and it is speculated that they may have engaged in human sacrifice. Druidic ritual was not preserved precisely because druids were superseded by Patrician Christianity, which, however, was characterized by accommodation with them. In recent years they have come to be regarded as benign high priests of Celtic spirituality. John O'Donohue, author of *ANAM CARA*, who was himself an ordained

Catholic priest, refers to ministers of religion like himself as 'druids', claiming an essential continuity of spiritual beliefs.

Druid Theatre. A theatre company formed in Galway in 1975 by Garry Hynes, Mick Lally and Máire Mullen. It has had its own theatre, Druid Lane Theatre, since 1979. The driving force has been producer Garry Hynes, who approached classic works of Beckett, Boucicault, Synge and Wilde with new vision and energy. The company also revived neglected works, and mounted new plays by Tom MURPHY, who wrote *BAILEGANGAIRE* (1975) specifically for them, and Vincent Woods (b.1960), notably *At the Black Pig's Dyke* (1992). Many of Druid's productions have been commercial successes, touring throughout Ireland and with runs in the ABBEY THEATRE and other Dublin theatres.

Druimceatt or **Druim Cett.** The site of an important convention held in 575, according to the ANNALS OF THE FOUR MASTERS. The place is taken to be the Mullagh, a grassy knoll 1.5 km (1 mile) south of Limavady, Co. Derry. It was the occasion of a rare visit home by COLUM CILLE, who was to act as honest broker between Aedan, the king of DÁL RIATA, and the Irish HIGH KING, Aed.

The discussion was about complicated dynastic matters, and no one is quite sure what was decided. Tradition has it, however, that it was at Druimceatt that Colum Cille, himself a poet, defended the FILID, the poet-class who, it was claimed, had become too numerous and turbulent. Among many other examples of their insolence was the demand for

> ... the gold bodkin that fastened the royal robes under the king's neck and was esteemed so sacred and unalienable, that it was carefully delivered from one prince to another ...
>
> SEATHRÚN CÉITINN (Geoffrey Keating): *Foras Feasa ar Éirinn* ('the general history of Ireland', completed 1634)

Things had got so bad that it was proposed that they be expelled from Ireland. Colum Cille reminded the representative assembly that the poets were the repositories of knowledge and that too much would be lost by their expulsion. They were allowed to stay under stringent new rules that dealt with numbers and recruitment:

> This agreement between St Cullum Cill [sic] and the king of Ireland is thus transmitted to us, in the lines of the old poet, called Maolruthuin:
> The poets were secur'd from banishment
> By Collum Cill who by his sage advice,
> Softened the king's resentment, and prevailed
> That every Irish monarch should retain
> A learned poet; every provincial prince,
> And lord of cantred, were by right allowed
> The same privileges and honour.
>
> Ib.; translated by John O'Donovan

The legend almost certainly glosses another example of the superseding of the older Celtic society: the older semi-priestly caste had to give way to the ministers of the new church. After Druimceatt the poets found their place in Irish society, but it was an acquiescent one and they had lost their semi-magical word power.

Drumcollogher Fire. A fire (5 September 1926) in the cinema in the village of Drumcollogher, Co. Limerick, in which 48 local people died. The fire began when a candle set the film reel alight (the film was *The Ten Commandments*) and quickly spread through the wooden building, which was built over a grain barn. An international relief fund raised £12,000, much of which went to support the 53 children who were left without providers because of the fire. The victims were buried in a communal grave in the local churchyard.

Drumcree Stand-offs. A series of confrontations in Portadown between ORANGE ORDER marchers returning from a service in Drumcree parish church on the Sunday preceding the TWELFTH OF JULY celebrations and the Nationalist residents of the Garvaghy Road, the traditional route of the 'walk'.

Though the return route was always contentious, serious trouble did not begin until 9 July 1995 when the RUC blocked the road and the marchers refused to disperse or take an alternative route. Eventually an uneasy compromise was reached and the marchers were allowed to walk silently down the road, although the triumphalist behaviour of Ian PAISLEY and David TRIMBLE at the scene helped to harden the residents' resolve.

During the year that followed attempts were made to broker an accommodation between marchers and Garvaghy Road residents, but without success. The 1996 stand-off on 7 July followed the same pattern, but widespread civil disturbances – including blocked roads, rioting, hijacking of vehicles and arson – during 9–11 July caused Sir Hugh Annesley, head of the RUC, to reverse his decision and to allow the RUC to force the marchers down the road. The result was equally serious disorder in Nationalist areas.

In 1997 the army and the RUC sealed off the road and allowed the marchers to walk silently through the estate. In the 36 hours that followed there were 584 attacks on the security forces, 691 petrol-bomb incidents and 15 gun and bomb attacks on the RUC.

In 1998 the PARADES COMMISSION insisted on a re-routing, and the army and police secured all access to the road with a steel barrier. The deaths of three Catholic children in a sectarian firebomb attack in Ballymoney were blamed on the heightened emotions over Drumcree; revulsion at this act caused many of the protestors to leave the scene.

Drumcree stand-offs continue each year as the return march continues to be re-routed and all attempts at finding a solution fail. Some believe the adamantine insistence of the Portadown Orangemen brings the order into even greater disrepute and seriously damages the institution, and millions of pounds are spent yearly maintaining the Parades Commission's instructions.

Drumlin (Irish *druim*, 'back', 'ridge'). An ice-age geological feature, found in the so-called 'Ulster Drumlin Belt', especially counties Leitrim, Cavan, Monaghan and Fermanagh. Drumlins often accompany lakes, which are formed in the hollows between them. They are small hills, elongated in the direction in which the glacier that deposited them was flowing and look rather like inverted spoons, although a drumlin landscape is more commonly referred to as 'basket of eggs' topography. A typical drumlin is about 30 m (100 ft) high, 150 m (500 ft) long and 60 m (200 ft) wide. It usually has a blunt nose pointing in the direction from which the ice approached, but is tapered more gently at the other end. Most drumlins have a base of gravel and sand, and a cap of glacial sediment. A look at the placenames of the towns of Leitrim alone will reveal the influence of drumlins: Drumahair, Dromad, Drumkeeran, Drumshanbo, Drumsna. There are hundreds of such placenames in the Drumlin Belt.

Drumm, James (1896–1974). Chemist and industrial technologist. He was born in Co. Monaghan on 25 January 1896. While professor of chemistry at University College Dublin he developed a type of battery that was capable of being very highly charged. The Great Southern Railway Company became interested in using them to power rolling stock, and two 'Drumm trains' travelling 130 km (80 miles) at 75 kph (47 mph) on a single charge and capable of carrying 130 passengers ran on the now disused Harcourt Street–Bray line between 1930 and 1950. Government support was withdrawn in 1940, and a promising project never properly developed. Drumm died on 18 July 1974.

Drumm, Máire (1920–76). Republican activist. She was noted when vice-president of Provisional SINN FÉIN (1972–6) for the inflammatory nature of her speeches in urging people to join the IRA. When Ruairí Ó BRÁDAIGH was arrested she became acting president of Sinn Féin (1971–2). Arrested several times during the 1970s, she resigned her position in Sinn Féin in October 1976 due to failing health. On 28 October, while a patient in the Mater Hospital in Belfast, she was shot dead by two UVF gunmen dressed as doctors.

Drummond, Thomas (1797–1840). Under-secretary for Ireland. He was born in Edinburgh, educated at Edinburgh University and joined the Royal Engineers. He initially achieved fame as the inventor of the 'Drummond limelight', which enabled surveyors to take measurements at times of poor visibility or inclement weather. He first came in Ireland in 1824 as a member of the ORDNANCE SURVEY team, and while he worked in rural areas he observed the appalling living conditions of the peasantry.

Drummond then brought a constructive and enlightened attitude to the position of under-secretary, which he held 1835–40, a period of TITHE WARS and other agrarian disturbance, implementing the measures agreed between Daniel O'CONNELL and the Whig government in what was known as the LICHFIELD HOUSE COMPACT. Drummond had little sympathy for landlords, famously pointing out to Tipperary magistrates that, 'Property has its duties as well as its rights; to the neglect of these duties in time past is mainly to be attributed that diseased state of society in which such crimes can take their rise.' By appointing stipendiary magistrates, who were independent of landlords, and reforming the collection of tithes in an act of 1838, he took some of the heat out of the Tithe War. He also passed an Irish Constabulary Act in 1836 that encouraged Catholics to enter the police force, and contributed to the establishment of the Poor Law in Ireland.

Drummond died in office after suffering some years of ill-health, and is buried in Mount Jerome cemetery in Dublin. What are said to have been his last words are inscribed on his gravestone:

> Bury me in Ireland,
> Land of my adoption.
> I have loved her well
> And served her faithfully.

Drumm train. *See* DRUMM, JAMES.

'Drunken Thady'. *See* BARD OF THOMOND, THE.

Druth. A HIBERNO-ENGLISH word for 'thirst', used in phrases such as: 'I'm gasping with the druth' (very thirsty). The word derives from 'drought'.

Dry money. A HIBERNO-ENGLISH phrase for readily available money, liquid assets.

Dry stone walls. A feature of the landscape of the west of Ireland, especially the BURREN and the ARAN ISLANDS. Stones were removed from the fields and skilled craftsmen constructed miles of walls with no mortar or other holding agent. In the Burren, houses, roofs and furniture were made of limestone flags, with upright flags being used for boundary walls. In the 19th century Cornelius O'Brien, an MP for Clare, won a bet by showing that his tenants could build a flag wall a mile long, a yard high and an inch thick by hand overnight, a task considered impossible.

Duanaire 1600–1900, An: Poems of the Dispossessed. An influential anthology (1981) created by the Irish-language poet and critic Seán Ó TUAMA and the English-language poet Thomas KINSELLA, featuring their own translations (unspecified as to which translator) of major Irish poems from the specified period, both literary and popular. It was published by the DOLMEN PRESS.

Dub. A native of Dublin, synonymous with JACKEEN but lacking the slightly dated, insulting feel of the latter. The term is used both by Dubliners themselves ('I'm a Dub') and to describe the Dublin GAA football team, which is often successful in championship matches, a context in which 'jackeen' is never used.

Dubhglas de híde. *See* HYDE, DOUGLAS.

Dubh Régles (Old Irish, 'black church'). A monastic church associated with the Columban foundation in Derry. Built at some time during the second half of the 6th century, probably *c*.590, it was burned twice, in 788 and again in 1166, but some ecclesiastical edifice remained on the site until plantation times, when an Anglican church was built on the site.

Dublin. The capital city of Ireland, called BAILE ÁTH(A) CLIATH in Irish. It is the seat of government, of most industries and commerce, contains the finest buildings and the richest cultural institutions. Although Ireland has traditionally considered itself a rural, agricultural country, by the end of the 20th century well in excess of a million people, nearly a third of the total population, lived in Dublin or its commuter belt.

Dublin was a VIKING settlement, originally a 9th-century LONGPHORT, and in succeeding centuries a trading centre. Before the Norman invasion of 1169 it was clearly regarded as a place of wealth and influence, supporting many churches and monasteries; so much so that in 1166 the Connacht king Ruaidrí Ua Conchobar (*see* LAST HIGH KING, THE) arranged for his inauguration not, as was traditional, in Tara, but in Dublin. When Dublin Castle (*see* CASTLE, THE) was built in the early 13th century it was clear that the town, shortly to become a city, was going to be the English centre of administration.

Dublin's golden age was the 18th century, when much of the city as we now know it, both buildings and streets, was laid out, although some of these fine Georgian houses in the later unfashionable northside were to become the worst tenement slums in Europe, even after the foundation of the state in 1922.

In the final decade of the 20th century the effects of the CELTIC TIGER and a very large population of young people led to Dublin becoming one of the 'fun' capitals of Europe, but in terms of infrastructure, especially transport, it lags far behind other European cities of its size.

> The City Dublyn, called Divelin by the English, and Balaclaigh (as seated on hurdles) by the Irish is the cheefe City of the Kingdome …
>
> FYNES MORYSON: *An Itinerary Containing His Ten Yeeres Travell* (1617)

> Dublin the beautie and eie of Ireland, hath beene named by Ptolome, in ancient time, Eblana. Some term it Dublina, others Dublinia, manie write it Dublinum, others of better skill name it

Dublinium. The Irish call it Ballee er Cleagh, this is, a towne planted upon hurdles. *For* the common opinion is that the plot upon which the civitie is builded, hath been a marish ground; and for that by the art or invention of the founder, the water could not be voided, he was forced to fasten the quake mire with hurdles, and on them build the citie.

> RICHARD STANIHURST: *De Rebus in Hibernis Gestis* in Raphael Holinshed's *Chronicles* (1577)

Dublin and Kingstown Railway. *See* WESTLAND ROW STATION.

Dublin and Monaghan Bombings. Linked atrocities associated in many peoples minds with the UWC (Ulster Workers Council) strike. On 17 May 1974 car bombs in central Dublin killed 25 people and a device in Monaghan killed 5, and of 150 people injured 3 died later of their injuries. Two of the three cars used in Dublin had been hijacked in Protestant areas of Belfast, but the UDA/UFF and the UVF denied involvement. Most people assumed that one or other of these groups was implicated and that British special operations forces were somehow involved. Investigation by the RUC and the GARDA SÍOCHÁNA produced no results and the issue continues to rankle. Several television programmes have been made about the events, and the bombings remain a mystery that will eventually require elucidation.

The long-awaited report by Judge Henry Barron set up in October 2000 was delivered to the Irish government on 29 October 2003 and made public on 11 December. He found that individual soldiers and police were probably involved, but that there was no evidence of collusion at senior level. He criticized the government of the day and noted that the forensic evidence and all the files had mysteriously disappeared. The relatives welcomed the report, but see it as a mere first step, and their campaign for a proper judicial inquiry continues.

'Dublin Bay'. A song lyric written by Helen Selina, Lady Dufferin (*see* HELEN'S TOWER) in appreciation of Dublin's magnificent bay, which has not unreasonably been compared with that of Naples. The lyric was published in *A Selection of the Songs of Lady Dufferin* (1895):

> O Bay of Dublin! My heart you're troublin';
> Your beauty haunts me like a fevered dream.
> Like frozen fountains that the sun sets bubblin'
> My heart's blood warms when I but hear your
> name.

Dublin Bombs. The detonation of two bombs on 1 December 1972 in central Dublin, killing two men and injuring 127 others. In the Republic the bombs were taken to be the work of British special operations. The atrocity contributed to the passage (by 69 votes to 22 at 4 a.m. on the following day) of the Offences against the State (Amendment) Bill because of the abstention of FINE GAEL deputies.

Dublin Castle. *See* CASTLE, THE.

Dubliners. A collection of short stories by James JOYCE, his first published prose work (1914). *Dubliners* is Joyce's take on the city of his birth. The dominant theme is middle-class, post-Parnellite paralysis, and the style is of its period. The occasional lushness of imagery is at times at variance with the nature of stories written 'with scrupulous neatness', as the author described them to his publisher Grant Richards. 'IVY DAY AT THE COMMITTEE ROOM' is an ironic tribute to the 'dead king' (Parnell), and the longest and closing story 'The DEAD' is a kind of epitome of the Ireland Joyce was sturdily rejecting.

Dubliners, The. A ballad and folk group that first performed for drinks in O'Donoghue's Pub in Merrion Row, Dublin, in 1962. The original members, all bearded, were Ronnie Drew (b.1934, vocalist), Barney McKenna (b.1939, fiddle and banjo), Luke KELLY (1940–84, vocalist) and Ciarán Burke (1935–88, guitar, tin whistle and harmonica), and they originally called themselves The Ronnie Drew Ballad Group after their lead singer. The story goes that it was Luke Kelly who suggested the name 'The Dubliners' in the back of a taxi on the way

to a gig in Howth, Co. Dublin; he was reading Joyce's DUBLINERS at the time. The group's first album, released in 1964, was called *The Dubliners with Luke Kelly*. In 1967 the single 'SEVEN DRUNKEN NIGHTS' was a major hit in Britain, and the group became popular performers there and in the USA as well as hugely successful in Ireland – their success due to the combination of the superb musicianship of McKenna and Burke, the talented gravel-voiced Drew and the superb vocalist Luke Kelly.

The line-up was fluid: John Sheahan (b.1939, fiddle and tin whistle) joined in 1964; Ciaran Burke left because of illness in 1974; Ronnie Drew was replaced by singer Jim McCann in 1974, but returned in 1979; Seán Cannon (b.1940) joined in 1982. Although feeling keenly the loss of Luke Kelly, who died in January 1984, the group continued to perform and record, and in 1987 a LATE LATE SHOW special marked their 25th anniversary. This show, which featured Christy MOORE and many other star performers, is remembered for the rendition of 'The Irish Rover' by The Dubliners and The POGUES – especially the combined voices of Ronnie Drew and Shane MCGOWAN. Drew himself closed the show with his trademark version of Brendan BEHAN's 'The Auld Triangle'. He left the Dubliners to pursue a solo career in 1995 and was replaced by Paddy Reilly of 'The FIELDS OF ATHENRY' fame. Barney McKenna is the only founder-member still performing with the group.

Dublin 4. The postal district number of the expensive and salubrious area of Ballsbridge, to the south of Dublin city centre. 'Dublin 4' has come to connote the sophisticated and opinionated inhabitants of that area, between whom and the PLAIN PEOPLE OF IRELAND there is perceived to be a great distance:

> ... a term to describe what was effectively a new
> class of people, whose principal characteristic
> was perceived as a stridently professed aversion
> to unreconstructed forms of Catholicism and
> nationalism, but in particular to Fianna Fail ...

people who, through their jobs in the media, the civil service and the professions, were in a position to influence the direction of society in an intravenous manner, and who were not shy about giving vent to their opinions at every available opportunity.

JOHN WATERS: *Jiving at the Crossroads* (1991)

'Dublin Jack of All Trades'. A popular 19th-century street (in every sense) ballad (*c.*1850) mentioning many of the significant places and occupations possible for the ingenious diversifier in the bijou city. In the ten verses the anonymous author mentions 42 occupations and their respective locations:

> In Summerhill a coacher, in Denzille Street a gilder,
> In Cork Street was a tanner, in Brunswick Street a builder,
> In High Street I sold hosiery, in Patrick Street sold all blades,
> So if you wish to know my name they call me Jack of all trades.

Dublin Metropolitan Police. *See* DMP.

Dublin Opinion. A humorous magazine that gently guyed the pretentiousness and inconsistencies of the Free State and the later forms of the developing country. It was begun in 1922, but did not take off until 1926 when Charles E. Kelly (1902–81) joined Thomas J. Collins (1894–1972) to co-edit. Kelly was a skilled artist and his political cartoons, especially of de Valera, were effective without savagery; de Valera was often seen in conversation with old statues of Queen Victoria as they compared notes on how things had changed. Others who shaped the character of the magazine were the Ulster artists Billy CONN (1895–1973) and Rowel Friers (1920–98). It was in its heyday (1925–60) a national institution, but was wound up voluntarily by its editors in 1968, by which time satire had become much more edged. An attempt to resurrect the magazine in 1987 proved vain.

Dublin Pipers Club (Na Píobairí Uilleann). A club for musicians and their pupils, based in Dublin's inner city. It was established in 1900, in the era of the CELTIC REVIVAL, and had a long history of cultural commitment. Although the club did not always have a formal existence or venue – at times of turbulence, such as the Anglo-Irish War, organizations that supported Nationalist culture were liable to be harassed – but it survived by meeting in the homes of members until it was revived by Leo ROWSOME in 1936. It was instrumental in establishing COMHALTAS CEOLTÓIRÍ ÉIREANN in 1951 and subsequently became the Leo Rowsome branch of that organization, continuing to teach the UILLEANN PIPES as well as other instruments.

Dublin Port and Docks Board. The body with responsibility for Dublin port. In May 1867 an act of Parliament reconstituted the Ballast Board of 1786 as the Dublin Port and Docks Board (the Ballast Board had itself succeeded the Ballast Office in 1786). The board was to have 25 members, including the lord mayor and three other members of the corporation, and representatives of business, ship owners and the COMMISSIONERS OF IRISH LIGHTS. It held its first meeting in January 1868. Later Port and Docks Acts changed the constitution of the board, as did the Harbour Act of 1946, which reduced the membership to 23.

Dublin University Magazine. A journal (1833–74) begun by a number of students and graduates of Trinity College Dublin to reflect the Irish Protestant and Unionist tradition. Its chief stimulus was reaction to CATHOLIC EMANCIPATION in 1829, and it maintained a strong opposition to Daniel O'CONNELL and his campaign for the repeal of the Act of UNION. Among its editors were Isaac BUTT, Charles LEVER and Sheridan LE FANU, who was proprietor from 1861. In spite of its uncompromising political stance and its conviction that Westminster's conciliation of Nationalists was undermining the loyal Unionist position (a complaint that still has an echo in 21st-century Ireland), its literary pages showed no bias and published work by James Clarence MANGAN, William CARLETON and John

O'DONOVAN alongside its more expected clients like Samuel FERGUSON, Caesar Otway, the proselytizer, and John Francis Waller (*see* 'SPINNING WHEEL, THE').

Dúchas. An Irish word meaning heritage, tradition or genetic predisposition. There is a famous Irish proverb, '*Briseann an dúchas tré shúile an chait*'('Nature breaks out through the eyes of a cat'). Dúchas was formerly the name of the Irish government's heritage service, the custodian of all the state's national monuments and parks. Dúchas is also the name of a traditional arts centre in Tralee, Co. Kerry, administered by COMHALTAS CEOLTÓIRÍ ÉIREANN.

Duck's meat. The hardened mucus in the eyes after sleep.

Dudeen (Irish *dúidín*, diminutive of *dúid*, 'stump'). A short-stemmed clay pipe.

Dufferin, Lady. *See* HELEN'S TOWER.

Duffy, Sir Charles Gavan (1816–1903). Journalist and patriot. He was born in Monaghan town, the son of a shopkeeper, on 12 April 1816, and was largely self-educated. From 1836 he worked as a journalist for the *Morning Register* in Dublin, thereafter on a new Belfast Catholic paper, *The Vindicator*, (1839–42). He was called to the Bar but did not practise in Ireland. In the summer of 1842 he returned to live in Dublin and met Thomas DAVIS and John Blake DILLON, both barristers, and with them he founded *The* NATION, the newspaper of the YOUNG IRELAND movement, which first appeared on 15 October of that year, its aim 'to create and foster public opinion in Ireland and to make it racy of the soil' (sic).

The paper was suppressed and Duffy, its editor, arrested in July 1848, ahead of the ill-considered rebellion of Smith O'Brien (*see* WIDOW MCCORMICK'S CABBAGE PATCH). When Duffy was released the following year he revived *The Nation* and became involved in the land-reform movement, founding the Tenant League with Frederick Lucas in 1850; he was

among the 40 MPs elected to Parliament for the league, a forerunner of the Irish Parliamentary Party, in 1852.

But when reform measures were blocked in the House of Lords, Duffy, who suffered from ill-health, emigrated to Australia, where he practised law in Victoria. He had a distinguished career of public service in his adoptive country: he became chief minister of Victoria in 1871 and was knighted in 1873. He moved to the south of France in 1880 and wrote several books, including a biography of Thomas Davis and an autobiography. He died in Nice on 9 February 1903 and is buried in GLASNEVIN CEMETERY in Dublin.

His son, George Gavan Duffy (1882–1951), practised as a lawyer in Dublin, and defended Roger CASEMENT; he was also a signatory of the TREATY of 1921 and, briefly, a CUMANN NA NGAEDHEAL minister.

Duffy, Louise Gavan (1884–1969). Patriot and educator, the daughter of Charles Gavan DUFFY. She was born in Nice and was one of the first women to attend University College Dublin, graduating in arts in 1911. She was a member of CUMANN NA MBAN and served in the GPO during the EASTER RISING of 1916. Her most enduring achievement was to found Scoil Bhríde, the first all-Irish school for girls, which survives as a GAELSCOIL in Ranelagh, Dublin.

Duffy's Circus. A term for a brief amorous encounter, originating in the wording 'For one night only' used on the posters for the circus. For rather more than a century, Duffy's Circus toured the country, staying for only a single night in the smaller rural towns. The term is still used, though its origin may not be known: 'I hardly remember him; it was only a Duffy's circus!'

Dúirt bean liom go ndúirt bean léi (Irish, 'a woman said to me that a woman said to her'). A term used in HIBERNO-ENGLISH to mean gossip or hearsay, especially of an unreliable nature. It is often used dismissively: 'That's only *dúirt bean liom go ndúirt bean lei*.'

Duke of Wellington, the. *See* WELLINGTON, ARTHUR WELLESLEY, 1ST DUKE OF.

Dul amú. An Irish verb meaning 'go astray', 'make a mistake', used as a noun in HIBERNO-ENGLISH to mean a stupid or misguided person. The word is usually applied to males, as in 'That fellow is a right *dul amú*.'

Dulse and yella man. The traditional specialities of the OULD LAMMAS FAIR. Dulse (*Rhodymenia palmata*) is a very tasty edible red seaweed and 'yella man' a lethal basalt-hard bright yellow toffee that used to be made at the fair. Dulse continues to be sold especially during the summer at seaside resorts.

Dún. *See* RING FORT.

Dún Aenghus. An Iron Age stone fort dramatically situated on the edge of a cliff on the southwest coast of Inis Mór, the largest of the ARAN ISLANDS. Below it the cliff drops 60 m (200 ft) sheer to the sea. In mythology it was described as having been been built by the FIRBOLGS who, after being defeated at the Battle of MAGH TUIREADH (Moytura), retreated to the far west of the country, Dún Aenghus being called after one of their chiefs. It is of the same type and period as the Grianán of AILEACH in Co. Donegal and STAIGUE FORT in Co. Kerry. It has four sets of defensive walls and beyond the third wall thousands of stones close together on the ground, forming a *chevaux-de-frise* (a defensive structure to stop cavalry).

Dunamaise, the Rock of (also spelt **Dunamase**). The ancient stronghold of the O'Mores, Gaelic chieftains in the area that is now Co. Laois. The 60-m (200-ft) high limestone fortification is situated 3 km (2 miles) from Portlaoise. It was marked on Ptolemy's map in the 2nd century AD, and the ruins of a 13th-century keep can still be seen on the rock. It was of great strategic as well as symbolic importance in a flat county. The county's new arts centre in Portlaoise is called the Dunamaise Centre.

Dunbar-Harrison Affair, the. In 1930 Letitia Dunbar-Harrison was appointed Mayo county librarian by the local appointments commission of the day. The Mayo Library Committee, a sub-committee of the county council, objected to her appointment on two grounds: that she was Protestant (she had studied at Trinity College Dublin) and that she had no Irish. When Mayo County Council refused to overrule its library committee, it was dissolved by the then minister for education, Richard MULCAHY. But the Catholic Church made clear its position that the people of Mayo had a right to a Catholic librarian, as did FIANNA FÁIL opposition leader Éamon de Valera, who said in the Dáil: 'I say the people of Mayo, where … over 98% of the population is Catholic, are justified in insisting upon a Catholic librarian.' Although Dunbar-Harrison was confirmed in the position, a boycott of libraries in the county made her position untenable and she was transferred to a library in Dublin. When Fianna Fáil came to power in 1932 the party reinstated the county council.

Dunbrody. The site of a large Cistercian abbey (now in ruins) in Co. Wexford, overlooking Waterford Harbour. The abbey was founded in 1170 by the Anglo-Norman lord Hervey de Montmorency, who was its first abbot.

Dunchadh (d.717). A saint who was abbot of IONA from 710 until his death. It was in the period of his rule that the Roman customs promulgated at the Synod of WHITBY in 664, such as the dating of Easter, were finally accepted by the Columban foundations. His feast day is 25 May.

Dun Emer Press. *See* YEATS, LILY.

Dungal. A scholar who left Ireland *c*.784 and lived as a recluse at St Denis, near Paris. After an eclipse of the sun in 810 he was asked by the Emperor Charlemagne to explain it. His letter, though still using the Ptolemaic system (with the earth as the fixed centre), shows independent astronomical observation. Either he or another Irishman of the same name was in northern Italy in the 820s. This man was made supervisor of education in the region by

Lothair I (795–855), the Holy Roman Emperor and grandson of Charlemagne. This Dungal was a kind of one-man Ofsted, to whom scholars from other schools would come for what we would nowadays call refresher courses. He left his library to COLUMBAN's abbey of BOBBIO where he ended his days, and, since it included a copy of the ANTIPHONARY OF BANGOR, it may be assumed that like the founder he was a pupil at COMGALL's Co.Down foundation.

Dungannon (Irish *Dún Geanainn*, 'Geanann's fort'). A town in southeast Co. Tyrone, population (1991) 8300. It is named after Geanann, the son of CATHBAD the druid. The site of the chief medieval fortress of the O'Neills, it retained its Nationalist aura even after it was planted by Arthur CHICHESTER. As such it was an appropriate place for the VOLUNTEER Dungannon conventions and for the title of Bulmer Hobson's DUNGANNON CLUBS.

Dungannon Clubs. The Nationalist movement launched in 1905 by Bulmer HOBSON and Denis McCullough (1883–1968), the name chosen as a tribute to the VOLUNTEERS. Unlike the IRB, which both men had joined, membership was open, attracting such constitutional Republicans as Robert LYND, who contributed articles and ideas for cartoons to the movement's journal, the *Republic*. Eventually the clubs became associated with SINN FÉIN.

Dún Laoghaire (Irish, 'Laoghaire's fort'). Dublin's major dormitory suburb, seaside resort, yachting centre and chief port for ferries between Britain and Ireland. Its population in the 1991 census was 190,000. Known originally as Dunleary, it became Kingstown to honour George IV who used it as his port of departure after his state visit to Dublin in 1821. The Laoghaire of its Irish name was a 5th-century king who built a fort there, of which no trace survives. It is the site of the FORTY-FOOT, the National Maritime Museum and the Martello tower where James Joyce once lived, and which features at the beginning of *Ulysses*; it is now a Joyce museum.

Dunlop, John Boyd (1840–1921). Inventor of the pneumatic tyre. He was born in Ayrshire, Scotland, and, after qualifying as a vet, set up a practice in Belfast in 1867. He developed the pneumatic tyre for the back wheels of the tricycle of his son, Johnny, in early 1888 and applied for a patent for his invention in July of that year: 'a hollow tyre or tube made of India-rubber and cloth, or other suitable material, said tube or tyre to contain air under pressure or otherwise and to be attached to the wheel or wheels in such a method as may be found most suitable.' Tyres of this type, popularly known as 'sausages', were used by the winner of the cycle races at the sports associated with Queen's College in the summer of 1888, and a Belfast firm, Edlin and Sinclair, began to sell the tyres the following year.

Dunlop moved to Dublin in March 1892, but he sold out his interest in the Dublin-based Pneumatic Tyre Company to his partner Harvey du Cros and retired from the board of Dunlop, as the company was by then called, in 1895. Although the Dunlop Rubber Company, under the management of du Cros *fils* Arthur (1871–1955), became a major international brand – with its headquarters in Coventry, the heart of UK bicycle manufacture and later car manufacture, and its own rubber plantation in Malaysia – John Boyd Dunlop had no shares in the enterprise at the time of this death. Dunlop was a major employer in Cork city until the 1980s.

Dunne, Ben. *See* BEN DUNNE KIDNAPPING; THANKS A MILLION, BIG FELLA.

Dunquin School. Dunquin, a small community in the far west of the west Kerry GAELTACHT, became famous when the FIANNA FÁIL government of Jack LYNCH and its minister for education, Pádraig Faulkner, outraged the local community and Irish-language enthusiasts by closing the school without consultation in the summer of 1970, claiming that the 23 remaining pupils did not constitute a viable unit and that they should be bussed to the nearest school, Ballyferriter. Local opinion mobilized, and at a meeting in Dunquin attended by language activists including Máirtín Ó CADHAIN it was resolved to keep the school open. For three years a committee raised funds nationally to pay an 'unofficial' although qualified teacher, Mícheál Ó Dubhshláine, until in 1973 the new coalition-government education minister Richard Burke, a fluent Irish speaker, reversed the decision of the previous government. In 2003 there was about the same number of pupils on the rolls as in 1970.

Dunsany, Lord (1879–1957). Writer and patron of the arts. Edward Martin Drax Plunkett, 18th Baron of Dunsany, was born in London on 24 July 1878, a nephew of Horace PLUN-KETT, and educated at Eton and Sandhurst, inheriting the Dunsany title and the family seat, Dunsany Castle, near Dunshaughlin, Co. Meath, in 1899. He became an officer in the Coldstream Guards and served in the Boer War. Among his early works were fantasy novels including *The Gods of Pegana* (1905), *The Sword of Welleran* (1908), *A Dreamer's Tales* (1910) and *Tales of Wonder* (1916), together with plays for the ABBEY THEATRE such as *The Glittering Gate* (1909) and *The Last Silk Hat* (1913). He was shot in the face near the Four Courts in Dublin during the EASTER RISING of 1916 as he went to report for duty with British forces. In later life he travelled widely and continued to produce an extensive body of work: poems, plays (many of them dealing with supernatural forces), novels, short fiction and memoirs. Sean O'FAOLAIN regarded him as a master of the short story. As a literary patron his best-known protégés were Francis LEDWIDGE, whom he discovered, and the short-story writer Mary LAVIN, who came to live in Co. Meath near his home. He supplied a foreword to her *Tales fom Bective Bridge* (1942). He died on 25 October 1957. Little of his prodigious output is currently known or read.

Dunt. *See* DINT.

Duodecimo Demosthenes. The nickname given to the Belfast politician Joe Devlin (*see* WEE

JOE) by Tim HEALY. The tribute celebrated his small stature and oratorical skills: duodecimo is the smallest size of book page, while Demosthenes (384–322 BC) was the greatest of the Athenian orators.

DUP. The Democratic Unionist Party, founded in 1971 by the Rev. Ian PAISLEY and Desmond Boal (b.1929), the MP for Shankill. Although Boal later left the party, Paisley remains as leader. Its main policy is absolute refusal to engage in any kind of power-sharing with Nationalists, and it has been strongly against any of the accommodations reached with them, including the ANGLO-IRISH AGREEMENT, the DOWNING STREET DECLARATION and the GOOD FRIDAY AGREEMENT. As a party it is greatly coloured by the charismatic energy of its leader, though in Peter Robinson (b.1948) it has an able second-in-command. Its showing in the Westminster elections suggested that because of its rural and working-class support it might supersede the UUP as the leading Unionist party in Northern Ireland. The elections held on 26 November 2003 fulfilled the prophecy: with 30 MLAs (Members of the Legislative Assembly), the DUP emerged as the party holding the largest number of seats; the UUP had 27.

Durationists. The name given to men enlisting in the Irish defence forces 'for the duration' of the EMERGENCY. They were also called E-men.

Dursey. *See* DORSEY.

Dwyer, Michael (1771–1815). United Irishman. He was born in the Glen of Imaal, Co. Wicklow. He took part in the REBELLION OF 1798 and afterwards he and a group of insurgents took refuge in the Wicklow hills, surviving there for five years, although there was a price of £1000 on Dwyer's head and £250 on each of his men. He was due to join in Robert EMMET's 1803 rising, but because the rising was premature he arrived too late. In December 1803 he gave himself up to the authorities and was sentenced to transportation to BOTANY BAY, where the governor was Captain William BLIGH. Because he was suspected of plotting another rebellion (*see* VINEGAR HILL²) he was sent for six months to the notorious NORFOLK ISLAND, thence to VAN DIEMEN'S LAND. Dwyer returned to Sydney and settled there after the departure of Bligh, rising to the position of high constable. He died there in 1815.

Dyddle. To provide an oral musical treatment or accompaniment – for instance for dancing in the absence of instruments or musicians – that is neither humming nor singing but the sound conveyed by the onomotopoeic 'dyddle'. In some parts of the country this skill is known as LILTING. Dyddling was also informally called puss-music or gob-music.

Dyddly-eye. A mocking phrase to convey the opinion that Irish traditional music is primi-tive, trivial or worthless, as in 'that dyddly-eye music'. It is a corruption of one of the sounds of dyddling (*see* DYDDLE) or LILTING.

Dyke, the. The popular name for the MARDYKE in Cork city.
See also BANKS, THE.

Dynamite War. A campaign originated in 1883 by the IRB in which significant targets in London were attacked with explosives. In 1884 four Fenians blew themselves up while trying to mine London Bridge, and on 24 January 1885 the campaign culminated in simultaneous explosions in the Tower of London, Westminster Hall and the House of Commons. Thomas CLARKE was one of the Fenians imprisoned for dynamiting. The dynamiters were the last Fenians to be released from prison, Clarke in 1898.

Earl Bishop, the. *See* HERVEY, FREDERICK AUGUSTUS.

Early, Biddy (1798–1874). Wise woman. She is famous in the folklore of Co. Clare as a healer, prophet and psychic, but little of verifiable fact is known about her. She is said to have been born in Faha, near Feakle in Co. Clare, to Thomas O'Connor and Ellen Early. Biddy kept her mother's name throughout her life because it was through her that she had received her gifts of healing and wisdom, although legend has it that she married six times. From the 1820s her reputation as a wise woman, especially as a healer of animals, began to spread. She had a famous blue bottle, which people believed had come from the SIDHE, and by looking into it she could tell the future. In 1828 Daniel O'CONNELL himself paid her a visit when he was contesting the Clare by-election. In 1840 she settled with a new husband in Kilbarron, Co. Clare, where she did not find favour with the local clergy. In 1865 she was finally charged with witchcraft in a court in Ennis, but the case against her was dropped for lack of evidence. Biddy herself maintained her Catholic faith and continued to say her ROSARY. She died in her home in Kilbarron in April 1874.

Eason and Son. A retail and wholesale bookseller and newsagent founded by Charles Malcolm Eason (1823–99) in 1886, when he bought the Dublin branch of W.H. Smith. Easons is now a major chain, with its flagship store in O'Connell Street, Dublin, and branches in almost every town and retail centre in Ireland, north and south.

Easter Duty. The requirement, also known as the eucharistic precept, placed upon all Catholics to visit the confessional and receive holy communion at Easter time in their own parishes. It was imposed to prevent neglect of the sacrament by various church councils from the 6th century, including the 4th Lateran (1215) and Trent (1545–63), and included in modern codes of canon law (1917 and 1983). Easter time was defined for Ireland as the period between Palm Sunday and Pentecost.

Easter Rising. The name given to the IRISH VOLUNTEER rebellion of 1916, because it began on Easter Monday, 24 April. It was a rebellion confined almost entirely to Dublin city (*see* ASHE, THOMAS), organized by a small caucus of IRB men within the Volunteers, notably Thomas CLARKE and Seán MCDERMOTT, and by James CONNOLLY and his IRISH CITIZEN ARMY, who collaborated with them. Because the general mobilization order for Sunday was cancelled by Volunteer leader Eoin MACNEILL, the number who participated was small.

The main rebel outpost was the GPO in O'Connell Street, from the balcony of which

Patrick PEARSE read the PROCLAMATION OF THE REPUBLIC. Various other strategic buildings, such as the College of Surgeons beside ST STEPHEN'S GREEN, the South Dublin Union and Boland's Mills, were also occupied. During the course of the week the British army threw a cordon around the city centre and attacked the rebel positions with artillery, forcing Pearse to offer an unconditional surrender on Saturday 29 April.

Between 3 May and 12 May, 15 rebel leaders were executed in KILMAINHAM JAIL. Although public opinion was initially hostile to the rebels, the executions of so many over so long a period aroused public sympathy. Among the rebels interned in FRONGOCH and other internment camps until the summer of 1917 there were many who would take part in the ANGLO-IRISH WAR of 1919–21.

East Link, the. The East Link Toll Bridge at the mouth of the River LIFFEY in DUBLIN, linking Fairview on the northside with Ringsend and Sandymount to the south. It was the third toll bridge in the history of Dublin (see HALF-PENNY BRIDGE). A public–private partnership project, the construction of the bridge began in April 1983 with design by McCarthy and Partners, and it was opened to the public on 24 October 1984. It was stipulated that shipping should still have access to the city quays, so the bridge has an opening span. The POINT concert venue is situated beside the East Link.

Eata (*fl.*7th century). The abbot of Melrose who, in spite of strongly supporting the Irish faction at the Synod of WHITBY, became Bishop of LINDISFARNE (Holy Island) after COLMÁN OF LINDISFARNE. He had been one of AIDAN's first neophytes when the monastery on Holy Island was founded. Recognizing the sanctity and diplomacy of Cuthbert, whom he had left at Melrose, he changed places with him and allowed him to continue with the task of reconciliation after Whitby.

Eating the gander. A pre-nuptial meal, normally in the bride's house, to allow the two parties to

a match (*see* MATCHMAKING) to get acquainted if they did not already know each other. The meal was a feature of traditional rural society until the mid-20th century. Roast gander and alcoholic drink were normally served, and there was dancing afterwards. The link between matchmaking and the rhythm of the agricultural year meant that in SHROVETIDE, when weddings took place, the geese were already hatching and the gander was redundant. *See also* GANDER².

Echo boys. The name given to the boys and youths who sold the evening paper published by the *Cork Examiner* (*see* PAPER, DE). They were part of the fabric of Cork city, calling their wares – '*Echo, Echo*, read all about it in the *Echo*' – on the streets, at road junctions and outside busy pubs.

Eclipse first. Part of the comment made at Epsom on 7 May 1769 by Dennis O'Kelly (*c.* 1720–87), the part-owner of the racehorse Eclipse. He is said to have remarked, 'Eclipse first, the rest nowhere,' when the horse won him a considerable sum of money. (Some historians give the occasion as the Queen's Plate at Winchester, but all agree about the now proverbial phrase.) Details of O'Kelly's early life are obscure, but he was born in Ireland and when he first came to London found employment as a sedan-chair carrier. He married Charlotte Hayes, a well-known lady of pleasure, and it was she who supplied the 650 guineas with which he purchased his share of the superlative animal. He later bought it outright for a further 1000 guineas, a large sum of money for the time. It was unbeaten in 18 races until October 1770 and its skeleton is preserved in the Royal Veterinary College. Its appropriate name came from its being born during a solar eclipse on 1 April 1764. Other horses that increased O'Kelly's wealth were Scaramouche and Gunpowder. O'Kelly himself sank into respectability by becoming a colonel of militia and obtaining the estate of the Duke of Chandos. Though he was unusually lucky as a gambler, his will provided that his heir should forfeit £400 for every bet he made. He died in his palatial house in Piccadilly on 28 December 1787.

Economic War. A trade war between Ireland and Britain that began in 1932 and lasted until 1938. The proximate cause was the withholding by the new FIANNA FÁIL government of Éamon de Valera of the LAND ANNUITIES that the Free State had contracted to pay the British exchequer in 1925, in the aftermath of the BOUNDARY COMMISSION report. To withhold the annuities was an election pledge of Fianna Fáil, strongly promoted by Republicans such as Peadar O'DONNELL.

In response the British government imposed special duties on Irish goods, particularly agricultural produce; the Irish government did the same for British products such as iron, steel, coal and machinery. The economic war caused great hardship, especially to farmers, who lost the main market for their livestock. It was said in rural areas that it was the first time that a wrapper came to be worth more than its contents. Farmers couldn't sell their stock, so day-old calves were skinned, the hides sold and the carcasses thrown away. It was during this period that someone trying to sell the IRISH PRESS in the fair field in Killarney received this reply from a local farmer, 'We've presses [i.e. cupboards] enough and nothing to put into them.'

The issues surrounding the economic war were gradually settled. The British were anxious that de Valera's new CONSTITUTION OF 1937 should not alter Ireland's position within the Commonwealth, especially since he had abolished the OATH OF ALLEGIANCE on coming to power in 1932. They were gradually reassured, and negotiations, mainly with Malcolm MacDonald, the Dominions secretary, resulted in an Anglo-Irish agreement in 1938 that ended the war.

Edenderry. A village in Co. Down, 6 km (4 miles) from Belfast. It is the usual site of the main Orange FIELD for the TWELFTH OF JULY celebrations.

Edgeworth, Maria (1767–1849). Novelist. She was the second of the 22 children of Richard Lovell EDGEWORTH, born in Oxfordshire to his first wife on 1 January 1767. Maria was educated in England but spent most of her life on the family estate in Edgeworthstown, Co. Longford, from early adulthood acting as secretary and companion to her adored 'critic, partner, father, friend' in his writings and his philanthropic and ameliorist endeavours on his estate, and after his death in 1817 managing the estate and supporting numerous half-siblings.

Maria's first publication, *Letters for Literary Ladies* (1795), advocated education for girls, and in 1798 she collaborated with her father on *Practical Education*, a Rousseauesque treatise. The rebellion of the same year saw a minor uprising ('a mixture of the ridiculous and the horrid' in Maria's words) in Edgeworthstown, but the Edgeworths escaped with nothing more than some broken windows, so high was their standing among their tenantry.

With the publication of her first novel CASTLE RACKRENT in 1800 Maria earned literary fame, and over the next 15 years she published 13 major works including *The Absentee* (1812), her novels implicitly criticizing members of her own class for lack of responsibility to the Irish. She edited her father's memoirs (published 1820), and earned the admiration of contemporary writers, including Wordsworth, Sir Walter Scott (who called her a 'very remarkable person ... the great Maria') and Lord Byron, all of whom visited her in Edgeworthstown. During the Great Famine she again proved herself a benevolent landlord, distributing food and raising relief money among her admirers in America. She died at home on 22 May 1849.

Edgeworth, Richard Lovell (1744–1817). Inventor and father of Maria EDGEWORTH. He was born in Bath and educated at Trinity College Dublin and Oxford. From his four marriages he had 22 children, of whom 19 survived infancy. He was an ameliorating landlord, improving cultivation systems and roads on his estates in Co. Longford and supporting CATHOLIC EMANCIPATION, legislative independence and the VOLUNTEERS. He voted against the Act of Union. His memoirs were published in 1820.

Ediphone. *See* IRISH FOLKLORE COMMISSION.

Eejit. The HIBERNO-ENGLISH pronunciation of 'idiot', a very common usage throughout Ireland. It is often used with intensifiers such as 'right', 'terrible', 'total', 'feckin', and pronounced with a good deal of emphasis: 'That fellow is a terrible eejit.' It is also pronounced 'eeja' in Dublin, with a typical dropping of the final consonant (*see* DELIRA AND EXCIRA).

Effin. A (slightly) euphemistic HIBERNO-ENGLISH (and British-English) version of 'fecking' (*see* FECK²), formed by articulating only the first letter of the word and adding the suffix 'in'. It is used as a derogatory adjective to strengthen a noun that may already be derogatory: 'effin EEJIT', 'the other effin driver'. Effin is also the name of a village in Co. Limerick, near the Tipperary border, a source of ribald jokes. For obvious reasons, 'Effin Effers' is an irreverant nickname for FIANNA FÁIL.

Egan, Pierce. *See* TOM AND JERRY.

Eggs. Every housewife in rural Ireland kept hens, so eggs were almost always to hand. For many housewives 'egg money', earned by selling eggs, was their only independent income. Eggs were frequently used to work PISHOGUES: they were buried in the hay, straw or rick of oats of the farmer for whom the spell was intended, sometimes marked with numbers or drawings. As with SPANCELS, burning destroyed the pishogue.
See also BOGÁN.

Eglinton, John. The pseudonym of William Kirkpatrick Magee (1868–1961), critic and polemicist. He was born in Dublin, a Presbyterian, and worked in the NATIONAL LIBRARY OF IRELAND from 1895 to 1921. In newspaper articles and several books of essays, such as *Bards and Saints* (1906) and *Anglo-Irish Essays*

(1917), he upheld the Unionist tradition and challenged the literary Nationalism of revivalists such as W.B. YEATS and Æ. In George Moore's *Hail and Farewell* (1911–14) he is depicted as the anti-Home Rule 'Contrary John', and in Joyce's *Ulysses* he appears as the effete librarian. He moved to England after independence, finding little to like about the new state.

Eigg. An island between Mull and Skye. It was the scene of the destruction of DONNÁN's monastery and the massacre of the monks on Easter Sunday 617 in what may have been an early, tentative Viking raid.

Eileen Flynn Affair, the. In April 1982, Eileen Flynn, a secondary teacher in Holy Faith School in New Ross, Co. Wexford, was dismissed from her post because she, a single woman aged 26, was pregnant with the baby of a separated local man, with whom she was living. The Employment Appeals Tribunal and the Circuit Court upheld the dismissal on the grounds that a Catholic school had the right to demand that its staff adhere to Catholic moral standards, although Eileen Flynn's salary was paid by the taxpayer. The Circuit Court judge, Noel Ryan, commented at the hearing in July 1984: 'Times are changing and we must change with them, but they have not changed that much in this or the adjoining jurisdiction with regard to some things. In other places women are being condemned to death for this sort of offence. They are not Christians in the Far East. I do not agree with this of course.' The Eileen Flynn case became a cause célèbre and another test of the compassion and tolerance of modern Ireland, in which the country was found wanting. The first ABORTION REFERENDUM took place the following year, but few among the pro-life campaigners saw any connection between it and the Eileen Flynn case.
See also ANNE LOVETT CASE; KERRY BABIES AFFAIR, THE.

Eircom. The name of the main Irish telecommunications company, formed after Telecom

Éireann (Irish, 'telecommunications of Ireland'), the telecoms branch of what was formerly the Department of Posts and Telegraphs, was privatized in 1999. There was a general share issue, in which hundreds of thousands of Irish people got their fingers burned, the price of the shares tumbling shortly afterwards.

Éire or **Eriu.** In Irish mythology the goddess who gives Ireland its name, though the names of her sisters FODLA and BANBA are used poetically. The three are members of the TUATHA DÉ DANAAN, the old gods of Ireland, and as they welcome the MILESIAN invaders each demands that the country be named after her. It is the poet AMERGIN who makes the decision, and Éire remains the Irish name for the country. Its genitive form *Éireann* is to be found in Saorstát Éireann (the Irish name for the Free State), and it was from the dative *Éirinn* that the anglicized form Erin, used in so many ballads, originated. De Valera's CONSTITUTION OF 1937 changed the name of Ireland from the Irish FREE STATE to 'Éire'.

Éirí in airde agus mór-chúis (Irish, 'pride', 'arrogance'). A term borrowed from Irish and used in HIBERNO-ENGLISH to mean hubris, overweening pride or HUMP OF GRANDEUR. Irish usage favours the emphasis provided by two synonymous phrases linked by *agus* ('and').

Elected. A HIBERNO-ENGLISH colloquialism meaning 'in a very good position'.
See also PIG'S BACK, TO BE ON THE.

Eleven Years' War. *See* CONFEDERATE WAR.

Elk, Irish. *See* IRISH ELK.

Ellis, John Fanshawe. The pseudonym used by Lady Jane Wilde (*see* SPERANZA) for her letters to *The* NATION. The name was derived from the initials of her own maiden name, Jane Frances Elgee.

Ellis Island. A 27-acre (11-ha) island in Upper New York Bay, close to the New Jersey shore, that was the entry point to the USA for 14

million immigrants, 500,000 of them Irish. Originally called Gibbet Island (it was the site of pirate executions as late as the 1850s), it became the main immigrant reception area on 1 January 1892, taking over from CASTLE GARDEN. The first client to be processed was Annie MOORE, a 15-year-old from Cork. A sculptural representation of this first-foot may now be seen in the Museum of Immigration that the forbidding place became in 1965. The walls are adorned with thousands of names of those so well described in the words inscribed on the base of the Statute of Liberty on nearby Liberty Island:

> Give me your tired, your poor,
> Your huddled masses yearning to breathe free ...
> EMMA GOLDMAN (1849–87): 'The New Colossus'
> (1883)

They were met by generally unsympathetic immigration clerks, inadequate interpreters and aggressive medical examiners, who made the place for many the 'Island of Tears'. During the Second World War, Ellis Island was an enemy-alien detention facility, and it finally closed in 1954.
See also AOH; DRAFT RIOTS; FIVE POINTS, THE; FRIENDLY SONS OF ST PATRICK, THE.

Ely O'Carroll. An historical area, a stronghold of the O'Carroll family, that comprised much of the modern Co. Offaly. The O'Carrolls occupied 40 castles in the area and intermarried with Irish and Anglo-Norman families. As part of the plantation of Ely O'Carroll in 1619 a grant of BIRR Castle and 1227 acres (497 ha) was made to Sir Laurence Parsons.

Emain Macha. The seat of the Ulster kings, second only to TARA in importance, and taking its name from the goddess MACHA. Its likely site is the enclosure at NAVAN FORT (*'n Emhain*) near Armagh city, where remarkable archaeological remains may be seen. Many of the events involving the RED BRANCH KNIGHTS in the Red Branch cycle took place in or near the enclosure at Emain Macha. It was said to comprise three richly appointed halls: the Craobh Ruadh ('red branch'), the Craobh

Dearg ('blood-red branch') and the Teite Brecc ('speckled house'). The first was the feasting and the sleeping quarters of the king and his warriors, the second was the treasury, and the third the armoury. Its resemblance to ARTHUR OF BRITAIN's Camelot is striking. Its most famous chatelain was CONCHOBHAR, but its regal history lasted 600 years, and it was the appropriate site for St PATRICK's ecclesiastical capital. The place figures prominently in the Ulster Cycle, also known as the Red Branch Cycle from the name of the feasting hall. The Cycle is a collection of heroic tales relating to the Ulaid, a prehistoric people from the north of Ireland who gave the province its name. The most famous of these is the TÁIN BÓ CUAILNGE (*Cattle Raid of Cooley*).

Emancipation. *See* CATHOLIC EMANCIPATION.

E-men. *See* DURATIONISTS.

Emer. The wife of CÚCHULAINN, who possesses the SIX GIFTS OF WOMANHOOD. To prevent the marriage Forgall, Emer's father, sends the young Cúchulainn for training to ALBA, but on his return Cúchulainn takes his willing bride by force, killing many of Forgall's warriors and causing him to commit suicide. The marriage is stormy but their love is never in doubt, and when, as befits a demi-god, her husband is loved by many women she is on the whole complaisant. When Cúchulainn falls in love with FAND the women settle matters between them, Fand eventually returning to her husband MANANNÁN MAC LIR. Just before his last battle Cúchulainn has a transferred prophetic vision of EMAIN MACHA in flames and Emer's body being thrown over the palisade. She falls dead into her husband's grave after uttering a heartbroken keen over his body.

'Emerald Isle, The'. The romantic coinage by William DRENNAN in his poem 'Erin' (1795):

> When Eire first rose from the dark-swelling flood,
> God blessed the green island, and saw it was
>   good;
> The emerald of Europe, it sparkled and shone,
> In the ring of the world, the most precious stone.
> *Fugitive Pieces in Verse and Prose* (1815)

Since then an element of irony has entered into its use. Robert EMMET, according to the balladeer, was happy to 'lay down [his] life for the Emerald Isle', but nowadays many would forego the title for a decrease in the rainfall that produces the mounting greenery.

Emergency, the. The name by which the period of the Second World War, in which Ireland remained neutral, was known (*see* NEUTRALITY). Frank AIKEN headed a new department for coordination of defensive measures: the regular army was greatly increased in size (*see* DURATIONISTS) and a LOCAL DEFENCE FORCE (LDF) established in September 1940, although when it became clear that Ireland was in no immediate danger of being attacked by Germany, numbers in the defence forces were allowed to drop again. There was a resurgence of IRA activity, the IRA having declared war against Britain in January 1939. De Valera dealt with this very severely: during the Emergency six men were executed, including the IRA chief-of-staff, the young Tralee man Charlie Kerins; three others died on hunger strike in the same period. For ordinary people the Emergency meant shortages of fuel and rationing of tea and sugar, although meat was plentiful. BORD NA MÓNA, the turf board, was established in 1944 to exploit Ireland's natural resources of peat.

See also COMPULSORY TILLAGE.

Emergency Response Unit. *See* ABBEYLARA SHOOTING, THE.

Emigration. *See* AMERICAN WAKE; CASTLE GARDEN; ELLIS ISLAND; MOORE, ANNIE.

Emmet, Robert (1778–1803). Revolutionary known as the DARLING OF ERIN, whose planned Dublin insurrection in 1803 ended in mob riot ('We were defeated and shamefully treated'). He was born in Dublin in 1778, the son of the state physician, and showed early the nature of his politics by his fiery speeches at debates at Trinity College Dublin and his leadership of the UNITED IRISHMEN there. Though not involved in the REBELLION OF 1798, he visited his revolutionary brother Thomas (1764–1827) in France in 1799 and met both Talleyrand and Napoleon.

In 1803, when Napoleon was expected to invade England, Emmet hoped to achieve what the 1798 rising had failed to do – to seize Dublin Castle and to generate a spontaneous countrywide insurrection. Such veterans of the earlier rising as Thomas Russell (*see* MAN FROM GOD KNOWS WHERE, THE) and Myles Byrne had also promised support. An explosion in his arms depot in Patrick Street (of which the authorities in fact seemed to have been unaware) caused him to bring forward the date of the attack to Saturday 23 July. The expected help did not arrive, and the attack on the castle fizzled out. The insurgents became mixed up with the usual Saturday night bravados, and with an abundance of pikes and muskets the rising became a drunken murderous riot. One of the 50 casualties was the liberal chief justice Lord Kilwarden (1739–1803), piked to death with his nephew in their coach.

Emmet could have escaped to France, but he wished to meet his sweetheart Sarah CURRAN, daughter of the advocate John Philpot CURRAN, once more before he left. He was apprehended by Major SIRR and publicly executed in Thomas Street, Dublin, on 20 October. *See also* LET NO MAN WRITE MY EPITAPH.

Emo Court. *See* MAD MARGARET'S WALK.

Enda (d.*c*.530). The father of Irish monasticism, who assimilated its principles at the CANDIDA CASA in Galloway. Like COMGALL he forsook a military career for the religious life and established Ireland's first foundation on Inis Mór in the ARAN ISLANDS. His monastery was noted for the severity of its rule, and mortification of the flesh took precedence over the usual monastic pursuits of study and copying. It was used as a place of spiritual retreat for other monks. Enda died *c*.530 at Killeany (Irish Cill Éinne), to which he gave his name. His feast is kept on 21 March.

Endymion. An eccentric 20th-century Dublin character who styled himself 'Endymion, whom the moon loved', after the mythical Greek king beloved by the moon goddess Selene. It was said that the Dublin Endymion 'went strange' after falling into an empty vat and breathing the fumes at the Guinness brewery where he used to work. His appearance is described by Oliver St John Gogarty in *AS I WAS GOING DOWN SACKVILLE STREET* (1937):

> Quaintly he came raiking out of Molesworth Street into Kildare Street, an odd figure moidered by memories, and driven mad by dreams which had overflowed into life, making him turn himself into a merry mockery of all he had once held dear. He wore a tail-coat over white cricket trousers which were caught in at the ankles by a pair of cuffs. A cuff-like collar sloped upwards to keep upright a little sandy head, crowned by a black bowler some sizes too small. An aquiline nose high in the arch gave a note of distinction to a face all the more pathetic for its plight. Under his left arm he carried two sabres in shining scabbards of patent leather. His right hand grasped a hunting-crop such as whipper-ins use for hounds.

He was also to be seen with a fishing rod which he poked through the railings of Trinity College. Gogarty wrote the best summary of Endymion in the same book:

> Dublin saw him only as a man gone 'natural', and Dublin has outstanding examples in every generation.

Englified. A HIBERNO-ENGLISH colloquialism synonymous with 'anglicized', but with a derogatory connotation when applied to a person who aspires to the habits or language of the English.

English Market. A covered meat, fish and vegetable market in Cork, traditionally famous for DRISHEEN and TRIPE, although since it was refurbished in the 1980s one is just as likely to find olives and mascarpone there.

English schools. *See* ERASMUS SMITH SCHOOLS.

Ennis, Séamus (1919–82). Traditional musician and music collector. A towering figure in traditional music, he played UILLEANN PIPES and tin whistle. He was also a gifted *SEAN-NÓS* singer, a collector of music and songs in all the GAELTACHT regions and a radio and television broadcaster. Ennis was born to musical parents in Finglas, then in north Co. Dublin, and worked for the THREE CANDLES PRESS in Dublin (1938–42). He collected music in the west of Ireland and in counties Cavan and Donegal for the IRISH FOLKLORE COMMISSION (1942–7), then worked as a broadcaster for RTÉ radio and BBC radio in turn, collecting material for and presenting the seminal AS I ROVED OUT (1951–60). Thereafter he lectured and performed in concert and on radio and television; he was celebrated particularly for slow airs. Ennis spoke Irish fluently and it was said of him that he could change from one CANÚINT (dialect) to another with no difficulty, depending on which Gaeltacht he was in.

Enniskillen (Irish *Inis Ceithleann*, 'Ceithleann's island'). The county town of Fermanagh, population (1991) 11,400, lying between Upper and Lower Lough Erne. Ceithleann, according to tradition, was the wife of BALOR OF THE EVIL EYE who swam for refuge to the island on which the town stands after inflicting mortal wounds on the king of the TUATHA DÉ DANAAN. Part of the castle of the Maguires has been preserved as a museum, containing relics of the two regiments of the British army to which the town gave its name, the Royal Inniskilling Fusiliers (*see* SKINS, THE) and the Royal Inniskilling Dragoons. The town was the scene of the Remembrance Day Provisional IRA bomb of 8 November 1987 when 11 people were killed and 63 injured.

Enterprise Ireland. The government organization charged with assisting the development of Irish business and commerce. It was established on 23 July 1988, replacing the existing Córas Tráchtála (Irish Trade Board).

Enya (b.1961). Singer and composer of popular music. She was born Eithne Ní Bhraonáin on 17 May 1961 in Gweedore in the Donegal GAELTACHT. She came of a musical family, members of whom formed the group CLANNAD

in 1970, and she sang with them in 1980–2. Since then she has pursued a solo career, releasing several highly successful albums, the material – a kind of 'new age' Celtic dreaminess – generally composed by her and painstakingly recorded, using synthesizers as well as traditional instruments. Her albums include *Watermark* (1988), *Shepherd Moons* (1991), *The Memory of Trees* (1995), *Paint the Sky with Stars* (1997) and *A Day Without Rain* (2000). She sometimes writes music for films, for example *The Lord of the Rings: The Fellowship of the Ring* (2001). Enya lives in a castle in Killiney, Co. Dublin, never performs live or appears on chat shows, and rarely gives interviews: her persona is ethereal and enigmatic, like her music.

Eoghan an Bhéil Bhinn (Irish, 'Eoghan of the sweet mouth') (1748–84). The nickname of the Jacobite poet Eoghan Rua Ó Súilleabháin. He was born at Meentogues, 13 km (8 miles) east of Killarney in Co. Kerry. He was the archetypal roistering poet, amorous, hard-drinking, generous-hearted and so talented that he was known for years after his death as 'Eoghan an Bhéil Bhinn'. Ó Súilleabháin studied at a bardic school at FAHA, west of Killarney, where poetry, music and the classics were taught, and when he was 18 he set up his own school at Gneeveguilla. This respectability did not last, and he took to the roads as a SPALPEEN (itinerant labourer). He spent the next decade labouring, writing poetry, schoolmastering and serving in the British navy and army. It was during this period of military service that he wrote his most famous AISLING, 'Ceo Draíochta', and it is for *aislingí* such as this and 'Ag Taisteal na Blárnan' that he is most celebrated. He is thought to have written 15 *aislingí* in all. He was discharged from the army and returned home to his beloved SLIABH LUACHRA in 1784. He opened a school at Knocknagree, offering a wide range of subjects from the classics to mathematics – all to be taught by himself – but died soon afterwards of fever caused by injuries inflicted in Killarney by the servants of a landowner whom he had satirized. He is one of the FOUR KERRY POETS commemorated in Killarney.

Epiphany, Feast of the. *See* WOMEN'S CHRISTMAS.

Epistola ad Milites Corotici. *See* CONFESSIO.

-er. A suffix common in HIBERNO-ENGLISH speech, especially in Dublin. It usually indicates familiarity or affection: a *chipper* is a fish-and-chip shop; *Croker* is CROKE PARK; *mortallers* are mortal sins.

Erasmus Smith Schools. The schools established throughout the country by the ERASMUS SMITH TRUST in the early 19th century, mostly in the decade 1810–20. There were nearly 200 of these schools, called 'English schools' because the medium of education was entirely English; the first was built on Valentia Island, Co. Kerry, the last in Ardee, Co. Louth. The local community paid half the teacher's salary and funded half the resources and repairs needed for the school, with the Erasmus Smith Trust paying the balance. Later in the 19th century many of the Trust schools became national schools.

Erasmus Smith Trust. A trust established by royal charter in 1669 at the behest of Erasmus Smith, a grocer who supplied Cromwell's army. As an adventurer he received 46,000 acres (18,600 ha) of land in the CROMWELLIAN SETTLEMENT, and he wished the revenue from these estates be used to educate children. The foundation deed of his trust, dated 1 December 1657, states:

> ... the great and ardent desire which he hath that the children inhabiting upon any part of his lands in Ireland should be brought up in the fear of God and good literature and to speak the English tongue.

The governors of the trust eventually established five grammar schools (Tipperary, Galway, Ennis, Drogheda and Dublin's High School, the last to be founded, in 1870) as well as endowing scholarships at Trinity College Dublin and funding accommodation for students. The trust was also involved in primary education, with the establishment of ERASMUS SMITH SCHOOLS. A valuable archive of trust material is held in Dublin's High School, Rathgar.

Erc (d.*c*.512). A learned member of the court of Laoghaire, HIGH KING of TARA. Erc was the traditional adversary of PATRICK, confronting the saint when he lit the fire on the hill of Slane in Co. Louth on the first Christian Easter Sunday in Ireland. However, he almost immediately gave Patrick homage. He was made a bishop by Patrick and established a hermitage at Slane, which flourished and grew as a monastic school. He is said to have been the tutor of BRENDAN THE VOYAGER. His feast day is 2 November.

Ere. A word used in HIBERNO-ENGLISH to mean anterior, earlier in time, as in 'ere yesterday' (the day before yesterday), 'ere last week', 'ere last year'.

Eremon. In Irish mythology, the son of Milesius (*see* MILESIANS) who is chosen by AMERGIN to be the king of Ireland. His brother Eber refuses to accept the ruling, and to keep the peace Eremon agrees to a partition of the country. This works for some time, but Eber keeps demanding more. Eventually in a struggle Eremon kills Eber and sets up at TARA the high kingship of all Ireland (*see* HIGH KING).

Eric (Irish *éraic*, payment). In early Irish society, the compensation paid to the extended family of a man killed deliberately. It was a fixed amount: the killer had to hand over seven slave women or the equivalent.

Erie Canal. A waterway, in the USA, that joins the Hudson River and Lake Erie. It was begun in 1817 and stretched for 581 km (363 miles) through the Mohawk Gap in the Appalachian Mountains. The finance came from New York state and was organized by De Witt Clinton (1769–1828), who served as governor for two terms (1817–22 and 1825–8), and in his unpleasant way strutted like a peacock at the opening of the canal on 25 October 1825.

The Erie Canal played a significant part in the drive of the American nation westwards, and it began a tradition of using an Irish labour force:

> I learnt the whole art of canalling; I think it an
> excellent trade.
> I learned to be very handy, although I was not
> very tall
> I could handle the sprig of shillelagh with the best
> man on the canal.
>
> ANON: 'Paddy on the Canal' (early 19th century)

Erin. A poetic name for Ireland (*see* ÉIRE).

Erin Go Bragh. A HIBERNO-ENGLISH patriotic slogan from the Irish *go brách*, 'for ever'. It and the other ubiquitous phrase CÉAD MÍLE FÁILTE were more regularly found on green banners abroad than at home:

> There came to the beach a poor Exile of Erin.
> The dew on his thin robe was heavy and chill.
> For his country he sighed, when at twilight
> repairing
> To wander alone by the wind beaten hill.
> But the day-star attracted his eyes' sad devotion
> For it rose o'er his own native isle of the ocean,
> Where once in the fire of his youthful emotion
> He sang the bold anthem of Erin go bragh.
>
> THOMAS CAMPBELL (1777–1844): 'The Exile of
> Erin' (1842)

Eriu. *See* ÉIRE.

Eriugena, John Scottus (*c*.810–*c*.877). One of the leading early medieval *docti* (scholars), who is named Irish (*Scottus*) in Latin and in Greek. He was born *c*.810 and reached maturity when the Viking raids in Ireland were at their height. By the early 840s he was at the court of CHARLES THE BALD, the grandson of Charlemagne. Charles encouraged scholars – although to a lesser extent than his grandfather – and employed the wandering Irishman to run the court school and translate Greek and Hebrew works into Latin, the lingua franca of western Europe.

It was at Laon, one of Charles's palaces, that Eriugena wrote in 851 his treatise *De Prae-destinatione* to counter the current heretical views, but this work was dismissed by critics as '*pultes Scottorum*' ('Irish porridge'). His greatest work *Peri Pheusis* (Greek, 'concerning nature', in Latin *De Divisione Naturae*) is in the popular form of a Socratic dialogue between master and pupil. It was condemned as pantheistic in 1225 and put on the *Index* of prohibited books in 1685. It is only since 1900 that his views have been considered tenable by Christians. His translation from Greek into Latin, commissioned by Charles, of the Neo-Platonist disquisition known as the *Pseudo-Dionysius*, had a profound effect on medieval thought. The excellence of the translation caused one savant to express surprise that a barbarian from the ends of the earth should be such a master of Greek.

Like all great personalities of the period, Eriugena attracted a number of legends: one such, that on the death of Charles he went to teach in the Wessex of King Alfred (849–99) as abbot of MALMESBURY, may be true, but its macabre tailpiece that he was stabbed to death by the pens of his pupils 'because he made them cogitate' is perhaps a piece of student wishful thinking. He died, probably in France, *c*.877. *See also* TABULA TANTUM.

Erris Head. *See* MULLET PENINSULA, THE.

Error of Judgement. The title of a book (1986) by the British Labour MP Chris Mullin, asserting the innocence of the BIRMINGHAM SIX. Mullin was among those who campaigned for years for the exoneration of the six.

Erse. A Lowland Scots pronunciation of the word 'Irish', applied to the Gaelic of the Western Highlanders. At the time of the linguistic diaspora in the 17th century the word was used to distinguish the residual Irish spoken peripherally from the stronger Scots Gaelic. It is now used mainly pejoratively or at least jocosely, especially because of its susceptibility to facile puns (*see* ERSEHOLE). It was one of the terms favoured by broadcaster Gay BYRNE on his radio show *The Gay Byrne Hour*.

Ersehole. The description by Brendan Behan of the *FÁINNE ÓIR* ('gold ring') worn by eager

Irish speakers on lapels and sweaters, to indicate a competency in the language.

Ervine, St John (1883–1971). Playwright, biographer and critic. He was born John Ervine, the son of deaf mutes, in Ballymacarret, and worked as an insurance clerk before joining the Fabian Society out of admiration for George Bernard Shaw. His first play, *Mixed Marriage* (1911), dealt with Ulster bigotry, and *John Ferguson* (1915), about Presbyterian rectitude, was produced during his time as manager of the ABBEY THEATRE, a post he left – after conflict with the company over the EASTER RISING – to join the Dublin Fusiliers. He lost a leg in France and settled down in Devon to become a trenchant but readable drama critic for several papers, including the *Observer*. Throughout the 1920s he wrote successful West End comedies and hagiographic biographies of CARSON (1915) and CRAIG (1949). His appraisal of Oscar WILDE (1951) shows a lack of sympathy with the subject unique among biographers. He will be chiefly remembered for his abrasive defence of the Northern Ireland state against the milder and better-mannered observations of Robert LYND, and for two Ulster plays, *Boyd's Shop* (1936) and *Friends and Relations* (1941). He died at his home in Devon on 24 January 1971.

> … with less complaint than a Sinn Feiner makes about his obsolete language which he cannot speak, will not write, and does not wish to learn.
> *Some Impressions of My Elders* (1922)

Esker (Irish *eiscir*, 'ridge of mounds'). A rounded hill or ridge formed by sand, gravel or rocks deposited by melting ice at the end of the last Ice Age. In the Irish Midlands the dissolution of the last ice sheet caused the formation of a large number of eskers, which form what is known as esker systems. The eskers are sometimes perfectly symmetrical and sometimes flat on top, and they have their own unique flora and fauna. They formed the roadways of early Christian Ireland, providing a dry, raised path and also a vantage point for look-out positions.

Esker Riada. An ESKER system running east–west across Ireland, dividing the country into a northern half and a southern half. It became the main thoroughfare, the *Slí Mór* (Irish, 'big way'), running from TARA in present-day Co. Meath, through what is now Offaly, to Connacht. The *Slí Mór* served the monastic settlement of Clonmacnoise, which was strategically situated in the middle of the country. The section of esker to the east of the monastic site is still known as the Pilgrim's Road.

Essex, Robert Devereux, 2nd Earl of (1567–1601). Elizabethan soldier, son of Walter Devereux, 1st Earl of ESSEX. A favourite of Queen Elizabeth I, he was appointed Irish lord lieutenant at the end of 1598, after the catastrophic defeat at the Battle of the YELLOW FORD had shown the English that Hugh O'NEILL, Earl of Tyrone, was an enemy to be reckoned with. Essex was an experienced and successful soldier and Elizabeth determined to give him ample military resources to defeat the northern chieftains, especially the traitorous Tyrone. He was assigned 16,000 foot soldiers and 1300 horsemen, although not all of these actually materialized. But he had enemies at court who undermined him at every opportunity, including Lord MOUNTJOY, his rival for the position of lord lieutenant.

Essex has traditionally been regarded as dilatory and incompetent in proceeding against Munster rather than going directly to Ulster as he had been commanded, but in fact the rebellion that became known as the NINE YEARS' WAR had by now spread to Munster, Connacht and Leinster, O'Neill and his ally Red Hugh O'DONNELL having instructed their confederates to attack the Pale and English supply lines. When Essex arrived in Dublin in April 1599 he received intelligence of this, and his campaigns in the southern half of Ireland were by way of being a pre-emptive strike. He met considerable opposition on his way through south Leinster, an indication that an alliance of Irish chieftains had been created that was ready and willing to support the

Ulster rebellion in expectation of a Spanish invasion.

At the end of August Essex finally turned towards Ulster, where he met O'Neill and arranged a truce. On his return to Dublin he received two highly critical letters from the queen and decided to return to London to make his case in person, fearing the influence of enemies at court. He was arrested when he arrived in London and eventually beheaded in 1601 after becoming involved in a plot against the queen. He was replaced as lord lieutenant of Ireland by his old rival Lord MOUNTJOY.

Essex, Walter Devereux, 1st Earl of (1541–76). Elizabethan nobleman and colonist. For services to Queen Elizabeth, particularly in suppressing the rebellion of 1569 in the north of England, he was made Earl of Essex in 1572. Ambitious to please the queen further, showing 'his good devotion to employ himself in the service of her majesty', he offered to colonize parts of central and eastern Ulster, at that time mainly under the rule of the O'Neills under Turlough Luineach and the MacDonnells led by Sorley Boy MACDONNELL. Essex departed for Ireland in July 1573 with 1200 soldiers and a group of colonists/adventurers, but his campaign was beset by problems including illness and lack of supplies. Failing to find an enemy to defeat in open battle, his campaign against the O'Neills and MacDonnells took the form of treachery and assassination – in 1574 he captured and executed Brian Mac-Phelim, a leader of the O'Neills. The deed for which he is most famous is the massacre of the followers of Sorley Boy MacDonnell on Rathlin Island on 26 July 1575. After the failure of his attempt to pacify Ulster, Essex returned to England later that year, but the following year the queen prevailed upon him to accept the position of earl marshal of Ireland. Three weeks after his fresh arrival in Dublin he died of dysentery, in September 1576. His son, Robert, 2nd Earl of ESSEX, campaigned in Ireland towards the end of the NINE YEARS' WAR.

Étain. In Irish mythology, the remarkably beautiful wife of the god MIDIR who figures in a complicated and sophisticated tale of many reincarnations. Midir uses AONGHUS ÓG, the love-god, as marriage broker, in his negotiations with Ailill, Étain's father, but he requires Aonghus Óg to clear 12 plains, drain the land by making 12 rivers and give him Étain's weight in silver and gold, before he will release her. Aonghus Óg succeeds in his tasks with the help of his father, the DAGDA, and brings Étain to Midir. They reckon without the jealousy of Midir's wife FUAMNACH, who changes Étain by turns into a pool of water, a worm and a fly to confuse Midir in his search for her. He recognizes her in that final form and as such she never leaves his presence. The jealous Fuamnach causes a magic wind to blow that tosses the fly about the sky for seven years until it is able to make its way to BRUGH NA BÓINNE, Aognhus Óg's home. He sends word to Midir, but Fuamnach, hearing the news, conjures up another magic seven-year wind. Finally the fly is swallowed by the pregnant wife of ETAR, and the daughter born to her is also called Étain. Though an avatar of the original, she is unaware of her previous history. When she grows up Midir tries to claim her as his wife, but yields her to her husband Eohaidh, to whom she bears yet another Étain.

Etar. In Irish mythology, one of CONCHOBHAR's Ulster champions whose pregnant wife swallows ÉTAIN in the shape of a fly. She produces a mortal daughter, a second Étain, whom MIDIR tries to claim as his lost spouse.

Ethlinn (also **Ethniu** or **Eithne**). In Irish mythology, the daughter of BALOR OF THE EVIL EYE, who is kept from the sight of men shut up in a crystal tower on TORY ISLAND by her father to prevent the fulfilment of a prophecy that he would die at the hands of his grandson. Balor steals the GLAS GAIBHLEANN, the magic cow that CIAN, the son of DIAN CECHT, is tending. Cian seeks help from a female druid called Birog who enables him, dressed as a woman, to penetrate Ethlinn's tower and make love to her while her female guardians are asleep. Having retrieved the cow Cian and Birog return to the mainland, leaving Ethlinn pregnant. In all she has three children, one of whom, LUGH Lámhfada, escapes the drowning imposed by Balor. He is fostered by the sea god MANANNÁN MAC LIR and becomes the god of arts and crafts. Ethlinn eventually marries NUADA and becomes an ancestor of FIONN MAC CUMHAIL.

Eucharistic Congress. The 31st in a series of such international assemblies, held in Ireland in 1932 (the supposed 1500th anniversary of the coming of PATRICK) by the Catholic Church to promote devotion to the Blessed Sacrament. It was held in Dublin 22–26 June in the presence of Edward Byrne, the Archbishop of Dublin, and the cardinal legate Lorenzo Lauri. Houses throughout the country were decorated with a specially designed Congress cross and a million people gathered in PHOENIX PARK to attend Mass and hear Count John McCormack sing 'Pange Lingua'. The events allowed the FIANNA FÁIL government, which had come to power for the first time in February 1932, to display its post-revolutionary fidelity to the Catholic Church: Éamon DE VALERA and Seán T. O'KELLY helped to bear the canopy for the papal legate.

The spectacles and the assembled crowds have been compared by some sceptics to the fascist rallies of the 1930s in continental Europe, and not until the visit of Pope John Paul II in 1979 did crowds like this gather in Ireland in the name of religion. The Catholic author G.K. Chesterton, who was present, wrote: 'There has never been a modern mass meeting, of anything like this size, that passed off so smoothly, or with so few miscalculations or misfortunes'; he also had the 'instantaneous thought: "This is democracy".'

The general pride in the event was not shared by all. Æ, no lover of de Valera's Free State, is recorded as sitting on a rock in Glengarriff, Co. Cork, on the day of the Phoenix Park Mass and calling out during a thunderstorm, 'Oh,

come on, come on, Manannan! You can do better than that. All I want you to do is wash out those damned Christian idolaters.'

Eureka Stockade. A battle in 1854 at Bakery Hill, just outside the township of Eureka in the Ballarat gold-mining area of Victoria, Australia. It was between some 300 policemen and soldiers and about 150 miners – mainly Irish, but also including Americans, Canadians and Italians and two Australian-born – who refused to pay a government licence fee that they considered unjust. (Gold was first discovered in Ballarat in 1851 and during the decade that followed it enticed about 84,000 Irish emigrants to this area.)

In the early hours of Sunday 3 December 1854 government forces attacked and captured the stockade – an area of about one acre (0.4 ha), roughly enclosed with slabs and carts, taking the defenders by surprise as they did not believe they would be attacked on the Sabbath. It is estimated that at least 40 insurgents were killed (some estimates put it as high as 60) and 4 members of the military.

The Eureka defenders had a flag called 'the Southern Cross' (blue, with a silver cross) and their password was 'Vinegar Hill!' (see VINEGAR HILL[2]). Irishman Peter Lalor (1823–89), brother of James Fintan LALOR, was the commander and administered a solemn oath: 'We swear by the Southern Cross to stand truly by each other and fight to defend our rights and liberty.' Eureka is now celebrated as a heroic piece of resistance to political repression by the fledgeling labour movement.

Some 120 men were captured at the stockade, but only 13 were charged with treason in Melbourne in 1855. Neither judge (Sir Redmond Barry, a Cork-born Protestant) nor jury would convict them. When, as a result of the agitation and a subsequent royal commission, the goldfields were granted parliamentary representation, Peter Lalor became the first member of the legislative council for Ballarat, and eventually speaker of the parliament for Victoria. He held a number of government posts and died in Melbourne on 10 February 1889.

Euro. The common European unit of currency adopted in Ireland on 1 January 2002. By exchanging its own currency (the Irish pound, or *punt* as it came to be called when it ceased to be linked with the British pound) for the euro Ireland strengthened its relationship with Continental Europe (where 11 other European Union states also adopted the euro) and weakened its financial ties with the UK, which did not adopt the euro. The changeover took place remarkably smoothly, the main adverse effect being the consequent stealthy inflation.

European Community / European Union. *See* COMMON MARKET.

Eurovision. Ireland embraced the Eurovision Song Contest with enthusiasm from 1965, the first year of its entry, when Butch Moore performed 'Walking the Streets in the Rain'. Notable Irish winners included DANA[2] in 1970 and Johnny Logan in 1980 and 1987. The country won Eurovision for three consecutive years (1992–4) – perhaps a little to the dismay of RTÉ because staging the contest consumed the great part of the station's annual light-entertainment budget – and again in 1996 with Emer Quinn singing 'I Am the Voice'.

See also 'CEOL AN GHRÁ'; *RIVERDANCE*.

Evans, E[myr] Estyn (1905–89). Archaeologist and geographer. Born in Shrewsbury and educated at Aberystwyth University, he was appointed to the geography department of Queen's University Belfast in 1928, and over the next 40 years revolutionized the way Ulster people looked at the province. He engaged in many archaeological surveys, cataloguing the extant ancient monuments and helping to found the Ulster Folk and Transport Museum at Cultra. In a series of publications and broadcasts he made the mundane details of Ulster rural life seem exciting, drawing on a mix of folklore, myth and the oral tradition. He became a kind of laureate of the local landscape, encouraging a new folk-in-environment approach to his subject. His illustrated books include *Irish Heritage* (1942), *Mourne Country* (1951), *Irish Folk Ways* (1957) and *The Personality of Ireland* (1973).

Eva of *The Nation*. *See* KELLY, MARY ANNE.

Evening. The word often used in HIBERNO-ENGLISH for afternoon, as in 'Two o'clock in the evening'.

Even the pigs are Protestants. A remark attributed to a visitor to the Co. Cork town of BANDON when he saw pigs being driven through the churchyard of the Church of Ireland. The town's religious affiliations are reflected in the first couplet below, which appeared in a notice on the walls of the town in the 17th century; the second couplet was the riposte of a Catholic wit:

> Jew, Turk or atheist
> May enter here, but not a papist.

> He who wrote this wrote it well
> For the same is written in the gates of Hell.

Examine my own heart. *See* DE VALERA, ÉAMON.

Exchange kings. A remark ascribed to Sir Teague O'Regan on being captured at the Battle of the BOYNE after James II (*see* SÉAMAS AN CHACA) had fled the field: 'Exchange kings and we will fight the battle over again.'

External association. *See* DE VALERA, ÉAMON; DOCUMENT NO. 2.

Eye. A negative intensifier in HIBERNO-ENGLISH. 'He did in his eye' expresses incredulity or scorn. It is very similar in meaning to 'He did in his arse' (*see* ARSE, TO DO IN ONE'S).

Faction fighting. The violence, often recreational, that characterized meetings between rival groups at PATTERNS and fairs, especially during the first three decades of the 19th century. These serial battles were eventually suppressed by the new Irish constabularies (*see* RIC). One of the most spectacular examples of faction confrontation was the so-called Battle of BALLYEAGH STRAND (1834):

> On the O'Hallaghans being driven to the churchyard, they were at a mighty inconvenience for weapons. Most of them had lost their sticks, it being the usage in fights of this kind to twist the cudgels from the grasp of the beaten men, to prevent them from rallying. They soon, however, furnished themselves with the best they could find, videlicet, the skull, leg, thigh, and arm bones, which they found lying about the graveyard. This was a new species of weapon, for which the majority of the O'Callaghans were scarcely prepared. Out they sailed in a body – some with these, others with stones, and making fierce assault upon their enemies, absolutely *druv* them back – not so much by the damage they were doing, as by the alarm and terror which these unexpected species of missiles excited.
>
>> WILLIAM CARLETON (1794–1869): 'The Battle of the Factions', in *Traits and Stories of the Irish Peasantry* (1830)

The widespread confrontations of the CARAVATS AND SHANAVESTS, long regarded as typical faction fights, are now seen as examples of class conflict. The faction protagonists are still celebrated in songs, current until recently in the USA and even finding a place in the *Scottish Students' Song Book* (1897):

> Oh, me fame wint abroad through the nation,
> And folks came a flockin' to see,
> An' they cried out widout hesitation
> You're a fightin' man, Billy McGee!
> Oh, I've claned out the Finnigan faction,
> An' I've licked all the Murphys afloat;
> If you're in for a row or a ruction
> Jist thread on the tail o' me coat!
>> ANON: 'Mush, Mush' (19th century)

Faha (also known as **Annagh**). A venue in SLIABH LUACHRA in Co. Kerry for an 18th-century court of poetry. A patron (*patrún*) or dancing festival was also held there.

Fáilte. The Irish word for 'welcome'. CÉAD MÍLE FÁILTE means 'a hundred thousand welcomes', and *Bhur gcéad míle fáilte anseo inniu* ('a hundred thousand welcomes to you all here today') is a common opening to a speech. *Fáilte is céad* ('a hundred welcomes') and *fáilte is fiche* ('twenty welcomes') are less fulsome versions of the same welcome. The National Tourist Development Authority created in 2001, is Fáilte Ireland (formerly Bord Fáilte). *See also* FIAL; FLAITHIÚIL; HOSPITALITY; *NUA GACHA BIA AGUS SEANA GACHA DÍ.*

Fáinne an Lae (Irish, 'dawn'). The first Irish-language newspaper. The first edition was issued on 8 January 1898 and edited by Bernard Doyle (*c.*1861–1933). It cost one penny and survived until March 1899, to be replaced by *An* CLAIDEAMH SOLUIS. The name was resurrected in the 1920s.

> The new journal will be a bona fide newspaper, intended to supply in Irish a summary of news, and miscellaneous interesting matter as weekly reading for the ordinary household. In fulfilling this purpose it will attain the great end of creating an Irish-reading public.
>
> EOIN MACNÉILL: *Irisleabhar na Gaedhilge* (November 1897)

Fáinne Óir (Irish, 'gold ring'). A lapel badge indicating both a competence in the Irish language and a desire to use it in conversation. It is pronounced 'fan-yuh ore'. The right to wear the *fáinne* is conferred after an oral examination, often at the end of an intensive summer course. A lesser competence is indicated by the *fáinne airgid* ('silver ring'), and a beginner's badge, known as the *fáinne daite* ('coloured ring') pronounced 'fan-yuh dye che', has recently been introduced.

See also ERSEHOLE.

Fair. A meeting place and venue for buying and selling livestock. In the days before the marts run by commercial companies, fairs were the only means for farmers to sell livestock they had raised. Jobbers (dealers) came from far afield – from the rich pastures of Meath and neighbouring counties – to fairs all over the south and west of Ireland. Fairs were held on a particular day each month in different towns; towns where fairs were held are recognizable to this day by their fair field or their very wide main street or by their large number of pubs – Knocknagree in Co. Cork and Castleisland in Co. Kerry are two examples. Farmers normally walked their animals to the fair – and sometimes home again if prices were too low (*see* ECONOMIC WAR). Pedlars and ballad singers were always to be seen in town on fair day, and, naturally, drink was taken (*see* DRINK TAKEN, TO HAVE).

Fair City. A popular home-grown soap opera shown on RTÉ television. It depicts the lives, loves and tribulations of a community in the fictional northside Dublin suburb of Carrickstown. The title comes from the opening line of 'Molly Malone' (*see* DISH WITH THE FISH):

> In Dublin's fair city,
> Where the girls are so pretty …

Fair day. *See* FAIR.

Fair dues. *See* FAIR PLAY.

Fair field. *See* FAIR.

Fair Head. A spectacular headland rising 194 m (636 ft) above the sea on the north coast of Co. Antrim, some 7 km (4 miles) northeast of Ballycastle. Its Irish name is An Bheinn Mhór ('the big hill'), anglicized as Benmore. The headland comprises sheer and gloomy dolerite cliffs (frequented by the bolder sort of rock-climber) perched above steep grass slopes and screes descending to the sea. Fair Head is one of the points from which the length of Ireland is measured: from here it is 486 km (302 miles) to MIZEN HEAD in Co. Cork. The GREY MAN'S PATH leads down a gully through the cliffs to the beach.

It was on the rocks of Carrig Uisneach (Irish, 'rock of Uisneach') beneath Fair Head that in the tragic old tale DEIRDRE, her lover NAOISE and the sons of Uisneach made their landing on their return from Argyll to Ireland, lured thither by false promises of safe conduct by the jealous King CONCHOBHAR. The sea below Fair Head, known as the Waters of Moyle, is the scene of another ancient legend, that of the Children of Lir (*see* FIONNUALA).

Fair People, a. The backhanded compliment by Samuel Johnson (whose doctorate was granted by Trinity College Dublin) when reassuring the Bishop of Killaloe that should he visit Ireland he would not treat the people 'more unfavourably than he had done the Scotch':

> Sir, you have no reason to be afraid of me. The Irish are not in a conspiracy to cheat the world by false representations of the merits of their

countrymen. No, sir; the Irish are a fair people – they never speak well of one another.

Quoted in James Boswell: *The Life of Samuel Johnson*, II (1775)

Fair play. The HIBERNO-ENGLISH expression 'fair play to' gives credit where credit is due, and might be seen as the opposite of begrudgery (*see* BEGRUDGER). It has also been adopted into Irish, in the expression, 'Fair play *dhuit*' ('Fair play to you'). 'Fair dues (doos)' has a similar meaning. 'Fair play' is the exact equivalent of the Irish *cothrom na féinne* (*see* O'BRIEN, FLANN).

Fairy shoemaker. A LEPRECHAUN. The leprechaun is sometimes depicted in stories sitting on a toadstool with a tiny last, hammer and awl.

Fairy thimble. A foxglove. It was believed that a pot of fairy gold was to be found at the root of a fairy thimble. A story is told of a woman who found such a pot of gold, only to have it disappear from her press (cupboard) later on that day. It was said that if you spat on the treasure the fairies could not subsequently take it back.

Faith. An exclamation or 'filler' used in HIBERNO-ENGLISH: 'Faith, I don't know' could be just as easily rendered as 'I don't know, faith'. It is now more likely to be used humorously or ironically. The variant 'faix' now seems very Oirish (i.e. STAGE-IRISH).

Faithful County, the. The GAA nickname for Co. Offaly, it is thought because the county produces respectable teams in both hurling and football. It is of fairly recent origin, thought to date from the time of the GAA's centenary celebrations in 1984.

Faith Healer. A play (1979) by Brian FRIEL, thought by some to be his most powerful. It gives us glimpses of the life (and death) of Frank Hardy, who is cursed with the gift of occasional healing. The action consists of four monologues, spoken by Hardy, his wife Grace and Teddy, the Cockney manager of their roadshow, with a coda by the now dead Hardy. The accounts differ in substantive detail –

a typical Friel device – but all are clear about Hardy's having been beaten to death by the disappointed brothers and friends of one of his failures in BALLYBEG. The experimental nature of the writing, the mantra of place-names visited on their endless journeys, the implicit discussion about the nature of artistic genius and the bleak characterization make it a remarkable piece of theatre.

> I'd get so tense before a performance, d'you know what I used to do? As we drove along those narrow, winding roads I'd recite the names to myself just for the mesmerism, the sedation, the incantation –
>
> Kinlochbervie, Inverbervie,
> Inverdruie, Invergordon,
> Badachroo, Kinlochewe,
> Ballantrae, Inverkeithing,
> Cawdor, Kirkconnel
> Plaidy, Kirkinner ...

Falconer, Edmund (1814–79). Actor-manager. He was born Edmund O'Rourke in Dublin and went on the stage as a boy. He was the original Danny Mann in Boucicault's *The* COLLEEN BAWN (1860) and author of plays and dramatic adaptations himself. He is remembered now as the writer of the song 'Killarney' (*see* HEAVEN'S REFLEX). He died in his house in Russell Square, London, on 29 September 1879.

Fall of ground. A HIBERNO-ENGLISH phrase for a downward slope. The phrase 'fall of the hill' is also used. Both expressions derive from the Irish verb *tit*, which means 'to descend' or 'to decline' as well as the more usual 'to fall'.

Falls Road. A district in west Belfast that is regarded as the chief Catholic/Nationalist enclave of the city, through which the named thoroughfare runs from the city centre to Andersonstown (*see* ANDYTOWN). Its lower part runs parallel to the mainly Protestant SHANKILL ROAD, though they diverge after about 1.5 km (1 mile). The two areas are separated by a peace line erected after the invasion of Protestant militants in August 1969 when many Catholic houses were set on fire.

Over the next 30 years the Falls (as the area is known) was the scene of many armed confrontations between the security forces and the Provisional IRA, and of the Official IRA's recurrent internecine struggles with the Provisionals and the INLA. It remains the spine of the West Belfast constituency, which is normally a safe seat for SINN FÉIN, held by Gerry ADAMS. (In the 1992 general election Dr Joe Hendron of the SDLP was elected in a surprise result thought to have been achieved by the tactical voting of some few thousand Loyalists who overcame decades of prejudice to keep Adams out.) President Clinton made a point of visiting the Falls on his visit on 30 November 1995 and very pointedly shook hands with Adams.

The Falls is as much metaphor as a topographical location, standing for resolute insistence on a sooner-rather-than-later united Ireland. In more peaceful times the two roads were the subject of an urban (if hardly urbane) compliment: 'Up the Falls and down the Shankill, you'll never see a neater ankle.'

Falmar (Irish *falmaire*). A HIBERNO-ENGLISH phrase still current in rural areas and meaning a big strong man.

False Surrender, the. *See* KILMICHAEL AMBUSH, and also *GUERRILLA DAYS IN IRELAND* and REVISIONISM.

Famine grass. *See* HUNGRY GRASS.

Famine Queen, the. The epithet applied to Queen Victoria by Maud GONNE, in an article vigorously opposing the queen's visit to Ireland in 1900. The article was published in Arthur Griffith's newspaper the *UNITED IRISHMAN*.

Famine road. *See* BÓTHAR NA MINE BUÍ.

Famous Knocker-Out, the. A title well earned by John L. SULLIVAN:

Oh! The chorus swell for bold John L.
We'll fling it to the breeze,
Yes, shout it loud, so England's crowd
Shall hear it o'er the seas.
The great and small, he's drowned them all
In many a clever bout;

Hurrah for John L. Sullivan,
The famous Knocker-Out.
ANON. (*c*.1885)

Fanchea (d.*c*.520). The daughter of a king of AIRGIALLA (Oriel) and sister of ENDA of Aran. She founded a convent at Rossory, on Lower Loch Erne near Enniskillen. According to tradition Enda helped Fanchea build the house. Later she established a sister convent to her brother's monastery at Killeany on Inis Mór and is buried there. Her feast day is 1 January.

Fand. In Irish mythology, the wife of the sea god MANANNÁN MAC LIR and mistress of CÚCHULAINN. During a period of estrangement from her husband her home in TÍR TAIRNIGIRI is attacked by FOMORIANS and she sends for Cúchulainn to defend her, offering him her bed in payment. He beats off the Fomorian threat and stays happily with Fand for a month; when he leaves for his home again he arranges to meet her on the Yew Tree strand on the Cooley (CUAILNGE) peninsula in Co. Louth. Cúchulainn's wife EMER finds out about the assignation and plots to kill Fand, but finding that the goddess genuinely loves her husband agrees to relinquish him. Manannán arrives and demands that Fand choose between him and the mortal. She returns with her husband to the OTHERWORLD, deciding that if she had gone with Cúchullain, Manannán could find no mate worthy of him, while Cúchullain still had Emer. The sea god shakes his cloak between the lovers so that they will never meet again, and so that the mortals be granted the gift of forgetting.

Farntickles or **ferntickles.** An Ulster word for freckles, as in the local rhyme recorded by Loreto Todd in *Words Apart* (1990):

Farntickles sware an oath but wan:
They'd never light on a yellow swan.

The reference is to the observation that people with sallow skins rarely get freckles.

Farquhar, George (?1677–1707). Playwright. The last and most decorous of the Restoration dramatists, Farquhar was born in Derry, son of the curate of Liscooley, near Castlefinn, Co. Donegal, and had his education at the Derry Free School interrupted by the SIEGE OF DERRY (1688–9). He may have been at the Battle of the Boyne, and certainly left Trinity College Dublin without a degree to join the SMOCK ALLEY company in 1696.

Farquhar's stage career was cut short after the stabbing of a fellow actor, and it was as a playwright he went to London with the script of *Love and a Bottle* (1698), the successful production of which at Drury Lane was followed by the equally successful *The Constant Couple* (1699). Other important works were *The Twin Rivals* (1700) and the ultimate breeches-part play, *The Recruiting Officer* (1704), based upon his own army experiences in the Low Countries.

Farquhar married a widow, Margaret Pennell, ten years his senior, having been persuaded by her that she was rich, but all she brought to the marriage was three children by her former husband. He bore her no ill will and she bore him two daughters. Though dying of tuberculosis he worked steadily at his last and best play, *The BEAUX' STRATAGEM* (1707), living just long enough to be aware of its triumph.

Farquhar's works, especially the three last-named plays, are part of the standard repertoire of British classical theatre, and his Irish characters, though fashionably anti-Catholic, tend like Charles MACKLIN's to be rather wittier and cleverer than their social betters.

Farrell, Mairéad (1953–88). Republican activist. She was born in Belfast and joined the IRA as soon as she left school at the age of 18. In 1976 she was sentenced to 14 years' imprisonment for bomb-making and served 10 years in Armagh women's prison, acting as the Republican leader there. On Sunday 6 March 1988 she and two IRA members, Seán Savage and Danny McCann, were shot dead by the SAS as they were walking down a street in Gibraltar. The SAS claimed that this pre-emptive strike was justified because they had certain intelligence that Farrell and her companions intended to plant a car-bomb to explode during a military ceremony a few days later. Although the three were on what the IRA called 'active service', they were unarmed at the time of their death.

The incident was controversial and its repercussions tragic: at the funeral of Farrell, Savage and McCann in Milltown Cemetery, west Belfast, on 16 March, a Loyalist killer, Michael Stone, opened fire on the vast crowd of mourners, killing three and wounding scores. At the funeral of one of his victims, three days later, two British soldiers in plain clothes who arrived on the scene were taken prisoner, beaten and then shot dead by the IRA. The violence of the two funerals in Belfast was relayed on television screens all over the world.

Farrell, Michael (1899–1962). Novelist. He was born in Carlow, the son of well-to-do parents. His medical studies at University College Dublin were interrupted by a spell in prison for possession of illegal documents during the Anglo-Irish War of 1919–21. He gave up medicine to run his wife's business. When Sean O'FAOLAIN started *The BELL* he was its amateur-drama correspondent and, as 'Lemuel Gulliver', ran 'The Open Window', its literary causerie, from 1943 till 1954. His autobiographical novel THY TEARS MIGHT CEASE (1963) was not published until after his death. It had been one of the myths of literary Dublin, in that its existence was known, but no one ever expected it to be completed; the published version was edited by Monk Gibbon.

Farrell, M.J. *See* KEANE, MOLLY.

FÁS (Foras Áiseanna Saothair). *See* ANCO.

Fastnet, the. A rock in the sea off Co. Cork, 6 km (4 miles) south of Cape Clear. It is the most southerly point in Ireland. It has a lighthouse, erected in 1854, whose beams are visible for 29 km (17.5 miles). The Fastnet Race is one of the best known of ocean yacht races, established in 1925 and held every two years.

The course starts at Cowes on the Isle of Wight, follows the coast of southwest England and then heads across the Celtic Sea to the Fastnet Rock, before returning to Cowes – a total distance of 984 km (615 miles). The race has been the final leg of the Admiral's Cup since 1957. In 1979 the 303 vessels competing in the race were hit by a violent storm, resulting in the deaths of 17 yachtsmen.

Fastook (Irish, *fásta suas*, 'grown-up'). A HIBERNO-ENGLISH word for a boy or young man who is grown-up enough to know better or to be treated differently. Often used with 'fine', as in: 'With that fine fastook in the house …' or 'Badly that fine fastook needs to be driven to school.'

FATDAD. An acronymic aide-mémoire for the six counties of NORTHERN IRELAND, namely Fermanagh, Antrim, Tyrone, Derry, Armagh, Down. For those who prefer the legally more precise name of Co. Londonderry the acronym becomes FATLAD.

Father of American Presbyterianism. *See* MAKEMIE, FRANCIS.

Father of the American Navy. The honorific title given to Commodore John Barry, who was born in Tacumshane, on the south coast of Co. Wexford, *c.*1745. He went to sea at age 14, made his home in Pennsylvania, USA, and by 1770 was a master mariner, trading with the West Indies.

> Blithe and bold and bred in the sea
> That beats and frets on Ireland's shore,
> He turned his face from a land unfree
> And westward over the ocean bore …
>> JOSEPH I.C. CLARKE (1846–1925): 'John Barry'

When the War of Independence began in 1775 all masters who supported the rebel cause became warship captains, though their vessels were merely converted merchantmen. Barry's ship, the *Black Prince*, became the *Alfred*. In 1776, as master of the *Lexington*, he secured the first prize of the war when he led the British ship *Edward* into Philadelphia harbour. In 1781, after many vicissitudes due to

his quick temper and the lack of resources of the Continental Congress, he was again given a command – as master of the *Alliance* – charged with securing the safe passage of Washington's emissary to Paris. On the way home he captured two British ships, though he was severely wounded in the actions.

After the war Barry left the sea, Congress deciding that the USA did not need a standing navy in peacetime. Barry continued to agitate for the establishment of a permanent marine force, becoming commodore in 1794, and finally persuaded President John Adams (in office 1797–1801) to build three warships. He died on 13 September 1803, having earned the title engraved on his memorial statue (by Wheeler Williams) on the quay at Wexford Harbour:

> So, first of our captains by your right,
> Long as the star-flag lights our land
> And justice rules with even might,
> John Barry, Father of our Navy.
>> JOSEPH I.C. CLARKE (1846–1925): 'Father of the Navy'

Father of the Irish Railways. *See* DARGAN, WILLIAM.

Father Prout (1804–66). The pseudonym of the humorist and journalist Francis Sylvester Mahony. He was born in Cork, the son of the owner of the prosperous Blarney Woollen Mills (8 km/5 miles from the city), and it was he who composed the lines about the BLARNEY STONE that gave it its worldwide reputation. He intended to train as a Jesuit but was asked to resign from the order as unsuitable – a drunken spree was mentioned as a probable cause – but was ordained as a secular priest in Lucca in 1832. He served heroically during a cholera outbreak in Cork, but having quarrelled with his bishop left Ireland and the ministry in 1834. He began to contribute to *Fraser's Magazine*, owned by his friend William MAGINN. His writings (including multilingual parodies) were published in 1837 as *The Reliques of Father Prout*, the name of the actual parish priest of Watergrasshill, who died in

1830. He became Rome correspondent of the *Daily News*, the paper founded by Dickens, in 1846 and finally settled in Paris, where he died. He is buried in the vaults of Shandon Church, the bells of which he made famous (*see* BELLS OF SHANDON, THE).

Father Ted. A Channel 4 comedy series written by Arthur Mathews and Graham Linehan and originally broadcast 1995–8. It starred Dermot MORGAN as Father Ted Crilly, Ardal O'Hanlon as his gormless room-mate Father Dougal McGuire, Frank Kelly as the violent semi-comatose alcoholic Father Jack Hackett (given to shouting 'Drrrink!' from his arm-chair) and Pauline McLynn as the long-suffering housekeeper Mrs Doyle, whose catchphrase, when pressing a cup of tea or other beverage on a resident or visitor was, 'Go on, go on, go on, go on, go on!'

The action takes place for the most part in the presbytery of bleak and windswept Craggy Island, apparently situated off Ireland's west coast. The basis of the show was not satire but surreal flights of fancy, such as an invasion of rabbits, Father Jack growing a great deal of hair on his hands or priests competing in races in full clerical garb or performing in the Eurovision Song Contest. The series became very popular in Ireland. Dermot Morgan died suddenly and prematurely just after completing the third and what he resolved would be the final series of *Father Ted*.

Father Trendy. A clerical character created (1979) by comedian Dermot MORGAN for the RTÉ comedy show *The Likes of Mike* and later developed into a stage show. Father Trendy, who was based on a cleric popular with the media, Father Brian D'Arcy, purveyed a mixture of unction, homespun theology and folk-group liberalism, and was the forerunner of the more famous FATHER TED. A book, *Trendy Sermons*, appeared in 1981.

FATLAD. *See* FATDAD.

Faughs. The nickname of the Royal Irish Fusiliers from their regimental motto 'Faugh-a-

Ballagh' (Irish *fág an bealach*, 'clear the way'). On 5 March 1811 at the charge of Barrosa in southern Spain during the Peninsular War the Irish-speaking 78th Foot:

> ... were already rushing forward, bayonets lowered, with wild cries of 'Faugh-a-ballagh' ('Clear the way!')
>
> MARCUS CUNLIFFE: *The Royal Irish Fusiliers 1793– 1950* (1952)

They were also known as BLAYNEY'S BLOOD-HOUNDS and have been part of the Royal Irish Rangers since 1968. There is a GAA club in Templeogue, Dublin, called 'Faughs'.

Faul, Monsignor Denis (b.1932). Catholic cleric and political campaigner. He was born in Co. Louth and educated at Maynooth, and it was while president of St Patrick's Academy, Dungannon, that he came to the fore as a critic of the treatment of people by the police and army in Northern Ireland. His charge that the judicial system was rigged against Catholics brought a reprimand from Cardinal William Conway. Equally critical of the violence of the IRA, he became chaplain to the hunger strikers during H-BLOCK HUNGER STRIKES of 1981. He strongly opposed the hunger strikes, and is regarded by many as the man who did most to end them, largely by persuading the families of the strikers that once a striker lost consciousness, it was the family of the striker that had the moral right to decide whether or not food should be given. He is now a parish priest in Pomeroy, Co. Tyrone, and continues to speak against injustice on both sides as he sees it.

Faulkner, Brian (1921–77). Unionist politician. He was born Arthur Brian Deane Faulkner at Helen's Bay, Co. Down, on 18 February 1921, the son of a wealthy shirt manufacturer, and educated at St Columba's, Dublin. He was the youngest MP when elected to STORMONT in 1949. He was minister for home affairs 1959–63 and successfully dealt with the IRA's BORDER CAMPAIGN. Always pragmatic in his approach to politics, he showed his business acumen as minister of commerce (1963–9).

He resigned from the government of Terence O'NEILL in 1969 in protest against the appointment of the CAMERON COMMISSION, and was an obvious successor to James CHICHESTER-CLARKE as prime minister in 1971.

Faulkner's introduction of INTERNMENT without trial on 9 August 1971 because of the deteriorating security situation, a measure effective in 1957, merely exacerbated the crisis, partly because it was seen as almost entirely directed against the Nationalist community. In December 1973 he signed the Sunningdale Agreement (*see* WHITELAW, WILLIAM), which set up a POWER-SHARING EXECUTIVE within Northern Ireland with himself as chief executive. Faulkner's political career essentially collapsed with the executive after the UWC strike. He retired from politics after his Unionist Party of Northern Ireland did badly in the 1975 election and became a life peer, as Lord Faulkner of Downpatrick, in 1977. He died after a hunting accident on 3 March 1977.

Though patronized by Ulster aristocrats as a 'little shirt maker', Faulkner was an astute politician who in a more normal society could have been a greater statesman. As it was, his strident membership of the ORANGE ORDER helped to reassure right-wing Unionists that Faulkner's were a 'safe pair of hands' in many crises.

Fay, Martin. *See* CEOLTÓIRÍ CHUALANN; CHIEFTAINS, THE.

FCA. *See* FREE CLOTHES ASSOCIATION.

Fear á Tí (Irish, 'man of the house'). A phrase, pronounced 'far a tee', meaning head of the household, but also used as the Irish version of master of ceremonies at a *CÉILÍ* or concert. The association comes from the folk practice of the AIRNEÁN, in which the head of the household played a significant part.

Feck¹. The Cork name for a game of pitch and toss.

Feck². A HIBERNO-ENGLISH euphemism for 'fuck', not used for copulation but as an exple-

tive or pejorative intensifier: 'Feck!', 'Feck that (for a lark)!', 'That fecking thing!', etc. The frequent use of the word in FATHER TED was seen by many as a symptom of the new liberal atmosphere of the 1990s.

Feck³. To steal or take what is not strictly yours. The word is not used for serious theft but for a misdemeanour such as slogging apples (*see* SLOG).

Feileastram. The Irish word for wild iris or yellow flag, a flower that grows plentifully in marsh and bogland in the south and west of Ireland. The word is widely used in HIBERNO-ENGLISH.

Feiritéar, Piaras (*c*.1600–53). Irish-language poet. He was chieftain of the Dingle peninsula in Co. Kerry (the village of Baile an Fheartéaraigh – Ballyferriter – still bears the family name) and a writer who, politics aside, would have fitted very comfortably with his Jacobean and Caroline contemporaries in England: his work bears strong resemblances to theirs and he may also have written in English. He is now best known for love poetry such as '*Léig Díot Th'airm*' ('Lay Down Your Arms'). In 1641 he supported the anti-English rising (*see* REBELLION OF 1641; CONFEDERATE WAR) for religious rather than for political motives. He continued the struggle for 12 years, but, although granted safe-conduct at the fall of ROSS CASTLE to the Cromwellian army, was treacherously hanged in Killarney in 1653. A 'poet's poet', he was highly trained in the traditional bardic techniques of syllabic poetry. He is one of the FOUR KERRY POETS, to whom a monument stands in Killarney.

Feis (plural *feiseanna*). The name for festivals at which competitions in traditional Irish music, song and dance are held. Originally music competitions organized by the GAELIC LEAGUE, *feiseanna* now often mean dancing competitions, whether local or national, at which elaborately costumed and ringleted young dancers, mostly female, perform complicated reels, jigs and hornpipes (*see* STEP DANCE). The first such *feis* was held in Macroom, Co. Cork, in 1899, a manifestation of the spirit of the CELTIC REVIVAL of the late 19th century.

See also KINGSHIP.

Feis Cheoil. A competition festival for young musicians and singers from 9 years upwards held in Dublin in the spring and now officially designated the Siemens Nixdorf Dublin Feis Cheoil. 'The Feis', as it is universally called, which has been in existence since 1897, was an offshoot of the GAELIC LEAGUE at the time of the CELTIC REVIVAL. Originally the Feis only featured traditional music, but of its 168 categories today, only a few for harp players maintain the link. Like its traditional counterpart, the FLEADH CHEOIL, the Feis has been a stepping-stone for many well-known performers, including John MCCORMACK, who won the tenor gold medal in 1902.

See also MCCALL, P[ATRICK] J[OSEPH].

Fellafellaffalary. A jokey but phonically accurate account of an Ulster accident, cherished by Robert LYND as a favourite joke. It disguises the sentence 'A fellow fell off a lorry.'

Female Oddity, the. A Dublin eccentric who wore only green-coloured clothes and had an equally eccentric diet, as described in the *Gentleman's Magazine* for 1780:

> … a fricasse of frogs and mice is her delight. Loves beef and mutton that is flyblown; when a child she was found eating small coal, and at night if her mother left her in a room by herself, she was seen to dispatch all the contents of the candle snuffers.
>
> Quoted in Peter Somerville-Large, *Irish Eccentrics* (1975)

Fenian Campaign of 1867. With the ending of the American Civil War in 1865 and the return to Ireland of a number of Irishmen who had become trained military officers, the time for a Fenian rising (*see* FENIANS) seemed to have arrived. A possible insurgency in 1865 was cancelled because promised arms did not arrive from the USA. (The Fenian movement was throughout its course bedevilled by internal rancour on both sides of the Atlantic, and it

was plagued by even more informers than the rebel ranks in the Rebellion of 1798.)

One of the American factions anxious to show its mettle engaged in an attempt to capture the Canadian island of Campo Bello in April 1866; however, the American authorities had been forewarned by the informer 'Red' Jim MacDermott, and the attempt was unsuccessful. Another foray across the Canadian border from Vermont (31 May–2 June) was hardly more successful, though in the briefly held Fort Erie a flag emblazoned with a gold harp and the letters IRA flew briefly from its flagpost.

Undaunted by failure, the Fenians in America and Ireland began to plan for a significant rising in 1867 that would involve several sites in Ireland and Britain. It was postponed from February until 5 March, and outbreaks in counties Dublin, Louth, Tipperary, Cork, Limerick and Clare proved unsuccessful, the British authorities, well primed by informers, having arrested most of the leaders. A specially chartered brig called the *Jacknell Packet*, renamed *Erin's Hope*, moored off the coast of Co. Waterford on 1 June, having been redirected from Sligo; the Fenian officers on board were put ashore at Cunigar, near Dungarvan, but were promptly arrested, and *Erin's Hope* sailed back to America.

> They both sat down together; then they rose to stand.
> A Fenian crew surrounded him and rowed him from the land.
> Then Patrick raised a Fenian flag and waved it near and far,
> And Bridget blessed her sailor boy on board the Man-O'-War.
>
> ANON.: 'The Fenian Man-O'-War' (1867)

Fenians. A secret revolutionary organization that had as its object making Ireland a republic and bringing English domination to an end. It was known more correctly and persistently as the Irish Republican Brotherhood (IRB), a name that outlasted 'Fenian', and was founded in 1858 by James STEPHENS (1824–1901) in Ireland and in America by John O'Mahony (1819–77), who took the term Fenian from the warrior band led by FIONN MAC CUMHAIL. Though its attempts in 1867 at risings on both sides of the Atlantic were farcical failures (*see* FENIAN CAMPAIGN OF 1867), the existence of the movement kept alive the PHOENIX FLAME, which enabled such old Fenians as Thomas CLARKE to influence younger men like Patrick PEARSE and his successors.

> I, A.B., in the presence of Almighty God, do solemnly swear allegiance to the Irish republic, now virtually established, and that I will do my utmost, at every risk, while life lasts, to defend its independence and integrity, and finally, that I will yield implicit obedience in all things, not contrary to the laws of God, to the commands of my superior officers. So help me God! Amen.
>
> Fenian oath, quoted in John O'Leary, *Recollections of Fenians and Fenianism* (1896)

Use of the word 'Fenian' by Ulster Protestants as a term of abuse for Ulster Catholics or Nationalists dates from the 1900s.

See also CLAN NA GAEL; EASTER RISING.

Ferdia or **Ferdiad.** In Irish mythology, the fellow student and closest friend of CÚCHULAINN, trained with him in ALBA in martial arts by SCÁTHACH. During the war of the TÁIN BÓ CUAILNGE he fights on the side of Medb, who goads him, although he is extremely reluctant, into combat with his friend. Their battle, which takes place near the modern town of ARDEE, reaches stalemate after four days, and Cúchulainn is forced to use the GAE-BOLG. The effect of Ferdia's death on him is such that he loses all his fighting spirit, and he too dies shortly afterwards.

Fer Doireach. *See* DARK DRUID, THE.

Fergal (d.784). An Irish monk, known also in the Latinate form as Virgil, who trained at CANICE's monastery at Aghaboe. He left on a pilgrimage to the Holy Land (*c.*740), but remained in Bavaria to continue the work of St Rupert (d.*c.*710) in evangelizing Austria. He was eventually placed in charge of the diocese of Salzburg, but was too humble to accept ordination as bishop. He was an intellectual, known as the 'Geometer', and was twice reported to Rome by St Boniface for his views on such matters as the nature of the earth's structure. His work of evangelizing Carinthia was thoroughly successful. His feast day is 27 November.

Fergus Mac Roth. In Irish mythology, the ruler of Ulster, who agrees to give up his kingship for a year at the insistence of his wife NESSA so that her son CONCHOBHAR can rule in EMAIN MACHA. At the end of the time the young man refuses to relinquish the throne, but Fergus continues to serve him as emissary to NAOISE and DEIRDRE in ALBA.

> So young Conor gained the crown;
> So I laid the kingship down;
> Laying with it as it went
> All I knew of discontent.
>
> SAMUEL FERGUSON (1810–86): 'The Abdication of Fergus Mac Roy', in *Lays of the Red Branch* (1897)

When he learns of Conchobhar's treachery. Fergus takes the side of MEDB in the TÁIN BÓ CUAILNGE war and fights the Ulstermen. According to tradition he is a scholar who sets down in OGAM an account of the fighting. He is killed by a spear thrown by AILILL, who finds him swimming naked with Medb.

Ferguson, Harry (1884–1960). Inventor and pioneer of agricultural machinery. He was born on 4 November 1884 at the family farm at Growell, near Hillsborough in Co. Down, but finding home life narrow and stifling, and farm work laborious, became a mechanic in Belfast at the age of 16. He showed a special aptitude for tuning engines and an inventive skill that led to modifications in the primitive motorcycles of the day, which he raced with such abandon that he became known as 'the mad mechanic'. He pioneered flying in Ireland (*see* FIRST IRISH FLIGHT, THE), but on his marriage in 1913 turned his genius to safer preoccupations.

Urged by the government during the First World War to devise machinery that would help the 'Grow More Food' campaign, Ferguson constructed a tractor with a mounted plough. Over the years he refined the product, eventually devising a tractor with hydraulic cab controls, which could plough, harrow and mow. In 1939 Henry Ford, impressed by the prototype, took Ferguson on as his only partner, agreeing after a 'handshake' to market the Fordson tractor, which had a profound effect on mechanized farming. In 1947 Henry Ford II, the grandson of the founder, reneged on the manual contract and Ferguson was driven to retaliate. He engaged in litigation that lasted four years; as he said, it was not for the money but for the rights of the small inventor against the big corporations. He intensified his campaign by opening a factory in Detroit close to Ford's major plant, which was recording annual sales of $33 million by 1949. In 1952 the case was finally settled with an award of $9.25 million.

Ferguson continued to interest himself in invention, working on automatic transmission and anti-locking devices in cars. He died suddenly on 25 October 1960 at his home in Stow-in-the Wold, England, having maintained an independence which precluded the acceptance of many offered honours, including a knighthood for inventive services to the Allies during the Second World War.

Ferguson, Samuel (1810–86). Poet and scholar. He was born in Belfast and educated at INST (where he learned Irish) and Trinity College Dublin, which he left without taking a degree. He attended Lincoln's Inn and was called to the Bar in 1838, becoming a QC in 1859. He retired from his law practice in 1867 to take up the appointment of deputy-keeper of Public Records. His work of reorganization of a neglected department was acknowledged by a knighthood in 1878.

Stimulated by the friendship of George PETRIE, John O'DONOVAN and Eugene O'CURRY, Ferguson became interested in Irish literature, and his translations of lyrics in *Lays of the Western Gael* (1864) have some of the power of the originals. They are still frequently anthologized, and were an early stimulus for the IRISH LITERARY REVIVAL.

Ferguson's rather tepid love affair with Irish Nationalism, a period to which his 'Lament for the Death of Thomas Davis' belongs, ended with his successful defence of Richard D'Alton Williams (see SHAMROCK²) on a charge of treason-felony after the Smith O'Brien rising of 1848 (*see* WIDOW MCCORMICK'S CABBAGE PATCH). Thereafter his instinctive Liberal Unionism reasserted itself; he wished to keep the link with Britain, but was in favour of limited self-government. He is buried in Dunegore churchyard in Co. Antrim, the home of his forebears.

> But I grieve not, eagle of the empty eyrie,
> That thy wrathful cry is still,
> And that songs alone of peaceful mourners
> Are heard today on Erin's hill.
> 'Lament for the Death of Thomas Davis'

Ferns Three. Three young men – Donnacha McGloin, Pat Jackmen and Colm O'Gorman – who were abused as children by Father Sean Fortune in the parish and diocese of Ferns in Co. Wexford. Their revelations about the response to their complaints by Bishop Brendan Comiskey led to his resignation as Bishop of Ferns in March 2002 (*see* BISHOP BRENDAN). The diocese of Ferns made a substantial out-of-court compensation settlement with Colm O'Gorman in 2003.

Ferntickles. See FARNTICKLES.

Festival of Kerry, the. *See* 'ROSE OF TRALEE, THE'.

Fetch. A preternatural vision of a living person, usually seen by a relative or friend. If occurring in the morning the visitation was a sign that the person, whose *doppelgänger* it was, would have a long and prosperous life; if in the evening it was a portent of imminent death:

> She only looked with a dead, dead eye
> And a wan, wan cheek of sorrow.
> I knew her Fetch; she was called to die
> And she died upon the morrow.
> JOHN BANIM (1798–1842): 'The Fetch' (1857)

Fethard-on-Sea. A village on the Hook Head peninsula in Co. Wexford that was the scene of an ugly sectarian confrontation in the late

1950s. Sean Cloney, a Catholic, and Sheila Kelly, a Protestant, had married against the wishes of their clergy, and Sheila had undertaken to bring their children up as Catholics, in accordance with the NE TEMERE decree. In 1957 their elder daughter, Ellen, was 6 and of school age. When a local priest ordered Sheila Cloney to send her daughter to a Catholic school she disappeared with the couple's two daughters, travelling first to the north of Ireland, thence to the Orkney Islands. After their departure local people, with the approval of the Catholic clergy, began a boycott of Protestant businesses and professionals in the village, including Sheila Cloney's father, who was a cattle dealer. The boycott lasted more than a year. The Cloneys were reconciled and eventually Sheila and her children came back to live with Sean in Fethard-on-Sea, but they educated the children at home. *A Love Divided* (1999) is a film about the experiences of the Cloneys and the village.

Fiachra (d.c.670). A 7th-century Irish hermit who unwittingly gave his name to the French four-wheeled cab (the *fiacres*, which first made their appearance on the streets of Paris in 1620 and had their stand outside the Hôtel Saint-Fiacre). He is traditionally the one who brought the last sacraments to St COMGALL, and is said to have brought Comgall's embalmed arm to his monastery at Ullard in Co. Kilkenny. On his arrival in France Fiachra set up his eremitical cell on the site of the town of Saint-Fiacre-en-Brie, near Paris (in the region famous for Brie cheese). He received so many visitors that he found it necessary to set up a hospice for Irish pilgrims, the first of its kind. His reputation as a gardener and as a curer of venereal disease made his shrine at Meaux greatly venerated long after his death. He is the patron saint of gardeners (because of the excellence of the vegetables that grew about his cells), with a feast day on 30 August.

Fial. The Irish word for 'generous', a very important concept in Gaelic society, and even for speakers of HIBERNO-ENGLISH, who have

adopted the word. *Fialtach* also has the connotation of a 'big strong man', a 'champion'. The word *fial* was often used in combination with FLAITHIÚIL (a synonym)– *fial flaithiúil* – or *fáilteach* ('welcoming') – *fial fáilteach*. *See also* FÁILTE; HOSPITALITY; RAIDHSE.

Fianna. In Irish mythology, a band of superlative warriors led by FIONN MAC CUMHAIL and said to date from 300 BC. Their purpose is to guard the HIGH KING of Ireland, CORMAC MAC ART, and their company includes Fionn's son OISÍN and his closest lieutenant DIARMAID UA DUIBHNE. They are attended by physicians, musicians, poets and DRUIDS, and their adventures form the material of the Ossianic Cycle, the source of the famous 18th-century imposture of James Macpherson (1736–96). These tales probably spring from a euhemerist memory of an historical military elite. It was extremely difficult to qualify for membership: almost-superhuman feats of athleticism and courage were required. The word *fianna*, meaning 'warrior-hunters', was used in Fianna Éireann (Countess Markievicz's revolutionary band of boy scouts; *see* REBEL COUNTESS, THE), and in the name of the political party FIANNA FÁIL ('band of warriors of Ireland'). The 19th-century insurrectionist FENIANS also took their name from the mythical Fianna.

Fianna Fáil (Irish, 'band of warriors of Ireland', though often mistakenly translated as 'soldiers of destiny'). A political party founded by Éamon DE VALERA on 16 May 1926, and described by Seán LEMASS as the SLIGHTLY CONSTITUTIONAL PARTY. On 12 August 1927 members of Fianna Fáil for the first time took the OATH OF ALLEGIANCE prescribed in the TREATY and so were able to enter the Dáil. Once the party came to power for the first time (9 March 1932) it was reluctant to lose it. In 1931 de Valera founded the IRISH PRESS, a propaganda tool for the party. Fianna Fáil has tended to be a populist party, in contrast to the party's main rival, FINE GAEL.

A list of Fianna Fáil administrations and taoiseachs follows:

1932–48: a series of Fianna Fáil administrations with de Valera as taoiseach;

1951–4: Fianna Fáil with de Valera;

1957–June 1959: Fianna Fáil with de Valera;

1959–66: Fianna Fáil with Seán Lemass as taoiseach (several administrations);

1966–73 and 1977–9: Fianna Fáil with Jack LYNCH as taoiseach;

1979–1981, March–December 1982, 1987–92: Fianna Fáil with Charles Haughey as taoiseach, in coalition with PEE DEES (PDs or Progressive Democrats);

1992–1994: Fianna Fáil with Albert REYNOLDS as taoiseach (two administrations, in coalition first with PDs, then with Labour);

June 1997 to date: Fianna Fáil with Bertie AHERN as taoiseach (in coalition with PDs).

Fiche Blian ag Fás. The title of an autobiographical work (1933) by the BLASKET islander Muiris Ó Súilleabháin (1904–50). Ó Súilleabháin was encouraged to write by English scholar George Thomson (1903–87), who in August 1923, on the advice of Robin Flower (see BLÁITHÍN), came to the Great Blasket to learn Irish. Thomson encouraged Ó Súilleabháin to become a garda (policeman) when he left the island rather then emigrate to the USA, like most of the islanders. Thomson also edited the text of _Fiche Blian ag Fás_ and co-authored (with Moya Llewelyn Davies) the English translation, _Twenty Years a-Growing._ Ó Súilleabhán drowned while bathing in Co. Galway, where he had made his home; he had written a second volume of autobiography, _Fiche Blian faoi Bhláth_, which was never published. The phrase _fiche blian ag fás_ forms part of a triadic Irish proverb: _fiche blian ag fás_ ('twenty years a-growing'), _fiche blian faoi bhláth_ ('twenty years in full bloom'), _fiche blian ag meath_ ('twenty years in decline').

Fidchell. An ancient Irish board game analogous with chess that is mentioned in many tales. It was invented by LUGH, and proficiency in the game was a requirement for both heroes and deities.

Field, John (1782–1837). Irish-born pianist and composer, celebrated as the inventor of the nocturne, a type of reflective character piece later adopted (and developed) by Frédéric Chopin. Born in Dublin, the son of a violinist at the city's Theatre Royal (see CROW STREET THEATRE), Field was first taught music by his grandfather, an organist. The young Field, a pianistic prodigy, made his performing debut as a ten-year-old (advertisements exaggerated his youth by describing him as 'a child of eight') at Signor Giordani's First Spiritual Concert at Dublin's ROTUNDA on Saturday 24 March 1792, playing 'Madame Krumpholt's difficult Pedal Harp Concerto'. By 1793 he was already composing for himself, his initial effort being an arrangement of an old Irish air entitled 'Go and Shake Yourself'.

In 1793 Field _père_ was offered a post in the orchestra of London's Haymarket Theatre, and the family moved to the British capital. Field _fils_ was apprenticed to Muzio Clementi, celebrated piano teacher, composer and proprietor of a successful piano and music business. Clementi employed Field at his warehouse to show off his instruments to prospective purchasers by improvisation. 1802 saw Field and Clementi embark on an ambitious European business trip to promote the publication of piano pieces by various contemporary composers, including Field himself. They spent time in Paris and Vienna (Field's interpretations of Bach and Handel taking the French capital by storm), and reached St Petersburg by the end of the year. Clementi left St Petersburg in the summer of 1803, but Field settled in the Russian city. He was fêted in aristocratic circles, and became much sought-after as a virtuoso and teacher (the composer Glinka was later one of his pupils). The first _Three Nocturnes_ were composed in the summer of 1814.

Field also travelled widely as a performing pianist. In response to an invitation from the Philharmonic Society, he visited London in 1832, meeting Mendelssohn and performing his own Concerto in F flat. He went on to play in France (again to rapturous acclaim), Switzerland and Italy. In Naples in 1834, however, he was taken seriously ill and languished in hospital for nine months until a Russian noble family, the Rachmanoffs, took him back to Moscow. He died just a few months after his return to Russia, on 11 January 1837. A deathbed anecdote records the ailing composer's somewhat laboured contribution to the stock of Irish confessional jokes. Field was asked, 'Are you a Catholic?' When he responded 'No,' he was asked, 'Are you a Protestant?' Again the answer was 'No.' He was then asked, 'Are you a Calvinist?' 'Not that either,' responded Field. 'Not a Calvinist – but a pianist!' Field wrote 7 piano concertos and a series of chamber compositions for piano and strings, but his chief claim on posterity lies in his 18 nocturnes.

Field, the. The generic term for sites of ORANGE ORDER rallies on the TWELFTH OF JULY where the marchers assemble to commemorate the Battle of the BOYNE, pledge loyalty to the queen and be reminded of their exclusiveness as protectors of Ulster traditions. The largest 'field' is that at Edenderry, just outside Belfast, consisting of 300 LOLs and attendant bands. An earlier 'field' was at Finaghy, closer to the assembly point at Carlisle Circus, but still requiring a trek of more than 10 km (6 miles).

See also ARCH; BANNER; SASH.

Field Day. A theatrical company founded in 1980 by Brian FRIEL and the actor Stephen Rea, and having on its board Seamus DEANE, David Hammond (film-maker and folk-music specialist), Seamus HEANEY and Tom PAULIN. Its purpose was to redefine Ireland's cultural identity through drama, pamphlets and the 4000-page, three-volume *Field Day Anthology* (1991). The plays written by Friel, Derek MAHON, Paulin, Heaney, Thomas KILROY, Stewart Parker and others gave Derry, the scene of the first productions, a dozen years of political drama and theatrical fame. In addition, the pamphlets generated sufficient

controversy to justify their writing, while the anthology (chiefly edited by Deane) – though attacked by revisionists as being too Nationalist and by feminists because of its under-representation of women – is a remarkable achievement that generally lives up to its brief of reappraisal. (Two further volumes were added in 2002 to correct the perceived lacunae in women's literature.)

'Fields of Athenry, The'. A ballad written in 1979 by Dubliner Pete St John, popularized by Paddy Reilly (b.1939) and recorded by countless artists. Although melancholy and traditional in style, it is very much in demand for dancing, both in its original quickstep tempo and livened to a disco beat. (The 'low' fields refers to the fact that Athenry is in flat east Galway countryside.)

> By a lonely prison wall
> I heard a young girl calling,
> 'Michael they are taking you away,
> For you stole Trevelyan's corn
> So the young might see the morn.
> Now a prison ship lies waiting in the bay.'
> *Chorus:*
> Low lie the fields of Athenry
> Where once we watched the small free birds fly.
> Our love was on the wing, we had dreams and
>   songs to sing,
> It's so lonely 'round the Fields of Athenry.

In recent years the song has been used as an anthem by Irish supporters at rugby internationals.

See also TREVELYAN'S CORN.

Fiesole. An Italian town, 6 km (4 miles) north of Florence, noted for its Etruscan remains. It was the bishopric of the Irish saint DONATUS (829–86), whose head, enclosed in a container of gilt bronze, is in the church of San Domenico, a village halfway between Fiesole and Florence.

Fighting Priest of Gweedore, the. The nickname of Canon James McFadden (1842–1917). He was appointed parish priest of Gweedore, Co. Donegal, in 1875 and ruled his parishioners with a rod of iron, using physical violence when he considered it necessary to combat the evils of drunkenness and CROSSROAD DANCES. Thus he earned another nickname, *an Sagart Mór* ('the big priest'), even though he was physically a small man. He supported his parishioners in agrarian agitation; he and they protested against evictions and did all in their power to prevent them from being carried out. He was arrested and, with 12 others, charged with murder in 1889, after an incident in which an RIC inspector died as a result of a scuffle. At the trial Peter O'Brien (*see* PETHER THE PACKER) was the prosecutor, while Tim HEALY was counsel for the defence. After two weeks a deal was struck with the prosecution: the defendants would plead guilty, Father McFadden would be released, and none of the others would be sentenced to death. The deal was done, but some of the other defendants were sentenced to 30 years in jail, and there was a great deal of public criticism of the actions of McFadden and Healy. McFadden later became parish priest of Iniskeel and died in Glenties, Co. Donegal.

'Fighting Race, The'. A poem by the prolific Joseph I.C. Clarke (1846–1925) inspired by the number of Irish names in the list of casualties in the *Maine* incident. The battleship had been sent to Havana in January 1898 to protect American citizens at risk during the Cuban revolution against Spain and to evacuate them if necessary. On 15 February the ship was sunk in an explosion, blamed on the Spanish, in which 260 officers and men out of the ship's complement of 350 were killed. Of these 64 were born in Ireland or had unmistakably Irish surnames. Clarke was a reporter and wrote this, his best-known piece of verse, for the *New York Sun*, where it appeared on St Patrick's Day 1898. It takes the form of a conversation between three Irish-Americans, Kelly, Burke and Shea, and demonstrates their innocent chauvinistic pride in their race's reputation. In the fourth verse Shea ('the scholar') recalls the battle feats of the WILD GEESE:

… We were at Ramillies,
We left our bones at Fontenoy
And up in the Pyrenees,
Before Dunkirk, on Landen's plain,
Cremona, Lille and Ghent,
We're all over Austria, France and Spain,
Wherever they pitched a tent.

'The Fighting Race' was said to be Michael COLLINS's favourite recitation.

Fighting 69th, the. A regiment of mainly Irish soldiers, forming part of the Irish Brigade recruited in New York state to fight in the American Civil War. Their first commander was Thomas Francis Meagher (*see* MEAGHER OF THE SWORD), and they suffered appalling casualties at the battles of Malvern Hill, Williamsburg, Antietam and Fredericksburg. Their flag had a harp at its centre set on a wreath of shamrock, with a scroll underneath carrying the Irish phrase, taken from a motto of the FIANNA, '*Riamh nar dhruid ó spairn lann*' ('Never part [us] from the clash of spears'). In the First World War the regiment was commanded by Colonel 'Wild Bill' Donovan and lost 3501 men, and it also played a significant part in the Second World War. In 1963 it was officially designated with its popular title by army decree and granted St Patrick's Day as its official regimental day. When President Kennedy visited Ireland in June 1963 he presented the regiment's original colours to the Irish people.

Our great Republic! Shall the kings behold,
Neath slavery's thrust, its overthrow?
Loud, righteous, quick our regiment's answer rolled
'The Irish Sixty-Ninth says, "No!"'
    JOSEPH I.C. CLARKE (1846–1925): 'The Ballad of the Sixty-Ninth'

Figure dances. *See* CÉILÍ DANCES; DANCING MASTERS.

Filid. The professional poet-class in ancient Ireland whose chief occupation was to compose eulogies to their aristocratic masters. The *file* – as a member of the *filid* was called – had an envied capacity with words, and having acquired knowledge of the past, especially the supposed genealogies of his masters, could construct mighty lays and perform them with skill and flattery. In pre- and early-Christian times they were thought to have something of the magical power of the DRUIDS (although their magic lay in their words) and they were the memory banks for the complicated system of BREHON LAWS. They were believed to have the capacity to raise blisters on their adversaries' foreheads and had, according to a tradition extant by the 6th century, acquired such power and arrogance that the various political and religious establishments wished to have them expelled (*see* DRUIMCEATT).

Finan (d.661). The saint who succeeded AIDAN at LINDISFARNE, and, like Aidan, was a monk of IONA. Finan managed to baptize not only Peada, the son of the unregenerate pagan Penda (?575–655), but also Oswy (d.670), who had killed Oswin (d.651), Aidan's second patron. Finan carried on the missionary work, bringing the faith – with a Celtic flavour – to the lands south of the Humber. He strongly resisted pressure from the English church to accept Roman instructions about the date of Easter, the monastic tonsure and other elements of divergence between the Celtic church and the Roman church. He died three years before the Synod of WHITBY ruled against the Irish practices. His feast day is 17 February.

Finbar(r). *See* FINDBAR.

Findan. *See* FINTAN OF RHEINAU.

Findbar or **Finbar(r)** (also called **Bairre**) (d. *c*.633). The patron saint of Cork. He was born near Crookstown, Co. Cork, the son of a Connacht father, a metalworker who moved to Munster to find work and married a slave girl. Findbar left home with three unidentified ascetics and spent much time in Scotland before establishing various hermitages in his native area, notably at Kilclooney and on an island in GOUGANE BARRA, which bears his name. Among many wondrous tales associated with him is one in which he is led by

an angel from the source of the River Lee at Gougane Barra to its marshy mouth, where he founded his most important monastery, out of which grew the see and city of Cork. Findbar died at Cloyne and his remains were taken to Cork to be enclosed in a silver shrine. His feast day is 25 September.
See also WHERE FINBARR TAUGHT, LET MUNSTER LEARN.

Findlater's Church. A Presbyterian church built at the northeast corner of Parnell Square, Dublin, in the 1860s by Alexander Findlater, one of the city's best-known grocers. The design was by Andrew Heiton of Perth.

Finea, Bridge of (also spelt **Finnea**). The site of a battle (1646) in Co. Westmeath during the CONFEDERATE WAR, in which the Irish leader Myles 'the Slasher' O'Reilly died on 5 August 1646 while defending the strategically important bridge over the River Inny at Finea against the Parliamentarian forces under General Munro:

> He fell but the foot of a foeman passed
> Not on the bridge of Finea …
>
> ANON.: incription on a plaque to O'Reilly on the site

Percy FRENCH's 'Come Back, Paddy Reilly' mentions the bridge of Finea when giving directions to Ballyjamesduff:

> The Garden of Eden is vanished they say
> But I know the lie of it still;
> Just turn to the left at the bridge of Finea,
> And stop on the way to Cootehill …

The body of Myles the Slasher followed the same route on its way to its burial place in the Francisan friary in Cavan town.

Fine Gael (Irish, 'tribe of Gael'). The name of a political party founded in 1933 when CUMANN NA NGAEDHEAL, the National Guard and the National Centre amalgamated. Its leaders have been: W.T. COSGRAVE (1935–44), Richard MULCAHY (1944–59), James DILLON (1959–65), Liam COSGRAVE (1965–77), Garret FITZGERALD (1977–87), Alan Dukes (1987–90), John BRUTON (1990–2001) and Michael Noonan (from January 2001).

Fine Gael has traditionally been the second largest party in the DÁIL, but suffered a serious decline in electoral fortunes in the general election of 2003, and is now trying to regroup. Traditionally centrist or (slightly) right-of-centre, as opposed to the populist FIANNA FÁIL, it had its conservative vote taken by the PEE DEES (PDs: Progressive Democrats) and its more liberal support stolen by Fianna Fáil and the LABOUR PARTY.

The party's participation in government is detailed below:

1948–51 and 1954–57: part of INTERPARTY GOVERNMENTS, with John A. COSTELLO as taoiseach (since CLANN NA POBLACHTA would not accept Richard Mulcahy);

1973–7: coalition with Labour, with Liam Cosgrave as taoiseach;

1981–2 and 1982–7: coalition with Labour, with Garret FitzGerald as taoiseach;

1994–7: part of RAINBOW COALITION with John Bruton as taoiseach.

Fingal[1]. The name by which FIONN MAC CUMHAIL is known in Scotland. His Caledonian fame, like that of his son Ossian (*see* OISÍN), began in the 18th century with the publication by the egregious James Macpherson (1736–96) of *Fingal, an Ancient Epic Poem in Six Books* in 1762. His invention, based loosely on old ballads, had for a time an electrifying effect on the leading European literary men of the day, including Goethe and Schiller, but not on Dr Johnson who rapidly dismissed it as Macpherson's own work and not a translation from the Gaelic. Its lasting contribution has been topographical rather than mythological, rendering the volcanic remains on the Inner Hebridean island of Staffa as 'Fingal's Cave'.

Fingal[2]. The name of a new Irish county, incorporating a populous region of the old north Co. Dublin. It extends from the River LIFFEY in the west, to the sea in the east and to the north as far as the county boundary. It is the fifth largest local authority, with a population of about 168,000. It came into being on 1 January 1994 when three new local authorities were established in place of the former Dublin County Council. The name Fingal is an anglicization of the Irish *Fine Gall* ('tribe or territory of foreigners'), so named because it was populated by VIKINGS (or what were later known as Hiberno-Scandinavians) and ruled by their kings.

Finn, Alec. *See* BOUZOUKI; DÉ DANANN.

Finn, Phineas. The Irish character in the Palliser sequence of seven political novels by Anthony TROLLOPE. *Phineas Finn* is the title of the second novel (1869), subtitled 'The Irish Member', while the fourth novel is titled *Phineas Redux* (1874); Phineas Finn also appears as a character in the last three novels. The character is based upon a number of successful Catholic politicians, notably John Sadleir (*see* POPE'S BRASS BAND, THE), though Trollope gives no suggestion of Sadleir's Grand Guignol end. There is more passion than politics in *Phineas Finn*, the second novel, but Finn does sacrifice his career over Irish TENANT RIGHT, and, though half in love with Madame Max Goesler, returns to Co. Clare to marry his childhood sweetheart Mary Flood. He reappears in *Phineas Redux*, having been relieved of uxorial duties by that convenience of the Victorian novel, the premature death. There is no lack of melodrama in Finn's life, including arrest for murder, from which he is saved by the assiduous detective work of Madame Max, whom he wisely marries. The part in the splendid BBC television dramatization of all seven novels (1975) was played by the Irish actor Donal MCCANN.

Finnbhenach. *See* TÁIN BÓ CUAILNGE.

Finnegans Wake. The title of James JOYCE's last novel (1939), borrowed from an Irish-American ballad but significantly lacking an apostrophe, making it sound like a kind of command. In the original song Tim Finnegan, a drunken hod carrier, dies after a fall, but at his wake revives when whiskey is accidentally spilt over his corpse (see 'TIM FINNEGAN'S WAKE').

The idea of indestructibility and resurrection ideally suited the author's theme of the cyclical pattern of history. The prose used by Joyce in the novel, full of multilingual wordplay, is a kind of comic *Encyclopaedia Hibernica*, moving freely through all history, myth and philosophies. The dreaming of Humphrey Chimpden Earwicker, a Dublin tavern-keeper – who has a wife Anna Livia Plurabelle (*see* ANNA LIFFEY) and children Shem and Shaun – uses the stream of consciousness technique used by Joyce in the earlier ULYSSES. (Earwicker's initials HCE has several avatars, including 'here comes everybody', the claim 'haveth childers everywhere', and the 'Howth Castle and Environs' of the opening sequence.) *Finnegans Wake* and *Ulysses* have been described, not entirely unfairly, as respectively the great unreadable and the great unread modern Irish novels. The last sentence of *Finnegans Wake*:

> A way a lone a last a loved a long the …

links up with its topographical beginning:

> riverrun, past Eve and Adam's, from swerve of shore to bend of bay, brings us by a commodious vicus of recirculation back to Howth Castle and Environs.

to complete the circle that encloses the reader.

Finnian of Clonard (d.*c*.549). A founding father of Irish monasticism, second only to St ENDA and more influential because of the convenient location of his foundations. He was born at Myshall, Co. Carlow, and educated at St Cadoc's monastery at Llancarfan in South Glamorgan, where he was a friend and fellow-student of St Gildas. At his monastery of CLONARD in Co. Westmeath he trained the TWELVE APOSTLES OF IRELAND. Like his Welsh master he emphasized the pre-eminence of study, and urged his pupils to set up their own establishments. Though ascetic in his own practice his rule was gentler than those of St COMGALL or St Enda. He died of plague *c*.549 and his feast day is 12 December.

Finnian of Moville (*c*.493–579). An Irish monastic father who did his early training at the great school of monks at CANDIDA CASA in Galloway. He spent 20 years in Scotland as a student and missionary, only leaving, it was said, because of the amorous advances of a Pictish girl. He went to Rome and obtained Latin copies of the Scriptures – the *Vulgate* – which he brought to Ulster in 540. For this reason his school at Moville, 8 km (5 miles) from BANGOR, in present-day Newtonards, was the leading school of biblical study. His feast day is 10 September.

Finn MacCool. *See* FIONN MAC CUMHAIL.

Fintan. In Irish mythology, the husband of CESAIR who survives the Flood by taking the form of a salmon. He eats the nuts of knowledge before going to live in a pool in the Boyne, and is greatly sought after as the Salmon of Knowledge (*see* FIONN MAC CUMHAIL).

Fintan of Clonenagh (d.603). A disciple of COLUM CILLE (Columba). When abbot of Clonenagh, Fintan made it the most rigorous of all the houses in Ireland. The monks ate no meat and did not use animals to help with their farm work. The most luxurious food was vegetables, and Fintan himself subsisted on stale barley bread and muddy water. Conditions became so bad that the monks in neighbouring houses objected. Fintan's feast day is 17 February.

Fintan of Rheinau (d.879). An Irish saint who was carried off from a Leinster abbey to Orkney as a slave by Norse raiders but who managed to escape to the mainland. He undertook a pilgrimage to Rome in thanksgiving and became a Benedictine monk, spending his last 22 years as an anchorite at Rheinau, near Schaffhausen on the Rhine in Switzerland. His feast day is 15 November.

Fionn Mac Cumhail (anglicized as **Finn MacCool**, and also known as **Fingal**[1]). A mythological Irish hero, chief of the FIANNA, the band of warriors whose purpose was to defend the

HIGH KING of Ireland. The deeds of his band and his own magical powers engendered the largest body of Irish wonder tales. There are many parallels with the legends of Arthur of Camelot, especially in the story of Diarmaid and GRÁINNE, in which the ageing king is betrayed by a young wife and his closest friend, echoing the tale of Lancelot and Guinevere.

Fionn outdoes even CÚCHULAINN in fame as a hero of Irish legend. He is the son of Cumal, a leader of the Fianna, and MURNA OF THE WHITE NECK, and is given the name Demna. Cumal is killed by GOLL MAC MORNA, who had become leader of the warrior band, and for most of Demna's childhood he is at risk from Goll. He establishes his reputation as a warrior early, slaying Lia and recovering the CRANE BAG he had stolen from the Fianna. He is sent for education to the druid Finegas, who lives beside the Boyne and hopes someday to hook FINTAN, the Salmon of Knowledge. One day he succeeds and gives the fish to Demna to cook. The boy, burning his thumb during the cooking, sucks it to ease the pain and unwittingly stores all Fintan's knowledge in a tooth, known in later stories as *fiacail feasa Fionn* ('Fionn's tooth of wisdom').

Now known as Fionn ('the fair one') and equipped with his father's magic spear, he defends TARA from an attack by a demon and is made head of the Fianna by CORMAC MAC ART. For many years he leads the Fianna in their golden age, faithfully served by Goll Mac Morna, Diarmaid Ua Duibhne and his son OISÍN.

Fingal (the cave on the Hebridean island of Staffa, celebrated in Mendelssohn's overture) is identified with him, and in later Ulster folktales (as Finn MacCool) he is the giant builder of the basaltic GIANT'S CAUSEWAY. In the story he is attempting to construct a path across the sea to Scotland so that he may fight a rival giant. The same story has him scooping up a piece of land from the centre of Ulster and tossing it at his rival, creating in an instant the ISLE OF MAN and LOUGH NEAGH. The Causeway's Irish name, *Clochán na bhFomaraigh*

('the stepping stones of the FOMORIANS'), suggests earlier builders.

Fionnuala. In Irish mythology, the daughter of LIR, who with her brothers, Aedh, Conn and Fiachra, are changed into swans by AOIFE[1], their stepmother and aunt. They languish for 500 years on the Western Ocean, for 500 more on the Sea of MOYLE and for a further 500 on Lough Derravaragh in Co. Westmeath. By then, as the later stories tell, Christianity had come to Ireland and the sound of a monastery bell restores them to very aged human form, giving them time to be baptized before their simultaneous deaths.

> Silent. O Moyle, be the roar of thy water,
> Break not, ye breezes, your chain of repose,
> While mournfully weeping, Lir's lonely daughter
> Tells to the night-star her tale of woes.
> THOMAS MOORE (1779–1852): 'The Song of Fionnuala', in *Irish Melodies* (1808)

Firbolg (Irish, 'bag-men'). In Irish mythology, the early inhabitants of Ireland who are enslaved by the TUATHA DÉ DANAAN and made to carry loads of fertile earth to rocky parts of the terrain. Historically they were pre-Celtic inhabitants with notable differences in physiognomy and stature from the tall, sandy-haired Celts. The word has persisted as a term of mild abuse.

Fireside, his own. *See* HIS OWN FIRESIDE.

First American Cardinal, the. John McCloskey (1810–85). He was born on 10 March 1810 in Brooklyn, New York, USA, to Irish parents who had emigrated from Dungiven, Co. Derry, in 1808. He was ordained in the old St Patrick's Cathedral in Queens, the first native New Yorker to be ordained as a diocesan priest. He was appointed to the staff of a new seminary in Nyack, New York, but was given permission to study in the Gregorian University (1835–7) in Rome after the college was destroyed in a fire. When he returned to New York he became pastor of Greenwich Village and president of St John's College, the forerunner of Fordham University.

In 1844 McCloskey was ordained bishop (on his 34th birthday) and placed in charge of the diocese of Albany in 1847. He replaced the dynamic John Hughes (*see* FIRST NEW YORK ARCHBISHOP, THE) as Archishop of New York in 1864, using a much more conciliatory approach in his public utterances, except in his admonishment of the FENIANS in 1866. His appointment as archbishop and later as cardinal (1875) was regarded by his detractors as the result of a supposed influence in Rome. It was only after his death that it became known that he had appealed to Popes Pius IX and Leo XIII to absolve him from the offices. He attended Rome for the First Vatican Council, and it was only with great reluctance that he was finally persuaded to vote for papal infallibility. By the time of his death on 10 October 1885 the archdiocese had a fine new cathedral, St Patrick's in Fifth Avenue, and a population of a million Catholics.

First Exile, the. A byname of COLUM CILLE (Columba).

First Irish flight, the. A 'hop' of 120 m (130 yds) at a height of 2.75 to 3.75 m (9 to 12 ft), achieved on 31 December 1909 by Harry FERGUSON in a monoplane of his own design. The flight, only six years after the Wright brothers' triumph at Kitty Hawk, North Carolina, took place in Hillsborough Park, Co. Down, the demesne of Lord Downshire, in very windy conditions. The aircraft was the first to have a tricycle undercarriage – a device that became common in the design of passenger aeroplanes 50 years later. A year later the 'Mad Mechanic', as he was known, made a successful flight of 30 km (20 miles). He gave up flying at the request of his wife, Maureen, whom he married in 1913.

First New York Archbishop, the. The honour granted to John Joseph Hughes, whose career took him from labouring in Chambersburg, Pennsylvania, USA, to being the leading Catholic cleric in the USA. He was born in Annaloghan, Co. Tyrone, on 24 June 1797 and educated locally. His father emigrated to Baltimore in 1816 and Hughes followed him a year later. He moved from employment as a gardener at Mount St Mary's seminary in Emmitsburg, Maryland, to being accepted as a clerical student at the age of 23.

Ordained in 1826 and appointed pastor in Philadelphia, Hughes founded the *Catholic Herald* and became known for his vigorous defence of Catholicism and, in particular, his care for the growing population of Irish-Americans. He became bishop of New York in 1842 and its first archbishop in 1850.

By then Hughes was known nationwide for his successful facing down of intermittent outbursts of nativism (the anti-immigrant and anti-Catholic movement that wished to keep America 'pure'; *see* KNOW-NOTHING PARTY). In 1844, during a period of anti-Catholic rioting, he organized armed gangs to protect his churches and hinted at retaliation. In 1841 he established St John's College, which later became the Jesuit Fordham University; he also founded the American College in Rome and in 1858 laid the cornerstone for St Patrick's Cathedral in Fifth Avenue, New York.

Essentially conservative, Hughes fought the radical Irish press established by political exiles and urged his flock to stay in the cities of the east where their religious needs would be catered for, rather than follow the spirit of the times and move west. He encouraged Irish-Americans to take part in the Mexican War (1846–8) and the American Civil War on the side of the Union, going to the Vatican at Lincoln's request to persuade Pope Pius IX not to recognize the Confederacy. He was a champion of independent schools, and in general the great architect of a proud Irish-Americanism. His last public appearance was to use his powerful oratorical skills to try to quell the DRAFT RIOTS of July 1863 in which Irish labourers were deeply involved. He died on 3 January 1864.

First New York Bishop, the. John Connolly, the second Catholic bishop to be consecrated for the United States. He was born in Slane, Co. Meath, in 1751 and ordained as a Dominican priest at Louvain. He lectured at San Clemente, the Dominican foundation in Rome, and acted as agent for the Irish church at the Vatican. When he was made bishop by Pope Pius VII on 6 November 1814 his diocese was the whole of New York state and part of New Jersey, with three churches and four priests. By his death in 1825 he had built six churches and several chapels along the ERIE CANAL to serve the predominantly Irish workforce. His body was discovered in an unmarked grave in 1976 and re-interred with proper solemnity in old St Patrick's Cathedral in the New York borough of Queens.

First Programme for Economic Expansion. *See* WHITAKER PLAN, THE.

First US Cardinal, the. *See* FIRST AMERICAN CARDINAL, THE.

Fishamble Street. A street that runs with a steep gradient between Dame Street and WOOD QUAY, Dublin. It was the official fish market (fish shambles) for Dublin until the end of the 17th century, when the city food markets were moved north of the River Liffey. Thereafter it became a residential street, and the city's general post office was situated there from *c.*1680 until *c.*1710. A popular tavern on the street was called The Bull's Head, and it was The Bull's Head Musical Society that was associated with the building of the street's famous Music Hall. The hall was opened in 1741 and George Frederick Handel, who lived in Dublin from November 1741 until August 1742, conducted the first performance of his *Messiah* there on 13 April 1742. So crowded was the auditorium (it is estimated that there was an audience of more than 700) that ladies were requested to leave their hoops and gentlemen their swords at home. The hall was a popular venue for musical and other entertainments throughout the rest of the 18th century.

Fitt, Gerry (b.1926). Republican Socialist politician. He was born in Belfast on 9 April 1926

and served in the merchant navy (1941–53). After a frustrating experience in civic politics as a member of the Irish Labour Party he managed to win the previously Unionist-held seat of Dock in the STORMONT election in 1962 and became Westminster MP for West Belfast in 1966. He was in Derry for the Civil Rights march on 5 October 1968 (*see* CIVIL RIGHTS MOVEMENT), a founder of the SDLP in August 1970 and deputy chief executive during the short-lived POWER-SHARING EXECUTIVE of 1974. A vocal critic of paramilitary forces and of the 1981 H-BLOCK HUNGER STRIKES, he lost his seat in West Belfast to Gerry ADAMS in June 1983 and was made a life peer (Baron Fitt of Bell's Hill) the following month. His public disapproval of the IRA led to his house in Belfast being several times attacked, forcing him to move to England. His slightly old-fashioned socialism was at odds with the 'green' Nationalism of even the SDLP, but during the 1960s he more than any other MP was responsible for making the British Labour Party take an interest in conditions in Northern Ireland.

Fit to rule all Ireland. A remark attributed to Henry VII concerning Gearóid Mór, the 8th Earl of Kildare (1456–1513) (*see* GREAT EARL, THE). He was suspected of plotting against Henry VII, especially in his supposed involvement in the conspiracy of Perkin WARBECK (d.1499) against the king. He was imprisoned in the Tower of London in 1494 on the instructions of the lord deputy, Sir Edward Poynings (1459–1521), but pardoned after two years and was made deputy. Henry is said to have replied to Poynings's charge that all Ireland was not fit to rule him: 'If all Ireland is not fit to rule this man, he is fit to rule all Ireland.'

Fitzgerald, Lord Edward (1763–98). United Irishman. He was born in the family seat, CARTON HOUSE, Co. Kildare, on 15 October 1763, the 12th child of the first Duke of Leinster. He joined the Sussex Militia in 1779 and served in America, where he was wounded in 1781, and in Canada. He became an admirer of the French Revolution and visited Paris in 1792, staying with Thomas Paine. At a dinner of British expatriates he toasted the abolition of all hereditary titles and as a result was dismissed from the army. He married Pamela, the ward of Madame de Genlis and the radical Duc d'Orléans, in December 1792 and returned to Dublin with his wife the following year, joining the Society of UNITED IRISHMEN in 1796 in despair at constitutional reform.

A militant, Fitzgerald sought French aid from General Hoche, but when this was delayed the United Irishmen committee decided to rise anyway in May 1798. In a pre-emptive strike in March 1798, based on information received, the members of the Leinster committee of the United Irishmen were arrested on the orders of Major SIRR in the house of Oliver BOND in Bridge Street, Dublin. Fitzgerald was absent and evaded arrest, but was a fugitive with a price on this head from then until 19 May, when he was apprehended by Major Sirr in the house of a supporter, Mr Murphy, a dealer in feathers in Thomas Street. He resisted arrest, killing one of the raiding party, but was himself gravely wounded in the shoulder. He died of his wounds in Newgate prison on 4 June. In Nationalist historiography he is a heroic figure, young, handsome and brave:

> ... For this Edward Fitzgerald died,
> And Robert Emmet and Wolfe Tone,
> All that delirium of the brave ...
>
> W.B. YEATS: 'September 1913', in *Responsibilities* (1914)

See also TAILORS' HALL.

FitzGerald, Garret (b.1926). Taoiseach (1981–2 and 1982–7). He was born in Dublin, the son of CUMANN NA NGAEDHEAL minister Desmond FitzGerald (1888–1947). He worked as an economist for Aer Lingus (1947–58), and lectured in economics in University College Dublin (1959–73). He entered politics in 1964, first as a FINE GAEL senator and from 1969 as a TD, representing the liberal wing of the party. In the national coalition with the

Labour Party (1973–7) he served as minister for foreign affairs. On Liam COSGRAVE's retirement in 1977 he was elected leader of Fine Gael, presiding as taoiseach over the coalitions of 1981–2 and 1982–7. His greatest achievement in foreign policy was the negotiation of the ANGLO-IRISH AGREEMENT with Margaret Thatcher in 1985. After the general election of 1987 FIANNA FÁIL formed a government, and FitzGerald resigned from party politics in 1992, maintaining an interest and public profile in European, economic and constitutional matters. His autobiography, *All in a Life*, appeared in 1991.

See also FLAWED PEDIGREE; OUT! OUT! OUT!

Fitzgerald, Maurice (b.1970). GAA footballer. He was born in Cahirciveen in the IVERAGH PENINSULA. A two-footed scorer from play and frees, he is an athlete of considerable skill and athletic grace, although in recent years he has become more famous for not playing than for playing for the county side. He began his inter-county career with Kerry in 1988. Among his best performances were the 1997 ALL-IRELAND final, where he scored nine points, and the Kerry All-Ireland victory of 2000.

Fitzgibbon, John, Earl of Clare (1749–1802). Lord chancellor of Ireland, nicknamed 'Black Jack' because he was so violently opposed to Catholicism. He was born in Dublin, the son of a wealthy lawyer who had converted to Protestantism, and educated at Trinity College Dublin and at Oxford. A student of distinction, he was called to the Irish Bar in 1772 and soon had a lucrative practice. He was appointed attorney-general in 1783, and in 1789 became lord chancellor of Ireland. Fitzgibbon was awarded the title Lord Clare in 1795, and in 1799 became a peer of Great Britain as Lord Fitzgibbon of Sidbury. With John BERESFORD and John FOSTER he formed a powerful kitchen cabinet known as 'the Three Jacks'.

Fitzgibbon resisted reform, particularly the alleviation of the POPERY LAWS against Catholics, and was also severely critical of reforming Protestant PATRIOTS like Henry GRATTAN, whose actions, he believed, threatened the connection with England on which the security and prosperity of his class depended. Lord Westmorland, who served as lord lieutenant (1790–5), said Fitzgibbon had 'no God but English government'. He earned the hatred of the Dublin mob for his role in the so-called FITZWILLIAM EPISODE in 1795. An advocate of stringent security measures in the face of the threat of rebellion by the UNITED IRISHMEN in the late 1790s, Fitzgibbon also played a leading role in the passage of the Act of UNION of 1800, remarking in a speech on 10 February 1801:

> … if it is to remain at the discretion of every adventurer of feeble and ostentatious talents, ungoverned by a particle of judgement or discretion, to dress up fictitious grievances for popular delusion and let loose a savage and barbarous people upon the property and respect of the Irish nation, what gentleman who has the means of living out of this country will be induced to remain in it?

He died in Dublin on 28 January 1802; his funeral cortège was followed by a hostile, jeering mob.

See also TAME AS DOMESTIC CATS.

Fitzgibbon Cup. The GAA hurling competition for third-level colleges, established in 1912.

Fitzmaurice, George (1877–1963). Playwright. He was born near Listowel, Co. Kerry, and worked in a bank and in the Land Commission before serving in the British army during the First World War. His later life was spent in seclusion in Dublin. His plays, 17 in number, were compared with those of Lady Gregory and Synge, but, except for the naturalistic *The Country Dressmaker* (1907) and *'Twixt the Giltinans and the Carmodys* (1923), never received the attention they deserved. Many of them were too fantastic for the audiences of the time; for example, *The Magic Glasses* (1913) concerns spectacles through which the owner can see marvellous sights, and *The Dandy Dolls* (1913) is about puppets and the world of the fairies.

Fitzmaurice, James. *See* BREMEN.

Fitzwilliam Episode, the. The political crisis concerning the recall on 21 February 1795 of William Wentworth, Earl of Fitzwilliam, appointed lord lieutenant in sucession to Lord Westmorland in December 1794 as part of a coalition agreement between the Whig government and its conservative wing. The reason given for his recall was that Fitzwilliam had unjustifiably dismissed senior holders of public office (including John BERESFORD), but a contributory factor was that he wished to support Henry GRATTAN's Catholic Relief Bill (*see* CATHOLIC RELIEF ACTS) of 12 February 1795. Fitzwilliam was replaced by the more hardline Earl Camden, a decision that contributed to the disaffection leading to the REBELLION OF 1798.

See also FITZGIBBON, JOHN, EARL OF CLARE.

Five Fifths, the. An ancient division of Ireland based upon the dynastic families of the areas Ulaid, Laigin, Mumu, Connachta and Mide. They correspond to the modern provinces of ULSTER, LEINSTER, MUNSTER and CONNACHT, and Co. Meath. In time Mide was assimilated into Laigin, thus producing the modern divisions. The redrawing of boundaries that led to the loss of this fifth is ascribed to NIALL OF THE NINE HOSTAGES and his sons. It resulted in the lexical anomaly that though there were now four provinces each was still called a fifth. The Irish phrase *Cúig Cúige na hÉireann* (pronounced 'cooig cooig-huh na hare-ann', literally meaning 'the five fifths of Ireland') is sometimes used as a phrase to describe Ireland as a whole.

Five Lamps, the. A Dublin landmark, named for its 19th-century five-branch cast-iron standard public lamp. It marks the junction of the North Strand, Portland Row, Seville Place, Amiens Street and Killarney Street in the north inner city.

Five Points, the. The five-cornered intersection of three Manhattan streets, Anthony (now Worth), Orange (now Baxter) and Cross (now

Mosco), which by 1855 was the worst slum in New York, with two-thirds of its denizens immigrant Irish. It was their first appalling experience of America and they were herded into basement lodgings, described by the *New York Tribune* as:

> ... without air, without light, filled with damp vapor from the mildewed walls, and with the vermin in ratio to the dirtiness of the inhabitants. They are the most repulsive holes that ever a human being was forced to sleep in.

Dickens mentions the locality in his *American Notes* (1842):

> ... and there is one quarter, commonly called the Five Points, which in respect of filth and wretchedness may be safely backed against Seven Dials ...[a district of London 'notorious for squalor, vice crime and degradation ...']

The chief building, known as the Old Brewery, because of its past use, was a brothel and thieves' kitchen, but many of the exploited people forced to live there were decent and respectable, and made every effort to get clear. Within twenty years most of the Irish had gone, their place taken by the next wave of immigrants, this time from Italy. The squalor was used by the Nativists (*see* KNOW-NOTHING PARTY) to damn Catholic immigrants, especially the Irish, aided by the one-sided brilliance of such artists as Thomas Nast (*see* 'I'M RISING IN THE WORLD').

The Five Points forms the backdrop to Martin Scorsese's film *Gangs of New York* (2002), itself based on Herbert Asbury's novel (1928) of the same name.

Fla. A Cork slang term meaning to have sexual congress, male to female; to fuck. In an apocryphal story a girl was overheard on a famous courting ground in Cork saying to her partner: 'Fla me nicely now.'

Fla'd out, to be. A Cork slang phrase, deriving from the verb 'to FLA' and meaning to be totally exhausted, especially from dissipation.

Flaithiúil. The Irish word for 'generous', 'open-handed'. It is pronounced 'flahool'. The word derives from *flaith*, the Irish for lord or nobleman, and shows the central importance of HOSPITALITY in Irish tradition. It is still a strong term of praise. *Flaithiúil* was often combined for emphasis with the synonymous *fial*, to give *fial flaithiúil*.

Flake. To 'hit' or 'punch'. The word is also used as a noun to signify a blow.

Flanagan, Father Edward J. *See* BOYS' TOWN.

Flannan (*fl.*7th century). A prince of the DAL CAIS. After much missionary work in the Hebrides, he was ordained bishop of his native diocese of Killaloe, Co. Clare, by Pope John IV in 640, and is the town's patron saint. He was noted for managing to recite the entire psalter each day in spite of all his labours. His feast day is 18 December.

Flatley, Michael (b.1958). Irish-American dancer, born in Chicago on 16 July 1958 of Irish parents – both of whom were talented in Irish music and dancing – who hailed from Sligo and Carlow. Flatley took up Irish dancing at the age of 11, studying at the Dennis Dennehy Dancing School in Chicago, and also mastered the flute, on which instrument he won two All-Ireland FLEADH CHEOIL titles, the first of them in 1975, the year in which he became the first American to win the Irish dancing world championships. After running his own dance school in Chicago, Flatley began to tour with The CHIEFTAINS, but it was as the male lead in, and choreographer of, RIVERDANCE from 1994 that he achieved international fame. After parting company with *Riverdance*, Flatley created two further Irish-dance spectaculars: *LORD OF THE DANCE* and *Feet of Flames*. Flatley has lived mostly in Ireland in recent years, having refurbished a BIG HOUSE, Castlehyde, near Fermoy in Co. Cork. His final public performance was in one of his own shows in Dallas, Texas, in 2001. Flatley is a dancer of astounding technical accomplishment, managing up to 28 taps a second in some of his more vigorous routines.

Flawed pedigree. During the Dáil debate on the nomination of Charles HAUGHEY as taoiseach to succeed Jack LYNCH in December 1979, Fine Gael leader Garret FITZGERALD declared of Haughey: 'He comes with a flawed pedigree.' This was considered a severe criticism under Dáil privilege: there had been rumours about Haughey's lifestyle and the source of his wealth for years, but nothing was known for sure until the revelations of the MCCRACKEN TRIBUNAL in 1997 (and the GUBU period was yet to come).

Fleadh Cheoil (Irish, 'music festival'). A series of music and singing competitions (often held in the open air) organized by COMHALTAS CEOLTÓIRÍ ÉIREANN, which has been a feature of Irish summer life since 1953. The word *fleadh* (pronounced 'fla') originally meant a drinking-feast, and the same spirit pervades the event; the All-Ireland Fleadh of August 2002, held in sunny weather in Listowel, Co. Kerry, attracted about 250,000 people. The event is characterized by spontaneous sessions in market squares, parks and very-late-night pubs. The idea spread to Britain and the USA, with *fleadhanna* being held in Finsbury Park, London, since 1990 (although cancelled in 2003) and in New York and Chicago:

> At the Fleadh Cheoil in Mullingar
> There were two sounds, the breaking
> Of glass, and the background pulse
> Of music. Young girls roamed
> The streets with eager faces
> Shoving for men. Bottles in
> Hand they rowed out a song:
> Puritan Ireland's dead and gone,
> A myth of O'Faolain and O'Connor.
>> JOHN MONTAGUE (b.1929): 'The Siege of Mullingar' (1963), parodying Yeats's 'Romantic Ireland's dead and gone, / It's with O'Leary in the grave.' ('September 1913')

Fleadh Cheoil an Raidió. See CEOLTÓIRÍ CHUALANN.

Fled Bricenn. See BRICRIU.

Fleischmann, Aloys (1910–92). Composer and pioneer in music education, born in Munich

but reared in Ireland. As professor of music in University College Cork (1934–80) he campaigned for music education in schools. He founded an orchestra and co-founded a ballet company in Cork and established the Cork International Choral and Folk Dance Festival (popularly known as the Choral Festival) in 1934. The academic staff of his department included, at different times, such leading exponents and champions of traditional music as Seán Ó RIADA, Pilib Ó Laoghaire and Mícheál Ó Súilleabháin. Among Fleischmann's enduring legacies is the *Sources of Irish Traditional Music* project, which set out to collect all the traditional tunes in printed and manuscript sources prior to 1855. The collection was completed before Fleischmann's death and published in 1998.

Flight of the Earls, the. The popular (if inaccurate) term describing the departure on 14 September 1607 from Ulster of Hugh O'NEILL, Earl of Tyrone, and Rory O'DONNELL, Earl of Tyrconnell. Together with their families and another supporter, Cúchonnacht Maguire, the Lord of Fermanagh (who procured the ship for them), they sailed from Rathmullen on LOUGH SWILLY, Co. Donegal, for Spain. Their ship landed in France, and after a laborious and protracted overland journey they finally settled in Rome as papal pensioners. The reasons for their departure remain imprecise, but fear of arrest by the English government was the most likely one. (O'Neill had been the main Irish leader in the NINE YEARS' WAR, which had ended in 1603.) The effect was to leave the northern Irish virtually leaderless and to prepare the way for the ULSTER PLANTATION.

Flit¹. A Dublin slang word for 'fellow', deriving from elided pronunciation 'f'lla'. 'Young flit' is also heard.

Flit². An Ulster (and Scots) word meaning to move house or lodging.

'Flitters, Tatters and the Counsellor: Three Waifs from the Dublin Streets'. A 'sketch' or short story (1879) based on the life of a street urchin;

it was the most popular work of May Laffan (1849–1916), a middle-class novelist with a Catholic father and a Protestant mother. Between 1882 and 1874, she published anonymously several novels with the background of land agitation and separatist politics, including the satirical *Hogan MP* (1876) and *Christy Carew* (1878), a story of Catholic middle-class Dublin. Married to an English-born academic, the chemist Walter Hartley (1846–1913), Laffan lived in Dublin and was committed to an asylum in 1910, where she remained until her death. Her husband was knighted in 1911 and their only son was killed at Gallipoli in 1915. She contributed to the RECESS COMMITTEE of 1895–6.

Floating Labyrinth, the. The unenthusiastic description of 'raine-soaked' Ireland by 'Lug-less' Will Lithgow, the crop-eared journeyman Scots tailor. Lithgow recorded his pluvial impressions in his autobiography *Rare Adventures* (1619):

> And this I dare avow, there are more rivers, lakes, brooks, strands, quagmires, bogs and marshes in this country than in all Christendom besides; for travelling there in the winter all my daily solace was sink-down comfort; whiles boggy-plunging deeps kissed my horse's belly; whiles, over-minded saddle, body and all; and often or ever set a swimming, in great danger, both I and my guides of our lives; that for cloudy and fountain-bred perils, I was never before reduced to such a floating labyrinth, considering that in five months' space I quite spoiled six horses, and myself as tired as the worst of them.

Flood, Henry (1732–91). Parliamentarian. He was born in Co. Kilkenny, the illegitimate son of Warden Flood, chief justice of the King's Bench in Ireland, and educated at Trinity College Dublin and at Oxford. He returned to live in Ireland in 1759, and was elected MP for Kilkenny and later for the borough of Callan. For many years he was the leader of the opposition in the Irish Parliament, and had a reputation as the House's finest orator. In 1769 he killed his election opponent, James

Agar, but was acquitted of the murder. In 1775 he accepted a government sinecure and become vice-treasurer of Ireland, but he never supported the government in Parliament and was removed from this post in 1781, by which time Henry GRATTAN had taken his place as opposition leader. He and Grattan had many differences of opinion, which led to a bitter personal quarrel on the floor of Parliament and the threat of a duel. Flood turned his attention to England and bought a seat in the House of Commons in 1783, but did not succeed in making an impact there. He retired from politics in 1790 and died in Kilkenny on 2 December 1791.

Flood Tribunal. *See* TRIBUNALS.

Floozie in the Jacuzzi. The popular Dublin nickname for the 1988 Dublin millennium fountain *Anna Livia Plurabelle* created by Sean Mulcahy and Eamonn O'Doherty. It was also nicknamed BIDET MULLIGAN. The fountain, originally sited in O'Connell Street, took the form of a reclining female figure of the *spéirbhean* type (literally 'sky woman', a goddess representing Ireland in AISLING poetry), decked with fronds and wavelets in celebration of the city's River Liffey. (Anna Livia Plurabelle was Joyce's version, in *Finnegans Wake*, of ANNA LIFFEY, the personification of the River Liffey.) The fountain became a target for vandalism (dyes and detergents were deployed) and also something of an unofficial litter bin, thereby earning another appelation, 'the Hoor in the Sewer'. It was eventually removed from O'Connell Street to a suburban park at Raheny.

Flower, Robin. *See* BLÁITHÍN.

Flúirseach (Irish, 'abundant'). A HIBERNO-ENGLISH term meaning 'plentiful', 'generous', for instance in relation to food or drink. There is also a noun, *flúirse*.

Fluthered. One of the legion of HIBERNO-ENGLISH words for 'drunk', common in Dublin but now seeming rather Oirish (*see* STAGE-IRISH).

Flying column. The combat unit most often used by the IRA in the guerrilla warfare that characterized the ANGLO-IRISH WAR of 1919–21. It usually consisted of a small group of some dozens of local men under a commandant, also local (Ernie O'MALLEY, who commanded in Limerick–Tipperary, was an exception). The pattern was for the column to engage with troops or policemen, usually AUXIES or BLACK AND TANS – who were recruited specially to deal with them – then melt back into the countryside, hiding in remote areas or taking refuge in out-of-the-way 'safe' houses. Many IRA men spent much of the war on the run.

The advantage of the flying column was its flexibility and speed; the disadvantage was that it was very difficult to exercise central control over local commanders. The first action of the war is generally accepted as being at SOLOHEADBEG, under the leadership of Dan Breen, on 19 January 1919; nobody at Volunteer headquarters in Dublin knew about it until it was over. Even Michael COLLINS, who supported the men of action against the more cautious de Valera, admitted that he could not control the flying columns. Among the other well-known commanders of flying columns were Tom BARRY (west Cork), Frank AIKEN (Louth–Armagh) and Seán McEoin (Longford; see BLACKSMITH OF BALLINALEE, THE).

Flynn, Eileen. *See* EILEEN FLYNN AFFAIR, THE.

Flynn, Pee (b.1939). FIANNA FÁIL politician and minister. From a home base in Castlebar, Co. Mayo, former teacher Pádraig Flynn built up a successful political career that culminated in a period as European Union commissioner for social affairs (1993–9). Able but arrogant and thoughtless, Flynn is remembered for two major PR gaffes: the first when he referred to Mary Robinson's new-found family values ('the new interest in her family') in a lunchtime radio discussion on 3 November 1999 during the presidential election campaign; the second when, on *The LATE LATE SHOW* of 15 January 1999 he referred patronizingly to property developer Tom Gilmartin, who had claimed to have given £50,000 to Flynn for Fianna Fáil in 1989. On the same show he forfeited all public sympathy by appealing for public understanding of the difficulty of maintaining three residences, in Castlebar, Dublin and Brussels. Flynn's chances of establishing a Fianna Fáil dynasty in Mayo were damaged when his daughter and successor as Mayo TD, Beverley Cooper Flynn, lost a libel action against RTÉ in 2001.

Fockle. A St John's Eve torch made of a sheaf of lit straw set on a long pole (*see* ÁINE; MIDSUMMER'S DAY). The name comes from the German word *Fackel*, which was brought to Limerick by the PALATINES.

Foclóir Gaeilge agus Béarla. *See* DINNEEN'S DICTIONARY.

Fodla. In Irish mythology a TUATHA DÉ DANAAN goddess whose name is used in poetry to represent Ireland.
See also BANBA; ÉIRE.

'Foggy Dew, The'. A patriotic ballad celebrating the EASTER RISING of 1916 and making an association between Catholicism and physical-force Republicanism that was quite unexceptionable even at the time of the 50th anniversary of the Rising in 1966:

> As down the glen one Easter morn to a city fair rode I,
> There armed lines of marching men in squadrons passed me by.
> No pipe did hum, no battle drum did sound its loud tattoo,
> But the Angelus bell o'er the Liffey's swell rang out in the foggy dew …

Foillán (d.655). The brother of St FURSA, who became abbot of BURGH CASTLE when his brother left for France. He was later obliged to leave when the Christian kingdom of East Anglia was attacked by the pagan Mercians. Mayor Pepin of Landen (whose wife Queen Itta had already founded a nunnery at NIVELLES in modern Belgium with her daughter Gertrude as abbess) gave him land at Fosses.

The two establishments kept close ties with each other and it was on a journey from Nivelles to Fosses that he was murdered by bandits in the forest of Seneffe. His feast day is 31 October.

Foinse (Irish, 'spring'). A national Irish-language weekly tabloid published in Indreabhán in the Connemara (Co. Galway) GAELTACHT since 1996. Owned by local businessman Pádraig Ó Céide (*see* AER ARANN), the newspaper takes a lively independent line on politics, and is a strong proponent of Irish-language and Gaeltacht interests. The circulation is about 9500 per week, and the paper is grant-aided by Foras na Gaeilge (*see* BORD NA GAEILGE) in the sum of €4500.

Foley, John Henry (1817–74). Victorian sculptor. His statues of Edmund Burke, Oliver Goldsmith and Henry Grattan stand at the front of Trinity College Dublin. Foley is also responsible for the O'Connell Memorial in O'Connell Street, Dublin, and the statue of Father Theobald Mathew in Patrick's Street in Cork (*see* STATUE, THE). He worked on the Albert Memorial in London and executed many other commissions in England.

Fomorians. In Irish mythology, a grotesque and malignant people, often with single arms, legs and eyes, located in the middle of their foreheads; they were the dark and evil forces of Irish myth. The element *fo* ('under') in their name confirms their ability to live under the sea, a convenience since PARTHOLÓN, having defeated their forces, drives them to exile in the Hebrides, the ISLE OF MAN and especially TORY ISLAND. Their most notable leader is BALOR OF THE EVIL EYE, but in spite of his powerful ocular weapon they are finally defeated by the TUATHA DÉ DANAAN at the second battle of MAGH TUIREADH (Moytura). They are driven from Ireland, but may still lurk in the outer islands.

Fools, the fools. A famous and much-quoted phrase from Patrick PEARSE's oration at the graveside of Cork-born Fenian Jeremiah

O'DONOVAN ROSSA in Glasnevin Cemetery, Dublin, on 1 August 1915:

> But the fools, the fools, the fools, they have left us our Fenian dead, and while Ireland holds these graves, Ireland unfree shall never be at peace.

Fooster (Irish *fústar*, 'fuss'). An onomatopoeic HIBERNO-ENGLISH word signifying 'hurry' or 'fluster'.

> Then Tommy jumped about elate,
> Tremendous was his fooster – O;
> Says he, 'I'll send a message straight
> To my darling Mr Brewster – O!'
>> Repeal song of 1843, quoted in P.W. Joyce, *English as We Speak It in Ireland* (1910)

Foot. To make a small stack of TURF, containing eight sods in all, by standing dry sods on their ends and leaning others systematically against them. The finished product was also called a 'foot'.

Foot and mouth. A disease that affects sheep and cattle. It is of grave concern to Ireland because of the size of the national herd and the central importance to the economy of beef exports. In 2001 a foot and mouth epidemic swept through England, Wales and southern Scotland, and threatened the Irish herd. When an outbreak of the disease was confirmed in the Cooley Peninsula, a border area in Co. Louth, shortly after an occurrence in Meaigh, Co. Tyrone, agricultural and security forces were mobilized to prevent the disease from spreading. Tourism and sporting events, as well as the movement and sale of livestock, were gravely affected. However, the threat was contained, and there was no epidemic in Ireland.

Foot and Mouth Final, the. During a 1941 outbreak of foot and mouth disease in Munster, travel into and out of the province was severely restricted. The ALL-IRELAND hurling final of that year was between two nominated sides, Dublin and Cork, because the Munster and Leinster provincial finals could not be completed.

Football. Despite the increased popularity of soccer, 'football' in most parts of Ireland still means Gaelic football. In the summer championship season, excitement reaches fever pitch for the provincial finals, the semi-finals and especially for the ALL-IRELAND football final, played in CROKE PARK in Dublin on the last Sunday of September. In general, counties are either football counties or hurling counties: Dublin, Kerry, Meath and the northern counties of Down, Armagh and Derry are football counties. Cork and Galway teams excel at both football and hurling, as does the FAITHFUL COUNTY, Offaly. Gaelic football is still an amateur sport, but over the past decades the professionalism of and commitment to training by players and managers have produced extremely high levels of fitness and athleticism. It has traditionally been a fast, high-scoring game with a lot of passing – 'catch and kick' is the epitome – but in recent years commentators have criticized players for neglecting these skills and for cynical fouling.

For all the world. A common intensifier and exclamatory expression in HIBERNO-ENGLISH: 'For all the world what did I see but ...' or 'He's for all the world like his mother.'

Foras na Gaeilge. *See* BORD NA GAEILGE.

Forbidden Fruit. The title of a book (1993) by Annie Murphy (b.1948) (with Peter de Rosa) detailing her relationship with Bishop Éamonn Casey (b.1927), with whom she had a son, Peter, while Casey was Bishop of Kerry in 1974. Murphy, an American divorcée, returned to the United States with her baby and Casey paid some money to support him. He was made Bishop of Galway in 1976, and remained one of the most visible, cordial and media-friendly members of the hierarchy, liberal on economic and development issues but conforming to the Catholic Church's line in the areas of personal morality, sex, abortion and divorce.

On 7 May 1992, the story of Casey's love-child broke in the Irish media, and also the fact that he had borrowed more than £70,000 of diocesan funds to pay off Annie Murphy, her partner and their son (the contributions

of wealthy patrons enabled him to repay this sum). Casey was obliged by the church to spend the next six years ministering in Ecuador and keeping a very low profile. He returned to live in England in 1998. When Annie Murphy went on *The LATE LATE SHOW* to publicize her book, it was clear from audience reaction that there remained among his fellow-countrymen a good deal of sympathy for Casey, although comments by him such as 'There is far greater need for parents to be available to their children than previously,' from a sermon in 1971, rang hollow in the light of his reluctance to acknowledge his son. The Éamonn Casey scandal was the first – but far from the worst – of many scandals to shake the Catholic Church in Ireland during the 1990s.

See also BISHOP BRENDAN; SINGING PRIEST, THE; WEAR ONE – JUST IN CASEY.

Ford, Battle of the. The battle that the mythic hero CÚCHULAINN fights near the present-day ARDEE, Co. Louth. It takes place near the end of the war of the TÁIN BÓ CUAILNGE when Ferdia, Cúchulainn's closest friend, is goaded by MEDB into single combat against the champion of Ulster. The battle lasts four days, and Ferdia weakens Cúchullain with a direct blow of his sword to his chest so that it is necessary for him to call for his ultimate weapon, the GAE-BOLG, to finish the job:

> My ribs are crushed in,
> my heart is all blood.
> I have not fought well.
> Hound I am fallen.
>> *Táin Bó Cuailnge*, translated (1969) by Thomas Kinsella (b.1928)

Ford, John (1895–1973). Irish-American film director. He was born John Martin Feeney on 1 February 1895 in Cape Elizabeth, Maine, USA, the son of a saloon-keeper and a hotel maid; he was not, as he claimed, born Sean Aloysius Ó Féinne in Ireland. He followed his older brother, who called himself Francis Ford, to Hollywood, and from 1917 made 127 feature films, including many movie classics: *The INFORMER* (1935), *Stagecoach* (1939; the film that made John Wayne a star), *The Grapes of Wrath* (1940), *How Green Was My Valley* (1940), *My Darling Clementine* (1946), *The QUIET MAN* (1952) and *The Searchers* (1956). During the Second World War he served as chief of the Field Photographic branch of the OSS (Office of Strategic Services), becoming a rear admiral during the Korean War in 1950.

As an Irish-American Catholic, a member of an often despised minority, Ford showed in his work general sympathy for the underdog. He had a romantic love of Ireland and of the American West, and he conveyed a sense of uncomplicated patriotism. His films are essentially artificial constructs, adult fairy tales, and outstanding examples of the medium. A complicated, not to say troubled, personality, he was noted for cruelty, rage and manipulativeness, but his repertory of favourite actors, including Wayne, Walter Brennan, Victor McLaglen, Ward Bond and Maureen O'HARA respected him greatly and called him 'Pappy'. He dismissed any suggestion of artistic pretension, saying on several occasions, 'It's no good talking to me about art.' When Orson Welles was asked by an interviewer from *Playboy* which were his favourite American directors, he replied, 'The old masters ... By which I mean John Ford, John Ford and John Ford.'

Ford of the Biscuits, Battle of the. A battle in the NINE YEARS' WAR, fought on the River Arney near Enniskillen in Co. Fermanagh (7 August 1594), in which Cormac O'Neill (brother of Hugh O'NEILL) and Hugh O'Donnell ambushed and defeated an English relief column heading for besieged Enniskillen. The name, given in the *ANNALS OF THE FOUR MASTERS*, derives from the supplies scattered in consequence of the fighting.

Forster, William Edward. *See* 'BUCKSHOT' FORSTER.

Fort Apache. A generic term used during the Northern Ireland Troubles for any police barracks or army post perceived as beleaguered

and under siege. The term came from the John FORD film of the same name (1948).

Fortune. The normal term for a dowry in Irish rural society until the mid-20th century. The fortune was a very important factor in marriage arrangements. Whether it was worth £50 or £300, it established the fitness of the young woman, both for the man she was about to marry and for the family and farm she was about to marry into. The dowry or part of it was paid over when the BINDINGS were signed. In a society where made matches (*see* MATCHMAKING) were the norm, the lack of a dowry could be an insuperable obstacle for a girl, be she ever so beautiful. Sometimes a young woman earned her own dowry in service in New York and came home to wed; the dowry she brought into the house would enable a sister of the groom, who might otherwise be condemned to spinsterhood, to make a good match.

Forty-Foot. A deep bathing pool at Sandycove, DÚN LAOGHAIRE, that used to be a male preserve. Nude swimming is now permitted only before 8.00 a.m. Its history is told in a witty monograph by the novelist Mervyn Wall (1908–97) entitled *Forty Foot Gentlemen Only* (1962), the ambiguous wording of the old notice placed at the pool's entrance.

Forty hours. A devotion, widespread in Irish churches, involving the exposition of the Blessed Sacrament for 40 continuous hours, honouring the time that Christ's body lay in the sepulchre. The altar of exposition is decorated with many candles and flowers, and there is an honour guard of watchers who kneel and pray for an hour before the monstrance. The devotion is commonly known by its Italian name *quarant' ore*.

'Forty Shades of Green'. The title – become proverbial – of a song written by American country singer Johnny Cash (1932–2003) in 1961, after a visit to Ireland. In the voice of an emigrant pining for home, it encapsulates the verdant rain-soaked charm of Ireland for

Irish-Americans, and also for many Irish people in the 1960s:

I close my eyes and picture the emerald of the sea,
From the fishing boats at Dingle to the shores of Donaghadee,
I miss the River Shannon, the folks at Skibbereen,
The moorlands and the meadows and the forty shades of green.
But most of all I miss a girl in Tipperary town,
And most of all I miss her lips,
As soft as eiderdown ...

Forty-Tens. The nickname of the Leinster Regiment, deriving from the response on parade of a soldier who was rather the worse for wear from the previous night's enjoyment; when his company was ordered to dress-off by numbers he called 'forty-ten' instead of 'fifty'. The name stuck, and was applied to the troopship that carried them to France in 1914.

Forum. *See* NORTHERN IRELAND FORUM.

Fossetts Circus. An Irish family circus that has toured the 32 counties annually since 1888 with its own clowns, acrobats and jugglers, and with imported large-animal acts. The season normally begins in March and concludes with a six-week run in Dublin at the end of the year.

Foster, John (1740–1828). One of the THREE JACKS who dominated the Irish political establishment at the end of the 18th century. He was born in Collon, Co. Louth, in 1740 and educated at Trinity College Dublin. Although his family had extensive estates, it was said that his grandfather had been a common farmer, and he was disparagingly nicknamed 'the Louth Mower'. He was elected to the Irish Parliament in 1761 and appointed chancellor of the exchequer in 1784, becoming speaker of the Houses of Commons in 1785. He opposed CATHOLIC EMANCIPATION and the Act of UNION, because he thought the latter would make the former inevitable. He also advocated ruthless repression of the REBELLION OF 1798. The Irish Parliament met for the last time on 2 August 1800 and on this day Foster refused to surrender the mace, the symbol of his office.

It is now in the Bank of Ireland arts centre in COLLEGE GREEN, the former Parliament building. He retired from public life in 1811 and died at Collon on 23 August 1828.

Foster, Vere Henry Lewis (1819–1900). Educationist and philanthropist. He was born on 26 April 1819 in Copenhagen, where his Irish father was a diplomat, and educated at Eton and Oxford, serving in the diplomatic service in South America. He first came to Ireland with his brother during the Great Famine, and worked for the welfare of emigrants, making three journeys on COFFIN SHIPS in order to document the appalling conditions and the exploitation of the wretched by shipowners, and to pressure for a change in regulations. It is estimated that later in the century, when famine again threatened, he personally paid the fares of 25,000 emigrants to America and the British colonies.

Working with emigrants convinced Foster of the need for an improved education system, and from the 1860s he devoted himself to this cause. From his own resources he funded hundreds of new parish schools, and refurbished many others. He is remembered now for his 'copybooks' (what would later be called 'headline copies'), in which pupils copied improving maxims line by line in order to develop a good style of copperplate handwriting. More than one million of these copybooks were sold from 1868. In that year Foster founded the Irish National Teachers' Association (later Organization), the INTO, which represents almost all Irish primary schoolteachers, north and south. In 1870 he moved to Belfast, where he spent the rest of his life helping the poor. His death in Belfast on 21 December 1900 went almost unremarked; of his fortune only £178 remained to him.

Fota House. A big house that was originally a hunting lodge, set in parkland in Fota 'island' about 19 km (12 miles) from Cork city on the way to Cobh (Queenstown). It was built by the Smith-Barry family, descendants of the Norman Philip de Barry, a brother of Giraldus de Barry (GIRALDUS CAMBRENSIS), who had their family seat in east Cork. In 1829 John Smith-Barry commissioned a Midleton-born architect, Sir Richard Morrison, and his son Vitruvius to enlarge the lodge. The Regency house became the centre-point of a magnificent ornamental estate. In 1975, when Mrs Dorothy Bell, last of the Smith-Barrys died, the 700-acre (280-ha) estate was bought by University College Cork, and Fota Wildlife Park was developed in collaboration with Dublin Zoo. In 1987 all but the wildlife park was sold and the parkland developed as a golf course. The arboretum and gardens were subsequently taken over by what was then called DÚCHAS, the government heritage service. The Fota Trust has undertaken the restoration of the house and domestic buildings, including a magnificent orangerie.

Found on, to be. To be found drinking in a public house after hours. The gardaí who raid the premises may take the names of those 'found on', but customers are rarely if ever prosecuted. A recidivist publican is, however, at risk of losing his licence.

Four Bones. An expression standing for the self: 'You care for nothing but your own four bones!' The bones are the arms and legs taken synechdochically.

Four Courts. The centre of the Irish judicial system. The Four Courts – Chancery, King's Bench, Common Pleas and Exchequer – were originally situated south of the river, in Dublin Castle (see CASTLE, THE) until the end of the 16th century, and from 1608 on St Michael's Hill, in the precincts of CHRIST CHURCH CATHEDRAL. Although the buildings and facilities were long considered inadequate, there was considerable public opposition to moving them: in 1684 and again in 1694 the city's lord mayors petitioned the lord lieutenant, citing the value to the 'old city' of the rental derived from properties 'sett to lawyers, attorneys and solicitors' and claiming 'if the courts be removed the heart of the cittie will be left destitute'. However, in 1762 a House of

Commons committee recommended relocation to the site on Inns Quay to the north of the River Liffey then occupied by the KING'S INNS society, and this site was acquired. The construction of the present building was begun to a design by the architect Thomas Cooley in 1776, and after his death in 1784 the architectural work passed to James GANDON, who was then also engaged in working on the CUSTOM HOUSE. Construction began in March 1786, courts first sat there in November 1796, and the building was substantially completed by 1802.

On 14 April 1922 forces of the Republican ANTI-TREATYITES occupied the Four Courts, a Dublin landmark and symbol of British administration. The CIVIL WAR is generally seen to have begun when, after the expiry of an ultimatum, Free State forces began to shell the building at 4.07 on the morning of 28 June 1922. The Republican garrison surrendered after two days, at 3.30 p.m. on 30 June (the surrender signed by Ernie O'MALLEY), but not before mining the public-records office attached to the courts (part of Thomas Cooley's original design), destroying thousands of documents dating from as early as the 12th century, an incalculable loss to scholars and genealogists. After the Civil War the building was restored by the Board of Works, who modified Gandon's central quadrangle and replanned the interior.

Four-Faced Liar, the. The four clock faces of St Anne's in Shandon in Cork city, the church that houses the famous BELLS OF SHANDON. It has been known for all four faces to show different times.

Four Green Fields. Ireland as a united country, the fields representing the four provinces: Ulster, Munster, Leinster and Connacht, and constituting the THIRTY-TWO COUNTIES of a united Ireland. In a popular ballad 'the poor old woman' (Ireland) insists that one of them, Ulster, is still 'in bondage'.

Four Kerry Poets, the. The collective name given to the 17th-and 18th-century poets,

Séafraidh Ó DONNCHADHA AN GHLEANNA, Piaras FEIRITÉAR, Aogán Ó RATHAILE and Eoghan Rua Ó Súilleabháin (*see* EOGHAN AN BHÉIL BHINN). In Killarney there is a monument to them in the form of a statue of a *spéirbhean* – an idealized figure of a goddess (literally 'sky-woman') representing Ireland and associated with *AISLING* poetry – sculpted by Séamus MURPHY and inscribed with a poem by Pádraig Ó Duinnín (*see* DINNEEN'S DICTIONARY). There is also a memorial to them in MUCKROSS ABBEY, near Killarney, where all except Feiritéar are buried.

Four Square Laundry. A cover believed to be used by British army for intelligence-gathering in Nationalist areas of Belfast in the early years of the TROUBLES. A Four Square van was attacked by the IRA on 2 October 1972 outside the Gemini Health Studios in Twinbrook and three men believed to be army agents were killed. The Gemini centre was thought to be part of the covert operation.

Foxer. A Cork term for a job done after-hours by a tradesman for another employer (usually domestic).
See also NIXER.

Foxford. *See* PROVIDENCE WOOLLEN MILLS.

Foxy. A common HIBERNO-ENGLISH adjective meaning red-haired.

Foxy boyo, the. A colloquial name for WHISKEY.

Foxy Kalmuck, the. *See* CULLEN, PAUL.

Foyle. The name of the river and the sea lough into which it flows in the northwest of Ireland. The river has three different names from its source in Co.Tyrone: the Strule as far as Newtownstewart, the Mourne to Strabane and the Foyle to where it meets the lough 6 km (4 miles) north of the city of Derry, which its divides. The lough, which separates Co. Donegal in the Republic of Ireland and Co. Derry in Northern Ireland, is noted for the variety of its sea birds.

Fraughan Sunday (Irish *fraochán*, 'bilberry'). A modern celebration of the feast of LUGHNASA held on the last Sunday of July. It is also known as Garland Sunday or Bilberry Sunday, and, in the GAELTACHT, as *Domnach Deireanach an tSamraidh* ('the last summer Sunday'). Its name in older Irish mythology was *Domnach Chrom Dubh* (literally 'the Sunday of the dark bent one'), referring to the pagan god named CROM DUBH and overcome, at least partially, by St PATRICK.
See also REEK, THE.

Free Clothes Association. The nickname under which the FCA (Forsaí Cosanta Áitiúil, 'local defence forces') was mockingly known. It was a scaled-down and restructured version of the LOCAL DEFENCE FORCE (LDF) formed in 1940 during the EMERGENCY. The personnel were trained in annual camps. When it became a separate organization in 1979 it had almost 20,000 personnel, officers and men.

Free Derry. The words 'You are now entering Free Derry' appeared on the gable of a house in St Columb's Wells on 5 January 1969, after the RUC incursion into the BOGSIDE following the BURNTOLLET AMBUSH. The words presaged the NO-GO AREA that the Bogside was to become on 12 August 1969. The house and those around it have since been demolished but the inscribed gable, enshrined as Free Derry Corner, has been preserved.

Free education. Education in Ireland since the foundation of the state had been hampered by lack of investment, by excessively large class sizes, by an inequitable two-tier secondary system whereby pupils in the vocational sector could not progress beyond the age of about 15, and by over-emphasis on compulsory Irish as a means to revive the language.

Donogh O'Malley (1921–68), who was FIANNA FÁIL minister for education in the last administration of Seán LEMASS, seized on the new prosperity of the 1960s to announce a scheme for free secondary education at a National Union of Journalists conference on 10 September 1966, claiming that the fact that 17,000 children were finishing their education for good at primary level was 'a dark stain on the national conscience'. (Although Jack LYNCH was minister for finance and the new scheme was set to cost a great deal of public money, O'Malley did not consult with or inform him, and announced the new measures while Lynch was out of the country.)

Free secondary education, along with free transport to school for all rural pupils, came into effect in September 1967, and that month there were 18,000 new enrolments in secondary schools. Grant-aid for third-level education was introduced the following year. Irish people enthusiastically benefited from these provisions, with the result that the country has one of the best-educated populations in Europe, a factor that proved useful in attracting high-tech industries to locate in Ireland a generation later (*see* CELTIC TIGER).

O'Malley's next, abortive, scheme was the amalgamation of Dublin's University College and Trinity College. He died suddenly in his home city of Limerick on 10 March 1968.

Freeman's Journal. A leading Irish newspaper which during its lifetime (1768–1923) had a variety of political stances, mostly liberal but occasionally pro-establishment, especially in its early years. (The title did not refer to a proprietor's name, but to men who are free.) One of its founders, Charles Lucas (1713–71), generally supported the PATRIOT anti-government views of Henry GRATTAN and his supporters, but after Lucas's death the newspaper was acquired by the political establishment at the Castle, who used it to attack Catholicism, the French Revolution and the UNITED IRISHMEN. From 1809 it became essentially constitutional-Nationalist, supporting Daniel O'CONNELL, CATHOLIC EMANCIPATION, the LAND LEAGUE and HOME RULE, though it turned against PARNELL at the time of the O'Shea scandal (*see* O'SHEA WHO MUST BE OBEYED). It supported the reconstituted Irish party under John REDMOND, and was not unexpectedly pro-TREATY. The latter view cost it dear, for on 29 March 1922 the anti-Treaty IRA destroyed its machinery. The paper

merged with William Martin MURPHY's *IRISH INDEPENDENT* in 1924.

Free Presbyterianism. The Free Presbyterian Church of Ulster was founded in 1951 by the Rev. Ian PAISLEY, after a dispute with the main PRESBYTERIAN church over the use of its facilities for a revivalist campaign. The first actual building associated with the church was at Crossgar, Co. Down, and now there are around 100 churches in Ireland and in various countries abroad. The 1991 census found that there were 12,500 members in Northern Ireland, attracted by the fundamentalism of the faith and the charisma of its founder. At the time of its opening on 4 October 1969 Paisley's Martyrs Memorial Church in Belfast was one of the largest Protestant places of worship in Europe.

Free State, the. The political unit, known officially as *Saorstát Éireann*, set up by the TREATY in 1921 and officially inaugurated on 6 December 1922, though its forces were engaged in a bitter CIVIL WAR with the ANTI-TREATYITES that lasted until 24 May 1923. By the CONSTITUTION OF 1937 the Free State became known as Éire.

Free trade or this. The threatening slogan of a demonstration of several thousand armed VOLUNTEERS in College Green, Dublin on 4 November 1779 to protest against restrictions imposed on Irish goods by the British Parliament to protect British trade. The following month Lord North, the prime minister, announced the lifting of the trade restrictions, giving Irish and British manufacturers a level playing field. The success of their resistance to trade restrictions encouraged the Volunteers to campaign for legislative independence in the early 1780s.

French, John Denton (Lord French of Ypres) (1852–1925). Lord lieutenant (viceroy) of Ireland (1918–21). He was born in Kent of a Co. Roscommon family, and entered the army in 1874. He became commander-in-chief of the British Expeditionary Force to France in 1914, and was created viscount in recognition of his war efforts in 1915. In 1918, at the time of the CONSCRIPTION CRISIS in Ireland, he boasted that he could enforce conscription 'with a slight augmentation of troops', and in May of that year he was appointed viceroy.

As the ANGLO-IRISH WAR gathered momentum during the following year, French wielded draconian powers under DORA, and martial law was declared in December 1920. Together with Sir Nevile Macready, commander-in-chief of the British army in Ireland, he pursued a military solution, playing into the hands of Michael COLLINS, who cleverly manipulated events like the killing of Tomás MACCURTAIN, the execution of Kevin Barry (*see* 'MOUNTJOY JAIL ONE MONDAY MORNING, IN') and the violent excesses of the AUXIES in particular to provide propaganda for SINN FÉIN and turn the general population against British rule. French became a hate figure among Republicans, and a dozen attempts were made on his life; after a particularly narrow escape on 19 December 1920 he became a virtual prisoner in the Viceregal Lodge in Dublin.

In the spring of 1921, as negotiations towards a truce continued with the IRA, French was replaced as lord lieutenant by a Catholic, Lord Fitzalan of Derwent. He returned to live in England and was created earl. On his deathbed in 1925 he refused to be reconciled with his sister, the socialist Republican Charlotte DESPARD.

French, Nicholas (1604–78). Bishop of the diocese of Ferns, Co. Wicklow, and influential CONFEDERATE CATHOLIC politician. He opposed the first peace with ORMOND, but in 1648, after a visit to Rome, he persuaded the bishops to agree to the second Ormond peace, a decision he later regretted. Ormond revoked his licence to return home and thereafter French became a severe critic of the Restoration settlement, imposed after Ormond again became lord lieutenant in 1662.

French, Percy (1854–1920). Entertainer, songwriter and watercolourist. He was born in Cloonyquin, Co. Roscommon, on 1 May 1852, and after a leisurely career as an undergraduate at Trinity College Dublin finally emerged to become 'Inspector of Drains', as one of his songs recalls, in Co. Cavan. Even as a student he had begun to write the mainly comic songs for which he is noted, including the often misascribed 'Abdul the Bulbul Ameer'.

When his work as an engineer finished in 1887 French edited (and largely wrote) the comic paper *The Jarvey*, and on its demise a year later collaborated with Houston Collisson (1864–1920) in a musical comedy, *Knights of the Road* (1888). Its success launched him on a career as a touring performer of his own material: songs (sometimes to his own accompaniment on the piano and usually with music by Collisson), monologues and sketches. He was a talented watercolourist, and lightning paintings became part of his act, including the extra trick of 'doubles', turning the canvas on his easel upside down to reveal a different picture.

French's songs are as popular now as when he wrote them: 'Come Back, Paddy Reilly', 'Phil the Fluter's Ball', 'The Mountains of Mourne' and 'Shlathery's Mounted Fut' are still widely sung. French died in Formby, Lancashire, on 24 January 1920 after a short illness. Collisson, who had taken orders in 1899 and officiated at his friend's funeral, died a week later.

French fiddle. An Ulster term for the mouth organ or harmonica. The epithet 'French', normally connoting something wicked, is here an indication of inferiority:

> Halfway out, the wind dropped and the men rowed on one side of the boat while I played treasonable music on a mouth-organ, or as it is called here, a 'French fiddle'. On our right spread many capes and the blue slopes of the Donegal mountains.
>
> AUSTIN CLARKE (1904–85): *A Penny in the Clouds* (1968)

Friar's Bush. A former cemetery off the Stranmillis Road in Belfast. It had been a significant site since early Christian times, with strong Patrician associations. The 'bush' was a spreading thorn, and it was used as a Mass shelter for the Catholics of Belfast during the PENAL DAYS. With the opening of St Mary's Church in 1784 the celebration of Mass there was discontinued, but the churchyard became the main Catholic burial ground after its consecration on 5 August 1829. From 1850 there were complaints of serious overcrowding, and the cemetery was finally closed in 1869 when the purpose-built Milltown was opened.

> In ancient times, as peasants tell,
> A friar came with book and bell
> To chaunt his Mass each Sabbath morn,
> Beneath Srath-milis trysting thorn.
>> JOSEPH CAMPBELL (1879–1944): 'Friar's Bush' (1905)

Fridian (d.588). The Irish founder of a monastery in Lucca, Tuscany. He became bishop there in 560 and was noted for his struggles against the heresy known as ARIANISM. He died on 18 March 588 and his relics, reconstituted as a wax image, are in a glass coffin in the church that bears his name in Lucca. He is credited with miraculously changing the course of the River Auser, which was once a tributary of the Arno but now flows directly into the Ligurian Sea. His feast day is 18 March.

Friel, Brian (b.1929). Short-story writer and playwright. He was born in Omagh and educated at his father's primary school, St Columb's, Derry, and at Maynooth. He taught for ten years in Derry and then became a full-time writer, scoring a notable success with *PHILADELPHIA, HERE I COME!* (1964). He had already published a volume of short stories, *The Saucer of Larks* (1962), and went on to publish *The Gold in the Sea* (1966). The stories, many of which had appeared in the *New Yorker*, deal with childhood, loss, the consolation of admitted illusion (a characteristic of some of his plays) and the individual's sense of fitness. The plays since *Philadelphia* (excluding versions of Chekhov, Turgenev and Charles MACKLIN) amount to more than 20, all noted for their humour, irony, the simple brilliance of the dialogue, and a sense of the tears of

things being kept at bay by a belief in the possibility of dreams someday coming true.

Friel is a restless experimenter in dramatic form, seeming to push the idea of the play to its furthest definition. He uses music, dance, time rearrangement, characters who detach themselves from the world of the play to address the audience directly and individual monologue rather than dialogue in such plays as *FAITH HEALER* (1979) and *Molly Sweeney* (1994), but his work is verbally precise and perfectly logical. His work *Afterplay* (2002) daringly brings together Andrey from Chekhov's *The Three Sisters* and Sonya from *Uncle Vanya*. In 2003 he presented *Performances* based upon the correspondence and second string quartet of Leoš Janáček (1854–1928).

Friel's work, though of universal appeal, is undoubtedly Irish: his Everyvillage is Ballybeg (Irish *Baile Beag*, 'little town'), and Irish history and politics are his primary material, either specifically as in *The Freedom of the City* (1973), *Volunteers* (1975), *TRANSLATIONS* (1980) and the ambiguously titled *Making History* (1988), or as part of the consciousness of the vocal and fragmenting families that often form the dramatis personae of his plays. Perhaps *DANCING AT LUGHNASA* (1990) – with its use of dance, ritual, compassion, Ballybeggary, a narrator who is one of the characters grown up, a clash of cultures, and the existential nature of memory – might crudely be taken as a representative play.

Friendly Sons of St Patrick, the. The longest-lasting of several 18th-century Irish fraternal and charitable societies that were founded before the American Revolutionary War. In 1768 in New York City a group came together as the Friendly Brothers of St Patrick, its membership consisting mainly of Irish-born officers in the British forces in North America. (In 1771 a similar brotherhood was established in Charleston, South Carolina.) The majority of Yankee Irish would then have been Ulster Presbyterians, though there would have been a number of latter-day Catholic WILD GEESE.

The name was partially taken over by the Friendly Sons of St Patrick established in Philadelphia that same year. Its members were almost entirely Protestant, which made the appointment of the Cork-born Catholic Stephen Moylan (*see* MOYLAN'S DRAGOONS) as president all the more remarkable. A New York branch with Daniel McCormick, a director of the Bank of New York, as its first president, was organized in 1784 in the now independent United States.

By 1790 the USA had 400,000 citizens of Irish birth, three-quarters of them Catholic, including an influx from the 17th-century penal colonies of the West Indies. Until the huge increase of Catholic immigrants after the Great Famine of the 1840s, the Irish connection of the Friendly Sons of St Patrick was sentimental rather than political, as the following quatrain suggests:

> May heaven's own breezes to Ireland's coast
> On invisible waves through the lightning and gale
> Bear our message of hope – our perennial toast:
> 'The Sons of St Patrick – the Knights of the Grail!'
>
> CLARE GERALD FENERTY (d. 1952): 'The Friendly Sons of St Patrick'

Frog-dancing. *See* KUTU-KUTU.

Frolic. A gathering of tenants, labourers and all hands to do emergency work.
See also MEITHEAL.

Frongoch. A prison camp in north Wales in which hundreds of SINN FÉIN activists, not all of whom had participated in the EASTER RISING, were interned in 1916. They included Michael COLLINS, Richard MULCAHY and many others who would be prominent in the Anglo-Irish War of 1919–21 and subsequently. Conditions were far from luxurious, but the prisoners trained and organized as a much more cohesive fighting force then heretofore while they were in Frongoch. The internees were released in time for Christmas 1916, and the sentenced prisoners the following June.

Fuadar (Irish, 'haste', 'rushed activity'). A term used in HIBERNO-ENGLISH for hurry or panic,

particularly an unnecessary hurry. It is used in a typical Hiberno-English formulation, 'What fuadar is on you?' (in Irish *Cén fuadar atá fúr?*)

Fuamnach. In Irish mythology, the first wife of MIDIR whose jealousy drives her to treat ÉTAIN, his chosen second wife, with great and ingenious cruelty. Fuamnach is finally bested by AONGHUS ÓG, who takes her head to his home at BRUGH NA BÓINNE as a trophy.

Fulacht fiadh or ***Fulacht Fiann*** (Irish, 'cooking place of the Fianna'). A cooking pit in which meat was cooked in water boiled by heated stones. The meat was wrapped in straw for cooking and the water was kept on the boil by the addition of further stones from the fire. Archaeologists believe that thousands of these pits are scattered throughout Ireland, and that they were in use from the end of the Stone Age until the 17th century. A modern experiment in a *fulacht fiadh* in Co. Cork proved that a leg of mutton could be cooked very satisfactorily using such an arrangement. *Fiadh* or *Fiann* in the term refers to the link that was believed to exist between these cooking pits and the mythological FIANNA.
See also CRAGGAUNOWEN.

Full, to be. An Ulster term meaning to be drunk, to have drunk enough.

Full and Plenty. A classic country cookery book (1960) by Maura Laverty (1907–66), with each section prefaced by a heartwarming story of romance or family life. Maura Laverty was born Maura Kelly in Rathangan, Co. Kildare, to a family of shaky fortunes. Part of her first novel, *Never No More* (1942) – a melodramatic and fragrant evocation of the idyllic country life of her heroine Delia Scully in her grandmother's Derrymore House outside Ballyderrig – was first published by Sean O'Faoláin in *The* BELL. Her third, autobiographical, novel, *No More than Human*, describes a period spent as a governess and writer in Spain in the 1920s. She returned from Spain to marry a journalist, James Laverty, and thereafter earned her living as a writer of novels and cookery books. One of her plays became the first Irish soap opera, *TOLKA ROW*.

Fuller, Stephen. The sole survivor of the BALLY-SEEDY MASSACRE of March 1923, during the CIVIL WAR. When the mines were detonated, Fuller was blown clear of the men to whom he had been tied and into a ditch. He escaped and made the story known. He was elected TD for FIANNA FÁIL in 1937 and 1938, but lost his seat in 1943. Fuller's personal testimony about Ballyseedy on Robert Kee's *Ireland: a Television History* in 1982 was one of the most sensational media events ever in Ireland. Many Irish people, without thinking too hard, might have thought that stories about Bally-seedy and other Civil War atrocities were Republican propaganda. However, it transpired that the protagonists, like Fuller, had preferred to keep quiet about these events, in order to avoid exacerbating old wounds.

Funeral customs. Because of their strong sense of the supernatural and their fear of the dead coming back to haunt them, Irish people were especially respectful of customs relating to funerals. Although these were religious events, some of the customs relating to them were very ancient and pagan in origin. The funeral procession took the longest way round from the house to the church and again within the graveyard, as it was considered disrespectful to the corpse to be in any hurry to bury it. The family or professional keeners performed at the grave, especially if it was the funeral of a young person, the mother of a family, or someone who had died in tragic circumstances. Then when the coffin was laid at the bottom of the grave one man would go down and unscrew all the nuts (at the time they used wing-nuts, which were easy to unscrew) and lay them on the lid in the form of a cross. This was to make sure that when the resurrection of the body occurred there would be no delay in the body being released from the coffin. It was the custom for the clothes of the dead person to be given away to a needy neighbour, who was

to wear them on three successive Sundays – otherwise the dead person would go naked in the next world.

See also TRIMMLIN' THE CHAIRS.

Funt. A HIBERNO-ENGLISH colloquialism for a kick to some part of the anatomy.

Fureys, The. A Dublin family of four musicians who together with Scotsman Davy Arthur (b.1954) formed a ballad/folk group known as The Fureys and Davy Arthur in 1981. Finbar (b.1946) became the best known member of the group, both for his heavily Dublin-accented vocals and for his playing of the UIL-LEANN PIPES. The group achieved great popular success, a melancholy ballad called 'When You Were Sweet Sixteen' reaching Britain's Top 20 in 1981, and a later recording of a First World War song, 'The Green Fields of France', becoming the definitive version.

Furrow, The. A journal founded in February 1950 by Canon James Gerard McGarry (1905–77), then professor of pastoral theology (1939–69) at Maynooth. The effect of the contents in the period when the Catholic Church in Ireland seemed least susceptible to change was remarkable. The editor's choice of topic and writer opened up the minds of Irish priests and concerned laity to continental thought, and prepared them for the changes that were to come through the Second Vatican Council (1962–5). McGarry also helped to bring about a minor revolution in ecclesiastical aesthetics, encouraging young painters, sculptors and especially architects. In 1969 he became parish priest of Ballyhaunis, Co. Mayo, and died in a car accident eight years later.

Fursa or **Fursey** (d.648). The *peregrinus* (*see PEREGRINI*) who after COLUMBAN was the best known of the Irish missionaries in 7th-century France. He gained such a reputation as a teacher that he decided, in the words of BEDE, 'to go on pilgrimage for the Lord [*peregrinatio pro Christo*] wherever opportunity offered.' He and his brothers FOILLÁN and ULTAN came to England some time after 630, and were welcomed by King Sigebert of East Anglia. Fursa founded the abbey of Cnobheresburgh (now BURGH CASTLE near Yarmouth in Suffolk) and ministered there with his brothers' help for ten years. Driven again into 'pilgrimage' and emulating his hero Columban he landed in NEUSTRIA, where Erchinoald, the mayor of the palace, gave him land to found a house at Lagny, near Paris, about the year 644. When he died at Mézerolles on his way back to England in 648 his uncorrupted body was brought by the mayor to be the centrepiece of the new church he had completed at PÉRONNE. Fursa's accounts of visions of the world of the spirits, both good and evil, of the fires of sin ready to consume the earth, and of the joyous state of the blessed, as chronicled by Bede, brought him lasting fame and became the main inspiration for Dante's *La Divina Commedia*. Fursa's feast day is 16 January.

G

GAA. The Gaelic Athletic Association. It was founded on 1 November 1884 in Hayes's Hotel in Thurles, Co. Tipperary, by Michael Cusack, a teacher from Co. Clare, Maurice Davin, a Co. Tipperary farmer, and five other men. This 'Irish Association', as it was originally called, had as its objectives the promotion of Irish identity, the bringing of athletics to Irish people of all classes and the revival of the traditional Irish sports of HURLING, FOOTBALL and HANDBALL. Charles Stewart PARNELL, Michael DAVITT and Dr Thomas Croke, Archbishop of Cashel (*see* CROKE PARK), became patrons of the association. The GAA quickly became politicized, and Irish Republican Brotherhood (IRB) members infiltrated county boards and club committees, and the IRISH VOLUNTEERS drilled with hurleys in the absence of guns. Many GAA members were interned after the 1916 EASTER RISING, and the British authorities banned GAA games in 1918. After independence, the GAA played a central life in the social, cultural and political life of the country. Every parish had a club, usually managed by the local clergy and teachers. In 2002 there were almost 2000 clubs affiliated to the association. Despite travel difficulties, championship matches became enormously popular. The GAA has rigorously enforced amateur status among its players, but team sponsorship was allowed in 1992 and from 1994 the hurling and football championships were also sponsored. *See also* ALL-IRELAND; BAN, THE; 'GHOST TRAIN FOR CROKE PARK, THE'.

Gabha (Irish, 'blacksmith'). A word (pronounced 'gowa') that is still to be found as a family nickname. In rural Ireland, blacksmiths, who made all the farm and garden tools and gates as well as shoeing horses, were skilful and respected craftsmen. The forge was a meeting place for all the people of the locality, as they waited for their horses to be shod. There was reputed never to have been a mean blacksmith, and smiths were also supposed to have healing powers. The water in which the horseshoes were cooled was believed to have curative powers, and to be a specific cure for warts. In the days when most people never saw a dentist, the blacksmith also extracted teeth.

Gabháil. The Irish word (pronounced 'gow-all') – also borrowed by HIBERNO-ENGLISH – denoting the amount that can be held between the outstretched arms, for instance of TURF or hay. The expression was commonly used in rural Ireland until the mid-20th century.

Gae-Bolg (Old Irish, 'belly-spear'). In Irish mythology, CÚCHULAINN's ultimate weapon, a spear that makes only one entry wound but which has thirty barbs that open inside the body. During his early training in ALBA his tutor SCÁTHACH presents it to him and shows him how to use it. Under her guidance Cúchulainn learns to throw it using his foot.

Gaelic Athletic Association. *See* GAA.

Gaelic football. *See* FOOTBALL.

Gaelic League (Irish, Connradh na Gaeilge). The last and most successful of 19th-century initiatives to revive Irish as a spoken language. It was founded on 31 July 1893 by a committee led by Eoin MACNEILL and Douglas HYDE, and for more than 20 years pursued successfully its apolitical purpose of language renewal. Teachers were encouraged to teach Irish in primary schools, and Irish became a popular subject for the Secondary Leaving Certificate. In addition, a series of festivals and literary competitions generated a Gaelic culture with a modern literature. The Gaelic League's greatest success was in the field of adult education, in which organizers and native-speaking TRAVEL-LING TEACHERS countrywide did much to make Irish a second language for a large proportion of the population. After 1915, under the influence of MacNeill and Patrick PEARSE, it became strongly associated with the IRISH VOLUNTEERS and the idea of seeking political independence by revolution. As such it strongly coloured the education policies of the Free State from 1922.

Gaelic Union. One of the precursors of the GAELIC LEAGUE, also known by its Irish name Aondacht na Gaeilge. It was founded in 1880 by certain members of SPIL, such as David Comyn, who, dissatisfied with the perceived lack of progress in the restoration of Irish as a living and unmarginalized language, formed the new society to concentrate upon literary and educational aspects of the movement. They succeeded in commissioning school textbooks and having Irish accepted as a subject for the Secondary Leaving Certificate.

Gael Linn (Irish, 'Irish pools'). An organization to promote the Irish language by means of the revenue earned on Gaelic football pools, established by An Comhchaidreamh, the association

of university Irish *cumainn* (clubs), in 1953. The trustees appointed then – including Máirtín Ó CADHAIN, Seán Ó Síocháin (later general secretary of the GAA), and Dónal Ó Móráin (later Director of Gael Linn) – effectively constituted the first board of the organization. Gael Linn supported the Irish language in a variety of novel ways, both economic and cultural: it established industries in GAELTACHT areas, and founded a label to record and market traditional music and Irish-language singing, an Irish-language theatre (An DAMER, 1955) and a weekly newsreel (AMHARC ÉIREANN, 1959). The first ever full-length feature film in Irish, MISE ÉIRE (1960), directed by George Morrison and with a soundtrack by Seán Ó RIADA, was funded by Gael Linn. The organization also awarded scholarships to primary-school children to spend a term living with a family in the Gaeltacht. Gael Linn is still active in the promotion of the Irish language and culture, and runs an all-Irish café in the centre of Dublin.

Gaelscoil. A primary or (less frequently) secondary school in which all classes and the other business of the school are conducted through the medium of Irish. Gaelscoils usually begin as a result of community demand and intense lobbying and fundraising by interested parents. Scoil Lorcáin in Monkstown, established in 1952, was the first of this type of publicly funded alternative to ordinary primary or secondary schools. In 1973 an umbrella organization, Gaelscoileanna, was formed and it is now funded by Foras na Gaeilge (*see* BORD NA GAEIGE), the 32-county development board for Irish that was established as a result of the GOOD FRIDAY AGREEMENT. By the end of 2003 there were 149 primary and 33 secondary gaelscoils throughout Ireland, north and south, with about 30,000 pupils. Education through Irish has been fervently espoused by members of Nationalist communities in Belfast, Derry and other urban areas in Northern Ireland.

Gaeltacht. A term meaning an area in Ireland where Irish is the vernacular of the majority of the people. Since the foundation of the state the numbers of people speaking Irish has declined inexorably, despite special grants and attempts to set up industries. Most of the Gaeltachts are situated on the western seaboard, and the very beauty of the scenery there has militated against the Irish language. The influx into these areas of BLOW-INS from other parts of Ireland or abroad, whose children may not speak the language, has rendered local schools English-rather than Irish-speaking for the majority. Some county councils have responded to this by granting planning permission to build houses in Gaeltacht areas only to those who can prove their proficiency in Irish. Census returns consistently show the number of native speakers of Irish to be lower than expected, and in some of what are called *breac-ghaeltacht* ('speckled Gaeltachts') the level of everyday use of the language is very low indeed.

See also DÉISE, THE; MEATH GAELTACHT, THE; MUSKERRY GAELTACHT, THE.

Gahan, Muriel. *See* COUNTRY MARKETS; *GRIAN-ÁN*.

Gaiety. A theatre in Dublin built in 1871 by the Gunn brothers in King Street, close to St Stephen's Green. It was (and still is) the home of pantomime and variety shows, notably those starring Jimmy O'Dea (*see* 'PRIDE OF THE COOMBE, THE').

Gaileen. A Co. Limerick dialect word for a bundle of rushes placed under the arms of a beginner learning to swim.

Gaisce. An Irish word for 'heroism', 'valour', used in HIBERNO-ENGLISH to mean praiseworthy deeds or an accomplishment. The phrase 'You did *gaisce*,' might praise anything from a cupboard cleaned out to a race won. 'Gaisce' is the National Challenge Award of the President of Ireland for young people aged 15 to 25, in the areas of community involvement, personal skills, physical recreation and adventurous activity.

Galar cam. An Irish phrase meaning 'crooked disease', used in HIBERNO-ENGLISH for staggers, the disease of sheep.

Gall (*c*.550–645). Saint. Gall was a student and one of the 12 companions of COLUMBAN, and went with him to the land of the Franks in 591. Gall seems to have been especially gifted linguistically, and was soon able to preach in local languages and dialects. In 612 Columban and he founded a monastery at Bregenz on Lake Constance, and it was here that the two men are supposed to have quarrelled. Columban's patron Theudebert had been killed by his brother Theuderic, a long-time enemy of Columban, and Columban was anxious to leave, partly to escape Theuderic but also to cross the Alps on the path to Rome. Gall, reluctant to leave the idyllic surroundings of their lakeside foundation, refused to go, claiming ill-health. The story is not to be found in JONAS's rather sanitized life of Columban, but Gall's biographer, Walafrid Strabo, records that the irascible missionary said to Gall: 'I enjoin on you before I go, that so long as I live in the body, you do not dare to celebrate Mass ...' (The story concludes with the arrival of Columban's abbatial staff five years later, sent by the dying monk to release Gall from the interdict.)

Gall quickly learned the Germanic language of the Alemanni, the local tribe, and preached Christianity to them with the approval of Duke Gunze and other local rulers. He died at the age of about 95, leaving behind a reputation of great sanctity and austerity of life, as well as fame as a skilful angler – the probable reason for the siting of his cell on the upper waters of the River Steinach. Gall is said to have attracted a significant 12 disciples and with their help to have converted the peoples of the territory of modern Switzerland by the time of his death in 645. The monastery (and town) of Sankt-Gallen, 70 km (45 miles) east of Zürich, named in Gall's honour, was founded by the Benedictine monk Otmar in 719, and the monastery survived until its suppression in 1797. It has a notable library begun by an Irishman, St Moengal, *c*.850. Gall's feast day is 16 October.

Gallagher, Patrick. *See* PADDY THE COPE.

Gallagher, Rory (1948–95). Blues guitarist. He was born in Ballyshannon, Co. Donegal, on 2 March 1948 but moved to Cork with his family in the early 1950s. He taught himself to play the guitar at the age of 9, and four years later formed his first band. When he was 16 he left school and joined the Fontana (later Impact) Showband, touring with them in Britain and Europe. In 1966 he formed a rhythm-and-blues group, Taste, which, with some changes of personnel lasted until 1970, at which time he formed the Rory Gallagher Band.

Gallagher released his first solo album, *Rory Gallagher*, in 1972, and over the next 20 years sold millions of albums and toured the world many times, including 25 tours of the USA. He guest-recorded with artists like Muddy Waters, Jerry Lee Lewis and Albert King as well as re-leasing his own successful albums, both studio and live, including *Against the Grain* (1975), *Photo Finish* (1978) and *Stage Struck* (1980). He continued to tour with a new band formed in 1993 until he became seriously ill in the Netherlands in January 1995. He died in King's College Hospital, London, on 14 June 1985, from complications following a liver transplant, and was buried in Cork, mourned by millions of fans throughout the world.

Gallaher's Blue. A popular make of cigarette invented by Thomas Gallaher, who was born in Templemoyle, near Derry, in 1840. He began his tobacco factory in Sackville Street in the city when he was just 17 and transferred it to Belfast in 1867. His huge factory in York Street, opened in 1896, processed many types of tobacco, cigarettes and snuff, including the milder Gallaher's Green and Park Drive, Woodbine's main rival in pre-filter days. Gallaher had his own estates in North Carolina, USA, and had become one of the city's leading manufacturers.

> The visitor to this model establishment if he be of the mighty army of smokers he will find pleasure in the reflection that he is one of the many millions whose devotion to the *celestial*

fume has brought into existence such a wondrous and unique industry as that which receives such excellent exemplification under Messrs. Gallaher & Company's influential auspices.
>
> > *The Industries of Ireland* (1891), quoted in Jonathan Bardon, *A History of Ulster* (1992)

'Gallant John Joe, The'. An anonymous ballad celebrating the exploits of Cavan footballer John Joe O'Reilly (b.1919), a commandant in the Irish army who died prematurely in November 1952. He was born in the Derries near Killeshandra and played Gaelic football for St Patrick's College, Cavan, and with his local club, Cornafean. He captained the Cavan team to victory in the ALL-IRELAND finals of 1947 (*see* POLO GROUND FINAL, THE), in which his brother 'Big Tom' O'Reilly also played, and again in 1948, the great Cavan team of that era winning every Ulster football final between 1937 and 1949. He also won four RAILWAY CUP medals, captaining the Ulster side in 1943 and 1950. He died at the Curragh Military Hospital on 21 November 1952:

> In the month of November 'twas a wild stormy day,
> I shut the front door and to town made my way,
> I met with a young man on the road I did go
> And he told me the news of the death of John Joe.
> ...
> He led Cavan to victory on a glorious day
> In the Polo grounds final when Kerry gave way,
> In Croke Park the next year when our boys bet Mayo
> Once again they were led by the gallant John-Joe.

The Gallant John Joe (2002) is also the title of a play by Cavan-born playwright Tom MACINTYRE, the soliloquy of the fictional widower John-Joe Concannon, a role created for and in collaboration with the actor Tom Hickey. Concannon occasionally breaks into a rendition of 'The Gallant John Joe'.

Gallogue (Irish *gallóg*). A HIBERNO-ENGLISH word for a big glassful, for instance of whiskey. The word is also used tautologically, as in 'a big gallogue'.

Galloping Hogan. The RAPPAREE (outlaw) said

to have led Patrick SARSFIELD and his men to the Williamite siege train they destroyed at Ballyneety in 1690.

See also SARSFIELD IS THE WORD.

Gallous. An adjective apparently deriving from 'gallows' and originally meaning 'fit for the gallows' (or likely to end up there). In HIBERNO-ENGLISH it can mean 'fine' or 'powerful', and also a daring person or act. (The similar Scots word *gallus* means 'fearless', 'bold', 'reckless'.) In J.M. Synge's *The* PLAYBOY OF THE WESTERN WORLD (1907), Pegeen's father, Michael Flaherty, tells Pegeen and Christy that the dispensation for Pegeen to marry Shawneen Keogh has come and that 'Father Reilly's after reading it in gallous Latin.' Later, Pegeen turns on Christy after he 'kills' his father for the second time, saying, 'there's a great gap between a gallous story and a dirty deed.'

Gallouses (Irish *gealasacha*). A HIBERNO-ENGLISH word for men's braces.

Gallowglass (Irish *gall-óglach*, 'foreign warrior'). A mercenary soldier from the Hebrides; such soldiers saw service in both Irish and Scottish armies. Gallowglasses are mentioned in Shakespeare's *Macbeth* (*see also* RUG-HEADED KERNS), and were imported into Ulster and Connacht, where they were used from the middle of the 13th century to help stop English colonization. Their leaders, usually clan chieftains, were paid in grants of land by the Irish lords who commissioned their services. In time the Boyles, Gallaghers, MacSweeneys, Mac-Donalds, MacCabes and MacLeods became part of the nobility of Ireland. The first three of these clans have retained nicknames because of perceived contemporary idiosyncrasies: Na Baoilligh Bheadaí ('the fastidious Boyles'); Gallachóirigh na gCipín Dóite ('the Gallaghers of the fire-tempered staves'); Clann tSuibhne na Miodóg ('the Sweeneys of the daggers').

Gallowglass Céilí Band. The most famous of all CÉILÍ BANDS in the golden era of such bands in the 1950s and 1960s. It was founded in Naas, Co. Kildare in 1950, and in 1955 the band achieved national prominence when it performed for the first time in the Mansion House in Dublin. Of the seven musicians, four were members of the McGarrs, a Naas family with Scottish origins – hence the band's name (*see* GALLOWGLASS). The instruments they played were piano, accordion, double bass, violin, saxophone and percussion.

Galltacht. The areas of the country where English is spoken, as opposed to the GAELTACHT. *Gall* means 'foreigner' but in Ireland it is usually taken to mean the English oppressor, so the term is a loaded one, suggesting cultural apostasy.

Gallybander. A home-made catapult, consisting of a stick and a band of elastic with which to project pebbles or other small missiles.

Galore. An English word meaning 'in abundance', from the Irish adverbial phrase *go leor* ('enough', 'plenty'). The word may have entered the English language through Scotland in the 17th century, before Scots-Irish had separated to become Scots-Gaelic (*see* ERSE). Its descriptive convenience and hint of joviality established it as part of ordinary English speech by 1800.

Galtymore, The. A dance hall in Cricklewood, north London, named after the highest peak in the Galtee Mountains in Co. Tipperary, and frequented by Irish immigrant building workers. Irish showbands and country singers were the staple fare.

See also NAVVIES; 'MCALPINE'S FUSILIERS'.

Galway. The capital city of the west of Ireland, known as the CITY OF THE TRIBES (after the 14 tribes of Galway), and also as 'the Limestone City', because of the stone used in many of its buildings. It is the gateway to Connemara and its GAELTACHT. Galway began as a fishing village, and was captured by the Normans in 1228, becoming the sole outpost of Anglo-Norman influence in the west of Ireland – 'the remotest town of European civilization'. The architectural flavour of the city was described by Sir Oliver St John in 1614:

The towne is small, but all is faire and statelie buildings, the front of the houses are all of hewed stone, uppe to the top, garnished with faire battlement, in a uniform course, as if the whole town had been built upon one model. It is built upon a rock, environed almost with the sea, and the river; compassed with strong walls and good defenses after the ancient manner ...

Galway surrendered to the Cromwellian army under Sir Charles Coote in April 1652, after a long siege. It was sacked by the army, and many of the finest buildings destroyed.

When Louis MacNeice visited the city before the Second World War it was still a provincial backwater:

O, the crossbones of Galway,
The hollow grey houses,
The rubbish and the sewage,
The grass grown pier,
And the dredger grumbling
All the night in the harbour;
The war came down on us here.

However, Galway is now a thriving modern city with a strong artistic identity: it is the home of the DRUID THEATRE and Macnas Street theatre company, and has a successful summer arts festival. It has recently been described as Europe's fastest-growing city, but its centre is small with medieval streetscapes and buildings. It is a very popular tourist destination, especially among young Europeans.

'Galway Bay'. A traditional song dripping with nostalgia and CELTIC TWILIGHT. Nothing is known of the composer or lyricist:

If you ever go across the sea to Ireland
Then maybe at the closing of your day
You will sit and watch the moon rise over
  Claddagh
And see the sun go down on Galway Bay.

Just to hear again the ripple of the trout stream,
The women in the meadows making hay,
And to sit beside a turf fire, five in the cabin,
And to watch the bare foot Gossoons at their
  play;

For the breezes blowing o'er the seas from Ireland
Are perfumed by the heather as they blow,

And the women in the uplands diggin' praties
Speak a language that the strangers do not know.

Galway Blazers. A celebrated hunt in Co. Galway, which, according to legend, took its name from the serious fire caused in Dooley's Hotel in BIRR by members of the group during a banquet in 1840. In their ASCENDANCY heyday the Blazers hunted over 3600 sq km (1400 sq miles) of central Galway, and the first hunt master was given the substantial sum of £450 per annum to maintain his field. The most celebrated master and dedicated hunter of all was Burton Robert Persse of Moyode, near Athenry, who held the office 1852–85. (Lady GREGORY belonged to another branch of the family, the Roxborough Persses.) Persse was a notable breeder of hounds as well as a fearless horseman, and he kept 20 hunters for his own use and that of his guests, who included British royalty. In 1881 local farmers blocked the hunt as a form of agrarian protest, although Persse was known to be a reasonable landlord, and he immediately sold his hounds and hunters, closed his house and went to hunt in England instead. Film-maker John Huston was a member of the Blazers when he lived in St Clerans.
See also KILRUDDERY HUNT, THE.

Galway hooker. A type of sailing cargo craft used by fishermen and traders of Connemara and the CLADDAGH. They have been called 'Galway's signature upon the water'. The name 'hooker' comes from the name of one of several types of Dutch craft. They have a distinctive design and there are four types: the *bád mór* ('big boat'), 10.5–12 m (35–40 ft) long, the *leath-bhád* ('half-boat') about 9.75 m (32 ft) long; the other, smaller craft are the *gleoiteog* (from *gleoite*, 'pretty', 'delightful', i.e. a neat and shipshape craft) and the *púcán* (literally 'pouch', 'small bag', i.e. a fishing smack). They are made of oak, and are sturdy and stable with a strong sharp bow and curving sides, specifically designed for navigation in narrow, difficult tracts of water while carrying heavy cargo of fish or other materials. The Claddagh fleet was said to number more than a hundred vessels in the years before the Great Famine.

Most of the hookers had gone from the water by 1975, and now they appear only on ceremonial occasions such as the Cruinniú na mBád ('gathering of the boats') festival in Kinvara, Co. Galway. It is thought that there are about 25 hookers in the area in seaworthy condition, most of them modern reproductions. *St Patrick*, one of only five original Galway hookers left on the water, was destroyed by gales in May 2002. It was built in 1910 as a working vessel by the Casey brothers of Carna and was called *Bád Chonroy* ('Conroy's boat') because it transported supplies from Galway to the Conroy shop in Connemara. In 1913 Patrick PEARSE travelled on the vessel from Rosmuc to the ARAN ISLANDS during the period of formation of the IRISH VOLUNTEERS. It sailed to America in 1986 – the only Galway hooker to do so – as well as to the Faroe Islands and Greenland. It was rebuilt in 1988–9.

Gam (Irish *gamal*, 'loutish silly person'). A word used commonly in HIBERNO-ENGLISH to mean a soft, foolish person. It usually refers to males, while gomalogue (Irish *gamalóg*) is a silly or stupid woman.

Game ball. A colloquialism arising from the name given to the last round in a game of HANDBALL and meaning very good, very satisfactory. The phrase is often used in answer to an enquiry: 'How are things?' 'Game ball.'

Gammon. *See* SHELTA.

Gander¹. A derogatory colloquialism in HIBERNO-ENGLISH, meaning a person, particularly a woman, of lanky ungainly appearance, reminiscent of a gander.

Gander². A HIBERNO-ENGLISH word meaning 'look'. To 'take a gander' at something means to check it out. A gander was also traditionally the party staged the night before a wedding, usually in the house of the bride-to-be.
See also EATING THE GANDER.

Gandon, James (1743–1823). The great archi-

tect of Georgian Dublin. He was born in London on 29 February 1743 to a family of French Huguenot origin. He was a pupil in the office of Sir William Chambers from 1758, and in 1765 started his own practice. He first came to Dublin in 1781, under the aegis of the Revenue Commissioners and John BERESFORD, with a remit to design the CUSTOM HOUSE, completed in 1791, which is regarded as his finest building. His remaining architectural work was mainly in Ireland. His other great buildings are the FOUR COURTS (1785–1802) and the King's Inns, begun in 1795 and completed by his partner Baker after he had resigned from the project in 1808. He was also responsible for St Stephen's Church on Upper Mount Street, nicknamed the PEPPERCANISTER. Thereafter he retired from professional life and lived until his death on 23 December 1823 in Canonbrook House in Lucan, which he had built for himself.
See also MAD MARGARET'S WALK.

Gansey. A common word in HIBERNO-ENGLISH for a pullover or sweater. It derives from the Channel Island of Guernsey, its original source. The word appears also in Irish as *geansaí*.

> They carried the curragh to the Point. Charlie kicked off his boots. 'Take off the gansey,' Manus advised.
> PEADAR O'DONNELL (1893–1986): *Islanders* (1927)

Gap of the North, the. A passage in south Armagh between Slieve Gullion and the Carlingford Peninsula, of great strategic importance in former times.

> The train rattled down through the Gap of the North, mystic country, fairy country, turn a stone and uncover a legend or a myth. Cuchullain the demigod to O'Hanlon the Rapparee, and highwaymen giving their ghosts to those moors and mountains and little fields.
> BENEDICT KIELY (b.1919): *Land without Stars* (1946)

Garda Síochána (Irish, 'guardians of the peace'). An unarmed police force established in the autumn of 1922. They were originally known as Civic Guards, but the name changed to

Garda Síochána soon afterwards. The Garda Síochána Act of 1958 allowed for the entry of women into the force (*see* BANGHARDA). The 'guards', as the force is popularly known, were in the early years of the state a widely-accepted community force, but the development of organized crime in the cities means that the work of the guards is now much more dangerous. An armed detective unit, the SPECIAL BRANCH, had, among its many functions, the fight against Republican subversives during the recent Northern Troubles. The plural form *gardaí* is commonly used: 'You'd better get a move on before the *gardaí* come.'
See also ABBEYLARA SHOOTING, THE; RIC.

Garden. A word used in Irish rural areas not for any floral area but for the potato patch that was to be found about most homesteads.

Garden County, the. The nickname for Co. Wicklow, presumably because of the impressive gardens of the county's many big houses, such as POWERSCOURT.

Gargle. A Dublin colloquialism for alcoholic drink.

Garland. A type of chapbook with eight folded pages containing songs or recitations and sometimes with a decorative woodcut on the top page. Garlands were popular in 18th-century Ireland.

Garland Sunday. *See* LUGHNASA.

Garnish Island. A island of 37 acres (15 ha) situated in Glengarriff Harbour in Bantry Bay, Co. Cork; it is also known as Ilnacullin ('island of holly'). It can be reached by boat from Glengarriff and is famous for its gardens. These were developed in the 1930s by Harold Peto, architect and garden designer, and the then owner, Anna Bryce. The island was bequeathed to the nation in 1953 and is now managed by the Office of Public Works. Because of the influence of the Gulf Stream, its sheltered situation and high humidity, the micro-climate of the island has been described as sub-tropical, and rare plants from many parts of the world flourish here. The gardens are famous also for

rhododendrons, azaleas and heathers. Garnish Island is open to visitors from March to November.

'Garryowen' (Irish *garraí Eoin*, 'John's garden'). The name of a marching tune, derived from a part of the city of LIMERICK. The tune is that of a late 18th-century drinking song popular with the young bloods in a town with woeful slums:

> Instead of Spa we'll drink brown ale
> And pay the reckoning on the nail
> No man for debt shall go to gaol
> From Garryowen in glory!

The tune of the song was adopted as a martial air by the US 7th Cavalry, who sung it as they rode to annihilation at the battle of the Little Bighorn (25–26 June 1876) in Dakota Territory.

A garryowen is also a particular kind of vertical kick forward used in RUGBY FOOTBALL, and is so named from the Garryowen Rugby Club in Limerick, where it was first deployed. A garryowen is also known as an 'up and under'. Finally, in James Joyce's novel ULYSSES (1922), Garryowen is the name of a 'mangy mongrel'.

Garsún. *See* GOSSOON.

Garvagh (Irish *garbh achadh*, 'rough field'). A village in Co. Derry founded by George Canning of the London Ironmongers Guild. George Canning (1770–1827), later prime minister of Britain, was born in Garvagh House. The village was also the birthplace of the harpist Denis O'HEMPSY (c.1695–1807).

Garvaghy Road. *See* DRUMCREE STAND-OFFS.

Gas. A word signifying something enjoyable, entertaining, intriguing. It may be used also as an epithet: 'He's a real gas man; the very best of gas!'
See also CRAIC.

Gasometer, the. A former Dublin landmark at the junction of Sir John Rogerson's Quay and Cardiff Lane on the south LIFFEY quays. It was built in 1934 by the Alliance and Dublin

Consumers Gas Company (established in 1866), was 82.4 m (270 ft) high and had a capacity of 85,000 cubic metres. It was demolished in 1993–4.

Gate Theatre. A theatre founded by Mícheál Mac Liammóir and his partner Hilton Edwards (*see* BOYS, THE²) in 1928. In 1930 it was established in a permanent building, in the converted supper-rooms of the old Assembly Buildings (1785) in Parnell Square, Dublin (*see* ROTUNDA, THE). Their intention was to present international drama and experimental theatre that would complement the ABBEY THEATRE's provision of mainly Irish and often rural plays. The theatre was chronically insecure financially, but Edward Pakenham, 6th Earl of Longford (1902–61), long a supporter of the theatre, became a ready provider of funds, helping to ease the financial insecurity. He joined the board in 1934, but after a disagreement about policy formed his own company, Longford Productions, which from 1936 occupied the theatre from April to September while the Gate company toured. Longford also maintained the fabric of the premises.

The theatre saw early performances by such actors as Cyril CUSACK and Orson Welles (1915–82), who at the age of 16 in 1931 played the lead in *Jew Süss*, an adaptation of the best-selling novel (1925) by Lion Feuchtwanger. The theatre was enlarged in 1993 and its present director, Michael Colgan, honourably and successfully carries on the traditions of the theatre's founders.

See also SODOM AND BEGORRAH.

Gathering, the. The name given to the first day of PUCK FAIR.

Gavin, Frankie (b.1956). Traditional musician. A Galway-born fiddler, flautist and tin whistler, Gavin has been associated with innovation and the cross-fertilization of traditional music since the 1970s.

See also DÉ DANANN.

Gawk. An onomatopoeic Cork slang word meaning to vomit.

Gaybo. The popular nickname of broadcaster Gay BYRNE.

See also LATE LATE SHOW, THE.

Gay Old Hag, the. *See* POOR OLD WOMAN, THE.

GBS. The initials used by the playwright George Bernard Shaw (1856–1950) and preferred to his full name. He was born in Dublin and educated, as he later said, at 'Lee's Musical Society [his mother's colleague and close friend, George Vandaleur Lee], the National Gallery [of Ireland] and Dalkey Hill'. (He recompensed the National Gallery by leaving the trustees a considerable proportion of all his copyright fees.) He left Ireland in 1876 and became involved in the gradualist left-wing politics of the Fabian Society that he founded with Beatrice (1858–1943) and Sidney Webb (1859–1947). He was an incisive and extremely funny drama critic with the *Saturday Review* (1895–8), and also a music critic (*see* CORNO DE BASSETTO), and became a brilliant if at times wearisomely wordy playwright.

Shaw's most popular plays are *Arms and the Man* (1894) – which, like *Pygmalion* (1916), was made into a successful musical comedy – *The Devil's Disciple* (1897) – which owes a great debt to BOUCICAULT's melodrama *Arrah-na-Pogue* (1864) – *Man and Superman* (1905), *Heartbreak House* (1921) and *St Joan* (1923). He was awarded the Nobel prize for literature in 1925, by which time he was more famous for his vegetarianism, causing his fellow-dramatist J.M. Barrie (1860–1937), sitting beside him at dinner, to ask whether he had eaten or was about to start.

Shaw remained a cranky supporter of Ireland, recklessly defending the various 20th-century insurrections and consoling Michael COLLINS's sister with the words, 'Let us all praise God that he did not die in a snuffy bed of a trumpery cough, weakened by age, and saddened by the disappointments that would have attended his life had he lived.' *JOHN BULL'S OTHER ISLAND* (1904) neatly turns the tables in what is now called the 'Shavian' style on jealously guarded national stereotypes.

Geaitsí. An Irish word for 'gesture', 'attitude', used in HIBERNO-ENGLISH for actions or gestures, particularly unusual or accentuated gestures or capers. The word might be used pejoratively of a melodramatic person, or a fidgety child might be asked to stop 'your old *geaitsí*'. From this has come the word *gatch*, meaning general demeanour or gait.

Geanc. The Irish word for 'snub nose', also borrowed by HIBERNO-ENGLISH. The adjective *geanncach* is also used.

Gearrcach. An Irish word for 'fledgling', 'nestling', borrowed by HIBERNO-ENGLISH, and still used commonly in rural areas.

Geis (Old Irish, 'taboo', 'prohibition'; plural *geasa*). In Irish mythology, a magical obligation superseding all other laws and moral imperatives. *Geasa* were imposed by the DRUIDS to ensure their authority and have their edicts implemented. Sometimes individuals would secure druidic help to put a person under several *geasa*. Disobedience was unthinkable since it meant social ostracism and inevitable death. CÚCHULAINN, when he kills Culann's mastiff, is put under a *geis* never to eat dog-meat, and GRÁINNE, with help from her druid Daire, imposes upon DIARMAID UA DUIBHNE the *geis* of coming away with her.

Geldof, Bob (b.1954). Rock singer and Third World activist. He was born in Dublin and educated at Blackrock College. In 1975 he became lead singer with a rock group that he helped to found, the Boomtown Rats, which as its name suggests excoriated the country's traditional religious and economic values in songs like 'Banana Republic', 'Rat Trap' (1978) and 'I Don't Like Mondays' (1979). Geldof's main claim to fame is his fund-raising for victims of famine in Ethiopia from 1984. With an array of pop stars he formed an ad hoc pop group in the autumn of that year to record the protest song 'Do They Know It's Christmas?', which became the biggest-selling single in British history, earning more than £8 million for the Ethiopia appeal. Even more successful world-

wide was the Live Aid concert organized by Geldof, which was held simultaneously in London and Philadelphia on 13 July 1985. The world's leading pop stars performed and the show was broadcast to millions of people worldwide, raising £50 million for Ethiopia. For his humanitarian efforts Geldof received an honorary knighthood in 1986. In the same year he published an autobiography *Is That It?* He continues to live in London, working in the entertainment business in that city.

General, the (1949–94). The nickname of Martin Cahill, a Dublin criminal. He was born in Crumlin, Dublin, and at the age of 16 was sentenced to two years' incarceration in an INDUSTRIAL SCHOOL in Daingean, Co. Offaly. When he was 20 he began a four-year sentence in MOUNTJOY JAIL for theft. After his release he formed a criminal gang that delighted in outwitting the gardai. His biggest heist was the theft in May 1986 of paintings worth £30 million from RUSSBOROUGH HOUSE, Co. Wicklow. So great was the threat posed by Cahill and his gang and so difficult was he to apprehend – he planned each operation carefully and was personally scrupulous, never drinking or taking drugs – that the gardai set up a special surveillance unit. However, although they succeeded in arresting some of Cahill's associates, they never got Cahill himself. His career came to an end on 18 August 1994, when he was shot dead in his car in Ranelagh, Dublin. His killer was a man posing as a council worker who escaped on a motorcycle; the IRA admitted responsibility for the killing.

Cahill became famous as a result of a best-selling book, *The General* by Paul Williams, published in 1995, the first in a series of documentary-type books about criminal figures in contemporary Dublin, which suspended any moral judgement, seeming instead to emphasize Cahill's successful jousts with the gardai. There have also been three films made about Cahill: *Vicious Circle* (1998), a film for TV; *The General* (1998) directed by John Boorman and starring Irish actor Brendan Gleeson as Cahill;

and the slightly less convincing *Ordinary Decent Criminal* (2000) starring Kevin Spacey and directed by the Irishman Thaddeus O'Sullivan.

General Assembly, the. The most senior body of the PRESBYTERIAN Church. It meets for a week each June, its membership representative of local presbyteries and so far as possible equally weighted with lay elders and clergy. It is at the assembly that the moderator is elected for the year and important church matters are discussed. Decisions passed at assembly still have to be approved by a majority of presbyteries at local level.

General Post Office (Dublin). *See* GPO.

Gentle. A HIBERNO-ENGLISH word suggesting mental inadequacy. Someone who is 'gentle' may be 'enchanted', 'fey', 'away with the fairies'.

Gentle Land, the. *See* OTHERWORLD.

Gentleman Jim. The nickname of the 'scientific' boxer James John Corbett (1866–1933), who defeated the great John L. Sullivan (the BOSTON STRONG BOY) in the 21st round at New Orleans on 7 September 1892. Corbett was born in San Francisco, USA, of Irish parents on 1 September 1866. He began as a bank teller but his father soon fixed him up with fights. His one weakness by the pugilistic standards of the time was his lack of a *heavy* punch, but he compensated by brilliant quick jabs and much feinting. In the great match with Sullivan he received no blows to the face. He lost the world championship to Bob Fitzsimmons (1862–1917) on 17 March 1897 in Carson City, Nevada. The fight was the first to be filmed and showed Corbett being lifted clear off the ground by the punch that knocked him out in the 4th round. Corbett's nickname was based upon his handsome appearance and fine clothes. He made several appearances on stage (including a version of GBS's *Cashel Byron's Profession*) and on film, and was the subject of the biopic *Gentleman Jim* (1942) in which he was played by Errol Flynn (1909–59). He died in New York City on 18 February 1933.

Gentleman who pays the rent, the. The terms by which the pig was referred to in the days of landlords and tenants. In a subsistence economy, the sale of a pig twice a year (a sow was kept for breeding) generated enough cash to pay the rent.

Geosadawn. A common HIBERNO-ENGLISH word for ragwort, from the Irish word for thistle or ragweed.

Geraldine League. *See* GREY, SIR LEONARD.

German and a genius, a. The ailing Swift's (*see* DEAN, THE) description of the German-born composer George Frederick Handel (*see* FISHAMBLE STREET) when the latter called to see him during his last days in Ireland in 1742:

> From then on he fell into a deep melancholy and knew nobody. I was told the last sensible words he uttered were on this occasion: Mr Handel, when about to quit Ireland, went to take his leave of him. The servant was a considerable time before he could make the Dean understand; which when he did, he cried, 'Oh, a German and a genius! A prodigy! Admit him.' The servant did so, just to let Mr Handel behold the ruins of the greatest wit that ever lived along the tide of time, where all at length are lost.
>
> LAETITIA PILKINGTON (?1712–50): *Memoirs* (1748–54)

German Plot. An alleged conspiracy between SINN FÉIN activists and German interests, described by the authorities in Dublin Castle in May 1918 as 'treasonable communication with the German enemy'. Almost all the leaders of Sinn Féin were arrested on 15 May. This was during the CONSCRIPTION CRISIS in Ireland and, since no evidence was ever produced of such a conspiracy, it is thought that it was a ploy by the British government to remove the leaders of the anti-conscription lobby from circulation and discredit their motives.

Germany calling. *See* LORD HAW-HAW.

Gerrymander. To redraw the boundaries of electoral districts in such a way as to give one political party undue advantage over others. The word is derived from Elbridge Gerry (1744–1814), governor of Massachusetts, USA, who did this in 1812 in order to preserve control for his party. Gilbert Stuart (1755–1828), the artist, looking at a map of the new distribution, with a little imagination converted the outline of one district in Essex County to a salamander and showed it to Benjamin Russell, editor of the Boston *Sentinel*. 'Better say a gerrymander,' said Russell, and the name caught on. The practice was in common use in Derry to maintain a Unionist majority in the city corporation until 1970.

'Ghost Train for Croke Park, The'. The title of a poem by Sigerson Clifford (1913–85) from his 1955 collection *The Ballads of a Bogman*, in which an emigrant in London reminisces about trips to CROKE PARK on the 'ghost train'. Steam trains left the more distant parts of Ireland at midnight on Saturday for the ALL-IRELAND Football championship in Dublin on Sunday:

And we gave the Kerry war-cry as we marched
    north two by two
To lep aboard the ghost train for Croke Park.

See also TOWN IT CLIMBS THE MOUNTAIN, THE.

Ghoti. An invention by GBS to underline his perceived need for a radical reform of English spelling. The word is pronounced 'fish': the 'f' as the 'gh' in 'tough'; the 'i' as the 'o' in women; and the 'sh' as the 'ti' in 'nation'.

Giant's Causeway. A remarkable geological formation that stretches for more than a mile on the coast of north Co. Antrim. It consists of cooled basalt in polygonal columns akin to Fingal's Cave on the Isle of Staffa in the Inner Hebrides of Scotland. This Fingal is associated with FIONN MAC CUMHAIL, and later folklore has it that the mythic Irish hero, transformed into a giant, built the causeway to allow him to reach Staffa. His purpose, depending upon the version of the story, was either to do battle with a Scots giant or to reach a female giant whom he wished to bed. In the former he scoops a piece of land from the centre of Ulster

and throws it at his rival, thus creating the Isle of Man and Lough Neagh, the largest lake in THESE ISLANDS. The causeway was dismissed by Dr Johnson in 1779 as 'Worth seeing? yes; but not worth going to see.'

For many a league along the quarried shore,
Each storm-swept cape the race gigantic tore;
…
Each mighty artist from the yielding rock,
Hewed many a polished dark, prismatic block:
One end was modelled like the rounded bone,
One formed a socket for its convex stone;
Then side to side and joint and joint they bound,
Columns on columns locked, and mound on
    mound
Close as the golden cells that bees compose …
    WILLIAM HAMILTON DRUMMOND (1778–1865):
    'The Giant's Causeway' (1811)

Giant's Ring. A Neolithic enclosure about 6 km (4 miles) south of Belfast. It is 7.4 acres (3 ha) in area, surrounded by a 4-m (13-ft) bank 200 m (640 ft) in diameter. The bank was originally made of small stones, and is now covered with earth and overgrown with grass. There is a dolmen covering a passage grave approximately at its centre.

Gibraltar Shootings. *See* FARRELL, MAIRÉAD.

Gibson, Mike (b.1942). Ireland's most-capped rugby union player. One of most talented players ever to represent Ireland, the Belfast-born Gibson won a total of 69 caps for Ireland (including 5 as captain), appearing 40 times at centre, 25 at outside half and 4 times on the wing. With Tony O'REILLY, he shares the Irish record for the longest international career (16 seasons). In addition, Gibson toured four times with the British Lions (as they were then known), in 1966, 1968, 1971, 1974 and 1977, winning 12 Lions caps. On the 1971 Lions tour of New Zealand he was the lynchpin of a back line that also included the Welshmen Barry John and John Dawes, and which cut the All-Black defence to ribbons. Gibson was once memorably described by the All-Black scrum-half Chris Laidlaw as a 'red admiral among cabbage whites'. He also represented Dublin

University, Wanderers and Cambridge University. In all he scored nine tries for Ireland and six drop goals.

Gifford, Grace (1888–1955). Cartoonist and Republican. She was born in Rathmines in Dublin, the daughter of a Protestant lawyer and his Catholic wife; all 12 children of the family were reared as Protestants. She studied at the Metropolitan School or Art in Dublin and at the Slade in London, and she and her sister Muriel (later wife of Thomas MACDONAGH) became members of INGHINIDHE NA HÉIR-EANN and the Irish Women's Franchise League (*see* SHEEHY-SKEFFINGTON, HANNA). Grace also joined SINN FÉIN.

Grace was engaged to Joseph Mary PLUNKETT in 1915; they were to be married on Easter Sunday 1916, but the wedding was postponed because Plunkett had to have an operation for glandular tuberculosis. His fiancée knew nothing of the EASTER RISING, or of Plunkett's involvment in it, until Easter Sunday itself. Grace Gifford and Joseph Mary Plunkett were married in his cell in Kilmainham Jail on 3 May 1916 with two soldiers as witnesses, but the couple were not allowed to spend any time together. Grace saw him for ten minutes the following morning before he was shot.

Gifford remained involved in Republican politics; she was elected to the Sinn Féin executive in 1917 and, like all the women activists, she was against the TREATY (*see* WOMEN AND CHILDERS PARTY). She was active in the Women's Prisoners Defence League and was imprisoned in 1923 during the civil war. While in prison, she painted a Madonna known as the 'Kilmainham Madonna' on the wall of her cell, and a replica of it can be seen in Kilmainham today. She published three books of cartoons and received a pension as a 'widow of the Rising' once Fianna Fáil came to power in the 1930s. She is buried in the Republican plot in GLASNEVIN CEMETERY.

Gill, Lough. *See* INNISFREE; LOUGH GILL.

Gimp. An urge or desire, as in, 'They won't have the gimp on them for it!' The derivation is obscure, but it may be from *gimp*, a coarse, stiff thread.

Ginkel, Godar van Reede, Baron van (1630–1703). A Williamite general who during the WILLIAMITE WAR assumed command of anti-Jacobite forces in Ireland in September 1690, when William III returned to London. Ginkel was born in Utrecht and accompanied the king to England in 1688. He was at the Boyne (1690), captured Athlone, defeated St Ruth at Aughrim (1691) and raised the Siege of Limerick later that year. He was created Earl of Athlone in 1692. He commanded the Dutch troops in Marlborough's army in the War of the Spanish Succession (1702–13).

Gintleman who brought so much money, the. The description of the poet Tennyson by the bugler who was employed at Killarney to 'set the wild echoes ringing' (*see* TORC WATERFALL). The story is recorded in William ALLINGHAM's *Diary* for 23 September 1880:

> T. – 'Yes it was Killarney suggested it ['Blow, Bugle, Blow']. The bugle echoes were wonderful – nine times – at last like a chant of angels in the sky. But when I was there afterwards I could only hear two echoes, – from the state of the air. I complained of this and said, "When I was here before I heard nine." "O!" says the bugler, "then you're the gintleman that brought so much money to the place"' [The 'Bugle Song' increased the number of tourists to Killarney.]

In spite of his pleasure in Killarney, Tennyson was no lover of Ireland:

> 'Couldn't they blow up that horrible island with dynamite and carry it off in pieces – a long way off?'
>
> William Allingham: *Diary* 19 September 1880

Giobal. An Irish word for 'rag', 'scrap of cloth', used in the plural in HIBERNO-ENGLISH to mean worn or frayed clothing; 'I'm in *giobals* today.' An adjective, *gioballach*, is also used.

Gíocs. An Irish word for 'sound', 'squeak', borrowed by HIBERNO-ENGLISH and, as in Irish, always used in the negative: *Ní raibh gíocs as*, is translated literally as 'There wasn't a *gíocs* out of him.'

Giraldus Cambrensis (Gerald of Wales; also known as Gerald de Barry) (?1146–?1223). The historian of the 12th-century Anglo-Norman invasion of Ireland, and, according to Irish apologists, the country's greatest traducer. He was born in Manorbier in Pembrokeshire, as the Latin sobriquet indicates, educated at Gloucester and Paris, and appointed archdeacon of Brecon (*c*.1175). An ambitious churchman – he claimed that, as a child at play on the beach, his brothers built sand castles, while he built sand churches – he failed to win a bishopric because of political unreliability (he backed the wrong faction). He first came to Ireland in 1182, and returned as a kind of English spin-doctor with Prince John in 1185.

The result of these visits was the publication of *Topographica Hibernica* (*The History and Topography of Ireland*, 1188) and *Expugnatio Hibernica* (*The Conquest of Ireland*, 1189). The general tenor of these documents is critical and propagandist. Giraldus set the pattern for British historians in regarding the Irish as a primitive race, sorely in need of proper religion, laws and culture (though he did praise Irish minstrels). The *Expugnatio* contains the only extant source of the vexed bull LAUDABILITER. As well as giving a detailed account of the invasions from the time of STRONGBOW, he has much to say about the minute details of Irish life, much of it written with a mixture of Welsh piety and exaggerated distaste. The brilliance of the writing gave the books an authority they might not otherwise have possessed. His view of Ireland was challenged in the *Foras Feasa ar Éirinn* of Seathrún CÉITINN, and by John Lynch in *Cambrensis Aversus* (1662) (*see* HIBERNICI IPSIS HIBERNIORES). Giraldus' cantankerousness led to a falling-out not only with the English but also with his Welsh countrymen, and by the time of his death he was a strong apologist for France.

Give every man his dew. *See* TULLAMORE DEW.

Give it a lash, Jack. An exhortation used by Irish soccer supporters in the World Cup campaigns of 1990 and 1994. 'Jack' is Jack CHARLTON, then manager of the national team. To 'give something a lash' means to 'give something your best shot'.
See also GREEN ARMY; JACK'S ARMY.

'Given Note, The'. *See* INIS ICÍLEÁIN.

Glacken, Paddy (b.1954). A Donegal-born fiddler who has played with the BOTHY BAND and with performers such as Donal LUNNY and Paul Brady. Glacken was the first traditional music officer with The Arts Council/An Chomhairle Ealaíon, Dublin (1985–90).

Gladstone, William Ewart. *See* GOM.

Glaise. An Irish word still commonly used in HIBERNO-ENGLISH and meaning a 'stream' or 'flowing water'.

Glám. An Irish word for 'grasp', 'clutch', used in HIBERNO-ENGLISH (especially in Ulster) to mean a handful or something that is snatched. It is also used as a verb, to *glám*:

> But he made a glam above me, an' a' hit the
> hingin' lamp, and the chimley fell aff it and broke
> into jibareens roun' his feet.
> TULLYNEIL (R.L. MARSHALL): 'Annie Ashypet', in
> *The Heart of Tyrone* (1940)

Glar. The heavy mud left at low tide on river or estuary shore:

> It'd be fine for her to have a day in the stran'
> where there's a glar, an'she'd be up to her waist in
> the dirt and wet.
> PEADAR O'DONNELL: *Islanders* (1927)

Glas Gaibhleann or **Gaibhneann.** In Irish mythology, the magic grey cow owned by CIAN which is stolen by BALOR OF THE EVIL EYE and taken to TORY ISLAND. It is in pursuit of this cow that Cian meets Balor's daughter, ETHLINN, and sires LUGH, who will fulfil the prophecy that Balor will be killed by his grandson.

Glasnevin Cemetery. The burial ground known to generations of schoolchildren as 'the dead centre of Dublin', and nicknamed CROAK PARK. Correctly called Prospect Cemetery, it was opened in 1831 and is thought to have received the remains of more than 11 million people, including Daniel O'CONNELL (who is commemorated by a round tower 50m (165 ft) high erected in 1869), John Philpot CURRAN, Gerard Manley HOPKINS, Barry Sullivan (*see* 2500 RICHARD IIIS), Charles Stewart PARNELL, Jeremiah O'DONOVAN ROSSA, Sir Roger CASEMENT, Arthur GRIFFITH, Michael COLLINS, James LARKIN and Éamon DE VALERA. Grim towers still to be seen at intervals along its outer walls once held the Cuban bloodhounds that were released into the grounds after dark to inhibit the activities of the resurrectionists, a practice which ceased in 1853. Nearby, on the banks of the Tolka River, was the site of the monastic school of St MOBHI, one of the TWELVE APOSTLES OF IRELAND.

> Mr Power's soft eyes went up to the apex of the lofty cone.
>
> He's at rest, he said, in the middle of his people, old Dan O' but his heart is buried in Rome. How many broken hearts are buried here, Simon!
>
> JAMES JOYCE: *Ulysses* (1922)

See also MOUNT JEROME.

Glass[1]. A word often used in HIBERNO-ENGLISH to mean a mirror or looking-glass.

Glass[2]. A half-pint of beer or stout (pub measure).

Gleek. An Ulster word meaning 'squint' or 'sideways glance', as in, 'I only had a quick gleek but it looks to be the job.'

Glenanaar. *See* SHEEHAN, CANON [PATRICK AUGUSTINE].

Glendalough (Irish *Gleann Dá Loch*, 'the valley of the two lakes'). One of the most picturesque of the Wicklow glens, with extensive remains of early Irish monasticism. It was the hermitage of Kevin in the 6th century, though the extant remains date from the 10th century. It contains the best remains of a monastic 'city', with a gatehouse, a 31-m (102-ft) round tower, and many churches, oratories and devotional sites associated with the saint, including the narrow cave excavated from the rock on the edge of

the upper lake, called St Kevin's Bed. The other saint associated with Glendalough is Laurence O'TOOLE, who was abbot there (1153–62) before becoming Archbishop of Dublin.

Gleninsheen Gorget. An exquisite necklet of gold, thought to date from about 700 BC, the period when goldsmiths did their finest work. It was found by a boy in Co. Clare in 1932, and identified and placed in the National Museum in Dublin some years later. It is a curved and ornamented sheet of gold with discs of gold at either end that were attached to the necklet with golden wires and decorated with bosses.

Glenroe. A long-running RTÉ rural soap filmed in Kilcoole, Co. Wicklow, axed with little warning in 2002. It took some of the characters from earlier rural soaps, *The Riordans* and *Bracken* (*see* BYRNE, GABRIEL), and combined humour, romance, country matters and social problems. The anchor family was the Byrnes, the father of which was the arthritic, choleric and devious Dinny, with obligatory heart of gold (played with gusto by Joe Lynch), and which also included his easygoing and slightly gormless son Miley (Mick Lally), and Miley's wife, the discontented, sharp-tongued Biddy (Mary McEvoy). Safe in its Sunday evening slot, *Glenroe* had the usual signs of under-rehearsal saved by good acting from the principals, and a following as faithful as its British counterpart *Emmerdale*.

Glenstal Abbey. A Benedictine establishment in Murroe, Co. Limerick, founded in 1927 and maintaining a boarding school for boys. (The only other Benedictines ministering in Ireland are the sisters of KYLEMORE ABBEY in Co. Galway.) Benedictines from Glenstal have been distinguished for the quality of their contribution to the intellectual discourse of modern Ireland, for their liturgy and music and, most recently, for *The GLENSTAL BOOK OF PRAYER*. *See also* NÍ RIAIN, NÓIRÍN.

Glenstal Book of Prayer, The. This slim volume of devotional pieces compiled by the monks of GLENSTAL ABBEY became, to the surprise of many, an enormous commercial success in

Ireland following its publication in 2001. Commentators variously attributed this success to a nostalgia for traditional certainties among Catholics buffeted by news of clerical misbehaviour, or alternatively to a kind of inherent and unchanging spirituality in the Irish psyche.

Glenswilly Decree. A warning issued by poteen makers in a society formed about 1800 that they were going to collect moneys owing to them. (Glenswilly is the area west of Letterkenny in Co. Donegal.) They distrained possessions, cattle and furniture. The practice ceased in 1850 after the death of a child smothered in a seized feather bed. The decree was used in general debt collecting among those who had no access to the laws of the land, and its authority may have rested in its being a survivor of the ancient BREHON LAWS.

Glib. The hair worn in a matted bush over brow and eyes. The practice was specifically forbidden by the 28th act of Henry VIII (1536–7), which was intended to regulate the dress and habits of the 16th-century Irish:

> That no person nor persons, the king's subjects within this land of Ireland, from and after the first day of May, which shall be in the year of our Lord God 1550, shall be shorn and shaven behind the ears, or use the wearing of hair upon their heads like unto long locks, called glibber, or have or use any hair growing on their upper lips, called or named a crommeal ...

The word 'crommeal' is an anglicized form of the Irish word *croiméal*, 'moustache'. The act did not become law until three years after Henry's death, when Edward VI was on the throne.

Gligeen. A HIBERNO-ENGLISH word for a chatterer, from the Irish word *cluigín*, 'little bell'.

Glimmer men. The nickname given to Dublin Gas company inspectors during the EMERGENCY. Fuel was so scarce that gas supplies were cut off for more than 14 hours in the day. To prevent the risk of possible explosions occasioned by the turning off and on of the supply, a little gas was allowed to stay in the pipes. The amount was small but might boil a kettle in, say, an hour. It was illegal to use this 'glimmer', and the inspectors had the license to test kettles and pots for evidence of use during the forbidden hours. At Christmas 1944 the THEATRE ROYAL pantomime *Mother Goose* starred the popular Dublin comedian Noel PURCELL, who in one scene was doing unmentionable things to a goose before cooking it when he was startled by a knock at the kitchen door. The ensuing dialogue went as follows:

> *Mother Goose:* Who's dere?
> *Voice:* I'm the Glimmer man.
> *Mother Goose:* Well I'm a glamour girl. Come in and we'll have a bit of gas!

There is a pub in Harold's Cross in Dublin called The Glimmerman.

Glocca Morra (Irish *clocha móra*, 'big stones'). The old Irish home of the immigrant Finian McLonergan as imagined by his daughter Sharon in the Broadway musical play *Finian's Rainbow* (1947) by Burton Lane, Yip Harburg and Fred Sady. The show was sharply satirical of many aspects of American life, including the question of colour, but most of the significance was lost on British and Irish audiences. The song, 'How Are Things in Glocca Morra?' was written by Harburg with tongue firmly in cheek. The mockery of its geographical imprecision when the song reached Ireland, though predictable, utterly missed the point, which was the extension of the satire to include unfocused Irish-American sentimentality about an Ireland most of them never knew:

> How are things in Glocca Morra?
> Is that little brook still leaping there?
> Does it still run down to Donny Cove?
> Through Killybegs, Kilkerry and Kildare?

Glór. A centre – concert venue and workshop space – for traditional Irish music in Ennis, Co. Clare, which was opened in November 2001. It is funded by central government and Clare County Council. The Irish word *glór* means 'voice' or 'sound'.

Glugar (also **gliogar**, **glogar**, **gluggar**). The Irish word for 'addled egg', used also in HIBERNO-ENGLISH and also by extension applied to any foolhardy or unsuccessful project; for instance, a book that does not sell might be described as a *glugar*. Sean O'FAOLAIN and Frank O'CONNOR were called 'CORKERY's glogars' because they did not fulfil their mentor's expectations.

G-Men. The members of the G-Division, the detective section of the DMP (Dublin Metropolitan Police). G-Division was subdivided into three areas of responsibility: crime, carriage supervision and political activism. Their headquarters was in Brunswick Street (now Pearse Street) and their system of intelligence was the simple but effective one of transferring all information from individual notebooks into a central register at the end of each duty. It was the political section that became Michael COLLINS's main urban adversary during the Anglo-Irish War of 1919–21.
See also BLOODY SUNDAY 1920; SQUAD, THE.

Go. A noun used in Ulster to mean an indeterminate number of objects: 'I took a go of eggs with me.'

Goats. It was believed that it was lucky for cattle to graze with a goat. 'The older the goat the giddier,' is a proverb that applies to more than goats.
See also 'POC AR BUILE, AN'; PUCK FAIR.

Go (a)way! An expression of incredulity.

Gob. A disparaging HIBERNO-ENGLISH term for 'mouth', from the Irish *gob*, 'beak'. (The British slang word *gob* for 'mouth' may also derive from the same source.) *Gob leathan* is a wide mouth. In J.M. Synge's *The Playboy of the Western World* (1907), Old Mahon describes his son Christy as having 'a murderous gob on him'. A children's rhyme goes:

> Twelve and twelve is twenty-four,
> Shut your gob and say no more.

Gobain (d.*c*.670). An Irish monk who accompanied FURSA to BURGH CASTLE and afterwards went with him to France. He was murdered in his hermitage, 24 km (15 miles) west of Laon, northern France, at the place now called Saint-Gobain, noted for its production of glass. His feast day is 20 June.

Gobán Saor. A mythological stonemason (a *saor* is a stonemason) who is credited in stories with building the ROUND TOWERS of Ireland.

Gobdaw (Irish *gabhdán*, 'gullible person'). A loose descriptive term used in HIBERNO-ENGLISH to convey general lack of respect. A gobdaw (although he may have public stature or wealth) is a person of no quality.

Gob-music. *See* DYDDLE.

Gobnait. An Irish abbess thought to have been born in Co. Clare in the 6th century and to have lived in Inisheer, the smallest of the ARAN ISLANDS, where there is a ruin called Kilgobnet. She was abbess of Ballyvourney, Co. Cork, appointed there by its founder ABBÁN. Among many legends associated with Gobnait is that she repelled a cattle raider by letting loose a swarm of bees on him. A much-worn 13th-century wooden statue of the saint used to be displayed in the church at Ballyvourney on 11 February, her feast day.

Go boys. Young men who dressed as women, painted their faces and arrived – uninvited but welcome – at wedding celebrations (traditionally held in the groom's house). Like the STRAWBOYS (synonymous with go boys in some parts of the country), they maintained anonymity, drank a toast to the bridal couple, danced a set – their leader dancing with the bride – and departed. The term 'go boys' is now applied in Dublin to delinquent youths.

Gobrónach (Irish *go brónach*, 'sad' or 'sorrowful'). A HIBERNO-ENGLISH borrowing from the Irish, used in sentences like 'You look very gobrónach today.'

Go by the wall. A HIBERNO-ENGLISH term for a hesitant, fearful or indecisive person. In Dublin the phrase has the connotation of someone devious or untrustworthy.

God direct me (us)! An appeal for wisdom, good counsel or inspiration, either real or pretended. A Clareman who had a fondness for drink and for bacon was admiring his fattened pig while leaning on his half-door one day and said, 'God direct me, I don't know whether to ate (eat) you or drink you.'

God never comes near Derry. A bitter description of the main port for Donegal seasonal workers *en route* to Scotland. Employment conditions were harsh and the misery seemed to begin with embarkation on the 'Scotch boat' onto which the workers were herded. It comes from the novel *The Rat Pit* (1915) by Patrick MACGILL:

PATRICK: 'God's choice about the company He keeps and never comes near Derry.'

'God Save Ireland'. A ballad written in tribute to the MANCHESTER MARTYRS by Timothy Daniel Sullivan (1827–1914) and published by his brother Alexander Martin (1830–84) in *The NATION* on 7 July 1867. Though strong opponents of the FENIANS, they shared the universal horror at the sentence and public hanging. The ballad's refrain:

'God Save Ireland!' said the heroes;
'God Save Ireland!' said they all;
Whether on the scaffold high
Or the battlefield we die,
O, what matter when for Erin dear we fall!'

incorporated the cry from the dock of Edward Condon, the fourth man whose American citizenship won him a reprieve. The ballad, set to a US marching tune, became the de facto anthem for Nationalist Ireland until it was superseded by 'The SOLDIER'S SONG' in 1926.

God's Beggar. *See* NAGLE, NANO.

God smiles... . The description of Ireland in the 1940s by Sean O'FAOLAIN. In the 'dreary Eden', as he called it in his biography of de Valera (1939), there seemed no moral maturity. O'Faolain summed up post-revolutionary Ireland scathingly in *The Month* (December 1949):

Our sins are tawdry, our virtues childlike, our revolts desultory and brief, our submissions

formal and frequent. In Ireland a policeman's life is a supremely happy one. God smiles, the priest beams, and the novelist groans.

Gogarty, Oliver St John (1878–1957). Wit, poet, memoirist and nose-and-throat surgeon. He was born in Parnell Square (then Rutland Square), Dublin, on 17 August 1878 and educated in many institutions, including Stonyhurst and Clongowes, and both the Royal University of Ireland and Trinity College Dublin. While an undergraduate he won prizes for poetry and was an intimate of the classical scholars John Pentland MAHAFFY and Robert Yelverton Tyrrell (1844–1914). After postgraduate work in otolaryngology in Vienna, he returned to Dublin to set up a lucrative medical practice, and went on to win a reputation as a wit, the owner of Ireland's first Rolls-Royce (a butter-coloured one), an aviator and a senator of the Irish Free State (1922–36).

The description of Gogarty as Joyce's 'stately plump Buck Mulligan' in *Ulysses* was far from accurate (*see* MULLIGAN, BUCK). Gogarty was proud of his athleticism; during the Civil War he escaped from Republicans by swimming the Liffey – and later presented the river with a pair of swans – a classical gesture celebrated in the prize-winning book of verse *An Offering of Swans* (1923). In spite of his Corinthian reputation he was a sincere patriot and a close friend of Arthur GRIFFITH, whom he tended in his last illness. He also performed the autopsy on Michael COLLINS.

Gogarty published several volumes of elegant if unreliable reminiscences including *AS I WAS GOING DOWN SACKVILLE STREET* and *It Isn't that Time of Year at All* (1954). He loathed de Valera, whom he described in the Senate as 'our Celtic Calvin' and in private as a 'cross between a corpse and a cormorant', and found the publicly pious Ireland of the 1930s suffocating. Most of his remaining years were spent in New York, where he died on 22 September 1957:

Our friends go with us as we go
Down the long path where Beauty wends,

Where all we love foregathers, so
Why should we fear to join our friends
...
Then do not shudder at the knife
That death's indifferent hand drives home;
But with the Strivers leave the Strife,
Nor, after Caesar, skulk in Rome.
　　'Non Dolet', in *Selected Poems* (1936)

See also LIFFEY SWIM, THE.

Goldenbridge Cemetery. The first Catholic cemetery in Ireland, established in Goldenbridge in Dublin in 1829, after a campaign by the CATHOLIC ASSOCIATION led by Daniel O'CONNELL. The 3-acre (1.2-ha) site purchased for £600 was open to all denominations and to the prayers of all denominations. Many victims of the cholera epidemic of 1832 are buried there. O'Connell also acquired Prospect Cemetery, later called GLASNEVIN CEMETERY, in the north of the city.

Golden Vale. An area comprising parts of north Cork, north Kerry, east Limerick and south Tipperary, famous for the fertility of the soil and its suitability for dairy farming.

Goldsmith, Oliver (1728–74). Poet, playwright and essayist. He was born in Pallas, Co. Longford, the son of an Anglican curate whom he immortalized as Dr Primrose in *The Vicar of Wakefield* (1766). He was educated in Athlone and attended Trinity College Dublin as a SIZAR (an undergraduate receiving a maintenance grant from the college). After a rackety career he graduated in 1749 but was refused ordination. He studied medicine in Edinburgh and at Leyden in Holland and, after a petit tour, became a teacher and hack in London in 1756. His plays *The Good-Natured Man* (1768) and *She Stoops to Conquer* (1773) show him outstripping his master FARQUHAR, and his long poem in heroic couplets, *The Deserted Village*, though ostensibly set in England in a place called Auburn, owes much of its inspiration to Lissoy, Co. Westmeath, where he spent nearly all his childhood, and which was devastated by a grasping landlord and the Penal Laws.

His *Manners and Customs of the Native Irish* (1759) show him as kindly but conservative towards his fellow countrymen. Though rather the butt of Dr Johnson's Club (an informal group founded by Johnson, and including Garrick and Boswell), he was loved for his sweet nature, valued for the excellence of his essays ('he wrote like an angel and talked like poor Poll') and infamous for his fecklessness.

Goll Mac Morna. In Irish mythology, the leader of the FIANNA before FIONN MAC CUMHAIL, having killed Fionn's father Cumhal to gain the position. He maintains a relentless enmity against the boy until Fionn's majority, when he surprisingly swears him allegiance. He continues to be a faithful member of the Fianna, even marrying Fionn's daughter, Cebha. He is responsible for the death of Cairell, Fionn's son, and when OSCAR, Fionn's grandson, tries to settle the matter, Goll throws a spear at him. His former comrades trap him in the Donegal peninsula of Rosguill ('Goll's headland') and he starves to death after 12 days. The name Goll signifies 'one-eyed'.

GOM. The complimentary sobriquet of William Ewart Gladstone (1808–98), standing for 'Grand Old Man'. It was first used by Lord Rosebery (1847–1929) in 1882. Gladstone had hoped to crown a career distinguished by high probity and liberalism with the successful realization of his mission 'to pacify Ireland', risking even the splitting of his Liberal Party. He failed, as have many well-meaning statesmen since, because of necessary caution (the ORANGE CARD could always be played) and a failure to appreciate both the intensity of Nationalist aspirations and the depths of Unionist intransigence, born of fear. His 'betrayal' of PARNELL over the O'Shea affair was born of his politician's awareness that his English Nonconformist supporters would not support Home Rule while the CHIEF remained leader of the Irish Parliamentary Party. Gladstone's open letter to John Morley (1838–1923), then chief secretary for Ireland, made it clear that 'notwithstanding the splendid

services rendered by Mr Parnell to his country, his continuance at the present moment in leadership would be productive of consequences disastrous in the highest degree to the cause of Ireland.'
See also KILMAINHAM TREATY.

Gombeen man (Irish *gaimbín*, 'interest'). An Irish moneylender (*fear a' ghaimbín*). The word was commonly applied in the late 19th century to shopkeepers, especially along the Atlantic seaboard, who extended credit at exorbitant rates to local country people. It was generally believed that the clients' dependency gave their creditors an amount of political and social control, and in some cases an unacknowledged alliance with the church put the dealers beyond clerical disapproval. The success of the cooperative movement (*see* PADDY THE COPE) helped mitigate the more extreme abuses. The phrase is still occasionally used as a generalized term of abuse for the mean-spirited in business, but, like 'souper' (*see* SOUPERISM), is not always precisely applicable.

Gone away, you know, they haven't. A remark made by Gerry ADAMS at a rally in Belfast on 13 August 1995 about the Provisional IRA, which was proved sadly prophetic when, on the following 9 February, the Provisionals ended their ceasefire with a massive explosion at CANARY WHARF in London. This remark and his statement that he could not deliver the IRA are significant factors in Adams's profile, and should not be ignored by commentators.

Gone Mad. *See* GONNE, MAUD.

Gonne, Maud (1865–1953). Republican activist. She was born in Surrey, the daughter of an army colonel of Irish descent, Tommy Gonne, and an English mother who died of tuberculosis when she was 4 years old. When she was 16, her father was stationed at the Curragh in Co. Kildare and Maud grew to maturity in Ireland, already the renowned beauty who was to inspire much of the early poetry of W. B. YEATS. After her father's death she lived unhappily in London for a period, and thereafter was taken

by an aunt to Paris, where she met Lucien Millevoye, a French journalist who fathered her two children, Georges (1890–1) and Iseult (1894–1954; she was to marry Francis Stuart, author of *BLACK LIST SECTION H*).

In June 1889 Maud met Yeats (she said that the Fenian John O'LEARY had sent her to Yeats's home), and the poet instantly fell in love with her and was to propose to her many times over the next quarter-century. In the 1890s she became involved in the campaign to release Fenian prisoners (*see* AMNESTY ASSOCIATION) and a humanitarian campaign for the relief of evicted tenants in Co. Donegal; she was influenced by John O'LEARY, by Arthur GRIFFITH, whose name for her was 'Queen', and by James CONNOLLY. On Easter Sunday 1900 she founded the first women's Nationalist organization, INGHINIDHE NA HÉIREANN ('daughters of Ireland'), a separatist pro-suffrage group that published a journal, *Bean na hÉireann* ('the Irish woman'), and which merged with CUMANN NA MBAN in 1914. In 1902 she played the leading role in Yeats's play CATHLEEN NÍ HOULIHAN, impressing the audience with the passion of her portrayal.

In 1900 Maud met John MACBRIDE and married him in 1903, although Griffith pleaded with her not to do so: 'I know you both, you so unconventional, a law to yourself, John so full of conventions.' The following year her son, Seán MACBRIDE, was born, and in 1905 the marriage was dissolved. However, on her return to Ireland after John MacBride was shot by the British in 1916 for his role in the Easter Rising, she styled herself Maud Gonne MacBride. Arrested with scores of other Republicans suspected of involvement in the so-called GERMAN PLOT of 1918, she spent six months in Holloway prison. She opposed the TREATY and in 1922 founded the Women's Prisoners Defence League (WPDL) to support and campaign for the release of Republican prisoners in Free State jails.

By now no longer either young or beautiful, but gaunt, middle-aged and always dressed in black, Maud Gonne continued as a public figure in Dublin, although she was now considered so eccentric that Dubliners referred to her as 'Gone Mad'. In January 1923 she was imprisoned for her WPDL activities, but released after 20 days of hunger strike. She died on 27 April 1953 and is buried in the Republican plot in GLASNEVIN CEMETERY. Partly because she was apostrophized so frequently in Yeats's poetry:

> For she had fiery blood
> When I was young,
> And trod so sweetly proud
> As 'twere upon a cloud.

and partly because of her own commanding and dramatic personality, she became a legend while still a young woman, but lived for several decades in an uncongenial independent Ireland. Her own autobiography, *A SERVANT OF THE QUEEN*, was published in 1938.

Good Behaviour. The first novel (1981) published by Molly KEANE under her own name (previously she had used the pseudonym M.J. Farrell), written when she was in her mid-70s. It is a black comedy, redolent with satire and irony, about the slow decline of the BIG HOUSE of the St Charles family. The narrator is the middle-aged daughter Aroon who, on the occasion of her widowed mother's death, recalls her childhood and adolescence and betrays an arrogant unawareness of what actually happened, failing to understand that the governess who committed suicide was her father's mistress or that her adversary, the remaining servant Rose, was also his sexual partner.

Goodbye money. A term deriving from HELLO MONEY and referring to the money that might be paid to unwelcome guests in contemporary Ireland, for instance to TRAVELLERS in an unofficial halting site, in order to prevail on them to depart.

Good Friday Agreement. The culmination of the so-called Northern Ireland peace process, when on 10 April 1998 a document detailing workable political structures was accepted by a majority on both sides. Properly called the Belfast Agreement, it represented a triumph for

the diplomatic skills of the American senator George MITCHELL, who had been appointed as peace adviser by President Bill Clinton. The agreement was generally welcomed, except by militant Republicans, who saw it as setting up a sanitized STORMONT, while right-wing Unionists saw it as the door to the dreaded united Ireland because of what they saw as the pervasive involvement of the Dublin government.

The main proposal of the agreement was for a cross-community assembly (the Northern Ireland Assembly) with a power-sharing executive elected by proportional representation. The executive had ten departments, to deal with trade, agriculture, health, finance, etc. Other elements were the setting up of a North–South ministerial council, a British–Irish intergovernmental conference, the right of all Northern Ireland citizens to be British or Irish or both, with the culture of each equally cherished, the DECOMMISSIONING of paramilitary arms, reform of the police service (*see* RUC), accelerated release of 'political' prisoners, and the removal of emergency powers and security installations. The legislative assembly has been prorogued several times and at the time of writing (August 2004) is in suspension because of a perceived delay in IRA decommissioning and the refusal of the Ulster Unionist Party (*see* UUP) to sit while this attitude is maintained. Sinn Féin, the party with IRA links, claims that decommissioning has been commensurate with 'demilitarization' on the part of the authorities. While in session the assembly worked very well and progress in other fields seems reasonable.

Goodman, Canon James (1829–96). Musician and collector of traditional music. He was born in Ventry, near Dingle, Co. Kerry, educated at Trinity College Dublin (TCD) and ordained a Church of Ireland priest in 1851. While a curate in Ardgroom in the Beara Peninsula of west Cork (1856–66) he collected the traditional music of the Dingle Peninsula from travelling musicians such as the famous blind Dingle fiddler, Thomas Kennedy. Four volumes of

1000 tunes, many of which have not survived in the folk tradition, are held in the Goodman Collection at TCD. Goodman was appointed professor of Irish at TCD in 1879; he translated St Luke's Gospel into Irish in collaboration with James Harnett Murphy, and produced a version in modern Irish of the popular prayer, 'ST PATRICK'S BREASTPLATE'. He also played the uilleann pipes.

Good Man, the. A euphemistic means of avoiding the actual use of the word 'God', practised by an older and more pious generation. A similar euphemism is 'the Man Above'.

> At length she spoke: 'I thank the Good Man yer father's no' living tae see this day.'
>
> SAM HANNA BELL (1909–90): 'This We Shall Maintain', in *Summer Loanen* (1943)

Goodnight, God bless and safe home. A valediction associated with Irish SHOWBANDS at the end of a night's dancing, and the title of a book (2002) about the showband era by Finbar O'Keefe. In the heyday of the showbands in the 1960s, thousands of people thronged dance halls such as the Lilac in Inniskeen in west Cork and Hayes's in Dromkeen, Co. Tipperary, often travelling for several hours from their home.

Good nor bad. A literal translation of the Irish *olc ná maith* ('bad or good'), used in HIBERNO-ENGLISH to mean 'not at all', as in 'He had no English good or bad.'

Good people (Irish *daoine maithe*). A HIBERNO-ENGLISH euphemism for the SIDHE or fairies, designed to placate a supernatural force of which ordinary individuals were afraid.
See also LITTLE PEOPLE.

Goody. A dish for children, invalids or the elderly, made by crumbling bread into warm milk and adding a sprinkling of sugar.

Goose Pie. A nickname for the Irish Parliament in COLLEGE GREEN invented by Dublin's inhabitants in the mid-18th century because of the rounded roof of James GANDON's building, and also because of their low opinion of the sense of the MPs.

Go raibh míle maith agaibh go léir. See A DHAOINE UAISLE.

Gore-Booth, Eva (1870–1926). Poet and feminist. She was born at Lissadell, Co. Sligo, and was one of the 'two girls in silk kimonos' of Yeats's poem 'In Memory of Eva Gore-Booth and Con Markievicz' (1933), the other being her sister Constance (*see* REBEL COUNTESS, THE). She moved to Manchester, England in 1892 and with her partner Esther Roper began a life-time commitment to feminism and pacifism, changing some of the belligerence of the originals in her versions of Irish myth. She wrote much poetry and unstageable drama and is chiefly remembered now for such lyrics as 'The Little Waves of Breffny':

> The grand road from the mountain goes shining to the sea,
> And there is traffic in it and many a horse and cart,
> But the little roads of Cloonagh are dearer far to me,
> And the little roads of Cloonagh go rambling through my heart …
> But the little waves of Breffny have drenched my heart in spray.

She died in Hampstead, London.

Gorgeous Gael, the. The nickname of the Irish boxer and performer Jack Doyle (1913–78). He was born in Cobh, Co. Cork, and enlisted in the Irish Guards at the age of 16. He became boxing champion of the entire Brigade of Guards and had achieved 28 successive wins when he decided to turn professional at the age of 19. In 1933 he fought the Welshman Jack Petersen for the British heavyweight title, but was disqualified, suspended for six months and fined for hitting Petersen below the belt. Disillusioned with boxing, Doyle turned to vaudeville and released more than a dozen records. He starred in a 1935 Elstree film, *McCluskey the Sea Rover*, and in two films in Hollywood. He decided to return to boxing – his publicity said 'He can sing like John McCormack and box like Jack Dempsey' – but had little success in either the USA or Britain. With his second wife, the Mexican actress Movita, he toured variety theatres in the USA, Britain and Ireland, but Movita left him for Marlon Brando in 1945. Doyle continued to have the charisma to attract an audience, whether he was boxing or singing, but his fortunes declined in his later years and he died penniless in a Notting Hill boarding house in December 1978.

Gorgeous Wrecks. The name given to the Irish Volunteer Defence Corps (IVDC), a reserve training body of the British army, consisting mainly of middle-class Irishmen over the age of military service. Their nickname came from the GR (Georgius Rex) on their armbands, and they were among the first forces to come under fire on Easter Monday, 24 April 1916, the first day of the EASTER RISING. At 4 p.m. in the afternoon a contingent consisting of members of various sub-corps of the IVDC – including the Dublin Veterans Corps, the Irish Rugby Football Corps and the City and Railway Corps – were returning from manoeuvres at Ticknock in the Dublin mountains. They were carrying unloaded rifles and were unaware of events in the city. As they approached Beggar's Bush barracks along Haddington Road they were fired on by IRISH VOLUNTEERS. Five men, including their sub-commandant F.H. Browning, were killed, and nine wounded.

Gormflaith. One of the 'wicked' women of the Irish past, who led a complicated matrimonial life in the 10th century. Her third husband was BRIAN BORU, and her serial polyandry is somewhat frowned upon in some of the Annals, which refer to her having made three leaps, 'jumps which a woman should never jump'. Appropriately she was very beautiful, but proud, vindictive and conniving. Brian's marriage to her may have been strategic, since she was the mother of Sitric, the king of the Dublin Danes, and her brother Máel Mórda was king of Leinster. She had earlier married Máel Sechnaill (the Malachy of Tom MOORE's song 'Let Erin Remember', who wore 'the collar of gold'). She is called Kormlada in the Viking saga *Burnt Njal*.

Gort cake. The large BARMBRACK that Lady GREGORY used to have baked at home in Coole Park to feed the company from the ABBEY THEATRE, who were in her aristocratic opinion undernourished:

> Tea was brewed and her vast Gort cakes – two feet in diameter and eight inches thick – were avidly consumed. Here too Lady Gregory provided sustenance for the players after rehearsals.
> HUGH HUNT (1911–93): *The Abbey* (1979)

Gossoon (sometimes **gorsoon**). A HIBERNO-ENGLISH word for 'boy', both in its usual sense but also as applied to a hired man. It comes from the Irish *garsún*, 'young boy', a word still current in Hiberno-English, especially in rural areas: 'That's a fine *garsún*.' The word has obvious connections with French *garçon* ('boy').

> An' down from the mountain came the squadrons an' platoons,
> Four-an'-twinty fightin' min, an' a couple o' sthout gossoons …
> PERCY FRENCH (1854–1920): 'Shlatery's Mounted Fut' (1889)

Gougane Barra. A beauty spot and place of pilgrimage near Ballingeary in Co. Cork. The valley has a lake that is the source of the River Lee. On the lake is an island, connected to the shore by a causeway, where St FINDBAR (also Finbarr or Bairre, the latter giving rise to 'Barra'), the patron saint of Cork, established his monastery in the 6th century. There is a well, St Finbarr's Well, an ancient cemetery and more modern STATIONS OF THE CROSS. A PATTERN is made to Gougane Barra on the Sunday nearest to the feast of St Findbar, which falls on 25 September.
See also MUSKERRY GAELTACHT, THE; *TAILOR AND ANSTY, THE*.

Gouger. A common HIBERNO-ENGLISH expression, especially in Dublin, for a ruffian or ne'er-do-well.

Government of Ireland Act. An act passed by the British government in December 1920 that granted HOME RULE to Ireland but on the basis of two separate parliaments, one for the six counties of the North, the other for the remainder of Ireland. The opposition of the Conservative partners in the coalition government of Lloyd George and of Northern Unionists led by James CRAIG both to a single parliament and to a nine-county Northern Ireland (that would lead, he believed, to Irish unity) meant that PARTITION of the six counties became a reality. Sinn Féin boycotted the elections in the South, and the North returned a Unionist majority. On 22 June 1921 the parliament of NORTHERN IRELAND was formally opened by King George V.

GPO. The General Post Office building in O'Connell Street, Dublin, which was the headquarters of the insurgents during the EASTER RISING of 1916. The building was designed and constructed by Francis Johnston (1814–8), but all that survives of the design is the severe classical façade, which was restored in 1929 after the building was destroyed in 1916 and 1922. The GPO is part of the mythology of Republicanism, since from its steps the PROCLAMATION OF THE REPUBLIC was read by Patrick PEARSE. Appropriately, the building houses a memorial to those killed there, in the form of the dying Cúchulainn by Oliver SHEPPARD (1865–1941), a piece actually completed before the event.

> When Pearse summoned Cuchulain to his side,
> What stalked through the Post Office? What intellect,
> What calculation, number, measurement replied?
> W.B. YEATS: 'The Statues', in *Last Poems* (1939)

Grace note. A note played either above or below the main melody in traditional music, to 'embroider' or ornament the tune.

Graces, the. Fifty-one 'Instructions and Graces' originally offered by Charles I in 1626 to the OLD ENGLISH in exchange for subsidies to maintain his army in Ireland. The details were negotiated by a delegation of eight Old English and three Protestant settlers in January 1628 and approved on 14 May in return for four quarterly subsidies of £40,000. The Graces were to include the right of Catholics to bear arms in self-defence, the right to have the title to their lands confirmed, and freedom of worship. The money was paid, but the Graces were never ratified. They were promised again by Lord Deputy WENTWORTH in 1634 in return for support from the Irish Parliament, but not granted. They were again offered by Charles I on 3 May 1641, but the outbreak of the REBELLION OF 1641 in October ended any further discussion.

Grace's card. In a deck of playing cards, the six of hearts. In 1689 emissaries of the Duke of SCHOMBERG called on John Grace (d.1690), Baron of Courtstown, Co. Kilkenny, asking him to join in the struggle against James II. The story goes that Grace picked up the playing card, which was lying on his table, and wrote on it what he also communicated verbally, 'Tell your master I despise his offer.' He promptly raised a regiment of foot and troop of horse for the true king. The six of hearts continued to be known as 'Grace's card' for at least a hundred years thereafter.

Gráinne. The Guinevere of Irish myth. She is the daughter of CORMAC MAC ART and betrothed to the aged FIONN MAC CUMHAIL. Seeing her future husband for the first time, she immediately turns her attentions to his son OISÍN as a more appropriate mate. Rejected by him, she puts DIARMAID UA DUIBHNE under a *GEIS* to compel him to run away with her, having drugged most of the guests at the wedding feast. A few, including GOLL MAC MORNA, are left undrugged to act as witnesses to Diarmaid's reluctant promise. The many 'beds' throughout Ireland called after the runaways are an indication of the fulfilment of Fionn's curse that they would not sleep in the same bed on consecutive nights. After Diarmaid's death, Gráinne returns with Fionn to TARA to suffer the continuing obloquy of the FIANNA. Her name signifies ugliness (clearly not of the physical kind), and she is always seen as a spoiled and wilful woman. Despite this, 'Gráinne' remains a popular name for Irish girls.

Graip. An Ulster word for a four-pronged farmyard fork; the same implement is called a pitchfork in Munster.

Grámhar. An Irish word for 'loving', pronounced 'gra-war', and formed from *grá* ('love'). It is borrowed by HIBERNO-ENGLISH to mean 'affectionate', 'loving', 'kind', especially of a child.

Grá mo chroí. An Irish phrase, literally 'love of my heart', and pronounced 'graw mo kree'. The phrase may be used as an endearment, but is now more likely to be a derogatory description of someone considered too sweet to be wholesome: 'She was very/too *grá mo chroí*.'

Grand. An adjective and adverb that in HIBERNO-ENGLISH may still have its original meaning of 'noble' or 'dignified', but is more likely to indicate modest satisfaction. 'I'm grand, thanks,' is a common answer to the greeting 'How are you?' Another use of grand (as also in Britain) is as a synonym of 'posh', with an implication of snobbery: 'She's very grand.'
See also HUMP OF GRANDEUR.

Grand Canal. Conceived as a major commercial route to link the River Barrow with the sea, the Grand Canal, to the south of Dublin's city centre, was completed in 1791 after nearly 50 years of work. The link with the Shannon was completed in 1805. Until the advent of the railways the canal was very successful, and it remained competitive until well into the 20th century. In the days of lighter traffic, the arterial road along the canal was Dublin's version of the *Boulevard périphérique* of Paris. 'Inside the canal' or 'outside the canal' are useful indicators of location, and the canal also separates Dublin's postal districts 2 and 8 from districts 4, 6 and 12. Patrick KAVANAGH's poem 'Lines Written on a Seat on the Grand Canal, Dublin' is inscribed in commemoration of the poet on a south-facing seat near Baggot Street Bridge:

> O commemorate me where there is water,
> Canal water preferably, so stilly
> Green at the heart of summer. Brother
> Commemorate me thus beautifully ...

See also CRANK ON THE BANK.

Grandeur, hump of. *See* HUMP OF GRANDEUR.

Grangegorman. An extensive complex near Phibsboro' on the north side of Dublin that was formerly a psychiatric hospital. 'You'd drive a body to Grangegorman' was a common sigh by Dublin mothers to recalcitrant children. Part of the complex was turned into a set for the EASTER RISING scenes of Neil Jordan's film (1996) about Michael COLLINS, and before the set was demolished the public was invited to visit the reconstruction of the GPO and the rest of Sackville Street. Now that psychiatric patients are increasingly being cared for in the community, negotiations are under way to sell Grangegorman to a university or other public enterprise.

Grangegorman Murders. Two psychiatric patients, Sylvia Shields and Mary Callanan, were killed in their sheltered home near Grangegorman on 6 March 1997. Dean Lyons, a heroin addict, who had been sleeping rough in the area, confessed to the murders after hours of questioning in the Bridewell garda station. He spent nine months in prison, even though two months after his arrest, Mark Nash, who was in custody for a double murder in Co. Roscommon, admitted that he was responsible for the killings. Dean Lyons died of a heroin overdose in Manchester, England, in September 2000.

Granuaile (1530–c.1603). Pirate-queen of Connacht. The name, pronounced 'gran-u-wail', is probably a version of Gráinne Ní Mháille, which is rendered into English as Grace O'Malley. She was a colourful character, with more than her share of myth-accretion. Her stronghold was Clare Island at the entrance to Clew Bay in Co. Mayo. She married twice, first Donal O'Flaherty, lord of Ballynahinch, and, when he died, Richard (of the Iron) Burke. Using fast-moving galleys, she attacked any ships that sailed near her maritime domain. She is said to have travelled to meet Elizabeth I to try to secure her inheritance rights, and to have spoken to her as one queen to another. Elizabeth's officials were less tolerant: Lord Deputy Sir Henry Sidney (1529–86) called her 'a most famous feminine sea-captain,' and Sir Richard Bingham (1528–99), the viceroy for Mayo, built a gallows especially for her benefit. However, she was pardoned, and, according to another legend, died in poverty and is buried on Clare Island. Over the centuries her name tended to be used almost as a type for Ireland in the long struggle for freedom, and she has now become a feminist icon.

> As through the hills I walked to view the hills and shamrock plain,
> I stood awhile where nature smiles to view the rocks and streams.
> On a matron fair I fixed my eyes beneath a fertile vale.
> As she sang her song it was on the wrong of poor old Granuaile.
>
> ANON.: 'Poor Old Granuaile' (mid-19th century)

Grattan, Henry (1746–1820). Parliamentarian and orator. He is in the public mind the politician most closely associated with the Patriot movement (see PATRIOTS) of the late-18th century that agitated for legislative independence for the Irish Parliament (see GRATTAN'S PARLIAMENT). He was born in Dublin on 3 July 1746 and educated at Trinity College Dublin. He was called to the Bar in 1773 and elected MP in 1775. The achievement of legislative independence (see YELVERTON'S ACT) was a triumph for Grattan: so grateful were his colleagues that they voted him a grant of £50,000 to buy an estate. But his rival Henry FLOOD achieved a greater degree of independence when the Renunciation Act, for which he had campaigned, was passed in 1783. This gave rise to an unseemly and bitter quarrel between the two men on the floor of Parliament.

After initial opposition Grattan, unlike Flood, became a strong advocate of CATHOLIC EMANCIPATION in the 1790s, warning the government of the dangers of adopting a policy of wholesale repression in response to the security threat of the UNITED IRISHMEN. In poor health, he withdrew from Parliament and went to live in Co. Wicklow, returning in 1799 to speak against

the Act of UNION. He was elected to the British House of Commons in 1805, and as a Whig continued to campaign for Catholic rights. He died in London on 4 June 1820 and is buried in Westminster Abbey.

Grattan's Parliament. The name given to the Parliament in Ireland between 1782, when it achieved legislative independence, and its extinction by the Act of UNION in 1800. The name honours the major role played in the achievement of that independence by Henry GRATTAN. It was not, however, a representative Parliament: it would be several decades before CATHOLIC EMANCIPATION was won, and most of the parliamentary boroughs were 'pocket' or corrupt. The fact of its achievement of independence and the prevailing economic prosperity of the 1780s and 1790s have caused Nationalists to look on this period more positively than it perhaps deserves.

Graves, A[lfred] P[erceval] (1846–1931). Poet and editor. He was born in Dublin on 22 July 1846, the son of Charles Graves (1812–99), professor of mathematics and later Anglican Bishop of Limerick. He was educated at Trinity College Dublin and later became a school inspector in England. He compiled many anthologies of Irish poetry and wrote some extremely popular song lyrics to traditional Irish tunes. These included 'Riding Double' (better known as 'Trottin' to the Fair'), 'The Little Red Lark' and the perennial 'Father O'Flynn', which, originally written for the *Spectator* in 1875, would have been very profitable had he not sold the copyright for a very small sum. His entertaining autobiography, *To Return to All That* (1930), is a light-hearted rebuttal of *Goodbye to All That* (1929), the controversial memoirs of his son, the poet Robert Graves (1895–1985). He died in Harlech on 27 December 1931.

> Of priests we can offer a charmin' variety
> Far renowned for larnin' and piety;
> Still I'd advance you widout impropriety,
> Father O'Flynn as the flower of them all.

Gray, Eileen (1879–1976). Designer. She was

born near Enniscorthy in Co. Wexford on 9 August 1879 of an ASCENDANCY family. She was educated at home and introduced to the arts by her painter father. As a young woman she was a society beauty, coming out from her mother's London home. She studied at the Slade from 1898 to 1902, then emigrated to Paris, living in France for the rest of her life. She originally created pieces of lacquer work, influenced by Japanese masters in that art, and had a successful interior-design business, but from the 1920s on she became increasingly interested in architecture, designing a modernist house for her own use in Roquebrune, Cap Martin, in collaboration with Jean Badovici (1893–1936), a Romanian-born modernist architect. This house, known as E.1027, was furnished with pieces in stainless steel, glass and aluminium, and was regarded as an avant-garde classic. She also decorated an apartment in St Tropez and retained a lifelong affection for the Côte d'Azur. After the Second World War her reputation was eclipsed by that of other architects and stylists, but from the late 1960s she was recognized as a modernist pioneer by architectural historians, and her pieces became very valuable. She died in her apartment in Paris on 31 November 1976. As well as being strikingly original in terms of her art, Gray was bisexual. She never lived in Ireland as an adult; at the end of her life she said, 'I am without roots, but if I have any, they are in Ireland.'

Gray, John (1815–75). Journalist and campaigner on public issues. He was born in Claremorris, Co. Mayo, and studied medicine at Glasgow, but practised medicine in Dublin for a short time only. He began to write for *FREEMAN'S JOURNAL* and by 1850 was the owner of that paper. A Protestant Nationalist, Gray favoured repeal of the Act of UNION and campaigned in his paper for the DISESTABLISHMENT OF THE CHURCH OF IRELAND. As chairman of Dublin Corporation's Waterworks Committee, Gray spearheaded the scheme to bring clean water to Dublin and nearby towns such as Dún Laoghaire and Bray from the

Vartry Reservoir in Roundwood, Co. Wicklow. Construction of the reservoir, dam and aqueducts took five years to complete (1862–7). He was knighted in 1863 and elected lord mayor of Dublin in 1868, but declined the honour. He died in Bath on 9 April 1875. His statue stands at the junction of O'Connell Street and Lower Abbey Street. In *ULYSSES* Leopold Bloom pays tribute to Gray when he fills his kettle at the sink after returning home to Eccles Street:

> Did it flow?
>
> Yes. From Roundwood reservoir in county Wicklow of a cubic capacity of 2400 million gallons, percolating through a subterranean aqueduct of filter mains of single and double pipeage constructed at an initial plant cost of £5 per linear yard by way of the Dargle, Rathdown, Glen of the Downs and Callowhill to the 26 cared reservoir at Stillorgan …

Great. In HIBERNO-ENGLISH to be great with someone means to enjoy a close friendship or long-standing intimacy with them. It derives from the Irish *bheith an-mhór le duine.*

Great Earl, the. The sobriquet of Géaróid Mór (Gerald Fitzgerald), 8th Earl of Kildare (1456–1513). The pre-eminent figure in Irish society from 1478 until his death, he served as governor of Ireland under five kings, although a supporter of the Yorkist side in the WARS OF THE ROSES. He formed alliances with Gaelic chiefs as well as OLD ENGLISH families, often by marriage, and his court included Irish *FILID* (poets). He died of a gunshot wound and was succeeded by his son Géaróid Óg.
See also LET HIM RULE ALL IRELAND.

Great Earl of Cork, the. *See* BOYLE, RICHARD, 1ST EARL OF CORK.

Great Escape, the. The mass escape from the MAZE on 12 September 1983 when 38 Provisional IRA prisoners absconded in the biggest break-out in British prison history. The escape involved the hijacking of a prison food lorry and led to the death of a guard, James Ferris, possibly from natural causes. The triumphalist nickname applied by Republicans to the break-out came from the 1963 John Sturges film about a mass escape of Allied prisoners-of-war from a German POW camp in the Second World War, and, as in the film, a number of the escapees were quickly rearrested, 15 almost immediately and 4 others within a few days. On 18 April 1988, 18 of the original number were imprisoned for a number of offences, including jailbreak. One of these was Gerard Kelly, now a Sinn Féin MLA (Member of the Legislative Assembly).

Great Famine, the. A vast human catastrophe, in effect lasting for a biblical seven years (1845–52). It was the cause of the reduction of the population of Ireland by death or emigration from an underestimated 8,177,744 (1841 census) to 6,554,074 (1851 census). Of the 1 million deaths, some were from hunger, but more succumbed to the various 'famine' plagues, mainly typhus and relapsing fever. The immediate cause was the failure in 1845, 1846 and 1848 of the potato crop, the main source of sustenance for 3 million people, through the fungal disease PHYTOPHTHORA INFESTANS. Since the prevailing economic ideology of the period was that of *laissez faire*, the government's response was lethally slow and half-hearted. Largely pointless schemes of public works (*see* BLACK '47; *BÓTHAR NA MINE BUÍ*; TREVELYAN, CHARLES), paid for in unappetising INDIAN MEAL, were inadequate for starving people used to the vitamin-rich potato, and eventually in 1847 kitchens supplying cooked food were established for those who had the strength to avail themselves of them.

The effect of the cataclysm was a vastly changed country, both economically and psychologically. The emigration, too, of 1 million Irish who passed on to their children horror tales of unburied corpses, increased eviction, proselytizing clergy using food as bait (*see* SOUPERS), COFFIN SHIPS and the continued export of other foods from Irish ports had a profound and continuing political effect. The best account of the catastrophe and the explanation for its tragic consequences are to be found in *The Great Hunger* (1962) by Cecil Woodham-Smith (1923–1984).
See also HUNGRY GRASS; LUMPER.

Great hooded cloak. *See* IRISH CLOAK.

Great Hunger, The. A 14-section poem (1942) about rural Irish life between the two world wars by Patrick KAVANAGH. It describes the sterile condition of his representative figure Patrick Maguire as he toils to make a small Co. Monaghan farm pay. The poem's title harks back to the aftermath of the GREAT FAMINE of the 1840s when parsimony and sexual inhibition, encouraged by a narrow-minded and authoritarian church, seemed to replace the gaiety of earlier times. The spiritual hunger for life and lack of love in such as Maguire are taken to be as devastating as the earlier cataclysm.

> He stands in the doorway of his house
> A ragged sculpture of the wind,
> October creaks the rotted mattress,
> The bedposts fall. No hope. No lust.
> The hungry fiend
> Screams the apocalypse of clay
> In every corner of this land.
> *The Great Hunger*, XIV

The Great Hunger was also the title of Cecil Woodham-Smith's famous 1962 account of the Great Famine.

Great little nation, this. In a letter to Charles HAUGHEY dated 11 December 1979 (shortly after Haughey was elected leader of FIANNA FÁIL and taoiseach), Michael Phelan, manager of the Dame Street, Dublin, branch of AIB, a bank to which Haughey owed a great deal of money that was never recouped, coined the phrase 'great little nation':

> To say the task you have taken on is daunting is an understatement but I have every faith in your ability to succeed in restoring confidence in this great little nation.

The irony of the fact that the 'great little nation' was in dire straits financially – and continued thus for more than ten years – while Haughey continued to spend millions of pounds beyond his means was not lost on the Irish public when this letter came to light.

Great North Wall. *See* BULL WALL, THE.

Greatrakes, Valentine (also **Greatorex**) (1629–83). Faith healer. He was born on 14 February 1629 on his father's estate at Affane, Co. Waterford and after fighting with Cromwell during his Irish wars was suitably rewarded. At the Restoration he was stripped of his offices of magistrate and clerk of the peace, and began to practise his own form of alternative medicine. He began to 'touch' for scrofula in 1662 – an odd presumption for a parliamentarian since medieval kings alone were held to have the power to cure 'the king's evil' – and soon extended his treatment to all kinds of other ailments. Now known as the 'Stroaker', he visited London in 1666 and 'cured' a number of patients by the laying-on of hands and the invocation of the deity. He took no money, and later wrote an autobiographical apologia in the form of a letter to Robert BOYLE (1627–91), the leading Irish scientist of his day, including 53 unsolicited testimonials from grateful eminences. He returned to Affane in May 1666 and died there on 28 November 1683.

Great South Wall, the. The construction of the (Great) South Wall that runs into Dublin Bay from Ringsend was conceived in order to provide shelter and make Dublin Bay safer for ships. It began with a timbered wall of just over 3 km (2 miles), commissioned by the Ballast Office (the predecessor of the Ballast Board, itself the predecessor of the DUBLIN PORT AND DOCKS BOARD) and constructed between 1716 and 1731. This quickly proved not to be strong enough to withstand wind and wave, but for the next 30 years attempt after attempt was made to keep it in repair until, in 1759, the Ballast Office petitioned Parliament for funds to build a stone wall. The POOLBEG LIGHT-HOUSE was first built at the extreme east end of the wall (completed 1767), and the wall itself was built gradually westwards over the next thirty years. The Ballast Board, which took over the functions of the Ballast Office in 1786, gave priority to the construction and it was completed in 1795. The Great South Wall

has remained to this day a popular resort for Dubliners.

For the Great North Wall, *see* BULL WALL, THE.

Grecian. A mildly mocking term applied to new Irish immigrants in Britain in the mid-19th century, the reference being to the perceived unintelligibility of their accents. The established immigrants were known as Irish Cockneys.

Grecian bend. A way of walking with the trunk slightly tilted forward, affected by some 19th-century ladies of fashion. It was in imitation of the Venus de Milo, the standard of ideal beauty, but the Dublin ladies were accused of using artificial means:

> Now the fashions of the ladies here, most
>   certainly are droll,
> They have things like tinkers budgets [i.e. 'bags'],
>   stuck behind upon their poll;
> They wear an artificial hump, upon their latter
>   end,
> Which makes them look like a Drommadery,
>   called the Grecian bend.
>   ANON.: 'Dublin in the Eighteen Eighties'

Green. The national colour of Ireland, a reflection of the rain-soaked greenery of the place. There is a tradition that Charles Stewart PAR-NELL attributed the country's misfortunes to its national colour, as green was always seen as an unlucky colour in folklore: it was believed to be the colour of the fairies or SIDHE, and that their displeasure at the appropriation of their colour by humans would cause bad luck. 'If you wear green you'll wear black before the year is out,' was one saying, and it was regarded as the height of folly for a bride to wear green: 'Married in green, not fit to be seen.' *See also* 'FORTY SHADES OF GREEN'; 'WEAR-ING OF THE GREEN, THE'.

Green Army. The name given to the supporters of the Republic of Ireland soccer team that qualified for the World Cup in 1990 and 1994. In Italy in 1990 and Florida in 1994, Irish soccer fans were known for their wholehearted support of the national side even in adversity, for the CRAIC they brought everywhere with them, and for their peaceable behaviour.

See also CAPTAIN FANTASTIC; CHARLTON, JACK; GIVE IT A LASH, JACK; JACK'S ARMY.

Greene, Gretta. The name, perhaps chosen with a comic hint of Gretna Green (Gretna on the Anglo-Scottish border being a traditional venue for runaway marriages), used by Nora BAR-NACLE to try to avoid publicity at the time of her marriage to James JOYCE in London on 4 July 1931. They had been partners for 27 years, ever since they went to live on the Continent on 8 October 1904. After the registry-office ceremony in Marloes Road, Kensington, they had lunch with Robert LYND and his family in Hampstead. The Lynds' daughters Sigle (21) and Máire (19) decided to hold a proper celebration, and a few days later they decorated the garden with Chinese lanterns, with the help of Cambridge friends Douglas Jay and Goronwy Rees. As Máire recalled in a piece written for *Writers & Hampstead* (ed. Ian Norrie):

> Sometime after midnight ... we all went into the drawing-room and then James Joyce went to the piano ... He sang 'Phil the Fluthers Ball' and I particularly remember the beautiful 'Shule Aroon'.

'Green Fields of France, The'. The title of a popular antiwar ballad by Eric Bogle, made famous by Dublin folk singer Finbar FUREY. The narrator addresses his questions and comments to 19-year-old 'Private Willie McBride', who is buried in a First World War graveyard:

> Well, how do you do, Private William McBride?
> Do you mind if I sit down here by your graveside,
> And rest for awhile in the warm summer sun,
> I've been walking all day, and I'm nearly done?
> And I see by your gravestone you were only nineteen
> When you joined the glorious fallen in 1916,
> Well, I hope you died quick and I hope you died clean
> Or, Willie McBride, was it slow and obscene?

Green grassy slopes. Words from the refrain of a popular Orange song of the same title, com-memorating the battle which has become a significant part of Orange tradition, recalled in the mantra, 'Derry, Aughrim, Enniskillen and the Boyne.' The association of Orangeism with the Battle of the BOYNE is entirely anachronistic, since the ORANGE ORDER was not founded for more than 100 years after the battle:

> On the green grassy slopes of the Boyne
> Where the Orangemen with William did join
> And fought for our glorious deliv'rance
> On the green grassy slopes of the Boyne.

Green Linnet. A record label specializing in folk and traditional music and now based in Danbury, Connecticut, USA. Since it was founded in 1973 it has issued recordings by many Irish musicians, including Martin HAYES.

Greeshy (also **greesh** or **greeshig**). The ashes of peat or small coal, from the Irish *gríosach*, often used for baking bread in a BASTABLE.

> The night the win' is risin', an' its comin' on to sleet,
> It's spittin' down the chimley on the greeshig at me feet.
>
> W.F. MARSHALL (1888–1959): 'Sarah Ann', in *Ballads and Verses from Tyrone* (1929)

Gregory, Lady (1852–1932). Augusta Gregory, writer, patron, co-founder of the ABBEY THEATRE, and one of the central figures, along with her friend W.B. YEATS, in the IRISH LITERARY REVIVAL. She was born Isabella Augusta Persse in Roxborough, Co. Galway, on 15 March 1852, and, unusually for a member of an ASCENDANCY family, developed a keen interest in the Gaelic culture of the people of the area. In this she was strongly influenced by her Irish-speaking nurse, Mary Sheridan, who counteracted the 'strict Orangeism of the drawing-room' with a great knowledge of folklore and stories from memory of the landing of the French at Killala in 1798 (*see* RACES OF CASTLEBAR). She married the Galway landlord Sir William Gregory (1817–92), deviser of the infamous GREGORY CLAUSE, in 1880, and it was not until after his death that she met Yeats and began a mutually rewarding lifelong friendship.

Yeats encouraged her to return to the Irish interests of her childhood, and it was she who introduced him to Edward MARTYN and helped to lay the foundations of the national theatre. She also taught Yeats the principles of dramaturgy, and contributed to CATHLEEN NÍ HOULIHAN and *The Pot of Broth*. She herself wrote 27 original plays, including SPREADING THE NEWS, *The Gaol Gate*, *The* RISING OF THE MOON and *The Workhouse Ward*, many couched in the local HIBERNO-ENGLISH dialect that became known as KILTARTAN. She also published Kiltartan versions of the old Celtic sagas in *Cuchulain of Muirthemne* (1902) and *Gods and Fighting Men* (1904), and of plays by the 17th-century French dramatist Molière, including *L'Avare*, *Le Médicin malgré lui* and *Les Fourberies de Scapin*.

Most of Lady Gregory's energies were devoted to the well-being of Yeats, who used her house at COOLE PARK as a regular retreat, and to the administration of what he tended to think of as *his* theatre (she sometimes arrived in Dublin with a large GORT CAKE to help feed the cast). Though grief-stricken at the deaths of the two young people closest to her – her only son Robert, shot down in Italy when serving with the Royal Flying Corps in January 1918, and her nephew Sir Hugh Lane, lost in May 1915 when the LUSITANIA sank – she involved herself vigorously in the matter of the LANE PICTURES. She died at Coole Park on 22 May 1932.
See also OLD LADY, THE.

Gregory Clause, the. An amendment to the Poor Law Act (1847), also known as the 'quarter-acre', forced upon the Whig government with the help of Irish MPs by Sir William Gregory (1817–92), husband of Lady GREGORY. According to the terms of the clause, relief was denied to those occupying more than a quarter-acre (0.1 ha) of land and to their dependants. (This latter refinement was rescinded in May 1848 when the authorities could not rebut the charge of imposing deliberate starvation upon the innocent.) The amendment, passed at the height of the GREAT FAMINE, caused appalling

hardship, but pleased those landlords (many of them ABSENTEE LANDLORDS) who wished to clear the accumulation of smallholders off their estates. Many of the COTTIERS, with their obsessional view of land-holding, preferred death to relinquishment, but the measure was virtually eviction under another name. Though Gregory was later regarded as a liberal, the 'quarter-acre' remained as a blot on his reputation. He wrote in his *Autobiography* (1894):

> Though I got an evil reputation in consequence, those who really understood the conditions of the country have always regarded this clause as its salvation.

Gretta Greene. *See* GREENE, GRETTA.

Grey, Sir Leonard (d. 1541). Elizabethan soldier. He arrived in Ireland as marshal of the English army in 1535 – he it was who suppressed the rebellion of SILKEN THOMAS (Thomas Fitzgerald, Earl of Kildare) – and the following year was appointed lord deputy in succession to Sir William Skeffington. Instructed by King Henry VIII to impose the oath of supremacy and demand submission from the Irish, he presided over the REFORMATION PARLIAMENT and pursued a belligerent policy, typical of what is known as the TUDOR RECONQUEST.

So perturbed were the Gaelic lords by Grey's militancy that they formed the Geraldine League, an alliance led by the Ulster chieftains Manus O'Donnell and Conn O'Neill that had the aim of restoring the power of the Earls of Kildare and maintaining the Catholic religion. In August 1539 Grey defeated an army of the League at the Battle of Bellahoe, on the Meath–Monaghan border, but the king was alarmed by the results of Grey's policy and recalled him to London in April 1540. He was executed for treason the following year.

Grey Man's Path. A chasm at FAIR HEAD in Co. Antrim. It plunges dramatically down a steep gully to the beach, and is recommended by guide books as more suitable for the foraging wild goats than for the inexperienced walker. The eponymous Grey Man in one account is a malevolent horse-like creature who lives under nearby Lough Dhu, and who may appear as a man with grey skin and green hair and horse's hooves.

Greysteel. *See* TRICK OR TREAT KILLINGS.

Grianán. Literally a 'solarium' or 'bower' (*grian* is Irish for 'sun') associated with feminine pursuits. An Grianán is the adult education centre of the IRISH COUNTRYWOMEN'S ASSOCIATION (ICA) in Termonfeckin, Co. Louth, established in 1954 with financial help from the Kellogg Foundation. The ICA holds residential courses in crafts and creative activities there for its members. Muriel Gahan (d.1995) was the project's driving force, and she was also behind in the foundation of a residential horticultural college for women, which opened in the same venue in 1968. A recently opened theatre in Letterkenny is called An Grianán.
See also AILEACH.

Griffin, Gerald (1803–40). Poet and novelist. He was born and educated in Limerick and went to England to become a playwright, but failed because of 'the fickleness of public literary taste'. He tried to make a living by hack work in London and at home, supported by a Quaker patron, Mrs Lydia Fisher, as all the while his religious fervour increased. In 1836 he became a CHRISTIAN BROTHER in Dublin, and he died in the monastery in Cork. He is famous as the author of *The* COLLEGIANS (1829), a novel of passion and murder based upon an actual case, which became very popular and provided Dion Boucicault with his first success, *The* COLLEEN BAWN (1860). Griffin also wrote the lyrics 'My Mary of the Curling Hair', 'Hy-Brasail' and 'Eileen Aroon'.

Griffith, Arthur (1871–1922). Nationalist politician, and co-founder of SINN FÉIN. He was born in Dublin on 31 May 1871 and became a printer, maintaining a wide and critical interest in Irish cultural affairs, helping to found the Celtic Literary Society and the Gaelic League. (His acidic view of the IRISH LITERARY REVIVAL was that of one who would have subjected

even art to the Nationalist cause.) He refused to support John REDMOND'S NATIONAL VOLUNTEERS, and was arrested in 1916, though he had no part in the EASTER RISING. He bore the privations of imprisonment cheerfully. In 1921, during the Anglo-Irish War, he led the delegation that negotiated the TREATY, and became a strong supporter of what had been wrested from Lloyd George. However, the strain of the struggle with the ANTI-TREATYITES and the bloody CIVIL WAR proved too much for his ailing body. He died on 12 August 1922, ten days before the other significant casualty of this turbulent period, Michael COLLINS.

Griffith, Richard (1784–1878). Engineer. He was born in Naas, Co. Kildare, and worked for the BOG COMMISSIONERS and the Board of Works. He is best known for the Primary Valuation, popularly known as GRIFFITH'S VALUATION.

Griffith's Valuation. A survey carried out county by county in 1848–60 by Richard GRIFFITH in order to provide a basis for the calculation of rates payable under the Poor Law. The information was arranged in printed volumes, showing the tenants, the landlords and the area and value of the holdings.

Grig. A HIBERNO-ENGLISH verb meaning to 'tease', to 'tantalize', from the Irish *griogadh*.

Gríosach. *See* GREESHY.

'Groves of Blarney, The'. A squib written by Richard Millikin (1767–1815), in burlesque of an anonymous effusion called 'Castlehyde', an attempt by someone whose first language was not English to celebrate the demesne:

> The grand improvements they would amuse you,
>   the trees are drooping with fruit all kind;
> The bees perfuming the fields with music, which
>   yields more beauty to Castlehyde.

Millikin was Anglo-Irish, educated and a member of the notorious Cork militia that put down the REBELLION OF 1798 with such cruelty. Hearing 'Castlehyde' sung at a party and unaware of its attempt to render into English something of Irish poetry, he boasted that he could do as well in 24 hours. He produced 'The Groves of Blarney', a tribute to a pleasure ground nearer home:

The Groves of Blarney
They look so charming,
Down by the purling
    Of sweet silent streams,
Being banked with posies
That spontaneous grow there,
Planted in order
    By the sweet Rock Close.

Interestingly Millikin does not mention the famous 'stone', and it was left to a native son, Francis Sylvester Mahony (FATHER PROUT) to incorporate a mention of Blarney Castle's most famous brick (see BLARNEY STONE).

Grubbed. A HIBERNO-ENGLISH adjective meaning 'trampled', 'trodden upon' (referring to soil or earth).

Grubb's Grave. A monument, in the VEE area of the Knockmealdown Mountains, to a landlord named Grubb. Legend has it that Grubb was buried standing with his dog and his gun.

Grudles. A concocted word in HIBERNO-ENG-LISH meaning any kind of food, but particularly of a fancy, special kind.

Gruelling. A HIBERNO-ENGLISH term for a severe scolding or reprimand. It is also hare coursing parlance for when a wily hare evades the hounds long enough to tire them out completely.

Gruel spooned up off a dirty floor. The harsh judgement by Jane BARLOW on *The UNTILLED FIELD* (1902), a collection of stories by George MOORE which, in their realism and subject matter, were considered daring at the time. Barlow wrote in a letter in November 1914: 'That old yahoo George Moore … His stories impressed me as being on the whole like gruel spooned up off a dirty floor.'

Grug. An Irish word, also used in HIBERNO-ENGLISH, denoting an angry attitude or a fighting pose.

GUBU. 'Grotesque, unbelievable, bizarre, unprecedented': the summing up by taoiseach Charles HAUGHEY of the events of July–August 1982, which culminated in the arrest of double murderer Malcolm MacArthur in the apartment of the FIANNA FÁIL government's (completely innocent) attorney-general, Patrick Connolly, on 13 August. In the Dáil, opposition TD Conor CRUISE O'BRIEN coined the acronym GUBU, which soon became the byword for Haughey's activities and misadventures during his nine months in government in 1982. MacArthur, a friend of Connolly's, had come to stay with him after committing two unprovoked and senseless murders, one of a nurse, Bridie Gargan, in Dublin's Phoenix Park on 22 July, in an abortive attempt to steal her car, the second of a Co. Offaly farmer, Donal Dunne, from whom he stole a shotgun and car, apparently with the intention of carrying out an armed robbery. Connolly resigned a few days after MacArthur's arrest, although not before he had exhibited, in the public mind at least, unpardonable *sangfroid* in leaving Ireland for a holiday in the USA. MacArthur was sentenced to life imprisonment in January 1983 for the murder of Bridie Gargan; he was prosecuted for one murder only.

See also BOOK OF EVIDENCE, THE.

Guerin, Veronica (1959–96). Journalist. She was born in Artane on the northside of Dublin, and after leaving school worked in her father's accountancy firm, becoming involved with the local FIANNA FÁIL party in a voluntary capacity. She married Graham Turley in 1985, and in 1990 their son Cathal was born. In 1990 she began to work as a journalist for the *Sunday Business Post*, but it was as the crime correspondent for Dublin's leading Sunday paper, the *Sunday Independent*, from 1993, that she made her name, investigating criminals of all types, especially wealthy drug barons and money-launderers. She worked alone and appeared to scorn danger, although she had received warnings: in 1994 shots were fired through the window of her house, and in 1995 a gunman shot her in the leg at her own front door. At lunchtime on 26 June 1996 she was shot dead by the rider of a motorbike that drew up beside her red sports car as she stopped at traffic lights just outside Dublin. Two men were subsequently convicted of her murder. In the months after her death Guerin achieved heroic status as a campaigner against crime. *Veronica Guerin,* a film about her life and death, directed by Joel Schumacher and starring Cate Blanchett, was released in 2003.

Guerrilla Days in Ireland. The title of an autobiographical book (1949) – necessarily subjective and partisan – by the War of Independence guerrilla leader Tom Barry (1897–1980). Barry was born in Rosscarbery, Co. Cork, the son of a policeman who had bought a pub on his retirement. He joined the army in 1915 and served at Ypres and later in Mesopotamia. In 1918 he was approached by the IRISH VOLUNTEERS as a man of known military experience. Soon he had trained his own highly disciplined west Cork FLYING COLUMN – a concept in guerrilla warfare he largely developed himself. On 28 November 1920 he led the KILMICHAEL AMBUSH, in which the AUXIES suffered their most serious defeat (15 were killed), and on March 1921, at Crossbarry, he successfully engaged a superior force from the Essex Regiment. Barry took the side of the ANTI-TREATY-ITES in the CIVIL WAR, and continued as a member of the IRA until 1938, when he resigned because he disagreed with the organization's bombing campaign in Britain. Revisionist historians, notably Peter Hart in *The IRA and its Enemies* (1998), have questioned Barry's version of events, particularly what is known as the 'false surrender' of the Kilmichael Ambush, after which a number of Auxiliaries were killed by the Republicans. Hart's views, cogently and convincingly argued, caused controversy among historians and aroused great anger in Barry's native west Cork.

Gug (Irish *gog*, 'syllable', 'tittle', 'tiny unit of speech'). A word used in HIBERNO-ENGLISH to mean 'speech'. It is usually used negatively, as in, 'There wasn't a gug out of her.' The word *gug* is also used as a child's term for a breakfast egg, as in 'Eat up your gug.' (The word probably derives from the sound made by a hen.)

Guildford Four, the. On 5 October 1974 two IRA bombs killed five people in two pubs in Guildford, Surrey. A month later two people were killed by an IRA bomb attack on a Woolwich pub. Paddy Armstrong, Gerry Conlon, Paul Hill and Carole Richardson, all Irish people living in England, were subsequently arrested and charged with murder in both incidents, and sentenced to life imprisonment. Irregularities in police evidence resulted in the release of all four in 1989. *In the Name of the Father*, a 1993 film based on the case, explored movingly the relationship between Gerald Conlon and his sick father, but was described by one critic as 'unashamed Irish myth-making' on account of the inaccuracies of its courtroom dénouement.

See also BIRMINGHAM SIX, THE; WINCHESTER THREE, THE.

Guinness. Ireland's national drink, a 'black liquidation with froth on the top', produced in Dublin since 1759. Arthur Guinness ('Uncle Arthur'), the founder of the James's Street brewery, was born in Celbridge, Co. Kildare, in 1725, son of the steward of the Celbridge estate of Archbishop Price of Cashel. In 1756 he started a brewery in nearby Leixlip with his brother Richard, his capital an inheritance of £200 from Archbishop Price. On 31 December 1759 he signed a 9000-year lease on St James's Gate Brewery, at £45 per annum. Arthur Guinness became a model citizen and ran the brewery until his death on 23 January 1803. His son Arthur inherited the business, as did his grandson Benjamin, and his great-grandsons Arthur (later 1st Lord Ardilaun) and Edward (later 1st Earl of Iveagh) jointly inherited the brewery in 1868. Guinness is now brewed in 50 countries, but the special ingredient on which all Guinness is based is produced only in St James's Gate. The drink has traditionally been regarded as a restorative or tonic (it is certainly calorific) and was sometimes prescribed by doctors. Robert Louis Stevenson had supplies brought to the Samoan Islands when writing *Treasure Island* (1883) Half the output of St James's Gate is exported: the first exports were in May 1796 when Arthur Guinness's opposition to the UNITED IRISHMEN caused the drink to be nicknamed 'Guinness's Black Protestant Porter', and a popular boycott was threatened. The brand is now owned by multinational giant Diageo, and 10 million glasses of Guinness are sold every day in 150 countries. Guinness became famous as much for its advertising posters and in particular for 'Guinness is good for you', its slogan from 1929, as for its other qualities, and the company also for many years published *The Guinness Book of Records*. Guinness is now also brewed in England, but the original Dublin plant still produces 18 million litres (4 million gallons) of the therapeutic liquor each day.

Guinness's Black Protestant Porter. *See* GUINNESS.

Gulliver's Travels. A prose satire (1726) by Swift (*see* DEAN, THE), originally titled *Travels into Several Remote Nations of the World*. It details the adventures of Lemuel Gulliver, a ship's surgeon, who visits various fantastic countries whose mores are thinly disguised versions of attitudes in Ireland and Britain. In LILLIPUT, the first landfall, the people are tiny and possess factional minds, in Brobdingnag they are gigantic and physically repellent, and in the land of the Houyhnhnms the vertical bipeds are called YAHOOS (one of several of Swifts' coinages that have become current), while the Houyhnhnms themselves are equine philosophers, and represent reason (their name is a

sound representation of a horse's whinnying). In an ironic development, which the author might well have relished, the tale, with Swift's obsessional scatological references removed, has become a children's classic.

> And he gave it for his opinion, that whoever could make two ears of corn or two blades of grass to grow upon a spot of ground where only one grew before, would deserve better of mankind, and do more essential service to his country than the whole race of politicians put together.
>
> 'A Voyage to Brobdingnag'

Gúm, An (Irish, literally 'the scheme' or 'the artifice'). The government publishing agency set up in 1925 by Ernest BLYTHE (1889–1975), the then minister of finance, to produce textbooks and literature in Irish. Much of its early work consisted in commissioning for minimal fees translations of works in English and other languages, but An Gúm did, not without much controversy, publish such important writers as Seosamh MAC GRIANNA and Máirtín Ó CADHAIN.

Gurrier. A Dublin slang word for a tough or lawless young man.
See also GOUGER; LATCHICO; MULLET.

Guthrie, Tyrone. *See* ANNAGHMAKERRIG.

Gutty. A term of class abuse applied to those perceived as low in morals and social standing. One possible source for the world is the suggestion that the favoured footwear of those thus designated was cheap tennis shoes, called gutties from the gutta-percha (waterproof rubber) once used in their manufacture. It also has connotations of 'gutter', and the term is still also used as the equivalent of GURRIER.

h

Hadji Bey (d. 1972). An Armenian who fled Turkey during the pograms of 1902 and set up a business in what became known as Cork's MacCurtain Street. His Turkish Delight was a Cork institution until his shop closed after its proprietor's death in 1972. The shop sign boasted 'A good name is worth millions.'

Haggard. An Ulster word meaning literally 'hay-yard', but used throughout Ireland for the kitchen garden or other unspecified parts of the farmyard.

> Butterfly, dear girl, we fixed the Longford lout. He'll never leave Longford again. The wife has him tethered and spancelled in the haggard. We wrote poison pen letters to half the town, including the parish.
>
> BENEDICT KIELY (b.1919): *A Ball of Malt and Madame Butterfly* (1973)

Hair-trigger Dick. *See* HUMANITY DICK.

Haitch. The pronunciation of the letter 'h' as 'haitch' rather than 'aitch' is a distinctive feature of HIBERNO-ENGLISH.

Half-mounted gentlemen. The largest and lowest category of Anglo-Irish gentry in the taxonomy devised by Sir Jonah Barrington (1760–1834) and printed in his book *PERSONAL SKETCHES of His Own Times* (1827–32):

> In those days the common people ideally separated the gentry of the country into three classes, and treated each class according to the relative degree of respect to which they considered

it was entitled. They generally divided them thus: 1 Half-mounted gentlemen; 2 Gentlemen every inch of them; 3 Gentlemen to the backbone.

Barrington's account is marvellously anecdotal and his own career was just as colourful as those he chronicled. He was gentry himself but impecunious, born in a once great house near Abbeyleix, Co. Laois, educated at Trinity College Dublin and called to the Bar in 1788. He was member in the Irish Parliament for Tuam (1790–7) and for Clogher (1798–1800). He was a vocal opponent of the Act of UNION (despite being promised, as he claimed, the post of solicitor-general), but was certainly a go-between in the elaborate system of bribery that sweetened its passing. He was appointed an Admiralty judge in 1798, knighted in 1807 and deprived of his office for peculation in 1830. Barrington spent his last years in Versailles, dying on 8 April 1834.

Half-note. A ten-shilling note. The Irish ten-shilling note was a distinctive orange and was considered to be of great value. After the introduction of decimal currency in 1971, the 50 pence piece never had the same buying power.

Half-one. A small measure (a half-glass) of whiskey.

Half past six. The age as announced by himself at which James JOYCE went as a boarder to

CLONGOWES WOOD college. He arrived at the school on 1 September 1888, and when asked his age replied, 'Half past six.' The phrase became his school nickname for a while.

Halfpenny Bridge. The most famous and recognizable of all Dublin bridges. The Halfpenny Bridge (pronounced 'Haypenny') is a single-span metal footbridge, which was opened for public use in May 1816. A toll of a halfpenny applied and was collected until about 1916. Although in its early days it was sometimes called Wellington Bridge (building of the bridge having been in progress at the time of the Battle of Waterloo), the Ordnance Survey called it Metal Bridge in 1938 and it is now officially known as (but never called) Liffey Bridge.

The Halfpenny Bridge is associated with the controversy about the Hugh Lane paintings (*see* LANE PICTURES, THE). In 1912, five years after Lane stipulated the erection of 'a permanent building on a suitable site' to house his bequest, it was proposed that this should be constructed on the bridge itself. Sir Edwin Lutyens created a handsome design of two buildings linked by a row of columns and topped by statues, which W.B. Yeats described as 'beautiful'. There was opposition on the grounds of expense, and public opinion in Dublin, expressed through the newspapers of William Martin MURPHY, rejected both design and paintings. The project was abandoned.

The strategically situated Halfpenny Bridge is still in constant use by pedestrians. Now expensively furbished, with its elegant lanterns and iron tracery, it has become the most identifiable symbol for the city of Dublin.

Hallowe'en. The eve of the feast of All Saints and a night of festivity throughout Ireland. At Hallowe'en parties there were games involving apples and nuts, both for children (such as bobbing for apples in a basin of water or trying to bite apples hung from the ceiling) and also for their older brothers and sisters, such as harmless DIVINATION techniques to discover future spouses. The main source of future fortune was to be found in the tokens found in the BARMBRACK that was the centre of the festivities. In Ulster the tokens tended to be hidden in apple tarts, as the second verse of 'MY AUNT JANE' makes clear:

> My Aunt Jane, she's awful smart;
> She bakes wee rings in an apple tart
> And when Hallowe'en comes around
> Fornenst that tart I'm always found.
> ANON. (late 19th century): 'My Aunt Jane'

Hall's Pictorial Weekly. *See* BALLYMAGASH.

Halpine, Charles (1829–68). Journalist and comic poet, using the pseudonym 'Private Myles O'Reilly'. He was born in Oldcastle, Co. Meath, the son of a clergyman. A supporter of YOUNG IRELAND, he emigrated to America in 1851 and was secretary to the great showman Phineas T[aylor] Barnum (1810–91) before becoming a journalist in New York. He joined the Federal army in 1861 and rose to the rank of brigadier-general in the Fighting 69th, having as a colonel commanded the first Afro-American regiment, which he had raised personally. Halpine wrote two historical novels and many songs and comic poems, including the anastronomical 'Irish Astronomy'. He died from an accidental overdose of chloral taken for chronic insomnia.

> So to conclude my song aright,
> For fear I'll tire your patience,
> You'll see O'Ryan every night
> Among the constellations.
> 'Irish Astronomy', in *The Life and Adventures, Songs, Services … of Private Myles O'Reilly* (1864)

Hames. A HIBERNO-ENGLISH word meaning a 'mess' or a 'hash', as in, 'He made a complete hames out of assembling the flat pack.' The literal meaning of the word refers to the pieces of a horse's collar, which are apparently difficult to assemble.

Hamilton, William Gerard. *See* SINGLE-SPEECH HAMILTON.

Hamilton, William Rowan (1805–65). Mathematician and astronomer. He was born in

Dublin on 4 August 1805 and showed early signs of prodigy. By the age of 12 he was fluent in 13 languages and had taught himself the geometry of Euclid in the original Greek. He entered Trinity College Dublin in 1823, and by 1827, while still an undergraduate, had been appointed professor of astronomy and director of Dunsink Observatory. He was knighted in 1835 for services to science, but all the while nursed a personal ambition to be a poet (he was a close friend of Wordsworth and Southey). One autumn day in 1843, while walking with his wife by the Royal Canal, he suddenly whipped out his penknife and scratched on the parapet of Broom Bridge the equation that was the basis for his theory of quaternions – essential for the development of quantum mechanics and nuclear physics. Hamilton died on 2 September 1865.

Hammond, David (Davy). *See* AS I ROVED OUT.

Hand, take a. A phrase used mainly in Ulster meaning 'tease', 'joke', as in 'Don't believe a word that fellow says; he's only taking a hand at you.' The person who attempts this nefarious deed is known as a 'take-a-hand'.

Handball. The least-known and least-played of GAA sports. It involves two or (less commonly) four players striking a small hard ball with the palm of the hand inside a four-walled court. In rural Ireland, handball was a very accessible sport, needing no equipment except a ball and the gable of a house or a high wall.

Handy. A useful HIBERNO-ENGLISH adverb with the meaning 'conveniently', 'easily', 'without too much exertion or speed', as in, 'Take it nice and handy on the road.'

Handy Andy. The eponymous main character of a comic STAGE-IRISH novel (1842) by Samuel LOVER (1797–1868). Written mainly for English readers and satisfying their stereotypical view of the Irish as stupid or obtuse, it was remarkably popular in Ireland, and the phrase is still current:

Andy Rooney was a fellow who had the most singularly ingenious knack of doing everything

the wrong way; disappointment waited upon all affairs in which he bore a part, and destruction was at his finger ends; so the nickname the neighbours stuck upon him was Handy Andy, and the jeering jingle pleased them.

Hanging. A Dublin colloquialism meaning 'exhausted'. 'Hanging drunk' is also used.

Hanging gale. A system of paying rent six months in arrears, the custom in Ireland in the 19th century. The word 'gale' as a day when rent is due may originate with the word 'gavel', an old word for 'tribute'. *The Hanging Gale* was the title of a BBC television series (1995) about the evils of landlordism in famine-stricken 1840s Donegal, conceived by and starring the four McGann brothers (Joe, Mark, Paul and Stephen).

Hankie, the priest with the. *See* DALY, EDWARD.

Hanna, Hugh (1824–92). Street preacher. He was born in Dromara, Co. Down, and ordained as a PRESBYTERIAN minister in 1851, having been a schoolmaster. His penchant for outdoor evangelical preaching earned him the deserved nickname 'Roaring Hanna', and he was prominent in the mixture of genuine spiritual experience and hysteria that characterized the revival of 1859. St Enoch's, the church specially built for him in 1872, was the largest Presbyterian building in Ireland, able to seat 2000 worshippers. He was also a fervent member of the ORANGE ORDER and a vigorous opponent of concessions to Catholics and the threat of HOME RULE. His inflammatory sermons were said to be responsible for anti-Catholic rioting in September 1857, and again in the summer of 1886 during the agitation against Gladstone's first Home Rule Bill, when a total of 50 people were killed. A statue erected in his honour in Belfast was blown up in 1970.

Hannay, Canon James Owen. *See* BIRMINGHAM, GEORGE A.

Ha o the Thane. An example of slightly artificial Ulster-Scots contrivance in its attempts at parity of esteem with English and Irish. It is urged as an alternative name of ÁRAS AN UACH-

TARÁIN, referring to the official residence of the President of Ireland.

Ha'penny place. A colloquialism meaning 'an inferior place', deriving from the low value of a ha'penny (halfpenny) coin. On hearing sensational gossip one might say: 'Well, that puts *my* story in the ha'penny place.'

Happy-careless. A HIBERNO-ENGLISH phrase meaning 'indifferent to' or 'detached from' a particular outcome, or 'not enthusiastic', 'placid by nature': 'I'm happy-careless whether we go or not.' The phrase may also be used negatively to denote someone seen as lacking in conscientiousness.

Happy English child, a. The last line in a quatrain required to be recited daily in Irish NATIONAL SCHOOLS (from 1831) where the Irish language was forbidden:

> I thank the goodness and the grace
> That on my birth have smiled,
> And made me in these Christian days
> A happy English child.
>> ARCHBISHOP RICHARD WHATELY (attrib.)

Hard chaw. Dublin slang for a 'tough nut', a GURRIER. Macho young Dublin boys might yearn to be considered 'chaws' or 'hard chaws', even superficially.

Hard drop, to have the. An Ulster expression meaning 'to be mean or parsimonious'.

Hardy. A HIBERNO-ENGLISH term used to describe weather that is harsh, particularly dry, cold weather: 'It's a hardy evening.' It also (as in British English) means 'resilient', 'able to endure hardship', 'physically capable' (although not necessarily strongly built). Of (Irish) Midlanders, considered to be phlegmatic, actor and comedian Niall Tóibín tells an apocryphal story of a countryman who, when asked about his reaction to the sight of a naked man running along a country road on a freezing Christmas Day, replied that, sure enough, he had remarked to his companion, 'Hardy man!'

Hare, William. *See* BURKE AND HARE.

Harland and Wolff. The Belfast shipbuilding firm founded in 1861 by Sir Edward James Harland (1831–95) and Gustave Wilhelm Wolff (1834–1913). Harland purchased Hickson's yard on Queen's Island (*see* DARGAN'S ISLAND) in 1858, and was partnered by the Hamburg-born Wolff three years later. They were joined in 1874 by William PIRRIE, under whose leadership the firm became 'shipbuilders to the world'. Pirrie became chairman in 1895 when Harland resigned, Wolff having taken over the Belfast Rope Works.

In 1899 the company built the *Oceanic* for the White Star Line, at 17,000 tons then the largest ship afloat, and the even larger TITANIC in 1912. The company prospered because of links with J[ohn] Pierpoint Morgan (1837–1913), the American magnate, and the Sheffield steel firm of John Brown. It opened yards at Govan, Liverpool and London. Under Pirrie's vigorous leadership the company survived recessions, helped by War Office contracts for warships, cargo vessels and aeroplanes in two world wars. After the Second World War the diversification into bulk carriers and oil tankers helped continue the firm's prosperity.

From the late 1960s, however, the company began to show losses and was bought out by the British government in 1975. It was privatized in 1989 and now survives with difficulty, catering for specialist markets such as the offshore oil business. The majority of workers throughout its history have been Protestant, and Catholic shipyard workers were at times of sectarian tension at risk of their lives (*see* BELFAST CONFETTI).

Harmonious Barry. The description by the playwright Arthur MURPHY of the Irish actor Spranger Barry. Barry was born in Dublin on 20 November 1719 and, after the family silversmith business failed, became an actor at SMOCK ALLEY, making his debut as Othello in 1743. In 1747 he repeated the role to Charles MACKLIN's Iago at Drury Lane, becoming David Garrick's (1717–79) chief romantic rival, taller, with a finer figure and beautiful speaking voice, but weak in interpretation. In 1758 he built CROW STREET THEATRE in Dublin with Henry Woodward (1717–77) and lost all his savings in its ruinous running, though his productions were splendid. He returned to London in 1767 and spent the rest of his career on the stages of Drury Lane, the Haymarket and Covent Garden, often acting with his second wife Ann Dancer (1734–1801). He died on 10 January 1777.

Harney, Mary. *See* PEE DEES.

Harp. The national symbol of Ireland, to be seen on all Irish coins and on government stationery. It has a long, romantic association with the country, and for foreigners harp music is often seen as being the most traditional of all – hence the harp entertainment at 'medieval' banquets at BUNRATTY CASTLE (although this is far from being genuine traditional music). The earliest representation of the familiar triangular harp is on the late 11th-century shrine of St Meadóg, suggesting that the instrument was in common use by then; the earliest Irish harp still in existence is the 'Brian Boru' in Trinity College Dublin, thought to date from the late 14th century. It is on this that the harp on Irish coinage is based.

Although the Gaelic harp tradition was not finally broken until the early 19th century, its fortunes were closely linked to the Gaelic way of life, where the *cruitire* (or harper) had a standing second only to that of the *filid* (poet) in the household of the chieftain. It is thought that at first poems were recited to the accompaniment of the harp, the harpist later singing to his own music. With the decline of Gaelic society in the 17th century, harpers depended for their livelihood on the generosity of the Anglo-Irish or foreign gentry, some, like CAROLAN, becoming itinerant.

By the early 19th century the traditional harp was in decline, to be replaced by the new 'Irish harp', taught to young ladies for self-accompaniment in convents and drawing rooms (this is the kind of harp music heard in Bunratty). There has been a revival in the tradi-

tional Irish harp in the last three decades, with harpers such as Gráinne Yeats and Máire Ní Chathasaigh re-establishing a link with the musicians of the 18th century by studying ornamentation and dance music from written sources and incorporating it into their own repertoire. These players have also been influential as teachers, and there is a new breed of traditional harper to be heard today.

Harrigan, Ned (1844–1911). Star of Irish-American vaudeville and comic theatre. Born in New York on 26 October 1844, he ran away from home to go on the stage. He teamed up with Tony Hart (Anthony J. Cannon, 1855–91), who played his wife Cordelia to his Dan Mulligan in a very popular series of shows (1872–84), which he wrote and directed. Harrigan wrote 39 plays and many songs including 'The Mulligan Guard' (1873), 'MULDOON, THE SOLID MAN' (1874) and 'MAGGIE MURPHY'S HOME' (1890), with music by his father-in-law Dave Barham. The first of these, 'The Mulligan Guard', though essentially comic, has darker overtones. The 'guards' were originally uniformed target companies, created in the aftermath of the American Civil War, but memories of the anti-Irish riots of the previous decade were still strong:

> We crave your condescension:
> We'll tell you what we know
> Of marching in the Mulligan Guard
> From Sligo Ward below.
> Our captain's name was Hussey
> A Tipperary man:
> He carried his sword like a Russian duke
> Whenever he took command.

Harrigan died in New York on 6 June 1911, having made his last stage appearance in 1908. The year before, in 1907, George M. Cohan (*see* 'YANKEE DOODLE DANDY') had written a popular song in tribute to the older songwriting performer:

> H–A-double R–I–G–A–N spells Harrigan,
> Proud of all the Irish blood that's in me;
> Divil a man can say a word agin me.
> H–A-double R–I–G–A–N spells Harrigan, you see;

It's a name that shame never been connected with.
Harrigan, That's me!
   'Harrigan'

Harrington, Pádraig (b.1971). Golfer. He was born in Dublin on 31 August 1971 and had an outstanding career as an amateur, making three Walker Cup appearances (including a victory at Royal Porthcawl in 1995). In September 1995 he turned professional, winning the Spanish Open in 1996 in his first year on the European Tour. He represented Europe in the 1999 Ryder Cup and in 2000 ended a run of nine second-place finishes by winning his second title, the Brazil Sao Paulo 500 Years Open. Victory in the Volvo Masters in Jerez followed in 2001. 2002 not only saw Harrington help Europe win the Ryder Cup, but also brought victories in the Dunhill Masters, and the Target World Challenge, in which he beat Tiger Woods. By 2004 Harrington was ranked eighth in golf's PGA world rankings

Harris, Richard (1930–2002). Actor. Born in Limerick in October 1930, Harris was a talented rugby player, but an attack of tuberculosis compromised his sporting career. He studied in London at LAMDA and in 1956 joined Joan Littlewood's Theatre Workshop, playing Mickser in her production of *The QUARE FELLOW*. His most memorable film roles were in *This Sporting Life* (1963) and as Bull McCabe in Jim Sheridan's film of *The Field* (1990). Harris was a kindly Professor Albus Dumbledore in the first two *Harry Potter* films. He once said, 'If I win an award for something I do, the London papers describe me as "the British actor, Richard Harris". If I am found drunk in a public place, they always refer to me as "the Irish actor, Richard Harris".' He died in London in October 2002.

Harrods Bombing. The 'Christmas' bombing, as the incident was afterwards remembered, in which two Provisional IRA car bombs were detonated with insufficient warning in Knightsbridge, London, at the back of Harrods department store on Saturday 17 December

1983. The streets were crowded with shoppers and five people were killed and 80 injured.

Harvester, Operation. *See* BORDER CAMPAIGN.

Harvey, [Beauchamp] Bagenal (1762–98). United Irishman and leader in the REBELLION OF 1798. Harvey, a Protestant, was born on his father's estate at Bargy Castle in Co. Wexford. He was educated at Trinity College Dublin and called to the Bar in 1782. Described as 'a man of liberal principles', he supported CATHOLIC EMANCIPATION and the reform of Parliament and became a member of the UNITED IRISHMEN in Dublin. On the night of 26 May 1798 he was arrested at his own house on the basis of information given under torture by Anthony Perry, a rebel colonel (*see* PITCH CAP) and imprisoned in Wexford jail.

After Wexford was taken by the rebels Harvey was appointed commander-in-chief of the rebel armies, despite his own alleged reluctance (used later in his defence), lack of military experience and manifest unsuitability for the job. His indecisive and dilatory leadership contributed to the rout of the rebel forces at the battle of NEW ROSS on 5 June; so overwhelmed was he by this disaster and by the SCULLABOGUE massacre of the same day that he left the army, replaced as commander-in-chief on 7 June by the no more effectual but noisier Father Philip Roche.

Harvey returned first to Wexford, thence, after the defeat at VINEGAR HILL[1], to his home at Bargy Castle, apparently confident of an amnesty or lenient treatment. When it became clear that this was not the case he left Bargy with his friend Dr John Colclough and took refuge in a cave on the SALTEE ISLANDS, intending to flee to France. Colclough and he were both betrayed, arrested, court-martialled and hanged on Wexford Bridge on 28 June 1798.

Hate. An Ulster word signifying a 'small amount', a 'whit'. It comes from the Scots phrase 'Deil hae it!' ('Let the devil have it!') and is found in such usages as 'Did you get much out of him? Dale a hate!'

Haughey, Charles J. (b.1925). Politician and taoiseach (1979–81, 1982, 1987–92). A charismatic but controversial leader, Haughey, who had been a TD since 1957, succeeded Jack LYNCH as leader of FIANNA FÁIL in December 1979. He was taoiseach during much of the recession of the 1980s, when he notoriously said that the Irish people would 'have to tighten [their] belts', while himself living in Georgian splendour on his north Dublin estate, Abbeville, the 18th-century former home of John BERESFORD. After a number of unsuccessful heaves against him, he finally resigned as taoiseach on 11 February 1992, claiming in his own vindication to 'have done the state some service'. There is no doubt that he was an able and imaginative legislator, but his reputation was irredeemably destroyed by the revelations of the MCCRACKEN TRIBUNAL in 1997 that he had received gifts of money from various individuals, notably £1.3 million from Ben Dunne (*see* THANKS A MILLION, BIG FELLA).
See also ARMS CRISIS; BOSS, THE; CAMORRA, THE; CHARVET SHIRTS; CHAS MAHAL; FLAWED PEDIGREE; GREAT LITTLE NATION, THIS; GUBU; LOW STANDARDS IN HIGH PLACES; *SCRAP SATURDAY*; TACA.

Haughton, Samuel (1821–97). Scientist. Born in Carlow and educated at Trinity College Dublin, graduating in mathematics, Haughton worked as a geologist and mineralogist, returning to TCD to study medicine in 1859. He became registrar of the medical school in 1862, and during the Dublin cholera epidemic of 1866 he recruited medical students to work among the poor. In the same year he published a formula for calculating the drop, based on the individual's weight, necessary to cause instantaneous death by hanging. He became President of the Royal Zoological Society and received many honours before his death in Dublin in 1897.

Hauling home, the. A marriage custom, observed in traditional rural society until the middle of the 20th century. Traditionally a young woman who 'married into' the farm of her husband was not supposed to go back to her old house for a month after the wedding. After the month had elapsed, a dance would be held at the parents' house, which was known as the 'hauling home'.

Hawarden Kite, the. The 'indiscreet' statement made privately to a journalist in December 1885 by Herbert Gladstone (1854–1930), the GOM's youngest son, that his father was about to declare for HOME RULE. (Hawarden Castle in present-day Flintshire was the Gladstone family seat.) His father repudiated the suggestion on 17 December, but it was clear that it was to be part of his ambition to 'pacify' Ireland.

Haw-Haw, Lord. The nickname of William Joyce (1906–46), the Nazi propagandist. Joyce made propaganda broadcasts in English from Germany on a nightly basis during the Second World War, and the nickname was coined by a *Daily Express* journalist a few weeks after the start of the war because of Joyce's manner of speaking 'English of the haw, haw, dammit-get-out-of-my-way variety'.

Joyce was born in New York to an Irish father and an English mother. The family returned to live in Ireland in 1909, first in Co. Mayo, then in Galway, where Joyce *père*, Michael, became manager of the Galway Bus Company. A Loyalist family, the Joyces moved to London after the foundation of the Free State. As a student in the early 1920s William Joyce became involved with various fascist groups. In 1934 he became head of research in Sir Oswald Mosley's British Union of Fascists, and in 1937 founded his own National Socialist League.

With his wife Margot, also a fascist supporter, Joyce travelled to Germany in September 1939 on a British passport (he claimed to be a British citizen, born in Galway) and they both began to broadcast in English: 'Germany calling, Germany calling. Here is the news and a talk in English...' He admitted his identity over the airwaves in April 1941. He and his wife were arrested by British troops in May 1945 and he was brought to London to stand trial for treason. His conviction was controversial since, although he had held an English passport since 1933, he was an American citizen. He was hanged on 3 January 1946.

Hayes, Martin (b.1962). Traditional fiddler. He was born in Feakle, Co. Clare, and like his father P. Joe played fiddle with the TULLA CÉILÍ BAND. He has travelled and performed extensively in the USA, and is regarded as one of the finest musicians of his generation.

H-Block Hunger Strikes. Two series of hunger strikes held in the winter, spring and summer of 1980–1 in protest at the loss of SPECIAL CATEGORY status by Republican paramilitaries in the MAZE prison. The hunger strikes resulted in ten deaths.

On 27 October 1980 seven prisoners, six from the Provisional IRA and one member of the INLA, began to refuse food. They held out until 18 December, when they began to take food following the presentation of a 34-page document by Humphrey Atkins, secretary of state for Northern Ireland (1979–81), which seemed to promise a more lenient prison regime.

On 25 January 1981, however, Bobby SANDS, the leader of the Provisional prisoners, claimed that moves for a resolution of the prisoners' difficulties had broken down. He began fasting on 1 March, the fifth anniversary of the start of the phasing out of special category status. The campaign that followed lasted seven months and in that time seven Provisionals and three members of the INLA died. The Provisionals who died were Bobby Sands (5 May, 66 days), Francis Hughes (12 May, 59 days), Raymond McCreesh (21 May, 61 days), Joe McDonnell (8 July, 61 days), Martin Hurson (13 July, 45 days), Kieran Doherty (2 August, 73 days), Thomas McElwee (8 August, 62 days). The INLA members who died were: Patsy O'Hara, the leader of the INLA prisoners (21 May, 61 days), Kevin Lynch (1 August, 71 days) and Michael Devine (20 August, 61 days).

Sands was elected MP in a by-election for Fermanagh–South Tyrone on 9 April, and

Kieran Doherty was elected TD in Cavan–Monaghan in the Irish general election in June. The British government of Margaret Thatcher refused to yield to any of the strikers' demands, in spite of intense local and international pressure, and much clerical lobbying. James Prior, the new secretary of state (1981–4), suggested through his junior Lord Gowrie that there might by some concessions if the campaign ended. On 3 October 1981 the six men still on strike began to take food, and three days later Prior announced that prisoners might wear their own clothes and that 50% of lost remission would be made up. The period of the 1981 strike was marked by generalized violence in Northern Ireland, with 64 deaths and many injuries.

From the Republican point of view the most significant aspect of the strikes, apart from the minor concessions, was the worldwide publicity and the galvanizing of general Nationalist opinion because of British government intransigence. They also led to the SINN FÉIN policy of the ARMALITE AND THE BALLOT BOX formulated at the end of 1981.

See also FAUL, MONSIGNOR DENIS; HUNGER STRIKE.

Headford Ambush (21 March 1921). The biggest engagement of the ANGLO-IRISH WAR in Co. Kerry took place at Headford railway junction (a junction of the Cork and Kenmare railway lines) between the Kerry No. 2 brigade FLYING COLUMN of the IRA and a party of some 30 British soldiers returning by train from Kenmare to Killarney. There were 30 men in the flying column under the command of Dan Allman and his second-in-command Tom McEllistrim. The fighting ended when a troop train arrived from Cork, the train the soldiers had been intending to take. There is disagreement as to the number of casualties: the British admitted 7 dead, the flying column claimed in excess of 20. There were also 3 civilian casualties; all of these were passengers who alighted from the train. A ballad by Joe Dinneen (1869–1928) (*see* DINNEEN'S DICTIONARY) celebrates the heroic deaths of Allman and another IRA man, Bailey.

Head-the-ball. A HIBERNO-ENGLISH phrase used to describe a person, usually a boy or youth, who is reckless or devil-may-care. It may also mean a boy who is chronically heedless or inattentive in school.

Health to wear. *See* WELL WEAR.

Healy, Cahir (1877–1970). Politician and journalist. He was born in Mountcharles, Co. Donegal, but moved to Enniskillen when he was 18. A member of SINN FÉIN, he was arrested in May 1922 and imprisoned on the ARGENTA and later in the notorious Larne workhouse. He wrote a series of articles on the condition of the internees which, when published in the *Sunday Express*, helped secure their release. Elected Westminster MP for Fermanagh–Tyrone in 1922, he could not take his seat and was one of the last of the Larne internees to be released, probably because of personal animus on the part of Dawson Bates, the minister of home affairs (*see* SPECIAL POWERS ACT). He was a Nationalist MP in what became the STORMONT parliament (1925–65), and his internment in Brixton for two years (1941–3) caused a storm of protest. He resigned from politics in 1965, an unrepentant Republican but personally popular with all sides in the House. Outside of politics he was a prolific contributor to newspapers, reviewing books and writing general articles. He died on 8 February 1970.

> John Redmond was driven from public life for even suggesting Partition for a period of five years. The new leaders agree to Partition forever.
>
> CAHIR HEALY: in the *Irish Independent* (5 December 1925) on the signing of the Boundaries Agreement

Healy, Tim (Timothy Michael Healy) (1855–1931). A politician whose career was marked by independence and shifting allegiances. He was born in Bantry, Co. Cork, on 17 May 1855 and left school at 13 to become a railway clerk in Newcastle-on-Tyne. By 1880 he had made such a name for himself in LAND LEAGUE agitation that he was elected unopposed for Wexford. (He was responsible for the 'Healy Clause' in the 1881 LAND ACT that protected tenants from rent increases on improvements – *see* THREE FS.) Thereafter he was rarely out of Parliament until he resigned his seat in 1918.

Healy was called to the Bar in 1884, and his intellectual prowess, aided by a prodigious memory and a scathing wit, made him one of the richest lawyers in Dublin. Although initially an admirer of PARNELL, coining the epithet the 'UNCROWNED KING', he became his greatest adversary at the time of the O'Shea divorce scandal in 1890 (*see* O'SHEA WHO MUST BE OBEYED), being anxious to retain the support of Gladstone (*see* GOM). Healy remained such a source of dissension that he was expelled from the Irish Parliamentary Party in 1902. He remained on terms with William Martin MURPHY and William O'BRIEN and with their help (and that of the Catholic Church) remained an MP.

Though unpopular with ANTI-TREATYITES and old Parnellites, Healy had sufficient support in the Free State administration to become the first governor-general (1922–8) (*see* UNCLE TIM'S CABIN). Apart from being the first to label Katharine as 'O'Shea who must be obeyed', he was the first to bring into the open the matter of Parnell's private life (*see* COMMITTEE ROOM 15). He died in Chapelizod, Co. Dublin, on 26 March 1931.

See also BANTRY BAND, THE; BEARA PENINSULA; FIGHTING PRIEST OF GWEEDORE, THE; TIM HEALY PASS.

Healy Pass. *See* TIM HEALY PASS.

Healy-Rae, Jackie. *See* PARISH-PUMP POLITICIAN.

Heaney, Seamus (b.1939). Poet. He was born in Mossbawn near Castledawson, Co. Derry, and educated at St Columb's College, Derry (where he was a classmate of Seamus DEANE), and Queen's University Belfast (QUB). He taught for some time in a Belfast school where the principal, Michael McLAVERTY, encouraged his writing. He later lectured in

English at St Joseph's College of Education and QUB (1966).

Heaney has published nearly a score of books of poetry and associated work, including a play, *The Cure at Troy*, a version of the *Philoctetes* of Sophocles, *Sweeney Astray*, a rendering of the medieval poem *Buile Suibhne* (*see* SUIBHNE GEILT), and *The Midnight Verdict*, a translation of parts of Merriman's 's CÚIRT AN MHEÁ-OÍCHE. As the award of the Nobel Prize for Literature (the culmination of many other awards) in 1995 proclaimed, he is one of the foremost poets writing in English, and Yeats's true successor as *the* Irish poet of the 20th century. The Nobel speech honoured him for 'works of lyrical beauty and ethical depth, which exalt everyday miracles and the living past'.

Heaney's early works, *Death of a Naturalist* (1966) and *Door into the Dark* (1969), reflect his precise observation of the country and the farm year he knew as a child. But already his artisans are becoming archetypes and the land that is worked is clearly the partitioned Ireland that had begun to show its sectarian sickness in the civil rights marches and the Protestant response, themes prominent in *Wintering Out* (1972) and especially NORTH (1975). Heaney, a Catholic Nationalist, has always resisted both the temptation and the pressure to 'speak' for any cause, apart from maintaining his rooted Irishness and preferring polite put-downs to thunder, as when in one of the pamphlets of FIELD DAY (of which he was a director) he refused the description of 'British poet'. Later work shows even deeper digging into Irishness but with worldwide referents, as *The Haw Lantern* (1987) indicates. *Station Island* (1984), about LOUGH DERG, calls to his table such significant figures as Joyce and William CARLETON, and *The Spirit Level* (1996), the first collection since his Nobel accolade, might be summed up by the title of one of its poems, 'Keeping Going'. *Opened Ground, Poems 1966–96*, was published in 1997.

Heaney moved to Wicklow in 1972 and now lives mainly in Dublin, when his responsibilities as Boylston professor of rhetoric at Harvard permit. His lectures as professor of poetry at Oxford (1989–94) appeared as *The Redress of Poetry* in 1995, and he has also published three volumes of excellent literary essays.

> I began as a poet when my roots were crossed with my reading. I think of the personal and Irish pieties as vowels, and the literary awareness nourished on English as consonants.
>
> SEAMUS HEANEY: attributed in *The Irish Times* (27 May 1971)

See also SEAMUS FAMOUS; SEAMUS HEANEY.

Heap, (up) in a. A useful HIBERNO-ENGLISH description of someone temporarily or permanently disorganized, confused or in a panic. *See also* TRÍNA CHÉILE.

Heart attack on a plate. *See* ULSTER FRY.

Heart of the rowl, the. The best part of something, a heart of gold. The origin of the phrase lies with Messrs Goodbody, who opened a tobacco factory in Tullamore in 1843, and whose first brand was called Irish Roll. The middle of the roll gave the juiciest tobacco, hence 'the heart of the rowl'. The phrase features in the anonymous Dublin ballad, 'Dicey Riley':

> Oh, poor old Dicey Riley she has taken to the sup,
> And poor old Dicey Riley she will never give it up.
> It's off each morning to the pop
> And then she's in for another little drop
> Oh, the heart of the rowl is Dicey Riley.

Heather Blazing, The. A highly praised novel (1993) by the Wexford-born writer Colm TÓIBÍN (b.1955), who took the phrase 'the heather blazing' from the third line of the ballad 'BOOLAVOGUE' ('A rebel hand set the heather blazing'). The context is the life of Lamon Redmond, a high court judge whose wife becomes terminally ill and who revisits some of his formative early experiences: the early loss of his mother, his father's lingering illness, the deaths of other family members and the crucial importance of history: 1798, 1916, the War of Independence and the foundation of Fianna Fáil, the party to which his father and he were both devoted. However neither humanity nor Republicanism is evident in his legal decisions: in a landmark judgement he finds for the defendants in a case brought by a pregnant teenage girl against a Catholic school that has expelled her; and as a member of the SPECIAL CRIMINAL COURT he is uncompromising towards those accused of IRA membership.

Heaven's reflex. The fulsome tribute to the lakes of KILLARNEY by Edmund FALCONER (1814–79) in his play *Inishfallen* (1862):

> Angels fold their wings and rest
> In that Eden of the west,
> Beauty's home, Killarney,
> Heaven's reflex, Killarney.

Heavy Gang. A phrase invented by the Irish media to describe a coterie among the GARDA SÍOCHÁNA alleged to have used violent and improper means (such as physical abuse and intimidation in the extraction of confessions) to achieve arrests and convictions among serious criminals and subversives, mainly in the 1980s. The *Irish Times* was the first to claim in early 1976 that a 'heavy gang' existed. *See also* SALLINS TRAIN ROBBERY.

Hedge schools. The paying schools conducted during the 18th and early 19th centuries in sheds, barns or hovels, or in the shelter of a hedge in summer weather. In the 18th century, Catholic schools were prohibited by the POPERY LAWS, and a schoolmaster might be punished by transportation. Schools had thus to be hidden away and run on an ad hoc basis. Pupils of all ages were in the same class, and their parents paid the master a small fee in coin or in kind. Despite the disadvantages under which they operated, hedge schools had varied curricula, including Latin and Greek, and some schoolmasters were reputed to be very learned. Although the hedge schools were by their nature a cottage industry, it is estimated that in the 1820s 300,000–400,000 children attended these schools, and that there were 9000 such schools in 1824. CATHOLIC EMAN-CIPATION and the introduction of the first NATIONAL SCHOOLS meant the end of hedge schools. William CARLETON was a hedge-school pupil and master, as were Brian MERRIMAN and Eoghan Rua Ó Súilleabháin (*see* EOGHAN AN BHÉIL BHINN).

He'd live in your eye and let the other one out in flats. *See* MIND MICE AT CROSSROADS.

He'd take the eye out of your head and come back for the lashes. *See* MIND MICE AT CROSSROADS.

Heel of the hunt, in the. A popular HIBERNO-ENGLISH phrase meaning at the tail-end of some event or episode.

Heel of the reel, in the. A rhyming version of HEEL OF THE HUNT, IN THE. A reel is one of the most popular Irish dances, played in common time, and some steps involve touching the heel to the ground. Brendan BEHAN, in 'The Confirmation Suit', says of his grandmother's pretend stockpot: 'In the heel of the reel it went out the same window as the sheep's head.'

Heeney, Patrick. *See* 'SOLDIER'S SONG, A'.

Heffo's Army. The nickname given to the devoted followers of Dublin's successful Gaelic football team in the 1970s, when they were managed by Kevin Heffernan. Under him, Dublin won the ALL-IRELAND championship in 1974, 1976 and 1977 and the National League in 1976 and 1978. 'Heffo' had also been a talented player, captaining Dublin to victory in the All-Ireland final of 1958.

> The Dubs are back, the Dubs are back,
> Let the railway end go barmy,
> For HILL 16 has never seen
> The likes of Heffo's Army.

Hegler Mail. The cry of the newsboys as they sold Dublin evening papers in Denis JOHNSTON's play *The OLD LADY SAYS NO!*. At the time when the play was written (1929) Dublin had two evening papers, the *Evening Herald* and the *Evening Mail*. In 1954 they were joined by the *Evening Press*. Now only the *Herald* survives.

Helen's Tower. A three-storey tower built by the 1st Marquess of Dufferin and Ava (1826–1902) on a hill in his estate in Clandeboye, Co. Down, in honour of his mother Helen Selina Sheridan, the granddaughter of Richard Brinsley SHERIDAN. It once held an extensive library, now dispersed, but the tower is still, in Tennyson's specially contributed words, a family memorial:

> Son's love built me, and I hold
> Mother's love engraved in gold …

(Browning and Kipling also contributed.) Helen was born in 1807, grew up in South Africa and lived at Hampton Court. She married Captain Blackwood, who succeeded to the barony of Dufferin in 1839. Though very widely travelled, she had little knowledge of Ireland before her marriage, but she wrote several famous Irish ballads including 'DUBLIN BAY', 'Terence's Farewell to Kathleen' and 'The Irish Emigrant':

> I'm bidding you a long farewell, my Mary, kind and true,
> But I'll not forget you darlin' in the land I'm going to.
> They say there's bread and work for all, and the sun shines always there,
> But I'll ne'er forget old Ireland, were it fifty times as fair.
> 'The Irish Emigrant' (1895)

She died in 1867.

Hellfire Club. A notorious group of 18th-century rakes who met in the Eagle Tavern in Cork Hill in Dublin, and perhaps occasionally at a hunting lodge on Montpelier Hill, at the foot of the Dublin Mountains. The latter belonged to Tom Conolly, a founder member, and its ruins have become known inaccurately by the club's title. Founded in 1735 by the first Earl of Rosse, the club anticipated by 20 years the more famous 'Monks of Medmenham' of Buckinghamshire in England, but it had the same, perhaps deserved, reputation for drink, debauchery, serial rape and diabolism. As reported by Justice Walsh in *Ireland Sixty Years Ago* (1847):

> … they set fire to the apartment in which they met, and endured the flames with incredible obstinacy, till they were forced out of the house; in derision, as they asserted, of the torments of a future state. On other occasions in mockery of religion, they administered to one another the sacred rites of the church in a manner too indecent for description …

Another rakish group, the Limerick Hell Fire Club, met at Askeaton Castle, where the master was Edward Croker of Ballinagarde; this club was singular in having one female member, Mrs Blennerhassett. The master had James Worsdale (*c*.1692–1767) paint the members, including the lady, and a poet, Daniel Hayes, left this tribute:

> But if in endless drinking you delight
> Croker will ply you till you sink outright,
> Croker for swilling Floods of Wine renowned
> Whose matchless Board with various plenty crowned
> Eternal scenes of Riot, Mirth and Noise
> With all the thunder of the Nenagh boys.
> We laugh, we roar, the ceaseless Bumpers fly
> Till the sun purples o'er the Morning sky
> And if unruly Passions chance to rise
> A willing Wench the Firgrove still supplies.

Hello money. The money paid by a supplier to a supermarket to 'encourage' the supermarket to stock the supplier's goods or display them prominently. The 1987 Groceries Order Act banned 'hello money' and other abusive practices, but some multiples devised ingenious ways to get around the ban.
See also GOODBYE MONEY.

Hell or Connacht, to. A phrase, supposedly coined by Oliver CROMWELL himself, to denote the deportation of old Irish and Norman-Irish landowners (all Catholics) to the west of the River Shannon after Cromwell ended Irish resistance in 1652. Their estates were allocated to Cromwell's soldiers and to those who had financed his campaign (mostly London merchants).
See also CROMWELLIAN SETTLEMENT.

Hennessy. The cognac distilled by the family of

Richard Hennessy (1720–1800). He was born in Ballymoy, Killavullen, Co. Cork. He settled in France in 1740 with relatives who had been among the WILD GEESE, joining DILLON'S REGIMENT and seeing action at Fontenoy in 1745 and in other engagements of the War of the Austrian Succession. Wounded, he retired from military service and married his cousin Ellen in 1763. Two years later he went to live in Cognac in western France, where he set up the distillery that still produces the Hennessy brand. The company sponsors the eponymous annual award for young Irish poets and fiction writers.

Henry, Paul (1876–1958). Painter. He was born in Belfast and educated at INST and at the Académie Julian in Paris. He was also a regular visitor to the studio of James McNeill Whistler (1834–1903), and came under the influence of the post-impressionists. Returning to London, he shared a studio in Kensington with his fellow-Belfastman, Robert LYND, who dedicated *The Sporting Life* (1922) to him 'because of the amusing days when we lived together in the same studio and owed money to the same milkman'. When Lynd and his wife Sylvia returned from their honeymoon on ACHILL in 1909 they enthused so much about the beauty and the quality of the light that Henry went there and stayed seven years. It is for his evocation of Connacht landscapes that he is known today, and a number of them were sold as posters to the LMS railway company and the Irish Tourist Board. He lost his sight in 1945 and died in Enniskerry, Co. Wicklow, on 28 August 1958.

Henry, Sam (1878–1952). Folksong collector. Details of his life are sketchy, but he worked as a pensions officer in north Ulster and was able because of the nature of his work to indulge his passion for collecting what he called the 'songs of the people'. They appeared regularly in the Coleraine newspaper, the *Northern Constitution* (1923–39), and Henry collected them into a manuscript, with music and lyrics (Henry was also a traditional fiddler) using his title

Songs of the People. He presented copies to libraries in Belfast, Dublin and Washington, but the songs remained unpublished until the musicologist and folksong expert Seán O'BOYLE was commissioned by Sam Hanna BELL, the radio producer, to edit and index them for use by BBC Northern Ireland. The entire Henry collection was published in 1990 by the University of Georgia Press.

Henry II (1133–89). King of England from 1154. He assented to the invasion of Leinster by STRONGBOW and the other Anglo-Norman adventurers to help Dermot MACMURROUGH recover his kingdom. Armed with the bull *LAUDABILITER* (1155), which gave papal sanction for the possible acquisition of the land of Ireland, he landed there in October 1171. By the time he returned to England the following April he had received submission from most of the Irish kings, established a putative authority over the Anglo-Norman colonists and reserved Dublin, Waterford and Wexford as his personal fief. In 1171 he designated his son Prince JOHN as Lord of Ireland.

Hen's kick. A phrase used in HIBERNO-ENGLISH as part of a negative expression: 'no further than a hen's kick' means not very far. *See also* ASS'S ROAR, WITHIN AN.

Herbert, Victor (1859–1924). Irish-American composer. He was born in Dublin on 1 February 1859, the grandson of Samuel LOVER. Educated in Germany, he was first cellist in the Stuttgart court orchestra before emigrating to America in 1886, where he became director of the 22nd New York regiment band. Though his ambition was to write serious classical music, his lasting fame lies in the 40 operettas he composed for the Broadway theatres, including *Babes in Toyland* (1903) and the perennial *Naughty Marietta* (1910), which featured the concert standards, 'I'm Falling in Love with Someone' and 'Ah, Sweet Mystery of Life' (the lyrics were by Rida Johnson Young, who also wrote 'Mother MACHREE'). He was one of the founders of ASCAP (American Society of Composers, Authors and Publishers), which protects musicians' copyrights. He died in New York on 24 May 1924.

Here goes in the name of God! The vow uttered by Theobald Mathew (*see* APOSTLE OF TEMPERANCE, THE) on 10 April 1838 as a formal renunciation of alcoholic liquor.

Herrema Kidnapping. On 3 October 1975 Republicans kidnapped a Dutch industrialist resident in Ireland, Tiede Herrema, and demanded the release of three Republican prisoners in Portlaoise prison. The kidnappers were tracked down to a small house in Monasterevin, Co. Kildare, and the gardai laid siege to the house. After 21 days Herrema was released unharmed. Herrema, who subsequently returned to live in Holland, showed great forbearance when speaking in public about his captors.

Hervey, Frederick Augustus (1730–1803). Church of Ireland bishop, peer, politician and noted eccentric. He was born in the family home at Ickworth, Suffolk, on 1 August 1730 and educated at Westminster and Corpus Christi, Cambridge. Taking orders at age 24, he had his ecclesiastical career significantly advanced when his brother, George, 2nd Earl of Bristol, briefly lord lieutenant of Ireland (1766–7), appointed him to the bishopric of Cloyne in 1767. From there it was but a leap to the much richer see of Derry in 1768 (*see* IN ONE LEAP). He increased the yearly income of his diocese by £13,000, not as commonly done by rack-renting, but by good accounting. His popularity with the people of Derry grew steadily. He contributed £1000 towards the building of the first bridge across the Foyle, and openly supported CATHOLIC EMANCIPATION (his Oath of Allegiance Act of 1774 was a significant step in the eventual dismantling of the POPERY LAWS).

Hervey combined eccentricity – making curates run races through boggy ground after gargantuan meals to see who would be appointed to a rich living – with aesthetic acquisi-

tiveness (he imported many treasures purchased in Europe). The great houses he built at DOWNHILL, Ballyscullion and Ickworth were filled with his acquisitions, but not much lived in. When his brother, the 3rd Earl of Bristol, died on 22 December 1779 he succeeded to the title, and his annual income was doubled to £40,000. He was also entitled to the unique title of Earl Bishop. His mildly scandalous private life, his liberalism – even his over-elaborate uniform as a colonel in the VOLUNTEERS – upset his chief rival Lord CHARLEMONT, who effectively frustrated a possible political career, describing Hervey as 'a bad father and a worse husband'. As it was, Hervey was temperamentally unfitted for the essential coarseness of public life, and he was happier on his many journeys on the Continent, giving his name to many Hotel Bristols. He died, not inappropriately, on the road to Rome on 3 July 1803.

Heth. An acceptable Ulster exclamation, cognate with 'Faith!':

> Heth, soree, an' it's gled I am to see ye, for I was feelin' a bit lonesome, and it being Hal'eve, too.
>
> ROBERT BRATTON: 'A Hal'eve Party', in *Round the Turf Fire* (1931)

Heuston Station. Dublin's main rail station for lines to the south and west, originally built as a terminus for the Great Southern and Western Railway and called Kingsbridge. The architect was Sancton Wood (1815–86) and the station was constructed 1846–7. The name was changed to Heuston on Easter Sunday 1966, in memory of Seán Heuston (1891–1916), one of the executed leaders of the EASTER RISING, but 'Kingsbridge' is still frequently heard. The station underwent large-scale refurbishment and modernization in the 1990s.

Hewitt, John (1907–87). Poet and museum director. He was born in October 1907 in Belfast, and educated at METHODY and Queen's University Belfast (QUB). He joined the staff of the Belfast Museum and Art Gallery in 1930, and like his friends E. Estyn EVANS,

John BOYD and Sam Hanna BELL, he was an active socialist. He was also an associate editor of LAGAN. In 1957 he left to become director of the Herbert Art Gallery and Museum in Coventry, believing that his radicalism was inhibiting his advancement in a Unionist-dominated institution. He returned to Belfast on retirement in 1972 and continued writing poetry and interesting himself in the arts. He was poet-in-residence at the New University of Ulster (1973–6) and at QUB (1976–9). His MA thesis was *Ulster Poets (1800–70)*, and among several anthologies edited by him are *The Poems of William Allingham* (1967) and *Rhyming Weavers* (1974). Hewitt's own work has the recurring theme of his forebears ('Once Alien Here') and the natives who were displaced to make room for them. In 1970 he and John MONTAGUE collaborated in the significantly named *The Planter and the Gael*. His volume of *Collected Poems* (1991), edited by Frank Ormsby, contains over 700 items. He wrote monographs on various Ulster artists and was co-editor with Bell and Nesca Robb (1905–76) of *The Arts in Ulster* (1951). He died in Belfast on 27 June 1987, and is honoured in the John Hewitt International Summer School held each year at Garron Tower on the Antrim Coast.

> Once alien here my fathers built their house,
> claimed, drained, and gave the land the shapes
>   of use
>
> …
>
> The sullen Irish limping to the hills
> bore with them the enchantments and the spells
> that in the clans' free days hung gay and rich
> on every twig of every thorny hedge…
>   'Once Alien Here', in *No Rebel Word* (1948)

Hi. A meaningless word that tends to appear frequently in Derry conversations with strangers, usually as the last word in a sentence: 'What time is it, hi?'

Hibernia. The Latin name for Ireland, one part of western Europe that the Romans never conquered. The name derives from the Greek *Iernoi* (later *Ierne*), a version of the Celtic *Érainn* (as in ÉIRE), with perhaps an admixture of Latin *hibernus* 'wintry'. Natives of Ireland are still sometimes poetically referred to as Hibernians, and the term appears in the name of various organizations, such as Edinburgh's Hibernian Football Club ('Hibs'), founded by an Irishman.

Hibernian Archipelago. *See* BRITISH ISLES.

Hibernici ipsis Hiberniores (Latin, 'more Irish than the Irish'). The epigrammatic description of the descendants of the Anglo-Norman invaders by Archdeacon John Lynch in 1662. It appears in *Cambrensis Aversus* (Latin, 'against the Welshman'), his answer to the propagandist writing of GIRALDUS CAMBRENSIS (Gerald of Wales), who had attempted to defend the 12th-century invasion.

Hibernicus. The pen name of James Arbuckle, the journalist and one-time friend of Jonathan Swift (*see* DEAN, THE). He was born (perhaps in Co. Down) in 1700, the son of a Presbyterian minister, and qualified as a physician in Glasgow, though his liberal views brought him into frequent dispute with the Calvinistic authorities. He worked as a teacher in Dublin and edited the *Dublin Weekly Journal*. In 1719 he published a mock-heroic poem on tobacco called *Snuff*, and two years later *Glotta*, a poem about the River Clyde, including an early description of the game of golf. His parody 'A Panegyric on the Rev D—n S——t' was for many years taken to be by Swift himself. His essay on Swift, *Momus Mistaken* (1735), caused him to fall out of favour with the Dean's circle. His date of death was probably 1742.

> When Jonathan was great at court,
> The ruined party made his sport,
> Despised the beast with many heads
> And damned the mob which now he leads
>
> …
>
> For Gulliver divinely shows,
> That humankind are all YAHOOS.
> Both envy then and malice must
> Allow your hatred strictly just.
>   'A Panegyric on the Rev D—n S——t' (1730)

Hiberno-English. The accepted term for English as it is spoken and sometimes written in Ireland, as distinct from standard or received English. It is also called Anglo-Irish or Irish English. It is partly the result of layers of colonization by peoples from different regions of England (and Scotland in the case of Ulster), who brought with them their own dialect, retaining words and usages that standard English has lost. But mainly it is the consequence of the influence of the Irish language – the vernacular of the majority of the Irish population until the late 18th–early 19th century – on the structure and vocabulary of English as it is spoken in Ireland.

Hiberno-English is ubiquitous in Irish speech, but the further one moves west and the nearer one comes both to the living GAELTACHT and to the areas in which Irish was spoken into the 20th century, the stronger its influence becomes. Many people in rural areas still use Irish vocabulary unconsciously for everyday items, and their speech is studded with constructions such as 'I am after doing' (*see* AFTER DOING SOMETHING, TO BE).

Hiberno-English has also supplied a literary language, although some playwrights and novelists – such as SHERIDAN, FARQUHAR and BOUCICAULT, who had 'Oirish' characters speak with strong BROGUES – may be considered as having created STAGE-IRISH characters and situations, a danger avoided in the work of J.M. SYNGE.

See also KILTARTAN.

Hidden Ireland, The. An influential work of historical criticism (1924) by writer and scholar Daniel CORKERY, which from a viewpoint unequivocally Nationalistic evokes the lives and society of many of the great Irish poets of the 18th century, including Aogán Ó RATHAILE and Eoghan Rua Ó Súilleabháin (*see* EOGHAN AN BHÉIL BHINN), and the remaining COURTS OF POETRY. Corkery's aim was to chart how 'the soul of the Gael' was revealed in the poetry of those who later came to be called the 'dispossessed':

The Ascendancy's creed is, and always has been, that the natives are a lesser breed and that anything that is theirs (except their land and their gold) is of little value.

Higgins, Aidan (b. 1927). Novelist and short-story writer. He was born in Celbridge, Co. Kildare, and educated at Clongowes. He had a number of temporary jobs, including touring with a marionette company in Europe and Africa. His collection *Felo de Se* (1960) contains, along with stories set in Europe, the novella 'Killachter Meadow', which was later developed into the novel *LANGRISHE, GO DOWN* (1966). Other novels include *Balcony of Europe* (1972), set in Andalusia, *Scenes from a Receding Past* (1977), which shows if nothing else the unreliability of memory, *Bornholm Night Ferry* (1983), a tale of a love affair between an Irish writer and a Danish poet told in letters, and *Lions of the Grünewald* (1995) with the by now common Higgins relationship of Irish man and European woman. He has also published three volumes of autobiography, *Donkey's Years* (1996), *Dog Days* (1998) and *The Whole Hog* (2001).

Higgins, Alex[ander Gordon] (b.1949). Professional snooker player known as 'Hurricane' Higgins because of the speed of his playing. He was born in Belfast on 18 March 1949 and turned professional in 1971 after a brilliant career as an amateur. In 1972 he became the youngest world champion at 23, beating John Spencer in the final in Birmingham. The sense of drama and whiff of danger that he brought to all his performances made him the game's greatest attraction, but erratic play and a somewhat rackety lifestyle meant that he did not regain the title until 1982, when he defeated Ray Reardon. He was part of the Ireland team that won the world cup 1985–7, and was Irish national champion four times (1972, 1978, 1980 and 1983). In recent years a drink problem and surgery for cancer have effectively finished his career. His biographer Bill Borrows asked him in an interview in August 2001 if he had enjoyed his life. Higgins's reply was:

'I haven't really had much to do with my life. All I've done is take part in it.'

Higgins, Francis. *See* SHAM SQUIRE, THE.

High, dry nor holy. A HIBERNO-ENGLISH negative intensifier, as in 'I couldn't find it, high, dry nor holy.'

High ball. A HIBERNO-ENGLISH term borrowed from Gaelic football – a high ball is difficult to field – and used figuratively in the context of conversation to mean a challenging remark or hard-to-handle question.

High Church, Low Steeple. Jonathan Swift's (*see* DEAN, THE) description of NEWRY, Co. Down:

> High church, low steeple,
> Dirty streets, proud people.

High king (Irish *ard rí*). The Ireland of the pre-Norman period was divided into *tuatha* (pronounced 'too acha'), territories of indeterminate size but ruled by a king (*rí*) and having a sufficiency of nobles and churchmen to give it a ruling class. Though many *tuatha* were in a constant state of war, each in a quixotic way gave a kind of allegiance to an overking (*ard rí*), often associated with the great UÍ NÉILL dynasty. A further sign of authentic royalty was a claim to rule the quasi-religious site of TARA, in Co. Meath. It is not clear just how much authority the high king had over local rulers, but the idea of a country united under an agreed leader, as in England and Scotland at the time, was unknown. Only BRIAN BORU achieved a working hegemony, but the concept of *Imperator Scottorum* ('emperor of the Irish', a title he used) died with him.
See also KINGSHIP; LAST HIGH KING, THE.

Hill, Noel. *See* CONCERTINA.

Hill 16. A standing terrace at the railway end of CROKE PARK, usually known simply as 'the Hill'. It has been home to generations of Dublin Gaelic football supporters. It is so called because it was constructed from the rubble of Sackville Street (now O'CONNELL STREET) after the destruction caused by the 1916 EASTER RISING.

Hillery, Patrick (b.1923). Politician; president of the Republic (1976–90). He was born on 2 May 1923 in Miltown Malbay, Co. Clare, and educated at University College Dublin, where he qualified as a medical doctor. Elected FIANNA FÁIL TD for Clare in 1951, he held the seat until 1973, serving in successive administrations as minister for education (1959–65), labour (1966–9) and foreign affairs (1969–73). He was involved in the negotiations leading to Ireland's entry into the COMMON MARKET in 1973 and served as Ireland's first European commissioner (1973–6), holding the social affairs portfolio. Hillery replaced Cearbhall Ó Dálaigh (*see* THUNDERING DISGRACE, A) as president of Ireland in 1976; he was an agreed all-party candidate, appointed without an election. He served a second seven-year term, again unopposed, from 1983 to 1990, and thereafter retired entirely from public life. A close associate of Jack LYNCH, Hillery is remembered for his robust support of his leader in the aftermath of the ARMS CRISIS.

Hill of Tara. *See* TARA.

Hillsborough Agreement. Another name for the ANGLO-IRISH AGREEMENT of 1985, signed at Hillsborough Castle, Co. Down.

Hillsborough Declaration. The joint statement in April 1999 by Tony Blair and Bertie Ahern, the respective British and Irish prime ministers, at Hillsborough Castle, Co. Down, formerly the seat of governors of Northern Ireland (1925–73) and now the residence of the secretary of state. It proposed a plan to break the impasse in the peace process by removing any connotations of surrender in the looked-for DECOMMISSIONING of weapons by the IRA. The latter rejected the plan. The 1985 ANGLO-IRISH AGREEMENT was signed at Hillsborough.

Hind, Gertrude. *See* SHANE, ELIZABETH.

Hiring fairs. A source of contract farm labour, hiring fairs were held in about 80 towns, mostly in Ulster. The largest fairs were held in Strabane, Omagh, Letterkenny and Derry (called there 'the rabbles'). They occurred twice a year, in May and November, on three consecutive Wednesdays. The first Wednesday was 'release' day when the hirelings of the previous semester could spend a week at home with their families (usually in Donegal). The second Wednesday was the hiring fair proper when new servants would be hired and new masters found. The third rabble was intended as a catch-up for farmers and clients who had not been suited the week before. The terms included basic accommodation, and, if the 'boy' or 'girl' was lucky, the same food as the farmer's family. First-time hirelings from west Donegal and Inishowen were advised by veterans to bind themselves to Presbyterian masters in order to avoid Sunday work. The practice had been largely discontinued by the mid-1930s, though the last recorded fair was held in Milford, Co. Donegal, in 1945.

> Strange farmers were looking us over. Soon a prosperous-looking gentleman approached and, addressing my father, inquired, 'What are ye esking for the wee boy?'
>
> 'Six pounds,' my father replied.
>
> 'He's a bit wee. How old is he? Can he milk? Is he any good with horses?' the man wanted to know.
>
> At last a bargain was struck for five pounds ten shillings. The stranger took my bundle, gave me a shilling and told me to meet him back on the Diamond at four o'clock sharp.
>
> P.J. DEVLIN (1909–86): *That Was the Way of It* (2001)

Hirple. An Ulster verb meaning 'limp', as in 'Since I got the arthuritis it's as much as I can do to hirple as far as the door.'

His own fireside. The brave reply made by the dramatist Richard Brinsley SHERIDAN in 1809, as he watched Drury Lane Theatre, of which he was the manager, burn to the ground. As he sat drinking in the street near the conflagration someone objected to his apparent indifference, to which he replied:

A man may surely be allowed to take a glass of wine by his own fireside.

Hobson, Bulmer (1883–1969). Nationalist politician and revolutionary. Hobson was a Quaker, born in Holywood, Co. Down, and educated at Friends School, Lisburn. He became a printer, but resigned to take part in revolutionary politics, founding the DUNGANNON CLUBS in 1905 and becoming vice-president of SINN FÉIN in 1907; he introduced the movement to the USA on the invitation of John DEVOY. He was a founder member of the IRISH VOLUNTEERS in 1913 and helped organize the HOWTH GUN-RUNNING, but so disapproved of the EASTER RISING that he had forcibly to be restrained by his own men until the GPO was occupied. After the setting-up of the new state he worked in the office of the revenue commissioners in Dublin Castle, retiring in 1948. He had been the main founder of the ULT (*see* DAMN YEATS, WE'LL WRITE OUR OWN PLAYS!) and continued his interest in drama by involving himself in the GATE THEATRE. His witty autobiography, *Ireland Yesterday and Tomorrow*, was written a year before his death in August 1969.

Hogan Stand, the. *See* CROKE PARK.

Hoggen Green. An area of central Dublin that began in the Viking era as an open area of pasturage in the vicinity of today's Dame Street and Exchequer Street. It contained the THING-MOTE or assembly place, and continued in existence for about 800 years (*c.*900–*c.*1700). Hoggen Green was also used as a recreation area, a burial ground and a dumping ground for refuse. Building on the site began early in the 17th century, and by 1728 most of the area had been built upon, with a street pattern very similar to that which exists in Dublin today. The derivation of the word 'hoggen' is unclear, but it is thought to relate to the burial mounds that were to be seen on the green.
See also MACTHORKIL, ASKULV.

Hold your whist. *See* WHIST.

Holland, John Philip (1841–1914). Inventor

of the submarine. He was born in Liscannor, Co. Clare, on 24 February 1841 and educated at Limerick's Christian Brothers school. Prevented by poor sight from a maritime career, he became a Christian Brother in 1858 and taught at various schools in Leinster and Munster. Released from his vows in 1872, he went to America and resumed his teaching career in New Jersey. In 1875 he built a small submarine, which was rejected as impractical by the US navy, but he continued his researches, financed by John DEVOY, who saw the craft as a means of attacking British shipping. The *Fenian Ram* was launched in 1881 and proved her underseaworthiness in the Hudson River. In 1898 the *Holland VI* so impressed the US navy at its trial under the Potomac that they accepted it for the fleet. So, ironically, did the British navy, ordering several of Holland's vessels. Holland was more successful as an inventor than as an entrepreneur, and though Russia, Japan and Germany developed his ideas he made little money. His design incorporated most of the features of the modern non-nuclear craft, with electric motors for submerged movement, retractable periscope, torpedo tubes and a rapid diving system. At the time of Holland's death on 12 August 1914 his invention was about to prove its deadliness as a weapon of modern warfare.

Holy Cross Abbey. A ruined abbey situated about 6 km (4 miles) from Thurles, Co. Tipperary, on the River Suir. It was founded by Donal Mór O'Brien *c*.1169 and occupied by a Cistercian community shortly afterwards. It takes its name from a relic of the true cross, which was displayed in a pillared shrine in the nave, making the church a popular place of pilgrimage. The church is cruciform and has many interesting features, including carvings, fine Gothic windows and mural paintings. It was restored 1970–5 and opened to the public. The abbey was suppressed in 1536 during the DISSOLUTION OF THE MONASTERIES; the abbot surrendered on condition that he would enjoy the revenues for his lifetime. Eventually Eliza-

beth I conferred the land and buildings on Thomas, Earl of Ormond.

Holy Ghost Fathers (Latin *Congregatio Sancti Spiritus*, abbreviated to CSSp). An order founded in Paris in 1703. Its connection with Ireland dates from 1859, when it was seeking English-speaking members for some of its African missions. The Archbishop of Dublin permitted the order to recruit in Ireland on condition that it provide education for young Catholic boys, Catholic schools still being in short supply 30 years after CATHOLIC EMANCIPATION. Blackrock College was the first Irish school of the Holy Ghost Fathers, and was known for many years as the 'French College' because of the provenance of its founders. Bishop Shanahan of Tipperary, a member of the society who ministered in Nigeria, is a candidate for beatification.

Holy Ground. The euphemistic and grossly inaccurate name for a low alehouse-cum-brothel that the Irish claim was situated in Cobh docks in Co. Cork. (The same claim has been made for Swansea and for the East River, Manhattan.) It became the subject of a raucous sea shanty, each verse ending with the refrain:

You're the girl I do adore
And still I live in hopes to see
The Holy Ground once more.

This was followed by the shout 'Fine girl you are!', *fortissimo* after the last verse.

Holy Island. *See* LINDISFARNE.

Holy wells. A feature of popular religion in Ireland, not always approved of by the institutional Catholic Church. It is estimated that there are about 3000 ancient holy wells dedicated to Our Lady (such as Lady's Well on Lady's Island in Co. Wexford) or local saints. In many cases the water, which can also be brought home in a bottle, is believed to provide cures for particular ailments, for instance the eyes, the ears or the limbs.

While many of these wells have fallen into disuse or have become inaccessible, others are still popular on the annual PATTERN or patron day of the saint. Many hundreds of people may attend the pattern of a popular or well-regarded saint, such as that of St Gobnait in Ballyvourney in west Cork, performing a certain ritual of clockwise 'rounds' while simultaneously reciting Catholic prayers by rote. Where trees – usually whitethorn, hazel or ash – overhang or adjoin a holy well, they may also be considered to have supernatural properties (and a taboo against damaging them remains) and they may be festooned with strips of flannel or rags as tokens. Stones in the vicinity of the well may also be regarded as sacred.

Many wells are of considerable antiquity: where they are named after local saints and have accompanying legends, many recounting the victory of Christianity over paganism, they date from the early Christian to the early medieval period. It is also likely that these were numinous places in pre-Christian times, and that the ritual has derived from an overlay of Christianity on a pagan ritual: the legendary physician DIAN CECHT used water from a holy well to treat the wounded at the Battle of MAGH TUIREADH (Moytura). Placenames containing the word *tobar* (pronounced 'tub-are'), such as Tobar na Mult ('well of the wethers') in the parish of Ardfert in north Co. Kerry, testify to the existence of holy wells.

> In the provinces of Munster and Connaught there were several fountains and wells, which in the early stages of Christianity were dedicated to some favourite saint, whose patronage was supposed to give such sanctity to the waters that the invalids who were immersed in them lost their maladies.
>
> ANON.: *Tour in Ireland* (1808)

See also CITY, THE; WELLS.

Home Rule. The aspiration to self-government that characterized constitutional Nationalists from 1870 to 1918. The term, which was advantageously vague, became current in 1873, when the Home Rule League superseded the Home Government Association founded by

Isaac BUTT in 1870. Home Rule bills were put before parliament in 1886, 1893 and 1912. They all offered local control of internal affairs, while foreign affairs, armed forces, currency and majority taxation were to remain with the Westminster Parliament; all these bills were met with absolute opposition by the Protestants of Ulster. The first two bills were defeated, but by 1912 the Lords' power of veto had been virtually removed and the Irish Parliamentary Party (see IRISH PARTY) held the balance in the Commons. The third bill was passed in 1914, and serious disturbance in Ulster was averted by the First World War and the agreement to postpone the bill's implementation until the end of hostilities. By 1918, however, the EASTER RISING and the rise of SINN FÉIN had changed Irish politics utterly. Ironically the only part of Ireland to be given Home Rule (*see* PARTITION) was the North that had done so much to oppose it. There is an apocryphal story of Gladstone (*see* GOM), then in his 80s, being knocked down by a mad cow near his home in North Wales; the cow was shot, but its head mounted in a local pub, the sign reading: 'This cow died in the campaign against Home Rule in Ireland.'

See also CARSON'S ARMY; CURRAGH INCIDENT; LARNE GUN-RUNNING; ORANGE CARD; ULSTER COVENANT; ULSTER WILL FIGHT; UVF.

Home Rule Party. *See* IRISH PARTY.

Homosexuality. Northern Ireland was the last part of the UK where homosexual acts in private remained a criminal offence, the Westminster Parliament only introducing reform for the province in 1982, 15 years after the rest of the UK. Homosexual acts only became legal in the Republic in 1993.

See also SAVE ULSTER FROM SODOMY.

Hone, Evie (1894–1955). Artist. She was born in Dublin on 22 April 1894. Although a semi-invalid after an attack of polio in her childhood, she was determined to be an artist, and studied in Paris with Mainie JELLETT between 1915 and 1921. In 1924 they held a joint exhibition of their abstract paintings in Dublin, but this met with a very cool reception. Hone had a strong religious sense, which led her to specialize in stained-glass work, and her first commission was for the Church of Ireland church in Dundrum, Dublin. Her talent was quickly recognized and she received commissions for religious work for both Catholic and Protestant churches as well as for secular institutions: one of her best-known works, entitled *My Four Green Fields*, was created for the CIÉ offices in O'Connell Street, Dublin, and is now in Government Buildings. Hone suffered from ill-health throughout her life but her output was considerable – she also painted in water colours and oils. She died in Dublin on 13 March 1955, more than ten years after the death of her friend Mainie Jellett.

Honest Jack. *See* LYNCH, JACK.

Honor Bright Case. Honor Bright was the working name of a 25-year-old prostitute named Elizabeth O'Neill, who was found murdered in the Dublin Mountains on the morning of 9 June 1925. The murder became a cause célèbre because two friends, Dr Patrick Purcell and Garda Superintendent Leopold Dillon, who had used the services of Honor Bright and her friend Bridie earlier in the morning, were charged with Honor's murder. They were acquitted by the jury.

Honourable, the Irish Society, the. The rather grand antique title (still in use) of the company set up originally in 1609 as 'The Society of the Governor and Assistants, London, of the New Plantation in Ulster, within the Realm of Ireland'. King James I intimated regally that the members of the London companies, descendants of the medieval guilds and immemorially jealous of their political and financial independence, should undertake the plantation of the county of Coleraine, which should become, with additions, a new county of Londonderry. Its chief town, which they should build, would have the same name. The new county was established in 1613 and towards the end of the century the company adopted

the name by which it is still known. The city of Londonderry, as they called it, was laid out in neat geometric lines, and on the highest ground they erected the first purpose-built Protestant cathedral in THESE ISLANDS. The original commemorative stone may still be seen in the porch, and acknowledges the society's contribution:

> If stones could speake
> Then Londons prayse
> Should sounde who
> Built this church and
> Cittie from the grounde.

The society still owns property in Derry and Coleraine, and is active in philanthropic and charitable projects. Any hope of a quick return for their large cash outlay was soon dashed, and one of the legacies of the original scheme is the continuing vexation caused by the conundrum of the city's name (*see* STROKE CITY).

Hooker. *See* GALWAY HOOKER.

Hook Head. A low-lying promontory in Co. Wexford, at the extreme south of Waterford Harbour. It is the location of Europe's oldest lighthouse still in use. The original tower was built at the end of the 12th century by the Norman Hervey de Montmorency on the site of an early Christian monastery where monks had kept a flame alight to warn shipping of the danger of reefs. In 1996 the lighthouse was automated. It now also serves as a visitors' centre.

Hooley. A word of uncertain derivation meaning a 'party' or 'celebration', usually involving CEOL AGUS CRAIC. It is usually associated with Irish people.

Hooligan. A loud, rough and even criminal type (usually young). The type is said to have been based on a gang of roughs led by one Hooley, hence 'Hooley's gang'. A more likely source was the performance of a late 19th-century Irish family called Houlihan who settled in Southwark.

> The original Hooligans were a spirited Irish
> family of that name whose proceedings enlivened

the drab monotony of life in Southwark towards the end of the 19th century.

ERNEST WEEKLEY (1865–1954): *The Romance of Words* (1922)

A further alternative may be the burlesque theatre in the eastern USA, in which a family by the name of Hooligan staged rowdy comic sketches.

Hoor in the Sewer. *See* FLOOZIE IN THE JACUZZI.

Hope, Jemmy (1764–1846). United Irishman. He was born in Templepatrick, Co. Antrim, on 25 August 1764 and became a linen-weaver. Though he left school when he was 10 he continued his education at night classes. Hope joined the UNITED IRISHMEN in 1795, and was sent to Dublin the following year to recruit members. While there he worked at his trade in the LIBERTIES, becoming friendly with Thomas Russell (*see* MAN FROM GOD KNOWS WHERE, THE) and Thomas Emmet (1764–1827), the elder brother of Robert. Returning north in 1798 he led the 'Spartan band' at the Battle of ANTRIM and fled to Dublin after the defeat. His family joined him there, and he continued to live in the city in spite of constant fear of arrest. After the amnesty of 1806 he returned to Belfast, and was still alive in 1846 when he was able to give an insider's information about the REBELLION OF 1798 to R.R. MADDEN.

Hopkins, Gerard Manley (1844–89). Poet and teacher. He was born in Stratford, Essex, and coming under the influence at Oxford of John Henry Newman (1801–90), 'poped' like him in 1866, and was ordained as a Jesuit in 1877. He burned all his poems before the final profession, but sent copies to his friend and fellow poet Robert Bridges (1844–1930). He was sent to Dublin in 1884 as professor of classics in the Catholic University. He was not happy in Ireland, feeling isolated, wracked by scruples and unwilling to give any hint about examination questions to his students. He died of typhoid fever and is buried in GLASNEVIN CEMETERY.

Tomorrow I shall have been three years in Ireland, three hard wearying years ... In those I have done God's will (in the main) and many many examination papers.

Letter to Robert Bridges, 1887

See also YES AND NO.

Hop the ball, to. A HIBERNO-ENGLISH phrase meaning to introduce a topic into a conversation in such a way, perhaps provocatively, as to elicit a response from the other party or ascertain his or her views.

Horan, Monsignor James. *See* KNOCK[1]; KNOCK INTERNATIONAL AIRPORT; KNOCK MARRIAGE INTRODUCTIONS BUREAU.

Horniman, Annie. *See* MISS HORNIMAN.

Hornpipe. A dance, not exclusively Irish, with maritime origins and in common (4/4) time. It is believed to have arrived in Ireland from Britain in the late 18th century. Traditional music accompanies the dance. It was taught by DANCING MASTERS as a STEP DANCE and it survives in this form; a hornpipe is also part of some set dances, often as the final movement. The hornpipe is a measured, emphatic dance and generally noisy, as it is danced with a hard-soled shoe – a buckled patent shoe in the case of modern step dancing.

Horrid. A HIBERNO-ENGLISH intensifier, usually negative or neutral, used predominantly in Co. Cavan, as in 'I was horrid busy all last week' or 'That house is horrid big.'

Horseman. The old five-shilling piece or crown, so called from the representation on the reverse side of a mounted St George battling with the dragon.

Horslips. A 'Celtic rock' group that performed and recorded 1970–9, having grown out of the previous decade's interest in traditional music and folk. The line-up included Eamonn Carr, Barry Devlin and Declan Sinnott, and the name was quarried out of 'Horsemen of the Apocalypse'. Their album *Happy to Meet Sorry to Part* (1973) was a major popular success, and, despite the disapproval of *echt*-traditionalists, their role was significant in popularizing traditional Irish music among a young audience.

Hospitality. The first duty of all individuals, rich or poor, in Celtic and early Christian Ireland, and a custom that has survived until today in rural Ireland, is to provide hospitality. Monasteries were open to all: travellers, the sick and the poor. To be called generous and lavish – *fial flaithiúil* (*see* FIAL; FLAITHIÚIL) – was the highest praise. In many rural houses, rich or humble, a bed was kept for travellers – the so-called *leaba na mbocht*, the bed of the poor – or a mattress made from straw in the kitchen if no other bed was available. Travellers were valued for the gossip they brought to a world without outside communication.
See also FÁILTE; *IRELAND OF THE WELCOMES.*

Houghers. An early example (1710s) of the kind of localized Irish agrarian SECRET SOCI-ETY that until the mid-1840s responded with violence to changes in agricultural practice. Typically secret, its threats uttered in the name of a mythical captain, it protested against the extension in Connacht of stock-rearing in what had been tilled land. The name came from the practice of hamstringing the sheep and cattle that they did not kill ('hough' being another word for hamstring).
See also CAPTAIN MOONLIGHT.

Hoult. A HIBERNO-ENGLISH corruption of 'hold', meaning a 'hug', an 'embrace' or a 'predica-ment'. 'He had her in a tight hoult.' A 'hard hoult' is a tight spot.

House dances. House dances were very popu-lar in rural Ireland until the 1930s and – un-officially at least – even into the 1950s, and were held on many occasions – a wedding, har-vest time, STATIONS or an AMERICAN WAKE. Unless for a particular occasion, such as an American wake, house dances were not nor-mally held on summer evenings; people danced on platforms at the crossroads instead (*see* CROSSROAD DANCES). Local musicians, usually fiddlers or pipers, would play or DYDDLE (lilt) for sets and other dances.

The clergy condemned house dances, as well as crossroads dances (and all dances in reality), as provokers of sins of the flesh because of the opportunities they offered for young people to consort with the opposite sex. Especially after the foundation of the state, when the clergy were allowed to assume greater and greater temporal and political power, they waged war against them, both in the local community and on a national level. There are many com-ical stories of parish priests lying in wait for courting couples or arriving at a house to scatter the dancers, for instance in the stories of Éamon KELLY. On 23 December 1933, in time for the frivolity of the Christmas season, the bishops published a statement about dances in the *Irish Catholic*, in which they alleged:

> During the intervals [between dances] the devil is busy; yes, very busy, as sad experience proves, and on the way home in the small hours of the morning, he is busier still.

In 1935, under the terms of the Public Dance Halls Act, the government of Éamon DE VALERA bowed to clerical pressure and out-lawed house dances, maintaining also that they were being used to collect funds for the IRA. The act decreed that running a dance required a licence, and the district justice had to approve the applicant. The loss of house dances meant the rise of parish dance halls, often run and supervised by the clergy; it also involved a change in the kind of traditional music played locally, and the rise (with the approval of the GAELIC LEAGUE) of the CÉILÍ BAND and other types of band to cater for larger public spaces.

Housefly Campaign, the. A campaign to tackle the health problem of houseflies which, because of poor sanitation, was acute in Dublin in the summer months. In 1911 the chief medical officer for the city, Sir Charles Cameron (1830–1921), had the corporation offer three pence for every bag of dead flies brought to the cleansing depot at Marrowbone Lane. The cor-poration supplied the bags, each of which – it was estimated – would hold at least 6000 flies. Unsurprisingly, the scheme was not a success, even among schoolboys. A scientist and journalist, Cameron also condemned thousands of tons of sub-standard food as unfit for human consumption, and the corporation had to withdraw the licence for the Clontarf oyster beds when he showed that they were responsible for the outbreak of enteric fever in the city. Cam-eron also designed an innovative ambulance for fever patients, and was responsible for the building by Dublin Corporation of three four-storeyed apartment blocks in Barrack Street (near the Royal Barracks, now COLLINS BARRACKS) in 1887, the first public housing in Dublin. He was associated with the development of BELLEEK china, having identified porcelain clay on the estate of a friend near Lough Erne. He received a knighthood in 1885 and was made an honorary freeman of Dublin in 1911.

Howanever. A HIBERNO-ENGLISH version of 'however', used as an indication of a pause or shortening of a narrative. It has something of the force of 'To make a long story short'.

How are ye! An extreme expression of disbelief as in, 'Scruples, how are ye! Thon fella wouldn't know a scruple if it hit him up the mouth!'

Howling of Irish wolves. The tongue-in-cheek dismissal by Rosalind in Shakespeare's *As You Like It* (1599) (V, ii) to halt the lovers' incantations that she herself had contrived:

> Pray you no more of this, 'tis like the howling of Irish wolves against the moon.

The phrase may originate from a belief among the English that the Irish were turned into wolves once a year. Its more likely source was the fact that though at the time of the writing of the play wolves had been extinct in England for 100 years, they did not disappear from Ireland until the 1760s.

Howth Gun-Running (26 July 1914). An incident in which the IRISH VOLUNTEERS successfully landed some 1500 German rifles at Howth from Erskine Childers's yacht *ASGARD*, in response to Edward Carson's open arming of

Ulster Unionists in April of the same year (*see* LARNE GUN-RUNNING). Soldiers sent to seize the arms only got hold of a few, and on their return to barracks were involved in an ugly incident in BACHELOR'S WALK, Dublin.

How to Play Gaelic Football. The first-ever GAA coaching manual (1914), written by Dick Fitzgerald (1884–1930), after whom Killarney's Fitzgerald Stadium (1936) is named. Fitzgerald, who played for Killarney's Dr Croke's Club, won five ALL-IRELAND medals for Kerry and was a member of the IRISH VOLUNTEERS, interned in Frongoch after the EASTER RISING of 1916. He died after a fall at Killarney courthouse two days before the Kerry–Monaghan All-Ireland final of September 1930.

'Hucklebuck, The'. A dance popularized by Brendan Bowyer and the Royal Showband which became a craze among dancegoers in the mid-1960s, and is still to be heard at the occasional wedding:

> You do the Hucklebuck, you do the Hucklebuck,
> If you don't know how to do it then you're out of
>   luck.
> Shove your baby in, twist her all around,
> Then you start a-shaking and a-moving all
>   around.
> Wriggle like a snake, waddle like a duck,
> That's what you do when you do the Hucklebuck.

Hughes, John Joseph. *See* FIRST NEW YORK ARCHBISHOP, THE.

Huguenots. The French Calvinists of the 16th and 17th centuries, who, though granted toleration under the Edict of Nantes (1598), were subject to increasing persecution, culminating in the revocation of the Edict in 1685. In the general flight from France thereafter an estimated 10,000 refugees came to Ireland, setting up 21 communities, the largest being in Portarlington in modern Laois, giving the town a distinct Gallic air. Other Huguenots played a part in the Ulster linen trade, and the la Touche family were prominent in Dublin's financial and political life. A small community existed in Dublin in the 17th century and was catered for religiously with a small chapel in St Patrick's Cathedral, and a Huguenot cemetery was opened in Merrion Row, Dublin, in 1693.

Humanity Dick. The nickname of Richard Martin (1754–1834), also known as 'Hair-trigger Dick' and the 'King of Connemara'. Educated at Harrow and Trinity College Dublin, he had an estate in Connacht that comprised 200,000 acres. His other two nicknames arose from his love of animals and his reputation as a duellist. The latter was perhaps exaggerated since duelling was part of the culture of the time, place and class. There is, however, no doubting the vigour of his efforts in respect of animal welfare, Martin spending his late 60s in getting anti-cruelty legislation through Parliament. On 16 June 1824 at Old Slaughter's coffee house in St Martin's Lane, London, at a meeting attended by Martin, the Society for the Prevention of Cruelty to Animals (now the RSPCA) was founded. He moved to Boulogne, having lost his parliamentary seat in 1827, and died there in 1834.

Humbert, General Jean Joseph Amable (b. 1767). The French officer who landed with a small force at Killala, Co. Mayo, on 22 August 1798, precipitating the last in the series of insurrections known collectively as the REBELLION OF 1798.

Hume, John (b.1937). Politician and winner of the Nobel Peace prize. He was born in Derry on 18 January 1937 and educated at St Columb's College and Maynooth. After some years as a teacher he became active in community affairs, helping found the local branch of the Credit Union and leading the campaign to secure a university for Derry. He involved himself in Nationalist politics from the beginning of the Civil Rights agitation (*see* CIVIL RIGHTS MOVEMENT), organizing non-violent protests, including a rent and rates strike in 1971. His winning of the Foyle seat in the STORMONT elections in 1969 was the beginning of a long parliamentary career; he was also an MEP from 1979 (in which his fluency in French was

a distinct advantage) and a Westminster MP from 1983.

One of the founders of the SDLP in 1970, John Hume served as minister for commerce in the short-lived POWER-SHARING EXECUTIVE in 1974. By the mid-1980s he was an internationally known and respected figure, especially in America, and one of the architects of the ANGLO-IRISH AGREEMENT of 1985. His long and patient discussions with Gerry ADAMS from 1988 were viewed with deep suspicion by most parties, but they played a key part in persuading the IRA to call their ceasefire in August 1994. The joint award with David TRIMBLE of the Nobel Peace Prize after the Good Friday Agreement in 1998 was felt in Hume's case to have been very well deserved.

Hump of grandeur. A criticism of a person with ideas above their station would be to say that they had a hump of grandeur.

Hunger and ease. A HIBERNO-ENGLISH description of the qualities of a dog's life. The phrase 'He has a dog's life: hunger and ease' might be applied to an idle, impecunious person.

Hunger strike. A protest tactic used at different periods of the 20th century by Irish prisoners, claiming an ancient Irish precedent in 'fasting upon' an enemy, but more likely following the example of the suffragettes. Force-feeding led to the death in 1917 of Thomas ASHE, on hunger strike because he refused to accept criminal status. After the deaths of Terence MACSWINEY and others in 1920, hunger-striking was suspended as a tactic during the ANGLO-IRISH WAR. Used intermittently since (and in several cases resulting in deaths), the tactic reached its grisliest culmination in the H-BLOCK HUNGER STRIKES of 1981, when ten Republican prisoners died in the MAZE.

Hungry for Home: Leaving the Blaskets (2000). The title of a book by London *Independent* journalist Cole Moreton (b.1947) about the end of the BLASKET ISLANDS community. Moreton gives a harrowing account of the hardships of the final years of life on the Great

Blasket, and interviews some of the emigrants in Springfield, Massachusetts, where all the former Blasket islanders settled.

Hungry Grass (Irish, *féar gorta*). The object of a superstitious and widespread belief that certain patches of greenery had the power to cause death by hunger if one stepped on them. The victim was seized by an overwhelming and unnatural hunger that had to be immediately appeased. Typically such patches were held to be the sites of the unmarked graves of famine victims or, in older belief, places where a meal had been taken and no share left for the people of the OTHERWORLD. The wary foot-traveller always carried a crust in his pocket in case of such an emergency.

Hunting Cap. The nickname of Maurice O'Connell (1728–1825), the uncle and guardian of Daniel O'CONNELL. He lived in the remote peninsula of IVERAGH, Co. Kerry, one of 22 children, and in spite of the POPERY LAWS he managed to become very rich, mostly by smuggling. He was frugal, not to say parsimonious by nature, and his nickname is due to the fact that he wore this type of headgear because a gentleman's beaver was taxed. He did not find his charge entirely congenial to his careful temperament, as a letter written to Daniel's father Morgan in 1790, when the boy was 15, suggests:

> Your son left this house ten days ago and took with him my favourite horse. Had it not been for that, I might have dispensed with his company. He is, I am told, *employed* at visiting the seats of hares at Kularig, the earths of foxes at Tarmon, the caves of otters at Bolus, and the celebration of Miss Burke's wedding at Direen – useful avocations, laudable pursuits, for a nominal student of law! The many indications he has given of a liberal mind in the expenditure of money has left a vacuum in my purse, as well as an impression on my mind, not easily eradicated.

Hunt Museum. A small but significant museum in Limerick endowed by John Hunt (1900–76). It contains more than 2000 precious works of art and antiquity, including such Irish treasures as the Cashel Bell and the Antrim Cross, and paintings by Renoir and Picasso. Since 2002 it has been located in the restored 18th-century custom house near St Mary's Church of Ireland Cathedral. John Hunt was a London-born antique dealer who became an authority on medieval art and began his collection in the 1940s. In 1939 he and his wife Gertrude (*née* Hartman, 1903–95) moved to LOUGH GUR in Co. Limerick where excavations were taking place under Professor Seán Ó Ríordáin of University College Cork. He also encouraged and advised on the restoration of BUNRATTY CASTLE. From 1950 the Hunts lived in Howth, Co. Dublin. *See also* CRAGGAUNOWEN.

Hurler on the ditch. A HIBERNO-ENGLISH phrase descriptive of the omniscient commentator who never did anything himself.

Hurling. A GAA game regarded in Ireland as perhaps the finest spectator sport: there are high scores, constant, speedy action and a great display of skills. It is the oldest game played in Ireland. *The* BOOK OF LEINSTER describes a battle that took place at MAGH TUIREADH (Moytura), near Cong in Co. Mayo, in 1272 BC between the native FIRBOLG and the invading TUATHA DÉ DANAAN. While preparing for battle the two sides agreed to play a game of hurling; the Firbolg proceed to win the game, and then slay their opponents. This is the earliest known reference to hurling. It was legislated for in the BREHON LAWS, and the story of the boy Setanta relates how he took the name CÚCHULAINN, the hound of Culann, after he had killed the actual hound of Culann by hitting his SLIOTAR into the dog's mouth with his CAMÁN. Two Irish high crosses – at MONASTERBOICE and KELLS – dating from around the 10th century show objects resembling a hurley and ball beside a depiction of the biblical story of David and Goliath. The design of the GAA cross, the organization's emblem, is based on these crosses. Among the great hurling counties are Kilkenny, Wexford, Tipperary, Cork, Clare and Limerick; among the great practi-

tioners of the past are Christy RING and the former taoiseach, Jack LYNCH. 'The hay saved and Tipp beaten' was the pinnacle of Cork hopes for the summer.
See also CAMOGIE; CLASH OF THE ASH, THE.

Hurricane Higgins. *See* HIGGINS, ALEX[ANDER GORDON].

Hy. The rendering in English of the Irish *í*, a literary word for 'island': for example, *Í Cholm Cille* is IONA. It is also used in older documents as the equivalent of *Uí*, the word for an historical sept-name: Hy-Neill is *Uí Néill* (the sept or clan O'Neill).

Hy-Brasil (Irish *Í Brasáil*, 'the island of BREA-SAL). A land to the west of the ARAN ISLANDS. It appears from under the waters of the Atlantic every seven years and brings death to the beholder. In later folklore it was thought to have been one of the many places of refuge for the TUATHA DÉ DANAAN after their defeat by the MILESIANS. Other stories have it as an earthly paradise, the land of eternal youth, the place where the souls of the dead experience everlasting bliss.

> Men thought it a region of sunshine and rest
> And they called it Hy-Brasail, the isle of the blest.
> GERALD GRIFFIN (1803–40): 'Hy-Brasail – The Isle of the Blest' (*c.*1830)

The name was internationally known and the place was marked on old charts. When the 15th-century Iberian mariners discovered South America, they called the most easterly region Brazil.
See also OTHERWORLD; TÍR NA NÓG.

Hyde, Douglas (1860–1949). Founder of the GAELIC LEAGUE and first president of Ireland (1938–45). He was born the son of the Anglican rector of Frenchpark, Co. Roscommon, on 17 January 1860, and educated at home because of childhood illness. He learned Irish as a boy and later studied it as part of the divinity course at Trinity College Dublin. Though he graduated LLD in 1886 his main academic concern was languages, and he was proficient in Latin, Greek, Hebrew, German and French.

(He served as professor of modern languages at the University of New Brunswick for the academic year 1891–2.)

However it was Irish, which he had learned, according to Yeats, from the COMPANY OF OLD COUNTRYMEN, that remained Hyde's main interest, and he published poems in Irish and in English, using his disarming pen name Craoibhín Aoibhinn (Irish, 'pleasant little branch'). (His name in Irish which he used for some of his writing and officially was Dubhglas de hÍde.) *Leabhar Sgeulaigheachta* ('book of stories', 1889), a collection of tales, rhymes and riddles, was followed by *Beside the Fire* (1890), a scholarly compilation of Irish folktales that had an obvious effect on the works of Yeats and Synge. Collaboration with the former led to the writing of CASADH AN TSÚGÁIN, the first play of any merit in modern Irish, in 1901, to be followed by nine others including the satire PLEUSGADH NA BULGÓIDE. *Love Songs of Connacht* appeared in 1893.

Two important works of Gaelic scholarship, *The Story of Early Gaelic Literature* (1895) and *A Literary History of Ireland* (1899) effectively refuted the slurs of MAHAFFY and others, who were bent upon belittling the language revival, and made Hyde the obvious choice for the chair of modern Irish at University College Dublin in 1905. In 1892 he became president of the National Literary Society, and his inaugural lecture, entitled *The NECESSITY FOR DE-ANGLICIZING THE IRISH PEOPLE*, paved the way for the founding of the GAELIC LEAGUE the following year. He remained its president until 1915, by which time, under the influence of such IRB members as MacNeill and Pearse, it had ceased to be the non-sectarian, non-political organization Hyde had intended at its foundation.

Hyde served as a Free State senator (1925–6) and retired from his university chair in 1932. In 1938 he was persuaded out of his retirement at Ratra, the house presented to him by the Gaelic League, to serve as the country's first president, which post he held until 1945. He died on 12 July 1949.

I

Ia (also **Hia** or **Ives**) (d.*c*.450). An Irish nun who crossed to Cornwall (on an ivy leaf, according to the story) as a missionary. She was martyred in her cell at the mouth of the River Hayle, and left her name to the town of St Ives. Her feast day is 3 February.

IACI. The Irish-American Cultural Institute, founded by Eoin McKiernan in St Paul, Minnesota, in 1964. McKiernan was born of Irish parents in New York in 1916, and after taking his PhD at Pennsylvania State became professor of English at Geneseo, New York State, and later at the College of St Thomas, St Paul, Minnesota. His first visit to Ireland was in his teens on a GAELTACHT scholarship to Rosmuc, Co. Galway, and he has retained a working knowledge of Irish. He has made more than 300 visits to Ireland, living in Dublin for a year with his wife and family in the 1960s.

The institute's journal of Irish studies, *Éire-Ireland* (founded 1966), covers all aspects of Irish heritage, especially literature and history. It was edited by McKiernan until his retirement, and more recently by Thomas Dillon Redshaw (b.1944).

IAOS. The Irish Agricultural Organization Society, founded in Dublin in 1894 by Sir Horace PLUNKETT to encourage the idea of cooperation among Irish farmers. Its most active field officer was Æ, and its most colourful local suc-

cess was the Templecrone Cooperative Society (*see* PADDY THE COPE).

See also KILLING HOME RULE WITH KINDNESS.

Ibar (*fl*.5th century). Traditionally the last of the pre-Patrician saints to yield to the apostle's authority. One story suggests that Ibar objected to PATRICK because he was foreign. When Patrick threatened to expel him he replied, 'Wherever I be I shall call it Ireland.' The two were reconciled, and Ibar set up a school on an island in Wexford Harbour, called Beggerin ('little Ireland'). His feast day is 23 April.

ICA. *See* IRISH COUNTRYWOMEN'S ASSOCIATION; IRISH CITIZEN ARMY.

ICC. *See* INDUSTRIAL CREDIT CORPORATION.

ICTU. The Irish Congress of Trade Unions, founded in 1959 when the Irish Trades Union Congress and the Congress of Irish Unions amalgamated. It is an umbrella body for trade unions, offering training and education, and negotiating with government and employers when general wage agreements are offered, such as happened in Ireland from the 1990s onwards. ICTU was responsible for healing the rift between the ITGWU and the WUI.

Íde. *See* ITA.

I die in a good cause. The reply made by Thomas ASHE to Laurence O'Neill, lord mayor of Dublin, when he asked him to give up his hunger strike shortly before his death on 25 September 1917. In the pantheon of Irish Nationalist heroes, Ashe occupies a revered place.

Ierne. One of many names for Ireland coming from Éirinn, the dative case of Eriú, the Old Irish word for the country (*see* ÉIRE). It is the name favoured by medieval geographers.

IFA. *See* IRISH FARMERS ASSOCIATION.

If it was a dog 'twould bite you. A colourful HIBERNO-ENGLISH riposte to someone on finding (easily) something they had lost or mislaid.

I hate thee, Djaun Bool. A line from a satirical piece translated, he claimed, from the Persian, by the Irish poet and opium eater, James Clarence MANGAN.

> *Thus writeth Meer Djafrit –*
>   I hate thee, Djaun Bool.
> Worse than Márid or Afrit.
>   Or corpse-eating ghoul.
> I hate thee like Sin,
>   For thy mop-head of hair,
> Thy snub nose and bald chin,
>   And thy turkeycock air.
> 'To the Ingleezee Khafir, calling himself Djaun Bool Djenkinzun'

I'll put you all on board again! The riposte made by US Commodore Charles Stewart (1778–1869) when the British captains of HMS *Cyane* and HMS *Levant* blamed each other for their capture by Stewart's ship the USS *Constitution* on 20 February 1815, during the later stages of the Anglo-American War of 1812. The Treaty of Ghent, ending land hostilities in the War of 1812, had been signed on Christmas Eve 1814, but because of the difficulty of communications the Battle of New Orleans was fought on 8 January 1815 (resulting in defeat for the British), and the sea war dragged on into the spring. It was then that Stewart met the British ships off Madeira and took them with minimal loss. When the captains insisted that if their tactics had been different the outcome might have been different also, Stewart interrupted:

> Gentlemen, there is no use in getting warm about

it; it would have been all the same whatever you might have done. If you doubt that, I will put you all on board again and you can try it over.

Stewart's father was born in Belfast and came to live in Philadelphia. Stewart himself joined the US navy at 13 and was a naval officer by 1800. After the war he commanded in turn the Mediterranean and the Pacific fleets, and became head of the Philadelphia navy yard. His daughter Delia was the mother of Charles Stewart PARNELL. The *Constitution* survived her battles so well that she was dubbed OLD IRONSIDES, a nickname inevitably also applied to the Commodore, who lived to be 91.

> A Yankee ship and a Yankee Crew –
> *Constitution*, where ye bound for?
> Whatever the British prizes be,
> Though it's one to two, or one to three, –
> 'Old Ironsides' means victory,
> Across the Western Ocean.
>   JAMES JEFFREY ROCHE (1847–1908): 'The *Constitution*'s Last Fight'

Image of Ireland, The. *See* DERRICK, JOHN; SHAGGY CLOAK.

Imbolg. The first day of the Celtic spring, now Christianized as St BRIGID's Day (1 February). The saint is conflated with a Celtic goddess of the same name who, as the deity in charge of farm animals, was invoked at lambing.
See also BEALTAINE; LUGHNASA; SAMHAIN.

Immram (Old Irish, 'voyage'). A tale-type of early Irish literature (8th–10th centuries) involving sea journeys to distant lands, where may be found the paradisiacal pleasures of beautiful women, a perfect climate enjoyed in perfect health by inhabitants and visitors, and where time seems to stand still. (It does not, of course, as those mortals who return to Ireland discover, turning to the ash of their true ages.) Sometimes the journeys take the voyagers to the OTHERWORLD. A typical example is the 8th-century *Immram Curaig Máele Dúin* ('the voyage of Mael Dun's craft'); this wonder tale, translated by P.W. JOYCE in *Old Celtic Romances* (1879), was the source of Tennyson's 'Voyage of Maelduine'.

Imperator Scottorum. See BRIAN BORU.

Importance of Being Oscar, The. A one-man entertainment (1960) devised and acted by Mícheál Mac Liammóir and directed by Hilton Edwards (*see* BOYS, THE²) about the life and work of Oscar WILDE. In the show biography is interlaced with commentary and excerpts from the subject's plays, prose and poetry. The Wilde presented is the public one that the man himself would undoubtedly have approved, even to the extent of a rather vulgar, pantomimic Lady Bracknell.

'I'm Rising in the World'. The caption of a cartoon by the brilliant US political cartoonist Thomas Nast (1840–1902) showing a simian immigrant Paddy climbing a ladder with an overloaded hod of bricks. Another Nast cartoon shows a slatterny, near-cretinous chambermaid with the caption, 'I'm stayin' in the Grand Hotel', while drawings of miserable Irish shanties are labelled with ironic accuracy: 'We're livng in Fifth Avenue.' Nast also invented the Republican elephant and the Democratic donkey, party symbols still in use. He was born in Landau, Germany, in 1840, and by the 1860s was a leading Republican protagonist and the darling of the Nativists (*see* KNOW-NOTHING PARTY). His pictorial campaign against the notoriously corrupt Democrat, William 'Boss' Tweed (1823–78), played a significant part in his exposure, but Nast's Nativist views inevitably led him to produce anti-Catholic, anti-Irish propaganda. Nast was already a well-known children's artist, and the benevolent image of Father Christmas was largely his invention. When he portrayed Catholic bishops, their mitres shaped into the jaws of crocodiles, emerging from the Vatican swamp about to attack idealized white Anglo-Saxon Protestant children, the effect was considerable. He ended his life as US consul in Ecuador, dying in 1902.

In a Glass Darkly. A collection of five highly effective horror tales (1872) by Sheridan LE FANU. The title comes from St Paul (I Corinthians 13). The stories are presented as case histories of Dr Martin Hesselius, a German specialist in psychic disorders. 'Green Tea' describes the lurch to suicide of a clergyman haunted by 'a small black monkey, pushing its face forward in mimicry to meet mine'; 'The Familiar' describes how an Irish Anglican clergyman is 'pursued with blasphemies, cries of despair, and appalling hatred'; 'Mr Justice Harbottle' is haunted by something 'crying with a voice high and distant as the caw of a raven hovering over a gibbet'; 'A Rope for Judge Harbottle' and 'The Room in the Dragon Volant' have the surprisingly modern theme of the effects of a drug that makes the recipient appear dead while actually remaining conscious and sentient. It is the vampire tale 'Carmilla', however, that is the most fascinating in the book, dealing remarkably frankly with what was then called Sapphic love and anticipating Bram Stoker's *Dracula* (*see* UNDEAD, THE) by 25 years (and supplying him in Hesselius with a readymade Van Helsing).

> It was like the ardour of a lover; it embarrassed me; it was hateful and yet overpowering; and with gloating eyes she drew me to her, and her hot lips travelled along my cheek in kisses; and she would whisper, almost in sobs. 'You are mine, you *shall* be mine, and you and I are one for ever.'

In Le Fanu's story the female narrator describes the dire consequences of meeting Carmilla, a beautiful young woman (with a strong line in nominal anagrams) who is to be her companion. The narrator discovers that Carmilla was Millarca in another avatar and was also the undying, undead Mircalla, the insatiable Countess Karnstein. It is clear that it was Le Fanu rather that Stoker who assembled what would become the perennial trappings of the vampire story: Carpathian castles, scared coachmen and stakes through the heart.

> The limbs were perfectly flexible, the flesh elastic; and the leaden coffin floated with blood, in which to a depth of seven inches, the body lay immersed. Here then were all the admitted signs and proofs of vampirism. The body, therefore, in accordance with ancient practice, was raised and a sharp stake driven through the heart of the vampire, who uttered a piercing shriek at the

moment, in all respects such as might escape from a living person in the last agony. Then the head was struck off, and a torrent of blood flowed from the severed neck. The body and head were next placed on a pile of wood, and reduced to ashes, which were thrown upon the river and borne away, and that territory has never since been plagued by the visits of a vampire.

In burgo Duno tumulo (Latin, 'In a grave in Down'). A phrase from a verse attributed to the Norman overlord John de Courcy (d.1219) about the supposed burial place of Ireland's three premier saints:

> In burgo Duno tumulo;
> Tumulantur in uno
> Brigida, Patricius
> Atque Columba Pius.
> (In Down three saints one grave do fill
> BRIGID, PATRICK and COLUM CILLE.)

The supposed grave is in the grounds of the Church of Ireland cathedral in Downpatrick, about 3 km (2 miles) from SAUL, traditionally the site of Patrick's first church and of his place of death. The site in Downpatrick lost so much earth during enthusiastic pilgrimages that in 1901 the antiquarian Francis J. BIGGER commissioned a monolith inscribed with the letters PATRIC to cover it.

Inchiquin, Murrough O'Brien, 1st Earl of. *See* MURROUGH OF THE BURNINGS.

Incorporated Law Society. A professional society for the regulation and representation of solicitors. It was originally established as the Law Society in 1830, and took its present name in 1888. It has its headquarters in Blackhall Place, Dublin, to the north of the River Liffey.

Indian meal. Maize, first used as a relief food in 1799 and widely distributed during the GREAT FAMINE. The poorly ground meal that was first offered was so deleterious to the digestion that it was called 'Peel's brimstone' (*see* PEEL, SIR ROBERT), but Indian or yellow meal, as it was called, became a popular cereal until the early 20th century, being used for the baking of bread (*see* CAKE).

Industrial Credit Corporation (ICC). A state-owned bank, established in 1933 with the aim of providing development funding to the industrial sector, which at the time was having difficulty in acquiring credit. Like the ACC it was chronically undercapitalized in its early years, but it was associated with some Irish business successes in the area of construction and manufacture, and helped to develop the Irish stock exchange in the 1930s.

Industrial schools. A system of residential care, originally for 'neglected, orphaned and abandoned children' according to the Industrial Schools Act of 1868, and broadened by the Children Act of 1908 to include young offenders. In Ireland these schools were run by nuns and CHRISTIAN BROTHERS. In 1929 the Free State government passed a new Children Act that allowed for children to be sent to an industrial school even if they had not committed a crime.

Although industrial schools were abolished in the UK in 1933 they survived in Ireland until the 1970s. Various reports in the 1930s and 1940s identified poor conditions, cruel treatment and undernourishment of children, but the schools were allowed to continue. The number of children committed to industrial schools by the courts steadily declined from 833 at the time that the Irish Republic was declared in 1949 to 162 in 1968–9, and in 1970 the Kennedy Report recommended closure of all these schools. Daingean in Co. Offaly was the last industrial school to close, in 1974.

The overwhelming cause of committal was 'lack of proper guardianship', which included imputed immorality on the part of a parent, for instance a mother who was widowed but 'keeping company' with another man. Only a small number were committed for inadequate school attendance, indictable offences and homelessness.

See also ARTANE; BOYS' TOWN; CAVAN ORPHANAGE FIRE; LETTERFRACK.

Infant of Prague. Copies of the statue at the shrine of the Infant or Child of Prague in that city (pronounced to rhyme with 'pray') were a feature of most Irish Catholic homes until the closing decades of the 20th century. A sixpenny piece tucked under the statue was believed to keep povety at bay. The statue was considered luckier if the head was broken off, an 'accident' arranged by some families.

Informer, The. The best-known novel of Liam O'FLAHERTY (1925), largely because of the atmospheric John FORD film (1935) and the performance of Victor McLaglen (1886–1959) as Gypo Nolan, a slow-witted fringe member of an IRA group who betrays his leader. The account of the self-delusion and murderous innocence of Gypo shows the author at his darkest.

Inghinidhe na hÉireann ('daughters of Ireland'). A separatist organization founded by Maud GONNE in 1900 for the purpose of improving national self-awareness. It was a cultural organization, providing Irish classes and staging plays of Nationalist interest, and also involved itself in propaganda, particularly through its newspaper, *Bean na hÉireann* ('women of Ireland', published 1908–11). It supported women's suffrage, and many of the Irish women who became prominent in national life and the struggle for suffrage were members, including Grace GIFFORD, Countess Markievicz (*see* REBEL COUNTESS, THE) and Helena MOLONY. *See also* CUMANN NA MBAN.

Ingram, John Kells (1823–1907). Scholar. He was born near Pettigo, Co. Donegal, and educated in Newry and at Trinity College Dublin (TCD), where he eventually held the chair of Greek. His famous ballad 'The Memory of the Dead', better known by its first line 'Who Fears to Speak of Ninety-Eight', was published anonymously in *The* NATION in April 1843, when Ingram was still a student:

> Who fears to speak of Ninety-Eight?
> Who blushes at the name?
> When cowards mock the patriot's fate,
> Who hangs his head for shame?
> He's all a knave or half a slave
> Who slights his country thus:

> But a true man, like you, man,
> Will fill your glass with us.

Ingram was the founding editor of *Hermathena*, the TCD journal (1874), and became president of the Royal Irish Academy (1892) and vice-provost of TCD (1898). He was a noted sociologist and, in spite of his fiery ballad – the authorship of which was not revealed until the publication of his *Sonnets and Other Poems* in 1900 – a Unionist in politics.

Ingram, Rex (1893–1950). Director of silent films. He was born Reginald Ingram Montgomery Hitchcock in Rathmines, Dublin, on 18 January 1893 and educated in St Columba's College in Rathfarnham. He emigrated to New York in 1911 as soon as he had finished school. In 1913 he began to work in the infant film industry, initially as an actor and scriptwriter, and he directed his first film, *The Great Problem*, in Hollywood at the age of 23. In 1920 he joined Metro, the company for which he directed the highly successful *Four Horseman of the Apocalypse*, starring Rudolf Valentino and Alice Terry (1899–1987), who was to become Ingram's wife. In 1924 Metro became part of MGM. Ingram was one of the most important directors of the silent era, directing nearly 30 films in all, including one sound film in 1931, and was greatly admired as a cinema stylist by later directors such as David Lean. He died suddenly in Hollywood on 22 July 1950.

In Great Haste. A collection of letters from Michael COLLINS to his sweetheart Kitty Kiernan, published in 1983 under this title because Collins was a man in a hurry when he wrote many of them. The letters cover the period of negotiations that led to the TREATY of 1921 and the CIVIL WAR of 1922–3. The letter quoted below, dated 2 August 1922, refers to the death of Harry BOLAND, Collins's former friend, also a former beau of Kitty Kiernan. Boland died on 2 August after he had been shot during an altercation with Free State soldiers in Skerries, Co. Dublin, a few days earlier. It conveys something of the bitterness of the civil war.

Last night I passed Vincent's Hospital and saw a small crowd outside. My mind went into him lying dead there and I thought of the times together, and, whatever good there is in any wish of mine, he certainly had it. Although the gap of eight or nine months was not forgotten – of course no one can ever forget it – I only thought of him with the friendship of the days of 1918 and 1919. They tell me the last thing he said to his sister Kathleen, before he was operated on, was 'Have they got Mick Collins yet?' I don't believe it so far as I'm concerned and, if he did say it, there is no necessity to believe it. I'd send a wreath but I suppose they'd return it torn up.

> *In Great Haste, The Letters of Michael Collins and Kitty Kiernan* (1983), ed. Leon Ó Broin

Inishowen (Irish *Inis Eoghain*, 'Owen's island'). A peninsula in northeast Donegal bounded on the east by Lough Foyle and on the west by Lough Swilly and containing Malin Head, the most northerly point of the island of Ireland. Owen was one of the sons of the semi-legendary NIALL OF THE NINE HOSTAGES; the other son, Conall, was granted the rest of the territory of Donegal, since known as Tír Chonaill (pronounced 'cheer conal'). In historical times Inishowen was the territory of the O'Dohertys until it was granted to Arthur CHICHESTER (1563–1625) as part of the ULSTER PLANTATION in 1605. It was this acquisition that led to the family's adoption of the title Donegall.

Inis Icíleáin (anglicized as **Innishvicillaun**). One of the BLASKET ISLANDS off the west Kerry coast. It was bought as a summer hideaway by Charles HAUGHEY, who built on it an elaborate and costly home based on the style of an Irish chieftain's fort. Inis Icíleáin is a source of much folklore, and the story of the air *'Port na bPúcaí'* or 'The Fairies' Tune' is one of the best known: the island was inhabited by members of the Ó Dálaigh (Daly) family, and Tomás Ó Dalaigh related the story of his encounter in the early 20th century with a *bean sí* or fairy woman, who gave him the tune. Seamus HEANEY's beautiful lyric 'The Given Note' is inspired by the story and the tune:

On the most westerly Blasket
In a dry-stone hut
He got this air out of the night ...

Inkle-weavers. The makers of broad linen tape. The expression was used as a measure of friendship (as in 'They are as GREAT as inkle-weavers') because the hands had to sit so close together at the loom.

INLA. The Irish National Liberation Army, a breakaway Republican group who refused to accept the Official IRA (*see* STICKIES, THE[1]) ceasefire in 1972. Founded in 1974 by Seamus Costello (1939–77), it tended to be left-wing and rather more ruthless even than the Provisional IRA. It was responsible for the killing of Airey NEAVE (1916–79), Conservative shadow secretary of state for Northern Ireland, on 30 March 1979, and the DROPPIN' WELL bombing in Ballykelly in 1982. The killing of the Loyalist paramilitary leader Billy Wright (*see* KING RAT) in the MAZE by INLA members in December 1997 had an unsteadying effect on the peace process, and resulted in a sectarian campaign of revenge that cost 18 lives. During its entire existence the group has been beset by (often bloody) internecine feuds. Its associated political wing IRPS (Irish Republican Socialist Party) has made no real attempt at serious political activity.

See also PLANET OF THE IRPS.

Innisfail (Irish *Inis Fáil*, 'the isle of Ireland'). One of many alternative names for Ireland, very popular in 19th-century sentimental verse, though the name appears in poetry as early as the 10th century.

Adieu! – the snowy sail
Swells her bosom to the gale,
And our bark from Innisfail
Bounds away
While we gaze upon the shore,
That we never shall see more
And the blinding tears flow o'er ...'

> R.D. WILLIAMS (1822–62): 'Adieu to Innisfail' (1842)

Innisfree. One of the smallest islands in Lough Gill, County Sligo. It is known around the world from one of W.B. YEATS's most popular poems, 'The Lake Isle of Innisfree', from his collection *The Rose* (1893):

> I will arise and go now, and go to Innisfree,
> And a small cabin build there, of clay and wattles made:
> Nine bean-rows will I have there, a hive for the honey-bee,
> And live alone in the bee-loud glade ...

Yeats wrote the poem in London after being inspired by the sound of a fountain in a shop window. Later Yeats's sister predicted that the island would be covered in signs such as 'The cabin is private' and 'Do not eat the beans'.

In one leap. The lighthearted response by Frederick Augustus HERVEY, 4th Earl of Bristol, on receiving the news in 1768 that he had been appointed bishop to the see of DERRY. He had already, as Bishop of Cloyne in Co. Cork, a reputation as being rather playful. The story goes that he was playing leapfrog with fellow clerics when the news came, and he announced to his friends: 'I have surpassed you all; in one leap I have jumped from Cloyne to Derry.'

In one year tamed. The phrase from 'An Horatian Ode upon Cromwell's Return from Ireland' (*c.*1650) by Andrew Marvell (1621–78):

> And now the Irish are ashamed
> To see themselves in one year tamed.

Inst. The name (short for 'institution') by which the Royal Belfast Academical Institution is universally known. It was founded in 1807 as the Belfast Academical Institution, a non-denominational college, by radical Presbyterians including William DRENNAN and John Templeton (1766–1825). It became in effect a Presbyterian seminary until the ARIANISM controversy of 1830 when such anti-Arianists as Henry COOKE accused many of the staff of heresy. After the foundation of Queen's College (*see* QUEEN'S COLLEGES) in 1845 and ASSEMBLY'S COLLEGE four years later, Inst became and has remained a leading boys' grammar school.

Intellect of the Game, the. The nickname applied to Danny Blanchflower (1926–93), the Belfast soccer player, partly because of his abilities as a wing-half and inspirational captain but mostly because of his articulate analysis of the game. He was born Robert Dennis Blanchflower on 10 February 1926, and after youth football and service with the RAF joined his local team Glentoran in 1954. As captain of Tottenham Hotspur he led the team to its famous League and FA Cup 'double' in 1961, retained the Cup the following year and won the European Cup Winners Cup in 1963. He was manager of the Northern Ireland squad (1976–9) and was sports writer for the *Sunday Express* for 25 years. Throughout his career and after retirement he was in demand as a loquacious but accurate analyst of the game. He also carved a special niche for himself as one of the very few celebrities who refused to accept the 'big red book' from Eamonn ANDREWS for *This Is Your Life*. His latter years were clouded by Alzheimer's disease, and he died in London on 9 December 1993. In 1968 he summed up what he saw as sport's core values:

> Sport is a wonderfully democratic thing, one of the few honourable battlefields left. It is a conflict between good and bad, winning and losing, praise and criticism. Its true values should be treasured and protected.

International Brigades. *See* RYAN, FRANK; SPANISH CIVIL WAR.

International Date Line. The punning title imposed upon the Bank Buildings, a department store in the centre of Belfast during the 1940s and 1950s, because of its popularity as a meeting place for the segregated students of the time.

International series. *See* AUSTRALIAN RULES; COMPROMISE RULES.

Internment. A quasi-legal device used from time to time by the authorities when it was impossible to imprison activists by conventional means. It was used extensively by the British against Republicans 1916–1921 and by the Free State government against ANTI-TREATYITES, during and after the CIVIL WAR, with a peak of

11,480 internees on 1 July 1923. In Northern Ireland internment was used 1922–4, during the Second World War (*see* EMERGENCY, THE) and the IRA's BORDER CAMPAIGN (1957–62). Internment was introduced again on 9 August 1971 in response to the increasing violence in the North. The sweep was based upon poor intelligence and accompanied by unacceptable interrogation methods that alienated the Nationalist community without notably lowering the level of violence. The murderous BLOODY SUNDAY 1972 began as an anti-internment march. Internment ceased in 1975. *See also* ARGENTA.

Interparty Government. The cumbersome name given to the coalition governments formed in 1948 and 1954, the major party in both being FINE GAEL and the taoiseach John A. COST-ELLO.

The 1948 coalition also included CLANN NA POBLACHTA, CLANN NA TALMHAN, the LABOUR PARTY and National Labour. Controversy over the MOTHER AND CHILD SCHEME led to the resignation of health minister Noël BROWNE and the collapse of the coalition in 1951. The first Interparty Government is also remembered for having passed the REPUBLIC OF IRELAND Act, formally declaring Ireland a republic, in 1948.

The 1954 coalition also included Labour and Clann na Talmhan, with Clann na Poblachta undertaking not to oppose the government. However after the BORDER CAMPAIGN broke out in 1956 Seán MACBRIDE proposed a vote of no confidence in the government, which was supported by FIANNA FÁIL, and the coalition fell in February 1957.

Fine Gael formed three coalitions with Labour in the 1970s and 1980s (*see* COSGRAVE, LIAM; FITZGERALD, GARRET), and Fianna Fáil went into coalition for the first time in 1985, with the Progressive Democrats (*see* PEE DEES). There has been no single-party government since then.

In the Shadow of the Glen. The first play of J.M. SYNGE, staged by the Irish National Theatre Society (forerunner of the ABBEY THEATRE) in Molesworth Hall, Dublin, on 8 October 1903.

The play's source was a story told to Synge by Pat Dirane, the SEANCHAÍ from Inis Meáin in the ARAN ISLANDS who had appointed himself Synge's mentor. In Dirane's tale he described how once, travelling from Galway to Dublin, he had sought shelter in a house in which a corpse was laid out on a table. The much younger wife of the dead man had plied him with food, tobacco and whiskey, leaving him with the corpse while she went visiting. The 'corpse' soon rose and told Pat that it was his intention to catch his unfaithful wife *in flagrante delicto*. She returned with a young man who was sent to rest in the bedroom and with the feeblest of excuses she soon joined him. The story concluded with a sentence as famous as any in the play:

> The dead man hit him a blow with the stick so that the blood out of him leapt up and hit the gallery.
>
> Quoted in J.M. Synge, *The Aran Islands* (1907)

In the play, originally called *Dead Man's Deputy*, the wife, equally disenchanted with her cold and ageing husband and her shuffling lover, goes off with a tramp, preferring his poetically described free life. The public's reaction to the play was mixed, many finding it improper. The reaction by Nationalists, especially Arthur Griffith in *The* UNITED IRISHMAN, was decidedly cool:

> Yet although Mr. Synge speaks Irish and resides for a period each year in Aran, this play shows him to be as utterly a stranger to the Irish character as any Englishman who has yet dissected us for the enlightenment of his countrymen.

This reception anticipated the much more violent response to Synge's *The* PLAYBOY OF THE WESTERN WORLD. In fact Synge was less concerned with the prevalence of loveless marriages than with the mystique of the free tramp and the deadliness of the settled life in 'the last cottage at the head of a long glen in Wicklow' where he sets his scene.

Invincibles, the. The extreme splinter group of the FENIAN movement formed with the intention of assassinating British officials who opposed the LAND LEAGUE. Their only significant venture was the brutal and counterproductive murder of Lord Frederick Cavendish (1836–82), the chief secretary, and Thomas Henry Burke (1829–82), his under-secretary, in Phoenix Park, Dublin, on 6 May 1882 (*see* PHOENIX PARK MURDERS).

In Vinculis. A sonnet sequence written by Wilfred Scawen Blunt while in Galway jail for inciting the tenants of Lord Clanricarde to resist eviction. The publication of the sequence in 1889 led Oscar Wilde to remark that 'prison has had an admirable effect on Mr Wilfred Blunt as a poet'. Blunt was born in 1840 in Sussex of an old Catholic family, and with his wife Lady Anne Wentworth, the granddaughter of Lord Byron, travelled widely in India and Egypt, becoming in the process a confirmed anti-imperialist. It was in Egypt that he met Lady GREGORY and they had an affair, Blunt later publishing her love letters to him as *A Woman's Poems* but not revealing the source. He published *Land War in Ireland* in 1912 and regularly boasted that he was the first Englishman to go to jail for Ireland's sake. He died in 1922.

> Galway's gaol was an old-fashioned rambling place with cells of various sizes, and the one I was given was well-lighted, showing a good patch of sky ... so that there was some pleasure to be had from watching the sea gulls overhead, and the jackdaws and sparrows, to which it was possible even to throw bread crumbs. The discipline was lax and the warders, most of them Nationalists, were friendly.
>
> *Memorandum on Prison Reform*, forwarded to the Home Secretary, Winston Churchill, 25 February 1910

Íochtar. An Irish word for 'low', used in HIBERNO-ENGLISH for a weak or sickly animal that might have to be hand-reared. The word also signifies skimmed milk (its opposite, cream, is *uachtar*).

Iona. A small island off the west coast of Mull in the Inner Hebrides where COLUM CILLE (Columba) founded a monastery in 563. Traditionally he sailed with 12 companions from Derry, which in medieval times was named after him as Doire Choluim Cille. Adamnán (*see* VITA SANCTI COLUMBAE) in his life of Columba refers to Iona as 'Iova Insula'. The island's name derives from the old Celtic word for 'yew tree', and the change from 'Iova' to 'Iona' was apparently the result of a mistranscription. Because of its sanctity it became a favourite burial place for Scottish kings, including Macbeth's predecessor, Duncan, who was buried there in 1040. It is still a place of pilgrimage.

> *Ross:* Where is Duncan's body?
> *Macduff:* Carried to Colmekill,
> The sacred storehouse of his predecessors
> And guardian of his bones.
> *Macbeth*, II.iv

Ir. In Irish mythology, one of the sons of MÍL. He is killed in a storm conjured up by the TUATHA DÉ DANAAN to prevent him from landing. His name, contrary to appearances, plays no part in the country's English name, the first syllable of which comes from Ériu (*see* ÉIRE).

IRA. The Irish Republican Army, a term that came into general use in the ANGLO-IRISH WAR (1919–21) and which has been used imprecisely since then as the acceptable English version of *Óglaigh na h-Éireann* ('Irish Volunteers'). The IRA emerged out of the IRISH VOLUNTEERS founded in 1913, and the Irish-language version, pronounced 'O-glee na herran', is used on all official documents and in correspondence. The initials IRA were first used in the Fenian invasion of Canada (*see* FENIAN CAMPAIGN OF 1867) to describe the army of the Irish Republican Brotherhood (IRB). The name 'IRA' was applied by the IRREGULARS to themselves during and after the CIVIL WAR. The movement was declared illegal in 1936 but resurfaced with bombings in Britain in 1939, again during the BORDER CAMPAIGN (1956–62), and opportunistically after the Civil Rights agitation of 1968 (*see* CIVIL RIGHTS MOVEMENT), leading to the latest and most long-lasting bout of the TROUBLES in Northern Ireland.

In 1969 the IRA split into two wings, one 'Official' and one 'Provisional'. The Officials (*see* STICKIES, THE[1]) ceased armed activity in 1972, but the Provisional IRA, commonly known as the Provos, continued a campaign of bombing and killing with the stated simplistic intention of securing British withdrawal from Ireland. After much tedious negotiation with no mitigation of activity, ceasefires were declared in August 1994 (ended by the CANARY WHARF bombs) and again in 1997. Provo activity has not been resumed since then and the Republican movement has concentrated on political activity embodied in SINN FÉIN. The old policy of political ABSTENTIONISM and of continuing the ARMED STRUGGLE has produced a number of dissident schismatic groups, notably the Continuity Army Council (*see* CONTINUITY IRA), still intermittently active, and the REAL IRA, which was responsible for the appalling OMAGH BOMB of 15 August 1998.
See also ADAMS, GERRY; ARMALITE AND THE BALLOT BOX, THE; DECOMMISSIONING; DISAPPEARED, THE; GOOD FRIDAY AGREEMENT; HILLSBOROUGH DECLARATION; PHYSICAL-FORCE REPUBLICANISM.

IRA – All the way! A slogan, often vocalized, used by NORAID in its fund-raising in America.

IRA and Its Enemies, The. The title of a book (1998) by the historian Peter Hart that challenges received wisdom about the IRA campaign in Cork city and county in the ANGLO-IRISH WAR (1919–21). Hart's narrative, which is compelling, provides a gloss on various incidents that is far from favourable to the IRA. It caused outrage, especially for its re-evaluation of the famous 'false surrender' of the KILMICHAEL AMBUSH of November 1920, described by Tom Barry in his *GUERRILLA DAYS IN IRELAND*.

IRA – I Ran Away. Graffiti found on walls in Nationalist areas of Northern Ireland in August 1969, indicating the disappointment felt that there was no Republican defence against Loyalist attacks.

IRB. The Irish Republican Brotherhood, a secret society associated with the FENIANS. It remained in existence during the LAND WAR, was occluded during the PARNELL hegemony, but was revived again in the early 20th century by Tom CLARKE and Seán McDERMOTT. It was the main force behind the 1916 EASTER RISING and (with an alphabetical change to IRA) in the ANGLO-IRISH WAR of 1919–21, providing the IRISH VOLUNTEERS with old military skills.

Ire. A HIBERNO-ENGLISH word (from Irish *oighear*) for irritation of the skin from wind or chafing.
See also WINDGALL.

Ireland Act (1949). An act passed by the British government in response to the Republic of Ireland Act 1948, passed by the INTERPARTY GOVERNMENT, which declared Ireland a republic and no longer a member of the British Commonwealth. The main provision of the British Act related to Northern Ireland, confirming the provisions of the GOVERNMENT OF IRELAND ACT of 1920:

> that Northern Ireland remain part of His Majesty's dominions and it is hereby affirmed that in no event will Northern Ireland or any part thereof cease to be part of His Majesty's dominions and of the United Kingdom without the consent of the parliament of Northern Ireland.

Ireland of the Welcomes. The concept of an Ireland that is hospitable and full of *CÉAD MÍLE FÁILTE* ('a hundred thousand welcomes'), which has always been a major selling point in the Irish tourism industry. It is also the title of the handsome bi-monthly magazine of Bord Fáilte, the Irish tourist board, published in Dublin since May 1952 and containing a mixture of information, advertising and features on Irish topics likely to be of interest to tourists, especially Americans. In its inaugural issue, Seán LEMASS, then minister for industry and com-

merce, wrote: 'I welcome the opportunity …
to offer the hospitality of Ireland in an everyday phrase from our native language – *céad
míle fáilte* … a hundred thousand welcomes.'

Ireland's Own. A weekly magazine founded in
1902 by Edward O'Cullen, proprietor of the
Wexford local newspaper *The People*. It is an
'easy-reading' magazine, presenting a mixture
of nostalgia, song words, short stories of Irish
interest and general features calculated to appeal
especially to emigrants. The 'Kitty the Hare'
ghost stories written by Victor O'D. Power
were especially popular and reprinted many
times.

Irish Academy of Music (now the Royal Irish
Academy of Music, or RIAM). A college begun
by a few music enthusiasts in 1848. It grew out
of the Antient Concerts Society, which met in
various hotels and private houses in Dublin
until it was able to buy and remodel a hall
in Brunswick Street as the ANTIENT CON-
CERT ROOMS. Classes were held there, and
with Queen Victoria's gracious patronage the
academy gained in prestige what it lacked in
funds. The initiative was greatly assisted by a
bequest from Elizabeth Coulson of £13,000 in
1861 and an annual government grant of £300
after 1870. The title 'Royal' was bestowed in
1872, and it has been known as the RIAM
since. It combines with Trinity College Dublin
and the Dublin City University to award
degrees and other qualifications.

Irish acre. A measurement of land almost twice
the size of the English acre.

Irish Agricultural Labourers Union. The Irish
branch of Joseph Arch's ALU, founded in
Kanturk, Co. Cork, in August 1873 with Isaac
BUTT as president.

Irish Agricultural Organization Society. *See* IAOS.

Irish ague. A disease – probably typhus – prevalent in Ireland in the 16th and 17th centuries.

Irish-American Cultural Institute. *See* IACI.

Irish bars. A phenomenon of the late 20th century. It was caused by the increased popularity

of Ireland as a tourist destination for young
Europeans and the perception that an Irish pub
was a good – indeed the best possible – place
for *ceol agus craic* ('music and CRAIC'). These
'Irish' theme pubs may be found in all the
European capitals and elsewhere on the Continent, bearing names of real or legendary Irishwomen such as MOLLY MALONE, Sally O'BRIEN
or Kitty O'Shea (*see* O'SHEA WHO MUST BE
OBEYED) and decorated to resemble an Irish
pub of the Ireland of 50 years ago: smoke-
darkened rafters, old bottles or artifacts and,
perhaps, traditional, folk or ballad music. If
there is demand, a rugby international or the
ALL-IRELAND hurling or football final is shown
on television. These pubs may have nothing
at all to do with Irish people, and the décor is
packaged and available commercially. As such
they are different from Irish pubs in America,
which, although they may bear similar names,
are usually owned and run by expatriate Irishmen or Irish-Americans. In an unconscious
irony, Dublin has seen the re-importation of
some 'Irish' pubs of this type in recent years.

Irish Bath, the. The vainglorious name given
to the town of Mallow, which lies athwart the
lordly Blackwater (*see* AWNIDUFF) in north Co.
Cork, about 30 km (20 miles) north-northwest
of the city. It was a leading watering place for
the second-city Anglo-Irish gentry and for
those of Limerick, 60 km (40 miles) to the
north. The birthplace of Canon SHEEHAN and
Thomas DAVIS, it still maintains an excellent
racecourse. The notorious RAKES OF MALLOW
were not native, but rather noisy seasonal
intruders. Mallow's spa was highly regarded,
as an anonymous early 19th-century song
(which rhymed perfectly at the time) suggests:

> All you that are,
> Both lean and bare,
> With scarce an ounce of tallow,
> To make your flesh
> Look plump and fresh
> Come, drink the springs of Mallow.

Irish Brigade, the[1]. A term applied through
history to bands of Irishmen in foreign armies.

An Irish Brigade of 1000 volunteers fought unsuccessfully for Pope Pius IX at Spoleto and Castelfiardo against the Piedmontese in 1860. There were Irish brigades in both the Federal and Confederate armies in the American Civil War (1861–5), and Eoin O'DUFFY led an Irish Brigade to fight for Franco in Spain in 1936 (*see* ANGELS OF MONASTEREVIN). However, the term is usually taken to refer to the 16,000 WILD GEESE who were part of the armies of France during the 17th and 18th centuries:

> They fought as they revelled, fast, fiery and true,
> And though victors they left on the field not a few;
> And they who survived, fought and drank as of yore,
> But the land of their hearts' hope they never saw more;
> For in far foreign fields from Dunkirk to Belgrade
> Lie the soldiers and chiefs of the Irish Brigade.
>
> THOMAS DAVIS (1814–45): 'The Battle-Eve of the Brigade' (1843)

Irish Brigade, the[2]. The name given to the group of Liberal MPs who united in Parliament in 1851 to oppose the Ecclesiastical Titles Bill. The group was better known under the nickname, the POPE'S BRASS BAND.

Irish bull. A seemingly self-contradictory remark, taken as characteristic of the Irish from the early 17th century by their colonial overlords. The oddity of expression, which the British took as evidence of native stupidity, was caused by the people's attempt to express themselves in a language notably different from their own tongue. In fact the most famous perpetrator, Sir Boyle ROCHE (1743–1807), was a member of the ASCENDANCY and knew no Gaelic. He is credited with the bulls:

> Why should we put ourselves out of our way for posterity; for what has posterity done for us?

and

> I smell a rat; I see him floating in the air and darkening the sky; but I will nip him in the bud.

It is perhaps as well to remember the remark of Sir John Pentland Mahaffy (1839–1919), (eventually) provost of Trinity College Dublin

and Oscar Wilde's mentor:

> An Irish bull is always pregnant.

Irish Bulletin, The. A propaganda news-sheet published by the DÁIL during the ANGLO-IRISH WAR of 1919–21 and circulated in America and other countries. Erskine CHILDERS, Desmond FitzGerald (father of Garret FITZGERALD) and Frank Gallagher, later first editor of the *IRISH PRESS*, were the writers most associated with it. The British government found it a diplomatic embarrassment and frequently tried to suppress it, confiscating the equipment used to produce it.

Irish Catholic Colonization Association. An experiment in emigration as a means of alleviating famine. In the years 1879–81 the potato crop failed in the parish of Carna, Co. Galway. The parish priest, Father Patrick Greally, wrote to various newspapers asking for help, and Bishop John Ireland of Minnesota suggested that assisted emigration to his Mid-West diocese might be a solution. In July 1880, 309 emigrants left the parishes of Carna and Carraroe and and were met by Ireland at St Paul, Minnesota. Most were conveyed to a region of northwest Minnesota called Graceville, where each man was given a farm of 160 acres (64 ha), with 12.5 of them cleared ready for the wheat crop, a house, a yoke of oxen and two horses. The experiment was not a success: the winter of 1880–1 was particularly severe; the Irish, used to living in more populated areas, found the loneliness intolerable; and they had no experience of growing wheat. They took to hanging about the town of Graceville blaming the bishop for having in some way deceived them. Eventually they were taken back to St Paul and found jobs on the railroad, living in Drayton's Bluff, which became locally known as Connemara Patch.

Irish Christian Brothers. *See* CHRISTIAN BROTHERS.

Irish Citizen, The. The official organ (1912–20) of the Irish Women's Suffrage Federation (*see* WOMEN'S SUFFRAGE). It was edited at first by James Cousins and his wife Margaret. Hanna

SHEEHY-SKEFFINGTON and her husband Francis were both very involved with it.

Irish Citizen Army (ICA). A body set up by the ITGWU on 23 November 1913 to protect workers and pickets from the DMP (Dublin Metropolitan Police) during the 1913 LOCK-OUT. James CONNOLLY became commandant in 1914 and LIBERTY HALL, the union's headquarters, became the centre of planning activity. The army, the first socialist militia, numbered about 350 and joined with the IRISH VOLUNTEERS in the EASTER RISING, digging trenches in St Stephen's Green and, finding the position untenable, occupying the nearby Royal College of Surgeons. A group also took over City Hall. Of its leaders Connolly and Michael Mallin were executed in Kilmainham Jail, while the death sentence handed out to Constance Markievicz (see REBEL COUNTESS, THE) was commuted to life imprisonment. Unlike the Volunteers, which tended to use the women of CUMANN NA MBAN merely as ancillaries, ICA women members had equal status with the men, and participated in the fighting.

Irish Civil War. See CIVIL WAR.

Irish cloak. A heavy full-length hooded cloak formerly worn by women – in some places in rural Ireland up to the beginning of the 20th century. The cloak was made of woollen broadcloth in a variety of colours. Black cloaks were worn by older women and widows, but these too had a colourful lining or braid. A young girl who was getting married would consider the cloak she acquired as a bride her most prized possession and would expect it to last her a lifetime. The variety known as the Kinsale cloak, with its elaborately worked hood, was particularly celebrated.
See also IRISH MANTLE.

Irish Cockneys. See GRECIAN.

Irish Code Duello. A series of rules devised at Clonmel, Co. Tipperary, in 1777 to cover the practice of duelling by 'Gentlemen delegates' from the Connacht counties of Galway, Mayo, Sligo and Roscommon. It was recommended

that a copy of the 25 rules should be kept in pistol cases, that 'ignorance might never be pleaded'. A typical entry was:

> 16. The challenged has the right to choose his own weapon, unless the challenger gives his honour he is no swordsman; after which, however, he cannot decline any second species of weapon proposed by the challenged.

Irish coffee. A fortified coffee containing a generous quantity of Irish whiskey and topped with cream to resemble a pint of GUINNESS. It is said to have originated in the Shannon House Hotel in Foynes, Co. Limerick, on a cold winter's night in 1942. A seaplane landed and the chef, one Jim Sheridan, poured whiskey into the coffee to warm the American travellers. One of them asked, 'Is this Irish coffee?'

Irish College. See COLLÈGE DES IRLANDAIS (Paris); PONTIFICAL IRISH COLLEGE (Rome).

Irish colleges. The general name used for the large number of summer schools that exist for the purpose of teaching Irish to teenage pupils. These are usually situated in the main GAELTACHT areas of Connemara, west Kerry and northwest Donegal, although there are also some to be found in non-Gaeltacht regions like Ballybunion, Co. Kerry, and Achill, Co. Mayo. Pupils normally stay for two-three weeks in the homes of local families (an important source of income for the women who act as BEAN A' TÍ); they attend classes taught by local teachers in the morning and participate in social or sporting activities in the afternoon. Summer courses in Irish colleges are an important rite of passage for many Irish 14–17-year-olds with attendant first love, loss and heartbreak.

Irish Confederation. A body set up by Smith O'Brien (see WIDOW MCCORMICK'S CABBAGE PATCH) and John MITCHEL of the YOUNG IRELAND movement on 13 January 1847, after they had seceded from Daniel O'CONNELL's Repeal movement. Though O'Brien was anxious for reform and reconciliation, militants like Mitchel and MEAGHER laid plans for a rising. The turmoil in Europe the following spring, especially the 1848 revolution in France, encouraged them further, and the Confederation clubs, stronger in urban areas than in the country, were advised to prepare themselves for what became the unsuccessful rebellion of 1848. The clubs were banned by the authorities on 26 July.

Irish Congress of Trade Unions. *See* ICTU.

Irish Convention (1917–18). A convention brought together by LLOYD GEORGE in July 1917 to discuss the difficulties relating to the granting of HOME RULE. It had 95 members under the chairmanship of Horace PLUNKETT and included representatives of Unionist and Nationalist opinion, including the Irish Parliamentary Party (*see* IRISH PARTY), but it was boycotted by SINN FÉIN and the LABOUR PARTY. The Irish Convention ended in failure in April 1918, issuing a report recommending self-government, which fewer than half the members endorsed. Another, minority, report warned the government of the dangers of trying to introduce conscription to Ireland (*see* CONSCRIPTION CRISIS). The irrelevance of the Convention to Nationalist Ireland was shown by the results of the election of December 1918, in which Sinn Féin won 73 seats, the Irish Parliamentary Party retaining only 6.

Irish Countrywomen's Association (ICA). Formed in 1910 as the women's branch of the cooperative movement, the aim of the ICA was to improve the life of women in rural Ireland by educating them in various crafts and skills. It is still a cooperative movement, with the broader aim of improving the standard of rural and urban life. A 26-county organization, with more than 1000 guilds and 20,000 members, it has sororial links with the Women's Institution in Northern Ireland.
See also COUNTRY MARKETS; GRIANÁN.

Irish dances. *See* CÉILÍ DANCES.

Irish disease. *See* TUBERCULOSIS.

Irish draught horse. When an Irish draught mare was bred with a thoroughbred stallion, the resulting half-breed provided excellent material for showjumping and eventing. Irish draughts have also been used for UK cavalry and mounted police.

Irish elk. A giant prehistoric deer (*Megaloceros giganteus*), identified from Pleistocene remains as 12,000–16,000 years old. It was 2 m (6.5 ft) high to the shoulder, with a 4-m (13-ft) antler span that in the thickly wooded island proved to be unwieldy and contributed to its extinction. The term 'Irish elk' is a misnomer; it is properly known as the Irish giant deer, and arrived in the country over the land bridges that existed before they were flooded at the end of the last Ice Age.

Irish Farmers Association (IFA). The largest, most vocal and most influential of Irish farmers' representative organizations, founded on 1 January 1970.

Irish Folklore Commission. A body established in 1935 by Séamus Ó Duillearga (*see* DELARGY, JAMES HAMILTON) to record and preserve the lore and traditions of rural Ireland. On a shoestring budget (in 1935 Éamon de Valera allowed a grant of £32,000, just £1000 for each of the 32 counties), the Commission employed five collectors who travelled the country, especially in the Irish-speaking western seaboard. The collectors recorded in writing (or later with machines with wax cylinders called ediphones) the SEANCHAS (stories) and the PISHOGUES and beliefs of old people. Under the indefatigable leadership of Delargy an enormous body of folklore was preserved and catalogued in the Commission's offices in University College Dublin at Earlsfort Terrace. Among the best known of the collectors in the years after the end of the Second World War were Kevin DANAHER, Seán Ó SÚILLEABHÁIN and Séamus ENNIS.

Irish Homestead. *See* Æ.

Irish Hospitals Sweepstakes. The Hospitals Sweepstakes, popularly known as 'the sweep', were founded in 1930 by Joseph McGrath (1887–1966), a former CUMANN NA NGAEDHEAL minister (*see* ARMY MUTINY), and two business associates, Richard Duggan and Spencer Freeman. They were by way of being a national lottery, at the same time supplying badly needed money for capital projects in Irish hospitals. The support of Irish immigrants in the USA who bought sweeps tickets through unofficial sources was crucial, such lotteries being illegal in most US states at the time. It has been calculated that in 1932 the income to Ireland from the Hospitals Sweepstakes was more than the government's net income-tax receipts. Joe McGrath's family also invested in the Dublin Glass Bottle Company and became involved in the revival of glassmaking in Waterford in 1950, establishing Waterford Glass as an international brand over the next 15 years. Irish Hospitals Sweepstakes went into liquidation in 1987 with a loss of 160 jobs, having failed to win the contract to administer Ireland's new national lottery.

Irish Hunger Memorial. A field in Battery Park, West Manhattan, New York, featuring a ruined cottage translapidated from its original site in Co. Mayo and a stone from each of the 32 counties of Ireland. The cottage was originally built at Attymass, near Ballina, Co. Mayo. The visitor may leave the site through a time tunnel, the entrance of which is inside the ruin and which leads to the exit at the Hudson River. The walls of the tunnel are lined with pictures and texts recording famines, old and contemporary, and music and actors' voices complete the multi-media effect. The field replicates the dereliction that was characteristic of Ireland in the years after the GREAT FAMINE (1845–52). The memorial was commissioned in 2000, and dedicated in 2002, on the 150th anniversary of the end of the famine.

Irish hyperbole. In the spoken language of HIBERNO-ENGLISH there has always been a tendency towards exaggeration and tautology. Many such hyperboles come straight from Irish, and are an inevitable result of exact translation from the latter to Hiberno-English. Here, for example, is a description of a leprechaun in a story in the *Irish Penny Magazine* (*c.*1870):

...a weeny deeny DAWNY little atomy of an idea of the small taste of a gentleman ...

Other examples include: 'every single one of them'; Diarmaid 'struck the giant and left him dead without life' (a direct translation of the Irish, *marbh gan anam*; 'I disown the whole family: seed, breed and generation'; Patrick greeting the squire: 'Your honour's honour is quite welcome entirely'; 'lend me the loan of your umbrella'; and an oral account of the death of a young man after a row:

It was dreadful about the poor boy: they made at him in the house and killed him there; then they dragged him out on the road and killed him entirely, so that he lived for only three days after.

Irish Independent, The. A newspaper founded by William Martin MURPHY in 1905, from a merger of Murphy's *Daily Nation* and Parnell's *Irish Daily Independent*, and incorporating the FREEMAN'S JOURNAL from 1924. It was determinedly modern, reflecting Catholic interests and directed at the middle ground of Irish politics. Until the foundation of the IRISH PRESS in 1931, the *Irish Independent*, together with its stable-mates the *Evening Herald* and the *Sunday Independent*, formed a virtual monopoly. (The IRISH TIMES had not yet become accepted as a liberal organ of general interest and was still perceived as the Unionist/Protestant paper.) The *Irish Independent* maintained its pro-TREATY, conservative, rather staid mien, often characterized as 'not so much a paper for parish priests as for parish priests' housekeepers', in contrast to the livelier and firmly pro-Fianna Fáil *Irish Press*. In 1973 the titles were bought by the entrepreneur Tony O'REILLY and the papers were visibly modernized and became less restrained in their coverage. The *Indo*, as it is affectionately called, is still the homegrown media leader, in so far as the term has any meaning in an increasingly globally owned press.

Irish joke. A generally mild racial gibe directed against the Irish, based on the perceived possession by the latter of old STAGE-IRISH characteristics. Such jokes, turning principally on the stereotype of the idiocy of the target, are similar in type to Polish and Bohemian jokes told in the United States. Some typical examples are as follows:

> Seamus and Sean start work at a sawmill. After an hour Seamus lets out a big yell:
>
> 'Help, Sean, I lost me finger!'
>
> Sean says, 'Now how did you go about doing that?'
>
> 'Sure I just touched the big spinning job here, just like thi-- Feck! There goes another one!'
>
> Seamus phones the airline to find out how long it takes to fly from Boston to Dublin.
>
> 'Er, just a minute, sir ...' says the man at the airline.
>
> 'Jasus, that's fast. Thank ye, sor.' And he hangs up.
>
> Seamus says to Sean, 'At me funeral be sure to pour a bottle o' whiskey over me grave.'
>
> 'Sure,' says Sean, 'but ye wouldn't mind if it was to pass through me kidneys first?'

Some of the best of all Irish jokes are those invented by the Irish themselves:

> *Foreman*: Mick, do you even knaw the difference between a joist and a girder?
>
> *Mick*: Sure, sor. Joyce wrote *Ulysses* and Goethe wrote *Faust*.

With perhaps the best of all being:

> Q: What's black and blue and lying in a hospital in Kilburn?
>
> A: The last Englishman to crack an anti-Irish joke.

See also KERRYMAN JOKES.

Irish Literary Revival. The term usually applied to the renaissance in all the arts in Ireland at the turn of the 19th–20th centuries. It had its remote origin in an 18th-century aristocratic interest in the antiquities of Ireland exemplified in Charlotte BROOKE's *Reliques of Irish Poetry* (1795), which was maintained in the more professional work of the ORDNANCE SURVEY scholars, the balladry of YOUNG IRELAND and the successful deliverance of both antiquarian knowledge and folklore by such writers as Samuel FERGUSON, James Clarence MANGAN and William CARLETON.

The movement is believed to have had its instinctive impetus in the political vacuum following the fall of PARNELL. The foundation of the GAA and the GAELIC LEAGUE, the publication of *Fairy and Folk Tales of the Irish Peasantry* (1888) and W.B. YEATS's *The CELTIC TWILIGHT* (1893), strongly primed by Douglas HYDE and Lady GREGORY, and the establishment of the IRISH LITERARY THEATRE (which led to a permanent national theatre at the ABBEY THEATRE) all played their part, and the cumulative effect was considerable.

Though the literary aspects were most obvious, other areas of the arts were not neglected, with affirmation of Irishness in architecture, the visual arts and even an opera in Irish when *Muirgheas* was staged in the GAIETY in December 1915. A renewed interest in ecclesiastical music and art was stimulated by Edward MARTYN, who was one of the leading figures of the revival. He founded the Palestrina Choir in the Pro-Cathedral in Dublin and was co-founder of the FEIS CHEOIL. Modern critics have decried the revival's dependence on peasant culture, mythology and rural settings, and question its relevance to modern Irish life.

> We all did something, but none what he set out to do. Yeats founded a realistic theatre, Edward [Martyn] emptied two churches – he and Palestrina between them – and I wrote *The Untilled Field* ...
>
> GEORGE MOORE (1852–1933): Preface, *The Untilled Field* (1914)

Irish Literary Theatre. The first phase (1899–1901) of the development of a national Irish theatre by W.B. YEATS, Lady GREGORY and Edward MARTYN and as such the forerunner of the ABBEY THEATRE. Their stated intention was

> to have performed in Dublin, in the spring of every year certain Celtic and Irish plays, which whatever their degree of excellence will be written with a high ambition, and so to build up a Celtic and Irish school of dramatic literature.

(For a fuller version, *see* STATEMENT OF INTENT.) In the three years they presented plays by Yeats, Martyn, George MOORE and the first performance of a play in Irish, *CASADH AN*

TSÚGÁIN by Douglas Hyde, on 21 October 1901. The first productions were staged in the ANTIENT CONCERT ROOMS in May 1899, and the others in the larger and more popular GAIETY theatre in February 1900 and October 1901.

Irish mantle. A fringed woollen cloak with a thick nap, universally used in medieval and early modern Ireland. It could be worn day and night, and many were exported to Britain between 1400 and 1700, in spite of government disapproval and heavy taxes. Edmund SPENSER summed up the establishment view in *A View of the Present State of Ireland* (1596):

> … a fit house for an outlaw, a meet bed for a rebel, and an apt cloak for a thief.

The mantle had been previously targeted by the 28th Act of Henry VIII in 1537 (*see* DRESS CODE):

> … no person or persons of what estate, condition or degree they be, shall use or wear any mantles, coat or hood after the Irish fashion …

Irish Melodies. A series of song lyrics by Tom MOORE, published in ten volumes between 1808 and 1824. They were composed with known Irish tunes in mind; these had been recorded by Edward BUNTING (1773–1843) at the BELFAST HARP FESTIVAL and had suffered a certain amount of prettification at his hands. Moore's 'ingenious coadjutor', Sir John Stevenson, was also accused of elaborating the musical arrangements and spoiling the simplicity of the original airs, especially in his florid operatic introductions. Yet for all their society elegance, especially when sung in Whig drawing rooms by their author, they were unquestionably Irish and played a significant part in keeping the ills of his country before the eyes of his political hosts. Almost immediately they became part of a general heritage of song, and were mentioned at least 20 times in Charles Dickens's novels. The continuing popularity of such numbers as 'Believe Me' (sung in *Bleak House* and *The Old Curiosity Shop*), 'The Harp that Once', 'The LAST ROSE OF SUMMER' and 'At the Mid-hour of Night' echoes the author's own prediction in a letter written to his publisher Thomas Longman in 1827:

> With what you say about Lalla Rookh being the 'cream of the copyrights', perhaps it may be in a *property* sense; but I am strongly inclined to think that in a race into future times (if *anything* of mine could pretend to such a run), those little ponies, the 'Melodies' will beat the mare Lalla Rookh hollow.

See also MUSICAL SNUFF-BOX.

Irish Mist. The first Irish liqueur, made from a combination of TULLAMORE DEW whiskey, honey and herbs. It was launched in 1948 by Desmond Williams, grandson of D.E. Williams, who gave his name to Tullamore Dew. It claimed to be based on 'the drink of the ancient Irish chieftains, heather wine'.

Irish National Foresters (INF). A friendly society for mutual insurance, founded in Cork in 1848 as a branch of the English organization known as the Ancient Order of Foresters. As Nationalist awareness increased, the INF broke away from its English affiliation and formed an entirely Irish society in Dublin in 1877. The members had green and gold dress uniforms and cocked hats, making their gatherings look like a Robert EMMET convention. But though they had banners decorated with shamrocks, harps and Celtic crosses like the AOH (and the ORANGE ORDER, *mutatis mutandis*), they were essentially a welfare society with little in the way of a political agenda. The need for private welfare insurance diminished with the Lloyd George Insurance Act of 1911, and the INF assumed an essentially social function, with clubrooms in many Irish towns:

> Peter is in full dress of the Foresters: green coat, gold braided; white breeches, top boots, frilled shirt. He carries the slouch hat with the white ostrich plume, and the sword in his hand.
>
> SEAN O'CASEY (1880–1964): *The Plough and the Stars* (1926), stage direction for Act I

Irish News, The. A Belfast Nationalist morning paper, first published in 1891. It grew out of the Belfast *Morning News,* founded in 1858 as a penny journal and stated by its rivals to be a paper for 'servants, street sweepers, peddlers and pot-hops'. The *Irish News* was strongly against PARNELL because of the revelations of his relationship with Katharine O'Shea (*see* O'SHEA WHO MUST BE OBEYED). Its first number was published on 15 August 1891 and it has remained the chief voice of Nationalist Ulster.

Irish of Vincennes, the. In August 1982 three Irish people – Mary Reid (1953–2003), Stephen King and Michael Plunkett – all members of the Irish Republican Socialist Party (the political wing of the INLA) were arrested on terrorism charges in an apartment in the Parisian suburb of Vincennes. The arrests were lauded as a success for a new anti-terrorism unit. It later emerged, however, that police had planted guns and explosives in the apartment and all three were cleared of the charges in October 1983, after spending nine months in prison.

Irish Parliamentary Party. *See* IRISH PARTY.

Irish Party. The name by which the Nationalist or Irish Parliamentary Party (also called Home Rule Party) in Westminster was known between 1882 and 1922. It grew out of Isaac BUTT's Home Rule League, but it was not until Charles Stewart PARNELL was elected chairman of the party in 1880 at the height of the LAND WAR that a cohesive party of loyal pledge-bound MPs began to take shape.

During the years until the split of 1890 Parnell exerted total control over the party, throwing its influence behind land agitation. He declined, however, to support militant movements like the PLAN OF CAMPAIGN, which he feared would threaten the alliance with the Liberals, formed in 1886 when the 86 Irish Party MPs held the balance of power in the House of Commons; Parnell had switched the party's allegiance from the Conservatives when it became clear that, unlike Gladstone, Conservative leaders would never support Home Rule.

Parnell also established a party newspaper, *United Ireland*, and a formidable constituency organization, the National League (*see* LAND LEAGUE), which attracted financial support from Irish interests at home and abroad. It was a considerable achievement for the leader and his party that a HOME RULE Bill was introduced by Gladstone as early as April 1886. The split in the parliamentary party in 1890 over Parnell's involvement in the O'Shea divorce case (*see* O'SHEA WHO MUST BE OBEYED; COMMITTEE ROOM 15) was seriously damaging for the cause of Home Rule, but until the Liberal Prime Minister H.H. Asquith (1852–1928) passed the Parliament Act of 1911 limiting the power of the House of Lords, there was no serious possibility of the passage of a Home Rule bill in any case.

The Irish Party, under its leader John REDMOND, did achieve the formal aim of Home Rule on 18 September 1914, although the implementation of the bill was postponed until after the end of the First World War, which had broken out the previous month. Also postponed was the Ulster question – a problem bequeathed by the parliamentarians, who had made efforts to solve it, to the Republicans of SINN FÉIN, who simply ignored the question until after the TREATY was signed. Until the success of Sinn Féin in the general election of 1918 – which came after the 1916 EASTER RISING and the CONSCRIPTION CRISIS – the Irish Party had overwhelming popular support in Nationalist Ireland and, a very significant factor, the support of the hierarchy and active participation of many parish clergy. By 1918 many of the men who were radicals and agrarian agitators in the 1880s had become elder statesmen – John DILLON was a notable example – and, although fine parliamentarians and dedicated public servants, they were out of touch with the zeitgeist.

Irish Press, The. A Dublin daily newspaper founded in September 1931 by Éamon DE VALERA and controlled by the de Valera family until it folded in 1995 as a result of union–management problems. Its first editor was Frank Gallagher (1893–1962), who had been deputy to Erskine Childers on the staff of the

IRISH VOLUNTEER propaganda news-sheet *The IRISH BULLETIN*. The *Irish Press* appealed to women, to Irish-language enthusiasts and in general to the working and lower middle classes. It was also the first paper to provide full coverage of the Sunday Gaelic games. Its sister newspapers, the *Sunday Press* (founded 1949) and the *Evening Press* (founded 1954) had very large circulations, the *Evening Press* being regarded as the voice of Dublin. Éamon KELLY tells the story of attempts made to sell copies of the *Press* to Kerry farmers in the fair field in Killarney during the ECONOMIC WAR: 'We have presses enough,' was the angry riposte of a harassed farmer, 'and nothing to put into them.'

Irish pubs. *See* IRISH BARS.

Irish Question, the. A phrase applied to the problem of what to do with Ireland, from the British point of view. It really only became an issue after CATHOLIC EMANCIPATION, when Irish Nationalists from Daniel O'CONNELL on showed themselves to be able parliamentarians seemingly not wholly incapable of some measure of self-government.

When Gladstone formed his first administration (1868–74) after an election fought solely on the issue of the DISESTABLISHMENT OF THE CHURCH OF IRELAND, he stated his commitment to resolving the Irish Question: 'My mission is to pacify Ireland.' Subsequently he tackled the land question (*see* LAND ACTS) and the question of denominational university education (*see* QUEEN'S COLLEGES; ROYAL UNIVERSITY OF IRELAND; NATIONAL UNIVERSITY).

After the introduction of universal male household suffrage in 1884 the IRISH PARTY became a force to be reckoned with, holding the balance of power in Westminster. Between the HAWARDEN KITE of 1885 and 1894, when he retired, Gladstone had introduced two HOME RULE bills, something that would have been unthinkable even twenty years previously. In the 1890s and the early 1900s the Conservative government's method of dealing with the Irish Question has been described as KILLING HOME RULE WITH KINDNESS or 'Constructive Unionism', a policy that did not permanently solve the Irish problem even if it did help to pacify the population.

It has been said that just when the British thought they had solved the problem, the Irish changed the question, and this is certainly true of the second decade of the 20th century: from a campaign for Home Rule to an acceptance of a TREATY that was, in Michael COLLINS's words, a stepping-stone on the way to complete independence.

Irish Republican Army. *See* IRA.

Irish Republican Brotherhood. *See* IRB.

Irish RM, Experiences of an. *See* SOME EXPERIENCES OF AN IRISH RM.

Irish Rugby Football Union. *See* RUGBY FOOTBALL.

Irish solution to a particularly Irish problem, an. The justification offered by Taoiseach Charles J. HAUGHEY for his Contraceptive Bill of 1979. The importation and sale of contraceptives had been banned in Ireland since 1935, and after skirmishes with the authorities such as the CONTRACEPTIVE TRAIN incident, a fatal blow against the legality of the ban was struck when the Supreme Court judged in favour of the appellant in the landmark MCGEE CASE in 1973. From 1973 to 1979 family-planning clinics could not sell contraceptives, but could give them to clients in return for a donation. Meanwhile doctors prescribed the Pill ostensibly as a means of regulating menstruation. When, finally and reluctantly, Charles Haughey's Fianna Fáil government grasped the nettle of contraceptive legislation, it was to make condoms available in pharmacies on prescription 'for bona fide family-planning purposes'. The bill caused a mixture of incredulity and derision, but the wily Haughey had ensured that contraception was no longer a contentious issue in Irish society, and increased liberalization of sale and supply followed over the next ten years. The contraceptive battle was yet another lost by the Catholic Church.

Irish stew. A traditional one-pot dish, such as is common in peasant or rural cultures worldwide; it involves cooking pieces of lamb or mutton (originally kid) with potatoes and onions, stock and herbs, over a slow heat or in an oven for several hours until the potatoes are thoroughly saturated. Purists decry the use of carrots, current in some parts of the country and used also to colour what is otherwise a very anaemic-looking dish. Ireland is not traditionally known for its cuisine, Irish stew being probably its most recognizable culinary export.

Irish Times, The. A daily newspaper, Ireland's first penny newspaper, founded in 1859 by Major Ronald Knox, a member of Isaac BUTT's HOME RULE Party. Initially published thrice-weekly, it had become a daily paper by the end of 1859. It was bought by the merchant Sir John Arnott in 1873. Even after the foundation of the Free State the paper, once dubbed 'that jaundiced journal of west-Britonism', continued to represent the ASCENDANCY and Protestant viewpoint. It took the editorship of Robert Smyllie (1935–54; see NICHEVO) to modernize and liberalize the paper. It subsequently became a voice of liberalism and general decency, contributing greatly to the debate about the nature of Irish society that raged from the 1960s onwards, regarding such issues as contraception, abortion and divorce. The more populist and energetic *Irish Independent* far exceeds it in terms of sales.

Irish Traditional Music Archive. A reference and resource centre funded by the arts councils of Ireland and Northern Ireland (see ACNI; CHOMHAIRLE EALAÍON, AN). Founded in 1987 and now with premises in Dublin's Merrion Square, it holds the largest collection of traditional music anywhere, and works with broadcasting organizations such as RTÉ and the BBC to archive recordings and collections.

Irish Volunteer Defence Corps. See GORGEOUS WRECKS.

Irish Volunteers. A military organization founded on 25 November 1913 as the result of an article by Eoin MACNEILL, 'The North

Began', in the GAELIC LEAGUE organ *An CLAIDEAMH SOLUIS* of 1 November. MacNeill suggested that Nationalist Ireland should imitate Northern Unionists, who had founded their own Ulster Volunteer Force (see UVF) in January 1913. The Irish Volunteers were established at a public meeting at the Rotunda in Dublin by MacNeill and Bulmer HOBSON, an IRB member. MacNeill read the Volunteer manifesto, which concluded:

> In the name of national unity, of national dignity, of national and individual liberty, of manly citizenship, we appeal to our countrymen to recognize and accept without hesitation the opportunity that has been granted them to join the ranks of the Irish Volunteers, and to make the movement now begun, not unworthy of the historic title which it has adopted.

(The latter reference was to the VOLUNTEERS of the 18th century.)

The Volunteers immediately attracted followers from among members of cultural Nationalist organizations such as the Gaelic League, the GAA and SINN FÉIN, as well as IRB members. By May 1914 the membership was 80,000 strong. The organization split after John REDMOND's speech at WOODENBRIDGE on 20 September 1914, urging Irish participation in the First World War, the majority supporting Redmond and forming the NATIONAL VOLUNTEERS. The more radical rump reorganized in November 1914, retaining the name 'Irish Volunteers'. The Irish Volunteers played a major role in the EASTER RISING, but by the time of the ANGLO-IRISH WAR of 1919–21 they were more commonly known as the IRA.
See also CUMANN NA MBAN.

Irish women, the. The name (Flemish *de Iershce damen*) given to the sisters of the Benedictine Abbey at Ypres in modern Belgium), founded in 1665, which was formally made an Irish monastery in 1682. During the 17th and 18th centuries, the daughters of the Irish nobility came to Ypres, first as students, with some returning later to become members of the community. It was these 'Irish women' who founded the Benedictine abbey at Kylemore in Co. Galway in 1920.

Irish Women's Franchise League / Irish Women's Suffrage Federation. *See* BENNETT, LOUIE; *IRISH CITIZEN, THE*; SHEEHY-SKEFFINGTON, HANNA; WOMEN'S SUFFRAGE.

Irish Women Workers' Union (IWWU). A trade union for women founded by Delia LARKIN (along with Helen Chenevix, Louie BENNETT and Helena MOLONY) in 1911 as a companion organization to her brother James LARKIN's new union, the ITGWU. Louie Bennett was its general secretary from 1917 to 1955. Among the union's important campaigns were opposition to the CONSTITUTION OF 1937 because of its denial of women's rights, and the laundry workers' successful strike in 1945 for the right to two weeks' paid holidays. The IWWU was amalgamated with the Federated Workers' Union of Ireland in 1984.

Irregulars. A term used especially by pro-Treatyites and Free-Staters to describe Republican soldiers in the CIVIL WAR, based on the premise that Republicans were irregular soldiers as opposed to the regular Free State army. This term was (not unnaturally) offensive to Republicans themselves, and is still offensive to their descendants.

Irvine, Alexander. *See* MY LADY OF THE CHIMNEY CORNER.

Irvine, Andy (b.1942). Musician. Irvine, who was born in London, came to Ireland in the early 1960s. He has played with a number of traditional groups including Sweeny's Men, DÉ DANANN and PLANXTY[2], and with such musicians and singers as Paul Brady, Donal LUNNY, Arty McGlynn and Christy MOORE. He plays guitar, bouzouki, mandolin and harmonica, most recently performing solo and with the group Patrick Street.

'I see His blood upon the rose'. *See* PLUNKETT, JOSEPH MARY.

Iseult or **Isolde.** The Irish princess in the Arthurian cycle who, betrothed to King Mark of Cornwall, falls in love with Tristan, the king's

nephew, who has been sent to fetch her from Ireland. It all ends badly. She gave her name to the Co. Dublin village of Chapelizod.

Isky Biaha. A version of *uisce beatha* (*see* USGUE-BAUGH) cited by Thomas Dineley (d.1695) in his *Tour in Ireland* (1681) as a cure for the 'Irish Disease, a dysenteria or bloody flux so called':

> … it is agreed on all hands, that the stronger cordial liquors, as brandy, *aqua vitae* (called here *isky biaha*), and vulgarly in England, *usquebath* … are good and proper. For besides the energy to make the blood more lively, they may also cause a propensity to sweating, whereby the badness of the blood may be thrown off into the habit of the body, so by a diaphoresis [artificially induced sweat] happily avert the humour.

Island, the. The universal nickname for the Queen's Island in Belfast (also once known as DARGAN'S ISLAND), especially when referring to the HARLAND AND WOLFF shipyard sited there.

> In a shipyard, boys do the work of men and men do the work of giants. In the Queen's Island they still talk of the worker who drove over three thousand rivets in nine hours.
>
>   SAM HANNA BELL: 'I Work down the Island', in *Erin's Orange Lily* (1956)

Island of Saints and Scholars. The exclusivist claim to fame for Ireland first mentioned in *Ireland's Ancient Schools and Scholars* (1893) by Archbishop John Healy, where he states that the country was known as *Insula Sanctorum et Doctorum* from the 12th century. It is a slightly dubious assertion where the '*et Doctorum*' is concerned. There is, however, plenty of evidence for the '*Sanctorum*'. MARIANUS SCOTTUS (OF COLOGNE) in his *Chronicon* (1083), a chronicle of events from the Creation to 1083, writes of

> *Hibernia insula sanctorum sanctis mirabilibus perplurimis sublimiter plena habebitur.*
> (Ireland, island of saints, is considered as exceptionally full of very wonderful holy men.)

In case this may seem chauvinistic, a non-Irish source, Jocelin of Furness (*c*.1180–85), confidently asserts:

Ita ut Hibernia speciali nomine insula sanctorum ubique terrarum iure nominaretur.

(Ireland is thus rightly described everywhere in the world by the special term 'Island of Saints'.)

A 9th-century text has the phrase: '*Scotia uber sanctorum patrum insula*' ('Ireland, an island abounding with holy fathers'), and by the early 1600s the title had become a commonplace. The tradition of Irish scholarship as an adjunct to sanctity is also quite old, as the careers of such *DOCTI* as SEDULIUS SCOTTUS, John Scottus ERIUGENA and CLEMENT SCOTTUS indicate. The combined phrase may be quite modern and deliberately formulated to counter 19th-century gibes about Ireland's lack of civilization. It convinced the fiery Walter Savage Landor (1775–1864), and he blazed forth in a comically savage poem in 1853:

> Ireland never was contented …
> Say you so? You are demented.
> Ireland was contented when
> All could use the sword and pen
> And when Tara rose so high
> That her turrets split the sky,
> About her courts were seen
> Liveried angels robed in green,
> Wearing by St Patrick's bounty
> Emeralds big as half the county.
>
> 'Ireland Never Was Contented'

Isle of Man. A large island roughly equidistant from England, Ireland, Scotland and Wales, as any traveller to the top of Snaefell, its highest point (616 m / 2064 ft) can confirm. The Manx name is *Ellan Vannin*, which, like the homophonic Irish *Oileán Mhanannán*, means 'Manannán's Isle'. The island figures little in early mythology apart from the belief that the rain and mist that blanket it from time to time is generated by MANANNÁN MAC LIR as a protection against enemies. It was British until the 4th century AD, but colonization from Ireland made the language clearly Gaelic. It was later settled by the Vikings, and then passed to the Scots in 1266, before coming under English control in 1341. Modern Manx is a form of Irish spelled phonetically as if it were English. According to later folktales, the island was formed by the earth scooped up from mid-Ulster that the giant (loosely associated with FIONN MAC CUMHAIL) who made the GIANT'S CAUSEWAY in Antrim used as a missile against the Scottish giant Fingal (who in some accounts is, confusingly, the same person as Fionn), thus simultaneously forming LOUGH NEAGH.

Istabraq. A celebrated steeplechaser, dear to the heart of Irish racegoers and the Irish public. He was owned by J.P. McManus, trained by Aidan O'Brien and ridden by Charlie SWAN. Three times winner of the Championship Hurdle at Cheltenham from 1998 (the Cheltenham meeting was cancelled in 2001 because of foot-and-mouth disease), he was a somewhat frail ten-year-old when he contested his fourth Championship Hurdle in 2002. He earned the applause of the crowd when he had to be withdrawn after the second fence.

Ita or **Íde** (b.*c*.480). The saint who after BRIGID was the most venerated in Irish hagiology. Like her she is the subject of many wonder tales, including one that claims she suckled the infant Jesus. The historical Ita was born in Drum, Co. Waterford, and was originally called Deirdre (the name Íde, meaning 'hungry for God', was an adopted one). She established the nunnery that bears her name at Killeedy (*Cill Íde*, 'Ita's church') in Co. Limerick. BRENDAN THE VOYAGER is believed to have been one of her pupils. Her fame spread beyond Ireland, and she featured in one of the poems of ALCUIN. Her feast day is 15 January.

> Tiny fosterling, I love thee,
> Of no churlish house thou art:
> Thou, with angels' wings above thee,
> Nestlest night-long next my heart.
>
> ANON.: 'Saint Ita's Fosterling' (8th century), translated by Robin Flower (1881–1946)

ITGWU. The Irish Transport and General Workers' Union, the trade union founded by James LARKIN in December 1908 after his suspension by the National Union of Dock Labourers, the group that had sent him to Dublin. Larkin, who was both a socialist and a Nationalist, was an inspired orator and an efficient organizer, appealing to workers' desires for improved conditions and for some measure of national self-determination. Union numbers reached 10,000 by 1913. It was to prevent workers from joining the ITGWU that Dublin employers locked them out in 1913 (*see* 1913 LOCKOUT).

After the failure of the strike Larkin left the demoralized union in the hands of James CONNOLLY and William O'Brien and spent almost seven years in America; in his absence membership grew to 120,000, many of this number being recruited from among the hitherto unorganized agricultural labourers. A split resulted from Larkin's attempts to regain control of the union on his return in 1923, and the union he founded in 1924, the Workers Union of Ireland (WUI), attracted 60,000 ITGWU members, almost all in Dublin.

The ITGWU continued to be a major force in Irish trade unionism and prospered especially after the Second World War, absorbing several smaller unions and finally healing the breach with the WUI when both unions were affiliated to the Irish Congress of Trade Unions in 1959. The ITGWU and WUI amalgamated in 1990 to form SIPTU (Services, Industrial, Professional and Technical Union), which currently has more than 200,000 members.

See also IRISH WOMEN WORKERS' UNION.

Ith. In Irish mythology, one of the MILESIANS. He is the grandson of MÍL, and sees Ireland from a tower in Spain and decides to visit it. He lands with 90 followers in Kerry just after the second battle of MAGH TUIREADH (Moytura), in which the TUATHA DÉ DANAAN have defeated the FOMORIANS. Asked, as an honest broker, to divide the land of Ireland between three Dé Danaan brothers – Mac Cecht, the husband of FODLA, Mac Cuill, the husband of BANBA, and Mac Greine, the husband of Eriu (or ÉIRE) – he waxes so enthusiastic about the place that they think he wishes to have it for himself. They kill him, and his followers take his body back to Spain. The invasion by the Milesians, who rout the Tuatha dé Danaan,

follows. (This invasion is taken to be the coming of the historical Celts, an event which lingered in the folk memory.)

'It's a Long Way to Tipperary'. *See* TIPPERARY.

Iveagh, 1st Earl of. *See* GUINNESS.

Iveragh Peninsula (Irish *Uíbh Rathach*). The most southerly and largest peninsula of Co. Kerry, an area of majestic beauty that includes most of the Ring of Kerry (*see* KERRY, RING OF), the MACGILLICUDDY REEKS (which have Ireland's highest mountain, CARRANTUOHILL), the small towns of Waterville and Cahirciveen, and the island of VALENTIA. Until recent years a GAELTACHT was centred around Ballinskelligs (the area is still officially a Gaeltacht), and a lively tradition of folklore and music remains. SCEILIG MHICHÍL and STAIGUE FORT are both popular tourist destinations, but an extensive archaeological survey, carried out from the mid-1980s to the mid-1990s, documented hundreds of little-known pre-Christian and early Christian monuments – forts, crosses, stone slabs, oratories, rock art and graves.

Ives. *See* IA.

'Ivy Day at the Committee Room'. A story in James Joyce's DUBLINERS (1914) written in 1905, heavy with the brooding presence of the dead PARNELL. There is a sense of departed glory as three canvassers prepare to help fight a municipal election, and as they chat they recall that it is the anniversary of Parnell's death (6 October 1891). Three bottles of stout are placed on the hearth and their popping corks are a mock-heroic version of a graveside salute. Before the end of the evening, Joe Hynes, an old Parnellite, recites a ballad called 'The Death of Parnell':

> He is dead. Our Uncrowned King is dead,
> O, Erin, mourn with grief and woe
> For he lies dead whom the fell gang
> Of modern hypocrites laid low.

IWW (Industrial Workers of the World). *See* JONES, MOTHER.

IWWU. *See* IRISH WOMEN WORKERS' UNION.

J

Jack. *See* JACKEEN.

Jack-acting. A term signifying 'playing the fool'.
See also ACT THE MAGGOT, TO.

Jackeen. A nickname for a native Dubliner (Jack and the diminutive 'een'), in use since the mid-19th century. The tautological 'Dublin jackeen' is also used. The word is used to convey, sometimes disparagingly, the distinction between a city slicker and a CULCHIE. The original meaning of the word seems to have had the same root as *seoinín* (*see* SHONEEN), a gaelicization of John Bull, meaning a pro-British person. Another suggestion is the miniature Union Jacks given to Dublin children to wave when Queen Victoria visited Ireland in 1900, hence 'jackeen'.
See also DUB.

Jacko. The nickname of Jack O'Shea (b.1957), a member of Kerry's Gaelic football team. He was born on 19 November 1957 in Cahirciveen, Co. Kerry. A star midfielder, he won seven senior ALL-IRELAND medals between 1978 and 1986 and six All Star awards in the same period. In the 1984 and 1986 COMPROMISE RULES series against Australia he was Irish captain.

Jack's Army. The name by which supporters of the Republic of Ireland soccer team managed by Jack CHARLTON (1986–95) were known.

Charlton's reign brought unprecedented success and acclaim to the Irish team, especially in the World Cup finals of 1990 (Italy) and 1994 (USA).

Jackson, William (1737–95). United Irishman. He was born in Dublin and took orders in London, gaining a considerable reputation as a radical journalist, vigorous in his support for the American War of Independence. He was chaplain to the notorious Duchess of Kingston, whom he followed into exile in France in 1792. There he was given the task of determining the chances of success of a French invasion of Ireland. He renewed acquaintance with John Cokayne, who had been the duchess's attorney, and who agreed to accompany him. Unaware that Cokayne was a government spy, promised a pension by William Pitt, Jackson confided the details of his mission to his travelling companion. To deepen the black comedy, their contact among the UNITED IRISHMEN was Leonard MCNALLY, the most successful and longest serving of the government agents. They arrived in Dublin in April 1794 and on the advice of Hamilton ROWAN contacted Wolfe TONE as the man best equipped to write the appraisal of the true state of feeling in the country. Tone completed his appraisal on 14 April and almost at once realized how vulnerable the existence of the document had left him. Jackson was arrested on 28 April, and by the time of his trial a year later Tone had decided it prudent to leave for America. Jackson played out the tragic farce: on 30 April 1795, the day he was due to be sentenced for high treason, he was found slumped in the dock, dead from the poison that his wife had smuggled into prison for him.

Jack White's. A pub in Brittas, Co. Wicklow, on the main Wickow–Gorey road. In a celebrated legal case, Catherine Nevin, dubbed 'the Black Widow' by the media, was convicted in 2000 of having arranged the murder of her husband Tom Nevin, the owner of Jack White's pub, by hired killers.

Jacob, Rosamund (1888–1960). Novelist and biographer. She was born in Waterford city to a middle-class Quaker family. As a Republican, she was a member of the GAELIC LEAGUE, INGHINIDHE NA HÉIREANN, SINN FÉIN and CUMANN NA MBAN. As a feminist, she was a member of the Irish Women's Suffrage League and a friend of Hanna SHEEHY-SKEFFINGTON, one of its founders. She opposed the TREATY and was imprisoned by the Free State government, but after the foundation of the state her attention turned to campaigning for civil liberties and for peace: she opposed the 1926 Censorship of Publications Act (*see* CENSORSHIP) and capital punishment, and became a member of the Campaign for Nuclear Disarmament (CND) in the final years of her life. As well as the feminist novels *Callaghan* (published under the pseudonym 'F. Winthrop' in 1920) and *The Troubled House* (1938), Jacob published a biography of Matilda TONE, *The Rebel's Wife* (1957).

Jacobite. A follower of JAMES II and his descendants, James the OLD PRETENDER and Charles Edward the YOUNG PRETENDER. The Catholic Irish continued to support the Stuarts in the hope of recovery of political power should the dynasty be restored to the British and Irish thrones. They fought with James II against William III (KING BILLY) in the WILLIAMITE WAR, and their poets wrote many poems in Irish and in English wishing for the coming of first his son James, then James's son Charles. This was especially true of the type of Irish poem known as the AISLING. Four of the 'seven men of Moidart' who landed with Bonnie Prince Charlie in Scotland in 1745 were Irish.

Jailic. *See* JAILTEACHT, THE.

Jail Journal. *See* MITCHEL, JOHN.

Jailteacht, the. Republican prisoners from Northern Ireland who acquired a knowledge of Irish while in jail for 'political' offences were said to have learnt 'Jailic' in the 'Jailteacht', be it the PORTLAOISE or the MAZE Jailteacht (the word puns on GAELTACHT). Whether or not the British government of the day admitted the reality of political status, de facto such prisoners were allowed free association with other Republicans, a good deal of leisure time and ample library facilities and educational opportunities. The association of the Irish language with PHYSICAL-FORCE REPUBLICANISM is a sensitive issue in both North and South.

Jakus. A euphemistic version of 'Jasus' (Jesus) used as an imprecation.

JAM. *See* MARRIAGE BAN, THE.

James II (1633–1701). King of England and Scotland from 1685. James had little of the statecraft of his brother Charles II in matters of religion and politics. He had become a Catholic in 1669 and remained an object of deep suspicion to the Protestant establishment. His use of the royal prerogative in nullifying the Test Act to advance Catholics in the army and civil administration deepened that suspicion, and the birth to him of a male child in June 1688 caused opposition forces to offer the throne to William of Orange (later William III), the Protestant husband of James's daughter Mary. When William reached London he allowed James a safe passage to France, whereupon James became a kind of pawn in the machinations of Louis XIV.

Louis sent James to Ireland, where a judicious restraint might have enabled him to retain sovereignty. The influence of James's Irish deputy TYRCONNELL proved too strong, and when he landed at Kinsale on 12 March 1689 the country was largely run by Catholics. James's demand for submission was rejected by the besieged Protestants of Derry in April, and with an uncharacteristic failure of nerve he fled the field at the Battle of the BOYNE in July 1690, thereby earning the contempt of both sides and the faecal nickname SÉAMAS AN CHACA. Shortly after, James left Ireland for good.

James's Street! A euphemistic interjection, deploying the name of the Dublin street where the GUINNESS brewery is located. The street was also once the site of a famous foundling hospital, and in the 18th century it formed part of the course of a whipping run for the punishment of wrongdoers.

Janey Mack! A Dublin interjection, used euphemistically instead of 'Jesus!' *Janey Mack Me Shirt Is Black* (1982) is the title of a book of Dublin street lore by Éamon MAC THOMÁIS, deriving from the children's rhyme:

Janey Mack me shirt is black!
What will I do for Sunday?
Go to bed and cover your head,
And don't get up till Monday!

Jansenism. A Catholic theological movement originating in the Netherlands and taking its name from Cornelius Jansen (1585–1638), Bishop of Ypres. Its central tenet is that all human nature is corrupt, that Christ died only for a few, and that all the rest are irredeemably condemned to hell. It was opposed by the papacy and the bull *Unigenitus* (1713) meant that it ceased to be a mainstream movement. It was also particularly disapproved of in France, where many Irish clerics studied for the priesthood in the 18th century. Irish Catholicism is often described as 'Jansenistic', but this is a loose description, often indicating the speaker's disapproval of the stern moral code and perceived sexual puritanism of Catholic clergy, even in the 20th century, rather than any more formal affiliation to the movement.

Jar. A measure of strong drink, the word deriving from the earthenware jar formerly used for beer and spirits. It is a very popular colloquialism in several forms: 'Going [out] for a jar' or 'a few jars' is a common Irish pastime. 'Jarred' is a Dublin slang word for 'drunk', and 'He has a few jars on him' is also used.

Musha ring dumma do dumma da
Whack fol de daddy-o
Whack fol de daddy-o
There's whiskey in the jar
ANON.: 'Whiskey in the Jar'

Jarlath (d.c.550). The patron saint of the archdiocese of Tuam. He was a disciple of Benen (who himself was taught by PATRICK) at Kilbennan, Co. Galway, and chose to stay close to his master when he founded his own monastery at Cluain Fois. One of his disciples, BRENDAN THE VOYAGER, is said to have advised him to travel east on his chariot and at the spot where a wheel should break he was to build a church and a school. The place was Tuam, 4 km (2.5 miles) away, and the archbishops of Tuam still wear a ring engraved with a broken wheel. The school founded there c.520 rivalled CLONMACNOISE as a centre of Celtic art in the 11th and 12th centuries. Jarlath's feast day is 6 June.

Jarvey, The. A humorous journal (1889–90) written and illustrated by Percy FRENCH. It was named after the drivers of jaunting cars, known universally as JARVEYS. It folded after two years, but it kept French afloat financially after he lost his job as inspector of drains for the Board of Works in Co. Cavan. The following morsel of deathless verse was reprinted from *The Jarvey* because of local interest by the *Sligo Independent* on 17 August 1889 (Mullaghmore is one of many Co. Sligo resorts):

Of all bewcheous situations
For tourists' recreations
(I make these observations
As I walk along the shore;)
The finest naval cinther
The Atlantic waves can inther,
In summer or in winther,
Is lovely Mullaghmore.

Jarveys. The name by which the drivers (usually male) of JAUNTING CARS in Killarney are known. The word may come from St Gervase, whose symbol was the whip. The archetypal jarvey speaks with a strong brogue and tells tall tales, even about local botany and topography, and the archetypal victim of jarvey-chat is an American tourist. Jarveys are commonly believed to be unscrupulous or at least avaricious, but this view does not take into account their long periods of inactivity, even during the short summer season, and the vicissitudes of the tourist trade. In 2001 Killarney jarveys celebrated the 250th anniversary of the first commercial jarvey activity in Killarney, but it seems likely that the mode of conveyance became popular for transporting passengers from the railway station to hotels in and near the town from 1850.
See also KATE KEARNEY'S COTTAGE.

Jaunting car. A light horse-drawn two-wheeler with a seat for the driver, usually known as a JARVEY, and side seats for the passengers, either facing inwards (in an inside car, more commonly called a trap) or outwards (in an outside car). Jaunting cars, punningly also known as 'tourist traps', still make a pleasant transport option for tourists in Killarney, the patter of the jarvey being a great part of the attraction. According to GBS in *John Bull's Other Island* (1898) they were the 'last survivors of the public vehicles known to earlier generations as Beeyankiny cars' (*see* BIANS):

> Make up your mind; don't be unkind
> And we'll drive to Castlebar.
> To the road I'm no stranger.
> To you there's no danger,
> So hop like a bird on me ould jaunting car.
>> ANON.: 'Come! Come, beautiful Eileen' (mid-19th cent.)

Jaw wages. A colloquialism used in Ulster meaning 'low (subsistence) wages'. The association with jaw is probably that of putting food in the mouth.

Jealous Wall, the. A Gothic folly or 'wall' built by Lord Belvedere in the 1750s between his own house and that of the neighbouring house of his brother, George Rochfort, in order that one house could not be seen from the other. The brothers were bitter enemies. Belvedere House, now restored, is near Mullingar, Co. Westmeath, and has magnificent gardens.

Jeanie Johnston. A perfect replica of a sailing ship (or COFFIN SHIP) from the period of the Great Famine, built over a period of 12 years (1988–2000) at Blennerville near Tralee in Co. Kerry. A 51-m (167-ft), 40-berth working vessel, with modern navigation aids and facilities, it had its first sea trial in early April 2002. The project emphasized North–South cooperation, but attracted unfavourable attention when it became clear that the final cost – €9.8 million of it paid by taxpayers – would be nearly €14 million instead of the €5.46 originally budgeted, although the vessel is thought to be worth no more than about €2 million. The *Jeanie Johnston* sailed both ways across the Atlantic in 2003.

Jellett, Mainie (1897–1944). Artist. She was born Mary Harriett Jellett in the family home in Fitzwilliam Square, Dublin. Her father was a barrister. She was educated at home – her teachers included Lolly YEATS – and attended the Metropolitan School of Art in Dublin and the Westminster School of Art in London, where she formed a friendship with the stained-glass artist Evie Hone and was taught by Walter Sickert. Her early paintings were post-impressionist oils, but in 1921 she and Evie HONE studied in Paris under André Lhote, a disciple of Picasso, who taught them cubism. At the first joint exhibition of their abstract work in Dublin in 1924 they were neither understood nor appreciated. Jellett devoted a good deal of time to non-representational religious art, seeing similarities between cubism and Celtic art, and taught, lectured, wrote and broadcast to promote modern art. She also worked with textiles, carpets, theatre sets and shop signs. By the 1940s she had become part of a circle of avant-garde artists in Dublin, including Norah McGuinness and Louis LE BROCQUY. In 1943 she was the first chair of the Irish Exhibition of Living Art (IELA), which set out to show work that was too experimental for traditional galleries. She died of cancer at the age of 47.

Jellybaby. A term used during the TROUBLES referring to the practice of concealing sticks of 'jelly' (gelignite) in a baby's buggy for transportation. The source is the popular gelatine-and-sugar sweet.

Jem or **jemmy** or (now more current) **jembo.** A word used in Dublin originally meaning a 'smart, dapper man' and now used to signify 'that fellow' or 'YER MAN': 'Look at jem over there with the cap.'

Jennings, Pat (b.1945). Soccer player. He was born on 12 June 1945 in Newry, Co. Down, and played professional football for Tottenham Hotspur (1964–77) and Arsenal. A world-class goalkeeper, he was capped 119 times for Northern Ireland (1964–86), retiring after that year's World Cup.

Jerpoint Abbey. The ruins of a Cistercian abbey situated just south of Thomastown, Co. Kilkenny. The abbey was built by the king of Ossory, Donal MacGillapatrick, around 1160. It was originally a Benedictine foundation, but was taken over by Cistercians from Baltinglass Abbey in Co. Wicklow in 1180. It was a totally self-contained and self-supporting community. At the time of the Dissolution of the Monasteries (1537–40), the abbey and its extensive estates were granted on lease to James, Earl of Ormond.

Jew, Turk or atheist. See EVEN THE PIGS ARE PROTESTANTS.

Jew that Shakespeare drew, the. The popular verdict on Charles MACKLIN's portrayal of Shylock at Drury Lane in February 1741. Expressed in the couplet –

This is the Jew
That Shakespeare drew

– it was a tribute to Macklin's recovery of the character from the sink of low comedy. His interpretation was the result of much research, but it succeeded beyond even the actor's hopes:

> At this period I threw out all my fire; and as the contrasted passions of joy for the Merchant's losses, and the grief for the elopement of Jessica, open a field for the actor's powers, I had the good fortune to please beyond my warmest expectations. The whole house was in an uproar of applause and I was obliged to pause between the speeches to give it vent, so as to be heard.
>
> *Memoirs of Charles Macklin* (1804), ed. William Cooke

The couplet has been ascribed to Alexander Pope, but without much authority since the chronically invalid poet died in 1744 and is unlikely ever to have seen any of Macklin's performances.

JFK. *See* KENNEDY, JOHN F[ITZGERALD].

Jib. A first-year undergraduate at Trinity College Dublin (TCD). Joyce mentions 'Trinity jibs in their mortarboards', but the origin of the word is obscure.

Jig. A lively, popular traditional dance and related music in 6/8 or 12/8 time. A jig can be double, single or KERRY SLIDE (a fast single jig used in polka sets, especially in SLIABH LUACHRA and west Kerry). The slip (hop) jig is in 9/8 time. Only REEL tunes are more plentiful than jigs in traditional music; most jig tunes date from the 18th and 19th centuries. Single jigs and slip jigs are commonly performed by solo dancers in soft shoes at *feiseanna* (*see* FEIS).

Jigs and the reels, the. A cause of the non-completion of some project because of confusion of intention, as in 'Between the jigs and the reels he never managed to tell her.' It is also used to indicate avoidance of unimportant detail in the recounting of an event.

Jildy. A term imported into the Irish army by soldiers with British army experience in India. It is both verb and adjective, as a verb meaning 'to smarten up' and as an adjective denoting the result of this action, equivalent to 'tidy', 'clean'.

Jimín. A comic children's novel (1921) by Pádraig Ó Siochfhradha (*see* SEABHAC, AN), enjoyed in primary schools by thousands of Irish children. The eponymous hero (*Mháire Thaidhg* is the matronymic) is accident-prone but engaging, his high spirits dampened only slightly at the end of the book when he decides he has a vocation to become a priest.

Jingbang. The 'total', the 'full complement':

> The Derryman, I hope, is proud
> Of Sperrin tops that touch the cloud;
> Still, when I see, behin' the barn
> The big, brown back of Mullagharn,
> I'd let him keep, while she's our own,
> The whole jingbang outside Tyrone.
>
> W[ILLIAM] F[REDERICK] MARSHALL (1888–1959):
> 'The Hills of Home' in *Ballads & Verses from Tyrone*
> (1929)

Jingle. A conveyance described by P.W. JOYCE in *English as We Speak It in Ireland* (1910) as 'one of Bianconi's long cars'. It carried six to eight passengers, was well-sprung and had a covered frame that could be removed in fine weather.

> The next improvement was the 'jingle', a machine rolling on four wheels, but so put together that the rattling of the works was heard like the bell of a waggon team.
>
> JOHN EDWARD WALSH (1816–69): *Ireland Sixty Years Ago* (1847)

See also BIANS.

Jiving at the Crossroads. The title of a book (1991) by Co. Roscommon-born journalist John Waters (b.1955) about the SHOWBAND culture and the mores of rural Ireland, offering trenchant criticism of what is known as 'DUBLIN 4'. Waters became an *Irish Times* columnist, expounding his sometimes provocative views on male–female politics, especially following a custody battle for his daughter Róisín with her mother, pop singer Sinéad O'CONNOR. In April 2002 he won substantial damages in a much-publicized libel case

against gossip columnist Terry Keane (*see* SWEETIE), the court having accepted that she had impugned his reputation as a father in her *Sunday Times* column.

JKL. The initials, standing for James, Kildare and Leighlin, with which James Warren Doyle, the Catholic bishop of that diocese, signed his frequent letters to newspapers and his political writings. He was born near New Ross, Co. Wexford, in 1786 and educated at the Augustinian seminary at Coimbra, Portugal. In 1806 he met Sir Arthur Wellesley, later Duke of Wellington, and acted as interpreter and highly successful peace negotiator between the Portuguese and the Peninsular army. Ordained as an Augustinian friar in 1809, he returned to Ireland, and after some years teaching in New Ross and Carlow became bishop in 1819. He was a vigorous apologist for the oppressed Irish Catholics, though his memories of the bloodshed of the 1798 rising made him a strong constitutionalist, believing that his wider flock's best protection against violence was British rule. A strong but not acquiescent supporter of Daniel O'CONNELL, he was a formidable critic of the Church of Ireland's social record, and played his part in its eventual disestablishment in 1869. His pamphlet *A Vindication of the Religious and Civil Principles of the Irish Catholics* (1824) and his *Letters on the State of Ireland* (1824–5) were closely studied by the government, and he was called to London on three occasions to give evidence before parliamentary committees. Throughout his career he was a vigorous pastoral reformer, establishing schools and libraries and building Carlow Cathedral. He died in his house, significantly named Braganza, on 16 June 1834.

Joan of Arc of the Prisons. The sobriquet given to Sister Sarah Clarke (1919–2002) by Paddy Hill, one of the BIRMINGHAM SIX, for whose release from prison she campaigned. Born in Eyrecourt, Co. Galway, Sarah Clarke entered La Sainte Union order and trained as a primary teacher in Carysfort College in Dublin. She taught in the order's schools in Ireland and England until 1974, when she became involved on a full-time basis in prison visiting and helping the relatives of prisoners after the introduction of the PREVENTION OF TERRORISM ACT in that year led to the arrest of large numbers of Irish people in the UK. She fought to clear the names of the Birmingham Six and the GUILDFORD FOUR, among others, before belief in their innocence became widespread. The title of her 1995 autobiography, *No Faith in the System*, underlined her later scepticism, in contrast to the acknowledged naïveté with which she began her campaigning. She did not discriminate between innocent and guilty prisoners, and replied to her critics by quoting the words of Christ: 'I was sick and in prison and you visited me.' An advocate for justice since she first visited an Irish prisoner in Brixton prison in 1971 at the request of a Belfast priest, she summed up her modus operandi as a civil rights activist: 'If you keep coming with little pins, some day you will make a big hole.'

Jobbers. *See* FAIR.

Jobbery. The awarding by politicians in government of positions in the judiciary and in state enterprises to their friends and supporters, also known as 'jobs for the boys'. If it has sometimes seemed that FIANNA FÁIL is the natural party of patronage, it now seems likely that this is merely a perception that arises because the party does not protest about jobbery when it is out of power. Even a leader of such high moral tone as Clann na Poblachta's Seán MACBRIDE was realistic enough to assert, at the time of the Battle of BALTINGLASS, that 'unsavoury matters are inseparable from politics'.

Jobs for the boys. *See* JOBBERY.

Jocelyn, Robert, 3rd Earl of Roden. *See* DOLLY'S BRAE.

Joe, Head, Heel or Toe. *See* BAMBRICK, JOE.

Joe Mooney Summer School. An annual COMHALTAS CEOLTÓIRÍ ÉIREANN (CCÉ) festival held in Drumshanbo, Co. Leitrim, in memory of Joe Mooney (d.1989), a native of the town, who

was a FIANNA FÁIL senator and the chair of CCÉ in Connacht. Comhaltas members give classes in all the traditional instruments, in SEAN-NÓS singing and in set dancing. The usual CÉILÍs and CEOL AGUS CRAIC follow in the evenings.

John (1167–1216). King of England from 1199. He was born in Oxford, the youngest son of Henry II (1133–1189), and was surnamed Lackland (having as a younger son no likely claim to either the land of England or the large part of France controlled by the Angevins). When he was 10 he was designated lord of Ireland by his father, and negotiations with the papacy resulted in his being granted the crown of Ireland in 1185. John's alienation not only of the Irish kings but also of the English in Ireland precluded his elevation at the time. He returned to Ireland in 1210 when, as king, he deprived many of the Anglo-Norman magnates of their land (they would successfully negotiate their recovery as part of the terms of Magna Carta (15 June 1215)). John's troubled reign at home prevented much involvement with Irish affairs, but he built many fine castles – in Dublin, Limerick and Carlingford – and set up an efficient bureaucracy, with coinage, a jury system and the early beginnings of a parliament.

John Bull's Other Island. The only full-length play by GBS about his homeland, written in 1904. In it Shaw characteristically reverses the stereotypes of the dreamy Irishman and the hard-headed Englishman. Originally called *Rule Britannia*, the final title was even cheekier, derived from *John Bull et son île* (1883) by the expatriate Frenchman Paul Blouet (1843–1903). Written for the ABBEY THEATRE at the request of Yeats, it was not staged until 1916, ostensibly because it was too large and difficult for the fledgling theatre to handle. The truth was that its debunking of romantic Ireland made it quite inappropriate for Yeats's and Lady Gregory's ideal of theatre.

In the play, Shaw's Irishman, Larry Doyle, a somewhat anglicized businessman, visits his home town with his partner, Thomas Broadbent. Broadbent becomes very popular with the villagers of Rosscullen, especially when they hear of his plans to build a new hotel and golf course. In contrast to the sour Doyle and the commercially preoccupied Broadbent, Shaw sets up a philosophical defrocked priest, 'Father' Keegan, whom he delineates with all the wistfulness of the stated unbeliever.

A command performance of the play, on 11 March 1905, caused King Edward VII to laugh so much that he broke the special chair provided by John E. Vedrenne (1867–1930), the manager of the Court Theatre.

> *Broadbent:* Never despair, Larry. There are great possibilities for Ireland. Home Rule will work wonders under English guidance.
>
> *Doyle:* Tom, why do you select my most tragic moments for your irresistible strokes of humour?

'Johnny I Hardly Knew Ye'. An earthy late 18th-century ballad upon which Gilmore's anodyne song 'When Johnny Comes Marching Home' (1862) was based (*see* LAMBERT, LOUIS). A reference to 'Suloon' (Ceylon) assigns it to the 1790s, and the line 'You're an eyeless, noseless, chickenless egg' must be as finely horrible as any in English:

> You haven't an arm and you haven't a leg,
>   Hurroo! hurroo!
> ...
> You're an eyeless, noseless, chickenless egg;
> You'll have to be put with a bowl to beg:
> Och, Johnny, I hardly knew ye!

Johnny I Hardly Knew You is also the title of a novel (1977) by Edna O'BRIEN (b.1932) in which an older woman ends up killing her younger lover.

Johnny Jump-up. The name of a strong cider brewed in Clonmel, Co. Tipperary, its potency credited to its being stored in whiskey barrels:

> 'Twas about twelve o'clock and the beer it was
>   high;
> The corpse he jumped up and he says with a sigh:
> 'I can't get to Heaven, they won't let me up
> Till I bring 'em a quart of the Johnny Jump-up.'
>
>   ANON. (late 19th-century): 'Johnny Jump-up'

John Scottus Eriugena. *See* ERIUGENA, JOHN SCOTTUS.

Johnson, Anna. *See* CARBERY, ETHNA.

Johnson, Lionel [Pigot] (1867–1902). Poet. He was born on 15 March 1867 in Broadstairs, Kent, the son of an Irish army officer. Educated at Winchester and New College, Oxford, he was strongly affected by Walter Pater's aestheticism. He converted to Catholicism in 1891 and in true *fin-de-siècle* style became a member of the Rhymers Club and an alcoholic. He was also attracted to the IRISH LITERARY REVIVAL through the influence of Yeats and wrote a verse prologue for the opening of the IRISH LITERARY THEATRE (8 May 1899). He published *Ireland and Other Poems* in 1894, but is now mainly remembered for his frequently anthologized piece, 'By the Statue of King Charles at Charing Cross' (1893). Dissipation and resulting insomnia had seriously weakened his health by 1897 and he died after a fall from a bar stool on 2 October 1902.

> The May fire once on every dreaming hill
> All the fair land with burning bloom would fill;
> All the fair land, at visionary light
> Gave loving glory to the Lord of Light.
> Have we no leaping flames of Beltaine praise
> To kindle in the joyous ancient ways?
>
>   LIONEL JOHNSON: Prologue to Yeats's *The Countess Cathleen*

Johnston, [William] Denis (1901–84). Playwright and war correspondent. He was born in Dublin on 18 June 1901, the son of a judge (later of the Supreme Court) and educated at Edinburgh, Cambridge and Harvard. He was called to the English (1925) and Irish (1926) Bars but became fascinated by the theatre, married the actress Shelah Richards (1903–85) and wrote *The OLD LADY SAYS NO!*, finally produced at the GATE THEATRE in 1929. *The Moon in the Yellow River* followed in 1931. Both were experimental plays reflecting disenchantment in the Free State after the glory days of the EASTER RISING and the ANGLO-IRISH WAR. Work as a pioneer television producer was interrupted by the Second World War, when Johnston became a war correspondent, being one of the first to discover the horrors of the Buchenwald concentration camp, which he first wrote about in *The* BELL in March 1951 and further described in his war autobiography *Nine Rivers to Jordan* (1953). Johnston was director of programmes for the BBC (1946–9) and after his resignation became a freelance writer and teacher. He wrote several plays and books about Jonathan Swift and in 1976 published *The Brazen Horn*, a philosophical treatise on time and theology. *The Scythe and the Sunset* (1958), about the Easter Rising, is a sardonic companion piece to O'Casey's *The PLOUGH AND THE STARS*. He died on 8 August 1984 at Ballybrack, Co. Dublin.

> As I drove through the woods the trickle of Displaced Persons grew in volume, until presently there was a continual stream of them – filthy emaciated creatures, many of them in those disgusting striped pyjamas in which the S.S. clothe their internees … Over the main gate I read a defiant inscription:
>
> Recht oder Unrecht – mein Vaterland.
>   'Buchenwald', in *The Bell* (March 1951)

See also JOHNSTON, JENNIFER [PATIENCE].

Johnston, Francis (1760–1829). Architect, 'after Gandon, the greatest name in Irish architecture', according to the architectural historian Maurice Craig. He was born in Armagh and came to Dublin in 1778 to train as an architect. His works in the classical style include Townley Hall in Co. Louth (1790s) and Dublin's General Post Office (1802–17) (*see* GPO). He also designed NELSON'S PILLAR. In 1805 he was made architect of the Board of Works and designed many public buildings such as asylums and penitentiaries. From 1824 until his death he served as president the Royal Hibernian Academy of Arts, which he had helped to found.

See also COLLEGE GREEN.

Johnston, Jennifer [Patience] (b.1930). Novelist. She was born in Dublin on 12 January 1930, the first child of Denis JOHNSTON and

the actress Shelah Richards (1903–85), and educated at Park House School and Trinity College Dublin. She has been recognized as a significant Irish writer since the publication of her first two novels *The Captains and the Kings* (1972) and *The Gates* (1973, although written first), both of which deal with the isolation of relicts of former ASCENDANCY families. In *How Many Miles to Babylon?* (1974), set mainly in the trenches of the First World War, the last hurrah of the BIG HOUSE feels the urgency of the new Ireland. Ireland is the background to her dozen novels, though she manages to confine it to the margins in more personal work such as *The Christmas Tree* (1981), about a woman dying of leukaemia, *The Illusionist* (1995), a case of who (precisely) is your father, *Two Moons* (1998), a story of three generations of women, and *This is Not a Novel* (2002). Johnston's characterization is universally faultless, her style lyrically spare, and the whole enlivened by humour.

Join. A west Ulster word meaning 'scold': 'She was all BROKE when her mother joined her.'

Joly, Jasper (1819–92). Bibliophile. He was born in Co. Offaly and entered Trinity College Dublin at 13, graduating at the age of 18. He took orders and was appointed vicar-general of the diocese of Tuam. He was a member of the ROYAL DUBLIN SOCIETY (RDS) and in 1863 executed a deed of trust bestowing his extensive library on the RDS, this collection to be transferred to a national library when such was established in Dublin. The NATIONAL LIBRARY OF IRELAND opened in 1890 with the Joly collection as its nucleus. The collection contains more than 20,000 printed books and manuscripts, many of them priceless.

Joly, John (1857–1933). Geologist and physicist. He was born on 1 November 1857, the son of a Church of Ireland rector, in Clonbulloge, in what was then King's County (now Co. Offaly). He was educated at Trinity College Dublin and appointed assistant to the professor of engineering on graduation in 1883. He became professor of geology in 1897, a post he held until his death. Like KELVIN he was both a practical inventor and a theoretical academic. In 1899 he estimated the age of the Earth at 80–90 million years, by measuring the sodium content of the sea, but as a pioneer in the study of radioactivity understood that better figures might be obtained from studying its level in rocks. In 1914 he was involved in the setting up of the Radium Institute with a view to using radium needles in the treatment of cancer. He also devised a means of colour photography. A Fellow of the Royal Society since 1892, he died in Dublin in 1933.

Jonas (b.*c*.600). The biographer of COLUMBAN. He was born in Susa in the Piedmont Alps and entered the monastery of BOBBIO in 618. It was the last foundation of his subject, who had died only three years earlier. Jonas was thus able to talk to witnesses who knew the saint intimately, including St GALL, with whom the saint had clashed over obedience. Jonas, a scholar in his own right, became secretary to a succession of abbots of Bobbio, and in travels with them gathered much information about his subject's life. The travels were extensive, and it was not until the years 640–2 that he settled to write his *Vita Columbani* ('life of Columban').

Jones, Mother (1830–1930). US labour agitator. She was born Mary Harris near Cork city and emigrated to America via Canada in 1835. She attended school in Toronto and worked as a teacher and dressmaker in Chicago and Memphis, Tennessee. In 1861 she married an iron moulder and active trade unionist, but lost him and their four children in a yellow-fever epidemic in 1867. Her home was burnt down in the Chicago fire of 1871 (*see* MRS O'LEARY'S COW). She resumed her work as a dressmaker but devoted her free time to the cause of labour, working with the Knights of Labor and later with the United Mine Workers. In 1877 she helped to organize railroad workers in Pittsburgh, Pennsylvania, and by 1880 she was a full-time activist, known for the incendiary nature of her oratory. Her organization

of coal strikes in Virginia, West Virginia and Colorado led to her being dubbed the 'angel of the miners'. She was a founding member of the 'Wobblies' – as members of the IWW (Industrial Workers of the World) were called. Tiny, dressed in unrelieved black, but with remarkably blue eyes, she was arrested four times before 1912, when she was imprisoned on a charge of conspiracy to murder. Pardoned by a new governor, she continued her work of agitation almost until her death, making her last platform appearance in 1924 at the Farmer-Labor Party convention. She wrote *Autobiography of Mother Jones* in 1925 in her 96th year. She died in Silver Spring, Maryland, soon after her 100th birthday.

Joog. A hyper-polite form of 'jug', used especially in Belfast, as in 'Don't dare put a milk bottle on the table. Where's the little china joog?'

Jordan, Eddie (b.1948). Owner of the Jordan motor racing team. He was born on 30 March 1948 in Bray, Co. Wicklow, and educated at Synge Street Christian Brothers school in Dublin. In 1980 he founded Jordan Racing, having himself been a successful racing driver at every level except formula one. In 1990 Jordan Grand Prix was established, and in 1991 the team entered the formula one championship for the first time, steadily improving its performances and winning 1st and 2nd at the 1998 Belgian grand prix (Damon Hill and Ralf Schumacher), and winning the 1999 French and Italian grands prix (Heinz Harald Frentzen). The Irish driver Eddie Irvine drove for Jordan (1993–5); other drivers who have raced for Jordan include Ayrton Senna, Jean Alesi and Michael Schumacher (who began his formula one career with Jordan in 1991).

Jordan, Neil (b.1950). Film director and writer. He was born in Sligo and educated at University College Dublin. After a collection of short stories, *Night in Tunisia* (1976), he published three novels, *The Past* (1980), *The Dream of a Beast* (1983) and *Sunrise with Seamonster*

(1994), the last being a vivid sensual tale set in the climate of betrayal of wartime Ireland and the Spanish Civil War. He is the best-known Irish film director of his generation. His films include *Angel* (1982), *Mona Lisa* (1984), *The Crying Game* (1992), *Interview with a Vampire* (1994), a film version of Patrick McCabe's *The Butcher Boy* (1997) and *The End of the Affair* (1999), but the film that received most publicity and reached the widest audience was his *Michael Collins* (1996; *see* COLLINS, MICHAEL). Conceived on an epic, romantic scale, it brought a version of a troubled period of Irish history before the world.

Jorum. A word that can mean an alcoholic drink, a generous measure, or a jug or vessel containing drink. It is of uncertain derivation.

Jot. A man of small stature, as in 'He's a jot of a fellow.'

Journal of Irish Literature (1972–94). A thrice-yearly journal published by Robert Hogan at Delaware University containing works by contemporary playwrights and novelists, reprints of neglected works, bibliographies and reviews.

Joxer Daly. *See* DALY, JOXER.

Joy, Francis. *See* BELFAST NEWS-LETTER.

Joy, the. A Dublin nickname for MOUNTJOY JAIL.

Joyce, James (1882–1941). Novelist and short-story writer. He was born in Dublin on 2 February 1882, the first child of a middle-class family that was already in difficulties owing to the egotism and fecklessness of the Cork-born father, who was, in the words of his sharp-tongued first-born, 'a praiser of his own past'. Though Joyce was born in the fashionable Brighton Square, Rathgar, and sent as a boarder (at 'HALF PAST SIX') to CLONGOWES WOOD, his family went through as many as 16 changes of address in the Dublin area in 20 years, during which they declined into abject poverty. In spite of this Joyce managed to graduate from University College Dublin in 1902 and began to fulfil his literary destiny, which he memorably described in early life as 'to forge in the smithy of my soul the uncreated conscience of my race', using the means of 'SILENCE, EXILE AND CUNNING'.

Joyce's first published prose work, DUBLINERS (1914), a collection of stories that he set in the Irish capital (the accounts of Dublin that it contains are essentially autobiographical), is written on the theme of bourgeois, post-Parnellite paralysis. More obvious autobiography is to be found in *A PORTRAIT OF THE ARTIST AS A YOUNG MAN* (1916). By the time of its publication Joyce had been a far-from-silent exile for 12 years and, though there were visits home, the rest of his life was spent out of Ireland – in Paris, Trieste and Zürich – with his mistress Nora BARNACLE, the chambermaid from Galway whom he finally married in 1931 (*see* GREENE, GRETTA).

ULYSSES (1922), Joyce's greatest work, a Homeric account of a single day's life in Dublin, 16 June 1904 (the day of his first date with Nora), has continued to be the subject of great critical and textual scrutiny. His last book, FINNEGANS WAKE, was not completed until two years before his death, though he had begun work on it as early as 1922. Joyce died – of a perforated ulcer – in Zürich on 13 January 1941 and was buried in Fluntern cemetery. He also published two books of lyrical poetry, *Chamber Music* (1907) and *Pomes Penyeach* (1927), and his play *Exiles* had its first performance in Munich in 1918.

Joyce, P[atrick] W[eston] (1827–1914). Gaelic scholar, musicologist and HIBERNO-ENGLISH lexicographer. He was born in Glenosheen, Co. Limerick, and, like his younger brother R.D. JOYCE, was educated in local HEDGE SCHOOLS. He became headmaster of the Model School, Clonmel, resigning in 1856, and graduated from Trinity College Dublin in 1861. He was employed in various capacities by the Commissioners for National Education from 1845, and became principal of the Marlborough Street Teachers Training College in 1874.

His anthology of old airs, *Ancient Irish Music* (1873), his *Grammar of the Irish Language* (1878) and his translation of the saga tales as *Old Celtic Romances* (1879) were of extreme importance in different aspects of the recovery of Irish culture. *The Origin and History of Irish Names of Place* (1869–70), his work on DINNSHENCHAS, has only recently been superseded. His *English as We Speak It in Ireland* (1910) was a pioneering work in Hiberno-English. He was a member of the Society for the Preservation of the Irish Language (SPIL), the ROYAL IRISH ACADEMY and president of the Royal Society of Antiquaries in 1906. He died in Dublin in November 1914.

Joyce, R[obert] D[wyer] (1830–83). Poet and physician. Younger brother of P.W. JOYCE, he had the same education at HEDGE SCHOOLS and replaced him as headmaster in Clonmel, resigning in 1857. He graduated as a physician from Queen's College, Cork, in 1865, having earned the money for his fees from poems and other writings for the chief periodicals of the period. His verse was published in *Ballads, Romances and Songs* (1861). He became professor of English literature in Newman's CATHOLIC UNIVERSITY and a member of the Royal Irish Academy, but found it expedient to flee to America in 1866 because of his known support for the FENIANS. He continued to interest himself in Fenian affairs as he practised medicine in Boston, lectured at the Harvard medical school and continued to publish stories and poems. He returned to Ireland a month before his death in 1883.

> 'I want no gold to nerve my arm to do a true
>   man's part –
> To free my land I'd gladly give the red drops from
>   my heart.'
> We are the boys of Wexford, who fought with
>   heart and hand
> To burst in twain the galling chain, and free our
>   native land!
>   'The Boys of Wexford', in *Ballads, Romances and
>   Songs* (1861)

Joyce, William. *See* HAW-HAW, LORD.

Jubilee mutton. A trivial amount. The expression comes from a distribution of small quantities of free mutton to the poor of Dublin on the occasion of Queen Victoria's diamond jubilee in 1897.

Judith Hearne. The original title of *The* LONELY PASSION OF JUDITH HEARNE.

Juke. An Ulster word with several cognate meanings associated with hiding and watching from concealment, as in 'Let's juke down here till we can see what they're at.' It can also be used to mean 'dodge' or 'avoid': 'The peelers was after me but I juked them by running up the cut.'

Jump. A word meaning to change religion, with the suggestion that it was done for profit rather than conviction.
See also SOUPERISM.

Jumped from Cloyne to Derry. *See* IN ONE LEAP.

Jump the besom, to. An Ulster expression meaning to have a common-law marriage. As with many similar expressions it was once a literal description of a significant ceremony, involving jumping over a broom or BESOM.

Juno and the Paycock. Sean O'CASEY's greatest play, set in a Dublin tenement during the CIVIL WAR. It was first staged at the ABBEY THEATRE in 1924, and the characters Captain BOYLE (the 'paycock' of the title), Juno BOYLE (his long-suffering wife) and Joxer DALY startled and delighted the Dublin audiences and joined Synge's Christy MAHON and PEGEEN MIKE in the pantheon of great characters of world theatre.

In a sense the play is a diptych, with Juno as the link. Her story and those of her daughter Mary and son Johnny supply the 'tragedy' of the subtitle ('a tragedy in three acts'), while the scenes with the bombastic work-shy Boyle and his parasite Joxer seem at times to have strayed from an appliqué pantomime. The serious plot is part melodrama and part true tragedy: the daughter is left pregnant; the family is deprived of an expected legacy by an incompetent clerk; and the son who had lost an arm during the EASTER RISING is hunted and finally killed by 'diehards' (ANTI-TREATYITES).

In spite of the melodrama, and a pause in the action for a singsong in Act II, the play is rich in language, atmosphere and characterization, the double act of Joxer and Boyle clearly influencing later playwrights, including BECK-ETT. The character of Juno, courageous and indomitable in the face of cruel adversity, is the chief of many tributes by O'Casey to his own mother. The play ends on an essentially nihilistic note in spite of superficial comic trappings:

> I'm telling you … Joxer … th' whole worl's … in a terr … ible state o'… chassis!

Juno Boyle. *See* BOYLE, JUNO.

Justiciar. The title held by the governor of Ireland on behalf of the king of England from the late 12th to the mid-14th century. The role combined military, legal and civil office. A court, called the Justiciar's Court, accompanied the justiciar or chief justice as he made visits to different parts of the country.

k

Kalashnikov. *See* AK-47.

Kate Kearney's Cottage. A celebrated café and pub situated at the entrance to the Gap of Dunloe, a beauty spot and Mecca for walkers, 8 km (5 miles) west of Killarney, Co. Kerry. The road through the 'Gap', as it is familiarly called, is surfaced, but the JARVEYS who preside over the area do their best to deter drivers from entering by claiming that it is unfit for motor traffic. In fact it is possible to drive through the Gap of Dunloe and emerge on Sneem Road at Moll's Gap, but the paucity of cars makes the route more pleasant for pedestrians and horse riders. Kate Kearney herself may have been invented by Lady MORGAN:

> Oh! should you e'er meet this Kate Kearney,
> Who lives on the banks of Killarney,
> Beware of her smile, for many a wile
> Lies hid in the smile of Kate Kearney.
>> LADY MORGAN (?1776–1859): 'Kate Kearney', in *Hibernian Melodies* (1801)

Kate Mac. *See* WEST CLARE RAILWAY.

Kathleen Mavourneen. A comic euphemism for a hire-purchase agreement. It comes from the line

> It may be for years and it may be for ever

from the ballad of that name by Julia Crawford. The ballad first appeared in the London *Metropolitan Magazine* in 1835 and was set to music by Frederick Nicholls Crouch (1808–96) in 1837. Crawford was born Louise Jane Matilda Montague, probably in Co. Cavan, in 1799. She wrote many songs and novels, all of which have sunk into obscurity except this song, which is still a platform piece. The word MAVOURNEEN, which gives it a dusting of greenery, is indicative of the popularity in Britain of romantic Irishness in the years before the harsh reality of the Great Famine. Crawford died in 1860.

> Kathleen Mavourneen! The grey dawn is
>   breaking,
> The horn of the hunter is heard on the hill;
> The lark from her light wing the bright dew is
>   shaking;
> Kathleen Mavourneen! what, slumbering still?
> Oh! hast though forgotten how soon we must
>   sever?
> Oh! hast though forgotten this day we must part?
> It may be for years and it may be for ever,
> Oh! why art though silent, thou voice of my
>   heart?

Kathleen ni Houlihan. *See* CATHLEEN NÍ HOULIHAN.

Kavanagh, Kruger. *See* KRUGER KAVANAGH.

Kavanagh, Patrick (1904–67). Poet and novelist. He was born on 21 October 1904 in Mucker (as he frequently reminded people), in the parish of Inishkeen, Co. Monaghan, the son of a small farmer and cobbler. He left school at 13 but began to 'dabble in verse', soon displaying an unsentimental view of his farm and parish, and an intellectual awareness of the wide world beyond. His work was published by Æ in the *Irish Statesman*, and by 1936 there was enough for a collection, *Ploughman and Other Poems*. This was followed, at Helen WADDELL's insistence, by *The Green Fool* (1938), a prose account of his childhood and young manhood, which was withdrawn because of a libel action by Oliver St John GOGARTY over a clearly innocent remark: describing an attempted visit to the Gogarty household, Kavanagh commented, 'I mistook Gogarty's white-robed maid for his wife or his mistress. I expected every poet to have a spare wife.' (The book was eventually republished in 1967.)

Kavanagh's extended poem *The GREAT HUNGER* (1942), the poetry collection *A Soul for Sale* (1947) and *TARRY FLYNN* (1948), an autobiographical and inevitably banned novel, marked Kavanagh as a significant Irish writer and perhaps the finest poet since Yeats. Living in Dublin from 1939, often in poor health and poverty, he scraped a living by casual journalism (including film criticism for the *Irish Press* as 'Piers Plowman'). In 1952 he and his brother Peter double-handedly produced the 13 issues of the polemical *KAVANAGH'S WEEKLY*, thereby decreasing their already diminishing store of goodwill.

Defeat in a famous libel case over a profile of him in the *Leader* magazine in 1954 left Kavanagh ill and penniless, but a post as lecturer in the extra-mural department of University College Dublin was arranged by John COSTELLO, who was taoiseach 1948–51 and 1954–7, and the all-too-successful defence counsel in the action. Surgery for cancer in 1955 did much to mitigate Kavanagh's endemic abrasiveness, and his subsequent work – such as *Come Dance with Kitty Stobling* (1960) and the new poems in his *Collected Poems* (1964) – is happier, more personal and less ideological. He died in Dublin on 30 November 1967, seven months after his marriage to Kathleen Maloney.

The sleety winds fondle the rushy beards of Shancoduff

While the cattle-drovers sheltering in the Featherna Bush
Look up and say: 'Who owns them hungry hills
That the water-hen and snipe must have forsaken?
A poet? Then by heavens he must be poor.'
I hear and is my heart not badly shaken.
'Shancoduff' (1934)

See also CRANK ON THE BANK; GRAND CANAL; O STONY GREY SOIL OF MONAGHAN.

Kavanagh, Rose (1859–91). Poet. She was born in Killadroy, Co. Tyrone, not far from the birthplace of William CARLETON, and educated at Loreto Convent, Omagh, and the Dublin Metropolitan School of Art. She wrote much patriotic verse and ran the children's section of the *Irish Fireside* and the *Weekly Freeman*. A close friend of Charles J. KICKHAM, she nursed him when he was blind and dying. Kavanagh died of tuberculosis at her home in Knockmany, near her birthplace.

Knockmany, my darling, I see you again,
As the sunrise has made you a King;
And your proud face looks tenderly down on the plain
Where my young larks are learning to sing.
'Knockmany', in *Rose Kavanagh and her verses* (1909)

Kavanagh's Weekly (1952). A polemical literary and political journal written and edited by Patrick KAVANAGH and designed and produced by his brother Peter, 13 issues of which appeared April–July 1952. It was bitterly critical of the FIANNA FÁIL government of the day, of the literary and social life of the country in general, and of individuals involved in any aspect of that life. The journal not surprisingly found it impossible to attract advertisers, and folded for lack of funds.

Keane, Dolores (b.1953). Singer. A member of a musically gifted Co. Galway family, she won All-Ireland FLEADH CHEOIL awards for singing in both Irish and English. She sang with DÉ DANANN in 1974–5 and again from 1981, and has made many recordings of traditional, folk and contemporary songs.

Keane, John B[rendan] (1928–2002). Playwright and fiction writer. He was born in Listowel, Co. Kerry, on 21 July 1928, the son of a teacher, and lived there most of his life, presiding over the small friendly pub that bears his name. His first play *Sive* (1959) was written for the local drama society and made a tremendous impact at the All-Ireland drama finals in Athlone. It deals with the clash of youth and age, greed and idealism, and, with the highly flavoured speech of north Kerry and a mixture of Brechtian and folk elements, it effectively regenerated the peasant play.

Most of Keane's work was first presented by the Southern Theatre Group in Cork rather than by the ABBEY THEATRE in Dublin, and *Sharon's Grave* (1960), *The Highest House on the Mountain* (1960) and *Many Young Men of Twenty* (1961), with its effective title song, its humour and genuine feeling for the wastefulness of emigration, all confirmed his position as the best-known Irish playwright of the period. His finest play *The Field* (1965) has a universality that lifts it out of purely regional appeal, and it was successfully filmed in 1990. Other successful plays include *The Year of the Hiker* (1963), about a 'shuiler' who comes home to die, and *Big Maggie* (1969), about a hyper-effective matriarch.

Keane also wrote poetry and a great deal of prose in the form of novels, short stories and epistolary fictions. His most enduring novels are likely to be *The Bodhrán Makers* (1986), *Durango* (1992) and *The Contractors* (1993). Although he was a fluent Irish speaker and a supporter of the language, he joined the short-lived and controversial LANGUAGE FREEDOM MOVEMENT in 1966. He was Ireland's favourite Kerryman and a raconteur of sometimes surreal genius, a treasured guest on Gay Byrne's LATE LATE SHOW. He suffered from poor health for a number of years and died in Listowel on 30 May 2002, his funeral attracting an enormous crowd of politicians, friends and literary associates.

Keane, Molly (1905–96). Novelist and playwright. She was born Molly Skrine in Co. Kildare, the daughter of the poet Moira O'NEILL, into a huntin', shootin', fishin' family of the kind that features in most of her fiction, both light and serious. Between 1928 and 1952, using the pen name M.J. Farrell (a name borrowed from a publican's fascia and meant to hide her artistic talent from her sporting friends), she wrote ten humorous novels, mostly dealing in a latter-day SOMERVILLE AND ROSS fashion with the life of the steadily diminishing ANGLO-IRISH and their often uneasy relations with the native Irish. Her first three plays, *Spring Meeting* (1938), *Ducks and Drakes* (1942) and *Treasure Hunt* (1949), were drawing-room comedies directed by John Gielgud, and were popular London West End successes. However, an adverse critical reaction to *Dazzling Prospect* (1961), in the period of the Royal Court Theatre's 'angry' revolution, ended her career as a playwright.

A lacuna of 20 years ended with the novel GOOD BEHAVIOUR (1981), the first book published under her own name. Its picture of the Anglo-Irish in greater decay changed the light-hearted books of M.J. Farrell to searing comedies with barely merciful analyses of an ASCENDANCY in a state of disintegration. *Time after Time* (1983) describes the disarray of the Swifts of Durraghglass, as the three sisters and their one-eyed gay brother are nearly destroyed by a malicious cousin. *Loving and Giving* (1988), about revenge for a childhood cruelty, and her last novel, *Conversation Piece* (1991), complete a fine quartet of late-flowering, black but beautifully written comedies.

Keane, Robbie (b.1980). Soccer player. He was born in Dublin on 8 July 1980 and joined Wolverhampton Wanderers from his Dublin soccer club, later playing for Coventry, Inter Milan and Leeds United before moving to Tottenham Hotspur in 2002. A striker of international calibre, he won his first cap for Ireland in March 1998 in a game against the Czech Republic and played a key role in Ireland's World Cup campaign in 2002.

Keane, Roy. *See* KEANO.

Keane, Terry. *See* JIVING AT THE CROSSROADS; SWEETIE.

Keano (b.1971). The nickname of soccer player Roy [Maurice] Keane. He was born in Cork city on 10 October 1971, and was signed by Nottingham Forest in 1990. As a Manchester United team member since 1994 (captain since 1998) he has become one of soccer's most successful and best-known players, also known for being obsessive, temperamental and demanding. He was first capped for Ireland against Chile in 1994 and the same year played for Jack Charlton's team in the World Cup finals in the USA. His relationship with the Irish team manager Mick McCarthy (*see* CAPTAIN FANTASTIC) was never cordial, and a confrontation at the start of the 2002 World Cup finals led to his being sent home. A subsequent media-fuelled public controversy ran and ran, dividing Irish opinion. Keane is a hero in his native Cork and among the many thousands of young Manchester United supporters in Ireland, and undoubtedly a footballer of great talent. *Keane: The Autobiography*, with Eamon Dunphy, appeared in 2002.

Kearney, Peadar (1883–1942). Songwriter. He was born in Dublin and educated at the Christian Brothers school at Marino. He became a house painter (like his famous nephew Brendan BEHAN), joined the GAELIC LEAGUE and the IRB and worked backstage at the ABBEY THEATRE. In 1911 he published 'A SOLDIER'S SONG' in *Irish Freedom* and it was adopted as a war song by the IRB – and eventually as the national anthem for the new state. After the CIVIL WAR Kearney returned to private life and his first occupation. Among his other songs are the Republican 'The Tri-Coloured Ribbon', the satirical 'Whack Fol the Diddle', Dublin songs such as 'Down by the Liffey Side', and 'Mrs McGrath', a comic anti-war song popularized by Ronnie Drew of The DUBLINERS:

Oh Mrs McGrath, the sergeant said,
Would you like to make a soldier out of your son
Ted?

With a scarlet coat and a big cocked hat
Now Mrs McGrath wouldn't you like that?

Kearney's songs gained renewed popularity in the BALLAD GROUP boom of the 1960s, especially among The Dubliners (the Dublin songs) and The WOLF TONES (the Republican songs).

Keating, Geoffrey. *See* CÉITINN, SEATHRÚN.

Keating, Ronan. *See* BOYZONE.

Keating, Sean (1889–1977). Artist. He was born in Limerick on 29 September 1889 and educated at St Munchin's College and the Royal College of Art in Dublin. A protégé of William ORPEN, he worked and studied with him in London. In 1916 he returned to Ireland and went to live in the ARAN ISLANDS, which were to inspire him for the rest of his life. He later taught at the National College of Arts and Design (NCAD) in Dublin and was president of the Royal Hibernian Academy. Although he designed a house in Dublin, he spent half of every year in Aran and painted many portraits of people of the islands. A traditionalist in style, he had little interest in modernism. He died in Dublin on 21 December 1977.

Keats and Chapman. A regular feature of CRUISKEEN LAWN, in which Chapman, the Elizabethan/Jacobean translator of Homer, is made magically contemporary with the poet Keats (no doubt via the alchemy of the latter's sonnet, 'On First Looking into Chapman's Homer'). The two have adventures that always end in atrocious puns:

Keats and Chapman once climbed Vesuvius and stood looking down into the volcano, watching the bubbling lava and considering the sterile ebullience of the stony entrails of the earth. Chapman shuddered as if with cold or fear.

'Will you have a drop of the crater?' Keats said.

The Best of Myles (1968)

Keegan, John (1809–1849). Poet. He was born in what was then Queen's County (now Co. Laios) and educated at a local HEDGE SCHOOL. He contributed verse to the available periodicals, *The* NATION, the *Irish Penny Journal* (*see* PENNY JOURNALS) and the DUBLIN UNIVERSITY MAGAZINE. His sentimental poems 'Bouchaleen Bawn' ('fair-headed little boy') and 'Caoch the Piper' are still known and recited. He died of cholera in Dublin and was buried in a common grave in GLASNEVIN CEMETERY.

> One winter's day, long, long ago,
> When I was a little fellow,
> A piper wandered to our door,
> Grey-headed, blind and yellow:
> And, oh! how glad was my young heart,
> Though earth and sky looked dreary,
> To see the stranger and his dog –
> Poor 'Pinch' and Caoch O'Leary.
>
> *Legends and Poems* (1907)

Keen (Irish *caoin*, 'cry'). A formal lamentation over the dead at a wake or at the graveside. The practice persisted into the early 20th century in rural areas, where there was a kind of semi-professional corps of keeners, vocal equivalents of the mutes of English funerals.

> When anyone lies a-dying, women hired on purpose, calling upon him with great outcries, and in an abundance of ridiculous expostulations, why he should depart from so many advantages. After he is dead they keep a mourning and loud howlings and clapping of hands together. When the corpse goes forth they follow it with such a peal of outcries that a man would think the quick as well as the dead, were past all recovery.
>
> EACHARD: *Exact Description of Ireland* (1691)

> The grief of the keen is no personal complaint for the death of one woman over eighty years of age, but seems to contain the whole passionate rage that lurks somewhere in every native of the island. In this cry of pain the inner consciousness of the people seems to lay itself bare for an instant, and to reveal the mood of beings who feel their isolation in the face of a universe that wars on them with winds and seas.
>
> J.M. SYNGE: *The Aran Islands* (1907)

Keenan, Brian (b.1950). Teacher, writer and kidnap victim. He was born in Belfast and educated at the New University of Ulster at Coleraine. While he was teaching in Beirut, Lebanon, he was kidnapped in April 1986 by Islamic

militants of the fundamentalist Hizbollah, and held in darkness for four and a half years in the Baalbek valley. He was eventually released on 24 August 1990 and in 1992 published the highly regarded *An Evil Cradling*, an account of his captivity (much of which he shared with the English journalist John McCarthy). A novel, *Turlough* (2000), was written in homage to the blind harper Turlough CAROLAN, whose courage in adversity comforted Keenan while in confinement.

Keep dick. An Ulster phrase meaning 'to keep a look out', as in: 'You shin over the wall and I'll keep dick.'

Keepers. A name given to men employed by landlords in the 1840s to protect their crops and stock against raids by the members of secret agrarian societies such as the CARDERS, HOUGHERS, MOLLY MAGUIRES, TERRY ALTS and WHITEBOYS.

Keep the Sabbath and everything else. The charge laid against the publicly pious who have also prospered in worldly matters.

Keher, Eddie (b.1941). Hurler. He was born in Inistioge, Co. Kilkenny, on 14 October 1941. One of the great scoring forwards of all time, between 1959 and 1977 he won six ALL-IRELAND medals with his county – scoring 14 points in the 1963 final – nine RAILWAY CUP medals and three NATIONAL LEAGUE titles.

Keimaneigh, Battle of (1822). The battle between local WHITEBOYS and a corps of YEOS (Yeomanry) in the scenic area of the pass of Keimaneigh in west Cork, described by Máire Bhui NÍ LAOGHAIRE in part of her long poem 'Cath Chéim an Fhia'. Despite the bravery of the boys and some casualties to the enemy, the day was with the yeos.

Kellett, Iris (b.1926). International showjumper. She was born in Dublin on 8 January 1926 and achieved early success on a horse called 'Rusty', winning the Queen Elizabeth Cup in 1949 and 1951. In 1952 she sustained a serious injury which kept her out of competition for nearly ten years, but in 1969 she became

Ladies European Champion. She ran a successful riding school at Mespil House near Dublin's Grand Canal.

Kells. A small market town in Co. Meath associated with the BOOK OF KELLS. There are remains of the monastic foundation: high crosses, a round tower and other fragments.

Kelly, Éamon (1914–2001). SEANCHAÍ (storyteller), actor and writer. He was born near Gneeveguilla in Co. Kerry on 30 April 1914, the son of a wheelwright and carpenter. He trained as a woodwork teacher and worked in Listowel, appearing in amateur productions with the local drama society before moving to Dublin to become an actor with RTÉ radio and later with the ABBEY THEATRE. He had a varied and successful career on the stage, acting in many of the classic plays of his era, including the works of Brian Friel, Tom Murphy and Sebastian Barry. His first professional stage role was as Gar's father S.B. O'Donnell in Hilton Edwards's production of *PHILADELPHIA, HERE I COME!* at the Gaiety Theatre in 1964, a role he reprised on Broadway in 1966.

Kelly published a series of books based on his one-man storytelling shows in the Abbey Theatre, including *In My Father's Time, Bless Me Father* and *English That for Me*, collected as *Ireland's Master Storyteller* in 1998, and two finely wrought volumes of memoirs, *The Apprentice* (1995) and *The Journeyman* (1998). His kind of traditional gathering for storytelling (*see* BOTHÁNTAÍOCHT) he called 'theatre of the hearthstone':

> In a gathering like this you had all the rude elements of the theatre. The storyteller provided the comedy and sometimes the tragedy because he could bring a tear when he spoke of the death of Naoise and the sons of Uisneach. The song was there, the music, the dance and the dressing up. I call this form of entertainment 'theatre of the hearthstone' – a diversion having its seed in the time when our forefathers sat at the mouth of a cave and listened to the happenings of a day's hunting.
>
> ÉAMON KELLY: Introduction to *Ireland's Master Storyteller* (1998)

Éamon Kelly continued to perform in public, both acting and storytelling, until shortly before his death on 23 October 2001.

Kelly, Hugh (1739–77). Dramatist. He was born in Killarney, Co. Kerry, but moved to London in 1760, becoming an editor of several fashionable magazines. His first play, *False Delicacy* (1768), was produced by Garrick at Drury Lane about the same time as GOLDSMITH's *The Good-Natur'd Man*, to the latter's disadvantage. He was a bitter critic of all things STAGE-IRISH and it is only in *A School For Wives* (1773) that he used Irish characters, notably Leeson, an Irish gentleman who is cured of duelling. Kelly quarrelled with Goldsmith, but was seen to weep at his funeral in 1774. He himself died three years later, probably of drink.

> Your people of refined sentiments are the most troublesome creatures in the world to deal with.
>
> *False Delicacy*, V.i

Kelly, Luke (1940–84). Singer and member of The DUBLINERS. He was born in Dublin on 17 November 1940 and was one of the founder members of The Dubliners, but after their first recording in 1964 he spent a year in England. There he met folk singer Ewan MacColl, from whom he learned a lot of songs and who influenced his singing style, which was passionately emotional, direct and engagé. He rejoined The Dubliners and sang with them, unless prevented from doing so by illness, until shortly before his untimely death from cancer on 30 January 1984.

Ultimately Kelly was a folk rather than ballad singer, among his most famous recordings being 'Raglan Road' (words by Patrick KAVANAGH to the tune of 'The Dawning of the Day'), the ballad 'Peggy Gordon' and two songs by Phil COULTER, 'The Town I Loved So Well' and 'Scorn Not His Simplicity'. He was undoubtedly the most popular of The Dubliners, appreciated for his bright red hair and his commitment to social justice as well as for the quality of his singing. Fellow Dubliner John

Sheahan said at the time of his death, 'Ronnie Drew was the daddy of the band, but Luke was the soul.'

Kelly, Mary Anne (1825–1910). Nationalist poet. She was born in Headford, Co. Galway, and, under the pen name 'Eva', was one of the leading female contributors to patriotic newspapers, becoming known as 'Eva of *The NATION*'. She became engaged to Kevin Izod O'Doherty (1823–1905), who was transported to Australia after imprisonment for his part in the Rising of 1848 (*see* WIDOW MCCORMICK'S CABBAGE PATCH). They finally married on his release in 1855 and lived for most of the rest of their lives in Brisbane, where O'Doherty had a medical practice.

Kelly, Michael. *See* SIGNOR OCHELLY.

Kelly, Ned (1855–80). Australian outlaw. His father John 'Red' Kelly (d.1866) was transported from Co. Tipperary in 1840; legend has it that his offence was to steal two pigs, but it seems more likely that he was a habitual thief. After serving time in Tasmania he crossed to Melbourne in 1848 and married Ellen Quinn. Ned, who was born in the state of Victoria, was in trouble with the law from 1871, but it was not until a policeman tried to arrest him and his brother Dan on allegations of cattle-robbery in 1877 that he, Dan and two others, Joe Byrne and Steve Hart, became outlaws in the Wombat Hills of Victoria, relentlessly pursued by the police, who alienated local opinion by harassing the innocent.

The Kelly gang carried out two daring robberies, in Eloroa and Jerilderie, but with a price on their heads they were betrayed in June 1880. The rest of the gang were killed in a shootout with police in Glenrowan, and Ned was arrested, having been shot in the leg because he was wearing homemade body armour. He was hanged in Melbourne on 11 November 1880, his last words reputed to be 'Such is life.' Kelly left behind two letters, the 'Cameron' and the 'Jerilderie', full of anti-English and anti-police invective and justifications for his life of crime

– although most of the policemen with whom he came into contact were Irish.

Kelly belonged to the Irish tradition of rural anti-property rebellion, but has a place in Australian mythology as a Robin Hood figure. With his distinctive home-made cylindrical helmet, Kelly became a frequent icon in the paintings of the Australian artist Sidney Nolan (1917–92), becoming part of what Nolan called 'the great purity and implacability' of the Australian landscape. A film called *Ned Kelly* (1970), directed by Tony Richardson, starred the Rolling Stones lead singer Mick Jagger as the outlaw, while the Australian novelist Peter Carey (b.1943) won his second Booker Prize for fiction with *True History of the Kelly Gang* (2001).

Kelly, Séamus (1912–79). Journalist. He was born in Belfast in August 1912 and educated at Queen's University Belfast and University College Cork, graduating from neither college. He was a boxing blue at Queen's and a part-time journalist while in Cork. He joined the Irish army in 1940 and was commissioned in the intelligence department the following year. In 1945 he replaced Brinsley MacNamara (*see VALLEY OF THE SQUINTING WINDOWS, THE*) as drama critic of the *Irish Times*, and in 1949 became the most permanent QUIDNUNC for that paper's 'An Irishman's Diary'. He continued as Quidnunc for nearly 30 years, making the column essential reading both for the 'gossip' and as a less surreal complement to CRUISKEEN LAWN. In 1954 he appeared as Flask in John Huston's film of *Moby Dick*, but returned to the paper, combining the exacting task of diarist with that of chief drama and ballet reviewer. He died on 10 June 1979.

Kelly, Sean (b.1956). Professional cyclist. He was born in Carrick-on-Suir, Co. Tipperary, on 21 May 1956 to a farming family, and began his cycling career by cycling the 5 km (3 miles) to and from school. He won the Irish junior championship in 1972 and 1973, and in 1979 he had the first win of his international career, the Grand Prix de Cannes, followed by the

Tour of Switzerland in 1982. From 1984 to 1989 he was ranked as the number-one cyclist in the world, despite never having won the Tour de France. He retired from professional cycling in 1988, having competed in up to 100 races a year for the previous 15 years.

Kelpie. The name of a yacht owned by Conor O'Brien and used as a companion vessel to the ASGARD for the gun-running by the IRISH VOLUNTEERS in July 1914. Because both owner and yacht were known to the authorities, the cargo was transferred to another boat and landed further down the coast, at Kilcoole, Co. Wicklow.

Kelts and Ultonians. The two ethnic groups into which the poet William ALLINGHAM, in a characteristically gentle way, divided his fellow Irish. A Protestant, he found much to admire in each group. The entry in his *Diary* (1907) for Saturday, 16 September 1848, which was written at Inver, on the north shore of Donegal Bay, includes this paragraph:

> Ultonians, in whom Scotch and English order and decency are blended with Irish heartiness, are a good kind of people, and the peculiar wild fun and tender fancy belonging to the Kelts are, not seldom, transfused among those who have lived so long in the midst of Irish customs, traditions, music and scenery ...

Kelvin, Lord (William Thomson, 1st Baron Kelvin of Largs) (1824–1907). Scientist and inventor. He was born William Thomson in Belfast on 26 June 1824, the son of the head of mathematics in INST. His father was appointed professor of mathematics at Glasgow University in 1832, and two years later his gifted son matriculated. He went to Cambridge at 16 and was elected a fellow of Peterhouse in 1846 when he was 22. (He was twice a fellow of Peterhouse: 1846–52 and 1872–1907.) In the same year, 1846, he was appointed to the chair of natural philosophy (physical science) at Glasgow and stayed for 53 years. On his retirement he was entitled to write more academic honours after his name than any man then alive. He adopted

the title Kelvin (taking the name from the river that flows past Glasgow University) on his elevation to the peerage in 1892.

Kelvin majestically combined theoretical and practical science, making the prototypes for his many inventions and insisting on the application of scientific discovery to utilitarian ends. His main claim to fame was his enunciation between 1851 and 1854 to the Royal Society of Edinburgh of the two laws of thermodynamics, which deal with the equivalence and capacity for transformation, one to the other, of heat and work. He campaigned vigorously for the standardization of scientific units, and in tribute to him the kelvin became the standard SI measure of temperature. (He had devised the absolute temperature scale in 1848; *see* KELVIN TEMPERATURE SCALE.) Kelvin's work on electricity, hydrodynamics and the compass made possible submarine telegraphy – and made sure that his house in Glasgow was the first to be lit by electric light. He was made a privy councillor in 1902 and was one of the first to be granted the new Order of Merit.

Kelvin was an ardent Unionist in politics and strongly religious throughout his long life. In his later years he became rather rigid in his attitudes, taking little interest in such advances in physics as radioactivity and X-rays. He died on 17 December 1907 in his mansion at Largs on the west coast of Scotland and was buried in Westminster Abbey on 23 December. A characteristic comment has been preserved. When his wife suggested an afternoon walk he is said to have replied: 'At what point does the dissipation of energy begin?'

Kelvin temperature scale. A measure of temperature proposed by Lord KELVIN in 1848, in which absolute zero is assigned the value 0 K. The freezing point of water (0° C) is 273.17 K, and conversion from Celsius to Kelvin is done by adding 273.17.

Kenmare. A small, pretty tourist town in Co. Kerry, beautifully situated on a wide ria (estuary) at the entrance to the BEARA PENINSULA, on a section of the Ring of KERRY. William

Petty, author of the DOWN SURVEY, wrote of the 270,000 acres (108,000 ha) granted to him in this area, that

> for a great man that would retire this place would be the most absolute, and the most interessant place in the world, both for improvement and pleasure and healthfulness.

William Petty-Fitzmaurice, 1st Marquess of Lansdowne, designed the original town plan in the 1770s, and what is now Main Street was called William Street in his honour. Petty, who was raised in Lixnaw in north Kerry, inherited the Lansdowne estates in Kenmare in 1761, and became prime minister of England 20 years later. The 2nd (1780–1863) and 5th (1845–1927) marquesses were also notable Liberal statesmen.

See also MOERAN, E[RNEST] J[OHN].

Kenmare River. The name given to the ria or estuary between the IVERAGH PENINSULA and the BEARA PENINSULA in Co. Kerry. It was called a river in legal documents by successive Lord Lansdownes (the local landowners) in order to preserve for themselves their vast and bountiful fishing rights along this coast.

Kennedy, Jimmy (1902–84). Song lyricist. He was born in Omagh on 20 July 1902, the son of Joseph Hamilton Kennedy of the RIC and brought up in Portstewart, Co. Derry, the north coast resort that was the inspiration for two of his most popular songs, 'Red Sails in the Sunset' and 'Harbour Lights'.

Kennedy graduated from Trinity College Dublin and spent some years as a teacher and an officer in the Colonial Service. A now forgotten piece, 'The Barmaid's Song', brought him to the attention of Bert Feldman, the sheet-music publisher, and he became a lyric editor, a lowly position with little fame. His novelty item 'The Teddy Bears' Picnic' (1932) sold 4 million records and many more sheets, but he did not receive any royalties for it until 1947. He accepted the inferior position of lyricist (somebody once told him, 'You can't whistle words'), but he is remembered for such songs as 'The Isle of Capri' and 'South of the Border' while

the composers, Wilhelm Grosz and Michael Carr, are forgotten.

By the outbreak of the Second World War (in which he served as an artillery captain) Kennedy was regarded as one of the world's leading songsmiths and an intimate of such stars as Bing Crosby (1904–77), who recorded nine of his songs. His wartime lyric contribution was the sadly optimistic 'We're Going to Hang Out Our Washing on the Siegfried Line', which enraged Hitler and featured in every victory street party in Britain in 1945. He also wrote the English lyric of 'Lilli Marlene', 'liberated' from German radio by the British 8th Army.

After the war Kennedy continued to work at his craft, writing in all more than 1000 popular songs (for some of which he also wrote music), until teenage record-based pop all but destroyed the sheet-music business. He still wrote occasional popular songs for the more mature market, notably 'Love Is Like a Violin' for the comedian Ken Dodd. He died in Cheltenham on 6 April 1984, having been given two Ivor Novello awards, an OBE (1983) and an honorary DLitt from the University of Ulster (1978). While working with Feldman, Kennedy wrote unashamedly for the market, as the following exportable piece makes clear:

> Did your mother come from Ireland?
> For there's something in you Irish.
> Can you tell me where you got those Irish eyes?
> And before she left Killarney,
> Did your mother kiss the Blarney?
> For your little touch of brogue you can't deny.
> 'Did Your Mother Come from Ireland?' (1936)

Kennedy, John F[itzgerald] (1917–63). The 35th president of the United States. The glamour of Camelot reached its peak with Kennedy's visit to Ireland in the summer of 1963. His Catholicism, plangent 'Irishness', rugged good looks and charm raised him to literally iconic status: in the cathedral of Our Lady Assumed into Heaven and St Nicholas in Galway city (built 1957–65) mosaic representations of his face and that of Patrick PEARSE decorate the mortuary chapel. His photograph joined that of

Pope John XXIII (1881–1963) on many Irish walls, and the death of both of these charismatic figures in the same year caused national grief. His visit (26–29 June) took in the remains of the KENNEDY HOMESTEAD in Co. Wexford, Dublin Castle, where he was given the freedom of the city and honorary doctorates from the National University of Ireland and Trinity College, and Leinster House, where he addressed the Dáil and Senate. His visit studiously avoided Northern Ireland, but gave a formal signal to the country that the ghosts of the Great Famine might finally be laid.

Kennedy Homestead. During his triumphant visit to Ireland in the summer of 1963 President Kennedy visited the homestead at Dunganstown, near New Ross in Co. Wexford, from which his great-grandfather Patrick Kennedy had emigrated in 1848. There he met his cousin, Mary Ryan. The cottage at Dunganstown has been preserved as a cultural museum and visitor centre. The extensive John F. Kennedy Park and Arboretum outside New Ross was also created in his memory and opened by Éamon de Valera on 26 May 1968.

Kennelly, Brendan (b.1936). Poet and academic. He was born in Ballylongford, Co. Kerry, and educated at St Ita's College, Tarbert, and Trinity College Dublin, to which he returned in 1973 as professor of modern English. A novel about village life, *The Crooked Cross* (1963), was followed by *The Florentines* (1967). Both showed a verbal fluency that was put to better use in a collection of poetry, *My Dark Fathers* (1964), about the wounds of history, especially those inflicted by the Great Famine and the conditions that caused it. His later work is more buoyant, more ribald, as if the absolute blackness had been exorcized; his Everyman Moloney is truly 'up and at it' (1984), and the title of the collection *Poetry My Arse* (1995) is self-explanatory. But there is room for tenderness and commitment, and a continuing worship of women. The Northern TROUBLES and the recurring nightmare of history produced two long poetry sequences about hate figures, *Cromwell*

(1983) and *The Book of Judas* (1991). *The Man Made of Rain* (1998) is a series of meditations on life and mortality inspired by his experience of serious heart surgery. His 2003 *Martial Art* consists of translations of Martial's *Epigrams*.

Kenneth. *See* CANICE.

Kent, Eamonn. *See* CEANNT, ÉAMONN.

Kentish fire. A signal of Orange opposition, consisting of a series of three rapid handclaps. The practice was common in Parliament and at public meetings before the ORANGE ORDER dissolved itself in 1836. The term arose from the protracted cheers given in Kent to the No-Popery orators in 1828–9. Lord Winchelsea took up the expression, and, when proposing the health of the Earl of Roden (*see* DOLLY'S BRAE) on 15 August 1834, added, 'Let it be given with the Kentish Fire.'

Kenyon, John (1812–69). Nationalist, priest and supporter of YOUNG IRELAND. He was born in Limerick and educated for the priesthood at Maynooth. While parish priest of Templederry, Co. Tipperary, he supported the policies of John MITCHEL and contributed to *The* NATION, but considered the Rebellion of 1848 (*see* WIDOW MCCORMICK'S CABBAGE PATCH) ill-conceived because of the recent hardship suffered in the GREAT FAMINE. In 1866, on a visit to Paris to meet Mitchel for the last time, he and Mitchel received a standing ovation from the students in the COLLÈGE DES IRLANDAIS.

Keogh, John (1740–1817). Catholic activist. He was born in poverty in Dublin but made a fortune in business. He was one of a number of self-made men who had the confidence to demand rights for the penalized Catholics of Ireland. In 1792 he went to London to petition George III for alleviation of grievances, and was the main driving force in the radicalization of the CATHOLIC COMMITTEE, which in turn led to the Relief Act of 1793. This gave a limited franchise and admitted Catholics to the Outer Bar, after the imposition of a degrading oath. Keogh joined the UNITED IRISHMEN, making his mansion in Mount Jerome available to them, and was briefly imprisoned in 1796. He was only intermittently involved in politics after this and died in Dublin on 13 November 1817.

Keogh, William. *See* POPE'S BRASS BAND, THE.

Kern. *See* RUG-HEADED KERNS.

Kerry. A county in the southwest of Ireland, adjoining Cork and Limerick, and nicknamed 'the KINGDOM'. It is famed for its scenery (the lakeside tourist resort of KILLARNEY as well as three magnificent peninsulas, DINGLE, IVERAGH and part of BEARA), its Gaelic footballers who have had more success in the ALL-IRELAND championship than any other county, and its cultural riches, which include the Irish language spoken in the Gaeltachts of Corca Dhuibhne (*see* DINGLE PENINSULA) and Iveragh, the literature of the BLASKET ISLANDS and north Kerry, and the traditional music and dance of SLIABH LUACHRA. Kerry is now a bustling, prosperous county, enriched by the tourist industry, by farming (particularly in fertile north Kerry) and by the success of enterprises such as the KERRY GROUP.

Kerry, Ring of. A circular tourist route, just over 160 km (100 miles) long, from KILLARNEY through KENMARE and around the IVERAGH PENINSULA, returning via KILLORGLIN. So popular is it in the tourist season, especially for American coach tours, that a one-way system operates for buses, essential on the narrow roads between Killarney and Kenmare and elsewhere on the route.

Kerry Babies Affair, the. On 14 April 1984 the body of a new-born baby was found on the shore at Cahirciveen in the Iveragh Peninsula of south Co. Kerry. It was found to have been stabbed. On 1 May gardai arrested Joanna Hayes, a young woman from Abbeydorney in faraway north Kerry, in connection with the killing. Joanna Hayes had secretly had a baby in the first half of April; the baby died and she

had buried it in a field near the family farm. Before long, however, she and her family were confessing to the gardai that she had in fact stabbed her baby to death and thrown it into the sea at Dingle, whence it had come to light at the other side of the Dingle Peninsula. However, blood tests on the body of the baby found in Cahirciveen revealed that Joanna and her partner could not have been its parents and the body of her own baby was later found near her home.

So many were the theories and such the speculation about this bizarre case and the role of the gardai in it that a tribunal of inquiry was established. The report of the tribunal was less than sympathetic to Joanna Hayes and her family, failing to explain the inconsistencies in the story and the fact that Joanna Hayes had confessed to a crime she had not committed; it also described a journey to Dingle to dispose of her dead baby that she had never made. Ireland of the 1980s (*see also* ANNE LOVETT CASE; EILEEN FLYNN AFFAIR, THE) presented the unedifying spectacle of a society allegedly 'pro-life' (*see* ABORTION REFERENDUMS) while exhibiting a singular lack of humanity towards women who were pregnant out of wedlock.

Kerry Blue. A breed of terrier, compact, powerful but graceful, originally used in Ireland and England for hunting small game and for retrieving. It is also known as the 'Irish Blue' terrier or simply the 'Kerry'. The coat of the Kerry Blue, which is dense and wavy rather than wiry, is blue mixed with silver, black or grey. For showing the head is usually clear, with whiskers left long. In 1924 an unidentified Kerry breeder wrote of his dogs:

> In the morn they herd the cattle; at noon they
> come in and tread the wheel to churn the butter;
> in the afternoon they herd again and after supper
> are turned out to guard the sheep, the chickens
> and geese and pigs. The last thing that they do
> before going to bed is to take off the pants of an
> Irishman.

The Kerry blue is related to the Irish terrier and the soft-coated wheaten terrier, but legend has it that the blue in their coat comes from a blue-grey spaniel that swam ashore after the wreck of the Spanish Armada in 1588. The breed has been recognized by the Kennel Club since 1922. Kerry blues are versatile animals, and have been used as police dogs and as guard dogs on military installations in Britain.

Kerry bog pony. A hardy chestnut pony, no higher than 100 cm (40 inches) – slightly bigger than a Shetland – and originally bred for work in the bog, where a small light animal was an advantage in wet, heavy ground. In coastal areas they also drew seaweed for use as fertilizer. They were known as 'farmer's workmaids', and survived longest in areas such as Glencar and Glenbeigh, mountainous parts of Co. Kerry. The ponies were registered as a rare breed by enthusiasts in the 1970s, when they were almost extinct, and a breeding programme has ensured their survival.

Kerry Cousins. A phrase referring to the various interconnected Kerry ASCENDANCY families that formed political dynasties in the 18th century, among them the Dennys (*see* TRALEE), Blennerhassets and Crosbies.

Kerry cow. A breed of small hardy black cow with downward-turning horns that is particularly suited to the land and weather conditions of the southwest of Ireland. Kerry cows have a long history, being said to descend directly from the herds kept by early Celtic farmers. Their milk was known to be exceptionally rich and creamy. Most have now been replaced by high-yielding Continental breeds, but a herd of them can be seen near MUCK-ROSS HOUSE by Killarney. There is a saying 'The Kerry cow knows Sunday', deriving from the time when people could not afford to eat meat, and instead supposedly bled the cow on Sunday and mixed the blood with oatmeal to make a kind of pudding.

Kerrygold. A world-famous brand of butter, aggressively marketed by the Irish Dairy Board (formerly Bord Bainne, the Milk Board, founded in 1961). It, GUINNESS and BAILEYS are Ire-land's three most widely recognized brands, and Kerrygold is exported to scores of countries.

Kerry Group. A multinational food and agri-business company with its headquarters in Tralee, Co. Kerry. The enterprise began in Listowel when north Kerry farmers established North Kerry Milk Products, which became in turn Kerry Cooperative and Kerry Group. The title of the 2001 company publication *The Kerry Way* conveys, perhaps somewhat tongue-in-cheek, the unique – and uniquely ambitious – ethos of the company, under the leadership of its founding chief executive Denis Brosnan (b.1944). Kerry Group is associated particularly with support of the LISTOWEL WRITERS WEEK, during which it sponsors a yearly fiction prize.

Kerryman jokes. A type of joke, very popular in the later decades of the 20th century, in which Kerry people, especially Kerrymen (hence the name) are the butt. These jokes, part of a common phenomenon whereby people from one county or province in a given country are singled out for ridicule, are a counterweight to the general perception that Kerry people are the cutest (*see* CUTE) in all Ireland. They are mostly taken in good part by Kerry people, who know better.

> Q: Why do you never get ice in a drink served in Kerry?
> A: Because the fellow with the recipe emigrated.
> Q: What does a Kerry bride wear on her wedding day?
> A: White Wellingtons.
> Q: How do you make a Kerryman laugh on Monday morning?
> A: Tell him a joke on Friday evening.
> Q: Did you hear about the Kerryman who had a brain transplant?
> A: The brain rejected him.

See also IRISH JOKE.

Kerry Mountain Rescue Team. A voluntary organization formed in 1966 for the purpose of saving the lives of climbers in the MACGILLI-CUDDY REEKS near Killarney, which includes

CARRANTUOHILL, the highest mountain in Ireland and the most popular among mountaineers. A fatality occurred on St Stephen's Day (Boxing Day) 2001 and a double fatality, the first in the team's history, near the Black Valley on 6 January 2002. To recover the bodies of the dead climbers, 24 members of the rescue team were airlifted to 180 m (600 ft) below the bodies. Some members of the team remained with the bodies overnight, honouring a Kerry mountaineering tradition, before they were brought down the following morning.

Kerry security. A derogatory term meaning a worthless pledge, dating from the early 19th century.

Kerry slide. A movement of the POLKA SET that is particular to the sets of SLIABH LUACHRA and west Kerry. It is frequently danced with great speed and verve, and is a showcase for fancy footwork. The music for the slide is a fast single JIG with a particular rhythmic emphasis.

Kerry witness. A derogatory colloquialism of unknown derivation, meaning an individual who will swear to anything.

Kesh (Irish *ceis*). A wattled bridge or causeway over a bog or as a footway to a CRANNÓG. The word occurs frequently in Irish placenames, the one most commonly heard in recent years being Long Kesh, the name Republicans used for the MAZE prison.

Kettle, Thomas (1880–1916). Politician and belle-lettrist. He was born in Artane in Dublin, the son of Parnell's lieutenant, Andrew Kettle, and educated at Clongowes and University College Dublin (UCD), graduating with a hardly used degree in law. He was Nationalist MP for East Tyrone (1906–9) and professor of economics at UCD (1909–16). He was active in trying to settle the 1913 LOCKOUT and saw the EASTER RISING as a betrayal of the SINN FÉIN movement, which, like Robert LYND, he regarded as the only effective means of achieving HOME RULE for all Ireland. During the

First World War he joined the Royal Dublin Fusiliers and was an active recruiter for the war 'for the freedom of small nations'; after the Rising he volunteered for service in Belgium. His essays, witty and profound, were published in *The Day's Burden* (1910), and his famous sonnet 'To My Daughter Betty, the Gift of God' was written shortly before his death at Guinchy on the Somme (*see* SECRET SCRIPTURE OF THE POOR, THE). His 'counsel to Ireland … that in order to become deeply Irish, she must become European' seems prophetic.

Kevin (Irish **Coemgen**) (d.*c*.618). The saint of the lonely but beautiful GLENDALOUGH. He was born in the mid-6th century in what is now Co. Wicklow, by tradition a nephew of St Eugene. He was educated by St Petroc of Cornwall, who was in Ireland at the time, and by the monks of Kilnamagh at Tallaght in Co. Dublin. He retired to a cell in Holywood, near Blessington, Co. Wicklow, but, finding it too worldly, retreated to Glendalough. So many flocked to be near him, however, that his wish for solitude was again denied him. With some reluctance, Kevin then founded an abbey with himself as abbot. He insisted on utter isolation during Lent. As with many charismatic figures there are many legends associated with Kevin, including his pursuit by a beautiful maiden (which Samuel LOVER turned to comic effect). Of all the early saints Kevin was the one regarded as being most in tune with nature. The story of his standing motionless, holding an egg laid by a blackbird in his hand until it hatched, is typical. His feast day is 6 June.

> At Glendalough lived a young saint,
>   In odour of sanctity dwelling,
> An old-fashioned odour, which now
>   We seldom or never are smelling;
> A book or a hook were to him
>   The utmost extent of his wishes;
> Now, a snatch at the 'Lives of the Saints';
>   Then a catch at the lives of the fishes.
>   SAMUEL LOVER (1797–1868): 'St Kevin' (1861)

Kibosh. A colloquial noun (also, less commonly, a verb) used in HIBERNO-ENGLISH (and also in Britain) in phrases such as 'to put the kibosh on …', to mean 'put an end to', 'finish off', 'do for' something. The derivation of the word is disputed, but it possibly comes from the Irish *caidhpín báis* ('death cap'), the black cap traditionally assumed by judges when pronouncing the death sentence, or perhaps referring to the black PITCH CAP used as a means of torture after the REBELLION OF 1798.

Kick. A sixpenny piece or tanner in pre-decimal money.

Kickham, Charles J[oseph] (1828–82). Novelist, poet and revolutionary. He was born in Cnoceenagaw near Mullinahone, Co. Tipperary, and made deaf at the age of 13 by an accident with gunpowder. He was a strong supporter of YOUNG IRELAND and became a FENIAN in 1860, editing the movement's newspaper, the *Irish People*. He was arrested as a Fenian in 1865, but served only 4 years of his 14-year sentence because of ill-health. He survived nearly blind and totally deaf for a further dozen years, writing his famous romance *Knocknagow, or the Homes of Tipperary*, in 1879. This achieved countrywide fame not because of any intrinsic merit but for its Irishness, its politics and its fulfilment of the subtitle. *Sally Kavanagh* (1869), a novel about rural hardship written in prison, also lived up to its grim subtitle *The Tenantless Grave*. Kickham wrote lyrics for many songs (some of them still current), including 'SLIEVENAMON' and 'Rory of the Hill'.

Kicking the Wall. The custom of kicking the wall at the end of the promenade in Salthill, a seaside resort outside Galway city. Salthill has been a popular tourist destination since the mid-19th century, with horse-drawn trams bringing holidaymakers from the railway station in Eyre Square in the centre of Galway. There are three beaches in Salthill: Blackrock (which was traditionally reserved for gentlemen), Ladies' Beach and Grattan Beach.

Kiely, Benedict (b.1919). Novelist, short-story writer and critic. He was born in Dromore, Co.

Tyrone, but brought up in Omagh, the scene of some of his novels. He was educated by the Christian Brothers and in 1937 entered a Jesuit novitiate in Co. Laois, but left because of tuberculosis. After convalescence he took a BA degree from University College Dublin. He was for many years one of the *personae* of the *Irish Press* diarist 'Patrick Lagan', and his traverse mainly of the northern part of the country increased his already large store of SEANCHAS. His first books were non-fiction, *Counties of Contention* (1945), a study of PARTITION, and *Poor Scholar* (1947), a lyrical evocation of the career of his fellow countyman, William CARLETON.

Kiely's first novel, *Land without Stars* (1946), was strongly autobiographical in topography, and its successor, *In a Harbour Green* (1949), also set in Omagh, is one of the finest evocations of small-town Irish life at the period. This was followed by *Modern Irish Fiction – A Critique* (1950), a remarkably astute and comprehensive survey of contemporary writing. Between 1950 and 1960 Kiely wrote five further novels: *Call for a Miracle* (1950), *Honey Seems Bitter* (1954), *There Was an Ancient House* (1955), *The Cards of the Gambler* (1955) and *The Captain with the Whiskers* (1960) – all wonderfully digressive and richly entertaining, and based upon the different backgrounds of the author's wide experience. Later novels, *Proxopera* (1977) and *Nothing Happens in Carmincross* (1985), are darkened by the extremism of both sides in the TROUBLES.

Kiely's collections of stories – *A Journey to the Seven Streams* (1963), *A Ball of Malt and Madame Butterfly* (1973) and *A Cow in the House* (1978) – seem to suggest that Kiely's real forte as a writer is as a kind of latter-day literary SEANCHAÍ who holds the reader with a voice as rich and allusive as the ancient mariner's eye was glittering. Two books of memoirs, *Drink to the Bird* (1992) and *The Waves Behind Us* (1999), confirm this judgement.

> From the top of Conn's Brae you can see, far away and on a clear day, to be sure, a blue pyramid and a blue pigback: Mount Errigal

and Muckish Mountain on the Atlantic shore. Nobody knows who Conn was: Conn Bácach Ó Néill, or Conn the Shaughran, or Conn of the Hundred Battles. Or some other Conn not mentioned in history apart from having that precipitous hill called after him. Which of us dare hope for so much of the immortal?

Drink to the Bird (1992)

Kierkegaard, Søren (1813–55). Danish philosopher and theologian. In spite of an emotional and troubled life Kierkegaard could be lighthearted and fanciful on occasion, as this excerpt from his *Journal*, written without authentication, in 1840 confirms:

> If I did not know that I was a true Dane, I might almost be tempted to suppose I was an Irishman in order to explain the contradictions at work within me. For the Irish have not the heart to baptize their children completely, they want to preserve just a little paganism and whereas a child is normally completely immersed, they keep his right arm out of the water so that in after life he can grasp a sword and hold a girl in his arm.
>
> (translated by Alexander Dru)

Kiernan, Tommy (b.1939). Rugby player. He was born in Cork on 7 January 1939 and is Ireland's most capped full-back – he played for his country 54 times between 1960 and 1973. Kiernan captained Ireland 24 times. He was national coach in the early 1980s and also coached the Munster team that memorably defeated the All Blacks in 1978 (*see* ALONE IT STANDS).

Kilburn. *See* NAVVIES.

Kildare, Géaróid Mór (Gerald Fitzgerald), 8th Earl of. *See* FIT TO RULE ALL IRELAND; GREAT EARL, THE.

Kildare Place Society (1811). A philanthropic society, the Society for Promoting the Education of the Poor, established in Dublin by a group of businessmen and professionals, some of them Quakers (*see* SOCIETY OF FRIENDS). It introduced the monitorial system (*see* MONITOR) and trained teachers at its headquarters in Kildare Place. The society received state fund-ing for a system of primary education that was ostensibly non-sectarian, and at first it attracted the support of Daniel O'CONNELL and other Catholic opinion-formers, but when it became clear that the society was either tacitly or openly supporting evangelical proselytizing (*see* SECOND REFORMATION) the Catholic Church became very critical. After the establishment of the NATIONAL SCHOOLS system in 1831, state funding was no longer given to such voluntary organizations. A single 'Kildare Place' school survives in Dublin, attached to the Church of Ireland teacher-training college in Rathmines.

Kildare Rebellion (1534–5). The rebellion that ended the dominance of the Fitzgeralds of Kildare among the OLD ENGLISH of the PALE. *See also* SILKEN THOMAS.

Kildare side. A colloquialism of uncertain derivation meaning the right-hand side, for instance one might wear an accessory or accoutrement on the 'Kildare side'.

Kilian (*c.*640–689). A saint, born at Mullagh, Co. Cavan, who preached Christianity to the Thuringians and Franconians, the occupiers of the lands of modern south and east Germany. One of his converts was Duke Gozbert, whom he persuaded to abandon his wife, Geilana, formerly his brother's wife. She is thought to have had Kilian and some of his fellow missionaries murdered. He was buried in the crypt of the cathedral of Würzburg which bears his name. His feast day is 8 July.

Kilkenny. The county town of Co. Kilkenny, with a population of 8500 (1996). It has played a significant part in Irish history. It was the site of the 6th-century monastery of St CANICE (hence its Irish name *Cill Chainnigh*) and it was in the Parliament meeting there in the 14th century that the Statute of Kilkenny (1366) was passed; this tried to keep separate the Anglo-Normans of the PALE and the 'mere Irish', forbidding intermarriage and even residence in the towns. The siting of the independent Irish parliament called the Confederation of Kilkenny (*see* CONFEDERATE CATHOLICS) in the town (1642–8) was an indication of its Catholic prosperity, largely due to the influence of the Butler family, the Earls of ORMOND whose castle still stands. Kilkenny had a notorious witchcraft trial in the 14th century when Dame Alice KYTELER's maid Petronilla was burned at the stake. The name of the town also features in the idiom 'to fight like KILKENNY CATS'. Kilkenny was created a city by James I in 1609, but later suffered a serious decline, especially in the 19th century, when with the coming of the railways it was no longer the main staging post on the Dublin–Cork road. But even in decline it had a vigorous social life:

Oh! the boys of Kilkenny are nate roving blades
And whenever they meet with the dear little
    maids,
They kiss them and coax them and spend their
    money free.
Oh! of all towns in Ireland, Kilkenny's for me!
    ANON. (early 19th century)

Today Kilkenny has become a Baedeker city, with a beautifully preserved cathedral, castle and an 18th-century town hall, and is now a leading provincial centre for the arts, crafts and design (see KILKENNY DESIGN).

Kilkenny, Confederation of. The alliance between Irish and OLD ENGLISH formed in KILKENNY city on 24 October 1642, properly known as the Confederated Catholics of Ireland (see CONFEDERATE CATHOLICS).

Kilkenny, Statute of. A statute determining the relations between the English and native Irish between its promulgation in 1366 and 1613 (in the reign of James I). The legislation was passed by the Parliament meeting in KILKENNY, the centre of Anglo-Norman power in the 14th century. There were 36 clauses in all, but the statute is remembered mainly for the measures put in place to prevent further contamination of the English colony by the 'Irish enemies' beyond the PALE. The preamble draws attention to the grievous state already persisting:

    …but now many English of the said land,
    forsaking the English language, fashion, mode

of riding, laws and usages, live and govern themselves according to the manners, fashion and language of the Irish enemies, and have also made divers marriages and alliances between themselves and the Irish enemies aforesaid; whereby the said land and the liege people thereof, the English language, the allegiance due to our lord the King, and the English laws there are put into subjection and decayed and the Irish enemies exalted and raised up contrary to right.

The enactments were essentially a defensive summary of existing statutes and were obeyed only to the same limited extent as *they* had been. Apart from specific injunctions covering the faults as indicated in the preamble, the native Irish were forbidden advancement in the church and admission into religious houses; intermarriage and concubinage were formally forbidden, as was the Irish language; the ancient Gaelic practice of fostering was banned; and even Irish entertainers from outside the lordship were to be forbidden entry:

    And whereas the Irish minstrels coming among
    the English spy out the secrets, customs and
    policies of the English whereby great evils have
    often happened, it is agreed and forbidden that
    any Irish minstrels, that is to say tympanours,
    poets, storytellers, babblers, rymours, harpers
    or any other minstrels shall come among the
    English; and that no English receive them or
    make them gift.

The provisions of the Statute of Kilkenny were not new: previous legislation had covered many of the same areas, and subsequent legislation reiterated the prohibitions on several occasions until the statute was repealed in the Parliament of 1613–15.

Kilkenny cats, to fight like. To fight till both sides have lost or are destroyed. The story is told that during the REBELLION OF 1798 Kilkenny was garrisoned by a troop of Hessian soldiers, who amused themselves by tying two cats together by their tails and throwing them across a clothes line to fight. When an officer approached to stop the 'sport' a trooper cut the two tails with a sword and the two cats fled. When asked to explain the two bloody tails, the trooper explained that two cats had been fighting and devoured each other, all but the tails.

Kilkenny Design. An affiliation of craft workers (originally Kilkenny Design Workshops) established by the Irish government in 1965 in the 18th-century stable of Kilkenny Castle to provide a creative environment for the promotion of graphic, industrial and craft design. Kilkenny Design shops, or Kilkenny Shops as they are now known, have an associated retail outlet in Kilkenny and an extensive shop in Dublin. The shops appeal to discerning tourists as well as Irish customers. The Crafts Council of Ireland relocated to Kilkenny in 1988.

Kill a Hessian for yourself. A phrase that comes from a story of the REBELLION OF 1798 when Hessian mercenaries were deployed against the insurgents. Their boots were noted for their excellence (and became fashionable after the Napoleonic Wars in Britain). In a skirmish an insurgent killed a trooper and secured his boots as a trophy. A comrade asked for the boots but was told, 'Kill a Hessian for yourself.' Subsequently the phrase was commonly used to quell someone seeking to obtain without effort something that cost the owner dear.

Killala. *See* REBELLION OF 1798.

Killarney. A justly acclaimed lakeside beauty spot in Co. Kerry. It inspired FALCONER to call it HEAVEN'S REFLEX and Tennyson to write a much better lyric, 'Blow, Bugle, Blow' (*see* TORC WATERFALL). Dion Boucicault transferred the action of Gerald Griffin's *The Collegians* to the lakes for his dramatic version, *The* COLLEEN BAWN (1860), and Julius Benedict (1804–85) called his opera on the theme *The Lily of Killarney*. The FOUR KERRY POETS are, it is claimed, buried in MUCKROSS ABBEY nearby, and there is a monument to them in the town. Killarney has been a tourist destination since the late 18th century, becoming especially popular after the coming of the railway, and the visit of Queen Victoria in 1861. The

town itself, architecturally undistinguished and crowded with hotels, many of them modern vulgarities, is surrounded by the thousands of acres of Killarney National Park, the gift of benefactors like the Bourne-Vincents, owners of MUCKROSS HOUSE. The park is an invaluable resource for climbers and walkers. Nearby are the highest mountains in the country (*see* MACGILLICUDDY REEKS and CARRAN-TUOHILL). Killarney is the departure point for touring the Ring of KERRY.

> Every rock that you pass by,
> Verdure 'broiders or besprints.
> Virgin there the green grass grows,
> Every morn springs natal day,
> Bright-hued berries daff the snows,
> Smiling winter's frown away.
> Angels often passing there
> Doubt if Eden were more fair,
> Beauty's home, Killarney
> Heaven's reflex, Killarney.
>> EDMUND FALCONER (1814–79)

See also JARVEYS; KATE KEARNEY'S COTTAGE; ROSS CASTLE.

Killarney Minstrel, the. The blind fiddler James Gandsey (1767–1857), who has been identified as an important source for the traditional music of SLIABH LUACHRA. Gandsey's mother was from Killarney, his father an English soldier stationed in ROSS CASTLE.

Killeen (Irish *cillín*, 'little churchyard'). A HIBERNO-ENGLISH word for a graveyard disused except for the occasional burial of unbaptized infants.

Killinchy muffler. An embrace in which a partner's arms are around one's neck. The name comes from a Co. Down village near Strangford Lough in Northern Ireland. The reason for the name is obscure.

Killing Home Rule with Kindness. The informal policy of such liberal Unionists as Sir Horace PLUNKETT (1854–1932) in the post-Parnellite years. They hoped that improved social conditions would deprive Nationalist agitation of

its impetus. Known more politely as 'Constructive Unionism', its principal elements were the solution of the land question by a series of successful measures, culminating in WYND-HAM's Land Act (1903) which facilitated land purchase, the extension of local government autonomy and the provision of government funding for Catholic universities. Though individually welcomed, the measures did little to reconcile Nationalists to the UNION.
See also IAOS; LAND ACTS.

Killing the messenger. A phrase of disputed origin. One version relates that in May 1487 a messenger came from the mayor of Waterford to the Earl of Kildare, Gearóid Mór Fitzgerald (*see* GREAT EARL, THE), with the news that the citizens of the town would not support the cause of the pretender to the English throne, Lambert SIMNEL. Gearóid Mór had the messenger hanged on the THINGMOTE in Dublin.

Killorglin. The small town in Co. Kerry associated with the annual PUCK FAIR; the town itself is sometimes itself called 'Puck' because of the notoriety of the event.

Killykeen Forest Park. An extensive amenity in Co. Cavan, situated 11 km (7 miles) from Cavan town on the shores of Lough Oughter. Clough Oughter Castle is within the park, although currently inaccessible; it was built by the local O'Reilly chieftains on an island in the lake, and it was here that Owen Rua O'NEILL died in 1649.

Killyman Wrackers. The nickname given to a particularly vicious corps of Yeomanry (*see* YEOS) who destroyed a number of Catholic homes in a village close to Dungannon, Co. Tyrone, in the aftermath of the REBELLION OF 1798. By a nice process of diminution the name was later given to a brand of local potatoes.

Kilmainham Jail. A jail built in 1792 in the Kilmainham district of western Dublin. Here Charles Stewart PARNELL was imprisoned in 1881–2, until the KILMAINHAM TREATY. Kil-

mainham Jail also witnessed the executions of the leaders of the 1916 EASTER RISING, shot by the British. The building is now a historical museum, housing, among other items, Erskine Childers's yacht *ASGARD*, used in the HOWTH GUN-RUNNING of 1914.

Kilmainham Treaty. The agreement between PARNELL and Gladstone (*see* GOM) in 1882 that marked the end of the LAND WAR. Kilmainham was the jail in Dublin where Parnell and his lieutenants had been incarcerated on 13 October 1881. As a contemporary ballad had it:

It was the tyrant Gladstone and he said unto himself,
'I nivir will be aisy till Parnell is on the shelf,
So make the warrant out in haste and take it by the mail,
And we'll clap the pride of Erin's isle into cold Kilmainham Jail.'

The rejection of the 1881 LAND ACT by the Land League had led to Parnell's arrest, and a wave of agrarian crime followed. (It was during this period that the chief secretary was given his nickname – 'BUCKSHOT' FORSTER.) The Act had granted many of the League's demands, including the THREE FS and the setting up of a LAND COMMISSION to adjudicate on rents and offer loans of 75% of the purchase price to tenants who wished to buy out their holdings. However, agitation had become a habit, and the question of rent arrears had not been dealt with. Under the terms of the treaty the provisions of the Act were extended to leaseholders and better terms offered to tenants in arrears.

Kilmichael Ambush (1920). The ambush of a party of Auxiliaries (*see* AUXIES) by 36 men of the West Cork Brigade of the IRA under Tom BARRY on 28 November 1920. It was one of the most successful actions of the ANGLO-IRISH WAR: 15 of the 16 Auxiliaries were killed and one wounded. REVISIONIST historian Peter Hart (*see* IRA AND ITS ENEMIES, THE) has drawn attention to the so-called 'false surrender' described by Tom Barry in *GUERRILLA DAYS IN IRELAND*, casting doubt on Barry's word and controversially suggesting that the second group of Auxiliaries were killed in cold blood. There were three IRA casualties. An anonymous ballad, 'The BOYS OF KILMICHAEL', celebrates the IRA victory.

Kilroot (Irish *Cill Ruaidh*, 'the church of the red land'). A village near Carrickfergus, Co. Antrim, that was Swift's (*see* DEAN, THE) first living (1694–6). He found an empty church owing to the large population of Presbyterians, and his congregations continued to be sparse. It was in Kilroot that Swift wrote *A Tale of a Tub* (1704).

Kilroy, Thomas (b.1934). Playwright and novelist. He was born in Callan, Co. Kilkenny, and educated at St Kieran's College and University College Dublin. He has held many academic posts in Ireland and America, relinquishing the chair of English at University College Galway in 1989 after ten years. He has written one novel, *The Big Chapel* (1972), based upon the same historical incident of 1870s clerical politics as inspired *The Greatest of These* (1943) by fellow-Kilkenny writer Francis MACMANUS. His first successful play was *The Death and Resurrection of Mr Roche* (1969), about the seedy life of Dublin flat-dwellers. This was followed by *The O'Neill* (1969), Kilroy's account of a historical character also brought to life by his FIELD DAY colleague Brian FRIEL; *Tea, Sex and Shakespeare* (1976), about the writing life; and the very popular *Talbot's Box* (1977), about the Dublin lay saint Matt TALBOT (1856–1925), which moved from the PEACOCK to the Royal Court in London. His plays for Field Day were *Double Cross* (1986) – in which the same actor played two peripheral characters from the Second World War, namely Brendan Bracken, Churchill's mysterious protégé, and William Joyce, the Nazi collaborator known as 'Lord HAW-HAW' – and *Madam MacAdam's Travelling Theatre* (1991), an uneasy attempt at social comment (on Ireland during the EMERGENCY) using farce. Kilroy has also written versions of Chekhov's *The*

Seagull (1981) and Ibsen's *Ghosts* (1989) set in Ireland.

'Kilruddery Hunt, The.' A celebration by Thomas Mozeen (1709–87) of the typically hard-riding, hard-drinking Anglo-Irish members of the Earl of Meath's hunt who chased a fox for five hours to the death through south Co. Dublin and over the county border into Wicklow in spite of its gallant efforts to evade the pack.

> In seventeen hundred and forty-four
> The fifth of December, I think 'twas no more,
> At five of the morning by most of the clocks,
> We rode from Kilruddery in search of a fox.
> …
> At his death there were present the lads I have
>   sung,
> Save Larry, who, riding a garron, was flung.
> Thus ended at length a most delicate chase
> That held us five hours and ten minutes space.
>   (A *garron* – Irish *gearrán* – is a gelding.)

Kiltartan. A village on the Gregory estate of COOLE PARK near Gort, Co. Galway, that gave its name to the idiom used by Lady GREGORY in much of her writings. It was based on the HIBERNO-ENGLISH of the district, and influenced by her growing knowledge of Gaelic forms. One of its characteristics is the so-called 'Kiltartan infinitive' that acts as a kind of absolute:

> The poor man to be deserted by his own wife,
> and the breath hardly gone out yet from his body
> that is lying bloody in the field.

The word appears in the titles of four of her books: *The Kiltartan History Book* (1909), *The Kiltartan Wonder Book* (1910), *The Kiltartan Molière* (1910) and *The Kiltartan Poetry Book* (1918), and she used the style in such prose works as *Cuchulain of Muirthemne* 1902), *Poets and Dreamers* (1903) and *Gods and Fighting Men* (1904), and in many of her plays. The style was satirized in Gerald MacNamara's play, *The* MIST THAT DOES BE ON THE BOG (1909).

> Going to Mass by the heavenly mercy,
>   The day was rainy, the wind was wild;

I met a lady beside Kiltartan
And fell in love with the lovely child ...

ANTAINE Ó RAIFTEIRÍ (c.1784--c.1835): 'Mary Hynes', translated by Frank O'Connor

Kiltartan also appears in the work of Lady Gregory's friend Yeats:

My country is Kiltartan Cross,
My countrymen Kiltartan's poor,
No likely end could bring them loss
Or leave them happier than before.

W.B. YEATS: 'An Irish Airmen Foresees His Death', in *The Wild Swans at Coole* (1919). The dead airman was Lady Gregory's son, Major Robert Gregory, killed in the First World War.

Kincora. The seat of BRIAN BORU in Killaloe, Co. Clare. Its position on the Shannon at the south point of Lough Derg made it easily accessible, and its position in the heart of country loyal to the king/emperor gave it a kind of Camelot-like magic, with as many legends attaching to it as to TARA. Kincora was destroyed in 1119 by Turlough O'Connor, who hurled its stones and timbers into the river.

Remember the glories of Brian the brave,
Tho' the days of the hero are o'er;
Tho' lost to Mononia and cold in the grave,
He returns to Kinkora no more!

THOMAS MOORE (1779–1852): 'Remember the Glory of Brian the Brave', in *Irish Melodies* (1808)

Kincora Scandal. A sexual-abuse scandal associated with a member of the ORANGE ORDER in Belfast, William McGrath (1916–91), who was housefather in the Kincora home for boys in east Belfast (1971–80). McGrath and two other care workers in Kincora were convicted of charges of sexual abuse in December 1981. At the same time McGrath had established a Loyalist ginger group called Tara, to which some individuals later to be prominent Unionists belonged. Because, it is believed, McGrath was a British intelligence agent, his activities as a sex offender were covered up and police investigations obstructed by the government.

King Billy. The often affectionate nickname of William III (1650–1702), who as Prince of Orange was concerned to keep Louis XIV of France (1638–1715) out of the Dutch Republic, and who accepted the throne of his father-in-law JAMES II as much to oppose the Sun King as to gain territory. His success at the Battle of the BOYNE (1690) caused both King Billy and the Boyne to become ORANGE ORDER icons, the king shown crossing the river on a white horse, a constant theme of BANNERS and ARCHES. As king he was not especially popular with his Protestant subjects, being tolerant of Catholicism and opposed to the POPERY LAWS that were insisted upon by Irish Protestants. His death in 1702 was caused by a fall from his horse Sorrell, reddish brown in colour, as the name suggests, and not the white of Orange insistence.

See also LITTLE GENTLEMAN IN VELVET, THE.

Kingdom, the. A nickname given to Co. KERRY, primarily for the purposes of sport or tourism, as in 'The Kingdom of Kerry'. It reputedly derives from a remark by John Philpot CURRAN that the magistrates of Kerry were a law unto themselves, a kingdom apart. A book on the successful Kerry football team of the 1970s and 1980s, published in 1989, was called *Kingdom Come*. John B. KEANE once remarked that 'Kerry people say there are only two kingdoms, the kingdom of Kerry and the kingdom of God.'

King John. *See* JOHN.

King John's Castle. A Norman castle in Limerick city, built 1200–02 during the reign of King JOHN, and repaired in 1226. It is five-sided, with one side giving directly on to the River Shannon. It was briefly captured by the O'Briens and MacNamaras in 1369, and put under the care of the city's mayor and citizens in 1423. During the wars of the 17th century the castle surrendered three times: to the CONFEDERATE CATHOLICS in 1641, to the Cromwellian General Ireton in 1651, and to the Williamite army of General GINKEL after the second siege of Limerick in 1691. It was used as a barracks in the 18th century, and many residences were built in it. In its present restored state it is one of Limerick's city main tourist attractions.

Kingkisheen (Irish *Cincgís*, Pentecost). A HIB-ERNO-ENGLISH word for someone born on or near Whitsun and fated to slay or be slain.

King of Dalkey. During the 18th century a custom developed that Dalkey Island, a small island near the south point of Dublin Bay, should declare itself an independent state and elect its own 'king'. An archbishop for the island and an admiral of the Muglins, a group of hazardous rocks northeast of Dalkey (now the site of the Muglins lighthouse) were also elected. Hugh Dempsey, who died in 1790, was one of these 'kings' of Dalkey.

King of Friday's Men, The. A play (1948) by M.J. MOLLOY about SHILLELAGH fighting and the assumed rights of some 18th-century Irish landlords over the daughters of their tenants. Bartley Dowd, a giant of a man and champion fighter, falls in love with Una Brehony, the latest TALLYWOMAN of the landlord Caesar French. Dowd finally kills French, leaving Una free to marry him. The play is written with great gusto and in slightly artificial sub-Syngean language.

King of Ireland. The title assumed, somewhat reluctantly, by Henry VIII in June 1541. Apart from acquisition by conquest, the English crown could point to the papal bull LAUDABI-LITER granted to HENRY II to give them moral right to the title. Mary Tudor (1516–58) had her position as queen confirmed by another papal bull when she acceded.

'King of Ireland'. *See* BERESFORD, JOHN.

King of Spain's daughter. A euphemism for Spanish wine current in Ireland in the 17th century. The trade between the two countries was a significant part of Ireland's alternative commerce up to the Act of UNION.

> Then the wet, winding roads,
> Brown bogs with black water,
> And my thoughts on white ships
> And the King o' Spain's daughter.
>
> PADRAIC COLUM (1881–1972): 'A Drover', in *Wild Earth* (1916)

King of the Beggars. The title of a biography of Daniel O'CONNELL (1938) by Sean O'Faolain (1900–91), suggested to him by fellow Cork-man Frank O'Connor (1903–66).

King of the Roads. *See* BIANS.

King Puck. The name given to the he-goat crowned 'king' and elevated on a platform in the town of KILLORGLIN, Co. Kerry, during the annual August festivities known as PUCK FAIR.

King Rat. The nickname of Billy Wright (1960–97), who became the leader of the Loyalist Volunteer Force (LVF), his own breakaway group of the UVF in Portadown. Suspected of involvement in the deaths of five Catholics in 1991 and 1992, he was expelled by the Combined Loyalist Military Command and ordered to leave Northern Ireland by 1 September 1996, an order he defiantly and successfully ignored. Imprisoned in March 1997 for threatening behaviour to a Protestant neighbour, he was held first in Maghaberry and then in the MAZE. It was there in December 1997 that he was shot and killed by three INLA prisoners, Chris McWilliams, John Kennaway and John Glennon, who surrendered themselves and their smuggled guns to the Catholic prison chaplain. The deaths of a number of Catholics in the following weeks were said to be reprisals for Wright's death.

King's County. *See* OFFALY.

Kingship. The CELTS, both pagan and Christian, believed that the ruler occupied a sacred position, propitiating the gods and the elements to protect his people from the forces of nature, such as drought, famine and disease, and from the arbitrary displeasure of the deities. If a king's reign was just, peace and prosperity would follow; if not, there would be conflict, famine, pestilence and all manner of disasters. The king was seen as the mate of the goddess of place. The ceremony in which the king assumed sovereignty and mated with the goddess, symbolically or otherwise, was called a *FEIS*. For instance, the king of TARA, a place of special mythic significance, mated with the goddess Medb Lethderg. The unreliable and anti-Hibernian chronicler GIRALDUS CAMBRENSIS records a story of a northern king mating publicly with a white mare on the occasion of his inauguration, the mare symbolizing the territory. She was then killed, cut up and boiled, and the meat eaten by the assembled people while the king bathed in the broth.

See also HIGH KING.

King's Inns. The name of the professional and training body of Irish barristers, and also of the premises used by this body. The society originated in about 1541, when 17 lawyers acquired premises in a former Dominican priory at Blackfriars at the junction of Church Street and the Liffey Quays; by 1611 the Society of the King's Inns, now firmly established, owned the property in perpetuity. During the 18th century the King's Inn acquired control of entry to the professions of barrister and solicitor alike, as well as disciplinary powers, although they subsequently lost power over solicitors to the INCORPORATED LAW SOCIETY. By 1730 the property at Blackfriars had deteriorated, and parts of it were occupied by impoverished individuals unconnected with the law. When the government made plans for a building programme on the Blackfriars site that included the FOUR COURTS on Inns Quay and a Public Records Office, the King's Inns Society bought a site further to the north of the Liffey, on Constitution Hill/Henrietta Street. James GANDON designed the handsome building, which is still in use by the society today, the foundation stone being laid by the lord chancellor, John Fitzgibbon, on 1 August 1800, the day the Act of UNION received the royal assent. The project was completed by Gandon's pupil and successor, H.E. Baker, after Gandon retired in 1808.

Kingsmills Massacre. The shooting on 5 January 1976 of ten Protestant workmen in south Armagh on their way home by van from work at Glenanne spinning mill. A mixed party of Republicans, INLA and Provisional IRA, stopped them at a fake checkpoint at Kingsmills near Bessbrook, lined them up and shot them. The operation was unauthorized and said to be in retaliation for the killing of five local Catholics the previous day.

King's shilling, the. A bounty offered to those enlisted by the recruiting sergeants of the British army 'by the beat of the drum' in the 18th and early 19th century. The derogatory phrase, 'taking the shilling' or 'taking the king's shilling' was used to describe those who took the bounty, and the phrase figures in many Irish songs and ballads.

Kinsale. A picturesque coastal town in Co. Cork, 30 km (20 miles) from Cork city. Famous in recent years for its gastronomy, it has derived much benefit from tourism. For over 300 years it was a garrison town and a port of consequence, and it therefore has a legacy of Georgian and Victorian architecture. Kinsale has long had a reputation as a popular resort, as an anonymous early 19th-century piece of doggerel makes clear:

> Then take my advice, if you've got boil or colic
> Only try what our baths and pure air will avail.
> Or if you're in health, just come here for the
>   frolic
> And abundant amusement you'll find in Kinsale.

See also CHARLESFORT.

Kinsale, Battle of (1601). The deciding battle of the NINE YEARS' WAR and a terminal defeat for the forces of Hugh O'NEILL and his allies. It was fought just outside the present-day town of Kinsale in Co. Cork, far from the territory of the Ulster Gaelic lords, and, for the first time in the war, on terrain not chosen by O'Neill for his own advantage. Although Lord Deputy MOUNTJOY had had some success in countering O'Neill's military achievements in Ulster, the war was far from over when the long-awaited Spanish expeditionary force landed at Kinsale in September 1601. It was encircled by Mountjoy's army, which was in turn encircled by the forces of O'Neill and his allies, who had made the long journey from Ulster. Mountjoy's soldiers were suffering from cold, wet and disease after the long siege, and it is said that the cautious O'Neill would have preferred to starve them into submission but was persuaded by the more impatient Red Hugh O'DONNELL to mount a dawn attack on 24 December. The English were forewarned and routed the Irish troops. On 2 January 1602 the Spanish were allowed to leave and the remnants of the Ulster forces made their way home. Although Hugh O'Neill did not submit to Mountjoy until March 1603, he spent much of the interim a fugitive in Ulster.

Kinsale cloak. *See* IRISH CLOAK.

Kinsella, Thomas (b.1928). Poet. He was born in Dublin and educated at the Model School at Inchicore, then at O'Connell School and University College Dublin, his degree completed as an evening student while he worked as a civil servant. His early collections include *Poems* (1956), *Another September* (1958) and *Downstream* (1962), wry looks at his country balanced by celebration of the wonder and danger of loving. He left the civil service in 1965 to serve as poet-in-residence at Southern Illinois University, and in 1970 became a professor in the English department at Temple University, Philadelphia, a college of which he opened in Dublin in 1976. His translation of the Old Irish Ulster epic *Táin Bó Cuailgne* ('The Cattle Raid of Cooley') as *The Táin* (1969), with illustrations by Louis LE BROCQUY, was hugely popular, as was *An Duanaire: Poems of the Dispossessed* (1981), an anthology of translations of Gaelic poems (with Seán Ó TUAMA). In 1972 he published *Butcher's Dozen*, a visceral reaction to Bloody Sunday in Derry and the whitewash of the Widgery Tribunal, as the first of his own PEPPERCANISTER pamphlets (called after the popular name for St Stephen's Church on Upper Mount Street, close to his home in Percy Place). Later collections of poems are *St Catherine's Clock* (1987), *Poems from Centre City* (1990) and *Madonna and*

Other Poems (1991). Now retired from academic life, he lives in Co. Wicklow.

Kip or **kip house.** A brothel or house of ill-repute, for instance in Dublin's MONTO. The madams were called 'kip-keepers'. 'The kips' was a general name for a red-light district. Today the word is applied to any less-than-salubrious establishment, such as a hotel that the speaker regards as a tawdry dump.

Kip of the reel. *See* CLIP O' THE REEL.

Kippen or **kippeen** (Irish *cipín*). A word used commonly in HIBERNO-ENGLISH for a small stick, such as is used for kindling.

Kirk session. The governing body of a local PRESBYTERIAN congregation, with members appointed for life. The minister acts as moderator at meetings.

Kist o' whistles. A dismissive description of a church organ or harmonium by traditionalist Ulster (and Scottish) Presbyterians. The controversy raged from 1868 until 1892, and when the 'kist' (a Scots word for 'chest') was finally accepted by a majority of kirks, a number of the sterner critics refused to attend church again.

> Is it not most amazing
> That such a fuss is all about
> A huge machine for praising
> – Or what is better far expressed
> Syne in the land of thistles:
> But whole in earnest, half in jest
> The 'Auld Wife's Kist o' Whistles'.
> VERITAS (*c*.1885)

Kitchen, to make. A culinary verb-phrase used in HIBERNO-ENGLISH meaning 'to make do with', 'to eat sparingly'. A woman might say to her hungry husband, 'You'll have to make kitchen of that.' The word 'kitchen' originally meant condiments or a sauce used to flavour food, the lack of which might be described in 'We ate it without kitchen.'

Kitchen comedy. A loose term applied to a series of popular plays that formed a genre of Irish theatre up until the 1950s. The term came from the usual set, a farm kitchen with access to the yard and the other downstairs rooms. There was usually a half-door and a substantial window that allowed the characters to see the lane leading to the main road, called a LOANEN or BOREEN, depending on whether the play was set in Ulster or otherwise. Along this lane would come the neighbours, wooers, postmen with letters from America, process-servers and clergymen – Catholic, Anglican or Presbyterian. The kitchen could for the nonce be set in a town, with a suggested lamp-post outside the window to establish the location. Such dramatists as Louis D'ALTON, Brinsley MacNamara (see VALLEY OF THE SQUINTING WINDOWS, THE), George SHIELS and Rutherford Mayne (see DRONE, THE) kept the theatres in Belfast, Cork and Dublin well supplied with entertaining well-made plays, which were seized upon avidly by the many local amateur companies that were such a feature of the Ireland of the time.

> Scene: The farm kitchen of John Murray. It is large and spacious, with a wide open fire-place to the right. At the back is one door leading to the parlour and other rooms in the house, also a large window overlooking the yard outside. To the left of this window is the door leading into the yard ...
>
> RUTHERFORD MAYNE: setting for The Drone (1908)

Kitchener, Horatio (Earl Kitchener of Khartoum) (1850–1916). Soldier. Kitchener was born in Gunsborough near Ballylongford in Co. Kerry on 24 June 1850, and educated in Switzerland and at the Royal Military Academy in Woolwich. He was commissioned in 1871 and served in the Middle East. As leader of the Egyptian army he won back the Sudan for Egypt in 1898, and from 1900 served as commander-in-chief of the British army in the Boer War. As a result he was decorated, made viscount and given a large grant of money. He was appointed secretary of state for war on 7 August 1914 and spearheaded the British army's early recruit-

ment drive. He was lost when HMS *Hampshire* was mined off the Orkneys in June 1916.

Kitty O'Shea's. *See* IRISH BARS; O'SHEA WHO MUST BE OBEYED.

Kitty the Hare. *See* IRELAND'S OWN.

Klondyke. The nickname of a 'character' in Cork city in the 1920s and 1930s (real name Jeremiah Healy), deriving from his claim to have dug gold in the Yukon. He also claimed to have had an illustrious and varied military career with the British forces. Little was known of him, but he was believed to have been shell-shocked in the First World War and in receipt of a disability pension from the British government. He was a gentle, courteous man, always formally dressed in a bowler hat and swallow-tailed coat. The title 'Dr Healy' by which he was also known was conferred on him by students from University College Cork during a rag week. In the late 1930s they organized a campaign to have him elected to Cork Corporation. A single-issue candidate, he agitated for the erection of a ladies' toilet in the city centre, allegedly claiming: 'Europe is in a turmoil. We are poised on the brink of a second world war. The nations of Europe are frantically re-arming. They are spending millions of pounds on arsenals – and all I ask is one urinal.' Klondyke/Dr Healy was duly elected to the corporation, and a toilet for ladies was erected on Lavitt's Quay, opposite the Opera House.

K.M.R.I.A. A sophisticated jokey expletive, based upon the qualification MRIA (Member of the ROYAL IRISH ACADEMY). It stands for 'Kiss my royal Irish arse' and in Joyce's ULYSSES it was used by Myles Crawford, the editor of the *Telegraph*, to intensify his rejection of Mr Keys's request, mediated by Bloom, 'for a little puff'. It occurs in the 'Aeolus' section of the Homeric novel, in which the text is broken up by typical newspaper headlines. At first Crawford's rejection is headlined 'K.M.A.', but when Bloom persists it is granted the more expansive strapline 'K.M.R.I.A.':

— He can kiss my royal Irish arse, Myles Crawford cried loudly over his shoulder. Any time he likes, tell him.

Knacker. A word originally meaning someone who bought decrepit horses for slaughter (also knacker's cart, knacker's yard). It now invariably has a negative connotation, meaning a n'er-do-well in Cork slang. In recent years the word has also taken on, in a very unpolitically correct fashion, the specific connotation of a member of the travelling community, particularly one engaging in casual roadside trading. *See also* TRAVELLERS.

Knauvshaul. *See* CNÁIMHSEÁIL.

Kneecapping. In Northern Ireland, a paramilitary punishment inflicted in Republican and Loyalist areas on those unfortunate residents deemed to have offended local mores. The intensity of the punishment varies with the angle of fire and the position of the entry wound. Over the years of the TROUBLES the frequency of such traumas led to the development of specific remedial techniques in Belfast hospitals.
See also SIX-PACK.

Knights of Columbanus. A Catholic lay organization for men, colloquially known as 'the Knights'. It was founded in Belfast in 1915 by Canon James O'Neill, with the aim of securing recognition for Catholicism and Catholic practices, opposing 'Orange ascendancy' and developing 'practical Christianity among its members'. It was established in Dublin in 1917 and recognized by the Catholic Church in 1934, drawing its membership mainly from the professional and business classes. Although the work of the association has mainly been charitable, it is linked in the common mind with ultra-conservative Catholicism and secrecy, and regarded as a kind of Catholic Freemasonry. It takes its name from the early Irish monk, St COLUMBAN, and is not to be confused with the Knights of Columbus, an American Catholic fraternal organization.

Knock¹. A Marian shrine in Co. Mayo that has been a popular place of pilgrimage since a large number of villagers reported an apparition of the Virgin Mary on the gable of the church on 21 August 1879. Many of the facilities currently available were constructed under the direction of Father (later Monsignor) James Horan (1912–86), parish priest of Knock from 1967; these facilities include a hostel, a rest-and-care centre for invalids, many of whom visit the shrine every year, and a basilica. Later Horan established a social-services centre, which included KNOCK MARRIAGE INTRODUCTIONS BUREAU. John Paul II visited Knock during his papal visit to Ireland in 1979 to celebrate the centenary of the shrine.

Knock². A verb used casually and variously in HIBERNO-ENGLISH to indicate movement, real or figurative, as in 'He knocked good use out of that car' or 'She knocked into me (my house) after Mass', 'That knocked a terrible fright out of me' or 'That will knock the TEASPACH out of him.'

Knockanure. *See* VALLEY OF KNOCKANURE.

Knock International Airport. An airport near the Marian shrine in KNOCK¹, Co Mayo. An example of the triumph of local will over bureaucracy, Knock International Airport was the brainchild of parish priest Monsignor James Horan (1912–86), and was officially opened by opposition leader Charles HAUGHEY in May 1986. Unlike the regional airports of Sligo, Galway and Donegal (Carrigfin), Knock can accommodate 320-seater jets, and has increasingly focused on international freight and passenger business as well as providing holiday flights to Continental sun-spots. In 2002, 200,000 passengers used the airport.

Knock Marriage Introductions Bureau. An introduction agency catering for more mature and rurally based people, founded by Father (later Monsignor) James Horan (1912–86) in 1968 and based at the Marian shrine of KNOCK¹ in Co. Mayo. The Bureau claims to have been instrumental in the contracting of more than 700 marriages.

Knockmealdown Mountains. A mountain range that extends in an east–west direction from just north of the town of Cappoquin in Co. Waterford, forming the border between Waterford and Tipperary, and extending into Co. Cork. The highest peak is Knockmealdown, 794 m (2604 ft). The range is divided in two by the mountain pass known as the VEE, which is one of the beauty spots of the southeast. It was in the Knockmealdowns that the last wolf in Ireland was slain in 1770 (or the second-last wolf, if Carlow's 1786 claim is to be believed).

Knocknagoshel Ambush (6 March 1923). A Republican ambush near the small village of Knocknagoshel in north Co. Kerry, at a time when the CIVIL WAR was being fought with particular ferocity in the southwest. A Free State lieutenant, two captains and two private soldiers were killed. A Republican statement issued after the ambush claimed that its intention was to kill a named lieutenant who allegedly 'had made a hobby of torturing Republican prisoners in Castleisland' (where a substantial Free State force was based). The ambush started a chain of vicious reprisals against Republican prisoners: 19 prisoners were killed over the next two weeks in various incidents, including the BALLYSEEDY MASSACRE and the COUNTESS BRIDGE KILLINGS. So many prisoners died while in custody in this period and there was so much public grief and outrage that the Free State army issued an edict declaring, 'Prisoners who die while in military custody in the Kerry Command shall be interred by the troops in the area in which the death has taken place.'

Knocknagow, or the Homes of Tipperary. A sentimental romance of 19th-century Irish life by Charles KICKHAM, published in 1879. It is strongly Nationalistic, disinclined to see much good in the current land system, and justly severe on cruel and avaricious landlords. Such characters as Mat the Thresher and Father Hannigan became as well known to a vast Irish readership as David Copperfield or Little Nell in Britain.

Knocknagree. A village in Co. Cork, in the SLIABH LUACHRA area on the borders of Cork and Kerry, famous for traditional music and SET DANCES, which are danced in one of the village's many pubs. The village was in the past also famous for its FAIRS and its extensive fair field. A particularly famous harvest fair was held on 25 July.

Knowe. An Ulster-Scots word for 'knoll', often used for the grassy summit of a small hill:

> If I rap and I call and I pay for all, my money is
>   all my own,
> I've never spent aught o' your fortune, for I hear
>   that you've got none.
> You thought you had my poor heart broke in
>   talking to me now,
> But I'll leave you where I found you, at the foot
>   of the Sweet Brown Knowe.
>> ANON.: 'The Maid of the Sweet Brown Knowe' (19th century)

Knowles, James Sheridan (1784–1862). Actor and playwright. He was born in Cork on 12 May 1784, the second cousin of Richard Brinsley SHERIDAN, and gave up a military career and medical studies to become an actor. When this proved unrewarding he opened a school in Belfast, and later another one in Glasgow. His plays *William Tell* (1825), *The Hunchback* (1832), *The Wife* (1833) and *The Love Chase* (1837) were extremely popular in their day, and Knowles became a close friend of Lamb, Coleridge, Hunt and Hazlitt. (He was the recipient of some of the letters in *Liber Amoris* (1823), Hazlitt's neurotic and ill-concealed account of his infatuation with Sarah Walker, his landlord's 19-year-old daughter.) In 1844 Knowles became a Baptist, publishing anti-Catholic pamphlets and attacking in particular Cardinal Wiseman (1802–65), whom he called 'the priest of the idol'. He was awarded a Civil List pension of £200 in 1848 and died in Torquay on 30 November 1862.

Know-Nothing Party. The name of an American political splinter group, once known as the Nativists, but who renamed themselves the Order of the Star-Spangled Banner. However, they were generally known as the Know-Nothings because of their curt reply to questions about what went on at their meetings: 'I know nothing about it.' They were a specifically anti-Catholic organization, and in the early 1850s gained power in several states. The *Cleveland Plain Dealer* (June 1854) tried to poke fun at them:

> When one Know-Nothing wishes to recognize another one, he closes one eye, makes an O with his thumb and forefinger and places his nose through it – which interpreted reads eye-nose-O, I knows nothing.

The party first appeared in 1849 to protest against the large influx of immigrants, most of them Irish, and its stated policy was to reserve political power to those whose families had lived in the United States for at least 50 years. As well as depriving immigrants of the right to vote or hold office, they wished to ban such rights for all Catholics. Some churches and convents were destroyed in rioting; in Louisville, Kentucky, on 6 August 1855 a Know-Nothing mob attacked Irish and German houses and public buildings, killing 20 people, and there was also trouble in Baltimore and St Louis. The immediate result was that Catholics, especially the Irish, developed their own subculture and an outsider mentality that took some time to thaw.

Knowth. *See* NEWGRANGE.

Knurls. An Ulster-Scots word meaning 'small protuberances', and hence used to denote chicken-pox, as in 'Thon scar on his forehead; that's where he scratched himself as a baby when he had the knurls.'

Köln. *See* COLOGNE.

Kossicks. A Dublin slang expression, now dated, for Wellington boots, presumably because of the association with Cossack boots.

Kruger Kavanagh. The nickname of Muiris Kavanagh (1894–1971), reportedly because, in childhood games, he played the part of Paul Kruger, the Boer leader. His pub, Kruger's, which was frequented by writers and artists,

among them Brendan BEHAN, who first wrote in Irish, still plies its trade in Dunquin in the far west of the Gaeltacht of Corca Dhuibhne (*see* DINGLE PENINSULA). Kruger was a colourful character who spun magnificent yarns, especially about his time in the United States, claiming to have been a close friend of John MCCORMACK and other celebrities. It was said about him 'He may be a fearful liar but all his lies are about himself.'

Kutu-Kutu. A social club for vigorous frog-dancing, as described by 'A late Professional Gentleman' on a visit to Kerry *c*.1820.

> Kutukutu was the glorious and prevailing fun by night. Galops, polkas and waltzes were not invented then; but they, to the other amusement I have mentioned, are innocent indeed. I'll describe it all as shortly and plainly as I can, first promising, in honour of the virtuous virgins of that day, that none but married ladies were members of this Kutu-Kutu Club, who had for partners young and old, married and unmarried men. The lady first led off, and crouching on her hunkers, she placed under each knee-cap a hand, and then hopping round the room as best she could, a gentleman following in her train as speedily as possible, and, overtaking her, jostled up against her, when both upset and went sprawling on the floor; and this exciting play was not confined to a single pair, but twenty couples at a time would become engaged therein.

Recollections of Ireland (c.1830)

Kyanize. To treat timber that is to be used for building purposes in advance for dry rot. It derives from the name of its inventor, John Ward Kyan (1774–1850), who was born in Dublin and managed his father's copper mines in Co. Wicklow. When the mines failed he went to work for a vinegar manufacturer in London. In 1832 he patented a system for preserving wood that was used for the building materials of many public buildings, such as the British Museum and the College of Surgeons in London. Kyanizing was later replaced by creosote. Kyan died in 1850 in New York, where he was working on a scheme to filter the public water supply.

Kybosh. *See* KIBOSH.

Kylemore Abbey. A Benedictine convent in Connemara, Co. Galway, with a day school for locals and an international boarding school. It is also a tourist attraction, with the romantic Victorian-Gothic convent building surrounded by mountains on the northern shore of Lough Pollacappul. The convent was built in 1866 as a country house for Mitchell Henry, a London surgeon-turned-businessman, replacing an earlier hunting lodge where he and his wife had spent their honeymoon. The estate comprised 13,000 acres (5200 ha) of mountain, rivers, lakes and bog with extensive shooting and fishing rights, and there was a 6-acre (2.4-ha) walled garden behind the castle. The neo-Gothic chapel near the castle was built as a memorial to Henry's wife Margaret, who died in 1874. Benedictine nuns from an Irish foundation in Ypres, Belgium, who wished to establish an abbey and school in Ireland, bought the building in 1920. The complex gives a good deal of employment locally to craftworkers, gardeners and those who manage the shop and restaurant.

Kyteler, Alice (*c.*1280–1330). A KILKENNY woman who was subjected to a witchcraft trial. Alice Kyteler was wealthy in her own right; she had already been married three times, and by the time of her trial she was married to a fourth husband, Sir John de Poer. In 1324 she was accused by her stepchildren of having bewitched and poisoned her first three husbands, and she, her personal servant Petronilla of Meath and several other women were charged with 'heretical sorcery', accused of having 'nightly conference with a spirit called Robert Artisson' and sacrificing to him 'in the highe waie nine red cocks and nine peacock's eies'. The Bishop of Ossory, Richard de Landrede, pursued the charge, and, having interrogated Alice Kyteler, found her guilty and handed her over to the civil authorities for flogging and execution by public burning. The night before she was to be executed she escaped to England with the help of influential friends, although her servant, Petronilla was burnt alive on 3 November 1324. Alice Kyteler's substantial house still stands as Kyteler's Inn in Kilkenny city.

L

Labour Party. An Irish political party founded in 1912 by James CONNOLLY and James LARKIN. Strictly speaking it is the oldest of the Irish political parties. (SINN FÉIN began as a Nationalist movement in 1905 but had no parliamentary existence until George, Count Plunkett, the father of the executed 1916 revolutionary Joseph Mary Plunkett, won a by-election in Roscommon North on 3 February 1917 (he did not take his seat)).

The Labour Party supported the Nationalist cause, agreeing with Sinn Féin not to put forward candidates in the 1918 general election in order to avoid splitting the Nationalist vote, and did not take a stand on the TREATY. In an essentially conservative and largely rural country, dominated by the Catholic Church, it was difficult for the party to make a breakthrough, although the general election of 1965 resulted in 22 Labour seats in the Dáil, prompting the slogan, 'The seventies will be socialist.' Neither the seventies nor subsequent decades were socialist, but the party often found itself holding the balance of power after the virtual demise of single-party government. It entered coalition governments with FINE GAEL in the 1970s and 1980s, and with FIANNA FÁIL in the 1990s, managing to be in government a great deal more than its numerical strength would suggest. The election to the presidency of Mary ROBINSON in 1990 was a great triumph for the party, and especially for its then leader, Dick SPRING.

Labraid Loinseach. In Irish mythology, the son of Ailill Áine, king of Leinster. The king is poisoned by his uncle, Cobhthach, who afterwards forces the boy Labraid to eat his father's heart. The trauma renders Labraid dumb, and he remains silent during a sojourn in Britain and Gaul, where he has fled to escape the machinations of the same great-uncle. He recovers his voice after being hit by a hurley stick in a game. While in Gaul Labraid falls in love with Moriath, the daughter of Scoriath, king of Fir Morc, but her mother guards her day and night, sleeping with one eye open. The girl teaches CRAIFTINE, Labraid's harpist, a magic tune that sends her mother and father to sleep, and the couple are able to make love. The parents accept the *fait accompli*, and Scoriath fits out Labraid with an army to invade Leinster and defeat his great-uncle. Cobhthach is lulled into a false sense of security when he hears that the captain of the Gaulish army cannot speak. Craiftine plays his sleep-music, and Cobhthach's army is easily vanquished.

In a more famous story Labraid was said to have horses' ears, a blemish which, if discovered, would have rendered him incapable of kingship. Each barber who cuts his hair is killed in order to keep the defect a secret. Once, however, the king, heeding the prayers of a

barber's mother, spares the barber after he swears that he will remain silent about the defect. However, the barber, unable to keep the secret, tells a tree, which in time is cut down to make Craiftine a new harp. When this harp is played it reveals the king's secret.
See also Ó LOINSIGH, LABHRAÍ.

Lá breá (Irish, 'fine day'). The term used by the local Irish-speaking people in the GAELTACHTS for someone who has come to the locality to learn Irish, the greeting *Lá breá* (pronounced 'law braw') being the perceived extent of the student's command of the language. In *Na hAird Ó Thuaidh* (1966), Pádraig Ó Maoileoin (PEAIDÍ AN DÚNA) referred to such students in the plural as '*laethanta breátha*'.

Lách. An Irish word meaning 'friendly', 'pleasant', used in HIBERNO-ENGLISH to indicate a person who is affable and kind, as in 'He's a fine *lách* boy.'

Lacy, Count Peter (1678–1751). Field marshal. He was born in Killeedy, Co. Limerick, on 29 September 1678, and by the age of 13 was engaged in the defence of Limerick against Williamite forces. He left in 1691 with Patrick SARSFIELD and joined the IRISH BRIGADE in the service of Louis XIV of France. In 1696 he went to Russia and was placed by Peter the Great in command of a special force of self-financing mounted aristocrats, called the Grand Musketeers. For the next 30 years he was active in many campaigns, until his appointment as governor of Livonia (an area now covered by Latvia and Estonia) in 1728. Created field-marshal in 1736, he saw further action against the Turks and Swedes until he retired in 1743 at the age of 65, having been a field campaigner for more than 50 years. He lived on his estates in Livonia for eight more years, dying on 11 May 1751. His career in its success and flamboyance has made him an archetypal member of the company of adventurers known as the WILD GEESE.

Ladar. An Irish word literally meaning 'ladle', 'spoon', and used metaphorically in both Irish

and HIBERNO-ENGLISH to indicate interference: to put your *ladar* in something (*do ladar a chur isteach i rud éigin*) means to offer unsolicited advice or intervention.

Ladies' Land League. An organization formed to support the National LAND LEAGUE in 1881. When it became clear to the leaders of the League that the organization was in danger of being proscribed, Anna PARNELL, sister of Charles Stewart PARNELL, supported by her sister Fanny PARNELL, and on the invitation of Michael DAVITT, founded the Central Land League of the Ladies of Ireland, known as the Ladies' Land League, 'to undertake the relief of evicted tenants after suspension of the habeas corpus act'. Anna, whom Davitt described as 'a lady of remarkable ability and energy of character', became president of the organization and spoke at its inaugural meeting in Claremorris on 31 January 1881. When Parnell and Davitt were imprisoned in Kilmainham, Anna and other women travelled the country to speak and organize, to attend evictions and to arrange for wooden huts to be built to accommodate the evicted families. At the same time, Fanny toured and raised public awareness in America. The women attracted censure from the Catholic hierarchy for behaving in so unfeminine a manner, and Parnell himself disapproved of the radical nature of their protest, especially as he was not in a position to control it. In December 1881 the government banned the Ladies' Land League and began to imprison its members. When Parnell was released after negotiating the KILMAINHAM TREATY with the government in May 1882, the organization was wound up. Anna Parnell, more radical than her brother, claimed that despite its popularity it did not have real power.

Ladies of Llangollen, the. The name given to two ladies of the Irish ASCENDANCY who set up home together near Llangollen on the River Dee in North Wales. Lady Eleanor Butler (1739–1829) and Sarah Ponsonby (1755–1831) ran away from their families – Eleanor from her family seat, Kilkenny Castle, and Sarah from the estate of her guardian, Woodstock, near Inistioge in Co. Kilkenny – sailed from Waterford with a servant, Mary Carryl, and built a house near Llangollen called Plas Newydd. There they lived for fifty years. They wore men's clothes and had their hair cropped and powdered; they lived simply, cultivating 13 acres (5 ha) of land, reading from their excellent library and engaging in artistic activities: Eleanor Butler was a musician and Sarah Ponsonby was an artist, and despite their mannish attire they were both talented embroiderers. The ladies and their gentle, eccentric way of life became famous, and they entertained many distinguished and cultured visitors, including William Wordsworth, Sir Walter Scott and the Duke of Wellington. Eleanor Butler died on 2 June 1829, Sarah Ponsonby on 9 December 1831. They and their servant Mary Carryl are buried in Llangollen. The Swan of Lichfield, Anna Seward, wrote *Llangollen Vale* (1796) in memory of her visit to the Ladies:

> Now with a Vestal lustre glows the Vale,
> Thine, sacred Friendship, permanent as pure;
> In vain the stern Authorities assail,
> In vain Persuasion spreads her silken lure,
> High-born, and high-endow'd, the peerless
>   Twain,
> Pant for coy Nature's charms 'mid silent dale, and
>   plain.

Ladra. The pilot of CESAIR's alternative ark; he is one of 3 men and 50 women that she brings to Ireland. Ladra accepts 16 of the women as concubines after a formal objection to his companions being assigned 17 each. He is said to have died 'of an excess of women'.

Lads, the. The often affectionate and usually wary means of referring to members of illegal organizations, particularly the IRA, especially used in the 1940s and 1950s when violent incidents were comparatively rare.
See also BOYS, THE[1].

Lady Betty (*c.*1750–1810). Hangwoman. A native of Kerry, an early widow and a woman of 'dark disposition', whose true name has been

lost, she was left to continue her life of grinding poverty when her only son and consolation emigrated to America. After some time, as the story goes, a strange man begged lodgings in her house and taunted her with stories of great wealth. She killed him in the night only to discover that he was her son. Sentenced to die for the murder in Roscommon jail, she escaped hanging as no executioner could be found. She promptly volunteered for the job and was granted clemency and a career, which she followed, it seems, with gusto. It is said that she decorated the walls of her apartment with pictures of her clients drawn by herself with a burnt stick.

Lady Morgan makin' tay. One of the sights of Dublin in the 1820s, as listed in a ballad attributed to Charles LEVER:

> Och, Dublin City, there is no doubtin',
> Bates every city upon the say:
> 'Tis there you'll see O'Connell spoutin'
> An' Lady Morgan makin' tay;
> For 'tis the capital of the finest nation
> Wid charmin' pisintry on a fruitful sod,
> Fightin' like devils for conciliation,
> An' hatin' each other for the love of God.

See also MORGAN, LADY.

Ladysmith. *See* MAKING A SHIFT FOR LADYSMITH.

Laffan, May. *See* 'FLITTERS, TATTERS AND THE COUNSELLOR: THREE WAIFS FROM THE DUBLIN STREETS'.

Lá Fhéile na Marbh (Irish, 'feast day of the dead'). The Irish name for All Souls Day, 2 November.
See also SAMHAIN.

Lagan. An annual literary magazine with four issues (1942–5) founded by Sam Hanna BELL and edited by John BOYD. A beacon of culture amid the encircling Philistine gloom, it was subtitled 'A Collection of Ulster Writings' and had such contributors as Bell and Boyd themselves, Michael MCLAVERTY, Joseph TOMELTY, John HEWITT, Michael James Craig (*see* MAY THE

LORD IN HIS MERCY BE KIND TO BELFAST) and Louis MacNEICE. William Conor (*see* MAKE NS MEET) provided many of the decorations.

Lake, Gerard (1744–1808). Soldier. He commanded the British army in Ulster in 1797, determined to suppress the UNITED IRISHMEN by military means. His poorly disciplined troops 'dragooned' Ulster, burning houses and arresting and hanging suspects. When he succeeded General Abercromby as commander-in-chief of the army in March 1798 he again imposed a reign of terror in the counties around Dublin, in order to flush out rebels and confiscate arms. On 25 May 1798, when rebellion had broken out in Wexford, he ordered his commanders to 'take no prisoners', and at VINEGAR HILL[1] on 24 June most of those killed were civilian camp followers and those who had already been wounded in the fighting. It is thought that there were about 29,000 rebel deaths in total, mostly in Wexford. In August General Lake's troops were routed at the RACES OF CASTLEBAR, after the French landing at Killala. According to a statement from Dublin Castle, dated 29 August:

> Advices were received last night from Lieutenant General Lake, by which it appears, that early on the morning of 27 {August} the French attacked him in his position near Castlebar, before his force was assembled, and compelled him, after a short action, to retire to Holymount. The Lieutenant General regrets that six field pieces fell into the enemy's hands; but states that the loss of the king's troops, in men, has not been considerable.

Lake, The. George MOORE's fictional farewell to Ireland, a novel (1905) extended from a short story originally meant for inclusion in *The UN-TILLED FIELD*. It deals with a recurring theme of the period, the Catholic Church's unchristian attitude to unmarried mothers, and features the unthinking and public denunciation of a pregnant schoolteacher by a priest (named, with mischievous glee, Oliver Gogarty), who comes to a realization of his own spiritual aridity. The book ends with a faked drowning in Lough Carra, as the priest literally and figuratively puts on new clothes before heading for America:

> There is a lake in every man's heart ... and he listens to its monotonous whisper, year by year, more and more attentive until at last he ungirds.

Lake County, the. The nickname of Co. Westmeath, which encompasses Lough Ree, a large lake on the River Shannon. Like other Irish county nicknames it is used particularly in the context of the ALL-IRELAND Gaelic football championship.

Lalor, James Fintan (1807–49). Young Irelander and agrarian reformer. He was born in Tillnakill, Queen's County, the son of a prosperous farmer, but had to leave school because of poor sight and hearing, physical malformation and chronic ill-health. His reading made him the most radical member of the YOUNG IRELAND movement, and his political philosophy of 'the land of Ireland for the people of Ireland' played a significant part not only in the thinking of the Ireland of his time but also informed the tactics and aims of the LAND LEAGUE. Inevitably he became part of the rhetorical arsenal of Patrick PEARSE and James CONNOLLY. In spite of his physical disabilities he was an active revolutionary, editing the *Irish Felon* when John MITCHEL was arrested. He was imprisoned for his part in the 1848 Rising (*see* WIDOW MCCORMICK'S CABBAGE PATCH), but was released in November after five months in broken health. He died a year later, on 27 December 1849.

Lalor, Peter (1823–99). Politician in Australia. The younger brother of James Fintan LALOR, he was educated at Trinity College Dublin and worked as a civil engineer before emigrating to Australia at the beginning of the Ballarat gold rush in 1852. He was the leader of the miners who defied government and police at the EUREKA STOCKADE of December 1854, and lost an arm as a result of the fighting. He was elected to the parliament of Victoria for Ballarat and held a number of government posts, including that of speaker of the house (1880–8). He died in Melbourne on 10 February 1889.

Lambeg Drum. The large drum, nearly a metre in diameter, which is a feature of the Orange celebration of the TWELFTH OF JULY. It is made of thin goatskin stretched over an oak frame. When it is played with a pair of Malacca canes the din can reach 120 decibels, the pain threshold of the human ear, while really enthusiastic timpanists glory in blood running down muscular arms in the contention of their drums. The first of the modern shell drums was made in 1870 for the Moira Orange Lodge (No.39) and played at an Orange demonstration in 1871 in the Co. Antrim linen village of Lambeg, between Belfast and Lisburn. It is from this initiation that the instrument takes its name:

> To a Lambegger his drum is always a 'bell', and 'tone' and 'ring' is the quality most sought after. The association can be traced in the names of such famous drums as *The Bell of Ballylisnahuncheon* and *The Chiming Bells*. But one man's imagery makes an iconoclast of the next; a drum-maker told me that he once had an order from a man who decided to name his drum *Roarin' Meg* after the famous cannon employed at the defence of Derry.
>
> SAM HANNA BELL (1909–90): 'To Chap the Lambeg', in *Erin's Orange Lily* (1956)

Lambert, Louis. The pseudonym of the Irish-born composer Patrick Sarsfield Gilmore (1829–92), whose most famous song, 'When Johnny Comes Marching Home', owes much to the more savage Irish original, 'JOHNNY I HARDLY KNEW YE'. Gilmore was born in Athlone, Co. Westmeath, and was established as a bandmaster in America by 1850. He and the entire Gilmore band enlisted in the Federal army at the outbreak of the Civil War in 1861, but by 1862 had been redeployed in the safer duties of troop entertainment. The song was written in the euphoria after the Gettysburg Address in anticipation of the boys (on both sides) coming home. It was a tribute to the 140,000 Irish soldiers who fought on the Northern side, and it became almost a second national anthem, even in the South. At the Peace Jubilee in Boston in 1869 Gilmore conducted the song with an orchestra of 1000 and a chorus of 10,000; among the guests was an approving younger Strauss. Gilmore died in St Louis, Missouri, in 1892.

> When Johnny comes marching home again,
>   hurrah, hurrah,
> We'll give him a hearty welcome then, hurrah,
>   hurrah;
> The men will cheer, the boys will shout,
> The ladies they will all come out.
> And we'll all feel gay,
> When Johnny comes marching home.

La Mon Restaurant Massacre. A Provisional IRA incendiary bomb attack on a Belfast restaurant on Friday, 17 February 1978, in which 12 people were burned to death and 23 seriously injured. Only a nine-minute warning was given, and the detonation of two incendiary devices caused a fireball, which razed the restaurant to the ground. Two scheduled events, the Northern Ireland Junior Motorcycle Club and the Northern Ireland Collie Club annual prize night, meant that there were 300 people in the restaurant that night.

Lancers. *See* SET DANCES.

Land. A word used in HIBERNO-ENGLISH to denote shock or surprise: to 'get a land' is to be unpleasantly surprised or disappointed – 'I got a terrible land when I heard about the accident.'

Land Acts. A series of ameliorative acts passed in the Westminster Parliament between 1881 and 1909 with the aims of quieting agrarian unrest (often in tandem with COERCION), improving the position of tenant farmers, and eventually facilitating the sale of land by landlords to tenants, thereby solving the land question for good (*see* LAND LEAGUE; LAND WAR). The most significant land acts were:

The 1881 Land Law Act, which gave legal status to the THREE FS and established a land court to which tenants could appeal their level of rent;

The Ashbourne Act of 1885 – named after the Conservative lord chancellor, Baron Ashbourne (1837–1913) – which offered the tenant loans of the full amount of the purchase price of land, and which led to the purchase of their holdings by more than 25,000 tenants;

BALFOUR's Land Act of 1891, which provided £33 million for land purchase in response to the PLAN OF CAMPAIGN;

The WYNDHAM Act of 1903, which offered landlords a bonus to sell their entire estates;

The BIRRELL Land Act of 1909, which for the first time compelled a landlord to transfer ownership of his land if a majority of his tenants wanted to buy their holdings.

Land Acts passed by governments of the Free State between 1923 and 1933 dealt with any remaining land still in the possession of landlords, and with the thorny question of LAND ANNUITIES still payable to Britain and arrears owed by the farmers.

Land Annuities. Sums of money payable to Britain in repayment of money advanced to Irish tenants for the purchase of their farms under various LAND ACTS. After the establishment of the Free State the moneys were remitted to London by the Irish exchequer, an unpopular measure, especially since arrears had accumulated during the period of disturbance 1916–23. Peadar O'DONNELL and other Republicans campaigned for the annuities to be withheld, and this was an election promise of the FIANNA FÁIL government which came to power in 1932. The withholding of annuities led to the ECONOMIC WAR.

Land Commission. A body established by the LAND ACT of 1881 to adjudicate on fair rents, and then given the further task of supervising the land-purchase schemes provided for in later acts. After the establishment of the Free State it also took over the work of the CONGESTED DISTRICTS BOARD. The Land Commission is still in existence, its main visible function now being the redistribution of land that has been left idle for years or for which no buyer is found on the open market. This normally occurs in relation to marginal land in the south and west of Ireland.

Landen. A battle in the WAR OF THE THREE KINGS (or, as some historians prefer, the War of the English Succession) at which Patrick SARSFIELD, Earl of Lucan, was killed in 1693. Landen lies halfway between Brussels and Liège, and Sarsfield and his WILD GEESE were fighting for Louis XIV against Dutch and British soldiers. He is credited with crying, as he watched the blood seep from his wounds, 'Oh that this were for Ireland!'

Land League. An organization founded in 1879 by Michael DAVITT, Charles Stewart PARNELL and Andrew Kettle (1833–1916) to fight the evils of landlordism and achieve better conditions for Irish tenant farmers. Its most celebrated tactic was the BOYCOTT, which was used against landlords, agents and any who rented a property from which another had been evicted. The main demands of the agitation were granted by the LAND ACT of 1881, and though in Parnell's eyes the Act was sufficient, it was rejected by the League. When he and the rest of the executive were imprisoned in Kilmainham (see KILMAINHAM TREATY) the agitation reached a climax, and it was not until their release and the passing of the Arrears Act of 1882 that peace of a sort was restored. The Land League was replaced by the National League, founded by Parnell, in October 1882. This was the constituency organization of the IRISH PARTY, not an agrarian organization, although it included among its aims the reform of the land system. It was Parnell's way of keeping the firebrands down.
See also LEPER OF OLD, AS A.

Land League Priest, the. The sobriquet of Father Eugene Sheehy (1841–1917). He was born in Broadford, Co. Limerick, and educated at the COLLÈGE DES IRLANDAIS in Paris, where he was ordained in 1868. While serving as a curate in Kilmallock he became president of the local Land League and was imprisoned in 1881. He was later parish priest in Bruree, Co. Limerick, where he knew Éamon de Valera as a boy. He resigned his parish because of ill-health and moved to Dublin, where he became involved in the IRISH VOLUNTEERS and the IRB. He visited the GPO during the EASTER RISING to minister to the occupants. He was a brother of Nationalist politician David Sheehy (1843–1932) and an uncle of Hanna SHEEHY-SKEFFINGTON.

Land of Cokayne, The. A HIBERNO-ENGLISH goliardic (ribald) poem, preserved in a 14th-century manuscript, which would confirm the extreme suspicions of anti-Catholic activists. The title probably means 'the land of cooking', and the poem describes a place where the appetites are readily satisfied, with a monastery and convent supplying all mutual needs. The monks are called to choir by the slapping of a girl's bottom, and the brothers and sisters swim naked in streams of just the right temperature. These extremely agreeable foundations are located in Clonmel, Co. Tipperary; the Irish version of Clonmel, *Cluain Meala*, means 'honey-meadow'.

> Ther is a wel fair abbei
> Of white monks and of gre.
> The beth bouris and halles;
> Al of pasteiis beth the walles,
> Of fleis, of fisse and rich met
> The likfullist that man may et.

Land of Ire, the. An exasperated punning nickname for Ireland, coined by Sir Robert Cecil (*c*.1563–*c*.1612), Queen Elizabeth I's secretary of state, in a letter to the lord admiral on 8 October 1600.

Land of Promise. *See* TÍR TAIRNGIRI.

Land of Spices, The. A novel (1941) by Kate O'BRIEN set in the Irish convent of a French order. It is based on the author's own experiences of her schooldays in Laurel Hill in Limerick, where she was sent as a young child after the death of her mother. There are two protagonists: the Reverend Mother, Belgian-born English intellectual Mère Marie Hélène Archer, who in the course of the novel hears of her beloved father's death and has to come to terms with the fact that she entered the religious life as a reaction to finding him with his student Etienne 'in the embrace of love'

(the phrase for which the novel was banned in Ireland); and her pupil, Anna, in whom Marie Hélène sees her talented and idealistic younger self. Anna comes under her care at the age of 6, and Marie Hélène oversees her development through family upheaval and tragedy, managing finally to ensure that she takes up a scholarship to study at University College Dublin rather than a job in a bank as her domineering grandmother would have her do. Anna is the first person Marie Hélène has truly loved since entering the religious life, and through her she manages to become reconciled to the changing Ireland in which she has served her order, the Nationalism and cultural complacency of which she has hitherto found repellent. Though there are moments of melodrama, the novel is a brilliant and moving study of the mind and character of Marie Hélène in particular, a veritable 'portrait of a lady'. The title comes from George Herbert's poem 'Prayer: the Church's Banquet' (1633):

> Church bells beyond the stars heard, the soul's
> blood,
> The land of spices; something understood.

Land of the Fish. *See* NEWFOUNDLAND.

Land of Women. *See* TÍR NA MBAN.

Land of Youth. *See* TÍR NA NÓG.

Land War. The name given to the agrarian disturbance and conflict between landlords, the authorities and tenants that began with the foundation of the LAND LEAGUE in 1879 and continued until 1903 (some historians say 1933). The term is most closely associated with the first phase of the struggle (1879–82), which began in Co. Mayo and spread to parts of Munster and Ulster. It involved general militancy in regard to landlords, demands for concessions in regard to tenure, and determined popular action to prevent or delay evictions by any possible means. The most famous single action taken in the entire Land War was the ostracizing of Captain BOYCOTT in 1880. The Land War was a great popular movement: for a brief period agrarian protest, constitutional Nationalism and physical-force separatism were united under PARNELL in the NEW DE-PARTURE of 1879–81. Violence was common, especially in the west of Ireland where the situation of tenant farmers was desperate. Gladstone's government put repressive measures in place, suppressing the Land League and imprisoning its leaders, and at the same time passed the LAND ACT of 1881, which granted some of the demands of the League, supplemented by an Arrears Act in 1882. Various acts were passed by the government until 1909, and in the early years of the Free State other provisions were enacted to deal with issues such as annuities (see LAND ANNUITIES).

Land without a Star. A description of Ireland after the loss of its Gaelic aristocracy by the Kerry poet Aogán Ó RATHAILE (c.1675–1729). The MacCarthy family had been his patrons:

Tír gan toradh, gan bhuinne, gan réilteann
(A land without produce, without a stream,
    without a star)
'Monuarsa an Charrth'-fhuil tráite tréithlag!'
('Lament for the MacCarthys, left powerless and
stranded!', c.1709)

Lane Pictures, the. The subject of the offer made by Sir Hugh Lane (1875–1915), nephew of Lady GREGORY and a successful art dealer, that his priceless collection of 39 impressionist works form the nucleus of an Irish gallery of modern art. The paintings had been exhibited in Dublin in 1908, but the proposal to house them in a Liffey-bridging gallery designed by Sir Edwin Lutyens (1869–1944) was rejected by the Dublin Corporation in 1913, partly upon financial but also upon 'moral' grounds. As the artist Sir William Orpen (1878–1931) records in his autobiography Stories of Old Ireland and Myself (1924):

Lane's Committee: We want some of your money
for Manet and Monet.
The Subscribers: Sure we haven't got any for
Monet and Manet.

Lane removed the paintings to the National Gallery in London and Yeats exploded into fine

vituperative poetry (see BLIND AND IGNOR-ANT TOWN). Relenting in 1915, Lane added an unwitnessed codicil to his will stipulating that should a suitable home be found for them by 1920 the paintings should be returned to Ireland. Lane was drowned in the sinking of the LUSITANIA in 1915 and the paintings remained with the National Gallery, even though 'a suitable home' – the Municipal Gallery of Modern Art – existed from 1929. It was not until 1960 that the current system of partial and alternate hanging was agreed between Dublin and London.

Lang, to be on the. A Cork colloquialism meaning to 'mitch (play truant) from school'.

Langers or **langered.** A word meaning 'extremely drunk', used mainly in the west and south of Ireland, as in 'Every Friday night he was langers' or 'It was the cider that had him langered.'
See also OSSIFIED; STOCIOUS.

Langrishe, Go Down. A novel (1966) by Aidan HIGGINS set in the 1930s, and dealing with the relationships between the three Langrishe sisters, remnants of an ASCENDANCY family, and Otto Beck, a mature German student who lives in their ancestral home, Springfield House. The sexual affair between Imogen and Beck, which leaves her shattered, is subtly described, and its symbolic relationship to the international situation of the period neatly pointed.

Language Freedom Movement (LFM). An organization established early in 1966 by Dublin architect Christopher Morris to campaign for the abolition of compulsory Irish in the education system – at that time a student could not pass the Leaving Certificate (school-leaving examination) without passing in Irish. John B. KEANE was one of the most prominent members nationally, although his espousal of this cause made him many enemies in his local Listowel:

Being a Gaelic footballer and a speaker of Irish,
some people could not understand why I should
join the movement. They failed to understand

that my motives were good and that I had nothing to gain from my involvement.

> Quoted in Gus Smith and Des Hickey, *John B. – the Real Keane* (1992)

Donegal writer Séamus Ó Grianna (MÁIRE) was also a member.

Many supporters of Irish were outraged even by the existence of the organization and meetings were repeatedly disrupted by activists such as Máirtín Ó CADHAIN and Seán Ó hEigeartaigh (*see* SÁIRSÉAL AGUS DILL) and members of GAEL LINN. About 1200 people attended a public meeting organized by the LFM in Dublin's Mansion House on 22 September 1966. They were almost all opponents of the organization, and they took the stage and dominated the meeting. John B. Keane and other LFM sympathizers later claimed to have been intimidated and physically assaulted; they were certainly greatly outnumbered. The LFM survived until 1969, and despite the apparent failure of its campaign it did have a liberalizing effect on public opinion and educational policy, highlighting the fanaticism of some of the more ardent revivalists.

See also REVIVAL, THE.

Lanna Macree's dog. A type of time-server, most neatly expressed in the play *The Eloquent Dempsey* (1906) by William BOYLE. In it the eponymous Dempsey, a publican with political ambitions, is chided by his wife:

> You're like Lanna Macree's dog – a piece of the road with everybody.

She elaborates:

> You'll go anywhere and subscribe to anything if they'll only let you make a speech about it. Jerry, you're a rag on every bush, fluttering to every wind that blows; and if you weren't the best husband and the best father that ever broke bread of life, I'd say you were the biggest rascal in the whole of Ireland.

Lanna Macree's dog had many relatives, demonstrating the need for the concept in Irish life: there were similarly obliging dogs owned variously by Billy Harran, Lanty McHale and O'Brien, while in Cork there was Dolan's ass:

> My fight for Irish freedom was of the same order as my fight for other sorts of freedom. Still like Dolan's ass, I went a bit of the way with everybody.

> FRANK O'CONNOR (1903–66): *An Only Child* (1961)

Lansdowne, Marquess of. *See* KENMARE.

Lansdowne Road. The location in Dublin of Ireland's national rugby stadium. It is due to be expanded and developed by 2008, following the demise of the proposed BERTIE BOWL.

Laois and Offaly, Plantation of. The first of the Tudor plantations, associated in the popular mind with the reign of Mary I (1553–8) but in reality carried out on a phased or incomplete basis between 1549 and 1563. The first step was to establish garrison forts to control the rebellious Irish landowners, the O'Mores and the O'Connors, then grants of land were made nearby, and the territory shired as Queen's County (Laois) and King's County (Offaly) in honour of Mary and her husband Philip II of Spain. The success of the plantation was fitful, with many colonists leaving and the former Irish landowners engaging in frequent revolts. The area remained a problem for the English administration until the end of the Tudor era.

Laon. A town in France, 120 km (70 miles) northeast of Paris. It was the seat of one of the palace schools of CHARLES THE BALD, noted especially for the presence of John Scottus ERIUGENA.

Lapadáil. An Irish word for 'wade', 'splash'. In HIBERNO-ENGLISH the verbal noun *lapadáling* has assumed the more general meaning of doing this and that or doing nothing in particular, such as the activities of small children around the house.

Lár, An (Irish, 'the centre'). The term that replaced 'The Pillar' to denote the destination of O'Connell Street for Dublin buses after NELSON'S PILLAR was destroyed by the IRA in 1966. It is sometimes mystifying to non-Irish-speaking tourists.

Larkin, Delia (1878–1949). Trade unionist. Two years younger than her brother James LARKIN, she gave up her work as a nurse to join him in Dublin and Belfast. She became the first general secretary of the IRISH WOMEN WORKERS' UNION, which she helped to found, and ran a soup kitchen at Liberty Hall during the 1913 LOCKOUT. After dissension arose between the Larkins and the ITGWU, James, Delia and another brother, Peter, founded the more left-wing Workers' Union of Ireland (WUI). James lived with Delia and her husband, Patrick Colgan, who had been a member of the Irish Citizen Army, for the last ten years of his life.

Larkin, James (1876–1947). Trade unionist and socialist. He was born in Liverpool on 21 January 1876 to a poor Irish family. At the age of five he was sent to live with his grandparents in Newry, Co. Down, returning to Liverpool at the age of nine. He worked as a labourer and seaman, and then as a foreman on the Liverpool docks. When he joined the men under him in striking he lost his job and became a full-time organizer for the National Union of Dock Labourers (NUDL). It was his union who sent him to Belfast in 1907, and in that city that he harnessed – if only for a brief period – worker solidarity across the sectarian divide by organizing a series of strikes, even a mutiny among the police. The NUDL leadership capitulated to the employers, however, and the following year transferred Larkin to Dublin, where he was within a short period suspended by the union for exceeding his brief.

Larkin's response was to form his own union, the Irish Transport and General Workers' Union (ITGWU) in late 1908–early 1909 to organize dockers, labourers and unskilled workers generally, as well as those who worked in the transport sector. At this time he earned the sobriquet 'Big Jim', for his charismatic personality and impassioned oratory as much as for his physical size. In the same year he founded a newspaper, *The Irish Worker*, which he used as a platform for unremitting attacks on em-

ployers. A series of separate strikes, the militancy of the ITGWU and the increasing hostility of employers represented by William Martin MURPHY, culminated in the 1913 LOCKOUT. The Lockout ended in failure for the workers and the union.

Larkin went on a fund-raising trip to America in October 1914 and stayed in the USA until 1923, becoming heavily involved with the militant International Workers of the World (IWW; *see* JONES, MOTHER). He was imprisoned in Sing Sing for his trade-union activities and released in January 1923 after serving three years for 'criminal anarchy'. He returned to the infant Free State, but failed to regain control of the ITGWU, founding instead the Workers' Union of Ireland. A socialist too radical for many of his trade-union colleagues and an activist to the end of his life, Larkin served on Dublin Corporation and as a TD 1927–32, 1937–8 and 1943–4. He was almost penniless when he died on 30 January 1947. His sister Delia LARKIN and sons James Jnr (1904–69) and Denis (1908–87) were also prominent trade unionists. There is a statue of Larkin in oratorical mode by Oisín Kelly in O'Connell Street, Dublin.

Lark in the Clare air. A punning plug for the lively MERRIMAN SUMMER SCHOOL, a summer school that has been held annually in various Co. Clare venues since 1967. It comes from one of the best known of Irish songs, 'The Lark in the Clear Air' (1834), with words supplied by Samuel FERGUSON to an exquisite native air called 'The Tailor':

> Dear thoughts are in my mind, and my soul soars enchanted,
> As I hear the sweet lark sing in the clear air of the day.

Larminie, William (1849–1900). Poet. He was born in Castlebar, Co. Mayo, and educated at Trinity College Dublin before joining the India Office in London. He had some knowledge of Irish and tried to incorporate Gaelic assonance into his own poetry, especially in *Fand and Other Poems* (1892), which contains the very moving 'Consolation'. (In Irish myth, Fand is the wife of Manannán Mac Lir and mistress of Cúchulainn.) This and his interest in folklore – collected in Connacht and Donegal and published as *West Irish Folk-Tales and Romances* (1893) – make him a kind of forerunner of the IRISH LITERARY REVIVAL. His poem 'The Nameless Doon' (earlier 'Ruin') about a dún in Lough Doon, Donegal, was admired by W.B. Yeats:

> Some one murdered
> We know, we guess; and gazing upon thee,
> And, filled by thy long silence of reply,
> We guess some garnered sheaf of tragedy;–
> Of tribe or nation slain so utterly
> That even their ghosts are dead, and on their
> grave
> Springeth no bloom of legend in its wildness;
> And age by age weak washing round the island
> No faintest sigh of story lisps the wave.

Larne (Irish *Latharna*, 'descendants of Lathar', referring to a pre-Christian prince). A port and industrial town (population 17,500) on the east Antrim coast, 30 km (20 miles) north of Belfast. It is the point of departure for ferries crossing the short sea route to Scotland (Cairnryan and Stranraer). South of the town is the Curran (Irish *corrán*, 'crescent'), a raised gravel beach rich in Neolithic flint implements. Regarded as a Unionist stronghold, it was the scene of the UVF gun-running in 1914.

Larne Gun-Running. The illegal importation of arms approved by the Ulster Unionist Council to arm the UVF in the case of imposition of HOME RULE. It was organized by F[rederick] H[ugh] Crawford (1861–1952), a Boer War veteran, who had arranged for 25,000 rifles and 3 million rounds to be brought from Germany in the *Fanny* and *Clyde Valley*. They landed on the night of 24–25 April 1914 at Larne, Donaghadee and Bangor, and were spirited away. The operation, planned and executed with exemplary precision, was a political triumph rather than a military success because of the relative scarcity of ammunition and the complexity of the weapons.

Several of my principal parishioners were absent all that night with their motors receiving their arms for distribution throughout the country, while various devices were resorted to for the purposes of diverting the attention of the police.

> E.D. ATKINSON: *Recollections of an Ulster Archdeacon* (1934)

See also HOWTH GUN-RUNNING.

Lartigue railway. *See* ONE-LINE RAILWAY.

Laserian (d.639). The Latinate name of the saint known also as Molaise (not to be confused with MOLAISE OF DEVENISH). Laserian was of Ulster origin, the grandson of Aidan, the Irish king of DÁL RIATA. He trained at CANDIDA CASA in Galloway, and after ordination by St Gregory the Great (540–604) founded the monastery and the ancient diocese of Leighlin in Co. Carlow. He travelled to Rome and was appointed by Pope Honorius I (d.638) as apostolic delegate to the synod of 630 that intended to settle divergences between the Celtic and Roman churches about such troublesome matters as the date of Easter – differences that in Britain were to cause such rancour and which were not settled until the Synod of WHITBY (and not even then). Laserian was largely successful in his efforts, and by 633 all Irish houses except Columban ones had conformed to Roman practice. He probably founded Teampall Mo-Laisse, the monastery on Inishmurray, off the Sligo coast, that bears his name. His feast day is 18 April.

Lash. A Cork slang term, of uncertain derivation, for an attractive girl.

Last High King, the. The unfortunately accurate description of Rory Ó Connor (Ruaidrí Ua Conchobar). He became ruler of Connacht in 1156, and in 1166 faced down the Ulster claimant, Mac Lochainn, to achieve the rank of HIGH KING (*ard rí*). His first task was to banish Dermot MACMURROUGH (Diarmait Mac Murchada), the turbulent king of Leinster. When MacMurrough returned with Anglo-Norman mercenary aid in 1167 he took no action, but after the main body of adventurers came in 1169 and 1170 he did what he could to rally the native Irish against them. He failed to dislodge them from Dublin, and showed what defiance he could by refusing to meet HENRY II when he arrived in 1171. He gradually lost authority, and was forced to abdicate in favour of his son in 1183. He died at CONG in 1198 after a few ineffectual attempts to recover his former status; some hold that he was buried at Cong, but others say he was buried in the cathedral at CLONMACNOISE.

'Last Rose of Summer, The'. One of Tom Moore's IRISH MELODIES, set to the popular tune of 'The Groves of Blarney'. It was appropriated by Friedrich Von Flotow (1812–83) for his comic opera *Martha, oder Der Markt zu Richmond* (1847). In it the aristocratic heroine (who has herself hired as a servant using the name Martha) sings it as an English folksong.

Latchico. A term for a useless inadequate, used mainly by building-site workers from the west of Ireland, as in 'Don't let that fellow come near me; he's a complete latchico!'

Late General Needham, the. *See* VINEGAR HILL[1].

Late Late Show, The. The longest-running television chat show ever, presented on RTÉ television by Gay BYRNE and running from 1964 to 1999. In May 1999, on the final show, U2 band members presented the host with a motorbike, in fulfilment of a longstanding dream of Byrne's.
See also BISHOP AND THE NIGHTIE, THE; FLYNN, PEE; NO SEX BEFORE TELEVISON; ONE FOR EVERYONE IN THE AUDIENCE; PHILBIN BOWMAN, JONATHAN; ROLL IT THERE, CO-LETTE.

La Tène. The name given by archaeologists – after a site in Switzerland – to the culture of the Continental Celts in the last five centuries BC; their curvilinear style of decoration is called the La Tène style. Two standing stones, the TUROE STONE and the Castlestrange in Co. Ros-

common, are decorated in this style, indicating the arrival in Ireland of La Tène Celts by this time.

Latin. For many centuries a second (and often preferred) language in Ireland, especially among clerics. It came with Christianity in the 5th century, and had to be learned as a foreign language because of an almost total lack of Roman influence in the country. The effect was for some time to preserve the precision of Ciceronian grammar and syntax. The oldest extant Latin writings are those of Patrick: his CONFESSIO and *Epistola ad Milites Corotici*, in which his apology for their awkward Latin should be taken *cum grano salis*, as a mark of humility rather than lack of grace. Latin continued to be used as a kind of scholarly vernacular until the 17th century. Even in the dark period of the HEDGE SCHOOLS the classics were still taught, and Latin was the prime subject in all secondary schools until the 1970s. The coming of the vernacular Mass effectively meant the end of Latin as the language of the Catholic Church, though in all its documents and its formal Vatican business it still uses the dead language.

Latin America. Irish involvement in Latin America originated as a by-product of the enlistment of the WILD GEESE in Catholic European armies, notably those of Spain. Typical was the career of Ambrose O'Higgins (c.1720–1801), who came from either Sligo or Meath (opinions differ); he went to Spain and, as Marquis de Osorno, became governor of Chile (1787–95) and viceroy of Peru (1795–1801). He died suddenly in Lima on 18 March 1801. His natural son Bernardo O'Higgins (1778–1842) is a Chilean national hero, being the man who won the country's freedom from Spain. Morgan O'Connell (1804–85), Daniel O'CONNELL's son, fought as an officer in the Irish South American Legion which supported Bolivar's (1783–1830) liberation of Venezuela. In the Mexican-American War of 1846–8, 200 Irish deserters, calling themselves St Patrick's Batallion, joined the Mexican side. Argentina received more than 10,000 Irish immigrants in the last quarter of the 19th century, mainly from Westmeath, Longford and Wexford.

Laudabiliter (Latin, 'praiseworthily'). The bull granted to Henry II during the pontificate (1154–9) of the English pope, Adrian IV, probably in the year 1155. It was not acted upon until 1172. Its authenticity has been the subject of much controversy even until modern times. It is thought to have originated with Theobald, Archbishop of Canterbury, who wished to stop his loss of control over the Irish church.

> Adrian, bishop, servant of the servants of God, to our well-beloved son in Christ the illustrious king of the English, greeting and apostolic benediction.
>
> Whereas then, well-beloved son in Christ, you have expressed to us your desire to enter the island of Ireland in order to subject its people to law and to root out from them the weeds of vice, and your willingness to pay annual tribute to the blessed Peter of one penny from every house, and to maintain the rights of the churches of that land whole and inviolate: We therefore … do hereby declare our will and pleasure that, with a view to enlarging the boundaries of the Church, restraining the downward course of vice, correcting evil customs and planting virtue, and for the increase of the Christian religion, you shall enter the island and execute whatsoever may tend to the honour of God and the welfare of the land; and also that the people of the land shall receive you with honour and revere you as their lord …
>
> Quoted in Giraldus Cambrensis, *Expugnatio Hibernica* ('the conquest of Ireland', 1189) II, vi

Lavelle, Patrick (1825–86). Nationalist clergyman. He was born near Louisburgh in Co. Mayo and educated for the priesthood at Maynooth and the COLLÈGE DES IRLANDAIS in Paris, abandoning scholarship and returning to Ireland after a dispute with the college's rector. He served as parish priest of Tourmakeady (Mount Partry), Co. Mayo (1858–69), becoming an outspoken opponent of the evangelical missionaries (*see* SECOND REFORMATION) who were operating in his parish with the support of the Church of Ireland bishop of Tuam,

Thomas Plunket. The dispute escalated when Lavelle condemned Plunket for evicting tenants on his estate on Tourmakeady, where the bishop's sister, Catherine Plunket, had an evangelical school. Plunket was denounced in a London *Times* editorial in November 1860 and questions were asked in the House of Commons, the episode becoming known as 'the War in Partry'.

Father Lavelle supported the IRB and gave the funeral oration at the grave of Terence Bellew MCMANUS, incurring the disapproval of the Archbishop of Dublin, Paul Cullen, who tried to have him disciplined; however, his own archbishop, John MACHALE of Tuam, supported him. He was parish priest of Cong (from 1869), when he and other Catholic clergy were strongly criticized by William Keogh (*see* POPE'S BRASS BAND, THE) in the Galway election petition of 1872, as a result of which the Nationalist candidate, John B. Nolan, who had been elected MP in the general election of the previous year, was deposed in favour of a Conservative, Captain le Poer Trench, on grounds of clerical intimidation. Father Lavelle took no further part in political life.

Laverty, Maura. *See* FULL AND PLENTY.

Lavery, Sir John (1856–1941). Painter and portraitist. He was born in Belfast on 17 March 1856, according to his autobiography *The Life of a Painter* (1940), but accounts of his early days are often conflicting. His father kept an unprofitable pub, which failed when John was three, and his attempt at emigrating to America ended when the ship sank off the coast of Wales. The tragedy was compounded when Lavery's mother died three months later. John and his brother Henry lived for the next seven years on an uncle's farm at Moira, Co. Down, before being sent to live with the aunt's cousin at Saltcoats in Ayr.

Lavery put an unhappy and restless childhood behind him when he got a job at 17 as a re-toucher with a Glasgow photographer and started to attend evening classes at the Haldane Academy of Art. In 1883 he spent the summer at the painterly village of Grez-sur-Loing, producing many pictures including *The Bridge at Grez*, which earned him a respectable reputation among his fellow artists. In 1885 his *The Tennis Party* was the success of the Royal Academy summer exhibition. His first wife was Kathleen McDermott, a Regent Street flower girl, whose portrait was another success. She died soon after the birth of a daughter, Eileen. By 1896 Lavery was in great demand as a society portraitist, and his marriage to the very beautiful Helen Trudeau, the widowed daughter of a Chicago industrialist, Edward Jenner Martyn, provided him with inspiration and stern criticism until her death in 1935. His painting of her appeared on Irish banknotes from 1928 until the coming of decimal coinage, and her image was still being used as a watermark until the advent of the euro.

When war broke out in 1914 Lavery joined the Artists Rifles, but he was now nearly 60 years of age and found he was unfit for army life. Instead he painted pictures of the Home Front, including *The First Wounded*. In 1921 the Laverys went to live in Ireland and became friendly with Michael COLLINS. Helen was an unofficial intermediary during the 1921 TREATY negotiations, and Lavery's painting of Collins's lying-in-state, called *Love of Ireland*, has great dignity and solemnity. Lavery had earlier also painted Terence MACSWINEY's lying-in-state and Sir Roger CASEMENT in the dock. He died in Rossenara House, Co. Kilkenny, on 10 January 1941.

Lavin, Mary (1912–96). Short-story writer and novelist. She was born in Massachusetts, where her Irish father was a land bailiff. Her mother returned to Ireland in 1920, taking Mary with her, and the family eventually settled in Bective, Co. Meath, where her father continued his work as estate manager. She was educated at Loreto College, St Stephen's Green, Dublin, and University College Dublin; her MA dissertation was on Jane Austen. She married William Walsh, a family friend, and on her father's death in 1945 bought Abbey Farm, also in Bective. Her husband died in 1954 and she supported her three daughters, her writing supplementing the uncertain farm income. She married Michael Scott, a laicized Jesuit, in 1969.

Mary Lavin's short stories, meticulously crafted but registering the inconsequentiality of life, place her in the highest rank of such fiction writers. She can make a drama out of the smallest domestic incident and is excellent in the portrayal of children, bereavement and women with women. Her stories (written between 1938 and 1985 and published in fourteen separate books) were collected into three volumes (1964, 1974 and 1985), and a *Collected Stories* appeared in 1971. She also wrote two novels: *The House in Clewe Street* (1945) and *Mary O'Grady* (1950). A new selection of stories, *In a Café*, was published in 1995, shortly before her death.

Law, Andrew Bonar (1858–1923). Leader of the British Conservative Party and prime minister for a brief period (October 1922–May 1923). He was born in New Brunswick in Canada but reared near Glasgow, the son of an Ulster Presbyterian minister. When he became Conservative leader in 1911, and until the end of his life, he strongly supported Ulster Unionist opposition to the third HOME RULE bill, also influencing the outcome of the negotiations leading to the Anglo-Irish TREATY of 1921.

Lawless, Emily (1845–1913). Poet and novelist. She was born in Co. Kildare, the daughter of Lord Cloncurry, but spent most of her youth in Co. Galway. She became one of the foremost of Irish writers, sympathetic to the people but regarding hopes of HOME RULE as chimerical. Her chief novels are *Hurrish* (1886), about the LAND WAR, *Grania* (1892), showing life in the Aran Islands, and two Elizabethan romances, *Maelcho* (1894) and *With Essex in Ireland* (1902). W.B. Yeats numbered *Hurrish* and *With Essex in Ireland* among the best Irish books. Her verse collection *With the Wild Geese* (1902) contains her justly anthologized pieces 'After Aughrim', mourning the WILD GEESE, and 'Clare Coast'. She moved to England for health reasons, but also because of the anti-Unionist campaign of Sinn Féin, and died in Surrey.

> She said, 'They gave me of their best,
> They lived, they gave their lives for me;
> I tossed them to the howling waste,
> And flung them to the foaming sea.'
>
> EMILY LAWLESS: 'After Aughrim', in *With the Wild Geese* (1902)

Lawnmower. The nickname applied by exasperated Irish soldiers on peace-keeping duties with the UN in the Lebanon to pilotless Israeli observation aircraft.

Lawyer's Nightcap. Pieces of toast dipped in wine:

> We did our best to be merry and jocund with the bad wine, putting sugar in it (as the senior lawyers are used to do with Canary wine), with toasted bread, which in English is called 'a lawyer's nightcap'.
>
> SIR JOSIAS BODLEY: *Description of a Journey to Lecale* (1603)

Laying hen. An inelegant description of the wife or partner of a farmer who has her own source of earned income.

Lazy bed. A ridge for the sowing of potatoes in which the grass sod was not removed but earth from either side was built on top of the grass and the line of seed potatoes. The work of making it was extremely hard, belying the name. The traces of such ridges can be seen in many parts of Ireland, and in the Highlands and Islands of Scotland.

Lazy, trifling... . Part of the description of Irish landlords by Arthur YOUNG (1741–1820), the agricultural theorist, in his *Tour of Ireland* (1780): '... lazy, trifling, negligent, slobbering, profligate'.

LE. The abbreviation of *Long Éireann*, Irish for 'ship of Ireland', and used as the mark of an Irish naval vessel, the equivalent of HMS or USS.

Leaba na mbocht. *See* HOSPITALITY.

Leadhb. An Irish word for 'rag', 'strip of mat-erial', 'leather', used in HIBERNO-ENGLISH for a useless or uncooperative person, particularly a woman.

Lead nor drive, neither. A colloquial phrase meaning to be without options, to be confined to one place, either literally or metaphorically: 'That fellow will neither lead nor drive.' The phrase derives from rural lore, in particular the difficulty of moving a wayward cow that will be neither led nor driven.

Leadránach. An Irish word for 'slow', 'dragging', used in HIBERNO-ENGLISH to convey the quality of something over-long or boring (for instance a book, film or story) or a person who is tedious, long-winded or slow.

League of Nations. The Irish Free State became a member of the League of Nations on 10 September 1923, although the application was opposed by the British government, which claimed that it represented all the Commonwealth countries, including Ireland. It was not until the 1930s, under Éamon de Valera, that Ireland began to play an active role in the politics of the League. De Valera was elected president of the council of the League in 1932, and acted as president of the League's assembly (1938–9). He supported the League's decision not to intervene in the SPANISH CIVIL WAR (1936–9) and also Neville Chamberlain's policy of appeasing Hitler.
See also LESTER, SEAN.

Leamh. A word, pronounced 'lav', with a wide range of meanings in Irish, such as 'insipid' or impotent'. In HIBERNO-ENGLISH it may be used to describe tasteless, dull or unsalted food, or applied to a book, an event or a person – anything or anyone considered dull or insipid.

Leather. An instrument of punishment for schoolboys associated particularly with the CHRISTIAN BROTHERS, used in such phrases as 'He gave me the leather' or 'I'm going to get the leather.' The leather was a wide leather band, perhaps originally a leather belt worn by the brothers over their soutanes. In Irish autobiographies there are numerous stories of children being severely – even sadistically – chastised or having academic material 'bet into them by the Christian Brothers'.

Lebarcham. A poet and the nurse of DEIDRE, her main female confidante in maturity. She tries to persuade CONCHOBHAR that her ward's striking beauty has faded during her sojourn with NAOISE in ALBA in the hope of his losing interest in her. One of the king's spies reports, however, that Deirdre is as beautiful as ever, and the tragic events are set in train.

Lebidjeh (Irish *leibide*). A HIBERNO-ENGLISH word for a foolish, slovenly softie.

Lebor Gabála Érenn. See BOOK OF INVASIONS.

Lebor na hUidre. See BOOK OF THE DUN COW.

Le Brocquy, Louis (b.1916). Artist. He was born on 10 October 1916 and educated at St Gerard's School in Bray, Co. Wicklow, and Trinity College Dublin. Although he studied art in England and on the Continent, for the most part he is self-taught. Along with Evie HONE and Mainie JELLETT, he founded the Irish Exhibition of Living Art in 1943 to showcase contemporary trends in painting and sculpture. In 1949 he was elected member of the Royal Hibernian Academy, where he had exhibited since 1937, and he has been a teacher of art and a consultant to artistic and cultural bodies. He once described his own paintings as palimpsests, ideas superimposed on ideas. He is one of Ireland's most respected modern artists, and his paintings now command enormous prices.

Ledwidge, Francis (1887–1917). Poet. Born in Slane, Co. Meath, in August 1887, Ledwidge is remembered for his much-anthologized assonantal elegy for Thomas MACDONAGH, one of the leaders of the EASTER RISING, who was executed in May 1916:

> He shall not hear the bittern cry
> In the wild sky where he is lain
> Nor voices of the sweeter birds
> Above the wailing of the rain …

When he wrote this poem, Ledwidge – who,

although a SINN FÉIN supporter, had joined the Royal Inniskilling Fusiliers in October 1914 – was on sick leave in Manchester, having served in the Dardanelles and on the Serbian front: 'I joined the British army, because she stood between Ireland and an enemy common to our civilization, and I would not have her say that she defended us while we did nothing at home but pass resolutions.' He was killed by a stray German shell near Ypres in July 1917 while repairing a road near the front. A collection, *Songs of the Field*, was published in 1915. *The Complete Poems*, edited by his patron Lord DUNSANY, was published in 1919 and re-edited by Alice Curtayne for publication at the same time as her biography, *Francis Ledwidge: A Life of the Poet* (1972). Seamus Heaney wrote of him:

> I think of you in your Tommy's uniform,
> A haunted Catholic face, pallid and brave,
> Ghosting the trenches like a bloom of hawthorn
> SEAMUS HEANEY: 'In Memoriam Francis Ledwidge',
> in *Field Work* (1979)

Lee-a-roady (Irish *liathróidí*, 'balls'). A faux-Irish contemporary term for 'balls' in the sense of 'testicles', metaphorically meaning 'nerve', 'bravery' or 'machismo' in risk-taking, particularly in business. The use of the word serves two purposes: it pays lip service to Irish uniqueness, suggesting that only Irishmen have *liathróidí* of quite this type; and it euphemistically avoids the vulgarity of the word 'balls'. (The real Irish word for testicle is *magairle*.) The term is not normally used by or about women.

> Have you no lee-a-roady at all, Cullen? You only want to buy one miserable garage off me. Why won't you buy the lot?
> BILL CULLEN: *It's a Long Way from Penny Apples* (2001)

Leestown. See RIORDANS, THE.

Le Fanu, [Joseph] Sheridan (1814–73). Author and editor. He was born in Dublin on 28 August 1814, the son of a clergyman of Huguenot extraction, his name pronounced 'leff-anew'. His forename of use was a tribute to his great-uncle Richard Brinsley SHERIDAN. He was educated at home and at Trinity College Dublin, where he read classics before being called to the Bar in 1839. He soon gave up law to become a full-time writer, and also became editor of the *Dublin University Magazine* (1861–9) and of the *Evening Mail*, which he created in 1840 out of three existing papers bought for the purpose (and which continued to be one of the city's evening papers until July 1962). His wife Susan Bennett died in 1858 after 14 years of marriage, and he became a virtual recluse in his Merrion Square house until his death on 7 February 1873.

Some of Le Fanu's best stories of mystery and obsession are to be found in IN A GLASS DARK-LY. He wrote many novels, including *The Cock and Anchor* (1845), *The House by the Church-yard* (1863), *Wylder's Hand* (1864) and the book by which he was best known, *Uncle Silas* (1864). Some are set in the Ireland of the previous century, and all use umbrous Irish topography to establish the menacing scene. Though no supporter of Daniel O'CONNELL Le Fanu was firmly Irish, as indicated by two early ballads, 'Shamus O'Brien' and 'Phadrig Crohore'.

> The soldiers run this way, the hangmen run that
> And Father Malone lost his new Sunday hat;
> And the sheriffs were both of them punished severely
> And fumed like the devil, because Jim done them fairly.
>
> 'Shamus O'Brien', in *The Poems of Joseph Sheridan Le Fanu* (1896)

Left foot, to dig with the. *See* DIG WITH THE LEFT FOOT, TO.

Legion of Cooks. The description by Lord Byron (1788–1824) of part of the entourage of George IV on his state visit to Ireland. In the 'Irish Avatar' (September 1821) he writes:

> But he comes! The Messiah of Royalty comes!
> Like a goodly Leviathan roll'd from the waves;
> Then receive him as best such an advent becomes
> With a legion of cooks and an army of slaves!

Legion of Mary. An association for lay members of the Catholic Church, founded in Dublin on 7 September 1921 by Frank Duff (1889–1980) and based on the teachings of the French theolo-gian St Louis Marie de Montfort. Members of 'the Legion', as it is popularly known, under-take to attend weekly meetings and to engage in practical mission or charitable work. The use of such terms as *praesidium* and *acies* for its subdivisions underline its militant aspect in its battle with evil. The organization has been very successful in Ireland and abroad, seeming to appeal particularly to women, and was frequently established in Catholic girls' schools as a sorority.

Le Gros, Raymond. A Welsh-Norman knight who with Miles de Cogan and others led the army that captured Dublin in September 1170. He was called 'le Gros' because he was 'of ample proportions'. He helped to break Ruaidhrí Ua Conchobair's siege of the city the following year, and married Basilia FitzGilbert, sister of STRONGBOW in 1173 or 1174.

Léine (Irish, 'linen garment', 'shirt'). The long tunic worn by Irish people until the decline of the Gaelic order in the early 17th century. It was always white, made of unbleached linen and simple in style, like a frock or long shirt pulled over the head. The *léine* was gathered at the waist by a CRIOS (belt) made of leather, which also provided a holder for a knife.

Leinster. One of the traditional provinces of Ireland, comprising the eastern and southeast-ern counties of Carlow, Dublin, Kildare, Kil-kenny, Laois, Longford, Louth, Meath, Offaly, Westmeath, Wexford and Wicklow. It takes its name from the Laigin (or Lageni) tribe, said to have come to Ireland in the 3rd century. In the early historical period Leinster extended from the Shannon to the Boyne, but was some-what reduced from the 6th century. The Mac-Murroughs were kings of Leinster until 1171, when Dermot MACMURROUGH died, passing on his kingdom to his son-in-law, the Anglo-Norman Richard de Clare, Earl of Pembroke (nicknamed STRONGBOW), who had helped to restore the exiled king to his throne. Strong-bow's assumption of the kingship of Leinster prompted HENRY II to invade Ireland, and

Leinster then came under the English crown. However, in reward for his services, in 1173 Henry granted Strongbow the lordship of Dublin, Waterford and Wexford, which became the core of the PALE, the area of Anglo-Norman settlement in Ireland. Further English settlement of Leinster occurred in the 16th and 17th centuries.

Leinster House. The home of the OIREACHTAS[1], Ireland's legislative houses, situated in Merrion Square, Dublin. It was originally the town house of the Duke of Leinster, designed in the Palladian style by Richard CASTLE in 1745. In 1815 it became the headquarters of the ROYAL DUBLIN SOCIETY (RDS). It adjoins the NATIONAL GALLERY OF IRELAND and the NATIONAL MUSEUM OF IRELAND, both of which were established by the RDS, as well as the nearby NATIONAL LIBRARY OF IRELAND. The DÁIL first sat in Leinster House in 1922, when the Free State government acquired part of the house; later the whole house was bought by the government.

Leitch, Maurice. *See LIBERTY LAD, THE.*

Lemass, Seán (1899–1971). Revolutionary and statesman; taoiseach from 1959 to 1966. He was born in Dublin on 15 July 1899 and educated by the CHRISTIAN BROTHERS at O'Connell's Schools. He and his older brother Noel fought in the GPO during the EASTER RISING of 1916; he escaped arrest and internment because of his youth and because he was recognized by a Dublin policeman who knew his family. After he finished school he worked in the family's drapery business in Capel Street, but remained active in the Volunteers. He was arrested and interned in December 1920, but released in July 1921 under the terms of the TRUCE. He opposed the TREATY and was a member of the Republican garrison that held the FOUR COURTS at the beginning of the CIVIL WAR. He was interned from December 1922 to December 1923, during which time his brother Noel was shot in an unofficial action by Free State forces and his body dumped in the Dublin Mountains.

Lemass was elected to the DÁIL in 1925 and sat for the same Dublin constituency until he retired in 1966, first taking his seat as a member of FIANNA FÁIL in 1927. During his time in government he served almost exclusively in one department, Industry and Commerce, until he became taoiseach after the retirement of Éamon de Valera in June 1959 (he had served as tánáiste – deputy to the taoiseach – from 1945). The economic and industrial policy of the Fianna Fáil government from its accession to power in 1932 was PROTECTIONISM: foreign investment was encouraged only in cases of absolute necessity, and Lemass was responsible for establishing what became known as semistate bodies, including AER LINGUS, BORD NA MÓNA, Irish Shipping, the INDUSTRIAL CREDIT CORPORATION and the Tourist Board. Protectionism clearly did not work in the 1950s, when Ireland suffered from an economic depression and massive emigration, despite the postwar boom in other European countries. Once he became taoiseach Lemass presided over a total change in economic policy, negotiating a free-trade agreement with Britain in 1965. With the help of T.K. WHITAKER he began the process of modernization and of opening the country to international investment.

Lemass's period as taoiseach was notable for the liberalizing of many aspects of Irish life, and, for the first time in over a century, the reversal of the trend of widespread emigration. Although he belonged to the old school of 1916 veterans and freedom fighters, his combination of vision and pragmatism was very influential. One of the most famous symbolic gestures of his term as taoiseach was his meeting with Northern premier Terence O'NEILL in Stormont in January 1965, the beginning of what he hoped would be a rapprochement with Unionists. This meeting, again masterminded by T.K. Whitaker, was the first de facto recognition of the Northern state by a leader of the Republic. Soon after this O'Neill made a return visit to Dublin. Lemass retired as taoiseach on 10 November 1966 and was succeeded by

Jack LYNCH. He died in Dublin on 11 May 1971.

Lemoner. A word, more common in the south of Ireland, meaning a let-down (referring to the bitterness of lemons):

> His wife left him to go to Paris with a woman.
> That must have been a right lemoner.
> BERNARD FARRELL (b.1941): *Canaries* (1980)

Leo. The pseudonym used by John Keegan Casey (1846–70) for material published in *The NA-TION*. He was born near Mullingar, Co. West-meath, the son of a teacher. He taught school himself and later worked as a clerk before his arrest as a Fenian. He contracted tuber-culosis in prison, and after his release his weakened health prevented him from recover-ing from injuries sustained in a traffic accident on the Dublin quays. His funeral was attended by 50,000 people – a tribute both to his politics and his verse. His most famous ballad 'The RISING OF THE MOON', which gave Lady Gregory the title for one of her most famous plays, was written when he was 15, and his love song 'Máire, My Girl' is still in the Irish recital repertory. 'The Rising of the Moon', written about the REBELLION OF 1798, is part of Irish vocal lore and still evocative of a revolutionary past:

> Out from many a mud-wall cabin eyes were
>   watching through that night;
> Many a manly heart was throbbing for the
>   blessed warning light.
> Murmurs passed along the valleys, like the
>   banshee's lonely croon,
> And a thousand blades were flashing at the Rising
>   of the Moon.

Captain James Kelly, one of the main players in the ARMS CRISIS, entitled his book on the affair *Orders for the Captain*, a slight twist of Casey's third line:

> I bear orders from the captain – get you ready
>   quick and soon.

Leonard, Hugh (pseudonym of John Keyes Byrne, b.1926). Playwright. He was born and brought up by adoptive parents in Dalkey and from 1945 worked as a clerk for the Land Com-mission. While thus engaged he built up an encyclopaedic knowledge of cinema, became heavily involved in amateur theatre and decided to become a writer. By the time he achieved his first local theatrical success, *Madigan's Lock* (1958), he had adopted the name of one of his own characters and left Ireland to work with Granada Television in Britain, dramatizing the works of authors as diverse as Dickens, Saki and Brian FRIEL. *A Walk on the Water* (1960), about a returned Irishman (a recurring theme of the time), was staged at the Dublin Theatre Festival, the first product of a very fruitful rela-tionship, and *STEPHEN D* (1962), mined from James Joyce's *STEPHEN HERO* and *A POR-TRAIT OF THE ARTIST AS A YOUNG MAN*, was such a success that it transferred to London, as did the author.

Leonard wrote many (often extremely fun-ny) plays over the next two decades, usually set and premièred in Ireland, turning a cold eye on his country and its murderous senti-mentality about Republicanism, its *nouveaux riches*, its attitude to its expatriates and its political corruption. This is especially true of *The Patrick Pearse Motel* (1971), *The Suburb of Babylon* (1977) and *Kill* (1982), where satire bubbles over into spleen. His greatest success was with *Da* (1973), a slice of authentic dram-atic autobiography, as the prose works *Home before Night* (1979) and *Out after Dark* (1989) confirm. Later came *A Life* (1980), which tells the elegiac story of Drumm, a minor character (and minor civil servant) from *Da*. Leonard is a master technician of the theatre and writes, as if to order, thrillers, fantasies, Chek-hovian threnodies and brilliant pastiche, as in *Time Out* (1980) and *The Mask of Moriarty* (1987).

> The climate is temperate, the birth rate relentless
> and the mortal ... the mortality rate is consistent
> with the national average.
> *A Life* (1980)

Leper of old, as a. The recommendation by PARNELL as to how those subject to a BOYcott should be treated. In a reply in Ennis, Co. Clare, on 19 September 1880, to a question from the crowd as to what should be done with a 'tenant who bids for a farm from which his neighbour has been evicted' he answered:

> Now I think I heard somebody say, 'Shoot him!' but I wish to point out to you a much better way – a more Christian, a more charitable way – which will give the lost sinner an opportunity of repenting. When a man takes a farm from which another has been evicted, you must show him on the roadside when you meet him, you must show him in the streets of the town, you must show him at the shop-counter, you must show him at the fair and in the marketplace and even in the house of worship, by leaving him severely alone, by putting him into a sort of moral Coventry, by isolating him from the rest of his kind as if he were a leper of old, you must show him your detestation of the crime he has committed.

Leprechaun (Irish *Leipreachán*). In late folklore a fairy shoemaker with a crock of gold, which he was bound to surrender, so long as the lucky discoverer could keep him in sight. He was easily identifiable by 'his scarlet cap and coat of green'. In all the stories the captor was out-witted.

> As quick as thought I grasped the elf,
> 'Your fairy purse,' I cried.
> 'My purse?' said he, ''tis in her hand,
> That lady by your side.'
> I turned to look, the elf was off,
> And what was I to do?
> Oh! I laughed to think what a fool I'd been,
> And the fairy was laughing too.
>
> ROBERT DWYER JOYCE (1830–83): 'The Leprahaun' (1861)

Statuettes of leprechauns and other items of leprechauniana have subsequently become one of the main staples (along with shillelaghs) of the tackier sort of Irish tourist shop. Their reputation has been somewhat salvaged, however, in the witty *Artemis Fowl* books by Wexford-born children's writer Eoin Colfer, in which the eponymous boy villain is taken on by the svelte but spunky heroine, Captain Holly Short of LEPrecon, a kind of SWAT squad of the SIDHE (fairies):

> The traditional image of a leprechaun is one of a small, green-suited imp. Of course, this is a human image. Fairies have their own stereotypes. The People generally imagine officers of the Lower Elements Police Reconnaissance squad to be truculent gnomes or bulked-up elves, recruited straight from their college crunchball squads.
>
> Captain Holly Short fits neither of these descriptions. In fact, she would probably be the last person you would pick as a member of the LEPrecon squad …
>
> EOIN COLFER: *Artemis Fowl: The Arctic Incident* (2002)

See also CLURICAUNE.

Leslie, Sir Shane (1885–1971). Man of letters. He was born John Randolph, a kinsman of Winston Churchill, at his ancestral home, Castle Leslie, Glaslough, Co. Monaghan, and educated at Eton, Paris and Cambridge. He became a Catholic in 1908, changed his name to an Irish form, interested himself in the IRISH LITERARY REVIVAL, stood twice as a Nationalist in Derry and conceived the impossible ambition of explaining the Irish to the English. He wrote verse, fiction, biography and history and became a world authority on LOUGH DERG and its pilgrimage, the main approaches to which were over his family's lands. His thinly veiled autobiographical novels – *The Oppidan* (1922), *The Cantab* (1926) and *The Anglo-Catholic* (1929) – are much more revealing than his discreet autobiographies, *The Passing Chapter* (1934) and *The Film of Memory* (1938). He was a connoisseur of ghost stories and no mean practitioner himself, publishing *The Shane Leslie Ghost Book* in 1955.

Lester, Sean (1888–1959). Diplomat and secretary-general of the League of Nations. He was born in Carrickfergus, Co. Antrim, and worked as a journalist before joining the Department of External Affairs of the Free State in 1922. In 1929 he was named Irish representative at the League of Nations, and from 1940 he served in Geneva as secretary-general of an organization that the war had made redundant. When the United Nations superseded the League of Nations in 1945, Lester wound up the League and retired to the west of Ireland, where he died in 1959.

Leth Cuinn and Leth Moga. The names for the two halves of Ireland, claiming to represent a prehistoric division dating from the time of the legendary MILESIANS. The half north of a dividing line from Dublin to Galway was Leth Cuinn, traditionally held to be dominated by the Uí Néill; the southern half, Leth Moga, was the territory of the Eóganacht of Munster. The division was aspirational rather than real, especially for the Munster kings, who did not usually have dominance over Leinster.

Let him rule all Ireland. The words attributed to Henry VII about the GREAT EARL – Géaróid Mór (Gerald Fitzgerald), 8th Earl of Kildare – when Sir Edward Poynings (1459–1521), the deputy-governor, having jailed Kildare in 1494, objected to his release from the Tower: 'If all Ireland cannot rule this man, let him rule all Ireland.'

Leth Moga. *See* LETH CUINN AND LETH MOGA.

Let no man write my epitaph. The words from Robert EMMET's speech from the dock that were for many years a Nationalist mantra, learned by heart as a kind of secular prayer. The speech, made just before Emmet's execution on Monday 29 September 1803, was continually interrupted by increasingly angry officials, including the judge, Baron Norbury (1745–1831):

> My lords, you are impatient for the sacrifice … be yet patient! I have but a few more words to say – I am going to my cold and silent grave – my lamp of life is nearly extinguished … My race is run – the grave opens to receive me, and I sink into its bosom. I have but one request to ask at my departure from this world, it is the charity of its silence. Let no man write my epitaph; for as no man who knows my motives dare now vindicate them, let not prejudice or ignorance asperse

them. Let them rest in obscurity and peace, my memory be left in oblivion, and my tomb remain uninscribed, until other times and other men can do justice to my character. When my country takes her place among the nations of the earth, then, and not till then, let my epitaph be written. I have done.

Let on. A widely used expression meaning both 'pretend' and 'admit to'. In Ireland it appears in the parody of a hymn to the local patron, once sung by Derry schoolchildren:

> St Columba broke a winda
> And he blamed it on St John,
> St John told St Patrick
> And St Patrick never let on.

Letterfrack. A notorious INDUSTRIAL SCHOOL in Connemara run by the CHRISTIAN BROTHERS. The building was retained after local opinion was canvassed, and Connemara West plc, established in 1971, now runs Letterfrack Furniture College there, in partnership with Galway-Mayo Institute of Technology.

Let the priest say Mass. An admonition against unnecessary advice.

Letts, Winifred M[abel] (1882–1972). Poet. She was born in Wexford, the daughter of the rector of Newton Heath, Manchester, and educated at Alexandra College, Dublin. Though she wrote for the theatre, achieving some success with *Hamilton and Jones* (1941) at the GATE THEATRE, she is best remembered as a poet for such memorable lyrics as 'A SOFT DAY', published in *Songs of Leinster* (1913) and much anthologized. She published a second collection, *More Songs of Leinster*, in 1926, and she also a wrote a memoir, *Knockmaroon*, about her grandparents' home, Knockmaroon House, near Dublin's PHOENIX PARK.

Lever, Charles [James] (1806–72). Novelist. Born in Dublin on 31 August 1806 and educated at Trinity College Dublin and the Royal College of Surgeons, he also studied medicine at Göttingen, in Lower Saxony. Returning to Ireland in 1832 he was in time to help stem a cholera outbreak in Kilrush, Co. Clare. He was then appointed dispensary doctor at Portstewart, near Coleraine, Co. Derry, the north-coast fishing village that was on the point of becoming a leading 19th-century watering-place, and where Lever House on the promenade still commemorates him. Lever's first 'military' novel, *The Confessions of Harry Lorrequer*, (1839) was influenced by his friend W.H. MAXWELL's *Wild Sports of the West* and established a genre of popular comic fiction describing the (mainly romantic) adventures of young subalterns in Ireland. The literary archetype of the devil-may-care, eloquent young Irishman is his original creation.

Lever wrote to supplement his professional earnings, pay his heavy gambling debts and help him take part in whatever highlife the CAUSEWAY COAST and trips to Dublin could supply. He left Ireland in 1839 to practice medicine in Brussels, and returned to edit the *Dublin University Magazine*, in which his novel *Charles O'Malley* (1841) was serialized (1842–5). He settled in Florence in 1847 then served as consul in Trieste from 1867 until his death on 1 June 1872.

Lever wrote 30 books in all, of which *Charles O'Malley* and *The Martins of Cro' Martin* (1856) are regarded as his best. The success of his work, particularly in his later increasingly serious treatment of politics, undoubtedly stimulated his friend TROLLOPE to write *The Macdermots of Ballycloran* (1847) and *The Kellys and the O'Kellys* (1848).

> Let some fortune-hunter carry off an heiress; let a lady trip over her train at the drawing-room; let a minister blunder in his mission; let a powder-magazine explode and blow up one half the surrounding population – there was but one expression to qualify all, 'How very Irish! how very Irish!' The adjective had become one of depreciation, and an Irish lord, an Irish member, an Irish estate, and an Irish diamond were held pretty much in the same estimation.
>
> CHARLES LEVER: *Our Mess: Jack Hinton, the Guardsman* (1843)

Leviathan of Parsonstown, the. A gigantic 180-cm (72-inch) telescope built by William Parsons,

3rd Earl of Rosse (1800–67) in the grounds of his home, BIRR Castle, in Co. Offaly, and still visible there. The astronomer-earl was the first to observe the spiral nature of nebulae and to recognize them as galaxies outside our own. The observatory at Birr, which was housed in a domed building, consisted of the Leviathan, a more versatile 90-cm (36-inch) telescope and a reflector. The Leviathan cost £20,000 to build (€1.27 million in today's money), and it was the earl's marriage to a Yorkshire heiress, Mary Field, in 1836 that allowed him to concentrate on building it. Between 1828 and 1845 he worked at developing the telescopes and built the observatory. The Leviathan was restored in 1996–7 at a cost of £1 million (€1.4 million).

Lia Fáil (Irish, 'stone of destiny'). A rectangular block of reddish-grey sandstone measuring 66 cm (26 inches) by 41 cm (16 inches) by 28 cm (11 inches), traditionally associated with the coronations of Scottish kings, and, before that, with the accession ceremony of the high kings of Ireland at TARA. Its only decoration is a simple cross, and it was said to crow with pleasure at the touch of the rightful king. In Scotland it is known as the Stone of Destiny or the Stone of Scone (*see below*). Another name for it is Jacob's Stone, from the legend that Jacob used it as a pillow when he dreamt of the angels ascending and descending the ladder (Genesis 28:11). In another story, the stone was COLUM CILLE's pillow.

According to the first legend the stone was given to a Celtic king who married the daughter of an Egyptian pharoah, and made its way to Tara in Ireland *c*.700 BC, where in ancient times the high kings were crowned. The Scots took it with them when they established the kingdom of DÁL RIATA in Argyll (although another story has Joseph of Arimathea bringing it to Scotland), and it was said that when the Dalriadan kings sat on the stone at their capital at Dunadd they took on royal power. The stone was later kept at Dunstaffnage Castle, until Kenneth MacAlpine unified Scotland in the 9th century and moved it and his court to Scone. Subsequently, all Scottish kings were crowned while sitting on the stone until 1296, when Edward I of England seized the stone and took it back to London. In 1307 it was placed beneath Edward's new Coronation Chair in Westminster Abbey as a symbol of Scotland's supposed subjugation to the kings of England.

On the night of 24–25 December 1950 Scottish Nationalists stole the Stone of Scone from Westminster Abbey, and later placed it on the high altar of Arbroath Abbey, symbolically reminding the world of the Declaration of Arbroath, Scotland's 'declaration of independence' of 1320. The stone was restored to its place in Westminster Abbey in February 1952, but officially returned to Scotland in 1996, when it was installed in Edinburgh Castle on 30 November, St Andrew's Day.

Liar, the. A Cork term for the *Evening Echo*, as in 'I saw it in the Liar this evening.'
See also PAPER, DE.

Liber Armachanus. *See* BOOK OF ARMAGH.

Liberator, the. The sobriquet of Daniel O'CONNELL, awarded because of his successful efforts to win CATHOLIC EMANCIPATION; however, he failed in his attempt to repeal the Act of UNION.

Liberties. The part of south Dublin formerly outside the jurisdiction of the medieval city, hence the name. The area had once been the property of the Great Abbey of Thomas Court, but after the Dissolution of the Monasteries by Henry VIII it was granted to Chancellor Brabazon, whose descendant, the Earl of Meath, in the early 18th century settled large numbers of Huguenot weavers, making it Protestant and prosperous (*see* LIBERTY BOYS AND ORMOND BOYS). By the end of the century the Liberties had become an appalling slum area and the degeneration was accelerated after the Act of UNION. An American doctor, James Johnson, visited the Liberties in 1844, and recorded his shock at the cohabitation of grandeur and squalor he found there with Dickensian irony:

Dublin – rent and split – worm-eaten, mouldering, patched and plastered – unsightly to the eye, unsavoury to the taste, and not very grateful to the olfactories – here there is but one step from magnificence to misery, from the splendid palace to the squalid hovel …

… winds and rain have *liberty* to enter freely through the windows of half the houses – the pigs have *liberty* to ramble about – the landlord has *liberty* to take possession of most of his tenements – the silk weaver has *liberty* to starve or beg.

Quoted in Thomas and Valerie Pakenham, *Dublin – A Travellers' Companion* (1988)

Liberty Boys and Ormond Boys. Rival factions in 18th-century Dublin. The Protestant tailors and weavers of the Coombe in the LIBERTIES area regularly battled with the Catholic butchers of Ormond Market. For days at a time the bridges and quays of the city were the scenes of fierce and bloody battles; the butchers would cut the leg tendons of the weavers and the latter would leave butcher prisoners hanging by the jaws on their own hooks. A sort of peace was arranged about 1748 with the terms published in the public prints, but outrages were recorded even as late as 1790:

The shops were closed; all business suspended; the sober and peaceable compelled to keep to their houses; while the war of stones and other missiles was carried on across the river. It will hardly be believed that for whole days the intercourse of the city was interrupted by the feuds of these factions. A friend of ours has told us that he has gone down to Essex Bridge [now Grattan Bridge] and stood quietly on the battlements for a whole day, looking at the combat in which over a thousand men were engaged …

(Justice) JOHN EDWARD WALSH (1816–69): *Ireland Sixty Years Ago* (1847)

Liberty Hall. The headquarters of the ITGWU, situated in Dublin on the corner of Eden Quay and Beresford Place to the north of the River Liffey. The union bought the original building, then a derelict hotel that had been called the Northumberland Commercial and Family

Hotel, in 1912, and named it Liberty Hall, and it was the centre of union activities in the 1913 LOCKOUT. During the EASTER RISING the IRISH CITIZEN ARMY marched the short distance from Liberty Hall to the GPO on Easter Monday 1916, and the building was badly damaged when it was shelled by British artillery from across the river. The new Liberty Hall, a modernist 16-storey tower, was erected by the ITGWU; construction began in 1961, to a design by Desmond Rea O'Kelly, and it was opened in 1965. The phrase 'This is Liberty Hall' was current in the 18th century and appears in *She Stoops to Conquer* (1773) by Oliver GOLDSMITH; Marlowe is trying to make his guests, who believe his house is an inn, feel at home:

> …pray be under no constraint in this house. This is Liberty-Hall, gentlemen. You may do just as you please here.
> II.i

Liberty Lad, The. The first novel (1965) of Maurice Leitch (b.1933), who was born in the mill village of Muckamore, Co. Antrim, and gave up teaching to work for the BBC in Belfast and London. Most of his novels, including *Poor Lazarus* (1969), *Stamping Ground* (1975), *Silver's City* (1981), and the novella *Chinese Whispers* (1987), are set in the south Antrim of his youth or in Belfast, a city of fascination and danger. Life in the North, even in 'peacetime', even for the educated young, is edged with the contagion of sectarian bitterness, diverting the working class from its appropriate support of radical change. This is most clearly felt in *The Liberty Lad*, which describes the slow maturing of Frank Glass, a young teacher from a mill village similar to the author's birthplace. He is impatient with his father's reverential attitude to the mill owners and his refusal to join a trade union. He objects too to his father's religious paranoia, though his own understanding of Catholics is necessarily limited:

> I began to think about Catholics, not about Catholics I know because I don't really know any but about them in general. Anything I found

out about them had been second-hand because, living in a community like this, one where the proportions are seventy-five for us, twenty-five for *them* (an inflammable mixture), division starts early – separate housing-estates, then separate schools, separate jobs, separate dances, separate pubs – a people with a past and no interest in the present.

Only *Silver's City* directly confronts the Belfast of the high Troubles, but Leitch's recent novel *The Smoke King* (1998) – set in 1942 and dealing with the investigation by an alcoholic RUC sergeant of the murder of a landlady by a black GI – indicates how deep the roots of sectarian hatreds lie. Leitch's bleak view of his native province is sometimes lightened by dark humour, and is energized by some lively writing.

Libya. A supplier of arms and money to the Provisional IRA in the 1970s and 1980s. The most spectacular evidence of this was the cargo of the Cypriot-registered *Claudia*, which on 28 March 1973 was seized in Waterford harbour by the authorities. Arms were confiscated, but a safe supposed to be carrying a million dollars was thrown overboard. This was later said to have been secured by IRA frogmen. Though the Libyan authorities were dismayed at the seizure they continued to supply arms and money. On 1 November 1987 the Panamanian-registered *Eksund* was intercepted by French customs, who found 150 tons of arms and explosives on board. It was clear that supplying was continuous and that rumours of IRA personnel being trained in subversive activities might well be true. The intention of Colonel Gaddafi, the Libyan leader, was to cause as much embarrassment to Britain as possible, and to this end he also, in the 1970s, established contacts with the UDA. At the beginning of the 1990s the Libyan authorities admitted that involvement with paramilitaries had been a mistake, and in July 1994 Said Mujbar, the Libyan foreign minister, said that his country would never supply arms to them again.

Lichfield House Compact. An informal agreement made at the town house of Lord Lichfield in the spring of 1835 between Daniel O'CONNELL and the Whigs to bring about the fall of Sir Robert PEEL's Tory government. Though both parties denied any agreement, O'Connell agreed to support a minority Whig government in exchange for mitigation of tithes, a new poor law and some limited reforms in municipal government (enabling O'Connell to become the first Catholic lord mayor of Dublin since 1690). O'Connell was not given an expected cabinet post, the suggestion having been blocked by two cabinet members who were Irish landlords. The most useful outcome of the compact was the appointment of Thomas DRUMMOND as under-secretary for Ireland. He increased the number of Catholics in the executive and caused the ORANGE ORDER to dissolve itself to avoid suppression.

Lick (Irish *leac*). A HIBERNO-ENGLISH term for a flagstone or slab. 'Lock' is another version.

Lick up to, to. A piece of common schoolboy (or perhaps more frequently schoolgirl) slang meaning to 'flatter', 'toady to' or 'fawn on' someone. To call someone a 'lick' is a serious term of abuse.

Liège. A Belgian city, cultural centre of the French-speaking part of the country, where SEDULIUS SCOTTUS ran the cathedral school.

Life of Riley. A term of uncertain derivation, meaning a life of ease, comfort, free of care: 'She has the life of Riley since her husband died.' Who Riley was isn't clear: Riley, usually spelled Reilly, is a common Irish surname, especially in Co. Cavan. The earliest recorded reference is in a 1919 song, 'My name is Kelly' by H. Pease:

> Faith and my name is Kelly, Michael Kelly,
> But I'm living the life of Riley just the same.

Liffey. The river on which DUBLIN was built. It rises in upland bog near the road between the Sally Gap and Glencree in Co. Wicklow, flows north and northeast through Co. Kildare, then passes through Chapelizod on the outskirts of Dublin, becoming tidal at Islandbridge, and

enters the sea at Dublin Bay. The basin of the Liffey has the lowest rainfall in Ireland, and it is being steadily urbanized as housing needs drive the city of Dublin ever further west.

The origin of the river's name is unclear, but the ANNALS OF THE FOUR MASTERS record its occurrence in the name of a king of Ireland, Cairbre Liffeachair, who reigned in AD 268 and was apparently fostered near the river. The name ANNA LIFFEY or Anna Livia, beloved by Dubliners and frequently found in song and story (as well as in the opening of Joyce's FINNEGANS WAKE), derives from the combination of Liffey with variations of the word *abha*, the Irish for river. 'Anna Liffey' was also used in official documents in recent centuries.

> 'Twas down by Anna Liffey my love and I did
> stray.
> There in the good old slushy mud the seagulls
> sport and play.
> We got a whiff of fish and ships and Mary softly
> sighed,
> 'Yerra John, come on, for a one and one, down
> by the Liffey side.'
> PEADAR KEARNEY: 'Down by the Liffey Side'

The earliest quays on the Liffey, including WOOD QUAY, were built by the Vikings. At present, 16 bridges cross the Liffey in Dublin, including two footbridges, the second of which – Blackhall Place Bridge, upriver from the HALFPENNY BRIDGE – was completed in 2003. Many bridges have had more than one name, some of these having been changed since independence. For instance, King's Bridge became Seán Heuston Bridge (*see* HEUSTON STATION) in 1941, having been SARSFIELD Bridge since 1922, although there is no evidence that anyone called it this; Richmond Bridge was changed to O'DONOVAN ROSSA Bridge in 1922; Queen's Bridge was changed to Queen Maeve Bridge (*see* MEDB) in 1922 and to Liam MELLOWS Bridge in 1942. Carlisle Bridge became O'CONNELL Bridge when it was reconstructed in 1880, and Essex Bridge became GRATTAN Bridge when it was rebuilt in 1875. There was a regular ferry service on the Liffey, from

Ringsend to where the POINT depot is situated, from the late 14th century until 1984, when the East Link Bridge was opened.
See also FLOOZIE IN THE JACUZZI.

Liffey Swim, the. A swimming race that has taken place for more than 70 years and attracts up to 100 competitors annually. One of the most devoted was a man named Jack Kearney, who is said to have first competed in 1950 and who finished in second place in 1995. *The Liffey Swim* (1923) is the title of a famous painting of this subject by Jack B. YEATS. Oliver St John GOGARTY won it several times, and on one such occasion responded to congratulations with the reply, 'I was just going through the motions.'

Liffey Valley. A large retail complex to the west of Dublin city that was opened in 2001. Before the complex was named, polls among local residents and potential customers established that 'Liffey Valley' was the brand name of choice.

Liffey water. Rhyming slang for 'porter' (Guinness). It was alleged that Liffey water was one of the essential ingredients of GUINNESS, accounting for its unique taste.

Lift. The conveying of a coffin on the shoulders of four bearers, either for the removal of the remains from house to hearse to church, or after the service for the funeral proper. The first lift was the prerogative of the immediate family, ideally husband and sons, and if possible those with the same name as the deceased. After an interval, usually determined by the undertaker, four men were selected for the second lift, with attention paid to degrees of kinship and friendship. The system of relays was continued for as long as was necessary. In rural areas up until the middle of the 20th century it was customary to take the longest possible route to the cemetery, passing, where feasible, the house of the deceased. Even today the coffin is carried an agreed distance before being placed in the hearse, and a cortège of friends and relatives walks another determined distance behind the hearse before the mourners take to their cars. Except in larger cities the procession of mourning cars still proceeds at a reverentially slow pace.

Like snuff at a wake. *See* SNUFF AT A WAKE, LIKE.

'Lillibuléro'. The song that – according to its composer Thomas, 1st Marquess of Wharton, (1648–1714) – whistled JAMES II out of three kingdoms. It was written in response to James's appointment of Richard Talbot, Earl of TYRCONNELL (1630–91), as lord deputy of Ireland, and the creation of a Catholic army and civil service. The refrain '*Lillibuléro bullen a la*' is a mocking parody of the Gaelic watchcry (a sort of war cry) used by Catholics in the REBELLION OF 1641. Its Irish original was most likely '*An lile bá léir é, ba linne an lá*' ('the lily prevailed; the day was ours').

> Ho brother Teig, dost hear the decree
> Lillibuléro bullen a la,
> Dat we shall have a new Debittie
> Lillibuléro bullen a la.

The song was sung and whistled by anti-Jacobite forces in the WILLIAMITE WAR – hence Wharton's claim for his composition.

Lilliput. The first land visited by Lemuel Gulliver in Swift's GULLIVER'S TRAVELS. The inhabitants of Lilliput are tiny and factionally minded, and their enmity with the neighbouring island of Blefuscu refers to the rivalry between Britain and France. In his diary, Wolfe TONE used Lilliput and Blefuscu to stand for Dublin and Belfast.

Lilting. A term for the traditional folk genre of wordless vocal music. It is synonymous with dyddling (*see* DYDDLE), gob music, mouth music and puss music. The skill of lilting is recognized in the FLEADH CHEOIL. Séamus Fay of Drumconnick in Co. Cavan is a celebrated third-generation lilter.

Lily of Killarney, The. An opera (1862) by Sir Julius Benedict (1804–85) with libretto by John Oxenford (William Arthur Dunkerley, 1852–

1941) and Dion BOUCICAULT, based upon the latter's melodrama *The COLLEEN BAWN*.

Lilywhites. The nickname of the Co. Kildare Gaelic football team, because their strip is totally white.

Limavady. A town in Co. Derry, originally known as Newtownlimavady when it was founded in 1610 by Sir Thomas Philips during the ULSTER PLANTATION. Its name in Irish, *Léim a' Mhadaigh*, signifies 'dog's leap', from a story that a hound managed to jump across the rocky gorge of the River Roe with a message under its collar from Ó Catháin, the local chieftain, and was thus instrumental in bringing help from the Dungiven branch of the clan, 11 km (7 miles) away. Limavady was the home of Jane Ross, who collected the music of the 'LONDONDERRY AIR', and when Thackeray (*see* TITMARSH, MICHAEL ANGELO) stayed at an inn in the Main Street while collecting material for *The Irish Sketchbook* in 1842 he was so impressed by the barmaid that he wrote a piece of pleasing doggerel, 'Peg of Limavaddy', in her honour:

> Riding from Coleraine
> (Famed for lovely Kitty)
> Came a cockney bound
> Unto Derry City;
> Weary was his soul,
> Shivering and sad was he
> Bumped along the road
> Leads to Limavaddy.
> …
> This I do declare
> Happy is the laddy
> Who the heart can share
> Of Peg of Limavaddy;
> Beauty is not rare
> In the land of Paddy,
> Fair beyond compare
> Is Peg of Limavaddy.

Limerick. A historic city on the Shannon, famous for KING JOHN'S CASTLE, its 17th-century sieges and treaty (*see* LIMERICK, TREATY OF), its rugby (GARRYOWEN and Shannon clubs), its CONFRATERNITY, its Soviet (*see* LIMERICK SOVIET) and *ANGELA'S ASHES*. It also earned notoriety in the late 20th and early 21st centuries for street violence and murders, caused in part by Mafia-like feuds between criminal families in socially deprived areas. The sobriquet 'Stab City' causes embarrassment and shame to the city's mostly law-abiding inhabitants.
See also ALONE IT STANDS; 'THERE IS AN ISLE'.

Limerick, Treaty of (3 October 1691). The treaty that ended the WILLIAMITE WAR in Ireland. After the disastrous Battle of AUGHRIM (12 July 1691) the Jacobite forces fell back on the city of Limerick, there to make a last stand. The city had been besieged by Williamite forces since July 1690, but the Jacobites under Patrick SARSFIELD held out strongly. Resistance to the first siege was aided by the morale-boosting destruction of William's siege train at Ballyneety on 11 August 1690 (*see* SARSFIELD IS THE WORD). However, in the second siege, it was clear by the autumn of 1691 that without further French help (which arrived a fortnight after the treaty was signed) the city could not hold out, and arrangements were made with General GINKEL for the most advantageous terms.

The treaty signed on 3 October 1691 allowed as many soldiers as wished to go to leave for France. Under this clause Sarsfield and 14,000 of his armies left to become the forerunners of the WILD GEESE. As far as civilians are concerned, those who took an oath of allegiance had the same religious freedoms as they possessed under Charles II and were confirmed in possession of their lands. The Protestant Dublin Parliament found these terms too generous and by the time they were confirmed by statute in 1697 they were so modified as to constitute a breach of the treaty's terms. Most of the concessions that were granted were later repealed as the POPERY LAWS were enacted. Limerick has been known since as the City of the Broken Treaty, and a limestone slab on Thomond Bridge, on which the treaty is said to have been signed, is a reminder of the dereliction (it was put on a pedestal in 1865).

Limerick Junction. A major railway junction between the Dublin–Cork mainline and lines to Limerick city and Waterford, situated not in Limerick but in Co. Tipperary, an unsign-posted 5 km (3 miles) from Tipperary town. It is said that the reason the junction (and train station) is situated outside the town is that the townspeople of Tipperary refused to have it, as they thought, foisted on them when it was first mooted.

Limerick Soviet. The workers' committee that briefly took power in Limerick in 1919 in pro-test at government policy in the early days of the ANGLO-IRISH WAR. Martial law had been imposed upon the city after the death of the RIC constable, Martin O'Brien, during the rescue of the IRA adjutant Robert Byrne from the Union hospital on 6 April. On 14 April the Limerick United Trades and Labour Council called a general strike in the city and set up a workers' soviet on the Russian model, as per-ceived by the idealists of the West. The work-ers took control of the city, published a *Daily Bulletin* and distributed essentials. They even had their own currency and a Peace Preserva-tion Force. The Limerick Soviet lasted until 25 April, when the strike was called off.

Limestone City. *See* GALWAY.

Lincoln's Avenger. The nickname given to Captain Edward P. Doherty (1809–65), a native of Co. Sligo, who was in command of the caval-ry patrol that is credited with capturing John Wilkes Booth, the assassin of President Lincoln, after an extensive manhunt (1865). Doherty is said to have pulled the dying Booth from a barn in which he and his accomplice had taken refuge and which had been set on fire by the pursuing troops.

Lindisfarne. The cradle of English Christianity, also known as Holy Island, which lies at the end of a 1.5 km (1-mile) causeway in Northum-berland, allowing access for a six-hour period between the tides. It seemed an ideal location for a Celtic monastery when AIDAN came from IONA in 635 at the invitation of Oswald, the Christian king of Northumbria. By 664 it was a well-established monastery and the mother house of several others, including MELROSE, Hartlepool, Coldingham, Tadcaster and Lich-field. St CUTHBERT – who in spite of his Anglo-Saxon name may have been Irish, and who was certainly trained by Irish monks – became abbot in 664. By then COLMÁN OF LINDIS-FARNE, in an irreconcilable quarrel over the decrees of the Synod of WHITBY, had led all the Irish monks and 30 British monks away.

Under Cuthbert the great Lindisfarne craft of illuminated manuscripts, which combined Celtic and Continental design, was developed. It is likely that the Book of Durrow (an illumi-nated manuscript of the Gospels) was compiled there *c.*650 and, like the later *BOOK OF KELLS*, was brought to Ireland for safekeeping when coastal sites like Iona and Lindisfarne became the object of Viking raids; it was preserved in the Columban monastery of Durrow, Co. Offaly, and is now in Trinity College Dublin. The *Lindisfarne Gospels* (*c.*700) are the auth-enticated glory of Aidan's foundation.

Linen Hall Library. An independent subscription library established in 1788 by the Belfast Reading Society, which became the BELFAST SOCIETY FOR PROMOTING KNOWLEDGE in 1792. Its second librarian was Thomas RUS-SELL of the UNITED IRISHMEN. The White Linen Hall (1784) was one of the architectural glories of the 18th-century city, and the grow-ing collection found a home there in 1802. It remained there – a non-sectarian and intel-lectual haven in a city not generally known for either of these qualities – until the Linen Hall was demolished in 1888 to make way for the ostentatious City Hall, symbol of Belfast's late Victorian prosperity. The library moved across to Donegall Square in 1892 and established itself in the former linen warehouse of Moore & Weinberg, retaining the familiar name. It has been treasured by such notable Ulster writers as Robert LYND, Forrest REID, Joseph TOMELTY,

Sam Hanna BELL and Seamus HEANEY. The library had a post-Second World War period of decline, but since 1988 it has been properly funded and now has the advantage of a fine modern building containing some important archives, notably of traditional Irish music and Ulster politics.

Line with, to do a. To date, to have a steady relationship with somebody.

Linfield. A Belfast association football club founded in March 1886 by a group of Sandy Row millworkers. They are known universally as the 'Blues' because of the striking colours of their jerseys, and their supporters sing a song to the tune of 'Come Friends, who Plough the Sea' from Act II of *The Pirates of Penzance* (1880):

> The Blues, the Blues, the Blues are here
> What the hell do we care ...

Traditionally Protestant in its support, its chief rival was BELFAST CELTIC, whose grounds were visible from Linfield's ground, Windsor Park on the Lisburn Road.

Linnaunshee (Irish *Leannán Sí*). A life-giving spirit, meaning literally 'fairy lover'. Unlike the Lhiannan-Shee of Manx folklore, who is a kind of personal vampire, the Irish version deals more in poetic inspiration.

> Where is thy lovely perilous abode?
>   In what strange phantom-land
> Glimmer the fairy turrets whereto rode
>   The ill-starred poet band?
>   THOMAS BOYD (1867–1927): 'To the Leanan
> Sidhe', in *Poems* (1908)

Lios. *See* RING FORT.

Lipton, Thomas Johnstone (1850–1931). Grocer. Born of Co. Monaghan parents in the Gorbals in Glasgow, Lipton emigrated at the age of 15 from the Broomielaw to New York, where one of his jobs was as a grocer's assistant. He consorted with the Irish and Scots in that city, saying,

> When there is any argument as to my real
> nationality, I come right into the open with the

declaration that I am a Scottish-Irishman or an Irish Scotsman, according to the leanings of the company I happen to be in at the moment.

On his 21st birthday Lipton opened the first of what would become a grocery empire of 300 shops across Clydeside. He employed a STAGE-IRISHMAN leading two pigs through the streets to publicize his shops, and used almost all Irish produce, most of which came by sea from Westport, Co. Mayo: each week he imported 6000 hams, 16 tons of bacon, 16,000 dozen eggs and 10 tons of butter. The company later became known as importers of tea, for which it is still known. At the turn of the century Lipton made the first of five attempts to win the America's Cup, using the Royal Ulster Yacht Club in Bangor, Co. Down, as his base; in 1930 he was presented with a special 'Loving Cup' by the Yacht Club of New York, in appreciation of his graciousness in defeat.

Lir. The ocean god whose name is immortalized as the ancient King Lear of Britain. In Irish mythology he is the father of FIONNUALA and her brothers in the story of the Children of Lir. One of these brothers is MANANNÁN MAC LIR, who replaces Lir as the Irish Poseidon.

Lisdoonvarna. A small town in north Clare famous for its seaweed baths, its matchmaking season and for the CEOL AGUS CRAIC engendered by the Lisdoonvarna Music Festival, which attracted up to 50,000 people annually in the six years of its existence (1978–83). Christy MOORE was the star performer, his song 'Lisdoonvarna' ('Oh Lisdoonvarna, Lisdoon, Lisdoon, Lisdoon, Lisdoonvarna') unforgettably epitomizing the era and the place. The CHIEFTAINS, Jackson Browne and Van Morrison (*see* VAN THE MAN) were among the other star turns. The festival became known as 'Grandson of Woodstock', and was revived in 2003, although Clare County Council refused to grant a site licence so the event had to be held in Dublin.

Lismore. A town in Co. Waterford beautifully situated on the Black River near the KNOCK-MEALDOWN MOUNTAINS. Originally a mon-

astic settlement under COLMÁN OF LISMORE, it was chosen as the site for his castle by JOHN, Lord of Ireland, in 1185. The castle has been owned for centuries by the Dukes of Devonshire.
See also BOOK OF LISMORE.

Lissadell. The home of the Gore-Booth family for some 400 years, in Co. Sligo. The present Lissadell House is an imposing neo-Grecian edifice dating from the 1830s. It was home to Eva (1870–1926) and Constance Gore-Booth (1868–1927); Yeats visited them here in their youth, and remembered them after their deaths in a fine poem (*see* REBEL COUNTESS, THE). The Gore-Booths sold the house in 2003.

Listowel Writers Week. An annual early-summer literary festival, founded in 1970 and held in the small north Kerry town of Listowel. It was the brainchild of Bryan MacMahon (*see* MASTER, THE), and includes writers' workshops, performances and competitions in the areas of fiction, poetry and drama. Every year during the closing days of May the town is filled to bursting with writers, critics and students, all of whom mingle most democratically. Listowel and its environs have been home to more than their fair share of writers, including George FITZMAURICE, John B. KEANE and Mac-Mahon himself. The town is also famous for its September race meeting.

'Little Bit of Heaven, A.' The quintessence of Irish-American song, with an alternative title 'Shure They Called It Ireland'. It was composed in 1914 by the prolific Ernest Ball (1878–1927) – also responsible for 'Mother Machree' – with lyrics by J. Keirn Brennan (1873–1948), an American of Irish extraction. It was incorporated into the play *The Heart of Paddy Whack* (1915) by Chauncey Olcott (*see* 'MY WILD IRISH ROSE'), and was dedicated to Olcott's wife Rita. Both of these 'Irish' songs were recorded profitably by, among others, John MCCORMACK and Bing Crosby:

> Shure a little bit of heaven fell from out the sky
>   one day

> And nestled on the ocean in a spot so far away;
> And when the angels found it, shure it looked so
>   sweet and fair,
> They said, 'Suppose we leave it, for it looks so
>   peaceful there.'
> So they sprinkled it with stardust just to make the
>   shamrocks grow;
> 'Tis the only place you'll find them, no matter
>   where you go.
> Then they dotted it with silver just to make its
>   lakes so grand
> And when they had it finished, shure they called
>   it Ireland.

Little Christmas. *See* BIG CHRISTMAS; WOMEN'S CHRISTMAS.

Little-endians. *See* BIG-ENDIANS.

Little Gentleman in Velvet, the. A JACOBITE toast during the reign of Queen Anne (1702–14), a tribute to the mole that raised the molehill that caused KING BILLY to fall from his horse Sorrell on 21 February 1702 and break his collar bone. His death on 8 March was attributed to the accident. A variant of the toast is 'the Little Gentleman in Black Velvet'.

Little Jerusalem. The area around the South Circular Road in Dublin's inner suburbs, including Clanbrassil Street, Lombard Street and Greenville Avenue, known for its Jewish population in the first half of the 20th century. There is an Irish-Jewish museum in Walworth Street in the same area.

Little People (Irish *daoine beaga*). A HIBERNO-ENGLISH euphemism for members of the SIDHE or fairy folk. Because they were believed to live inside the mounds of ring-forts, they needed to be smaller than mortals. They were also called, in propitiatory fashion, *daoine maithe* ('good people').

Live Aid. *See* GELDOF, BOB.

Live on, to. Part of a number of HIBERNO-ENGLISH phrases indicating meanness. Some of the sharpest descriptive phrases in contemporary Hiberno-English are reserved for those who are frugal and parsimonious, either by nature or out of necessity. Examples include: 'To live on the smell of an oil rag', 'To live on the clippings of tin', 'To live on the skin of a rasher'. These phrases may convey an element of reluctant admiration.

See also MIND MICE AT CROSSROADS.

Lloyd George, David (1863–1945). Liberal prime minister during the most crucial period of modern Irish history (1916–22). He became prime minister in succession to Asquith in December 1916 and was anxious to find a peaceful solution to the IRISH QUESTION, convening the IRISH CONVENTION in 1917. Acting against the advice of some of the participants (and his own better judgement) he tried to introduce conscription to Ireland in April 1918 (*see* CONSCRIPTION CRISIS), although he had accurately opined the previous year: 'You would get them at the point of the bayonet and a conscientious objection clause would exempt by far the greater number.' This and the terror imposed by the BLACK AND TANS and the AUXIES during the ANGLO-IRISH WAR meant that the majority of Irish Nationalists, even moderates, supported SINN FÉIN and tolerated the IRA, so Lloyd George was forced to negotiate with men like Michael COLLINS, whom he had previously called the 'leader of a band of assassins'. Nationalist history demonized him for what was perceived to be his cunning and treachery in the TREATY negotiations, especially for his ultimatum of 5 December 1921 that persuaded Collins and Arthur Griffith that they should agree to the terms.

Loaf bread. *See* SHOP BREAD.

Loanen. A word meaning a 'small country lane', the diminutive of the Scots 'loan'.

> The boy in the corduroy kneebreeches moved slowly down the sunny gnat-hung loanen, searching the sheughs for sourleek or wild strawberries.
>
> SAM HANNA BELL (1909–90): *Summer Loanen* (1943)

Local Defence Force (LDF). An auxiliary (reserve) army formed in September 1940 dur-

ing the EMERGENCY. It was under the command of the regular chief of staff, but with a local directorate. In all, 100,000 men were recruited, armed and uniformed. After the war this auxiliary force was scaled down and restructured as Forsaí Cosanta Áitiúil (FCA; an exact translation of LDF, except that *forsaí* is plural).

See also FREE CLOTHES ASSOCIATION.

Locke, Josef. The stage name of the tenor Joseph Mclaughlin (1917–2001). He was born in Derry on 23 March 1917 and joined the Irish Guards at 16. He was hired by Jimmy O'Dea (*see* 'PRIDE OF THE COOMBE, THE') for his shows, and then moved to London in 1944. His name was regarded as too cumbersome for variety bills and so it became Josef Locke. He was one of the highest-paid stars of the circuit, playing 19 consecutive seasons in Blackpool. His recordings of 'Blaze Away', 'Goodbye' (from the 1936 musical *The White Horse Inn*) and especially 'Hear My Song' were extremely profitable. Tax problems, which took ten years to settle, required that he go back to Ireland in 1958, but he returned to Blackpool for a further three years in 1968. He retired to Ireland in 1971, but continued to make guest appearances. A film based on Locke's life, *Hear My Song*, appeared in 1991.

Locke's Distillery. A distillery established in the village of Kilbeggan, Co. Westmeath, in 1757. It came to public notice when in 1947 an international consortium called Trans-World, based in the Swiss city of Lausanne, made an attempt to buy the distillery from the remaining family owners, although it seemed not to have funds to do so. Contacts between shady members of the consortium, a government minister who supported their bid and President Seán T. O'KELLY resulted in a scandal and an investigative tribunal. It emerged that the putative buyers were anxious to acquire and sell not the distillery itself but its store of whiskey – spirits being in short supply after the Second World War. The consortium left the country as soon as they were uncovered and the tribunal cleared the politicians and the president of wrongdoing, but criticized an official who had arranged the visit of the consortium members to ÁRAS AN UACHTARÁIN (the residence of the president).

Lock of, a. A large, indeterminate number of things or people, a phrase common in the HIBERNO-ENGLISH of Ulster: 'I'll bring a lock of sticks and we can light a bonfire.'

Logan, James (1674–1751). Colonial statesman. He was born on 20 October 1674 at Lurgan, Co. Armagh, the son of a Quaker schoolmaster who provided his son's education. He sailed for Pennsylvania with William Penn (1644–1718) as his secretary in 1699 and became in effect governor of the colony. From 1731 he was chief justice of the supreme court of the colony and maintained friendly relations with local chiefs. An amateur botanist, Logan was granted recognition by Linnaeus (1707–78), who named the Loganiaceae after him. He died on 31 October 1751. Coincidentally, Tah-gah-jute (c.1725–80), a Native American also from Pennsylvania who turned against whites when his family was massacred, was also called James Logan.

LOL (Loyal Orange Lodge). A local chapter of the ORANGE ORDER, meeting in a hall usually adorned with the legend LOL followed by its number. The network of LOLs provided, and still provides, a rapid-response mechanism for rallying forces. The formation of the UVF in 1913 and the LARNE GUN-RUNNING were greatly facilitated by the existence of the lodges. There are currently about 2000 lodges in Ireland, 60 of them in the Republic, and for most of the time they fulfil the ordinary social purposes of village halls.

Lombard, Peter (c.1554–1625). Absentee archbishop of Armagh. He was born in Waterford and educated at Oxford and LOUVAIN, becoming professor of philosophy and theology there. In Rome (1598–9) he acted as Hugh O'NEILL's agent with Pope Clement VIII (d.1605) and wrote *De Regno Hiberniae Sanctorum Insula Commentarius* ('observation on the kingdom of Ireland, island of saints') hoping for papal support. Clement appointed him archbishop of Armagh instead of O'Neill's candidate. Conservative in outlook (he condemned the heliocentric theories of Copernicus), he was anxious to avoid dissension with the English authorities in the hope of ameliorating the condition of Catholics. In 1621 he made arrangements to return home, but stayed in Rome until his death. *De Regno*, published in 1633, was suppressed by Charles I.

London Assurance. An early play (1841) by Dion BOUCICAULT, using the pseudonym Lee Moreton. It reverses the usual stereotype by having the rustic characters superior in every way to the city-dwellers. It describes the ultimate success of the wooing of Grace Harkaway by Charles Courtly, and that of the worldly Lady Gay Spanker by the devious Dazzle. A successful Royal Shakespeare Company revival in 1972 set the play in the Regency period, giving its Victorian characters a more spacious ambience, and was memorable for Donald Sinden's performance as the rake Sir William Harcourt Courtly.

Londonderry. *See* STROKE CITY.

Londonderry, Siege of. *See* MAIDEN CITY.

'Londonderry Air'. The exquisite tune collected at a fair in LIMAVADY, Co. Derry, in 1851 by Jane Ross (1810–79) from a travelling fiddler called MacCormack. The composer is thought to have been the 17th-century harpist Ruairí Dall Ó Catháin, a member of the Dunseverick branch of the clan, who also wrote the famous love song 'Tabhair Dom Do Lámh' ('Give me your hand'). The epithet *Dall* indicates that he was blind, which may explain his profession. He was the inspiration for the character Rory Dall McMurrough in Sir Walter Scott's first novel *Waverley* (1814). Several songs have been written for the air, but the most successful was 'Danny Boy' (1913) by the prolific English lyricist Fred[eric] E[dward] Weatherly (1848–1929):

O Danny Boy, the pipes, the pipes are calling

From glen to glen and down the mountain
    side ...

This has become one of the most famous of Irish
songs, heard in karaoke bars from Tokyo to
Timbuctu.

Lone bird. A person who is completely alone
or abandoned. There is a proverb 'A lone
bird's a coward.'

'Lonely Banna Strand, The'. The title of a popular ballad about the landing of Roger CASE-
MENT an a beach near Tralee on Good Friday
1916 (Good Friday was, of course, in April,
not May, despite the following lines):

'Twas on Good Friday morning,
All in the month of May,
A German ship was signalling,
Beyond there in the bay,
We've twenty thousand rifles
All ready for to land,
But no answering signal did come from
The lonely Banna Strand.
        ANON.

Lonely Passion of Judith Hearne, The. The first
literary novel (1955) of Brian MOORE, written
in Canada after the author's long apprentice-
ship to his craft by means of journalism and
pulp fiction. The original title was plain *Judith
Hearne*. Judith Hearne is middle-aged, genteel,
impoverished and bibulous, surviving on an annuity bequeathed her by an aunt to whom she
has devoted her life. She loses her few remaining piano pupils, moves from cheap digs to
cheaper and pins her last hopes for romance on
a crude and exploitative 'returned Yank', James
Madden, her landlady's brother. When he shat-
ters her illusions – he too had illusions, that
she was a wealthy woman – she suffers a
crisis of faith (in which the craw-thumping, i.e.
ostentatiously and aggressively devout, priest
of the parish fails her utterly), followed by a
complete nervous breakdown. The novel, which
is bleak and deterministic, is complex and technically ambitious, combining many different
narrative modes, including the free indirect
style that became Moore's trademark – as did

his remarkable insight into the psyches of his
female protagonists.

Long acre. A term for the grassy verges by
the roadside used by impecunious farmers to
provide fodder for their cows, sometimes over
long distances.

Long Fellow, the. One of the nicknames of
Éamon DE VALERA, because of his height. Unlike the LONG HOOR, it is not exactly disparaging, but all Dev's nicknames, in one way
or another, attempt to bring him down to size.
See also DEV; BIG FELLOW, THE.

Long finger, to put on the (Irish *cur ar an méar
fhada*). A HIBERNO-ENGLISH phrase meaning
to 'postpone' or 'procrastinate'.

Long Hoor, the (i.e. whore). A nickname used
by Michael COLLINS (the BIG FELLOW) to describe Éamon DE VALERA (aka DEV or the LONG
FELLOW), a colleague in revolution. In January
1921 de Valera, himself recently returned from
a publicity and fundraising tour in the United
States, tried to persuade Collins to go to America in his place so that Collins could see for
himself the negative effect IRA violence was
having on the minds and hearts of Americans.
De Valera complained to Richard MULCAHY
on Christmas Eve 1920:

Ye are going too fast. This odd shooting of a
policeman here and there is having a very bad
effect, from the propaganda point of view, on
us in America. What we want is one good battle
about once a month with about 500 men on each
side.

Collins was not impressed by this argument,
so de Valera proposed that he should go to
America, flattering Collins about 'how moderate and full of commonsense' he was. Collins
was not taken in, feeling that Dev was just
trying to get him out of the way:

That long whore won't get rid of me as easy as
that.

Long Kesh. *See* MAZE, THE.

Longley, Michael (b.1939). Poet. He was born
in Belfast of English parents and educated at

INST and Trinity College Dublin, graduating with a degree in classics. After some years teaching he joined ACNI, retiring as director of combined arts in 1991. He has been linked with Seamus HEANEY and Derek MAHON as a member of a supposed 'Ulster School', originally associated with Philip Hobsbaum of Queen's University Belfast, but like each of them he has gone on to find a distinctive voice. His published work includes *No Continuing City* (1969), *An Exploded View* (1973), *The Echo Gate* (1979), *The Gorse Fires* (1991), *The Ghost Orchid* (1995), *Broken Dishes* (1998) and most recently *The Weather in Japan* (2000), for which he won the T.S. Eliot Prize. Other awards have included the Whitbread, the Hawthornden and the Queen's Gold Medal (2001). His work has neither ignored the Northern Ireland Troubles (and other greater evils like the Holocaust) nor been obsessed by them. His poems reflect his closely observed world, both urban (as in his native city) and rural (as in his second home in Co. Mayo). One might describe his work as having elegant immediacy.

> He would have been a hundred today, my father,
> So I write to him in the trenches and describe
> How he lifts with tongs from the brazier an
> ember
> And in its glow reads my words and sets them
> aside.
> 'Broken Dishes'

Long March, the. The name given to the cataclysmic journey made by Donall O'SULLIVAN BEARE, his family and retainers from west Cork to Leitrim in 1602–3. In Nationalist history the march has been a potent symbol of the tragic death of the Gaelic order.
See also PEOPLE'S DEMOCRACY.

Long Note, The. A lively and influential traditional music series broadcast on RTÉ radio (1974–90), produced initially by Tony McMahon (b.1939). McMahon, who was born near Ennis in Co. Clare, is an ACCORDION player of note, a musicologist and a sometimes trenchant critic of contemporary trends in

traditional music. He worked as a radio and television presenter with RTÉ (1974–98). Bill Meek (b.1937) succeeded him as presenter of *The Long Note* in 1975.

Longphort. An Irish term, literally meaning 'harbour for ships', which is used to denote the settlements established by VIKINGS in the 9th century in Dublin and Annagassan, Co. Louth, and in the following century in Waterford and Limerick. The word later came to mean any Viking fortified settlement.

Long, slow swim through a sewage bed, a. The description by Frank O'CONNOR of the Senate debate about the banning of *The TAILOR AND ANSTY* (from the preface to the 1948 edition).

Long Stone, the. A pillar erected by the VIKINGS near the place they came ashore in Dublin. It may have had a practical function (as a landmark for sailors), a symbolic function (by laying claim to the place) or even a ritual function (as an offering to the god Thor). The Long Stone was situated near the junction of modern-day Pearse Street and Townsend Street, and was described in 1663 as 'the longe stone over against the colledge' (i.e. Trinity College). It was known to be still standing in 1679, but its subsequent fate is not known. In 1986 a granite pillar sculpted by Cliodhna Cussen was erected on the presumed site of the Long Stone.

Looby. A HIBERNO-ENGLISH noun of uncertain derivation used colloquially to mean a 'clown', an 'idiot', either constitutionally or because of a particular action: 'You're an awful looby to lose your shirt,' a frustrated mother might say to her son.

Loodheramaun (Irish *lúdramán*, 'lazy, idle fellow'). A term of mild abuse in HIBERNO-ENGLISH, usually directed at a boy or young man less diligent than he might be.

Loody (Irish *liúdaí*, 'shirker'). A noun or adjective used in HIBERNO-ENGLISH to convey disapproval of a person who is idle or good-for-nothing. The word is also used to describe clothes that are loose or ill-fitting: 'That coat is very loody on you.'

Looka or **lookit.** A colloquial form of the word 'look', used in Dublin as an interjection or introductory word: 'Looka, that's my glass you're drinking out of.' It is also used for admonishment, 'Lookit, didn't I tell you to stop doing that?' Sometimes 'lookit here' is used for emphasis. It is an example of the characteristic Dublin tendency to add a suffix to a word to indicate familiarity, rather than abbreviating it (*see also* -ER).

Lops (Irish *lapa*, 'paw', 'flipper'). A HIBERNO-ENGLISH word for the paws of an animal or (disparagingly) the hands.

Lord deputy. The title of most of the chief governors of Ireland from the time of Henry VIII until the end of the 17th century. In the 16th and early 17th century the holders of the office were local lords, notably the Earls of Kildare (*see* FIT TO RULE ALL IRELAND). After the Kildare Rebellion of 1534–5 (*see* SILKEN THOMAS) Englishmen such as Sir Leonard GREY, Sir John PERROT and Thomas WENTWORTH were favoured. Some lord deputies, such as MOUNTJOY and Wentworth, were promoted to LORD LIEUTENANT while serving as governors of Ireland.

Lord French's Bodyguard. A nickname of the South Irish Horse because some of its members were assigned as personal guards to John Denton FRENCH during his period as lord lieutenant of Ireland (1918–21).

Lord Haw-Haw. *See* HAW-HAW, LORD.

Lord lieutenant. The title given from the end of the 17th century to the chief governor of Ireland (previously generally known as the LORD DEPUTY). The post was held by British politicians or sometimes, in the 19th century, by Irish peers. After the Act of UNION, the absence of a parliament in Dublin meant that the job of lord lieutenant was less onerous and less significant than before, and the British Parliament discussed the abolition of the office on several occasions. However, the office survived until the foundation of the Free State in 1922; the Vice-Regal Lodge in Phoenix Park was the home of the incumbent. The lord lieutenant was also known as the viceroy.

Lord of Cheltenham. *See* ARKLE.

Lord of the Dance. A spectacular post-RIVERDANCE Irish dance show, devised by and starring the Irish-American dancer Michael FLATLEY. It opened at the POINT in Dublin in June 1996. The show's title is derived from that of a religious folk song by the English songwriter Sidney Carter (1915–2004), sung in Ireland by the CLANCY BROTHERS and other groups. The music for *Lord of the Dance* was composed by Ronan Hardiman, and the story is based on Irish folk legend.

Lorry into, to. A Dublin colloquialism meaning 'to eat with gusto, greedily', usually pronounced 'lurrying': 'She really lorried into the chocolates.'

Lose the run of oneself, to. A popular colloquial phrase meaning 'to get carried away', 'to lose control of oneself'. It is sometimes used with intensifiers, such as 'to lose the run of oneself entirely/badly'.

Losset (Irish *losaid*, 'kneading tray'). A term used in HIBERNO-ENGLISH to mean a table spread with food, or a breadboard.

Lotto. Ireland's national lottery, first introduced in 1987 and administered by An Post (the post office). It proved immediately popular among Irish people. Lottery funds are distributed among charitable, voluntary and cultural organizations. The idea of an Irish lottery, however, is hardly new. One George Cooper in *Letters on the Irish Nation* (1795) noted that:

> The public streets of Dublin are filled with lottery offices beyond even the conception of a Londoner. These shops are adorned with everything which can catch the eye and delude the mind of the unwary. They are furnished with the most gaudy trappings, are generally papered with green and gold, and lighted up with such a profusion of the most expensive cut-glass chandeliers and girandoles, which throw the streets at night into a blaze, and glitter which cannot fail of surprising

the stranger ... I have often heard of the families of industrious mechanics and manufacturers driven by their frauds into the streets to beg for bread; but yet these are all trifles compared with the extent to which the evil of lottery offices is carried on in Ireland.

By the end of the 18th century, the government responded to pressure to tighten controls on lottery offices. It became more difficult to bet and it was illegal to 'insure' tickets for the poor, so lotteries declined as a result.

Lough Derg. A lake in southeast Co. Donegal, 8 km (5 miles) from Pettigo. The island of Oileán na Naomh (or Station Island) on the lake is famous as a place of austere pilgrimage, and has attracted pilgrims from Ireland and abroad since early Christian times. The island was the scene of St Patrick's Purgatory, in which he is said to have fasted for 40 days and was granted visions of Purgatory and Hell. Pilgrims are taken to the island by boat during summer weekends (the church and dormitories are maintained by the diocese and a small fee is payable) and spend one night without sleep, eating only dry bread, drinking only tea and performing prescribed penitential excercises. On the second night they are allowed to sleep, and they leave the island on the next afternoon, although they are not allowed to eat until after midnight. In an increasingly secular society, Lough Derg now attracts visitors for different reasons from before: it promises individuals an ascetic spiritual experience and a connection with other people of similar mind.

Lough Derg has figured in the work of such Irish writers as William CARLETON, W.B. YEATS, Sir Shane LESLIE (whose family owned the approaches), Sean O'FAOLAIN, Patrick KAVANAGH and Seamus HEANEY. In his 1942 poem 'Lough Derg' Patrick Kavanagh acidly comments on the motives of contemporary pilgrims:

Solicitors praying for cushy jobs
To be County Registrar or Coroner,

...

Mothers whose daughters are final medicals,

Too heavy-hipped for thinking,
Wives whose husbands have angina pectoris,
Wives whose husbands have taken to drinking.

'Lough Derg Pilgrim, The' (1828). The first published work of William CARLETON, which originally appeared as 'A Pilgrimage to Patrick's Purgatory' in the *Christian Examiner*. It is a picaresque account of the author's trip to Lough Derg, during which he is robbed by a confidence trickster. He deplores the superstitious religious content of the pilgrimage while admiring the scenery. The piece was reprinted in *TRAITS AND STORIES OF THE IRISH PEASANTRY* (1843–4) with some of the more anti-Catholic passages removed.

Lough Foyle (Irish *Loch Feabhail*, perhaps 'estuary of the lip'). A large sea lough in northwest Ireland into which the River Foyle flows at Culmore, 6 km (4 miles) from Derry. The 'lip' is the sandy bar of Magilligan Point, Co. Derry, which is less than a mile from Greencastle in Co. Donegal and which seems to want to make the estuary into an inland lake.

Loughgall. A village some 8 km (5 miles) north of Armagh. It was the scene of an ambush by the SAS of an ASU (active-service unit) of the Provisional IRA on 8 May 1987. The eight-man unit was wiped out when it attacked the unmanned RUC station. A passing motorist also died in the shooting, and his brother was wounded. The ASU included some of the most experienced IRA members of the East Tyrone–Monaghan Brigade. The inquest (not held until May 1995) heard that 600 bullets were fired by the SAS unit. The coroner abandoned the inquiry after the IRA families withdrew their counsel and walked out because they had been refused access to information.

Lough Gill. A small lake in Co. Sligo, just east of Sligo itself. One of its islands is INNISFREE, immortalized by Yeats. There is a novel (1883) by Patrick G. Smyth called *The Wild Rose of Lough Gill*, the title of which has given its name to one of the tourist boats on the lake. (Nearby Manorhamilton holds an annual Wild Rose Festival, a beauty contest.) The novel itself is subtitled 'a tale of the Irish war in the 17th century' and is more historical than romantic. It does feature, however, Kathleen Ny (sic) Cuirnin, fragrant granddaughter of the seanachie of Lough Gill, and after many adventures (including being abducted by a heinous Englishman), the last scene finds her arm-in-arm at a state ball in the Escorial with her Irish love, Don Edmundo O'Tracy of the WILD GEESE, as his lovely wife, Doña Kathleen.

Lough Gur. A horseshoe-shaped lake 18 km (11 miles) southeast of Limerick city. Lough Gur is also the name given to the area around the lake, which is rich in archaeological remains. The many Neolithic dwellings and burial places, dating from between 3000 and 2000 BC, were exposed in the 19th century when the water table was lowered by drainage: they include gallery graves, standing stones, stone circles, megalithic tombs, a RING FORT and a CRANNÓG in the lake. There are also some early Christian remains. The area was part of the lands of the Fitzgeralds of DESMOND, and the ruins of two Desmond castles can be seen. According to legend the last of the Desmonds is doomed to live under the waters of Lough Gur, emerging fully armed at daybreak each morning of one year in seven, until his horse's silver shoes are worn away. Mary Carbery's *The Farm by Lough Gur* (1937) is a retelling of the life story of Sissy O'Brien, whose family lived in Knockfennell beside the 'enchanted lake', recounted to the author when Sissy was an old woman.

Lough Neagh (Irish *Loch nEathnach*, 'Eochu's lake'). The largest lake in either Great Britain or Ireland (396 sq km / 153 sq miles). There are several legends about how it got its name; one suggests that Eochu was a horse god, lord of the OTHERWORLD beneath the lake, another that it was the name of a Munster prince who was drowned when a well overflowed to form the lake. Its central position means that five counties of Ulster – Derry, Antrim, Down, Armagh and Tyrone – touch it.

See also GIANT'S CAUSEWAY; ISLE OF MAN.

Loughryman (Irish *lucharachán, luchramán*, 'elf'). In Ulster folklore, a benevolent little person with magical powers:

> One pleasant day in June time
> I met a loughryman,
> His feet and hands were wizened
> His height was not a span.
> Says he, 'My lad you're lucky,
> I wisht I was like you;
> You're lucky in your birth star
> And in your fidil too.'
>
> JOSEPH CAMPBELL (1879–1944): 'The Ninepenny Fidil', in *Songs of Uladh* (1904)

Lough Swilly (Irish *Loch tSúilí*). A long sea inlet that separates INISHOWEN from the rest of Donegal. The name comes from the Swilly river (Irish *An tSúileach*, 'the one with eyes'). Known as the 'Lake of Shadows' because of the remarkable variation of the light, it was a useful anchorage for the Royal Navy up until 1938 when, as one of the TREATY PORTS, it was unconditionally returned to Irish sovereignty. It was in Lough Swilly that the FLIGHT OF THE EARLS began and Wolfe TONE was captured.

Louvain or **Leuven.** The provincial capital of Brabant in Belgium, site of a university (founded in the 15th century) that played a significant part in the Counter-Reformation. In 1606 Flaithrí Ó Maoilchonaire (?1560–1620), the Franciscan Archbishop of Tuam, persuaded Philip III of Spain to establish St Anthony's College, which was regarded as a kind of academic home from home for Irish scholars. Among notable members of the college were Aodh Mac an Bhaird (1593–1635), who became guardian of the college in 1626 and conceived the idea of collecting and collating all the surviving historical and hagiographical information about Ireland, inspiring Mícheál Ó Cléirigh to begin the ANNALS OF THE FOUR MASTERS in Ireland and John COLGAN to publish *Acta Sanctorum Hibernae* (1645) and *Trias Thaumaturga* (1647). St Anthony's was suppressed during the French Revolution and many of the manuscripts transferred to the Royal Library in Brussels.

Love in a Village. The best-known ballad play (1762) of Isaac Bickerstaffe (1733–c.1812), with music by Thomas Arne (1710–78). It is regarded as the first comic opera in English, and contains the song about the flagrantly self-sufficient Miller of Dee ('I care for nobody, no not I, / If no one cares for me'). Bickerstaffe was born in Dublin in 1733, and from 1755 to 1772 was a leading figure of the London theatre scene, regarded as the new John Gay (1685–1732). He was a friend of GOLDSMITH and may have suggested some elements of the plot of *She Stoops to Conquer*, elements also to be found in *Love in a Village*. An earlier ballad opera, *Thomas and Sally; or the Sailor's Return* (1760), includes an early example, if not the first mention, of a universally held nautical slander:

> How happy is the sailor's life
> From coast to coast to roam;
> In every port he finds a wife,
> In every land a home.

In 1772 Bickerstaffe was forced to flee to France, accused of sodomy, then a hanging offence, and spent the rest of his life in deliberate, if penurious, obscurity.

Lover, Samuel (1797–1868). Novelist and songwriter. He was born in Dublin and, resisting pressure to work in the family stockbroking firm, trained as a painter, specializing in seascapes and miniatures from 1818. A competent singer, he began writing songs and stories for the Dublin magazines. One of these was the ballad 'Rory O'More', which he extended into a popular if somewhat STAGE-IRISH novel and from which he devised a very popular and definitely Stage-Irish play.

Lover moved to London in 1833 where he became a well-known figure in the literary circles of the capital and a friend of Dickens, with whom he founded *Bentley's Miscellany* (1837–68) and for which he wrote HANDY ANDY. When his eyesight began to fail in 1844 Lover gave up miniature work and devised a one-man show which featured songs and monologues written and performed by himself,

rather in the manner of Percy FRENCH 40 years later. Of his 300 songs, many – including 'The Low-Backed Car', 'Molly Bawn', 'The Angel's Whisper' and 'Barney O'Hea' – are still performed. He received a civil-list pension in 1856 and died in St Helier, Jersey, on 6 July 1868.

Lover, like Charles LEVER, was disapproved of in the early years of the 20th century for his exploitation of 'comic Paddery', but the charge has caused the literary worth and genuine Irishness of both men to be overlooked.

> 'Now, Rory, leave off, sir: you'll hug me no
>   more,
> That's eight times to-day that you've kissed me
>   before.'
> 'Then here goes another,' says he, 'to make sure,
> For there's luck in odd numbers,' says Rory
>   O'More.
>   'Rory O'More' (1826)

See also LOW-BACKED CAR.

Lovett, Anne. *See* ANNE LOVETT CASE.

Low-backed car. A primitive wagon without wheels consisting of a platform set on the shafts and sloping towards the back for ease of entry and exit.

> When first I saw sweet Peggy, 'twas on a market
>   day;
> A low-backed car she drove, sat upon a truss of
>   hay,
> But when that hay was blooming grass
> And decked with flowers of spring
> No flow'r was there that could compare
> With the blooming girl I sing.
>   SAMUEL LOVER (1797–1868) 'The Low-backed
>   Car' (1844)

Low drop. A phrase meaning 'bad blood'. Unbecoming behaviour in a young lady might result in the criticism: 'There was always a low drop in you.' In *No More than Human* (1944), Maura Laverty's third novel about her period spent as governess with a wealthy Spanish family, she imagines her mother's strictures on her behaviour as taking this form. The term 'bad drop' is also used.

Low standards in high places. In May 1967,

minister George Colley addressed the FIANNA FÁIL cumann (branch) at University College Galway:

> Do not be dispirited if some people in high places appear to have low standards.

He was presumed to be referring to Charles HAUGHEY and TACA, and although he denied this after being reprimanded by Taoiseach Jack LYNCH, everyone continued to believe it. Colley opposed Haughey for the leadership of Fianna Fáil when Lynch resigned as taoiseach in 1979 and was roundly defeated. Haughey appointed him tánaiste (deputy to the taoiseach) and minister for finance in his first administration, but Colley made it clear that he would not give his loyalty to Haughey.

Loyalists. A term originally used during the American Revolution (1775–83) to describe those Americans who supported continued links with Britain. In Northern Ireland 'Loyalist' has come to denote a militant and vociferous (and often working-class) Unionist (*see* UNIONISM). The terms 'Loyalist' and 'Loyalism' are used by these Unionists as counterpositives to their polar opposites of 'Nationalist' and 'Nationalism'. They also frequently crop up in the media: a Protestant housing estate might be described as a 'Loyalist stronghold', or terror groupings such as the UDA and UVF as 'Loyalist paramilitaries'. When, as often happens, however, Loyalists do not approve of Her Majesty's government's policies and attack police and army, media voices will tend to ask, often in large headlines, 'Loyal to whom or what?'

LUAS. A light-rail (essentially tramway) network for Dublin, the construction of which was initiated after years of debate and official prevarication. It is expected to be completed, well behind schedule, in 2004. The construction of one of the two lines, to Sandyford to the south of the city, has meant in effect the restoration of the old Harcourt–Bray line, which was closed by a short-sighted government in 1962. In the years of the CELTIC TIGER Dublin's traffic problems had become so intractable that the LUAS, as well as making traffic much worse during construction by closing and blocking roads, seemed too little too late. *Luas* is the Irish word for 'speed' (though not for 'speedy'); its capitalization to LUAS is a piece of branding.

Lucca. A town in Tuscany 20 km (12 miles) from Pisa. Its patron is FRIDIAN.

Luck of Barry Lyndon, The. The first novel of the English writer William Makepeace Thackeray (*see* TITMARSH, MICHAEL ANGELO), written in tribute to Henry Fielding and serialized in *Fraser's Magazine* in 1844. Its picaresque, 18th-century anti-hero is an Irishman who begins life as Redmond Barry and becomes a 'gentleman' by marrying the Countess of Lyndon. He is finally ousted by his stepson and dies in Fleet Prison. Barry has elements of the STAGE-IRISH outlaw or fortune hunter and is shown by Thackeray to be completely lacking in morality or self-awareness. The novel was elegantly filmed by Stanley Kubrick as *Barry Lyndon* in 1975.

> Thackeray's *Barry Lyndon* is a very accurate sketch of the sort of thorough-paced scoundrel Ireland can produce, not when she is put to it, but quite wantonly, merely for the fun of being mischievous.
>
> GEORGE BERNARD SHAW, writing in 1913

Luck penny. A sum of money ranging in value from a few pence to a couple of pounds given back to the buyer of cattle, sheep or pigs at a fair or on the occasion of a financial transaction such as the letting of land.

Luckstone of the Butlers. A small sphere of rock crystal in a gilded copper mount that was a talisman of the Butlers of ORMOND for many centuries. It is now in the HUNT MUSEUM in Limerick.

Lúdramán. *See* LOODHERAMAUN.

Lugh. One of the greatest of the Celtic gods, known as Lámhfada ('long-handed'). Sun god and patron of art and craft, and foster-son of MANANNÁN MAC LIR, he is the grandson and slayer of BALOR OF THE EVIL EYE, whom he kills at the second battle of MAGH TUIREADH. The father of CÚCHULAINN by the mortal DECHTIRÉ, he fights by the Ulster hero's side when he has grown weak with hunger and the wounds inflicted by his friend FERDIA. His name is found in Lugdunum, the Celtic name for London, and in Ludgate, and in such place-names as Lyons and Leiden.

Lughnasa. The third quarter-day in the Celtic year, closely related to the British Lammas and celebrated on 1 August. The name comes from LUGH, a Celtic sun-god, whose bounty brought forth the harvest. The festival, which was celebrated on either the last Sunday of July or the first Sunday of August, was characterized by dancing and the wearing of berries and fruits, and survives in the modern Irish name Lúnasa (the month of August). It gave Brian FRIEL the title for his most successful play DANCING AT LUGHNASA (1990). Lughnasa is also called Garland Sunday, Whortle Sunday, Bilberry Sunday and FRAUGHAN SUNDAY. It was a popular day for local PATTERN days or visiting HOLY WELLS.
See also BEALTAINE; IMBOLG; REEK, THE; SAMHAIN.

Lúidín. An Irish word for 'little finger', used in HIBERNO-ENGLISH to indicate diminutive size: 'He was no bigger than my lúidín.'

Lump. A word used in HIBERNO-ENGLISH to denote a person, particularly a woman, of stout, sturdy build.

Lumper. The 'famine' potato, high in water content and poorly resistant to blight. The Irish had begun to sow this variety from about 1810 because of its high yield. The better quality 'apple' and 'minion' that had formed the usual seeds were gradually discarded.
See also GREAT FAMINE, THE.

Lundy. A name applied to any perceived traitor to the Ulster Protestant cause. Lieutenant-Colonel Robert Lundy was sent to Derry as commander of the garrison in December 1688, and after the closing of the gates by the APPRENTICE BOYS soon renounced his allegiance to JAMES II. He was appointed governor of the city in February 1689, but at the approach of James II's army in April advised surrender (see SIEGE OF DERRY). Dismissed from his post and in some danger of his life, he was allowed to leave the city in disguise. (One story has him, dressed as a woman, climbing down a pear tree that grew beside the walls.) He was detained for some time in the Tower of London, but maintained his allegiance to William III and afterwards served with distinction with the British army at Gibraltar. He died in 1717.

The association of Lundy's name with treachery is clearly unjust. His advice to the citizens to surrender was the correct one from a military point of view, and he assumed that no injury could be offered against the king's quasi-divine person. When the Apprentice Boys began their yearly celebration of the siege in 1814 Lundy became the chief scapegoat. A persistent and totally inaccurate piece of local folklore had it that he gave the keys of the city to the besiegers for a bap and a herring to ease his hunger. So in the way of such things his is the effigy that is burnt in the city each 18 December in memory of the shutting of the gates; at about 3 o'clock in the afternoon a giant moustachioed figure dressed in a rough approximation of the military dress of the period and stuffed with fireworks is set on fire. Meanwhile the more vigorous of Loyalist orators use the colonel's name to malign any who would deviate from current Protestant thinking.
See also MAIDEN CITY.

Lunny, Donal (b.1947). Musician. He was born in Newbridge, Co. Kildare. Successively a member of Emmet Spiceland, a late-1960s ballad group, PLANXTY[2], the BOTHY BAND and MOVING HEARTS, he plays bouzouki, guitar and bodhrán, and he has also been influential as an arranger and producer. He has collaborated with musicians of all kinds, contributed to many recordings and been a major force in folk and traditional music for over 30 years.

Luscan (Irish loscádh, 'burning'). A Munster

word for an area cleared from heath by burning; like so many words from the rich rural heritage it is now archaic.

Lusitania. A liner that was torpedoed by a German submarine off the south coast of Ireland on 7 May 1915, with the loss of 1198 passengers, including Sir Hugh Lane (*see* LANE PICTURES, THE) and 128 Americans, The sinking produced an outcry in the neutral USA and undoubtedly led to its entry into the First World War in 1917. Many of the victims were buried in Cobh and there is a memorial on the town's promenade.

Luttrell, Henry (*c.*1655–1717). Supposed traitor to the JACOBITE cause. A member of the Luttrell family whose seat was at Luttrellstown House at Castleknock near Dublin, Colonel Luttrell earned the contempt of his countrymen for his alleged betrayal of his comrades at the Battle of AUGHRIM in July 1691. After the Treaty of LIMERICK he joined his regiment to the Williamite army, thereby ensuring that he kept his estates – hence the subsequent allegations that he had entered into secret negotiations with the Williamite General GINKEL at the time of Aughrim. On the night of 3 November 1717 he was shot dead while being carried home in his sedan chair to his town residence in Dublin. A reward was offered but the perpetrator was never caught.

> If Heaven be pleased when mortals cease to sin,
> And Hell be pleased when villains enter in,
> If earth be pleased when it entombs a knave,
> All must be pleased – now Luttrell's in his grave.
> ANON.

Luxeuil. The site of COLUMBAN's most important monastery, founded *c.*590. The town lies 370 km (230 miles) southeast of Paris, its full modern name being Luxeuil-les-Bains. One of the great mother houses of European monasticism, it later adopted the Benedictine rule and survived until the French Revolution. The monastic buildings have been incorporated into a seminary and the church was granted the status of basilica in 1926.

Lynch. A verb meaning to execute summarily without due process, especially by hanging. The word is reputed to have originated with a member of the Lynch family, the most important of the Tribes of Galway (*see* CITY OF THE TRIBES). An apocryphal story tells of a 15th-century mayor of Galway, James Lynch, whose son had killed a Spaniard in the city in a dispute over a woman. The mayor, who was also the chief magistrate, executed his son himself because no one else would carry out the sentence he imposed. This story has the force of legend for tourists to Galway, although it has never been substantiated, and historians do not believe it to be true. Another story, preferred by Galway people, is that the word comes from Captain William Lynch of Virginia, who was indicted in 1782 for illegally punishing people. Lynching has traditionally been associated with the frontier states of the American West and with areas of racial tension in the South.

Lynch, Eliza (1835–86). Consort. She was born in Cork and emigrated to Paris with her family while still a child. After a short-lived early marriage to a French army vet she became a courtesan in Paris, the mistress of Don Francisco Solano Lopez, the eldest son of the president of Paraguay. When Lopez returned to Paraguay in 1855, Eliza accompanied him and bore him four sons. He became president after his father's death but never married Eliza. In 1864, during the bloody war in which Paraguay fought against Brazil, Argentina and Uruguay, she is reputed to have formed and led a female regiment, and was appointed regent of Paraguay by Lopez. He and her son were killed on the battlefield and Eliza was said to have buried them both with her bare hands. She was captured and later released, and returned to Paris where she died in 1886. Paraguay later declared her a national hero, and her body was re-interred in the capital, Asunción.

Lynch, Jack (1917–99). Political leader. He was born in Cork city and first found fame as a sportsman. A gifted footballer and hurler, he won senior ALL-IRELAND medals in a record six successive years, in hurling in 1941–4 and 1946 and in football in 1945. Elected to the Dáil for FIANNA FÁIL in 1948, he served in various ministries (*see* MARRIAGE BAN, THE) before becoming the surprise successor to Taoiseach Sean LEMASS on the latter's retirement in 1966. He led the country during a period of modernization (including entry to the COMMON MARKET) and turbulence (the Northern Troubles broke out in 1969). The most difficult and controversial period of his career was undoubtedly that of the ARMS CRISIS of 1970. He was out of office during the period of the Fine Gael–Labour coalition (1973–7), a period when he was dubbed 'the REAL TAOISEACH'. He was replaced as leader of Fianna Fáil and taoiseach by a rehabilitated Charles HAUGHEY in 1979 and retired from the Dáil in 1981.

'Honest Jack', as he was called, was undoubtedly the most popular politician of the century (since Daniel O'Connell, according to Fine Gael's Liam Cosgrave), liked for his integrity, his mild geniality, his possession of the common touch, his sporting prowess, his fondness for a glass of PADDY² and, not least, his ability to sing 'The Banks of My Own Lovely Lee' (*see* BANKS, THE) with feeling among his own people in Cork. His funeral oration by his protégé Des O'Malley in 1999 elevated his standing almost to sainthood.

See also FREE EDUCATION; STAND IDLY BY, WE CANNOT; TACA.

Lynch, Liam. *See* REAL CHIEF, THE.

Lynch, Patricia (1898–1972). Writer of children's books. She was born in Cork but was brought up and educated in London, Scotland and Belgium. She became a journalist and feminist, covering the EASTER RISING for Sylvia Pankhurst's *Worker's Dreadnought*. She married the socialist R.M. Fox in 1922 and settled in Dublin. Her children's stories, beginning with *The Turfcutter's Donkey* (1935), the first of a series, became international favourites, as did the 'Brogeen the Leprechaun' stories from 1947. She published nearly 50 books, including

a slightly fictionalized autobiography, *A Story-teller's Childhood* (1947).

Lynchehaun, James (*c*.1858–1937). Fugitive. Having assaulted his English landlady Agnes MacDonnell on 6 October 1894 because of a threatened eviction in Achill Island, Lynchehaun managed to avoid arrest with the help of local peasant women. He escaped to America and was tracked down to Indianapolis by British agents. Irish-American patriotic organizations took up his case and persuaded the American authorities not to extradite him, on the grounds that he was a political prisoner. Lynchehaun returned to Achill disguised as a priest and again eluded the RIC. The incident provided Synge with one of the elements of *The* PLAYBOY OF THE WESTERN WORLD and with the character of Christy MAHON. In an earlier draft of the play Synge made one of the characters say,

> If they did itself I'm thinking they'd be afeared to come after him. Sure they never laid a hand to Lynchehaun from the day they knew the kind he was.

Lynd, Robert [Wilson] (1879–1949). Essayist and critic. He was born in Belfast on 20 April 1879, the son of a Presbyterian minister, and educated at INST and Queen's College before becoming literary editor of the *Daily News* (the *News Chronicle* from 1930) in London. He was strongly influenced by James CONNOLLY and became an active member of Arthur Griffith's SINN FÉIN. He had also joined the GAELIC LEAGUE at its foundation. It was as a teacher of Irish in London in 1904 that he met his wife, the poet Sylvia Dryhurst (1888–1952), who was nine years his junior. (Their two daughters Sigle and Máire were brought up speaking Irish.)

Though bitterly regretting the EASTER RISING, Lynd campaigned vigorously for the reprieve of his friend Roger CASEMENT. He wrote a weekly essay for the *New Statesman* (using the pseudonym YY) and was a regular contributor to *John O'London's Weekly* (a magazine of mainly middlebrow literary articles and book reviews), which he edited in the five years before his death. Though he lived in England for more than 50 years, Lynd maintained a close interest in Irish affairs. He published more than 30 books, consisting mainly of collections of his elegant occasional essays, but his output also included a critically astute and deservedly popular account of 18th-century literary life, *Dr Johnson and Company* (1927).

The Lynds' house at 5 Keats Grove, Hampstead, became a gathering place for literary London and for Irish expatriates down on their luck. When James Joyce and Nora Barnacle were married in 1931 (*see* GREENE, GRETTA) the wedding feast was held at Keats Grove. Lynd died on 6 October 1949 and was buried at his own request in Belfast. At the funeral the Irish government was represented by Seán MACBRIDE, who was then minister of external affairs

Lyndon, Barry. *See* LUCK OF BARRY LYNDON, THE.

Lynn, Kathleen (1874–1955). Physician, Republican and reformer. She was born in Cong, Co. Mayo, the daughter of a Church of Ireland clergyman, and was one of the first women in Ireland to be awarded a degree in medicine – by the Royal University, Dublin – in 1899. She failed to find a hospital to accept her residency, the Adelaide Hospital in Dublin claiming that lack of 'female accommodation' prevented it from employing her. Because of this she set up her own general practice in her home in Belgrave Road in Rathmines and gradually became a supporter of the suffragist movement and – for humanitarian reasons – of the ITGWU.

In 1913 Lynn joined the IRISH CITIZEN ARMY and was appointed its chief medical officer before the EASTER RISING of 1916. During the Rising she and Helena MOLONY held City Hall for the rebels after the death of the officer commanding the building, Molony's fiancé Seán Connolly. She was imprisoned until the general amnesty of 1917 and again in 1918 as a member of the SINN FÉIN executive. She opposed the TREATY, and when she was elected to the Dáil in 1923 did not take her seat; there-

after devoting her time to medicine rather than politics. In 1919 she and a friend, Madeleine ffrench-Mullen, opened a hospital for children, St Ultan's, in Charlemont Street in Dublin, which employed only women (it is no longer in existence). She held clinics there until close to the time of her death in 1955.

Lynott, Phil (1951–86). Popular musician. He was born in England to a Dublin mother and a Brazilian father, and reared by his grandmother in Dublin. In 1969 he, Eric Bell and Brian Downey formed a rock band called Thin Lizzy, which had a breakthrough single in 1973 with a heavy rock version of the Irish folksong 'Whiskey in the Jar' (*see* JAR). A 1976 album, *Jailbreak*, and a single, 'The Boys Are Back in Town', marked the pinnacle of their success in Ireland and in Britain. Lynott married Caroline Crowther and wrote and sang a moving song to his baby daughter, 'Sarah', but the marriage foundered. Thin Lizzy split up in the summer of 1984 and Lynott died on 4 January 1986 of heart and liver failure after a drug overdose. He was buried in Dublin.

Lyons, F[rancis] S[teward] L[eland] (1923–83). Historian and biographer. He was born in Derry and educated at Trinity College Dublin, becoming provost of that university in 1974. He had previously held the chair of modern history at the University of Kent (1964–9). His best-known historical works are the admirable survey *Ireland Since the Famine* (1971) and his biography *Parnell* (1977). *Culture and Anarchy in Ireland 1890–1939*, his last published work (1979), was influenced by the outbreak of the Northern Troubles and has been both praised and excoriated as a REVISIONIST text. Before his sudden death he had been named official biographer of W.B. Yeats, a task that passed to his former student and great admirer, Roy Foster.

Lyreacrompane. A remote upland area between Castleisland and Listowel in the Stacks Mountains of mid-Kerry, the repository of much folklore and tradition. John B. KEANE spent his childhood holidays there and used the story of the Lyreacrompane matchmaker Dan Paddy Andy O'Sullivan as the basis of his book *Dan Pheaidí Aindí* (1977), translated as *Man of the Triple Name* (1984). He found the language of Lyreacrompane to be a mixture of Irish and English, and said in an interview:

> It had an extraordinary influence on my early plays and on my speech thereafter. For all its raciness it was still a very measured language.

Lyric Players Theatre. A theatre founded in Belfast in 1951 by Mary O'Malley and her husband Pearse, first in their own house then in an annex and finally from 1968 in a custom-built theatre in Ridgeway Street. Its ghostly patron is W.B. Yeats, all of whose plays have been staged there, giving rise to the gibe 'Hail Mary, full of Yeats'. It continues to offer work by most significant writers, Irish and international. The journal THRESHOLD, first published in 1957, is associated with the theatre.

Lysaght, Edward. *See* PLEASANT NED.

Maamtrasna Murders. The murder on 8 August 1882 of five members of the Joyce family, the parents and three children, in Maamtrasna, Connemara, Co. Galway, allegedly because of a dispute over grazing rights and internal SEC-RET SOCIETY politics. Of those accused of the crime, three were hanged and five sentenced to life imprisonment, it was claimed on perjured evidence.

Mac Ádhaimh, Roibeárd (1808–95). Irish-language scholar. He was born in Belfast to a prosperous Presbyterian family, and educated at INST, where he came under the influence of Gaelic and classical scholar William Neilson. In 1833 he was among the founders of the Ulster Gaelic Society (*Cuideachta Gaeilge Uladh*), and later both founded and edited the *Ulster Journal of Archaeology* (1853–62). Among the scholars to whom he was patron was Aodh Mac Dómhnaill. Their valuable work of collecting and studying Irish manuscripts was in preparation for an English–Irish dictionary, which was, however, never published.

Mac Aingeal, Aodh (1571–1626). Irish-language poet and religious writer. He was born in Downpatrick, Co. Down and became tutor to the sons of Hugh O'NEILL, Earl of Tyrone. He joined the Franciscan order in Salamanca in 1600, and in 1618, at the order's house at Louvain, wrote and published in simple and clear Irish, the text *Sgáthán Shacramuinte na hAithridhe* ('mirror of the sacrament of penance'). Mac Aingeal was very much a Counter-Reformation philosopher of his time, as his works on Duns Scotus show. Among his best-known pieces is the popular Christmas song, '*Dia do bheatha, a naoidhe naoimh*'.

McAleese, Mary (b. 1951). Eighth president of Ireland. She was born Mary Leneghan in west Belfast on 27 June 1951 and educated at Queen's University Belfast (QUB). A member of the Bar in both the Republic and Northern Ireland, she became Reid professor of law at Trinity College Dublin in 1975 in succession to Mary ROBINSON. She was also a current-affairs presenter on RTÉ television (1979–85). In 1987 she was appointed director of the Institute of Professional Legal Studies at QUB, a post she held until she was elected president of Ireland in 1997. She was also pro-vice chancellor of QUB (1994–7). In 1997 she secured the FIANNA FÁIL nomination to run for the presidency, although opposed by former taoiseach Albert Reynolds. She was inaugurated as president on 11 November 1997.

McAliskey, Bernadette. *See* DEVLIN, BERNA-DETTE.

'McAlpine's Fusiliers'. The title of a song by Dominic BEHAN, most famously rendered by Ronnie Drew in a recording by The DUBLI-

NERS. It evokes the life of Irish NAVVIES who built the Great North Road and other parts of Britain's transport infrastructure during the 1940s and 1950s when there was widespread emigration from Ireland. (A spoken prologue dates the poem in 1939.) McAlpine is Sir Robert McAlpine, a building contractor.

As down the glen came McAlpine's men with
　their shovels slung behind them,
'Twas in the pub that they drank their SUB and
　out in the Spike you'll find them.
They sweated blood and they washed down mud
　with pints and quarts of beer,
And now we're on the road again with
　McAlpine's fusiliers.
I stripped to the skin with Darkie Finn way down
　upon the Isle of Grain,
With Horse Face O'Toole, we knew the rule, no
　money if you stopped for rain.
McAlpine's God was a well filled hod, your
　shoulders cut to bits and seared,
And woe to he who looked for tea with
　McAlpine's Fusiliers.

Mac Amhlaigh, Dónal (1926–89). Irish-language journalist and novelist. He was born in Galway. His family moved to Kilkenny and it is from that city that he emigrated, leaving a bleak and impoverished Ireland for England in 1951. He spent the rest of his life in Northampton where he worked as a navvy (labourer; *see* NAVVIES). *Dialann Deoraí* (*The Diary of an Exile*) was published in 1960 and is the work for which he is best known. Although giving naught for the reader's comfort, it provided a welcome change from the predominantly rural style of prose writing in Irish, and became a modern classic. Mac Amhlaigh's other works include the short-story collections *Sweeney agus Scéalta Eile* (1970) and *Deoraithe* (1986). He contributed a column in Irish to the *Irish Times* for many years.

McAnally, Ray (1926–89). Actor. He was born in Buncrana, Co. Donegal, on 30 March 1926, the son of a bank manager, and left Maynooth seminary to join the ABBEY THEATRE company in 1947. He became one of Ireland's lead-

ing actors, appearing in 150 plays, including the role of Columba in *The Enemy Within* (1962) by Brian Friel. (He later played Hugh in the same author's TRANSLATIONS for the FIELD DAY company in 1980.) In a long career, which balanced stage, film and television, he proved himself a memorable actor, playing award-winning roles as the beleaguered Labour prime minister in *A Very British Coup* (1984) and as Cardinal Altamirano in the film *The Mission* (1986). He died on 15 June 1989.

Macánta (Irish, 'honest'). An Irish word, also used in HIBERNO-ENGLISH, and meaning 'honest', 'trustworthy', 'kind-natured': a child who is *macánta* is easy to mind; a dog that is *macánta* will not bite when approached; a cow that is *macánta* will not kick while being milked.

Macardle, Dorothy (1899–1958). Novelist and historian. She was born in Dundalk, the daughter of a well-known brewing family. She was educated at Alexandra College and University College Dublin, then taught at her old school until her arrest for Republican activities in 1922. *The Irish Republic* (1937), her account of the years 1916–23, though written from the Republican point of view (as is her booklet *TRAGEDIES OF KERRY*), is the fullest documentary account of the period. Apart from anti-Free State propaganda work, she wrote *Children of Europe* (1949), an account of the fate of refugee children after the Second World War. She also wrote novels and plays, one of which, *Uneasy Freehold* (1942), about a revenant, was filmed in 1944 as *The Uninvited* (its American title) with Ray Milland and Gail Russell. *Earth-Bound* (1924) is a collection of short stories that she wrote in prison; they are set in Ireland and reflect her usual themes, the fight for freedom and the supernatural.

Macaronic verse. A kind of verse in which words of a foreign language intrude into a native one. It was popularized by a monk of Mantua called Teofilo Folengo (1491–1544), who thought it the literary equivalent of macaroni ('a gross, rude and rustic mixture of flour, cheese and butter'). It existed in Ireland before the coming of the Anglo-Normans in the 12th century, but its mixing of languages was especially appropriate to a time in the late 18th and early 19th century when Irish was giving way to English as the vernacular of the majority of the population.

The Irish form of macaronic verse usually involved alternate lines or alternate verses of English and Irish, though sometimes the Irish or the English was reserved for the refrain. The mood, as with the 16th-century European form, was often comic, or at least light-hearted, but the macaronic topics covered the full spectrum of ballad material – love, roistering, crime and exile. In 19th-century examples of the genre such contemporary personalities as Daniel O'CONNELL and Father Matthew (*see* APOSTLE OF TEMPERANCE, THE) figure prominently. Wanting a means of writing what was essentially an oral tongue, the broadsheet printers used a form of crude phonetics in which the Irish is all but buried as in, for example, the last line of the refrain of 'SHULE AROON': 'Gotheen mavourneen slaun' for '*Is go dtéidh tú a mhúirnín slán*' ('may you be ever safe, my darling').

A typical example of the jollier macaronic is '*Slán agus beannacht le buaireamh an tsaoil*':

> There's an alehouse near by
> *Agus beimid go maidin ann.*
> [And we'll stay there till morning.]
> If you are satisfied
> *A ghrá gheal mo chroí*
> [Bright love of my heart]
> Early next morning we'll send for the clergyman
> *Agus béimidne ceangailte i nganfhios don tsaol.*
> [And we'll be united unknown to the world.]
> *Beimid ag ól fad a mhaireas an t-airgead*
> [We'll carry on drinking as long as the money lasts]
> Then we'll take the road home with all speed.
> When the reckoning is due, boys, who cares for the landlady?
> *Slán agus beannacht le buaireamh an tsaoil.*
> [A hearty farewell to the woes of the world.]
> ANON. (18th century)

Some macaronic verse combined Latin and Irish, appropriately in the hymn '*Deus Meus*':

> *Deus meus, adiuva me,*
> *Tuc dam do sheirc, a meic mo Dé;*
> *Tuc dam do sheirc, a meic mo Dé;*
> *Deus meus, adiuva me.*
> [My God, come to my aid,
> Give me your love, O Son of my God.]
>
> *Domine, Domine, exaudi me,*
> *M'ainim rop lán dot grad, a Dé*
> *M'ainim rop lán dot grad, a Dé*
> *Domine, Domine, exaudi me,*
> [Lord, Lord, listen to my pleas,
> May my soul be full of love for you, O God.]
> MÁEL ÍSU ÚA BROLCHÁN (d.1051)

Macartan (d.505). An early disciple of St Patrick, said to have been his bodyguard. Patrick ordained him as abbot-bishop of the see of Clogher, which once stretched from the Irish Sea to Donegal and still takes in much of southwest Tyrone and Monaghan. Macartan is the patron saint of the diocese and his feast day is 24 March.

Mac Art's Fort. An univallate ringfort on the edge of Cave Hill (440 m / 1200 ft) in Belfast where Wolfe TONE with Samuel Neilson, Henry Joy MCCRACKEN and Thomas Russell (*see* MAN FROM GOD KNOWS WHERE, THE) spent 48 hours in June 1795 before Tone went to America. There they vowed 'never to desist in our efforts until we have subverted the authority of England over our country and asserted our independence.' Later generations fancying that the hill viewed from the side had a resemblance to the profile of *l'empereur* named the peak 'Napoleon's Nose'.

McAteer, Eddie (1914–86). Nationalist leader. He was born in Coatbridge in Scotland but his father, who came from Fanad in Co. Donegal, soon moved the family to Derry. He worked as a civil servant (1930–44) before becoming an accountant. He was returned unopposed to Stormont as an anti-partitionist for Mid-Derry in 1945 and 1949, and as member for Foyle in 1953. After the O'Neill–Lemass meetings in 1965 he agreed to accept the role of leader of the official opposition Nationalist party. This he relinquished when the CIVIL RIGHTS MOVEMENT changed the nature of Northern Ireland politics. He was defeated by John HUME in the general election of 1969, and shortly afterwards retired from politics. He died on 28 March 1986. A burly, witty man, known universally as 'Big Eddie', he urged restraint during the rougher politics of the late 1960s and insisted that if Unionists had had the wisdom and grace to grant concessions earlier much trouble could have been avoided.

MacAuley, Catherine (1778–1841). Founder of the Sisters of Mercy. She was born on 29 September 1778 at Stormanstown House, near the site of Dublin Airport, but was later the ward of the Callahans of Coolock House. They at first disapproved of her 'Romish practices' but became Catholics themselves and left her the family fortune in 1822. She had become aware of the dire situation of the urban poor and in 1827 bought a 'house of mercy' in Baggot Street, Dublin, to provide a refuge for women and children. She had a band of volunteer helpers, but meeting clerical opposition at every turn decided to formalize the community. It was difficult for the rich 55-year-old to submit to the discipline of novitiate training (undertaken at the Presentation Convent) but her Order of Mercy was permitted by Pope Gregory XVI (1765–1846) on 24 March 1835 and given final approval five months before its founder's death on 10 November 1841. She lived up to her aims: 'to educate poor little girls, lodge and maintain poor young ladies who are in danger, that they may be provided for in the proper manner, and to visit the sick poor'. The order has spread worldwide, and with 23,000 sisters is the largest congregation of women in the Catholic Church. The process for the canonization of Mother Catherine is well advanced.

McAuley, John Henry (d.1937). Songwriter. He was born on a farm in Glenshesk, one of the NINE GLENS of Antrim, but was disabled in a childhood accident. He was taught to carve wood by the woman who employed his mother as a cook, and he was able to make a living at his craft in his workshop in Ballycastle. A skilled fiddle-player, he is remembered as the author of the ballad 'The Ould Lammas Fair':

> But the scene that haunts my memory is kissing Mary Ann,
> Her pouting lips all sticky from eating yellow man
> As we crossed the silvery Margey and strolled across the strand
> From the Ould Lammas Fair at Ballycastle-O!

MacBride, John (1865–1916). Revolutionary, husband of Maud GONNE and father of Seán MACBRIDE. He was born in Westport, Co. Mayo, on 7 May 1865, and as a young man was a member of the IRB and involved in the foundation of the GAA. On the outbreak of the Boer War in 1899 he joined an Irish brigade and fought on the Boer side against the British, rising to the rank of major, a title by which he was thereafter known. He married Maud Gonne in Paris in 1903, and after the end of the marriage returned to Dublin where he had a job with the Dublin waterworks. At the outset of the EASTER RISING of 1916 he joined the forces commanded by Thomas MACDONAGH at Jacob's factory, although he was not a member of the IRISH VOLUNTEERS. After the rising he was courtmartialled, and executed on 5 May 1916 – one of the more arbitrary decisions of the British, as he was not a leader of the rebels. It is thought by some historians that it was by way of reprisal for his having fought on the Boer side in 1899.

> The other man I had dreamed
> A drunken, vainglorious lout.
> He had done most bitter wrong
> To some who are near my heart,
> Yet I number him in the song;
> He, too, has resigned his part
> In the casual comedy;
> He, too, has been changed in his turn,
> Transformed utterly;
> A terrible beauty is born.
>
> W.B. YEATS: 'Easter 1916', in *Michael Robartes and the Dancer* (1921)

MacBride, Seán (1904–88). Politician and international jurist. The son of Maud GONNE and John MACBRIDE, Seán MacBride had a long and distinguished career as a Republican politician and human-rights campaigner, and was awarded both the Nobel Peace Prize (1974) and the Lenin Peace Prize (1977). He founded CLANN NA POBLACHTA in 1946 and was minister for external affairs in the first INTER-PARTY GOVERNMENT (1948–51). MacBride left politics in 1961 and subsequently became celebrated for his work as chairman of Amnesty International (1961–75) and UN commissioner for Namibia (1973–7).

McBride, Willie John (b.1940). Rugby player. He was born in Toomebridge, Co. Antrim, on 6 June 1940 and played for Ballymena rugby club. Capped 63 times for Ireland, 12 times as captain, he played in 17 tests on Lions tours to Australia, New Zealand and South Africa. He was coach to the Irish rugby team in 1983–4.

McBurney, William. *See* 'CROPPY BOY, THE'.

McCabe, Eugene (b.1930). Playwright and novelist. He was born in Glasgow and returned with his family to Ireland when he was nine. He was educated at Castleknock and University College Cork, and in 1964 took over the running of the family farm on the worrisome territory of the Monaghan–Fermanagh border. His play *King of the Castle* (1964), one of two hits at the 1964 Dublin Theatre Festival (the other being Brian Friel's *PHILADELPHIA, HERE I COME!*), is the story of a childless couple in which the husband arranges to have his wife impregnated by another man. In 1976 he wrote *Victims*, a trilogy of contemporary plays for RTÉ about the Northern Troubles in his violent area; he later developed the plays as prose fiction. His novel *Death and Nightingales* (1992), though set in the 1880s, is full of contemporary resonances.

McCabe, Patrick (b. 1955). Novelist. He was born in Clones, County Monaghan, and taught in Balbriggan and London. He won the Hennessy Award for a short story in 1979 and began writing novels, producing *Music on Clinton Street* (1986), about the breakdown of the old order of Irish life among young people. He followed this with *Carn* (1989), an anatomy of a Southern border town; having suffered a slump with the closing of the railway the town is restored to temporary boom by the entrepreneurial ability of a native son, but succumbs again to hopelessness as the Northern Troubles seep south. The townspeople are drawn with a raw sympathy, and the IRA characters have an appropriate cold ruthlessness.

The *Butcher Boy* (1992) was shortlisted for the Booker Prize and won the *Irish Times*/Aer Lingus Award. It became a play – both hilarious and grotesque – with the title *Frank Pig Says Hello*, and was made into an outstanding film (1997) by Neil Jordan. The character of Francie Brady, the ultimate victim of rogue genes, parental neglect and small-town prejudice, survives sexual abuse and various institutions to wreak a logical revenge on the town. *The Dead School* (1995) is also about madness and conscious mental deterioration. McCabe's humour takes some of the sting out of his black vision of Irish life. Recent novels are *Breakfast on Pluto* (1998) and *Emerald Gems of Ireland* (2001); *Mondo Desperado* (1999) is a collection of short stories.

McCall, P[atrick] J[oseph] (1861–1919). Ballad-maker. He was born in Dublin and educated at the Catholic University. Later he kept a pub that was frequented by Douglas HYDE and other members of the IRISH LITERARY REVIVAL, and he was one of the organizers of the first FEIS CHEOIL in 1897. His *Fenian Nights' Entertainment* (1897) was serialized in the *Shamrock*, the heroic tales told in racy modern language. He is remembered for his ballads of 1798, written for the centenary celebrations, notably 'BOOLAVOGUE', 'Kelly from Killane' and 'Follow Me Up to Carlow'. His *In the Shadow of St Patrick's* (1894) is a volume of reminiscences of old Dublin. He was a son of John McCall (1822–1902), who, although a grocer in Dublin, collected songs from his own home area of Clonmore on the Carlow–Wexford border: a manuscript containing more than 150 unpublished pieces is in the NATIONAL LIBRARY OF IRELAND.

McCann, Donal (1943–99). Actor. He was born in Dublin, the son of John McCann, a playwright and politician, and educated at Terenure College and the ABBEY THEATRE School of Acting. He worked on the stage, on television and in film in England and in Ireland, and is remembered in his own country for his mesmerizing performances as Frank Hardy in Brian Friel's FAITH HEALER in 1979 and as Thomas Dunne in Sebastian Barry's The STEWARD OF CHRISTENDOM. After fighting a long battle with alcoholism, McCann died of cancer on 18 July 1999.

McCann, Michael Joseph (1824–83). One of many writers for The NATION whose name is forever associated with one particular contribution, in this case the poem 'The Clan Connel War Song', which appeared on 28 January 1843 and which has been known since as 'O'Donnell Abu!' (abú is Irish for 'forever'). It celebrates a period in 1597 when Red Hugh O'DONNELL briefly controlled Donegal and most of northern Connacht during the NINE YEARS' WAR. McCann was born in Galway and taught at St Jarlath's, the junior seminary in Tuam. He later went to London and became a journalist, editing the short-lived periodical The Harp. He died in London.

> Bonnought and gallowglass
> Throng from each mountain pass!
> On for old Erin – O'Donnell Abu!

McCann Affair, the. A notorious case (1910), perceived as arising out of the recently promulgated NE TEMERE decree. A Belfast Catholic husband named McCann left his Protestant wife and took his children with him, with the approval of the Catholic Church. Coming as it did during the growing agitation against HOME RULE it seemed to prove that the Orange cry 'Home Rule – Rome Rule!' was the simple truth.

McCarthy, Justin (1830–1912). Nationalist politician and novelist. He was born near Cork city on 22 November 1830, and at the age of 17 became a journalist with the Cork Examiner (see PAPER, DE). He worked as a journalist in Liverpool and London, becoming editor of the Morning Star in 1864 and publishing several successful novels, which were especially popular in the United States. From 1871 he supported the IRISH PARTY under Parnell and was elected MP for Longford in 1879; at the same time he worked as a journalist and writer of novels, biographies and works of popular history, such as History of Our Own Times (1879). As vice-chairman of the party, he was among Parnell's chief opponents in the split of 1890, leading the majority of the MPs out of COMMITTEE ROOM 15 and holding the chairmanship of the party until 1896. Despite this, he maintained cordial personal relations with Parnell until the latter's death. McCarthy became almost completely blind in 1897 and left political life in 1900, continuing his literary work right up until the year before his death. In all he published almost 20 novels, including A Fair Saxon (1873), Miss Misanthrope (1878) and The Right Honourable (1886), with English as well as Irish themes. He died in Folkestone on 24 April 1912.

McCarthy, Mick. See CAPTAIN FANTASTIC.

MacCarthy Cup. The trophy presented to the ALL-IRELAND hurling champions, named after Liam MacCarthy, a businessman who had supported the GAA in Britain.

McCloskey, John. See FIRST AMERICAN CARDINAL, THE.

McClure, Sir Robert John Le Mesurier (1807–73). Arctic explorer. He was born in Wexford on 28 January 1807, the extra nominal appendages coming from his adoptive father General Le Mesurier, who sent him to Eton and Sandhurst. He joined the British navy in 1824, went to the Arctic in 1836, returning in 1845 in the expedition led by Sir John Ross to find Sir John Franklin and his crew who had disappeared in their search for a Northwest Passage. There were 15 such expeditions between 1848 and 1854, and in the one that left in 1850 McClure commanded the ship *Investigator*. It was separated from Ross's ship and was ice-bound until the spring of 1851, but during that year he discovered that there actually was a Northwest Passage. The *Investigator* was trapped again for two years and McClure was forced to lead his men across the ice on foot. They were eventually rescued by a Captain Kellett, and on his return to England McClure was knighted, given a bounty of £10,000 and had a strait in Canada named after him. He was later made an admiral and wrote an account of his Arctic expeditions in *Voyages* (1884). He died in England on 17 October 1873.

Mac Conmara, Donncha Rua (1715–1810). Irish-language poet. Details of his life are obscure and confused, but it is thought that he was born in Co. Clare and spent much of his life teaching in Co. Waterford, with a short period working as a clerk for the Church of Ireland. One of his best-known works, *Eachtra Ghiolla an Amaráin* ('adventures of an unfortunate fellow'), is a description of an emigrant's trip to Newfoundland, a trip he himself may have made in about 1745. In the popular mind he is most associated with the exile's lament '*Bánchnoic Éireann Ó*' ('the white hills of Erin, oh'), a feature of many Irish academic courses, recorded in an unaccompanied version by the group CLANNAD in the 1970s.

> *Beir beannacht óm chroí go tír na hÉireann*
> *bánchnoic Éireann Ó*
> *chun a maireann de shíolrach Ír is Éibhir,*
> *ar bhánchnoic Éireann Ó*
> *An áit úd 'narbh aoibhinn binnghuth éan*
> *mar shámhchruit chaoin ag caoineadh Gael;*
> *'sé mo chás bheith míle míle i gcéin*
> *ó bhánchnoic Éireann Ó*
> (Take a blessing from my heart to the land of Erin
> to the white hills of Erin oh,
> to all who remain of the descendants of Íor and Éibhear,
> on the white hills of Erin oh

to the place where the sweet voice of the birds sounds so lovely
like the gentlest of harps lamenting for the Gael;
It is my plight to be a thousand miles away from the white hills of Erin oh.)

McCooeys, The. A BBC Northern Ireland radio drama series based upon a working-class Belfast family. It ran (with short intermissions) from 1949 until 1957 and proved to be the most popular of all the region's offerings. (Lord Brookeborough, the prime minister, once rang Harry McMullan, programme director, asking him to change the time of the Saturday-evening slot to 7.30 because, since it was compulsory listening for all his household, his dinner was served half-an-hour late.) Its brilliant comic script was by Joseph TOMELTY, who also played the unadventurous grocer, Bobby Greer, and it advanced the careers of J.G. Devlin and Stephen Boyd (1928–77), the latter of whom appeared in many Hollywood movies including *Ben Hur* (1959). Soon catchphrases such as 'You're a comeejan' and 'Slup up your shloup' were heard everywhere about the province. Because of the nature of what was called 'the most contrary region', the programme, in other details remarkably true to Belfast life, made no mention of either religion or politics. Tomelty was involved in a serious car accident in 1957, radically limiting his career as a writer and actor, and the series closed.

McCormack, John (1884–1945). Tenor. He was born in Athlone, Co. Westmeath, on 14 June 1884. In 1902 he won the gold medal at the FEIS CHEOIL, and after a short tour of America in 1903 studied in Milan under Vincenzo Sabatini. He made his operatic debut in Savona in 1906, using the assumed name Giovanni Foli (his wife's name was Lily Foley). His British debut was at Covent Garden in 1907, when he sang Don Ottavio in *Don Giovanni*, afterwards making one of the best ever recordings of 'Il mio tesoro'.

McCormack appeared in opera houses all over the world with the leading stars of the day, but he admitted that he had little skill as an actor, and found a more satisfying career as a recitalist, in which role he was acclaimed as the leading lyric tenor of his time. Though his singing of tenor arias was impeccable, his programmes were filled with popular songs, including such favourites as 'Ireland, Mother Ireland', 'Mother Machree', 'I Hear You Calling Me' and 'The Old House' with which he finished his concerts. Rachmaninov, hearing him singing one of these at a New York party, said, 'John, you sing a good song well but you sing a bad song *magnificently*!'

McCormack was a source of tremendous pride to his fellow countrymen, especially exiles, and there were few Irish homes that did not have copies of some of his 500 records. He was made a hereditary papal count in 1928. Though an American citizen from 1919, he spent much of his time in Ireland. He died in Dublin on 16 September 1945.

McCourt, Frank. *See* ANGELA'S ASHES.

McCracken, Henry Joy (1767–98). United Irishman. He was born in Belfast on 31 August 1767 into a family of Huguenot extraction and was a manager at the family factory at 21. He founded the Society of UNITED IRISHMEN with Thomas Russell (the MAN FROM GOD KNOWS WHERE) in 1791 and was imprisoned in Kilmainham Jail (1796–7) for being a member of the society. On his release he returned to Belfast and assumed command of the insurgents at the Battle of ANTRIM on 7 June 1798 (*see* REBELLION OF 1798). Driven off by General Nugent, he and some companions hid out on Cavehill (*see* MAC ART'S FORT) in Belfast while his sister Mary arranged for a ship to take him to America. While on his way to embark he was arrested by the Carrickfergus Yeomanry and brought to Belfast. Refusing to inform upon his comrades, he was sentenced to death, and was hanged in the Cornmarket on 17 July 1798.

McCracken, Mary Anne (1770–1866). Radical and philanthropist. She was born in Belfast and was well educated for a woman of the time, being particularly interested in mathematics

and literature. She ran a muslin business with her sister Margaret (*c*.1780–1815), but found time for political, cultural and philanthropic activities. She was active in her brother Henry's UNITED IRISHMEN, and after his execution did her best to succour Thomas Russell (the MAN FROM GOD KNOWS WHERE) in the weeks following Robert EMMET's abortive revolt of 1803. After Russell's execution Mary realized that revolutionary feeling was at an end in Belfast and gave herself to a variety of good causes. She helped Edward BUNTING organize the BELFAST HARP FESTIVAL while he lodged in her house, and was secretary of the Belfast Charitable Society (1832–51). She was active in famine relief in 1845–7, and was one of the chief sources for R.R. MADDEN's history of the United Irishmen. She died, aged 96, on 26 July 1866.

McCracken Tribunal. A tribunal of inquiry into Ben Dunne's payments (*see* THANKS A MILLION, BIG FELLA) to Fine Gael TD Michael Lowry and to Charles HAUGHEY. The tribunal, chaired by Mr Justice Brian McCracken, was established on 7 February 1997 and reported on 25 August of that year. The report stated that it was 'quite unacceptable that a member of Dáil Éireann, and in particular a cabinet minister and taoiseach, should be supported in his personal lifestyle by gifts made to him personally'. There would be 'enormous' potential for bribery and corruption. Charles Haughey, after months of stonewalling, had begun to cooperate with the tribunal on 9 July.

See also CHARVET SHIRTS; FLAWED PEDIGREE; LOW STANDARDS IN HIGH PLACES.

McCrea-Magee College. A third-level educational establishment opened in Derry on 10 October 1865 as a Presbyterian seminary. It had been endowed by Martha Maria Magee (d.1846), a philanthropist, who left part of her fortune of £60,000 to the founding of a seminary that would be more convenient for northwest postulants than ASSEMBLY'S COLLEGE in Belfast. By 1909 it had a considerable number of non-divinity students and had begun to admit women. In 1905 Basil McCrea, one of the college's trustees, provided £7000 to endow a chair of natural philosophy, and on his death left £70,000 subject to his sister's life interest. She left a further £5000 in 1911, and in recognition of this generosity the college incorporated her name in the title. By arrangement with Trinity College Dublin, Magee students completed the final two years of their degrees there, an arrangement that led to some difficulties after 1920 and diminished the number of divinity students. In 1970 the college became a constituent part of the New University of Ulster, now known simply as the Ulster University (UU).

Mac Cuarta, Séamus Dall (*c*.1650–1715). Irish-language poet. He was born in Omeath, Co. Louth. As the *Dall* in his name implies, he became blind as an adult, but before that he laboured on farms in his own area. He spent his life in northeast Leinster, in the region between Carlingford Lough and the Boyne. Although educated in the classics and trained in the bardic tradition, his nature poetry and feeling for living things makes him unusual among the more formal poets of his time. The lyrics '*Fáilte don Éan*' ('Welcome Sweet Bird') and '*An Lon Dubh Báite*' ('The Drowned Blackbird') are his best-known poems, the former especially much anthologized. Like his friend CAROLAN the harpist, who had the same disability, he depended upon patrons for survival. In the dark years of the early 18th century, with the native Irish aristocracy in decline, he was reduced to beggary, but lived to what was in his era a great age.

Mac Cumhaidh, Art (*c*.1738–73). Irish-language poet. He was born in the Creagán area of Co. Armagh, the son of an impoverished small farmer. He had a HEDGE SCHOOL education and worked for some time as a teacher, but spent most of his life as a farm labourer and gardener. Known locally as 'Art of the Tunes', he wrote satires, AISLINGs and poems in praise of benefactors, and some of his poems remained alive as traditional songs for many generations. '*Máire Chaoch*' ('Blind Mary') is a mocking poem he wrote about the sister of the local parish priest. His most famous poem, '*Úirchill an Chreagáin*' ('The Churchyard of Creagán'), is an aisling in which he laments the demise of the O'Neills of the Fews, Gaelic patrons of literature:

Is é mo ghéarghoin tinnis gur theastaigh uainn
    Gaeil Thír Eoghain
Agus oidhríbh an Fheadha, gan seaghais faoi léig
    'ár gcomhair
Géagaibh glandaite Néill Fhreasaigh nachar
    dhiúlt do cheol
Chuirfeadh éide fá Nollaig ar na hollaimh bheadh
    ag géilleadh dóibh.
(The lack of the Irish of Tyrone is a cause of great
    grief and pain to me
And the heirs of the Fews mournfully buried in
    front of me,
The illustrious descendants of Niall Frasach who
    were always open to poetry
Would present robes at Christmas to the learned
    ones who served them.)

Mac Cumhaill, Fionn (pseudonym of Maghnas Mac Cumhaill, 1885–1965). Irish-language novelist. He was a native Irish speaker, born near Annagry in the Rosses of Donegal and educated at St Eunan's, Letterkenny, and for a time at University College Dublin, which he left to travel to America. He returned to Ireland in 1913 to help run the GAELIC LEAGUE summer school at Cloghaneely in Donegal and begin writing. His best-known book, *Na Rosa go Bráthach* (*The Rosses for Ever!*, 1939), was for many years a secondary school textbook, valued more for the quality of its Irish than as literature. Other novels were *Sé Dia an Fear is Fearr* (*God is the Best Man There Is*, 1928) and *Lascaire na gCiabh-Fholt Fionn* (*The Dandy with Golden Hair*, 1955). Books for children include *Maicín* (*Little Mac*, 1946) and *An Dochartach* (*O'Doherty*, 1935). *Gura Slán le m'Óige* (*Farewell to My Youth*, 1974) is a posthumously published memoir of childhood.

MacCurtain, Tomás (1884–1920). Revolutionary. He was born in Ballyknockane, Co. Cork, and became a member (and teacher) in the GAELIC LEAGUE. With Terence MACSWINEY he organized the IRISH VOLUNTEERS in Cork in preparation for the EASTER RISING, although no fighting took place in that city. After his release from internment he was active in the movement, becoming the first SINN FÉIN lord mayor of Cork. He was assassinated in his home by a gang of masked raiders – almost certainly Northern members of the RIC – in the early hours of 20 March 1920. The coroner's verdict blamed, among others, RIC District Inspector Swanzy for his death. (The hated Swanzy was shot dead by the IRA in Lisburn, Co. Antrim, in August 1920.) MacCurtain's assassination caused widespread outrage as an affront to democracy and gave a valuable propaganda weapon to Sinn Féin.

Macdara (*fl.*5th century). A saint who gave his name to an island off Carna, Co. Galway. Until recent times local boats dipped their sails thrice when passing it. There used to be pilgrimages to the island on 16 July and 25 September, both taken as the saint's feast days.

McDermott, Seán (1884–1916). Revolutionary, also known as Seán Mac Diarmada. He was born in Kiltyclogher, Co. Leitrim, on 28 February 1884 and in 1900 emigrated to Glasgow, where he worked as a conductor on the trams. After two years he moved to Belfast, where he became involved in the GAELIC LEAGUE and through meeting Bulmer HOBSON was drawn into the DUNGANNON CLUBS. He joined the IRB in Belfast in 1906 and the following year became a full-time organizer for SINN FÉIN, setting up branches throughout the country. Although lame after an attack of polio in 1912 he was an indefatigable worker, elected to the leadership of the IRISH VOLUNTEERS in 1913 and a member of the IRB military council that planned the EASTER RISING of 1916. He was a signatory of the PROCLAMATION OF THE REPUBLIC, fought in the GPO and was executed on 12 May 1916. McDermott is a shadowy historical figure in comparison to his colleagues CONNOLLY, MACDONAGH and PEARSE, but he is now regarded as having been an extremely influential figure in the planning and execution of the Rising.

MacDiarmada, Seán. *See* MCDERMOTT, SEÁN.

Mac Domhnaill, Aodh (1802–67). Irish-language poet, philosopher and scientist. He was born in Lower Drumgill in Co. Meath but spent much of his life in the north of Ireland. After a spell as a Protestant Bible instructor, he worked in Belfast from 1842 under the patronage of the scholar Riobeárd MAC ÁDHAIMH, teaching Irish and transcribing manuscripts. He wrote an Irish primer and a book on natural philosophy but is now best remembered for his poem '*I mBéal Feirste Cois Cuain*' ('In Belfast by the Harbour'). He later went to live in Co. Donegal and died in poverty in Co. Cavan.

MacDonagh, Donagh (1912–68). Poet and playwright. He was born in Dublin, as his poem 'Dublin Made Me' proclaims, the son of Thomas MACDONAGH, the poet and revolutionary, and educated at Belvedere and University College Dublin, where he was part of a gifted and witty circle that included Flann O'Brien, the actor Cyril Cusack and the poet Dennis Devlin. After six years at the Bar he became a district justice in 1941, but he continued his interest in folk ballads, poetry and versedrama, as well as broadcasting. His *Happy as Larry* (1946), a ballad-opera after the manner of John Gay, uses contemporary tunes, including a splendid song for Clotho, Lachesis and Atropos, 'Three Young Ladies from Hades', sung to the tune of 'Three Lovely Lasses from Bannion'. He also wrote *God's Gentry* (1951), a study of travellers, and *Step-in-the-Hollow* (1957), an Irish version of Kleist's *Der Zerbrochene Krug* (1808). He was co-editor with Lennox Robinson of the important *Oxford Book of Irish Verse* (1958).

McDonagh, Martin (b.1971). Playwright. He was born in London to parents from the west of Ireland, and spent holidays in Easkey, Co. Sligo, where his mother came from, and Connemara, his father's birthplace. He remained in

London after his parents returned to live in Connemara. *The Beauty Queen of Leenane* was first staged by the Druid Theatre Company in Galway in February 1996, with Marie Mullen playing the main role. It had a successful run at London's Royal Court, and McDonagh was made writer-in-residence at the Royal National Theatre. Three subsequent plays, all premièred in 1997 – *The Cripple of Inishmaan, A Skull in Connemara* and *The Lonesome West* – were staged together in Galway as the 'Leenane Trilogy' in June 1997, and subsequently in London and New York. With Conor MCPHERSON, McDonagh is regarded as the leading Irish playwright of his generation.

See also STAGE-IRISH.

MacDonagh, Thomas (1878–1916). Poet, playwright and revolutionary, father of Donagh MACDONAGH. He was born in Cloughjordan, Co. Tipperary, and educated at Rockwell. He was for some time a postulant but left in 1901 to become a teacher in Kilkenny, Fermoy and finally in Patrick PEARSE's ST ENDA'S SCHOOL. By 1911 he had graduated from University College Dublin and was appointed lecturer in English. Disenchanted with the GAELIC LEAGUE, he joined the IRB in 1913 and was one of the signatories of the PROCLAMATION OF THE REPUBLIC during the EASTER RISING. During the Rising he was in command of the forces in Jacob's factory and was executed with Patrick and Willie PEARSE on 3 May.

MacDonagh's poetry, strongly influenced by his Catholicism and the IRISH LITERARY REVIVAL, was published in various volumes, notably *The Golden Joy* (1906) and *Songs of Myself* (1910), which includes the much anthologized 'John-John', an admiring address by a settled wife to a traveller husband:

> I turned my face to home again,
> And called myself a fool
> To think you'd leave the thimble men
> And live again by rule,
> And go to mass and keep the fast
> And till the little patch;
> My wish to have you home was past
> Before I raised the latch

And pushed the door and saw you, John,
Sitting down there.

> THOMAS MACDONAGH: 'John-John', in *Songs of Myself* (1910)

Lyrical Poems (1913) contains 'The Yellow Bittern', a sprightly version of Cathal Buí Mac Giolla Gunna's '*An* BONNÁN BUÍ' which gave Francis LEDWIDGE the cue for his threnody for MacDonagh: 'He shall not hear the bittern's cry.' In his play *Metempsychosis* (1912) MacDonagh satirized W.B. Yeats as Lord Winton-Winton de Winton, but to Yeats, after the birth of the 'terrible beauty' at the Easter Rising, he was one who:

> ... might have won fame in the end,
> So sensitive his nature seemed,
> So daring and sweet his thought.

> W.B. YEATS: 'Easter 1916', in *Michael Robartes and the Dancer* (1921)

MacDonnell, Finola (*fl.*16th century). The mother of Red Hugh O'DONNELL. She came from Islay in the Inner Hebrides, the daughter of a powerful Highland chieftain, and was brought up at the court of Mary Queen of Scots. She married Hugh O'Donnell, Lord of Tír Chonaill in 1569, bringing with her as dowry a band of REDSHANKS. She was known as *Iníon Dubh* ('dark daughter') because of her reputation for ruthlessness in furthering her own power and the political career of the eldest of her four sons (b.1572). He was kidnapped in 1587 by Sir John PERROT and kept in Dublin Castle for four years. Unable to rely upon her prematurely senile husband, Finola became the effective ruler of the O'Donnell lands, arranging for the death of Red Hugh's rivals: Hugh Gallagher was murdered in 1588, and she defeated and killed Donnell O'Donnell in battle in 1590. Her private army, consisting mainly of Scottish mercenaries, ensured her son's inauguration as the O'Donnell in 1592. After the FLIGHT OF THE EARLS and the death of her son, she implicated Niall Garbh O'Donnell, her remaining sons' enemy, in Cahir O'DOHERTY's rebellion and was granted 600 acres (240 ha) at the time of the ULSTER PLANTATION.

MacDonnell, Sorley Boy (*c*.1505–90). Antrim chieftain. He was born of Scottish descent in Dunanayne Castle, Ballycastle, Co. Antrim, his forename in Gaelic, *Somhairle Buí*, translating as 'Samuel the sallow'. Most of his subjects were Hebridean Scots, and being one himself he had two sets of enemies, the native Antrim Irish and the English. In spite of frequent bloody encounters he usually managed to come to terms again with the latter, if only after stalemate.

MacDonnell's worst moment was the RATHLIN MASSACRE when on 26 July 1575 he had the grief of knowing that the Earl of ESSEX had sent Francis Drake to kill his family and confiscate all his treasure on the island where they had been sent for safety. Essex later reported to Elizabeth I that he 'was likely to run mad for sorrow, tearing and tormenting himself … and saying that he then lost all he ever had'. Essex had taken possession of the north Antrim territory of the Mac Quillans, a territory known as the Route, with relative ease, but the O'Neills proved more formidable adversaries.

Both the O'Neills and the MacDonnells, woefully ignorant of *realpolitik*, tried to use the Tudors, particularly Elizabeth I, to win local supremacy, and at different times Shane O'NEILL and Sorley made public submission, the latter describing his obeisance before a portrait of the queen in Dublin Castle as 'kissing the pantofle of the same' (a pantofle being a kind of slipper). The lord deputy, Sir John PERROT, though aware that in spite of all his efforts Antrim was 'a second Scotland', agreed to a wary truce in 1586 with the 81-year-old Sorley. The latter admitted that he had no legal rights in Ulster, and lived on in a kind of peace as constable of Dunluce and lord of the land between the Bann and the Bush until his death in the same house that had seen his birth. He was buried in Bonamargy Abbey in Ballycastle.

McDyer, James (1911–87). Self-help advocate. He was born on 14 September 1911 in Kilraine, near Glenties, Co.Donegal, and educated at St Eunan's College, Letterkenny, and at Maynooth. Ordained priest in 1937 he spent the war years in London and Brighton, served with initial reluctance on Tory Island and spent 20 years (1951–71) as curate in Glencolumbkille. When he arrived the area had no modern amenities, not even tarred roads, and, drained by emigration (with only five marriages a year), there was a dearth of young people. Largely by voluntary labour he built a community hall, and, using work camps staffed by university students on vacation, he began a group water scheme. His 20-year campaign was marked by both success and failure, not to mention bitter struggles with politicians, but the name of Glencolumbkille was emblazoned across the world. As the result of his efforts a dying region, refurbished as a holiday resort and heritage area, with appropriate small industries involving tweed, wool and fish, began to have a viable existence. The rugged curate became a household word throughout Ireland as a community restorer, and he was made parish priest of the district in 1971. He died at the presbytery in Carrick on 25 November 1987.

MacEntee, Seán (1889–1984). Politician. A native of Belfast, MacEntee took part in the EASTER RISING, was sentenced to death, reprieved and imprisoned. He was with the anti-treatyites in 1922 and was minister for finance in every Fianna Fáil administration 1937–54 and minister for health 1957–65. He also served, sometimes simultaneously, in the departments of health and social welfare, local government and for a short period during the EMERGENCY in industry and commerce. The poet Máire MHAC AN TSAOI (b. 1922) is his daughter.

MacEoin Seán. *See* BLACKSMITH OF BALLINALEE, THE.

Mac Gabhainn, Mící (1865–1948). Irish-language autobiographer. He was born in Cloghaneely, Co. Donegal, and hired as a spalpeen (itinerant worker) from the age of 9. By 15 he was a labourer in Scotland, and when he was 20 he emigrated to America, working the silver mines in Butte, Montana, and lighting out for the Yukon in the Klondyke gold rush after 1896. He returned home in 1902, a comparatively rich man. His reminiscences, recorded by the folklorist Seán Ó hEochaidh, became a book, *Rotha Mór an tSaoil* (1959) ('the great wheel of destiny'), from which he emerges as a shrewd, witty, engaging man. The book was translated as *The Hard Road to the Klondyke* (1962) by Val Iremonger (1918–91).

McGahern, John (b. 1934). Novelist and short-story writer. He was born in Dublin but brought up in Co. Leitrim, where his father was a garda sergeant. This provided the material for his first novel *The Barracks* (1963). He was educated at St Patrick's College, Dublin, and University College Dublin, and taught in the city until the publication of his controversial novel *The DARK* (1965) caused him to be dismissed. Though he was refused reinstatement, the notoriety attached to the case virtually finished the system of narrow literary censorship that had bedevilled the state since 1929. After much time spent travelling and teaching abroad, he is again resident in rural Leitrim.

Other novels include *The Leavetaking* (1974),which has some elements of autobiography, and AMONGST WOMEN (1990), which was a critical and commercial success, being shortlisted for the Booker Prize. Like his excellent short stories, collected in 1992, his novels are remarkable for the sociological accuracy of their rendering of Irish provincial life and for their unrelenting honesty, occasionally mitigated by quirky humour.

That They May Face the Rising Sun (2002) recounts the small happenings of a year in a lakeside community, in which the BLOW-INS, Joe and Kate Ruttledge, learn about life and death – and evil too – from the actions of members of the community and the wisdom of their neighbours.

When they were gathering the tools to go to the village for the customary gravediggers' drinks, Ruttledge asked Patrick Ryan, 'Does it make a great difference that his head lies in the west?'

'It makes every difference, lad, or it makes no difference.'

'In what way?'

'You should know, lad,' he said, enjoying such full possession of the graveyard that even John Quinn's presence went unheeded. 'You went to school by all accounts long enough to know.'

'The world is full of things I don't know,' Ruttledge said.

'He sleeps with his head in the west ... so that when he wakes he may face the rising sun.' Looking from face to face and drawing himself to his full height, Patrick Ryan stretched his arm dramatically towards the east. 'We look to the resurrection of the dead.'

JOHN MCGAHERN: *That They May Face the Rising Sun* (2002)

MacGearailt, Piaras (1702–95). Irish-language poet. He was born in the Ballymacoda area of Co. Cork, to a family that had lost its estates in the previous generation. He received a good education, perhaps in Spain. The POPERY LAWS obliged him to convert to the Protestant religion to keep possession of the family farm, but he nevertheless wrote religious poetry and conveys his remorse in '*A Chogair, a Charaid*' ('Listen, Friend'). The poem for which he is best known is the Jacobite anthem, '*Rosc Catha na Mumhan*' ('The Battle Song of Munster'), in which he envisages a French fleet invading Ireland, with a Jacobite monarch (Caesar in the poem) on board. It is sung to a rousing martial tune.

D'aithníos féin gan bhréig ar fhuacht
's ar anfa Théitis taobh le cuan
ar chanadh na n-éan go séanmar suairc
go gcasfadh mo Shaesar glé gan ghruaim.
Measain gur subhach don Mumhain an fhuaim
's dá maireann go dubhach de chrú na mbua
torann na dtonn
le sleasaibh na long
'tá ag tarraingt go teann 'nár gceann ar cuaird
(I recognized for sure by the cold,
and by the storm Thetis made by the harbour,
by the birds singing their songs so sweetly,

that my bright Caesar would come back exultant.
I know the sound is sweet to Munster
And to the descendants of the mighty who now
   live in servitude;
The noise of the waves
Along the sides of the ships
That are drawing strongly on their way to us.)

McGee, Thomas D'Arcy (1825–68). Poet and Young Irelander. He was born in Carlingford, Co. Louth, on 13 April 1825 and reared in Wexford. He emigrated to America at age 17 and was editor of the *Boston Pilot* by 1846. His writings on Ireland were described by Daniel O'CONNELL as 'the inspired utterances of a young exiled boy'. He returned to Ireland to engage strongly in the YOUNG IRELAND movement, writing for *The* NATION and having to escape in disguise after his involvement in the Smith O'Brien rising of 1848 (*see* WIDOW McCORMICK'S CABBAGE PATCH). During the next decade he lost his belief in revolutionary politics, moved to Canada and became a prominent constitutional reformer. He was assassinated on 7 April 1868 in Ottawa after a vigorous denunciation of a threatened FENIAN invasion of Canada.

> Long, long ago, beyond the misty space
> Of twice a thousand years,
> In Erin old there dwelt a mighty race,
> Taller than Roman spears.
>
> THOMAS D'ARCY MCGEE: 'The Celts' (1869)

McGee Case, the. A constitutional case around the issue of contraception. In 1973 Mary McGee brought a constitutional case after some spermicide she had ordered from the UK was confiscated by customs officials: the privacy of married couples was at issue. The Supreme Court found in her favour in a landmark decision: Mr Justice Walsh decided that Articles 41–3 of the CONSTITUTION OF 1937 meant that 'the individual has natural human rights over which the state has no authority; and the family, as the natural primary and fundamental group of society, has rights as such which the state cannot control.'
See also IRISH SOLUTION TO A PARTICULARLY IRISH PROBLEM, AN.

McGeeney, Kieran. *See* THERE'S ONE FAIR COUNTY IN IRELAND.

MacGill, Patrick (1889–1963). Novelist. He was born in Maas, near Glenties, Co. Donegal, the 'Glenmornan' of his novels. He was hired out in Tyrone at 12 and went to Scotland as a tattie-hoker (someone who pulls potatoes) at 14. As he grew older and stronger he worked as a navvy on railways and building sites, filling his sparse leisure with wide reading and writing.

MacGill's early poetry, *Gleanings from a Navvy Notebook* (1911), *Songs of a Navvy* (1911) and *Songs of the Dead End* (1912), which he hawked from door to door, earned him the sobriquet the 'Navvy Poet'. His verse is effective and accessible, but his real literary achievement is to be found in the companion novels *Children of the Dead End* (1914) and *The Rat Pit* (1915), describing the life that he and other migrant workers experienced. These caused a sensation on publication; their strong socialist and anticlerical material had them denounced from many pulpits. The first, which autobiographically ends on a fairly optimistic note, describes the appalling conditions under which the Donegal lad Dermod works. *The Rat Pit*, which tells the story of his sweetheart Norah, is much more grim, describing her seduction, prostitution and death.

MacGill was appointed editor of ancient manuscripts in the library of Windsor Castle but served as a stretcher-bearer with the London Irish Rifles during the First World War and wrote about its horrors in the novels *The Great Push* (1916) and *The Red Horizon* (1916). *Glenmornan* (1919) is also autobiographical, describing the reaction in Ireland to the scandalous work of the writer, while *Lanty Hanlon* (1922) is a rural comedy set on the Gweebarra River, near his birthplace. MacGill went to America, married there and died of multiple sclerosis in Massachusetts on the same day as Aldous Huxley, C.S. Lewis and John F. Kennedy. The Patrick MacGill Summer School (established in 1981), dedicated to literature and politics, is held annually in Glenties.

Bad cess to the boats! For its few they take back
of the many they take away.

Children of the Dead End (1914)

MacGillicuddy Reeks. A mountain range west of
Killarney in Co. Kerry, known locally simply
as 'the Reeks'. It contains the highest peaks in
the country, including CARRANTUOHILL. The
mountains are very popular among climbers,
both amateur and professional, combining technical challenge with unsurpassed scenery. The
'Reeks Walk', held on a suitable Sunday in
summer, encompasses all twelve main peaks
of the range.

See also KERRY MOUNTAIN RESCUE TEAM.

McGilligan, Patrick (1889–1979). Politician. He
was born in Coleraine, Co. Derry, and educated
at Clongowes Wood and University College
Dublin (UCD). A barrister, he was professor
of law at UCD from 1934. He was elected TD
in successive general elections (1923–51) and
became minister for industry and commerce in
succession to Joseph McGrath (*see* ARMY
MUTINY), promoting the Shannon hydroelectric scheme at ARDNACRUSHA that became
known as 'Mr McGilligan's White Elephant',
and also promoting the ESB – the Electricity
Supply Board, a state monopopy established by
the CUMANN NA NGHAEDHEAL government in
1927 to run the country's electricity generating
stations; it is still the main supplier of electricity in Ireland. He was minister for finance in
the first INTERPARTY GOVERNMENT (1948–
51) and established the Industrial Development
Authority (IDA). After he retired from the
cabinet, he served as attorney-general.

Mac Giolla, Tomás (b.1924). Politician. He was
born in Nenagh, Co. Tipperary, and educated
at University College Dublin, becoming president of Official SINN FÉIN after the split with
the Provisionals in January 1970. He was elected TD for the Dublin West constituency for
Sinn Féin the Workers' Party in November 1982
and held this seat (for the WORKERS' PARTY
after 1983) until the general election of 1992,
refusing to follow Proinsias DE ROSSA and the

other Workers' Party TDs into Democratic Left.
Mac Giolla was a tireless constituency worker,
and no one could doubt his earnest commitment to working-class socialism. He served as
lord mayor of Dublin in 1993.

Mac Giolla Gunna, Cathal Buí. *See* 'BONNÁN
BUÍ, AN'.

McGowan, Shane (b.1957). Pop singer and songwriter. He was born on Christmas Day 1957 in
Kent, when his parents were visiting relatives.
The first six years of his life were spent on a
farm in Puckhaun, Co. Tipperary, before the
family moved to London. In 1972 he was expelled from school for possession of drugs.
After seeing *The Sex Pistols* in concert in 1976
he became involved in the punk movement,
playing and recording with various punk bands
while working in a record store. One of these
bands, the Millwall Chainsaws, developed into
POGUE MAHONE, a name derived from the
Irish vulgarism; the band were later known as
The POGUES. They had their first gig in October 1982, playing a manic hybrid of punk
and Irish folk (often with a Republican edge),
and achieved considerable success and media
notoriety for their originality, for McGowan's
passionate, gravelly voice, and also for his unremitting abuse of alcohol and other substances. His association with The Pogues ended
in November 1991 on a tour in Japan, during
which he either left the band or was sacked.
Over the years McGowan has collaborated with
a variety of leading singers, including Christy
MOORE, Kirsty McColl (with 'Fairy Tale of
New York'; *see* ARSE, TO DO IN ONE'S) and
Sinéad O'CONNOR, and recorded with a backing band called The Popes.

McGrath, Joseph. *See* ARMY MUTINY; IRISH
HOSPITALS SWEEPSTAKES; WATERFORD GLASS.

Mac Grianna, Seosamh (1901–90). Novelist and
short-story writer. He was born in Rannafast,
the brother of MÁIRE (pseudonym of Séamus Ó
Grianna, the different surnames resulting from
a family feud). He qualified as a teacher at St
Patrick's College, Drumcondra, Dublin, in 1921

and taught for some time at home. He took the anti-Treaty side in the CIVIL WAR and, interned by Free State forces, found teaching jobs hard to get on his release in 1924. He worked for An GÚM as a translator of English books, most of them pretty undistinguished, *Muintir an Oileáin*, his version of Peadar O'DONNELL's *Islanders* (1927), being an honourable exception. *An Grá agus an Gruaim* ('love and gloom', 1929), his collection of short stories with a historical novella, showed a command of literary Irish that did not depend upon local lore as did the popular work of Máire. He wrote literary criticism in *Padraig Ó Conaire agus Aistí Eile* ('Padraig Ó Conaire and other Essays', 1936), historical biography in *Eoghan Rua Ó Néill* (1931) and a novel *An Droma Mór* ('the big drum') which languished in the Gúm files from 1933 till 1969 when a revival of interest in his work led to its publication and an award from the Irish-American Cultural Institute. Mac Grianna's last book, the autobiographical apologia *Mo Bhealach Féin* ('my road', 1940), contains the words that marked the end of his writing life: '*Thráigh an tobar sa bhliain 1935*' ('the well dried in 1935'). Thereafter his health failed and he spent the next 50 years in St Conall's mental hospital, Letterkenny.

> *Is óg i mo shaol a chonaic mé uaim é, an ród sin a bhí le mo mhian, an bealach cas geal a raibh sleasa cnoc ar gach taobh de, a ba deise ná aon cnoc dá bhfuil i gceol.*
>
> (I was young when I saw before me the road of my wishes, a glittering highway that wound its way through sloping hills, more beautiful than any celebrated in song.)
>
> *Mo Bhealach Féin* (1940)

McGuinness, Frank (b.1953). Playwright. He was born in Buncrana, Co. Donegal, and educated at University College Dublin, taking an MPhil in medieval studies, and then became a member of the staff of the English department at Maynooth. His early plays – *Factory Girls* (1983), set in a Buncrana shirt factory with a cast almost entirely of women, and OBSERVE THE SONS OF ULSTER MARCHING TOWARDS

THE SOMME (1985), a sympathetic study of soldiers of the Ulster Division in the First World War – might be called conventional, but later work is more experimental: *Innocence* (1986) about the troubled life of the painter Caravaggio (1573–1610); *Carthaginians* (1988), taking its inspiration from the events of BLOODY SUNDAY 1972; and *Someone Who'll Watch over Me* (1992), inspired by Brian KEENAN's book *An Evil Cradling* (1992) based upon his experiences as a hostage in Beirut. McGuinness has also produced versions of plays by Ibsen, Chekhov and Lorca, and wrote the scenario for the film (1998) based upon Brian Friel's DANCING AT LUGHNASA.

McGuinness, Martin (b.1950). Republican activist. He was born on 23 May 1950 in the Nationalist area of Derry, loosely called the BOGSIDE, and worked as a butcher until becoming involved the Troubles. He has been vice-president of SINN FÉIN since 1983, and though active for many years in the armed struggle became like Gerry ADAMS a strong supporter of the political process. His reputation was such that he was included in the delegation that met William WHITELAW (1918–99), secretary of state for Northern Ireland, in July 1972, a meeting that led to a brief ceasefire. He became leader of the Provisional IRA in Derry in 1971, and, along with Adams (his equivalent in Belfast), he gradually shifted control of the movement away from Dublin.

As the peace process, in which McGuinness played a major part, continued on its tortuous and snail-paced way, his public profile – neat in appearance and terse in conversation – increased significantly. By the time of the GOOD FRIDAY AGREEMENT, he and Adams had emerged as the public figures of the movement, adept at defining, to their own satisfaction, their complicated relationship with the IRA. He is the Sinn Féin liaison representative with General John de Chastelain of the DECOMMISSIONING body. In 1998 he was elected to the Northern Ireland Assembly (set up by the Good Friday Agreement), and holds the education portfolio; he has proved himself an able if controversial minister when the power-sharing executive is not in suspension. He has been Westminster MP for Mid-Ulster since 1997, but under the policy of ABSTENTIONISM has not taken his seat.

> Martin was standing at the bottom of the stairwell surrounded by women. He looked like a pop-star standing there blinking at them. The guy undoubtedly has charisma and presence. It was remarkable; he went from being bogeyman to getting accepted by people and being found fascinating on that human level.
>
> LIAM CLARKE AND KATHRYN JOHNSTON: *From Guns to Government* (2001)

McGurk's Pub. A pub in North Queen Street, Belfast, which was the scene of an early UVF explosion. A bomb placed in the bar exploded without any warning on 4 December 1971, killing 15 people and injuring 13. It was the city's worst fatality-count up to that date. Responsibility was claimed by 'Empire Loyalists'.

Macha. In Irish mythology, a goddess who appears in several incarnations: as a deity, another name for the MÓRRIGÁN; the wife of NEMED; and the mysterious wife of Cruinniuc Mac Agnomian, the builder of EMAIN MACHA and the founder of the first hospital in Ireland, a deed commemorated by a sculpture at the Northwest Hospital, Altnagelvin, Derry. Cruinniuc is an Ulster chieftain who after being widowed takes in a mysterious stranger as his second wife. When pregnant with twins (*emain* in Irish) she is made to race against the king's horses because of an unfortunate boast of her husband. She wins the race but dies giving birth at Emain Macha; her dying curse condemns all Ulster males for 81 generations to suffer the pangs of childbirth for five days and four nights at the times of Ulster's greatest peril. As a result of Macha's curse CÚCHULAINN, not being of Ulster birth, was alone able to fight the forces of Connacht during the TÁIN BÓ CUAILNGE war. Macha Mong Ruadh (Red-haired Macha), then high queen, is credited with the building of NAVAN FORT in 337 BC and Árd Macha (ARMAGH).

Máchail. An Irish word for 'stain', 'defect' or 'disfigurement' (for instance on a baby). The word is now used in HIBERNO-ENGLISH to mean an 'inconvenience', an 'unfortunate turn of events', a 'damage' or 'grievance'. It derives from the Latin *macula*, 'stain'.

MacHale, John (1791–1881). Nationalist archbishop. He was born in the Irish-speaking district of Tirawley, Co. Mayo, on 6 March 1791 and baptized by a priest who was hanged after the Rebellion of 1798. After ordination in Maynooth in 1814 he remained as professor of theology until appointment as Bishop of Killala in 1825. While at Maynooth he published a number of public letters, signed 'Heirophilos', attacking the TITHE system. It was obvious that he and Daniel O'CONNELL should find common ground, and he was vocal in his support of CATHOLIC EMANCIPATION and of general non-compliance with British administration. His opposition to the NATIONAL SCHOOLS system, which the other bishops accepted, was a miscalculation based upon his fears of proselytism and the loss of the Irish language.

Appointed Archbishop of Tuam in 1834 (despite strong government opposition) MacHale was Paul CULLEN's chief adversary in the Irish hierarchy, holding out against Newman's appointment as head of the CATHOLIC UNIVERSITY because he was English, and opposing the doctrine of papal infallibility at the First Vatican Council (1870). His charismatic but headstrong leadership and his deliberately direct and undiplomatic style in public affairs showed him out of step with the *zeitgeist*, especially as he grew older and his influence diminished. His writings, mainly in Irish, included poetry, textbooks and works of devotion. He translated the *Iliad* (1844–71) and the *Irish Melodies* of Thomas MOORE (1871). At 90 he still preached a Sunday sermon in Tuam cathedral and died there on 7 November 1881.

> For forty-six years the people of Ireland have been feeding those of England with the choicest

produce of their agriculture and pasture; and while they thus exported their wheat and their beef in profusion, their own became gradually deteriorated in each successive year, until the mass of the peasantry was exclusively thrown on the potato.

Letter to Lord John Russell, 15 December 1846

Machree (Irish *mo chroí*, 'my heart'). A still common HIBERNO-ENGLISH term of endearment, notoriously preserved in the Irish-American song 'Mother Machree' (1910) by Rida Johnson Young (1869–1926), with music by Ernest Ball (1878–1927) in collaboration with Chauncey Olcott (*see* 'MY WILD IRISH ROSE'). It was a favourite with the tenor John MCCORMACK, who invariably used it as an encore in his concerts:

Sure I love the dear silver that shines in your hair
And the brow that's all furrowed and wrinkled with care.
I kiss the dear fingers so toilworn for me.
Oh, God bless you and keep you, Mother Machree.

MacIntyre, Tom (b.1931). Playwright, fiction writer and poet. He was born in Balieborough, Co. Cavan, and educated at University College Dublin. He taught English at Clongowes and creative writing at Ann Arbor, Michigan, and in Massachusetts. His first book *Dance the Dance* (1969), a collection of often ribald stories, was followed by *The Charollais* (1969), a novel about a bull from the sea that stirs up an Irish community into extremes of sexuality. It is funny and nicely satirical about an Ireland on the brink of change. His drama, best interpreted by the actor Tom Hickey and directed by Patrick Mason, is experimental, with effective use of dance and mime. The most successful play was *The* GREAT HUNGER (1983), based upon Patrick Kavanagh's famous poem. Others include *Dance for Your Daddy* (1987) and *Rise Up, Lovely Sweeney* (1985), the title of the latter from an Ulster ballad but the theme from *Buile Shuibhne*, the luminous 12th-century text (*see* SUIBHNE GEILT). *Caoineadh Airt Uí Laoghaire* ('lament for Art O'Leary', 1998) is a

bilingual dramatic account of the background to Eibhlín Dhubh NÍ CHONAILL's famous lament for her husband. MacIntyre's poetry collections include *Blood Relations* (1972), *I Bailed Out at Ardee* (1987) and *Fleur-du-lit* (1991). *The* GALLANT JOHN JOE, a play written for and in collaboration with Tom Hickey, was first staged in 2002.

See also CHIRPAUN.

McKee, Dick. *See* BLOODY SUNDAY 1920.

McKelvey, Joe. One of four Republican prisoners executed by a Free State firing squad in MOUNTJOY JAIL on 8 December 1922, during the CIVIL WAR.

See also MELLOWS, LIAM; O'CONNOR, RORY.

Macken, Walter (1915–67). Novelist and playwright. He was born in Galway, where he spent most of his life. At 17 he joined An TAIBHDHEARC, and there learned the whole craft of theatre. After some years as an insurance salesman in London he became a member of the ABBEY THEATRE company. He also acted in films, notably in Brendan Behan's *The Quare Fellow*. Although he began his writing career as a playwright, it is for his novels, which combined literary worth with popularity, that he is remembered: for instance *Rain on the Wind* (1950), his third book, about the life of a fisherman in the CLADDAGH. His greatest success was with his historical trilogy: *Seek the Fair Land* (1959), about Ireland in the time of Oliver Cromwell; *The Silent People* (1962), about the Great Famine; and *The Scorching Wind* (1964), about the Anglo-Irish War of 1919–21. *Flight of the Doves* (1971), a children's story, was successfully filmed.

McKenna, Barney. *See* BANJO; DUBLINERS, THE.

McKenna, Siobhán (1923–86). Actor. She was born in Belfast on 24 May 1923 into an Irish-speaking household: her father, a Cork-born mathematician, lectured at Queen's University Belfast, and her mother was from Longford. The family moved to Galway when she was eight and her father was appointed professor of mathematics at University College Galway (UCG). She was educated at St Louis Convent in Monaghan and studied languages at UCG.

From the beginning of her college days McKenna became deeply involved with An TAIBH-DHEARC, the small Irish-language theatre in Galway, originally translating modern plays into Irish for production there, then acting in them herself. Because the plays were in Irish, her parents considered that she was engaged in a worthwhile activity, so they did not object too much until it became clear that acting was her chosen profession. She completed her degree with honours before moving to Dublin, where she eventually got a small part in the ABBEY THEATRE.

McKenna achieved international fame as Joan of Arc in Shaw's *Saint Joan*, which played in Dublin in 1950 and opened in London in 1954, but the part for which she is still remembered is that of Pegeen Mike in Synge's *The PLAYBOY OF THE WESTERN WORLD* in the 1951 Dublin production and the 1962 film. Her last major role, undertaken some months before her death, was as the matriarch in a production by DRUID THEATRE, Galway, of Tom Murphy's *BAILEGANGAIRE*, a play written specially for her. Her final performance was on 24 May 1986, and she died of lung cancer on 16 November of that year.

MacKenna, Stephen (1872–1934). Translator of the *Enneads* of Plotinus (*c*.AD 205–270). He was born in Liverpool of Irish parents on 15 January 1872. He worked in a Dublin bank, and later as a journalist in London and Paris where he met J.M. SYNGE, Maud GONNE and John O'LEARY. In 1897 he fought for the Greeks in the war against Turkey, an experience he described as like 'waiting for a train in Mullingar'.

MacKenna became European correspondent of Joseph Pulitzer's *New York World* and covered the Russo-Japanese War (1904–5), interviewing Tolstoy while he was in Russia. It was a very well-paid job but he grew tired of

the 'yellow' journalism associated with Pulitzer and resigned in 1907. He returned to Dublin and worked for the FREEMAN'S JOURNAL, becoming an active worker for the GAELIC LEAGUE and a friend of many of the writers of the IRISH LITERARY REVIVAL. During the EASTER RISING MacKenna was turned away from the GPO by Patrick Pearse because of his obvious ill-health.

MacKenna began his life's work in 1908, with the publication of the first book of Plotinus's text 'On Beauty'. The *Enneads* ('the nines') are six books of nine essays each, detailing the philosopher's neoplatonism, and the Greek text is extremely difficult to follow because of the complexity of the concepts and the abrupt transitions of thought. The complete translation took 13 years (1917–30), and it is regarded as the finest translation of any Greek classic. After his wife died in 1923 he went to England and earned a poor living by casual journalism. He died in England on 8 March 1934.

Mackey, Mick (1912–82). Hurler. He was born in Castleconnell, Co. Limerick, and played for the Ahane club, winning 15 county senior championsip medals in hurling and five in football. He was captain of the victorious Limerick hurling team in the ALL-IRELAND finals of 1936 and 1940, also winning an All-Ireland medal in 1934, and is remembered for having scored five goals and three points in the 1936 Munster final against Tipperary. He was trainer of the Limerick hurling team in the 1950s.

McKiernan, Catherina (b.1969). Athlete. She was born on 30 November 1969 in Cornafean, Co. Cavan, achieving international success in 1992 when she finished second in the world cross-country championships in Boston. That year she also broke the Irish record for the 10,000 metres and reached the 10,000 metres final in the world athletics championship in Stuttgart. In 1994 she again came second in the world cross-country championships and won a European championship cross-country gold medal.

Macklin, Charles (?1699–1797). The adopted name of the great 18th-century Irish actor, who was born Charles Mac Lochlainn, probably in Derry of Inishowen stock, his family coming from the seaside village of Culdaff. His date of birth has never exactly been determined, but one of many legends associated with him is that he lived to be 100, and since he died in 1797, 1697 is often taken as his year of birth, though the likely year is 1699. He was conscious of his Irish ancestry, boasting to Johnson's Boswell that if he could have proved himself to be the son of his father he might have claimed an estate in Ireland.

At some stage his mother married Luke O'Meally, a tavern keeper from Islandbridge in Dublin, and Charles began to play small parts in the Dublin theatres. He grew big and burly, and at 17 tried his fortune as a strolling player in England. He gradually lost his brogue and, despairing of anyone taking the trouble to pronounce his name properly, shortened it to Macklin. By 1730 he was an established member of the Theatre Royal company in Drury Lane, already with a reputation as a hard drinker and great lover. His ungovernable temper once caused him to kill a fellow actor in a quarrel over a wig. He was found guilty of manslaughter and sentenced to be branded; the sentence was carried out with a cold iron, and Macklin reappeared on the Theatre Royal stage to great applause.

Macklin continued to dominate the theatre of London and Dublin for 50 years, and his greatest part was that of Shylock, which he first played in 1741. The rhyme 'This is the JEW THAT SHAKESPEARE DREW' expressed the popular verdict. Macklin was the first to see pathos and dignity in the character that up till then had been played as a low comic part. He was David Garrick's only rival in both comic and tragic roles, and is supposed to have lived with him and Peg Woffington (*see* WOFFINGTON, THE) in a *ménage à trois*.

The Science of Acting, Macklin's book on his art, was lost in manuscript in an Irish Sea shipwreck. He did much in his writing and teaching to decry the tradition of stylized acting that was the rule at the time, and introduced a naturalness that was regarded as revolutionary. He stressed clear and natural diction, and the use of pauses to suggest intellectual turmoil and decision. Sometimes these periods of silent acting were rather long; once he berated an over-zealous prompter for 'interrupting me in my grand pause'.

Macklin wrote ten plays, including *The True-born Irishman* (1762), which Brian FRIEL adapted as *The London Vertigo* (1990), the very popular *Love-à-la–Mode* (1759) and *The Man of the World* (1781). Failing memory caused him to retire from the stage in 1789 when he was nearly 90. He lived for eight more years, dying on 11 July 1797.

MacLaverty, Bernard (b.1942). Novelist and short-story writer. He was born in Belfast and worked for ten years as a medical laboratory technician before taking a degree at Queen's University Belfast and moving to Scotland. His four collections of stories, *Secrets* (1977), *A Time to Dance* (1982), *The Great Profundo* (1987) and *Walking the Dog* (1994), are full of piquant characters: prostitutes, amateur musicians, bewildered adolescents and even sword-swallowers. The last-named collection contains short experimental pieces interleaving more conventional stories. One story, 'My Dear Palestrina', is about a boy and his music teacher in a war-torn Ulster, also the background of his novel *Cal* (1983), which describes the relationship between a young terrorist and the widow of his victim. It was successfully filmed, as was an earlier novel, *Lamb* (1980), about a delinquent boy and a teaching brother. His recent novels include *Grace Notes* (1997), about an expatriate Ulster composer, which was shortlisted for the Booker Prize, and *The Anatomy School* (2001), a novel about family and rites of passage in Belfast.

McLaverty, Michael (1904–92). Short-story writer and novelist. He was born in Carrickmacross, Co. Monaghan, but brought up in Belfast, where he taught for many years after graduating with a BSc from QUB in 1927 and qualifying as a teacher in 1928. He began writing short stories for such journals as the *Capuchin Annual*, and a first collection, *The White Mare*, was published in 1943. He was already known as a novelist, having written the ever-popular *Call My Brother Back* (1939), a novel of childhood and youth, partly set in Rathlin Island, and *Lost Fields* (1941), a thematic account of the reluctant settling of country people in the city. Six novels published between 1945 and 1965 were written out of a strong Catholicism which determined the nature of the material and its treatment. To some this professional decision seemed a severe limitation for any artist since his themes were the great ones of good and evil. McLaverty's greater talent lay in his stories, which, written in a beautifully spare style, dealt with the dilemmas of unheroic people as they lived their unexceptional lives. *Collected Stories* (1978), with an introduction by Seamus HEANEY, contains his finest work.

Mac Liammóir, Micheál. *See* BOYS, THE².

Maclise, Daniel (1808–70). Painter. He was born the son of a shoemaker on 2 February 1808 in Cork, then a prosperous city with a strong intellectual and artistic life. He left a position in a bank to open up a studio where he drew pencil portraits. One of these was a profile of Sir Walter Scott done during the novelist's visit in 1825. Two years later in London he found that the sketch had made his name known in the appropriate circles. He won gold and silver medals at the Royal Academy School and soon was in demand for caricatures for *Fraser's Magazine*, which had been co-founded by William Maggin and would have other Irish editors including Francis Sylvester Mahony (*see* FATHER PROUT) and William ALLINGHAM.

Maclise became friendly with Thomas MOORE, Dickens and Thackeray (*see* TITMARSH, MICHAEL ANGELO), and illustrated their work. One of his paintings in the City of Manchester Gallery, *The Origin of the Harp* (1842), an illustration of Tom Moore's poem,

features a nymph whose sensuality is remarkable given the mores of the time. He also was the best illustrator of William CARLETON.

Maclise's *Marriage of Strongbow and Eva* (1854), a huge canvas, is one of the treasures of the National Gallery of Ireland and as authentic as contemporary scholars could make it. It demonstrates his continuing preoccupation with things Irish. Other mammoth projects were frescoes for the House of Commons on Nelson and Wellington (1859–64). He refused the presidency of the Royal Academy in 1866 and later also refused a knighthood. One of his last paintings, the beautiful *Madeline after Prayer* (1868), based on Keats's 'The Eve of St Agnes' (1818), shows a strong Pre-Raphelite influence. He died of pneumonia in his house in Cheyne Walk, Chelsea, on 15 April 1870.

Mac Lochlainn, Charles. *See* MACKLIN, CHARLES.

MacMahon, Bryan. *See* MASTER, THE.

MacMahon, Heber (1600–50). Bishop and military leader. He was born at Farney, Co. Monaghan, educated at Douai and ordained in LOUVAIN in 1625. He was vicar-general for his native diocese of Clogher before being appointed Bishop of Down and Connor in 1642 and later translated to Clogher, consecrated on 2 June 1643. MacMahon was deeply involved in the politics of the time: he was a delegate at the Confederation of KILKENNY in 1642, and later acted as advisor to Owen Rua O'NEILL. On O'Neill's unexplained death in 1649 he assumed command of the Confederation's northern forces. He took the garrison at Dungiven and, in a change from O'Neill's successful delaying tactics, insisted on a pitched battle with Sir Charles Coote (d.1661), the lord president of Connacht, at Scarrifhollis, near Letterkenny on 21 June 1650. The defeat for the Confederates was crushing, with only the cavalry surviving in any numbers. MacMahon led the remains of his army towards Enniskillen and was severely wounded in a skirmish with a party from the garrison. Taken prisoner, he was beheaded and his head set on a spike above the castle. He was buried on DEVENISH ISLAND, an old monastic site.

McMahon, Tony. *See* LONG NOTE, THE.

MacManus, Francis (1909–65). Novelist and broadcaster. He was born in Kilkenny and educated at St Patrick's College and University College Dublin. He taught for 18 years before joining Radio Éireann in 1948, eventually becoming the driving force behind the remarkable series of Thomas Davis lectures. His first fiction was the trilogy *Stand and Give Challenge* (1934), *Candle for the Proud* (1936) and *Men Withering* (1939), about the life and grim 18th-century times of the Gaelic poet Donncha Rua MAC CONMARA. A second trilogy, about 20th-century life in his native county, *This House Was Mine* (1937), *Flow On Lovely River* (1941) and *Watergate* (1942), shows him to be one of the finest of Irish realist novelists, his firmly rooted Nationalism and Catholicism enabling him to write with critical charity about both those 'isms'. *The Greatest of These* (1943) deals, with greater terseness and austerity, with the clerical scandal in Callan in the 1870s that also inspired *The Big Chapel* by Thomas KILROY. His finest novel (and the only one published outside Ireland), *Fire in the Dust* (1950), describes small-town Irish prudery in the 1940s. MacManus wrote biographies of Boccaccio (1947) and the fiery COLUMBAN (1963), as well as a travel book, *Seal ag Ródaíocht* ('a while on the road', 1955).

MacManus, Seumas (1869–1960). Storyteller and novelist. He was born in Inver, Co. Donegal, and educated at Glencoagh National School, to which he returned as principal in 1888. His stories and verse appeared in the *Shan Van Vocht*, the Belfast Nationalist magazine founded by Alice MILLIGAN and Anna Johnson, who wrote poetry as 'Ethna CARBERY' and whom he married in 1901. He went to America in 1899 (returning home each summer), and in America found a ready market for his kind of folksy Irish material. Over a long career he produced many popular novels describing Donegal childhood, such as *A Lad of the O'Friels* (1903), *Bold Blades of Donegal* (1935) and *The Little Mistress of Eskar Mór* (1960); there were also many books of collected fairy tales and tales of local life, full of high humour and a significant measure of STAGE-IRISHness; a number of one-act plays, including *The Townland of Tamney*, which was presented by the Irish National Theatre on 4 January 1904 on the same bill as Yeats's *By Shadowy Waters*; an epic history, *The Story of the Irish Race* (1921); and a lively autobiography, *The Rocky Road to Dublin* (1938). In the late 1930s he edited and largely wrote a weekly magazine called *Chimney Corners*. He died in his 90s by falling from a nursing-home window in New York.

> It was fine, footing it over the hills of Banagh on a September morning. All the more enjoyable when, alone on a journey, you trot it at a trot that times to the beating of the eager heart, skip the ditches and leap the streams, take braes and hills upward with vim, and downward with abandon, listening to the soul singing in you as you go.
>
> *Three Knights of Knockagar* (1938)

McManus, Terence Bellew (1823–61). YOUNG IRELAND activist. The details of his early life are obscure, but it is thought that he was born in Tempo, Co. Fermanagh. He became a shipping agent in Liverpool and joined Young Ireland on his return to Ireland in 1843. In July 1848 he was involved with Smith O'Brien in the engagement known as WIDOW MCCORMICK'S CABBAGE PATCH, and was arrested in Cork while trying to escape to America. He was sentenced to death but instead transported to VAN DIEMEN'S LAND for life. In 1852 he escaped to America with James Francis Meagher (*see* MEAGHER OF THE SWORD) under circumstances of extreme hardship – 'little short of what you can imagine of hell's flames', he wrote in a letter to Charles Gavan DUFFY – and settled in San Francisco. McManus died in poverty, and his body was brought home for burial in GLASNEVIN CEMETERY on 10 November 1861. The FENIANS orchestrated a major display of solidarity: about 70,000 people lined the route or attended the funeral, and the funeral oration was by Father Patrick LAVELLE.

MacMaster, Anew (1894–1962). Actor-manager. He was born in Monaghan and educated in England, where he became an actor appearing in such popular melodramas as *The Scarlet Pimpernel* (1911) and as leading man in the long-running *Paddy the Next Best Thing* (1920). He formed his own Irish fit-up company in 1925 and for years toured the country presenting Shakespeare plays and other dramas in village halls to capacity audiences. Among the actors who formed part of his company were Micheál Mac Liammóir (whose sister he married), Hilton Edwards and Harold Pinter. Tall and handsome, he was noted for his Shylock, Richard III and Coriolanus, and he was a memorable Hamlet at Stratford in 1933. He died in Dublin on 24 August 1962.

Mac Mathúna, Ciarán (b.1925). Collector and broadcaster of traditional music. He was born in Limerick city. After taking an MA on the subject of Irish folk songs at University College Dublin, he worked for the Placenames Commission, then in 1947 he got a job with Raidió Éireann, his duties including the collection of music and songs from all over Ireland with an outside broadcast unit. He presented *A Job of Journeywork* on Sunday afternoons from 1957 and became a popular radio personality, his pace calm and unhurried, his broadcasting personality genial. In 1970 he began to compile and present *Mo Cheol Thú* (meaning literally 'you are my darling', but with an obvious pun on *ceol*, 'music'), a mixture of traditional music and poetry with a folk theme, which is broadcast on RTÉ radio early on Sunday morning. He is married to Dolly MacMahon, a traditional singer.

Mac Meanmain, Seán (1886–1962). Irish-language writer. He was born in Iniskeel near Glenties, Co. Donegal, and educated at Coláiste Uladh, the GAELIC LEAGUE school

founded in 1906. He became a teacher at the McDevitt Institute in Glenties. He wrote many books of stories, often in the first person and based upon his own experience, in the lucid, unaffected Irish of central Donegal, including *Scéalta Goiride Geimhridh* ('short winter tales') (1915), *Fear Siúil* ('travelling man') (1924) and *Ó Chamhaoir go Clapsholas* ('from dawn to dusk') (1940). His collected work was edited in three volumes (1990–2) by Séamus Ó Cnáimshí.

> *Deirtí roimhe seo go raibh seacht cineál meisce ann: meisce chaointe, meisce bhrúine, meisce chrábhaidh, meisce gháirí, meisce stangaireachta, meisce breallánachta agus meisce chodlata.*
>
> (It has been said that there are seven kinds of drunkenness: lachrymose, sorrowful, pious, giggling, argumentative, foolish and sleepy.)

Mac Murchada, Diarmait. *See* MACMURROUGH, DERMOT.

MacMurrough, Dermot (Irish **Diarmait Mac Murchada**) (d.1171). King of Leinster from about 1132. He was a strong supporter of his century's religious reform, endowing several Cistercian and Augustinian foundations in Leinster, and establishing ALL HALLOWS PRIORY monastery in Dublin. In 1166 he was banished from Ireland by the high king, Ruaidhrí Ua Conchobair, allegedly for abducting DERVORGILLA, the wife of his rival Tigearnán Ua Ruairc, king of BREFFNI (or Breifne; the modern counties of Leitrim and Cavan), after which Ua Ruairc burned MacMurrough's castle in Ferns, Co. Wexford. The real reason seems more likely to be MacMurrough's own failed attempt to win the high kingship (*see* HIGH KING). He received permission from Henry II, whom he visited in Aquitaine, to recruit forces within his dominions. In South Wales he made an ally of STRONGBOW and other Anglo-Norman lords, who arrived in Ireland in 1169. After the capture of Waterford he gave Aoife, 'his daughter whom he so much loved', to Strongbow in marriage. In Nationalist history Diarmait has always received a bad press as the man responsible for letting the Anglo-Normans in, but it is possible that his sobriquet Diarmait na nGall ('Dermot of the foreigners') predates his association with Strongbow and friends and refers to his supremacy over the Viking kingdom of Dublin. He died in Ferns in 1171.

McNally, Leonard (1752–1820). Lawyer, playwright and government spy. He was born in Dublin and educated at Trinity College Dublin. He kept a fashionable grocery shop in Capel Street, but still managed to be called to the Irish Bar in 1776 and the English Bar in 1783. One of the founder members of the Society of UNITED IRISHMEN, he was revealed as an informer when at his death his son wanted to know if his father's annual government dole of £300 would pass to him. His defences at the trials of Napper TANDY, Wolfe TONE and Robert EMMET were regarded as brilliant, if unsuccessful. This may have been due to his practice of conveying to the prosecution in advance the details of his defence. He wrote 12 popular plays for Dublin and London theatres and a number of comic operas for Covent Garden. One of his pieces, *Robin Hood* (1784), was playing in Dublin on the night that he betrayed the whereabouts of Lord Edward FITZGERALD to the authorities. His song, the concert-platform classic, 'The Lass of Richmond Hill' (1789), was written for Miss L'Anson of Hill House in Richmond, Yorkshire, who afterwards became his wife. His successful and profitable career as a mole may have begun in self-protection and continued in genuine dismay at the revolutionary tendencies of the United Irishmen. He died in Dublin on 13 February 1820.

> On Richmond Hill there lives a lass,
> More bright than Mayday morn,
> Whose charms all other maids surpass,
> A rose without a thorn.

MacNamara, Brinsley. *See* VALLEY OF THE SQUINTING WINDOWS, THE.

MacNeice, Louis (1907–63). Poet and playwright. He was born in Belfast 'between the mountains and the gantries' on 12 September 1907 and educated at Marlborough and Merton College, Oxford. He graduated with a double first in classics and philosophy, and his poetry is irradiated with classical attitudes. (His 1936 version of Aeschylus's *Agamemnon* is a classic in its own right.) He taught classics at Birmingham (1929–36) and Greek at Bedford College in London (1936–40) but, after the break-up of his marriage, joined Laurence Gilliam's features department at the BBC in 1941, staying more than 20 years and contributing to its reputation for excellence.

MacNeice wrote a number of memorable radio plays, notably *Out of the Picture* (1937) and *The Dark Tower* (1946). *One for the Grave*, his modern *Everyman*, was part of the 1966 Dublin Theatre Festival. He was primarily a poet, and a prolific one, equally at home in love lyrics and prophecy. His *Autumn Journal* (1939), a long poem recording London life after the Munich Crisis, combines art with readability, and even the less successful *Autumn Sequel* (1946), three times as long, is marvellously readable.

Ireland, which both amused and exasperated him, recurs as a theme for verse, sometimes savagely chided, as in 'Neutrality', but always fascinating him and claiming his love and allegiance: 'The woven figure cannot undo its thread.' He never lost a salutary fear of 'darkest Ulster' but, by appointing the liberal Sam Hanna BELL as features producer for BBC Northern Ireland in 1946, hoped to thaw intransigent attitudes. He died on 3 September 1963 after contracting a viral infection while looking for a special sound effect deep in a coal mine. His autobiography to 1940, *The Strings Are False*, was published posthumously in 1965.

MacNeill, Eoin (1867–1945). Scholar and revolutionary. He was born in Glenarm, Co. Antrim, on 15 May 1867 and educated at St Malachy's Belfast and the ROYAL UNIVERSITY OF IRELAND. With Douglas HYDE and others he founded the GAELIC LEAGUE in

1893, immersing himself in Irish history, and was appointed professor of early Irish history at University College Dublin in 1908.

MacNeill was instrumental in founding the IRISH VOLUNTEERS in 1913, and later became chief of staff. He was opposed to the EASTER RISING of 1916, which he thought had no chance of success, but the Rising was organized by a combination of IRB elements in the Volunteers and James Connolly's IRISH CITIZEN ARMY. On Easter Sunday 1916, having heard about the failure of Roger CASEMENT's mission to land German arms in Co. Kerry, he issued orders countermanding previous orders for the mobilization of the Volunteers. After the Rising, in which he took no part, he was arrested and sentenced to life imprisonment.

MacNeill supported the TREATY and became minister for education in the Free State government, but was forced to resign his ministry after the findings of the BOUNDARY COMMISSION emerged in 1925. He lost his seat in the Dáil in the general election of 1927, and thereafter devoted his time to scholarship. His best-known scholarly works are *Phases of Irish History* (1921) and *Celtic Ireland* (1921). He died in Dublin on 15 October 1945.

McPherson, Conor (b.1972). Dramatist. He was born in Dublin to a family with Co. Leitrim roots, and educated at University College Dublin. His first major work, *The Weir*, was commissioned by the Royal Court Theatre in London and opened in 1998. Like *Port Authority* (2001) it is a series of monologues, described by the playwright as being 'about a breakthrough. Lots under the surface coming out.' The powerful monologues of McPherson's plays testify more to the characters' misunderstandings of themselves and others than to illumination, what McPherson calls 'the poetry of inarticulacy': 'an awful lot of inarticulacy in my plays; very often the most inarticulate character is the one that people are drawn to more and more ...'

McQuaid, John Charles (1895–1973). Archbishop of Dublin. He was born in Cootehill,

Co. Cavan, on 28 July 1895, studied at Clongowes, University College Dublin and Rome, and was ordained a Holy Ghost priest in 1924. He became president of Blackrock College, a foundation of the Holy Ghost Fathers, in 1931, and in 1940 he was appointed Archbishop of Dublin.

An able and energetic administrator and an astute politician, McQuaid spearheaded an extensive building programme of churches and schools in the expanding Dublin diocese. He held strong conservative views and was responsible in 1944 for introducing a ban on Catholics studying at Trinity College Dublin, a ban that was not lifted until 1970, and for orchestrating clerical opposition to Noël BROWNE's MOTHER AND CHILD SCHEME in 1950. He promoted Catholic social and moral teachings at all times and took a strong view on the evils of contraceptives and divorce, saying in April 1971, 'To speak of a right to contraception on the part of an individual ... is to speak of a right that cannot even exist.'

It was perceived, even by a compliant faithful, that McQuaid was hand-in-glove with Éamon DE VALERA's FIANNA FÁIL party, which was in power for most of the period of his archbishopric, so that at this time Ireland was effectively a confessional – and repressive – Catholic state. After the death of both men it emerged that McQuaid had had a significant influence on the drafting of de Valera's CONSTITUTION OF 1937 while he was still president of Blackrock College, de Valera's alma mater. McQuaid was a reluctant apologist for the modernizing Second Vatican Council in the 1960s, and retired early in 1972. He died on 7 April 1973 in Loughlinstown hospital, and de Valera was seen to weep over his body.

Macra na Feirme (Irish, 'children of the farm'). A voluntary organization established in rural areas in 1944 to promote the personal and professional development of individual farmers, by providing occasions for social contact and opportunities to learn additional skills and improved farming methods.

Macready, [Cecil Frederick] Nevil (1862–1945). Commander-in-chief of British forces in Ireland (1920–3) during the ANGLO-IRISH WAR. He was chosen for the job by the lord lieutenant, Lord FRENCH, having been commissioner of the Metropolitan Police from 1918. He claimed to disapprove of the lawless tactics of the BLACK AND TANS and the AUXIES, stating that he would 'break any officer who was mixed up in reprisals', but, perhaps lacking a viable alternative response to the IRA's guerrilla campaign, did not prevent the recurrence of such reprisals. On 8 July 1921 he met IRA leaders in the Mansion House in Dublin to agree the TRUCE of 11 July, undertaking as a condition of the truce to release the IRA leader, Seán MACEOIN, at that time under sentence of death. He oversaw the withdrawal of British troops from Ireland in January 1922 and retired from active service the following year, publishing a memoir, *Annals of an Active Life*, in 1942.

Mac Stiofáin, Seán (1928–2001). Republican and Provisional IRA chief of staff from 1970. He was born John Edward Drayton in London. In 1953 he and Cathal Goulding (1922–1998), an IRA member since the Second World War and chief of staff of the Official IRA (1969–72), were sentenced to eight years in jail for carrying out an arms raid on a Suffolk school. He was a key figure in the IRA in the early days of the Northern TROUBLES, and was instrumental in its split into the Official IRA and the more militant Provisionals. Although he met William WHITELAW for talks in London in 1972, he ordered an intensification of the IRA bombing campaign which peaked with the BLOODY FRIDAY atrocities of 21 July 1972, in which nine people were killed and more than 100 injured. Later that year Mac Stiofáin was jailed for six months in the Curragh after being convicted of IRA membership in the Republic. He went on hunger strike, and the IRA made an unsuccessful attempt to free him when he was being treated in a Dublin hospital. In January 1973 he ended his hunger strike on the orders of the Provisional leadership, and it is believed

that he ceased to be chief of staff at this time. In 1981 he resigned from Provisional SINN FÉIN after the ARMALITE AND THE BALLOT BOX strategy proposed by Danny Morrison was adopted. He died in hospital in Navan on 18 May 2001.

MacSwiney, Mary (1872–1942). Republican activist. The elder sister of Terence MACSWINEY by five years, she was born in London and reared in Co. Cork by her English mother after her Irish-born father abandoned the family. She was educated at Queen's College in Cork and as a young woman taught at a convent school in Kent, but in 1904, on her mother's death, she returned to Cork. As well as continuing to teach in Cork, she became involved in Republican politics, joining the GAELIC LEAGUE and INGHINIDHE NA HÉIREANN (later CUMANN NA MBAN) and becoming what she herself called a 'conservative suffragist'. When she lost her teaching job in Cork as a result of her support for the EASTER RISING of 1916, she opened St Ita's, a school for girls in her home in Rathmines in Dublin, modelled on Patrick Pearse's ST ENDA'S SCHOOL.

With her brother, Mary MacSwiney was involved in campaigning against conscription in 1918, and when he went on hunger strike and died in prison in 1920 she helped to maximize the propaganda impact of his death. With Muriel, his widow, she went on a lecture tour in the USA, her political views becoming more and more intransigent. She was elected TD for Cork city in 1921 and spoke for three hours in the Dáil against the TREATY, describing the agreement as 'the grossest act of betrayal that Ireland ever endured'. In 1922 and 1923 she was imprisoned on two occasions for Republican activity, on both occasions being released after going on hunger strike. After her release she joined Maud GONNE's Women's Prisoners Defence League (WPDL). Loyal to the end to an ideal and unattainable republic, she rejected DE VALERA's decision to reenter constitutional politics when FIANNA FÁIL was founded in 1926, refused to recognize the Free State and gave her support to the military wing of the IRA. She died in Dublin in 1942.

MacSwiney, Terence (1879–1920). Revolutionary. He was born in Cork and educated at the ROYAL UNIVERSITY OF IRELAND, becoming a technical instructor. He was active in the GAELIC LEAGUE, SINN FÉIN and the IRISH VOLUNTEERS, mobilizing Volunteers for an EASTER RISING that did not happen in Cork. He was elected to the first Dáil for the constituency of mid-Cork, and succeeded Tomás MACCURTAIN as mayor of Cork on 30 March 1920. Arrested under DORA, he was courtmartialled on 16 August and sentenced to two years' imprisonment. He immediately went on hunger strike in Brixton prison and died after 73 days without food, on 24 October 1920.

The publicity surrounding MacSwiney's protracted death was very damaging to Britain's reputation in Europe, Australia and America. MacSwiney's funeral in London had a guard of honour of Volunteers in prohibited uniform and the streets were filled with mourners, not all of them Irish exiles. Two bishops and some 400 clergy filled St George's Cathedral for the funeral Mass. MacSwiney's martyr's death and the execution of Kevin Barry (see 'MOUNTJOY JAIL ONE MONDAY MORNING, IN') in Dublin a week later were a major propaganda coup for Michael COLLINS and Sinn Féin. Furthermore, HUNGER STRIKE now entered the lexicon and tactics of Republicanism, to emerge most strongly with the H-BLOCK HUNGER STRIKES of 1981.

Mac Thomáis, Éamonn (1927–2002). Republican and writer. He was born in Rathmines, Dublin, on 13 January 1927. His father died when he was 5 and he left school at the age of 13 to work as a delivery boy for White Heather Laundry, thereby becoming familiar with the topography of Dublin. He was interned in the Curragh during the IRA campaign of 1957–9, and imprisoned for IRA membership in 1973–4. His first book of informal lore and observation of the capital was *Down Dublin Streets* (1966); *Gur Cakes and Coal Blocks* (1976),

The Labour and the Royal (1978), and *Janey Mack Me Shirt is Black* (1982) followed. He also became well known as a broadcaster, introducing two series on RTÉ television of *Dublin: a Personal View* (1979; 1983). He died in August 2002.

MacThorkil, Askulv (d.1171). The Viking ruler in Dublin at the time of the capture of the city by the Normans. When the city fell it is recorded that many of the inhabitants made their escape by sea, taking with them their most precious belongings. The following year Askulv returned with boatloads of soldiers, but was sorely defeated after a day's furious fighting in the Battle of HOGGEN GREEN. Miles de Cogan, the Norman leader, offered to spare his life in return for a ransom, but Askulv instead threatened further Norse attacks, whereupon he was summarily beheaded. There is a Dublin public house called MacTurcaill's in Townsend Street, not far from the site of Hoggen Green.

Macushla (Irish *mo chuisle*, 'my pulse'). Like MACHREE, a persistent HIBERNO-ENGLISH endearment. The term is preserved in the eponymous Irish-American recital standard by Josephine V. Rowe (of whom nothing else is known). It was, like 'Mother Machree', a regular 'finisher' for the Irish tenor John McCormack:

> Macushla! Macushla! Your sweet voice is calling
> Calling me softly again and again.
> Macushla! Macushla! I hear its dear pleading,
> My blue-eyed Macushla, I hear it in vain.

Macushla Revolt (1961). A revolt by gardai in Dublin, which took its name from the Macushla ballroom, where a protest meeting attended by 815 gardai was held on 5 November 1961. A pay award had been granted to the force in October 1961 and accepted by the representative body, but gardai with less than three years' service were not included in the award. It was the younger gardai who revolted, in protest against this perceived injustice and because they felt the representative body was not promoting their interests adequately. A few days after the protest meeting at the Macushla ballroom, the commissioner asked that 11 of the ringleaders of the revolt, which by then involved a 'go slow', be dismissed. Charles HAUGHEY, who was FIANNA FÁIL minister for justice at the time, defused the revolt with the help of the Archbishop of Dublin, John Charles MCQUAID, and promised that there would be no victimization of its leaders.

Madden, R[ichard] R[obert] (1798–1886). The historian of the UNITED IRISHMEN. He was born in Dublin on 20 August 1798 and qualified as a physician after studies in Paris, London and Naples. He served as a liberal magistrate in the West Indies and Africa (1833–43) and from 1846 to 1850 was colonial secretary for Western Australia, where, as in his other posts, he tried to improve the condition of the native inhabitants. From 1843 to 1846 he lived in Portugal as special correspondent for the *Morning Post*, and it was there that he wrote the seven-volume *The Lives and Times of the United Irishmen*, a sympathetic account that helped establish the heroic myth of the REBELLION OF 1798. He had earlier (1840) written a life of Robert EMMET and a fascinating account of the pathologies of Burns, Byron, Shelley and others in *The Infirmities of Genius* (1833). He became secretary of the Loan Fund Board in Dublin (1850–80) and died on 5 February 1886.

Madden, Samuel (1686–1765). Philanthropist, known as 'Premium' Madden because of his establishment of a fund to help students at Trinity College Dublin, his alma mater. He was born in Dublin on 23 December 1686 and, taking holy orders, became vicar of Newtownbutler, Co. Fermanagh, near family estates that he inherited in 1703. He was also co-founder of the Dublin Society, the forerunner of the ROYAL DUBLIN SOCIETY. He died in Fermanagh on 31 December 1765.

Mad Dog. The nickname of two men who achieved notoriety during the Northern Ireland Troubles, though active on opposite sides of the sectarian divide. The name was given largely because of the number of deaths accredited to them.

Dominic McGlinchey (1954–94) from Co. Derry joined the Provisional IRA at 17 after severe treatment by the security forces, and was chief of the INLA from 1982. He was believed to have been responsible for many atrocities, including the DROPPIN' WELL and DARKLEY killings, and was imprisoned several times (once for the killing of a 67-year-old postmistress). On 31 January 1987, while he was in Portlaoise prison (1985–93), his wife Mary (1954–87) was shot dead in front of her children at her home in Dundalk, Co. Louth. When Dominic was released in 1993 he elected to stay in Ireland in spite of warnings about his safety. He was shot dead outside a public telephone box in Dundalk on 10 February 1994 by members of an INLA splinter group.

The other 'Mad Dog' is Johnny Adair (b. 1964). He is credited with the deaths of many Catholics as head of the UFF, and was expelled from the UDA as a cause of internal dissension (*see* UDA/UFF). Released from prison under the terms of the Good Friday Agreement, he was returned there by two different secretaries of state for Northern Ireland, Peter Mandelson and Paul Murphy, because of his presumed direction of Loyalist in-fighting and of violent involvement at DRUMCREE. He is believed to have been the target of the IRA bomb in Frizzell's fish shop in the Shankill Road on 28 October 1993 and to have had some involvement in the TRICK OR TREAT response the following week at Greysteel, Co. Derry. In prison at the time of writing, he has seen members of his family go into voluntary exile in England for their own safety.

Mad Dog Coll. The nickname of a gangster, Vincent Coll (1908–32), who was born in Gweedore, Co. Donegal, and who became notorious as the most vicious of a number of Irish criminals in the Upper West Side of Manhattan (hence known as 'Westies'). He was given the nickname after a spate of murders that decimated a rival gang; in one shoot-out he killed a small child and injured several other children.

Mad Ireland. The description of Yeats's native country by W.H. Auden (1907–73) in his memorial poem 'In Memory of W.B.Yeats' (1940):

> You were silly like us; your gift survived it all;
> The parish of rich women, physical decay,
> Yourself. Mad Ireland hurt you into poetry.
> Now Ireland has her madness and her weather still,
> For poetry makes nothing happen …

Mad Margaret's Walk. A walkway in the grounds of Emo Court in Co. Laois, so called because legend has it that a maid of that name hanged herself there. The neo-classical mansion at Emo Court was designed by James GANDON and was constructed between 1790 and 1800. The formal gardens were designed by Capability Brown, the informal by William Brown. They are famous for rare trees and classical statuary.

Mad Mechanic, the. *See* FERGUSON, HARRY.

Mad Sweeney. *See* SUIBHNE GEILT.

Mael Dúin. The hero of the fabulous IMMRAM (voyage-tale) *Curaig Maile Dúin*, which was the source for Tennyson's *Voyage of Maeldune* (1880) and inspired the medieval *Navigatio Brendani*. Mael Dúin is the son of a raped nun who died in childbirth. His father was from the ARAN ISLANDS and died at the hands of sea raiders. When Mael Dúin becomes a man he gathers round him 60 Irish warriors and with them sets sail to find his father's murderers. During this Irish Odyssey, made in a CURRACH made of skin, they visit 33 islands, each of which is filled with wonders: giant ants, demon horses, talking birds, intoxicating fruit, protective walls of flame and a lake whose waters have the power to restore youth. Most popular with the seafarers is TÍR NA MBAN ('the land of women'), which is ruled by a queen and where a partner is provided for each man and there is an endless supply of

food, drink and entertainment. Eventually the mortals grow tired of timeless beauty and sail for home. When they finally find their quarry, instead of killing them they make peace.

Mael Fhothartaig. *See* ÁEDÁN.

Maelruain (d.792). A disciple, as his name suggests, of RUADHAN of Lorrha. He was the founder of the monastery of Tallaght, Co. Dublin, *c*.775, and his austere rule made him the obvious leader of the CULDEE movement that reformed the Irish monastic system in the 8th and 9th centuries. His feast day is 7 July.

Maelrubha (*fl*.7th–8th centuries). A member of the BANGOR community. He left for IONA and spent nearly 50 years (673–722) as a roving missionary in northern Pictland. He founded the monastery of Applecross in Wester Ross, near Skye, and his name is remembered in that of Loch Maree. His feast day is 21 April.

Maeve. *See* MEDB.

Magairle Annraoi Rí (Irish, 'King Henry's testicles'). The origin of the Anglican church, as starkly suggested by a 19th-century Irish-speaking priest from the pulpit:

> *Ná thrácht ar an mhinistéir Gallda,*
> *Ná ar a chréideamh gan bheann, gan bhrí,*
> *Mar níl mar bhuan-chloch dá theampuill*
> *Ach magairle Annraoi Rí.*
> (Don't speak of your alien minister,
> Nor of his church without meaning or faith,
> For the foundation stone of his temple
> Is the ballocks of Henry the Eighth.)
> Translated by Brendan Behan

Magdalen(e) home. The name given to a home founded in Leeson Street, Dublin, by Lady Arabella DENNY for the purpose of rehabilitating fallen women. This home survived until the mid-20th century. More recently the term has come to mean institutions run by religious orders in which young women were incarcerated and made to work in laundries without payment until as late as the 1970s. They were called 'Magdalen' homes after Mary Magdalen, the repentant prostitute of the New Testament. Research in the 1990s and thereafter by television and print journalists (a film on the same subject, *The Magdalene Sisters*, directed by Peter Mullan, was released in 2002) revealed that while there was no legal basis to this incarceration and the women were at all times free to leave, many of them did not realize this or simply had nowhere to go.

Young women were admitted to Magdalens if they were pregnant out of wedlock (their babies taken from them and given for adoption), if they were orphaned or considered to be in danger of falling into immoral behaviour, or simply if they were so pretty as to be considered a temptation to men. They were committed by family, by their local priests or by other institutions such as orphanages. In 1996, when a laundry run by the Sisters of Our Lady of Charity in Sean MacDermott Street in Dublin was about to close, 40 'penitents', most of them elderly, all completely institutionalized, were still working there (150 women had worked there in its heyday). The Magdalen institutions were another example of the misogynistic abuse of power by the Catholic Church with the connivance of the civil authorities during the first 50 years of the Irish state. *See also* ARTANE; INDUSTRIAL SCHOOLS.

Magee, Patrick (1922–82). Character actor on stage, film and TV. He was born in Armagh city, and after experience with the ULSTER GROUP THEATRE in Belfast moved to London. Noted for his gravelly voice and the intensity of his performances, he was a fine interpreter of Pinter and of Peter Weiss in *Marat/Sade* (1964). Beckett wrote *Krapp's Last Tape* (1958) specially for him. He made many films and appeared often on television, but it was believed that this work was mainly undertaken to finance his stage appearances.

Magee, William Kirkpatrick. *See* EGLINTON, JOHN.

Magee College. *See* MCCREA-MAGEE COLLEGE.

'Maggie Murphy's Home'. A typical song of the Irish-American communities, written by Ned

HARRIGAN for his play *Reilly and the Four Hundred* (1890). The 'Four Hundred' were the only people in New York City that could claim to be 'society', according to Ward McAllister, the self-appointed arbiter. No Reilly was likely to have had anything to do with such a society. In spite of this the song shows the slow beginnings of upward mobility. The word 'home' here carries the connotations of the grander 'At Home':

On Sunday night, 'tis my delight
And pleasure, don't you see:
Meeting all the girls and all the boys
That work downtown with me.
There's an organ in the parlour
To give the house a tone:
And you're welcome every evening
At Maggie Murphy's home.

Maggie Ryan. A Dublin slang term for margarine.

Maggoty. A colloquial and rather crude or critical term meaning 'very drunk'. It is roughly synonymous with MOULDY.

Maggymore (Irish *margadh mór*, 'big market'). A term used in the HIBERNO-ENGLISH of Ulster to mean a big market or fair. 'Maggiemen' or 'maggymen' were the hucksters, three-card-trick men or stall operators at the fairground or market.

Magh Dhá Cheo. *See* OTHERWORLD.

Magh Meala. *See* OTHERWORLD.

Magh Tuireadh (Irish, 'plain of the towers'), anglicized as **Moytura**. In Irish mythology the site of two important battles, the first near Cong in Co. Mayo between the native FIRBOLG and the TUATHA DÉ DANAAN, led by NUADA, the second in north Sligo between the Tuatha dé Danann and the FOMORIANS. Nuada is slain by BALOR OF THE EVIL EYE in this battle.

Maginn, William. *See* O'DOHERTY, SIR MORGAN.

Maglone, Barney (*c*.1820–75). The pen name of R[obert] A[rthur] Wilson, the poet and comic writer. He was born in Dunfanaghy, Co. Donegal, and after some years teaching emigrated to America. He returned to Ireland in the 1840s, acting as sub-editor for *The* NATION and contributing many comic sketches to the *Belfast Morning News* in the 1860s.

Magrath, Meiler (*c.*1523–1622). Reformation ecclesiastic. He was born in Co. Fermanagh, entered the Franciscan Order and was appointed Bishop of Down and Connor by the pope in 1565. However, five years later, after professing loyalty to the reformed church, he was made Anglican Bishop of Clogher, and in 1571 Archbishop of Cashel. He maintained both Catholic and Anglican sees for many years, also becoming involved in politics, informing on rebels against the crown while simultaneously conspiring with them. At one point he held four bishoprics (although the pope deprived him of Down and Connor in 1580 for 'heresy and many other crimes'), extorting the maximum revenue but completely neglecting them all. He retained the see of Cashel and is buried in the cathedral there.

Maguire, Leo (1903–85). Music and choral teacher, compère and broadcaster. Born in Dublin, Maguire sang at the age of 10 in an IRISH CITIZEN ARMY rally. He presented the WALTONS sponsored lunchtime programme on RAIDIÓ ÉIREANN from 1952 to 1981, ending with the exhortation 'If you feel like singing, do sing an Irish song.'
See also PURCELL, [PATRICK JOSEPH] NOEL.

Maguire, Sam (1879–1927). A Republican after whom the SAM MAGUIRE CUP is named. Born in Dunmanway, Co. Cork, like his friend Michael COLLINS he worked in the Post Office in London, and was a keen sportsman, captaining the London Gaelic football teams that contested the ALL-IRELAND football finals of 1900, 1901 and 1903. He was Collins's director of intelligence in London and a major force in the IRB. After independence he returned to a civil service job in Dublin. He died of TB in February 1927. Peader KEARNEY wrote of Maguire:

Your kindly generous smile gave strength to all
Who grasped your hand in that great
  brotherhood
Waiting throughout the years for Eire's call.

Mahaffy, Sir John Pentland (1839–1919). Scholar. He was born in Switzerland on 26 February 1839, to an Irish family and educated at Trinity College Dublin, where he read classics. He was professor of ancient history at that university from 1869, and provost from 1914 to 1919. Although a clergyman he was knighted in 1918. A brilliant conversationalist in theory (his *Principles of the Art of Conversation* was published in 1887) as well as in practice, he was dismissive of Nationalist and Irish-language literature. He was famous for epigrams such as his comment on the IRISH BULL ('always pregnant') and his description of Ireland as a place 'where the inevitable never happens and the unexpected always occurs'. His publications include books on philosophy and the ancient Greeks, as well as *An Epoch of Irish History* (1903), about the origins of TCD. Mahaffy helped to establish the Irish Georgian Society, and was elected president of the ROYAL IRISH ACADEMY in 1911.

Maharajah of Connemara, the. The name by which Prince Ranjitsinhji (or 'Ranji') of Nawanagar (1872–1933), a celebrated cricketer who settled in Co. Galway, was popularly known. He was born in the Indian province now known as Gujarat and educated at Trinity College, Cambridge. One of the most famous cricketers of the age (he scored 3000 runs in first-class cricket in 1899), he succeeded his cousin as Prince of Nawanagar in 1906. He maintained a lavish house in Staines, near London, where his hospitality and capacity for living beyond his means were legendary, and rented Ballynahinch Castle near Roundstone in Co. Galway for two years before buying it in 1926 for £30,000. (Ballynahinch Castle was the former seat of the Martin family; *see* HUMANITY DICK.) Prince Ranjitsinhji was by then a passionate angler, and he made extensive improvements to the castle and grounds, constructing jetties and fishing huts. Ranji returned to Connemara every summer until his death in 1933 at his palace in Jamnagar, the capital of Nawanagar. Ranji's was one of a number of cricketers' names that appeared in punning versions in Joyce's FINNEGANS WAKE:

> At half-past quick in the morning. And her lamp was all askew and trumbly-wick-in-her, ringey-singey.

Mahogany gaspipe. A mocking version of characteristic sounds in Irish by those who have little or none. Another version, 'Jeyes fluid as condensed milk', is used because of the first word's phonic resemblance to *caidé*, the Irish for 'what'?

Mahon, Christy. The name of the cowering anti-hero of J.M. Synge's *The* PLAYBOY OF THE WESTERN WORLD (1907), who becomes a hero in actuality:

> Ten thousand blessings upon all that's here, for you've turned me a likely gaffer in the end of all, the way I'll go romancing through a romping lifetime from this hour to the dawning of the Judgement Day.

The idea that a man who had killed his father should be regarded with awe and affection by the people of Mayo in a place where there is 'not a decent house for four miles, the way every Christian is a bona fide' is a typical piece of Syngean subversion, but the germ of the idea came from the LYNCHEHAUN case in which a criminal was hidden from the police.

Mahon, Derek (b.1941). Poet. He was born in Belfast and educated at INST and Trinity College Dublin, where he studied classics. He worked as a teacher and journalist, and was writer-in-residence at Coleraine (1978–9) and Trinity College (1988); and now divides his time between Dublin and New York. He has published many collections of poetry, among them *The Hunt By Night* (1982) and *Antarctica* (1985). A *Selected Poems* was published in 1990, *The Hudson Letter* in 1996 and *The Yellow Book*, a meditation on decadence in literature and culture, in 1997; a *Collected Poems* appeared in 1999. He has also published a selection of journalistic writings, *Journalism: Selected Prose* (1996). Because of the coincidence of place and date of birth, Mahon's name was conveniently linked with his near coevals Seamus HEANEY and Michael LONGLEY, although the three writers have very distinct voices. *Night Crossing* (1968) portrays a kind of spiritual exile, cut off not only from home but also from history. The mocking, ambivalent lines from his poem 'Rage for Order' (which gave Frank Ormsby the title for his poetry anthology of the Ulster Troubles; the phrase originally comes from Wallace Stevens's 1935 poem 'The Idea of Order at Key West': 'Oh! Blessed rage for order, pale Ramon, / The maker's rage to order words of the sea…') will serve as an interim testament:

> Somewhere beyond the scorched gable and the
>   burnt-out buses
> there is a poet indulging
> his wretched rage for order
> or not as the case may be …

John Banville has described Mahon's poem 'A Disused Shed in County Wexford' as 'the most beautiful single poem produced by an Irishman since the death of Yeats'. *High Time*, his version of Molière's *L'École des Maris* (1661), had its première in a FIELD DAY production in 1994. His *Collected Poems* appeared in 1999.

Mahonia. The pinnate-leaved shrub of the evergreen barberry family called after Bernard McMahon, an Irish-American botanist. He arrived in Pennsylvania, said to have been 'driven out of Ireland for political reasons'. He opened a seed shop and nursery in East Philadelphia and in 1804 published a catalogue offering at least 1000 different items. His *American Gardener's Calendar* (1806) was a bestseller, and Thomas Nuttall (1786–1859), the English-born botanist who was to become curator of the Botanical Garden at Harvard in 1822, named the shrub in his honour. He died in 1816.

Mahony, Francis Sylvester. *See* FATHER PROUT.

Maicín. The Irish word for 'son' with the addition of the diminutive *ín*. The word is used as a term of affection in HIBERNO-ENGLISH for a boy or youth.

Maide briste. An Irish phrase literally meaning 'broken stick', used in HIBERNO-ENGLISH to signify a pair of tongs.

Maiden City. A sobriquet applied to Derry/Londonderry (*see* STROKE CITY) in tribute to its successful withstanding of several sieges, especially that by Jacobite soldiers in 1689 (*see* DERRY, SIEGE OF). The most notable laureate of the siege was Charlotte Elizabeth Tonna (1790–1846) whose poems, especially 'No Surrender' and 'The Maiden City' helped reaffirm the city's special position:

> That hallowed grave-yard yonder
> Swells with the slaughtered dead –
> O brothers! Pause and ponder –
> It was for us they bled;
> And while their gift we own, boys –
> The fane that tops our hill –
> Oh! The Maiden on her throne, boys,
> Shall be a Maiden still!
>> 'The Maiden City'

Maidstone, HMS. A ship of the Royal Navy, which was pressed into service as a prison ship following the reintroduction of INTERNMENT in 1971. It had been used for a similar purpose during the Second World War. Conditions on the ship, anchored in Belfast Lough, were so appalling that after a 13-day hunger strike it ceased to be used as a holding centre. Before this seven prisoners escaped by jumping over the side and swimming ashore.

Maigue Poets (Irish *Filí ma Máighe*). A group of Limerick poets of the 18th century, so called because of their local river, the Maigue. The group included Seán Ó Tuama (SEÁN AN GHRINN) and Aindrias Mac Craith (An MANGAIRE SÚGACH).

Mainland, the. A term used deliberately by Unionists in Ulster, and either carelessly or tendentiously by others, to refer to the island of Britain (comprising England, Wales and Scotland). Irish Nationalists never use it, resenting the implication that Ireland is some kind of off-shore island.

See also BRITISH ISLES; HIBERNIAN ARCHIPELAGO; THESE ISLANDS.

Máire. The pseudonym of Séamus Ó Grianna (1889–1969), Irish-language novelist and short-story writer. He was born in Rannafast in the Rosses of Donegal into a family renowned for its SEANCHAS. His brother Seosamh MAC GRIANNA was also a writer, the difference in their names coming from a family disagreement, and another brother Seán Bán and his sister Máire Bhán were noted *seanchaithe*. A teacher from 1912, he took the ANTI-TREATYITE side in the CIVIL WAR, and was interned in 1924. In 1932, under the Fianna Fáil government, he was reinstated in the civil service. He was a contributing editor to both de Bhaldraithe's and Ó Donaill's dictionaries. He wrote many novels and short stories about his native place, using his mother's name and with her often as narrator; these tales were treasured for their idioms and picture of the Donegal GAELTACHT life at the turn of the 20th century. He set his face against the Nua-litríocht (modernism, anathema to traditionalists and supporters of literature rooted in native experience like Máire's), and refused to allow his best novel CAISLEÁIN ÓIR to be standardized (*see* CAIGHDEÁN). Other significant works are *Cioth is Dealán* ('sunshine and shower', 1927) a collection of short stories, and an autobiography *Saol Corrach* ('troubled times', 1945). *See also* LANGUAGE FREEDOM MOVEMENT.

Máire Rua (1615–86). Woman of property. She was born in Bunratty Castle, Co. Clare, granddaughter of the 3rd Earl of Thomond. Her first husband was Daniel Neylon, who died when she was still in her twenties; they had four children and Máire inherited his estate at Dysert O'Dea in Co. Clare. She was tried for his murder but acquitted. Her second husband was her cousin, Conor O'Brien. In the 12 years of their marriage Máire bore her husband eight children and the couple extended their estates and rebuilt the family's tower house at

Leameneh (*Léim an Eich*, 'leap of the steed') on the edge of the Burren in Co. Clare. In 1651 Conor was shot in a skirmish with Cromwellian troops. It is said that his widow drove at top speed to Limerick, requested an interview with the Cromwellian leader, General Ireton, and offered to marry one of his officers on condition that the family estates should pass to her son. The officer who volunteered for this duty was a Coronet Cooper. Family tradition reports that the marriage was a happy one and that Máire Rua's children became fond of their stepfather. After the Restoration she was obliged to sell her estates and leave Leameneh. She went to live in Drumoland Castle, the home of her son, Donogh O'Brien. He was made a baronet by James II in 1685 and Drumoland (now a luxury hotel) became the seat of the barons of Inchiquin.

Maith go leor (Irish, 'good enough'). An Irish phrase meaning 'good enough', used euphemistically in HIBERNO-ENGLISH as an adjectival phrase meaning 'drunk'. It is roughly synonymous with NICELY.

Make. A halfpenny in pre-decimal coinage, in use until the late 1960s. The word, universal throughout Ireland, was also to be found in Scotland.

Makem, Sarah (1898–1985). Traditional singer. She was born in Keady, Co. Armagh, and had an extensive repertoire of songs from Irish, English and Scottish sources. She made only one album but was a very great influence on scores of students and other singers who recorded her material. Her son, Tommy Makem, sang with the CLANCY BROTHERS.
See also AS I ROVED OUT.

Makem, Tommy (b.1932). *See* CLANCY BROTHERS, THE.

Makemie, Francis (1658–1708). Presbyterian missionary. He was born in Ramelton, Co. Donegal, and trained for the Presbyterian ministry in Glasgow. Ordained there in 1682 for his native Laggan presbytery, he volunteered to go to America the following year and preached

in Virginia, Maryland and North and South Carolina. He hoped to unite the non-conformist churches against the moves made by the established church to suppress them. He was an astute businessman, doing well in land deals and adding to his store by marrying a rich wife. They owned a large estate in Accomac County in Virginia, but Francis's missionary zeal was as strong as ever. In 1706, the year he set up the first American presbytery, he was arrested for preaching on Long Island without a licence, imprisoned and forced to defend himself in court. Though he won his case he was required to pay the cost both of the defence and the prosecution. The trauma of imprisonment and the legal battles had a serious effect on his health and he died in 1708. He is regarded as the founder of PRESBYTERIANISM in the USA.

Make ns meet. The thing that the Belfast artist, William Conor, claimed he was never able to do, when asked to explain the unusual spelling of his surname. He was born on 6 May 1881 in the Old Lodge Road in Belfast and became an apprentice poster designer for the firm of David Allen, which covered the hoardings of the city with its garish advertisements. Though his wages were only four shillings and sixpence a week, he was able to save enough to study art in Dublin and Paris. His chief concern was the representation of the people and streets of his native city: shipyard workers, shawlies, children queuing for matinees, tired people huddled in a jaunting car, the City Hall under snow. He was also in demand as a portrait painter, his sitters including Douglas Hyde and Robert Lynd. With his soft felt hat, large bow tie and silk handkerchief cascading from the breast pocket of a velvet jacket, he was an obvious Bohemian in a non-Bohemian city. He once wrote:

All my life I have been completely absorbed and with affection in the activities of the Belfast people and surrounding country ... I trust these paintings and drawings will recall a world that is quickly disappearing and could soon be forgotten.

He was awarded the OBE in 1952 and a Civil List pension in 1959. He died from hypothermia in the large house he shared with his brother and sister on 6 February 1968.

Making a shift for Ladysmith. A story relating to the Second Boer War (1899–1902), during which the British garrison at Ladysmith was besieged by the Boers. An Irish youth wrote in a letter to his mother that he was 'making a shift for Ladysmith', to his mother's surprise, as he had never previously shown any interest in sewing. Ladysmith was relieved on 1 March 1900. A shift is a woman's undergarment, as mentioned in *The PLAYBOY OF THE WESTERN WORLD*.

Malachy or **Maelmaedoc** (1095–1148). Reforming Archbishop of Armagh, and one of the few incumbents to have been born in the see. Ordained at 25 by CEALLACH, he was given the task of reviving the abbey at Bangor in 1123 and the neglected diocese of Connor the following year. He lived the ascetic life of a monk of Bangor until a hostile Ulster chief drove him and his monks out to seek peace and seclusion in Kerry in 1127. His appointment to the primatial see in 1132 plunged him into local politics again. Ceallach had been determined to break the hereditary succession, and his relatives opposed Malachy, putting his life in danger several times and retaining the diocese's treasure, including Patrick's staff and the priceless *BOOK OF ARMAGH*.

Having wrought the necessary reforms, Malachy relinquished his post to the abbot of Derry and returned to Connor, setting up an Augustinian foundation at Downpatrick. His greatest achievements were the final reconciliation of the Celtic church with Rome, the establishment of the canonical hours and the revival of the administration of the sacraments that had fallen into disuse. Formal papal recognition could come only with the presentation of *pallia*, lambswool collars, which would mark authority, so Malachy went to Rome to seek them for Armagh and Cashel. On the way he stopped with Bernard (1090–1153), the founder of the Cistercian order, at Clairvaux. The two men became friends and after Malachy's death Bernard wrote his biography.

Pope Innocent decreed that the *pallia* would be conferred only at the request of a national synod, but made the saint his delegate. Malachy returned home bringing with him enough monks to establish the first Irish Cistercian abbey, at Mellifont, and hastily summoned a synod at Inispatric near Skerries. He was dispatched by the synod to Rome to bring home the *pallia*, but died at Clairvaux on the way. Bernard buried him in his own habit and wore Malachy's for the remaining five years of his life. He was canonized in 1190, the first papal canonization of an Irishman. Malachy is patron of the diocese of Down and Connor, and his feast day is 3 November.

Malachy, High King of Ireland (d.1022). A king of the southern branch of the Uí Néill of Meath. He became HIGH KING in 980 when he defeated the forces of the Viking leader, Olaf Cuarán (Olaf of the Sandals), at Tara. During the next two decades he successfully attacked Dublin three times, in 981, 989 and 995, imposing a tribute of one ounce of gold for each garden in the city. In 995 he plundered the Norse Ring of Thor, a ceremonial armband of precious metal, believed to be the 'collar of gold' metioned in Thomas MOORE's melody 'Let Erin Remember':

When Malachy wore the collar of gold
Which he won from the proud invader.

Malachy was engaged in constant rivalry with BRIAN BORU; in 997, at a meeting in Clonfert, each recognized the other's authority in his own half of the country, but in 1002 Malachy was forced to submit to Brian's supremacy as high king after a number of successful attacks on his territory. Malachy was formally an ally of Brian's in the Battle of CLONTARF in 1014 against the Norse and Maelmordha, the king of Leinster, but he withdrew his forces before the battle. The death of Brian Boru left him undisputed high king.

Mallon, Seamus (b.1936). Nationalist politician

He was born on 17 August 1936 in Markethill, Co. Armagh, and trained as a teacher. A headmaster, he was actively involved in the CIVIL RIGHTS MOVEMENT of the late 1960s, joined the SDLP and was eventually elected as MP for Armagh in 1986. By then he was deputy leader and the party's spokesman on law and order. He was bitterly critical of RUC shootings and the apparent covers-up that followed; he was equally scathing about the Provisional IRA's continuing campaign of violence. After the GOOD FRIDAY AGREEMENT he became deputy first minister in the Northern Ireland legislative assembly, though often visibly at odds with David TRIMBLE, the first minister. He resigned from politics in 2001. A man of straight-faced humour, he described the agreement as 'Sunningdale for slow learners' (*see* POWER-SHARING EXECUTIVE).

Mallow Defiance. A calculatedly dissonant speech made by Daniel O'CONNELL in the town of Mallow, Co. Cork, on 11 June 1843. It was in the middle of his sequence of monster meetings calling for repeal of the Act of UNION, and at a public dinner in Mallow O'Connell rose to berate the British authorities, urging the reporters present to note exactly what he said. He suggested that Sir Robert PEEL and the Duke of WELLINGTON *might* be second Cromwells, and indicated that *if* they repeated the 17th-century monster's massacres the Irish would respond. It was a typical CUTE Kerryman's speech, since any analysis of the text kept him 'o' th' windy side of the law' but marvellously inflamed his hearers – and seemed to make him more fiery than YOUNG IRELAND.

> They prayed to the English for humanity, and Cromwell slaughtered them. I repeat it. Three hundred of the grace, the beauty, the virtue of Wexford slaughtered by those English ruffians. But, I assert, there is no danger to the women of Ireland, for the men of Ireland would die to the last in their defence. We were a paltry remnant in Cromwell's time. We are nine millions now!

Malmesbury. A town in Wiltshire, near Swindon, site of a 7th-century abbey founded by Maeldubh, a learned monk from Ireland. His most famous pupil, Aldhelm, took charge of the monastic school *c*.675. William of Malmesbury (*c*.1090–*c*.1143), the first significant English historian after BEDE, was a monk there. His writings, especially *Gesta Pontificum Anglorum* ('deeds of English pontiffs') contains useful information about the Irish PEREGRINI. He is also the source of anecdotes about the career of John Scottus ERIUGENA.

Malone, Edmund (1741–1812). Shakespearean scholar. He was born in Dublin on 4 October 1741 into a legal family that claimed descent from the kings of Connacht. Educated at Trinity College Dublin, he was called to the Bar in 1767 and practised on the Munster circuit until 1777. Then, on the death of his father and the inheritance of a modest income, he went to London and turned his attention to literary matters. He became a friend of Dr Johnson and a member of his 'club', and was to give Boswell considerable help with his *Life* (1791). He exposed the work of Thomas Chatterton (1752–70) as forgeries, but his main preoccupation was Shakespeare, and he strove to establish the chronology of the plays and publish a scholarly text. The chronology *An Attempt to Ascertain in which Order the Plays were Written* (1778) was a monumental work and places Malone in the forefront of Shakespearean scholars. His history of the English stage followed in 1780 and the first part of his scientifically edited *Complete Works* appeared in 1790. The unfinished *Life of Shakespeare* and the remaining volumes of the *Works* were completed after his death by James Boswell Jr, repaying some of his father's editorial debts. Malone died in London, but is buried near CLONMACNOISE.

Malone, Molly. *See* DISH WITH THE FISH.

Malt, a ball of. A HIBERNO-ENGLISH term for a glass of whiskey.

Man above, the. *See* GOOD MAN, THE.

Manannán Mac Lir. The Irish Neptune, who can drive his chariot over the waves and change his shape like the Homeric Proteus. A great lover of women, he uses the latter facility to visit them at night, often in the shape of a heron. Always seen as a handsome warrior, he has a self-propelled ship called *Wave-Sweeper* and lives with his wife FAND in TÍR TAIRNIGIRI (the Land of Promise), a country beyond the waves. After a quarrel he leaves her unprotected against attacks by the FOMORIANS. She summons CÚCHULAINN as her champion and they become lovers. Manannán has children (including MONGÁN) by mortal women and is the presiding deity of the ISLE OF MAN. The frequent mists that cover the island are explained (by the Manx tourist board) as Manannán's making it safe from invasion.

Manchester Martyrs, the. The name popularly given to William O'Meara Allen, Michael Larkin and William O'Brien, who were hanged publicly at Salford on 23 November 1867 for their complicity in the killing of the unarmed Sergeant Charles Brett during the rescue of the FENIAN prisoners Colonel Thomas Kelly and Captain Timothy Deasy on 18 September. Kelly and Deasy were being taken by unaccompanied police van from the courthouse to Belle Vue jail when it was surrounded by a party of 30 Fenians under a railway bridge. A shot fired through the ventilator of the van by Peter Rice was probably intended merely to burst the lock but it mortally wounded Brett. A female criminal in her terror opened the door with keys from the sergeant's belt and the prisoners (and Rice) eventually escaped to America. Under English law the three captured men were guilty but the harshness of the sentence and the nature of the execution caused outrage among Irish Nationalists. (A fourth man, Edward Condon, escaped the gallows as an American citizen after pressure from the US embassy.) They were immortalized in the ballad 'GOD SAVE IRELAND', published in *The NATION* on 7 December. A contemporary broadsheet ballad recalls that

> One cold November morning in eighteen sixty-seven,

> These martyrs to their country's cause a sacrifice were given.
> 'God save Ireland,' was the cry, all through the crowd it ran.
> The Lord have mercy on the boys that helped to smash the van.

Mandates policy. *See* BARNEWALL, SIR PATRICK.

Man from God knows where, the. The name given in the 1918 poem of the same title by Florence Wilson (*c*.1870–1947) to United Irishman Thomas Russell (1767–1803). The narrator is a farmer who witnesses Russell's execution in Downpatrick, Co. Down, after Robert EMMET's failed rebellion of 1803:

> Then he bowed his head to the swinging rope,
> While I said 'Please God' to his dying hope
> And 'Amen' to his dying prayer
> That the wrong would cease and the right prevail,
> For the man they hanged at Downpatrick gaol
> Was the man from God knows where.

Thomas Russell was born near Mallow in Co. Cork, where his father, a regular soldier, was stationed. He served in the British army (1783–91) and as an officer in Belfast associated with radical families like the MCCRACKENS and the Simms. He met Wolfe TONE while serving in Dublin in 1790. He became part of a middle-class largely Protestant Republicanism, separatist, inclusive and committed to human rights. He spent time among the poor people of Ulster and travelled extensively in that province to establish clubs for the Society of UNITED IRISHMEN and to consolidate existing clubs. Hence the sobriquet 'The man from God knows where'.

Arrested for sedition in Dublin in 1796, Russell spent two years in Newgate prison and missed the REBELLION OF 1798 and the execution of his friends, Henry Joy McCracken and Wolfe Tone. After a further period in prison in Fort George in Scotland, he went to France and then returned to Ireland to try to incite the peasants of the north to support Robert Emmet. His part in that rebellion saw him convicted of treason and hanged on 23 October 1803 in

Downpatrick, Co. Down. Russell was religious and idealistic: he described his soul as being 'on fire' against injustice.

Mangaire Súgach, An (Irish, 'the merry pedlar'). The nickname of Aindrias Mac Craith (1710–90), Irish-language poet. He was born near Kilmallock in Co. Limerick and worked for a while as a teacher, but later became a wandering minstrel and one of the most regular clients of Seán Ó Tuama (another of the MAIGUE POETS; see SEÁN AN GHRINN) at his inn at Croom. He was briefly a Protestant, but was expelled from the congregation for conduct unbecoming. He was expelled from Croom for similar reasons by the local parish priest, who remembered his brief apostasy. The poem '*Slán is Céad ón dTaobh Seo Uaim*' ('A Hundred Farewells from Me'), popularly known as '*Slán le Máighe*' ('Goodbye to the Maigue') was written about this time and describes the loneliness of his condition in later life, '*ó seoladh me chun uaignis*' ('since I was sent into loneliness'). It has a plangent beauty and may be sung to the air of '*The BELLS OF SHANDON*'. Mac Craith wrote a fine elegy on the death of his friend Seán Ó Tuama in 1775. He is buried in Kilmallock, Co. Limerick.

Mangan, James Clarence (1803–49). Poet. He was born on 1 May 1803 in Dublin, the son of a small grocer who went bankrupt. He was taught by a Father Graham, who gave him a smattering of the modern languages in which he later became proficient. From the age of 15 to 30, in spite of great talent, he was forced to work as a drudging copy clerk. After this he managed to survive by his writing, occasional work in the library of Trinity College Dublin and in the offices of the ORDNANCE SURVEY (1833–9), where he won the friendship of George PETRIE, Eugene O'CURRY and John O'DONOVAN.

Under such pseudonyms as 'Clarence', adopted from *Richard III* as a 'poetic' name, and 'The Man in the Cloak' (a literal description) he wrote much prose and poetry for periodicals such as the *Dublin Magazine*, his most popular poems being versions of prose translations from the Irish made by the Ordnance Survey scholars. He also published translations from German. With such poems as 'Dark Rosaleen', 'The Nameless One', 'Twenty Golden Years Ago' and 'Gone in The Wind', which show great imagination and technical proficiency, Mangan is now regarded as the significant Irish poet of the mid-19th century. His work and life show a remarkable affinity with that of the American Edgar Allan Poe (1809–49). An early contributor to *The NATION*, he greatly admired the vigorous politics of John MITCHEL. Worn out by malnutrition and opium addiction, he died on 20 June 1849 during a cholera epidemic.

See also I HATE THEE, DJANN BOOL.

Mangy. A derogatory colloquial term used to describe a mean, parsimonious person. It derives from 'mange', a parasitic skin disease that affects dogs.

Manly. A HIBERNO-ENGLISH usage, deriving from the word 'manly' in its original sense but here meaning 'cheeky', 'impertinent' or 'precocious'. It is often used of children or of macho young men.

Mannikin traitor. *See* O'DONOGHUE, DANIEL.

Mannix, Archbishop Daniel (1864–1963). Catholic Archbishop of Melbourne. He was born in Charleville, Co. Cork, on 4 March 1864 and ordained to the priesthood at Maynooth in 1890. A brilliant scholar, he was appointed professor of theology in 1894 and president of Maynooth in 1903. In 1911 he was sent to Australia and became Archbishop of Melbourne in 1917. An ardent Nationalist, he became spokesman for the Irish community in his adoptive country, opposing conscription during the First World War and from afar supporting the movement for Irish independence. He championed the cause of Catholic denominational education in Australia, and established Newman College for men as well as St Mary's Hall for women students at the University of Melbourne. He also spearheaded the establishment of Catholic parishes, institutions, schools and churches all over Australia. Like most clerics of his time he was conservative in social matters and was supportive of Catholic Action, a movement in which Catholics involved themselves in politics with a view to promoting their church's values in legislation and in society as a whole. He was a significant figure in Irish-Australia, helping to give that community its identity, although there was never in that country the same degree of support for physical-force Republicanism as existed in the United States. In 1920 Prime Minister Lloyd George prevented him from landing in Ireland and from visiting centres of Irish population in Britain, so incendiary were his political utterances at the height of the ANGLO-IRISH WAR – such as 'All Ireland asks of England is this – take one of your hands off my throat and the other out of my pocket.' Mannix made a famous public condemnation of the atomic bombing of Hiroshima in 1945. He died in Melbourne on 6 November 1963, still archbishop of that diocese.

Manntach. An Irish word for 'gapped', 'gummy', 'toothless', used in HIBERNO-ENGLISH for someone toothless or with gaps in the teeth. It is often used of children who are losing their milk teeth, but also of old people.

Mansion House, the. The official residence of Dublin's lord mayor. Situated in Dawson Street near St Stephen's Green, it is also used for public functions, such as Ard Fheiseanna (annual conferences of political parties; *see* ARD FHEIS). The mansion was originally built by Joshua Dawson, after whom the street is named, in 1710. Dawson sold the house to Dublin Corporation in 1715 at a cost of £35,000 as a residence for the lord mayor. The first Dáil met there in January 1919.

Man Who Won the War, the. On 19 December 1921, while formally proposing the adoption of the TREATY in the Dáil, Arthur GRIFFITH described Michael COLLINS as 'the man who won the war'. In reply Cathal BRUGHA, an anti-

treatyite who had little time for Collins, asked whether Collins 'had ever fired a shot at any enemy of Ireland'. In fact, there *is* no record of Collins ever having fired a shot during the Anglo-Irish War of 1919–21.

Mara, P.J. (b.1942). Charles HAUGHEY's colourful and popular public relations consultant. He was born in Drumcondra, Dublin on 16 March 1942. Haughey had always recognized the importance of PR, and most other politicians followed suit during the 1980s and 1990s, so that Ireland became a nation of SPIN DOCTORS. P.J. Mara was repeatedly satirized (as 'Mara') during Dermot MORGAN's impersonation of Charles Haughey in SCRAP SATURDAY. After Haughey retired, Mara was supremely successful as FIANNA FÁIL's director of elections in 1997 and for part of the 2002 campaign.
See also UNO DUCE, UNA VOCE.

Marble City. A nickname for KILKENNY, because of the quarrying of marble in the area.

Marcus, David (b.1924). Editor and writer. He was born in Cork and educated at University College Cork and King's Inns, Dublin. Though qualified in law he rarely practised, preferring to write and edit; he was editor, with Terence Smith, of *Irish Writing* (1946–54), and also editor of *Poetry Ireland* (1948–54). He then worked in London for 13 years, returning to Ireland in 1967. For 20 years (1968–88) he ran a 'New Irish Writing' page in the Saturday edition of the *Irish Press*, discovering and publishing many talented young Irish writers who had no other outlet, and reminding readers of the excellence of the continuing work of established writers. (One of these new writers was the writer Ita DALY, who became his wife.) He also ran a fresh and exciting book page.

In 1954 Marcus published a semi-autobiographical novel *To Next Year in Jerusalem*, but did not return to serious writing for more than 30 years, when he produced two historical novels, *A Land Not Theirs* (1986), the story of the Jewish community in Cork during the Anglo-Irish War of 1919–21, which, in Sean

O'Faolain's phrase, 'gave Cork its epic', and *A Land in Flames* (1987), set in Kerry and ending with the burning of a big house and the coming of the BLACK AND TANS. A book of excellent short stories, *Who Ever Heard of an Irish Jew?*, was published in 1988. He has also produced a marvellously witty version of Merriman's CÚIRT AN MHEÁN-OÍCHE (*The Midnight Court*), written in modern colloquial English verse. Well known for his advocacy of the Irish short story as a superb literary form, he has continued to edit many anthologies that resoundingly prove his case. He published *Oughtobiography*, a witty book of memoirs, in 2001.

Mardyke. A pleasant tree-lined avenue to the west of Cork city centre. Edward Webber, a public official, was responsible for its creation in 1720.

> When my heart was as light as the wild winds that blow,
> Down the Mardyke by each elm tree …
> JONATHAN HANRAHAN: 'The Banks of My Own Lovely Lee'

Unfortunately the elm trees fell victim to Dutch elm disease and had to be felled and replaced in the 1980s.
See also BANKS, THE.

Maria Duce (Latin, 'with Mary as leader'). A Catholic movement founded in 1942 by Father Denis Fahey (1883–1954) of the HOLY GHOST FATHERS to advance the church's social teachings. In practice it was an anti-communist, fundamentalist society anxious to make Catholic teaching a part of the national constitution. It eventually lost any support it might have had from the Irish clerical hierarchy because of its noisy extremism.

Marianus Scottus (of Cologne) (1028–82/3). The name by which the Irish missionary Máel Brigte was known in 11th-century Europe (*Scottus* being medieval Latin for 'Irish'). He entered the monastery of Moville near Strangford Lough in Co. Down in 1052. Four years later the abbot, Tighernach Bairrcec, sentenced him to exile for a reason now unknown. Marianus

Scottus became a Benedictine monk in 1056 at St Martin's in Cologne, remaining there until 1058. In 1059 he was ordained a priest in Würzburg, prior to being voluntarily walled up as an 'incluse'. Ten years later he moved to Mainz in the Rhineland, and assumed a similar walled-up position. In spite of this extreme mortification he managed to write the *Chronicon Universale*, which tells the story of the world from the Creation until the year 1082. It includes a great deal of Irish ecclesiastical history and has much information on the Irish scholars of the period.

Marianus Scottus (of Ratisbon) (d.1084). The Latin name ('Marianus the Irishman') of Muiredach Macc Robairtig, an Irish monk. He was born in Donegal and left on pilgrimage for Rome in 1067. At RATISBON he and his companions were persuaded to stay and were offered the church of Weih Sankt Peter. As the numbers of the Irish community increased, Muiredach, by now known by his Latin name, began the building of the larger monastery of St James, which was completed in 1111, years after his death. It became the mother house of a number of Benedictine foundations in Germany and Austria that were known as the *Schottenklöster* ('Irish monasteries').

Marie Antoinette. *See* RICE HOUSE, THE.

Markievicz, Countess. *See* REBEL COUNTESS, THE.

Marriage Ban, the. The ban on married women continuing to teach in the country's national schools, introduced by the FIANNA FÁIL government in October 1933, despite the strong objection of the primary teachers' union. This was at the height of the Depression, when jobs were scarce, and it was also alleged that the Catholic hierarchy, which by then had considerable political power, favoured the ban on the grounds that pregnant teachers might give a bad example to pupils. When Jack LYNCH became minister for education in 1957 there was a shortage of 3000 trained teachers. Lynch wanted to reduce the size of classes and increase the school-leaving age, neither of which he could do without extra teachers. Meanwhile, JAMS (junior assistant teachers with minimal training) were employed at a very low wage, whether married or not, a practice that Lynch called 'educationally indefensible'. Lynch wisely cleared the move with Dublin's Archbishop John Charles MCQUAID before lifting the ban from 1 July 1958.

Marriage customs. In folklore, there are many traditional customs connected to the wedding day: Saturday was considered unlucky, as was the colour green, as was a bride wearing pearls; neither bride nor groom should sing at their own wedding, but they should dance the first dance with the bridesmaid and groomsman; a man should be the first to wish the bride joy; it was good luck to meet a cuckoo on the way from a church; it was bad luck to meet a funeral; it was unlucky for the wedding ring to slip off the finger of the bride; and a couple that married in harvest time would be forever gathering.

Marry in. The term used to describe the phenomenon whereby the groom moved into the bride's house and took over the bride's farm rather than vice versa. The Irish phrase for the man who 'marries in' is *cliamhain isteach* (*cliamhain* is from the same root as *cleamhnas*, Irish for 'match', and means a relative by marriage).

See also MATCHMAKING.

Marsh, Narcissus. *See* MARSH'S LIBRARY.

Marshall, W[illiam] F[rederick] (1885–1959). Poet and novelist. He was born in Dereband, Co. Tyrone, and brought up in Sixmilecross, where his father was a schoolmaster. He was educated at the Royal School in Dungannon, University College Galway and Assembly's College in Belfast, where he was ordained a Presbyterian minister, spending the main years of his ministry in Castlerock, Co. Derry. He was an authority on the Ulster dialect, and one of the drama highlights of pre-war BBC Northern Ireland was his production of *A Midsummer Night's Dream* in Tyrone accents.

His best known dialect poem, 'Me a' Me Da', was included in *Ballad and Verses from Tyrone* (1929), and his novel *Planted by a River* (1948), set in the reign of Queen Anne, considers the Ulster Plantation from the point of view of the austere industrious settlers. *Ulster Speaks* (1936) is a collection of essays on dialect, and *Ulster Sails West* (1950) describes the 18th-century Protestant emigration to the New World.

> I'm livin' in Drumlister
> An' I'm getting very oul',
> I have to wear an Indian bag
> To save me from the coul'.
>
> 'Me an' Me Da'

Marsh's Library. The oldest public library in Ireland, built (1701–4) in the garden of St Sepulchre's, St Patrick's Close, Dublin, by Narcissus Marsh, the Archbishop of Dublin. He was born in Cricklade, Wiltshire, on 20 December 1638, and after education at Magdalen Hall, Oxford, and a successful career in the Church of Ireland, became archbishop in 1694. He became primate of Ireland with his seat in Armagh in 1703 and died on 2 November 1713. Swift (*see* DEAN, THE) always blamed him for his own lack of advancement, and in *The Character of Primate Marsh* (1710) pilloried him as 'the first of the human race, that with great advantages of learning, piety and station escaped being a great man …' His library, which grew out of his own collection, has many early manuscripts and a fine collection of printed books. It was, however, to be used by a limited public, as the Visitation Book (1704) makes clear:

> All Graduats and Gentlemen shall have free access to the said Library on the Dayes and Houres before determined, Provided They behave Themselves well, give place and pay due respect to their Betters, But in case any person shall carry Himself otherwise (which We hope will not happen) We order Him to be excluded, if after being admonished He does not mend his manners.

Martello towers. A series of defensive towers

constructed during the Revolutionary and Napoleonic Wars, at a cost of about £1800 each, around the coast of Ireland and southeast England (and also in Jersey, the Cape coast of South Africa and in Ontario). They take their name from Cape Mortella on the northwest coast of Corsica, where a stone defensive tower repelled a British attack in 1794. Nine Martello towers were built in the area of Dublin Bay in 1804, all but Sutton on the south shore, and including Sandymount, Sandycove and Seapoint. Seven of these are still standing. The first floor provided living quarters for the garrison, while the ground floor housed the kitchen, stores and magazine. The towers varied in size and the garrisons in strength: 16 men were garrisoned in Sutton, while Sandycove seems to have been used mainly as a lookout tower. None of the garrisons were ever deployed on active service. Sandycove Martello Tower, which provides the setting for the opening of James Joyce's ULYSSES, is now in use as the James Joyce Museum.

Martin, Richard. *See* HUMANITY DICK.

Martin, Violet. *See* SOMERVILLE AND ROSS.

Martinmas. *See* BLEEDING FOR ST MARTIN.

Martyn, Edward (1859–1923). Dramatist of the IRISH LITERARY REVIVAL. A wealthy Catholic landlord, he was born in the family home, Tulira Castle near Ardrahan in Co. Galway, and later studied at Oxford. He was a member of the GAELIC LEAGUE and an important figure in the literary revival of the 1890s: in 1894 he encouraged George MOORE to return to live in Ireland, and in 1896 he introduced W.B. YEATS to his neighbour Lady GREGORY, and from this meeting developed the IRISH LITERARY THEATRE, the first productions of which were Yeats's *The Countess Cathleen* and Martyn's own *The Heather Field* (1899).

Martyn was also passionately interested in music, and in 1899 in Dublin's Pro-Cathedral he established the Palestrina Choir – in which John MCCORMACK sang, and which continues to this day; he was also a founder of the FEIS CHEOIL. He served on the first board of the ABBEY THEATRE in 1904, but later became disillusioned with its artistic policy of promoting peasant drama. Instead he founded, with Thomas MACDONAGH and Joseph Mary PLUNKETT, the more literary but shortlived Irish Theatre in Hardwicke Street, Dublin, in 1914. His play *The Dream Physician* (1914) has a character, George Augustus Moon, who is a caricature of George Moore, apparently in revenge for Moore's cruel depiction of his erstwhile friend in *Hail and Farewell* (1911–14). Martyn, who suffered from ill health, spent the final years of his life as a virtual recluse in his Galway home. He willed his body to a Dublin medical school for dissection and instructed that the remains be given a pauper's burial.

Marya. *See* MORYA.

Massey, William Ferguson (1856–1925). Prime minister of New Zealand. He was born in Limavady, Co. Derry, and educated at a private school in Derry. His farming parents had settled near Auckland in 1864 and he joined them in 1870. He became a Conservative politician in 1894 and premier in 1912. He had the unique record of holding that post for the remaining 13 years of his life, seeing his country through the First World War and representing it at Versailles in 1919. During his time in Europe ten cities, including Derry and Belfast, made him a freeman. He died in Wellington on 10 May 1925.

Massive. A HIBERNO-ENGLISH colloquialism meaning 'very fine', 'excellent'; the term is used in relation to clothes, appearance, a job or the weather.

Mass Rock. A rooted part of Irish folklore associated with the 18th-century POPERY LAWS. The popular view was illustrated by a frequently reproduced print showing a fully vested priest saying Mass in the open air on a flat rock in a remote region. Watchmen are placed apart from the main congregation, and at the bottom of the picture can be seen redcoats advancing on the priest who would have had a price on his head. In fact worship was not prescribed at the period and ordinary priests were free to say Mass; the use of Mass rocks, of which many survive, may have had more to do with lack of amenities rather than persecution. The tradition of the hunted priest belongs rather to the brief intense period of Cromwellian violence.

Master, The (1992). An autobiographical work by the essayist and fiction-writer Bryan Mac-Mahon (1909–98). MacMahon spent all his working life as a national school teacher in his home town of Listowel, Co. Kerry – 'the master' was the term always used for the (almost invariably male) school principal in rural Ireland. In the book the author charts the course of his teaching and writing career, and describes his successful efforts – corroborated by many of his former pupils – to awaken imagination and creativity in those he taught during the years of poverty, poor resources and emigration. He described his efforts (in the title of one of his short stories) as helping to open the 'windows of wonder'; in the story the young teacher touches the imagination of the children by recounting Irish legends to them: 'The windows I speak of are the legends of our people. Each little legend is a window of wonder.'
See also 'VALLEY OF KNOCKANURE'.

Master McGrath. The famous coursing greyhound that won the Waterloo Cup in 1868, 1869 and 1871, and was only once beaten on 37 courses. It is celebrated by a memorial, erected in 1873, at Ballymacmague crossroads 5 km (3 miles) from Dungarvan, Co. Waterford. Inevitably the dog became the subject of a famous and persistent ballad:

> The hare she led on with a wonderful view,
> And swift as the wind o'er the green field she flew,
> But he jumped on her back and he held up his paw;
> 'Three cheers for old Ireland,' says Master McGrath.

Matchmaking. The art of arranging marriages ('making matches'), a common phenomenon in rural Ireland until the second half of the 20th century. Matches were made between marriageable young men and women of the locality, and sometimes older people too, by a local person, man or woman, perhaps someone who ran a shop or pub and was in the way of knowing who was in need of a wife – or simply someone who had a talent for the calling. If a couple liked each other and were considered a suitable match from the point of view of social standing and income, no obstacle would be put in their way. The problems arose when a young man from a comfortable farm wanted to marry a girl with no dowry or vice versa.

There are stories in folklore of girls being forced to marry men who were much older, toothless, blind, lame or in some other way undesirable. In John B. Keane's play *Sive* (1959) a match is arranged between the schoolgirl Sive and the ageing Seán Dóta, although she loves a young man named Liam. The evil genius is the matchmaker, Thomasheen Rua, described as 'shifty-looking, ever on his guard'. Matches were often drawn down BETWEEN THE TWO CHRISTMASES in order for the wedding to take place the following SHROVETIDE.

Mater, the. The name by which the Mater Miserocordiae ('mother of mercy') Hospital in Dublin's Eccles Street is universally known. It was founded by Catherine McAuley and the Sisters of Mercy in 1861. It is now a major acute hospital and a teaching hospital for University College Dublin.

Mathew, Theobald. See APOSTLE OF TEMPERANCE, THE.

Mat(t) the Thresher. A character in Charles KICKHAM's novel *KNOCKNAGOW, OR THE HOMES OF TIPPERARY*. He has become something of a bucolic type, and has given his name to a famous inn in Birdhill, Co. Limerick, on the Cork–Limerick road.

Maturin, Charles Robert (1782–1824). Novelist and playwright. He was born in Dublin of

Huguenot stock, educated at Trinity College Dublin and ordained for the Church of Ireland in 1803. His plays were not successful, but of his six novels *Melmoth the Wanderer* (1820) is regarded as a Gothic classic, one of the last of its kind. It was written during its author's long curacy (1805–24) of St Peter's in Aungier Street in South Dublin. The narrative voice is that of John Melmoth, a 19th-century Dublin student who tells in five interlinked episodes the story of an earlier Melmoth who sold his soul to Satan for an extended life. He may be relieved from the debt if he can find someone sufficiently wretched who might be persuaded to take on the Faustian debt. When Oscar Wilde was released from Reading jail and was in exile in France he used the name Sebastian Melmoth (Maturin was a relation of his mother and the Sebastian was suggested by the arrowheads on the prison garb). Maturin died in Dublin on 30 October 1824.

Maudling, Reginald. *See* ACCEPTABLE LEVEL (OF VIOLENCE); BLOODY AWFUL COUNTRY; MURDERING HYPOCRITE.

Maum (Irish *mám*, 'handful'). A word used in HIBERNO-ENGLISH to mean a handful (sometimes the full of the two hands) or a hand of cards. It is also the word for a gap or mountain pass: Maam Cross in Co. Galway is a striking example of the latter.

Mavourneen (Irish *mo mhuirnín*, 'my pet'). A HIBERNO-ENGLISH term of endearment synonymous with 'my beloved'. It is to be found in the title of such songs as 'KATHLEEN MAVOURNEEN' and 'Come Back to Erin' (1866) by CLARIBEL.

Mavrone. *See* MO BHRÓN.

Maxwell, W[illiam] H[amilton] (1792–1850). Novelist. He was born in Newry and educated at Trinity College Dublin. It is unlikely that he served, as he claimed, as Captain Hamilton Maxwell in the Peninsula War and at Waterloo, though his rollicking novels with dashing Irish officers are full of impressive military lore. His

family insisted on the other resort of younger sons, and he was ordained an Anglican minister in 1820. He was given the sinecure of Balla, Co. Mayo, which left him free to hunt over Lord Mayo's estates and produce the book for which he is still known, *Wild Sports of the West* (1832). This farrago of sketches and ripe gossip about hard-riding country gentlemen provided his friend Charles LEVER with the material for his more successful novels – Maxwell's *Hector O'Sullivan and His Man Mark Antony O'Toole* (1842) and *Luck is Everything, or The Adventures of Brian O'Linn* (1848) are weak and stiff by comparison. Maxwell also wrote a life of Wellington (1839–41) and a history of the Rebellion of 1798. He died in Musselburgh in poor circumstances on 29 December 1850.

> I verily believe that no people upon earth are more easily satisfied in roads than the natives of Ballyveeney. A narrow strip of rough ground along the sea-beach, a mountainous watercourse, tolerably disencumbered of its rocks, or a practicable passage across a bog, provided it be but a fetlock deep, are considered by the inhabitants of this wild peninsula to be excellent horse-ways.
> *Wild Sports of the West* (1832)

May Day. *See* BEALTAINE.

May fayner. *See* MÉ FÉINER.

Mayne, Rutherford. *See* DRONE, THE.

Maynooth. The name by which St Patrick's College in Maynooth, Co. Kildare, is universally known. It is the national seminary for the education of secular Catholic priests for all the Irish dioceses, and is fed by the diocesan seminaries. Founded by the Irish Parliament in 1795 in order to win over moderate Catholic opinion, it was in use as a university for lay students until 1817. The college was originally given annual grant-aid by the British government, but after the DISESTABLISHMENT OF THE CHURCH OF IRELAND this was replaced by a capital sum. Maynooth now consists of a seminary, a pontifical university (since 1899) and a lay college (since 1966), and has been a recognized constituent college of the NATIONAL UNIVERSITY since 1910. Maynooth was originally independent of the Irish bishops, but episcopal control increased during the 19th century. For many years the Irish bishops have met there to issue statements on moral issues; it is therefore synonymous in the public mind with episcopal power and – sometimes – unwarranted interference into political matters.

Maynooth Mission to China. *See* COLUMBAN FATHERS.

Maynooth pardon. In March 1535, during the Kildare Rebellion of SILKEN THOMAS, the lord lieutenant, Sir William Skeffington, laid siege to the castle of Maynooth, the seat of the Fitzgerald earls of Kildare. While Silken Thomas went in search of reinforcements for his garrison, the castle was betrayed to Skeffington by the constable, Christopher Paris, in exchange for a sum of money. When Skeffington took the castle, however, he had Paris and 25 of the garrison executed as an example to the others. A 'Maynooth pardon' means, therefore, a pardon that is no pardon at all – a breach of trust. Silken Thomas himself met the same fate after surrendering to Sir Leonard GREY later the same year.

Maynooth Resolution (1884). An agreement between the INTO (Irish National Teachers' Organization) and the Catholic hierarchy concerning the treatment of teachers in national schools, all of which were individually controlled by the local parish priest. For moral turpitude, real or imagined, for drinking or company-keeping, or simply for disagreeing with his/her clerical boss, up to the time of the resolution any teacher could be dismissed with three months' notice and have no redress. The resolution stated that no teacher could be dismissed without the bishop of the diocese being informed and giving his assent, and that the teacher had a right to be heard in his/her own defence. Despite the resolution, there were incidences of clerical abuse of teachers until the 1960s.
See also MCGAHERN, JOHN.

Mayor of the Bullring. An 18th-century Dublin official who was elected on Mayday and who had the unlikely and presumably laborious office of punishing those frequenting brothels. The Bullring was in the Corn Market and the 'mayor', as the guardian of bachelors, was entitled to approve any marriages. The practice was recalled in *Ireland Sixty Years Ago* (1847) by John Edward Walsh (1816–19): 'After the marriage ceremony, the bridal party were commonly conducted to the ring by the "mayor" and his attendants, when a kiss from "his worship" concluded the ceremony…'

May the Lord in His Mercy Be Kind to Belfast. The refrain from a much-quoted 1930s squib, 'Ballad to a Traditional Refrain', by Maurice James Craig (b.1919). The title came from a conversation he had with James Joyce when they met in Paris in 1938. Joyce, who had an enormous store of Irish ballads, asked Craig, as a native of the city, to try to find the source of the title. (It came from a tribute to the people who had treated the UNITED IRISHMEN so well.) The refrain led to a splendid, loving attack on the northern city:

> Red brick in the suburb, white horse on the wall,
> Eyetalian marbles in the City Hall:
> O stranger from England, why stand so aghast?
> *May the Lord in His Mercy Be Kind to Belfast.*

Apart from its aesthetics the author also had occasion to rap its backwoods politics:

> O the bricks they will bleed and the rain it will weep,
> And the damp Lagan fog lull the city to sleep;
> It's to hell with the future and live on the past:
> *May the Lord in His Mercy Be Kind to Belfast.*

Maze, the. A high security prison for the incarceration of the most dangerous Republicans and Loyalists near Lisburn in Co. Antrim. Originally known as Long Kesh, it is still called 'the Kesh' by older Republicans. It became notorious for its H-blocks, the cell compounds that had the shape of the letter H when seen from the air. Their use marked the end of SPECIAL CATEGORY status in 1977. The H-blocks became familiar to the world at large as the location of the BLANKET PROTEST and DIRTY PROTEST that later evolved into the H-BLOCK HUNGER STRIKES (1980–1). Most of the remaining inmates left the Maze in the summer of 2000 in accordance with the early release scheme agreed as part of the GOOD FRIDAY AGREEMENT.

McGrath, Paul. *See* OOH AH! PAUL MCGRATH.

Meadhrán. An Irish word for 'dizziness', 'migraine', used in HIBERNO-ENGLISH for dizziness, confusion or noise in the head: 'I have a *meadhrán* from listening to that noise all day.'

Meagher of the Sword. A nickname devised by William Makepeace Thackeray (*see* TITMARSH, MICHAEL ANGELO) in *Punch* for Thomas Francis Meagher, who in a speech to the Repeal Association (agitating for the repeal of the Act of UNION) on 28 July 1846 hailed the sword as 'a sacred weapon':

> Abhor the sword and stigmatize the sword? No, my lord, for in the cragged passes of the Tyrol it cut in pieces the banner of the Bavarian, and won the immortality for the peasant of Innsbruck. Abhor the sword and stigmatize the sword? No, my lord, for at a blow a giant nation sprung up from the waters of the far Atlantic, and by its redeeming magic the fettered colony became a daring free republic.
>
> Quoted in *The Nation*, 1 August 1846

Meagher was born in Waterford in 1823, and though intended for the Bar took up politics. He was a founder member of the IRISH CONFEDERATION, and like the other leaders of the 1848 Rebellion (*see* WIDOW MCCORMICK'S CABBAGE PATCH) had his death sentence for treason-felony commuted to transportation for life to VAN DIEMEN'S LAND. He escaped in 1852 with Terence Bellew MCMANUS and made his way to America.

Meagher worked as a journalist in New York until the outbreak of the American Civil War in 1861, when he assumed command of the Irish Brigade (*see* FIGHTING 69TH, THE) in the Federal army. He had plenty of opportunities to consider the sacredness of the sword since his men were all but annihilated at Fredericksburg and Chancellorsville, largely due to his military incompetence, and he himself was wounded. He was appointed temporary governor of the Montana territory in 1866, and was drowned in a riverboat accident on the Missouri on 1 July 1867.

Mealychreeshy. An Ulster dish, once popular, made of oatmeal fried in fat:

> Now he pushed his plate away after mopping up the last of the *mealychreeshy* which had been their evening meal.
>
> SAM HANNA BELL (1909–90): *December Bride* (1951)

Meanness. There are a number of colourful Irish phrases indicating meanness, including 'He's so mean he wouldn't give you the itch' and 'He wouldn't give you the steam off his piss.'
See also LIVE ON, TO; MIND MICE AT CROSSROADS.

Mearning (also **mearing** or **mering**). A term used in Ulster for the boundary between two farms, from the Old English *mere* ('boundary'; *see also* MERESMEN). The term is still used in its practical sense, but is also used metaphorically or even poetically, as in Joseph Campbell's title *Mearing Stones* (1911).

Meas. An Irish word for the act of measuring, estimating, evaluating. In HIBERNO-ENGLISH the term is commonly used for respect or regard. The sentence 'I have no *meas* on him' (meaning 'I have no respect for him') is a direct translation of the Irish '*Níl meas are bith agam air*.'
See also MISE LE MEAS.

Meath. A county in the province of Leinster, known as Royal Meath because of the presence within its boundaries of TARA, the site associated with the high-kingship of Ireland (*see* HIGH KING). It has a population of 109,700 (1996 census). Its rich grassy acres were happily seized by the invading ANGLO-NORMANS and it was an important part of the PALE. The town of Kells gave its name to the *BOOK OF KELLS*, which was taken there for safety from IONA during the Viking terror.

... let you go off till you'd find a radiant lady
with droves of bullocks on the plains of Meath.

J.M. SYNGE (1871–1909): *The Playboy of the
Western World* (1907)

Meath Gaeltacht, the. The areas of Baile Ghib
and Reath Cairn in Co. Meath, which were
settled with families from the GAELTACHT in the
1930s, thanks to the pressure group Muinntir na Gaeltachta ('people of the Gaeltacht').
The idea of moving people from poor Gaeltacht areas along the western seaboard and
settling them further east in order to establish
new Gaeltachtaí was mooted under the CU-
MANN NA NGAEDHEAL government (1922–32).
When FIANNA FÁIL came to power in 1932
there was an expectation that de Valera would
take positive action on behalf of Irish. When
this did not materialize, Gaeltacht communities established the pressure group Muinntir
na Gaeltachta, particularly popular in Connemara. Members came to Dublin by bicycle to
meet de Valera at Easter 1934 and a decision
was finally reached to establish a Meath Gaeltacht.

The LAND COMMISSION made holdings ready
for Connemara people in Ráth Cairn and
bought the Baile Ghib estate of landlord Tom
Gerard in 1935. Families came there from
south and west Kerry, Connemara, Mayo and
Donegal. Unlike Ráth Cairn, in Baile Ghib
settlers were mixed in with local families, every
second holding being given to a Gaeltacht
family and a local family – a great disadvantage
in language terms. Irish was not established
permanently in Co. Meath, although for some
years it was known as an Irish centre with
its own IRISH COLLEGE. Some families went
back to their home places, and it is said that
the older people were lonely and that fishing
nets could be seen hanging as decoration in
houses far from the sea. In 1953 some families
from Connemara were settled in Delvin, Co.
Westmeath.

Medb (in modern Irish, 'Méabh', pronounced
'Maeve', which is also the anglicized version of
the name). In Irish mythology, a goddess who
has an incarnation as the devious, acquisitive
and much-married queen of Connacht, conferring kingship on her spouses. She is chiefly associated with the epic TÁIN BÓ CUAILNGE ('the
cattle raid of Cooley'), which tells of the discovery that Finnbhenach, the white bull, will
not join a herd owned by a woman and that
therefore the herd of her husband AILILL is
greater than hers. She persuades Ailill to lead
with her an army to obtain the BROWN BULL
OF CUAILNGE, the fabulous Brown Bull of Ulster. The war that follows results in the deaths
of many warriors, including CÚCHULAINN, who
confronts her armies alone because the Ulster
warriors have been debilitated by the curse of
MACHA. Medb is, in true goddess fashion, free
with her sexual favours, and is killed (whatever that may mean for an immortal) by a brain
ball from the sling of Forbaí, the son of her
former husband, CONCHOBHAR, while swimming in Lough Ree. She is said to be buried
under the great cairn on the summit of Knock-
narea, near Sligo:

> The wind has bundled up the clouds high over
>   Knocknarea,
> And thrown the thunder on the stones for all that
>   Maeve can say.
>
> W.B. YEATS: 'Red Hanrahan's Song About Ireland',
> in *In the Seven Woods* (1904)

Medium. A term for a half-pint of stout, pronounced 'meejum'.

Meeting house. The former name for a Presbyterian place of worship, the surviving buildings
still retaining the older name. They were simple
in style with a gallery round three sides and
generally undecorated, though stained glass
was permitted for the windows. The word is
still in use by the Society of Friends (Quakers)
as the location for weekly meetings.

> Ravara meeting-house mouldered among its
> gravestones like a mother surrounded by her
> spinster children.
>
> SAM HANNA BELL (1909–90): *December Bride*
> (1951)

Meeting of the Waters. The picturesque conflu-
ence of the Avonmore and Avonbeg rivers, near

Avoca in Co. Wicklow, immortalized in verse by Thomas MOORE in 1806. He insisted:

> There is not in this wide world a valley so sweet
> As that vale in whose bosom the bright waters meet;
> Oh! the last rays of feeling and life must depart,
> Ere the bloom of that valley shall fade from my heart.

The area achieved fame as the location of the BBC television series *BALLYKISSANGEL*.

Mé Féiner. A media invention of the 1990s, deriving from SINN FÉIN(er) and meaning a person who thinks only of himself, who is a selfish or self-regarding. The term is also used, by liberal or radical commentators, to suggest an undesirable type of materialism (especially among the young) that arrived on the whiskers of the CELTIC TIGER.

See also SHINNERS.

Megalith. A word literally meaning 'great stone' and used in its adjectival form 'megalithic' to denote the archaeological remains of the inhabitants of Ireland during the Neolithic period of 3000–2000 BC, particularly the tombs or passage graves constructed with such massive stones.

See also CARROWKEEL; LOUGH GUR; NEWGRANGE.

Meigeall. The Irish term for the whiskers of a goat, and also for a man's beard. The word is also used in HIBERNO-ENGLISH.

Meitheal. The Irish word for 'gang', 'party', and hence a group of men assembled to do a specific job, particularly in the bog or for haymaking at harvest-time or for building or maintaining farm buildings or fencing. Originally these men were employed, but in recent and current HIBERNO-ENGLISH the term has come to mean unpaid work that is returned in time of need. In some areas, the term *comhar(ing)* was used for this. The word is now used to denote the participants on any cooperative project, even one including women.

Mel (d.*c*.490). A saint contemporary with Pat-

rick, who made him Bishop of Ardagh with a 'cathedral' near Mostrim, Co. Longford. The saint's staff is now in St Mel's Diocesan Museum in Longford. One significant story concerns his supposed error during the profession of Brigid when he made her a bishop and insisted that the conferring should stand. Mel is the patron of the diocese of Ardagh and Clonmacnoise, and his feast day is 6 February.

Melia murder! *See* MÍLE MURDER.

Melk. An Austrian town about 64 km (40 miles) west of Vienna. It has a Benedictine abbey set on a fortified crag overlooking the Danube, and is connected with COLMÁN OF STOCKERAU, who on a pilgrimage to Rome in 1012 was tortured and hanged in Stokerau near Vienna. When miracles were ascribed to the corpse, the remains were taken by the local ruler Henry the Fowler (*c*.876–936) to his stronghold in Melk. His grandson, Holy Roman Emperor Henry II (973–1024), built an ornate tomb to house the relics, and the place became a regular place of call for Irish pilgrims. The emperor was later canonized in 1146.

Melleray, Mount. A Cistercian monastery in Co. Waterford, situated at the foot of the Knockmealdown Mountains near Cappoquin in exceptionally beautiful countryside. It was founded in 1832–3 by Irish Cistercian monks who had been expelled from the Abbey of Mellerey in France, during the upheaval that had accompanied the accession of Louis Philippe to the throne in 1830. They were given land for the foundation by Sir Richard Keane, a local landlord. In the 1950s there were as many as 140 monks at Melleray, but this number has greatly declined. There is a guesthouse in the grounds and the monastery has become popular as a place of solitude and contemplation, even for individuals who would not profess to be Catholics.

Mellifont, Treaty of (1603). The treaty negotiated by Hugh O'NEILL and Lord Deputy MOUNTJOY that brought a formal end to the NINE YEARS' WAR. Queen Elizabeth's death a short time before was kept secret by the English negotiators, but in any case O'Neill appears to have struck a good bargain: he was pardoned for his rebellion and was given a new grant of his lands. However, the FLIGHT OF THE EARLS in 1609 may have been an indication that the new order was more fraught for O'Neill and the other Ulster chieftains than anticipated.

Mellifont Abbey. The remains of a Cistercian abbey near Drogheda, Co. Louth, founded by St Malachy of Armagh in 1142. Malachy was granted lands by Donogh O'Carroll, Prince of Uriel, and brought monks from the mother house at Clairvaux, as well as a French architect to build the church, which was consecrated in 1157. Little of the church remains, but there are graceful cloisters and an unusual two-storey lavabo or wash house, in which the monks washed their hands before going into the refectory.

Mellows, Liam. One of four Republican prisoners executed by firing squad by the Free State government in MOUNTJOY JAIL jail on 8 December 1922. The four were chosen – ostensibly one representative of each province – from among the body of Republican prisoners, and, with only a semblance of a trial, were executed in reprisal for the killing by Republicans of Cork TD Seán Hales. 'My dearest mother,' Mellows wrote shortly before his death:

> Though unworthy of the greatest human honour that can be paid to Irishman or woman, I go to join Tone and Emmet, the Fenians, Tom Clarke, Connolly, Pearse, Kevin Barry and Childers. My last thoughts will be on God and Ireland and you … I had hoped that some day I might rest in some quiet place, but if it be prison clay it is all the sweeter, for many of our best lie there.

See also O'CONNOR, RORY.

Melly Tlismas. A phrase typical of the 'baby' language that Swift used with Stella (see DEAN, THE). A letter written by him on 25 December 1711 begins

> A melly Tlismas; meli Tlismas, I sd it first. I wish oo a sousand zoll, with halt and soul.

Melrose. An abbey in the Scottish Borders. The original abbey (subsequently known as Old Melrose) was a little to the east of the present town of Melrose, on a bare promontory in the River Tweed. It was founded from LINDIS-FARNE c.640, and EATA, the first abbot, was a Northumbrian pupil of AIDAN. Melrose was the school of Cuthbert, whose life and work resembled that of PATRICK in Ireland. In 1136, at a new site where the town of Melrose now stands, David I founded the first Cistercian house in Scotland, which survived until the Reformation.

'Men Behind the Wire, The'. A west Belfast Republican song by Paddy McGuigan marking the introduction of INTERNMENT in Northern Ireland on 9 August 1971. It was recorded, with considerable commercial success, by a ballad group called Barleycorn.

> *Chorus:*
> Armoured cars and tanks and guns
> Came to take away our sons,
> But every man will stand behind
> The Men Behind the Wire.
>
> Through the little streets of Belfast
> In the dark of early morn
> British soldiers came marauding
> Wrecking little homes with scorn.
>
> Heedless of the crying children,
> Dragging fathers from their beds,
> Beating sons while helpless mothers
> Watched the blood flow from their heads.

Mendicity institutes. The name given to voluntary associations established in the early 19th century, particularly in urban areas, in response to poverty, destitution and homelessness. They were funded by donations and administered by voluntary committees, distributing food and money and sometimes providing accommodation, although usually to small numbers of people. The Poor Law Act of 1838 meant that most of the mendicity institutes were replaced by workhouses.

Mercier Press. A Cork-based publishing house established in 1994 by John M. Feehan. It originally only published books of religious interest, but gradually built up a reputation as a publisher of Irish-interest paperbacks, especially history and folklore. Authors included Kevin DANAHER, John B. KEANE and Éamon KELLY.

Merciful hour. A mock piety, originating in Dublin but given a wider currency thanks to its frequent use by Gay BYRNE in his radio programmes.
See also DELIRA AND EXCIRA.

Meresmen. A term used for local people paid two shillings a day to guide officers of the ORDNANCE SURVEY along local townland and parish boundaries (*see also* MEARNING).

Merries, the. A colloquial Cork term for a fairground, amusement park; the word is abbreviated, in characteristic Cork fashion, from 'merry-go-round'.

Merriman, Brian (?1745–1805). Irish-language poet. He was born near Ennistimon in Co. Clare, the son of a stonemason, or perhaps the illegitimate son of a gentleman. He taught school in Feakle in his home county and after 1790, married and with two daughters, continued his profession in one of Limerick's schools. He died suddenly in 1805, his death notice referring to him as a teacher of mathematics. Such a calling does not necessarily preclude literary talent, and certainly *CÚIRT AN MHEÁN-OÍCHE* (*The Midnight Court*), written about 1780, is an original and exuberant work. Very few of his other poems are known. For several decades now there have been MERRIMAN SUMMER and MERRIMAN WINTER schools (the former in the poet's own county), which provide a forum for academic and cultural lectures and discusions.

Merriman Summer School. A summer school held in various towns in Co. Clare. Cumann Merriman/The Merriman Society was founded in 1967 to commemorate the work of Brian MERRIMAN and to promote interest in Irish culture and history. The first Merriman Summer School was held in Ennis in 1968, and every year the school is held in a different town in Co. Clare. The week-long programme, which includes lectures, discussions and workshops, takes a different theme every year, and is very popular among students, journalists, visiting academics and observers of Irish life. Set-dancing workshops, *céilís* and *craic* also form part of the week's activities.

Merriman Winter School. A weekend of literary, historical or cultural activities held in January–February each year. The first was in Nenagh in 1969 and the 35th in Bunratty, Co. Clare, in 2003. The usual *CEOL AGUS CRAIC* applies.

Merry dancers, the. An Ulster expression, imported from Scotland and still current, for the aurora borealis or northern lights.

Mespil House. An elegant country house built in 1751 near a bridge (now known as Leeson Street Bridge) over the Grand Canal in Dublin. It was built by a Dr Barry in 1751 and was famous for the elegance of three plaster ceilings. It was the last home of Sarah PURSER, and here she held one of Dublin's more famous at-homes, over which she presided with astringently witty authority. The site is now a block of flats, but the ceilings have been re-erected elsewhere: *Jupiter and the Elements* in ÁRAS AN UACHTARÁIN and *Hibernia* and *Arts and Sciences* in Dublin Castle (*see* CASTLE, THE). The house gave its name to Mespil Road.

Messenger, killing the. *See* KILLING THE MESSENGER.

Messiah, first performance of. *See* FISHAMBLE STREET.

Metal Man. The name of two statues used as markers for ships, the best-known indicating TRAMORE Bay, Co. Waterford (the other is on Perch Rock near Sligo.) The Metal Man in Tramore carries an effigy of a sailor, arm outstretched to warn ships off the rocks, and was constructed in 1816 after a troop ship sank in Tramore Bay with the loss of about 363 lives. According to legend, any 'eligible maiden' who hopped three times around the base of the Tramore Metal Man (a distance of about 73 m/80 yds) would find a good husband within the year.

Metcalfe's coins. In 1926 the Free State government announced a competition for the design of the country's new coinage, and the selection committee was chaired by W.B. Yeats. The winner was Percy Metcalfe (1894–1970), a sculptor from Yorkshire. The new coins were issued in 1928. The front of each bore the HARP, the back an animal or fowl: a woodcock on the farthing (quarter-penny); a sow and piglets on the halfpenny; a hen and chickens on the penny; a hare on the threepenny piece, a wolfhound on the sixpenny piece; a bull on the shilling; a salmon on the florin (two shillings) and a horse on the half-crown (2/6). Each coin bore the minuscule initials 'PM'. Little about the new state garnered as much praise as the coinage. According to a writer on the *Manchester Guardian*:

> I think that the Irish coinage will be
> acknowledged as the most beautiful in the
> modern world. I doubt if any country but Ireland
> would have the imagination that made such
> designs possible.

When decimal currency was introduced in 1971 most of Metcalfe's designs were retained on the new coins. The one-pound coin, first issued in 1990, carried a red deer designed by Thomas Ryan in the style of Percy Metcalfe. Sadly, since the introduction of euro coins in 2001, the Metcalfe designs are no longer in circulation.

Methodism. A Protestant denomination with up to 23,000 adherents in Ireland. It is governed by the Annual Conference, which is held each June before the church's year begins on 1 July. The conference is attended by ministers and lay representatives from each of 125 circuits and they elect a president, the equivalent of the moderator in the Presbyterian Church. Methodism came to Ireland with John Wesley, who first arrived on 9 August 1747 and made 20 more visits over the next 40 years. His preaching and lively social conscience brought

him and his steadily growing following into conflict with the established Church of Ireland, but the combination of piety and concern for justice is still as strong now as it was at the church's admirable beginning.

Methody. The affectionate name for Methodist College in Belfast, which began its scholastic life as the Wesleyan Methodist Collegiate Institution in 1868. Its first headmaster desired that the institution should be coeducational, and 'young ladies' were admitted early in the school's life. In 1885 the name was simplified to its present form. One wing of the original college housed a theological seminary, which in 1918 was moved to separate premises called 'Edgehill' in Lennoxvale, about half a mile away; this became Edgehill College in 1928, and in 1951 was made into a constituent college of Queen's University Belfast. The lay school in its original site in Malone Road is one of the largest and finest 'maintained' grammar schools in the United Kingdom.

Mhac an tSaoi, Máire (b.1922). Irish-language poet, critic and translator. She was born in Dublin but immersed from childhood in the Irish of Dunquin, in the west Kerry GAEL-TACHT. The daughter of politician and minister Seán MACENTEE and niece of poet and scholar Monsignor Pádraig de Brún, she was educated at University College Dublin and the Sorbonne, and worked with Tomás de Bhaldraithe on his *English-Irish Dictionary* (1959) and abroad with Ireland's Department of External Affairs. Her poetry unites the best of the traditional and the modern, and she is capable of great lyric intensity. Her collections include *Margadh na Saoire* (1956), *An Galar Dubhach* (1980) and *An Cion go dtí Seo* (1987). Her autobiography, *As Old as the State*, was published in 2003. She is married to the politician and journalist Conor CRUISE O'BRIEN.

Mhuire Mháthair! Irish for 'Mother Mary!' The imprecation is used in HIBERNO-ENGLISH on hearing shocking or distressing news.
See also WIRRASTHRUE.

Miach. In Irish mythology, the more talented son of DIAN CECHT. He replaces the silver hand that his father has fashioned for NUADA with one of flesh and blood, and thus enables Nuada to recover the kingship of the TUATHA DÉ DANAAN. He also manages transplants, once giving a human the eye of a cat. His father, envious of his medical skills, attacks him three times, but Miach is able to cure his own wounds. He finally succumbs to a lesion in the brain. After his death 365 herbs – with the power of healing even mortal wounds – grow out of his grave. These are gathered by Miach's sister, Airmid, but the relentless Dian Cecht scatters them so that no one knows which is which.

Mí-ádh. An Irish term for 'ill luck', used in HIBERNO-ENGLISH to mean a 'misfortune', a 'curse': 'What *mí-ádh* was on you that you did such a thing?' ('*Cén mí-ádh a bhí ort gur dhein tú an rud sin?*'); 'That fellow is nothing but a *mí-ádh*.' 'There's some class of a *mí-ádh* on him, Doctor,' remarked the father of the infant Gabriel BYRNE (b.1950) after the latter had given his baby brother turpentine to drink (*Pictures in My Head*, 1994).

Michael Angelo Titmarsh. *See* TITMARSH, MICHAEL ANGELO.

Mick. A generic, frequently pejorative, term for an Irishman in England. It is of older provenance than PADDY[1], and it is believed that this term came into currency after the public execution (the last such in Britain) of Co. Fermanagh-born FENIAN Michael Barrett, who was hanged in front of Newgate Gaol in London in May 1868. He had been the only person found guilty, on what is now believed to be flimsy evidence, of blowing up the wall of Clerkenwell House of Detention in 1867 in an attempt to free IRB member Richard O'Sullivan; at least six people were killed in the explosion and many others were injured. The soldiers of the Irish Guards regiment are also popularly known as 'the MICKS'.

Mick McQuaid. A brand of plug tobacco popu-

lar among traditional pipe-smokers. The name probably derives from *The Adventures of Mick McQuaid* (1875) by Galway-born Colonel William Francis Lynam (1845–94) – initially serialized in Lynam's periodical *Shamrock*; McQuaid appears to have been a 'devious schemer'.

Micko. The name by which Kerry footballer Mick O'Connell (b.1937) was known. O'Connell, whose sporting prowess at mid-field was legendary and who was one of the great sporting figures of his age, was born on VALENTIA island on 4 January 1937 and played in nine ALL-IRELAND finals for Kerry, on the winning side in 1959, 1962, 1969 and 1970. He also won the NATIONAL LEAGUES and RAILWAY CUP medals. An autobiography, *A Kerry Footballer*, appeared in 1974.

> Whenever I am asked what was the greatest game I have played, I am never stuck for an answer. Without reservation, that charmed hour was the national league final of 1961 against Derry. Everything, and I really mean everything that I contested in the air I won and every kick must have seemed guided by some supernatural control. And so effortless was the whole operation that I must have, that day, reached the pinnacle of my physical form.
>
> MICK O'CONNELL: *A Kerry Footballer* (1974)

Micks, The. The nickname of the Irish Guards, who were also known as Bob's Own because Lord Roberts of Kandahar (1832–1914) was the regiment's first colonel. According to Army Order No. 77, 1 April 1900:

> Her Majesty the Queen having deemed it desirable to commemorate the bravery shown by Irish regiments during the operations in South Africa in the years 1899 and 1900 has been graciously pleased that an Irish Regiment of Foot Guards be formed to be designated the 'Irish Guards'.

Mick the Miller (1926–39). A famous greyhound. He belonged to a Father Martin Brophy, who named him after an employee, Mick Miller. After outstanding wins in Ireland, he was entered for the English Derby, which he won in 1929 and 1930, the first time that any greyhound had won the English Derby in two consecutive years. In 1929 Father Brophy sold him to an English bookmaker for 800 guineas. Mick the Miller played the leading role in the film *White Boy* in 1935. Mick, now stuffed, may be viewed at the Rothschild Zoological Museum in Tring, Hertfordshire.

Midir. In Irish mythology, the son of the DAGDA, and an important member of the TUATHA DÉ DANAAN. He is the husband of ÉTAIN (who suffers several metamorphoses at the hand of FUAMNACH, his first – and understandably jealous – wife). Étain becomes in turn a pool, a worm and a fly that is swallowed by the pregnant wife of the Ulster warrior ETAR. The child is a daughter, a second Étain, whom Midir tries to claim as his wife. He first attempts to win her from her husband Eochaidh Eiream in a game of FIDCHELL, and then abducts her, the two flying out of the chimney in the form of swans. He takes her to his palace at Brí Leith near Ardagh in Co. Longford, but eventually yields her to Eochaidh, to whom she bears yet another Étain. When the Dagda relinquishes his leadership of the gods, Midir refuses to accept BODB DEARG as the new ruler. It is in the titanic war that follows that the Tuatha dé Danann, torn apart by dissension, lose their divine power, literally go to ground and are degraded into the fairies of later folklore.

Midnight Court, The. *See* CÚIRT AN MHEÁNOÍCHE.

Midsummer's Day. One of the four great traditional feast days, celebrated on St John's Eve, 23 June. Herbs gathered on this day, especially that dedicated to its patron, St John's wort, were thought to be especially powerful. St John's wort, called the 'faery herb', was used to make a balm for wounds and to treat rheumatism. Long before what are now called 'alternative' remedies became popular it was used as a remedy for depression, 'the AIRY FIT' being supposedly a condition caused by witchcraft.

Migrant workers. *See* NAVVIES; SPALPEEN; TATIE-HOWKERS; TUNNEL TIGERS.

Míl (sometimes **Míl Espaine**). The name in Irish mythology of the mysterious figure who organizes the last invasion of Ireland. His followers, many of them blood relations, conquer the Ireland of the TUATHA DÉ DANAAN, though Míl does not actually set foot in the desirable country seen by his son (in some stories grandson or nephew) ITH from a tower in Spain. (There is some confusion as to whether this is the actual Hispania of the Romans or a synonym for the Land of the Dead; *see* OTHERWORLD.) According to the myth, Míl is of the 35th generation in direct line from Adam, and Milesius, the latinized version of his name, suggests he was a soldier (Latin *miles*). *See also* MILESIANS.

Míle murder. A HIBERNO-ENGLISH phrase meaning a 'big fuss', 'conflict' or 'disturbance' (Irish *míle*, 'a thousand'). It is an example of the common linguistic phenomenon of combining English and Irish words in one phrase. It is sometimes given as 'melia murder'.

Milesians. In Irish mythology, the last tribe to invade Ireland, identified with the historical Celts. Called after their leader MÍL or Milesius, who came from Spain, they superseded the TUATHA DÉ DANAAN. Míl never reached Ireland, but his wife SCOTA and his son IR did (although in some versions Ir dies in a storm before landing); despite appearances, neither played a part in the naming of the conquered country.

Milesius. *See* MÍL.

Militia. *See* RIC; YEOS.

Milk Rás. *See* RÁS TAILTEANN.

Millennium Spire, the. *See* NELSON'S PILLAR.

Millennium Wing. An extension to the NATIONAL GALLERY OF IRELAND in Dublin, designed by Benson and Forsyth and officially opened in 2002. The wing provides the gallery with an entrance on Clare Street and houses a wide range of European as well as Irish masterpieces, including Caravaggio's *The Betrayal of Christ*, which was donated to the museum by a Jesuit community in Dublin, who, while it was in their possession, had believed it to be a copy.

Millie. A Belfast abbreviation of 'mill worker', denoting a woman who worked in a mill.

Milligan, Alice (1886–1953). Poet and editor. She was born in Omagh, Co. Tyrone, in September 1886 and educated at Methodist College in Belfast, Magee College in Derry, and King's College London. On her return to Belfast she was an active worker for the GAELIC LEAGUE (and its laureate). She and Ethna CARBERY edited the *SHAN VAN VOCHT* (1896–9) and she composed the first dramatic scene in modern Irish for the Letterkenny FEIS in 1898. *The Last Feast of the Fianna*, produced at the GAIETY by the IRISH LITERARY THEATRE on 19 February 1900 was the fourth play of the IRISH LITERARY REVIVAL to be staged. Her patriotic poems were published in *We Sang for Ireland* (1950). She grew silent after Partition and wrote little, dying in the Omagh house where she was born on 13 April 1953.

'Come in for it's growing late,
And the grass will wet ye!
Come in! or when it's dark
The Fenians will get ye.'
...
But one little rebel there,
Watching all with laughter,
Thought, 'When the Fenians come
I'll rise and go after.'

'When I Was a Little Girl', in *We Sang for Ireland* (1950)

Milligan, Spike (1918–2002). Comedian. Terence Alan Milligan was born in Poona, India, where his Sligo-born father served in the Royal Artillery. Although holding an Irish passport, he joined his father's old regiment in the Second World War and served in North Africa, where he met Harry Secombe. From 1946 until *The Goon Show* was reluctantly taken on by a conservative BBC (it ran from 1951 until 1960), he performed in a group and wrote comedy, 'wandering around', in his own words, with Peter Sellers and Harry Secombe, his

collaborators on the Goons. After the Goons broke up, Milligan had marital difficulties and the first of many serious nervous breakdowns, but he recovered to be a successful playwright and stage and film actor. He also wrote a number of bestselling comic books that drew on his experience in the war: *Adolf Hitler, My Part in His Downfall* (1971), *Monty, My Part in His Victory* (1976) and *Mussolini, His Part in My Downfall* (1978). A comic novel *Puckoon* (1963) concerned a fictional Irish village that is split down the middle by the BOUNDARY COMMISSION. Acerbic and iconoclastic to the end, Milligan was a popular but never comfortable chat-show guest. He declared his last words would be 'I told you I was sick.'

Milliken, Richard [Alfred]. *See* GROVES OF BLARNEY, THE.

Mind mice at crossroads. An expression indicating parsimony, always used in the conditional, as in 'She said her landlord was so mean he'd mind mice at crossroads.' Other phrases expressive of meanness include: 'He'd live in your eye and let the other one out in flats' and 'She'd take the eye out of your head and come back for the lashes.'
See also LIVE ON, TO; MEANNESS.

Mind the dresser! A cry uttered more out of devilment than necessity at country dances, which were often held in private houses.
See also AIRNEÁN.

Minging. An Ulster (and Scots) word still commonly used to describe extreme dirtiness and smelliness, as in 'I need a shower; I feel minging!'

Minker's torri. *See* SHELTA.

Minstrel Boy, The. The title of several biographies of the poet and song lyricist Thomas MOORE, and of one of the most popular of his *Irish Melodies* (1807–34).

Miracle Worker, The. The title of the Broadway play (1959) by William Gibson and the film (1962) made from it, about the work of the partially sighted Anne Sullivan, who taught the deaf and blind Helen Keller (1880–1968) to speak. Anne Sullivan was born of Irish parents in Feeding Hill, Massachusetts, in 1866 and was educated at the Perkins Institute at Waltham in the same state. She returned as a teacher in 1887 and met the 7-year-old Keller, who had been blind and deaf from the age of 19 months after a bout of scarlet fever. She became Keller's governess and undertook the exhausting task of teaching her the manual alphabet by tapping the palm of her hand; she also taught her a method of touch lip-reading by placing her fingers against the speaker's face. Her pupil became a successful academic and writer, and Sullivan as companion and mentor shared her life of campaigning for the blind and deaf. Sullivan died in 1936, leaving a temporarily bereft Keller. The account of her coping with the crisis is told in *Helen Keller's Journal* (1938). Sullivan's name is perpetuated in the Anne Sullivan Foundation, an Irish charity catering for the deaf and blind.

Miraculous medal, the. An oval silver-coloured medal with an image of the Blessed Virgin Mary on one side, and on the other a cross and a representation of the hearts of Jesus and Mary. It was worn on a blue ribbon as the insignia of the CHILDREN OF MARY. It apparently has the name and reputation of 'miraculous' because its appearance was revealed miraculously to Catherine Labouré, a Sister of Charity of the Society of ST VINCENT DE PAUL in 1830. In Ireland there was great popular devotion to the miraculous medal: it was pinned to clothes or baby's bedclothes or attached to ROSARY beads. Like many devotional rituals, the habit of wearing the miraculous medal has fallen into disuse.

Mise Éire (Irish, 'I am Ireland'). The first ever full-length feature film in Irish, funded by GAEL LINN, directed by George Morrison and released, to considerable acclaim, in 1960. Its sweeping theme was the struggle for independence of the Irish nation. Seán Ó RIADA wrote the score, which became celebrated in its own right.

Mise le meas (in full *is mise le meas*, Irish, 'it is I, with respect'). A formal phrase meaning 'yours respectfully', 'truly', 'sincerely', at the end of a letter. It is often used at the end of official letters, for instance to and from government departments, even being used in letters written in English.

'Mise Raifteirí an File' (Irish, 'I am Raftery the poet'). A poem once ascribed to its subject but now known to have been composed by Seán Ó Ceallaigh, an expatriate Irishman living in Oswego, New York state, from phrases associated in folk memory with Antaine Ó Raifteirí (BLIND RAFTERY). The poem was published in the journal *An Gaodhal* in 1882:

> Mise Raifteirí an file, lán dóchas is grá,
> Le súile gan solas, le ciúnas gan crá
> ...
> Féach anois mé, is mo chúl le balla
> Ag seinm ceoil do phócaí folamh.
> (I am Raftery the poet, full of hope and of love,
> With eyes without seeing, peace without pain.
> ...
> See me now with my back to the wall
> Playing music for empty pockets.)

Miss Horniman. The rather formal title used for Annie Elizabeth Frederika Horniman (1860–1937), whose financial patronage enabled W.B. Yeats to establish the Irish National Theatre Society in a permanent home in the ABBEY THEATRE. She had met the poet when she was a student at the Slade School of Art at meetings of the mystical Order of the Golden Dawn, and began an emotional friendship with him that was but pallidly returned. Heiress to the riches of an English tea-merchant and passionately interested in theatre, she began – after appropriate psychic consultations including the tarot cards – to subsidize the society in 1903, and purchased and equipped at a cost of £13,000 the building in Abbey Street, Dublin, that was to become Ireland's national theatre. She paid the salaries of the full-time actors and promoted the company in England, but began to find the society's staging of such Nationalist plays as *The RISING OF THE MOON* by Lady

GREGORY offensive. (Her relations with the author herself were also strained, mainly because of her intimacy with Yeats.)

Miss Horniman broke completely with the society when the theatre was kept open during the period of official mourning for Edward VII in 1910, but sold her holdings to the directors on advantageous terms. Still fascinated with theatre she moved to Manchester, buying and equipping the Gaiety Theatre and managing there an excellent repertory company until 1917. She encouraged such local playwrights as Stanley Houghton (1881–1913) and Harold Brighouse (1883–1958), respectively authors of such popular standards as *Hindle Wakes* (1912) and *Hobson's Choice* (1916). She also did much to encourage the establishment of repertory theatres in other provincial cities, by which time she was known as 'Queen Horniman'.

Missing, the. *See* DISAPPEARED, THE.

Mission. A visit to a parish by one or several priests who were members of an order for the purpose of reviving spiritual fervour and attendance at the sacraments among the laity. The mission, which would come about once every five years, would last for a week or even two, with men and women attending on alternate evenings or alternate weeks. The preachers emphasized the renewal of baptismal vows and confession. Originally missioners were Franciscans or Dominicans, but in the 20th century they were more likely to be Jesuits or Redemptorists, whose stock-in-trade was hellfire sermons. Missions were one of the many means used by the Catholic Church to maintain domination over and the fear of God in the laity. They are still held in some areas, and Redemptorists are still among the most popular preachers, but the tone and content of the sermons have changed beyond recognition.

> Two holy fathers that used to come here, and even though of saintly appearance, they were well versed you may say in every description of villainy. They'd light the chapel with language, bringing their voices down very low and then making a tremendous shout that'd frighten the living daylights out of everyone. People used to be afraid to go up near the altar. And we'll say a shy man sitting there, if the holy father fixed his eye on him, and he in a rage, the poor man'd pass out.
>
> Even down near the door where we used to be, you'd be shivering in your shoes, for each night they'd go from one evil to another, from the sins of life to death, from death to judgement, and judgement, as was only natural, to the place below! Oh glory! The fires of hell would be described down to the very last detail, the smoke and the steam and the gnashing of teeth! Poor old women sitting there in the chapel, no more sin on them than the child in the cradle, only trying to make ends meet, and the tears rolling down their cheeks at the thought of all those people suffering on the hobs of hell for all eternity.
>
> ÉAMON KELLY: 'The Hereafter', in *Ireland's Master Storyteller* (1998)

Missionary Settlement, the. 'The first missionary settlement which was ever established among the native Irish using the Irish language,' as the *Achill Missionary Herald and Western Witness* printed in its first number on 31 July 1837. Since the paper was written mainly by the Irish-speaking Rev. Edward Nangle, the founder of the experiment on ACHILL island, a certain triumphalism was permitted.

Nangle was born near Athboy, Co. Meath, in 1799 and educated at Trinity College Dublin. In 1831, under the aegis of the Sunday School Society of Ireland and encouraged by the Protestant Bishop of Tuam, he set up a missionary colony at Doogort at the foot of Slievemore mountain on the north coast of Achill. He persuaded a number of Protestant families from the mainland to help in his foundation. Unquestionably conversion of the local, poverty-stricken Catholic population was part of his mission, and the establishment of a church (1835), school (1834) and printing press (1837) in the first six years was a tribute to the energies of the missionary whose purpose was 'to bear a faithful and uncomplimentary testimony against the superstition and idolatry of the Church of Rome'. Nangle was a fluent Irish speaker, realizing the importance of the language in gaining converts in the west of Ireland, and he published an *Introduction to the Irish Language* in 1854.

Though Achill had been somewhat neglected by the diocese, Archbishop MACHALE of Tuam, fearing wholesale conversions, established his own mission using Franciscan priests and opened a national school at Bunacurry. By the beginning of the Great Famine Nangle had created a substantial village, and though he was as assiduous in famine relief among Catholics as among his own flock there were inevitable accusations of SOUPERISM. The mission lost some of its energy when Nangle was appointed to a parish on the mainland, and it was defunct by 1879. Nangle himself died in 1883. An attempt to colonize an area called Mweelan by first building houses came to nothing, and the roofless relics form a kind of ghost village:

> ... *graue Steinmauern, dunkle Fensterhöhlen, kein Stück Holz, kein Fetzen Stoff, nicht Farbiges, wie ein Körper ohne Haare, ohne Augen, ohne Fleisch and Blut: das Skelett eines Dorfes* ...
>
> (... grey stone walls, dark window holes, not a flake of wood or rag of material, utterly colourless, like a body without hair, without eyes, without flesh and blood – the skeleton of a village ...)
>
> HEINRICH BÖLL (1917–85): *Irisches Tagebuch* ('Irish Journal', 1961)

See also SECOND REFORMATION.

Mistress Murphy's Chowder. The final resting place of 'the overalls' in an Irish-American comic vaudeville song written as a one-hit wonder in 1898 by George L. Geifer. The full title of the song was 'Who Threw the Overalls in Mistress Murphy's Chowder'. It was featured in a Phil Silvers film, *Coney Island* (1943), and recorded by Bing Crosby. The fact that a threatened Hibernian 'ruckus' did not take place is an indication that the American Irish could at last laugh at themselves and had accepted American cuisine.

> 'Who threw the overalls in Mrs Murphy's chowder?'

Nobody spoke – so he shouted all the louder:
'It's an Irish trick that's true;
I can lick the Mick that threw
The overalls in Mistress Murphy's chowder.'

Mist that Does Be on the Bog, The. A squib by Gerald MacNamara (*see* THOMPSON IN TÍR NA NÓG) satirizing the idiom of the plays of J.M. SYNGE and Lady GREGORY. It was first staged at the ABBEY THEATRE on 26 November 1909, and its barbs were taken in good part by both patrons and management. The author called the play 'a fog in one act', and the following is a typical piece of dialogue:

> *Clarence:* And you think, kind ladies, that I have the gift of the bards upon me?
>
> *Cissie:* Sure it's as plain as the staff of a pike, for the beautiful words pour from your lips like a delf jug and it full of buttermilk.

The title has remained in currency as a dismissive phrase for the kind of pseudo-poetic, literally-translated-from-Irish dialogue that characterized some lesser Abbey plays.

Mitchel, Charles (1920–96). RTÉ newsreader. He was the face of the television newsroom from its inception on 1 January 1961 until he retired in 1984, and a familiar personality in most Irish homes. In 1962 he won a Jacob's broadcasting award.

Mitchel, John (1815–75). YOUNG IRELAND activist and felon. He was born in Dungiven, Co. Derry, the son of a Trinitarian minister who afterwards turned to Unitarianism and was called to Newry, Co. Down. Mitchel was educated there and at Trinity College Dublin, and after a period working in his uncle's bank in Derry became apprenticed to a solicitor. He came under the influence of Thomas DAVIS and succeeded him on the staff of *The NATION* after his premature death. The Great Famine of the 1840s, which he regarded as British-inflicted genocide, persuaded him that only armed insurrection would bring about the remedy for Ireland's miseries. In 1847 he co-founded the IRISH CONFEDERATION, and in 1848 he decided that *The Nation* was too tame and founded his own paper, *The United Irishman*, in which he advocated the 'treason' that caused him to be arrested in May of that year.

Mitchel was sent to VAN DIEMEN'S LAND (Tasmania) via Bermuda, where he had nearly died in confinement. Things were better in Tasmania; he was able to send for his wife and six children, and escaped with them to America in 1853. He became a strong supporter of the Southern States and of slavery; his eldest and youngest sons died in the Civil War, and he was arrested in New York because of newspaper articles in defence of Jefferson Davis and the Confederate stance.

Returning to Ireland in 1875 Mitchel was elected as member for Tipperary in February unseated as an undischarged felon and promptly re-elected in March a few days before his death in Newry, where he is buried. His *Jail Journal*, published in America in 1854, is one of the holy books of 19th-century Nationalism. He also wrote *The Last Conquest of Ireland (Perhaps)* (1861).

> Good night, then, Ireland and Irish tumults, strugglings and vociferations, quackery, puffery and endless talk.
>
> *Jail Journal* (1854)

See also SEND WAR IN OUR TIME; SILVER TONGUE AND SMILE OF WITCHERY.

Mitchelburne, John (also **Michelburne**) (1647–1721). Governor of Derry during the siege (*see* DERRY, SIEGE OF). He was born in Sussex and had an active career in the army. As colonel of a regiment of foot he played a significant part in the defence of Derry during the siege (1688–9) and served briefly as governor of the city. It was he who set the red flag on the cathedral steeple, giving later generations the 'Derry crimson' icon. Like several other anti-Jacobite heroes he was not recompensed, even though he had lost his wife and children, and held IOUs for £1000 of his own money given to the city defenders. He was not as promised made mayor of the city in 1690 nor governor of Culmore, and spent time as a debtor in the Fleet in 1709, while suing for money he believed was owed him by Parliament.

Mitchelburne is thought to be the author of a play, *Ireland Preserved, or the Siege of Londonderry* (1705), which features such historical characters as Conrade d'Rosin, the Rev. George WALKER and a 'third governor, Mitchelburne, called Granade', as well as two comic hangmen on opposite sides, Black Jack and Teague. The play, which may have been polished by George FARQUHAR, remained popular, and William CARLETON recalls having seen it done by a barnstorming company in his boyhood (early 19th century). Mitchelburne died in Derry on 1 October 1721, leaving money 'for maintaining the flag in the steeple of Derry'.

Mitchell, George (b.1933). American Democrat senator. He was born in Maine and educated at Georgetown University, where he took a degree in law. He was a member of the US senate (1980–94), serving on the select committee on the Iran-Contra Affair in 1987 and becoming majority leader of the senate in 1988. In November 1995 President Bill Clinton appointed him special adviser for economic initiatives in Ireland. He was the author of the Mitchell Report, released in 1996, which laid out six principles concerning democracy and non-violence, and he played a major part in the peace process leading to the signing of the GOOD FRIDAY AGREEMENT on 12 April 1998; for this he received many honours, including the UNESCO Peace Prize. He also served on a fact-finding committee about Israeli-Palestinian relations, and has written several books on political themes.

Mitchell, Susan [Langstaff] (1866–1926). Editor and satirist. She was born in Carrick-on-Shannon, Co. Leitrim, on 5 December 1866, but was brought up by Dublin aunts after her bank manager father died in 1872. In London for an ear operation she stayed with the Yeats family and soon found herself in the thick of the IRISH LITERARY REVIVAL, acting as George MOORE's secretary and sub-editor of the *Irish Homestead* and the *Irish Statesman*. Her collection of satirical verse portraits, *Aids to the Immortality of Certain Persons in*

Ireland Charitably Administered (1908), is still fresh. By the time of her death on 4 March 1926 she was known as one of Dublin's literary hostesses.

> Jove thunders from Olympus, and Moore from Ely Place,
> I damn respectability and call it a disgrace;
> ...
> But WB was the boy for me – he of the dim, wan clothes;
> And – don't let on I said it – not above a bit of a pose;
> And they call his writing literature, as everybody knows.

Mitchelstown Cave. An extensive cave now open to the public on the Mitchelstown road near Cahir, Co. Tipperary. It was discovered accidentally in 1833 by men quarrying for stone. It has impressive formations, such as that called 'the Tower of Babel'.

Mitchelstown Massacre. An incident that occurred in Mitchelstown, a town in north Co. Cork, on 9 September 1887. Two local MPs, William O'BRIEN and John Mandeville (1849–88), a tenant leader in Co. Tipperary, were ordered to appear before magistrates in connection with the organization of tenant resistance as part of the PLAN OF CAMPAIGN. They refused to comply, but a large angry crowd assembled in the town. Chief Secretary Arthur BALFOUR had ordered the RIC to take a hard line against all such agrarian disorder, and on this occasion police fired into the crowd, killing three people and wounding others. A subsequent investigation forced the resignation of RIC County Inspector Brownrigg, and Balfour acquire his sobriquet 'Bloody Balfour' as a result.

Mi Wadi. A dilutable orange squash very popular in Irish families before the advent of American-style carbonated soft drinks. It derives its name from Mineral Water Distributors, the company that has produced the drink since 1927.

Mizen Head. The most southerly mainland point in Ireland, in southwest Co. Cork. This sea area was notorious for wrecks, and a signal fog station was built there in 1909–10 on the island of Cloghane, which is connected by a footbridge to the mainland at the far end of the Mizen Peninsula, beyond the village of Schull. The fog station was demanned in 1993 and subsequently converted into a heritage centre. *See also* FASTNET, THE.

Mná na hÉireann (Irish, 'women of Ireland'). A fashionable, sometimes ironic term meaning the women of Ireland in general or perhaps the women who have a consciousness of a collective feminist destiny. It came into vogue in 1990 when Ireland's first woman president, Mary ROBINSON, was elected, and already appears dated.

Mobhi (d.*c.*545). One of the TWELVE APOSTLES OF IRELAND. He was trained by FINNIAN OF CLONARD and with his master's encouragement set up his own school at Glasnevin in Dublin. It was a kind of graduate school for other masters, and among his mature students were COLUM CILLE, COMGALL, CIARÁN OF CLONMACNOISE and CANICE. He died in the mid-6th-century plague and his foundation did not survive his death, nor are there any archaeological remains. Mobhi's feast day is 12 October.

Mo bhrón. Irish for 'my grief', an interjection conveying regret, sometimes anglicized as 'mavrone'.

Mo Cheol Thú. See MAC MATHÚNA, CIARÁN.

Mockeyah. A colloquial Cork adjective or (more usually) adverb suggesting pretence or a joke: 'He was dressed as a priest mockeyah.' The word is also used as an exclamation or a question.

Model County, the. The nickname of Co. Wexford, because of its progressive farming methods and model farms (the county is fertile and prosperous and the villages well maintained). The first agricultural college in Ireland was established in Bannow, Co. Wexford, in the 1850s. Like all nicknames for counties, it comes into its own during the GAA championship season, hurling in the case of Wexford (*see* YELLOWBELLIES).

Model schools. Training schools for teachers established from the 1830s as part of the infant NATIONAL SCHOOLS system. The first model school for males and females opened in Dublin in 1834, and by 1850 there were 25 model schools throughout Ireland, each equipped to house and train teachers for a six-month period. Because they were controlled directly by the national-school commissioners and no training was given in the teaching of religion, the Catholic hierarchy were dissatisfied with them, and in 1866 Catholics were forbidden to attend. Some 'model' schools survive in name, now part of the normal primary education system.

Modest Proposal, A. A pamphlet (published anonymously in October 1729) by Jonathan Swift (*see* DEAN, THE) at his most mordant and ambivalent. The full title continues:

> *For Preventing the children of the Poor People in Ireland from being a burden to their Parents or Country; and for making them beneficial to the Publick*

Written while he was staying in Co. Armagh, the pamphlet proposes as a solution to 18th-century Ireland's economic ills that its infants be raised for food:

> I have been assured by a very knowing American of my acquaintance in London, that a young healthy child well nursed is at a year old a most delicious, nourishing and wholesome food, whether stewed, roasted, baked or boiled, and I make no doubt that it will equally serve as a *fricassée* or a *ragoût*.

It is hard to tell whether it simply represents Swift in his comic misanthropic vein, or whether it is meant as a crushing indictment of English rule, or even as a display of distaste for the feckless native Irish who were soon to be the models for his YAHOOS. The aptness of the symbolism to English mismanagement is patent: the system of absentee landlordism and economic deprivation was another form of cannibalism. The contrast between the feline prose and its gross content marvellously heightens the satiric effect:

> Those who are more thrifty (as I must confess the times require) may flay the carcase; the skin of which, artificially dressed, will make admirable gloves for ladies, and summer boots for fine gentlemen.

Moengal or **Marcellus** (d.871). The saintly monk who established the library at Sankt-Gallen (*see* GALL) *c*.850. It housed an outstanding collection of manuscripts written by Irish scribes. He may have been the same Moengal (also Marcellus) who ran the cloister schools at BANGOR and had as his pupil Notker Balbus (*c*.840–912), the early composer of church music and compiler of a *Martyrology* (891–6) containing much information about Irish saints. In the *Necrology* of St Gall Moengal's death is recorded (in Latin) as that of 'the best and most learned of men' and in the ANNALS OF ULSTER it is recorded for the year 871 that 'Moengal the pilgrim, abbot of Bangor, brought his old age to a happy close'. His feast day is 27 September.

Moeran, E[rnest] J[ohn] (1894–1950). Composer. Moeran's music belongs to the English pastoral tradition, but he was, like his fellow-composer Arnold Bax (*see* O'BYRNE, DERMOT), increasingly influenced by the culture and landscape of Ireland as his career progressed.

The son of a Dublin-born Protestant clergyman, Moeran was born in Isleworth, Middlesex and brought up in rural Norfolk before studying at the Royal College of Music. Following the First World War (during which he sustained a head injury that required the insertion of a metal plate into his skull) he continued his musical studies with the composer John Ireland. Moeran composed prolifically in the early 1920s, Norfolk and its folk-song being a key influence. In the mid-1920s he became friendly with fellow-composer Philip Heseltine (better known under his pen name of Peter Warlock). Their three-year tenancy of a house in Eynsford, Kent was allegedly a time of bohemian riotousness that on more than one occasion attracted the attentions of the local constabulary. Drink would, from now on, be an increasing problem for the unfortunate Moeran. An effect of his war wound was to make him appear drunk even after very small amounts of alcohol and, whatever the true extent of his drinking, his inability to tolerate alcohol led many to see him as a chronic alcoholic.

A more positive influence was Moeran's growing interest in his Irish roots. His song settings of poems by JOYCE, *Seven Poems of James Joyce* (1929), marked his emergence from the boozy barrenness of the Eynsford years. From now on Ireland as much as Norfolk would be a major source of musical inspiration for him. He became particularly attached to KENMARE, Co. Kerry, and sojourns in the West of Ireland would punctuate the remainder of his life. (Moeran's Irish literary friends included Seamus O'SULLIVAN. The song settings *Six Poems of Seamus O'Sullivan*, for solo voice and piano, completed in 1944, are a highlight of his song output.)

Moeran spent much of the 1930s working on his Symphony in G Minor – a vast, gloomy work completed in 1937. Most of the symphony was written in Co. Kerry. Bax referred admiringly to 'the unwordly Western-Irish lights that seemed to glimmer down on the pages of ... [the] symphony' and 'the delicately distilled suggestions of native folk-idiom heard [there].' Moeran's Violin Concerto – a work shot through with Irish lyricism – followed in 1942. In 1945 he married the cellist Peers Coetmore, for whom he composed a Cello Concerto and Cello Sonata. The marriage was not a success, a lengthy period of separation beginning in spring 1947. Moeran spent the first half of 1948 in Kenmare, 'roughing it' for part of the spring amongst the tents of a group of Travellers. His *Songs From County Kerry* were published the following year.

As well as being a source of inspiration, Ireland was the scene of some of Moeran's heaviest drinking. A drinking bout in Ireland in October 1948 led to a complete breakdown in his health. In September 1949 Moeran 'disappeared' to Ireland for a further period of hard drinking, resurfacing sick and depressed in England in December. He left England for the last time in March 1950. A visit to a specialist in Dublin diagnosed a brain disorder, and Moeran began to fret that his growing mental instability might lead to his being certified insane. In June he was back in Kenmare. On 1 December 1950, during a heavy storm, Moeran was seen to fall from the pier at Kenmare. He was dead by the time he was recovered from the sea. He was buried in the town's Old Churchyard.

Moiley. A HIBERNO-ENGLISH word for a hornless cow, coming from the Irish *maol*, 'bald'. It is also used figuratively:

> Robbie Art, nicknamed Moiley, because of his high bald forehead
>
> SAM HANNA BELL: *December Bride* (1951)

Molaise of Devenish (d. late 560s) One of the TWELVE APOSTLES OF IRELAND, instructed by their master FINNIAN OF CLONARD to set up their own hermitages. Molaise chose the tiny DEVENISH, an island in Lower Lough Erne 5 km (3 miles) from Enniskillen, where he continued his friendship with COLUM CILLE. He is believed to have made the arduous journey to Rome and brought home sacred relics. The monastery that he founded used to hold the Soiscél Molaise, a book shrine now housed in the National Museum in Dublin. Molaise's feast day is 12 September.

Mo léir. Irish for 'my ruin', 'my woe', an expression used to convey grief or regret. The phrase is more likely to be used in HIBERNO-ENGLISH with a sense of philosophic acceptance rather than lament: 'He wanted to study medicine but *mo léir* he didn't study hard enough for his exams.' The intensified verions *mo léir cráite* (Irish *cráite*, 'troubled', 'tormented') and *mo léan géar* (Irish *géar*, 'sharp', 'grievous') are also used, although not in casual conversation.

See also MO BHRÓN.

Moling (d.697). A Wexford saint who studied at GLENDALOUGH and set up a monastery known as Tech Moling (Moling's house) in Co. Carlow, which continued for many centuries as St Mullins, one of the premier Leinster foundations. His name is also to be found in Timolin in Co. Kildare and in Tigh Moling, near Inishtiogue in Co. Kilkenny. Among many tales associated with the saint was that he could walk on water and that he introduced rye to Ireland. He became Bishop of Ferns, and his feast day is 17 June.

Moll Doyle's Daughters. A codename for a secret agrarian society of the late 18th and early 19th century, used in the phrase 'Moll Doyle and her daughters …' The phrase 'to give [someone] a Moll Doyle' means to administer physical or verbal punishment.

Molloy, M[ichael] J[oseph] (1917–94). Playwright. He was born at Milltown, Co. Galway, and educated at St Jarlath's College in Tuam. His studies for the priesthood were terminated because of illness and he became a farmer, but he retained a love of drama and fine language that had begun with a childhood visit to the ABBEY THEATRE. His best-known works are *The King of Friday's Men* (1948), an evocation of late-18th-century Irish peasant life, and *The Wood of the Whispering* (1953), which mixes fantasy with the Connacht depopulation.

Molloy, Matt (b.1947). Traditional musician. A virtuoso tin-whistle and flute player, he was born in Ballaghadereen, Co. Roscommon. He was a member of the original BOTHY BAND in 1974 and has been a member of The CHIEFTAINS since 1979. He has recorded several solo albums and collaborated with other traditional musicians. His bar in Westport, Co. Mayo, is famous for SESSIONS of *CEOL AGUS CRAIC*.

Molly Maguires. A short-lived SECRET SOCIETY organized in 1843 to resist evictions for non-payment of rent. The members, young Irishmen, dressed up as women and manhandled landlords' agents. They were active during 1844, especially in the counties of Leitrim, Roscom-mon and Longford. The name was later adopted by a secret society of Irish-American anthracite miners in Pennsylvania (*c*.1865–77), founded to seek better conditions; however, their tactics eventually included intimidation of English and German miners, and they were accused of killing members of the company's police force. A number of members were hanged in 1877 in Scranton after a ruthless pursuit by members of the Pinkerton detective agency. The Irish-American society was the subject of the film *The Molly Maguires* (1970), starring Richard HARRIS and Sean Connery. The story also inspired Arthur Conan Doyle's novel *The Valley of Fear* (1915).

'Molly Malone'. The song most strongly associated with Dublin. It is also called 'Cockles and Mussels', but it is more often known by the name of its heroine, a beautiful young fishmonger called Molly Malone who, regrettably, 'died of a fever'. It is the anthem of Dublin city (and Dublin's GAA football team).

> In Dublin's fair city,
> Where the girls are so pretty,
> I first set my eyes on sweet Molly Malone.
> She wheeled her wheelbarrow
> Through streets broad and narrow,
> Crying, 'Cockles and mussels, alive alive, oh!
> *Chorus:*
> 'Alive alive, oh!
> Alive alive, oh!'
> Crying, 'Cockles and mussels, alive alive, oh!

The origins of the song are obscure but it is now believed to have been written as a comic song in the late 19th century by an Edinburgh man, James Yorkston. Not much is known about Molly Malone apart from the information in the ballad, though she was probably active around the end of the 18th century and may be buried in St Audoen's Church.

See also DISH WITH THE FISH; *FAIR CITY*.

Moloney, Paddy (b.1938). Traditional musician. A Dubliner, Moloney, who plays UILLEANN PIPES and tin whistle, has since the group's inception been leader of The CHIEFTAINS.

See also CEOLTÓIRÍ CHUALANN.

Molony, Helena (1884–1967). Feminist, Republican and trade unionist. She joined INGHIN-IDHE NA HÉIREANN in 1903, and in 1908 she became editor of *Bean na hÉireann*, a militant separatist magazine founded by Maud GONNE. The following year she was instrumental, with Constance Markievicz (*see* REBEL COUNTESS, THE), in founding the Fianna Éireann ('warriors of Ireland', a revolutionary version of the boy scouts). At around the same time she joined the ABBEY THEATRE and was an actor there until 1920. She participated in protests organized by SINN FÉIN against the visit of King George V in 1911 and was imprisoned. James CONNOLLY asked her to become secretary of the Irish Women Workers' Union (IWWU) in 1915; she joined the IRISH CITIZEN ARMY and took part in the 1916 EASTER RISING, after which she was imprisoned in Dublin. She took the Republican side against the TREATY, later returning to work with the IWWU and serving as president of the Irish Trade Union Congress. She died in Dublin on 28 January 1967.

Moluag (*c.*592). A Pictish saint from DÁL RI-ATA, who studied at BANGOR and established a monastery at Mortlach on the shores of Loch Linnhe in Argyll. He died at Rosemarkie on the Moray Firth and his feast day is 25 June.

Molyneux, William (1656–98). Scientist and political economist. He was born in Dublin on 17 April 1656 and educated at Trinity College Dublin and the Middle Temple in London. He was surveyor-general and chief engineer (1684–8) and during the Williamite War of 1689–91 lived in Chester, where he became friendly with the philosopher John Locke. His work on optics, *Dioptrica Nova*, was for a long time the standard work on the subject. In terms of his importance in Irish history, his major work was *The Case of Ireland's Being Bound by Acts of Parliament in England Stated*, a 'patriotic' pamphlet published in 1698 and challenging the constraints on the legislative independence of the Irish Parliament (*see* POYNING'S LAW). The pamphlet was denounced in Westminster as 'of dangerous consequence' and a copy burned by the common hangman. Molyneux died on 11 October 1698.

Monasterboice. A monastic site in Co. Louth. It includes a round tower, the remains of churches, and, most notably, one of the most perfect surviving high crosses, the 10th-century Cross of Muiredach, thought to be named after an abbot of that name who died in 922. There is another high cross, called the 'Tall Cross', and a third in the monastery's graveyard. The round tower, which it is possible to climb to the top of (although this is not permitted), suffered damage from a fire in 1097, when the monastery's library and treasures were lost.

Mongán. The son of MANANNÁN MAC LIR and Caintigerna, a mortal queen of the land around LOUGH NEAGH. When the child is three nights old, his father takes him to his palace in TÍR TAIRNIGIRI ('the land of promise') and invests him with magical powers. When he reaches maturity he marries the beautiful Dubh Lacha, his exact coeval. Later, in a burst of irrational generosity, he offers his friend Brandubh, king of Leinster, any wish he has the power to grant. Brandubh, who had long desired Dubh Lacha, asks for her as his wife. Mongán cannot in honour refuse, but uses his inherited power to sleep with his wife in the guise of a monk and trick Brandubh into accepting a withered old hag, temporarily made beautiful, rather than Dubh Lacha. Though later killed in battle, Mongán is believed to have returned to earth as FIONN MAC CUMHAIL.

Monitor. A young man or woman who, once he or she had finished primary education, worked in his or her own national school as a teacher's assistant. Many monitors went on to the teacher-training colleges.

Monks of the Screw. The members of a literary and social club (1780–95) which met at a house in Kevin Street in the Dublin LIBERTIES, and later at the home in Rathfarnham of the 'prior', John Philpot CURRAN, the liberal advocate. Its members, though mainly Protestant, were strong opponents of the Act of UNION (1801). A piece of verse written by Curran best indicates the temper of the club's proceedings:

When St Patrick this order established
He called us the 'Monks of the Screw';
Good rules he revealed to our abbot
To guide us in what we should do:
'My brethren be chaste! – till you're tempted,
When sober be grave and discreet
And humble your bodies with fasting
As oft as you've nothing to eat.'

Monster Meetings. A means of indicating to reluctant British governments that the time was ripe for the repeal of the Act of UNION. The tactic was devised by Daniel O'CONNELL in 1843. The first meeting, held on 9 March 1843 at Trim, Co. Meath, attracted 30,000 people; at Mullingar on 14 May the numbers had increased to 100,000; and in Cork a week later the crowd had swelled to half a million. The effect was greatly to increase the 'repeal rent', the weekly contribution made by supporters of the cause, from a norm of £50 a week to £3100 after the MALLOW DEFIANCE. The meeting at TARA held on 15 August was said to have attracted a full million people, though how the count was made is uncertain.

The culmination of the campaign was to be a meeting on Sunday 8 October near Dublin at CLONTARF (another name to conjure with from Ireland's glory days), and this was to make the host at Tara look 'like a caucus'. On the Saturday evening, when many protesters would already have started for the capital, Sir Robert PEEL proscribed the meeting. Warships rode at anchor in Dublin Bay beside the venue and Clontarf itself was ringed with cavalry. O'Connell immediately cancelled the meeting; to a man with a lifelong policy of non-violence the prospect of nearly a million people converging on the fields and strands of the bay being met by armed soldiers – and within range of naval guns – was unthinkable. He had the agreement of the YOUNG IRELANDers, though they afterwards denied it. Peel had O'Connell, his son and seven supporters arrested for sedition, and arranged for an entirely Protestant

jury at the trial. As a result O'Connell spent a comfortable three and a half months in the Richmond Bridewell in Dublin until he was released on appeal to a rapturous populace. It was to be his last hour of triumph.

Montague, John (b.1929). Poet. He was born in Brooklyn, New York, but brought up in Garvaghey, Co. Tyrone ('From the Rough Field I went to school / In the Glen of the Hazels'). He was educated at University College Dublin and at Yale, and taught at Berkeley and University College Cork, retiring in 1988. He has published more than a dozen collections of poetry, notably *Poisoned Lands* (1961), *The Rough Field* (1972), *A Slow Dance* (1975), *The Great Cloak* (1978) and *The Dead Kingdom* (1988). His work reflects his Nationalism, his pleasure in the Gaelic past and regret for its passing, and the intensity of personal relationships. *Death of a Chieftain* (1964) and *A Love Present* (1997) are collections of short stories, while the novella *The Lost Notebook* (1987) recalls a love affair in and with Italy. Montague edited *The Faber Book of Irish Verse* (1974), and his criticism is available in *The Figure in the Cave* (1990). In 1998 he was appointed to the chair of Irish poetry, to be held for a year each in Queen's University Belfast, University College Dublin and Trinity College Dublin.

Montez, Lola (1816–61). The professional name of the dancer Marie Dolores Gilbert. She was born in Limerick, the beautiful daughter of a British army officer. After eloping with another army officer, from whom she was subsequently divorced, she began her career as a dancer in London in 1843, calling herself 'Lola Montez, Spanish dancer'. She enjoyed success in the main cities of Europe, after a few years becoming the favourite of King Ludwig of Bavaria, who saw her dancing in Bavaria. She wielded considerable power in Bavaria, but was banished after a rebellion in 1848, which public opinion blamed on her. Subsequently she performed in Australia (1851–3), then settled in New York, where she devoted herself to charitable causes. She died in that city on 17 January 1861.

Montgomery, Henry (1788–1865). Presbyterian minister. He was born in Killead, Co. Antrim, and educated at the University of Glasgow. In 1810 he was ordained for the Presbyterian Church, and combined the post of English master at INST with the living of Dunmurry, near Belfast. An opponent of Henry COOKE, he led the Arian section of the synod (*see* ARIAN- ISM), but was defeated and formed the Remon- strant Synod of Ulster in 1829. (In 1910 the movement became the Non-Subscribing Pres- byterian Church, consisting of members who refused to subscribe to the 17th-century West- minster Confession of Faith.) Montgomery's known liberalism (he supported CATHOLIC EMANCIPATION) and his Arianism meant that mainstream Presbyterianism, led by the politi- cally astute Cooke, inevitably prevailed.

Montgomery, Leslie Alexander. *See* DOYLE, LYNN.

Month's mind. A Requiem Mass, to which neigh- bours and relatives are invited, said in the house of the deceased or in the local church a month after the death.

Monto. A Dublin nickname for Montgomery Street, an area east of O'Connell Street that was a red-light district from the 19th century until well after the foundation of the state, the area being close to British army barracks and the docks. The main focus for vice was not Montgomery Street itself, but rather Mecklen- burgh Street Lower (now Railway Street) and the lanes round about it (such as Little Martin's Lane, interestingly renamed Beaver Street). Among Monto's more illustrious clients was the future Edward VII, and the illegitimate con- sequences of such liaisons were known as 'Monto babies'. The LEGION OF MARY largely did for Monto in the 1920s, leaving in its wake reform schools and Magdalene laundries (*see* MAGDALEN(E) HOME).

> When the Czar of Rooshia, and the King of
>   Prooshia
> Landed in the Phoenix in a big balloon,

> They asked the Garda band to play 'The Wearin'
>   o' the Green'
> But the buggers in the depot didn't know the
>   tune,
> So they both went up to Monto, Monto, Monto
>   ...
> ANON.: song 'Take Me Up to Monto' (the reference
> is to Dublin's Phoenix Park)

Montrose. An estate in Donnybrook, south Dub- lin, the specific location of RTÉ since 1972. The now outdated expressions 'here in Mon- trose' or 'the people out in Montrose', were sometimes used ironically or negatively, even by station staff, to indicate their sense of an ivory-tower attitude among RTÉ management.

Monument of Light. *See* NELSON'S PILLAR.

Mooney, Joe. *See* JOE MOONEY SUMMER SCHOOL.

Mooney, Ria (1904–73). Actress and stage pro- ducer. She was born in Dublin and began to act at the age of six, as a teenager singing with the Rathmines and Rathgar Musical Society. In 1924 her performance at the Dublin Arts Club in Chekhov's *Proposal* attracted the attention of ABBEY THEATRE management, and she was invited to join the theatre, playing the part of Rosie Redmond in the first production of *The Plough and the Stars* (1926), for which she was the choice of the playwright Seán O'CASEY. After spending some years in England and America, both acting and producing plays, she returned to Ireland in the 1930s. In 1944 she was appointed director of the Gaiety Theatre School of Acting, and she was also the first woman producer at the Abbey. She died in Dublin in January 1973.

Moonlighter. A 19th-century cattle rustler, espe- cially of landlords' herds. There were a number of self-styled CAPTAIN MOONLIGHTS in pre- Famine Ireland.

Moonshine. A fanciful or euphemistic name for illicit liquor such as POTEEN, so called because it was brewed by moonlight:

> I'm a rambler, I'm a gambler, I'm a long way from
>   home,

And if you don't like me, well, leave me alone.
I'll eat when I'm hungry, I'll drink when I'm dry,
And if the moonshine don't kill me, I'll live till I
die.
I've been a moonshiner for many a year,
I've spent all me money on whiskey and beer.
I'll go to some hollow, I'll set up my still
And I'll make you a gallon for a ten shilling bill.

ANON.: traditional ballad 'I've Been a Moonshiner for Many a Year'

Moore, Annie. An emblematic figure, a young Cork girl who emigrated from Cobh to America in 1891 with her two brothers (their parents had already settled in New York). On 1 January 1892, Annie's 15th birthday, she was the first immigrant to be processed at the new Immigrant Landing Station on ELLIS ISLAND, and to mark the occasion she was presented with a $10 gold coin by officials. This event was reported in New York newspapers and in the *Cork Examiner* of the day. About 12 million immigrants, 580,000 of them Irish, passed through Ellis Island over the next 60 years. In February 1993 President Mary Robinson unveiled a sculpture of Annie and her brothers by Jeanne Rynhart in Cobh, and Cobh Heritage Centre opened at the same time. The same sculptor created another memorial on the occasion of the Centennial and Rededication of Ellis Island in 1992. This statue was unveiled on Ellis Island, also by President Robinson.

Moore, Brian (1921–99). Novelist. He was born in Belfast on 25 August 1921 and educated at St Malachy's College. He emigrated to Canada in 1948 and settled in Montreal, where he became a successful journalist and writer of pulp fiction. His first literary novel, *The LONELY PASSION OF JUDITH HEARNE* (1955), was a critical success on both sides of the Atlantic. He went to live to New York in 1959, the recipient of a Guggenheim fellowship, and moved to California in 1965, spending the rest of his life there. Moore's 21 novels deal with emigration and displacement, family ties and the search for identity, and the quest for meaning by people in a post-Christian world. Among his major early

novels are *An Answer from Limbo* (1963), which conveys his disillusionment with the commercialization of New York literary life, and *I Am Mary Dunne* (1968), in which he brilliantly captures the feelings and neuroses of a female protagonist.

Always an experimenter in theme and style, Moore set out never to write a similar novel twice. In the 1970s and 1980s his work varied from a Borges-style fable, *The Great Victorian Collection* (1976), to a metaphysical thriller, *Cold Heaven* (1983), and the historical *Black Robe* (1987). Three of his later works, written as thrillers, mark a return to settings that he experienced as a young man: *The Colour of Blood* (1987) is set in Poland; *Lies of Silence* (1990) is the novel of the Northern Ireland Troubles that he said he would never write; and *The Statement* (1996) focuses on the guilt of members of the collaborationist French Catholic Church during the Second World War. Moore's final novel, *The Magician's Wife* (1997), set in Algeria, highlights both the ethical blindness of European colonial powers and the fanaticism of Islam. *The Lonely Passion of Judith Hearne* and *Black Robe* have been filmed. Brian Moore died in Malibu, California, on 11 January 1999.

Moore, Christy (b.1945). Singer and songwriter. A traditional, folk and modern singer of great talent and an *engagé* songwriter in a way that is unusual in Ireland, Moore was born in Newbridge, Co. Kildare. He first performed with Donal LUNNY, and spent the formative period 1966–71 playing and singing in folk clubs in England. On his return to Ireland he recorded the successful album *Prosperous* (1972) with Lunny, Andy IRVINE and Liam O'Flynn. These four musicians made up the group PLANXTY[2]. After Planxty, Moore formed MOVING HEARTS with Donal Lunny, but since 1982 he has pursued a successful solo career, performing and recording a large number of albums. There are few Irish performers of any generation who command as much public adulation and warm affection as Moore.

Moore, George [Augustus] (1852–1933). Novelist. He was born on 24 February 1852 at Moore Hall, Ballyglass, Co. Mayo, the home of his Catholic landlord father. He went to Paris to become a painter but, admitting to a lack of talent, moved to London and eventually became a slightly shocking novelist with such works as the popular *Esther Waters* (1894). His cousin Edward MARTYN, another Catholic landlord from Connacht, invited him to be part of the IRISH LITERARY REVIVAL.

Moore had some experience of modern drama, and he was able to whip Martyn's play *Tale of a Town* into shape for the stage and change its title to *The Bending of the Bough* for performance at the Gaiety Theatre, Dublin (1900). He also collaborated with Yeats in a dramatized version of the story of *Diarmuid and Grainne* (1901). His temperament was really unsuitable for collaboration, and he could be extremely difficult socially, having a reputation for scandalous and usually untrue gossip. Sarah PURSER said of him: 'Gentlemen kiss and never tell. Cads kiss and tell. George doesn't kiss but he tells.'

Moore left Ireland for good in 1911 and celebrated his Irish adventures in his autobiographical *Hail and Farewell* (1911–14). This account may have been his best contribution to the Revival, although *The* UNTILLED FIELD (1903), whatever its lofty pretensions, contains some fine short stories. Moore died in London on 21 January 1933, having made an international reputation with *The Brook Kerith* (1916), a novel about a Christ who survives the crucifixion, and *Heloise and Abelard* (1921), a romantic account of the 12th-century star-crossed lovers.

> We all did something, but none did what he set out to do. Yeats founded a realistic theatre, Edward emptied two churches – he and Palestrina between them – and I wrote *The Untilled Field*, a book written in the beginning out of no desire of self-expression, but in the hope of furnishing the young Irish of the future with models.
>
> Introduction to *The Untilled Field*

Moore, Thomas (1779–1857). Poet and song lyricist. He was born on 28 May 1779 in Aungier Street in Dublin to a prosperous grocer and a very ambitious mother who saw to it that her son would have the best possible education. He entered Trinity College Dublin in 1794, the year after Hobart's Catholic Relief Act permitted Catholics to enter the university for the first time, and became a close friend of Robert EMMET – who did Moore the service of not involving him in any of his subversive activities. Moore thus avoided the REBELLION OF 1798, and in 1803, when Emmet was brutally executed, he was busy preparing to embark from London for Bermuda to take up his sinecure as an admiralty registrar, a post obtained by his patron Lord Moira (1754–1826). He subsequently spent most of his time in London.

Moore was intended for the law, but patronage, a fine tenor voice and a genuine skill with light verse provided an agreeable alternative. After two non-duels he became fast friends with his adversaries, Lord Jeffrey (1773–1850), the savage critic of the *Edinburgh Review* (who had called Moore 'the MOST LICENTIOUS OF MODERN VERSIFIERS'), and the poet Byron, whose *Memoirs* he censored and whose biographer he became. His pseudo-oriental romance *Lalla Rookh* (1817) was wildly popular, but he lives on in his IRISH MELODIES and a few other song lyrics. He died on 26 February 1857 having outlived all his children. Though not an aggressive man, he maintained his Irishness (*see* MUSICAL SNUFF-BOX) and was critical of Daniel O'CONNELL's compliance with various British governments.

See also ANACREON MOORE; MINSTREL BOY, THE.

Moran, D[aniel] P[atrick] (1869–1936). Editor and phrasemaker. He was born in Waterford and educated at Castleknock, near Dublin. He worked for some time as a journalist in London before returning home to become an active and usually strident Nationalist and GAELIC LEAGUE supporter. In his periodical the *Leader* (founded in 1900, and continuing until 1971) he vigorously attacked any aspect of Irish life that was not Catholic and Gaelic. A vituperative flair caused him to label Æ as 'the hairy fairy', Protestants as 'sour-faces', the Anglo-Irish as 'WEST BRITONS' and apers of English manners 'SHONEENS'. He invented the isolationist phrase 'Irish Ireland' in a series of articles published in *The Philosophy of Irish Ireland* (1905). He died in Sutton, Dublin, though his paper, becoming steadily more reactionary, survived him by 35 years.

> Since Grattan's time every popular leader, O'Connell, Butt, Parnell, Dillon and Redmond, has perpetuated this primary contradiction. They threw over Irish civilization whilst they professed – and professed in perfectly good faith – to fight for Irish nationalism.
>
> *The Philosophy of Irish Nationalism* (1905)

More Irish than the Irish. *See* HIBERNICI IPSIS HIBERNIORES.

More power to you. A general expression of approval and appreciation, used punningly as a slogan by Northern Ireland Electricity. A variant is 'More power to your elbow.' *See also* POWER.

Morgan, Dermot (1952–98). Comedian. He was born in Dublin on 31 March 1952 and educated at University College Dublin. He worked as a teacher until 1980, when he left the job to tour the country with the FATHER TRENDY show that had begun life on the RTÉ television comedy series *The Live Mike* (1979–84; the title referring to Mike Murphy). In the early 1990s he and writer Gerry Stembridge created a satirical radio show, SCRAP SATURDAY, again for RTÉ. It was enormously popular, shaping the public's perceptions and memories of politicians like Charles HAUGHEY and Pee FLYNN. He achieved fame in Britain as the eponymous FATHER TED on the Channel 4 situation comedy, a role for which he received several awards. He died suddenly in London on 28 February 1998.

Morgan, Lady (?1776–1859). Novelist. She was born Sydney Owenson at sea, the daughter of an unsuccessful actor-manager who had been born MacOwen and a Catholic. Sydney became a governess and turned to writing, anticipating Tom MOORE's *Irish Melodies* by seven years with *Hibernian Melodies* (1801). She drew upon her Irish-speaking relatives from Mayo to write her best-selling *The Wild Irish Girl* (1806), which, though a romance with the author as heroine, is sound on such matters as women's freedom and CATHOLIC EMANCIPATION. She was taken up by the Marchioness of Abercorn, who urged her surgeon Charles Morgan to marry the young writer, and who arranged a knighthood for him as a wedding present. The salon of Lady Morgan (as she now was) in her Kildare Street house became one of the highlights of Dublin society, and her books, whether fiction or accounts of her frequent travels, made her a rich woman. Her will included a benevolent fund for actors and governesses. She died on 14 April 1859 in London, to which she had moved in 1837 on the receipt of a pension of £300 granted by Lord Melbourne.

> Lady Singleton had, however, something to blame or rectify with every step she took. At Belfast where they remained a day, she proved as she stood on the bridge, that it should have erected upon twenty arches instead of twenty-one ... that the canal which connects the harbour with Lough Neagh was formed against every principle and system of inland navigation. At Carrickfergus where they were shown the spot where King William landed, she discovered he had chosen the worst place on the coast.
>
> LADY MORGAN: *The O'Donnel* (1814)

See also KATE KEARNEY'S COTTAGE; LADY MORGAN MAKIN' TAY.

Moriarty, Biddy. An early 19th-century street trader who kept a stall on the Liffey quays opposite the Four Courts in Dublin. She was notorious for her belligerence and abusive tongue, and some friends of the young Daniel O'CONNELL thought that he should meet her and engage her in a verbal duel. Though reluctant, O'Connell finally agreed and eventually vanquished her, somewhat surrealistically. Her thrusts were perhaps predictable: 'May the divil fly away with you, you micher from

Munster, and make celery-sauce of your rotten limbs, you mealy mouthed tub of guts.' (A *micher* is one who plays truant.) O'Connell's exotic, geometric reponses finally silenced her: 'Look at her, boys! There she stands – a convicted perpendicular in petticoats! There's contamination in her circumference, and she trembles with guilt down to the extremities of her corollaries. Ah, you're found out, you rectilineal antecedent, and equiangular old hag! 'Tis with the devil you will fly away, you porter-swiping similitude of the bisection of a vortex!' Biddy sensibly reached for a saucepan and O'Connell and his friends made their excuses and left.

Moriarty, John (b.1936). Writer and philosopher. His unique style – dense, allusive, mystical and playful – has earned him hundreds of aficionados. Something of a professional Kerryman, he was born in Moyvane in north Kerry and has lived for many years 'near the foot of Mangerton', a mountain close to Killarney. His most important publications include *Dreamtime* (1994) and the first two volumes of *Turtle was a Long Time Gone: Crossing the Kedron* (1996) and *Horsehead Nebula Neighing* (1997).

Moriarty Tribunal. *See* ANSBACHER DEPOSITS; TRIBUNALS.

Mórrigán or **Morrigú** (sometimes referred to as **the Mórrigán**). The chief goddess of war and slaughter, synonymous with ghastliness in the Celtic pantheon. She favoured the form of a raven or a carrion crow, giving those birds an evil reputation. She was active on the side of the TUATHA DÉ DANAAN at the battles of MAGH TUIREADH (Moytura), and had intercourse with the DAGDA astride a river. Her relentless animosity against CÚCHULAINN was based on his rejection of her advances, and when he managed to wound her in the form of a she-wolf, he realised that he would not survive in the final struggle. As he died at the Battle of FORD she perched in the form of a crow on his shoulder and watched as a beaver lapped his blood.

Morrison, Danny. *See* ARMALITE AND THE BALLOT BOX, THE.

Morrison, Van. *See* VAN THE MAN.

Morrison visa. A visa for permanent residence in the United States that was made available to a certain quota of Irish people on a lottery basis in the early 1990s. It was the product of an immigration-reform bill introduced in the US House of Representatives by Connecticut Congressman Bruce Morrison.

Mortler or **mortaller.** A Dublin colloquialism for a mortal sin, used (although not exclusively) by children to mean a grievous sin they must confess to the priest in confession. The suffix -ER is a common means of expressing familiarity or even affection in Dublin speech.

Morya or **marya** (Irish *mar dhea*). A common and useful expression in HIBERNO-ENGLISH, used ironically to convey the realization of pretence. The original Irish *mar bh'eadh*, or *mar bhadh eadh* literally means 'as if it were so'. The phrase is often used to express doubt or irony, as in 'He's a musician morya' (i.e. he's pretending to be a musician to avoid doing anything else).

Moryson, Fynes (1566–1630). Elizabethan writer. After travelling extensively in Europe he joined the establishment of Lord MOUNTJOY in Ireland and later became Mountjoy's personal secretary. He is best known for the description of the NINE YEARS' WAR contained in *An Itinerary* (1617), including eyewitness accounts of some events. Moryson was hostile to the Irish and all things Irish, with the exception of whiskey, and very much disposed to exaggerate the achievements of his patron, so his testimony, although valuable, needs to be read with caution.

Mossa. *See* WISHA.

Most distressful country. *See* 'WEARING OF THE GREEN, THE'.

Most Inquisitive People. A description of Irish gossips by Sir John Davies (c.1570–1626), solicitor-general of Ireland, who went on to describe the penalty accruing:

> Besides, all the common people have a whining tune or accent in their speech, as if they did still smart or suffer some oppression. And this idleness, together with fear of imminent mischiefs, which did continually hang over their heads, have been the cause that the Irish were ever the most inquisitive people, of any nation in the world. As St Paul himself made observation upon the people of Athens; that they were an idle people, and did nothing but learn and tell news. And because News-carriers did by their false intelligence many times raise troubles and rebellions in this realm, the Statute of Kilkenny [*see* KILKENNY, STATUTE OF] doth punish News-tellers (by the name of Skelagher [from Irish *scéalach*, 'gossiping']) with Fine and Ransom.
>
> *Discovery of the True Causes Why Ireland Was Never Entirely Subdued until the Beginning of His Majesty's Reign* (1612)

Most licentious of modern versifiers, the. A description of Thomas MOORE by Francis Lord Jeffrey (1773–1850), editor of the *Edinburgh Review*, in his critical article on the poet's third book *Epistles, Odes and Other Poems* in July 1806. He concluded with a fine Edinburgh finish:

> To us, indeed, the perpetual kissing and twining and panting of these amorous persons is rather ludicrous than seductive; and their eternal sobbing and whining raises no emotions in our bosoms save those of disgust and contempt.

Moore, for all his diminutive size (1.55 m / 5 ft 2 in), was not one to allow such a personal attack to go unchallenged. He at once called Jeffrey out, and the duellists met at Chalk Farm on the early morning of 15 August. It was clear that neither of them had ever handled a pistol before. In the delay that followed while their seconds tried to sort out the charges, the adversaries chatted with great amity, and when at last they were ready to aim a party of police officers arrived and carted them off to Bow Street. There in the same cell they discussed Ireland, Scotland and literature – and became friends for life.

The matter did not end there; the gadfly Lord Byron had got to hear of the debacle and in his satire *English Bards and Scottish Reviewers* (1809) he fittingly commemorated it:

> Health to great Jeffrey! Heaven preserve his life,
> To flourish on the fertile plains of Fife,
> And guard it sacred in its future wars,
> Since authors sometimes seek the field of Mars!
> Can none remember that eventful day,
> That ever-glorious almost fateful fray,
> When Little's leadless pistol met his eye
> And Bow-street myrmidons stood laughing by?

Moore, whose second book had been published as the *Poetical Works of 'Thomas Little'* in 1801 immediately challenged Byron, but the latter was out of the country when the note arrived and when the two men eventually met their mutual admiration led to a lasting friendship, with Moore named as Byron's literary executor and biographer.

Mot. A colloquial Dublin term for a girl or girlfriend ('the mot'), often pronounced 'moth' or 'moh'. The derivation of the world is uncertain.

Mothall. An Irish word for 'fleece', 'shaggy hair', used in HIBERNO-ENGLISH for a mop of hair, or hair that is too thick or over-long.

Mother and Child Scheme (1950–1). A controversial scheme that proposed free health care for all women and children up to the age of 16. The scheme was associated with the then CLANN NA POBLACHTA TD and minister for health, Noel BROWNE, but when the Catholic hierarchy, especially Archbishop John Charles MCQUAID of Dublin, rejected the scheme as being an unwarranted interference into family life, the leader of the Interparty Government, John A. COSTELLO, and Browne's own party leader, Seán MACBRIDE, declined to support him. Browne resigned in March 1951. The ruling politicians' slavish acceptance of the political power of the hierarchy damaged Irish public life for decades, and gave ammunition to Northern Unionists for their ritual denunciation of the Republic as a place of 'Rome rule' (as in the old slogan 'Home Rule is Rome Rule').

A longer perspective has laid at least some of the blame for the debacle on the Irish Medical Organization, whose members were no more enthusiastic about 'socialized medicine' than the bishops. Treading more softly, the Fianna Fáil government that succeeded the Interparty administration introduced a similar though means-tested scheme in 1953.

'Mother Machree'. *See* MACHREE.

Mother of all the Behans. The name by which Kathleen Behan (1889–1984) was known. She was born Kathleen Kearney (sister to Peadar KEARNEY) into a working-class family in Capel Street, Dublin. After the death of her father when she was 9 she was sent to Goldenbridge orphanage, where she stayed until she was 15. She joined CUMANN NA MBAN and acted as a courier in the EASTER RISING of 1916. Her first husband, Jack Furlong, fought in the Rising and survived it, but died in the flu epidemic of 1918, leaving her with two small children. Her second husband. Stephen Behan, was another Republican. The couple had five children, including Brendan and Dominic. They first lived in a tenement building in Russell Street, but in 1939 they were given a corporation house in a new housing estate in Crumlin. At the end of her life, Kathleen Behan achieved fame as a character in her own right, and as the mother in particular of Brendan BEHAN.

Motions, just going through the. *See* LIFFEY SWIM, THE.

Motte and bailey. A type of fortification composed of mounds, ditches and wooden structures, introduced by the Anglo-Normans who first came to Ireland at the end of the 12th century. The 'motte' or mound, created from the soil excavated from the surrounding ditch or 'fosse', had a wooden dwelling tower and a wooden fence around its edge. The 'bailey' was a lower, larger area, connected to the motte by a wooden bridge, and was also enclosed by a wooden fence and encircled by a ditch. There were about 350 examples of motte and bailey in the east of Ireland. By the beginning of the following century the Anglo-Normans' characteristic stone castles had begun to take their place.

Mouldy. A colloquial and rather crude or critical term meaning 'very drunk'. It is roughly synonymous with MAGGOTY.

Mountain. The term used for rising bogland or rough moorland in the SLIABH LUACHRA area of counties Kerry and Cork. The word *sliabh* ('mountain') in the placename has this meaning.

Mountain dew. A name for illicit liquor such as POTEEN, often brewed on mountainside farms in remote areas.

> Let the grasses grow
> And the waters flow in a free and easy way,
> But give me enough of the rare old stuff
> That's made near Galway Bay.
> Come gangers all from Donegal,
> Sligo and Leitrim too,
> Oh, we'll give 'em a slip
> And we'll take a sip of the rare old mountain dew.
> SAMUEL LOVER (1797–1868): 'The Rare Old Mountain Dew'

Mountainy. A word used in HIBERNO-ENGLISH to describe a person from a remote area, particularly a person considered backward or uncouth. There is a popular saying: 'Marry a mountainy woman and you'll marry the whole mountain.' 'Mountainy' as applied to animals (such as sheep) means a smaller hardier variety than the lowland variety. The term 'mountainy men' usually associated with sheep, is also used.

> Down by the lough I shall wander once more
> Where the wavelets lap lap round the stones on the shore:
> And the mountainy goats will be wagging their chins
> As they pull at the bracken among the Twelve Pins.

Mountbatten (of Burma), Earl (1900–79). Last viceroy of India. As a lateral member of the Royal family and great uncle and confidante of

Prince Charles (who was a regular visitor to his holiday home at Classiebawn, Mullaghmore, Co. Sligo), Earl Mountbatten was always a potential target for the IRA. On 27 August 1979 he died when his boat was blown to pieces by a radio-triggered bomb, which also killed his 14-year-old grandson and a local boy who was a member of the boat's crew. The Dowager Lady Brabourne died later from her injuries. Coming as it did on a day when 18 soldiers were killed by bombs in WARRENPOINT, Co. Down, it had a dubious propaganda value for the Provisional IRA. Thomas McMahon was found guilty of the killings on 23 November and sentenced to penal servitude for life.

Mounted Micks. *See* ARRAN'S CUIRASSIERS.

Mount Jerome. A cemetery at Harold's Cross, Dublin, which includes the city's largest Protestant burial ground. It holds the remains of, among others, Thomas DAVIS, Thomas DRUMMOND and J.M. SYNGE:

> There'll come season when you'll stretch
> Black boards to cover me:
> Then in Mount Jerome I will lie, poor wretch,
> With worms eternally.
>
> J.M. SYNGE (1871–1909): 'To the Oaks of Glencree',
> in *Poems and Translations* (1911)

Mountjoy, Lord (Charles Blount, 1563–1606). Elizabethan soldier and administrator. He was appointed lord deputy in the place of the 2nd Earl of ESSEX in 1600, and it was he who brought the NINE YEARS' WAR to a close, harrying Hugh O'NEILL and his allies in south Ulster and north Leinster, burning crops and laying waste to land, while leaving a great deal of latitude to Henry DOCWRA in northwest Ulster and George CAREW in Munster to pursue war on their own terms. Before the Battle of KINSALE, it was clear that Mountjoy's strategy had paid dividends and that the Irish chieftains had come under serious pressure. It was Mountjoy who defeated O'Neill, Red Hugh O'DONNELL and their allies at Kinsale, and he who agreed the Treaty of MELLIFONT with O'Neill. In recognition of his services James I made him Earl of Devonshire and lord lieuten-

ant of Ireland, effectively the same office as that of lord deputy but with a more prestigious title. Fynes MORYSON, who acted as Mountjoy's private secretary at this time, wrote an account of the Nine Years' War and Mountjoy's victories that was very favourable to his patron.

Mountjoy Jail. A prison on Dublin's North Circular Road, colloquially known to its inmates as 'the Joy'. A purpose-built prison dating from 1850 with a capacity of about 550, it is the main committal prison in the state for males aged 18 years and over serving sentences up to life. Chronic overcrowding in Mountjoy has led to the contemporary 'revolving door' phenomenon, whereby offenders are released after serving only a small part of their sentence only to re-offend, be re-arrested and re-sentenced. Mountjoy is associated with imprisonment and execution of Irish rebels at the hands of the British, especially the execution of Kevin Barry in 1920 (*see* 'MOUNTJOY JAIL ONE MONDAY MORNING, IN'), and also with the imprisonment and execution of Republicans by the Free State government during the CIVIL WAR (*see* MELLOWS, LIAM; O'CONNOR, RORY). The prison was named after Lord Deputy Mountjoy.
See also RASHERHOUSE.

'Mountjoy Jail one Monday morning, In'. The title and opening line of an anonymous patriotic ballad about the execution of 18-year-old medical student Kevin Barry (1902–20) in the hanghouse in MOUNTJOY JAIL on 1 November 1920. IRA Volunteer Barry was sentenced for his part in an attack on an armed convoy in Church Street in Dublin on 20 September 1920, during which three British soldiers were killed or fatally wounded.

Barry's case excited great public attention and sympathy because of his youth, because his defence was disabled by his refusal, as a Volunteer, to recognize the court, and because he was the first political prisoner to be executed since the 1916 EASTER RISING. This sympathy and the revulsion caused by the death of

Terence MACSWINEY from force-feeding while on hunger strike in Brixton Prison on 25 October 1920 were exploited by Michael COLLINS to foment disaffection and hostility to crown forces on the day of the execution and during subsequent weeks.

Barry's arrest and imprisonment were handled by regular soldiers, who were much better disciplined than either the BLACK AND TANS or AUXIES, but Barry nevertheless issued a statement alleging that he had been mistreated while in custody. Hence the lines in the ballad:

Just before he faced the hangman
In his gloomy prison cell,
British soldiers tortured Barry
Just because he would not tell.

Most telling is the final verse of the ballad:

Another martyr for old Ireland,
Another murder for the crown,
Whose brutal laws may kill the Irish
But can't keep their spirit down.

Barry's end was described as 'a brave and beautiful death' by an emotional Canon Waters, who ministered to him before his execution. Along with those of eight other men executed in Mountjoy during the ANGLO-IRISH WAR, Barry's remains were exhumed in October 2001 and, after a state funeral that attracted a considerable attendance, reinterred in the Republican plot in GLASNEVIN CEMETERY in Dublin. The relatives of a ninth man, Patrick Maher, brought his remains home to Tipperary for reinterment in accordance with his own wishes. In Nationalist iconography, Kevin Barry occupies an honoured place.

Mount Sandel. The site on the east bank of the Lower Bann, near Coleraine, Co. Derry, of the earliest human habitation in Ireland, dated from *c*.7000 BC. These aboriginal people were hunter-gatherers, and they had come to Ireland in skin-covered boats on journeys slighter shorter than those of today. They subsisted mainly on fish and fowl, wild pig, and apples and nuts in season, and lived in communal circular huts.

Mourne, Mountains of. A range of granite mountains in the south of Co. Down, extending from Newcastle to Carlingford Lough. They are the highest mountains in Ulster, the tallest, Slieve Donard (852 m / 2795 ft), rising from the sea near Newcastle. They can be seen on clear days from the Isle of Man and from north Dublin. They have had a continual fame thanks to one of the best-known songs of Percy French, written in 1896. French had no especial connection with Co. Down, but he glimpsed the Mournes on a clear day from Skerries in Co. Dublin:

Oh, Mary, this London's a wonderful sight,
Wid the people here workin' by day and by night,
They don't sow potatoes, nor barley, nor wheat,
But there's gangs o' them digging for gold in the street –
At least, when I axed them, that's what I was told:
So I just took a hand at this diggin' for gold,
But for all that I found there, I might as well be
Where the Mountains o' Mourne sweep down to the sea.

Mouth. A Dublin colloquialism for an over-talkative boastful person, or a person who cannot keep a secret: 'She's a real mouth. Don't tell her anything.'

Mouth music. A HIBERNO-ENGLISH term for a form of singing, but without recognizable words, using the mouth like an instrument. It is synonymous with DYDDLING, gob music, LILTING and puss music.

Moutre. An Ulster term (from Scots *multure*) for payment in kind for milling of corn, usually in the form of one tenth of the ground corn.

Moving Bog Disaster. At Christmas 1896 the Donnelly family – father, mother and six children – were swept away when a landslide swept mountainous quantities of material from a bog into the Abhann Uí Chriadha river in the SLIABH LUACHRA area of Co. Kerry. The seventh Donnelly child, Katie, survived because she was visiting relatives.

Moving Hearts. A group that fused traditional

and folk music with rock and jazz, founded in 1981 by Donal LUNNY and Christy MOORE. Among the line-up at various stages before the group broke up in 1984 were Declan Sinnott, Mick Hanly and Davey Spillane.

Moving statues. A phenomenon associated with the village of Ballinspittle, near Kinsale in Co. Cork. A statue of Our Lady in the local grotto was said to have moved in 1985 and for some years thereafter the village became a place of pilgrimage for thousands of people. The 'moving statue' itself was damaged later in 1985 by members of a Christian sect from California and, although repaired, has not since been seen to move.

Moylan's Dragoons. A light cavalry unit led by the Cork-born Stephen Moylan (1737–?). With the young French general, the Marquis de Lafayette (1757–1834), Moylan's Dragoons forced the surrender of Lord Charles Cornwallis (1738–1805) at Yorktown, Virginia, on 19 October 1781, thus effectively ending the American Revolutionary War. Moylan had arrived in Philadelphia in 1768, the unusually rich immigrant son of a successful shipping merchant. Though a Catholic he was elected first president of the largely Protestant FRIENDLY SONS OF ST PATRICK, and when the war began in 1775 became Washington's secretary. He resigned because of adverse reaction to his attempts to reform the War Office, and, demonstrating the same asperity, he was court-martialled after a charge of insubordination by his commander, Count Casimir Pulaski (killed on 28 October 1779 at the Battle of Savannah, Georgia). Acquitted, Moylan resumed charge of his 4th Pennsylvania Light Dragoons, wearing his eccentric and militarily undesirable uniform of red waistcoat, bright green coat, bearskin hat and buckskin breeches.

> And here at Yorktown now they yield
> And our career is o'er,
> No more thou'lt flutter oe'r the field,
> Flag of the brave! – no more …
> Comrades farewell; may heaven bestow
> On you its richest boons!

> So let us drink before we go
> To Moylan's brave Dragoons.
>   THOMAS D'ARCY MCGEE (1825–68): 'Moylan's Dragoons' (1869)

Moyle, Sea of. The stormy part of the North Channel off the north coast of Antrim. It was the location of the 300-year exile of the Children of Lir (*see* FIONNUALA). The name Moyle is used as the title of the local government region of northeast Antrim, with Ballycastle as its administrative centre:

> Sadly, O Moyle! to thy winter-wave weeping,
> Fate bids me languish long ages away;
> Yet still in her darkness doth Erin lie sleeping,
> Still doth the pure light its dawning delay.
>   THOMAS MOORE (1779–1852): 'The Song of Fionnuala', in *Irish Melodies* (1808)

Moyne, Lord. A title bestowed on sons of the Earls of Iveagh of the GUINNESS family. The name derives from a placename of a small inlet in Lough Corrib in Co. Mayo, near the family estate at Ashford Castle. The 1st Lord Moyne was Walter Edward Guinness (1880–1944). Bryan Guinness (1905–92), 2nd Lord Moyne, was a writer whose first wife was Diana Mitford, who went on to marry Oswald Mosley, leader of the British Union of Fascists.

Moyne's a Guinness. A Dublin version of 'mine's a Guinness', punning on the title borne by members of the Guinness family (*see* MOYNE, LORD) and depending also on the characteristic Dublin pronunciation of the vowel in 'mine' as 'oy'.

Moynihan, Johnny. *See* DÉ DANANN.

Moytura. *See* MAGH TUIREADH.

Mr Dooley. A character invented by Finley Peter Dunne (1867–1936), the Chicago-born son of Irish immigrants, and featured from 1893 to 1900 in the *Chicago Evening Post*. Mr Dooley was a saloonkeeper in the Irish working-class district of Bridgeport and achieved national fame for his wit and wisdom and subtle use of language, expressed in an apparently impenetrable Irish brogue. His reminiscences of 'th' ol' country' and his often mordant comments on the American-Irish gently satirized his fellow expatriates, but all the same Dunne's column made the brogue respectable and showed its speakers to be as clever, righteous and as patriotic as their White Anglo-Saxon Protestant detractors – the WASPs of later years. A typical response (to the threatened war with Spain over Cuba) was:

> 'I don't know,' said Mr Dooley. 'But if there is, I'm prepared for to sacrifice th' last dhrop iv Hinnissy's blood an' th' last cint iv Hinnissy's money before surrindhring.'
> *Chicago Evening Post*, 21 December 1895

Mr Hutton. The name used by Wolfe TONE to refer to himself in his diary, the source being the second syllable of Hutton. A typical entry is that for July 1792, when the journal was begun:

> Journal of the proceedings of John Hutton, Esq, on his third journey to the North of Ireland; including the artful negotiations with the Peep-of-day-boys and sundry peers of the realm ...

Mr McGilligan's White Elephant. See ARDNACRUSHA; MCGILLIGAN, PATRICK.

Mr Russell of *The Times*. William Howard Russell (1820–1907), called 'the first and greatest of war correspondents' in his epitaph in St Paul's Cathedral, London. He was born in Dublin and attended Trinity College Dublin before moving to London in 1841. He was offered a position with *The Times* as a result of his reporting of the 1841 Longford election campaign. The first campaign he covered as war correspondent was the Danish-Prussian war over Schleswig-Holstein in 1850, but it was his eyewitness reporting on the army's mismanagement of the Crimean War (1853–6) that made his name and led to the resignation of the prime minister, the Earl of Aberdeen, in 1855. He is credited also with exposing the conditions of army hospitals: 'there was not the least attention paid to decency or cleanliness – the stench was overpowering ... men died without out the least effort to save them'; he is also

credited with inventing the phrase 'the thin red line' as a description of British soldiers standing against the Russian cavalry. Russell went on to report on British atrocities in the Indian Mutiny (1857–8), and on the American Civil War, denouncing 'the peculiar institution of slavery'. Though criticized as unpatriotic at the time of his Crimean and Indian reports, Russell later became a friend of the future King Edward VII and of Dickens and Thackeray, who appreciated his wit and storytelling abilities. He was knighted in 1895.

Mrs Delany's Collages. An *oeuvre* comprising nearly 1000 collages composed of hundreds of pieces of coloured paper, each rendering a different flower in intricate detail. Mary Granville Delany (1700–88) was regarded as one of the wittiest, most charming and most creative women of her time, and was a friend of royalty and nobility. She married Patrick Delany, Dean of Down, in 1743, and lived in Dublin and Downpatrick until after her husband's death in 1768. She was a gifted needlewoman and artist; her famous collages were made when she was aged between 73 and 82.

Mrs Desperate. See DESPARD, CHARLOTTE.

Mrs Doyle. The housekeeper for FATHER TED and his fellow priests on Craggy Island, played by comedienne Pauline McLynn. An inveterate maker of cups of tea – 'Go on, go on, go on, go on!' (have a cup of tea) is her trademark refrain – she seems airily oblivious of the idiosyncrasies and deficiencies of her employers.

'Mrs McGrath.' See KEARNEY, PEADAR.

Mrs Mulligan. See MULLIGAN, BIDDY.

Mrs O'Leary's Cow. The almost certainly incorrectly reported cause of the great Chicago fire of 8–10 October 1871. It certainly started in the small dairy of Catherine O'Leary (1836–95) in De Koven Street, and the likely but unprovable cause was a match that had lit the pipe of Daniel (Peg-Leg) Sullivan, one of her employees. At the time Irish people made up 20% of the city's population (and formed a third of the police force). The story of the cow kicking over the lantern was invented by reporters to sell papers, negative stories about the Irish still being regarded as good copy. In 1997 the Chicago city council passed a resolution entirely exonerating Mrs O'Leary, 102 years after her death. Not unexpectedly her later years were unhappy, and she became a recluse emerging from her home only to go to Mass. The fire was particularly damaging in a city of 334,000 people, built mainly of wood, with only 17 horse-drawn fire appliances and 185 firefighters. In the previous 95 days only an inch (25 mm) of rain had fallen, and when the fire started convection winds of 100 kph (60 mph) caused firestorms lasting for a day and a half. $190 million of damage was done (a huge amount by contemporary standards) and 90,000 people were made homeless, but the death toll at 300 was regarded as small. The sparing of the industrial and railroad sectors of the city helped to contribute to a remarkable and rapid recovery, so that by 1893 the city was able to host the highly successful World Columbian Exposition.

M60. A type of US machine gun. During the Northern Ireland Troubles a few were obtained illegally by Irish-American activists and were used in south Armagh, often against British army helicopters.

Muckross Abbey. A ruined Franciscan abbey beautifully situated beside Lough Leane, 5 km (3 miles) from the town of KILLARNEY, Co. Kerry. It is thought to have been founded by local leader Donal McCarthy for the friars in 1448 and completed in about 1475. There is a church containing a number of tombs, and a cloister with an old yew tree in the centre, as well as accommodation on the first floor for the monks. The friary was suppressed in 1541 (*see* DISSOLUTION OF THE MONASTERIES) but restored at the beginning of the 17th century and reopened in 1612. The friars were finally expelled by Cromwellian forces in 1652. Three of the FOUR KERRY POETS are said to be buried in Muckross Abbey.

Muckross House. A Tudor-style mansion, now a tourist attraction, about 6 km (4 miles) south of the town of KILLARNEY, Co. Kerry, on the Kenmare road. The house, which has splendid views of Lough Leane and celebrated gardens, was built in 1843 by Henry Arthur Herbert, a local landlord. An American family, the Bourne-Vincents, acquired the house and made a gift of the whole estate to the people of Ireland. This extensive area of lakes, upland, woodland and moor, in combination with land bequeathed by other philanthropists, forms what is known as Killarney National Park, an enormously important resource for the area. Queen Victoria stayed in Muckross House on her 1861 visit, and the Herbert family bankrupted themselves to make house and grounds ready for her visit. They expected recompense in the form of title or office, but Victoria's husband Albert (1815–61) died not long after the royal couple's return to London and she appeared to forget entirely about her Irish hosts. Muckross House has been restored and furnished and is open to the public; nearby is a recent development, Muckross Traditional Farm, where different types of dwellings and farm buildings have been reproduced, and animals and people may also be seen going about their daily business as if in the rural Ireland of a century ago.

Muintir na Gaeltachta. *See* MEATH GAELTACHT, THE.

Múinteoirí taistil. *See* TRAVELLING TEACHERS.

Muintir na Tíre (Irish, 'people of the country'). A community development organization based on the principles of cooperation and Christian charity, founded in 1931 by Canon John Hayes (1887–1957), later parish priest of Bansha, Co. Tipperary. It is an educational and social organization and has been responsible for a great deal of development in rural areas, including the expansion of rural electrification, group water-supply schemes, local industries and provision of leisure facilities for young people, much of this achieved by voluntary labour. In the 1970s the organization received substantial funding from the European Social Fund of the COMMON MARKET.

Muirchú. A fishery protection vessel, originally the *Helga*, which as a British naval vessel had shelled the centre of Dublin on the Wednesday of the 1916 EASTER RISING, destroying LIBERTY HALL and the upper storey of the GPO. The Irish name, pronounced 'murra-who', means 'sea hound', and the vessel became the first ship of a hastily assembled marine service at the outbreak of the Second World War.

Mulcahy, Richard (1886–1971). Revolutionary and statesman. He was born in Waterford and fought with Thomas ASHE in north Co. Dublin in the 1916 EASTER RISING. He became chief of staff of the Irish Volunteers in March 1918 and worked with Michael COLLINS to try to maintain control over the IRA units scattered around the country during the ANGLO-IRISH WAR of 1919–21.

Mulcahy succeeded Collins as commander-in-chief of the Free State army in August 1922, and it is said that the shock of Collins's assassination contributed to the severity of his treatment of Republicans during the CIVIL WAR. His pejorative nickname 'Seventy-Seven' derived from the number of Republican prisoners executed by the Free State during this period; he was also called 'Dirty Dick'. Mulcahy was more of a hate figure than Kevin O'HIGGINS among Republican sympathizers, perhaps because he was at the military coalface during the Civil War – it was maliciously alleged of him that he was the only individual who would shoot a woman in cold blood – although it was O'Higgins rather than Mulcahy who ended up as the victim of an unsanctioned IRA revenge killing.

Later Mulcahy served in various CUMANN NA NGAEDHEAL/FINE GAEL ministries, and he was leader of Fine Gael from 1944 to 1959. However, the opposition of his party's CLANN NA POBLACHTA partners prevented him from becoming taoiseach in the INTERPARTY GOVERNMENT of 1948–51, in which he served instead as minister of education. Richard Mul-

cahy's writings on the period of the Anglo-Irish War, the Civil War and his later life in politics were published by his son Risteárd Mulcahy under the title *Richard Mulcahy: a Family Memoir* (1999).

See also ARMY MUTINY.

Muldoon, Paul (b.1955). Poet. He was born near Moy in Co. Armagh and educated at Queen's University Belfast. He worked as a producer on Radio Ulster until the late 1980s, before moving to America where he is director of the creative-writing programme at Princeton University. His published work includes *New Weather* (1973), *Mules* (1977), *Quoof* (1983), *Meeting the British* (1987), *Madoc: A Mystery* (1990) and *Hay* (1998). He published a *New and Selected Poems* (1996) and was editor of *The Faber Book of Contemporary Irish Poetry* (1986). His poetry is obstinately personal and wittily allusive, though as a child of the Northern Troubles he cannot altogether avoid political considerations. He is regarded as one of the finest of the younger Irish poets, and his work has been honoured with many awards. He was elected to the Oxford chair of poetry in 1999 and his collection *Moy Sand and Gravel* (2002) won the 2003 Pulitzer Prize.

'Muldoon, the Solid Man'. The best-known song (1874) of the prolific Ned HARRIGAN, the great star of Irish-American vaudeville and comic theatre. 'Muldoon' is the archetypal Tammany ward-heeler (an unscrupulous follower of a political boss) who 'came here when small from Donegal' and is now in a position of power from which he can distribute favours:

> I control the Tombs, I control the Island
> My constituents, they all go there
> To enjoy the summer's recreation
> And the refreshing East River air.
> I'm known in Harlem; I'm known in Jersey;
> I'm welcome hearty on every hand;
> Wid my regalay on Patrick's Day
> I march away like a solid man.

Mulkerns, Val[entine] (b. 1925). Novelist and short-story writer. She was born in Dublin and educated at the Dominican College, Eccles

Street. She became a drama critic and associate editor of *The* BELL under Peadar O'DONNELL. Two lyrical novels, *A Time Outworn* (1951) and *A Peacock Cry* (1954), partly based upon her own life, showed her as a writer of controlled passion and the possessor of a lucid, witty style. Though she continued to write for Dublin papers, she published nothing until 1978 when *Antiquities*, a series of linked stories, showed a new maturity. Later collections, *An Idle Woman* (1990) and *A Friend of Don Juan* (1988), are witty, sympathetic and slightly mournful about the deteriorating quality of life in her native city, one of the themes of her novel *Very Like a Whale* (1986). *The Summerhouse* (1984), a faultless study of south-coast life, won the Allied Irish Bank Prize for Literature.

Mullen, Karl (b.1926). Rugby player. He was born in Co. Wexford and played for the Old Belvedere club in Dublin. A hooker, he was capped 25 times for Ireland (1947–52) and captained Ireland to its only grand slam in 1948 and to the triple crown in 1949. Mullen also captained the first Lions team to tour Australia and New Zealand after the Second World War.

Mullet. A contemporary Cork slang term for a GURRIER or blackguard.

Mullet Peninsula, the. A remote and beautiful peninsula (Irish *Béal an Mhuirthead*, the 'mouth of the sea') on the northwest coast of Co. Mayo, usually known simply as 'the Mullet'. It is separated from the interior by great stretches of bogland. Its most northerly point is Erris Head, and the town of Belmullet is situated on the narrow spit of land joining the peninsula to the mainland. The Mullet, noted for storm winds and high tides, has four lighthouses: Ballyglass on the north coast, Eagle Island and Black Rock on the west, and Blacksod on the south. Lighthouse keepers on Eagle Island reported a freak wave 67 m (220 feet) high on 11 March 1861. The Inishkea Islands, 4 km (6 miles) west of the mainland and uninhabited since 1937, carry evidence of Bronze Age settlement (*c.*2000 BC).

The population of the Mullet has been in unremitting decline since the Great Famine, when large numbers of emigrants left Blacksod Bay for Canada or took the more expensive passage to Boston: in the 1840s, the population density was 155 per sq km (400 per sq mile), now it is 4.8 (12.5). Between 1908 and 1922 it became the only centre for industrial whaling in Ireland, when two Norwegian companies operated whaling stations here for the capture of fin and blue whales. The English writer T.H. White (1906–64) had a close association with the area in the late 1940s: *The Godstone and the Blackymoor* (1959) is his story of the Mullet.

Mulligan, Biddy. The chief persona of the brilliant comedian and actor Jimmy [James Augustine] O'Dea. He was born in Dublin in 1899, the son of the proprietors of a little toyshop in Lower Bridge Street that ran down to the Liffey opposite the FOUR COURTS. His home was close to the street known as the Coombe, a name that he helped to make more famous (*see below*). At school in Rathmines his best friend was Seán LEMASS and both were startled on the return from a hike in the Dublin Mountains on Easter Monday 1916 to discover that the Volunteers had taken over the GPO. O'Dea was later to be Lemass's best man. He trained as an optician in Edinburgh, and by 1921 he had opened premises in South Frederick Street, Dublin. Always interested in theatre, he turned professional in 1927 and formed a partnership with the writer Harry O'Donovan (1896–1973), who, in a series of hilarious sketches, developed the character of Mrs Mulligan, the eponymous 'PRIDE OF THE COOMBE' who kept a street stall in the LIBERTIES of the south inner city. Her anthem was adapted from a much older song by the prolific songsmith 'Seamus Kavanagh', of whom nothing can be discovered, except that his name is almost certainly a pseudonym:

I sell apples and oranges, nuts and split peas,
Bananas and sugarstick sweet,
On Saturday night I sell second-hand clothes
From the floor of my stall on the street.

You may travel from Clare to the County Kildare,
From Francis Street on to Macroom:
But where would you see a fine widow like me,
Biddy Mulligan, the pride of the Coombe.

For more than 30 years O'Dea was the star of Christmas pantomimes and variety shows at the Theatre Royal and the Queen's, Olympia and Gaiety theatres. He also toured the main variety theatres in Britain and Ireland and was regularly on radio and television. He appeared in 12 films, 8 of them made before the Second World War, his film career culminating with a starring role as King Brian in Walt Disney's *Darby O'Gill and the Little People* (1959). His BBC wartime series *Irish Half Hour* caused some chagrin at STORMONT, provoking an indignant letter from John M. Andrews, the Northern Ireland prime minister, in November 1941. His last performance was as Finian McLonergan in *Finian's Rainbow* on 5 September 1964. He died on 7 January 1965. Mícheál Mac Liammóir, one of his lifelong admirers, remembered the first time he saw him in pantomime:

> Incredible is the word that springs to mind for that dauntless, beetle-black, razor-sharp yet strangely benevolent little demoness of an Ugly Sister. Of course he wasn't ugly at all; he was ravishing; one couldn't for a moment understand why Prince Charming didn't fall for such impish impudent enchantment; what had a thousand Cinderellas to offer in place of this dazzling radiance …
>
> *All for Hecuba* (1947)

See also BIDET MULLIGAN.

Mulligan, Buck. One of the fellow tenants of STEPHEN DEDALUS in the Martello Tower at Sandycove in Joyce's novel ULYSSES. In reality Mulligan is a hardly disguised portrait of Oliver St John GOGARTY.

Mulligan Stew. A rough stew made by American tramps from whatever ingredients were available. The name seems to have come about by association with IRISH STEW:

> I've wined and dined on Mulligan stew
> And never wished for turkey

As I hitched and hiked and grifted, too
From Maine to Albuquerque …
LORENZ HART (1895–1943): 'The Lady is a Tramp', in *Babes in Arms* (1937)

Mullingar. A large and prosperous town in Co. Westmeath with an equally prosperous agricultural hinterland, of which the following was written by Edinburgh-born W. J. Rankine in 1874:

> And then there's Main Street
> That broad and clean street
> With its rows of gas lamps that shine afar.
> I could spake a lecture on the architecture
> Of the gorgeous city of Mullingar.

Mullingar heifer. 'Beef to the heels like a Mullingar heifer' or simply 'Beef to the heels' is an epithet sometimes unflatteringly applied to women. It derives from a popular anonymous 19th-century ballad:

> There was an elopement down in Mullingar,
> But sad to relate the pair didn't get far,
> 'Oh fly!,' said he 'darling, and see how it feels.'
> But the Mullingar heifer was beef to the heels.

Mullins, Brian (b.1954). GAA footballer. A gifted footballer and member of St Vincent's club and the Dublin team, he won four ALL-IRELAND medals with his county, in 1974, 1976, 1977 and 1983 (despite a serious car accident in 1980), and played on the losing sides in the 1975, 1978, 1979, 1984 and 1985 finals. He was briefly co-manager of the Dublin team (1985–6) and manager of Derry (1995–8).

Mullock. A HIBERNO-ENGLISH verb of obscure derivation meaning to 'mess around', to 'do untidy, slovenly work' or to 'do no work at all'.

Mulready envelope. An envelope resembling a half-sheet of letter paper when folded, having on the front an ornamental design by William Mulready (1786–1863), an artist born in Ennis, Co. Clare. These were the stamped penny-postage envelopes introduced in 1840, but the Mulreadies remained in circulation for one year only, because of public ridicule of their design. They are prized by stamp collectors.

Mummers. *See* BIDDY BOYS.

Munchee (Irish *móinte*, 'areas of bog or moor'). An Ulster HIBERNO-ENGLISH term for bogland, deriving from the typically soft Ulster pronunciation of *móinte*.

Municipal Gallery of Modern Art. A gallery located in Charlemont House in Parnell (formerly Rutland) Square, Dublin, to the north of O'Connell Street. Charlemont House was the handsome Georgian townhouse of James Caulfeild, 1st Earl of CHARLEMONT, the construction of which was begun in 1770. The gallery has a fine collection of modern Irish art, including paintings by Jack B. YEATS and Sarah PURSER. It also shares the Lane Collection with London's National Gallery (*see* LANE PICTURES, THE).

> Heart-smitten with emotion I sink down,
> My heart recovering with covered eyes;
> Wherever I had looked I had looked upon
> My permanent or impermanent images:
> Augusta Gregory's son; her sister's son,
> Hugh Lane, 'onlie begetter' of all these …
>
> W.B. YEATS: 'The Municipal Gallery Revisited', in *Last Poems* (1939)

Múnlach. An Irish word for a puddle of dirty water, animal urine or excrement. The word is still current in the HIBERNO-ENGLISH of rural areas.

Munro, Henry (1758–98). Revolutionary. He was born in Lisburn, Co. Antrim, and became a linen-draper. An adjutant in the VOLUNTEERS in 1778, he joined the Society of UNITED IRISHMEN in 1795. Though a Freemason and head of the Lisburn lodge, he was a strong advocate of relief from the POPERY LAWS. At the outbreak of the REBELLION OF 1798 he was chosen to command the insurgents in Co. Down, and seized Ballynahinch on 11 June. The town was taken again by Colonel Nugent's troops on the 13 June and looted by the soldiers. Munro was arrested, tried by court-martial and hanged opposite his own house in Lisburn in sight of his family on 15 June. His body was then decapitated and exhibited in the centre of Lisburn.

> The army came up and surrounded the place
> And they took him to Lisburn and lodged him
>   in jail.
> They took him to Lisburn without more delay,
> Stuck his head on a spear that very same day.
>
> ANON.: 'General Munroe [sic]' (early 19th century)

Munster. The most southerly province of Ireland, the name deriving from the tribal name Mumha. It comprises counties Waterford, Cork, Kerry, Clare, Limerick and Tipperary, and has a mild climate and plentiful rainfall. The province includes the Gaeltachts of the DÉISE and Corca Dhuibhne in the DINGLE PENINSULA. Munster was one of the ancient FIVE FIFTHS or kingdoms of Ireland. Later in the Middle Ages, Munster comprised the two kingdoms of DESMOND and THOMOND, whose rulers took it in turn to be king of Munster. Anglo-Norman infiltration began under Henry II, and powerful families such as the Butler earls of Ormond and the Geraldine earls of Desmond became increasingly Gaelicized and independent. *See also* ORMOND.

Munster Plantation (1583). A plantation carried out when the lands of the rebels became forfeit after the second of the DESMOND REBELLIONS. In all 35 undertakers (soldiers and administrators serving in Ireland and gentlemen recruited in England) received estates of up to 12,000 acres (4800 ha) each; in all nearly 300,000 acres (120,000 ha) were granted in an area extending from Cork to Limerick; grantees included Sir Walter RALEIGH (whose estates were eventually bought by Richard BOYLE) and Edmund SPENSER. The NINE YEARS' WAR spread to Munster in 1598, and during the rebellion many of the estates were reclaimed by the Irish; the planters, small in number and poorly defended, fled to England. The plantation was successfully re-established after the Battle of KINSALE in 1601.

Munster plums. A nickname for potatoes.

Murder by the throat. A comment made by British prime minister David LLOYD GEORGE in a major public speech about the security situation in Ireland on 9 November 1920. The BLACK AND TANS had arrived on 25 March 1920, the Auxiliaries (*see* AUXIES) had taken up duty in September; the ANGLO-IRISH WAR had settled into a pattern of ambushes by the IRA, reprisals by the police and the terrorization of the civilian population – who, not surprisingly, had decided that they preferred their own terrorists to British terrorists; and Kevin Barry had been hanged on 1 November (*see* 'MOUNTJOY JAIL ONE MONDAY MORNING, IN'). Lloyd George declared that it was essential 'to break the terror before you can get peace ... We have murder by the throat. We had to reorganize the police and when the government was ready we struck the terrorists and now the terrorists are complaining of terror.' There is no doubt that the heavily armed and well-equipped force of Auxiliaries in particular were formidable adversaries for the IRA.

Murder Capital of Ireland, the. *See* ROS NA RÚN.

Murdering hypocrite. A verbal attack – followed by a physical assault – by Bernadette DEVLIN on Reginald Maudling, British home secretary, in the House of Commons on 31 January 1972, the day after Derry's BLOODY SUNDAY: 'I have a right as the only representative who was a witness, to ask a question of that murdering hypocrite.' Later she said to journalists, 'I am just sorry I did not go for his throat.'

Murder Machine, The. *See* PEARSE, PATRICK [HENRY].

Murna of the White Neck. In Irish mythology, the descendant of NUADA and ETHLINN and mother of FIONN MAC CUMHAIL.

Murph, the. The name by which Ballymurphy, a Nationalist/Republican district of west BELFAST, is generally known. It was the scene of numerous confrontations with the security forces during the 1970s, and also of internecine squabbles between PROVOS, STICKIES[1] and the INLA.

Murphy. The most common surname in Ireland.

'Murphy' is sometimes also used as a term for 'potato', reflecting that item's popularity in the Irish diet, but this usage is dated.

Murphy, Annie. *See* FORBIDDEN FRUIT.

Murphy, Arthur (1727–1805). Actor and author. He was born in Co. Roscommon on 27 December 1727 and educated at St Omer, in Northern France, later working as a clerk in Cork and London. His first stage appearance was as Othello at Covent Garden in October 1754, and, although he was successful in the role, he retired from acting after two years and was called to the Bar, at which he practised until 1788. His first play, *The Apprentice* (1756), produced in Drury Lane, earned him £800. He was a popular author for the stage, producing mainly farces in the French style – including *The Way to Keep Him* (1760), *No One's Enemy but His Own* (1763) and *Three Weeks after Marriage* (1776) – but also some tragedy and comedy. He also wrote biographies of David Garrick and Doctor Johnson, together with poetry and criticism. Despite his earnings from his writings he was frequently in debt, and George III granted him a pension of £200 a year in 1798. He died in his home in London on 18 June 1805.

Murphy, Delia (1902–71). A ballad singer with a distinctive and robust Nationalist style. She was born in Claremorris, Co. Mayo, and educated at University College Galway, where she graduated BComm. She married a diplomat, Tom Kiernan, and lived abroad with him on various postings, but developed a performing and recording career before the Second World War. The songs she made her own and with which she is still associated include the melancholy 'Dan O'Hara' and 'The Spinning Wheel', and the more upbeat 'Three Lovely Lassies from Bannion' and 'I'll Live Till I Die'. She returned to live in Dublin in 1969 and died in February 1971, having appeared once on *The* LATE LATE SHOW.

Murphy, Denis. *See* DENIS THE WEAVER.

Murphy, Dervla (b.1931). Travel writer. She was born in Lismore, County Waterford, and educated at the Ursuline Convent in Waterford. Her first book, *Full Tilt* (1965), best described by its subtitle 'Ireland to India on a Bicycle', was a bestseller because of the skill, humour, curiosity and intrepidity of the author, and her many other books have the same virtues. A worldwide traveller, she turned her rover's eye on Northern Ireland in *A Place Apart* (1978), like *Full Tilt* a prizewinner, with interesting results. Her autobiography is aptly called *Wheels within Wheels* (1979), and recent work includes *Transylvania and Beyond* (1992), *The Ukimwi Road* (1993), which follows the AIDS trail in Central and South Africa, *South from Limpopo: Travels through South Africa* (1997) and *Through the Embers of Chaos: Balkan Journeys* (2002). She lives a simple, bookish life at home in Lismore when she is not travelling, and still uses a bicycle as her sole means of locomotion, even for long distances.

Murphy, Father John (c.1753–98). One of the leaders of the Wexford rebels (*see* REBELLION OF 1798), celebrated in the ballad 'BOOLA-VOGUE'. Murphy and a companion, James Gallagher, were captured in Tullow, Co. Carlow, on 3 July 1798. They were publicly flogged in the town square, hanged and decapitated. Father Murphy's body was then set on fire in a barrel of pitch, but later rescued and secretly buried in the town graveyard. There is a monument to the two men in the square in Tullow, the site of their execution:

And the Yeos at Tullow took Father Murphy
And burned his body upon the rack.
    P.J. MCCALL (1861–1919): 'Boolavogue'

Murphy, Michael J. *See* AT SLIEVE GULLION'S FOOT.

Murphy, Richard (b.1927). Poet. He was born in Milford House, his family home in Co. Galway. His father was in the British colonial service and his boyhood was spent in Ceylon and the Bahamas. He was educated at Wellington, Magdalen College, Oxford, and the Sorbonne.

He ran a school in Crete before coming to live on Inishbofin off the Connemara coast, which is the inspiration for much of his poetry. *Sailing to an Island* (1963) contains many of the poems for which he is famous, notably the title poem, 'The Last Galway Hooker' and 'The Cleggan Disaster'. *The Battle of Aughrim* (1968) contains a commentary on the aftermath of the WILLIAMITE WAR. Other work includes *High Island* (1974) and *The Price of Stone* (1985). A *Collected Poems* appeared in 2000, and a memoir, *The Kick*, in 2001.

Murphy, Seamus (1907–75). Sculptor and stonemason. He was born near Mallow, Co. Cork, on 15 July 1907. Daniel CORKERY was his teacher and encouraged him to study at the School of Art in Cork. He went to Paris on a scholarship to study sculpture, and when he returned to Cork he opened his own studio. As well as being a monumental sculptor, creating fine, unadorned gravestones – including the headstone of his friend Seán Ó RIADA in Cúil Aodha (in the MUSKERRY GAELTACHT) – he quickly earned a reputation as a portrait sculptor. He sculpted heads of politicians, writers and public figures, creating bronze heads of all the presidents of Ireland from Douglas Hyde to Cearbhall Ó Dálaigh; these are now in ÁRAS AN UACHTARÁIN (the official residence of the president). Murphy's autobiography, with the punning title *Stone Mad*, was published in 1950; in it he describes the idiosyncrasies of some of the stonemasons ('stonies') with whom he carved. He exhibited, taught (as professor of sculpture at the Royal Hibernian Academy) and worked at his sculpture until the end of his life. He died suddenly in Cork on 2 October 1975.

Murphy, Tom (b.1935). Playwright and novelist. He was born in Tuam, Co. Galway, and educated at the local Christian Brothers school before becoming a metalwork teacher. *On the Outside* (1959), his first play, written with Noel O'Donoghue, is set outside a dancehall and deals with the violent frustration of young men too poor to enjoy the pleasures within, a neat symbol for the Ireland of the time. Violence and inarticulacy (in an Irish family in England) are also the themes of *A Whistle in the Dark* (1961), which, like *A Crucial Week in the Life of a Grocer's Assistant* (finally produced in 1969), was rejected by the conservative ABBEY THEATRE management of the time. Later work, distinguished by great power and some experimentation, includes *The Morning after Optimism* (1971), *The White House* (1972), *The Sanctuary Lamp* (1975), *The Gigli Concert* (1983), BAILEGANGAIRE (1985) and *Too Late for Logic* (1989), all of which deal in some way with Irish people and their troubled engagement with their distressful country. *The Seduction of Morality* (1994), Murphy's first novel, concerns the effect of the return of a prostitute who inherits a family business. It formed the basis of *The Wake*, which was produced at the Abbey in 1998.

Murphy, Tom Billy. *See* TOM BILLY.

Murphy, William Martin (1844–1919). Businessman and Nationalist politician. He was born in Bantry, Co. Cork, the son of a building contractor, and educated at Belvedere College Dublin. A builder and railway magnate in the UK and abroad, after he returned to Ireland he was the leading shareholder in the Dublin United Tramways company and owned Clery's department store, together with the *Irish Catholic* and *Irish Independent* newspapers. He was Nationalist MP for St Patrick's Ward in Dublin (1885–92) and with Tim HEALY opposed Parnell, becoming a member of the so-called Bantry Band, Healy's political machine.

Murphy was also one of the leading opponents of the Lane Bequest (*see* LANE PICTURES, THE), earning the contempt of Yeats, with whom he had a public feud:

> For how can you [Lady Gregory] compete,
> Being honour bred, with one
> Who, were it proved he lies,
> Were neither shamed in his own
> Nor in his neighbours's eyes?
>
> W.B. YEATS: 'To a Friend whose Work has come to Nothing' in *Responsibilities* (1914)

In the *Irish Independent* of 17 January 1913 Murphy wrote: 'Speaking for myself I admire good pictures and I think I can appreciate them but as a choice between the two, I would rather see in the city of Dublin one block of sanitary houses at low rents replacing a reeking slum than all the pictures Corot and Degas ever painted.'

Murphy organized a federation of employers against James LARKIN's ITGWU, and in August 1913 demanded that his own workers sign an undertaking not to join the ITGWU, calling Larkin an 'unscrupulous man, who used men as tools to make him the labour dictator of Dublin'. Larkin responded by calling a strike and in September Murphy and other employers locked out the workers (*see* 1913 LOCKOUT), earning the opprobrium of liberal opinion (he appears as a character in James Plunkett's STRUMPET CITY). Murphy recruited for the British army in the First World War, and wrote *The Home Rule Act 1914 Exposed* (1914), advocating that Ireland have colonial status.

Murphy's Irish Open. Ireland's premier international golf tournament, held at various courses throughout Ireland and sponsored by Murphy's Brewery since 1994. It was known as the Carroll's Irish Open (sponsored by a cigarette manufacturer) between 1975 and 1993.

Murphy's Law. An expression generally taken as meaning 'If anything can go wrong it will go wrong.' It is linked with Ireland because of the ubiquity of the surname but is, in fact, of American origin. The original Murphy's Law was 'If there are two or more ways to do something, and one of those ways can result in a catastrophe, then someone will do it'. The Murphy who formulated the theory (but not the exact words) was an aerospace engineer on a US air force project to test human acceleration tolerances in 1949. In one experiment 16 accelerometers were to be connected to different parts of the subject's body and there were two ways in which each sensor could be attached to its mount. Murphy formulated the law after someone managed to attach all

16 sensors the wrong way around. 'Murphy's Law' had its first lexicographical outing in *Webster's Dictionary* in 1958.

Murray, Laurence Patrick (Lorcán Ó Muireadhaigh; 1883–1941). Irish-language activist. He went as a student to Maynooth in 1901, but an impressive academic career was interrupted when he was asked to leave the college in 1908 because of supposed involvement in a protest against the visit of Edward VII to Maynooth and other instances of indiscipline. He went to the College of St Thomas in St Paul, Minnesota, was ordained a priest there in 1910 and became a mathematics teacher in the college. When the IRISH COLLEGE at Omeath, Co. Louth, was opened in 1912 he became part of the summer staff, using his free time to collect local Irish lore. In 1917, when America joined in the First World War, he refused to take a loyalty oath to an ally of the British and lost his job. Returning home again he did parish work in his native diocese of Armagh, and in 1921 was appointed religious inspector for the diocese. In 1924, supported by Comhlatas Uladh ('Ulster association') he founded the monthly magazine *An tUltach* ('the Ulsterman') dedicated to the furtherance of Ulster Irish. The following year under the same auspices he founded the summer school Coláiste Bhríde in Ranafast, an Irish-speaking region of west Donegal. The school still flourishes and is his best memorial.

Murray, Ruby (1935–96). Singer. She was born in Belfast and toured Northern Ireland as a child star, already possessed of the characteristic husky voice that gave her her special appeal. She went to London in 1954 and became the resident singer on the BBC television show *Quite Contrary*. Her first record single 'Heartbeat' made the UK top five in 1954, and 'Softly, Softly' was number one in 1955. That year she had five singles in the Top 20. Basically shy, she was unable to handle the stresses of stardom, and, though voted the most popular female vocalist in Britain, she became more and more dependent on alcohol. With the radical change in popular music in the 1960s her career went into eclipse. In 1982 she was arrested for being drunk and disorderly and spent the last eight months of her life in a nursing home with a badly affected liver. She died in Torbay on 17 December 1996. Her name is remembered in a piece of neo-Cockney rhyming slang, a 'Ruby' being a curry, as in 'Let's go down the pub and then get a Ruby.'

Murray, T[homas] C[ornelius] (1873–1959). Playwright. He was born in Macroom, Co. Cork, on 17 January 1873 and trained as a teacher at St Patrick's College, Drumcondra, Dublin, graduating in 1893. From 1909 he contributed plays to the ABBEY THEATRE, the best and most successful being *Autumn Fire* (1924), which has a Phaedra theme. The realism of his dialogue and the daring choice of subjects brought him some clerical criticism, and he was happy to leave Cork and accept the post of headmaster of Inchicore Model School (1915–32) in Dublin. He was called 'the doyen of the Munster realists', a description derived from such grim dramas as *Maurice Harte* (1912) about a clerical student without a vocation, and *Michaelmas Eve* (1932), in which a young man, on the advice of his mother, jilts the girl he loves to marry a woman with land. His services to literature were recognized in 1949 with an honorary DLitt from the National University of Ireland. He died in Dublin on 7 March 1959.

> Hearing the cows gadding in the heat and they making a little boom of thunder with their hoofs on the sod and myself in a little room under the roof and no better than a breathing corpse.
> *Autumn Fire* (1924)

Murrough of the Burnings (Irish *Murcha na dTóiteán*). The nickname given to Murrough O'Brien (1614–74), 1st Earl of Inchiquin, who in a colourful career converted to Protestantism as a youth, allied himself with the Parliamentarians in the English Civil War and became infamous as a formidable opponent of the CONFEDERATE CATHOLICS in the CONFEDERATE WAR, defeating them at Knockanuss, Co. Cork, in 1647. He evicted Catholics from Cork in 1644 and massacred the defenders of

Adare and Cashel in 1647. He rejoined the Royalist side, and after the Royalist defeat in 1650 went into exile in Spain, where he became governor of Catalonia. He returned to Catholicism in 1657, and to his Munster estates after the Restoration. In DINNEEN'S DICTIONARY he is described as 'a terrorist of the civil [i.e. Confederate] war'.

Museum of Country Life. The first branch of the NATIONAL MUSEUM OF IRELAND outside Dublin, opened in September 2001 in Turlough Park, 6 km (4 miles) east of Castlebar in Co. Mayo. The main building of the estate, Turlough Park House (1865), was designed by Thomas Newenham Deane, who also designed the National Museum Building in Kildare Street, Dublin. The Museum of Country Life, the first new building to be commissioned by the National Museum since 1890, houses a collection of artefacts and utensils that represent the traditions of rural life throughout Ireland.

Mush and **Musha.** *See* WISHA.

Musical snuff-box. A characteristically irascible dismissal of the IRISH MELODIES of Tom Moore by William Hazlitt (1778–1830) in *The Spirit of the Age* (1825):

> If these prettinesses pass for patriotism, if a country can heave from its heart's core only these varnished sentiments, lip-deep, and let its tears of blood evaporate in an empty conceit, let it be governed as it has been. There are here no tones to awaken liberty, to console Humanity. Mr Moore converts the wild harp of Erin into a musical snuff-box.

Hazlitt's radicalism would have been temperamentally alien to Moore, but in spite of these strictures his melodies did speak for Ireland. The first volume contains a clear tribute to his friend Robert EMMET in 'O Breathe Not His Name' (taken from Emmet's speech from the dock in October 1803), while 'Let Erin Remember' was said by its author to have wrested from Emmet the cry:

> Would that I were at the head of twenty thousand men and marching to that tune!

Music of what happens, the. There is a legend that one day FIONN MAC CUMHAIL is in discussion with some of his followers about the sweetest music in existence. Fionn's son OISÍN suggests the song of the cuckoo, his grandson OSCAR the ring of a spear on a shield, while other warriors suggest many other things. But Fionn says, 'The music of what happens, that is the finest music in the world.'

Muskerry Gaeltacht, the (Irish *Gaeltacht Mhúscraí*). An area of west Cork in which Irish was the dominant spoken language until after the Second World War (it is still an official GAELTACHT). It includes small towns such as Ballingeary, GOUGANE BARRA, Ballyvourney and Coolea, and the parishes of Cill na Martra and Uíbh Laoghaire. The area produced a fine corpus of songs in Irish, some love songs, some AISLINGÍ, among them *'Cois Abhann na Séad'* and *'Bean Dubh an Ghleanna'*, which are still performed in the traditional manner today. A celebrated IRISH COLLEGE, Coláiste na Mumhan, was established in Ballingeary in 1904, and from then until the foundation of the state it taught Irish-language enthusiasts, *Timirí* (Gaelic League organizers of adult education) and TRAVELLING TEACHERS. In 1922, when it was decreed that all schoolchildren should study Irish, it was discovered that 80% of teachers did not have the ability to teach it. Large numbers of mainly Anglophone teachers came to Ballingeary and other Irish colleges – in the process, it is alleged, contributing to the decline of spoken Irish among the host families in this and other of the weaker Gaeltachts, as did the holidaymakers who followed them to such scenic and unspoilt areas. A theory has been advanced that women abandoned Irish more quickly than their menfolk – the Tailor's wife Ansty (*see TAILOR AND ANSTY, THE*), who had worked in a hotel in Gougane Barra and met foreigners there is given as an example – but this phenomenon has never been adequately investigated.

Mussenden Temple. A domed rotunda commissioned and designed by the Earl Bishop, Frederick Augustus HERVEY. It was constructed 1783–5 on top of the cliffs at DOWNHILL, Co. Derry, and is all that has survived intact of the grandeur of that eccentric demesne. Based on the temple of Venus at Tivoli, it was built for his beautiful cousin Mrs Frideswide Mussenden, who, however, died at the age of 22, before the building was completed. Hervey used it as his summer library, and in a typically liberal gesture made the vault available to the Catholics of the neighbourhood as a place of worship. The inscription on the frieze, from *De Rerum Natura* (11, 1, 2) by Lucretius (*c.*99–*c.*55 BC), is appropriate to its windswept position on the very edge of the sea cliff:

> *Suave mari magno turbantius aequora ventis*
> *E terra magnum alterius spectare laborem.*
> (It is pleasant when the wind stirs up great waves to watch from the land the plight of someone else.)

Mutton dummies. An Ulster slang term for plimsolls, perhaps in approximate phonetic imitation of the dated HIBERNO-ENGLISH term 'rubber dollies'.

'My Aunt Jane'. A Belfast street song (also adopted in Derry and other towns) dating from the late 19th century. It enshrines a feature of the back streets of the 'Red Brick City', namely the 'wee shop'. This was converted from the spotless, unused front parlour, and sold 'candy apples, hard green pears, CONVERSATION LOZENGES':

> My Aunt Jane she took me in,
> She gave me tea out of her wee tin:
> Half a bap, sugar on the top,
> Three black lumps out of her wee shop.

My Fight for Irish Freedom. *See* BREEN, DAN.

My heart to Rome. A part of a mantra learned by many generations of Irish schoolchildren about the spiritual legacy of Daniel O'CONNELL. He died in Genoa on 15 May 1847 on a pilgrimage to Rome and his heart was, on his instruction, placed in a shrine and taken to the city by his chaplain, Dr Miley, and his fourth son, Daniel. It was placed in the Irish College at Santa Agata dei Goti, while his body was taken home to Ireland and buried in GLASNEVIN CEMETERY. O'Connell is claimed to have said in a typical rhetorical flourish: 'My soul to heaven, my heart to Rome and my body to Ireland.'

My Lady Bountiful. A character in George Farquhar's last play *The BEAUX' STRATAGEM* whose name has become archetypal. She is described in the Dramatis Personae as 'An old, civil, Country Gentlewoman, that cures all her neighbours of all distempers, and foolishly fond of her son, Squire Sullen.' The expression had attained proverbial status by the middle of the 18th century, denoting a person of great generosity and kindness.

> Come, sir, your servant has been telling me that you are apt to relapse if you go into the air: your good manners shan't get the better of ours – you shall sit down again, sir. Come, sir, we don't mind ceremonies in the country – here, sir, my service t'ye. You shall taste my water; 'tis a cordial I can assure you, and of my own making – drink it off, sir.
> IV. i

My Lady of the Chimney Corner. A memoir (1913) by the evangelist Alexander Irvine (1862–1941) of his mother Anna Gilmore, with whom he had a remarkably happy childhood, in spite of terrible poverty. They lived in a house in Pogue's Entry in Antrim town, and the building is now the Irvine Museum. The Catholic wife of a Protestant shoemaker who lost his trade to cheap factory products, Anna Gilmore managed by imaginative stories and unaffected piety to inspire her talented son, the ninth of 12 children, to a life of service. He was a coal miner in Scotland and later served in the Royal Marines. He became a champion boxer, a skill that doubtless stood him in good stead while doing missionary work among the derelicts of the Bowery in New York. Uncompromising in both his Christianity and his socialism, he served as a padre in the First World War (the basis of one of his autobiographical volumes,

God and Tommy Atkins, 1918), and was asked to mediate in the British General Strike of 1926. He began writing with the encouragement of the American novelist Jack London (1876–1916), and wrote two further accounts of his charismatic mother, *The Souls of Poor Folk* (1921) and *Anna's Wishing Chair* (1937). The title of his last book, another volume of autobiography, *The Fighting Parson* (1930), adequately describes his life.

> 'Me an' Jamie wor pirta sack people, purty d – d rough, too, but yer ma was a piece of fine linen from th' day she walked down this road wi' yer Dah.'

My Left Foot (1954). The title of an autobiography by Christy Brown (1932–81), which he typed by foot. Brown was born into a large family in Crumlin, Dublin, severely handicapped with athenoid paralysis. He revealed a remarkable intelligence when, after being for years considered mentally handicapped, he began drawing on the floor with a piece of chalk gripped between his toes. He was taught to speak by his mother, and later given effective speech and coordination training. *Down All the Days* (1970) is a novel of childhood, and was followed by a volume of poetry, *Come Softly to My Wake* (1971). Jim Sheridan's film of *My Left Foot* (1989), starring Daniel Day-Lewis as Christy Brown, won many awards.

Myles the Slasher. *See* FINEA, BRIDGE OF.

My name is O'Hanlon. *See* PATRIOT GAME, THE.

My New Curate. The best-known novel (1900) of Canon SHEEHAN, about a parish priest and his new curate, and how they learn from each other. The younger man is full of ideas about improving the lot of his parishioners, but his schemes tend to go awry: a shirt factory fails and an uninsured fishing boat is lost. He is saved from bankruptcy by the people, and leaves the parish to become the bishop's secretary. The novel provides a useful picture of post-Land War, pre-revolutionary Ireland.

> It is all my own fault. I was too free with my tongue. I said in a moment of bitterness, 'What can a bishop do with a parish priest? He's independent of him.' It was not grammatical and it was not respectful. But the bad grammar and the impertinence were carried to his Lordship, and he answered, 'What can I do? I can send him a curate who will break his heart in six weeks!'

'My Wild Irish Rose'. A popular Irish-American song written in 1899 by Chauncey Olcott. He was born John Chancellor Olcott on 21 July 1860 in Buffalo, New York, and began his stage career in 1876 as a member of a black-faced minstrel troupe. He went to London to study music, appearing several times on stage there, and on his return home began to star in a number of Irish musical plays that he also wrote. He collaborated with Ernest R. Ball on the music for 'Mother Machree' (1910; *see* MACHREE) and 'WHEN IRISH EYES ARE SMILING' (1913). 'My Wild Irish Rose' (1899) was all his own work, and he incorporated it into a typical Irish show of the period, *A Romance of Athlone*. The title was suggested to Olcott on his single visit to Ireland when, it is said, in order to stop his young Killarney guide from singing SEAN-NÓS Gaelic songs, he asked him the name of a flower growing by Lough Lene. The boy answered, ''Tis just a wild Irish rose.' It was used as the title for the 1947 biopic based on Olcott's life, with Denis Morgan (1910–94) in the lead. Olcott died in Monte Carlo on 18 March 1932.

> My wild Irish Rose, the sweetest flower that
>   grows;
> You may search ev'rywhere but none can
>   compare
> With my wild Irish Rose.
> My wild Irish Rose, the dearest flower that
>   grows,
> And someday for my sake, she may let me take
> The bloom from my wild Irish Rose.

N

Ná bac leis. An Irish phrase meaning 'Don't bother with it'. In HIBERNO-ENGLISH the phrase, sometimes anglicized as 'nabocklesh', is used to advise discretion or to let well alone.

Nagle, Nano (1728–84). Religious founder. She was born Honoria, the eldest child of Ann Mathew and Garret Nagle, a prosperous landowner and merchant of Balgriffin, near Mallow, Co. Cork. Educated in Paris, she returned to an Ireland in which the POPERY LAWS effectively deprived the Catholic poor of education. (She herself had earlier attended a HEDGE SCHOOL near Castletownroche, in which one of her fellow pupils was Edmund BURKE.) Appalled at the lack of education of Catholic children in Cork city she opened a school in Cove Lane in 1754, and by 1758 several hundred children were being educated in her seven schools, the work aided by a considerable legacy in 1757. Until then she was regularly seen about the city wrapped in a black cloak and carrying a lantern, so sweetly persistent in her search for alms that she became known as 'God's Beggar'. Her health began to fail in the face of a relentless workload, and she persuaded the Ursuline Sisters to come to the city in 1771. The Ursulines proved willing but unsuitable since their experience in education had previously been with the daughters of the rich. In 1777 Nano (as she was universally known) and three companions – Mary Collins, Eliza-beth Burke and Mary Tuohy – pronounced their final vows before Bishop Moylan on 24 June to become the founder members of the Order of the Presentation Sisters of the Blessed Virgin Mary, a community of nuns devised by her to meet the needs of the poor. By the time of her death on 26 April 1784 the order and its rule, which 'excluded every exercise of charity which was not in favour of the poor', was well established. It has since spread to England, America, Australia and India.

Nairac, Robert (1948–77). A British army captain who seems to have been allowed a free rein in undercover intelligence work in strongly Republican south Armagh (*see* BANDIT COUNTRY). Nairac took the considerable risk of frequenting local pubs and learnt the words of rebel songs. Inevitably he came to the attention of local IRA members, who kidnapped him at the Three Step Inn, Drumintee, in south Armagh on 14 May 1977 and later killed him, probably disposing of his body in the nearby Ravensdale Forest Park. On 9 November 1977 Liam Townsend was tried and convicted of his murder. Nairac, still one of the DISAPPEARED, was posthumously awarded the George Cross. He seemed to belong to a certain British tradition of the maverick solo operator, more suited to escapist fiction than to the unromantic truth of the Northern Ireland TROUBLES.

Nale in the Pail. A nickname for the Millennium Spire, which stands on the site of NELSON'S PILLAR.

Naming names. A term associated with media investigations and tribunals into irregularities around planning and payments to politicians in the 1990s and later. The threat to 'name names', for example of recipients of payments, is often met with matching threats to seek an injunction to stop publication or sue for libel.

Namurs, the. The nickname of the Royal Irish Regiment, in tribute to their being the first regiment in the British army to be awarded a battle honour; this was earned at the Battle of Namur in 1695 during the War of the League of Augsburg (1688–97). They were also known as Paddy's Blackguards, a name garnered when they were in the army of JAMES II. They survived the 'Glorious Revolution' that deposed James and put William III on the throne, and were not disbanded until 1922.

Nangle, Edward. *See* MISSIONARY SETTLEMENT, THE.

Naoise. In Irish mythology, the consort of the tragic heroine DEIRDRE, and eldest of the three sons of USNA. He and his brothers AINLÉ and ARDÁN are RED BRANCH KNIGHTS in the service of CONCHOBHAR. When he meets Deirdre, the betrothed of his master, she realizes that he fulfils her criteria of male beauty; they fall in love and flee to the safety of Glen Etive in ALBA. Returning home under the parley of FERGUS MAC ROTH – against Deirdre's advice – he and his brothers are killed as a result of the usual mixture of betrayal, magic and misdirected loyalty. He is buried by a little lake opposite Deirdre's grave, and the branches of the pines that grow out of their graves mesh to form a lovers' arch, as in the Greek myth of Baucis and Philemon.

Naomhóg. A type of coracle or CURRACH used throughout the Dingle Peninsula and especially associated with the BLASKET ISLANDS. The *naomhóg*, which is light enough to be handled by two men, is constructed by stretching canvas over laths of wood and painting the canvas with pitch to make it waterproof. Until the 1960s it was the universal mode of maritime transport in the area, used for fishing, and for transporting goods, people and even animals across the treacherous passage of water between Dunquin Pier and the landing places on the Blaskets. The word *naomhóg* itself is related to the old Irish words *noe* and *nai*, cognate with the Latin *navis*, 'ship'. There appears to be no connection with *naomh* (saint), although this is a common misconception.

Napoleon's Nose. *See* MAC ART'S FORT.

Nast, Thomas. *See* 'I'M RISING IN THE WORLD'.

Nation, The. A weekly paper, the organ of YOUNG IRELAND, owned and edited by Charles Gavan DUFFY with strong support from John Blake DILLON and Thomas DAVIS. The last supplied much of the cultural material – essays and patriotic ballads – advocating a pride in Ireland's glorious past and a wish for its re-establishment as an independent nation. Founded in October 1842, *The Nation* played a major part in the political and general education of the Irish people until its suppression in 1848. It was revived by Duffy again in the following year and continued until 1897. An anthology entitled *The Spirit of the Nation*, containing the most popular poems and ballads and first published in 1843, was still in print in the 1930s. The following less-than-deathless verse was printed in the first edition:

> 'Tis a great day, and glorious, O Public! For you –
> This October Fifteenth, Eighteen Forty and Two!
> For on this day of days, lo! *The Nation* comes
>   forth,
> To commence its career of Wit, Wisdom, and
>   Worth –
> To give Genius its due – to do battle with Wrong –
> And achieve things undreamed of as yet, save in
>   song.
> Then arise! fling aside your dark mantle of
>   slumber,
> And welcome in chorus *The Nation's* First
>   Number.

National Gallery of Ireland. A gallery situated in Merrion Square, Dublin, beside Government Buildings. When the ROYAL DUBLIN SOCIETY had Leinster House as its headquarters it also owned the land, called Leinster Lawn, on which the gallery was built. In 1853 a great industrial exhibition was held there, masterminded by railway magnate William DARGAN. Admirers of Dargan subscribed to a testimonial to him and he suggested that the funds be used to establish an art gallery. It opened to the public in 1864, just a few years after the complementary Natural History Museum (*see* NATIONAL MUSEUM OF IRELAND) on the other side of Leinster Lawn. The original building was extended in 1903, and again in 1968. George Bernard Shaw bequeathed one-third of his estate to the gallery. Among the treasures of the gallery is a fine collection of the works of John B. YEATS and Jack B. YEATS, the father and brother, respectively, of the poet. The gallery has also been home to the National Portrait Collection since 1884.
See also MILLENNIUM WING.

Nationalism/Republicanism. Two terms that in subtly different ways are used to describe those people in Northern Ireland whose political goal is a reunited Ireland. Republicans (such as supporters of SINN FÉIN) at their most rhetorical make the term Nationalist an inclusive one, while suggesting that they are the truest kind. Other Nationalists (such as supporters of the SDLP) are at pains to distance themselves from Republicanism which carries the connotation of intransigence and violence when necessary (*see* PHYSICAL-FORCE REPUBLICANISM). The former, while yielding nothing in their genuine wish for reunification, prefer (and have preferred) to use constitutional means of attaining their goal.
See also LOYALIST.

Nationalist Party. *See* IRISH PARTY.

National League. *See* LAND LEAGUE.

National Leagues, the. A GAA inter-county HURLING and FOOTBALL league initiated in 1925 to provide competition during the winter months. The first games were played in October 1925, and the first finals the following May. The leagues have never attained the same popularity as the championship (*see* ALL-IRELAND).

National Library of Ireland. A library established in 1877 by the Science and Art Museum Act. It developed from the ROYAL DUBLIN SOCIETY Library (which included 30,000 books), and has been located next to where the DÁIL now is, in Kildare Street, Dublin, since 1891, in a purpose-built premises designed by Thomas Deane. It holds six million items of Irish interest, including manuscripts, photographic material, maps and archives, and has been a legal deposit or copyright library for all material published in Ireland since 1927.

National Museum of Ireland. A museum established by the Science and Art Museum Act of 1877 (*see* NATIONAL LIBRARY OF IRELAND), and including the Natural History Museum in Merrion Square and the National Museum (of antiquities) in Kildare Street, beside the Dáil. It holds such priceless treasures as the TARA BROOCH, the ARDAGH CHALICE and the Cross of CONG. In 1997 the National Museum acquired additional accommodation, in the former COLLINS BARRACKS, which opened in 1997.

National schools. The primary education system supported by the British government from 1831. In that year the government established a Board of Commissioners for National Education, which included representatives of the Church of Ireland, the Catholic Church and the Presbyterian Church, under the chairmanship of the Duke of Leinster. The commissioners provided most of the cost of building schools, paid most of the salaries of teachers and provided textbooks, while local sponsors, such as landlords or clergymen, provided the site and contributed to the cost of maintenance and the salaries of teachers, whom they appointed. Inspectors appointed by the commissioners supervised the schools. The schools were intended to be non-denominational, with

Catholic and Protestant children being educated together for the most part but separately for religious instruction. Initially the Catholic Church was supportive, but gradually became disillusioned with aspects of the system, while the Church of Ireland and Presbyterian churches disapproved from the beginning. Gradually the schools became in practice denominational, a reality that was recognized by the Powis Commission in 1870. There were half a million pupils in Irish national schools by the end of the 19th century, and although the national schools have been blamed for contributing to the decline of the Irish language and culture (*see* TALLYSTICKS) and for being excessively narrow in their pedagogy, they contributed greatly to literacy in English, preparing young people for emigration to America and Britain.

National University. The final solution of the British government to the vexed question of denominational university education. The National University of Ireland (NUI) – comprising University College Cork, University College Galway and University College Dublin (reconstituted) – was established by the Irish Universities Act of 1908, while the Queen's University of Belfast became a separate college. The act put an end to the ROYAL UNIVERSITY OF IRELAND. MAYNOOTH became a recognized college of the NUI, as it is universally called, in 1913, and a constituent college in 1966. The NUI was in theory non-denominational, and the colleges were forbidden to have chairs of theology or scripture, but it was stipulated that the composition of the governing body of each should be acceptable to the majority religion of the students, thus ensuring that the Catholic hierarchy was given a major role in the governing body of the three southern colleges. The three universities in question remain constituent colleges of the NUI, although there was in the 1970s discussion of the possibility of making UCD (University College Dublin) independent, and the country's new universities of the 1970s and 1980s, UL (University of Limerick) and DCU (Dublin City University), have not formed part of the NUI. Individual universities emphasize or downplay the NUI connection: for instance UCG (University College Galway) has recently rebranded itself NUI Galway or NUIG.

National Volunteers. A majority breakaway group from the IRISH VOLUNTEERS, who after John REDMOND's speech at WOODENBRIDGE in September 1914 were prepared to join the British army. The National Volunteers numbered about 170,000, and many of them fought on the Western Front, although, unlike the UVF, they were not allowed to form their own regiment, and were in general undervalued by the War Office. The minority group in the Irish Volunteers kept the name, and it was they who, with the help of the IRB, organized the 1916 EASTER RISING.

'Nation Once Again, A'. The title of the best known patriotic ballad by Thomas DAVIS (1814–45), published in *The NATION*. Davis's aim was as much educational as inspirational; *The Nation*'s pages were intended to be the Irish peasant's academy. It is somewhat ironic that, while the author was anxious to make his readers aware of the glory of Ireland's own past, he saw no need to gloss the 'three hundred men and three men' of the first verse – he could rely on their having, because of attendance at HEDGE SCHOOLS, at least an oral acquaintance with the glory and grandeur of classical antiquity. Later generations need to be informed that the 'three men' were Horatius, Herminius and Lartius who kept the bridge against the Etruscan army of Lars Porsena in the 6th century BC, and the 'three hundred' were the Spartans under Leonidas who held the pass of Thermopylae against the might of the Persians led by Xerxes in 480 BC:

When boyhood's fire was in my blood
I read of ancient freemen
For Greece and Rome who bravely stood –
Three hundred men and three men.
And then I prayed I yet might see
Our fetters rent in twain,

And Ireland, long a province be
A nation once again.

The ballad was used by Winston Churchill in an offer to de Valera of Irish unity in exchange for use of the TREATY PORTS by the British after Pearl Harbor. The telegram, sent on 8 December 1941, was brought personally by the British ambassador, Sir John Maffey (1877–1969), later Lord Rugby, though it was very late in the evening:

> Now is your chance. Now or never. 'A nation once again.' Am ready to meet you at any time.
>> Quoted in Joseph T. Carrol, *Ireland in the War Years 1939–45* (1975)

See also URINATION ONCE AGAIN.

Native speaker. A person for whom the Irish language is the mother-tongue, normally reared in a GAELTACHT area or in an Irish-speaking household elsewhere. The Irish term is *cainteoir dúchais*, meaning exactly the same.

Natural party of government, the. A description of the FIANNA FÁIL party, made by its then leader Charles HAUGHEY with the arrogance that comes from having been too long in power. With the exception of two brief periods of rule by INTERPARTY GOVERNMENTS (1948–51 and 1954–57), Fianna Fáil was in single-party government from 1932 until 1973. The party also had a monopoly on the presidency until Mary ROBINSON was elected to that office in 1990.

See also CORE VALUE; TEMPORARY LITTLE ARRANGEMENT.

Navan Fort. A late Bronze Age enclosure 3 km (2 miles) west of Armagh city that has been identified as the probable site of EMAIN MACHA, the seat of the ancient kings of Ulster, named after a princess or goddess MACHA. In mythology Emain Macha was the stronghold of King CONCHOBAR and his RED BRANCH KNIGHTS, and here CÚCHULAINN spent his youth, before leaving to fight the army of Queen MEDB of Connacht. At the site, a low hill-top is surrounded by a bank with a ditch inside, and there is a large mound in the middle which was excavated 1963–71, revealing that a ditched enclosure, some 150 m (165 yds) in diameter, had been built in the late Bronze Age. Subsequently nine successive groups of of dwellings were built on the site, which was abandoned in the early Christian era. However, some of the old traditions seem to have remained: BRIAN BORU camped here when he visited Armagh in 1005, and Niall O'Neill built a house here in the 14th century. An extensive interpretive centre has been created beside the archaeological remains.

Navvies. The name by which Irish labourers in Britain in the 1950s and 1960s were generally known (the word itself has no Irish connections, deriving from labourers who worked in navigation waterways or canals in the 19th century). The Irish navvies, most of them uneducated and unprepared, were forced by poverty at home to take the boat (*see* TAKING THE BOAT) and come to London and other British cities where construction work on roads and houses was plentiful in the postwar era. (Women also emigrated in large numbers, to work in factories, shops and hospitals.)

Many left their local railway station in Ireland with a label tied to their coat bearing the name of the builder for whom they were going to work, and he or a representative would meet them at London's Euston Station. Others were picked up at the station by agents, who got a commission from big builders like McAlpine (*see* MCALPINE'S FUSILIERS) and WIMPEY for each labourer they acquired. Still others queued every morning at Camden Underground station or the Crown on Cricklewood Broadway to be selected by a ganger for that day's casual work.

Irish people tended to congregate in areas like Kilburn, Camden Town and Cricklewood, and the lucky ones settled down, bought houses and raised children who became much better educated than their parents. The not-so-lucky lived in digs, drank too much in the Crown in Cricklewood and danced in the GALTYMORE or another of the legion of Irish ballrooms in London at the time – until they were too old to dance, longed for home but never made it back and never put down roots in Britain. The unluckiest of all worked 'ON THE LUMP' for unscrupulous contractors, many of them Irish, 'following the work' around Britain for years and finding themselves homeless and marginalized, without social-insurance entitlements.

The money sent home by navvies and other emigrant workers in Britain – usually in the form of a weekly ten-shilling postal order to their families – contributed enormously to Ireland's domestic economy during the 1950s. In today's terms they sent back a sum estimated to have been between €650,000 and €1 million each year. Almost 80% of those born in Ireland between 1931 and 1941 had to emigrate; 89% of those went to Britain. Half a million Irish people emigrated during the 1950s alone. *See also* TATIE-HOWKERS; TUNNEL TIGERS.

Navvy Poet, the. *See* MACGILL, PATRICK.

Naygur. In HIBERNO-ENGLISH a form of the word *niggard*, denoting an unusually wretched miser.

> In all my ranging and serenading,
> I met no naygur but humpy Hyde.
>
> > Quoted in P. W. Joyce, *English as We Speak It in Ireland* (1910)

Neave, Airey (1916–79). Politician. Neave, famous for being the first British officer to escape from the German POW camp Colditz (1942) – a feat described in *They Have Their Exits* (1953) – was not only the politician who masterminded Mrs Thatcher's election as Conservative Party leader in place of Edward Heath in 1975, but was also her hard-line shadow secretary of state for Northern Ireland. This the INLA regarded as sufficient reason for his elimination, which was arranged by a mercury trembler switch on a device in his car as he drove out of the Members' car park of the House of Commons on 30 March 1979. The assassination took place the day after the defeat of the Labour government on a no-confidence motion had made a UK general election certain and a Conservative victory likely.

'Necessity for De-anglicizing the Irish People, The'. *See* DE-ANGLICIZING THE IRISH PEOPLE, THE NECESSITY FOR.

Neck of the Butlers, the. *See* AFFANE, BATTLE OF.

Neill's Blue Caps. The nickname for the Royal Dublin Fusiliers (who like so many other groups from the city were known as Dubs). During the Indian Mutiny (1857–8) the 1st battalion wore blue caps and was commanded by a Colonel Neill. Another nickname-honour, the Old Toughs, was granted to the 2nd battalion during the mutiny.

Neilson, Samuel (1761–1803). United Irishman. He was born at Ballyroney, Co. Down, the son of a Presbyterian minister. Apprenticed at 16 to a woollen draper, he had his own business eight years later and had by 1790 amassed a fortune (for those years) of £8000. He gave up business for politics and conceived the idea of a political society that would welcome Irishmen of all creeds and classes. In 1791, with the help of Henry Joy MCCRACKEN and Wolfe TONE, he founded the Society of UNITED IRISHMEN, and in 1792 established the *The* NORTHERN STAR as the society's organ, with himself as editor. Though very popular and with a circulation of 4000, it ceased publication when its offices were wrecked by the Monaghan militia in 1797. By then Neilson was in prison; he had been arrested in 1796 and was imprisoned in Kilmainham Jail, in Dublin. Imprisonment had a deleterious effect on his health, and he was released in February 1798 on the condition that he would abstain from 'treasonable conspiracy'.

Neilson immediately began planning for a rising with Lord Edward FITZGERALD, and was himself arrested trying to rescue Fitzgerald from Newgate Prison, being severely wounded in the affray. He was detained until 1802 at Fort George on the Moray Firth, near Inverness in Scotland, with other members of the society including Thomas RUSSELL and Thomas Addis Emmet. Deported to the Netherlands, he made secret visits to Belfast and Dublin in December

1802 before sailing to America. His last political action was to advise Robert EMMET against his planned rising. He settled in Poughkeepsie in New York and was in the process of launching a new evening paper when he died suddenly on 29 August 1803.

Neither Profitable nor Popular. 'The Man who spoke Irish at a Time when it was neither Profitable nor Popular' was (complete with laudatory upper-case letters) one of the heroes of the satirical column CRUISKEEN LAWN, a column that also feted 'The Brother', 'The Da' and 'The Plain People of Ireland'.

Nelson's Pillar. A monument honouring Horatio Nelson, victor of Trafalgar, that stood in Dublin's O'CONNELL STREET (formerly Sackville Street) from 1809 until 1966. On 18 November 1805 the Corporation of Dublin passed a resolution congratulating King George III on his victory at the Battle of Trafalgar. A meeting of the 'nobility, clergy, bankers, merchants and citizens of the city' was held to discuss a means of honouring the hero of that victory, Lord Nelson. The committee established at that meeting, which included Arthur Guinness, decided to build a pillar with a statue of Nelson, and £4000 was quickly collected to advance the project. Building work began in February 1808 – the architect was Francis JOHNSTON – and Nelson's Pillar was opened to the public on the anniversary of the Battle of Trafalgar, 21 October 1809. The outside was of Wicklow granite and the interior of black limestone. Pillar and statue were 41 m (134 ft) high and visitors could climb 168 interior steps to the top. Nelson's Pillar was blown up by the IRA on 9 March 1966, and while clearing away the remains of the pillar, the Irish army damaged property in O'Connell Street. Nelson's head can now be viewed in the Civic Museum in South William Street in Dublin.

After years of discussion, consultation and controversy, a spire (it was originally known as the 'Monument of Light' and then as the 'Millennium Spire') was constructed in Waterford and finally, on 22 January 2003 the final section was erected on the site of Nelson's Pillar. A stainless steel structure, illuminated at the top and the bottom, it is 120 m (394 ft) high, 3 m (10 ft) in diameter at the base, and 15 cm (6 ins) in diameter at the top. Some claimed that the 140-m (459-ft) crane – the tallest in Ireland – used in the erection of the spire was of more interest than the monument itself and should be retained. One Moore Street trader quipped, 'We got the Bertie pole instead of the BERTIE BOWL.' Alternative nicknames include the 'Nail in the Pale' and the 'Stiletto in the Ghetto'. The cost of the project was estimated to be in the region of €4.6 million.

Nelson's Pillar Time Capsule. The foundations of the destroyed Pillar were left untouched until 2001 when archaeologists were sent in to investigate in advance of construction work for the controversial Millennium Spire (*see* NELSON'S PILLAR). They found a cut granite block with a sealed cavity but – to great public disappointment – the cavity was empty. There was a myth that a treasure trove was concealed at the base of Nelson's Pillar because a book published in 1818 by Warburton, Whitelaw and Walsh and called *History of the City of Dublin* recorded that 'various coins' had been deposited in a recess covered by a brass plate.

Nemed. In Irish mythology, as recorded in the BOOK OF INVASIONS, the leader of the third of the waves of supposed invaders of the island of Ireland. He is a descendant of Japhet, the son of Noah, and arrives from Scythia with 32 ships. Many of the passengers die at sea of famine, but magically, when the survivors land their numbers increase sufficiently to defeat the FOMORIANS three times. After Nemed's death his followers become the Fomorians' slaves, but mount a revolt against their grisly rule (including an attack on the Fomorian stronghold of TORY ISLAND). The insurrection is put down with great ruthlessness: only 30 of the 16,000 followers of Nemed are left alive, and these few leave Ireland to find a kinder shore.

Ne plus ultra. A Latin phrase meaning '(go) no further', words traditionally supposed to have been written on the Pillars of Hercules (the straits of Gibraltar) as a warning to ships. It was deployed in a slightly obscure piece of rhetoric by Charles Stewart PARNELL in a speech in Cork on 21 January 1885:

> No man has a right to say to his country: 'Thus far shalt you go and no further,' and we never attempted to fix the *ne plus ultra* to the progress of Ireland's nationhood, and we never shall.

The speech was made in response to Joseph Chamberlain's attempt to kill the demands for HOME RULE by setting up a central board, which would have limited legislative powers applicable only to local government. The speech became his most quoted piece of oratory, and some of it was inscribed on the plinth of his memorial statue, which stands between O'Connell Street and Parnell Square in Dublin. Its significance is not entirely clear, and it certainly suggested to later generations more than Parnell had ever intended.

Nessa. The mother of CONCHOBHAR. She conceived the child with the druid CATHBAD while married to Fachtna, king of Ulster. On Fachtna's death, his half-brother FERGUS MAC ROTH accedes to the throne, but in return for Nessa's sexual favours allows Conchobhar to reign for a year. She advises her son so well about the duties of kingship that he is able to remain on the throne while retaining the full support of the people. Nessa's power gradually decreases as her son becomes the most notable of all the Ulster kings, the only serious blot on his character being his betrayal of DEIRDRE and the SONS OF USNA.

Ne temere (Latin, 'lest rashly...'). A decree (1908) by St Pope Pius X (1835–1914) that insisted that Catholics marrying Protestants must agree to their children being reared as Catholics. It was a reaffirmation of long-standing church teaching, but its effect in Ireland, especially in the North, was significant. It was seen as a further example of the growth of Catholic power and a demonstration of little charity towards Protestants.

See also MCCANN AFFAIR, THE.

Neustria. The western Frankish kingdom that was carved out of the realm of Clovis (465–511), the Merovingian king, and eventually ruled by his grandson Charibert. It comprised modern Normandy and some of the lands to the south and east, and had Paris as its capital. It became a mission field for Irish PEREGRINI.

Neutrality. Much has been written and argued on the subject of Irish neutrality, especially in the Second World War, since for many a failure to take a stand against Hitler was morally inexcusable. DE VALERA's visit of condolence to the German ambassador in Dublin after the death of Hitler in 1945 was cited as proof that Ireland was really neutral on the German side, or that, yet again, 'England's difficulty was Ireland's opportunity.' In reality, from the outbreak of the war, the country adopted a position of 'benevolent neutrality' towards the Franco-British Allies: although military commitment was withheld, resources such as manpower and shipping were provided to the UK; German military personnel and agents were interned, but Allied airmen repatriated; and it was Irish weather forecasts that determined the timing of the Normandy landings in June 1944. This policy suited the Allies – Ireland was of more use to them as a neutral country – and the generosity of Marshall Aid provisions to the Republic after the war was evidence of the approval of the USA. After the war Ireland did not join NATO, retaining a foreign policy of non-alignment, but it has been active in the UN since its inception, and committed large numbers of troops to UN peacekeeping missions in the Congo, Cyprus, Lebanon and Somalia, and special forces to East Timor. Some scores of Irish troops were killed on these missions. There is little doubt that Ireland's traditional neutrality has been eroded both by closer identification with Continental Europe and participation in the European Union and by close economic links and ties of friendship with the USA. Over-flight of US military aircraft was allowed during the Gulf War of 1990–1, during the attack on Afghanistan of 2001–2 and during the preparations for war against Iraq in 2003. Neutrality was a major issue in the NICE REFERENDUM campaigns of 2001 and 2002.

New Departure. A tactical agreement (1879) between Charles Stewart PARNELL, Michael DAVITT and the Fenian leader John DEVOY that proved the basis for the ultimate success of the LAND WAR. Essentially it was an agreement for extremists and parliamentarians to work together to obtain agrarian reforms and eventually the abolition of landlordism. The FENIANS were bitterly divided about the idea, and the protagonists' motives were far from identical: Devoy, believing incorrectly that the Westminster government would never compromise on the land question, hoped to drive the tenants to Republican activism; Davitt wished to settle the question of land ownership once and for all; and Parnell hoped for a middle way that would satisfy the tenants and win support for his essentially constitutional search for HOME RULE. By giving unspecific support to the New Departure he managed to rally all shades of Nationalist feeling behind him.

New English. *See* OLD ENGLISH.

Newfoundland. A large island off the east coast of Canada, known to the Irish as *Talamh an Éisc*, meaning 'land of the fish' (and pronounced 'tallow an aisk'). Its rich grounds, especially the Grand Banks, attracted hardy fishermen from southeast Ireland from the middle of the 17th century. The voyages were seasonal and the stay on the island temporary, but the place remained in the folk memory of Co. Waterford. This quasi-familiarity was perhaps the main reason why, in the years 1800–30, some 30,000–35,000 people from the southern coast of Ireland settled in Newfoundland. The effect has been to give 'Newfie' culture and even its oddly accented English a distinctly Irish flavour.

Newgrange. A megalithic passage tomb dating from about 3200 BC. It is situated in the BOYNE VALLEY, near Slane in Co. Meath. The grave-mound, which is kidney-shaped, is about 11 m (36 ft) high and 90 m (300 ft) in diameter, and has been reconstructed with materials found on the site after a major excavation that began in 1962. The inner passage, about 4.5 m (15 ft) long, leads to a cruciform chamber with a corbelled roof about 6 m (20 ft) high. It is estimated that the construction of the passage tomb at Newgrange would have taken a workforce of 300 at least 20 years, many of the materials having been brought considerable distances. The most famous features at Newgrange are the spiral decorations on the entrance stone and on a stone in the burial chamber (popularly regarded as 'Celtic' but predating the Celts by 2500 years), and the astrological alignment: during the winter solstice (19–23 December), a shaft of sunlight (weather permitting) enters through the roofbox over the entrance and illuminates the inner chamber for about 17 minutes. Newgrange is Ireland's best-known prehistoric monument and receives about 200,000 visitors each year. There is an extensive interpretive centre, called BRUGH NA BÓINNE, which also offers a visit to the nearby passage tomb of Knowth. The third tomb in the immediate complex is Dowth, which is not accessible from Brú na Bóinne. Whether Newgrange and other passage tombs were used for sacred rituals other than burial is still a subject of speculation. In mythology Newgrange was said to be the home of AONGHUS ÓG, the god of love.

Newman, John Henry (1801–90). The most famous Catholic convert of his day, who on 15 April 1851 received a letter from Paul CULLEN, Archbishop of Dublin, asking him for advice on how to set up his CATHOLIC UNIVERSITY and requesting that he deliver a number of lectures against the 'mixed education' offered by the QUEEN'S COLLEGES. Cullen formally invited him to become rector of the new university on 12 November; Newman readily agreed and was installed on 4 June 1854. However, Newman's idea of a university and that envisioned by the Irish hierarchy were somewhat at odds, and he resigned in 1858. Out of the experiment grew the modern University College Dublin.

> It is almost a definition of a gentleman to say that he is one who never inflicts pain.
>
> 'Knowledge and Religious Duty', in *The Idea of a University* (1852)

New Ross. A town in Co. Wexford. It was built on a steep hill on the River Barrow near the border with present-day Co. Kilkenny. The town was founded by William Marshall, Earl of Pembroke, and his wife Isabella in 1204. Although it is nearly 30 km (20 miles) from the sea, at one time it was the most important port in Ireland, and it still has a busy trade. The most famous emigrant from the area was Patrick Kennedy, great-grandfather of John F. KENNEDY, 35th president of the United States, who returned to visit his ancestral home in June 1963 (*see* KENNEDY HOMESTEAD). On 5 June 1798 a major engagement took place in New Ross when the Wexford rebels captured the town, only to lose it again later in the day. Over 2000 people died during this battle – far more than at VINEGAR HILL[1] – and most of the thatched buildings of the town were burned.

Newry. A town in Co. Armagh and Co. Down (population 19,400). The name is an anglicized pronunciation of the Irish, *An tIúr*, 'the yew tree'. It was earlier known as *Iúr Cinn Trá*, 'the yew tree at the head of the strand'. Newry was the terminus of the first navigational canal to be built in these islands, stretching from Lough Neagh to Carlingford Lough. It had a mainly Catholic population, suffered economic slump because of PARTITION, was the scene of active, not to say violent, CIVIL RIGHTS agitation in the late 1960s, and was frequently targeted by the IRA during the TROUBLES. It was designated a city in 2002.
See also HIGH CHURCH, LOW STEEPLE.

Newry Mortar Attack. A Provisional IRA attack on the RUC station in Edward Street, Newry, on 28 February 1985. Nine officers, including two women, were killed, making it the worst single incident in the history of the force.

Next Parish, Boston. A descriptive phrase applied to many Atlantic seaboard communities, from which emigration to that 'next parish' was invariably high.

Niall Glúndub ('Niall of the Black Knee'; *fl.*896–919). King of the Cenél Eogain (northern Uí Néill), who extended his power base from Ulster and Connacht and became King of Tara and HIGH KING of Ireland (916–19). He died in a battle with the Vikings in Dublin.

Niall of the Nine Hostages (A translation of his Irish name, Niall Noigiallach). A semi-mythical HIGH KING, who supposedly flourished in the early 5th century and who is said to have been the ancestor of the Uí Néill. His dates are given confidently by the annalists as 380–405. He is remembered in the folk tradition as a raider of the British and French coasts – the 'nine hostages', whose details are obscure, have been associated with several coasts. Claudian (d.*c.*404), the last of the Latin poets in the classical tradition, mentions him in his panegyric on Flavius Stilicho (*c.*365–408), who sent troops against Niall on the orders of Emperor Theodosius the Great (347–395). His name was once on every Irish schoolchild's lips, though they knew little more than the name.

Niall of the Nine Sausages. The inevitable nickname of Niall Boden, the presenter in the 1950s of a commercial on Radio Éireann for Donnelly's sausages:

> With two wrappers for double protection
> The best that your money can buy ...
>
> ...
>
> So the next time you visit your grocer
> Tell him no other sausage will do,
> To his other suggestions say, 'No, sir!'
> It's Donnellys' sausage for you.

Nicely. A euphemistic HIBERNO-ENGLISH term meaning 'drunk' or at least 'tipsy', as in 'He was nicely last night.'
See also MAITH GO LEOR.

Nice Referendum (2001, 2002). A plebiscite, controversially held twice, to enable the Irish government to ratify the Treaty of Nice. This was an EU agreement to allow the enlargement of the community and the formulation of a common defence policy, which was at variance with the declaration of the country's NEUTRALITY in the CONSTITUTION OF 1937. Article 1.2 of the Treaty of Nice states: 'The common foreign and security policy shall include all questions relating to the security of the Union, including the progressive framing of a common defence policy, which might lead to a common defence, should the European Council so decide. It shall in that case recommend to the Member states the adoption of such a decision in accordance with their respective constitutional requirements.' This proposal to amend the Constitution – the 24th such amendment – was narrowly defeated on 7 June 2001, but passed, also by a narrow margin, when put before the people again on 7 November 2002.

Nichevo (Russian, 'nobody'). The pseudonym used by R[obert] M[aire] Smyllie (1894–1954), the charismatic editor of the IRISH TIMES. He was born in Glasgow, attended Sligo grammar school and began a university education at Trinity College Dublin (TCD), but was interned during the First World War as an enemy alien, having unfortunately chosen Germany as a suitable place for a walking tour in the summer of 1914. Too short of funds to continue at TCD, he covered the 1919 Paris Peace Conference for the *Irish Times* (securing a scoop interview with Lloyd George). He stayed with the paper, and eventually became its editor in 1934. He did much to reconcile the paper to its Irishness, and made it liberal and politically independent. He began the feature 'An Irishman's Diary', which still continues, suggested to Flann O'Brien that he write CRUISKEEN LAWN, and had the w-wit to employ P-Patrick CAMPBELL as third-leader writer. He was a noted figure in Dublin's literary life, holding court each evening in the Palace Bar, Fleet Street, and writing his own lithe column as Nichevo. He died – still in post – on 11 September 1954.

> Troglyditic myrmidons; moronic clodhoppers; ignorant bosthoons; poor cawbogues whose only claim to literacy was their blue pencils.
>
> Smyllie's description of the Government censorship office during the EMERGENCY, quoted in Dónal Ó Drisceoil, *Censorship in Ireland during the Second World War* (1996)

Nicholson, John (1821–57). Indian governor and cult figure. He was born in Dublin but was taken to Lisburn, Co. Antrim, on the death of his father in 1830. Educated at the Royal School, Dungannon, he became an ensign in the Indian army in 1837. He had the horrific experience of discovering the murdered body of his brother Alexander in 1842, three days after meeting him during the First Afghan War. He went on to become assistant to Sir Henry Lawrence, the British resident at Lahore, and in 1849 he was deputy commissioner at Lahore, before his appointment as governor of the Punjab (1850–7). During the Indian Mutiny he fought valiantly at Peshawar, staying in the saddle for 20 hours, according to reports. About this time a Hindu guru deified Nicholson as an avatar of Brahma, and he was subsequently worshipped by devotees calling themselves 'Nikalsainis'. Nicholson somewhat ungraciously had them punished and imprisoned, but the worship continued. He died soon afterwards, during the storming of Delhi.

Ní Chonaill, Eibhlín Dubh (*c*.1743–*c*.1780). Irish-language poet. She was born in Derrynane, Co. Kerry, one of the 22 children of Dónall Mór Ó Conaill, the grandfather of the Liberator, Daniel O'CONNELL. In 1767, against the wishes of her people, she married Colonel Art Ó Laoghaire of the Hungarian army, who had returned from the Continental wars. The couple settled near Macroom in Co. Cork, and there he fell foul of Abraham Morris, the high sheriff. It is said that Morris demanded Ó Laoghaire's fleet bay mare at a price of £5, as he was entitled to do under the largely inactive but still binding POPERY LAWS. Ó Laoghaire set out to kill Morris on 4 May 1773, but was himself killed by the sheriff's military bodyguard in Carriganima, Co. Cork. Legend has it that the blood-spattered mare galloped home to Eibhlín and that she then rode to Carriganima to grieve over her husband's body. The traditional 'keening' or lament ascribed to her, '*CAOINEADH AIRT UÍ LAOGHAIRE*', is written in elegant but simple language. Eibhlín contrived to have the members of the picket who shot her husband transported, although Morris was acquitted, and Morris himself was later killed by Ó Laoghaire's brother. Recent scholarship has suggested that the poem is not after all the work of his widow, nor belonging to the category of folk poetry known as *amhráin na ndaoine* ('songs of the people'), and that the killing of Art Ó Laoghaire was the last in a series of politically motivated murders of the Catholic landowning class that took place in 18th-century Cork.

NICRA (Northern Ireland Civil Rights Association). *See* CIVIL RIGHTS MOVEMENT.

Ní Dhomhnaill, Nuala (b.1952). One of the finest Irish-language poets of her generation. She was born in Lancashire, but spent much of her childhood in the Kerry GAELTACHT, near Ventry. She was educated at University College Cork at the time of the remarkable flowering of Irish-language poetry involving Michael Davitt, Liam Ó Muirthile and *Innti* magazine. Her first collection, *An Dealg Droighin* (1991), features the Munster fertility goddess Mór – Ó Domhnaill's themes have always included femaleness, sexuality and fertility. Her style is uncluttered and direct, but also at times very lyrical. She is one of the most popular and accessible of the younger poets in Irish, being a formidable performer of her own work, with the capacity to reach even those who do not understand the language in

which she writes. Other collections include *Féar Suaithinseach* (1984) and *Feis* (1991). She has attracted translators of the highest rank, including Michael Hartnett, Seamus Heaney, Michael Longley, Paul Muldoon, Eiléan Ní Chuilleanáin and Medbh McGuckian, and in collaboration with translators has published bilingual collections, such as *Pharaoh's Daughter* (1990), *The Astrakhan Cloak* (1992) and *The Water Horse* (2002).

Ní Ghráda, Máiréad (1899–1971). Irish-language writer. She was born near Ennis, Co. Clare, and educated at University College Dublin. She was a member of CUMANN NA MBAN and then worked, successively, as a teacher, an announcer for Raidió Éireann and a publisher's editor. She achieved notoriety for her play *An Triail (The Trial)*, first performed in the Dublin Theatre Festival in 1964 – despite the hope of one of the adjudicators of the Irish Life competition that 'it would never be performed', so shocked was he by its theme. The heroine Máire Ní Chathasaigh is driven to despair when she is rejected by her married lover, schoolteacher Peádraig Mac Ceárthaigh, who has wooed her with honeyed words; after she bears his child, she kills her baby and herself. The play, an onslaught on the false piety and hypocrisy of Irish society of the 1960s, has since achieved classic status.

'Night before Larry Was Stretched, The'. The title of a famous late 18th-century or early 19th-century Dublin lowlife ballad, rich in the cant of the period. It was probably written by Robert Burrows (1756–1841), later Dean of Cork, who was one of the MONKS OF THE SCREW. The term has become semi-proverbial. Larry is to hang for murder, but his friends are allowed to cheer him up with a pre-execution party. To lay this on they have to 'sweat their duds' (pawn their clothes), but then

... Larry was ever the lad
When a boy was condemned to the squeezer
Would fence all the duds that he had
To help his poor friend to a sneezer
And warm his gob 'fore he died.

The last verse – with its mention of the 'numbing chit' (gallows) and the 'rumbler' (cart) – is a chilling reminder that in the days before the use of the trapdoor the condemned died slowly of strangulation and relied on friends to swing from his feet to hasten the end.

When we came to the numbing chit
He was tucked up so neat and so pretty,
The rumbler jogged off from his feet,
And he died with his face to the city;
He kicked, too – but that was all pride,
For soon you might see 'twas all over;
Soon after the noose was untied,
And at darkee we waked him in clover
And sent him to take a ground sweat.

Nijinsky (1967–92). Racehorse. Owned by Charles Englehard and trained at the Vincent O'BRIEN stables at Ballydoyle, Co. Tipperary, Nijinsky (named after the Russian ballet dancer, 1890–1950) came to be known as 'the king of flat racing'. In the 1970 season, as a three-year-old, he was the first horse since 1935 to win the 2000 Guineas, the Derby and the St Leger – his 11th consecutive win – in the same year. He was narrowly defeated in that year's Prix de l'Arc de Triomphe, and after another defeat he was retired to stud in the United States. His jockey Lester Piggott considered him the most talented horse he had ever ridden, although he also thought him very temperamental.

Niland Gallery. A gallery owned by Sligo local authority. It includes more than 40 paintings by Jack B. YEATS, as well as works by Irish artists such as Estella SOLOMONS, George Russell (Æ) and Gerard DILLON. It was established by Nora Niland, Sligo's county librarian (1945–79), who decided to create a focal point for the study of the poet W.B. Yeats. Primarily interested in literature, she established the Yeats Memorial Collection in 1957 and the Yeats Summer School in 1960. For the first summer school she borrowed three paintings by Jack B. Yeats, which, when purchased by the local authority, formed the nucleus of the collection; many others were donated or purchased with donated funds. A major benefactor

was James Healy of New York, who presented 37 works by Irish artists to the gallery. Jack B. Yeats himself said, 'From the beginning of my painting life every painting which I have made has somewhere in it a thought of Sligo.'

Ní Laoghaire, Máire Bhuí (1774–*c*.1849). Irish-language poet and songwriter. She was born near Inchigeelagh in the Muskerry area of west Cork and lived after her marriage in the district of Ballingeary near Céim an Fhia, the place she has made famous. She had little formal education but a great store of traditional learning. Her poetic output – comprising AISLINGS, ballads and laments about the distressful state of the Ireland of her time – were handed down orally in her locality. Her most famous work, '*Cath Chéim an Fhia*' ('Battle of KEIMANEIGH') is a vigorous, rousing and partisan account of a battle between local WHITEBOYS and a battalion of yeomanry in 1822. Her last work, '*A Mháire Ní Laoghaire*' (an address to the poet), is a collaboration with a local poet, Donncha Bán Ó Loinsigh.

Ní Mháille, Gráinne. *See* GRANUAILE.

Nimmo, Alexander (1783–1832). Engineer and surveyor. He was born in Kirkcaldy in Fife, Scotland. He came to Ireland as an engineer for the BOG COMMISSIONERS, and until his early death in January 1832 carried out a great number of public and private engineering projects all over the country from his home and office in Marlborough Street, Dublin. A pier in Galway's docks is named after him, and he also designed Dunmore East mail harbour in Co. Waterford and the village of Roundstone in Connemara. He made extensive surveys of Irish coastal waters, and in 1831 he was commissioned to design the Dublin–Kingstown (Dún Laoghaire) railway line, which was built, largely to his specification, in 1834 (*see* WESTLAND ROW STATION).

Nine Fridays. A Catholic devotion to the Sacred Heart, once extremely popular in Ireland. The client was required to attend Mass and take Holy Communion on the first Fridays of nine consecutive months. An hour spent meditating on the Sacred Heart in front of the tabernacle was also recommended. The devotion was begun after four visions reportedly experienced between 1673 and 1675 by the French mystic Margaret Mary Alacoque (1647–90), who said that Christ had appeared to her with the words: 'Behold this heart, which has loved men so much and is loved so little in return.' She had to put up with much opposition in her Convent of the Visitation in Paray-le-Monial, but it had ceased by the time of her death. A feast of the Sacred Heart was established in France by Clement XIII in 1765 and made universal by St Pius IX in 1856, to be held within the octave of the feast of Corpus Christi, then nine weeks after Easter. Those who faithfully fulfilled the conditions were promised that they would not die without the comforts of the last sacraments.

Nine Glens, the. A remarkable topographical feature of Co. Antrim. Two of the valleys run north into Ballycastle Bay, and the remaining seven run from southwest to northeast, towards the North Channel. Their names reading from the north are Glentaisie, Glenshesk, Glendun, Glencorp, Glenaan, Glenballyeamon, Glenariff, Glencloy and Glenarm. There is some disagreement among scholars about the significance of their Gaelic names – as often happens when the name in question is very old. Glentaisie (*Gleann Taise*) is taken to mean 'Taise's glen', commemorating the prehistoric, if not actually mythical, Princess Taise, the daughter of the king of Rathlin who avoided capture by a Norwegian king when her lover Congal beat off the invading force. It is also known as Glentow after the river that flows through it. Glenshesk (*Gleann Seisc*) may be 'barren glen', and its river is joined by the Tow, just east of Ballycastle. Glendun (*Gleann Doinn*) is the 'glen of the Dun', the river which meets the sea at Cushendun (in Irish *Cois Abhann Doinne*, 'foot of the river Dun'), the little town designed by Clough Williams-Ellis (1883–1978) of Portmeirion fame. Glencorp

(*Gleann Corp*) is 'glen of the bodies', almost certainly celebrating a battle long ago. Glenaan (*Gleann Athain*) may mean 'glen of the burial chamber', and Glenballyeamon (*Gleann Bhaile Éamainn*) is simply the 'glen of Ballyeamon', the name of a settlement. The remarkably beautiful Glenariff (*Gleann Airimh*), the queen of the nine, is the 'glen of the arable land', a true description of its lower reaches. Glencloy is *Gleann Cloíche* ('glen of the megalith') or *Gleann Claí* ('glen of the ditch') or *Gleann Claíomh* ('glen of the sword'). Glenarm (*Gleann Arma*), the most southerly, is 'glen of the army', and the town of the same name was the site of a find of prehistoric flint tools.

1913 Lockout. The Dublin employers' response to trade-union militancy. Led by William Martin MURPHY, the employers insisted that their employees leave the ITGWU or face dismissal. The union called out other workers, and by September 20,000 were locked out or on strike. The workers' leaders, Jim LARKIN and James CONNOLLY, were arrested for sedition, and since many of the employers, including Murphy, were Catholic, the Church tended to take their side, even to the extent of declaring some of the relief operations communistic. The DMP (Dublin police) were heavy-handed in breaking up pickets and protests, using sabres as well as batons. Two men died in one such action on 31 August, and violence involving workers, 'scabs', pickets and police continued throughout the autumn and winter, while the families suffered extreme privations. The formation of the IRISH CITIZEN ARMY on 23 November, ostensibly to protect pickets from the police, marked a significant development in the national struggle. The workers, having reached the end of their resources by January 1914, returned to work, having gained nothing from their ordeal but humiliation, though the employers' aim in breaking the union had not been achieved. Murphy urged his fellow employers to pay them enough to live 'in frugal comfort', a phrase taken from the encyclical *Rerum Novarum* (1891) of Leo XIII (1810–1903).

Nine Years' War (1594–1603). The name given to the war between Hugh O'NEILL, Earl of Tyrone, and his Ulster allies, notably his son-in-law Red Hugh O'DONNELL, and the crown. At the beginning O'Neill played a double role, displaying loyalty to the state in the conflict over the division of the MacMahon lordship in Monaghan, while at the same time supporting rebels like his brother Cormac; it was not until 1595 that he was declared a traitor.

The early battles of the war consisted of guerrilla-like ambushes of crown forces, the rebels making good use of mid-Ulster's boggy, mountainous and inhospitable terrain; engagements included those at the FORD OF THE BISCUITS (1594) and CLONTIBRET (1595). The Battle of the YELLOW FORD (1598) in Co. Armagh was a superb victory for O'Neill against his bitter enemy, Henry BAGENAL.

Early attempts to stop the advance of the Ulster rebellion were ineffectual, and it spread to Connacht and Leinster in 1595 and to Munster in 1598 (when insurgents burnt Edmund SPENSER's castle at Kilcolman). After the failure of the expedition of the Earl of ESSEX in 1599, O'Neill and his allies controlled most of Ireland, and at the end of that year he unsuccessfully sought the help of the OLD ENGLISH to the fight for the Catholic faith.

The rebellion was eventually defeated by a combination of factors: Henry DOCWRA and Lord Deputy MOUNTJOY established garrisons in Ulster to weaken the position of O'Neill and his allies by destroying crops and burning land; and O'Neill and O'Donnell were forced to fight a pitched battle far from home and on terrain not of their choosing, when the Spanish landed at Kinsale in Co. Cork at the end of 1601 (*see* KINSALE, BATTLE OF). In September 1602 Mountjoy destroyed the sacred inauguration stone of the O'Neills at Tullahogue, and in March 1603 the Treaty of MELLIFONT ended the war.

The war was financially ruinous for the Tudor exchequer, costing near £2 million, but it was the last time that an Irish rebellion seriously threatened the English presence in the country. In Nationalist history, defeat in the Nine Years' War is seen as the death-knell of Gaelic Ireland – a defeat consolidated by the subsequent FLIGHT OF THE EARLS.

Ninidh (*fl.*6th century). One of an early group of Irish saints known as the TWELVE APOSTLES OF IRELAND. Little is known of his life, but he is associated with Inishmacsaint, one of many islands in the lovely Lower Lough Erne, Co. Fermanagh, where he founded a monastery. His name is recalled in a hill called Knockninny ('Ninidh's hill'), 16 km (10 miles) south of Enniskillen.

NIPPLIEs. A media invention of the 1990s, reflecting the era of the CELTIC TIGER, when emigration to London by Irish professionals and artists was a matter of choice, not necessity. The acronym stands for 'New Irish *p*rofessional *p*erson *l*iving *i*n England'. A variant interpretation is 'Northern Ireland professional *p*erson *l*iving in England'.

Ní Riain, Nóirín (b.1951). Traditional singer. She is well known as an interpreter in her own right, particularly of traditional songs of the DÉISE, as revealed in the album *Stór Amhrán* (meaning a collection or store of songs) (1991) and the book of the same name. She has also performed Gregorian chant with the monks of GLENSTAL ABBEY, and the album *Vox de Nube* (1989) is the fruit of this collaboration.

Nits make lice. The alleged cry of the English and Scots soldiers as they killed Catholic Ulster children in 1642 in revenge for the Protestant massacres of the previous year (*see* REBELLION OF 1641).

Nivelles. A Belgian town 30 km (20 miles) south of Brussels, site of the monastery founded by FOILLÁN for Irish monks. The relics of the saint, who was slain by robbers near Fosses in 655, are paraded every seven years in *La Marche de Saint Feuillen*.

Nixer. A job done after-hours by a tradesman for another employer (usually domestic), the income not being declared to the revenue commissioners (*see also* FOXER).

No addition. A HIBERNO-ENGLISH phrase meaning 'of no benefit': 'That hammer (the one with the handle hanging off) is no addition.' The phrase is common in the northern half of Ireland.

Nobel prizewinners. Ireland's Nobel laureates for literature are W.B. YEATS (1923), George Bernard Shaw (GBS; 1925), Samuel BECKETT (1969) and Seamus HEANEY (1995). The Nobel Peace Prize was awarded to Seán MACBRIDE (1974), Betty Williams and Mairead Corrigan of the Northern Ireland Peace movement (*see* PEACE PEOPLE), and jointly to John HUME and David TRIMBLE in 1998.

No better man. A phrase used in HIBERNO-ENGLISH to indicate approval, deriving from 'No better man for the job': 'I had Jack to do my plastering and no better man.' The phrase is sometimes used as an exclamation – for example, if one heard of a mountain climbed or a Nobel Prize won, one might exclaim 'No better man!', or, indeed, 'No better woman!'

No capital offence. The licence granted to the English in the early 17th century in dealing with the 'mere Irish', as recounted by Sir John Davies (*c*.1570–1626), the Irish solicitor-general:

> The mere Irish were not only accounted aliens, but enemies; and altogether out of the protection of the law; so as it was no capital offence to kill them, and this is made manifest by many records. Wherein we may note that the killing of an Irish man was not punished by our law as manslaughter, which is felony and capital (for our law did neither protect his life nor revenge his death) but by a fine or pecuniary punishment.
>
> *Discovery of the True Causes Why Ireland Was Never Entirely Subdued until the Beginning of His Majesty's Reign* (1612)

No-go areas. A term used of certain areas of Derry and Belfast between the summers of 1969 and 1972; in such areas the security forces had no writ and paramilitaries (usually Provisional IRA) held sway. The most notable example was the BOGSIDE in Derry, where, until OPERATION MOTORMAN (31 July 1972),

barricades marked the peripheries of the area. Some parts of west Belfast and Ardoyne intermittently established themselves as no-go areas, and were answered by similar limited retaliative action by Loyalists, especially in the Shankill and Woodvale districts, which lie between the two Nationalist areas.
See also FREE DERRY.

No more bother to you. An exclamation of approbation or congratulation in HIBERNO-ENGLISH, for example on hearing of an achievement or a successful conclusion to a project – for instance, on hearing that a son has won a scholarship, a mother might say, 'No more bother to you!' It means something like 'Why am I not surprised?'

Noody Nawdy (Irish *niúdar neádar*, 'indecision' or 'an indecisive reply'). A HIBERNO-ENGLISH term for a weak, insipid or indecisive person.

Noraid. The acronym by which the Irish *Northern Aid* Committee was usually known. It was set up in the USA in 1969, ostensibly to provide funds for Nationalist families suffering deprivation during the early years of the Northern Irish TROUBLES. The committee had raised around $5 million by 1987, drawing its main support from cities with significant Irish-American populations, such as New York, Boston, Philadelphia and Chicago. (In 1981, the year of the H-BLOCK HUNGER STRIKES, the amount collected was $400,000, double the annual average.) Though its benevolent intentions were not questioned by the British government, the latter argued that the existence of such funds released others for subversive use. Besides, it was generally believed that a portion of Noraid money was removed either in Dublin or the USA to buy arms for the Provisional IRA.

The chairman and founder of Noraid, Michael Flannery (b.1902), was a veteran of the ANGLO-IRISH WAR of 1919–21, and when he was acquitted in 1982 of gun-running by a New York court he said that such activities would always have his blessing. His choice as marshal of the St Patrick's Day parade in 1983 was controversial, but he left the organization in 1988 because of SINN FÉIN's decision to take seats in the Dáil if elected (thus reversing the old policy of ABSTENTIONISM).

In the 1980s the most public figure in Noraid was Martin Galvin, who gained a colourful reputation because of the number of occasions on which he flouted a British government exclusion order, appearing in Belfast in 1984, Derry in 1985 and visiting the relatives of the IRA men killed at LOUGHGALL in 1987. He later split with the organization because, it was thought, of the IRA's calling of a ceasefire in 1994. With the coming of the peace process, Noraid ceased to be a significant agency.

Nore. A river of southeastern Ireland, rising in the Slieve Bloom Mountains of Laois, and flowing southeastward through Kilkenny to meet the Barrow just north of New Ross. It is one of the so-called THREE SISTERS.

Norfolk Island. A cliff-bound island with coastal reefs 1600 km (1000 miles) from BOTANY BAY, Australia. Norfolk Island was a natural prison, and was used as a place of punishment for a dozen UNITED IRISHMEN convicts paranoically suspected of conspiring to rebel in Parramatta near Sydney in 1800 (*see* VINEGAR HILL[2]). These and the many Irish convicts already on the island fell foul of the commandant, the sadistic Major Joseph Foveaux (1765–1846), who was known to have ordered one convict to be given more than 2000 lashes in all, so that finally he had to be lashed on the soles of his feet, all other skin having been removed. The only ways to escape the island, called the 'old hell' by the convicts, were by death or by committing a crime that would entail trial in Sydney on the mainland. The colony in Norfolk Island was abandoned in 1814, VAN DIEMEN'S LAND (Tasmania) becoming the new penal island of choice.

Normalization. The state of cordial relations between Britain and Ireland that resulted from the acceptance by Britain that the Republic of Ireland has a valid interest in the affairs of Northern Ireland. Relations were strained during the ECONOMIC WAR and the EMERGENCY and more recently at the beginning of the Northern TROUBLES and as a result of events such as the introduction of INTERNMENT in 1971, BLOODY SUNDAY in 1972, and the H-BLOCK HUNGER STRIKES of 1981. Relations between the two countries steadily improved during the 1990s, helped by the more conciliatory style of John Major and his successor Tony Blair, and by the warm personal relationship between Blair and Bertie AHERN. The arrival of Prince Charles on a two-day visit to Dublin on 14–15 February 2002 'signifies further normalization between our two countries,' said British ambassador, Sir Ivor Roberts, and the Prince of Wales used the occasion to deliver a speech that focused on reconciliation: 'I am only too aware of the long history of suffering which Ireland has endured, not just in recent decades but over the course of its history … We need no longer be victims of our difficult history with each other.'

Normans. *See* ANGLO-NORMANS.

Norse. The language of the VIKINGS, who, in Ireland, were mainly Norwegian. The name is also applied to the invaders themselves, particularly when referring to the settlements they founded. After the Vikings began to intermarry with the Irish, particularly in Dublin and other Viking cities, Irish borrowed many words from Norse, especially in relation to trade and marine activities, such as *margadh* ('market'), *fuinneog* ('window') and place-names like Wicklow and Howth.

North (1975). The fourth poetry collection of Seamus HEANEY, in which he addresses both obliquely and directly the political realities of his own province, Ulster. The book is divided into two parts, and carries also two separate introductory poems in celebration of peaceful rural rituals. 'Funeral Rites' takes up the theme of healing ritual, evoking the ancient burial-place of NEWGRANGE:

Now as news comes in
of each neighbourly murder
we pine for ceremony,
customary rhythms ...

The collection is rich and allusive, making reference to the long-buried in 'The Bog Queen' and 'The Grauballe Man', and to the Vikings. 'Whatever You Say, Say Nothing' and 'The Ministry of Fear' contrast a militarized Northern Ireland with the gentler former days of 'A Constable Calls', while in the final poem the poet, in ironic commentary on his own situation, describes himself as a wood-kerne, camouflaged, 'escaped from the massacre'.

Northern Ireland. That part of Ireland that remains part of the United Kingdom, and which enjoys a limited amount of devolution. Originally it was intended to include the nine counties of the historical Ulster, but James CRAIG and the Unionists who won the right to dismember the country believed that with the inclusion of Donegal, Monaghan and Cavan, permanent Unionist hegemony could not be guaranteed. The six counties chosen (*see* FAT-DAD) were thought to be just sufficient to maintain a working entity, but the exclusion of the border counties also excluded a number of loyal Unionists, and the inclusion of the city of Derry and parts of counties Tyrone and Fermanagh meant that many Nationalists felt betrayed into alien hands. The state of Northern Ireland came into formal existence with the GOVERNMENT OF IRELAND ACT in September 1920.

Northern Ireland Assembly. *See* GOOD FRIDAY AGREEMENT.

Northern Ireland Civil Rights Association. *See* CIVIL RIGHTS MOVEMENT.

Northern Ireland Forum. A sort of interim peace-process representative body elected by proportional representation on 30 May 1996. It was one half of the twin-track approach, the other half being DECOMMISSIONING. Although SINN FÉIN won 17 seats they were excluded because the IRA ceasefire had broken

down with the CANARY WHARF explosion of 9 February. All parties had to accept the principles set down by Senator George MITCHELL concerning democracy and non-violence. Sinn Féin were allowed back in September 1997 after the second IRA ceasefire, but at this point the DUP and UK Unionist Party abandoned ship. The Forum held its final session on 24 April 1998 to debate the GOOD FRIDAY AGREEMENT.

Northern Star, The. The newspaper (1792–7) of the Ulster UNITED IRISHMEN, edited by Samuel NEILSON (1761–1803). Highly popular, it ceased publication when its offices were wrecked by the Monaghan militia.

North Mon. The North Monastery in Cork, a Christian Brothers school on the northside of the city known for its enthusiasm for Irish and all things national. Jack LYNCH received his education there.

North/South. The political and geographically inaccurate division of the country of Ireland. The two divisions – the six counties of NORTHERN IRELAND and the twenty-six of the Republic of Ireland – represent a deep psychological split that is stronger that any territorial division. The North is seen as LOYALIST and Unionist, though the steadily growing minority of northern Nationalists makes this increasingly untrue. Equally the South is less monochrome than the public pronouncements of politicians might suggest.

North Wall. An embankment built to reclaim lands north of the Liffey in Dublin – including North Strand and Amiens Street – from the tidal river, begun in 1717 and completed in 1729 with the erection of the North Wall itself. It gave its name to the port of Dublin. All the great Irish railway companies had stations at the North Wall as most of the passenger and goods traffic of Dublin port was carried on there. For many years the North Wall was the departure point for the steam packets that took so many abroad as emigrants, and it is still a passenger and cargo port of considerable importance. The North Wall Generating

Station was built by the ESB (Electricity Supply Board) in 1947.

Norton, Graham (b.1963). Comedian and broadcaster. He was born Graham William Walker in Dublin on 4 April 1963. Because of his father's job the family moved a good deal. He was educated at Bandon Grammar and University College Cork, then spent some time in San Francisco before moving to London to study drama at the Central School. He began to perform as a comedian in a London pub after completing drama school; for several years from 1991 he took part in the Edinburgh Festival Fringe; he also played a small part in FATHER TED in 1995. In 1997 he was nominated for the Perrier award. In 1996 he began to work as a television presenter, with the late-night Channel 4 programme *Carnal Knowledge*. His own show, *So Graham Norton*, began in 1998, changing to the five-nights-a-week *V Graham Norton* (still on Channel 4) in January 2002 after he had turned down a lucrative offer from the BBC. He has won several BAFTA awards and in 2001 appeared as a waxwork in Madame Tussauds.

No sex before televison. Oliver J. Flanagan (1920–87), Fine Gael TD for Laois-Offaly, declared in 1963, in response to various controversial items on *The LATE LATE SHOW*, that 'There was no sex before television.'
See also BISHOP AND THE NIGHTIE, THE.

No surrender! *See* DERRY, SIEGE OF.

Not a bother. A phrase used currently, particularly in Dublin, to indicate good health or good spirits, often in answer to the opening enquiry of a conversation: 'How are you?' 'Not a bother, thanks.'

Not a child in the house washed. A phrase used commonly even in current HIBERNO-ENGLISH to describe a state of unpreparedness, of having nothing done, especially in the evening time – a sort of verbal hand-wringing. The addendum '… or a cow milked' was sometimes added in rural areas.

Not a word of a lie. A phrase used commonly in HIBERNO-ENGLISH to emphasize the truth of a narration, particularly in the case of a surprising or outlandish tale.

Not right. An expression meaning 'a bit simple', 'slightly mad', 'away with the fairies'. It is short for 'not right in the head', and may be accompanied by a finger pointing thither.

Not to put a tooth in it. *See* PUT A TOOTH IN IT.

NT. The title traditionally used for a primary school (national) teacher. 'She's an NT' was the designated way for talking about such a teacher.
See also OS.

Nuabhéarsaíocht. *See* SÁIRSÉAL AGUS DILL; Ó TUAMA, SEÁN².

Nuada. The first leader of the TUATHA DÉ DANANN, at the time of their wresting of Ireland from the FIRBOLG. He loses his hand at the great first battle of MAGH TUIREADH (Moytura), even though he wields the invincible CLAIDEAMH SOLUIS ('sword of light'). This imperfection makes it impossible for him to continue as the dé Danann king, even though DIAN CECHT makes him a serviceable hand of silver; hence his sobriquet *Argetlámh* ('silver-handed'). When the latter's son MIACH (whom his father later kills out of envy at his greater medical skill) creates a hand of flesh for him he is able to resume his position as king. He and his wife Macha are slain by BALOR OF THE EVIL EYE at the second battle of Magh Tuireadh.

Nua gacha bia agus seana gacha dí (Irish, 'the freshest of food and the oldest of drink'). The ancient recipe for the best hospitality.
See also FÁILTE.

NUI. *See* NATIONAL UNIVERSITY.

Nun of Kenmare, the. The nickname of Margaret Anna Cusack (1829–99), writer and polemicist. She was born in Dublin on 6 May 1829 to a Protestant family; her parents separated, and she left Ireland with her mother and brother to live in Exeter. She became engaged to a friend of her brother, but the young man died and she turned to religion. She originally entered an Anglican convent and worked with the poor in London, but was received into the Catholic Church on 2 July 1858. She joined the Poor Clare order in Ireland in 1860 and, now known as Sister Frances Clare, was sent to Kenmare, Co. Kerry, in 1861 to open a convent. During the famine of 1879–80 she raised funds to help the poor and destitute. The rest of Margaret Cusack's life brought repeated difficulties, reversals and disagreement with episcopal authorities. After leaving Kenmare she wanted to establish a convent in Knock, Co. Mayo, but the local bishop refused her permission. In England she founded a new congregation, the Sisters of Peace, and went almost immediately to America, starting a foundation in New Jersey to help young immigrant girls. In 1891 she left the congregation, believing that her continued personal involvement would be a hindrance to its work, and returned to England. At the end of her life she returned to her original congregation of Anglican sisters. She reverted to Anglicanism, and died in Leamington on 6 June 1899. She published two autobiographies, *The Nun of Kenmare* (1888) and *The Story of My Life* (1893), the former severely critical of the shortcomings of the Catholic Church; she also wrote biographies of Daniel O'CONNELL, Father Mathew Theobald (*see* APOSTLE OF TEMPERANCE, THE), St PATRICK, St COLUM CILLE and St BRIGID, and many pamphlets on social and educational subjects. She is regarded by some as a pioneering feminist.

O

Oath of Allegiance. One of the requirements (Article 4) laid down by the 1921 TREATY for members of the Free State parliament. It was the provision most resented by ANTI-TREATY-ITES, who felt unable after the ANGLO-IRISH WAR of 1919–21 to swear allegiance to the king, but attempts to exclude it failed. When DE VALERA was elected to the DÁIL he reluctantly went through the form of the wording, and when his FIANNA FÁIL party came to power in 1932 one of his first actions was to introduce a bill abolishing the oath.

O'Beirne, Brian Oswald. *See* BYRNE, DONN.

Obemdub. A placename, probably representing the Irish *abhainn dubh*, 'black river', which could have been pronounced 'oven doov'. It was never precisely identified, but was likely to have been in Donegal. It is mentioned in a letter from Diego Brochero to Philip III of Spain as a suitable place for a landing of a Spanish expeditionary force. In fact the force landed at Kinsale in September 1601 and were quickly besieged by the English forces under Lord Deputy MOUNTJOY (*see* KINSALE, BATTLE OF). The letter is quoted in *Naming Names* (2001) by Bernard Share:

> ... *que sea en las costas del norte en el puerto que llaman Obemdub.*
>
> (... that it should be on the northern coastline at the port called Obemdub.)

O'Boyle, Seán (1908–1979). Song collector and Irish scholar. He was born in Belfast and educated at St Malachy's College and Queen's University Belfast. Appointed to the staff of St Patrick's College, Armagh, on graduation, he taught there until retirement in 1973. Encouraged initially by Sam Hanna BELL, he made a number of 'explanatory surveys of the Ulster town and countryside' (as Bell put it in an unpublished autobiographical sketch), along with Peter Kennedy of the English Folksong Society. In this way between 1952 and 1954 an important archive of local folksongs was gathered. Working with Kennedy and Séamus ENNIS, O'Boyle assembled enough material for two important BBC Northern Ireland radio series, *As I Roved Out* and *Music on the Hearth*, which he compiled and introduced. He also chaired many discussions about folk music. His publications included *Cnuasacht de Cheoltaí Uladh* ('a collection of Ulster music') and *The Irish Song Tradition*.

Ó Brádaigh, Ruairí (b.1932). Republican. He was born in Longford and educated at University College Dublin. He joined the IRA as a student and was active in the BORDER CAMPAIGN. He was IRA chief of staff (1958–9 and 1961–2) and was elected to the Dáil as a SINN FÉIN TD for Longford–Westmeath in 1957. At the time of the Republican split in 1970 he became the first president of Provisional Sinn

Féin, but acquiesced in the shift of power to the activists in the North. He lost the leadership to Gerry ADAMS in 1983, but as a strong supporter of the policy of ABSTENTIONISM left the party when the policy was dropped in 1986. He left to form the faction Republican Sinn Féin, and had the doubtful satisfaction of having his direst prophecy fulfilled when Sinn Féin accepted the GOOD FRIDAY AGREEMENT and confirmed the political survival of Northern Ireland.

O'Brien, Conor Cruise. *See* CRUISE O'BRIEN, CONOR.

O'Brien, Edna (b.1930). Novelist and short-story writer. She was born in Tuamgraney, Co. Clare, and educated at Loughrea, Co. Galway, and in Dublin, where she qualified as an assistant pharmacist. She followed this profession for some time before marrying Ernest Gébler (b. 1915) in 1951. She went to live in London in 1958, and they were divorced in 1967. Her (automatically) banned novels about the 'country girls' Kate and Baba – *The Country Girls* (1960), *The Lonely Girl* (1962) and *Girls in Their Married Bliss* (1963) – were extremely successful, as much for their black humour and deceptively untutored style as for their rejection of puritan Ireland. Subsequent novels, including *August Is a Wicked Month* (1964), *A Pagan Place* (1971), *Johnny, I Hardly Knew You* (1977), *The High Road* (1988) and *Time and Tide* (1992), usually have as protagonist a sensual woman who suffers for love. *House of Splendid Isolation* (1994) is based on the story of INLA killer, Dominic McGlinchey (*see* MAD DOG), whom she interviewed.

O'Brien's short-story collections include *The Love Object* (1968), *A Scandalous Woman* (1974), *Returning* (1982) and *Lantern Slides* (1990). Her play *The Gathering*, about the apparently put-upon mother of a family, was staged in the ABBEY THEATRE in 1974. In her most recent work she has drawn some of her material from meticulously researched actual events: *Down by the River* (1997) is based on the X CASE and *In the Forest* (2002) on the

Brendan O'DONNELL murders of 1994. Edna O'Brien is a popular chat-show guest and is often invited to her country of birth, seeming to belong totally to Ireland and her own county of Clare, despite her many years living in London.

O'Brien, Edward (1880–1952). Yachtsman and author. He was born in Limerick, a grandson of the Young Ireland rebel Smith O'Brien (*see* WIDOW McCORMICK'S CABBAGE PATCH). He was educated at Winchester, Trinity College Dublin and Oxford. In 1914 he landed a consignment of arms from his yacht *Kelpie* for the IRISH VOLUNTEERS at Kilcoole, Co. Wicklow. He served in the British navy during the First World War. An enthusiastic mountaineer and yachtsman, he was the first Irishman to sail around the world in his own yacht, *Saoirse*. He wrote more than a dozen books, including sailing books *Across Three Oceans* (1926) and *From Three Yachts* (1928), and adventure stories for boys.

O'Brien, Flann. The pseudonym used by the Irish satirist Brian O'Nolan (1911–66). He was born into an Irish-speaking household in Strabane, Co. Tyrone, on 5 October 1911, the son of a customs officer who moved to Dublin in 1923. He graduated in Celtic languages from University College Dublin in 1932 and became a civil servant in 1935. He began to write as an undergraduate, finding an outlet for his polyglottal, paronomastic humour in the magazine *Comhthrom Féinne* ('fair play'), and published his first book, an uncategorizable novel-complex, AT SWIM-TWO-BIRDS, in 1939. The Second World War prevented the publication of *The Third Policeman* (written in 1940), but by then he had begun in the *Irish Times* the column CRUISKEEN LAWN ('full jug'), which he signed Myles na Gopaleen, from a character in Dion Boucicault's *The COLLEEN BAWN*, a pseudonym he also used for the Irish squib *An BÉAL BOCHT* (1941). By comparison with the searing surrealist wit of the column, the post-war novels *The Hard Life* (1961) and *The Dalkey Archive* (1964) were less inventive, and at times distinctly sour. A series of television playlets with Jimmy O'Dea (*see* MULLIGAN, BIDDY) and David Kelly (b.1935) called *O'Dea's Your Man* introduced him to a wider audience. *The Third Policeman* was published a year after O'Nolan's death from cancer on 1 April 1966.

> The gross and net result of all this is that people who spend most of their natural lives riding iron bicycles over the rocky roadsteads of this parish get their personalities mixed up with the personalities of their bicycles as a result of the interchanging of the atoms of each of them and you would be surprised at the number of people in these parts who are nearly half people and half bicycles.
>
> *The Third Policeman* (1940)

O'Brien, Kate (1897–1974). Novelist and playwright. She was born in Limerick to wealthy parents and educated at Laurel Hill and by scholarship at University College Dublin, the family business having failed with the death of the father. O'Brien worked as a journalist in London and in Spain as a governess, married a Dutch journalist, Gustaaf Renier, in 1923 and quickly divorced. After her play *A Distinguished Villa* (1926) was a success in London she became a full-time writer.

O'Brien's first novel *Without My Cloak* (1931) describes the rise to economic success of a family like her own, painting an unusual picture of 19th-century Catholic Ireland; the *The Ante-Room* (1934) develops the story of some minor characters from her first book. The protagonists in her remaining (implicitly feminist) novels are women, Irish or Spanish, the Irishwomen facing the clash of passion and morality (or rather what they have been trained to accept as morality). Her books were given the accolade of banning by the mean-minded, unctuous members of the Censorship of Publications Board, but she responded with scorn: *Pray for the Wanderer* (1938) was a riposte to the banning of *Mary Lavelle* (1936), and *The Last of Summer* (1943) was written when *The* LAND OF SPICES (1941), a novel

about women in the religious life, was banned because of a single sentence.

As well as novels, O'Brien wrote highly personal travel books, including *Farewell Spain* (1937) about the country from which she was banned for 11 years because of her portrayal of Philip II in *That Lady* (1946), a novel that describes the clash between Philip and a free-souled aristocrat, Aña de Mendoza, with whom he was in love. After living for much of the 1950s in Roundstone in Connemara, Co. Galway, Kate O'Brien returned to England in 1961 and spent the rest of her life near Faversham in Kent. Her work was rediscovered by a new generation of readers and feminist critics during the 1980s and 1990s.

O'Brien, Murrough. *See* MURROUGH OF THE BURNINGS.

O'Brien, Peter. *See* PETHER THE PACKER.

O'Brien, Sally. A character created by Frank Sherwin for a 1980s advertising campaign for Harp, the Guinness-brewed lager. Sally O'Brien, sultry in a wholesome Irish sort of way 'and the way she might look at you' (a deliberately archaic PADDYISM) epitomizes all that is good about the damp green fields of home for the male character working in the relentless heat of a Gulf state, where 'you could sure sink a pint of Harp' – if you had one, that is.
See also IRISH BARS.

O'Brien, Vincent (b.1917). Racehorse trainer. Born in Churchtown, Co. Cork, he was an amateur jockey before becoming a trainer. From his headquarters, Ballydoyle House in Co. Tipperary, where he moved in 1951, he has had notable success with both national hunt and flat racers; horses from his stables won three Grand Nationals, four Cheltenham Gold Cups, and Hatton's Grace won the Championship Hurdle four times. On the flat the Vincent O'Brien stables won 16 English classics, including six Epsom Derbys, and 27 Irish classics, and were three times winner of the Prix de l'Arc de Triomphe. NIJINSKY was one of the most famous horses Vincent O'Brien ever trained, and Lester Piggott the jockey most associated with his stables. He retired from training in 1994.

O'Brien, William (1852–1928). Nationalist politician. He was born in Mallow, Co. Cork, on 2 October 1852 and educated at Cloyne Diocesan College (well realized in his novel WHEN WE WERE BOYS) and Queen's College, Cork. He worked as a journalist, and in 1881 was appointed editor of the LAND LEAGUE journal *United Ireland* by PARNELL, and soon afterwards began the first of nine prison terms, one of which he spent naked in Tullamore Jail because he would not wear prison garb. While in Kilmainham Jail he worded the No-Rent Manifesto, which was to be such a potent part of the PLAN OF CAMPAIGN, and which he elaborated with John DILLON.

O'Brien became MP for Mallow in 1883, and did what he could to heal the party during the divorce scandal (*see* O'SHEA WHO MUST BE OBEYED). He saw that the only lasting solution to the Irish Question was some kind of reconciliation between Unionists and Nationalists, and it was largely due to his efforts that WYNDHAM's Land Act (1903), the measure that finally ended the land agitation, became law.

Like many others of the old IRISH PARTY his style of politics, with its threes Cs – conference, conciliation, consent – was overtaken by SINN FÉIN in 1918. He died suddenly in London on 25 February 1928, and was buried in Mallow. His writings were consciously literary and of an unimpeachable patriotic and moral quality. His *Recollections* (1905), for example, contains no mention of Katharine O'Shea.

See also MITCHELSTOWN MASSACRE.

O'Brien, [William] Smith. *See* WIDOW MCCORMICK'S CABBAGE PATCH.

Ó Brolcháin, Flaithbhertach (d.1175). Abbot and church builder. He was appointed as chief ecclesiastic in Derry in 1150 and given the prestigious title of coarb (successor) of COLUM CILLE by Muircentach Mac Locheainn, king of the Cenél Eógain, the powerful dynasty that controlled Inishowen and most of Derry and Tyrone. This required a little bit of rewriting of history, since it is only tradition that associates the saint with the city. The political element in the appointment was not unusual, and a strong Derry was intended as proof of the king's suitability for the office of HIGH KING. Under Ó Brolcháin's rule Derry enjoyed an early period of high prestige. It was from his time that the place previously known as Doire Calgach ('oak wood of Calgach', an ancient local pagan chieftain) took its modern name of Doire Columcille. He built the Tempull Mór ('great church') in 1164, which later became the cathedral when Derry was confirmed as the diocesan centre, and which also supplied the modern name of the parish of Templemore.

Ó Bruadair, Dáibhí (*c*.1625–98). Irish-language poet. He was born in east Cork to a family of comfortable means, and had a good education in English, Latin, Irish and history. He was also trained in bardic poetry and genealogy. From about 1660 he lived in Limerick, and his poetic output was prodigious. As the century progressed the destruction of the Gaelic world he represented became more certain. Indeed his consciousness of the cataclysm makes his poetry a valuable historical source for the period: for example, 'Caithréim Phádraig Sáirséal' ('the victory of Patrick Sarsfield') celebrates SARSFIELD's famous if minor victory over the Williamites, while 'An Longbhriseadh' ('the shipwreck') laments his country's plight after the Treaty of LIMERICK and the flight of the WILD GEESE. His patrons, the Fitzgeralds, left with the other Wild Geese, and Ó Bruadair was reduced for a time to working as a farm labourer. His distaste for the louts who replaced the old aristocracy is clearly seen in the poem 'Mairg nach fuil 'na dhubhthuata' ('a pity not to be an utter boor'). He died in January 1689, sustained at the end by some of the older Irish families who still had property.

Observe the Sons of Ulster Marching towards the Somme. The most successful and best known of the plays of Frank McGUINNESS. It was first produced in the Peacock Theatre, Dublin, in February 1985. It is mediated through the memories of Kenneth Pyper, the only survivor of a group of soldiers in the 36th (Ulster) Division in the First World War who took part in the Battle of the SOMME. Their courage, fanaticism, companionship – and the ideal for which they fought – are splendidly conveyed. The play's climax shows them heading across No Man's Land wearing, by special permission, their Orange COLLARETTES over their uniforms.

> The sons of Ulster will rise and lay their enemy low, as they did at the Boyne, as they did at the Somme, against any invader that will trespass on their homeland. Fenians claim a Cuchullain as their ancestor, but he is ours, for they lay down for centuries and wept in their sorrow, but we took up arms and fought against an ocean. An ocean of blood. His blood is our inheritance. Not theirs. Sinn Féin? Ourselves alone. It is we the Protestant people, who have always stood alone. We have stood alone and triumphed, for we are God's chosen.

See also CARSON'S ARMY; REDMOND, JOHN [EDWARD]; UVF.

Obstructionism. *See* BELFAST QUASIMODO.

O'Byrne, Dermot. The pseudonym used by Sir Arnold BAX, the English composer, for his writings about Ireland. Bax was born in London on 8 November 1883. He won prizes for composition and piano at the Royal Academy of Music, and eventually became a distinguished composer and Master of the King's Musick (1942). After reading Yeats's *The Wanderings of Oisin* in 1902, according to his own account, 'in a moment the Celt within me stood revealed. I knew that I too must follow Oisin and Niamh into the sunset.'

Bax came to Ireland in 1905 with his playwright brother Clifford (1886–1962) and 'began to write Irishly', producing verse, plays and stories about Ireland under the name 'Dermot O'Byrne' (his friend Æ once sent him a press cutting declaring Arnold Bax to be the pseudonym of the poet Dermot O'Byrne). He became friendly with Patrick PEARSE and other 1916 leaders, responding to the EASTER RISING with 'A Dublin Ballad – 1916', which the authorities suppressed in 1918 as subversive:

> O write it up above your hearth
> And troll it out to sun and moon,
> *To all true Irishmen on earth*
> *Arrest and death come late or soon.*
> …
> Well, the last fire is trodden down,
> Our dead are rotting fast in lime,
> We all can sneak back into town,
> Stravague about as in old time,
> And stare at gaps of grey and blue
> Where Lower Mount Street used to be
> And where flies hum around muck we knew
> For Abbey Street and Eden Quay.

His autobiographical sketch *Farewell My Youth* (1943) confirms that in the early Dublin years he was regarded as much as a writer as a composer. He was knighted in 1937. In his later years he acted as external examiner in music for University College Cork. He died in Cork on 3 October 1953.

See also MOERAN, E[RNEST] J[OHN].

O'Byrne, Feagh MacHugh (*c*.1544–97). Wicklow chieftain. He became head of the O'Byrnes of Wicklow in 1580 and was a constant source of trouble to the English of the Pale. He was relatively safe in the fastness of the long Wicklow valley of Glenmalure and defeated a number of attempts to winkle him out. After tactical submissions to Lord Deputy PERROT in 1584 and to his successor William Fitzwilliam in 1588, he was eventually proclaimed a traitor. O'Byrne was captured by Sir William Russell, the lord deputy, on 8 May 1597 and summarily executed by a Sergeant Milborne.

> Curse and swear, Lord Kildare!
> Feagh will do what Feagh will dare –
> Now Fitzwilliam, have a care;
> Fallen is your star low!
> Up with halbert, out with sword!
> On we go; for, by the Lord!
> Feagh MacHugh has given the word:

'Follow me up to Carlow.'

P[ATRICK] J[OSEPH] McCALL (1861–1919): 'Follow Me up to Carlow', in *Irish Fireside Songs* (1911)

Ó Cadhain, Máirtín (1906–70). Irish-language novelist and short-story writer. He was born in the Connemara Gaeltacht area of Cois Fharraige and educated at St Patrick's College in Dublin, qualifying as a primary schoolteacher in 1926. Over the following ten years as a teacher in Co. Galway he began to write fiction. A fervent Irish-language activist and campaigner for the development of the GAELTACHT, he was often embroiled in controversy. He became a member of the army council of the IRA and was interned in the Curragh during the EMERGENCY for his Republican activities. It is likely that his later fiction was influenced by his period of internment and the opportunity for wide reading it gave him.

The theme and atmosphere of Ó Cadhain's finest and best-known work, *Cré na Cille* (1948; translated in 1984 as *Churchyard Clay*), are very far from a traditional view of Gaelic Ireland. The novel is set in a Connemara graveyard, and in it a number of gravebound characters – some long dead, others recently arrived – converse. The main character is Caitríona Pháidín, who had an acrimonious relationship with her sister Nell. Ó Caidhin is showing the pettiness and unpleasantness of rural Gaeltacht life, far from the idyll imagined by aspiring Irish scholars. It is also humorous at times. *Cré na Cille* and the short-story collections *An tSraith ar Lár* (1967) and *An tSraith Dhá Thógáil* (1970) are modernist works in which the protagonists are at sea in a hostile world.

Ó Cadhain found it difficult to get congenial employment after his internment, but he was appointed lecturer in Irish at Trinity College Dublin in 1956 and professor of Irish in that university the year before his death.

Is mise Stoc na Cille. Éistear le mo ghlór.
Caithfear éisteacht …
(I am the Graveyard Trumpet. My voice must be heard. You must listen…)
Cré na Cille (1948)

O'Cahan, Rory Dall. *See* 'LONDONDERRY AIR'.

O'Carolan. The name by which the harper and composer Turlough CAROLAN is sometimes known, as in the popular piece 'O'Carolan's Concerto'.

O'Casey, Sean (1880–1964). Playwright. He was born in Dublin into a Protestant working-class family on 30 March 1880 and christened John Casey. The death of his father in 1886 left the large family penniless, and he was forced to leave school at 14. In spite of a painful eye condition, which had made his attendance at school sporadic, he was an omnivorous reader and he soon became convinced of the need for a radical reform of a society that tolerated the kind of conditions in which the poor of Dublin lived. He became an active supporter of Jim LARKIN and remained a socialist all his life. As a member of James CONNOLLY's IRISH CITIZEN ARMY (ICA) he took part in the 1913 LOCKOUT, but left the ICA when Connolly formed an alliance with Patrick PEARSE in 1914. His first published work was *The Story of the Irish Citizen Army* (1919) written as by P. Ó Cathasaigh (the Irish form of the name 'Casey'), a pseudonym he also used for contributions to various journals. The colourful account of his childhood in a series of garrulously impressionistic *Autobiographies* (1939–54) is morally if not factually accurate, the verbal exuberance being the mark of the relentless and uncontrolled autodidact.

O'Casey learned his dramaturgy, like Shaw, from the generally melodramatic and sentimental fare provided at the Queen's Theatre, for which he had free passes. As a slum-dweller and a labourer with the Great Northern Railway he knew the facts of working-class life, and his brilliantly shocking Dublin trilogy, *The SHADOW OF A GUNMAN, JUNO AND THE PAYCOCK* and *The PLOUGH AND THE STARS*, did for the poor of Dublin what Synge had done for the peasants of Connacht and Wicklow, earning the same gratitude. Dismayed by the ABBEY THEATRE's rejection of his next play *The Silver Tassie* (1928) because of its expressionistic treatment of scenes about the First World War, O'Casey went into permanent exile in Devon. Later plays – *The Star Turns Red* (1940), *Red Roses for Me* (1942), *Purple Dust* (1945) and *Oak Leaves and Lavender* (1947) – combine socialist propaganda, anticlericalism and farcical humour. A further trio *Cock-a-Doodle Dandy* (1949), *The Bishop's Bonfire* (1955) and *The Drums of Father Ned* (1959) (the latter withdrawn from the Dublin Theatre Festival because of the perceived interference of Archbishop McQUAID), are rather experimental and allegorical, and their occasional staging is more a mark of respect than of worth. They suggest a man out of touch with the theatre and the Irish roots that gave him inspiration. He died on 18 September 1964.

Ó Catháin, Ruairí Dall. *See* 'LONDONDERRY AIR'.

Ó Cathasaigh, P. *See* O'CASEY, SEAN.

Ó Ceallaigh, Seán T. *See* O'KELLY, SEÁN T.

'Ochón! a Dhonncha' ('lament for Donncha'). The title of one of the most popular and most anthologized laments in the Irish language. The poem was written by Pádraig Ó hEigeartaigh, (1871–1936), who was born in the Iveragh peninsula of Co. Kerry. He was taken to America when he was 12 and went to work in a cotton mill in Massachussetts. 'Ochón! A Donncha' was written on the death of his small son in a boating accident, and published by Patrick PEARSE in *An CLAIDEAMH SOLUIS*:

> Ochón! a Dhonncha, mo mhíle cogarach, fén
>   bhfód so sínte;
> fód an doichill 'na luí ar do cholainn bhig, mo
>   loma-sceimhle!
> Dá mbeadh an codladh so i gCoill na Dromad ort
>   nó in uaigh san Iarthar
> Mo bhrón do bhogfadh, cé gur mhór mo dhochar,
>   is ní bheinn id' dhiaidh air.

> (My grief, Donncha, a thousand times my dearest
>   love, stretched under the clay;
> The inhospitable sod lying on your little body
>   tortures me cruelly!
> If you were sleeping in the cemetery of Dromad or
>   in a grave in the west

It would soften my unbearable grief, and I
  wouldn't hold it against you.)

Ochone (Irish *Ochón*, 'alas'). The principal cry of the KEEN. The word's use is now entirely jocose.

> Why did ye die? – why did ye die?
> Laving us to sigh! Och, hone!
>   DION BOUCICAULT (1820–1890): *The Shaughraun*
>   (1875)

Ó Cléirigh, Mícheál. *See* ANNALS OF THE FOUR MASTERS.

Ó Coileáin, Seán (*c.*1754–*c.*1816). Irish-language poet. He was born near Clonakilty, Co. Cork, to a family who had enough wealth to have the boy sent to Spain to study for the priesthood. He gave up his clerical studies and returned to Ireland to set up a HEDGE SCHOOL at Myross, near Union Hall in west Cork. He was known as the 'silver tongue of Munster', and is most famous now for '*An Buachaill Bán*' ('the white-haired boy'), the last of the Jacobite AISLINGS, and for the romantic '*Machtnamh an duine dhoilíosaigh*' ('musings of a melancholy man', 1813), set in the atmospheric ruins of Timoleague Abbey. Some scholars believe the latter poem may be a translation of a friend's English poem, and there is a strong tradition that it was written as a Gaelic response to Gray's *Elegy* (1751). Ó Coileáin was prone to melancholy anyway, a not unexpected condition for a poet of the period, especially one who sensed that he was the last of his kind.

Ó Conaire, Pádraic (1883–1928). Irish-language novelist and short-story writer. He was born in Galway but reared in Ros Muc in the Connemara Gaeltacht and educated at Rockwell and Blackrock College (*see* HOLY GHOST FATHERS). He went to work as a civil servant at the Ministry of Education in London and there became a teacher for the GAELIC LEAGUE and involved socially with the Irish expatriate community, including at the time Michael COLLINS. He was also made welcome in cultured English homes, and was a good friend of Robert LYND. His best writing was done in London; he spent the last decade of his life back in Ireland, much of it homeless and in poverty. The short-story collections *Nóra Mharcuis Bhig agus Sgéalta Eile* ('Nora Marcus Beag and other stories', 1909) and *An Chéad Chloch* ('the first stone', 1914) and his novel *Deoraíocht* ('exile', 1910) are considerable achievements, owing more to the influence of the Russian writers Dostoievski and to modernist trends than to any vision of a rural Gaelic Utopia. His best stories were collected as *Scothscéalta* ('finest stories') and translated by Eoghan Ó TUAIRISC and others as *The Finest Stories of Pádraic Ó Conaire* (1982).

O'Connell, Daniel (1775–1847). Constitutional Irish leader and lawyer, who succeeded in obtaining emancipation for Catholics from the last of their penal disabilities in 1829 (*see* CATHOLIC EMANCIPATION), so earning the byname 'The Liberator'. However, his hitherto successful method of peaceful MONSTER MEETINGS, which he addressed with brilliant demotic eloquence, failed to obtain the repeal of the Act of UNION (1801). In spite of this failure, O'Connell had recreated an Irish nation, endowing an underclass, for two centuries debased, with a sense of worth, and begun the process that led ultimately to independence.

O'Connell was born in Co. Kerry on 6 August 1775 and spent his first years in a mode of life that had changed little for centuries. The Kerry mountains and rocky shores were remote enough to prevent undue interference from the authorities, and O'Connell's uncle HUNTING CAP, with whom he had been fostered, lived an almost feudal life. Born just before the POPERY LAWS began to be slowly repealed, the young O'Connell was sent to France to be educated, and there saw at first hand the excesses of the Terror. The result was to make him a relentless enemy of violence, summarizing his view in a speech delivered on 28 February 1843:

> Not for all the universe contains would I, in the struggle for what I conceive my country's cause,

consent to the effusion of a single drop of human blood, except my own.

This was the cause of his breaking with YOUNG IRELAND in 1846, but by then failing health and the GREAT FAMINE had changed everything. He died in Genoa on 15 May 1847 on a last journey to Rome, thus generating the mantra that was known to many generations of Irish schoolchildren (*see* MY HEART TO ROME).

See also BIG BEGGARMAN, THE; DARLING LITTLE QUEEN, THE; MORIARTY, BIDDY; O'CONNELL'S BLACK GLOVE.

O'Connell, Maura. *See* DÉ DANANN.

O'Connell, Maurice. *See* HUNTING CAP.

O'Connell, Mick. *See* MICKO.

O'Connell's black glove. The glove that, according to a widely held legend, Daniel O'CONNELL wore on his right hand whenever he took communion as a penitential gesture following his duel with John D'Esterre. It was for him a rare departure from moral force and grew out of an apparently trivial affair. Dublin Corporation had petitioned against the granting of CATHOLIC EMANCIPATION, and in a speech on 22 January 1815 O'Connell referred to it as 'the beggarly Corporation of Dublin'. John D'Esterre, a failing merchant and member of the corporation, called him out. One of several conspiracy theories suggests that D'Esterre, known as a crack shot, was primed by the authorities to remove a serious troublemaker. They met across the county line in Kildare on 1 February. D'Esterre's bullet hit the ground in front of O'Connell's foot. O'Connell aimed low and shot his adversary in the thigh. Assured that he did not seem to be seriously wounded O'Connell returned to Dublin, but D'Esterre died the next day of loss of blood. O'Connell's remorse was genuine; he offered to share his income with the young widow and when years later he heard that D'Esterre's daughter was involved in litigation he represented her free of charge and won her case.

O'Connell Street. Dublin's main thoroughfare, originally named Sackville Street after Lionel

Cranfield Sackville, 1st Duke of Dorset, who was lord lieutenant (1730–1 and 1750–5). The WIDE STREET COMMISSIONERS enlarged the street in the 1780s and built Sackville (now O'Connell) Bridge in 1790. Three-quarters of the street was destroyed during the EASTER RISING of 1916, and many of the commercial buildings date from the 1920s. Sackville Street was officially renamed O'Connell Street in May 1924, although Dublin Corporation had voted to change the name as early as 1884 (but were prevented by an injunction taken out by residents). There is a monument to Daniel O'CONNELL at the southern end of the street and the PARNELL monument stands at the top. In recent decades there has been a proliferation of fast-food restaurants and seedy souvenir shops in O'Connell Street; there is also a perception among natives and tourists alike that it is the most dangerous street in Dublin from the point of view of personal injury. Dublin Corporation has unveiled plans to upgrade the area and improve its image.
See also GPO; NELSON'S PILLAR.

O'Connor, Arthur (1763–1852). United Irishman. He was born Arthur Conner in Mitchelstown, Co. Cork, of partial English descent, educated at Trinity College Dublin and called to the Irish Bar in 1788. He became an MP (1791–5) for the parliamentary borough of Philipstown, in what was then King's County, which his uncle controlled, and tended while in the House to support the government. A meeting with Lord Edward FITZGERALD in 1796 resulted in his joining the UNITED IRISHMEN and adopting a more Irish form of his name. He proved hot-headed and was arrested on 28 February 1798 with James COIGLEY at Margate as they made their way to France. He was acquitted of treason, perhaps by incriminating his colleague. Arrested on new charges in Ireland, he was deported to France in 1802 and spent the rest of his life there. He was made a general by Napoleon and became bitterly anticlerical, condemning Daniel O'CONNELL as a priest's lackey.

O'Connor, Feargus (1794–1855). Chartist leader. He was born at Connorsville, Co. Cork, on 18 July 1794, the son of the United Irishman Roger O'Connor (1762–1834), and was called to the Bar after education at Trinity College Dublin. He was elected MP for Co. Cork in 1832 on a platform of repealing the Act of UNION, but was soon at odds with Daniel O'CONNELL and lost his seat in 1835. He moved to England and with the help of his newspaper the *Northern Star*, which he had founded in 1837, he presented himself as leader of the Chartist movement. Elected MP for Nottingham in 1847 he helped draft the People's Charter, which was presented at a huge Chartist meeting in London in 1848. Personally eccentric (he claimed descent from the ancient kings of Ireland), O'Connor was a successful mob orator but was weak in organizational skills and had no clear policy. He became insane in 1852 and died in an asylum on 30 August 1855.

O'Connor, Frank (1903–66). The pseudonym of Michael O'Donovan, short-story writer and translator, who was born and reared in Cork and educated locally. He was given early adult education by Daniel CORKERY, who taught him (and his slightly older colleague Sean O'FAOLAIN) Irish and national culture. Like O'Faolain he took the Republican side in the CIVIL WAR and like Peadar O'DONNELL was interned in 1923. His paramilitary experi-ences provided the material for his first book of stories, *Guests of the Nation* (1931), the title story of which is one of his best, and a somewhat slanted biography of Michael COLLINS, *The Big Fellow* (1937).

After release O'Connor joined the library service and soon made his name as a literary gadfly (eternally at odds with the Censorship Board, of which he became an implacable and effectual enemy) and as the finest short-story writer Ireland has produced (the only near rival being William TREVOR). Between 1936 and 1969 he published six collections of stories, the early ones earning him the label 'anticlerical', but few people have written with such accuracy about priests – as can be seen in *The Collar* (1993), an anthology edited by his widow Harriet Sheehy. By the end of the 1940s O'Connor had had enough of tight little Ireland and began a successful career as a maverick, heretical academic in the USA.

O'Connor's translations from early Irish verse in *A Golden Treasury of Irish Poetry 600–1200* (1967), done with David Greene (1915–81), and of Middle and Modern Irish verse in *Kings, Lords and Commons* (1959) did much to stimulate interest in an unrecognized treasure. His 1945 translation of Merriman's CÚIRT AN MHEÁ-OÍCHE (*The Midnight Court*) had as a matter of course been banned. His two volumes of autobiography *An Only Child* (1961) and *My Father's Son* (1967) provide a fascinating account of a somewhat wayward life. He died on 10 March 1966.

> At the age of twenty I was released from an internment camp without money or job. The Civil War had just ended, and since I had taken the loser's side I found that ex-jailbirds like myself did not get whatever positions were available under the new government. But all teachers were now required to learn the Irish language, so for a few months I taught Irish to the teachers at the local Protestant school in Cork – St Luke's. This brought in only a few shillings a week, but I now knew how to teach and I liked the work.
>
> *My Father's Son* (1968)

O'Connor, James Arthur (1792–1841). Landscape painter. He was born in Dublin, the son of an engraver and print-seller. Largely self-taught, he began to exhibit successfully at the Dublin Society in 1809, and for the next 13 years painted topographical scenes in the west of Ireland, often on commission from local gentry. Some of his work, notably *View of Lough Derg with Portumna Castle in the background* and *The Grounds, Ballinrobe House*, show a strong influence of the French classical painter Claude Gelée (1600–82), but other work shows him to have been remarkably eclectic in style. In spite of these commissions he found it difficult to make a living, and

moved with his wife Anastasia to London in 1822. He travelled widely in Britain and France, painting for King Louis-Phillipe (1773–1850), who had been a client in 1826 when he was an exile in England. Prosperity still eluded him, and, with his eyesight failing and his essential neatness and clarity unfashionable, he died in London in such poverty that a group of Irish artists had to raise a subscription to purchase a small annuity for his widow.

O'Connor, Pat (b.1943). Film director. He was born in Ardmore, Co. Waterford, on 30 December 1943 and was educated locally and in Los Angeles and Toronto, where he took a degree in film and video. After his return to Ireland he worked with RTÉ (1971–83), directing the award-winning television dramatization of William Trevor's *The BALLROOM OF ROMANCE*. *Cal* (1984), based on a novel by Bernard MACLAVERTY, was his first feature film, followed by *A Month in the Country* (1987). In Hollywood O'Connor directed *Circle of Friends* (1995), an adaptation of the Maeve Binchy novel, and *Dancing at Lughnasa* (1997), based on the play by Brian FRIEL.

O'Connor, Rory (1883–1922). Republican. He was born in Dublin and educated at Clongowes and University College Dublin, where he graduated in arts and engineering. He worked in Canada as a railway engineer (1911–15), returning to Dublin in time to take part in the EASTER RISING of 1916, in which he was injured. After being released from internment he was active in the IRA, becoming director of engineering during the Anglo-Irish War of 1919–21. He rejected the TREATY and repudiated the authority of the Dáil in March 1922, later playing a leading part in the establishment of the Republican garrison in the FOUR COURTS. He was captured when Free State forces attacked the building on 28 June 1922 and held captive until, on 8 December, he was one of the four Republicans – the Leinster representative – executed in MOUNTJOY JAIL as a reprisal for the killing of TD Seán Hales. The execution of O'Connor was regarded as particularly poignant because he had been the best man at the wedding the previous year of Kevin O'HIGGINS, the Free State minister who sanctioned the executions.

O'Connor, Sinéad (b.1966). Pop diva. A woman of considerable beauty, talent and flair for publicity, O'Connor was born in Dublin on 8 December 1966, but lived for many years in London before returning to her native city. During a concert tour of the USA she refused to allow the American national anthem to be played at one of her shows, and caused a sensation on a US television show in 1992 by tearing up a picture of the pope, saying, 'Fight the real enemy.' In April 1999 she was ordained a priest in Lourdes by the rebel bishop Michael Cox, calling herself Mother Mary Bernadette and taking a vow of celibacy in which, she later reported, she 'failed miserably'. Her greatest hit was a version of Prince's song 'Nothing Compares to U' from the successful album *I Do Not Want What I Haven't Got* (1990).

O'Connor, T[homas] P[ower]. *See* TAY-PAY.

O'Connor Snr, Christy (b.1924). Golfer. He was born in Knocknacarragh, Co. Galway, on 21 December 1924, and began to play professional golf only in his late 20s. As a professional golfer he won 24 competitions, finishing seven times in the top five of the British Open, although he was never the winner. With Harry Bradshaw he won the World Cup in 1958, and he also played a large number of Ryder Cup matches. Christy O'Connor Jnr, also a professional golfer, is his nephew.

O'Connor's Van. The key phrase in a line from Thomas Davis's ballad 'A NATION ONCE AGAIN', which is often taken out of context for would-be jocose effect, and which has proved dismaying to generations of children who have heard the joke too often before. It is usually sung by fathers as they drive through the winding roads of Connacht. The ballad, entitled 'The West's Asleep', so moved Yeats that he 'could never hear it without great excitement'. Such couplets as

> Be sure the great God never planned
> For slumbering slaves, a home so grand

were intended to rouse, and combined with its dramatic music the ballad is still a very potent patriotic instrument:

> When all beside a vigil keep,
> The West's asleep, the West's asleep –
> Alas! and well may Erin weep,
> When Connaught lies in slumber deep.
> There lake and plain smile fair and free,
> 'Mid rocks – their guardian chivalry –
> Sing oh! Let man learn liberty
> From crashing wind and lashing sea.

The anti-climax of

> For often in O'Connor's van
> To triumph dashed each Connaught clan

(if one were to regard the van as a modern motor vehicle) is considerable. The triumph referred to was the occasional victories over the Anglo-Normans by the heirs of Rory Ó Connor, the LAST HIGH KING.

O'Conor, Charles (1710–91). Catholic activist and antiquary, known as 'O'Conor of Belanagare'. He was born in Co. Sligo and educated by a Franciscan priest. He could show direct descent from the O'Connors who had been kings of Connacht before the Anglo-Norman invasion. In 1720 his father regained possession of the confiscated family estate of Belanagare in Co. Roscommon to which Charles succeeded in 1749.

O'Conor, John Curry (*c.*1710–80), a Dublin doctor, and Thomas Wyse (*c.*1700–70), a member of an aristocratic family from Waterford, founded the CATHOLIC COMMITTEE in 1760. It was concerned to rally a fairly prosperous Catholic middle class who had escaped the net of the Penal or POPERY LAWS, to assert their rights as quiescent not to say loyal citizens, and to obtain some relief for their less fortunate co-religionists. Their pamphlets were mild affairs, convincing people that they had been written by liberal Protestants. Curry was anxious to counterbalance the received wisdom about the REBELLION OF 1641 while O'Conor, who collaborated with Curry in

An Historical and Critical Review of the Civil Wars in Ireland (1755), was concerned to show the economic inadvisability of the Popery Laws and to demonstrate that Ireland, far from being a colony with a barbaric under-class, was heir to an ancient civilization. His main work in this was *Dissertations: An Account of the Ancient Government, Letters, Sciences, Religion, Manners and Customs of Ireland* (1753).

O'Conor's detestation of the Popery Laws had a strongly personal aspect: he remem-bered as a young man having to attend Mass in a cave, and in his later years he was forced to pay a large security to his Protestant young-er brother who brought a DISCOVERY suit against him. In 1760, when his eldest son mar-ried, he passed the estate to him and lived in a cottage in the demesne, where he died on 1 July 1791.

O'Conor, Roderic (1860–1940). Post-impres-sionist painter. He was born on 17 October 1860 in Roscommon on a family estate, which, when he sold it to the Land Commission in 1910, provided him with a steady income for the rest of his life. He was educated at Ample-forth, in Dublin at the Metropolitan College of Art and in Antwerp. He made his home permanently in France after 1885 and began to incorporate into his painting the striations he found in the work of Van Gogh, most clearly seen in his *Field of Corn, Pont Aven* (1892) and *Breton Peasant Knitting* (1893). In 1892 he went to Pont-Aven in Britanny, where he became a close friend of Gauguin and helped him financially, but decided not to accompany 'that maniac' to Tahiti. His later years were spent in seclusion with his wife Renée Honta, who was 34 years his junior. This absence from the marketplace caused his reputation to be occluded, but he is now regarded as one of the most international of Irish-born painters. He died on 18 March 1940 at Neuilly-sur-Layon, Maine-et-Loire, and was buried locally.

O'Conor of Belenagare. *See* O'CONOR, CHARLES.

Ó Criomhthain, Tomás. *See* OILEÁNACH, AN T-.

Ó Cuinneagáin, Gearóid. *See* RESURRECTION AR-CHITECTS.

O'Curry, Eugene (1794–1862). Gaelic scholar. He was born in Dunaha near Kilkee in Co. Clare into a family which, though lacking in formal education, was steeped in Gaelic tradi-tion. He spent his youth working at a variety of occupations in Clare and in Limerick city, and moved to Dublin in about 1835. There he began to work for the ORDNANCE SUR-VEY under George PETRIE, who spearheaded a topographical section from 1830 to 1841.

Petrie had assembled a number of Irish scho-lars, including John O'DONOVAN (O'Curry's relative-by-marriage) and Samuel FERGUSON, to do fieldwork and research on manuscripts. O'Curry also came in contact with other scholars based at Trinity College Dublin (TCD) and the Royal Irish Academy (RIA) who were deeply interested in the manuscript sources for Gaelic culture. At various stages he studied and catalogued Irish manuscripts in the RIA and the British Museum, and edited the legal text, *The Book of Achill*, held in TCD. Thereafter he became an expert on Gaelic law and customs, basing his research on manuscript sources. He and John O'Donovan worked together on an edition of *Senchas Mór* ('great book of lore'), another legal text. In 1854 O'Curry was made professor of Irish history and archaeology at the Catholic University (now University College Dublin).

O'Curry's most significant contribution to Gaelic scholarship were the volumes based on a series of lectures he delivered there and pub-lished as *Lectures on the Manuscript Materials of Ancient Irish History* (1861) and *On the Manners and Customs of the Ancient Irish* (1873), in which he reconstructed Gaelic life and customs from the evidence of the manu-scripts. He edited versions of stories from the heroic cycle, such as *The Sick Bed of Cuchu-lainn* and *The Only Jealousy of Emer*, and translated from the Irish love poems such as '*An Cuimhin Leat an Oíche Úd?*' ('Do You

Remember that Night?'). With George Petrie, he collected traditional music and songs in the Aran Islands, which Petrie published in *The Ancient Music of Ireland* (1855).

The influence of his pioneering work on manuscript sources is incalculable; he and scholars like him paved the way for the GAELIC LEAGUE and language revival, and recreated the concept of an ancient and sophisticated Gaelic society. His *Musical Instruments of the Ancient Irish*, part of a three-volume work published in 1873, proves him to have been among the first and most influential of what would now be called ethnomusicologists.

> Do you remember that night
> When you were at the window,
> With neither hat nor gloves
> Nor coat to shelter you?
> I reached out my hand to you,
> And you ardently grasped it;
> I remained to converse with you
> Until the lark began to sing.
>> 'Do You Remember That Night?'

ODC. An expression used during the Northern Ireland TROUBLES by police, prison guards and other law enforcers to stand for 'ordinary decent criminals' as opposed to 'subversives', from whom they were kept strictly apart.

O'Dea, Jimmy. *See* MULLIGAN, BIDDY.

Odious. An intensifier, both positive and negative, pronounced 'ojus' and used predominantly in Co. Cavan. A job might be 'odious' hard; food might be 'odious' plentiful. Comedian Niall Tóibín memorably characterized Cavan people, who are seen as having entrepreneurial skill in construction and the pub trade, as being 'odious good at turning a buck'.

Ó Direáin, Máirtín (1910–88). Irish-language poet. He was born on Inis Mór, the largest of the ARAN ISLANDS. As a young man he went to work in the post office in Galway, later moving to the civil service in Dublin, where he spent the remainder of his working life until retirement in 1975. One of the finest and most assured of modern Irish poetic voices, Ó Direáin was recognized as a major poet by Seán ó Tuama in his anthology *Nuabhéarsaíocht* (1950), a year after the publication of Ó Direáin's *Rogha Dánta* ('selected poems', 1949). Ó Direáin's verse is beautifully lyrical and rhythmic; in many of his poems he uses a language that denotes the natural features of his native Aran Islands both to celebrate their unchanging beauty – in lyrics such as '*An tEarrach Thiar*' ('western spring') and '*An Nollaig Thiar*' ('western Christmas') – and to point up the contrast with the bleakness of contemporary urban life. Later collections included *Ó Morna agus Dánta Eile* ('Ó Morna and other poems', 1957) and *Ceacht an Éin* ('the bird's lesson', 1980). *Tacair Dánta* ('selected poems') was published in 1984.

O'Doherty, Cahir (1587–1608). The last Gaelic lord of INISHOWEN. As a boy of 14, having made submission to Elizabeth I, he was confirmed in his position as a chief of the O'Doherty clan by Sir Henry DOCWRA, the Tudor lord of Derry. He joined Docwra in his campaign against Hugh O'NEILL and fought so bravely at Augher that he was recommended to the lord deputy for a knighthood. He lived the life of a Tudor aristocrat and was allowed by his patron to practise his Catholic religion. He might have had a long career as the queen's loyal Derryman if his patron had remained. Docwra, however, left Derry in 1606, having in disappointment sold his interests to George Paulett. The successor was vain and quarrelsome, and soon made an enemy of the hot-headed O'Doherty, publicly striking him during an argument over ownership of a piece of land. It was the end of O'Doherty's 'loyalty'. He marched on the city, killed Paulett and was condemned as a traitor by the lord deputy, Arthur CHICHESTER. His rising was supported by O'Hanlons, O'Cahans and Sweeneys, and the fighting continued as far to the northwest as Aranmore and Tory Island. O'Doherty was killed in a skirmish at Doon Rock, near Kilmacrenan, Co. Donegal, on 5 July 1608 and his head was spiked outside Dublin Castle. Arthur Chichester graciously accepted the grant of his Inishowen lands.

O'Doherty, Sir Morgan (1793–1842). The pseudonym of William Maginn, poet and journalist. He was born in Cork on 10 July 1793 and was an undergraduate at Trinity College Dublin by the age of 12. He taught in his father's school and ran it when he died in 1813. He began writing for *Blackwood's Magazine* (1819), suggesting the inclusion of the series of popular dialogues *Noctes Ambrosianae* (1822–35) and writing some of them himself. In 1830 he founded *Fraser's Magazine*, contributing a successful series of pen portraits called 'Gallery of Literary Characters', which, with illustrations by Daniel MACLISE, repeated the popularity of the *Noctes Ambrosianae*. The death of his longtime mistress, the writer L.E.L. (Letitia Elizabeth Landon, 1802–38), from a probably accidental overdose of prussic acid affected him badly, aggravating the racketiness of a lifestyle already rackety. He was imprisoned for debt in 1837, and died on 21 August 1842. He was the origin of the character Captain Shandon in his friend Thackeray's *Pendennis* (1848–50).

> The safety of women consists in one circumstance – men do not possess at the same time the knowledge of thirty-five and the blood of seventeen.
>
> *Thoughts and Maxims* (1855–7)

Ó Doirnín, Peadar (*c*.1704–69). Irish-language poet. He is thought to have been born near Dundalk, Co. Louth, and to have been a schoolmaster. There is considerable confusion about his life, as Seán de Rís, the editor of his surviving poems, makes clear in *Peadar Ó Doirnín, a Bheatha agus a Shaothar* ('his life and work', 1969). He may have been destined for the priesthood, but is thought to have become tutor to the family of one Arthur Brownlow, a Protestant from Lurgan, who had then in his possession the *Book of Armagh*. Ó Doirnín may have taught Brownlow Irish. They parted after some years because of inevitable

disagreements about politics, and Ó Doirnín married Rose Toner and settled near Forkhill, Co. Louth, where he became a teacher. He wrote satirical verse and came in for constant persecution by a local government agent known as Johnston of the Fews. Among Ó Doirnín's best known works are 'Úr-Chnoc Chéin Mhic Cáinte' ('the lovely hill of Cian Mac Cáinte') and '*Mná na hÉireann*' ('the women of Ireland'), love poems with a strong element of fantasy and exaggeration. Ó Doirnín died in his classroom on 3 April 1769 and is buried at Urney churchyard near Dundalk. Seosamh MAC GRIANNA's story 'Codladh an Mháistir' ('the master's sleep') is based on the circumstances of Ó Doirnín's death.

Ó Donnchadha, Tadhg. *See* TORNA.

Ó Donnchadha an Ghleanna, Séafraidh (*c*.1620–78). Irish-language poet. He was born in Killaha Castle near Killarney, Co. Kerry, the seat of the O'Donoghues of the Glens, of which family he became chief on the death of his father in 1643. Although he participated in the REBELLION OF 1641, taking part with his three sons in an attack on Tralee Castle, he retained his patrimony and made Killaha Castle a haven both for fugitives from the fighting and for men of letters and poets. He is one of the four FOUR KERRY POETS apostrophied 'Aogán, Séafraidh, Piaras, Eoghan' by Pádraig Ó Duinnín (*see* DINNEEN'S DICTIONARY) on a Killarney memorial, and his poetry was edited by Ó Duinnín, who published a collection in 1902. Although he composed poetry mainly in the formal *dán díreach* syllabic style, he also wrote more personal lyrics. '*Do chuala scéal do chéas gach ló mé*' ('I heard news that tortures me every day') is a heartfelt lament for the passing of the Gaelic and Catholic order:

> … Ní bhfuil cliar in iathaibh Fódla
> Ní bhfuilid aifrinn againn nó orda,
> Ní bhfuil baiste ar ár leanaibh óga…
> (We have no clergy in Fodla's [Ireland's] land
> We have neither Mass nor monks
> We have no means to baptize our children …)

O'Donnell, Brendan. Murderer. In May 1994

a young woman, Imelda Riney, her small son Liam and a local priest, Father Joseph Walsh, were abducted by local man Brendan O'Donnell in Co. Clare. A few days later their bodies were found by a search party in Cregg Wood in the same county. O'Donnell was arrested after abducting another young woman, Fiona Sampson from Whitegate (who survived), tried for murder and imprisoned for life. He died in prison. The multiple killings devastated Ireland, especially as O'Donnell was already known to gardai as being antisocial and potentially dangerous.

See also O'BRIEN, EDNA.

O'Donnell, Daniel (b.1963). Popular Irish singer. He was born in Kincasslagh in the Rosses region of west Donegal and educated locally. He began singing in the local church choir and started on the circuit already followed by his sister Margo, who was also a singer. A combination of an easy-listening repertoire, an easier manner, a very presentable appearance, a genuine charm, a squeaky-clean reputation and a remarkable memory for names and faces have made him extremely popular with his target audience, mainly middle-aged women. A typical joke about O'Donnell runs: 'What has 100 legs and no teeth? The front row of a Daniel O'Donnell concert.' There are regular coach parties to his home in the Rosses and until recently he held a kind of annual 'at-home', which attracted hundreds of fans. The O'Donnell phenomenon was the theme of the popular West End and Broadway play, *Women on the Verge of HRT* (1997) by the Belfast playwright Marie Jones.

O'Donnell, Peadar (1893–1986). Writer and socialist. He was born at Meenmore near Dungloe, Co. Donegal, and became a teacher and union organizer, using his personal knowledge of the migrant workers in Scotland. He took the Republican side in the CIVIL WAR, recording his experiences in *The Gates Flew Open* (1932). His agitation against the LAND ANNUITIES helped bring down the Cosgrave government in 1932, and he was a local recruiter for the International Brigade during the Spanish Civil War. In 1940 he persuaded Sean O'FAOLAIN to edit *The Bell*, and took over as editor (1946–54) when O'Faolain retired. Of O'Donnell's novels, three – *The Storm* (1925), *Islanders* (1928) and *Proud Island* (1975) – are set in the islands of the Rosses of Donegal, which he knew from boyhood and where he taught. *The Big Windows* (1955) – set in the heart of the Donegal Mountains, which O'Donnell remembered from a time spent 'on the run' when he was nursing a wound – is about a woman who has left her bright island home for the dark interior glens. *The Knife* (1930) and *On the Edge of the Stream* (1934) are about small-town Irish life, the former dealing with the lot of Protestant farmers caught on the Free State side of the border after PARTITION. *Adrigoole* (1929) is based on a true incident in which a mother and child died of starvation in a pro-TREATY area while her Republican husband was imprisoned. For most of the 93 years of his life O'Donnell was a fighter for social justice, his writings in fiction implicitly furthering his undoctrinaire socialism. He died in a Dublin hospital on 13 May 1986.

O'Donnell, Red Hugh (Aodh Rua Ó Dónail, *c*.1571–1602). Lord of Tír Chonaill. He was the son of Sir Hugh O'Donnell and Finola MACDONNELL. He saw military action when he was 12, and his betrothal at 15 to a daughter of Hugh O'NEILL, Earl of Tyrone, caused Sir John PERROT to have him kidnapped by luring him on to a Spanish liquor vessel in Lough Swilly. O'Donnell's second attempt at escape, on Christmas night 1591, was successful, though one of his companions died of the bitter cold. He eventually made his way safely to Ballyshannon, and in 1592 replaced his prematurely senile father as chieftain.

During the NINE YEARS' WAR O'Donnell overran Connacht, and with O'Neill inflicted a heavy defeat on the English forces under Henry BAGENAL at the Battle of the YELLOW FORD in August 1598. In 1601 help from Spain came in the shape of 3400 soldiers, who landed at

Kinsale on Co. Cork. O'Donnell led his army over the Slievefelim Mountains in Co. Limerick, eluding Sir George CAREW, who tried to block his passage at Cashel. After the defeat at KINSALE Red Hugh was sent to Spain to seek further help from Phillip III. He was well received but died suddenly on 10 September 1602 at Simancas, possibly by poison. He was buried with royal honours at the church of the Franciscan monastery in Valladolid.

> They brought
> His blackening body
> Here
> To rest
> Princes came
> Walking
> Behind it
> And all Valladolid knew
> And out to Simancas all knew
> Where they buried Red Hugh.
>
> THOMAS MCGREEVY (1893–1976): 'Aodh Ruadh Ó Domhnaill', in *Poems* (1934)

O'Donnell, Rory, 1st Earl of Tyrconnell (Ruairí Ó Dónaill, 1575–1608). Younger brother of Red Hugh O'DONNELL. He accompanied Red Hugh to Kinsale (*see* KINSALE, BATTLE OF) and took over the leadership when his brother went to Spain. He submitted to Lord Deputy MOUNTJOY in 1602 and went with him to England in 1603 to show his allegiance to the new king. James I received him cordially and arranged for him to be knighted the following year in Christ Church Cathedral in Dublin and created Earl of Tyrconnell. However, he was dissatisfied with the land grant and feared that the government intended to depose the Ulster earls, using the recusancy laws as the excuse. He tried to persuade Hugh O'NEILL, Earl of Tyrone, and Maguire (a chieftain of what is now Co. Fermanagh) to join him in an attack on Dublin Castle, but, fearing that his plans had been discovered, joined them in the so-called FLIGHT OF THE EARLS in 1607. He died the following year in Rome, on 29 July 1608.

'O'Donnell Abu'. *See* MCCANN, MICHAEL JOSEPH.

O'Donoghue, D[avid] J[ames] (1866–1917).

Literary historian and biographer. He was born in Chelsea on 22 July 1866 to Cork parents, and educated locally to primary level only, completing his own education at the British Museum Reading Room. He began to work as a journalist and became involved in the IRISH LITERARY REVIVAL in London and later in Dublin, where he moved in 1896. He was appointed librarian at University College Dublin in 1909, and continued to contribute to literary journals. A researcher and writer of great industry and energy, he compiled *Poets of Ireland* (1892–3), which contained biographical entries on 2000 poets and which was reissued in a revised and enlarged edition in 1912. He wrote biographies of William CARLETON (1896) and James Clarence MANGAN (1897), and prepared editions of the works of many Anglo-Irish authors, including James Fintan LALOR, Samuel LOVER, Thomas DAVIS and John Keegan CASEY. Yeats wrote a comic sketch of O'Donoghue, which was published in *Autobiographies* (1955), but there is no doubt that he performed a valuable service to those poets W.P. RYAN called 'the forgotten bards', as well as to the 19th-century writers whose work he edited.

O'Donoghue, Daniel (1833–89). Parliamentarian. He was born in Co. Kerry, where he was the head of the O'Donoghue family of Glenflesk, thereby being known as 'The O'Donoghue of the Glens'. A great-nephew of Daniel O'CONNELL, he was educated at Stonyhurst. In 1857 he was elected Independent Opposition MP for Co. Tipperary in succession to John Sadlier, but represented Tralee for the Irish Party from 1865 to 1885, committed to the alliance between Charles Stewart PARNELL and the Liberals under Gladstone. He challenged Sir Robert Peel, 3rd Baronet, to a duel for calling him a 'mannikin traitor'. He retired from politics in 1885.

O'Donoghue of the Glens. *See* O'DONOGHUE, DANIEL.

O'Donohoe, John. *See* ANAM CARA.

O'Donovan, Gerald (1871–1942). Novelist and

reforming priest. He was born Jeremiah Donovan on 15 July 1871, the son of a Cork pier-builder, and was educated at Maynooth, being ordained for the diocese of Clonfert in 1895. He was a white blackbird among the clergy: liberal, aesthetically inclined and a strong supporter of the GAELIC LEAGUE and the IAOS. He made Loughrea Cathedral, of which he was administrator, a centre for culture as well as liturgy. He was the inspiration for George Moore's aesthetic priest in the story 'Fugitives' in *The* UNTILLED FIELD (1903) and for his Father Gogarty in *The Lake* (1905). Though the diocesan clergy's choice, he was passed over for bishop by the Vatican because of his 'modernist' views, and relations between himself and Dr Thomas O'Dea, the new bishop, soon deteriorated. He resigned in 1904 and eventually went to live in London, supporting himself with hack work until he married in 1911 Beryl Verschoyle, the daughter of an Anglo-Irish colonel. She was able to support him until he joined the Italian desk in the War Office in 1914, becoming its head in 1918. It was there that he met the novelist Rose Macaulay (1881–1958) with whom he had a relationship until his death of cancer on 26 July 1942 and whose literary mentor he became. His first and best novel *Father Ralph* (1913) is largely autobiographical, and four others – *Waiting* (1914), *Conquest* (1920), *Vocations* (1921) and *The Holy Tree* (1922) – deal with Irish themes, religious and political.

> The Carmelites will do their best to get him. He would be wasted with them – the boy ought to be a scholar, not a pulpit windbag.
>
> *Father Ralph* (1913)

O'Donovan, John (1806–61). Scholar and antiquary. He was born on 9 July 1806 at Atta-teemore, Co. Kilkenny, the son of a prosperous Catholic farmer, and educated in Dublin. He joined the ORDNANCE SURVEY in 1829 as Gaelic adviser, having been earlier employed to teach Irish to Lieutenant Thomas Larcom, the head of the Survey in Ireland. He catalogued more than 140,000 placenames, recorded in letters

that were published in 50 volumes (1924–32) as he travelled the length and breadth of Ireland. The *Ordnance Survey Letters* were edited and published by Father Michael O'Flanagan between 1924 and 1932. (Larcom reprimanded O'Donovan for defacing official documents with 'ribaldry', and O'Donovan agreed to make all his future communications 'very serious, cold and unIrish'.) A typical letter written from Raphoe in east Donegal on 1 October 1835 begins:

> This day we travelled through the rich Presbyterian country lying between this and Strabane, but found it useless to consult the inhabitants about the significations of the Townlands.

O'Donovan's greatest achievement was his edition and translation of the ANNALS OF THE FOUR MASTERS (1848–51) in six volumes. He was tireless in his work of translation of Irish manuscripts, yet still found time for a host of other activities: he wrote *A Grammar of the Irish Language* (1845), was called to the English Bar (1847), became a studentless professor of Celtic at Queen's College Belfast (1850), and in 1852 began to work with his regular collaborator and brother-in-law, Eugene O'CURRY, on the ancient laws of Ireland. The two men quarrelled and grew so suspicious of each other that they tried to conceal their work from each other. O'Curry claimed that O'Donovan's death was caused by a chill caught when seated at a window so that O'Curry might not read what he was writing. O'Donovan died on 9 December 1861. His work in all aspects of Irish history, language and culture played a significant part in the cultural revival of the late 19th century.

O'Donovan Rossa, Jeremiah (1831–1915). Fenian. He was born Jeremiah O'Donovan in Rosscarbery, Co. Cork, in September 1831 and at a later stage added the Irish word *Rossa* ('headlands') to give his name a more distinctive Gaelic aura. While running a grocery shop in the Co. Cork town of Skibbereen he set up the Phoenix Literary and Debating Society in

1856. It was implicitly revolutionary, strongly influenced by YOUNG IRELAND and welcomed into the IRB in May 1858. He became business manager of the FENIAN organ the *Irish People*, which published its first number on 28 November 1863.

Along with other Fenians, O'Donovan Rossa was arrested on 15 September 1865 and sentenced to 20 years imprisonment under extremely harsh conditions (*see* SPECIAL MEN) He was elected to Parliament at a by-election on 27 November 1869, but disqualified as a convicted felon. He was released with other Fenians on 'exile licence' in 1871 and spent the rest of his life in the USA. (He and four other Fenians, John DEVOY, Charles Underwood O'Connell, Henry Mulleda and John McClure, travelled to America on the SS *Cuba*, thus earning themselves the surprisingly modern nickname 'the Cuba Five'.)

O'Donovan Rossa continued in active Fenianism, editing the *United Irishman* and setting up in March 1876 a 'skirmishing fund' to finance terrorist activity in Britain. Though he became 'head centre' of the Fenian Brotherhood in February 1877 he was often at odds with his fellow expatriates, mainly because of personal attacks and bouts of drunkenness. He left Devoy's CLAN NA GAEL, setting up a rival organization, the United Irishmen of America, in Philadelphia in June 1880. After the failure of his UK dynamiting venture in 1885 he became less extreme, offering grudging support to PARNELL and reluctantly trying the constitutional alternative.

The O'Donovan Rossa legend, however, continued to burn with a PHOENIX FLAME; he died in New York on 30 June 1915 and his body was brought home. His burial in GLASNEVIN CEMETERY on 1 August gave Patrick PEARSE the opportunity for his most famous (if largely inaudible) speech (*see* FOOLS, THE FOOLS). He published two volumes of reminiscences: *O'Donovan Rossa's Prison Life* (1874) and *Rossa's Recollections, 1838–1898* (1898).

> Gladstone starved me till my flesh was rotten for want of nourishment, Gladstone chained me with hands chained behind my back for thirty-five days at a time, Gladstone leaped upon my chest, while I lay on the flat of my back in a black-hole cell in his prison. Peori [the Italian revolutionary] didn't experience such treatment as that in the Italian prison. Yet the great Englishman could cry out his eyes for him. No wonder those eyes got sore in the end.
>
> *Recollections*

O'Dowda, Brendan (1925–2002). The leading contemporary interpreter of Percy FRENCH. His first album included two of French's songs, 'Darling girl from Clare' and 'Bridget Flynn', and thereafter he became a mainstay of RTÉ radio. His Percy French one-man show attracted large audiences.

O'Driscoll, Brian (b.1979). Dublin-born, Blackrock College-educated rugby union player for Leinster, Ireland and the British and Irish Lions. A centre of prodigious skill and strength, O'Driscoll won his first international cap against Australia in June 1999, and established himself in the Irish side during that year's World Cup. It was his performances in the 2000 Six Nations championship, however, that transformed him from youthful talent into Irish sporting icon. He scored tries against Scotland and Italy and achieved a memorable hat-trick of tries against France as Ireland won their first victory in Paris in 28 years. O'Driscoll went on to tour Australia with the Lions in the summer of 2001, playing in all three test matches and scoring a superb individual try in Brisbane. By now he was being hailed as the most gifted centre in world rugby and the most talented Irish rugby player since Mike GIBSON. O'Driscoll assumed the Irish captaincy in November 2002 in place of the injured Keith WOOD, presiding over an 18–9 win over the then world champions Australia in Dublin (Ireland's first win over the Wallabies in 23 years). O'Driscoll helped Ireland reach the quarter-finals of the 2003 World Cup (where they had the misfortune to come up against a French team in rampant mood), in the process adding a further three to his growing tally of international tries. He resumed the Irish captaincy following Keith Wood's retirement, and led Ireland to a shock victory over World Cup-winners England at Twickenham in March 2004. At the time of writing (September 2004) O'Driscoll has played 52 times for Ireland (13 times as captain) and has scored 25 tries for his country, an Irish record.

O'Duffy, Eimar [Ultan] (1893–1935). Novelist. He was born on 29 September 1893, the son of a society dentist, and educated at Stonyhurst and at University College Dublin. Though a member of the IRB he strongly opposed the EASTER RISING, becoming Eoin MACNEILL's informant of PEARSE's intentions, and was dispatched to Belfast to call off the mobilization there. This unfashionable attitude is reflected in his novel *The Wasted Island* (1919, revised 1929) and his future in the new bourgeois state looked bleak, though he managed to keep a job with the Department of External Affairs, supplementing his income with earnings from such novels as *The Lion and the Fox* (1922), about Hugh O'NEILL at the time of the Battle of Kinsale, and two lighter books, *Printer's Errors* (1922) and *Miss Rudd and Some Lovers* (1923).

O'Duffy lost his civil service job in 1925 and moved with his wife Kathleen Cruise O'Brien and their two children to England. He supported his family by writing detective stories and began the trio of satirical fantasies about the unregretted Ireland he had left and upon which his literary reputation rests: *King Goshawk and the Birds* (1926), *The Spacious Adventures of the Man in the Street* (1928) and *Asses in Clover* (1933). These novels use Celtic mythology and Swiftian savagery to pillory all aspects of the Free State, including its economics and acquiescence in clerical domination. His later years were clouded by failing health and money worries, and he died in New Malden, Surrey, on 21 March 1935. The text of an unfinished autobiography, *The Portrait Gallery*, was destroyed on his instructions after his death.

You should have seen Cuchulain playing tennis with the gentry and the ladies of the Bon Ton suburb. He learnt the whole art and skill of the game in ten minutes, and straightway beat the Champion of Ireland six-love, six-love, and six-love. Never had such strength and agility been seen before. He could cross the court in one leap; he never served a fault, and none but the Champion ever returned his service; he would take any stroke on the volley; and at the net his smash invariably burst the ball.

King Goshawk and the Birds (1926)

O'Duffy, Eoin (also Eoghan) (1892–1944). Politician and BLUESHIRT leader. He was born near Castleblayney, Co. Monaghan, on 20 October 1892 and trained as an engineer, later working as an auctioneer. He took part in the Anglo-Irish War and supported the TREATY, becoming commissioner of the Civic Guard (later GARDA SÍOCHÁNA) when the force was founded in 1922. When FIANNA FÁIL came to power in 1932, Éamon DE VALERA found Duffy's politics uncongenial and had him dismissed from his post as commissioner in 1933, whereupon O'Duffy refused another public-service position and instead devoted himself to politics.

In 1933 O'Duffy was elected leader of the Army Comrades Association, an association of ex-Free State soldiers that had been founded the previous year, and the name of which he changed to the National Guard. It was this organization that became known as the Blueshirts because of the uniform and the fascist-style salute and ideology. Its demonstrations were banned by the government. O'Duffy was elected first president of FINE GAEL when the party was formed in September 1933, but resigned the following year, launching instead a more overtly fascist political party, the National Corporate Party. The Blueshirts, a short-lived phenomenon, had their last outing when in 1936–7 O'Duffy organized an Irish Brigade (*see* ANGELS OF MONASTEREVIN) to fight on the Nationalist side in the SPANISH CIVIL WAR. Most of the soldiers were back in Ireland within a year and O'Duffy retired from public life. He died on 20 November 1944.

O'Faolain, Eileen (1900–88). Writer of folktales and children's books. She was born Eileen Gould in Cork city, like her husband Sean O'FAOLAIN, whom she met at Ballingeary IRISH COLLEGE and whom she married in Boston in 1927. She wrote lively fairy stories for children, including *The Little Black Hen* (1940), *The King of the Cats* (1941) and *Miss Pennyfeather and the Pooka* (1949). Her classic *Irish Sagas and Folktales* (1954) and *Children of the Salmon* (1965) tell the old stories in a mode as acceptable to adults as to children.

O'Faolain, Julia (b.1932). Novelist and short-story writer, the daughter of Sean and Eileen O'Faolain. She was born in Twickenham, where her father was a lecturer, and was educated at University College Dublin, Rome and the Sorbonne. Her first books, *We Might See Sights* (1968), *Man in the Cellar* (1974) and *Daughters of Passion* (1982), are short-story collections. *Women in the Wall* (1975) is a spare and beautiful account of the remarkably autonomous life of nuns in Merovingian Gaul. *The Judas Cloth* (1992) deals with the papacy of Pius IX. All her later novels rehearse, sharply and sometimes cruelly, her themes of women, the church and life in academic America and a still medieval Europe. She is a member of AOSDÁNA.

O'Faolain, Sean (1900–91). Novelist and short-story writer. Ireland's foremost 20th-century man of letters, he was born John Whelan in Cork, the son of an RIC constable and a theatrical landlady. He graduated from University College Cork in 1921, using the Irish form of his name, having been a student by day and a revolutionary at night. He took the Republican side in the CIVIL WAR, but gradually turned against violence and extremism. O'Faolain's first book of short stories, *Midsummer Night Madness* (1932), was given the honour of being banned in Ireland. He went to live in Wicklow, supporting himself there by his pen for the rest of his long life. He wrote many short stories, some of the finest for *The BELL*, which he edited from 1940 to 1946 with genial kindness to its often unprofessional contributors and for which, with righteous wrath, he wrote editorials excoriating 'our bourgeoisie, Little Islanders, chauvinists, puritans, stuffed-shirts, pietists, Tartuffes, Anglophobes, Celtophiles, et alii hujus generis'.

O'Faolain also wrote biographies, travel books about Italy (his second favourite country), works of criticism, including *The Short Story* (1947), and one stage comedy, *She Had to Do Something* (1938). His novels, *Bird Alone* (1936) and *Come Back to Erin* (1940), are not as successful as his stories. His autobiography *Vive Moi!* was first published in 1964, and in the updated (1993) version, at his daughter Julia's behest, he recounted his affairs with Elizabeth BOWEN and Honor TRACY. No other writer of the period had O'Faolain's cultural breadth, his moral courage or his sense of nationhood.

Ó Farachháin, Roibeárd (Robert Farren) (1909–84). Poet. He was born in Dublin and educated at St Patrick's College Drumcondra, and at University College Dublin. He taught for ten years before joining RAIDIÓ ÉIREANN in 1939, becoming controller of programmes (1953–74) and a director of the ABBEY THEATRE. In 1940, with Austin CLARKE, he founded the Dublin Verse-Speaking Society, which grew into the Lyric Theatre Company in 1944, presenting verse-dramas biannually at the Abbey until 1951, supplying a felt need in the capital. His own work for the company included *Convention at Druim Ceat* (1943), about the assembly near Limavady, Co. Derry, attended by Colum Cille to settle, among other matters, the succession of the kingdom of Dál Riata and the position of poets in Ireland, and *Lost Light* (1943). His best-known books of verse are *Rime, Gentlemen, Please* (1945) and an epic version of the career of Colum Cille, *The First Exile* (1944). His mildly chauvinistic but entertaining *The Course of Irish Verse* was published in 1948.

Offaly. A Midlands county, formerly known

as 'King's County' after Philip II of Spain, husband of Queen Mary at the time of the PLANTATION of Laois and Offaly. Philipstown, originally the administrative centre and also named after Philip, is now the town of Daingean. The county town is Tullamore. The following description of the county appeared in the *New London Gazetteer* in 1826:

> King's county, a county of Ireland, bounded north and east by Westmeath, Meath, east by Kilkenny and Queen's county, south by Tipperary, and west by Galway; 43 miles long and 39 miles broad, containing 707 square miles. More than 1/3 of the county is occupied by bogs and mountains; the soil of the arable lands is very fertile, and consists either of a deep moor, or a shallow gravely loam. Principal rivers, the Shannon, Little Brosna, and Greater Brosna. It sends 2 members to parliament. Pop. 132,319. Chief town, Phillip's town.

The notable physical features (and tourist attractions) of the county are the Slieve Bloom mountain range, which stretches for 77 km (48 miles) across the southeastern part of the county, the Bog of Allen, the River Shannon and the Grand Canal. A significant proportion of the county is covered by peatlands, and the tracts of milled peat are often described as the 'brown gold' of Offaly.
See also BIFFO.

Offences against the State Act. Security legislation introduced by Fianna Fáil in 1939 in response to the IRA bombing campaign in Britain. The clause permitting internment without trial was declared unconstitutional, but was reintroduced on amendment in 1940. The act was used during the EMERGENCY, the BORDER CAMPAIGN and from 1972 during the Northern Ireland TROUBLES.

Official IRA. *See* STICKIES, THE[1].

Ó Fiach, Tomás (1923–90). Archbishop of Armagh, cardinal and historian. He was born near Crossmaglen, Co. Armagh, on 23 November 1923 and educated at St Patrick's College in Armagh and at Maynooth, University College Dublin and Louvain. Ordained in 1948, he became lecturer in history at Maynooth in 1953, professor in 1959 and president of the college in 1974. He was elevated to the primatial see in 1977 and made cardinal two years later. Until then he was known primarily as a scholar – an authority on the early Christian missionaries to Dark-Age Europe – as his two most significant publications *Gaelscrínte i gCéin* ('Irish shrines abroad', 1960) and *Irish Cultural Influences in Europe* (1966), attest. His appointment as leader of the Catholic Church in Ireland at the height of the Northern Ireland TROUBLES inevitably brought a political dimension to his career. He remained uncompromisingly a Nationalist – a republican with a small 'r' – and he was evenhanded in his condemnation of the IRA and of the countermeasures of the security forces, a stance that did little to increase his popularity, especially in Britain. Within the church he was a moderate with a commitment to ecumenism. Ó Fiach died on pilgrimage to Lourdes on 8 May 1990.

Ó Fiannachta, Pádraig (b.1927). Poet, scholar and translator. He was born near Dingle in Co. Kerry and educated at St Brendan's College in Killarney, University College Cork and Maynooth. He was ordained a priest in 1953. An authority on Welsh as well as early and modern Irish, he was professor of modern Irish at Maynooth from 1981 to 1992. He wrote (with Thomas P. O'Neill) a biography of de Valera (1968 and 1970), and his collections of poetry include *Ponc* (1970), *Donn Bó* (1976), *Rúin* (1971) and *Deora Dé* (1988; the title literally means 'God's tears', but in Munster is used for the common shrub fuchsia); he is also a novelist, literary historian and travel writer. Editor and main translator of the new Irish Bible, *An Bíobla Naofa* (1981), he was also editorial director of An Sagart, Maynooth's Irish-language imprint and editor of the periodical *Irishleabhar Mhá Nuad* ('Maynooth periodical'). After retiring from his academic post he became parish priest of Dingle.

O'Flaherty, Liam (1896–1984). Writer. He was

born on 28 August 1896 on Inis Mór, the largest of the ARAN ISLANDS. He was educated at Rockwell College, Co. Tipperary, where he was a postulant of the Holy Ghost Fathers. He had been enrolled by the order in University College Dublin when he decided he had no vocation; instead, in 1915, he joined the Irish Guards, as Bill Ganly (his mother's maiden name). Wounded and badly shell-shocked in 1917, he took several years to recover; during this period he was involved in the seizure of the ROTUNDA in Dublin to set up a socialist state, and fought on the Republican side in the CIVIL WAR.

O'Flaherty left Ireland in 1922 to become a full-time writer, producing over the next 30 years many remarkable novels and short stories in English, including *The Neighbour's Wife* (1923) and *The Black Soul* (1924), which gives a memorable picture of Aran life. A long novella, *The Return of the Beast* (1929), describes how the humanity of ordinary men is eroded under a bombardment in no-man's land, much as Gypo Nolan in *The INFORMER* (1929) changes from a slow-witted, decent man to a shambling animal in whom a dawning conscience comes too late. *Spring Sowing* (1924), O'Flaherty's first collection of stories, deals as much with animals and even inanimate nature (as in 'The Wave') as with humans. A historical trilogy *Famine* (1937), *Land* (1946) and *Insurrection* (1950) shows the best and worst of the author.

Æ once summed up O'Flaherty's work as follows: 'When O'Flaherty thinks, he is a goose; when he feels, he is a genius.' His sympathetic delineation of the mute and inarticulate is his greatest strength; his artistic 'agony', though sincere, rings false. His women, apart from mothers, are unconvincing, and his admiration for cold-blooded fanatics such as Gallagher, the IRA commander in *The Informer*, Tyson in *The Martyr* (1933) and Dwyer in *Land* may be an indication of his own mercurial temperament.

O'Flaherty's short stories, nearly 200 in number, are better than his novels, and there is a marvellous appropriate terseness in the language of *Dúil* ('desire', 1953), a collection of stories in Irish, some of them versions of earlier English ones. *Shame the Devil* (1934) is a striking first volume of autobiography and, considering the length and drama of O'Flaherty's life, one could wish that he had written about his next 50 years with the same frankness and elegance. He returned to live in Ireland in the 1960s and died in Dublin on 7 September 1984.

> … then just as suddenly her anger vanished like a puff of smoke, and she burst into wild tears, wailing, 'My children, oh my children, far over the sea you will be carried from me, your mother.' And she began to rock herself and she threw her apron over her head.
>
> 'Going into Exile', in *Spring Sowing* (1924)

Ó Flynn, Liam (Liam Óg, b.1945). Traditional musician (*see also* BRENDAN VOYAGE, THE; PLANXTY[2]).

Ó Gallachair, Réamonn (1518–1601). 'Last' Bishop of Derry. He was born in Raphoe, Co. Donegal. In 1545, at the age of 27, he was appointed Bishop of Killala, and on 22 June 1569 was translated to Derry. He was acting Primate of Ireland for most of his time in Derry, and performed at least one ordination. He is thought to have aided Armada survivors in 1588, and during the NINE YEARS' WAR he was under the protection of Red Hugh O'DONNELL. When Cahir O'DOHERTY made submission to Sir Henry DOCWRA, Ó Gallachair felt himself to be in danger. On 7 March 1601 he left Derry for the protection of Domhnall Ballach Ó Catháin, who was lord of north Co. Derry, and was killed near the city by a band of raiding English soldiers under the command of Sir John Holles. Bishop Montgomery, his Anglican replacement, noted with equanimity that 'Reimundus, the last Irish bishop, was slain … by the English.' The Catholic see was vacant from 1601 until 1720, and it was not until 1780 that a Catholic bishop, Philip McDevitt (*c.*1726–97), who served for 31 years, actually lived again in the city.

Ogam or **ogham.** An alphabet for the Irish language using groups of one to five strokes, which were represented as notches on the equivalent of a tallystick or on the edges of standing stones or vertical posts. There are over 300 ogam stones in Ireland, mainly in the southwest, but they are also to be found in other Celtic regions – Wales, the Isle of Man, Cornwall and Scotland. The characters, 20 in all, were represented by parallel lines touching a central base line. Five of these drawn vertically from above stood for h, d, t, c, q (h represented by a single stroke, d by a double stroke, etc); five drawn from below gave n, s, v, l, b; five crossing the base line vertically were the vowels; while the five that crossed the line diagonally gave m, g, ng, z and r. They had names associated with trees: for example, a (the single vertically crossing stroke) was named after the elm, and b (the single inferior stroke) named after the birch. They were read upwards on the left and downwards on the right of the stone or post. The extant inscriptions date from the 4th to the 6th centuries AD and are usually of personal names in the genitive case. The alphabet is associated mythologically with OGMA of the TUATHA DÉ DANAAN.

Óglaigh na hÉireann. The Irish name for the IRISH VOLUNTEERS, deriving from the plural of *óglach*, meaning literally a 'youth of military age'. The newspaper published intermittently by the Irish Volunteers between 1918 and 1922 was called *An tÓglach* ('the volunteer'). Its editors included Ernest BLYTHE.

Ogma. In Irish mythology, the TUATHA DÉ DAN-AAN god of eloquence, a son of the DAGDA. Ogma is cognate with the continental Celtic god Ogmios, whom the Greek writer Lucian (*c.*AD 115–after 180) claims as the Celtic Hercules. He is credited with the invention of the OGAM alphabet. He performs well in the Second Battle of MAGH TUIREADH (Moytura), claiming the talking sword Orna, which was able to narrate its heroic deeds and was the property of the sea god Tethra, a colleague of Manannán Mac Lir.

Ó Gnímh, Fearflatha (*c.*1540–*c.*1630). Irish-language bardic poet. He was head of the Gnímh family, bards to the O'Neill family in Co. Antrim, and much of his poetry was written to honour one or other branch of that family – of Antrim, Down or Tyrone. He saw the effective end of the Gaelic order in Ulster, and his poetry – '*Beannacht ar Anmain Éireann*' ('my blessing on the soul of Ireland', 1609) is one example – mourns the passing of the native aristocracy and the Gaelic traditions of learning that were part of that culture. Another well-known lament is '*Mo Thrua mar Táid Gaidhil*' ('my grief that they are foreigners'), written about 1612.

O'Grady, Standish James (1846–1928). Novelist. Often confused with his cousin Standish Hayes O'Grady (1832–1915), the Gaelic scholar, he was born in Castletown Berehaven, Co. Cork, the son of the Anglican rector who was also a viscount. He was educated at Trinity College Dublin and called to the Bar in 1872. His interest in Irish myth led to the intensive research that produced *History of Ireland* (1878–80) and made him one of the enablers of the IRISH LITERARY REVIVAL; he had a profound effect on W.B. Yeats in particular. This was especially true of his rewriting of the saga tales as adventure novels: a trilogy about CÚCHULAINN, *The Coming of Cuculain* (1894), *In the Gates of the North* (1901) and *The Triumph and Passing of Cuculain* (1920), and a similar treatment of FIONN MAC CUM-HAIL and the FIANNA in *Finn and His Companions* (1894). Other novels, written with children in mind, include *The Bog of Stars* (1893), *Lost on Du-Corrig* (1894), *Ulrick the Ready* (1896), *In the Wake of King James* (1896) and *The Flight of the Eagle* (1897) about Red Hugh O'DONNELL. O'Grady, a Liberal Unionist who correctly anticipated the coming resort to arms, left Ireland in 1918 and spent the rest of his life in the Isle of Wight, dying there on 18 May 1928.

Ó Gramhna, An tAthair Eoghan (Father Eugene O'Growney, 1863–99). Irish enthusiast, scholar and grammarian. He was born in Ballyfallon, Co. Meath, and educated at St Finian's College in Navan and at Maynooth, where he was ordained a priest in 1889. His enthusiasm for Irish dated from his youth, and as a student he spent summers in GAELTACHT areas. He was appointed curate in a parish in Co. Westmeath and wrote articles for *Irisleabhar na Gaedhilge*, the periodical of the GAELIC UNION (a precursor of the GAELIC LEAGUE). In 1891 he became its editor and professor of Celtic literature and language at Maynooth. When the Gaelic League was founded in 1893, with his friend Douglas HYDE as its president, he became vice-president. His book *Simple Lessons in Irish* (1894), based on a series of lessons he wrote for *Irisleabhar na Gaedhilge* and the *Weekly Freeman*, was a great popular success. Chronic ill-health caused him to leave Ireland for America and led to his premature death in Los Angeles. He was reinterred in Maynooth in 1901.

Ó Grianna, Séamus. *See* MÁIRE.

O'Growney, Eugene. *See* Ó GRAMHNA, AN TATHAIR EOGHAN.

O'Hanlon, Ardal (b.1965). Comedian and actor. He was born on 8 October 1965 in Carrickmacross, Co. Monaghan, the son of the Fianna Fáil TD and government minister Rory O'Hanlon. While he was at university in Dublin he began a career as a comic after-dinner speaker, and after college he and friends set up the Comedy Cellar in Dublin. In 1994 he won the Comedy Newcomer of the Year competition at the Hackney Empire in London and subsequently performed as a stand-up comic in Britain. He was cast as Father Dougal McGuire in the successful Channel 4 sitcom FATHER TED, and has also starred in the television series *My Hero* and *Big Bad World*. He still tours as a stand-up comic and has acted in films and in straight theatre. His novel, *The Talk of the Town*, was published in 1998.

O'Hanlon, Fergal. *See* PATRIOT GAME, THE.

O'Hanlon, Redmond (1640–81). Ulster TORY (Irish *tórai*, 'raider'). Though a historical character, his career became the subject of romantic stories. He is regarded as a kind of Robin Hood, believed to succour the Irish poor with money stolen from the foreign rich and capable of heroic deeds. Born near Poyntzpass, Co. Armagh, he used the vaunted rank of count, and probably had some military experience in France. His family was dispossessed of lands near Tandragee, and about 1670, as head of a band of outlaws, he was an alternative ruler of the counties of Tyrone and Armagh. In 1676 a reward of £100 was offered for his body, alive or dead, and in 1681 his foster brother Arthur O'Hanlon shot him as he lay sleeping in a hideout in Eightmilebridge, Co. Down. His head was spiked outside the jail in Downpatrick and his body buried in the graveyard of Relicarn, near his birthplace.

> By Douglas Bridge I met a man
> Who lived adjacent to Strabane,
> Before the English hung him high
> For riding with O'Hanlon.
>
> The eyes of him were just as fresh
> As when they burned within the flesh;
> And his boot-legs were wide apart
> For riding with O'Hanlon.
>> FRANCIS CARLIN (1945): 'The Ballad of Douglas Bridge'

O'Hara, Maureen (b.1921). Actress. She was born Maureen Fitzsimons in Dublin on 17 August 1921, and educated at the ABBEY THEATRE school of acting and the London College of Music. Her first American film was a dramatization of Daphne du Maurier's *Jamaica Inn* (1939) and she appeared in *The Hunchback of Notre Dame* with Charles Laughton and in *How Green Was My Valley*, also in 1939. In Ireland her best-known film role was as Kate Danaher in *The QUIET MAN*, in which John Wayne also starred.

Ó hÉanaigh, Seosamh (Joe Heaney, 1919–84). SEAN-NÓS singer. He was born in Carna in Connemara and showed great vocal promise as a young man, winning first prize at the

OIREACHTAS in 1942. He was a building worker in England for some years, performing with other traditional musicians in clubs and pubs. In the early 1960s he returned to Dublin and played a part in the ballad and traditional flowering of those years. In 1966 he emigrated to New York and worked for more than a decade as an elevator operator, until he was given teaching positions in folklore departments in American colleges. He made a number of recordings for GAEL LINN and also performed in concert in Dublin a few years before his death.

O'Hehir, Mícheál (1920–96). Sports commentator. He was born in Glasnevin, Dublin, on 2 June 1920. He began to do radio commentaries on GAA matches when still a schoolboy, demonstrating at the All-Ireland semi-final at Mullingar on 14 August 1938 a prodigious knowledge of the game and the history of the players. In 1944 he began to work as a sports sub-editor at the *Irish Independent*, and three years later was appointed the newspaper's racing correspondent, meanwhile doing radio sports commentary for RTÉ and BBC (*see* POLO GROUND FINAL, THE). He became head of sport at the newly established RTÉ Television in 1961. He had abandoned engineering studies at University College Dublin to become a full-time commentator and his capacity to convey the atmosphere at important matches, especially ALL-IRELAND finals, made him the best-known voice in Ireland. He was accused with some justice of making even bad matches sound good, and he was an equally precise and exciting racing commentator. He covered President KENNEDY's spectacular visit to Ireland in June 1963 and his funeral the following November. He resisted many offers of work outside of Ireland and continued in broadcasting after resigning as head of sport at RTÉ in 1970. He was debilitated by a stroke in 1985 and died on 24 November 1996.

Ó hEigeartaigh, Seán. *See* SÁIRSÉAL AGUS DILL.

Ó hEithir, Breandán (1930–90). Writer in Irish and English. He was born on Inis Mór in the ARAN ISLANDS, where his parents were schoolteachers, and was the nephew of Liam O'FLAHERTY. He was educated locally and at Coláiste Éanna in Galway, the school being evacuated during the EMERGENCY. (This and other diverting episodes of his first 20 or so years are drolly recounted in his 1984 sporting memoir *Over the Bar*, which ostensibly deals with his lifelong obsession with Galway hurling.) He spent a brief ill-starred period on a scholarship at University College Galway – which provided him with material for the partly autobiographical *Lig Sinn i gCathú* (1976; translated by the author as *Lead Us Into Temptation* in 1978) – and after some years working at a variety of occupations, including that of travelling salesman, turned to writing.

Ó hEithir was a gifted political journalist in Irish and in English, and in the three decades' span of his varied career was at different times Irish editor of the *Irish Press* (1957–63), editor of *Comhar*, presenter of RTÉ's Irish current-affairs programme *Féach*, a long-standing columnist with the *Irish Times* and a scriptwriter for film and TV. The cynical and amusing *The Begrudger's Guide to Irish Politics* (1986) was another product of his immersion in Irish politics. His second novel, *Sionnach ar Mo Dhuán* (1988), was both controversial and successful. He settled in Paris with his German-born wife in the period before his death, maintaining his professional, personal and sporting links with Ireland and his reputation as a brilliant talker and shrewd observer. An autobiographical book for children, *An Nollaig Thiar* (1989; the title, meaning 'western Christmas', is that of a poem by Máirtín Ó DIREÁIN), was the last he published before his death.

O'Hempsy, Denis (*c*.1695–1807). Harper. Also known as Hempson, he was born near Garvagh, Co. Derry, but went blind when he was 3 because of smallpox. He began to play the harp when he was 12, and at 18 travelled through Ireland and Scotland with his own instrument, presented by local benefactors. It was made from white willow with a back of bog fir. One of his star appearances was before Bonnie Prince Charlie at Holyrood in 1745. The Earl-Bishop, Frederick Augustus HERVEY, provided him with a house on the episcopal property at Magilligan, and he was one of the more exotic performers at the BELFAST HARP FESTIVAL of 1792. Among many unlikely biographical details ascribed to him is that he married in 1781, when he was 86, a woman from Inishowen, who bore him a daughter. He died at the reputed age of 112, the repository of the oldest Irish harp music.

O'Herlihy, Nora (1910–88). Founder of the credit-union movement in Ireland. She was born in Ballydesmond, in the SLIABH LUACHRA area of the Cork–Kerry border, where her father was a primary schoolteacher. With Seamus McKeown she founded the first credit union in Ireland, Dunore, in 1958, and went on to establish the Irish League of Credit Unions in 1963, having studied the practicalities of money cooperatives with the Credit Union National Association (CUNA) in America.

Ó hIfearnáin, Liam Dall (c.1720–1803). Irish-language poet. He was born at Shronell near Tipperary town and spent his whole life in the same area. He wrote personal poetry, laments and patriotic verse, Jacobite in sympathy like that of his contemporaries, and the poem by which he is probably best remembered, the AISLING 'Pé in Éirinn í' ('whoever she is'). 'Ar Bhruach na Coille Móire' ('on the edge of the great wood'), as well as being beautiful and lyrical, is an energetic political composition in which the poet claims that if he heard that the English were defeated, he would rise from the grave itself. He was a regular participant at the court of poetry that was held at the home of Seán Clárach Mac Dohhnaill at Kiltoohig. and is credited with having invented the name CATHLEEN NÍ HOULIHAN for Ireland.

O'Higgins, Bernardo (1778–1842). Chilean revolutionary. He was born on 20 August 1778 in Chillán, the illegitimate son of Ambrose O'Higgins (c.1720–1801), the Irish-born governor of Chile and viceroy of Peru. He was educated in Peru and later in England, where he met activists in the struggle for Latin-American independence. Returning to Chile in 1802 after his father's death, he became an active member of the revolutionary movement, leading an unsuccessful uprising in 1814 and being forced to flee to Argentina. A second attempt (1817–18) proved successful, and independence from Spain was announced on 12 February 1818. O'Higgins was virtual dictator of the country until 1823. His reforms in education and land-ownership and his attempts to limit bull-fighting and gambling met with opposition, especially from the church, old nobility and economic interests, and he was deposed in January 1823. O'Higgins lived for the rest of his life in Peru, dying there on 24 October 1842.

O'Higgins, Kevin (1892–1927). Statesman. A native of Stradbally, Co. Laois, O'Higgins was elected MP for Laois in the general election of November 1918 and was an able, even if sometimes self-righteous minister for home affairs (later justice) in the CUMANN NA NGAED-HEAL government from 1922. O'Higgins, who was staunchly pro-TREATY, supported the reprisal execution of four Republicans in MOUNT-JOY JAIL on 8 December 1922, although one of them was Rory O'CONNOR, who had been best man at his wedding a year previously. O'Higgins's father was murdered by a party of Republicans at his home in February 1923, and he himself was assassinated while on his way to Sunday Mass on 10 July 1927. Although no one was ever charged for his murder and the action was not sanctioned by the IRA, his killers were assumed to have been Republicans determined to extract revenge for O'Higgins's hardline behaviour during the CIVIL WAR and thereafter.

See also PUBLIC SAFETY ACTS; SMILE LIKE MOON-LIGHT ON A GRAVESTONE.

Oh that this was for Ireland. Words attributed to Patrick SARSFIELD on being fatally wounded at the Battle of LANDEN in 1693, where he fought for the French.

Ó hUiginn, Tadhg Dall (1550–91). Irish-language poet. He was born in Co. Sligo, a member of the famous Ó hUiginn family of bards or hereditary poets. Tadhg Dall, blind as his name suggests (Irish *dall*, 'blind'), had several patron families among the Gaelic aristocracy of the region, including the Burkes, the O'Rourkes and the O'Haras. His poetry is mostly of the conventional bardic type, written in praise of his patrons and urging them on to heroic feats of arms against one another or against the English, but very fine of its kind, lucid and sophisticated. Tadhg Dall settled in some style with his family near his home place of Leyney in Co. Sligo. There, it is said, members of the O'Hara family killed him, his wife and child in revenge for his having satirized them in a poem: 'six men of the O'Haras', he had alleged, had come and eaten all the food and drink in the house.

Oideas Gael (Irish, 'instruction in Irish'). An organization for the teaching of Irish to adults, usually in courses of one week's duration, established in 1984 and based in Glencolumbcille in Co. Donegal.

Óige, An (Irish, 'the young'). The Irish Youth Hostel Association. It was founded in 1931 by a group that included Thekla BEERE. At the end of that year it had two hostels and 215 members; now it has 32 youth hostels countrywide, catering for families and people of all ages. Many An Óige hostels are situated in very scenic areas, such as Dunquin in the DINGLE PENINSULA, Glanmore Lake on the BEARA PENINSULA and Glencolumbkille in Co. Donegal.

Oileánach, An t- (Irish, 'the islandman'). The autobiography (1929) of Tomás Ó Críomhtháin, which gives an account of all aspects of the harsh but culturally rich life on the BLASKET ISLANDS. The book, regarded as a classic, is dignified and elegiac in tone, its author

conscious of preserving a record of a way of life that was coming to an end. He was born on the Great Blasket in 1856, and was the first islander to be able to read and write Irish. He was encouraged to write by Irish and foreign visitors who came to the island to study one of the few unsullied remnants of Gaelic oral culture. Chief among these visitors were Brian Ó Ceallaigh from Killarney and the Englishman Robin Flower, who was taught Irish by Ó Críomhtháin. Ó Ceallaigh assembled his day-by-day accounts of island life and had them edited by An SEABHAC as *Allagar na hInise* (1928), translated by Tim Enright as *Island Cross-Talk* in 1986. Ó Críomhtháin died in 1937, having lived to see his work translated by Flower as *The Islandman* in 1934.

Scríobhas go mioncruinn ar a lán dár gcúrsaí d'fhonn go mbéadh cuimhne i poll éigin orthú agus thugas iarracht ar mheon na ndaoine a bhí i mo thimpeall a chur síos chun go mbéadh a dtuairisc i nár ndiaidh, mar ná beidh ár leithéidí arís ann.

(I have written in detail of much that we did because I wished that some record should be preserved; I have tried to capture the character of the people I knew so that some memorial may survive us, for our likes will never be seen again.)

Óinseach. An Irish word meaning 'foolish, silly person'. It normally refers to a woman, although the definition is not rigid, and in HIBERNO-ENGLISH it may also refer to a male. In a family situation the comment 'You're a right *óinseach*' may convey an affectionate frustration rather than serious criticism.

Oireacht. An assembly or court in early Gaelic society. By the 11th and 12th centuries the term had developed to refer to a regional council under a king. From the 14th century, an *oireacht* ('urraght' in English) was a collective noun taken to mean the leading nobles of a district under a Gaelic king. *Oireachtas*, the term for the actual council meeting in Gaelic Ireland, was brought back into use by both the GAELIC LEAGUE at the end of the 19th century and by de Valera's CONSTITUTION OF

1937 (*see* OIREACHTAS, AN T-1; OIREACHTAS, AN T-2). In the form 'iraght' the word may still be seen in placenames, such as Iraghticonnor (Oireacht Uí Chonchubhair) in Co. Kerry.

Oireachtas, An t-1 (Irish OIREACHT, 'assembly', 'court'). The name given to the legislature of the Republic of Ireland, consisting of the DÁIL, the assembly of deputies (TDs), the SEANAD or senate, and the president, who is not allowed to be a member of either assembly.

Oireachtas, An t-2. An annual festival of Gaelic culture initiated by the GAELIC LEAGUE in 1897 on the models of the Scottish Mod and the Welsh Eisteddfod. In music the most popular competitions are for men's and women's SEAN-NÓS singing, and also for the Corn Uí Riada (Ó Riada Cup, called after Seán Ó RIADA), a singing award for which men and women are eligible to compete. Its literary competitions have played a significant part in the establishment of a modern Gaelic literature, journalism and other media.

Oirghialla. *See* AIRGIALLA.

Oirish and Oirishness. *See* STAGE-IRISH.

Oisín (anglicized as **Ossian**). The son of the hero FIONN MAC CUMHAIL. The name signifies 'fawn', a reminder that his mother SADB was for a time a deer. He marries a fair-haired stranger called Eibhir, and their son OSCAR is a significant warrior in his grandfather's band, the FIANNA. Oisín is carried off to *Tír Tairnigiri* (the 'land of promise') by Niamh, the daughter of the sea god MANANNÁN MAC LIR. According to one of the legends his stay lasts three weeks, but when he returns on a visit on a magical white steed he finds that 300 earthly years have passed: Ireland has become Christian, and all the great champions of the Fianna are dead. His stirrup breaks as he tries to help some men raise a mighty stone, and his foot touches the ground in spite of Niamh's warning. He reverts to his mortal age, and before he succumbs is able to tell PATRICK, who baptizes him, of the high deeds of his father, his son and the

other members of their band. Oisín is thus celebrated as the poet of the Fianna, and his dialogue with the saint becomes on occasion quite acrimonious. Since the time of the fabrications of James Macpherson (1736–96), so trenchantly condemned by Dr Johnson, the Fionn Cycle or *Fiannaíocht* has tended to be called the Ossianic Cycle.

Oisín i ndiaidh na Féinne (Irish, 'Oisín after the Fianna'). A proverbial expression (pronounced 'usheen in yea na faynuh') describing a person who has survived long after his compeers have gone – referring to the story of OISÍN.

O'Keeffe, John (1747–1833). Irish dramatist. He was born in Dublin on 24 June 1747 and began a career as an artist, but gave it up to become part of the SMOCK ALLEY company in 1767. He spent the next dozen years as an actor, mainly on tour. During this time he married the daughter of Tottenham Heaphy, the manager of the theatre in Limerick, but they parted in 1780. In all he wrote 68 theatrical pieces, mostly comic, and continued to dictate his work when totally blind in 1790 after 20 years of failing sight. Immensely popular in his time, he managed to assert the dignity of his fellow Catholic Irishmen without alienating his British following. He is remembered now for the phrases '*Amo, amas* – I love a lass' from *The Agreeable Surprise* (1781), 'You should always except the present company' from *The London Hermit* (1793), 'Fat, fair and forty' from *The Irish Mimic* (1795), and the still current concert piece 'I Am a Friar of Orders Grey' from his comic opera *Merry Sherwood*. *Wild Oats* (1791), full of apt Shakespearean quotations, was based upon his experiences as a strolling player, and was his most popular play during his lifetime. When it was revived for the Royal Shakespeare Company in the mid-1970s by Clifford Williams, it ran for two years in London. A further revival for the National Theatre in 1996 was also successful. He died in Southampton on 4 February 1833.

I'm clothed in sackcloth for my sin,
With old sack wine I'm lined within,
A chirping cup is my matin song,
And the vesper bell is my bowl's ding dong.
What baron or squire
Or knight of the shire
Lives half so well as a holy friar.

'I Am a Friar of Orders Grey'

O'Keeffe, Pádraig (1887–1963). Traditional musician. A gifted fiddler and highly influential music teacher from the SLIABH LUACHRA area of counties Kerry and Cork, he was born in Glounthane, near Ballydesmond, the son of a schoolteacher. He succeeded his father as teacher in the local school but lost his job in 1920 because of various derelictions of duty, and thenceforth earned his living as an itinerant fiddle teacher (he was called 'the last of the fiddle masters'.) It was his custom to travel on foot all over Sliabh Luachra, instructing pupils and writing music down for them in his own system of notation. He taught all the great Sliabh Luachra fiddlers of the second half of the 20th century, including DENIS THE WEAVER (Denis Murphy) and Julia Clifford, and also the accordionist Johnny O'LEARY. A colourful character with a clever tongue, and given to drink, he lived alone until the end of his life. He died of pneumonia in the exceptionally cold February of 1963.

O'Kelly, Dennis. *See* ECLIPSE FIRST.

O'Kelly, Seán T. (1882–1966). Statesman; president (1945–59); the Irish form of his surname is Ó Ceallaigh. He was born in Dublin on 25 August 1882 and educated at O'Connell's Schools. His path followed the common trajectory of membership of the GAELIC LEAGUE (1898) followed by involvement in the IRB and SINN FÉIN, of which he was a founder-member in 1905. In the EASTER RISING of 1916 he served under Patrick PEARSE in the GPO, and was interned in England as a result. He was elected MP for the College Green ward of Dublin in the general election of December 1918 (and thereafter represented a Dublin constituency until 1945), and ceann comhairle (speaker) of the first Dáil in January 1919. During the Anglo–Irish War of 1919–21 he served as a Republican envoy to the Paris Peace Conference and to Washington.

An opponent of the TREATY, O'Kelly was one of the founders of FIANNA FÁIL in 1926, and when the party came to power in 1932 he was appointed minister for local government and public health. He also served as minister for finance (1941–5), relinquishing this position when he was elected president in 1945, in succession to Douglas Hyde. Returned to the presidency without opposition in 1952, he was succeeded by de Valera on the latter's retirement as taoiseach in 1959. He died in Dublin on 23 November 1966.

O'Kelly, Seumas (?1875–1918). Playwright and fiction writer. He was born near Loughrea, Co. Galway, and, although he had minimal formal education, he became editor of the *Leinster Leader*, which he took over when his brother was arrested in 1916. He also took over the editorship of *Nationality*, replacing Arthur GRIFFITH when he was deported in 1918. It was in the premises of *Nationality* that he died, after the invasion of the office by British soldiers and their wives celebrating the Armistice by attacking SINN FÉINers. O'Kelly wrote two novels, *The Lady of Deerpark* (1917) and *Wet Clay* (1922), which are very much melodramas of their time, a children's book, *The Leprechaun of Kilmeen* (1920), and several plays for the ABBEY THEATRE, including *The Shuiler's Child* (1909). His masterpiece – which when adapted as a play for radio by Mícheál Ó hAodha won the Prix Italia in 1961 and was later filmed for television – was the novella *The Weaver's Grave* (1919), which shares the theme of 'The Widow of Ephesus' by Petronius Arbiter (d. AD 65).

The widow was left alone with the other grave-digger. He drew himself up out of the pit with a sinuous movement of his body which the widow noted. He stood without a word beside the pile of heaving clay and looked across at the widow.

She looked back at him and suddenly the silence became full of unspoken words, of flying, ringing emotions.

The Weaver's Grave (1919)

Olaf Cuarán. *See* MALACHY, HIGH KING OF IRELAND.

Olcott, Chauncey. *See* 'MY WILD IRISH ROSE'.

Old-age pension. The Old Age Pensions Act of 1908, during the premiership of Herbert Asquith, introduced the first non-contributory pension to Ireland. Administered by the Local Government Board, it gave a means-tested pension of five shillings a week to those over the age of 70. As many people at the time did not know their age, claimants' bona fides were established by asking them if they remembered the night of the BIG WIND of 1839. In the austerity budget of 1932 minister for finance Ernest BLYTHE, took a shilling off the (already modest) old-age pension: this measure was popularly believed to have cost CUMANN NA NGAEDHEAL the general election of that year.

'Old Bog Road, The.' A noted song of exile, popular on both sides of the Atlantic. The author, Teresa Brayton, had experience of exile, for though she was born near Cloncurry, Co. Kildare, in 1868 and qualified as a teacher, she lived for many years in America. She managed to visit Ireland during the years leading up to the Easter Rising and was a personal friend of Patrick PEARSE. She died in Co. Wicklow in the 1920s.

> My feet are here on Broadway this blessed harvest morn,
> But O the ache that's in them for the spot where I was born.
> My weary hands are blistered from work in cold and heat
> And O to swing a scythe today thro' fields of Irish wheat.

Old English. The name applied to the descendants of the Anglo-Norman conquerors of Ireland (*see* STRONGBOW). These descendants tended to think of themselves as English people who happened to be born in Ireland. They were mainly Palesmen (*see* PALE, THE)

– those who lived in the safety of the fortified counties of English rule (Dublin, Kildare, Meath and Louth) – and the burgers of the various towns, like Cork and Galway, which they had helped to foster. They were loyal to the English throne and to the Catholic faith, and this presented them with a serious dilemma after Henry VIII's break with Rome. Their position was gradually eroded by the coming of the 'New English' – Protestant, arriviste and, like most Tudors in Ireland, ruthless in their methods. The distinction between the Old and the New English gradually weakened during the CONFEDERATE WAR, and by the time of the Restoration of Charles II it had lost a great deal of its significance.

Old fellow, the (also **the auld** or **ould fella**). An informal but not necessarily disrespectful Dublin manner of referring to one's father. 'Old lady' is also used of an elderly female parent.

Old God's time. An expression indicating a period beyond memory, as in:

> Royal Dublin Fusiliers, the old Toughs. Joined up in old God's time.
>
> JAMIE O'NEILL: *At Swim Two Boys* (2001)

Old IRA. The name given to members of the IRA who fought in the Anglo-Irish War of 1919–21, as opposed to those involved in the movement after the foundation of the Free State, during CIVIL WAR, the EMERGENCY, the BORDER CAMPAIGN or the Northern TROUBLES since 1969. The FIANNA FÁIL government eventually made available an 'IRA pension' to needy elderly veterans, leading inevitably (there being little documentation relating to the activities of the Anglo-Irish War) to allegations that there were many undeserving recipients.

Old Ironsides. The nickname given to the USS *Constitution* after its fight with the British ship HMS *Guerrière* on 19 August 1812. Though the *Guerrière* was wrecked, the *Constitution* sustained so little damage that she was called 'Old Ironsides' thereafter. In time, and inevitably, the nickname was also applied to its famous skipper, Commodore Charles Stewart who lived to be 91.

See also I'LL PUT YOU ALL ON BOARD AGAIN!

Old lady. *See* OLD FELLOW, THE.

Old Lady, the. The mildly disrespectful but affectionate appellation used by the members of the ABBEY THEATRE staff and company for Lady GREGORY.

Old Lady of d'Olier Street. *See* OLD LADY OF WESTMORELAND STREET.

Old Lady of Westmoreland Street. The nickname of *The* IRISH TIMES, a newspaper perceived as being reliable, stable and respectable, until the 1940s. The address of the newspaper is now d'Olier Street, the former rear entrance, so the nickname has changed to 'Old Lady of d'Olier Street'. The nickname is now used only occasionally.

Old Lady Says No!, The. A satirical play by Denis JOHNSTON (1901–84). It uses many lines of HIBERNO-ENGLISH drama and poetry that had formed part of the oral treasury of 19th-century Ireland to satirize the unheroic and hypocritical Free State of the 1920s. The play, originally called *Shadowdance*, begins with a melodrama about Robert EMMET in which the actor playing the hero is concussed and wanders out, still in character and in costume, into the unromantic Dublin of the 1920s. The play was first offered to the ABBEY THEATRE but returned with the pencilled comment that became its new title. The insistent story that the old lady in question was Lady GREGORY (nicknamed the Old Lady) has never been disproved, and it was exactly the kind of play that the partners of the GATE THEATRE were looking for. Its production in the PEACOCK in 1929 with Mac Liammóir in the lead was to be the first of many.

> Strumpet City in the Sunset …
> Wilful city of savage dreamers
> So old, so rich with memories!

Old Light and New Light. The names applied to rival parties in 18th-century Irish PRESBYTERIANISM. The term originated when members of the liberal Belfast Society were accused by the older Calvinistic ministers of offering 'new light' to the world. For most of the century the New Light subscribers dominated Presbyterian affairs, effectively routing the Old Light adherents of the rigid Westminster formularies. In the early 19th century the liberal New Light ministers became tainted with ARIANISM and were driven out of the synod. The doctrinal controversies were thought to have an element of political rivalry, especially between the rival figures of the liberal Henry MONTGOMERY and the conservative Henry COOKE.

Old Mister Brennan. A character created in the 1990s to advertise Brennan's bread. Mr Brennan, an elderly Dubliner, represented the comfortable traditional values of old Dublin while promoting sliced pan that promised to be 'today's bread today'.

Old Mother Riley. A character devised by Arthur Lucan (1887–1954), whose real name was Arthur Towle, for music-hall and film appearances. Old Mother Riley was a comic Irish washerwoman who permanently wore a ridiculous bonnet on a wig, which was nearly all bun. The act required a great deal of racing about and grotesque bodily positions. The character had a pretty daughter Kitty, played by Lucan's wife, the Dublin-born Kitty McShane (1898–1964). She helped smother his native Lancashire accent with a passable, if unspecific, Hibernian accent. Oral history suggests that the partnership was not especially happy.

Old Pretender, the. The name given to James III (1688–1766), as he legitimately was from 1701, after the death of his father JAMES II. His birth made the prospect of another Catholic king of Britain seem likely, and moves were begun to seek a Protestant king. Many believed that he was not the queen's son but had been smuggled in in a warming pan. (This is thought by some to be the source of the Mother Goose rhyme, 'Hushabye baby'.) His two attempts to recover his throne, in 1708 and 1715, were unsuccessful. The first, which involved a substantial French army with many Irish WILD GEESE officers, was not landed on the orders of the French admiral. The second rising of Scottish Highland Jacobites fizzled out after the indecisive battle at Sheriffmuir, Perthshire on 15 November 1715. Known dismissively by non-Jacobites as the 'Pretender', from the French *prétendre* ('to claim as a right'), James did not become the 'Old' until the career of Charles Edward his son gave him the nickname of the 'YOUNG PRETENDER'. (Jacobites referred to George I equally dismissively as the 'Elector'.) As James III he reserved the right to appoint Irish bishops.

Old Red Socks. A not entirely vicious appellation applied to a current pope by Ulster Protestants. It used to be part of the vocabulary of the Rev. Ian PAISLEY.

Old Sow. The personification of Ireland, according to Stephen Dedalus in *A PORTRAIT OF THE ARTIST AS A YOUNG MAN*:

– Do you know what Ireland is? asked Stephen with cold violence. Ireland is the old sow that eats her farrow.

Old Toughs, the. *See* NEILL'S BLUE CAPS.

Old Year's Night. An alternative expression for New Year's Eve, no longer current but still heard occasionally.

O'Leary, John (1830–1907). Nationalist. He was born on 27 July 1830 in Co. Tipperary and gave up law studies at Trinity College Dublin when he realized that barristers had to swear allegiance to the British crown before they could practise. He later abandoned medical studies at Cork and Galway. Initial brushes with the police as a member of YOUNG IRELAND led to a short spell in Clonmel jail, and he was obvious FENIAN material, though in fact he never took the oath. In 1863 he became editor of the Fenian journal, the *Irish People*. He was arrested as a subversive in 1865 and served 9 years of a 20-year sentence, agreeing to exile for the reminder of the sentence. He returned to Dublin in 1885 and became literary mentor to a group of young people including W.B. YEATS and Katharine TYNAN. His reminiscences were published as *Recollections of Fenians and Fenianism* in 1896. He died in Dublin on 16 March 1907.

We hear constantly of the dimunition of disaffection in Ireland, and even of late we have been hearing of the growth of affection, but all that is very idle talk. Disaffected we have been, disaffected we are, and disaffected we shall remain, till the English let go their grip of us.
Recollections of Fenians and Fenianism (1896)

Romantic Ireland's dead and gone,
It's with O'Leary in the grave.
W.B. YEATS: 'September 1913', in *Responsibilities* (1914)

O'Leary, Johnny (1923–2004). Traditional musician. An ACCORDION player usually known as 'Johnny Leary' from the SLIABH LUACHRA area on the borders of counties Kerry and Cork, he learned his music from his uncle, Dan O'Leary, and from fiddle master Pádraig O'KEEFFE. He played with fiddler Denis Murphy (DENIS THE WEAVER) in Gneeveguilla in the early years of his career and again on a regular basis in Dan Connell's pub in Knocknagree from 1965 until Murphy's early death in 1974. He continued to play for weekly set dances in Dan Connell's until shortly before his death in February 2004.

'Oliver's Advice'. The best-known – perhaps the only read – Orange ballad by William Blacker (1777–1858), in which he applies Cromwell's supposed military advice to the Ulster of his time, after the fracas at DOLLY'S BRAE. The story has it that during his Irish campaign Cromwell, while urging his platoon across a stream to engage the enemy, advised them to trust in God but to make sure to keep their gunpowder dry. Blacker was born in Carrickblacker, near Portadown, Co. Armagh, in 1777, the son of a yeomanry captain, and educated at Trinity College Dublin. Tradition places him at the Battle of the DIAMOND (1795), and much of his life was spent in support of all things Orange, while holding the rank of colonel in the militia. Blacker's verse-sequence *Ardmagh* (1848) purported to tell the story of Armagh Cathedral from earliest times.

Characteristically his attitude to the Great Famine was that its source was 'the Lord's correcting hand'. He died in 1858.

> For 'happy homes', for 'altars free', we grasp the ready sword –
> For freedom, truth and for our God's unmutilated word.
> These, these the war-cry of our march, our hope the Lord on high;
> Then put your trust in God, my boys, and keep your powder dry.
>
> 'Oliver's Advice' (1849)

Ó Lochlainn, Colm. *See* THREE CANDLES PRESS.

Ó Loinsigh, Labhraí. A HIGH KING of legend who has donkey's ears. Afraid to reveal his secret, he has all the barbers who cut his hair killed, until one day a young boy comes to cut his hair. When the boy pleads for his life the king spares him on condition that he tells his secret to no one. The boy keeps his promise but, burdened by the secret, whispers it to a tree one day. The story of the king's ears spreads on a sighing of the leaves and the singing of the wind, and when the king himself hears it he realizes that it would be better for him and his subjects if he no longer hid the truth about his donkey's ears. This myth is associated with the beautiful setting of Loughine, an inland salt lake near Skibbereen in Co. Cork. *See also* LABRAID LOINSEACH.

Omagh (Irish *An Ómaigh*, 'the virgin plain'). The county town of Tyrone, with a population of 17,300 (1991). It was the scene of the worst atrocity of the Northern Ireland TROUBLES.

Omagh Bomb. An attack by the REAL IRA on the Co. Tyrone town during Civic Week on 15 August 1998, when a car bomb exploded without warning, killing 28 people and wounding 310 (a 29th victim died later). The effect was to accelerate the peace process and to cause all but the CONTINUITY IRA to declare a ceasefire. In spite of a massive investigation on both sides of the border no one has been arrested for the atrocity.

O'Mahony, John. *See* FENIANS; STEPHENS, JAMES KENNETH.

O'Malley, Des. *See* CONDUCT UNBECOMING; PEE DEES; REYNOLDS, ALBERT; TEMPORARY LITTLE ARRANGEMENT.

O'Malley, Donogh. *See* CAMORRA, THE; FREE EDUCATION; TACA.

O'Malley, Ernie (1898–1957). Republican. He was born in Castlebar, Co. Mayo, but the family moved to Dublin when he was eight and he was educated at O'Connell's Schools and University College Dublin (UCD), where he studied medicine. He participated in the EASTER RISING and was interned. During the ANGLO-IRISH WAR of 1919–21 he acted as an organizer for the IRA, and saw action in several regions, including counties Tipperary and Kilkenny. He was imprisoned for three months in 1920–1, but never revealed his identity; as soon as he escaped from prison he took charge of the Second Southern Division. *On Another Man's Wound* (1936) is his account of the period 1916–21, and is regarded as the finest work to emerge from those particular Troubles.

O'Malley opposed the TREATY, and was responsible for detonating the explosion that destroyed the public records office in the FOUR COURTS at the beginning of the CIVIL WAR. During the Civil War he was appointed assistant chief-of-staff of the ANTI-TREATYITES and imprisoned in MOUNTJOY JAIL (November 1922–July 1924). Wounds incurred in the fighting and a long hunger strike in 1923 undermined his health, but he recovered and lived abroad, in Spain and America, from 1924 to 1935. A sequel to his first book, *The Singing Flame*, dealing with the Civil War, was published posthumously in 1978. His papers, a valuable resource for students of the period, are held at UCD. There is a study of O'Malley by Richard English, *Ernie O'Malley: IRA Intellectual* (1998).

O'Malley, Grace. *See* GRANUAILE.

O'Malley, Tony (1913–2003). Artist. A self-taught painter who became one of the leading Irish artists of the late 20th century, he was born in Callan, Co. Kilkenny, on 23 September 1913. After leaving school he joined the Munster and Leinster Bank and worked in provincial towns in Ireland from 1933 to 1958, painting in his spare time – despite an atmosphere he described as 'suffocating', lack of congenial company and several bouts of TB in the 1940s. From 1955 he spent holidays painting in Cornwall, where he formed relationships with other artists and found creative freedom for the first time, and, having retired from the bank on health grounds in 1958, he lived there permanently from 1960. He and his artist wife returned to live near Callan in 1990. In 1993 he was elected SAOI of AOSDÁNA, and was awarded many public honours before his death.

Ó Maoileoin, Pádraig. *See* LÁ BREÁ.

O'More, Rory (*fl.*1620–52). Leader of the REBELLION OF 1641. An army officer, he was descended from the Gaelic kings of Co. Laois. Because of his marriage to a member of the family of Sir Patrick BARNEWALL, he was a bridge between the Irish and the OLD ENGLISH in the CONFEDERATE WAR. It was he who commanded the Ulster army in the successful engagement at Julianstown on 29 November 1641, and he subsequently negotiated the alliance with the Old English of the Pale. A commander during the subsequent war, he was last seen when making his escape to an island off the west coast after the Irish defeat.

Ó Muircheartaigh, Mícheál. Radio and television sports commentator. He was born in Dingle, Co. Kerry, and educated at St Patrick's College, Dublin. He worked as a primary school teacher in Dublin, commentating for RTÉ radio on a part-time basis from 1949, and full-time from the early 1980s. He succeeded Mícheál O'HEHIR as the media voice of the GAA, being associated in particular with the football championship matches. His trademark style is bilingual in English and Irish, and he is famous for his digressive remarks:

Pat Fox out to the forty and grabs the sliotar, I

bought a dog from his father last week. Fox turns and sprints for goal, the dog ran a great race last Tuesday in Limerick. Fox to the 21 fires a shot, it goes to the left and wide … and the dog lost as well. …

Sean Óg Ó hAilpín … his father's from Fermanagh, his mother's from Fiji, neither a hurling stronghold.

… and Brian Dooher is down injured. And while he is, I'll tell ye a little story. I was in Times Square in New York last week, and I was missing the championship back home. So I approached a newsstand and I said, 'I suppose ye wouldn't have the *Kerryman*, would ye?' At which the Egyptian behind the counter turned to me and he said, 'Do you want the north Kerry edition or the south Kerry edition?' He had both so I bought both. And Dooher is back on his feet …

Ó Muirgheasa, Énrí (1874–1975). Folklorist. He was born in Co. Monaghan and educated at St Patrick's College in Dublin. While working as a primary teacher and later as a schools inspector he collected folklore and folksongs, and encouraged others to do likewise; he did valuable work among some of the last native Irish speakers in parts of Ulster. His published collections include *Céad de Cheoltaibh Uladh* (*A Hundred Ulster Songs*, 1915) and *Dánta Diadha Uladh* (*Religious Songs of Ulster*, 1936). His extensive manuscript collection is housed in the Department of Irish Folklore, University College Dublin.

On. A part of a phrase indicating that someone has finally and perhaps not very tidily got dressed, as in 'Have you not on you, yet?', 'Get on you!' Another common associated phrase is 'I pulled on me', meaning 'I got dressed', perhaps in a hurry.

One and one. A bag of chips and a portion of fish, bought in a chip shop and pronounced 'wan and wan'. The term is said to derive from the Italian *uno e uno*, shorthand for *uno di questo, uno di quello* ('one of this – chips, one of that – fish') used by staff in the immigrant chip shops of the later 19th century. *See also* LIFFEY; SINGLE.

'One Day for Recreation'. A celebrated MACA-RONIC courting song from the Killarney area (local placenames Clydagh and Muckross are mentioned), in which the ardent wooer discovers that his young love is the daughter of a minister and 'a pupil of Jack Lahey's':

One day for recreation,
Is gan éinne beo i m' chuideachta,
I spied a charming fair maid
'Na haonar is í i siopa istigh.
She was singing like an angel
'S mé ag éisteacht lena binneghuth
I whispered soft and aisy
'Sé dúirt sí stad den radaireacht.
(One day for recreation,
When there was no one with me,
I spied a charming fair maid
All alone in a shop.
She was singing like an angel,
I was listening to her sweet soft voice,
I whispered soft and aisy
She said to me to stop my flirting.)

One for everyone in the audience. A saying by Gay BYRNE, host of *The LATE LATE SHOW*, that became something of a catchphrase. The show became increasingly commercial, involving itself in promoting personalities and products – so giveaways of products and services were part of the experience for the studio audience.

One-handled adulterer. The description by Stephen Dedalus in the 'Aeolus' episode of ULYSSES of Admiral Horatio Nelson (1758–1805), who once stood atop NELSON'S PILLAR in Dublin's O'Connell Street. Nelson lost his right arm in 1796 at Santa Cruz, and after the Battle of the Nile in 1798 became the lover of Emma Hamilton (*c.*1761–1815), the wife of Sir William Hamilton (1730–1803), the British ambassador to Naples.

– And settle down on their striped petticoats, peering up at the statue of the onehandled adulterer.
– One handled adulterer! the professor cried. I like that. I see the idea. I see what you mean.
JAMES JOYCE (1882–1941): *Ulysses* (1922)

O'Neill, Captain Francis (1848–1936). Collector and publisher of traditional Irish music. He was born near Bantry in Co. Cork, and after several years of travel and adventure joined the police force in Chicago, rising to become general superintendent of police in that city (1901–05). He began a project to write down tunes which he and a colleague collected from immigrants from all parts of Ireland. In 1903 he published *The Music of Ireland*, a major collection of 1850 tunes, classified according to type; in 1907 *The Dance Music of Ireland – 1001 Gems* appeared. Among his other publications are *Irish Minstrels and Musicians* (1913), a directory of musicians.

O'Neill, Hugh, 2nd Earl of Tyrone (*c.*1550–1616). Gaelic leader during the TUDOR RECONQUEST. He was born in Dungannon, the stronghold of the O'Neills, and raised in the Pale after the death of his father Matthew in 1558. At first he remained loyal to the crown, who used him to curb the power of Turlough Luineach O'Neill, another Gaelic chieftain, but he gradually increased his own power and influence, achieving domination in Ulster with the help of his son-in-law Red Hugh O'DONNELL. In 1591 he eloped with Mabel Bagenal, sister of Henry BAGENAL, but this attempt to form an alliance with the New English misfired when Bagenal refused to pay Mabel's dowry, and O'Neill was soon unfaithful to his new wife.

The conflict known as the NINE YEARS' WAR (1594–1603) was slow to ignite, and during the early years O'Neill managed to retain an appearance of loyalty to Elizabeth while training his armies in the fastness of Ulster. Tyrone, as he was called by the English, was an able, astute politician and a brilliant military tactician, exploiting the boggy and wooded terrain of his province to his advantage. The English administration feared the loss of Ireland, especially after the Battle of the YELLOW FORD, and the prosecution of the war was proving ruinous to the exchequer. There is some evidence that O'Neill saw himself as a defender of Catholicism: he tried unsuccessfully to enlist the support of the OLD ENGLISH of the Pale in a Counter-Reformation crusade – but this was not to come about until a generation later (*see* O'NEILL, OWEN RUA).

After the defeat at the Battle of KINSALE, O'Neill made peace with Lord Deputy MOUNTJOY at MELLIFONT in 1603, and left Ireland with his followers in what is known as the FLIGHT OF THE EARLS in 1609. He never returned to Ireland, and died in Rome in 1616.

O'Neill, Máire. *See* ALLGOOD, MOLLY.

O'Neill, Moira. The pseudonym of the poet [Agnes] Nesta Skrine (née Higginson, 1865–1955). She was born in Cushendun at the foot of one of the Nine Glens of Antrim, which were the inspiration for her popular two-volume *Songs of the Glens of Antrim* (1901, 1921). She was the mother of the writer Molly KEANE.

O'Neill, Owen Rua (*c*.1582–1649). Gaelic leader of the CONFEDERATE CATHOLIC army during the CONFEDERATE WAR. A nephew of Hugh O'NEILL, Owen Rua had a successful career in the Spanish army in the Netherlands, distinguishing himself especially in the defence of Arras, besieged by the French in 1540. After the beginning of the REBELLION OF 1641 he returned to Ireland to fight for his patrimony and for the Catholic religion, and was appointed general in place of Phelim O'Neill by an assembly of Ulster Irish. In November 1642 he swore the oath of confederacy in Kilkenny, and put together a strong army, with which he won the Battle of BENBURB on 5 June 1643.

Like Hugh O'Neill after the Battle of the YELLOW FORD, Owen Rua did not press home his advantage, nor did he cooperate well with the OLD ENGLISH generals, Preston and Castlehaven. With the support of Papal Nuncio Rinuccini, he opposed the first peace with ORMOND in 1646, and again sided with Rinuccini in accepting a controversial truce with Murrough O'Brien, Earl of Inchiquin (*see* MURROUGH OF THE BURNINGS). In 1649, after the victory of Parliament in the English Civil War and the departure of Rinuccini, he

finally committed his army to an alliance with Ormond, but a month later, on 6 October 1649, he died in Clogh Oughter Castle in Co. Cavan while on his way south to joint Ormond's forces. Cromwell had arrived in Dublin in August 1649 and was already on his way to total domination of the country, but in Nationalist history the death of Owen Rua at his crucial juncture has always been seen as a cruel twist of fate:

> Wail, wail for him through the Island! Weep, weep for our pride!
> Would that on the battle-field our gallant chief had died!
> Weep the Victor of Benburb – Weep him, young men and old;
> Weep for him, ye women – your Beautiful lies cold!
> We had thought you would not die – we were sure you would not go,
> And leave us in our utmost need to Cromwell's cruel blow.
> Sheep without the shepherd, when the snow shuts out the sky –
> Oh! why did you leave us, Eoghan! – why did you die?
>> THOMAS DAVIS (1814–45): 'Lament for the Death of Eoghan Ruadh O'Neill', in *The Poems of Thomas Davis* (1846)

O'Neill, P. The name used on all statements issued by the Provisional IRA since the creation of that organization in 1970, whether justifying or threatening attacks or even on occasion expressing regret at unintended fatalities or injuries. It is thought that the name was invented by the then chief-of-staff, Seán MAC STIOFÁIN. With the development of the peace process the tone of the statements has become more conciliatory, and as the IRA stance on decommissioning and future violence is crucial to the process, a great deal of attention is paid to them by media and politicians alike. To date the British government and northern Unionists have wanted more clarity from P. O'Neill than he appears willing to supply. A statement in July 2002 apologized for killing innocent civilians:

The future will not be found in denying collective failures and mistakes or closing minds and hearts to the plight of those who have been hurt.

O'Neill, Shane (*c*.1530–67). Ulster chieftain, known as Seán an Díomais ('Shane the Proud'). As the eldest legitimate son of Conn O'Neill (*c*.1484–*c*.1559), 1st Earl of Tyrone, he declared himself The O'Neill in 1559, having killed his half-brother Matthew, who had been nominated as heir by his father. In 1562 he persuaded Elizabeth I to recognize his hegemony, and when his exotic entourage arrived in London she greeted him as 'Captain of Tyrone'. The maintenance of the 'captaincy' meant that the remaining years of his life were spent in the field against the other Ulster chiefs, plundering the territories of Fermanagh, Cavan and Armagh. He attacked the PALE, starved Sorley Boy MACDONNELL into submission at Dunluce Castle in 1565 on the north coast, and attacked the Scots settlements on the northeast coast. He was defeated at Farsetmore, in the sloblands of Lough Swilly, by the O'Donnells in 1567, with many of his men being drowned by the incoming tide. In desperation he threw himself on the mercy of his old enemies the MacDonnells at Cushendun, Co. Antrim, perhaps believing that his holding of Sorley Boy as hostage would save him. The MacDonnells murdered him at a feast given in his honour on 2 June 1567, more because of collusion with Lord Deputy Sidney (1529–86) than out of ancient revenge.

O'Neill, Terence (1914–90). Northern Ireland premier. He was born on 10 September 1914, the son of the member for Mid-Antrim, who was the first Westminster MP killed in the First World War, when Terence was only three months old. Educated at Eton, he served in the Irish Guards in the Second World War (in which both his elder brothers were killed) and was elected to the STORMONT Parliament (1946–70). He served as finance minister (1956–63) and then replaced Lord BROOKEBOROUGH as prime minister.

From the start of his premiership O'Neill was anxious to improve community relations, and set the province on the path of economic recovery. He realized that economic cooperation with the Republic of Ireland was desirable, and caused a sensation when he invited Sean LEMASS to Stormont on 14 January 1965 and went himself to Dublin on 9 February. This was followed after Lemass's death by mutual visits with Jack Lynch in 1967 and 1968. The effect was to stir up the worst of extreme Unionist recalcitrance, now with a charismatic and adamantine young leader, the Rev. Ian PAISLEY.

The CIVIL RIGHTS campaign, which began in 1968, led to O'Neill's offer of a five-point plan of political reform. A snap general election called in February 1969 did not provide him with the mandate that he had hoped for, and facing mounting Unionist opposition he resigned on 28 April 1969. He was made a life peer in 1970, taking his title – Lord O'Neill of the Maine – from a river in his Bannside constituency. He died in Lymington, Hampshire, on 12 June 1990. He was not the first to underestimate the resolute nature of Unionist absoluteness, and his detached paternalism pleased no one.

I have tried to break the chains of ancient hatreds. I have been unable to realize during my period of office all that I sought to achieve. Whether now it can be achieved in my lifetime I do not know. But one day these things will be and must be achieved.
Television resignation address, 28 April 1969

One-line railway. The name applied with slight inaccuracy to the Listowel and Ballybunion railway that covered the 15 km (9 miles) between the two Kerry towns from 1888 to 1924. The monorail (or more accurately three-rail) system was patented by Charles Lartigue, a Frenchman. It was the only Lartigue railway that was in service commercially (another was built in France but never used). It was inspired by Lartigue's observation of camels in Algeria carrying heavy loads in panniers. Trestles carried a single rail at waist height on which carriages were balanced; special bridges were built to carry roads over the line as level crossings were not possible. The system was cheap to lay because it did not need a heavy bed for the track, but intersections were rather more expensive. The railway was noisy, uncomfortable – pitching from side to side like a camel – and slow, taking 40 minutes to travel between Ballybunion and Listowel. It used to be said that, in the event of difficulties, first-class kept their seats, second-class got out and walked, and third-class pushed. The 'Lartigue', as it was called, never paid, being in financial trouble from as early as 1897, but it was an object of curiosity to visitors. The line was damaged during the CIVIL WAR and the railway closed in 1924. Enthusiasts recently rebuilt a short stretch of the Lartigue line and commissioned a special locomotive.

One man – one vote. The demand of the Northern Ireland Civil Rights Association (NICRA) in 1966–9 for universal suffrage and abolition of the multiple franchise enjoyed by certain businesses in local-government elections. *See also* CIVIL RIGHTS MOVEMENT.

One satiric touch. A part of Swift's (*see* DEAN, THE) legacy to his country, expressed poetically:

> He gave what little wealth he had
> To build a house for fools and mad:
> And showed by one satiric touch
> No nation wanted it so much.
> 'Verses on the Death of Dr Swift' (1739)

The 'house' is St Patrick's Hospital in Bow Lane, Dublin, built 1749–57 and now an important psychiatric centre with a fine collection of Swiftiana and other 18th-century memorabilia.

One wing. *See* BIRD NEVER FLEW ON ONE WING, A.

One word borrowed another. A phrase used in HIBERNO-ENGLISH to indicate a situation of unintended verbal conflict. It means that one word led to another, with the result that the speaker went much further than he had in-

tended, for instance along the road of confrontation with a neighbour.

O'Nolan, Brian. *See* O'BRIEN, FLANN.

On the blanket. *See* BLANKET PROTEST.

On the lump. Working 'on the lump' was the term used by Irish NAVVIES in Britain for doing casual work for cash, without paying tax or a stamp. Many Irishmen spent a lifetime on the lump, 'following the work' around Britain, exploited by unscrupulous contractors, some of them also Irish. This meant that they had no security, health-and-safety protection, insurance or social-welfare entitlements; the short-term advantage for the men was that they received their pay without deductions, although this advantage was often more apparent than real. They often received their pay in a pub; another reason for the drink problems common among the Irish immigrant community in Britain.

On the run. A phrase (used particularly since the outbreak of the TROUBLES in Northern Ireland) to describe the situation of an individual wanted by the police under suspicion of having committed terrorist offences, and who has to resort to hiding in various places outside his own home or even outside the jurisdiction. The phrase was also used during the Anglo-Irish War of 1919–21: all guerrilla fighters were permanently on the run and sometimes had to stay hidden for several week to avoid the reprisals of the BLACK AND TANS or AUXIES.

On the sick. A Dublin colloquialism for being in receipt of sickness or disability benefit from the Department of Social Welfare, whether for a real or pretended illness.

Ooh Ah! Paul McGrath! The chant of soccer supporters for Paul McGrath (b.1959), Irish international soccer player and popular personality. McGrath was born in Middlesex of an Irish mother and a Nigerian father and grew up in Co. Dublin. In 1982 he signed for Manchester United from St Patrick's Athletic, a Dublin club, and later played for Aston Villa, Derby County and Sheffield United. He first played for the Republic of Ireland in 1985, and a member of the World Cup squad in 1990 and 1994, in all winning 83 caps for Ireland before he retired from international football in 1997. Although he normally played in defence, he scored eight goals for Ireland. McGrath won general respect and sympathy by speaking in public about his alcoholism and by devoting time to philanthropic work.

Operation Green (German *Der Fall Grün*). The Nazi plan to invade Ireland during the Second World War. The German plan consisted of an invasion of southern Ireland (suggested by Hitler to coincide with the 25th anniversary of the Easter Rising) after an invasion of Northern Ireland. The west coast of Britain would then have been vulnerable. The British had contingency plans to occupy the TREATY PORTS by force if necessary. *Der Fall Grün* was shelved because of the invasion of Russia in 1941.

Operation Harvest. *See* BORDER CAMPAIGN.

Operation Motorman. The code name of the operation of the security forces to clear barricades in NO-GO AREAS in Derry and Belfast on 31 July 1972. On that day 1500 troops with armoured cars cleared the Bogside and Creggan areas of Derry, meeting little opposition, although two people were shot by the army. The intention to dismantle such areas had been very well telegraphed, and Republican areas in Belfast made barely a token resistance. Loyalists in Belfast removed their own obstructions, which they claimed with some unction had only been set up in response to Republican barricades.

Opus Dei (Latin, 'the work of God'). A conservative Catholic organization for lay people established in Spain in 1928 by José Maria Escrivá. The movement came to Ireland in 1947. Members, who retain their own work, commit to a routine of prayer and good works, some also committing funds to the organization. In Ireland Opus Dei runs a number of its own schools and university residences for students.

Ó Raifteiri, Antaine. *See* BLIND RAFTERY.

Orange Card. The phrase used by Lord Randolph Churchill (1849–94) in a letter to Lord Justice Fitzgibbon on 16 February 1886 suggesting that the extreme Ulster Protestants, especially those of the ORANGE ORDER, should be used to defeat Gladstone's first Home Rule Bill: 'I decided some time ago that if the GOM went for Home Rule the Orange Card would be the one to play. Please God it may be turn out to be the ace of trumps and not the two.'

Orange juice. The name given to electricity flowing North–South in the cross-border electricity-exchange scheme.
See also PADDY POWER.

Orange lily. A flower that was once part of the regalia of members of the ORANGE ORDER on their walks.

> Then heigho the lily-o,
> The royal, loyal lily-o;
> There's not a flower in Erin's bower
> Can match the Orange lily-o.
> 'The Orange Lily-o' (early 19th century)

Orange Order. A Protestant political society established in 1795 after the Battle of the DIAMOND in Co. Armagh. The first lodge was formed in the inn of James Sloan near Loughgall, and the movement spread rapidly, attracting membership among the yeoman bands and even the gentry. The order was named after William III (KING BILLY), the Dutch Prince of Orange who had supplanted his Catholic father-in-law JAMES II in 1688 and was regarded thereafter as a kind of patron saint of Protestantism. As an aid to secrecy the members joined local lodges known as LOLs (Loyal Orange Lodges), the title LOL 1 being granted to the lodge in Dyan, Co. Armagh, in tribute to the creation there in 1793 of a group known as the Orange Boys.

The Orange Order became a significant element in Irish politics, helping with the brutal suppression of the REBELLION OF 1798 (when there were 470 lodges), but eventually became such an embarrassment to the British authorities that it was suppressed in 1825. It was soon revived with strong support from the Duke of Cumberland, William IV's brother, who was Master of the Grand Lodge of Great Britain, but it dissolved itself in 1836 because of the threat of a coup d'état involving the duke. It reappeared in 1845, and greatly increased its membership at the time of the HOME RULE agitation in the 1880s.

The Order has since been the adamantine backbone of unrelenting Unionism. Its generally triumphalist, often provocative, marches – mainly to celebrate William III's victory over the Jacobites at the Battle of the BOYNE in 1690 – have continued to be a source of affront to Ulster Nationalists (*see* DRUMCREE STANDOFFS; TWELFTH OF JULY). There are now 2000 Irish lodges, including 60 in the Republic, with 80,000 active members. A Grand Orange Council of the World was founded in 1867, and its members in England, Scotland, the USA and throughout the Commonwealth meet every three years.

See also ARCH; BANNER; ORANGE CARD; ORANGE LILY; ORANGE TOAST; PEEP O' DAY BOYS; ROYAL BLACK INSTITUTION; SASH; 'SASH MY FATHER WORE, THE'; SCARVA.

Orange Peel. The nickname imposed upon Sir Robert PEEL by Daniel O'CONNELL at his most effectively vituperative. On 29 May 1813, at a meeting of the Catholic Board (a forerunner of the CATHOLIC ASSOCIATION formed after the suppression of the CATHOLIC COMMITTEE in 1811) he referred to 'Orange Peel' as

> a raw youth [Peel was 27] squeezed out of
> the working of I do not know what factory in
> England [Peel's father was a rich Lancashire
> cotton magnate], who began his parliamentary
> career by vindicating the gratuitous destruction
> of our brave soldiers in the murderous expedition
> to Walcheren [disastrous amphibious attack on
> Antwerp in 1809 to encourage an anti-Napoleon
> rising in Germany, which cost the lives of at least
> 4000 men] and was sent over here before he got
> rid of the foppery of perfumed handkerchiefs and
> thin shoes … a lad ready to vindicate anything,
> everything.

Orange toast. The supposed toast used at early meetings of the ORANGE ORDER, especially at its headquarters in Dublin, and printed in Sir Jonah Barrington's *PERSONAL SKETCHES*:

> The glorious, pious and immortal memory of the
> great and the good King William: – not forgetting
> Oliver Cromwell, who assisted in redeeming
> us from popery, slavery, arbitrary power, brass
> money, and wooden shoes. May we never want
> a Williamite to kick the a**e of a Jacobite! and
> a f**t for the *Bishop of Cork*! And that he won't
> drink this, whether he be priest, bishop, deacon,
> bellows-blower, grave-digger, or any other of the
> fraternity of *the clergy*; may a north wind blow
> him to the south, and a west wind blow him to the
> east! May he have a dark night – a lee shore – a
> rank storm and a leaky vessel, to carry him over
> the river Styx! May the dog Cerberus make a meal
> of his rump, and Pluto a snuff-box of his skull;
> and may the devil jump down his throat with a
> red-hot harrow, with every pin to tear a gut, and
> blow him with a *clean* carcass to hell! *Amen*!

Orange Young Ireland. A joking description applied to such writers as Isaac BUTT and Sir Samuel FERGUSON, Protestant contributors to the *Dublin University Magazine* (1833–77) who cherished cultural aspects of Irish life and heritage and, while strongly defending the Act of UNION, were critical of British mismanagement of Irish affairs. The term alludes to the opposing aspirations of the ORANGE ORDER and YOUNG IRELAND.

Ó Rathaile, Aogán (1675–1729). Irish-language poet. One of the FOUR KERRY POETS and regarded by many as the greatest of all Gaelic poets, he was born at Screathan a' Mhíl in the SLIABH LUACHRA district of east Kerry. He belonged to a family of small landowners that owed fealty to the native chieftains, the MacCarthys, who were supplanted by the JACOBITE Brownes. Much of Ó Rathaile's poetry is the mournful cry of the client who fell with the fall of his master. Frank O'CONNOR, who translated some of his best work, described him as 'one of the great snobs of literature', and certainly '*Vailintín Brún*' ('Valentine Browne'), written in satirical disparagement of his would-be patron, who failed to restore him to his lands when he himself was reinstated, shows considerable disdain from a beggar. But the sense of degradation and the hardship he suffered are the more poignant because he was conscious of his superior education, obtained at what was the period's equivalent of a university at Killarney. '*Mac an Cheannaí*' ('the merchant's son') and '*Gile na Gile*' ('brightness of brightness') are among the finest of all the AISLING poems. It is said that '*Mac an Cheannaí*' is the first *aisling* every written, and for that reason Ó Rathaile is sometimes called 'the father of the *aisling*'. In '*Gile na Gile*', Ireland, more beautiful than any woman, is apostrophized and consoled with the hope of a Jacobite success. Ó Rathaile combined the highest skills of bardic poetry and the conventions of *aisling* and satire with immense rhythmic power and intensity of personal and political feeling. He died in poverty in Corca Dhuibhne (*see* DINGLE PENINSULA) and is buried with his true patrons, the MacCarthys, in MUCKROSS ABBEY in Killarney.

Order of St Patrick. A now defunct order of chivalry established by George III in 1788, with its chapel in ST PATRICK'S CATHEDRAL, Dublin. Since 1922 the only people appointed to the order were the then Prince of Wales and his brother the Duke of Gloucester, the induction being carried out by their father, George V.

Ordnance Survey. The decision to survey Ireland and improve the standard of its mapping arose in the first instance from the need to establish the precise boundaries of the country's *c*.60,000 TOWNLANDS for the purpose of equitable taxation. A scale of six inches to the mile was adopted because of the smallness of these local divisions. The operation was led by Colonel Thomas Colby of the Royal Engineers based in London and his assistant Lieutenant Thomas Larcom, whose headquarters were in PHOENIX PARK. They employed a staff of 2000, which included such scholars as John O'DONOVAN, Eugene O'CURRY, George PETRIE and

Thomas DRUMMOND. Starting with a baseline marked on Magilligan Strand in Co. Derry in 1828 they triangulated the entire country, noting all aspects of topography – rural, urban and archaeological – social conditions and folk practices, and such hitherto ignored repositories of old language as placenames. The translations of these, mainly by O'Donovan, gave an early stimulus to interest in Irish, and provided Brian FRIEL with the theme of one of his finest plays, *TRANSLATIONS* (1980).

O'Reilly, Alexander. *See* BLOODY O'REILLY.

O'Reilly, John Boyle (1844–90). Poet and FENIAN. He was born in Dowth Castle, the son of a schoolmaster, and worked as a printer and journalist in Drogheda before joining the British army in 1863. He was arrested as a Fenian mole and, after much harsh treatment, transported to Australia. He escaped to America and became editor of the *Boston Pilot*, which became a kind of transatlantic version of *The NATION*. He wrote *Moondyne* (1879), a novel about his convict life in Australia, and many patriotic ballads and love lyrics. A witty liberal, he opposed anti-Semitism and racial prejudice against Afro-Americans and could rely on regular contributions to the *Pilot* from Douglas HYDE, T.W. ROLLESTON, Katharine TYNAN and W.B. YEATS. He died in Boston Harbour in August 1890, from an accidental overdose of chloral, taken for chronic insomnia.

> 'You gave me the key of your heart, my love;
> Then why did you make me knock?'
> 'Oh that was yesterday, saints above!
> And last night – I changed the lock!'
>   'Constancy' (1878)

O'Reilly, Private Myles. *See* HALPINE, CHARLES.

O'Reilly, Tony (b.1936). Rugby player, businessman and philanthropist. He was born in Dublin and educated at Belvedere, University College and Trinity College Dublin, playing school and club rugby and winning 29 international caps between 1955 and 1970. He first showed entrepreneurial talent as managing director of

Bord Bainne, the Irish dairy (literally 'milk') board, later becoming president and chief executive of the Heinz Corporation at its US headquarters, a post he held until 1998. He is chairman of Independent Newspapers, which owns the *Independent* and *Herald* titles in Dublin (*see* IRISH INDEPENDENT, THE), and has numerous other business, media and telecommunications interests. As chairman of the Ireland funds of the USA, Canada, Britain and several European countries he has been involved in funding community and cultural projects north and south of the border. He also endowed the O'Reilly Institute for Computer Science at Trinity College Dublin.

Ó Riada, Seán (1931–71). Composer, teacher, and musician. He was born John Reidy in Adare, Co. Limerick, but during his final years became identified with the GAELTACHT area of Cúil Aodha in west Cork. He taught in the Department of Music at University College Cork, and is remembered particularly for his sweeping orchestral scores for the films MISE ÉIRE and *Saoirse,* and for his *Mass* in Irish, which was based on traditional tunes and is widely sung by congregrations throughout Ireland to this day. He also famously arranged 'The Banks of My Own Lovely Lee' (*see* 'BANKS, THE') for orchestra for a Radio Cork celebration of the Munster city in 1958. Ó Riada was an iconic figure, symbolizing a new national pride and self-esteem in the 1960s, and he made a significant contribution to the development of traditional Irish music by bringing the techniques of jazz and classical music to bear on his arrangements.
See also CEOLTÓIRÍ CHUALANN.

Ó Ríordáin, Seán (1917–77). Irish-language poet. He was born in Ballyvourney in west Cork, at that time a GAELTACHT area, but moved with his family to Iniscarra, nearer to Cork city, when he was a teenager. He worked in an administrative capacity for Cork Corporation from 1937, but he suffered from ill-health, including the TB which he contracted while still a young man, and retired early from his position in 1965. His first collection, *Eireaball Spideoige* ('a robin's tail', 1952), broke new ground in Irish poetry with its tone of isolated personal inquiry (often *angst*), its obsessive search for an authentic language and its broad philosophical speculations married to a deep attachment to the integrity of the Gaelic tradition. Further collections enhanced Ó Ríordáin's reputation as both a poet and a highly original thinker; these included *Brosna* ('twigs', 1964), *Línte Liombó* (1976) and *Tar Éis Mo Bháis* ('after my death', 1978), published posthumously. A collected poems, *cáthán Véarsaí,* was published in 1980. Ó Ríordáin was a major poet; his integrity evidenced by everything he wrote. He was also a long-standing columnist for the *Irish Times.*

Ormond. An ancient territory of eastern Munster, and the title taken by the Anglo-Norman family of Butler. The name Butler itself originated in the French word *botellier* – butler or wine-opener – an office held by Theobald Walter in the 12th century. The family grew steadily in importance, receiving grants of land in Tipperary, Kilkenny, north Munster and parts of south Leinster and the title Earl of Ormond in 1329. In 1391 they acquired Kilkenny Castle, their main seat, but there is also a surviving Butler castle in Cahir, Co. Tipperary, and an Elizabethan manor, called castle, in Carrick-on-Suir in the same county. In the 15th century the 3rd and 4th Earls of Ormond, both called James, acted as the king's lieutenants and held other important administrative roles, effectively being allowed to rule Ireland, although the 4th Earl found a bitter enemy in Richard TALBOT. James Butler (1610–88), 12th Earl and 1st Duke of ORMOND, was the most influential Irishman of his day.

Ormond, James Butler, 12th Earl and 1st Duke of (1610–88). Royalist lord lieutenant of Ireland (1644–50, 1662–9 and 1677–85). He was reared a Protestant and married the heiress to the estates of another branch of the Ormonds, Elizabeth Preston. A protégé of

Thomas WENTWORTH, Ormond commanded the army in Ireland when he was only 30. After Wentworth's execution Ormond was appointed lord lieutenant in 1644, the first Irishman to hold this post since the rebellion of SILKEN THOMAS. He was head of the king's army in Ireland during the REBELLION OF 1641 and the CONFEDERATE WAR, but he made no concessions to Catholics until the second Ormond Peace of 1649, after Charles I had been defeated in the English Civil War (*see* O'NEILL, OWEN RUA). Ormond too was defeated at the Battle of RATHMINES in August 1649, and in December 1650 he left Ireland, following Charles II into exile. After the Restoration the Butler lands that had been confiscated (some were left in his wife's possession in Kilkenny) were restored to Ormond and he was made a duke. As lord lieutenant again he imposed the Restoration settlement in Ireland, satisfying neither the Catholics who wanted their lands restored nor the Cromwellian adventurers who faced losing some of the land they had been given. Ormond knew that it was impossible to satisfy all the parties that were clamouring for redress, and he concentrated most of all on serving his own interests. In his final period as lord lieutenant he laid out ST STEPHEN'S GREEN in Dublin and commissioned the ROYAL HOSPITAL in Kilmainham.

Orpen, Sir William (1878–1931). Painter. He was born in Stillorgan, Dublin, on 27 November 1878 and, showing an early promise in drawing, attended the Dublin Metropolitan School of Art from the age of 13 and the Slade from 17. Elected an associate member of the Royal Academy (1910) he soon became one of the most fashionable and wealthy portrait painters of the day. He also painted lyrically erotic nudes, noted for their humanity as well as their sensuality, especially *A Woman* (1906), *Early Morning* (1925) and *Sunlight* (*c*.1925). He moved freely between Britain and Ireland, finding time in spite of many society commissions for the strange canvas *The Holy Well*, one of the quixotic glories of the National Gallery of Ireland. He became a bitterly effective war artist in 1917, and was an official pictorial recorder of the peace conference at Versailles (1919). He was made a KBE in 1918 and an RA in 1921. His later years were darkened by drink and the sense of a lost pleasure in work that while still expert had become mechanical. He died in London on 29 September 1931, having written two volumes of reminiscence, *An Onlooker in France (1917–1919)* (1921) and *Stories of Old Ireland and Myself* (1924).

> ... old Ireland that Romantic Lady who slumbered and dreamt her way along to the music of the laughter and tears of her people.
> *Stories of Old Ireland and Myself* (1924)

OS (Irish *oide scoile*, 'schoolteacher'). A courtesy title used by the authorities for communication with primary teachers.
See also NT.

Osborne, Walter (1859–1903). Painter. He was born at 5 Castlewood Avenue, Rathmines, Dublin, on 18 June 1859 and educated at the Royal Hibernian Academy and Metropolitan School of Art. A scholarship (1881–2) won for his painting *A Glade in Phoenix Park* allowed him to study in Antwerp, and from then on he lived by his brush. He painted many commissioned portraits but preferred the rural and domestic scenes experienced in regular summer visits to England and at home. He is best known now for *The Ferry* (1889–90), which won him a prize at the World Columbian Exhibition in Chicago, *Near St Patrick's Close* (1887) and a study of old scholars in *Marsh's Library* (1898). He died of pneumonia on 24 April 1903 in the house in which he had spent his whole life.

Oscar. In Irish mythology the son of OISÍN and grandson of FIONN MAC CUMHAIL. The 'os' element of the name means 'deer', a reminder of the story of his grandmother SADB. Though earlier noted for clumsiness he becomes a famous warrior, at times reaching the level of CÚCHULAINN in battle-frenzy. He dies in single combat at the last great battle of the FIANNA at Garristown in Co. Dublin (the equivalent of Camlan in the Arthurian cycle), but not before inflicting a fatal wound on his mortal enemy CAIRBRE, the high king who succeeded his father CORMAC MAC ART. Oscar's wife AIDÍN dies of grief and is buried on Beann Eadair (Howth Head).

Ó Sé, Seán. *See* CEOLTÓIRÍ CHUALANN; '*POC AR BUILE, AN*'.

Ó Searcaigh, Cathal (b.1956). Irish-language poet. He was born in Gortahork in the Co. Donegal GAELTACHT and educated at the National Institute of Higher Education (now the University of Limerick) and Maynooth. In his collections, which include *Miontraigéide Cathrach* ('small city tragedy', 1975), *Súile Shuibhne* ('Sweeney's eyes', 1983), *An Bealach 'na Bhaile* ('the road home', 1991) and *Ag Tnúth leis an tSolar* ('Waiting for the Light', 2000) he unites the traditions of the great Irish poets with modern cultural influences and a kind of personal Celtic spirituality. His work has been translated into English by Séamus Heaney, Gabriel Fitzmaurice and others. *Na Buachaillí Bána* ('the white boys', 1996) treats sexual themes frankly and in a way that is highly original for writing in Irish. He was writer-in-residence at the University of Ulster and Queen's University Belfast in the 1990s.

> Anseo ag Stáisiún Chaiseal na gCorr
> d'aimsigh mise m'oileán ruin
> mo thearmann is mo shanctóir.
> (Here at Caiselnagore station
> I have secured my secret island,
> My refuge, my sanctuary.)
> 'Anseo ag Stáisiún Chaiseal na gCorr', in *An Bleacach 'na Bhaile* (1991)

O'Shannon, Cathal (1889–1969). Journalist and trade unionist. He was born in Randalstown, Co. Antrim, but was brought to Derry when he was six months old. Educated at St Columb's College, he worked as a shipping clerk in Belfast, and in keeping with the spirit of the times joined the GAELIC LEAGUE and the IRB. On Holy Saturday 1916, in preparation for the EASTER RISING, he mobilized the 100 IRB members in Coalisland, but stood them down when no orders arrived. He was arrested a week later, released in 1917, arrested again in 1920 but let go after a 17-day hunger strike. Elected Labour TD for Louth–Meath in 1922, he was active in negotiations to settle the CIVIL WAR. He continued to work as a trade-union officer, becoming secretary to the Irish TUC in 1941. From 1946 he served at the Labour Court as a workers' representative. He died on 4 October 1969.

O'Shea Who Must Be Obeyed. A pun made by many in the Irish Party about Katharine O'Shea (1845–1921), the mistress of Charles Stewart PARNELL, and notably used as a caption for a *Vanity Fair* cartoon. It plays on 'She Who Must Be Obeyed', the by-name of Ayesha, the main character in *She* (1887), the popular romance by H. Rider Haggard (1856–1925). The joke also clearly establishes that her surname had the less usual pronunciation 'O'Shee'.

Katharine O'Shea was born Katharine Wood on 31 January 1845, daughter of the Rev. Sir Page Wood. The family were upper-middle-class Whigs, and an uncle had been lord chancellor in Gladstone's first administration. Her husband, William Henry O'Shea (1840–1905), was Irish, Catholic, spendthrift and feckless, and by 1875 the marriage was effectively over. Katharine met Parnell on 30 July 1880, and by the time he was arrested (*see* KILMAINHAM TREATY) she was pregnant with their first child.

In order to keep O'Shea complaisant Parnell forced him upon the reluctant electors of Galway in 1886. (He had decided on a career in politics but had been rejected, to no one's surprise but his own, by the electors of a Liverpool constituency.) Even then he voted against the Home Rule Bill. Katharine had since the 1870s been the loved companion of her rich Aunt Ben (Mrs Benjamin Wood) at Eltham, near London. When Aunt Ben died, aged 96, in May 1888, she left her fortune of £140,000 to Katharine, and at once her siblings, who had tried to have the aunt found incompetent even while she lived, began to contest the will. The effect was to delay probate for three years and leave the impecunious O'Shea neither a legatee nor bribable.

With his usual mixture of mischief and fecklessness it seemed to O'Shea that divorce was a possible means of further income, and so the writ was issued with results both tragic and farcical (*see* COMMITTEE ROOM 15). The three children Katharine had by Parnell (1881, 1883, 1884) were all registered under the name O'Shea. She was divorced from O'Shea in 1890 and married Parnell the following year, but he died in October 1891. She suffered poor health for the rest of her life and did not have any further connections with Ireland. She survived her husband of three months by 30 years, dying on 5 February 1921.

Katharine O'Shea was known as Katie to her family and husband, and as Queenie or Wifie to her lover. The disparaging 'Kitty' or 'Kitty O'Shea' – the name by which she is still remembered in Ireland – was used only by the anti-Parnellite Irish press, clergy and public, as in this denunciation by a Father Murphy, in a sermon to his congregation in Bondyke in January 1891:

> Parnell is a debased wretch and a low scoundrel and Ireland would be very badly off if they could not find a better leader ... He has been living in sin with Kitty O'Shea since 1880.

It is likely that publicans who call an IRISH BAR at home or abroad 'Kitty O'Shea's' are unaware of the prejudicial origins of the name.

Ó Siochfhradha, Pádraig. *See* SEABHAC, AN.

Ossian. *See* OISÍN.

Ossianic Cycle. *See* FIANNA; OISÍN.

Ossian's Grave. A megalithic court grave in Glenaan, Co. Antrim, associated with OISÍN, the son of FIONN MAC CUMHAIL.

Ossified. One of many slang terms for 'drunk', suggested by the rigidity as cartilage turns to

bone after the introduction of calcium salts, as in, 'He wasn't so much stocious as ossified.'

O stony grey soil of Monaghan. The apostrophe of the poet Patrick KAVANAGH to the earth of his native county:

> O stony grey soil of Monaghan
> The laugh from my love you thieved;
> You took the gay child of my passion
> And gave me your clod-conceived.
>
> 'Stony Grey Soil', in *A Soul for Sale* (1947)

Ó Súilleabháin, Amhlaoibh (1780–1837). Diarist. Considered to be the first diarist in the Irish language, Amhlaoibh was born in Killarney, Co. Kerry, but his father, a teacher in a HEDGE SCHOOL, moved the family to Co. Kilkenny. He later became a teacher and also ran a shop in Callan after his marriage. His *Cín Lae* ('diary') is a lively mixture of reflection, observation and social commentary by a man who had read widely in English and Irish. A selection from this very lengthy work was edited by Tomás de Bhaldraithe as *Cín Lae Amhlaoibh* (1970) and translated into English by the same author as *The Diary of Humphrey O'Sullivan* (1979).

Ó Súilleabháin, Eoghan Rua. *See* EOGHAN AN BHÉIL BHINN.

Ó Súilleabháin, Seán (1903–96). Folklorist and writer. He was born in Tuosist on the Beara Peninsula in south Co. Kerry, and worked as a primary schoolteacher before joining the IRISH FOLKLORE COMMISSION on its establishment in 1935. His published work includes *A Handbook of Irish Folklore* (1942) as well as his definitive *Caitheamh Aimsire ag Tórraimh* (1964), published in English as *Irish Wake Amusements* (1967). He devised the SCHOOLS COLLECTION, carried out by the Commission in the 1930s.

Ó Súilleabháin, Tadhg Gaelach (1715–95). Irish-language poet. He was born near Drumcollogher in Co. Limerick. He was a lighthearted wanderer about south Munster, writing occasional political verse of a pro-Jacobite nature that earned him a spell in Cork jail. In middle age he settled in Dungarvan, Co. Waterford, and as a result of a sudden religious conversion subsequently wrote mainly confessional poetry. His *dánta diaga* ('religious poems') were published in 1802 as *Timothy O'Sullivan's Irish Pious Miscellany*. The book was reprinted 40 times, and the poems, set to folk tunes, were sung as hymns in churches throughout the 19th century. '*Duan Chroí Íosa*' ('hymn of the heart of God') is his best known religious poem.

O'Sullivan, John Marcus (1891–1948). Academic and government minister. He was born in Killarney, Co. Kerry, and educated locally, at Clongowes Wood and at University College Dublin (UCD). He was professor of modern history at UCD and served as CUMANN NA NGAEDHEAL TD for North Kerry (1924–32). After a time as parliamentary secretary to the minister for finance (1924–6) he was minister for education (1926–32). He introduced a Vocational Education Act, which established 38 vocational education committees (VECs) to take responsibility for vocational (or what was then known as technical) education. When FREE EDUCATION was introduced in 1967, VECs retained charge of second-level schools that had no connection with the religious or voluntary sector.

O'Sullivan, Maureen (1911–98). Actress. She was born on 17 May 1911 in Boyle, Co. Roscommon, and as a young woman emigrated to the United States. In Hollywood she starred with John McCormack in *Song o' My Heart* (1930), but she is best-known for playing Jane to Johnny Weissmuller's Tarzan in the series of films produced before the Second World War. She also starred in *The Barretts of Wimpole Street* (1934), *David Copperfield* (1934) and *Pride and Prejudice* (1940). She died in Arizona on 23 June 1998. Her daughter Mia Farrow (b.1945) is also a celebrated actress.

O'Sullivan, Seamus. The pseudonym of James Sullivan Starkey (1879–1958), poet, essayist and editor. He was born in Dublin and educated at home and briefly at Wesley College and the medical faculty of the Catholic University. He became an apprentice to his pharmacist father. He was a minor figure in the IRISH LITERARY REVIVAL, producing several books of verse. *The Earth-Lover* (1909) contains unforgettable pictures of his city, including 'Nelson Street' and the popular 'A Piper'. He founded the *Dublin Magazine* (1923–58), which complemented the *Irish Statesman* (*see* Æ) and *The* BELL in forming the main cultural outlets for the new state. His collections of essays include *Essays and Recollections* (1944) and *The Rose and the Bottle* (1946). He was married to the artist Estella SOLOMONS.

> A piper in the street today,
> Set up, and tuned, and started to play,
> And away, away, away on the tide
> Of his music we started ...

See also MOERAN, E[RNEST] J[OHN].

O'Sullivan, Sonia (b.1969). Athlete. She was born on 28 November 1969 in Cobh, Co. Cork, and studied on an athletics scholarship at Villanova University in the USA. From the early 1990s she has been Ireland's leading female athlete, winning many international competitions and breaking all previous Irish records in distances from 1500 metres to 5000 metres. In some major competitions, notably the Olympics, her performance has been disappointing: she came fourth in the 3000 metres race at the Barcelona Olympics of 1992, dropped out of the 5000 metres final at the Atlanta Olympics of 1996, and again performed poorly at the Sydney 2000 Olympics. She has won many European Championship gold medals, competing at various distances, and was the world champion at 5000 metres in the Gothenburg World Championships of 1995 and again in Budapest in 1998. She has also achieved success as a cross-country runner. O'Sullivan is a very popular sporting figure in Ireland.

O'Sullivan Beare, Donall (1560–1618). Gaelic

chieftain. He was the chief of the O'Sullivans on the BEARA PENINSULA in west Cork and joined the rebellion of Hugh O'NEILL against the English (*see* NINE YEARS' WAR). After the Battle of KINSALE in 1601 and the fall in 1602 of his last outpost, Dunboy Castle (near the modern town of Castletown Beare) to Sir George CAREW, he took refuge in the remote hills of the Cork–Kerry border until it became clear that no further Spanish aid was forthcoming. In desperation he set out for Ulster, leaving Glengariff on 31 December with 400 soldiers and 600 women, children and retainers. On the long journey north he lost much of the group through illness and exposure; many were also killed by English soldiers or by the armies of Gaelic chieftains loyal to the crown. Only 35 reached the haven of Leitrim Castle, home of O'Rourke of Breffni. O'Sullivan Beare sailed for Spain in 1603 with his wife and children, and was given a knighthood and pension by Philip III. He was killed by an Irishman in Madrid. The 'Long March' of O'Sullivan Beare has been re-enacted by a group from the Beara Peninsula.

Otherworld. In Irish mythology, the realm of the gods and the resting place of mortal souls before reincarnation. The place was visible only once a year – at SAMHAIN, the beginning of the Celtic winter and now associated with Hallowe'en, when the powers of evil have licence before yielding to the sanctity of all the saints in heaven. Aspects of the Otherworld are found in TÍR TAIRNGIRI, TÍR NA NÓG and HY-BRASIL. The Celts believed that the spirits of the dead went to another, heavenly world (they did not believe in a hell). This was variously called called Hy-Brasil, the Gentle Land, the Land of Shadows, Magh Dhá Cheo (the 'plain of two mists'), Magh Meala (the 'honey plain') or Tír na Nóg (the 'land of youth'). In his introduction to *Irish Sagas* (1959), Myles Dillon (1900–72) describes the Otherworld as follows:

A country where there is no sickness nor age nor death; where happiness lasts for ever, food and

drink do not diminish when consumed, to wish for something is to possess it; where a hundred years are as one day. This Land of the Living is in the Western Sea.

The Otherworld was also the term used to describe the provenance of people or events believed to be not of the natural or everyday world.

See also GOOD PEOPLE; OVERLOOKED, TO BE; PISHOGUES; READ OVER, TO BE; SIDHE.

O'Toole, Laurence (*c.*1128–1180). Archbishop of Dublin. Known in Irish as Lorcán Ó Tuathail, he was one of only three canonized Irish saints. He was born in Co. Kildare, son of local ruler Maurice O'Toole, and educated at GLENDALOUGH, becoming abbot in 1153. In 1162 he was consecrated Archbishop of Dublin, the second person to occupy that position, which *The* ANNALS OF THE FOUR MASTERS described as 'archbishop of the foreigners [i.e. Vikings] and of Leinster'.

In 1170, when an Anglo-Norman army led by STRONGBOW, Miles de Cogan and Raymond le Gros and assisted by O'Toole's own brother-in-law Dermot MACMURROUGH laid siege to Dublin, O'Toole attemped to negotiate terms of surrender, but the Anglo-Normans took the city by force while he was doing so. The following year he again tried to negotiate when Ruaidhri Ua Conchobair in turn besieged the city. Ruaidhri refused to grant terms and the Anglo-Normans routed his army in Castle-knock.

Thereafter the pragmatic O'Toole managed the *realpolitik* of being spiritual leader of an Irish-Norse city under Anglo-Norman rule, mediating between HENRY II, who spent the winter 1171–2 in Dublin, and Irish leaders. He participated in the Lateran Council of 1179 and was appointed papal legate in Ireland; when he returned to Ireland he convened a reform synod for Connacht in Clonfert. When O'Toole visited Henry on yet another mission of mediation in 1180 Henry refused him permission to return to Ireland. He followed Henry to Normandy in an attempt at reconciliation and died there in Eu in November 1180.

O'Toole's leadership of the Dublin church coincided with an enormous change in the governance of this part of Ireland. He was represented by his own biographers as a champion of the 12th-century church reform movement and canonized in 1226 by Honorius III (d.1227). He is the patron saint of Dublin and his feast day is 14 November.

Ó Tuairisc, Eoghan (Eugene Watters) (1919–82). Poet and novelist, who wrote in both Irish and English. He was born in Ballinasloe, Co. Galway, and served as an officer in the army during the EMERGENCY. He taught in Dublin until 1961 when he became a full-time writer. *L'Attaque* (1962), his first significant work, is a novel written in Irish and set in Co. Mayo during the REBELLION OF 1798. Strongly influenced by Tolstoy's *War and Peace*, the novel portrays the inhumanity of war, making ironic use of Irish heroic myths that glorify conflict. It was followed by *The Weekend of Dermot and Grace* (1964), a long poem based on the epic *Tóraigheacht Dhiarmada agus Ghráinne*. With his second wife, Rita Kelly, Ó Tuairisc produced a sizeable body of work, including a joint poetry collection, a play about Patrick Pearse, *Fornocht do Chonac* (1981), and *The Road to Bright City* (1981), brilliant translations of early short stories by Máirtín Ó CADHAIN.

Ó Tuama, Seán¹. *See* SEÁN AN GHRINN.

Ó Tuama, Seán² (b.1926). Irish-language poet, playwright and critic. He was born in Cork and educated at University College Cork (UCC), where he was taught by Daniel CORKERY. He became professor of modern Irish at UCC and an influential teacher and apologist for the Irish language. His anthology *Nuabhéarsaíocht* ('new verse') (1950) recognized the quality of rising Irish poets such as Seán Ó RÍORDÁIN, Máirtín Ó DIREÁIN and Máire MHAC AN TSAOI. In 1960 he published a major scholarly work, *An Grá in Amhráin na*

nDaoine ('love in the songs of the people'), in which he studied the traditional love poetry of the ordinary people as both a French and an Irish phenomenon. He subsequently produced volumes of criticism, essays and poetry. He collaborated with Thomas KINSELLA on *An DUANAIRE 1600–1900: POEMS OF THE DISPOSSESSED*.

Ould Biddy. An ageist term of disapproval, using the diminutive of the name Brigid to characterize a meddling old woman.

Ould decency. A term used to signify something past its best but still serviceable. Often applied to articles of dress, such as an old pair of comfortable shoes: 'These are the remains of oul' decency.'

Ould Lammas Fair. The oldest popular fair in Ireland held in Ballycastle, Co. Antrim, each August (as the name implies) since 1606. It used to last a week but now it is held over two days at the end of the month. The social aspects have always taken precedence over the sale of sheep and ponies, and it achieved countrywide and emigrant fame because of a ballad written by John McAULEY, a local woodcarver. Most Irish people can sing the refrain:

> Did you treat your Mary Ann
> To dulse and yellow man
> At the ould Lammas fair in Ballycastle-O.

(*See* DULSE AND YELLA MAN.)

Louis J. Walsh (*see* POPE IN KILLYBUCK, THE) described the atmosphere between the wars in a local journal:

> But once a year at least, all Ballycastle – old and young, Catholic and Protestant, rich and poor, gentle and simple, Orange and Green – foregathered on the Diamond for the three nights of the Lammas Fair, and joked and gambled and chatted and made merry together. All differences of class or creed were for the time being forgotten. You were all just Ballycastle folk – not unfortunate people like those who could only claim Cushendall or Ballymoney or Ballymena, or cold Portrush as their *civitas* – and this was your

own Lammas Fair, and you meant to make the most of it. Thus we got to know each other in an intimate way that seems impossible in any other township, and though we might have our quarrels and rivalries and feuds we never forgot that we were Ballycastle people, and when we met in 'far foreign fields' we clave to each other like children of the same hearthstone.

'The Lammas Fair in Ballycastle', in *The Glensman*, January 1932

'Ould Orange Flute, The'. A popular 19th-century comic song celebrating the intense loyalty of members of the ORANGE ORDER. It tells of a Protestant flautist who becomes a Catholic, forsaking 'the ould cause / That gave us our freedom, religion and laws'. Attempting to play his flute in a Catholic church, he finds that the loyal flute will play nothing but Loyalist songs. Like the heretic it has proved to be it is sentenced to be burned at the stake. The song has been sung with gusto ever since its anonymous composition by all shades of political persuasion:

So the ould flute was doomed and its fate was pathetic;
'Twas sentenced and burned at the stake as a heretic.
As the flames roared around it they heard a strange noise:
Th' ould flute was still playing 'The Protestant Boys'.

Ould ShAbbey. The affectionate name for the ABBEY THEATRE in its unimpressive original building in Abbey Street, Dublin (1904–51). After the fire in 1951 the company moved to the much larger Queen's Theatre in Pearse Street and stayed there in an inappropriate setting until its return to Abbey Street and a new building in 1966.

No longer could the Dubliners make a date with their favourite remark 'See you at the oul' shAbbey tonight.'

SEAN MCCANN: *The Story of the Abbey Theatre* (1967)

Ould Sod. A nickname for Ireland in the mouth of exiles, used mostly with genuine affection but in recent times with a strong element of mockery. The word 'sod' is the equivalent of the English 'turf', and one of the legends associated with COLUM CILLE is that when he left in exile in Iona he brought a green sod with him.

The mere suspicion that the landlord wished to get rid of them has driven many an Irish family far away from the 'old sod'.

CHARLES KICKHAM (1828–82): *Knocknagow* (1879)

The expression may lead to the possibility of misunderstandings, as recorded by Dominic Cleary:

When President Reagan came to Ireland, he was greeted with a beautifully ambiguous banner which read 'Welcome to the Ould Sod'.

'Ould Triangle, The'. The title of a melancholy song from Brendan Behan's play *The QUARE FELLOW* (1954), in which a prisoner is executed in MOUNTJOY JAIL. The reference in the second line is to the geographical situation of Mountjoy, beside the Royal Canal:

And the ould triangle went jingle jangle
Along the banks of the Royal Canal …

Our Exagmination. The first apologia for James Joyce's FINNEGANS WAKE by an apostolic 12 writers including Samuel Beckett (1906–89), the Irish poet Thomas McGreevy (1893–1967) and the American poet William Carlos Williams (1883–1963) in May 1929. The full mock-portentous title, *Our Exagmination round His Factification for Incamination of Work in Progess*, was suggested by Joyce himself.

Outdoor Relief Protests. A campaign organized in Belfast 4–14 October 1932 by unemployed workers for an improvement in welfare benefits, which were much lower than in British cities. (The term 'outdoor' referred to poor relief granted outside of workhouses.) The campaign was unusual in that its support crossed the sectarian divide and that it was organized by communists who had split from the Northern Ireland Labour Party, notably Tommy Geehan and Betty Sinclair, but characteristic in that the demonstrations led to serious rioting with two deaths. Relief was improved from 8 to 20 shillings a week at the minimum level and from 24 to 32 shillings at the maximum. Geehan correctly described the outcome as 'a glorious victory', but the cross-community support was never again in evidence.

> For many years the workers of Belfast had been divided by artificial barriers of religion and politics but the past two months had witnessed a wonderful spectacle because the workers were now united on a common platform demanding the right to live.
>
> TOMMY GEEHAN: 10 October 1932

Out! Out! Out! The media summary of Margaret Thatcher's absolute dismissal on 19 November 1984 of the options for an agreed peace in Ulster as suggested by the New Ireland Forum on 3 May:

> … a unified Ireland was one solution. That is out. A second solution was a confederation of the two states. That is out. A third solution was joint sovereignty. That is out. That is a derogation from sovereignty.

The Forum had been the idea of John HUME, and there were delegates from the main Irish Nationalist parties, north and south, when they first met in Dublin in May 1983. The British reaction greatly dismayed the Irish government; Garret FITZGERALD, who was then taoiseach, described Mrs Thatcher as 'gratuitously offensive'. In spite of the rancour and the gloom, the summit eventually led to the ANGLO-IRISH AGREEMENT.

Outside car. *See* JAUNTING CAR.

Ouzel Galley. The barque *Ouzel* left Dublin with a crew of 40 on a voyage to Smyrna (now Izmir) on the west coast of Turkey in 1695. When, after three years, nothing had been heard of the ship, her owners, the merchant company of Ferris, Twig and Cash, presumed her lost, and their insurers settled with them. Then, almost exactly five years after she had sailed, the *Ouzel* returned, complete with captain, crew and a valuable cargo. The ship

had been captured by pirates but the crew had managed to regain control of the vessel and all the booty seized by their captors. On its return the question arose as to who owned the goods, the insurers having already settled with the owners. Five years of litigation ensued until at length it was agreed that the valuables should be used to fund a benevolent society for needy merchants. From this came the establishment of a board called the Ouzel Galley Society (known as the Ouzel Galley), with 40 members to represent the number of crew on the original ship, which arbitrated in disputes relating to trade and business. Over the next century the society dealt with 364 cases. It was wound up in 1899, and distributed its remaining assets among six Dublin hospitals.

Overlooked, to be. To be the victim of a spell or curse cast by a neighbour or by a representative of the OTHERWORLD.

Over right someone out. A HIBERNO-ENGLISH phrase meaning to be right in front of someone: 'I/She came out the door at ten o'clock and there he [the ghost, the fugitive, someone surprising] was over right me/her out.'

Over the bar. The means of scoring a point in the two main GAA games, FOOTBALL and HURLING (also CAMOGIE, the women's version of hurling). A point is awarded for kicking, striking or fisting the ball over the bar, and a goal (three points) for putting the ball in the net in the expected way. 'It's over the bar for a point' is the mainstay of GAA commentary and a phrase familiar to every Irish person. *Over the Bar* is the title of a 1984 memoir by writer and journalist Breandán Ó HEITHIR (1931–90), subtitled 'A Personal Relationship with the GAA'. In counties where the high-scoring hurling is popular, 'one goal and three points' in the family context means one girl and three boys.

Over the limit. Having more than the legal amount of alchohol in one's bloodstream while driving. There is a constant battle between

Irish motorists and the law on the subject of drink-driving. If a driver is breathalyzed (there is no random testing in Ireland: a garda may breathalyze a driver only if he has reason to suspect that he has too much drink taken) and found over the limit by a blood or urine test, there is automatic disqualification from driving. But despite a very high level of road-accident fatalities and injuries, many Irish people still have a sneaking sympathy for those put off the road. PARISH-PUMP POLITICIANS have been known to interfere with the administration of justice in cases of drink-driving.

Owain. The hero of a 12th-century lay, *The Descent of Owain*, written by Henry of Saltrey, an English Cistercian. Owain was an Irish knight of the court of Stephen (*c*.1097–1154), who by way of penance for a wicked life, entered and passed through St Patrick's Purgatory at LOUGH DERG.

Owens, Blackburne E. (1845–94). The pseudonym (built out of her forenames) of the novelist and feminist biographer Elizabeth Casey. She was born on 10 May 1845 in Slane, Co. Meath, lost her sight in childhood but had it restored by Sir William WILDE. She worked as a journalist in London from 1873 and wrote copybook sentimental Victorian novels, including *A Woman Scorned* (1876), which was serialized in *The* NATION, *The Glen of the Silver Birches* (1880) and *The Hearts of Erin* (1883). These were, however, atypical, in that her resentment of the attitude to women in a male-dominated society is a constant theme. *A Bunch of Shamrocks* (1879), a collection of tales, slips a little into HIBERNO-ENGLISH condescension. Most interesting to modern readers is her *Illustrious Irishwomen* (1877), a two-volume dictionary of feminist biography, the first of its kind, from the earliest times (she begins with MACHA, but does not include any of her living contemporaries, probably for legal reasons). After her literary career failed she returned to Ireland and died in a house fire in Fairview, Dublin, in April 1894.

Oxter. The word commonly used in Ireland (and Scotland) for 'armpit' as in, 'He appeared at the barn door with a bale of hay under every oxter.'

Oxygen of publicity, the. The phrase used by Margaret Thatcher (b.1925), the British prime minister, to describe the media coverage that she believed was benefiting the IRA and which she intended to prevent. It was first heard at a speech to the American Bar Association in London on 15 July 1985 when she announced in general terms: 'We must try to find ways to starve the terrorist and hijacker of the oxygen of publicity on which they depend.' The expression was repeated by Douglas Hurd (b.1930), who had been her Northern Ireland secretary (1984–5), when as home secretary he instituted in 1988 stringent censorship rules covering not only the contents but also the vocalization of SINN FÉIN statements. This led to the often risible (and self-defeating) use of actors' voices to dub over broadcast statements from such figures as Gerry ADAMS and Martin MCGUINNESS. Both the British and the Irish governments (*see* SECTION 31) ceased their media restrictions on Republicans in 1994.

p

Pachal (also **pauchle** or **pachle**). A somewhat vague Ulster term of abuse, still current, applied to men who seem to combine physical ungainliness, unreliability and laziness. It may be heard in the dismissive phrase, 'the pachal frae Ahoghill', partly because of the exact rhyme and partly because the Co. Antrim village, like its near neighbour Cullybackey, is unfairly pilloried because of its name.

Pack. A HIBERNO-ENGLISH word indicating close acquaintance, as in, 'That pair! Oh they're very pack allthegether!'

Paddies, Priests and Pigs. *See* ALLINGHAM, WILLIAM.

Paddy[1]. A fit of anger, named after the diminutive of Patrick, the name by which Irishmen are universally (and usually derogatorily) known. The word comes from the Irishman's supposed tendency to sudden bursts of rage. An allied phrase is 'getting his Irish up', as in the eponymous Irish-American song: 'Whenever they got his Irish up / Clancy lowered the boom.'
See also BARNEY.

Paddy[2]. A brand of Irish whiskey favoured by traditionalists. It was said to be the drink of choice of 'the Real Taoiseach' Jack LYNCH, perhaps because both were products of the city of Cork.

'Paddy and Mr Punch'. The title of an essay (1991) by Roy Foster (b.1949), Carroll professor of Irish history at Oxford University, examining the usually murky view of Ireland from Bouverie Street (location of *Punch*'s offices in London) during the 19th century. The simian appearance of the 'Paddies' in the English periodical are reminiscent of Thomas Nast's cartoons across the Atlantic (*see* 'I'M RISING IN THE WORLD'), and Daniel O'CONNELL is brilliantly if unfairly excoriated in 1845 as 'The real potato blight of Ireland'.

Paddy Clarke, Ha, Ha, Ha. The title of a Booker Prize-winning novel (1993) by Roddy DOYLE, set in 1968. The eponymous hero, a 10-year-old Dublin boy in whose words the novel is told, realizes that his father has left home for good, and the taunting rhyme of local children gives the book its title:

> Paddy Clarke –
> Paddy Clarke –
> Has no da.
> Ha ha ha!

Paddyism. A term of mild abuse or self-irony to describe an action or speech that is perceived as being STAGE-IRISH or based on an exaggerated display of so-called national characteristics, such as excessive drinking, the gift of the gab or the use of an IRISH BULL. There is a less commonly used adjective, 'Paddyish'. The term Paddyism may also be used, more seriously, to indicate a negative perception of Irish people and institutions abroad, especially in Britain:

> Malignant anti-Paddyism in the British media or among some of Abbey's [Abbey National Building Society] institutional investors could, of course, scupper BoI [Bank of Ireland].
>
> *Sunday Business Post*, 23 June 2002

Paddy power. The name given to electricity flowing South–North in the cross-border electricity-exchange scheme. Paddy Powers is the name of a well-known firm of book-makers. *See also* ORANGE JUICE.

Paddy's Blackguards. *See* NAMURS, THE.

Paddy the Cope. The nickname of Patrick Gallagher (1873–1964), founder in 1906 of the Templecrone Co-operative Society in Dungloe, in remote and rocky west Donegal. In spite of the opposition of local traders and merchants he instituted a system of bulk buying of foodstuffs and fertilizers, thus breaking the power of local GOMBEEN MEN, who responded with a smear campaign suggesting that his scheme was financed by Protestants. (This charge had some truth in that Sir Harold Plunkett and his deputy Æ, the founders of the Irish Agricultural Organization Society, the IAOS, who lent him some support, were not Catholic.) The term *cope* came from the local pronunciation of 'co-op'. In time Gallagher expanded the society, establishing a general store, developing a local weaving industry, setting up a glove factory, building a pier in Dungloe and instituting street lighting.

Padhsán. An Irish word, also used in HIBERNO-ENGLISH, for a puny, scrawny, insignificant person. The word also suggests meanness or pettiness of character.

Padraic-what-do-you-colum. The manner in which James JOYCE referred to the poet and playwright Padraic COLUM. *See also* COLUM, MARY.

Paisley, Ian [Richard Kyle] (b.1926). Clergyman and politician. He was born in Armagh and educated at Ballymena Model School and South Wales Bible College. Ordained by his Baptist father in 1946, he founded his own denomination, the Free Presbyterian Church of Ulster, in 1951. Until the mid-1960s his political activities were fairly low-profile, consisting of vociferous denunciation of any compromise with the principles of extreme and unyielding Unionism and – from the pulpit of his church, Martyrs' Memorial, and in his newspaper, the *Protestant Telegraph* – a sustained and offensive anti-Catholicism (his usual description of the current pope was 'old Redsocks'). He reacted predictably to the talks in 1965 between Terence O'NEILL and Seán LEMASS, but it was his opposition to the CIVIL RIGHTS MOVEMENT that gave him his entrée into Parliament, running O'Neill so close in Bannside that the latter resigned in 1969. Paisley became a STORMONT MP in 1970 and a Westminster MP the following year. His Democratic Unionist Party (DUP) dates from this election. He was heavily involved in the UWC strike in May 1974, and continues to have a solid base of support both in urban working-class and rural areas. His rough rhetorical skills and ripe humour make him an unignorable figure, but many wonder at the apparent inconsistency of his (and his party's) relentless opposition to the GOOD FRIDAY AGREEMENT and their participation in the Northern Ireland Assembly.

Palatines. Calvinist German refugees from the Rheinland-Pfalz (Rhenish Palatinate). After the French occupation of their homeland, 820 families (more than 3000 persons) were sent by the British authorities to Ireland in 1709. They were settled mainly in Limerick and Wexford, though their original intention was to seek religious freedom in New England (and indeed many used the first opportunity to emigrate there). Only the Limerick Palatines remained in significant numbers, endogamous and culturally separate from the often hostile Irish. An area between Adare and Rathkeale is still known as the Palatinate, and there are residual German names, such as Bovenizer, Switzer and Teskey. All had either emigrated or been assimilated into the native population by the end of the 19th century.

Pale, the (also **the English Pale**). The territory round Dublin that in the Middle Ages was the only part of Ireland where the crown's writ unquestionably ran. It was known in England as a 'land of peace', in contrast to the turbulent remainder. Its area fluctuated in size from its greatest extent in the 14th century, when it comprised large areas of Louth, Meath, Kilkenny and Kildare as well as Dublin, to its condition in 1500 when it had contracted to a band 80 km (50 miles) north of Dublin and 50 km (30 miles) inland. The word *pale* (from the Latin *palum* 'stake', via Middle English *pale* 'fence of stakes') indicated a ring of defensive forts amounting to a *palisade*, but such exclusiveness was never achieved. It gave rise to the still current phrase 'beyond the Pale', meaning beyond the bounds of what is acceptable (morally or socially).

Pale moon was rising, The. The opening line of 'The ROSE OF TRALEE', a romantic ballad by William Mulchineck (1820–64).

Palm. *See* CYPRESS.

Pana. A nickname for Patrick Street, the main street in Cork city: 'I was in Pana and I met Theresa.' 'Doing Pana' is a ritual for young people resembling the Spanish *paseo*. It involves parading up and down Patrick Street with one's friends and with an eye to members of the opposite sex, for instance on a Saturday afternoon or Christmas Eve. Much of Patrick Street was burnt down by the AUXIES on the night of 11 December 1920, as a reprisal for an IRA ambush at Dillon's Cross, near Victoria Barracks, earlier that day.

Pande palmam. *See* PANDYBAT.

Pandy. A colloquial name for mashed potatoes.

Pandybat. The instrument used for corporal punishment in Jesuit establishments, notably at CLONGOWES WOOD, as recorded in *A POR- TRAIT OF THE ARTIST AS A YOUNG MAN.*

It was usually made of strips of leather, though the pupils believed that whalebone or even lead was sewn inside. It lasted longer than a cane.

> Fleming held out his hand. The pandybat came down on it with a loud smacking sound: one two three four five six – Other hand!
>
> JAMES JOYCE (1882–1941): *A Portrait of the Artist as a Young Man* (1916)

The pandybat probably took its name from the Latin *Pande palmam*, ('Put out your hand').

Papal Brigade. A brigade of Irish volunteers who arrived in Rome in the summer of 1860 in response to an appeal by Pope Pius IX for help in defending the Papal States against the forces seeking to unify Italy. The Irish unit was composed of eight companies with about 1100 volunteers, and was known as the Battalion of St Patrick. The Papal armies, which were badly organized, were quickly defeated, and the Irish volunteers returned home after little more than four months.

Paper, de. The nickname used in Cork for the local paper, the ('de') *Cork Examiner*, which, in an effort to broaden its readership, changed its name first to the *Examiner* in 1996 and then to the *Irish Examiner* in 1999. An advertising jingle in the 1970s exploited this pronunciation:

> Down south the Cork Examiner is the one they call de paper …

The *Cork Examiner* was founded in 1841 by John Francis Maguire (1815–72) as an evening paper published three times a week. It had 'one great, one paramount object – the service of Ireland'. Maguire was a constitutional Nationalist who served as an MP from 1852 until his death, and his newspaper supported Daniel O'CONNELL's movement to repeal the Act of UNION and the DISESTABLISHMENT OF THE CHURCH OF IRELAND. His partner, Thomas Crosbie, succeeded him as owner and manager of the company, and Examiner Newspapers is still a Crosbie family business. Crosbie made the *Cork Examiner* into a daily morning paper and launched a new paper, the *Evening Echo* (*see* ECHO BOYS).

Papish. A term of abuse regularly applied by hostile Protestants. It is a form of the word 'papist', which had a brief 19th-century respectability with some writers. Today the terms FENIAN or Taig or TEAGUE are more likely to be used in streets gibes and graffiti. An Orange song from 1849 recalls that 'we knocked five hundred papishes right over DOLLY'S BRAE'.

Paps, the. A pair of mountains near Shrone, Co. Kerry. In Irish they are *Dhá Chích Danainn* ('the two breasts of DANA¹'). At their foot lies the CITY.

Parades Commission. A body set up in March 1997 to determine whether certain contentious parades in Northern Ireland should take place. The personnel, four members under the chairmanship of Alastair Graham, a former trade unionist, were chosen to represent both sides of the community divide, but in the last number of years there have been several resignations and necessary reconstitutions of membership. At the beginning of its existence a mediation role was envisaged, but when this was replaced by that of simple decision the Rev. Roy Magee, who had helped bring about the Loyalist ceasefire, resigned. The most difficult decisions are usually those concerning the yearly walk from Drumcree Church down the Garvaghy Road back to Portadown (*see* DRUMCREE STAND-OFFS), but other flashpoints, including the Lower Ormeau Road in Belfast, have also been adjudicated upon. Though severely criticized by involved parties, the decisions of the commission are becoming generally acceptable.

Parish-pump politician. The kind of elected representative to whom a local funeral or a local social-welfare claim is more important than DÁIL legislation of national or international significance. Although public representatives of this type arouse the ire of Dublin journalists, they are usually first past the post when it comes to being re-elected. So popular are they that they often manage to be elected as independents when the Dublin-based party headquarters, out of touch with the grass roots, declines to have them nominated on the party ticket. South Kerry's Jackie Healy-Rae is the supreme example of the successful parish-pump politician. The activities of the parish-pump politician are described by critics as clientelism. In April 2002 a junior minister, Bobby Molloy, resigned after revelations that he had attempted to make contact with a judge in a rape and incest case on behalf of a constituent. In the *Irish Times*, Denis Coghlan referred to Molloy as 'the quintessential constituency politician, oiling the parish pump and providing a direct interface between the voters of Galway West and officialdom'. Pat Shortt (b.1967), half of a popular comedy act called d'Unbelievables (the other half, Jon Kenny, has since gone his own way), caricatured on stage for many seasons the appearance and exploits of Maurice Hickey, a parish-pump politician par excellence.

Park, the. PHOENIX PARK, Dublin. Because the president's residence ÁRAS AN UACHTARÁIN is located here, 'Going for the park' means aspiring to the office of president

Parke, Thomas Heazle (1857–93). Doctor and explorer. He was born on 27 November 1857 in Clogher House, near Drumsna, Co. Leitrim. After qualifying as a doctor, he joined the British army and was posted to Egypt. He volunteered to travel with H.M. Stanley on his expedition up the Congo to relieve Emin Pasha in the Sudan after the death of General Gordon in 1885. Parke's diary details the smallpox, dysentery and other diseases that ravaged the members of the expedition, of whom only 100 survived of the 800 who set out. Stanley himself said that without Parke the expedition would not have achieved its goal. In May 1890 Parke returned to England to great acclaim, but his health was compromised and he died suddenly in Argyll three years later. He is buried in the family graveyard in Kilmessan, Co. Leitrim. His statue, showing him in active-explorer pose, stands outside the Natural History Museum in Dublin.

Parknasilla. A luxury hotel beautifully situated outside Sneem on the Ring of Kerry. It was built in 1890 by the Great Southern and Western Railway Company to exploit business generated by the railways – although in this case guests had to be conveyed by horse and carriage the not inconsiderable 24 km (15 miles) from the nearest railway station, Kenmare. Great Southern hotels were also built in Killarney, Kenmare, Galway and Rosslare; all but that in Kenmare are still in business. The land for the hotel was acquired from Bishop A.P. GRAVES, who used the original house at Parknasilla as a summer residence.

Parnell, Charles Stewart (1846–91). Leader of the Irish party at Westminster, whose possible success in obtaining HOME RULE was severely compromised when the hitherto complaisant husband of his mistress Katharine O'Shea (*see* O'SHEA WHO MUST BE OBEYED) sued for divorce in December 1889, naming him as co-respondent.

Parnell was born on 27 June 1846 into a Protestant landlord family in Avondale, Co. Wicklow, educated at Magdalene College, Cambridge, and went against his class to become a Home Rule MP for Meath (1875–1880) and for Cork city (1880–91). He and Joe Biggar (*see* BELFAST QUASIMODO) perfected obstructionist tactics that made the business of the House of Commons all but impossible. By 1880 he had become, in rapid succession, deviser with Davitt and Devoy of the NEW DEPARTURE, president of the LAND LEAGUE and chairman of the IRISH PARTY. The KILMAINHAM TREATY allowed him to sue for Home Rule by entirely constitutional means, and the election in 1885, which returned 86 Nationalist MPs, gave Gladstone (the GOM) the Commons majority to introduce his first Home Rule Bill – which was, however, defeated owing to the dereliction of Joseph Chamberlain (1836–1914).

By 1890 Parnell had been exonerated of involvement in terrorism (*see* PARNELLISM AND CRIME), had united all shades of Nationalist opinion and was ready with Liberal help to get Gladstone's second Home Rule Bill through the lower house when the bombshell of the divorce action split his party (*see* COMMITTEE ROOM 15). His death on 6 October 1891 only three months after his marriage to Katharine was a serious setback for the Nationalist cause. *See also* UNCROWNED KING, THE.

Parnell, Fanny (1849–82) and **Anna** (1853–1911). Feminists and land agitators. They were born on the family estate at Avondale, Co. Wicklow, the younger sisters of Charles Stewart PARNELL, and were educated in Paris and New Jersey, the home of their mother Delia. From her they inherited a detestation of British rule in Ireland, and when they settled with her in New Jersey in 1879 they raised funds for the LAND LEAGUE, later forming the LADIES' LAND LEAGUE at Davitt's suggestion. Anna also wrote about the agrarian struggle for American publications. When Fanny Parnell died suddenly of a heart attack in July 1882, Parnell refused to have her body brought for burial to Ireland lest her funeral should cause a public disturbance, and Anna and he became totally estranged. She moved to Cornwall, changed her name to Cerisa Palmer and devoted her life to painting, although still supporting Republican organizations like INGHINIDHE NA HÉIREANN and SINN FÉIN. She drowned at Ilfracombe in Devon in 1911.

Parnellism and Crime. The general title of a series of articles published in *The Times* between March and December 1887, which suggested that PARNELL, as indicated by a series of letters purportedly written by him, was involved in terrorism. One letter in particular, dated 15 May 1882 and published in the paper on 18 April, was particularly damning, suggesting that he approved of the PHOENIX PARK MURDERS on 6 May 1882:

> I am not surprised at your friend's anger, but he and you should know that to denounce the murders was the only course open to us. To do that promptly was plainly our best policy. But you can tell him that, though I regret the accident of Lord F. Cavendish's death, I cannot

refuse to admit that Burke got no more than his deserts. You are at liberty to show him this, and others whom you can trust also, but let not my address be known. He can write to the House of Commons.

Parnell's reaction was typically disdainful. He denounced the letter as a bare-faced forgery, and would have let the matter drop had not the Conservative government set up a special commission, hoping to implicate the whole Nationalist movement.

From the start the commission had little success in establishing a link between Nationalism and violence. Then on 21 February 1889 Richard Pigott (*c.*1828–89), a failed Nationalist magazine editor, who had supplied information, including the damning letters, to the Irish Loyal and Patriotic Union, the leading anti-Home Rule society, was called as witness. He was blisteringly cross-examined by Parnell's counsel, Sir Charles Russell (1832–1900), the first Catholic lord chief justice since the Reformation. It became clear that Pigott had forged the letter; in one of them, dated 9 January 1882, the word 'hesitancy' had been incorrectly spelled. At the end of the day's hearing he fled to Spain and a week later shot himself in a Madrid hotel. The reputation of the paper was seriously impugned, and Parnell emerged unscathed, although in its report, published on 13 February 1890, the commission censured him for his failure to denounce the perpetrators openly.

Parsons, Charles. *See* BIRR.

Parsons Bookshop. A bookshop on Baggot Street Bridge much frequented by Dublin writers, especially in the 1950s and 1960s. Run by two literary ladies, Mary King and May Flaherty, it stocked some unusual titles, but its clientèle was more esoteric. As Mary LAVIN wrote in the visitors book: 'Parson's where one met as many interesting writers on the floor of the shop as on the shelves.' It was a favourite stamping ground for such literary eminences as Frank O'Connor, Patrick Kavanagh, Ben Kiely and Brendan Behan.

Parsonstown. *See* BIRR; LEVIATHAN OF PARSONSTOWN, THE.

Partholón. In Irish mythology, the leader of the second invasion of Ireland. He, like NEMED and MÍL, is of Biblical ancestry, being a descendant of Japhet, the son of Noah. He leads his followers to Munster, at that time occupied by FOMORIANS. He is credited with introducing agriculture to Ireland, bringing with him ploughs and ploughmen. He and his followers succumb to the plague. The elements of folk memory of actual colonization are particularly obvious in this account.
See also BOOK OF INVASIONS.

Partition. The establishment of the Northern Ireland state, which by the GOVERNMENT OF IRELAND ACT became law on 23 December 1920. The idea of establishing a separate state in Ireland to which HOME RULE would not apply had been discussed as early as 1912, but it was not until LLOYD GEORGE met Edward CARSON and John REDMOND after the EASTER RISING in May 1916 that the six-county partition was first floated. Antrim, Armagh, Derry and Down had secure Protestant majorities, but a four-county unit was regarded as too small for devolution. Tyrone, Fermanagh and Derry City, in spite of their problematic Nationalist majorities, were added to the Loyalist four, and the seeds of continuing political unrest were planted. Michael COLLINS and Arthur GRIFFITH were criticized for not breaking off negotiations at the TREATY talks over the question of partition. They naïvely hoped that the BOUNDARY COMMISSION of 1924–5 would render Northern Ireland ungovernable.

Partry, War in. *See* LAVELLE, PATRICK.

Passing Day, The. The most significant play (1936) of the Ulster dramatist, George SHIELS. It was chosen by Tyrone Guthrie as one of the Festival of Britain productions in the Opera House in Belfast in 1951, and deals with the last day of life of a miserly Ulster general dealer named Phibbs, who like a latter-day Molière character is visited by many clients who hope to benefit from his will. These include his doctor, his solicitor and the town gravedigger, all possible characters of a modern morality. Though some sympathy for Phibbs is generated by revelations about his early life, his character remains unpleasant and grasping. The play moved to London and its leading actor Joseph TOMELTY was launched on a new career as a character actor in film.

> I told him I'd pay nothing. Says I, I'll spend my last shilling in the High Courts before I'd pay you a penny. I don't know, says I, what we're coming to. Armies of high-paid officials living like fleas on a dog's back.
>
> *The Passing Day* (1936)

Patalogue (Irish *patall*, the young of an animal or bird). A term used in HIBERNO-ENGLISH for a chubby child.

Patrick. The chief apostle and patron saint of Ireland. Born *c.*390 of Roman British origin he spent six years in Ireland as a slave, and in maturity returned there to preach Christianity to the pagan Celts. He was ordained bishop in Auxerre sometime before 432, the traditional date of his arrival in Ireland. His mission field was the northern half of the country, with headquarters at Armagh, near the longtime centre of worship at EMAIN MACHA. He made Armagh the primatial see *c.*444, but the pattern of Irish church rule was to be for many years abbatial rather than episcopal or diocesan. Uniquely among the Irish saints of the period he left two personal documents, CONFESSIO and *Epistola ad Milites Corotici*, which show a man of humility, stern piety and righteous anger against the followers of a so-called Christian prince who killed Irish captives. According to tradition he is buried in the same grave as COLUM CILLE and BRIGID in DOWNPATRICK, near the supposed site of his first church at SAUL. His feast day of 17 March is celebrated worldwide, both sacredly and profanely (*see* ST PATRICK'S DAY).

> You've heard, I suppose, long ago,
>   How the snakes in a manner most antic,
> He marched to the County Mayo,

> And trundled them into th'Atlantic.
> Hence not to use water for drink
>   The people of Ireland determine
> With mighty good reason, I think,
>   Since St Patrick has filled it with vermin,
> And vipers and other such stuff.
>
> WILLIAM MAGINN (1793–1842): in *Blackwood's*, December 1821

See also LOUGH DERG; REEK, THE.

'Patriot Game, The'. The title of a ballad by Dominic BEHAN commemorating the death of 18-year-old Co. Monaghan Republican Fergal O'Hanlon, who with Seán South (*see* 'SEÁN SOUTH FROM GARRYOWEN') was killed in an IRA raid on Brookeborough RUC barracks in Co. Tyrone on New Year's Day 1957. The ballad wrongly gives O'Hanlon's age as 16, and in his voice boasts:

> My name is O'Hanlon, I'm just gone sixteen,
> My home is in Monaghan, that's where I was a wain.
> I gave up my boyhood to drill and to train
> And to play my own part in the patriot game.

See also BORDER CAMPAIGN.

Patriot Parliament. The name given by Young Irelander Charles Gavan DUFFY, many years after the event, to the Parliament of May–July 1689, summoned by JAMES II on his arrival in Ireland. The Earl of TYRCONNELL, James's representative in Ireland, had ensured that the Parliament was overwhelmingly Catholic, and it restored lands to those who had owned them in 1641 (annulling the CROMWELLIAN SETTLEMENT) and denied the right of the English Parliament to legislate for Ireland. James, anxious to retain the support of Irish Catholics, particularly the OLD ENGLISH, for the coming conflict with William III, reluctantly agreed to these measures, but refused to repeal POYNING'S LAW. After the Williamite victory, an act of 1695 repealed all the measures of the Patriot Parliament.

Patriots. A term applied to late-17th- and 18th-century Protestants like Lord CHARLEMONT, Henry FLOOD, Henry GRATTAN and William MOLYNEUX, whose greatest achievement can be seen as legislative independence from 1782 in what is inaccurately known as GRATTAN'S PARLIAMENT.

See also POYNING'S LAW; YELVERTON'S ACT.

Patron. *See* PATTERN.

Patronage, political. *See* JOBBERY.

Patten Report. The report (1999) of Chris[topher Francis] Patten (b.1944), chairman of the Independent Commission on Policing set up by the GOOD FRIDAY AGREEMENT. The report proposed sweeping changes, including a name change with new insignia, an independent police board, a police ombudsman, and a smaller force with equal recruitment of Catholic and Protestants. Many of Patten's recommendations were implemented when the RUC was replaced by the Police Service of Northern Ireland (*see* PSNI), but some Nationalists, including SINN FÉIN, felt that the ur-Patten had been diluted and refused to appoint members to local partnership boards.

Pattern. A particular form of devotion at a church, a HOLY WELL or some other place of pilgrimage. The word 'pattern' derives from *pátrún* ('patron'); in past centuries each parish observed the feast day of its own patron saint. Different sites had different pattern days: the great pagan feast days of IMBOLG (1 February, St BRIGID's Day), BEALTAINE (May Day; *see* CITY, THE), MIDSUMMER'S DAY and LUGH-NASA were associated with different saints and popular throughout the country. People came and did rounds of varying complexity by walking around the perimeter or within the site while reciting prayers according to a given formula. Miracles were attributed to pattern days, and crutches were occasionally left behind by those who claimed to be able to walk again after doing the rounds. Writers of the 18th and 19th century described the drinking and fighting that sometimes occurred during pattern days, and in 1704 an act of the Irish Parliament forbade people to attend patterns: the penality was a whipping or a fine of ten shillings. During the same period the Catholic Church too con-demned large assemblies at patterns because of the risk of violence, but it has ceased to disapprove of holy wells and pattern days and some local clergy now participate in the pilgrimage, for instance saying Mass on the site. John O'DONOVAN researched holy wells and pattern days all over the country as part of his work for the ORDNANCE SURVEY.

> On the anniversary of each saint numbers flocked round these wells for the united purpose of devotion and amusement; tents and booths were pitched in the adjoining fields; erratic musicians, hawkers and showmen assembled from the neighbouring towns, and priests came to hear their confessions; the devotees, after going round the holy well several times on their bare knees, the laceration of which had a marvellous effect of expiating offences, closed the evening by dancing, and at their departure fastened a small piece of cloth round the branch of the trees or bushes growing near these consecrated waters, as a memorial of their having performed these penitential exercises.
>
> ANON.: *Tour in Ireland* (1808)

Paulin, Tom (Thomas Neilson Paulin, b.1949). Poet, playwright and critic. He was born in Leeds but grew up in Belfast. Educated at Hull and Lincoln College, Oxford, he is a director of FIELD DAY, for which he wrote *Riot Act* (1985), a version of Sophocles's *Antigone*, and a pamphlet 'A New Look at the Language' (1983). He has also written *Seize the Fire* (1983), based upon Aeschylus's *Prometheus Bound*. His first collection of poetry, *A State of Justice* (1977), won a Somerset Maugham award, and it was followed by such other collections as *Liberty Tree* (1983), *Fivemiletown* (1987), *Walking a Line* (1994), *The Wind Dog* (1999) and *The Invasion Handbook* (2001). These show Paulin's versatility, vernacular strength and intellectual independence. Though raised as an Ulster Protestant he abominates sectarianism, finding spiritual identification with the Republican ideals of the Rebellion of 1798 and taking as a model of radicalism William Hazlitt, whose biography he wrote as *Day-Star of Liberty: Hazlitt's Radical Style* (1998). A frequent panellist on late-night discussion television programmes, he tends to express trenchant views on the arts and the politics of Ireland and the Middle East so firmly that he risks sounding at times intemperate.

> In the violet light
> You watch a helicopter
> Circling above the packed houses,
> Probing streets and waste ground.
>
> 'Surveillances', in *The Strange Museum* (1980)

Peace People. A movement begun in August 1976 when three children of the Maguire family from the ANDERSONSTOWN area of Belfast were killed by a car driven by a runaway gunman. The founders of the movement were Mairead Corrigan, the children's aunt, Betty Williams and Ciaran McKeown, a local journalist. Peace rallies were held throughout Ireland, in London and abroad, and each of the founders made efforts to counter violence by visiting scenes of possible confrontation, often at risk to themselves. Financial support came from Norway, Germany and America, and Williams and Corrigan were joint recipients of the Nobel Peace Prize in 1976. Disputes over how the money should be spent and what future tactics should be eventually split the movement, though without personal recrimination. The Peace People ceased to exist as a formal movement by the end of the 1970s, but each of the participants has continued efforts for peace.

Peace Preservation Force. *See* PEEL, SIR ROBERT; PEELER.

Peacock, The. The smaller adjunct to the ABBEY THEATRE that has tended to be used for 'alternative' theatre: verse drama, satirical review and experimental plays. It staged the first productions of the GATE THEATRE (1928–31) and now as a fully equipped theatre with flexible seating arrangements continues to stage 'downstairs' plays regarded as less suitable for the main auditorium.

Peaidí an Dúna ('Paddy of the fort'). The nickname of Pádraig Ó Maoileoin (1913–2002).

Ó Maoileon, a native of Couminole near Dunquin in the Corca Dhuibhne Gaeltacht (*see* DINGLE PENINSULA) and a grandson of Tomás Ó Criomhthain (*see* OILEÁNACH, AN T-), worked for 30 years as a garda in Dublin before becoming part of the editorial team of Ó Domhnaill's Irish–English dictionary. He was regarded as an expert on the CANÚINT of his own area.

See also LÁ BREÁ.

Pearce, Edward Lovett (*c.*1699–1733). Architect of the Palladian school. He was born in England of Irish extraction, and after serving in the army arrived in Dublin around 1726. He collaborated with the Italian architect Alessandro Galilei on the design of CASTLETOWN HOUSE, Co. Kildare, and in 1728 was commissioned to design the House of Parliament in COLLEGE GREEN, Dublin. In 1730 he was appointed surveyor-general. He died suddenly in 1733 and Richard CASTLE took over his practice.

Pearse, Margaret[1] (d.1932). Republican and mother of Patrick and Willie PEARSE. She and all the other women TDs in the Dáil (WOMEN AND CHILDERS PARTY) were vehemently against the TREATY, probably in the case of Kathleen CLARKE, Mary MACSWINEY and Margaret Pearse out of reverence for their heroic dead. She toured America May–October 1924, mainly to raise funds for the impoverished ST ENDA'S SCHOOL's but also to promote the Republican viewpoint. Her speeches began: 'Don't sympathize with me over the loss of my sons. Congratulate me. It is a grand thing to know that I have had the privilege of being the mother of two young men who died battling for our dear old land.'

Pearse, Margaret[2] (1878–1969). Teacher and elder sister of Patrick PEARSE. She was born in Dublin and educated at the Holy Faith Convent in Glasnevin. She taught with her brothers at ST ENDA'S SCHOOL and with her mother, also Margaret PEARSE, strove to keep the school open after the deaths of Patrick and William.

In 1926 she undertook a lecture tour in the United States to raise funds. She was TD for Co. Dublin (1933–7) and from 1938 until her death a member of the senate. The school passed into her possession on her mother's death in 1932 but closed in 1935 for lack of funds. She died in Dublin on 7 November 1969 and was given a state funeral. She bequeathed the house and grounds of St Enda's to the state; the building, in Rathfarnam, Dublin, now houses the Pearse Museum.

Pearse, Patrick [Henry] (1879–1916). Poet, educationalist and revolutionary, also known as Pádraic Pearse. He was born in Dublin and educated at Westland Row Christian Brothers School, the Royal University and the King's Inns. A cultural Nationalist from an early age, he joined the GAELIC LEAGUE in 1896 and was editor of An CLAIDEAMH SOLUIS (1903–9) before resigning to work full-time at ST ENDA'S SCHOOL, the Irish-speaking school he had founded the previous year, which was based upon his own educational theories (published in *The Murder Machine*, 1912). He was one of the founders of the IRISH VOLUNTEERS in 1913 and a member of the IRB. His graveside oration at the funeral of the Fenian Jeremiah O'DONOVAN ROSSA on 1 August 1915 is much quoted, particularly by PHYSICAL-FORCE RE-PUBLICANS:

Life springs from death and from the graves of patriot men and women spring living nations. The defenders of this realm have worked well in secret and in the open. They think that they have pacified Ireland. They think that they have purchased half of us and intimidated the other half. They think that they have foreseen everything, think they have provided against everything; but the fools, the fools, the fools they have left us our Fenian dead, and while Ireland holds these graves Ireland unfree shall never be at peace.

Pearse was commander-in-chief of the Volunteers during the EASTER RISING. He was a signatory of the PROCLAMATION OF THE REPUB-LIC and president of the provisional government, and it was he who signed the order for the unconditional surrender of the rebels. He was court-martialled and executed by firing squad in Kilmainham on 3 May 1916, and his brother William PEARSE, who had fought with him in the GPO, was executed on 4 May.

Political and educational writings occupied Pearse most, but he found time to write stories, poems and plays in English and Irish. Of his English poems, 'The Mother', 'I Am Ireland', 'Renunciation', 'The Fool' and 'The Wayfarer' (written on the day before his death) are the best known and frequently anthologized:

Lord, thou art
hard on mothers:
We suffer in their coming and their going;
And tho' I grudge them not, I weary, weary
Of the long sorrow – And yet I have my joy:
My sons were faithful and they fought.

PATRICK PEARSE: 'The Mother'

His play *The Singer* (1915) is about his self-fulfilling prophecy of the blood sacrifice that obsessed him. *Íosagán agus Sgéalta Eile* ('little Jesus and other stories', 1907) and *An Mháthair agus Sgéalta Eile* ('the mother and other stories', 1916) are collections of stories, while *Suantraidhe agus Goltraidhe* ('lullabies and laments', 1914) contains his poems in Irish, some of which are versions of his English poems. His *Collected Works* were edited by a former pupil and secretary, Desmond RYAN, and published 1917–22.

See also PEARSE, MARGARET[1].

Pearse, William (1881–1916). Revolutionary. He was born in Dublin, the younger brother of Patrick Pearse, and educated at Westland Row Christian Brothers School. He worked for some time in his father's stone-masonry business and studied art in Dublin and in Paris. A fluent Irish speaker, he later taught art at ST ENDA'S SCHOOL, as time went on shouldering more and more responsibility for the running of the school. He joined the IRISH VOLUNTEERS and although he played no part in organizing the EASTER RISING he fought with the rank of captain in the GPO, and was arrested at the end of Easter Week and court-martialled. He was executed by firing squad in Kilmainham on 4 May, a day after his brother's death. By executing the younger Pearse brother, it was believed by many out of simple vindictiveness, the British created 'another martyr for old Ireland' (*see* 'MOUNTJOY JAIL ONE MONDAY MORNING, IN').

Pearse Station. *See* WESTLAND ROW STATION.

Peat. *See* BOG[1]; TURF.

Peata. An organization with headquarters in Dublin that provides animals for institutions caring for the elderly. 'Pet therapy' is found to be especially of value to patients suffering from dementia, and Peata (the Irish word for 'pet') supplies teams of visiting dogs with their handlers. It is reckoned that the actual stroking of a quiet animal may be beneficial.

Peatachán (Irish *peata*, 'pet'). A pettish or peevish child.

Peck, Gregory (1916–2003). Film star. He was born Eldred Peck on 5 April 1916 in La Joliffe, the son of an Irish father whose name he took professionally. Tall, almost too handsome and with an irresistible voice, the essence of slightly stiff integrity, he was a star from the time he appeared as a priest in a film of A.J. Cronin's novel *The Keys of the Kingdom* (1944). He played General MacArthur (1977), Captain Ahab (1956), Captain Horatio Hornblower (1951), many gritty cowboys and fighting men, and Audrey Hepburn's honourable squire in *Roman Holiday* (1953). He won an Oscar as Atticus Finch in *To Kill a Mocking Bird* (1962). Peck was a regular visitor to Ireland and would have been US ambassador if Lyndon Johnson had run for a second term. He was named Irish-American of the year in 1997 and made a DLitt of the National University of Ireland in 2000. He died on 12 June 2003.

Pee Dees. The Progressive Democrats, a political party founded by Des O'Malley and Mary Harney in late 1985 with the stated objective of 'breaking the mould' of Irish politics. The party adopted liberal social policies, arguing for the separation of church and state, and liberal economic policies also, promoting competition and the market economy. Despite achieving fairly modest electoral support, the Pee Dees have been in government, in coalition with Fianna Fáil, from 1996 to date.
See also TEMPORARY LITTLE ARRANGEMENT.

Pee Flynn. *See* FLYNN, PEE.

Peel, Sir Robert (1788–1850). Tory politician. He was born the son of a self-made cotton millionaire, and could afford not only a Harrow and Oxford education but also the rotten borough of Cashel, which first enabled him to sit in Parliament in 1809. He was chief secretary for Ireland (1812–18) and his vigorous defence of the Union and bitter opposition to CATHOLIC EMANCIPATION earned him the inevitable nickname ORANGE PEEL, probably from his lifelong adversary Daniel O'CONNELL (with whom he almost fought a duel), though it is not absolutely certain that O'Connell described Peel's smile as 'like the silver plate on a coffin'.

Though naturally conservative (and defensive as 'new money' in a landowning party), Peel was essentially pragmatic and, to the unbiased, a reformer of Irish life. His Peace Preservation Force (1814) and the PEELERS that succeeded it established a rule of law that protected the weak in what had been an unruly country. His measures during the potato failure of 1817 (a kind of dress rehearsal for the ghastliness of the Great Famine) were effective, as was his handling of the first winter of the 'hungry Forties', though his importation of the alien American corn or INDIAN MEAL caused it to be known as 'Peel's brimstone'. He eventually supported Emancipation, but effectively killed O'Connell's tactic of the MONSTER MEETING, banning the Clontarf meeting in October 1843, which was to be the greatest of all. He died after a fall from a horse.

Peeler. A member of the Royal Irish Constabulary (RIC). The nickname derived from the mistaken belief that Sir Robert PEEL (1788–1850) had founded the Irish (later Royal Irish)

Constabulary in 1836. He had, in 1814, introduced a forerunner, a Peace Preservation Force, that was to be dispatched to disturbed counties.

'Peeler and the Goat, The'. A poem by Darby Ryan (*see* BARD OF BANSHA, THE) about an incident in 1830 when a goat was arrested by an officious member of the Royal Irish Constabulary in Bansha's main street, allegedly for 'roistering' and butting another policeman. Ryan, on horseback, is reputed to have read the poem in public outside Bansha's Old Church on a Sunday morning.

> The Bansha peeler went out one night on duty
>   and patrolling-O
> He spied a goat upon the road, who seemed to be
>   a strolling-O
> With bayonet fixed he sallied forth and seized
>   him by the wizen-O
> Swearing out a mighty oath he'd send him off to
>   prison-O.
> 'Oh mercy! Sir,' the goat replied. 'Pray let me tell
>   my story-O
> I am no rogue or ribbon man, no croppy, whig or
>   tory-O
> I'm guilty not of any crime ne'er petty nor high-
>   treason-O
> And I'm sorely wantin' at this time, for 'tis the
>   rantin' season-O.'

'The Peeler and the Goat' is also a figure-dance from the COUNTY BOUNDS area of Kerry and Cork.
See also PEELER.

Peel's brimstone. *See* INDIAN MEAL; PEEL, SIR ROBERT.

Peep o' Day Boys. A Protestant society spawned by the rise in religious tension in Co. Armagh in the mid-1780s. The immediate source was Protestant dismay at the repeal of some of the anti-popery legislation (*see* POPERY LAWS), but latent paranoia and the perceived rise of a Catholic merchant class in the larger towns also played their part. In particular, Catholic involvement in the changing cottage linen industry, previously exclusively Protestant, led to raids on Catholic houses, burning of looms

and the seizure of defensive arms, which Catholics were theoretically not entitled to hold. The formation of the Catholic DEFENDERS in 1788 increased sectarian tension and led to the establishment in 1795 of the ORANGE ORDER, which most of the Peep o' Days joined.

Peg. A verb used in HIBERNO-ENGLISH, meaning 'throw': 'She pegged the book out the door after him.'

Pegeen Mike. The female protagonist of J.M. Synge's *The PLAYBOY OF THE WESTERN WORLD* (1907), and much the strongest character in the play. The daughter of Michael James Flaherty, a SHEBEEN keeper, she is entranced by the wild poetry of the hero, Christy Mahon, and shown to be capable of it herself in spite of being 'a girl you'd see itching and scratching, and she with the stale stink of poteen on her from selling in the shop', according to her older rival, the earthy Widow Quin:

> Well the heart's a wonder; and, I'm thinking,
> there won't be our like in Mayo for gallant lovers,
> from this hour to-day.

When Christy's prevarications are revealed she leads those who punish him, burning his leg with a sod of peat, and it is she who closes the play with cries of sorrow at his loss:

> Oh, my grief, I've lost him surely. I've lost the
> only Playboy of the Western World.

Peggy's leg. A stick of hard boiled sweet, a cheap piece of confectionery popular among children.

Pegh or **pech.** An ULSTER-SCOTS verb meaning 'pant', 'breathe loud and fast'.

> But there wos John, he had his two hands up,
> Scared like an' peghin', with no hat or coat.
>   W.F. MARSHALL (1895–1952): 'John the Liar', in
>   *Ballads and Verses from Tyrone* (1929)

Peig (Peig Sayers, 1873–1958). Irish-language SEANCHAÍ and autobiographer. She was born in Dunquin on the DINGLE PENINSULA in west Kerry. She went into service in Dingle as a young girl, then lived much of her life on the Great Blasket (*see* BLASKET ISLANDS) after her marriage to islander Pádraig Ó Gaoithín in 1892. She bore ten children, only five of whom survived, most to emigrate to the United States, and was widowed while still a fairly young woman. She became famous as a *seanchaí*, attracting folklorists and scholars to the Blaskets – her stories were published in a collection called *Scéalta ón mBlascaod* ('stories from the Blaskets') – and was persuaded to dictate her own story *Peig: Tuairisc a thug Peig Sayers ar a beatha féin* ('an account given by Peig Sayers on the events of her own life', 1936) to her son Mícheál. For decades the book was a fixture on the Irish curriculum, its context becoming increasingly remote to the growing number of urban students, and its content considered to be sanitized by scholars familiar with Peig's more earthy stories from folklore. A translation by Bryan MacMahon was published in 1973. Peig Sayers's second book, *Machtnamh Sean-Mhná* (1939), was translated by Seamus Ennis as *An Old Woman's Reflections* (1962). Peg moved to the mainland in 1942 in advance of the general resettlement of the islanders (1953), and after a long illness died in hospital in Dingle.

Penal Days. The loose and generally emotive term applied to the years of Irish Catholic disadvantage in the 17th and 18th centuries. Religious persecution was real, notably from 1649 until the Restoration in 1660, during the 'Popish Plot' (1678–81) agitation of Titus Oates (1649–1705), and after the WILLIAMITE WAR, when POPERY LAWS gave legal respectability to local zealots. The folkloric memory of the MASS ROCK, with priests at risk of their lives celebrating the liturgy in the open air in remote areas – together with the notion that the same bounty was paid for the head of a wolf as of a priest – were part of the 19th-century catalogue of infamy associated with Britain, as in Thomas DAVIS's ballad quoted below. These aspects were probably exceptional rather than general, certainly in the 18th century, when the POPERY LAWS were rather concerned with the social and political emasculation of Catholics than the prevention of religious practice. There

was no general ambition to convert Papists to the true faith; it was sufficient to make them politically and socially null. The tradition of true horrors so sedulously handed down in the oral history nearly all belong to the period of Cromwellian measures.

> They bribed the flock, they bribed the son,
> To sell the priest and rob the sire;
> Their dogs were taught alike to run
> Upon the scent of wolf and friar ...
> THOMAS DAVIS (1814–45): 'The Penal Days' (1842)

Penal Laws. *See* POPERY LAWS.

Penny journals. Weekly magazines written to satisfy an increase in literacy and renewed interest in Ireland's past. The *Dublin Penny Journal* (30 June 1832–25 June 1836) and the *Irish Penny Journal* (4 July 1840–26 June 1841) had articles on Irish legends, saints, archaeological remains and beauty spots, plus stories, articles and poems by leading writers of the times. The name chiefly associated with both journals is George PETRIE, who wrote about Irish antiquities and arranged for illustrative engravings. The views of the editors of each showed a remarkable consonance: the *Dublin Penny Journal* was described as 'a purely national journal, utterly free from all taint of party bias or feeling', while the *Irish Penny Journal* described itself as 'a cheap literary publication for the majority of people in the country, combining instruction with amusement and staying away from polemic or political issues'.

Penny whistle. *See* WHISTLE.

People's Democracy. A radical civil rights movement formed by Bernadette DEVLIN, Michael Farrell and Eamonn McCann at Queen's University Belfast in October 1968 as a result of RUC suppression of a march in Derry. Like their American student counterparts, the members of People's Democracy (PD) knew the value of publicity, and the cameras and eyes of the world were on them when a small PD group marched from Belfast to Derry – the so-called 'Long March' – on 1 January 1969. They were ambushed by Loyalists under Major

Ronald Bunting at Burntollet bridge in Co. Derry on 4 January, and members of the police force, far from protecting the marchers, showed themselves to be openly sectarian (*see* BURNTOLLET AMBUSH). The march and the ambush – the PD members were described as 'mere hooligans' by prime minister Terence O'NEILL – had the effect of further polarizing opinion in Northern Ireland. In the general election of 1969 PD candidate Bernadette Devlin won a seat in Westminster for the Mid-Ulster constituency, and the party as a whole took 4% of the popular vote. PD soon transmogrified into a small group of Republican socialists, losing its general radical appeal.

Peppercanister. A nickname for St Stephen's Church on Upper Mount Street, near the Grand Canal, Dublin, referring to the church's tower, which is shaped like a pepperpot. The church was designed by the great Georgian architect James GANDON. Its fine acoustics means that it is regularly used for classical concerts as well as for Church of Ireland worship. The poet Thomas KINSELLA, whose Dublin home is nearby, published pamphlets under his own 'Peppercanister' imprint.

Peppergrass, Paul. The pen name of the novelist and priest John Boyce (1810–64). He was born in Donegal town in 1810, the son of a magistrate and leading hotelier. He was ordained in Maynooth in 1837, served as a curate in Fanad and Glenties, and emigrated to the United States in 1845. He joined the staff of Holy Cross College in Worcester, Massachusetts, in 1846, and while there achieved considerable fame as a lecturer on history and literature, and was a correspondent of Dickens, Charles LEVER and the French novelist Eugène Sue (1804–57). He wrote novels from a strongly Catholic point of view, including *Shandy M'Guire* (1848), about the Ireland he had left behind, *The Spaewife* (1853), an historical romance of Tudor England, and *Mary Lee* (1859), surely the earliest satire on a 'Yankee' in Ireland. He died on 1 January 1864 after a long illness.

Peregrinatio pro Christo. *See* FURSA; PEREGRINI.

Peregrini (Latin, 'pilgrims', 'wanderers', 'resident foreigners'). The term used to describe those Irish monks who imposed upon themselves the WHITE MARTYRDOM of exile from their beloved country to carry the faith to Dark Age Europe. The first of such who made the *perigrinatio pro Christo* ('the pilgrimage for Christ') was COLUM CILLE, who left for Scotland in 563 and spent the rest of his life there. Other notable *peregrini* were COLUMBAN, GALL and FURSA.

Per O atque Mac. A traditional means of distinguishing the native Irish:

> *Per O atque Mac veros cognoscis Hibernos*
> ('By O and Mac you will recognize the true Irish.')
>
> Quoted in William Allingham, *Diary* (1907), autobiographical introduction

Péronne. A town in northern France on the River Somme, the site of a monastery founded by Irish monks at the shrine of St FURSA. Fursa's brother ULTAN was abbot there, and it was known as *Peronna Scottorum* ('Péronne of the Irish') until its destruction by Norsemen in 880.

Perrot, Sir John (*c.*1527–92). Lord deputy and agent of the TUDOR RECONQUEST. He was president of Munster (1571–3) and ruthlessly suppressed the first DESMOND REBELLION. After his return as lord deputy (1584–8) he tried to impose SURRENDER AND REGRANT and English law, particularly in Ulster but also in Leinster and Connacht, but he clashed with the Gaelic chieftains and both the Old and New English (*see* OLD ENGLISH) because of his methods of achieving these aims. The corrupt William Fitzwilliam (1526–99), his successor as lord deputy (1588–94), invented evidence to have him charged with treason, but, although he was convicted, Queen Elizabeth did not have him executed. Perrot was rehabilitated after his death.

Personal Sketches. The highly colourful and entertaining account of the twilight of the 18th-century Anglo-Irish ASCENDANCY by one of its more rackety members, Sir Jonah Barrington. *Personal Sketches of His Own Times* in three volumes (1827–32) gives a valuable and witty, if naïvely nostalgic, account of his class from the inside.

> At the great house all disputes among the tenants were then settled – quarrels reconciled – old debts arbitrated: a kind Irish landlord reigned despotic in the ardent affections of the tenantry, their pride and pleasure being to obey and support him.
>
> *Personal Sketches of His Own Times*, I (1827)

See also HALF-MOUNTED GENTLEMEN.

Perverts. *See* SOUPERISM.

Pete Briquette. The stage name of Pat Cusack, a member of The Boomtown Rats rock group (*see* GELDOF, BOB). Peat briquettes are a fuel made from compressed peat, manufactured by BORD NA MÓNA and widely sold in Ireland.

Peters, Mary (b.1939). Athlete. She was born near Manchester but her family moved to Ireland when she was very young, and she was educated at Ballymena Academy, Portadown College and Belfast College of Domestic Science. She won a gold medal in the pentathlon and shot in the 1970 Commonwealth Games and an Olympic pentathlon title in the 1972 games in Munich, with a world-record score of 4801 points. An athlete of great endurance and determination, she set British records in the shot, 100-metre hurdles and pentathlon. She was awarded an MBE in 1973 and a CBE in 1990, and has been an athletics trainer and a member of the sports councils of both Northern Ireland and Britain.

Pether the Packer. The nickname of Peter O'Brien (1842–1914), lord chief justice of Ireland (from 1889), who had a reputation for packing juries and spoke with a marked lisp. He was born on 29 June 1842 in Co. Clare and educated at Clongowes and Trinity College Dublin. Called to the Bar in 1865, he became attorney-general in 1888 and, though a Cath-

olic, was assiduous in administering the government's coercive measures. He was raised to the peerage in 1900 and died in Stillorgan, Co. Dublin, on 7 September 1914. The 'packing' was made possible because of an oddity in Irish law, which enabled the crown to reject individuals summoned for jury service in criminal cases. In a case concerning the sale of a crab unfit for human consumption, recorded by Maurice Healy (1873–1943) in *The Old Munster Circuit* (1939), he could scarcely control his amusement at a witness who had been too well prepared by her solicitor:

> The young lady took up her tale. 'Well, then … he selected one and gave it to me. So I relying on his skill and judgement, took it ' – 'Thtop, thtop!' cried Pether. 'You used thothe words also?' 'Yes, my Lord. 'Where were you educated?' 'At the Ursuline Convent, Blackrock, my Lord.' 'And thinth when have the UrthulineThithters included Thection Fourteen of the Thale of Goodth Act in their curriculum?'

Petrie, George (1790–1866). Antiquarian and scholar. He was born in Dublin and educated at the Royal Dublin Society art school. His conversion to a passionate interest in Irish antiquities dated from his travels as an illustrator of guide books, when he became acquainted with some of the great archaeological treasures of the country. In 1833, the year of publication of his *Essays on the Round Towers of Ireland*, he was employed by the ORDNANCE SURVEY, along with John O'DONOVAN and Eugene O'CURRY. When funding for his work at the Ordnance Survey ceased in 1841 he continued to strive for the preservation of relics of ancient life, writing of Irish antiquities in *The Dublin Penny Journal* and later in *The Irish Penny Journal* (*see* PENNY JOURNALS). To him must be given credit for the preservation of manuscripts like the ANNALS OF THE FOUR MASTERS and such treasures as the Cross of CONG in museums and public institutions in Ireland.

Petty, William. *See* DOWN SURVEY; KENMARE.

Pfizer riser. A nickname for the drug Viagra,

which is prescribed for erectile dysfunction and has been manufactured by the Pfizer Pharmaceutical Corporation at Ringaskiddy near Cork city since 1998.

Philadelphia, Here I Come! The first play (1964) by Brian FRIEL, written after he had become a full-time writer. It had a successful Broadway run and indicated that Ireland had a significant new playwright. It details the last night at home of a young man, Gar O'Donnell, who is due to leave for America. The chief part is played by two actors, who delineate Public Gar and Private Gar, the second showing how insecure and scared Gar really is. In scenes with his taciturn father, his loutish but innocent mates, his teacher, his one-time girlfriend, the local priest and Madge the housekeeper who helped rear him after the death at his birth of his mother, he tries desperately to find a reason for staying. The play is uproariously funny and heart-wringing at the same time, as his last attempt to talk tenderly to his father fails and he prepares himself for flight:

> *Private:* Watch her carefully, every movement, every gesture, every little peculiarity; keep the camera whirring; for this is a film you'll run over and over again – Madge Going to Bed On My Last Night At Home ... Madge ... [*Public and Private go into bedroom.*] God, Boy, why do you have to leave? Why? Why?
> *Public:* I don't know. I – I – I don't know.

Philbin Bowman, Jonathan (1969–2000). Journalist and media personality. He was born in Dublin on 6 January 1969 and educated at Newpark Comprehensive School, which he left at the age of 16, appearing on the The LATE LATE SHOW to explain his reasons. He was co-presenter of a radio programme, *The Rude Awakening*, on a Dublin station and became a provocative columnist for the *Sunday Independent*. He died in his home as the result of an accident on 6 March 2000.

Phillips, Molesworth (1755–1832). Royal marine and explorer. He was born in Swords, Co. Dublin, on 15 August 1755 and commissioned second lieutenant in the Royal Marines in 1776. He was appointed to the marine complement on the *Discovery*, one of the ships on Captain Cook's last voyage (the other being the *Resolution*), and sailed from Plymouth in July 1776 for the South Pacific. On 14 February 1779 Cook and a party of marines landed in Kealakekua Bay, Hawaii, to repossess one of the *Discovery's* boats. The natives, once friendly, had become hostile, and during the operation Cook was clubbed to death from behind. Phillips, himself wounded, managed to swim to another boat. On his return to England he was promoted to captain and in 1792 married a sister of Fanny Burney (1752–1840), thereby becoming part of Dr Johnson's literary circle. He died of cholera at his Lambeth home on 11 September 1832.

Phineas Finn. *See* FINN, PHINEAS.

Phoblacht, An. *See* AN PHOBLACHT.

Phoenix Flame, The. A book (1937) by Desmond Ryan that gives the history of the FENIANS. The title (apart from its age-old metaphorical connotation) came from the small Co. Cork town of Skibbereen where Jeremiah O'DONO-VAN ROSSA began his Phoenix National and Literary Society in 1857. With a motto 'Ireland for the Irish' and the conviction that 'the Saxon' would never 'relax his grip except by the persuasion of cold lead and steel,' it was almost inevitable that its active members should soon be subsumed into Fenianism.

Phoenix Park. The beautiful 1752-acre (709-ha) park on Dublin's north side, one of the largest urban amenities in Europe. It was enclosed in 1662 to make a deer park of greater than 2000 acres (800 ha) around the Phoenix, the viceregal country residence, and received its present boundaries in 1744. The origin of the name is not Greek in spite of appearances but rather Irish: *fionn uisce* ('clear water'). The demesne contains ÁRAS AN UACHTARÁIN, the residence of the president of Ireland, together with the Zoological Gardens (1830), the Department of Defence and the home of the US ambassador. Because of its great size it has been able to accommodate the crowds for such events as the Eucharistic Congress (1932), the visit of President Kennedy (1963) and the one million people who came to see Pope John Paul II in 1979.

Phoenix Park Murders. The assassination with surgical knives on 6 May 1882 of Lord Frederick Cavendish (1836–82), the recently appointed chief secretary, and Thomas Burke (1829–82), the under-secretary, by a FENIAN splinter group who called themselves the IN-VINCIBLES. The eight-man group was led by James Carey (1845–83), who after his arrest in 1883 turned queen's evidence. Five of the party were publicly hanged, while Carey was spirited out of the country to South Africa. He was traced by Patrick O'Donnell, an Invincible, who on 29 July 1883 shot him dead on board the liner *Melrose* on a voyage from Cape Town to Natal. O'Donnell was hanged at Newgate in London on 17 December 1883. PARNELL was horrified and offered to apply for the Chiltern Hundreds (i.e. resign his parliamentary seat), but his followers and Gladstone persuaded him to stay and do what he could to save the situation. The savage and counterproductive event led to the establishment of the Special Irish Branch at Scotland Yard (the forerunner of the present-day anti-terrorist force).
See also PARNELLISM AND CRIME; SKIN-THE-GOAT.

Phoney or **phony.** An American slang word meaning 'fraudulent', 'spurious' or 'insincere', also current in Ireland and Britain from about 1920. It is said to derive from 'fawney', an obsolete cant word meaning the imitation gold ring used by confidence tricksters, itself from the Irish *fáinne*, 'ring'.

Phrases make history here. The rueful comment made by Sir John Maffey (1877–1969), the British ambassador during the Second World War, on the CHURCHILL–DE VALERA RADIO EXCHANGES in May 1945. In a letter to the Dominions Office on 21 May, Maffey wrote,

'There was balm for every Irishman in this, and with the Irish people today, Mr de Valera is as great a hero as the Irishman who scores the winning try at Twickenham ... This temperamental country needs quiet treatment and a patient, consistent policy. But how are you to control Ministerial incursions into your china shop? Phrases make history here.'

Physical-force Republicanism. The name given to the conviction held by various separatist groups from the UNITED IRISHMEN at the end of the 18th century to today's REAL IRA and CONTINUITY IRA that the only way to achieve national self-determination (or in the case of the IRA since 1922, the reunification of the country) is by waging war on the oppressor. The manifestations of physical-force Republicanism have included the ineffectual skirmishes of YOUNG IRELAND; the bombing campaigns of the FENIANS; the heroic sacrifices of the EASTER RISING of 1916; the guerrilla and propaganda warfare orchestrated with some success by Michael COLLINS during the ANGLO-IRISH WAR of 1919–21, and the terrorist and propaganda campaign waged by the Provisional IRA in Northern Ireland from 1970 to 1997. In the Republic, many resent the appropriation of the mantle of Wolfe TONE and Patrick PEARSE by the contemporary IRA, while for some REVISIONIST historians, the IRA of our time is an inevitable outcome of the glorification of 1916.

Phytophthora infestans. The fungal infection, originating in the Americas, that causes potato blight, turning the tubers into a black and noisome pulp. It was the chief cause of the GREAT FAMINE of the 1840s. The potato plants are infected by spores blown onto the leaves, and washed into the tubers by the prevalent Irish rain. Though efforts were made to discover a remedy, it was not until the 1880s that it was found that a mixture of lime and copper sulphate sprayed on the leaves prevented the blight.

Pickled Earl, the. The nickname given after his

death to Richard Southwell Burke (1822–72), 6th Earl of Mayo. He served as chief secretary of Ireland and was appointed viceroy of India in 1868. While carrying out an inspection of a penal colony he was murdered in 1872. He had requested that he be buried in his home village of Johnstown in Co. Kildare, and in order to transport his body on the long sea journey from India it is said that it was immersed in a barrel of rum. At his funeral, toasts were drunk to the 'Pickled Earl'.

Picts. The inhabitants of Scotland before the 5th-century invasion of Argyll (DÁL RIATA) by Scots from Ulster. Because of the short sea journey (32 km / 20 miles) there was regular traffic between Ireland and Scotland. One result was that there were Picts living in the north of Ireland, some of them becoming Christian, and some included in the list of Irish saints. When COLUM CILLE established his monastery on IONA he used it as a base to spread the Christian gospel among the pagan Picts. The Pictish territory survived in the northeast of Scotland until the 9th century, when it was more or less peaceably taken over by Kenneth MacAlpine (d.858), the Dalriadan king, to form a united kingdom of Scotland. The name, once thought to come from the Latin *Picti*, 'painted ones', is now held by modern scholars to have its roots in ancient Pictish, a Celtic language.

Pigeonhouse Fort. An area at the inner edge of what became known as the GREAT SOUTH WALL, Dublin, on which a blockhouse was built for storing materials and goods in about 1760. It takes the name by which it is known from John Pigeon (sometimes Pidgeon), who was resident caretaker of the blockhouse from 1761. He and his wife and daughters ran a business in the house, providing rest and refreshments for passengers disembarking from ships from England and Wales and for Dubliners visiting the construction site of the Great South Wall. After Pigeon's death in 1786, a bigger blockhouse was built by the Ballast Board that controlled Dublin Port, and in 1793, as a result of the increase in the number of passengers passing through the

area, the Pigeonhouse Hotel was constructed; it was an imposing structure, managed by a Mrs Tunstall.

In response to the REBELLION OF 1798, the government requested the use of the Pigeonhouse area as a temporary military post, and occupied what came to be called the Pigeonhouse Fort until 1897, the hotel being used for officers' quarters and the other buildings for various military uses. It was one of the barracks targeted in Robert EMMET's plans for rebellion in 1803. In 1897 the army vacated the fort and Dublin Corporation bought the complex for £65,000, the army retaining a right of way in perpetuity. From 1906 the Corporation used the Pigeonhouse harbour for the treatment and disposal of sewage, and in 1902 the foundation stone was laid for the Corporation's own generating station to supply the needs of Dublin. In 1971 the generator was taken over by the Electricity Supply Board, and now uses natural gas or oil to generate electricity.

Pigott Forgeries. *See* PARNELLISM AND CRIME.

Pig's back, to be on the. A HIBERNO-ENGLISH phrase meaning to be in a position of advantage. It is a literal translation of the Irish, *ar muin na muice*.

> Someone remarked: 'Henry's on the pig's back now'. It did not seem to me to be a particularly enviable position, but they seemed to imply that Father had just had a stroke of luck.
> ROBERT GREACEN (b.1921): *The Sash My Father Wore* (1997)

Pike Theatre. A small, experimental theatre in Dublin's Pembroke Street, established by Alan Simpson and Carolyn Swift in 1953. In the eight years of its existence, the Pike staged one of the first English performances of Beckett's *WAITING FOR GODOT*, the première of Brendan Behan's *The QUARE FELLOW*, and English-language premières of works by Jean-Paul Sartre and Eugène Ionesco.
See also ROSE TATTOO AFFAIR, THE.

Pilgrim's Way. An ESKER between Shannonbridge and the great monastic settlement of

Clonmacnoise in Co. Offaly; it became a road for medieval pilgrims.

Pilibeen (Irish *pilibín*). The green plover. Plovers were never harmed by farmers as it was believed that they ate from the fields the liver flukes that were the scourge of cattle and sheep.

Pilkington, Laetitia (1712–50). A friend of Jonathan Swift (*see* DEAN, THE). She was born in Dublin and at the age of 17 married a parson, Mathew Pilkington, who was made chaplain to Lady Charlemont. Laetitia began a friendship with Swift who procured for her husband a job in London, but the marriage ended because of her infidelity. Her *Memoirs*, which were published in Dublin in 1748, contain an account of the last days of Swift. She opened a bookshop in London, and when that venture failed returned to Dublin, where she died on 29 August 1750.

Pin, the. *See* PIONEERS.

Pincher. A term used in HIBERNO-ENGLISH for a whinger, a petty, CRABBID individual.

Pinkindindies. The members of the HELLFIRE CLUB who used to cut off the points of their scabbards and prick or 'pink':

> The persons with whom they quarrelled with the naked points, which were sufficiently protruded to inflict considerable pain, but not sufficient to cause death. When this was intended, a greater length of blade was uncovered.
>
> JUSTICE JOHN EDWARD WALSH: *Ireland Sixty Years Ago* (1847)

They were also known as Sweaters (as they made their victims sweat).

'Pint of Plain, A'. The paean of tribute to stout from Flann O'Brien in AT SWIM-TWO-BIRDS (1939):

> When money's tight and is hard to get
> And your horse has also ran,
> When all you have is a heap of debt –
> A pint of Plain is your only man.

Pioneers. The term used to describe members of the Pioneer Total Abstinence Association of the Sacred Heart. It was founded in 1898–1901

by Father James Cullen (1841–1921) and was intended as an exemplary rather than an actively crusading society. Yet it became a significant feature of Irish life, with 300,000 members, each required to wear the Pioneer lapel badge, known as 'the pin', which featured a representation of the Sacred Heart as described by St Margaret Mary Alacoque (*see* NINE FRIDAYS). Display of the pin was seen as very desirable in a prospective male partner until the 1970s. The association published a magazine that featured on its front cover a media or sporting celebrity wearing a pioneer pin. The pub culture of modern Ireland and the rise of teenage drinking have caused the number of Pioneers greatly to diminish from 50% of the population in 1968 to 13% in 2000, most members being older women.

Pip, the. A disease that causes poultry to waste away. The HIBERNO-ENGLISH phrase 'to give someone the pip' means to irritate or annoy.

Pirn. A Scots word once common in Ireland meaning 'reel', 'bobbin', 'spool', especially used by linen workers. It is used by Yeats as a verb with the spelling 'perne', meaning to wind thread on to a spool, and therefore analagous to his favoured word 'gyre':

> O sages standing in God's holy fire
> As in the gold mosaic of a wall,
> Come from the holy fire, perne in a gyre,
> And be the singing-masters of my soul.
>
> W.B. YEATS: 'Sailing to Byzantium' (1927), in *The Tower* (1928).

Pirrie, William James (1847–1924). Shipbuilder. He was born on 24 May 1847 in Quebec and brought home to Belfast on the death of his father when he was two. He attended INST from 1858 and four years later was apprenticed as a shipbuilder at HARLAND AND WOLFF's yard. There he rose quickly, becoming chief draughtsman and a partner in the firm in 1874. For the next 50 years the company was his life, and the statement that Harland and Wolff were 'shipbuilders to the world' was no idle boast. He became chairman in 1895 and helped the firm weather several periods of depression.

He had been a liberal in politics, supporting HOME RULE, and though he became more conservative as he grew older he dealt pragmatically with the sectarian and trade-union difficulties that the coming of the Northern Ireland state had brought to the shipyard. He was made a member of the new Northern Ireland senate, and created a viscount in 1922. He probably held on too long to office, for when he died of pneumonia on 7 June 1924 the company was found to be almost bankrupt. He was the greatest Irish businessman of his day, the epitome of the industrial competence of Belfast.

Pishogues or **pishrogues** (Irish *piseog*). A HIBERNO-ENGLISH word originally meaning 'charms' or 'spells' used for good or ill: to cure diseases or inflict injuries, to conserve or increase farm produce, or to bring bad luck to the produce. If two farmers were at loggerheads one might put the evil eye on the other ('work a pishogue') by taking meat or an egg from his neighbour and burying it on the boundary of the two farms. When the food rotted the crops would fail or farm animals sicken and die. Alternatively a farmer might seek to rid himself of a misfortune such as a sick animal by passing it on to his neighbour (*see* EGGS; SLING CALF; SPANCEL). Love charms were also pishogues (*see* DIVINATION). BEALTAINE (May Day) was the best day of the year to work any pishogue, for good or ill.

Pishogues also reflected a belief-system in which events are controlled by superhuman powers – in this sense, a pishogue is closer in meaning to the English term 'superstition'. For example, it was believed that a fisherman should not go out to sea if he met a red-haired woman on his way to his boat, that fire should not leave the house while butter was being churned, and that a grave should not be opened (for a funeral) on a Monday. There were many pishogues applying to birth, marriages and death. The phrase 'Ah, it's only an old pishogue' dismisses such a belief.

Pitch cap. An instrument of torture and means of extracting confessions or information used by the YEOS and militias, particularly before and during the REBELLION OF 1798. It consisted of a mixture of boiling pitch and tar, which was applied to the victim's head to make a kind of 'cap'. Anthony Perry, a Wexford Protestant who commanded the rebels in the northern parts of the county, was pitchcapped by the brutal North Cork militia at the start of the Rebellion and revealed to them some of the plans of the insurgents.

Pitchfork. *See* GRAIP.

Plain People of Ireland, the. The intermittent commentators in CRUISKEEN LAWN who react with a deflationary lack of enthusiasm to some of Myles na Gopaleen's wilder flights:

> *The Plain People of Ireland:* Did you really go to Clongowes?
> *Myself:* Certainly.
> *The Plain People of Ireland:* Isn't that a fancy place, gentlemen's sons and all the rest of it?
> *Myself:* It is. That's what I mean.
> *The Plain People of Ireland:* Um. Did they teach you spelling there at all?
> *Myself:* They taught me anything you like to mention.
> *The Plain People of Ireland:* How about the word 'judgement' above? Unless I am very much mistaken, that should be JUDGMENT.
> *Myself:* It is unthinkable that you should be very much mistaken, but if you take the trouble to look up any dictionary, you will find that either form is admissible, you smug, self-righteous swine.
> (*Half to Myself:* The ignorant self-opinionated sod-minded suet-brained ham-faced mealy-mouthed streptococcus-ridden band of natural gobdaws!)
> *The Best of Myles* (1968)

Plain set. *See* SET DANCES.

Plámás. The Irish term for 'flattery', 'soft words', frequently used in HIBERNO-ENGLISH, as in 'You're full of old *plámás*.'

Planet of the Irps. The nickname applied to the Divis Street tower blocks in the Lower Falls district of west Belfast during the Northern Ireland TROUBLES, playing on the 1968 film *Planet of the Apes*. The complex was regarded as a stronghold of the INLA and its political wing, the Irish Republican Socialist Party, known as the IRSP and by metathesis as Irps.

Plan of Campaign. The name given to a tactic adopted by the National League (successor of the LAND LEAGUE) between 1885 and 1893 as part of the continuing agrarian struggle. Although the LAND ACT of 1881 had brought about some improvement, by 1885 an agricultural depression meant that tenants had fallen behind with rents and evictions were again becoming commonplace.

At a meeting in Monaghan on 4 October 1885, Tim HEALY suggested that tenants in a given area ask a reasonable abatement of rent from their landlord. If they were refused they should lodge the proposed rent in a bank in the names of several local trustees of good standing, including the local parish priest, and use the funds raised by this means to help evicted tenants (the support of the Catholic Church was crucial to the Plan of Campaign). Healy also suggested that in order for this tactic to be successful it should be adopted on a national scale, making it impossible for landlords to evict large numbers of tenants. But it was not until the following autumn, after the number of evictions had continued to grow, not just on the west coast but throughout much of the country, that the plan gained general acceptance, with the publication of a document entitled 'A Plan of Campaign' in *United Ireland* on 23 October 1886.

The Plan of Campaign was first put into practice with maximum publicity by local tenants led by John DILLON and William O'BRIEN in Portumna, Co. Galway, the following month. The Plan was 'proclaimed' on 18 December 1886 as 'an unlawful and criminal conspiracy', and Dillon and other exponents were charged with criminal conspiracy (although not convicted). By the early spring of 1887 Dillon estimated that 116 estates had been affected. But the Plan of Campaign faltered on two

grounds: opposition by PARNELL, who feared it would damage the Liberal–Nationalist understanding at Westminster; and the passing of a severe COERCION Act in March 1887, which was implemented by a tough new chief secretary, Arthur BALFOUR. Balfour suppressed branches of the National League and imprisoned its leaders, while soothing agrarian dissent by passing a LAND ACT the same year that brought a further 100,000 tenants within the scope of the provisions of the Act of 1881. He also managed, working both openly and in secret, to turn the Catholic Church against the Plan, and in April 1888 a papal rescript condemned it. The Plan foundered after the Parnell split in the IRISH PARTY, and was effectively over by 1893; it had, however, secured favourable terms for tenants on more than 70% of the estates involved in the campaign.

Plantation. The Tudor and Jacobean policy of settling people from England and Scotland in Ireland. It was intended ostensibly for the imposition of 'civility' upon the 'barbarous' native Irish, but also provided an opportunity for economic growth, increased control, security from foreign invasion and a means of disposing of surplus population. The authorities' instinctive attitude was to regard the land of Ireland as a micro-version of the American colonies, offering similar possibilities of advancement for landless younger sons, who would be subject to the same risk from the savage natives. The most successful plantations were the informal ones, as in the 17th-century investment of counties Antrim and Down in the north of the country with a large number of unassimilable Lowland Scots (*see* ULSTER PLANTATION).

The first attempt at planted colonization was made in 1556 in Laois and Offaly, the territories of the O'Connors and the O'Mores, during the reign of Mary Tudor – Laois and Offaly were named Queen's County and King's County in honour of Mary and her husband Philip II of Spain. Like the late-16th-century MUNSTER PLANTATION it proved troublesome and unproductive, especially at the beginning. The greatest confiscation occurred after the 1653 CROMWELLIAN SETTLEMENT, and with the final defeat of JAMES II in 1691 the Irish were left owning a mere 15% of the land. Even this was at risk owing to the POPERY LAWS. The recovery of Irish lands was to be the great pre-occupation of Ireland's 19th-century history (*see* LAND ACTS; LAND LEAGUE; LAND WAR).

Planxty¹. A piece of music written in honour of a patron. Turlough CAROLAN wrote a number of these pieces, the best known being 'Planxty O'Rourke' and 'Planxty Irwin'.

Planxty². A successful and innovative tradi-tional-folk group of the 1970s that included in its line-up at various times the finest of musi-cians and singers. Founded in 1972, the origi-nal group consisted of Andy IRVINE, Donal LUNNY, Christy MOORE, and Liam Ó FLYNN. It flourished until 1975 and again, after a split and a reunification, in 1978–81. The original four members reassembled for a series of Planxty concerts in January–February 2004.

Plastic Paddies. A mocking term applied to those children of first-generation immigrants to Britain who respond vigorously and noisily to things Irish – such as Guinness, folk music, St Patrick's Day and RIVERDANCE – with rather more enthusiasm than the folks in what they often call the OULD SOD.

Playboy of the Western World, The. The greatest play of J.M. SYNGE, first staged on Saturday, 26 January 1907 by the Irish National Theatre Society at the ABBEY THEATRE, the scene by the following Monday of the violent protests since known as the '*Playboy* Riots'. The term 'playboy' was one of slightly watchful approval, since it designated a latter-day hero with skills, physical attraction and a hint of danger, in contrast to the pedestrian peasants that were the norm, especially in the 'western world' of Connacht. The play, set in Co. Mayo, deals with the effect of Christy MAHON, a self-confessed parricide, on the people of a seaside village, parti-cularly PEGEEN MIKE, the daughter of Michael James Flaherty, the local publican. Christy at the start is of rather unprepossessing material, but grows to fill the role of playboy because of his reception.

The respect for Christy's 'gallous deed' among the people, especially the women, had an actual precedent in the James LYNCHEHAUN case, but it was the love-scenes (with imagery culled from Hyde's translations of the *Love Songs of Connacht*) and the implication that the murder had increased Christy's erotic appeal for the local women that caused Nationalist institu-tions, including the GAELIC LEAGUE, to object to another slur on the Irish nation. Neither did they did approve of the portrayal of the men coming from a funeral, 'stretched out retching speechless on the holy stones', but when W.G. Fay, the actor playing Christy, fluffed the line, 'It's Pegeen I'm seeking only, and what'd I care if you brought me a drift of chosen females, standing in their shifts itself, maybe, from this place to the eastern world?' the place erupted. At the time the word 'shift' was formally inde-cent anyway, and 'drift' had been used earlier as a collective noun for heifers, but Fay in his nervousness at the growing tension in the theatre substituted the words 'a drift of Mayo women in their shifts' for Synge's actual text. The disturbances lasted for a week, many of them generated as much by mischief as moral-ity. Similar disturbances occurred with greater or lesser intensity in England and America – the Irish-Americans were if anything more puritanical, more defensive and more vigorous in their reactions than the folk at home.

In time the play became the jewel in the Abbey's crown; in 1968 when the Abbey com-pany had an audience with Pope Paul VI they presented him with a rare edition of the play bound in white leather. In its time and place, however, it was quite an inflammatory piece; what the regular playgoers could sense, shifts aside, was the play's wildness, its anthropo-logical tap-roots, its parodic elements of anc-ient Irish myth, and the richness and uninhib-itedness of its language. Synge's great discovery as a Dublin member of the Ascendancy was, as he wrote in its introduction to the play, that

In a good play every speech should be as fully flavoured as a nut or an apple, and such speeches cannot be written by any one who works among people who have shut their lips on poetry. Ireland, for a few years more, we have a popular imagination that is fiery, and magnificent, and tender...

Even in the 21st century the *Playboy* holds its remarkable power, achieving a near-Shakespearean capacity for re-interpretation.

Pleasant Ned. The nickname of Edward Lysaght (1763–1810), an Anglo-Irish poet. He was born in Brackhill, Co. Clare, and educated at Trinity College Dublin and at Oxford, being called to both the Irish and English Bars. His main occupation was as a Dublin police magistrate. A strong supporter of the VOLUNTEERS, he celebrated them in verse and was a vocal opponent of the UNION. He was a member of the MONKS OF THE SCREW, famous for impromptu verse, bons mots and impersonations of John Philpot CURRAN, Henry GRATTAN and other notables of the period. He wrote a number of popular love songs, including 'On Lovely Kitty's Singing' and 'Kate of Garnyvillo', and is suggested as the author of the superlative 'Kitty of Coleraine'. Lysaght died impoverished in 1810, but so popular was 'Pleasant Ned' that £2000 was collected for his wife and family.

> While other nations tremble, by proud oppressors gall'd,
> Our hustings we'll assemble, by Erin's welfare call'd.
> Our Grattan, there we'll meet him, and greet him with three cheers;
> The gallant man, who led the van of Irish Volunteers.
> 'The Man who led the Van of Irish Volunteers', in *Poems* (1811)

Pledge, the. A phrase used both of the general confirmation pledge administered by the bishop willy-nilly to all the pupils in the church (to abjure alcohol until the age of 21) and of the voluntary promise made to become a member of Father Mathew's temperance movement (*see* APOSTLE OF TEMPERANCE, THE) or of the

PIONEERS (the Pioneer Total Abstinence Association). For a boy or man to 'take the pledge' was an outcome devoutly wished for by all mothers and by the wives and families of habitual drinkers.

Pleidhce. An Irish word for a 'stump' or 'stake', or a 'bundle of rolls of carded wool', used in HIBERNO-ENGLISH to mean a fool (male) or worthless person.

Pleusgadh na Bulgóide. A bilingual satirical dramatic squib (1903) by Douglas HYDE, pillorying the Trinity College dons who attacked Irish, especially Sir John Pentland MAHAFFY and Robert Atkinson, who had denounced the language before the Intermediate Education Commission in 1899. The title means 'the bursting of the bubble', and in the play Hyde uses the word *bulgóid* ('bubble') to stand for *Tríonóid* ('Trinity'). The plot describes how the faculty of 'Bubble College' are cursed by Ireland in her persona of the Sean-Bhean Bhocht (*see* POOR OLD WOMAN, THE) so that the only language they can speak is Irish. This occurs on the day when the college is being visited by the lord lieutenant and his entourage. The characters Mac Eathfaidh (Magaffy) and Dr Mac Aitchinn (Hatkin) are clearly based on the detractors, guying especially the former's affected lisp, and the dialogue describing Irish is only a slight exaggeration of their evidence before the commission:

> *Mac Eathfaidh:* I have the beth pothible reason for knowing that what they call their modern language is an appalling jargon. It's really only a theries of grunts and thqueals and snorts and raspings in the throat.

Plough and the Stars, The. An anti-heroic play by Sean O'CASEY about slum life in Dublin around the time of the EASTER RISING. The play's realistic account of the urban majority's reaction to the events, including looting and jeering at IRISH VOLUNTEER prisoners, and the inclusion of the character Rosie Redmond, a prostitute, caused a famous ABBEY THEATRE riot when the play was first produced there in

1926. The citizens of the Free State were not in the mood to face the reality of Dublin's actual response to happenings that ten years on had assumed an almost religious significance. In spite of cries that there were no prostitutes in Dublin, Yeats addressed the audience with the oft-quoted remark, 'You have disgraced yourselves again.'

As ever with O'Casey the play is rich in character and exuberant speech, which happily distracts from the sentimentality of some of the dialogue. Jack Clitheroe, a Volunteer, and his new wife Nora share a tenement with a ripe collection of characters, including Fluther Good, a bibulous carpenter, who never wishes 'to say anything derogatory', the Covey, a slogan-repeating socialist, Bessie Burgess, a Protestant woman whose son is fighting in France, and Mrs Gogan and her consumptive daughter Mollser. Clitheroe is greatly influenced by a speech given by 'the Man', heard from off-stage, calling for blood sacrifice, and is killed during the fighting. Fluther brings home the pregnant and miscarrying Nora who had gone out into the war-torn city to try to find her husband, and Bessie is shot trying to drag the now demented Nora from the window. The play ends with the ironical singing of 'Keep the Home Fires Burning' by British Tommies, as Dublin itself burns – a neat summary of the play's pacifist message. The title refers to the flag of the IRISH CITIZEN ARMY (*see* STARRY PLOUGH, THE), a pictorial version of the well-known constellation.

Plubaire (Irish *plobaire*). A HIBERNO-ENGLISH word for a person (often a child) with round, fleshy cheeks.

Plucking the Geese. 'They're plucking the geese in Connacht' – said when flakes of snow begin to fall. Plucking goose and duck feathers was a staple of work in CONGESTED DISTRICTS, unusually prevalent in the west.

Plucks (Irish *pluc*, 'cheek'). A word used in HIBERNO-ENGLISH for the cheeks, especially plump cheeks, for instance a baby's or child's.

Plunkett, Horace (1845–1932). Pioneer of the cooperative movement in Ireland. The son of Lord Dunsany, he first set up a cooperative shop on the family estate, and gained further experience of farming by ranching in Wyoming for ten years. He returned to Ireland in 1888, began the cooperative movement and became the first vice-president of the Department of Agriculture and Technical Instruction. Between the 1890s and 1914, more than 800 cooperative societies were established in Ireland, including cooperative creameries, supply centres and credit societies. Plunkett was associated with the policy known slightly maliciously as KILLING HOME RULE WITH KINDNESS. In 1894 he set up the IAOS (Irish Agricultural Organization Society), which helped to change the attitudes of the new Irish farmers. He appointed Æ as organizer and editor of the society's journal, *The Irish Homestead*. Plunkett's book *Ireland in the New Century* (1904) displeased many people because it was critical of certain aspects of the Catholic Church's influence in Ireland. Plunkett was a Unionist MP for Dublin, and was subsequently appointed a senator of the Free State, but after the burning of his house by Republicans in 1923 he left Ireland for good. He died in Weymouth in Dorset.

Plunkett, James (1920–2003). Fiction writer. He was born James Plunkett Kelly in Sandymount, Dublin, and educated at Synge Street Christian Brothers School and at the College of Music. After a clerkship in the Gas Company he became a trade unionist, working for James LARKIN, whose career he dramatized in *The Risen People* (1958). He was one of the writers who received encouragement from Sean O'FAOLAIN, and the October 1954 edition of *The BELL* included a novella and four stories by Plunkett, which were later published as *The Trusting and the Maimed* (1955). Plunkett is best known for his Dublin trilogy: STRUMPET CITY (1969) – the title borrowed from Denis Johnston's play *The OLD LADY SAYS NO!* – *Farewell Companions* (1977) and *The Circus Animals* (1990). These novels give an account of the changing fortunes of the city, from the dramatic days of the 1913 LOCKOUT to the mean-minded 1950s. Plunkett's *Collected Short Stories* was published in 1977. He died on 28 May 2003.

Plunkett, Joseph Mary (1887–1916). Poet and revolutionary. He was born in Kimmage, Dublin, but had poor health and spent much time abroad, living in Mediterranean countries including Algeria. He was a signatory of the PROCLAMATION OF THE REPUBLIC during the EASTER RISING and was executed on 4 May 1916, having married Grace GIFFORD on the eve of his execution. His poetry is in two volumes: *The Circle and the Sword* (1911), showing Arabic influences, and the posthumous *Poems* (1916). He is best known for lyrics with a strong mystical strain such as 'My Lady Has the Grace of Death' and the much-anthologized 'I See His Blood upon the Rose', which has also been set to music.

> I see His blood upon the rose
> And in the stars the glory of His eyes.

Plunkett, Oliver (1629–81). Canonized saint. He was born on 1 November 1629 at Loughcrew, near Oldcastle, Co. Meath, and ordained for the priesthood in Rome in 1654. He remained as professor of theology at the *Collegium de Propaganda Fidei* until 1669, when he was ordained Archbishop of Armagh. He was welcomed by his fellow OLD ENGLISH Catholics of the Pale, but viewed with suspicion by the Irish clergy of the greater part of the archdiocese. The post-Cromwellian church was in need of reform, and Plunkett was full of Counter-Reformation fervour. His work of reform was possible, if difficult, until the anti-Catholic frenzy that shook Britain after the fictitious 'Popish Plot' (1678), concocted by Titus Oates (1649–1705), caused the Dublin authorities to arrest the Archbishop of Dublin while Plunkett went into hiding. He was arrested in 1679 on trumped-up charges of treason, the evidence being provided by renegade clergymen. His trial in Ireland collapsed, but at a second trial in London the jury found him guilty. He was

executed at Tyburn on 1 July 1681 (since kept as his feast day), the last Catholic to be martyred in England. His disembowelled, quartered body lies at Downside Abbey, and his head is preserved in St Peter's Church in Drogheda, Co. Louth. He was canonized on 12 October 1975, the third and latest Irish saint so to be honoured.

Poc. *See* PUCK[2].

'Poc ar Buile, An' ('the raging buck-goat'). A very well-known comic song in Irish, with a rousing chorus. It was written by Donal Mullins (of whom nothing else is known) and originated in Kerry, as the placenames in the song indicate. It was made famous by Cork singer Seán Ó Sé, who sang it with CEOLTÓIRÍ CHUALANN, and is often performed in pubs by people whose store of CÚPLA FOCAL is very small indeed.

> *Ar mo ghabháil dom siar chun Droichead Uí*
> *Mhórdha*
> *Píce im dhóid 's mé ag dul I meithil*
> *Cé chasfaí orm I gcumar ceoidh*
> *Ach pucán crón is é ar buile*
>
> *[Curfá:]*
> *Ailliliú puilliliú,*
> *Ailliliú tá'n poc ar buile.*
> *Ailliliú puilliliú,*
> *Ailliliú tá'n poc ar buile.*
>
> (As I was going west to Moore's Bridge
> My pike in my fist as I went to work on a
>   MEITHEAL
> What should I meet in a foggy valley
> But a very angry tan buck-goat?
>
> *[Chorus:]*
> Ailliliú puilliliú,
> Ailliliú the goat is raging.
> Ailliliú puilliliú,
> Ailliliú the goat is raging.)

Pogue mahone (Irish *póg mo thóin*, 'kiss my arse'). A humorous HIBERNO-ENGLISH catch-phrase, conveying disrespect or incredulity, also sometimes used to trick foreigners into using a vulgarity.

Pogues, The. A successful punk/folk group led by Shane McGOWAN between 1982 and 1991. The name of the band, originally POGUE MA-

HONE, derives from the HIBERNO-ENGLISH catchphrase.

Point, the. A venue for theatre, musicals and concerts that opened in 1989. It has the largest audience capacity in Dublin. The building, which is situated at the junction of North Wall Quay and East Wall Road, near the EAST LINK Bridge, was formerly a goods terminal for the Great Southern and Western Railway Company, constructed 1875–8.

Point-to-point. A horse race, usually a steeplechase (see STEEPLECHASING), in which amateur jockeys take part, not on a formal racecourse but from one point to another on an improvised or temporary circuit, over fields or on a beach. Point-to-points often form part of a summer festival or sports day in Ireland. Point-to-pointing is also popular in England.

Poison. An adverb used in HIBERNO-ENGLISH to describe a quality, even a desirable quality, taken to excess, as in 'She's poison neat.'

Police Service of Northern Ireland. See PSNI.

Polka set. A dance that had its origins in Bohemia and spread throughout Europe in the 19th century. The polka came to Ireland at the end of that century and was absorbed into some of the country's SET DANCES. The SLIABH LUACHRA set is known as the polka (locally pronounced 'polkay') set; it has six movements, finishing with a KERRY SLIDE and hornpipe, and takes about 30 minutes to dance. A half-set with two couples can be danced if there is a shortage of space.

Polkay. See POLKA SET.

Polluted. A HIBERNO-ENGLISH slang word, common in Dublin, meaning 'very drunk'.
See also OSSIFIED; SCATTERED; STAVING; STOCIOUS.

Polo Ground Final, the. The ALL-IRELAND football final of 1947 between Kerry and Cavan; it was, uniquely, played at a baseball stadium called the Polo Grounds in New York to commemorate the centenary of the GREAT FAMINE and the emigration of hundreds of thousands of Irish people to the United States. Cavan won the match, and one of several outstanding Cavan players, Peter Donoghue, who scored eight points in all, was dubbed the 'Babe Ruth of Gaelic football' by American sports writers (Babe Ruth was the premier baseball star of the era). The match was broadcast live on Raidio Éireann, with a memorable commentary by Micheál O'HEHIR.
See also 'GALLANT JOHN JOE, THE'.

Polybus. The pen name of Eaton Stannard Barrett (1786–1820), the poet and novelist. He was born in Cork, educated at Trinity College Dublin and practised law in London. His sequence of satirical verses *All the Talents* (1807) gave the Whig government formed after the premature death of the Younger Pitt the name by which it is known to history – 'the Ministry of All the Talents'. He became a newspaper proprietor, and wrote a satire on the Gothic novels of the time. His most famous poem is about the biblical Mary Magdalene.

> Not she with traitorous kiss her Saviour stung,
> Not she denied Him with unholy tongue;
> She, while apostles shrank, could dangers brave,
> Last at the cross and earliest at the grave.
> 'Woman' (1810)

Ponny. A drinking mug made out of enamel or tin, and by extension any small receptacle. The word, still in frequent use in the HIBERNO-ENGLISH of Munster, is of obscure derivation.

Pontifical Irish College. The Irish College in Rome, founded on 1 January 1628 by Father Luke WADDING and the Roman cardinal, Ludovici Ludovisi, for the education of Irish priests. Originally under the care of the Irish Franciscans, the college passed into the control of the Jesuits from 1635 until 1772. The college reopened after the Napoleonic Wars in 1826; since then it has been run by the Irish hierarchy, and all the rectors of the college have been Irish. The college is currently used mainly by postgraduate students, and has also became known as a venue for the marriage of Irish couples; about 300 couples marry here each year. During the summer holidays the college operates as a pilgrim centre. The building contains a monument to Daniel O'CONNELL, who famously left his heart to Rome.

Pooka (Irish *púca*). In Irish folklore, a mischievous demon that used to lead travellers astray, often taking the form of a horse that would thrust itself between its quarry's legs and carry the victim on a wild ride across country. It would lie in wait at natural breaks: bridges, crossroads, streams and other boundaries. The pooka was believed to spoil blackberries that remained after SAMHAIN (31 October), so these should never be picked. It was also used as a bogeyman by parents: 'Go to sleep or the pooka will come for you.' It figures in the proverb *An rud a scríobhann an púca, léann sé féin é* ('What the pooka writes the pooka can read'), used in relation to indecipherable writing or of obscure text.

Pookeen (Irish *púicín*, 'mask', 'eye-covering'). The HIBERNO-ENGLISH name for the game of blindman's buff.

Poolbeg Lighthouse. A lighthouse at the end of the GREAT SOUTH WALL in Dublin Bay, completed in its original form in 1767, 'a truncated cone of hewn granite cemented with the best tarras', and strengthened against the elements throughout the 18th and 19th centuries. The Poolbeg Lighthouse had a resident keeper until 1968; since then it has been automated. It is a popular landmark in the Dublin area.

Pooley. A HIBERNO-ENGLISH word for urine, especially of a domestic animal.

Poor Mouth, The. See *BÉAL BOCHT, AN*.

Poor Old Woman, the. The translation of the Irish *An tSeanbhean Bhocht* (often anglicized as Shan Van Vocht), one of the more desponding personifications of Ireland, used especially between 1750 and 1900. In Yeats's play CATH-LEEN NÍ HOULIHAN (1902), the old woman at a time of revolution turns into a young girl with 'the walk of a queen'. An alternative version was the more upbeat late 19th-century 'Gay Old Hag':

> Remember '98, says the gay old hag,
> When our Boys you did defeat, says the gay old hag;
> Then our Boys you did defeat but we'll beat you out compleat,
> Now you're nearly out of date, says the fine old hag.

See also CÁIT NÍ DHUIBHIR; RÓISÍN DUBH.

Poor Poll. *See* GOLDSMITH, OLIVER.

Popehead. A derogatory term applied to Catholics, especially in Loyalist areas of east Ulster. *See also* FENIAN; PROD.

Pope in Killybuck, The. The best-known of the plays of Louis [Joseph] Walsh (1880–1942). He was born in Maghera, Co. Derry, and practised as a solicitor in Ballycastle, Co. Antrim, and various towns in his home county, becoming a district justice in Co. Donegal. He was imprisoned in Derry jail as a member of SINN FÉIN in 1921 and recorded his experiences in *In My Keeping – and in Theirs* (1921). His best-known prose work is the humorous *Yarns of a Country Attorney* (1925). *The Pope in Killybuck*, a rural comedy (sometimes referred to as *The Auction in Killybuck*, depending upon the prevailing political temperature), was first staged by the Dalriada Players in Ballycastle in 1915. It describes the machinations of Alexander McCracken, a Protestant farmer, as he sets potential local buyers of different political persuasions in competition to improve the price of his farm. As he boasts at the end of the play, 'Here's to the Pope in Killybuck, and may there be strife between Orange and Green so long as Alexander McCracken has a bad farm of land to sell.'

Popemobile. The car, enclosed with bulletproof glass, used by Pope John Paul II on his visit to Ireland in 1979. It was christened on its first appearance at PHOENIX PARK on 29 September when the Pope said Mass before a congregation of 1.3 million people.

Popery Laws or **Penal Laws.** A series of anti-Catholic measures enacted between 1695 and 1709, following the end of the WILLIAMITE WAR. Their main source was the predominantly Protestant Irish Parliament, still reeling from the perceived vulnerability of earlier land settlements while the Catholic JAMES II briefly held power. The 1695 acts prohibited Catholics from carrying arms, from keeping horses valued at more than £5 (no Catholic could refuse to sell his horse for that price), from sending their children abroad for education and from joining the army. In 1697 'all papists exercising ecclesiastical jurisdiction and all regulars of the popish clergy' were given nine months to leave the kingdom. From 1704 Catholics were prevented from buying land or holding leases for more than 31 years. On the death of a Catholic father all the sons (or, if necessary, daughters) were given equal shares, though the eldest could inherit if he conformed to the established religion. Even more miserably unjust was the right granted to even distant conforming cousins to bring a DISCOVERY suit and claim the land from a papist owner. All professions except medicine were closed to Catholics, and inevitably many lawyers and members of other professions rushed to conform. In the same way a large number of the remaining Catholic landlords took the necessary oaths. By the end of the reign of George I (1714–27) it was possible to say that 'the law does not suppose any such person to exist as an Irish Roman Catholic'.
See also PENAL DAYS.

Pope's Brass Band, the. The nickname, imposed by their adversaries, of a caucus of Catholic MPs at Westminster in the 1850s, led by George Henry Moore, the father of the writer George MOORE; they themselves preferred the more neutral term 'Irish Brigade'. After the 1852 election they numbered 40, including Frederick Lucas, the founder of the Catholic periodical, *The TABLET*, and though they decided not to embark on the policy of parliamentary obstruction suggested by Moore (in astute anticipation of PARNELL's tactics), they were in a position to make demands because of the delicate balance of the British parties. They found to their chagrin that two of their more prominent members, William Keogh (1817–78) and John Sadleir (1814–56), had become members of Lord Aberdeen's Whig cabinet as, respectively, solicitor-general for Ireland and a junior lord of the treasury, in spite of their pledge of independent opposition.

Keogh later became a judge (1856) and showed himself notably stern with FENIAN leaders. Execrated by Nationalists and in failing health he went to Germany in 1878, where in Bingen-am Rhein on 30 September he attacked his valet and then cut his own throat. Sadleir's end was even more dramatic. He was known internationally for his financial dealings, owning railway companies in England, France and Switzerland, and when his Tipperary Joint-Stock Bank failed after he had overdrawn his personal account by £200,000 in 1856 he poisoned himself on Hampstead Heath on 17 February, a silver tankard smelling strongly of prussic acid at his side. He was the main source of the character Mr Merdle in Dickens's *Little Dorrit* (1857), the crooked financier who, although he gave lavish dinners, 'hardly seemed to enjoy himself much, and was mostly to be found against walls and behind doors'. Sadleir was also one of the inspirations of Trollope's character Phineas FINN in the Palliser novels.

Popular music. A growth industry in Ireland in recent decades; the country ranks fourth in the world after the USA, UK and Canada in terms of music sales, obviously benefiting from sharing the world language of popular music.
See also CLANNAD; CORRS, THE; ENYA; GELDOF, BOB; SHOWBANDS; O'CONNOR, SINÉAD; U2; VAN THE MAN.

Portadown. *See* TOWN POLITICALLY RELIABLE, A.

Portadown Saint. A geographically inaccurate, if hagiographically sound, description of Æ by John Butler YEATS (1839–1922), father of the poet. He called him 'a saint but born in Porta-down', when, in fact, he came from Lurgan, a town then 10 km (6 miles) distant.

Porter. A black beer, originally a weaker version of GUINNESS (Single X). The word derived from the association of the brew with porters and other labourers. The term is now synonymous with Guinness or with stout, although relatively little used by younger people.

Portlaoise. The county town of Co. Laois (formerly QUEEN'S COUNTY) in the Midlands, called Maryborough until 1922 after Queen Mary I. A large prison complex on the outskirts of the town (nicknamed the BOG) was used for the incarceration of Republican subversives from the North and the Republic during the Northern TROUBLES.

'Port na bPúcaí'. See INIS ICÍLEÁIN.

Portrait of the Artist as a Young Man, A. James JOYCE's (1916) fictionalized spiritual autobiography, using the name Stephen DEDALUS and describing his childhood, schooldays at Clongowes and Belvedere, consideration and rejection of a vocation to the priesthood, discovery of sex with prostitutes, Thomistic disputations with staff and fellow undergraduates at the Royal University, rejection of family and Ireland ('the old sow that eats her farrow'), his personal aesthetic to be achieved by 'SILENCE, EXILE AND CUNNING' and assorted 'epiphanies' (including that of the girl on Sandymount Strand: '– Heavenly God! cried Stephen's soul, in an outburst of profane joy'). The title is that of Rembrandt's painting in the Uffizi Gallery in Florence, and the total seriousness of the book should not be taken as absolutely literal. Joyce was 34 when it was published and he practically invites the reader to supply necessary and salutary ironies.

Post, An. The national postal service of the Republic of Ireland, established in 1984 when the post and telegraphs service was divided into postal and telecommunications units. It is a state-owned corporate entity. An Post has

operated LOTTO, Ireland's first national lottery, since its inception in 1987.

Potato. A vegetable, *Solanum tuberosum*, introduced into Ireland from the Americas – probably not by Sir Walter Raleigh (*c*.1584–1618), though he used to be given the credit. The first documentary reference is in the *Montgomery Manuscripts* (1606), which mentions land being granted to Scots immigrants in Co. Down for the cultivation of flax and potatoes. During the next two centuries the potato gradually became the staple diet of the very poor, requiring little but intensive labour for a short period of the year and being easy to cook. By the start of the 19th century 2 million acres (800,000 ha) were under the crop, yielding between 12 and 18 million tons annually. Each adult would eat up to 6.5 kilos (14 lbs) per day, which when supplemented by milk or herrings provided a perfectly nutritious diet. Three million people depended on the potato for existence, so that the triple failure of the crop due to the fungal infection PHYTOPHTHORA INFESTANS between 1845 and 1849 meant inevitable famine (*see* GREAT FAMINE, THE).

> Sweet roots of Erin, we can't do without them.
> No tongue can express their importance to man.
> Poor Corporal COBBETT knows nothing about them;
> We'll boil them and eat them as long as we can.
> REV. JOHN GRAHAM *Poems, Chiefly Historical* (1829)

Poteen (Irish *poitín*, 'little pot'). An illicitly distilled alcoholic drink made usually from a mash of potatoes, grain and yeast, and often flavoured nowadays with apple or orange. The spirit was also known as 'the crater' or 'crathur' ('creature') and was claimed to be superior to licit liquors by its steady drinkers. Its manufacture increased rapidly after the Revenue Act of 1779, which banned small stills and imposed duties on others. Though regarded as a necessary feature of wakes and weddings, especially as reported in songs and stories, its popularity was greater in the northern half of the country. Like much else in Ireland its peak production ended with the GREAT FAMINE, though its manufacture and even its consumption remained 'reserved sins' (one requiring confession to the bishop) in certain dioceses until the late 20th century. The successful enforcement of the law by the RIC (from 1857) and the RUC and Garda (from 1922) has severely confined its manufacture to offshore islands and remote mountain districts. *See also* CALAMITY WATER; DOUBLE; GLENSWILLY DECREE; SINGLINGS; WRECK.

Pothole. A term for a deep hole in the road, sometimes very extensive, occurring especially after frost or rain. Potholes have long been the bane of the Irish driver's life. They occur particularly in Co. Cavan, where the poor subsoil causes the road surface to sink or crack, so much so that Cavan is sometimes called 'pothole county'.

Pot oven. *See* CAKE.

Potts, Seán. *See* CEOLTÓIRÍ CHUALANN; CHIEFTAINS, THE.

Potts, Tommie (1912–88). Traditional musician. Born in the Coombe in Dublin, he was a traditional fiddler, improviser and composer who made only one recording, *The Liffey Banks* (1972), and rarely performed in public, yet had a significant influence on other musicians.

Poulnabrone. A portal dolmen, estimated to be more than 5000 years old, standing 6 km (4 miles) from Ballyvaughan in the BURREN area of Co. Clare. In 1986 excavations revealed a burial chamber under the dolmen containing the remains of at least 23 people – 16 children and 7 adults – buried between 3200 and 3000 BC. Poulnabrone is in a popular tourist area, and is one of the most celebrated single monuments in Ireland, attracting more than 100,000 visitors a year.

Poundies. A term for mashed potatoes with milk or butter, deriving from the pounding motion used to mash them. *See also* CHAMP; PANDY; THUMP.

Power. A popular HIBERNO-ENGLISH term for a great deal or a large number or quantity of people or things: 'That glass of punch did my flu a power of good,' or 'There was a power of people in town.' The expression 'More power to you!' or 'More power to your elbow' is one of admiration or encouragement, the opposite of begrudgery (*see* BEGRUDGER).

Power, John O'Connor (1848–91). Fenian and Nationalist politician. He was born in Ballinasloe, Co. Galway, and emigrated to America, where he joined the IRB. He was involved in the raid on Chester Castle in 1867. After his return to Ireland he joined Isaac BUTT's Home Rule League in 1873 and was elected MP for Co. Mayo. In Parliament he became a prominent obstructionist. Although ordered by the IRB to leave Parliament he refused, and was expelled from the Supreme Council in 1877. He was the first MP to offer support to the tenant farmers of Co. Mayo in 1879, joining the LAND LEAGUE on its inception. A rival of Charles Stewart PARNELL for the leadership of the IRISH PARTY in 1880, he became estranged from Parnell after the KILMAINHAM TREATY, supporting more radical initiatives on behalf of small tenant farmers, and stood as a Liberal in the general election of 1885 against Parnell's wishes. He lost his seat and retired from politics.

Powers. A brand of Irish whiskey that has many aficionados; it is a rival of PADDY² for the traditional whiskey market.

Powerscourt. A country house designed for Viscount Powerscourt by Palladian architect Richard CASTLE and constructed 1731–1740. Powerscourt is situated on a magnificent estate of 14,000 acres (5600 ha) outside the village of Enniskerry in Co. Wicklow, about 20 km (12 miles) from Dublin, which was granted to Richard Wingfield, 1st Viscount Powerscourt, in 1618. The gardens, which extend over 45 acres (18 ha), consist of formal gardens, walled gardens, lakes and terraces, and contain many fine marble and bronze statues and fountains. It is said that the terraced Italian garden took 100 men 12 years to finish. Powerscourt House was totally gutted by fire in 1974, but the building has since been partially restored and some of it is open to the public.

Powerscourt Waterfall, 3 km (2 miles) away, is, at 120 m (400 ft), the highest in Ireland, and the second highest in the British Isles after Eas a'Chùal Aluinn (200 m/658 ft) in the Scottish Highlands. An anecdote tells how Viscount Powerscourt dammed the waterfall so that he could entertain the visiting King George IV (1762–1830) by releasing a torrent while the two stood on a bridge built across the falls below. When the water was released the viewing bridge was totally washed away, but luckily it had not been possible to persuade the king to leave the banquet at Powerscourt House in order to see the spectacle.

> Looping off feline through the leisured air
> Water, a creature not at home in water,
> Takes to the air. It comes down on its forepaws,
> changes
> Feet on the rockface and again extended
> Bounds.
>
> DONALD DAVIE: 'The Waterfall at Powerscourt' (1955–6)

Power-sharing executive. The Northern Ireland executive set up at the Sunningdale Conference (6–9 December 1973). It contained Unionists led by Brian Faulkner with 24 seats, the SDLP led by Gerry Fitt with 19 seats, and the Alliance party led by Oliver Napier with 8 seats. The principal points were the insistence of the government of the Republic and the SDLP on the legitimate aspiration to Irish unity, but by consent and with the agreement of a majority of Northern Ireland people. A Council of Ireland would be set up to consider matters of trade and industry, tourism, culture, roads and such matters in which the two parts of Ireland might be considered interdependent. The executive took office on 1 January 1974, but was brought down by the UWC strike on 28 May. The term has also been revived for the (intermittently suspended) executive that emerged from the GOOD FRIDAY AGREEMENT.
See also WHITELAW, WILLIAM.

Poyning's Law (1494). A law enacted by Sir Edward Poynings, the English lord deputy (1494–5), by which the approval of the king had to be sought by the lord deputy to summon the Irish Parliament and to draft bills. Originally envisaged as a restriction on the power of the lord deputy (the Earl of Kildare having used the Parliament to support the Yorkist pretender Lambert SIMNEL in 1487), the law became, under WENTWORTH, a weapon against Parliament. In practice, during the late 17th and early 18th century, Poyning's Law was used by the English executive to amend bills drafted in the Irish Parliament rather than to refuse them. The PATRIOTS saw in Poyning's Law a serious obstacle to legislative independence, and YELVERTON'S ACT of 1782 modified it: although the royal assent could still be withheld, this power was used judiciously in the period up to the Act of UNION.

PR. The standard abbreviation of proportional representation.
See also SINGLE TRANSFERABLE VOTE.

Práiscín. The Irish word for a square of leather worn on the thigh of an uilleann piper (*see* UILLEANN PIPES) and used to control the wind by pressing the end of the chanter against it; it is also known as the 'piper's apron'. Modern pipes have instead a stop valve at the end of the chanter.

Praiseach. An Irish word for a porridge or gruel of Indian meal. In HIBERNO-ENGLISH 'to make *praiseach*' means to make a mess of something, to spoil or destroy something: 'You'll make *praiseach* of that bread if you cut it with a blunt knife.'

Praiser of His Own Past. The last gibe in a series of criticisms of Simon Dedalus by his exasperated son Stephen in *A PORTRAIT OF THE ARTIST AS A YOUNG MAN*. The model for Simon was, of course, JOYCE's own father, James Stanislaus Joyce (1841–1931), who danced a mocking yet stately rigadoon behind his staider son and died a mere ten years before him:

A medical student, an oarsman, a tenor, an amateur actor, a shouting politician, a small landlord, a small investor, a drinker, a good fellow, a story-teller, somebody's secretary, something in a distillery, a tax-gatherer, a bankrupt and at present a praiser of his own past.

> JAMES JOYCE (1882–1941): *Portrait of the Artist as a Young Man* (1916)

Prátaí or **preátaí.** *See* PRATIES.

Praties. A common HIBERNO-ENGLISH word for POTATOES, deriving from the Irish *prátaí*.

> Oh! the Praties they are small over here – over here.
> Oh! the Praties they are small over here.
> Oh! the Praties they are small, and we dug them in the fall,
> And we ate them skins and all, full or fear – full or fear.
>
> ANON. (mid-19th century)

Preab san ól. An Irish phrase meaning the light-hearted enjoyment of drink.

> *Níl beart níos críonna*
> *Ná bheith go síoraí ag cur preab san ól.*
> (There's no better practice
> Than carousing forever without a care.)
>
> RIOCARD BAIRÉAD (1740–1819): 'Preab san Ól'

Premier County. The nickname given to Co. Tipperary for the purposes of the ALL-IRELAND hurling championship. There is no clear reason for this, except perhaps the undoubted prosperity of the county, occupying as it does the greater part of the GOLDEN VALE.

Presbyterianism. The faith of about 300,000 Irish people, the second-largest denomination in Northern Ireland. It had its Irish origins about 1640 among the Scottish settlers in Ulster, and its members as nonconformists were debarred from public office by an act of 1704 that required holders to take Anglican communion at least once a year; marriages made in a Presbyterian church were not regarded as legal until 1845. Local congregations are run by a KIRK SESSION made up of elders, including the minister. A GENERAL ASSEMBLY (lay and clerical) meets once a year and elects a moderator, who acts as spokesman. Highly distrustful of central ecclesiastical authority, Presbyterians value the democratic nature of their faith. Many Presbyterians emigrated to America during the 18th century and played a significant part in the War of Independence (1775–83) and in the principles behind the Declaration of Independence (4 July 1776).

See also ARDENS SED VIRENS; ARIANISM; ASSEMBLY'S COLLEGE; BLACK OATH; MAKEMIE, FRANCIS; MEETING HOUSE; OLD LIGHT AND NEW LIGHT.

Presidents of Ireland. The presidency in its current form was established by de Valera's CONSTITUTION OF 1937, when it replaced the old office of governor-general of the Free State. At the same time the office of president of the executive council of the Free State (i.e. the head of government) became that of TAOISEACH. The president, or head of state, has only very limited powers, and is elected every seven years. Douglas HYDE was the first president (1938–45) and until the election of Mary ROBINSON in 1990 all subsequent presidents were members of FIANNA FÁIL: Seán T. O'KELLY (1945–59); Éamon DE VALERA (1959–73); Erskine Hamilton CHILDERS (1973–4); Cearbhall Ó Dálaigh (1974–6; *see* THUNDERING DISGRACE, A); and Patrick HILLERY (1976–90). Mary MCALEESE succeeded Mary Robinson in 1997. The presidency is clearly the political area in which Irishwomen have been most successful. 'Going to/for the park' (the PHOENIX PARK, where the president's residence, ÁRAS AN UACHTARÁIN, is situated) is a phrase used to indicate an aspiration to the office of president, and 'in the park' describes the happy situation of the incumbent.

Press. A HIBERNO-ENGLISH (and Scots) term for a cupboard.

See also IRISH PRESS, THE.

Prevention of Terrorism Act (PTA). A series of measures rushed through the UK Parliament after the Birmingham pub bombings in 1974 (*see* BIRMINGHAM SIX, THE). Its two main powers were:

(1) that of excluding from Britain persons alleged to be involved in Northern Ireland terrorism and

(2) that of arresting suspected persons and detaining them for 48 hours, with the possibility of extending detention for a further five days on the authority of the home secretary or the secretary of state for Northern Ireland.

Price, Leslie. *See* DE BARRA, LESLIE.

'Pride of Sweet Clogheen, The.' An anonymous ballad in praise of Mary Bowles, an IRISH VOLUNTEER from Clogheen, just outside Cork city, who is said to have ridden up Blarney Street (her route home) with a machine-gun over her shoulder during the Anglo-Irish War of 1919–21:

> Never yet was known a lady, not yet was known a queen,
> To match the deeds of Mary Bowles, the Pride of Sweet Clogheen.

'Pride of the Coombe, The'. The song most closely identified with the comedian Jimmy O'Dea (*see* MULLIGAN, BIDDY). It was originally called 'The Queen of the Coombe' (the Coombe is a street on the south side of the Liffey in Dublin, in the area known as the LIBERTIES), and was written especially for a GAIETY pantomime, a version of *Aladdin* called *Taladoin, or The Scamp with the Lamp*, which opened on 26 December 1889. Sung by Richard Purdon, who played Widow Twankey, in true panto style it bristled with local allusions:

> I'm a dashing young widow that lives in a spot
> That is christened the Dublin Coombe,
> Where the shops and the stalls are all out on the street,
> And my palace consists of one room.

The chorus held to the script and title:

> You may ramble through Clare and the County Kildare
> And from Drogheda down to Macroom,
> But you never will see a widow like me,
> Mrs Twankey, the Queen of the Coombe.

It proved extremely popular, and over time was slightly modified by the elusive Seamus Kavanagh, whose name appears as the author of many popular Irish songs. The chorus known and sung by most Irish people over 30, at home or abroad, was adapted from the original by O'Dea in his first appearance in the character in April 1930:

> You may travel from Clare to the County Kildare,
> From Francis Sreeet down to Macroom:
> But where would you see a fine widow like me,
> Biddy Mulligan, the pride of the Coombe.

The stuff sold by the ebullient street trader had changed little in 40 years:

> I sell apples and oranges, nuts and split peas,
> Bananas and sugarstick sweet
> On Saturday night I sell second-hand clothes
> From the floor of my stall on the street.

See also BIDET MULLIGAN.

Priest with the hankie, the. *See* DALY, EDWARD.

Princess Grace Irish Library. A library founded in Monaco in 1984 as a memorial to Princess Grace (1929–82) and her attachment to her Irish roots; before marrying Prince Rainier III in 1956 she had been the US film star Grace Kelly. The library shares a building with the Princess Grace Foundation in the city of Monaco, and provides a comprehensive biographical and bibliographical website.

Private Myles O'Reilly. *See* HALPINE, CHARLES.

Proclamation of the Republic (1916). At noon on Easter Monday, 24 April 1916, rebels occupied the GPO in Dublin's O'Connell Street. This was the beginning of the EASTER RISING. A few minutes later Patrick PEARSE read the Proclamation of the Republic to a small, unenthusiastic crowd outside. The proclamation is indicative of the idealism and hubris of the small unelected band of IRB conspirators – the 'secret revolutionary organization' mentioned in the second paragraph – that took up arms against Britain. It begins:

> Irishmen and Irishwomen, in the name of God
> and of the dead generations from which she

receives her old tradition of nationhood, Ireland, through us, summons her children to her flag and strikes for her freedom.

Asserting the right of Irish people to the ownership of Ireland and their duty of allegiance to the new Republic, the proclamation was signed 'on behalf of the Provisional Government' by seven leaders, all to be executed the following month for their part in the Rising. In addition to Pearse himself, they were Thomas J. CLARKE, Seán MCDERMOTT, Thomas MACDONAGH, Éamonn CEANNT, James CONNOLLY and Joseph PLUNKETT.

Prod or **proddy.** A derogatory term used of Protestants by Catholics. It is not an entirely unkind word, as POPEHEAD is in the other direction; it may even have an element of social classification.

> When I was a very small boy we used to sing at passing Protestants:
> Proddy, proddy dick
> Your ma can't knit
> And your da
> Won't go to bed
> Without a dummy tit.
>> EAMONN MCCANN (b.1943): *War and an Irish Town* (1974)

Progressive Democrats. *See* PEE DEES; TEMPORARY LITTLE ARRANGEMENT.

Property has its duties. *See* DRUMMOND, THOMAS.

Proportional representation. *See* SINGLE TRANSFERABLE VOTE.

Prosperous. A small town in Co. Kildare established by Robert Brooke in 1776 as a centre for cotton manafacture, supported by generous grants and loans from the Irish Parliament. The venture failed within a decade but the town survives.

Protectionism. An economic policy originally advocated by SINN FÉIN and pursued particularly by successive FIANNA FÁIL governments under the intensely Nationalist and separatist leadership (1932–59) of Éamon DE VALERA.

The policy involved using tariffs to protect Irish industry and agriculture, and the establishment of state enterprises (*see* SEMI-STATES) to exploit natural resources and to supply domestic needs. Protectionism also existed on the cultural plane, with the government and Catholic Church colluding to enforce CENSORSHIP and prohibit contraception and divorce. It continued after the Second World War, despite the manifest failure of the policy, and was abandoned only after the resignation of de Valera as taoiseach in 1959 and the adoption of the WHITAKER PLAN by his successor Seán LEMASS. The Anglo-Irish Free Trade Agreement of 1965 and Ireland's entry into the COMMON MARKET in 1973 meant that, far from being protected, Ireland's economy was now an open one.

See also CELTIC TIGER.

Protestant Action Force. A cover name occasionally used by the UVF since its regeneration in 1966.

'Protestant Boys'. A popular but anonymous 'party' song of the late 18th century, congenial rather than minatory in spirit – as the line about papists insists: 'We hate them as masters – we love them as men.' The use of the word 'Orange' was common before the founding of the ORANGE ORDER in 1795.

> In Orange and Blue
> Still faithful and true,
> The soul-stirring music of glory they'll sing;
> The shades of the Boyne
> In the chorus will join
> And the welkin re-echo with 'God save the king'.

Protestant parliament for a Protestant people. The statement 'We are carrying on a Protestant parliament for a Protestant people' was made in a speech by Sir Basil Brooke – later 1st Viscount BROOKEBOROUGH – at Stormont on 21 November 1934. It has been often quoted since as exemplifying the rationale of the state of NORTHERN IRELAND established in 1921.

Prout, Father. *See* FATHER PROUT.

Proverbs. The Irish word for proverb is *seanfhocal* ('old saying'), and the Irish language lends itself easily to the proverbial:

Breeding is stronger than training. (*Is treise dúchas ná oiliúint.*)

Breeding breaks through the eyes of the cat. (*Briseann an dúchas trí shúile an chait.*)

Company shortens the road. (*Giorraíonn beirt bóthar.*)

A drink first and then a story. (*Is túisce deoch ná sceál.*)

It's often a person's mouth broke his heart. (*Is minic a bhris béal duine a chroí.*)

A little tastes better than a lot. (*Bíonn blas ar an mbeagán.*)

No man is an island. (*Ar scáth a chéile a mhaireas na daoine.*)

Praise young people and they will follow you. Scold young people and they will fall by the wayside. (*Mol an óige agus tiocfaidh sé. Cáin an óige agus titfidh sé.*)

There's no place like home. (*Níl aon tinteán mar do thinteán féin.*)

What's rare is wonderful. (*An rud is annamh is iontach.*)

Providence Woollen Mills. A woollen mill founded in 1892 by a Sister of Charity, Agnes Morogh-Bernard (d.1932), also known as Mother Arsenius, in the impoverished Mayo town of Foxford. In April 1891 she established the Convent of Divine Providence on the site of an old corn mill on the River Moy, from where her community went about their work of educating children and ministering to the poor. Mother Arsenius persuaded John Charles Smith, a Protestant mill owner from Caledon, Co. Tyrone, to help her to set up a spinning and weaving plant in Foxford. In May 1892, with support from the CONGESTED DISTRICTS BOARD, the new factory went into production, harnessing the power of the River Moy. By the early 20th century Providence Woollen Mills in Foxford employed several hundred people, and its products were in use all over Ireland: until the advent of continental-style duvets every home possessed distinctive blue- or pink-striped Foxford woollen blankets. In 1988 declining sales forced the mills to close, but they have reopened under new management on a much smaller scale. Tourists are now the main market for fine Foxford rugs, tweeds and knitwear.

Provos or **Provies.** The Provisional IRA.

Proxy operation. The Provisional IRA's tactic of using a prisoner in fear of his own life or of those close to him to deliver a bomb to a target. The most appalling example occurred on 14 October 1990 at a border checkpoint at Coshquin near Derry in which six soldiers and the civilian driver of the car bomb died. Outrage at the savagery contributed to the ending of the practice.

Prunty, Patrick (1777–1861). The given name of the father of the Brontë sisters who had the misery of outliving all his six children. He was born at Emdale, Ballynaskeagh, Co. Down, on St Patrick's Day 1777, the son of a Protestant father and Catholic mother, who inculcated in him a respect for learning and solaced him when, apprenticed as a weaver at 15, he would rise at 4 a.m. to con the lessons in the classics provided by the Rev. Andrew Harshaw. After losing a job as a teacher because of an innocent over-intimacy with a reciprocating girl pupil he gained a scholarship to St John's, Cambridge. There he changed his name to Brontë, and on graduation found a number of livings, marrying a Cornish girl, Maria Branwell, in 1812 and moving with their children to Haworth Rectory in Yorkshire in 1820. His wife died of cancer a year later, and for the next 40 years he lived in the storm-tossed house with four geniuses and four tragic deaths, which, as the critic Walter Allen (1911–95) said in *The English Novel* (1954), would in any romance be 'three too many of each'. He bore stoically the scandalous behaviour of 'th' vicar's Pat', his only son, and with true Ulster egalitarianism supported striking Yorkshire weavers. He died on 7 June 1861, six years after his daughter Charlotte.

PSNI (Police Service of Northern Ireland). The police force that replaced the RUC under the terms of the partially implemented PATTEN REPORT on 1 November 2001.

Ptolemy (Claudius Ptolemaeus) (*c*.AD 90–168). Greek geographer and astronomer. He was born Ptolemaeus Hermion in Egypt and worked in Alexandria, mainly as an improver and corrector of other men's work. His *Geography* (*c*.150) of the world contains a kind of coordinate representation of the western edges of known Europe, including Ireland, which is called *Ivernia*. The work is extant in a 15th-century Latin translation, and though there is no map of the country as such it lists 60 geographical features by latitude and longitude, and a rough map may be drawn from the position of the promontories, estuaries and coastal towns. Dublin appears as *Eblana* and Lough Foyle to the north as *Vidua*. It gave the Chevalier Sir Charles Wogan (*c*.1698–1754) a chance to complain about the behaviour of the Irish ASCENDANCY in a letter to Jonathan Swift on 27 February 1732:

> As for the new nobility and gentry of Ireland, they pass currently for English abroad; and Dublin, the fourth city in Christendom, is taken for no more than the Eblana of Ptolemy.

Pub crawl. A pastime that requires an individual or (more usually) a group to go from pub to pub, having one or more drinks in each establishment. Sometimes records – most pubs in least time – are set for a particular occasion, for example the beginning of the Christmas holidays for a group of workers. There are pub crawls for charity, and in Dublin and other cities literary pub crawls (pubs associated with, for example, James Joyce or Patrick Kavanagh) and musical pubs crawls.

Public Dance Halls Act. *See* HOUSE DANCES.

Public Safety Acts. A series of acts passed or renewed between 1923 and 1928 granting the government emergency powers and suspending habeas corpus. The measures were introduced by the CUMANN NA NGAEDHEAL government in the aftermath of the CIVIL WAR in an effort to deal with continued Republican violence and the general disorder resulting from several years of armed conflict. Kevin O'HIGGINS, minister for justice (home affairs until 1924) was the person most strongly associated with this repressive legislation, and he was murdered by Republicans on 10 July 1927. After his death the government passed an even more severe Public Safety Act, giving the GARDA SÍOCHÁNA extensive powers of search and detention and the courts powers to hand down sentences of death or life imprisonment for unlawful possession of arms. This act remained in force until the end of 1928.

Puck[1]. The town of Killorglin, Co. Kerry, by association with its famous PUCK FAIR: 'Are you going to Puck today?'

Puck[2] (Irish *poc*). A he-goat or buck-goat, also called a puck-goat (*see* PUCK FAIR).

Puck[3]. A HIBERNO-ENGLISH word for a sharp blow or stroke. It comes from the Irish *poc*, 'puck', i.e. a stroke of the hurley. In hurling the ball is put back into play after a score by means of a puck-out.

Puck Fair. An annual three-day festival held in the small town of Killorglin, Co. Kerry, in which a white he-goat is crowned 'King Puck' and much revelry, dancing, CEOL AGUS CRAIC ensue. Puck Fair, or 'Puck' as it is commonly known, is now largely a tourist event, but it was originally a horse fair, attracting TRAVELLERS in particular. The first day of the fair is known as 'the Gathering', the third as 'the Scattering'.

Puckoon. *See* MILLIGAN, SPIKE.

Puncán (Irish *ponncán*). A HIBERNO-ENGLISH word for American or Yank. It is sometimes used in a derogatory sense to mean a loud, talkative American.

Punt. The standard Irish currency after Ireland joined the European Monetary System in 1979. Until then the Irish pound had kept parity with the British pound. The currency disappeared with the coming of the euro on 1 January 2002.

Purcell, [Patrick Joseph] Noel (1900–85). Actor and comedian. He was born on 23 December 1900 in Dublin and became a callboy in the Gaiety Theatre at the age of 12, and then trained as a joiner and shopfitter. In the 1930s he joined the company of Jimmy O'Dea (*see* MULLIGAN, BIDDY), his build – 1.9 m (6 ft 4 ins) tall and thin as a rake – making him an ideal grotesque to play pantomime dames. In 1947 he played McGinty, the rabble-rousing teacher in *Captain Boycott*, and began a career in films that lasted for 30 years, appearing in *The Blue Lagoon* (1948), *Moby Dick* (1956) and *Mutiny on the Bounty* (1962) and many others. He met his wife Eileen Marmion, who was 18 years his junior, when he played Dame Longshanks to her Red Riding Hood in 1930. They were married in January 1941 – as he put it, 'Eileen waited for me to grow up.' 'The Dublin Saunter', his theme tune, was written especially for him by Leo Maguire (d.1986). Purcell was made a freeman of his beloved native city in 1984, a year before his death on 3 March 1985.

> Grafton Street's a wonderland, there's magic in the air;
> There are diamonds in the lady's eyes and gold dust in her hair;
> And if you don't believe me, come and meet me there,
> In Dublin on a sunny summer morning.
> 'The Dublin Saunter' (1954)

Purser, Sarah (1848–1943). Artist. She was born in Dún Laoghaire, Co. Dublin, to a middle-class Protestant family, reared in Dungarvan, Co. Waterford, and educated in Switzerland, the Metropolitan School of Art in Dublin and the Académie Julian in Paris. To earn her living she took up painting portraits of members of the British aristocracy, through which she progressed, as she put it herself, 'like a dose of measles'. In the 1890s famous Irish literary figures like Douglas HYDE, Maud GONNE, Edward MARTYN and W.B. YEATS also sat for her, and their portraits have remained among their best-known visual representations. She became a wealthy woman and stood guarantor for the IRISH LITERARY THEATRE established by Yeats and Martyn in 1898.

Sarah Purser shared with Edward Martyn an interest in church art, particularly stained glass, and set out to revive the craft of stained glass in Ireland, founding a cooperative stained-glass studio, An TÚR GLOINE ('the glass tower'), in Pembroke Street in Dublin in 1903. She herself made windows for the ABBEY THEATRE and Loughrea Cathedral. Artists working in An Túr Gloine included Evie HONE and Harry CLARKE, and all artists were responsible for both design and execution of the glass.

From 1911 Sarah Purser lived with her unmarried brother in Mespil House near Dublin's Grand Canal, where she held a monthly second-Tuesday salon. She became influential in Irish cultural life, appointed to the board of the National Gallery and becoming the first female associate member of the Royal Hibernian Academy, and she campaigned for the establishment of Dublin's MUNICIPAL GALLERY OF MODERN ART. She painted and played an active part in An Túr Gloine until her death at the age of 95, but she had only one solo exhibition in her long and successful career – in 1923, when she was 75.

Purties. A HIBERNO-ENGLISH term for pretty things, cosmetics, jewellery, such as a little girl might find on her mother's dressing table.

Puss (Irish *pus*, 'mouth', 'lips'). A HIBERNO-ENGLISH word for a pout or sulky expression. Children or teenagers might be described as 'having a puss on them'.

Puss music. A HIBERNO-ENGLISH term for the tunes played for a house dance with the mouth and a comb in the absence of any other instrument. It is also used as a synonym for gob music, DYDDLING or LILTING.

Puss Sunday. The first Sunday of Lent, so called because young people not married at SHROVE-TIDE would not now have the chance of marrying until the following year, and would thus have a PUSS on them.

Put a tooth in it. A HIBERNO-ENGLISH verbal phrase meaning to speak tactfully or diplomatically. It is always used negatively, to indicate blunt or direct speech: 'She didn't put a tooth in it when asked her opinion'. It is frequently used as an introductory remark: 'Not to put a tooth in it ...'

Put him in to get him out. The slogan used in the by-election in Longford in May 1917 when Joe McGuinness, an IRB prisoner from Longford who had been in Lewes jail since the 1916 EASTER RISING, stood for election. This publicity tactic was masterminded by Michael COLLINS, against opposition from Éamon DE VALERA and others, in order to highlight the plight of Republican prisoners in British jails. All the prisoners sentenced after the Rising were released the following month.

Put manners on. A HIBERNO-ENGLISH phrase meaning to teach a lesson, correct or discipline or bring down a peg or two: 'That'll put manners on him.' It is sometimes used to express *schadenfreude*, for instance of a TD who has lost his seat in the Dáil or an individual who has lost her job.

Put the heart across or **crossways.** A common HIBERNO-ENGLISH phrase meaning to startle or frighten: 'You put the heart across me!' The phrase derives from the sensation of having the heart leap so much that it seems to change its place in the body.

Put to the pin of one's collar. A HIBERNO-ENGLISH phrase deriving from the pin that attached a man's collar to his shirt and meaning 'challenged', 'stretched to the limit': 'I'll be put to the pin of my collar to finish the dress in time.'

Pygmalion. The best-known play (1914) of George Bernard Shaw (GBS), largely because of the success of the musical *My Fair Lady* (1954) derived from it by Lerner and Loewe. It is a modern version of the story of the eponymous Cypriot king who falls in love with a statue he has created and to which Aphrodite gives life as Galataea. In Shaw's version, Henry Higgins, a phonetician, wins a bet that it is only her speech that prevents a personable woman of any class from being taken for a duchess. (The idea probably came from the effect of Shaw's own elegant Dublin accent.) The imposture succeeds, but at great cost to Eliza Doolittle, the Cockney flower-girl who is declassed by the process. The other great character, apart from the bustlingly offensive Higgins, is Eliza's father Alfred Doolittle, who, as 'one of the undeserving poor', is punished by becoming a millionaire. The sentimental contra-Shavian ending of the musical play is its only weakness.

q

Quakers. *See* SOCIETY OF FRIENDS.

Quarant' ore. *See* FORTY HOURS.

Quare Fellow, The. A genuinely humorous play by Brendan BEHAN about prison life and the convicts' reactions to the hanging of a prisoner, 'Silver-top', who has killed his wife. The play was first performed in Dublin's PIKE THEATRE in 1954, and was then staged by Joan Littlewood at the Theatre Royal, Stratford East, on 24 May 1956. The eponymous fellow is never seen, but his inevitable fate darkens the atmosphere. Though very funny and having the authentic atmosphere of prison life, based upon the author's own experiences, the play is an effective protest against judicial killing. A typical passage is the following exchange between the compassionate warder Regan and Holy Healey, the unctuous prison visitor:

> *Healey:* Well, we have one consolation, Regan, the condemned man gets the priest and the sacraments, more than his victim got maybe. I venture to suggest that some of them die holier deaths than if they had finished their natural span.
> *Regan:* We can't advertise, 'Commit a murder and die a happy death,' sir. We'd have them all at it. They take their religion very seriously in this country.

Quare gunk (Irish *gonc*, 'rebuff', with 'quare', the dialect version of 'queer', acting as an intensifier). A common Ulster expression indicating severe and unusual disappointment: 'Didn't he get the quare gunk when she said she wouldn't touch him wi' a graip.'

Quark. A term in physics indicating any elementary particle (such as those that make up protons within the nucleus of the atom) with a positive electric charge equal to one-third or two-thirds that of the electron's negative charge. The term was coined by the physicist Murray Gell-Mann (b.1929) from the phrase in Joyce's *FINNEGANS WAKE*, 'three quarks for Muster Mark', because there were originally thought to be three quarks.

QUB. The Queen's University of Belfast, originally one of the Queen's Colleges set up by Sir Robert PEEL in 1845 under the general title of the Queen's University of Ireland in a bid to palliate the agitation for repeal of the UNION. The colleges in Belfast, Cork and Galway were denounced as 'godless' by both Presbyterian and Catholic leaders (including, to YOUNG IRELAND's dismay, Daniel O'CONNELL). With the 1908 Irish Universities Act the college in Belfast became known by its present title, Cork and Galway becoming incorporated in the new NATIONAL UNIVERSITY of Ireland.

'Queen of the Combe, the'. *See* 'PRIDE OF THE COOMBE, THE'.

Queen's Colleges. The first government-funded universities in Ireland. Colleges in Belfast, Cork and Galway were established by Sir Robert PEEL under the Provincial Colleges Act (1845) and linked in 1850 to form the Queen's University of Ireland. They were non-denominational, but had denominational residence halls, and the teaching of theology was strictly controlled. These 'Godless colleges' were immediately condemned by Catholic churchmen such as John MACHALE, Archibishop of Tuam, who went to Rome in 1847 to seek the official condemnation of the pope, and by Daniel O'CONNELL. The Catholic hierarchy resented its lack of influence over appointments in the universities, and MacHale condemned them as an attempt 'to bribe Catholic youth into an abandonment of their religion'. Cardinal Paul CULLEN attempted unsuccessfully to establish a CATHOLIC UNIVERSITY, and the Queen's Colleges in Cork and Galway had only a few hundred students. The hierarchy agitated for a denominational university system for Catholics until the NATIONAL UNIVERSITY of Ireland, founded in 1908, went some way to satisfying their demands. At that time Belfast's Queen's College became the Queen's University of Belfast (*see* QUB).

Queen's County. The former name given to modern Co. Laois during the 16th-century PLANTATION of Laois and Offaly in honour of Queen Mary I (ruled 1553–8). The county town was called Maryborough until in 1922 the Free State changed its name to PORTLAOISE.

Queen's Island. *See* DARGAN'S ISLAND.

Queenstown. The name assigned to the old Cove of Cork in 1849 in honour of the post-Famine visit of Queen Victoria (1837–1901). It reverted to Cobh, the Gaelic version of its old name, in 1921. The queen described her visit in a letter to her Uncle Leopold, King of the Belgians:

> Our visit to Cork was very successful; the mayor was knighted *on deck* (on board the *Fairy*), like in times of old. We had previously stepped ashore at Cove, a small place, to enable them to call it Queen's Town; the enthusiasm was immense, and at Cork there was more firing than I remember since the Rhine … *En revanche*, the women are really very handsome – quite in the lowest class – as well at Cork as here: such beautiful black eyes and hair and such fine colours and teeth.
>
> Letter from the Lodge, Phoenix Park, 6 August, 1849

Queen's University. *See* QUB.

Querist, The. A series of 900 epigrammatic and didactic questions about the condition of Ireland, published anonymously in Dublin in three parts (1735–7) by George BERKELEY.

> Whether there be upon earth any Christian or civilized people so beggarly wretched and destitute as the common Irish?
> Whether, nevertheless, there is any other people whose wants may be more easily supplied from home?
> Whether there be not every year more cash circulated at the card-tables of Dublin than at all the fairs of Ireland? Whose fault is it if poor Ireland continues poor?

Quick Pick. A random selection of numbers for LOTTO, the twice-weekly Irish national lottery. Participants usually select six numbers based upon personal choice, suggested by birthdays, significant dates, momentary inspiration – even by close study of frequencies. For those who cannot be bothered the quick-pick option saves time and recrimination.

Quidnunc (Latin, 'what now?'). A word meaning 'gossip' or 'newsmonger' – used as the name of the chief character in the farce *The Upholsterer or What News* (1757) by the Irish playwright Arthur Murphy (1727–1805) – and therefore an appropriate cover-name for the diary writers of *The IRISH TIMES*. The feature was started by R.M. Smyllie (*see* NICHEVO).

Quiet Man, The. A film (1952) directed by John Ford (1895–1973) starring John Wayne, Maureen O'HARA and Victor McLaglen and based on the short story by Maurice WALSH. Wayne stars as Paddy Bawn Enright, a local man returned after 15 years in America where, unknown to the local people, he has achieved fame as a boxer under the name of 'Tiger' Enright ('For he was a quiet man, not given much to talking about himself and the things he had done.'). Maureen O'Hara is Ellen Roe O'Danaher, the young woman he loves and marries. Victor McLaglen is her brother, the mean and cunning Red Will, whom Paddy Bawn is eventually obliged to fight to save his honour and his marriage. The location most associated with the making of the film is the village of CONG in Co. Mayo on the shores of Lough Conn. Cong boasts a 'Quiet Man' bar and other film memorabilia.

Quiet pint. A campaign (2000) for the removal of piped music from bars and the restoration of the quiet needed to enjoy a peaceful pint (of GUINNESS).

Quill, Thady. The subject of a famous 19th-century ballad that celebrates a rather more vigorous and joyous way of life than one normally associates with the Victorian age. Timothy 'Thady' Quill (1860–1932) was a real person, an itinerant labourer of great strength who was known as a human hydraulic lift, and also known as a very good bowler (*see* BOWLING).

> For rambling and roving, for gambling and courting
> For drainin' a bowl e'en as fast as you'd fill,
> In all your days roaming you'll find none so jovial
> As our Muskerry sportsman, the Bould Thady Quill.
>
> JOHN THOMAS (JOHNNY TOM) GLEESON (b. 1853): 'The Bould Thady Quill', in *GAA Ballads of Rebel Cork*. Muskerry is the attractive wooded country that lies to the west of Cork City and is best seen from the tower of Blarney Castle.

Quinn, Edel (1907–44). Missionary. She was born near Kanturk in Co. Cork. Because her father was a bank manager the family often moved, and she was educated in various convent schools in Ireland and England. In 1926 she began to work as a secretary in Dublin, although intending to enter the Poor Clare convent in Belfast as a contemplative nun, and soon afterwards joined the LEGION OF MARY. In 1932 tuberculosis prevented her from joining the convent and she spent 18 months in a sanatorium in Co. Wicklow. In October 1936 she went to Africa as a volunteer for the Legion, and served in Kenya, Mauritius and Nyasaland (now Malawi), establishing praesidia (Legion associations) in these countries. Her tuberculosis recurred and she spent two years (1941–3) in sanatoria or convalescent homes, returning to work in Kenya in 1943. She died in Nairobi on 12 May 1944 and is buried there. For Catholic Ireland, and especially for Catholic girlhood, Edel Quinn was a shining role model as a pioneering lay missionary.

Quiz. A word invented (according to a popular story) by one Daly, the 18th-century manager of a Dublin theatre who wagered that he could introduce a new word of no meaning into the language within 24 hours. Accordingly on every wall, and indeed on all accessible places, were chalked up the four mystic letters, and all Dublin was inquiring what they meant. The wager was won and the word became part of the language. The word in fact already existed as in 'quizzing-glass', with which the grand viewed the eccentric, or vice versa.

R

Ra, the. A slang term for the Provisional IRA; its use is confined to Republican areas of Belfast.

Rabble. The word used for a HIRING FAIR in northwest Ulster.

Races of Castlebar. The initial success in Co. Mayo of the 31-year-old General Jean Humbert's Franco-Irish forces on 27 August 1798, when they routed government troops under General Gerard LAKE (1744–1808). Lake later surrounded the revolutionary force at Ballinamuck, Co. Longford; he accepted Humbert's surrender but massacred his 2000 Irish followers.

Rackrent. An excessive or extortionate rent, as charged by some Irish landlords, especially during the 19th century. The metaphor comes from the medieval torture instrument, with rent being stretched to its absolute limit, the amount being the rough equivalent of the land's value on the open market. If a tenant by extra labour and prudence made improvements in the property, thus increasing its value, it was common practice for the landlord (or his agent) to increase the rent accordingly. It was this last turn of the rack-wheel that caused most bitterness and made 'fair rent' the first of the THREE FS that the LAND LEAGUE demanded.

Raftery, Antaine. *See* BLIND RAFTERY.

Raic. An Irish word for 'quarrel', 'mêlée', 'noise', 'disturbance', pronounced 'rack'; it is common in HIBERNO-ENGLISH. The phrase 'making *raic*' is also used.

Raidhse. An Irish word meaning 'abundance', 'plenty', commonly used in HIBERNO-ENGLISH. There is also an adjective *raidhsiúil*. To say that there is *raidhse*, for instance at a meal or on a visit to someone's house, is a great compliment.

Raidió Éireann. *See* RTÉ.

Raidió na Gaeltachta. A radio station established by RTÉ to serve the people of the GAELTACHT areas. It began transmission on 2 April 1972. It has gradually increased its coverage and broadcasting time, and has become an important part of the life of the Irish-speaking audience in Ireland as a whole. This has, however, allowed the number of Irish-language programmes broadcast on national radio and television to decrease steadily over the past 30 years. Raidió na Gaeltachta is broadcast from the three main Gaeltachts, with its headquarters and news and current affairs divisions based in Casla (Costello) in Connemara, and stations in Baile na nGall (Ballydavid) in west Kerry and Na Doirí Beaga (Derrybeg) in Co. Donegal. It also broadcasts programmes from the smaller Gaeltacht areas of Uíbh Rathach (the IVERAGH PENINSULA in Co. Kerry), Múscraí (the MUSKERRY GAELTACHT of west Cork) and Gaeltacht na DÉISE (the Ring area of Co. Waterford).

Railway Cup. An interprovincial GAA football and hurling competition that was held from 1927 until the mid-1980s, the final traditionally being played in CROKE PARK on St Patrick's Day. It was so called because the Great Southern Railway Company was the first sponsor.

Ráiméis. The Irish word for 'nonsense', 'foolish talk', used commonly in HIBERNO-ENGLISH: 'Will you give over with your old *ráiméis*.'

Rainbow Coalition (1994–7). The name given to the coalition comprising three parties of varied political hues: the centre-right FINE GAEL party, led by John BRUTON, who became taoiseach; the Labour Party, led by Dick SPRING, who became tánaiste (deputy taoiseach) and minister for foreign affairs; and the more radical Democratic Left (successor to the WORKERS' PARTY), led by Proinsias DE ROSSA, who became minister for social welfare. The coalition was formed without a dissolution of the Dáil (and hence without an election) after Labour had withdrawn from a coalition with FIANNA FÁIL, under the leadership of Albert REYNOLDS, of which it had been part since 1992. Although Reynolds resigned as leader, shouldering responsibility for the BRENDAN SMYTH AFFAIR, and Bertie AHERN took his place, Dick Spring declined to work with Ahern. After protracted negotiations, the Rainbow Coalition was formed. In an inspired move (and generous on the part of Fine Gael, the major partner), Ruairí Quinn of Labour was made minister for finance, preventing disagreements on budgetary policy such as had bedevilled the coalitions of the 1980s. The Rainbow administration can claim credit for several significant achievements, perhaps not all entirely of its making: the beginning of the economic miracle that became known as the CELTIC TIGER; significant progress towards agreement in the Northern TROUBLES; and the abolition of the constitutional ban on divorce (1995).

Rajah from Tipperary, the. The nickname of

George Thomas (1756–1802), a soldier and adventurer in India. He was born the son of a small farmer in Roscrea, Co. Tipperary, and joined the British navy. In 1781 he deserted at Madras and enlisted as a mercenary in the service of the Nizam of Hyderabad. During a colourful career in India he served in turn the Begum Sumra of Sirdhana and Appa Rao, the Muhratta governor of Meerut, eventually becoming ruler of Meerut, a large territory with substantial revenues. With the help of the French, the Sikhs deposed him in 1802, and he died of fever in Bengal as he was about to return to Ireland.

Rake. A large number or quantity of something or of people: 'There was a rake of people in the house.' The term is of uncertain derivation, perhaps originating in the load that could be carried on a rake, a farmyard or haymaking implement.

'Rakes of Mallow, The'. A ballad about less worthy visitors to the town of Mallow in Co. Cork, which was a popular resort for the Anglo-Irish gentry in the 18th and early 19th century. Built astride the beautiful Blackwater, the town and its chalybeate spa attracted many visitors, and caused it to be dubbed the IRISH BATH. Its racecourse completed the list of attractions. It was visited by Sir Walter Scott and was the home for some years of Anthony Trollope (1815–82), when he worked as a Post Office surveyor. Its notoriety sprang from its popularity with young gallants who came for the season. The ballad has been ascribed with little likelihood to PLEASANT NED Lysaght:

> Beauing, belling, dancing, drinking,
> Breaking windows, damning, sinking,
> Ever raking, never thinking,
> Live the rakes of Mallow.
> Spending faster than it comes,
> Beating waiters, bailiffs, duns,
> Bacchus' true begotten sons,
> We're the rakes of Mallow.

Raleigh, Sir Walter (*c*.1584–1618). Elizabethan courtier and adventurer. After serving against the Spanish at SMERWICK HARBOUR, he was given the largest tract of land in the MUNSTER PLANTATION – 40,000 acres (16,000 ha). He settled the estate with English tenants and exploited native woodland, mostly from a distance, but eventually sold his lands to Richard BOYLE after having come into conflict with the lord deputy, the corrupt Sir William Fitzwilliam (1526–99).

Rambling house. A house where people were given to congregating, for gossip and story-telling and perhaps for a song or dance late in the night. It was normally the men who rambled, except at WOMEN'S CHRISTMAS, when the men stayed at home. The rambling houses served an important function in the days before radio, television and cars, and were responsible for preserving much traditional lore and stories. SEANCHAÍ Éamon Kelly described a rambling house as a place 'where the affairs of the day were debated, where entertainment mingled with education' (*The Apprentice*, 1995). On a fine summer's evening it was not unknown for the rambling house to convene in the lee of a suitable hedge or at the mouth of a limekiln. RTÉ radio's popular weekly programme of the 1950s, *The Rambling House*, featured Éamon KELLY as the host, with singers Teresa Clifford and Seán Ó Síocháin and actor Éamon Keane to recite poems and ballads. The programme began with the invitation:

> The rick is thatched, the fields are bare,
> Long nights are here again.
> The year was fine, but now 'tis time
> To hear the ballad men.
> Boul in, boul in and take a chair,
> Admission here is free.
> You're welcome to the rambling house
> To hear the seanchaí.

The concept of the rambling house was recently revived on Limerick local radio: since 1998 Joe Harrington has recorded more than a thousand contributors for a weekly *Rambling House* programme.
See also AIRNEÁN; BOTHÁNTAÍOCHT; BOWL (IN), TO; CÉILÍDHING.

Ranjitsinhji of Nawanagar, Prince. *See* MAHARAJAH OF CONNEMARA, THE.

Rann (Irish, 'quatrain'). A quarterly Ulster journal of poetry, edited by Roy McFadden (1921–90) with Barbara Edwards. It ran from 1948 to 1953, having some of the energy of LAGAN and with the same liberal and regionalist stance. About the middle of its career it included odd bits of prose and reviews. Its final number included a useful mini-dictionary of Ulster writers compiled by John BOYD.

Rapparees. Bandits or outlaws who, singly or in groups, attacked houses, farms and travellers in Ireland in the 17th and early 18th century. The name derived from *rapaire*, a kind of pike, and is largely synonymous with TORY, although the latter term is thought to predate it. In Nationalist history, rapparees were regarded as a hybrid of freedom fighters and Robin Hood figures, Catholics whose lands had been stolen and had no alternative but to take to the woods. More recent research has, however, suggested that rapparees were for the most part simply robbers, similar to outlaws in other remote areas of Europe (*see* REVISIONISM). *The Rapparee* (1870) is a historical melodrama by Dion BOUCICAULT concerning a group of defeated JACOBITE gentry after the Treaty of LIMERICK.

Rare Oul' Times. A phrase, confined to Dublin, suggesting a lost golden age. It became the title of a song (1977) by Pete St John, painting a nostalgic, idealized picture of a LIBERTIES childhood:

> Ring a ring a rosie, as the light declines;
> I remember Dublin city in the rare oul' times.

Rasherhouse. A Dublin nickname for the women's prison in MOUNTJOY JAIL, deriving from 'rasher', a term for sexual intercourse. *The Rasherhouse* (1997) is a book about Mountjoy by Alan Roberts.

Rás Tailteann. A national multi-stage bicycle race that first took place in 1953. It was the brainchild of Joe Christie, who was race director for many years. The race derived its name from the Tailteann Games (*see* AONACH TAILTEANN). It was replaced by the FBD 'Milk Rás', sponsored by farm insurers FBD, which takes place annually in May.

Rath. *See* RING FORT.

Rathcroghan. The burial place in Co. Roscommon of ÉIRE, FODLA and BANBA, the legendary ancient queens of the TUATHA DÉ DANAAN. It is situated in the Cemetery of the Kings on the hill of Rathcroghan, near Frenchpark in Co. Roscommon. This hill was the investiture site of the kings of Connacht.

Rathlin. (Irish *Reachlainn*, meaning uncertain). An L-shaped island in the Sea of Moyle, 10 km (6 miles) north of Ballycastle, Co. Antrim, famous for its cliff scenery and variety of sea birds. The first part of Ireland to be raided by Vikings (790), it was later occupied by Mac-Donnells from Scotland. It was the refuge of Robert Bruce (1274–1329), king of Scotland, in 1306, and legend places the story of Bruce and the spider there (a basalt cave is pointed out as the arachnophile Bruce's place of shelter). The island was later the scene of the RATHLIN MASSACRE.

Rathlin Massacre. The slaughter on 25 July 1575 of the inhabitants of the island by John Norris and Francis Drake on the orders of the Earl of ESSEX. Some 200 were killed on the surrender of Bruce's Castle, and 400 other victims were found around the caves and cliffs of the island. The dead included the family of Sorley Boy MACDONNELL, who had to watch helplessly from the Antrim Coast. Elizabeth I congratulated Essex on his success.

Rathmines, Battle of (1649). In 1649 the Royalist Duke of ORMOND laid siege to Dublin, which was held for the Parliamentarians by the governor of the city, Colonel Michael Jones. Ormond originally set up camp in Finglas, to the northwest, then in later July moved camp to an area south of the city, between the modern suburbs of Ranelagh and Rathmines. When

on 1 August Ormond sent a party to capture Baggotrath Castle, nearer to the city centre, Jones ordered troops out to prevent this. The battle that developed the following day, 2 August, was disastrous for the Royalists, who were driven back southwards from the city. Ormond escaped on horseback. CROMWELL arrived in Dublin on 15 August.

Ratisbon. The French name (current until the 19th century) of the Bavarian city of Regensburg, which lies on the Danube about 100 km (60 miles) northeast of Munich. It was the site of the Irish Benedictine monastery of St James, which was begun by MARIANUS SCOTTUS (OF RATISBON) in 1076. It became the mother house of other *Schottenklöster* ('Irish monasteries') in Würzburg, Nürnburg, Constance, Vienna and Eichstätt.

'Rattle the Hasp'. The title of a jig originating from the practice of providing a dance floor in a marquee by laying a number of doors, lifted off their hinges – hasps and all – side by side:

> But they couldn't keep time on the cold earthen
> floor
> So to humour the music they danced on the door.
>> THOMAS CROFTON CROKER (1798–1854): *The Popular Songs of Ireland* (1839)

Raymond le Gros. *See* LE GROS, RAYMOND.

RDS. *See* ROYAL DUBLIN SOCIETY.

Reading in the Dark. *See* DEANE, SEAMUS.

Reading societies. A number of societies founded in Ulster in the late 18th and early 19th centuries whereby members subscribed for the purchase of a library. Social events and discussion groups formed part of these libraries. The LINEN HALL LIBRARY in Belfast grew out of such a society, the Belfast Reading Society.

Read over, to be. To be exorcized (read over by a priest). In rural Irish society, which was much given to superstitions (*see* PISHOGUES) and belief in the OTHERWORLD, it was not uncommon for people to believe themselves or their homes to

be possessed by a spirit or for their family or neighbours to believe it of them.
See also CLEARY, BRIDGET.

Real Charlotte, The. A novel (1894), still popular and convincing, by SOMERVILLE AND ROSS. It delineates middle-class Protestant Ireland and its subtle relationship with the aristocratic BIG HOUSE as no other work has done. Its chief character, Charlotte Mullen, the ruthless aspiring protagonist – whose capacity for effective evil is somewhat mitigated by an unexpected softness for Roddy Lambert, the worthless man she loves and loses – is one of the most memorable in all of Irish fiction.

Real Chief, the. The sobriquet of the Republican leader, Liam Lynch (1890–1923), who was one of the most diehard of the ANTI-TREATYITES in the CIVIL WAR. Lynch was commander of the 1st Southern Division of the IRA in the Anglo-Irish War of 1919–21, and was an important and influential opponent of the TREATY. He became chief of staff of the Republicans and refused to accept that defeat by Free State forces was inevitable. After Lynch's death in an action in the Knockmealdown Mountains in Co. Waterford on 10 April 1923, Frank AIKEN was able, on behalf of the Republicans, to announce a cessation of hostilities – from 30 April 1923.

Real goat's toe, the. A laudatory HIBERNO-ENGLISH term meaning 'the real thing', 'the tops'.

Real IRA. A dissident Republican group formed by members of the Provisional IRA who did not assent to the Northern Irish peace process of the 1990s. Its members are mainly from the border counties, especially Armagh and Louth. A 225-kg (500-lb) bomb that devastated the centre of Banbridge, Co. Down, on 1 July 1998 was claimed by them, as was the OMAGH BOMB, which killed 28 people on 15 August of that year. The outrage was so great that the Provisional IRA paper *An Phoblacht* advised that they should disband. They reformed in 2000 and are intermittently active.

Real Taoiseach, the. The satirical nickname of the Fianna Fáil leader Jack LYNCH, awarded to him by *Hall's Pictorial Weekly* (*see* BALLYMAGASH) during the term of the Fine Gael–Labour coalition government of 1973–77, as if the actual taoiseach, Liam COSGRAVE, were an imposter.

Rebel Countess, the. The nickname of Constance Markievicz (1868–1927), revolutionary and labour leader, because of her adoption of radical causes despite her ASCENDANCY birth and marriage to a Polish count. She was born Constance Gore-Booth on the family estate at LISSADELL, Co. Sligo, and as a child was active and tomboyish, a noted horse-rider:

> The light of evening, Lissadell,
> Great windows open to the south,
> Two girls in silk kimonos, both
> Beautiful, one a gazelle.
> But a raving autumn shears
> Blossom from the summer's wreath;
> The older is condemned to death,
> Pardoned, drags out lonely years
> Conspiring among the ignorant.
>
> W. B. YEATS (1865–1959): 'In memory of Eva Gore-Booth and Con Markiewicz', in *The Winding Stair and Other Poems* (1933)

Constance Gore-Booth came out at the court of Queen Victoria in London in 1887, and, after studying art at the Slade, went to live in Paris in 1897. There she pursued her studies among avant-garde friends and there she met and married (in 1900) Count Casimir Markievicz, an aristocratic Catholic Pole and an artist like herself. They had one daughter, Maeve Alys, who was born in 1901 and who was reared mainly at Lissadell while her mother pursued political and labour activities in Dublin. The couple parted amicably after Constance, or 'Madame' as she was now called, became involved in politics.

In 1908 Constance Markievicz joined INGHINIDHE NA HÉIREANN and wrote for the organization's magazine, *Bean na hÉireann*, coming into contact with feminists, Republicans and labour leaders like James LARKIN. In 1909 she founded Fianna Éireann ('warriors of Ireland'), a Republican boy-scout movement named after the legendary FIANNA, intended as a training ground for martial skills. This was one of the activities she most enjoyed, and in time she devoted her home and all her money to her 'boys'. During the 1913 LOCKOUT she worked in a soup kitchen that provided food for the starving workers and their families, and she became a member of both CUMANN NA MBAN and the IRISH CITIZEN ARMY, in which she was given the rank of staff lieutenant.

During the EASTER RISING of 1916 Constance Markievicz was second-in-command to Michael Mallin in St Stephen's Green. She was court-martialled and sentenced to death (Michael Mallin was executed), but her sentence was commuted because of her sex. (Con Colbert and Seán Heuston, two of the executed men, had been Fianna boys.) Countess Markievicz was imprisoned in England and released under the terms of the general amnesty of 1917. In 1918 she was again in jail for protesting against conscription, and it was while she was in jail that, standing for SINN FÉIN in the election of that year, she became the first woman to be elected to the Westminster Parliament, although she never took her seat.

During the ANGLO-IRISH WAR of 1919–21 Constance Markievicz was minister for labour in the alternative Republican administration, often on the run and twice imprisoned, in Dublin and in Cork. She opposed the TREATY – she was then in the influential position of president of Cumann na mBan – and fought in Dublin at the opening stages of the CIVIL WAR in 1922. She was elected TD in the elections of 1923 but did not take her seat, and the same year was imprisoned by the Free State government for campaigning for the release of political prisoners. She worked among the poor in the tenements of Dublin during the last years of her life, owning very little and poorly dressed. After the foundation of FIANNA FÁIL she campaigned for the party and retained her own seat in the elections of 1927 as a Fianna Fáil candidate. She died of cancer later that same year in a public ward of a Dublin hospital.

The poor of Dublin whom she had served for much of her life lined the route of her funeral.

Rebel County, the. A nickname for Co. Cork. It is commonly believed to have earned this sobriquet during the Anglo-Irish War of 1919–21 – the centre of the city was burned by the AUXIES on the night of 11 December 1920 – but it is more likely to be a far older appellation, deriving from the fact that the city briefly supported the Yorkist pretender, Perkin WARBECK against Henry VII in 1495. The nickname is used as an alternative to the county's name by media commentators during the Gaelic football and hurling championship.

Rebellion of 1641. A rebellion led by Catholic gentry dispossessed in the ULSTER PLANTATION, such as Rory O'MORE. It began on 22 October 1641, provoked by fears of a Puritan administration in Ireland and the rise of a Puritan Parliament in England. The rebellion was initially successful, taking the Ulster planters by surprise, but involved uncontrolled sectarian killings of, it is estimated, about 4000 Protestants by poorly controlled rank-and-file. These figures were later greatly exaggerated, especially in *History of the Irish Rebellion* (1646) by John Temple, master of the rolls, and this contributed to centuries of distrust of Catholics by Ulster Protestants. Having gained control of Ulster, the rebels captured Dundalk and defeated a government army at Julianstown in Co. Louth on 29 November 1641. Within a week the OLD ENGLISH, fearing harsh Puritan rule and disappointed at not having been granted the GRACES promised by Thomas WENTWORTH, joined the rebellion. This led in turn to the CONFEDERATE WAR.

Rebellion of 1798. An insurrection – in reality a series of separate insurrections – that occurred in three of Ireland's four provinces during the summer of 1798, inspired for the main part by the radical philosophy of the UNITED IRISHMEN, but also (particularly in Co. Wexford) by agrarian and sectarian grievances.

There were four main outbreaks. The first

occurred in the north Leinster counties of Kildare, Dublin and Meath during the last ten days of May, apparently intended as the beginnings of an attack on Dublin. British troops stamped out the rebellion in engagements at Carlow (25 May), Tara, Co. Meath (26 May), and the Curragh (29 May).

In Co. Wexford rebels overcame forces of yeomanry at Oulart on 27 May and captured Enniscorthy and Wexford town. After this initial success the insurgents, brave fighters but poorly led, were unable to extend the rebellion outside their own county and were comprehensively defeated at NEW ROSS (5 June) and VINEGAR HILL[1] (21 June).

The third rebellion took place the following month in the United Irishmen's heartland of east Ulster. Henry Joy MCCRACKEN and his 4000 men captured Ballymena, but were defeated in Antrim town on 7 June; Henry MUNRO, at the head of an even larger army, was overcome at Ballynahinch on 13 June.

The final act of the drama was sparked off by the arrival of a small French force under General Humbert in Killala Bay, Co. Mayo, on 22 August. Some 3000 local people joined the thousand French soldiers, and the combined army defeated the forces of General LAKE on 27 August (see RACES OF CASTLEBAR). But on 8 September, at Ballinamuck, Co. Longford, the French–Irish army itself was heavily defeated.

Rebellion of 1848. The rising of the YOUNG IRELAND group, originally planned to take place in Dublin and the countryside. However, it ended up being restricted to a few rural areas because of the repressive measures taken by the well-informed British authorities in Dublin. Although the rising initially attracted the support of large numbers of peasants, this dissipated after an encounter with troops in Killenaule, Co. Tipperary, on 28 July 1848. The only real engagement of the rebellion was that at WIDOW MCCORMICK'S CABBAGE PATCH in Ballingarry, Co. Tipperary, on 29 July, under the leadership of Smith O'Brien, in which two rebels were killed. Although farcical in its

inefficacy, the Rebellion of 1848 did perform the function of passing the torch of romantic physical-force Republicanism from Robert EMMET to the FENIANS.

Recess Committee. A cross-party committee of influential Irish people from various walks of life that met during the parliamentary recess of 1895–6 to discuss local administration, agriculture and education in Ireland. The idea of the committee was suggested by Sir Horace PLUNKETT, and its membership included John REDMOND and Timothy Harrington of the Irish Parliamentary Party and the Unionist Lords Mayo and Mounteagle, as well as the writer May Laffan (see 'FLITTERS, TATTERS AND THE COUNSELLOR: THREE WAIFS FROM THE DUBLIN STREETS'). The establishment in 1899 of the Department of Agriculture and Technical Instruction, with Plunkett as its first vice-president, was the result of the recommendations of the committee, contained in its report of July 1896.

Red Branch Knights. In Irish mythology, the band of warriors who defended Ulster during the reign of CONCHOBHAR. They were known in Irish as An Chraobh Rua (pronounced 'an creeve rooa'), and were believed to have been founded by Conchobhar's grandfather, Ross the Red. CÚCHULAINN was their greatest champion. Members of the fellowship began their training at the age of seven at the headquarters at EMAIN MACHA.

Redbreasts. The nickname of the 5th (Royal Irish) Lancers, so called from the scarlet facings of their uniforms. The regiment was amalgamated in 1922 with the 16th Lancers and now is part of the Queen's Royal Lancers.

Redbrick City. An appropriate nickname for the city of Belfast because of the many red-brick terrace houses that were built during the 19th century to cater for the rapidly increasing working-class population. The right kind of clay was plentiful around the southern shores of Lough Neagh, and the Coalisland brickworks were kept busy:

Redbrick in the suburbs, white horse on the wall
...
> MAURICE JAMES CRAIG (1919–99): 'Ballad to a
> Traditional Refrain' (1938)

Redd. An Ulster verb meaning 'tidy', or, as a past participle, 'finished'. It is often used with 'up', as is 'tidy'. In the sentence, 'Have you the kitchen redd yet?' the word is analogous with the Irish word *réidh*, ('ready'), as in *'An bhfuil an chistín réidh agat go fóill?'*

> Usually four or five neighbouring families joined in the trip and shortly after breakfast, when the house had been redd up ... all the family would pack into the trap ...
> SAM HANNA BELL (1909–90): 'To Crack by the Hearth', in *Erin's Orange Lily* (1956)

'Red Flag, The'. The socialist anthem, normally sung to the tune of 'O Tannenbaum' and written by Irishman Jim Connell (1852–1929):

> The People's Flag is deepest red,
> It shrouded oft our martyred dead.

Connell was born in Co. Meath. He joined the IRB in Dublin in 1867 and after he went to England to look for work, he became a member of the national executive of the National League, successor to the LAND LEAGUE. He left the IRB and in 1883 joined the Social Democratic Federation (SDF).

'The Red Flag', reputedly written on one 15-minute train journey between Charing Cross and New Cross, was published in *Justice*, the SDF weekly paper, in 1889. Connell later recounted that the song was inspired by the London dockers' strike of 1889, the LAND WAR in Ireland, the persecution of revolutionaries in tsarist Russia, and the Chicago Martyrs (four anarchist leaders who were hanged because of unproven complicity in the throwing of a bomb in Haymarket Square, Chicago, on 4 May 1886, during a protest meeting about police brutality).

Although Ramsay MacDonald, the leader of the British Labour Party, disliked 'The Red Flag', a competition held in 1925 with 300 entries, adjudicated by John MCCORMACK and Sir Hugh Roberton, the founder of the Glasgow Orpheus Choir, failed to produce a better party anthem. The song's finest hour was in 1945 when 393 Labour MPs assembled in Westminster sang it after their general election victory. Connell died on 8 February 1929. A communal rendition of the song forms the traditional ending of the Labour Party's annual conference, which has proved something of an embarrassment to some in the 'New Labour' leadership.

Red Hand Defenders. A title of convenience used by members of the UDA/UFF, UVF and other Northern Ireland Loyalist paramilitary organizations, especially when carrying out sectarian atrocities. Another version is Red Hand Commandos.

Red Hand of Ulster. The device, originally part of the heraldic bearings of the O'Neills, incorporated into the arms of Ulster, usually as dexter but also as sinister. Its couped gules representation is said to come from an ancient folktale about two chieftains who were racing their boats to establish ownership of the rich lands of Ulster. They had agreed that whoever touched the beach first could claim all the territory. The O'Neill, seeing that his rival was winning, cut off his hand at the wrist and tossed it on to the strand. According to the adamantine rules of such tales he was granted ownership. The story would seem to suggest that, statistically at least, the bloodied representation should be of a left hand.

Redmond, John [Edward] (1856–1918). Statesman. He was born in Co. Wexford on 1 September 1856, the son of the Catholic MP for Wexford, and educated at Clongowes, Trinity College Dublin and Gray's Inn. He was called to both the Irish and English Bars but did not practise, and was an MP from 1881 until his death. A strong supporter of PARNELL, he helped to heal party rancour, and in 1900 became leader of the entire IRISH PARTY. In 1911 he found himself holding the balance of power in the Commons and able to introduce the third HOME RULE Bill. His patient work on Wyndham's LAND ACT of 1903 and in the negotiations leading to the establishment of the NATIONAL UNIVERSITY showed his temper. He was startled by Unionist intransigence (*see* CARSON'S ARMY; CURRAGH INCIDENT; ULSTER COVENANT), but responded with near saintly patience.

Redmond agreed with characteristic generosity of spirit and lack of political acumen to a postponement of the implementation of the Home Rule Bill until after the First World War, and suffered continual humiliation from the government and the War Office: he was not given an Irish division to match the honour granted to Ulster (*see* OBSERVE THE SONS OF ULSTER MARCHING TOWARDS THE SOMME), his son was refused a commission at the first time of application, and his suggestion that the IRISH VOLUNTEERS could defend Ireland, thus releasing British soldiers to fight in France, was mockingly refused. His speeches encouraging young Irishmen to join the army (*see* WOODENBRIDGE) caused a rift in the Volunteers (*see* NATIONAL VOLUNTEERS) and increased the numbers who took part in the EASTER RISING.

The 1916 Rising took Redmond totally by surprise. He pleaded in vain for clemency for the leaders and strove to devise a dominion structure for Ireland, but the temper of Irish politics had passed him by. His brother Willie, who had joined the army at the outbreak of the war, was killed on 7 June 1917, and Redmond himself died suddenly on 6 March 1918. In the election of December that year, his party lost all but six of its seats to SINN FÉIN.

Red Rum. A celebrated steeplechaser who was bred in Co. Kilkenny by the McEnery family, trained by Ginger McCain, and who won the Aintree Grand National three times, in 1973 and 1974, ridden by Brian Fletcher, and in 1977, ridden by Tommy STACK. Red Rum came second in the race in 1975 and 1976. In 1978 he did not start. Like ARKLE, 'Rummy', as he was popularly known, was considered by his fans to be almost human. He was a special guest at the BBC Sports Personality of the Year Awards in 1977, in which year Björn Borg won Wimbledon, Liverpool the European Cup and Tom Watson the British Open. Red Rum is buried beside the finishing post at Aintree.

Redshanks. The nickname of the Jacobite soldiers (1200 plus camp followers) of Lord Antrim who in 1688 were ordered by the Earl of TYRCONNELL to replace the Protestant garrison who had left Derry for Dublin. The mocking name was a memory of the previous century's Scottish mercenaries, who wore kilts. When they arrived the city was alive with rumours of the COMBER LETTER, and when the advance party came across the River Foyle by boat and marched up the hill to the Ferry Gate, 13 of the London apprentices in the city, having wrested the city keys from the garrison, shut the gate against the soldiers. The other three gates in the elegantly designed city were also slammed, and the Redshank party threatened with cannon. The king's army had been defied and the situation was ripe for the historic siege (*see* SIEGE OF DERRY; MAIDEN CITY).

Reek, the. The familiar name given to Croagh Patrick (765 m / 2510 ft), a mountain that rises steeply from the southern shore of Clew Bay, Co. Mayo. PATRICK is said to have fasted on its summit for the whole of Lent in the year 441 until he had won from heaven the right to act as defence counsel for his adopted Irish on Doomsday. Each year, on FRAUGHAN SUNDAY, thousands of pilgrims, many of them barefoot (particularly painful on the bare scree of the upper quartzite cone), make the journey to the summit. There are a number of 'stations' where set prayers are recited on fixed DEISEAL circuits, and Masses are said in an oratory at the top. Croagh is an anglicization of the Irish word *cruach* ('haystack' or 'rick'), hence the popular name.

Reel. A solo or group SET DANCE and the associated music, which is played in 4/4 time. Reels are the most numerous of traditional music tunes. They are thought to have come from France via Scotland, and many of the older traditional reels have Scottish roots.

Reels, to be in the. To be out of your mind, to have lost your senses.

Reenafureera (Irish *Rinn na Foraire*, 'headland of the lookout'). The location of a small hotel called Heron Cove, near Sneem in Co. Kerry, where General Charles de Gaulle and also the Dutch royal family stayed on holiday in the 1950s and 1960s.

Ree-raw. *See* RÍ-RÁ.

Reformation. The period 1536–47 in the reign of Henry VIII marked the beginning of the Reformation in Ireland with the enactment, by the Parliament in Dublin (*see* REFORMATION PARLIAMENT), of the Act of Supremacy and a law ordering the DISSOLUTION OF THE MONAS-TERIES. It was not, however, until the reigns of Edward VI (1547–53) and Elizabeth I (1558–1603) that an attempt was made to impose a reformation of doctrine and worship. This happened particularly with the Act of Uni-formity of 1560, by which all clergymen were required to use the English Prayer Book at all services and all lay people were required to attend Anglican Sunday worship. A fine of one shilling was levelled on recusants. However, the Irish wars (*see* TUDOR RECONQUEST) of Elizabeth's reign made clear to the English that the Gaelic Irish, in particular, had no in-tention of adopting Protestantism; they sought instead the help of Catholic Spain to fight the English (*see* NINE YEARS' WAR). There is some evidence that Hugh O'NEILL saw himself by the end of the 16th century as a defender of Catholicism as well as of his Gaelic patrimony. It was in the reign of James I (1603–25) that uniformity was imposed most harshly, par-ticularly among the OLD ENGLISH of Dublin (*see* BARNEWALL, SIR PATRICK), and by the 1630s, religious attitudes in the country had hardened on both the Catholic and Protestant sides. The CONFEDERATE WAR of the 1640s was the result of the momentous recognition by the Old English that they could no longer be loyal simultaneously to England, particularly with a Puritan Parliament, and to Catholicism.

Reformation Parliament. The Irish Parliament that in 1536 passed the Act of Supremacy, declaring Henry VIII to be the supreme head of the church in Ireland, and that in the follow-ing year passed a law ordering the dissolution of all Irish religious houses (*see* REFORMATION; DISSOLUTION OF THE MONASTERIES).

Regency Crisis (1789). The crisis that arose from the mental instability of George III; it had a distinct effect in Ireland. The Irish Parliament, which by then had gained a measure of legis-lative independence (*see* GRATTAN'S PARLIA-MENT; YELVERTON'S ACT) voted independent-ly on 19 February 1789 to ask the Prince of Wales, the future George IV, to assume the regency of Ireland, believing him to be more sympathetic to its independence than his father. This action by the Irish Parliament alarmed the British government, confirming their view that legislative independence for Ire-land was dangerous (*see* UNION, ACT OF). The king quickly recovered his mental capacity and no regent was appointed.

Regensburg. *See* RATISBON.

Reginald's Tower. A landmark public building in Waterford city, located at the junction of the Quays and the Mall. Thought to be the oldest tower of mortared stone in Europe, it was erected by and gets its name from Reginald MacIvor, Danish governor of Waterford in 1003 (*see* VIKINGS). In 1463 it contained a mint, and in the 19th century it was used as a prison. Waterford City Museum is now housed in the tower, and the exhibits include the colourful regalia of Waterford Corporation and a collection of 19 royal charters bestowed on the city by eleven English kings.

Regium donum (Latin, 'royal grant'). A block grant from the government (literally the king) for the payment of Presbyterian ministers. It varied from £600 per annum at its inception in 1672 to £1600 from 1718. It was initiated in the reign of Charles II, suspended under James II, restored under William III, and suspended briefly in 1714–15 because of the opposition of the Anglican Church. It was abolished in 1869 at the time of the DISESTABLISHMENT OF THE CHURCH OF IRELAND, and the Presbyterian Church received a capital sum of £770,000 as compensation.

Religion. The Republic of Ireland has traditionally been seen as an overwhelmingly Catholic country, and indeed only a very small percentage of the population belongs to other faiths. Since 1980, as a result of scandals such as clerical sexual abuse (*see* BISHOP BRENDAN), abuse of power by the hierarchy (*see* FORBIDDEN FRUIT), the role of the clergy in institutional abuse and a conservative, out-of-touch hierarchy appointed by Pope John Paul II, there has been a huge decline in church attendance. In 1983 it was estimated that 87% of Irish people attended Sunday Mass, but in 2000 an *Irish Times* survey revealed that only 40% of people believed it was important to attend Mass, and in the 18–24 age-group only 14% believed it to be so. In the same period recruitment to seminaries and convents has declined catastrophically.

Religious, silly or indecent. A comment by J.P. MAHAFFY, provost of Trinity College Dublin (1914–19) about literature in Irish. A member of the Intermediate Education Committee in 1899, he claimed that it was impossible to find a Gaelic text that was not 'either religious, silly or indecent'.

Repeal Movement. The movement, led by Daniel O'CONNELL, for the repeal of the Act of UNION of 1801.

Repeal rent. *See* MONSTER MEETINGS.

REPS. The Rural Environmental Protection Scheme funded by the European Union and adopted by many Irish farmers. The scheme was introduced in 1994 as Ireland's response to an agri-environment regulation by the Council of the European Union. The primary objectives of the scheme are: to establish farming practices and controlled production methods that reflect the increasing concern for conservation, landscape protection and wider environmental problems; to protect wildlife habitats and endangered species of flora and fauna; and to produce quality food in an extensive and environmentally friendly manner. REPS is a very important source of funding for many cash-strapped Irish farmers, although there is some concern among environmentalists about the extent to which the scheme is genuinely of benefit to the environment.

Republicanism. *See* NATIONALISM / REPUBLICANISM.

Republic of Ireland. Ireland was declared a republic by the enaction of the Government of Ireland Act of 1948, under the first INTER-PARTY GOVERNMENT, led by John A. COSTELLO. The act declared that Ireland was no longer a member of the British Commonwealth, and that 'the description of the state shall be the Republic of Ireland'. On Easter Monday 1949 the Republic of Ireland formally came into existence. The British government passed the IRELAND ACT in response. Although the CONSTITUTION OF 1937 declares the name of the country to be 'Ireland' or (in Irish) Éire, the term 'Republic of Ireland' is frequently used to distinguish the southern state from Northern Ireland, for instance in sport, business and telecommunications.

Resign–Marry–Return. A cabled message from Cecil Rhodes (1853–1902) to PARNELL during the O'Shea scandal (*see* O'SHEA WHO MUST BE OBEYED).

Resurrection Architects (*Ailtirí na hAiséirí*). One of the factions in the Irish-language movement of the 1940s, used as a basis by Flann O'BRIEN for his short play in Irish, *An Sgian* (*The Knife*), which was first performed as part of a variety show in the Gate Theatre at Christmas 1944. The faction was an offshoot of CONNRADH NA GAEILGE, and was established by Gearóid Ó Cuinneagáin in Dublin in 1941. It became a considerable national movement, with 1200 members, employing street protest and agitation and contesting the general elections of 1943 and 1944. It is alleged that Ó Cuinneagáin envisaged the establishment of a fascist regime with himself as leader. When Ó Cuinneagáin's supporters became disenchanted with their leader's political aspirations, a rival organization, the Victory Generation (*Glún na Buaidhe*) was established by Pronsias Mac an Bheatha. Seán South (*see* 'SEÁN SOUTH FROM GARRYOWEN') was a member of the organization, and some members were later active in CLANN NA POBLACHTA. Some of the activities of the *Ailtirí* are described from a child's point of view in Hugo Hamilton's (b.1953) memoir, *The Speckled People* (2003).

Retreat from Moscow. A phrase coined to describe the emigration to Ireland of some of the wealthy individuals of postwar Britain who wished to escape from the high-taxation welfare state introduced by the Labour government of Clement Attlee (1945–51). They perceived Ireland as a conservative country where food and servants were plentiful, and often settled in properties acquired cheaply on the scenic south and west coasts. Many returned to Britain after the 1951 election re-established the Conservatives in power. During the same period of postwar building boom, hundreds of thousands of Irish workers emigrated to Britain (*see* NAVVIES).

Returned Yanks. *See* YANKS.

'Revenge for Skibbereen'. The name by which a famous, anonymous 19th-century ballad properly called 'Old Skibbereen' is known, the final, rousing words being, 'And loud and high we'll raise the cry / Revenge for Skibbereen!' The song takes the form of a father's account of his home in response to a question posed by his son (father and son are exiles, presumably in America). It is a harrowing and angry account of landlords, evictions, poverty and hunger:

Oh well I do remember the black December day
The landlord and the sheriff came to drive us all
    away;
They set my roof on fire with their cursed English
    spleen,

And that's another reason why I left old
    Skibbereen.

In the public mind, Skibbereen is regarded as having seen the very worst of the GREAT FAMINE: 28,000 people are estimated to have died there, and a further 8000 to have emigrated. It is thought that 8000–10,000 victims of famine and disease were buried in one mass famine pit at Abbeystrewery on the outskirts of the town. Lord Dufferin visited this graveyard in 1847 and wrote:

The bodies had been daily thrown in, many without a coffin, one over another, the uppermost being only hidden from the light of day by a bare three inches of earth, the survivors not even knowing where those most dear to them lay sleeping.

Skibbereen WORKHOUSE, which was built to accommodate 800, often held several thousand inmates. The senior physician of the workhouse, Daniel Donovan (1808–77), worked heroically with the starving and the dying, and did much to highlight the plight of his patients in the English press, as well as arranging passage out of Ireland for many of the survivors.

Michael COLLINS is said to have sung 'Old Skibbereen' in the Imperial Hotel in Cork on the night before his death on 22 August 1922.

Revisionism. A term used, particularly by its critics, to denote a particular kind of anti-Nationalist historiography current in Ireland since about 1970. Before 1970 the popular teaching of Irish history was based on the premise that the British were always evil, the Irish always heroic and idealistic and that the struggle for national self-determination had begun with BRIAN BORU and proceeded in a direct line of succession to Éamon DE VALERA. Up to and including the national celebrations of the 50th anniversary of the EASTER RISING in 1966, the country's national complacency was largely undisturbed, but the beginning of the Northern TROUBLES in the late 1960s forced Irish historians and Irish people, faced with a renewal of paramilitary violence claiming to be in their name, to look again at their history.

Two key texts in the development of what is now called 'revisionism', both published in 1972, were written not by academic historians but by politicians with intellectual leanings: Garret FITZGERALD's *Towards a New Ireland* and Conor CRUISE O'BRIEN's *States of Ireland*. Both books averred that the predominant separatist strain in Irish history was closer to the parliamentary Nationalism of Daniel O'CONNELL and HOME RULE than to Republicanism, and developed what has become known as the 'two nations' theory: that there are two distinct cultural entities in Ireland, both valid and both deserving of the name 'Irish': the Gaelic Nationalist 'nation' and the Protestant Unionist 'nation'.

Among academic historians Leland (F.S.L.) LYONS (1923–83) of Trinity College Dublin posited the 'battle of two civilizations' theory in *Culture and Anarchy in Ireland 1890–1939*, a collection of essays first delivered in Oxford in 1978 and published in 1979. His pupil Roy Foster assumed his mantle after his premature death, and for Nationalists such as historian Brendan Bradshaw, Foster is the *bête noire*. Foster's works include *Modern Ireland 1600–1972* (1988) and a two-volume biography of W.B. Yeats (the first volume *The Apprentice Mage*, appeared in 1988, and the second, *The Arch-Poet*, in 2003). In a critique of *Modern Ireland*, Seamus DEANE wrote:

> Revisionists are [Unionists] despite themselves; by refusing to be Irish nationalists, they simply become defenders of Ulster or British nationalism, thereby switching sides.
>
> SEAMUS DEANE in *Revising the Rising* (ed. Máirín Ní Dhonnchadha and Theo Dorgan, 1991)

Revisionism has made it possible, and even desirable, to think the unthinkable, to question the sacred texts: Catholic sectarianism in the Rebellion of 1798 (*see* SCULLABOGUE, BARN OF); Republican torture and violence in the 1919–21 Anglo-Irish War; even the veracity of Tom Barry's account of the false surrender at the KILMICHAEL AMBUSH (*see* IRA AND ITS ENEMIES, THE).

Revival, the. The proposed revival of the Irish language, close to the heart of Éamon DE VALERA, who dominated Irish political life from 1932 until the late 1950s. One of the great mysteries of Irish life is why since independence the revival failed so dismally, and why children who study Irish in school every day of their school career for perhaps 14 years end up having very little knowledge of it and indeed – many of them – cordially detesting it. Among other factors, commentators blame over-reliance on the education system as a means of revival, compulsion, poor pedagogy, and the hypocrisy of leaders of the state who paid lip-service to the language and produced the CÚPLA FOCAL on state occasions but who did not lead by example. Nor was the revival always well served by the revivalists. Flann O'BRIEN was particularly acidulous on the subject, and there may have been a grain of truth in his assertion that 'the revivalists do not seek merely to revive a language ... They seek to propagate the thesis that to be Irish (through and through) one must be a very low-grade peasant ...'
See also LANGUAGE FREEDOM MOVEMENT.

Reynolds, Albert (b.1932). FIANNA FÁIL politician. He was born in Roosky, Co. Roscommon, on 3 November 1932 and educated at Summerhill College, Sligo. As a businessman he was involved in dancehall promotion and pet food, founding a company called C&D Foods. He became a member of Longford County Council in 1974, and in 1977 was elected to the Dáil. From 1979, under Charles HAUGHEY he served as minister for posts and telegraphs, then as minister of transport and power, before taking over industry and commerce (1987–8) and finance (1988–1991).

When Charles Haughey resigned as taoiseach in February 1992, Reynolds was elected party leader and taoiseach. He was an ambivalent head of the Fianna Fáil–Progressive Democrat (PEE DEE) coalition government of that year, which he had earlier described as 'a TEMPORARY LITTLE ARRANGEMENT'. Relations further deteriorated during the BEEF

TRIBUNAL hearings of 1992 to which he and coalition partner Des O'Malley, Progressive Democrat leader, presented contradictory testimony. When the PDs withdrew from government Fianna Fáil assembled a new coalition with the Labour Party early in 1993.

There is no doubt that Reynolds played a significant role as a broker in the Northern peace process. He and Prime Minister John Major signed the DOWNING STREET DECLARATION in December 1993, and an IRA ceasefire was announced in September 1994. At the end of that year in a controversy centring on the extradition of a paedophile priest (*see* BRENDAN SMYTH AFFAIR), the Labour–Fianna Fáil coalition collapsed. Reynolds resigned as taoiseach and leader of the party, succeeded by Bertie AHERN as leader.

Reynolds, Thomas (1771–1836). Informer. He was born in Dublin, the son of a prosperous merchant, and educated at a Jesuit college in Liège, Belgium. Although he inherited valuable property from his father, business misfortune and extravagance left him almost bankrupt. Himself a member of the UNITED IRISHMEN, he became an informer in 1798, although he was married to the sister of Matilda TONE. As a result of his information, members of the Leinster directory were arrested in the house of Oliver BOND in March 1798 (*see also* FITZGERALD, LORD EDWARD). Reynolds was paid £5000 and given £1000 a year for life, but obliged to leave Ireland. He lived first in Britain, then in Paris, where he died on 18 August 1836.

RHA. *See* ROYAL HIBERNIAN ACADEMY.

RIA. *See* ROYAL IRISH ACADEMY.

Ribbonmen. A highly ritualistic Catholic/Nationalist SECRET SOCIETY, which was active during the early decades of the 19th century in the northern half of Ireland. It was seen as a recrudescence of Defenderism (*see* DEFENDERS, THE) and engaged intermittently in largely defensive sectarian clashes with Orangemen in Ulster (*see* ORANGE ORDER). It was said to have taken its name from an insignia worn by members. Ribbonism was both a rural and urban phenomenon, existing in Dublin and other parts of Leinster, Ulster and north Connacht, and was manifestly Catholic-sectarian; Ribbonmen clashed with members of Orange lodges in Ulster. In rural areas they took part in the TITHE WAR and protested, usually by means of violence and intimidation, at the exploitation of tenant farmers. It ceased to be active by 1840, the energies of its members being taken up by O'Connellism and YOUNG IRELAND.

RIC. The Royal Irish Constabulary, Britain's police force throughout most of Ireland at the time of the Anglo-Irish War of 1919–21. It was founded as the Irish Constabulary by an act of Parliament of 1836, which united earlier local police forces. It was given the prefix 'Royal' by Queen Victoria in 1867, in recognition for having suppressed the FENIAN CAMPAIGN OF 1867. The constabulary was centrally controlled, hierarchical and subject to military-style discipline. During the first decades of its existence it was used to impose public order in cases of agrarian or TITHE disputes, and to assist in carrying out evictions. Gradually, however, the force took on the characteristics of a civilian police force and included many Catholics and Nationalists of tenant-farmer stock, particularly from the west of Ireland. On the outbreak of the Anglo-Irish War, the early engagements of which specifically targeted RIC barracks in the search for arms, members of the force found themselves in an impossible situation, especially after BLACK AND TANS and AUXIES were recruited to bolster their falling numbers. Many resigned; others collaborated with the IRA, Michael COLLINS having realized how useful they were as sources of information about the movement of troops and armaments. At the end of the war those who did not collaborate found it difficult to return to civilian life, and some had to leave the country. Others joined the new police force of the free state, the GARDA SÍOCHÁNA. *See also* DMP; RUC.

Rice, Edmund Ignatius (1762–1844). Founder of the CHRISTIAN BROTHERS. He was born to a prosperous farming family in Callan in Co. Kilkenny on 1 June 1762, and was educated locally. He then moved to Waterford city to work in his uncle's export business, which he inherited and in which he prospered. His wife, whom he had married in 1785, died in 1789 as a result of a riding accident, leaving a premature and handicapped infant daughter, and this appears to have been the turning point in Rice's life. He retired from business with the intention of entering an enclosed order, but realized that his vocation lay in helping his own people. He opened a school for poor boys in Waterford city in 1800 and later, with a fledgling community, moved to a purpose-built school and monastery called Mount Sion, which is still a school for boys. The order he founded, officially called the Institute of the Brothers of Christian Schools in Ireland but universally known as the Christian Brothers, was approved by Pope Pius VII in 1820, and comprised 22 houses in Ireland and England by the time Rice retired in 1838. He died in Mount Sion on 29 August 1844.

Rice House, the. An 18th-century wine merchant's house in Dingle, Co. Kerry, also known as 'the Presbytery' because it was owned by the Catholic church in the 19th century. Count James Louis Rice, son of a wine merchant, was a co-officer of the future emperor Joseph II, brother of Marie Antoinette, in the Austrian army. When Marie Antoinette was imprisoned during the French Revolution, Rice visited her in the guise of a Frenchman, and hatched a plan to bribe her jailers, rescue the queen and bring her to his father's house in Dingle, where rooms were made ready to receive her. Marie Antoinette, however, refused to leave the prison without her husband.

Rice House Barracks. *See* ASHE, THOMAS.

Richard II (1367–1400). King of England. During his reign (1377–99) he made two expeditions to Ireland, the first (1394–5) with the aim of subordinating the Gaelic chieftains and extracting greater revenues from the country by reforming the civil administration. When the Gaelic chiefs submitted, Richard treated them leniently. During his second expedition in 1399 his cousin Henry Bolingbroke claimed his throne. He returned to England but was deposed at the end of 1399.

Riddle of the Sands, The. *See* CHILDERS, [ROBERT] ERSKINE.

Ride. A Dublin slang term originally denoting a female free with her sexual favours (from the verb 'to ride', signifying 'to have sexual intercourse'), whose meaning has become extended to include someone who displays lively, extrovert or daring behaviour. The exclamation 'You're a ride!' is suggestive more of admiration than of censure.

Riders to the Sea. The second (short) play by J.M. SYNGE, which was first staged by the Irish National Theatre Society in the Molesworth Hall, Dublin, on 25 February 1904. It was the only one of Synge's plays actually set in ARAN ISLANDS, and its portrayal of the bitter hardness and fatalism of island life and the apparent inevitability of tragedy there made it unpopular at the time. The central figure, Old Maurya, has already lost her husband and five of her six fishermen sons to the sea. In an attempt to prevent her last son, Bartley, from making a journey to the mainland to sell horses she withholds her blessing. He too is drowned before he is able to board the hooker that will take him to Connemara. The play, which replicates in its mood and structure the rhythmic surge and withdrawal of waves on the seashore, ends on a note of cathartic acceptance and a kind of desperate victory over the elements: 'They're all gone now and there isn't anything more the sea can do to me.' Maurya's last line was adapted from a letter written by an islander to Synge: 'No man at all can be living for ever, and we must be satisfied.' It has since been appreciated as one of the finest short plays ever written. Ximinez translated it into Spanish as *Jinetes hacia el Mar*, and it provided the germ for Bertolt Brecht's *Die Gewehre der Fraülein Carrara*. The composer Ralph Vaughan Williams set the text unchanged for his short opera of the same name (1937).

Rift. An Ulster slang verb meaning to 'belch'. The tautological 'rift gas' is also used.

Rightboys. An agrarian society of the late 18th century, originating in Co. Cork and spreading into the neighbouring counties Tipperary, Kerry, Limerick and Waterford. The society was named after its mythical leader, 'Captain Right' and engaged in violent protest against the infringement of tenant rights and the payment of TITHES to the Church of Ireland and dues to Catholic clergy. Rightboys are thought to have been more widespread than WHITE-BOYS.

Ring, Christy (1920–79). Hurler. He was born in Cloyne in east Co. Cork and made his début for his county team in 1939. He was the first hurler to win eight ALL-IRELAND medals, three as Cork captain; he also won 18 RAILWAY CUP medals. His exploits are the stuff of legend, and include scoring three goals in three minutes in the Munster Final of 1956, and scoring six goals and four points in a game against Waterford in 1959, at the age of 39. He retired from hurling in 1963. Of the many (anonymous) ballads written to celebrate his exploits, the following is sung to the air of 'The Bould Thady QUILL':

> For lifting and striking, for doubling like lightning,
> For points or goal-scoring his praises we'll sing.
> He's hurling's most glorious, he's always victorious,
> He's Cork's darling hurler, the bold Christy Ring.

A more formal ballad by Bryan MacMahon (*see* MASTER, THE) bestows heroic status on the sportsman ('Slaney' refers to the Wexford hurling team):

> When we were young we read at school that in the days of old

> The young Setanta showed his worth with shield and spear of gold
> As hurling hard on royal sward he'd Red Branch heroes fling
> But Slaney's plan must find a man to equal Christy Ring.

A GAA park in Cork city, Páirc Uí Rinn ('Ring park'), is named after Christy Ring.

Ring barrow. A circular earthen mound surrounded by a bank. Such barrows are human burial mounds dating from the late Bronze Age (*c.*1500 BC).

Ring fort. A circular enclosure, normally comprising an earthen bank with a single or double ditch topped by a wooden fence; stone was also used where plentiful, such as in the BURREN or on the ARAN ISLANDS. Ring forts were the secure homes of farming communities from pre-Christian or early Christian times, and it is estimated that there were in all more than 40,000 of them in Ireland; the vast majority have never been excavated. Some have fallen prey to developers, although in rural communities a strong taboo on destroying ring forts remained until recent decades, a taboo reinforced by their association with the SIDHE (the remnants of the TUATHA DÉ DANAAN, who after their defeat by the FOMORIANS were said to have fled underground into these ring forts); many forts had a particular feature thought to represent the interests of the Sidhe, such as a blackthorn tree. Some forts have souterrains (underground passages), which were used for storage or as places of refuge, rather in the manner of air-raid shelters. Local lore also claims that souterrains were used to link a series of forts in a particular locality.

Ring forts are toponymically important: the usual Irish word is *rath*, but *lios* (pronounced 'liss'), *caher*, *dún* (pronounced 'doon') and *cashel* also occur; *caher* signifies a stone construction, while *dún* and *cashel* denote a larger, more fortified structure. All these words occur frequently in Irish placenames.

Ring of Kerry. *See* KERRY, RING OF.

Ringsend car. A hackney vehicle with one horse,

so called because the coastal area of Ringsend in Dublin was once a bathing resort for Dublin gentry, and these hackneys were used to bring them to and from the city.

Ringsend uppercut. A kick in the groin; the origin of the phrase is obscure.

Riordans, The. A popular weekly rural soap opera produced and broadcast by RTÉ 1965–80. Broadcast on Sunday evenings, it was the first television drama ever to mirror the lives of the people of rural Ireland. Leestown, a fictional village in Co. Kilkenny, was the home of the farming Riordan family and Wesley Burrows the scriptwriter most associated with the series, which featured actors Tom Hickey, Martin Cowley, Biddy White Lennon and Anne D'Alton. Because the show was early-evening family viewing and because the events were seen to be unfolding in a 'real' Irish setting, RTÉ management was very sensitive to adverse criticism and exercised a kind of auto-censorship: contraception, extra-marital sex and adultery were among the topics *not* dramatized during the life of the serial.

Rí-rá. An Irish term for 'fuss and excitement', 'reckless merriment', 'revelry'. In HIBERNO-ENGLISH (anglicized as *ree-raw*) it is often used with the roughly synonymous RUAILLE BUAILLE.

Rising of the Moon, The. A play by Lady GRE-GORY first staged at the ABBEY THEATRE on 9 March 1907. It takes its title from a ballad about the REBELLION OF 1798 by John Keegan Casey (1846–70) (*see* LEO), who was a member of the FENIANS. The play is essentially a duo-logue between an RIC sergeant and a 'ragged man', as the dramatis personae puts it, and it deals very subtly with the ambivalence that often afflicted members of the paramilitary force. It is clear from the poster pasted to the barrel on which both characters sit that a fugitive is being sought: a reward of £100 is being offered for his capture, and it is expected that he will try to escape from the quay by boat. The sergeant is slow but not

unkind and the man, claiming to be Jimmy Walshe, a ballad singer, is allowed to stay. He passes the time by singing Nationalist songs in which the sergeant eventually joins, having had essentially the same upbringing as the man. The man is soon able to demonstrate that but for fate the sergeant could have grown up to be a rebel like the wanted man. When the man begins the title song he is answered by a whistle from a boat and the sergeant allows him to escape. The closing line shows him perplexed yet oddly euphoric:

> A hundred pounds! A hundred pounds! *(Turns towards audience)* I wonder, now am I as great a fool as I think I am?

Rising Sun bar. *See* TRICK OR TREAT KILLINGS.

Rising tide will lift all boats, the. The phrase used by Seán LEMASS to describe his view of economic growth, often used since to justify tax cuts for the higher paid and favourable tax rates for industry and banking. This is another version of the 'trickle-down theory' of national economics.

See also WHITAKER, T[HOMAS] K[ENNETH].

Riverdance. An Irish dance show, first seen as a remarkably dramatic interval entertainment during the Eurovision Song Contest in 1994, featuring the talents of Michael FLATLEY, the Irish–American dancer, his professional part-ner Jean Butler and dance company, the chor-al group Anúna and the music and lyrics of Bill Whelan. The seven-minute spectacular was to give Irish hard-shoe step-dancing and its ac-companying music a global success, largely owing to the dynamic, and sometimes troubled, talents of Flatley.

Although some of the developments of *River-dance* had been heralded by the performances of the national folk theatre SIAMSA TÍRE, for most Irish people it was a revelation of how sensuous and energetic – and internation-ally appealing – Irish dancing could be. Con-ceived on a massive Broadway-like scale, the show used scores of Irish step dancers as chor-us, even more when it divided into separate touring shows with different principals. *Riverdance*, which ran for months in large venues in Europe, America, Australia and Japan, became an international cultural phenomenon and contributed in no small measure to the popularity of Ireland as a tourist destination in the 1990s. For the most part it was accepted with enthusiasm by teachers and theorists of Irish dancing, to whose pupils the show offered unprecedented employment opportunities. Flatley dissociated himself from the *Riverdance* project to devise and choreograph two further dance spectaculars, LORD OF THE DANCE (1996) and *Feet of Flames* (1998), which are noted both for their brilliance and for a sensuality hitherto untapped in the medium of Irish dance.

Riverrun. The first word of Joyce's FINNEGANS WAKE (1939), and subsequently the name of a publishing company established by Allen Figgis of Dublin in the 1960s.

Roadwatch. A radio traffic slot on RTÉ, sponsored by the AA (Automobile Association) and called 'AA Roadwatch'. The pronunciation of placenames by some of the (Dublin-born) presenters caused media commentators to coin the phrase 'Roadwatch accent' or 'DORT-speak' (*see* DART, THE).

Roaring Hanna. *See* HANNA, HUGH.

Roaring Meg. The best known of the cannon used during the Siege of DERRY. Cast in 1642, it got its name because of its size (it was the largest of the siege guns) and thunderous report, and later gained an iconic value with Ulster Protestants.

Robinson, [Esmé Stuart] Lennox (1886–1958). Playwright and theatre manager. He was born on 4 October 1886 in Douglas, Co. Cork, and educated intermittently, for reasons of health, at Bandon grammar school. In spite of fervent Nationalism, caught when the ABBEY THEATRE company played *The RISING OF THE MOON* at the Cork Opera House in 1907, he remained, as he wrote in *The Bell* in June 1944, 'a hopeless case from the Catholic point of view'. As manager of the Abbey he decided in May 1910 not to close the theatre when Edward VII died, and thus helped speed MISS HORNIMAN on her way back to Manchester for good. He joined the Carnegie Trust as organizing librarian in 1915 but returned to the Abbey in 1919 and became a director in 1923.

Robinson's novel *A Young Man from the South* (1917) is a witty, semi-autobiographical account of literary life in pre-1916 Dublin, but it is as a prolific playwright who could handle realistic drama, light comedy, Ibsenite exposure of provincial mores and fantasy with equal skill that he is remembered. His work includes *The Clancy Name* (1908) about the prevalence of respectability over common sense, *The Lost Leader* (1918) about Parnell, *The Whiteheaded Boy* (1916) about lighthearted small-town intrigue, *Drama at Inish* (1933), and two plays about the ascendency class, *The Big House* (1926) and *Killycreggs in Twilight* (1937). His *Ireland's Abbey Theatre, 1899–1951* (1951) is a useful, matter-of-fact history. He died in Monkstown, Co. Dublin, on 14 October 1958.

> It is common knowledge that the leading newspapers employ as dramatic critics journalists who are excellent on a racecourse or a football field but who are hopelessly astray – or asleep – in the stalls of the Gaiety or the Abbey.
> *A Young Man from the South* (1917).

Robinson, Mary (b.1944). Lawyer and head of state. She was born Mary Burke in Ballina, Co. Mayo, where both of her parents were doctors, and educated at Mount Anville in Dublin and at Trinity College Dublin (TCD). After graduating in law she went on a scholarship to study at Harvard, where she came in contact with the American civil rights and feminist movements of that time. After her return to Ireland she practised at the Bar and was appointed to a professorship in constitutional and criminal law at TCD in 1969, remaining active as a lawyer and commentator in the areas of constitutional and human-rights law. She was elected to the Senate for TCD. In

1976 she joined the Labour Party and twice stood unsuccessfully for election to the Dáil, but resigned from the party in 1985, in protest at the ANGLO-IRISH AGREEMENT of that year, which, she said, would alienate Unionists. She resigned from the Senate in 1989, and in 1990 was selected as Labour candidate for the presidency of Ireland. After a professionally run campaign she easily topped the poll and was inaugurated president in December 1990, promising in her speech to promote a tolerant and pluralist Ireland. From 1997, after her term as president ended, until 2002 Robinson was United Nations High Commissioner for Human Rights.

Roche, Adi (b.1955). Campaigner for children of Chernobyl. She was born in Clonmel, Co. Tipperary, worked for Aer Lingus (1975–83) and then for CND (Campaign for Nuclear Disarmament). She came to national prominence as founder and director of the Chernobyl Children's Project, a charity established in 1990 to help child victims of the disaster at the Chernobyl nuclear plant in Ukraine on 26 April 1986. The project arranges for children from Belarus to spend summer holidays with Irish families, and sends humanitarian and medical aid to Belarus and Ukraine, as well as providing long-term medical care in Ireland for children seriously affected by radiation. A book by Adi Roche, *Children of Chernobyl*, was published in 1996. In 1997 Roche was persuaded by the Labour Party to run for the presidency in succession to Mary Robinson, but after a bitter and personalized campaign she was placed fourth among the contenders (*see* MCALEESE, MARY).

Roche, Regina (1764–1865). Novelist. She was born Regina Dalton in Waterford, where she lived for the rest of her life. She wrote more than 15 works of sentimental and Gothic fiction, set in Ireland and Europe. *Children of the Abbey* (1796) was her greatest success; her other novels include *The Munster Cottage Boy* (1820) and *The Tradition of the Castle* (1824).

Roche, Sir Boyle (1743–1807). An 18th-century Irish politician with a particular taste for IRISH BULLS. He served in the army in America, returning to Ireland before the outbreak of the War of Independence. He first entered parliament in 1776 and continued to sit for a number of constituencies including Tralee, Gowran, Portarlington and Old Leighlin (the Irish equivalent of the 'rotten borough' Old Sarum) until the Act of UNION. His constant support of the government was exemplary – and profitable. He was given a pension, a peerage and a position as master of ceremonies in the CASTLE. He strongly opposed CATHOLIC EMANCIPATION and supported the union, saying his love for the two countries was such that 'he would have the two sisters embrace like one brother'. He died in his elegant house in Eccles Street on 5 June 1807. He was also known by the nickname 'Sir Boyle Balderdash'.

Roche, Stephen (b.1950). Cyclist. He was born in Dundrum, Dublin, on 20 November 1950. In 1987, his *annus mirabilis*, he won the Giro d'Italia and the world cycling championship, and was the first Irish winner of the Tour de France, on 24 July. Two days before he had been taken away by an ambulance at the end of the day's racing, unconscious and suffering from exhaustion. In the end Roche defeated Spanish favourite Pedro Delgado by less than 30 seconds.

Rockall. A small rock in the Atlantic about 370 km (230 miles) west of the Hebridean island North Uist. It is 24 m (80 ft) at its widest and was separated from Greenland 60 million years ago. It lies in an area rich in oil and gas and was annexed by Britain in 1955. In 1984 Deputy Patrick Donal Harte (b.1932), then TD for Donegal Northeast, urged the Irish government to assert its right to sovereignty over Rockall.

Rock of Cashel. A dramatic limestone outcrop (aka St Patrick's Rock) rising 60 m (200 ft) above the Golden Vale in Co. Tipperary at the town of Cashel. The site of the stronghold of the MUNSTER kings in the 5th century, it was donated to the Church in 1101. The marvellous remains that make it such an architectural jewel are all of ecclesiastical origin; they include a round tower, a cathedral and the magnificent 12th-century Cormac's chapel:

To hear in piety's own Celtic tongue
The most heart-touching prayer
That fervent suppliants e'er was heard among;
O, to be then and there.

There was a time all this within thy walls
Was felt and heard and seen;
Faint image only now thy sight recalls
Of all that once had been.

THE REV. DR. MURRAY: 'The Rock of Cashel'

Rodden. An ULSTER name for a narrow road, from the Irish *róidín* ('little road').
See also BOREEN; CASÁN; LOANEN.

'Roddy McCorley'. A popular patriotic ballad by Ethna CARBERY. It is sung in march time, and is a favourite with marching bands. Roddy McCorley was hanged in Toomebridge in Co. Antrim during the REBELLION OF 1798, some time after the Battle of Antrim in June 1798:

Ho! See the hosts of fleetfoot men
Who speed with faces wan,
From farmstead and from fishers' cot
Upon the banks of Bann.
They come with vengeance in their eyes
Too late, too late are they,
For Roddy McCorley goes to die
On the bridge of Toome today.

Roddy the Rover. The journalistic tag used by Aodh DE BLÁCAM (1890–1951) for his diary column in *The IRISH PRESS* (1932–49).

Rodgers, W[illiam] R[obert] (1909–69). Poet. He was born in Belfast into a strict Presbyterian family, which he magically evoked in his often repeated radio feature *The Return Room* (1955). He was educated at Queen's University Belfast and Assembly's College, and called as minister to the parish of Loughgall, near Armagh (1935–46). He began to broadcast talks on Raidio Éireann, and in 1946 was recruited

by Louis MACNEICE for the Features Department of the BBC in London. One result was a flagship series of *Irish Literary Portraits* (1947–65) for the Third Programme, focusing on Yeats, Synge, Shaw and others. In 1966 Rodgers went to America and was writer-in-residence on several campuses. His poetry, in which sensuality and asceticism, the Bible and the ancient classics clash to produce marvellous, troubled statements, was published in *Awake! And Other Poems* (1941), *Europa and the Bull* (1952) and *Collected Poems* (1971). He died in Los Angeles in 1 February 1969 and is buried in Loughgall.

Son of Adam; Sin of Adam;
I was heir of all that Adamnation
And hand-me-down of doom: the old newcomer
To the return room.
The apple blushed for me below Bellevue;
Grey Lagan was my Jordan, Connswater
My washpot, and over Castlereagh
I cast out my shoe.

The Return Room, 23 December 1955, BBC Northern Ireland

ROI. A convenient acronym for REPUBLIC OF IRELAND, used regularly as part of a postal address.

Róisín Dubh (Irish, 'little black rose'). A poetic personification of Ireland. 'Dark Rosaleen', the famous poem by James Clarence MANGAN (1803–49), is a notably free version of the 18th-century poem of this title. Originally a love poem, its first verse has the old theme of the hope of help for the stricken island from Catholic Europe:

A Róisín, ná bíodh brón ort fár éiri duit.
Tá na bráithre ag teacht ag sáile agus iad ag triall
*   ar muir.*
Tiocfaidh do phardún ón bPápa is ón Róimh
*   anoir*
Is ní spáralfar fíon Spáinneach ar mo Róisín dubh.
(Róisín, do not grieve for all your sad past.
The friars are aboard and come by sea to you.
Your pardon will come from the pope in Rome
And the Spanish wine will not be skimped for my
    Róisín Dubh.)

Mangan's version reads

> O, My Dark Rosaleen,
> Do not sigh, do not weep!
> The priests are on the ocean green,
> They march along the Deep.
> There's wine from the royal Pope
> Upon the ocean green;
> And Spanish ale shall give you hope,
> My Dark Rosaleen!

See also CÁIT NÍ DHUIBHIR; CATHLEEN NÍ HOULI-HAN; POOR OLD WOMAN, THE.

Rolleston, T[homas] W[illiam] (1857–1920). Poet and translator. He was born at Glasshouse, Shinrone, Co. Offaly, the son of a county court judge. He was educated at St Columba's College and Trinity College Dublin, and spent four years (1879–83) in postgraduate study in Germany. He was founding editor of the *Dublin University Review*, compiler of *Poems and Ballads of Young Ireland* (1888) and secretary of the influential Irish Literary Society in London (1892). In January 1896 he suggested in the Press Club that 'Irish was an inadequate instrument for the expression of contemporary thought', but when Douglas HYDE successfully translated an article chosen by him from a scientific journal he became a member of the GAELIC LEAGUE. He became sufficiently competent at Irish to translate back into English some of George MOORE's stories from *The UNTILLED FIELD*. An authority on German literature, he became German editor of the *Times Literary Supplement* in 1908. During the First World War he worked in the censor's office responsible for letters written in Irish as well as German. His poetry, including the much anthologized 'The Dead at Clonmacnoise', is contained in *Sea Spray: Verses and Translations* (1909). He died in London on 5 December 1920.

> There beneath the dewy hillside sleep the noblest
> Of the clan of Conn,
> Each below his stone with name in branching
> Ogham
> And the sacred knot thereon.
>
> 'The Dead at Clonmacnoise' (1909)

Roll it there, Colette. A phrase associated with the *The* LATE LATE SHOW and its presenter Gay BYRNE, who used it whenever a film clip was to be shown.

Ronan (d.664). An abbot of Dromiskin, a monastery near Castlebellingham, Co. Louth, believed to have been founded by PATRICK. Ronan appears in the legend of SUIBHNE GEILT, the king driven mad by the noise of the battle of Mogh Rath (Moira, Co. Down), as the holy man who curses him. The saint's relics were placed in a shrine in 801, but it disappeared in the 10th century. The name is found in Kilronan on Inishmore, the largest of the ARAN ISLANDS. His feast day is 18 November.

Ronán. *See* ÁEDÁN.

Ronnie Barker. Rhyming slang for 'Parker', used for the ballpoint pen refills, inside which messages were smuggled in and out of prison by and for Republican prisoners during the Northern Troubles. The expression derives from the name of the British comedy actor (b.1929).

Rooney, William (1873–1901). Journalist and language revivalist. He was born in Dublin. A member of the GAELIC LEAGUE, he wrote many articles for Nationalist periodicals in the 1890s and travelled throughout the country as an Irish teacher, despite having poor health. In 1899, with his long-term colleague Arthur GRIFFITH, he founded *The United Irishman*, with Griffith as editor. It was Griffith who after his death edited his *Poems and Ballads* (1902) and his *Prose Writings* (1909) for publication.

Rooting around. A phrase in the HIBERNO-ENGLISH of Ulster used to indicate desultory, ineffective or inconclusive activity.

Rory O'More. A sentimental novel (1837) by Samuel LOVER with a background of the REBELLION OF 1798. The hero is a good-hearted stage Irishman (*see* STAGE-IRISH), and there is a love interest and a gallant Frenchman doing preparatory work for a French invasion. Tyrone Power (1797–1841), the great-grandfather of the Hollywood actor, starred in Lever's own stage adaptation, and a 1911 film version was shot in Ireland by Sydney Olcott.

Ros, Amanda McKittrick (1860–1939). Novelist and poetaster. She was born in Drumaness near Ballynahinch, Co. Down, became a schoolteacher and married Andrew Ross, the stationmaster at Larne, Co. Antrim. (The 'Ros' she regarded as more romantic than her husband's proper name.) She is notorious for her oddly phrased and alliteratively charged romances *Irene Iddlesleigh* (1897) and *Delina Delaney* (1898), which elevated bathos into high art. Her verse in *Poems of Puncture* (1913) and *Fumes of Formation* (1933) contains surreal vituperation against her favourite targets, lawyers ('Mickey Monkeyface McBlear'). She also wrote occasional poems, as in 'On Visiting Westminster Abbey', which begins:

Holy Moses! Take a look!
Flesh decayed at every nook,
Some rare bits of brain lie here,
Mortal loads of beef and beer.

Her work exercised an appalling fascination on such writers as Aldous Huxley and Louis MacNeice, who started a Ros cult.

Rosary. A Marian devotion consisting of three sets of meditations – Joyful, Sorrowful and Glorious – on the life, death and Resurrection of Christ. (In October 2002 John Paul II added the 'Mysteries of Light' for use on Thursdays.) Each meditation involves five decades (set of ten) of Hail Marys, preceded by an Our Father and followed by a Gloria. Traditionally the Rosary was recited by the whole family on its knees before bedtime, family members reciting the decades aloud in turn; in larger households the master or mistress would recite the Rosary with all the servants. Additional prayers before or after the decades, particularly common in the religious seasons of Lent or Advent, were called 'trimmings' (*see* TRIMMIN'S ON THE ROSARY). A set of Rosary beads was used to count the prayers of the decade, and until relatively recently every Catholic adult and child

in Ireland would have owned a set of rosary beads. Beads were made of more or less valuable material as circumstances dictated: metal, bakelite or plastic (in more recent years); materials such as mother-of-pearl or semi-precious stones would be used for a special set. Children were customarily given a set of white beads at their First Communion, and Rosary beads blessed at Knock, Lourdes, Fatima or other Marian shrines were held in particularly high esteem.

Rosary beads. *See* ROSARY.

Roscommon, 4th Earl of. *See* DILLON, WENTWORTH, 4TH EARL OF ROSCOMMON.

Roscrea. A small town in Co. Tipperary associated with the production of breakfast rashers and sausages.

'Rose of Mooncoin, The'. A song of disappointed love, said to have been composed by Watt Murphy, a teacher who came to Mooncoin, Co. Kilkenny, in 1826 and fell in love with Elizabeth, the daughter of the local rector. The rector, disapproving of the match, sent Elizabeth (the 'Molly' of the song) to England. Francis MACMANUS took the title of his novel *Flow on Lovely River* (1941) from the chorus:

How sweet 'tis to roam by the sunny Suir stream
And hear the doves coo neath the morning's sunbeam,
Where the thrush and the robin their sweet notes combine
On the banks of the Suir that flows down by Mooncoin.
Chorus:
Flow on, lovely river, flow gently along
By your waters so sweet sounds the lark's merry song
On your green banks I'll wander where first I did join
With you, lovely Molly, the Rose of Mooncoin.

'The Rose of Mooncoin' is the anthem of the often successful Kilkenny hurling team in the ALL-IRELAND championship.

'Rose of Tralee, The'. A romantic ballad by

William Mulchineck (1820–64). Mulchineck, a gentleman, loved a beautiful girl called Mary O'Connor whose father made shoes in Brogue Lane, Tralee, and who herself worked as a servant in his mother's house. Although he asked her to marry him and she accepted his proposal, he was falsely accused of murder and had to flee the country in 1833. When he returned after six years in India, Mary's funeral was taking place (the cause of her death is not recorded but it seems likely that she died of a broken heart).

> The pale moon was rising above the green
> mountains,
> The sun was declining beneath the blue sea,
> When I strayed with my love to the pure crystal
> fountain
> That stands in the beautiful vale of Tralee.
>
> She was lovely and fair as the rose of the summer,
> Yet 'twas not her beauty alone that won me;
> Oh no, 'twas the truth in her eyes ever dawning,
> That made me love Mary, the Rose of Tralee.

The story, which may be true, is commemorated in the town park with a monument to Mulchinock and his Mary. The song, set by Charles Glover (1806–63), was made known internationally by John McCORMACK, who sang it in the film *Song o' My Heart* (1930) and at many farewell concerts. Legend has it that the 'pure crystal fountain' or well referred to by Mulchineck still exists in a place called Sceathanach on the outskirts of Tralee.

The Festival of Kerry, which takes place in late August, and was established in the 1950s in order to attract tourists and sightseers to a depressed Tralee, has as its centrepiece the Rose of Tralee contest, which was initiated in 1958. Communities of the Irish diaspora, as well as the cities and counties of Ireland, select attractive young women to compete: thus there will be a Manchester Rose, a Sydney Rose, a Holyoke (a city in Massachusetts that has an extensive Irish community) Rose. Officially at least it is no Miss World contest: the personality, charm, performance and aspiration of the contestants are taken into account. The show has been televised by RTÉ since 1978, and for many years, Gay BYRNE's skills as compère lifted the standard of the proceedings. 'The Rose of Tralee' is also Kerry's anthem for the purposes of the ALL-IRELAND football championships, and is the tune played on the pitch at half-time by the ARTANE BOYS' BAND.

Roses, Wars of the. *See* WARS OF THE ROSES.

Rose Tattoo Affair, the. A controversy about censorship of the stage that erupted in the late 1950s when Tennessee Williams's play, *The Rose Tattoo*, was staged at the PIKE THEATRE, the experimental theatre of Alan Simpson and Carolyn Swift. On 23 May 1957 Simpson was arrested at the theatre and jailed, having a few days earlier refused to withdraw the play, alleged indecent by complainants. The case against Simpson was finally dismissed by the Supreme Court over a year later, but the Pike never recovered from the crippling legal expenses incurred in the case. This represented one of the last contortions of the CENSORSHIP Board, which traditionally interfered only with the written word: a less ultra-Catholic board was quietly constituted as a result.

Rosmorkyn. The site on the northeast coast of Scotland in modern Caithness of a Columban abbey, founded by the 7th-century Irish monk Curitan. Little is known about him except that he attended the Synod of Birr in 697 when the *Cáin Adamnáin* (*see* VITA SANCTI COLUMBAE) was promulgated.

Ros na Rún. A successful long-running Irish-language soap opera broadcast twice-weekly on TG4; it is subtitled and has about 200,000 viewers. It is set in a sleepy Connemara village of the same name (the Irish name means 'headland of the secrets', or 'headland of the sweethearts'), but with a storyline so full of incident, scandal and violence that Ros na Rún has been called 'the murder capital of Ireland'. It was first broadcast on 4 November 1996 as a pilot drama project by what was then known as T. na G. (Teilifís na Gaeltachta) and is produced by a combination of two production companies, one Irish-language, one

English, employing about 100 people in the Connemara GAELTACHT. The drama is sponsored by Foras na Gaeilge (successor to BORD NA GAEILGE) and, although it has been accused of sloppy grammatical standards, a pilot project has brought it and its accompanying educational apparatus into transition-year classes in 100 schools.

Ross, Martin. *See* SOMERVILLE AND ROSS.

Ross Castle. A tourist attraction on the shores of Lough Leane about 1.5 km (1 mile) from the town of Killarney, Co. Kerry. The castle, which has recently been restored, comprises a 16th-century tower surrounded by a BAWN[3] with rounded turrets, and a much later extension on the southern side of the tower. It was built by a chieftain of the O'Donoghue Ross and held by the Royalists under Lord Muskerry in the Cromwellian wars. There was a legend that the castle would never be taken except from the water and, hearing this, Ludlow, the Cromwellian commander, brought a boat up the River Laune from the sea at Killorglin and through Lough Leane. When the defenders saw a boatload of soldiers approaching they knew that all was lost and abandoned their posts.

Rosse, 3rd Earl of. *See* LEVIATHAN OF PARSONSTOWN, THE.

Rosses, the. A heavily indented coastal area of northwestern Co. Donegal; the name, in Irish Na Rosa, means 'the headlands'. The main settlement is Dunglow.

> High on the hill-top
>   The old King sits;
> He is now so old and grey
>   He's nigh lost his wits.
> With a bridge of white mist,
>   Columbkill he crosses,
> On his stately journeys
>   From Slieveleague to Rosses ...
>   WILLIAM ALLINGHAM: (1824–89) 'The Fairies' ('Up the airy mountain, / Down the rushy glen ...')

> My sorrow that I am not by the little dún
> By the lake of the starlings at Rosses under the hill,

And the larks there, singing over the fields of dew
...
    SEAMUS O'SULLIVAN: 'The Starling Lake', in *Collected Poems* (1940)

Rosslare. A passenger port and adjacent beach resort in Co. Wexford. Car ferries to Fishguard in Pembrokeshire, Wales, and to Roscoff and Cherbourg in France sail from the port. The resort is famous for a family-run hotel, Kelly's of Rosslare.

Rossville Flats. High-rise flats in Derry's BOGSIDE, since demolished, that were the scene of much confrontation and actual violence during the Northern Ireland Troubles. During the Battle of the BOGSIDE in 1969 the roofs of the flats made such an excellent site for the throwing of bricks and petrol bombs that after OPERATION MOTORMAN in 1972 the British army kept a permanent observation post there. Nearby was 'Aggro Corner', where William Street and Rossville Street met, always a scene of potential trouble and so named by the British army. Both places were the scenes of the civilian deaths on BLOODY SUNDAY 1972.

Rothe House. An Elizabethan house in Kilkenny, built by John Rothe (1560–1620) in 1594. It currently houses Kilkenny's tourist office on its arcaded ground floor and a museum on the second and third floors. It is one of the best preserved examples in Ireland of a rich merchant's house of the 16th century. Rothe House is linked to the National Ecclesiastical Assembly convened by Bishop Rothe, a cousin of John Rothe, in May 1642. This led to the formation of the parliament of the confederation (*see* KILKENNY, CONFEDERATION OF; CONFEDERATE CATHOLICS) in October 1642. The Rothe family paid dearly for the association: the house was confiscated and the family deported to Connacht in 1653. The house was restored to them after the Restoration, in 1660, and finally passed from the family in 1691. Rothe House became a school in the 18th century; among the pupils were the BANIM brothers, who describe the building in one of their novels. The Kilkenny Archaeological Society bought the house in 1962, restored it and opened the museum in 1966.

Rotunda, the. A lying-in or maternity hospital, the first of its kind in Ireland or Britain, founded by Dr Bartholomew Mosse (1712–59) in 1745. The hospital moved to its current location, a building specially designed by Richard CASTLE in the Palladian style, in 1757. A pleasure garden and a rotunda were built on the site in the 1760s, and an assembly room (*see* GATE THEATRE) in the 1780s, with a view to fundraising for the hospital by providing entertainment for the wealthy. In the 1770s the hospital became a training centre for midwives, both male and female. In January 1922, at the head of a group of unemployed dockers, the writer Liam O'FLAHERTY as 'Chairman of the Council for the Unemployed' took over the Rotunda Rooms and held out for four days until they were ejected.
See also FIELD, JOHN.

Round, to stand a. The Irish custom by which each member of a group in a pub in turn buys drinks for all the group. The bigger the group, therefore, the more drink consumed. There is evidence that drink-driving laws (*see* OVER THE LIMIT) and changing mores among the urban young have begun to modify the round system.

Round about Our Coal-fire, or Christmas Entertainments. The title of a chapbook published by an 18th-century Dublin printer, anticipating Dickens by 110 years. Unfortunately no copy has survived, but we know from the following advertisement that it contained

> ... stories of fairies, ghosts, hobgoblins, witches, bull-beggars, rawheads and bloody-bones, besides several curious Pieces relating to the History of old Father Christmas. Adorned with many diverting cuts. Price 3d. Lately Published and to be sold by James Hoey, at the Sign of Mercury in Skinner-Row, opposite the Tholsel, Dublin, 1733.

'Bull-beggars', 'rawheads' and 'bloody-bones' were all forms of hobgoblins, used to frighten children.

Rounds, to do. *See* CITY, THE; HOLY WELLS; PATTERN.

Round towers. A feature of Irish monasteries dating from the 10th–13th century. These plain stone towers were five storeys high or more, with windows at the top level from which a bell would be rung to summon the monks to prayer or food (the Irish term is *cloigtheach*, 'bell house'). The doorways were normally about 3 m (10 ft) from the ground, giving to the structures a defensive value, as personnel could climb up with valuable possessions and the access ladder be pulled up behind them, for instance during a Viking raid. It is also thought that the position of the doorways was a means of strengthening the base of the towers because the foundations were weak. One of the best surviving examples of a round tower is that at Ardmore, Co. Waterford; it is 29 m (95 ft) high and is thought to date from the 12th century. Like the ARDAGH CHALICE and the TARA BROOCH, round towers have often served as symbols of Nationalist Ireland, for instance on children's copybooks or on souvenirs.

Rowan, [Archibald] Hamilton (1751–1834). United Irishman. He was born in London on 12 May 1751, and inherited considerable wealth from his grandfather. He was educated at Westminster and Cambridge and settled on an estate in Co. Kildare in 1784. A member of the VOLUNTEERS, he attended the Dublin Convention of 1784. He joined the UNITED IRISHMEN in 1791. Like Wolfe TONE he was compromised by association with the Rev. William JACKSON and sentenced to two years' imprisonment for sedition. He escaped to France and thence to America where he again met Tone but, horrified by what he had witnessed of the Terror in France, refused to join with Tone and Napper TANDY in rebellion. In 1803 he was pardoned and returned to Ireland to settle on his estate at Killyleagh Castle, Co. Down. He remained a supporter of liberal causes, particularly CATHOLIC EMANCIPATION. He died in Dublin on 1 November 1834.

Rowley, Richard. The pseudonym of Richard Valentine Williams (1877–1947), poet, playwright and publisher. He was born in Belfast on 2 April 1877 and managed the family cotton-handkerchief manufacturing business until it collapsed in 1931. He then became chairman of the Assistance Board, and in 1943 founded the Mourne Press, which published his own work and the short stories of Michael MCLAVERTY and Sam Hanna BELL. His poetry, about 'ordinary Ulster folk', was published in *The City of Refuge* (1917) and *Ballads of Mourne* (1940), and his verse play *Apollo in Mourne* (1926) describes the effect of the high-spoken god – banished by Jove from Olympus – on Co. Down peasants. He died in Loughgall, Co. Armagh, on 25 April 1947.

> *Jove:* There shall you wander
> Amidst a barbarous people, harsh of speech
> And of fierce aspect, dwelling in huts of stone,
> Seeing the sun but seldom, eating strange meats,
> And never tasting wine, or fruits, or oil.
>
> *Apollo in Mourne* (1944)

Rowsome, Leo (1903–70). Musician. A player and maker of UILLEANN PIPES, Leo Rowsome was born in Dublin and took over the family business of making and repairing pipes. He was a very important figure in the revival of traditional music and the achievement of recognition for the pipes as a serious and worthy instrument; he re-established the DUBLIN PIPERS CLUB and was a founder member of COMHALTAS CEOLTÓIRÍ ÉIREANN. He wrote a tutor for the pipes and made a large number of recordings.

Royal Arch Purple. A loyal chapter that is part of the ORANGE ORDER outside of Ireland but at home was formed into a separate group in 1911. Known as the Grand Loyal Arch Purple Chapter it is part of the Orange hierarchy, and most members are eventually initiated into the chapter after suitable scriptural instruction.

Royal Belfast Academical Institution. *See* INST.

Royal Black Institution. An organization like the ORANGE ORDER but tending in the past to draw its officers from the working classes rather than the aristocracy. It was founded as the Imperial Grand Black Chapter on 16 September 1797, and its local units are called preceptories. The Orange Order and all such quasi-religious organizations were prohibited in the decade 1836–46, but in 1846 at a meeting in Portadown, Co. Armagh, the institution was re-established. Ties with the Orange Order are strong, the Black Men, as they are colloquially called, often using the LOLs for their meetings. Candidates for admission have to be already members of the Orange Order and the ROYAL ARCH PURPLE, and there is a complicated hierarchy within the institution. Though their annual celebration is in commemoration of the relief of Derry (TWELFTH OF AUGUST 1689; *see* MAIDEN CITY) and the Battle of Newtownbutler (31 July 1689), preceptories hold their annual processions on the last Saturday of August, a trade holiday since 1967.

Royal County. The nickname of Co. Meath, because the Hill of TARA is situated in that county, between Dunshaughlin and Navan. The county is also known as 'Royal Meath'. The use of the nickname is associated particularly with the Gaelic football championship, and is often used by radio and television commentators in search of variety.

Royal Dublin Society (RDS). An organization founded as the Dublin Society on 25 June 1731 with the aim of 'improving husbandry, manufactures and other useful arts and sciences'; it has been called 'Royal' since 1820, when George IV became its patron. Its remit originally included the provision of grants for livestock breeding, fisheries and scientific research, and it has also been associated with the establishment of many major cultural institutions, including the NATIONAL LIBRARY OF IRELAND, the NATIONAL MUSEUM OF IRELAND, the NATIONAL GALLERY OF IRELAND and the Botanic Gardens in Dublin. From 1831 the RDS, as it is universally known, has held a spring show for the exhibition of livestock and agricultural manufacture – until 1924 at the organization's headquarters, LEINSTER HOUSE (now home of the Dáil) in Kildare Street, Dublin; thereafter in its larger premises at Ballsbridge, 3 km (2 miles) from the city centre. The other highlight of its calendar, held in August, is the international horse show (initiated in 1868), which includes the Nations Cup competition, popularly known as the 'Aga Khan Cup'. The society also organizes lectures, recitals and concerts in Ballsbridge for the benefit of members, and has a fine library.

Royal Hibernian Academy (RHA). An institution for the encouragement of the fine arts. It was founded by royal charter in 1823 and provided with a school and gallery in Abbey Street in Dublin by Francis Johnston (1760–1829), the leading architect of the day, who was president for the last five years of his life. Its first secretary, Martin Cregan (1788–1870), contributed 334 paintings to academy exhibitions while he lived, including 26 portraits for the first showing. His family piece of Johnston, his wife and nephews was one of the highlights of 1827. Exhibitions have been held annually since 1826, not excepting 1916, the year of the Easter Rising, when its premises and some of its paintings were destroyed. Until 1939, when a specially designed building was opened in Ely Place, the academy was housed in the National College of Art in Kildare Street. Exhibitions have been held in Ely Place since 1985.

Royal Hospital, the. A hospital for old and disabled soldiers built in Kilmainham, Dublin, between 1680 and 1687 (with additions in 1701) to the design of Sir William Robinson, the surveyor-general during the lord-lieutenancy (1661–84) of Richard Talbot, Duke of ORMOND. It was to be the Dublin equivalent of the Royal Hospital, Chelsea, which was finished in 1691 to a design of Sir Christopher Wren on the instruction of Charles II. The king was also the patron of the Dublin facility, as his letter to Ormond in 1679 makes clear:

... And we do hereby give unto you full power

and authority from time to time to issue and employ the same towards the building and settling an hospital for such aged and maimed officers and soldiers as shall be dismissed out of our army as unserviceable men, and for making provision for their future maintenance, in such way and manner as you shall think fit.

The Royal Hospital was in use as a retirement home until 1927, and also contained the residence of the commander-in-chief of the British army in Ireland. The hospital buildings became the headquarters of the GARDA SÍOCHÁNA in the 1920s, but in 1949 it was vacated as being unsafe. The complex now houses Ireland's Museum of Modern Art (IMMA).

Royal Irish Academy (RIA). An organization for study and the advancement of knowledge founded by the Duke of CHARLEMONT in 1785 and granted a royal charter in 1786. It has occupied its present headquarters in Dawson Street in Dublin since 1825. It became best known in the 19th century for the scholarship of members such as the mathematician William Rowan HAMILTON, the antiquarian George PETRIE and the Celtic scholar Eoin MACNEILL. It has an extensive library and a priceless collection of more than 2500 Irish manuscripts. The contemporary academy has some 300 members, in many disciplines, both humanities and sciences.
See also K.M.R.I.A.

Royal Irish Academy of Music. *See* IRISH ACADEMY OF MUSIC.

Royal Irish Constabulary. *See* RIC.

Royal schools. A number of 'royal free' schools were established by James I in the early 17th century as part of the ULSTER PLANTATION; they later came under the auspices of the CHURCH OF IRELAND. Further schools were established by Charles I. These grammar schools existed in most of the planted counties of Ulster: Tyrone, Fermanagh, Cavan, Donegal and Armagh, as well as in Offaly (then King's County) and Co. Wicklow. Portora Royal School in Enniskillen,

Co. Fermanagh, and The Royal in Cavan town, now a Church of Ireland secondary school, are examples of surviving royal schools.

Royal Ulster Constabulary. *See* RUC.

Royal University of Ireland. An examining body that replaced the QUEEN'S COLLEGES according to the terms of the University Education (Ireland) Act of 1879. The existing Queen's University was dissolved and the Royal University fellowships were divided between the existing Queen's Colleges, Magee College in Derry and the Catholic University in Dublin, henceforth called University College, Dublin. Degrees from the Royal University were available to all who passed the university's exams, including, for the first time, women.

RTÉ (Raidio Telefís Éireann). The name of Ireland's public-service broadcaster. It currently transmits radio programmes on five channels – RTÉ 1, 2 FM, Lyric FM, RAIDIÓ NA GAELTACHTA and Ceolnet (an internet broadcasting channel for traditional music) – and also has two television channels. RTÉ is a statutory corporation with headquarters in Donnybrook, a south Dublin suburb. It has been providing service on radio since 1926 and on television since 1961. Under the terms of the Broadcasting Act 1960 and subsequent legislation, the corporation is governed by the RTÉ Authority, a nine-member board appointed by the government. The National Symphony Orchestra, the RTÉ Concert Orchestra and the Philharmonic Choir are all the responsibility of RTÉ.

Ruadhan (d.584). A Munster saint, one of the TWELVE APOSTLES OF IRELAND, who after training by FINNIAN OF CLONARD set up his own abbey at Lorra in Co. Tipperary, 15 km (9 miles) west of Birr. This became one of the foremost of Munster abbeys, boasting a miraculous food-producing tree and a scriptorium where the 9th-century Stowe Missal was crafted. The manuscript of the missal is in the ROYAL IRISH ACADEMY and its metal shrine in the NATIONAL MUSEUM OF IRELAND. St Ruadhan's bell is now housed in the British Museum. Ruadhan's feast day is 15 April.

Ruaille buaille. An onomatopoeic Irish phrase used in HIBERNO-ENGLISH to mean confusion, noise or helter-skelter activity.
See also RÍ-RÁ.

RUC. The Royal Ulster Constabulary, the police force of Northern Ireland before the establishment of the Police Service of Northern Ireland (PSNI) on 1 November 2001. It replaced the RIC in 1922, having recruited 50% of its membership from that force and having a large intake from the Ulster Special Constabulary (USC) set up in 1920 (*see* B-SPECIALS), who were mostly past members of the UVF. It was originally intended that one third of the force should be Catholic, but after five years of its existence the fraction of Catholics was less that a fifth and by 1970 a tenth. Always regarded by Nationalists as a partisan force only slightly more respectable than the USC, it was severely criticized for its handling of CIVIL RIGHTS marches in 1968–9. A number of reforms were put in place, including the disarming of ordinary members of the force, but since they became targets of the IRA early in the Troubles they soon became the most heavily armed police force in the UK. By the time of the GOOD FRIDAY AGREEMENT they had become more transparently even-handed, thereby alienating some sections of the Protestant community. Under the terms of the PATTEN REPORT they were replaced by the PSNI.

Rugby football. A team game with 15 players a side, introduced to Trinity College Dublin by pupils of the English public school Rugby. The Trinity Rugby Club was founded in 1854, and in 1879 the Irish Rugby Football Union (IRFU), which still regulates the game, was formed. Except in Limerick (*see* ALONE IT STANDS), rugby in Ireland is a middle-class sport, popular in boys' schools; it has to compete for players and audiences with soccer in the towns and with GAELIC LEAGUE football in both rural and urban areas. Since 1995 rugby players have been allowed professional status. The Six Nations Championship (Ireland, England, Scotland, Wales, France and Italy), played in the winter season, is now very popular, and the Irish supporters' anthem is 'The FIELDS OF ATHENRY'. Rugby is an All-Ireland sport (i.e. players are drawn from the Republic and the North), and home internationals are held in Dublin's Lansdowne Road stadium.

See also GIBSON, MIKE; KIERNAN, TOMMY; McBRIDE, WILLIE-JOHN; O'DRISCOLL, BRIAN; WOOD, KEITH.

Rug-headed Kerns. The description by Shakespeare, in *Richard II* (II.i), of 14th-century Irish soldiery:

> Now for our Irish wars.
> We must supplant those rough rug-headed kerns
> Which live like venom where no venom else
> But only they have privilege to live.

The word comes from the Irish *ceithearn*, 'band of warriors' (the word for an individual member being *ceithearnach*). The Anglo-Irish, blurring the distinction, used the word *kerns* for native Irish mercenaries who from the 12th century offered themselves at need. They were lightly armed independent groups unsuitable for pitched battles but ideal for harrying populations upon whom they leeched in time of peace. They obviously offered their services to their neighbours across the North Channel, since they are mentioned in *Macbeth* (I.ii):

> From the Western Isles
> Of kerns and gallowglasses is supplied.

See also GALLOWGLASS.

Rundale. A system of land tenure (also known as 'runrig') common in the western parts of the country in the century before the GREAT FAMINE, whereby land was held in collective tenancy by extended family groups, and arable land divided among individual farmers in such a way that all had use of both good and bad sections of land for subsistence (potato) and cash crops. A related system was that of 'changedale', which meant that tenants alter-

nated areas of good and bad land from year to year. The total acreage being small, rundale strips were often very small indeed, and a tenant could have some dozens of strips scattered over many different fields. As there were no fences, there were frequent disputes in the system. Historians now see rundale as a response to the rapid population growth of the late 18th century and the increasing dependence on the POTATO.

Runrig. *See* RUNDALE.

Rural electrification. The term by which the extension of electric power to rural Ireland in the 1950s was known. In the rural electrification scheme, Ardmore in Co. Waterford was the first village to receive a supply, on 24 May 1954. Throughout the 1950s electricity gradually became available in the rest of the country, the erection of poles providing much-needed employment to local men. At the time the cost to a family was £1/10/- (about €2) for each light and £2 (€2.50) for each socket. Most families took only a few lights and maybe one socket because of the expense and the unfamiliarity. The Sacred Heart lamp was the first and most important item to be electrified in most rural homes. Another consequence of electrification was that the bright electric light revealed to housewives the shabbiness of their traditional furniture – the dresser, the SETTLE bed, the scrubbed deal table – and there was a rush to apply paint. When stripped-pine country furniture became fashionable in Ireland in the 1970s, the paint applied in the 1950s was painstakingly removed.

Rural Environmental Protection Scheme. *See* REPS.

Rush light. A type of light made by peeling a rush, dipping it in melted wax or tallow and clamping it in a holder. A great number of rushes was needed to provide any degree of illumination over a long winter night. Rush lights were commonly used in rural Ireland until the advent of TILLY LAMPS in the 1920s.

Russborough House. A fine Palladian mansion 5 km (3 miles) from Blessington in Co. Wicklow. It was designed by Richard CASTLE and constructed 1741–51 for Joseph Leeson, later Earl of Milltown. It is built of granite quarried at Ballyknocken and consists of a central colonnaded block with two wings. The garden contains an extensive maze. After the death of the last Earl of Milltown, the Milltown Collection was presented to the NATIONAL GALLERY OF IRELAND. Sir Alfred Beit bought the house in 1952 to provide a home for the Beit Collection of Dutch, Flemish and Spanish masterpieces. In 1978 Russborough House was opened to the public and part of the collection was presented to the National Gallery in 1988. Paintings have twice been stolen from the house: in 1974 Rose Dugdale stole 16 paintings to raise funds for the IRA, but all the paintings were recovered; of the paintings stolen by Dublin criminal Martin Cahill (*see* GENERAL, THE) and his gang in 1988, only one has been recovered.

Russell, [William] George. *See* Æ.

Russell, Seán (1893–1940). The IRA chief of staff who masterminded the organization's bombing campaign in Britain 1939–40. He was born in Dublin and educated at the Christian Brothers School in Westland Row. Interned for his part in the EASTER RISING of 1916, he became a member of the headquarters staff of the IRA during the Anglo-Irish War of 1919–21. He rejected the TREATY and fought on the Republican side in the CIVIL WAR, breaking with de Valera and the other Republicans who founded FIANNA FÁIL in 1927. When de Valera outlawed the IRA in 1936, Russell demanded outright war against Britain. Although the organization was split, he spearheaded the plans for the bombing campaign in Britain, which began on 16 January 1939 and culminated in the Coventry explosion of 25 August of that year. He went to America to seek aid, and was prevented by the outbreak of the Second World War from returning to Ireland. He went instead to Ger-

many where the navy arranged for him and Frank RYAN to be transported to Ireland by submarine. Russell died en route on 14 August 1940 and was buried at sea; Ryan was returned to Germany.

Russell, Thomas. *See* MAN FROM GOD KNOWS WHERE, THE.

Russell, William Howard. *See* MR RUSSELL OF THE TIMES.

Ryan, Connie. *See* SET DANCES.

Ryan, Darby. *See* BARD OF BANSHA, THE.

Ryan, Desmond (1893–1964). Republican writer and journalist. He was born in London, the son of W.P. RYAN, and educated at ST ENDA'S SCHOOL in Dublin. He later worked as secretary to Patrick PEARSE. During the 1916 EASTER RISING he fought in the GPO, and after release from internment became a journalist. His books about Republicanism and the labour movement include *The Man Called Pearse* (1919), *James Connolly* (1924), *The Phoenix Flame* (1937) and *The Rising* (1949). He also edited the *Collected Works of Patrick Pearse* (1917–22).

Ryan, Frank (1902–44). Republican and socialist. He was born in Co. Limerick and interned as a Republican during the CIVIL WAR. An energetic propagandist and agitator, he was active in the IRA during the 1920s, and joined the propaganda section of the International Brigades in the Spanish Civil War. He was captured by the Nationalists in 1938 and sentenced to death, but instead spent two years in prison in Burgos, during which time his health deteriorated. Refusing to release him, Franco instead had him handed over to German military intelligence on the French border. DE VALERA made it clear that Ryan was not welcome back in Ireland – his return 'would entail all sorts of complications'. Ryan stayed in Germany during the war after an abortive attempt to come back to Ireland by submarine (*see* RUSSELL, SEÁN), although he became increasingly disillusioned with Nazism after Hitler's attack on the USSR. He died in Berlin in 1944.

Ryan, W(illiam) P(atrick) (1867–1942). Socialist and writer in Irish and English. He was born in Templemore, Co. Tipperary, and worked as a journalist in London. In 1906 he returned to edit the *Irish Peasant* in Navan, Co. Meath, but the journal was suppressed by Cardinal Logue for alleged anticlericalism and socialism. The following year Ryan established his own *Peasant*, which he published 1907–8; in 1909 it became the *Irish Nation*. In 1910 he returned to London, where he worked for many years in labour journalism. An enthusiastic supporter of the CELTIC REVIVAL, he also edited for some years *An t-Éireannach* ('the Irishman') for the London GAELIC LEAGUE. His published works encompassed drama, fiction, essays and poetry, and included *The Heart of Tipperary* (1893), *The Pope's Green Island* (1912) and *The Irish Labour Movement* (1919). He died in London. He was the father of writer Desmond RYAN.

Ryan's Daughter. A film (1970) belonging to the genre of historical melodrama, directed by David Lean and starring Robert Mitchum and Sarah Miles, and shot largely in the spectacular landscape of the DINGLE PENINSULA in Co. Kerry. It is set in 1916, and tells the story of the wife of the local village schoolmaster who falls in love with a British officer, with predictably unpleasant consequences. The ruins of the 'village' of Kirrary that were specially constructed near Dunquin remained in place for many years. For the people of the area the making of the film was a revelation, especially as many of them, used only to fishing and subsistence farming, earned what were to them colossal wages as construction workers or extras. The release of the film also brought an influx of tourists to the area.

S

Sacred Relics. The locks of Swift's remaining hair that were clipped from his head at his death on 19 October 1745 (*see* DEAN, THE). The rape of the locks is described by his godson Thomas Sheridan (1719–88) in *The Life of the Rev. Dr. Swift* (1784):

> Though he had been, for so many years, to all intents and purposes dead to the world, and his departure from that state seemed rather a thing to be wished than deplored, yet no sooner was his death announced, than the citizens gathered from all quarters, and forced their way in crowds into the house, to pay the last tribute of grief to their departed benefactor. Nothing but lamentations were heard all round the quarter where he lived, as if he had been cut off in the vigour of his years. Happy were they who first got into the chamber where he lay, to procure, by bribes to the servants, locks of his hair, to be handed down as sacred relics to his posterity. And so eager were numbers to obtain at any price this precious memorial, that in less than an hour, his venerable head was entirely stripped of all its silver ornaments, so that not a hair remained.

Sadb. In Irish mythology, the mother of OISÍN, poet son of FIONN MAC CUMHAIL. The name is pronounced 'sive' in English. She is the daughter of BODB DEARG and is turned into a deer by the DARK DRUID. Out hunting Fionn would have killed her except that his hounds will not approach her. (In one account Fionn, sensing human elements, crushes his hound BRAN[1]

between his legs to prevent it attacking her.) That night she comes to Fionn in human form and becomes his mistress, having discovered that the Dark Druid has no power within the FIANNA compound. Later, when Fionn is off hunting, the Dark Druid again turns her into a fawn, and she disappears. Fionn searches for her for seven years, and finally, at the foot of Ben Bulben in Co. Sligo, he finds a naked boy who has been raised as a deer. He recognizes the boy as his son, calling him Oisín ('little deer'). *Sadb* is the title of J.B. KEANE's first play (1959).

Sadlier, John. *See* POPE'S BRASS BAND, THE.

Saeva Indignatio. Dean Swift's phrase (*see* DEAN, THE) in his self-composed epitaph, cited as the main cause of his lifelong heartbreak:

> *Ubi saeva indignatio*
> *Ulterius*
> *Cor lacerare nequit.*
> (Where fierce rage can no longer tear his heart.)

The epitaph concludes with a typical Swiftean admonition:

> *Abi Viator*
> *Et imitare, si poteris*
> *Strenuum pro virili*
> *Libertatis vindicatorem.*
> (Go wayfarer and match if you can this active champion of human freedom.)

Saffron. A species of crocus, *Crocus sativus*,

which provided the orange-yellow dye for Irish shirts (often using as much as 35 yards of linen) and women's kirtles and tunics. The exotic colour, which the English traduced as being coloured by 'man's stale', was one of the main targets of Henry VIII's DRESS CODE.

SAG. Saint Anthony Guide, the initials sometimes written by the pious on the back of the envelope for posting. This St Anthony was a Dominican of Padua, also patron of lost property.

Sagairt Óir. A woeful comparison of 17th-century Ireland with the age of St PATRICK, attributed to St Oliver PLUNKETT.

> *Sagairt óir is cailísí crainn*
> *Bhí le linn Phádraig in Éirinn;*
> *Sagairt chrainn is cailísí crainn*
> *In ndeire an domhain dearóil.*
> (Golden priests and wooden chalices
> In Ireland in the time of Patrick;
> Golden chalices and priests of wood
> In this latest miserable age.)

Sagart Mór, an. *See* FIGHTING PRIEST OF GWEEDORE, THE.

'Said the King to the Colonel'. The first line of the octet 'The Irish Colonel' by Sir Arthur Conan Doyle (1859–1930), born in Edinburgh of Irish parents, about the Irish Brigade in the French army of Louis XV (1710–84), the king in question. The colonel is unnamed but was one of the WILD GEESE, and the incident occurred at the siege of Rehl in 1732 during the War of the Polish Succession:

> Said the king to the colonel,
> 'The complaints are eternal,
> That you Irish give more trouble
> Than any other corps.'
> Said the colonel to the king
> 'This complaint is no new thing,
> For your foemen have made it
> A hundred times before.'

St Brigid's Cross. *See* ST BRIGID'S DAY.

St Brigid's Day. The first day of February, regarded in Irish tradition as the first day of

spring and hence the first day of the year. It was celebrated with a mixture of pagan and Christian customs (*see* IMBOLG). Butter was always freshly churned on this day, and a cake as big as a cartwheel with curds and eggs was baked. The Cros Bhríde (St Brigid's Cross, woven from rushes) was hung over the kitchen door and the byre to invoke the protection of the saint. A slice of bread and a sheaf of straw were left on the window sill near the front door for the saint and her pet cow, who were thought to travel the roads of Ireland on St Brigid's Night. A length of ribbon was left outside for the saint's blessing: this was believed to cure toothache and headache.
See also BEALTAINE; BRIGID; LUGHNASA; SAMHAIN.

St Columba broke a winda. *See* LET ON.

Saint Denis. The site near Le Bourget, north of Paris, of the medieval abbey that became the cemetery of the French kings. It held the cell of DUNGAL, who lived there from 784 to 827.

St Enda's School. A boarding school for boys founded by Patrick PEARSE in 1909. It was known in Irish as Scoil Éanna. St Enda's adopted a strongly Gaelic curriculum and ethos, rejecting what Pearse called the 'murder machine' of rote learning and rigid teaching methods. The legendary hero CÚCHULAINN was the model for the boys, their motto taken from the FIANNA: 'Courage in our hands, truth in our tongues and purity in our hearts'. Pearse's brother Willie PEARSE and his sister Margaret PEARSE also taught there. The school was originally located in Cullenswood House in Ranelagh, Dublin, and after moving in 1910 to a house with a 50-acre (20-ha) site, the Hermitage in Rathfarnham, it was always strapped for cash; it was largely funded by CLAN NA GAEL donations in the period 1914–16, when Pearse's reputation for advanced Nationalism deterred the parents of would-be pupils. Despite the efforts of Pearse's mother Margaret PEARSE[1] and appeals for funding to DE VALERA, it closed in 1935. The building passed to

Margaret (junior) after her mother's death in 1932, and after her own death to the state. The Hermitage, which is set in pleasant parkland, now houses the Pearse Museum.

St George's Church. The bells that Leopold Bloom heard ringing in ULYSSES (1922) were those of St George's Church, Hardwicke Street, east of O'Connell Street in Dublin. St George's, which was consecrated in 1814, is recognized as the masterpiece of Francis Johnston, the architect of the GPO and the Chapel Royal in Dublin Castle (*see* CASTLE, THE). The steeple, the highest in Dublin, is the only one that can be seen from O'Connell Bridge. The church was deconsecrated in 1991, after the Church of Ireland had failed to raise the large sums necessary to restore the steeple and portico. The bells were removed to the church in Taney Road, in the city's southern suburbs.

Saint-Gobain. *See* GOBAIN.

St John's Eve. *See* MIDSUMMER'S DAY.

St John's wort. *See* MIDSUMMER'S DAY.

St Patrick, Order of. *See* ORDER OF ST PATRICK.

St Patrick for Ireland. A play (1639) by one of the leading Caroline dramatists, James Shirley (1596–1666), who lived in Dublin in the years 1636–40, to escape the plague, it was said. It is the first Irish play of the modern theatre, written with all the confidence and flattering inaccuracy of the visitor. It features Patrick's struggle with the Druids, his expulsion of the serpents that attacked him and his establishment of Christianity in place of a barbaric paganism (a theme close to the heart of Shirley, who ruined a promising career as an Anglican divine by becoming a Catholic in 1625). Apart from its theme there is nothing especially Irish about the play; it is typical of the drama of its period, with much rhyme and an absence of the dark psychology of the Jacobeans.

> A man shall come unto this land
> With shaven crown, and in his hand
> A crooked staff ...

'St Patrick's Breastplate'. An 8th-century poem in Old Irish to which the name of St Patrick has been attached, but which combines pre-Christian sentiments of love of place and of nature with devotion to the Trinity:

> I bind unto myself today
> The virtues of the starlit heaven,
> The glorious sun's life-giving ray,
> The whiteness of the moon at even ...

The best-known part, often set to music, is an exhortation:

> Christ be with me, Christ within me,
> Christ behind me, Christ before me,
> Christ beside me, Christ to win me,
> Christ to comfort and restore me.

St Patrick's Cathedral. A cathedral of the Church of Ireland, in Patrick Street, Dublin. A collegiate church was built here, outside the city walls, in 1192, on the site of an earlier parish church. Although much of the fabric of the current church dates from the 13th and 14th centuries, large portions are also the result of rebuilding work begun under the auspices of Sir Benjamin Guinness in 1864. During the 13th century rivalry continued between St Patrick's, called 'cathedral' from 1213, and neighbouring CHRIST CHURCH CATHEDRAL, until in 1300 the pope issued a decree granting supremacy to Christ Church. During the Reformation St Patrick's was downgraded to the status of parish church, but elevated again under the reign of the Catholic Queen Mary in 1554–5. Jonathan Swift was dean of St Patrick's from 1713 to 1745 (*see* DEAN, THE).

St Patrick's Cross. A flag devised by Dublin Castle (*see* CASTLE, THE) in the 17th century as a parallel to St George's Cross, and briefly used in the 1930s as an emblem by the BLUESHIRTS. A saltire red cross on a white background, it was incorporated into the Union flag from 1801. It had neither national significance nor connection with St Patrick.

St Patrick's Day. Ireland's national festival, celebrated with a bank holiday, parades and (recently) fireworks and other events on 17

March. The feast day of the national saint is celebrated with different spectral intensities of green in many venues throughout the world. It was early on a holiday in America, being declared such by some Irish Protestants in Boston in 1737, and the first St Patrick's Day parade was held there in 1779. It did not become a public holiday in Ireland until 1900, largely through the efforts of the GAELIC LEAGUE. The League's success in having all public houses closed on St Patrick's Day from 1904 was less popular. The biggest parade of all is traditionally in New York. It is customary for the Irish taoiseach to be in the USA on this day, and for him to present a bowl of SHAMROCK[1] to the US president. Since the arrival of the CELTIC TIGER, efforts have been made to lift the standard of the parade in Dublin by including street theatre, mime and dancing, as well as the traditional fare of American marching bands and commercial floats.

> So I fetched me Sunday bonnet and the flag I love
> so well
> And I bought meself a shamrock just to wear on
> me lapel.
> Don't you know that today's March seventeen?
> It's the day for the wearing of the green!
>> ROGER EDENS: 'It's a Great Day for the Irish', from
>> the film *Little Nelly Kelly* (1940)

St Patrick's Day (or the Scheming Lieutenant). A farce by Richard Brinsley SHERIDAN, staged in the THEATRE ROYAL in Dublin in 1775. The eponymous Lieutenant O'Connor impersonates a German quack in order to win the hand of Lauretta, whose father Justice Credulous is implacably opposed to their marriage.

St Patrick's Purgatory. *See* LOUGH DERG.

St Ruth, Marquis de. *See* AUGHRIM, BATTLE OF.

St Stephen's Green. A large park in the centre of a Georgian square in Dublin, taking its name from St Stephen's Church, built here in the middle of the 13th century. The area was a grazing common outside the city until 1664, when, during the lord-lieutenancy of the Duke of ORMOND, the Corporation enclosed part of

it and divided the 30 acres (12 ha) outside this enclosure into building plots, at first supporting a mixed population but by the end of the 18th century becoming one of the most fashionable areas in Dublin. Some of the houses fell victim to development in the 1960s; of those remaining the best known is probably the 19th-century Shelbourne Hotel. The two finest houses on the square are on the south side: Iveagh House, built in 1730 and now occupied by the Department of Foreign Affairs, and Newman House (1765), which housed the CATHOLIC UNIVERSITY. The bijou University Church is beside Newman House. St Stephen's Green witnessed some fierce fighting during the 1916 EASTER RISING.

St Ultan's. *See* LYNN, KATHLEEN.

St Vincent de Paul, Society of. A Catholic charitable organization founded in Paris in 1833 by Antoine Frédéric Ozanam (1813–53) and named for St Vincent de Paul (1580–1660), who established the Vincentian order, zealous in carrying out good works. The society was established in Dublin in 1844 and played a part in relief efforts during the GREAT FAMINE. It now has more than 10,000 members in Ireland and continues to respond successfully to poverty and want, particularly in urban areas in Dublin.

Sáirséal agus Dill ('Sarsfield and Dill'). An Irish-language publishing house established in 1945 by civil servant Seán Ó hEigeartaigh (1917–67) and his wife Bríd Ní Mhaoileoin (b.1920) to promote literary writing in Irish, after the work of some important emerging writers was rejected by An GÚM. *Nuabhéarsaíocht 1939–49*, edited by Seán Ó TUAMA[2] in 1950, and *Nuascéalaíocht*, edited by Tomás de Bháldraithe in 1952, were ground-breaking anthologies, the former poetry, the latter short stories. The imprint subsequently published the leading Irish writers of the day, including Máirtín Ó CADHAIN – *Cré na Cille* sold 2000 copies within three weeks of its publication in 1949 – and Máirtín Ó DIREÁIN. Seán

Ó hEigeartaigh died suddenly in 1967, but his wife continued to publish literature in Irish until 1980, when she sold the company to Caoimhín Ó Marcaigh. Thereafter it became known as Sáirséal Ó Marcaigh.

Sáirséal Ó Marcaigh. *See* SÁIRSÉAL AGUS DILL.

Salach (Irish, 'dirty'). A word used in HIBERNO-ENGLISH to describe weather that is wet and miserable: 'That's a *salach* old day.'

Sallins Train Robbery. On 31 March 1976 the mail train was held up near Sallins in Co. Kildare and more than £200,000 stolen. Gardaí arrested 40 members of the Irish Republican Socialist Party (IRSP) on suspicion of involvement in the robbery; all but 6 were released without charge after a period in detention, some claiming that they had been mistreated and had signed statements under duress. Four men were charged with the robbery, and three were found guilty: Osgur Breatnach, Nicky Kelly and Brian McNally. Breathnach and McNally spent 17 months in jail before being released on appeal on the grounds that their confessions were acquired under 'oppressive circumstances'. Kelly, although protesting his innocence, was sentenced to 12 years' imprisonment after the release of Breatnach and McNally, but was released after serving 4 years in 1984 and was eventually granted a state pardon and financial compensation. He has since been a Dáil candidate in Co. Wicklow for the LABOUR PARTY.
See also HEAVY GANG.

Sally O'Brien. *See* O'BRIEN, SALLY.

Sally rod. A stick cut from a willow tree (sally) and used for the chastisement of children by parents and teachers.

Sally's Bridge. A minor bridge over the GRAND CANAL in Dublin, officially named Parnell Bridge but always known as Sally's Bridge, allegedly because an old woman named Sally collected the tolls there at a time when tolls were payable.

Salmon of Knowledge. *See* FINTAN.

Saltee Islands. Two small uninhabited islands off Kilmore Quay in Co. Wexford, privately owned but accessible from Kilmore and popular among ornithologists because of the wide range of unusual bird life they support. It is thought that the name, deriving from the Norse *Saly Ey* ('salt islands'), dates from the middle of the 12th century.

Salthill. *See* KICKING THE WALL.

Salt Monday. The first Monday in Lent, on which, in certain areas in the west of Ireland, salt was sprinkled on bachelors and spinsters – those who might have been expected to get married during SHROVETIDE – to preserve them until the next Shrovetide.

Salzburg. The central Austrian city, about 240 km (150 miles) of Vienna, famous as the birthplace of Wolfgang Amadeus Mozart. The Irishman FERGAL, known in Austria as Virgil, was appointed abbot of St Peter's monastery there by Duke Odil of Bavaria in 742.

Sam. *See* SAM MAGUIRE CUP.

Sam and Ella. Cartoon characters (derived from the word salmonella) representing germs in a health education video for children.

Samhain. The Celtic feast of the dead and the coming of winter. It is now known as HALLOWE'EN since the church Christianized 1 November as All Hallows and the following day as the feast of All Souls. At Samhain, even more so than at BEALTAINE, the door between the natural and supernatural worlds (*see* OTHERWORLD) was believed to be ajar, the SIDHE (fairy hosts) were abroad and the dead, especially the unhappy dead, were free to walk again on earth. Even in modern times doors were left unlatched and food laid ready for these unearthly visitors. The feast was marked with light-hearted divination games and, as at Bealtaine, with bonfires, lit now to counter the approaching dark.
See also IMBOLG; LUGHNASA.

Samhain. The journal published each autumn by the members of the IRISH LITERARY THEATRE (1901–6; 1908). The text consisted largely of statements of policy by YEATS and the scripts of the theatre's early plays: *CASADH AN TSÚGÁIN* (1901), *CATHLEEN NÍ HOULIHAN* (1902), *RIDERS TO THE SEA* (1903) and *IN THE SHADOW OF THE GLEN* (1903).

Sam Maguire Cup. The trophy, named after the Republican and footballer Sam MAGUIRE, awarded to the winners of the ALL-IRELAND Senior Football final and as such the most coveted in the GAA. The cup, known colloquially as 'Sam', is a copy of the celebrated ARDAGH CHALICE, and was first presented to Kildare, who defeated Cavan in the championship in 1928. On the last Sunday of every September (unless the game is drawn) the captain of the winning team raises aloft the Sam Maguire Cup and, beginning with '*A DHAOINE UAISLE*', makes a speech of thanks to manager, selectors and supporters. The Cup, after being filled with whiskey and emptied, tours the schools of the winning county and finds a home in that county until the following year's final.

Samson and Goliath. The nickname of two giant cranes in the HARLAND AND WOLFF shipyard in Belfast.

San Clemente. The beautiful basilica of San Clemente in the Via San Giovanni in Laterano in Rome has been in the care of the Irish Dominicans since 1677. Father Joseph Mullooly (1812–80), an amateur archaeologist from Lanesboro, Co. Longford, undertook excavations in the building in 1857, uncovering the original 4th-century church and a series of medieval frescoes dating from the 7th to the 11th centuries.

Sancti. *See* ISLAND OF SAINTS AND SCHOLARS.

Sands, Bobby (1954–81). Republican hunger striker. He was born in Rathcoole in north Belfast and apprenticed as a coachbuilder. His family were intimidated out of their home by Loyalists in 1972, and Sands became an active member of the Provisional IRA, serving several terms for possession of illegal weapons. In 1976 he joined the protest about the removal of SPECIAL CATEGORY status and became leader of IRA prisoners in the MAZE in 1980. When promised concessions were not granted he led the H-BLOCK HUNGER STRIKES of 1981, beginning on 1 March and dying on 5 May, the 66th day of his fast. He was elected MP in the Fermanagh–South Tyrone by-election on 9 April. Since his death he has achieved iconic status as a Republican martyr.

San Isidoro. The church and friary of San Isidoro in Via degli Artisti in Rome has been used as an Irish Franciscan college since it was granted to the order at the instigation of Father Luke WADDING in 1625, except for brief periods when it fell into the hands of invading French forces in 1798–9 and in 1810. From 1625 until his death in 1657 Wadding worked to establish and extend the college.

Saoi (Irish, 'expert', 'master'). A savant or master of the arts in Gaelic society. To be named *saoi* is an honour bestowed by the contemporary AOSDÁNA on artists of distinction.

Saorstát Éireann. *See* FREE STATE, THE.

Saor Uladh. *See* BORDER CAMPAIGN.

Sapphira. The pen name of Mary Barber (*c*.1690–*c*.1757), the poetic protégé of Jonathan Swift (see DEAN, THE). She was probably born in Dublin and married Jonathan Barber, a woollen draper of Capel Street. Her verse, which she began 'chiefly to form the Minds of my Children' (Preface to *Poems on Several Occasions*, 1734), attracted the attention of the Dean, and he became her patron. Her work brought her little money, but she benefited from the publication of Swift's *Polite Conversation* (1738), the royalties from which he made over to her.

> I pity poor *Barber*, his wife's so romantic:
> A letter in rhyme! – Why the woman is frantic.
> This reading of poets has quite turned her head!

On my life, she should have a dark room and
  straw bed.

'Conclusion of a Letter to the Rev. Mr. C—' (1734)

Saratoga Sharpshooter, the. The nickname given
to Timothy Murphy, the Irish-American sniper
who during the American War of Independence
shot Brigadier-General Simon Fraser at the Battle of Saratoga in October 1777, thus preparing
the way for the surrender of General John Burgoyne (1723–92):

'Twas then brave Morgan lowered his glass,
And pointing where Fraser stood,
Cried, 'Woodsmen say when a man must pass,
"He's the log that jams the flood."
Six thousand men of the new-born states –
American, Irish, Dutch – are we.
One man holds back the flood of the fates
That sweeps us on to be free;
Let Heaven open for him its gates,'
And Tim Murphy climbed a tree.

JOSEPH I.C. CLARKE (1846–1925): 'Saratoga'
(Daniel Morgan (1736–1802) was commander of the
Virginia Riflemen.)

Sarsfield, Patrick (Lord Lucan, *c*.1650–93).
Jacobite military leader. He was born in Lucan,
Co. Kildare, of an OLD ENGLISH family with
connections to the Gaelic aristocracy, and
inherited the family estate in 1675. He was
educated at a French military academy and
served in the Duke of Monmouth's regiment in
France and England (1678–85), later fighting
for JAMES II against Monmouth during the
latter's rebellion. At this point he returned to
Ireland and served James's Catholic viceroy,
Lord TYRCONNELL, in the king's army in
Ireland, being promoted colonel in 1686.

During the WILLIAMITE WAR, when he was
known as 'the Darling of the Army', Sarsfield
played a major role, having his greatest success
at the first Siege of Limerick in 1690 (*see* SARS-
FIELD IS THE WORD). D'Avaux called him '*Un
fort brave homme, qui n'avoit point de tête*',
reflecting, perhaps harshly, the general view
that, although the bravest of the brave, he was
not the cleverest. He was made Earl of Lucan
by James in 1691 and promoted to lieutenant-
colonel. After the crucial battle and heavy

losses at AUGHRIM, Sarsfield led the remnants
of the defeated Jacobite army back to Limerick,
which surrendered to the Williamites on 3
October 1691. In keeping with the terms of the
Treaty of LIMERICK, which he played a large
part in negotiating, Sarsfield and about 12,000
Jacobite soldiers went into the service of Continental armies (*see* WILD GEESE, THE). He continued to serve James II in the Irish Brigade in
France, and, after hope of a second Stuart
restoration faded, remained in the French army
until he was fatally wounded at the battle of
LANDEN in Belgium. He died on 23 July 1693.
In Nationalist mythology Sarsfield occupies an
honoured place for his courage and charisma.

Sarsfield is the Word. The usual version of a
cry attributed to Patrick SARSFIELD during
his successful raid on the Williamite baggage
train on 11 August 1690 at Ballyneety, Co.
Limerick, during the first Siege of Limerick (*see*
LIMERICK, TREATY OF). Having learned that
his name was being used as the password, at
his charge his forces shouted: 'Sarsfield is the
watchword – Sarsfield is the man!'

Sash. The original regalia worn by members
of the ORANGE ORDER and the ROYAL BLACK
INSTITUTION on ceremonial occasions. Like
the collarette, which largely replaced it, the
sash displays a badge showing the number of
the member's lodge. It was large, worn across
the left shoulder and caught with a pin at the
top of the right thigh. Formerly those who
were members of both institutions wore both
sashes crossing at the chest. Members of the
AOH used to wear similar sashes but coloured
green and white.

'Sash My Father Wore, The'. Perhaps the best
known of Orange songs (*see* ORANGE ORDER),
sung happily by all sides in Northern Ireland.
It spite of its happy adoption by Ulster Orangemen, it actually originated in Glasgow.

It is old but it is beautiful, and its colours they
  are fine,
It was worn at Derry, Aughrim, Enniskillen and
  the Boyne,

My father wore it in his youth in the bygone days of yore,
And on the Twelfth I love to wear the sash my father wore.

See also TWELFTH OF JULY.

Sassenach. A derogatory term, deriving from the Irish *Sasanach* ('English person', from Late Latin *saxones*, 'Saxons') and denoting not only British people but Protestants, members of the ASCENDANCY, indeed anyone not considered *echt*-Gael. (In Scotland the word is simply a derogatory word for an English person, although formerly it could also denote a Lowland Scot.)

Saul (Irish *Sabhall*, 'barn'). The traditional site of Patrick's first church, 3 km (2 miles) northeast of DOWNPATRICK. According to the legend, when Patrick landed in 432 (responding to his dream summons 'to return and walk with us again'), the local chieftain gave him a barn that was to serve as his place of worship, and which later became known as *Sabhall Pádraig* ('Patrick's barn'). Patrick is said to have returned to Saul to die in 461.

Saunderson, Edward James (1837–1906). Unionist politician. He was born in Castle Saunderson, Belturbet, Co. Cavan, and began his public career as a Liberal MP (1865–74) and a concerned if paternalistic landlord. The LAND WAR and threats of HOME RULE made him an aggressive defender of the status quo. He joined the ORANGE ORDER in 1882 and was soon deputy grand master for Ireland. Like many Protestant leaders who followed him, Colonel Saunderson could speak to supporters with a strong mixture of broad humour and emotionally minatory rhetoric. (His military title came from membership of the militia battalion of the Royal Irish Fusiliers.) He was Conservative MP for North Armagh from 1885 until his death, and he was the main instigator of the Unionist caucus within that party, determined to match the Parnellite faction and to secure a voice for Ulster Loyalists.

'Save the Harvest' Final. In 1946 the ALL-IRELAND football final, which would normally have been played on the last Sunday in September, was delayed until 6 October to allow the nation to save a harvest that had been threatened by a long spell of bad weather. Kerry and Roscommon drew in the final and Kerry won the replay.

Save Ulster from Sodomy. The banner head of a campaign organized by the Rev. Ian PAISLEY in 1977 in response to an increase in gay rights. The graffitoed response on banners and walls was: 'Save Sodomy from Ulster'.

Sayers, Peig. *See* PEIG.

Scairbhín. An Irish word that literrerally means 'rough or rocky seabed', but is applied in HIBERNO-ENGLISH to the last two weeks of April and the first two weeks of May, or (more usually) to a cold and blustering east wind that is typical of this period, as in 'This is the time of the *scairbhín*.' The period is also called *scairbhín na cuaiche*, as this is the time of year when the cuckoo's (*an chuach*) song is first heard.

Scald. A pest or nuisance. Scald is also a verb; a parent might exclaim to a mischievous child: 'You have me scalded' (i.e. my heart broken).

Scallon, Dana Rosemary. *See* DANA².

Scallops. *See* THATCH.

Scalp or **scolp.** A rough cabin often roofed with grass sods, from Irish *scáilp*, 'fissure in rock'; hence both the sod and earthen hut. The diminutive form is scalpeen (Irish *scáilpín*).

Scalped, to be. To be grievously overcharged or done out of money, for instance by an unscrupulous tradesman.

Scapular. A religious emblem consisting of two pieces of decorated material connected by cord and worn, as the name implies, over the shoulder or round the neck under other garments. Once extremely common in Ireland (*c.*1850–*c.*1950), they were often the mark of membership of lay orders, notably the Third Order of St Francis. Members who had died were laid out in a scapular brown garment.

Scarlet fever. A mocking description of the rush of the urban and rural middle class to join the VOLUNTEERS in 1778–9, deriving from the brilliance of their often self-designed uniform jackets.

Scarva. A village on the Newry Canal, 12 km (8 miles) from Tandaragee, the site of the Sham Fight, an annual pageant in which members of the ROYAL BLACK INSTITUTION re-enact the Battle of the BOYNE each 13 July. Scarva was a rallying point for the Williamite forces on their march south to meet the Jacobites. The 'battle' is fought in full 17th-century costume, and the highlight is a joust between the two kings, with 'James' most agreeably falling from his horse. *See also* THOMPSON IN TÍR NA NÓG.

Scáthach. In legend, a female expert in martial techniques who lives in a Hebridean island, usually identified as Skye. Her most famous pupil is CÚCHULAINN, whom she teaches the famous battle leap and whom she provides with the GAE-BOLG. Her sister AOIFE[2], whom Scáthach defeats with Cúchulainn's help in a struggle to decide the best of female warriors, later becomes his mistress and bears him the son CONLAÍ, who is later killed by his father.

Scattered. Very drunk.

Scattering. The third day of PUCK FAIR, the day of the dispersal of the attendance.

Scattery Island. *See* SENAN.

Sceilig Mhichíl. A barren and rocky island off the Iveragh Peninsula in Co. Kerry, the larger of the SKELLIG ROCKS, on which the remains of an early Christian monastery and beehive huts may be seen. Weather permitting, boats from Portmagee and Derrynane bring tourists to the island during the summer. The monastery is said to have been founded by St FINAN, and it is thought that a foundation survived there until the 13th century, when the monks moved to Ballinskelligs, on the mainland. The remains of the monastery are 170 m (550 ft) above sea level, reached by steps cut into the steep rock, and a church, two oratories and six BEEHIVE HUTS are situated on a series of terraces lower down.

Sceilp or **skelp** (Irish *scealp*, 'blow' or 'portion'). In HIBERNO-ENGLISH a blow or slap, such as a parent might administer to a child: 'I'll hit you a sceilp if you don't do what you're told.' The word can also mean a slice or portion of food: 'Give me a sceilp of that meat.'

Sceolan. One of the hounds of FIONN MAC CUMHAIL. The hound is also his nephew and twin brother of his hound BRAN[1]. Their mother Tuireann, Fionn's sister (though some stories say his aunt), is changed into a bitch by a druidess, the jealous mistress of her husband Ullan. She is pregnant at the time and she subsequently gives birth to the twin hounds.

Sceon. An Irish word for 'terror', 'panic', used in HIBERNO-ENGLISH particularly to describe a person's demeanour: 'She had a *sceon* on her when she thought she had seen a ghost.' One might say that someone habitually has a 'sceoned' look.

Schomberg, Frederick Herman, Duke of (1615–90). A German mercenary with a formidable reputation, and the first Williamite commander in the WILLIAMITE WAR. He landed at Bangor, Co. Antrim, with an army of nearly 15,000 men in August 1689, but after reaching Dundalk decided to winter near Lisburn in Co. Antrim rather than fight the Jacobite army. Over the winter he lost almost half of his men to disease, losing the king's favour as a result. He was killed at the Battle of the BOYNE.

School for Scandal, The. The finest play (1777) of Richard Brinsley SHERIDAN. It describes the difficulties of leading an honest life in a polite London society that is dominated by the salon of the malicious Lady Sneerwell. The main characters are the brothers Joseph and Charles Surface, the first a mean, sanctimonious villain, the other an honest, likeable spendthrift, who are tested by their rich uncle Sir Charles Surface as to their worth when he returns from India. Joseph woos Maria, the ward of Sir

Peter Teazle, who has married a young wife, and he is revealed as a scoundrel when, at the behest of Lady Sneerwell, he tries to seduce Lady Teazle.
See also HIS OWN FIRESIDE.

Schools Collection, the. In the winter of 1937–8 the IRISH FOLKLORE COMMISSION recruited children in national schools to record their local folklore. They were relieved from homework on condition that they interview elderly relatives or neighbours about particular themes and write down their stories in specially provided copybooks. More than a thousand volumes of the Schools Collection are preserved in the Department of Irish Folklore at University College Dublin. These provide invaluable insight not just into the stories of the older people at the time but also into their perception of events like the Great Famine. The Schools Collection was the brainchild of Kerry-born folklorist Seán Ó SÚILLEABHÁIN.

Sciollán. The Irish word for 'potato set', a piece of potato with a seed eye for setting. The word is used universally in the HIBERNO-ENGLISH of rural Ireland.

Sciortán or **sceartán.** An Irish word, commonly used in HIBERNO-ENGLISH, for a parasitical insect or tic often found embedded in the skin of those working in the bog or meadow, or in the coat of their dogs. It is also a term of abuse: a *sciortán* is a worthless person.

Scoil Éanna. *See* ST ENDA'S SCHOOL.

Scoil Éigse (Irish, 'school of poetry or learning'). A weeklong summer school offering classes in the main traditional instruments and SEAN-NÓS singing in Irish and English. Scoil Éigse is held in the same town as the All-Ireland FLEADH CHEOIL, the week before the *fleadh*. SESSIONS follow in the evening. Scoil Éigse has been run by COMHALTAS CEOLTÓIRÍ ÉIREANN since its establishment in 1972.

Scoraíocht. A social evening, evening visiting or entertainment. The term is roughly synonymous with AIRNEÁN, BOTHÁNTAÍOCHT and CÉILÍDHING.

Scota. The wife of MÍL and the mother of IR. She dies fighting the TUATHA DÉ DANAAN in Kerry. She is reputed to be buried in Scota's Glen near Tralee.

Scotia. A Latin name for Ireland in use until the 12th century. Its inhabitants were known as *Scotti* or *Scoti*. The name transferred to Scotland following the settlement of the latter country by the *Scotti* of DÁL RIATA.
See also TABULA TANTUM.

Scran. *See* BAD SCRAN!

Scrap Saturday. A satirical radio show broadcast on RTÉ for two years, 1990–2. It was written by Dermot MORGAN and Gerry Stembridge and performed by Morgan, Owen Roe and Pauline McLynn. Although very popular it was axed by RTÉ; critics claimed that this was self-censorship, and Morgan called it 'a shameless act of broadcasting cowardice and political subservience', but since the politicians it satirized were among its greatest fans, this seems unlikely. The most famous politician targeted by *Scrap Saturday* was Charles HAUGHEY, then taoiseach (played by Morgan), who always featured in tandem with 'Mara', his press secretary P.J. MARA (played by Owen Roe); Pee FLYNN and his wife 'Wilma' provided a glimpse of prehistoric family life. The final outing of the team was a live *Scrap Ireland* show in Dublin in 1997.

Scratch a convict. The first words of an anti-Irish editorial published in the *Chicago Evening Post* in 1868:

> Scratch the skin of a convict or pauper and the chances are you tickle the skin of an Irish Catholic made a criminal or a pauper by the priest and politician who have deceived him and kept him in ignorance, in a word, a savage as he was born.

The whole-hearted involvement of the Irish in the Civil War (on both sides) established them as being as patriotic as any other ethnic group, but anti-Irish (and wider anti-Catholic) attitudes persisted among the white Anglo-Saxon Protestant establishment. The experience of social dysfunction among many Irish immigrants, especially in the years during and immediately after the GREAT FAMINE, reflected the trauma suffered by many paupers (many of them knowing only Irish) in their transition from rural Ireland to urban America. It was inevitable that a proportion should find themselves in jails, hospitals, orphanages and mental institutions.

Scraw. A thin sod dried for use as fuel or roof covering, coming from the Irish word *scraith*, as in *Chuir siad scraitheanna ar an dteach* ('they roofed the house with scraws').

Scullabogue, Barn of. The site near Carrigbyrne in Co. Wexford, of a massacre by rebels of Loyalist prisoners, including many women and children, on 5 June 1798, during the REBELLION OF 1798. After the defeat of the insurrectionists by the garrison at NEW ROSS, retreating rebels brought stories of army atrocities back to the camp at Carrigbyrne. The burning of the barn at Scullabogue, carried out by the rank and file, was in reprisal for these reported atrocities. The next day the commander-in-chief of the UNITED IRISHMEN, Bagenal HARVEY, issued a proclamation threatening the death penalty for those who 'killed, murdered, burned or plundered'.

For Protestants the victims of Scullabogue became martyrs at the hands of the sectarian rebels. George Cruickshank (illustrator of Dickens's novels) provided illustrations of the barn of Scullabogue and another 1798 incident on Wexford Bridge, where unarmed Loyalists were piked and thrown into the river, for Maxwell's *History of the Rebellion* in the 1840s. Although entirely imagined and not based on any contemporary source, these illustrations were to become emblematic of Catholic evil for Loyalists. Loyalist leader Henry COOKE declared:

> The unhappy men and women who fell victims at Scullabogue barn have been the political saviours of their country. They live in our remembrance. Their deaths opened the eyes of many thousands in Ulster.

Scum condensed of Irish bog. The opening words of a versified broadside against Daniel O'CONNELL by *The Times* in 1832; it continues:

> Ruffian, coward, demagogue,
> Boundless liar, base detractor,
> Nurse of murders, treason's factor.

Scunner or **scunder.** An ULSTER-SCOTS word for a sudden loathing, often inexplicable, and even giving rise to nausea:

> Well, soree, till the day he died Jimsey Boxty
> never could thole the sights of bains [beans]
> for it always give him a sort of fash or scundher.
>> ROBERT BRATTON (*fl.* 1925-35): 'Beans and Buttermilk', in *Round the Turf Fire* (1931) (Ulster-Scots *thole*, 'endure', 'tolerate')

Scut. A HIBERNO-ENGLISH term for 'blackguard' or 'reprobate', sometimes used in disparagement of a male child or youth. A scut is the tail of a rabbit or hare.

Scut under the Butt. An irreverent Dublin rhyming nickname for the statue of James CONNOLLY opposite LIBERTY HALL, which is dwarfed by the nearby Butt Bridge (*see* SCUT; BUTT, ISAAC).

SDLP. The Social Democratic and Labour Party, founded in 1970 as an amalgam of constitutional anti-Unionist parties in Northern Ireland. Its chief constituents were the CIVIL RIGHTS MPs John HUME and Austin Currie and their large following, and the Republican Socialist Party led by Gerry FITT. Fitt led the party until 1979, resigning as leader because of the insistence by Hume and Seamus MALLON that the 'Irish dimension' should be part of political progress. The SDLP, led by Hume, has maintained a consistent opposition to violence, causing it to be graffitied by Republicans as the 'Stoop Down Low Party'. The politicization of SINN FÉIN after 1982 has weakened the SDLP's Catholic following. Fitt lost his seat in West Belfast to Gerry ADAMS in June 1983, having forfeited a great deal of support because of his vocal opposition to the H-BLOCK HUNGER STRIKES. Results in the 2001 UK general election showed a continued erosion of support for the SDLP, with strong electoral gains for Sinn Féin among new voters. Mark Durkin (b.1961) became leader of the party on the resignation of Hume. The image of the party has tended to be middle-class and/or middle-aged. The Assembly elections in the autumn of 2003 showed further losses to Sinn Féin.

Seabhac, An (1883–1964). The pseudonym (meaning 'the hawk') of the Irish-language writer Pádraig Ó Siochfhradha. He was born in Dingle, Co. Kerry, where his father worked on the estate of Lord Ventry. He became a teacher and later an editor for the GAELIC LEAGUE, and as a member of the IRISH VOLUNTEERS was interned during the Anglo-Irish War of 1919–21. After the establishment of the Free State he became a civil servant, then editor for the Educational Company of Ireland, where he produced many textbooks, plays and versions of Irish stories. Apart from JIMÍN, his best-known work is *An Baile Seo 'Gainne* ('our town', 1913), a series of gentle, humorous sketches – a sort of Lake Wobegon of GAELTACHT life.

Seachrán, Ar. The Irish term for 'astray', 'lost', 'wandering'. The title of Dion Boucicault's play *The* SHAUGHRAUN (1875) is an anglicization, with Conn the Shaughraun ('wanderer') in the title role. The word is now more likely to be used in its anglicized form.

Séadna. A lively novel (1904) by an t-ATHAIR PEADAR that became a classic text in schools and for the teaching of Irish. The eponymous hero sells his soul to the devil (*an fear dubh*, 'the black man') for financial gain, but manages to avoid fulfilling his part of the contract after the granted 13 years of reprieve have elapsed.

Séamas an Chaca (Irish, 'James the shit'). A scornful nickname applied to JAMES II after his dereliction at the Battle of the BOYNE. According to the lore of the time the king railed at Lady Tyrconnell, the wife of Lord TYRCONNELL, his lord lieutenant, when he met her in Dublin: 'The Irish have run well.' She is said to have replied, 'You, sire, seem to have beaten them!'

Seamus Famous. The nickname of the future Nobel Prizewinning poet Seamus HEANEY, as guyed by Clive James in *Peregrine Prykke's Pilgrimage through the London Literary World* (1974).

Seamus Heaney. Neo-Cockney rhyming slang for 'bikini', as in 'We're going to the beach; bring your Heaney.'

Seanad (Irish, 'senate'). The upper house of the OIREACHTAS[1], essentially subordinate to the DÁIL, but theoretically capable of initiating legislation and possessing a greater power of modification of bills because of the increased use of parliamentary committees.

Seán an Ghrinn ('Seán of the fun'). The nickname of the Irish-language poet Seán Ó Tuama (?1707–75). He was born near Kilmallock in Co. Limerick, and was briefly a schoolteacher, before becoming keeper of an inn at Mungret Gate in Croom at which all poets were said to have been served without charge. He was one of the MAIGUE POETS, and it was he who gathered the southern poets together on the death of their leader Seán Clárach in 1754 to see how both poetry and the Irish language should be preserved. An ardent JACOBITE like other Gaelic poets of his time, Ó Tuama is now best known for '*A Chuisle na hÉigse*' ('Oh pulse of poetry'), which anticipates the return of the Stuarts and the support they will receive from the Gaelic poets (*see* AISLING). Ó Tuama's concerns and hospitality cost him his livelihood, and he experienced periods of financial hardship.

Sean-Bhean Bhocht, An. *See* POOR OLD WOMAN, THE.

Seanchaí. The Irish word for a storyteller and repository of tradition. The *seanchaí* was a welcome visitor in most rural homes, especially in the long winter nights when most CÉILÍDHING or BOTHÁNTAÍOCHT took place. Stories as ancient as those of the pre-Christian FIANNA survived in the repertory of Irish-language storytellers until the 20th century, as well as many other stories of more local interest. In the SLIABH

LUACHRA area on the borders of counties Kerry and Cork, accounts of exploits of the great 18th-century Gaelic poets, especially the colourful Eoghan Rua Ó Súilleabháin (*see* EOGHAN AN BHÉIL BHINN), were current until the middle of the 20th century, although it was not then an Irish-speaking region. Storytelling was primarily a male pursuit, both for practitioners and audience, with the notable exception of West Kerry's Peig Sayers (*see* PEIG). The most famous contemporary *seanchaí* was Éamon KELLY, who was born in Gullaune, Co. Kerry, in April 1914 and died in October 2001. His training as a professional actor, his feeling for tradition and local lore and his humour made him a supreme practitioner of the art of storytelling. The texts of his many solo performances were published in book form.

Seanchas. The Irish word for the material – lore and tradition – related by the SEANCHAÍ. The term also has the meaning of gossip or chat between individuals.

Sean-nós (Irish, pronounced 'shan noas' and meaning, literally, 'old-style'). A form of unaccompanied traditional singing current to this day in Irish-speaking areas, especially the Connemara Gaeltacht. The singer, male or female, performs with an appearance of detachment or preoccupation that signals, paradoxically, intense concentration, a narrative song, a lyric or a lament, to name but a few of the many types, to an attentive audience in a house, at STATIONS or at a private party. These days *sean-nós* singing can be heard in SESSIONS, at summer schools or in competition at the FLEADH CHEOIL or OIREACHTAS². The end of a *sean-nós* song (sometimes signalled by the singer's speaking rather than singing the final line) is more likely to be met by murmurs of appreciation than by rapturous applause, even when it has been performed by the best of singers. The *sean-nós* repertoire varies from Gaeltacht to Gaeltacht (*see* DÉISE, THE), but some of the so-called *amhráin mhóra* ('major' or 'big songs') are common to all regions. Exponents of the calibre of Máire Áine Nic Dhonnchadha, Seo-

samh Ó HÉANAIGH and Nioclás TÓIBÍN show the form at its very best. There exists also a distinct traditional style of singing in English and MACARONIC. The term *sean-nós* is also used to designate a type of traditional stepdancing practised mainly in the Connemara Gaeltacht.

'Seán South from Garryowen'. The title of a ballad, sung to the air of 'Roddy McCorley', celebrating the exploits and martyrdom of Limerick-born Republican Seán South (1929–57). South took part in an IRA raid on Brookeborough RUC barracks in Co. Tyrone on New Year's Day 1957, as part of the BORDER CAMPAIGN, in which he and Fergal O'Hanlon were killed:

> There were men from Dublin and from Cork, Fermanagh and Tyrone
> But the leader was a Limerick man, Seán South from Garryowen.

South's death was the one occurrence of the Border Campaign that attracted widespread public sympathy: there were tens of thousands of mourners at his funeral in Limerick.
See also 'PATRIOT GAME, THE'.

Second Reformation. The general name given by historians to a number of evangelical initiatives by Protestant agencies between 1790 and 1860 to convert Irish Catholics. The desire to save Catholics from their damnable ignorance was accompanied by a political awareness that this hitherto acquiescent majority was beginning to demand rights.

The poorer parts of the Atlantic seaboard, largely Irish-speaking, were early seen as ripe for reformation, and a Methodist operation using bilingual missionaries was mounted in 1790. Other efforts included the MISSIONARY SETTLEMENT on Achill Island and the work of Alexander Dallas (1791–1869) and his Society for Irish Church Missions (1849) who saw the GREAT FAMINE as a heaven-sent opportunity for the promulgation of the true religion (*see* SOUPERISM). Agencies such as the Hibernian Bible Society (1806), the Sunday School Society (1809) and the Religious Tract and Book Society

(1810) flooded town and country with free bibles and a million tracts. There was even an Irish Society for Promoting the Education of the Native Irish through the Medium of their Own Language (1818).

The societies made impressive gains, especially in the west, but by 1860 their foundations had all but disappeared. The Catholic Church, realizing the danger, had established stronger parochial structures, reconverted the strayed sheep with their own missionaries and gained control of schools. The 'reformation' naturally increased religious bitterness and made the Catholic Church more than ever determined to insist upon denominational education at all levels.

Secret scripture of the poor, the. The best known, if slightly obscure, line of Thomas KETTLE (1876–1916), the politician and belle-lettrist. It comes from the sonnet 'To My Daughter Betty, the Gift of God', written shortly before his death in September 1916 at Guinchy on the Somme. His body was never found.

Know that we fools, now with the foolish dead,
Died not for flag, nor King, nor Emperor,
But for a dream, born in a herdsman's shed,
And for the secret Scripture of the poor.

'In the field, before Guillemont, Somme, September 4, 1916'

Secret societies. There were essentially two kinds of secret society in the Ireland of the 18th and 19th centuries: those of a political/sectarian nature, and the more common kind who engaged in agrarian protest.

The latter were a phenomenon of Irish agricultural life for about 80 years from the first appearance of the WHITEBOYS in Tipperary in 1761 (though the HOUGHERS had appeared earlier in the century). Other groups included the Hearts of Steel, Oakboys, TERRY ALTS, CARDERS and MOLLY MAGUIRES. The societies were characterized by elaborate oaths and the suggestion of a mysterious leader, with names like CAPTAIN MOONLIGHT and Captain Rock. The members were usually Catholic peasants, and the formation of specific societies was usually

in response to such developments as enclosures of common land, increase of taxes and the farming out of TITHES to middlemen. The societies – whose activities included destruction of property, killing or maiming of livestock and occasional violence, including assassination – tended to die out after the GREAT FAMINE.

Regarding political/sectarian secret societies, the decade before the REBELLION OF 1798 saw the formation of a Catholic society known as the DEFENDERS as a counter to the Protestant PEEP O' DAY BOYS, who soon reassembled themselves as the ORANGE ORDER. Many of the Defenders joined the UNITED IRISHMEN, while the Defenders' new avatar in the 19th century was as RIBBONMEN.

See also IRB; LAND WAR; TITHE WAR.

Sectarian, mono-ethnic, mono-cultural. A description of the Republic of Ireland by Ulster Unionist leader David TRIMBLE at a party meeting in Belfast on 9 March 2002:

Contrast the United Kingdom state – a vibrant, multi-ethnic, multi-national liberal democracy, the fourth largest economy in the world, the most reliable ally of the United States in the fight against international terrorism – with the pathetic sectarian, mono-ethnic, mono-cultural State to our south.

Section 31. Section 31 of the Broadcasting Act 1960 was first invoked by the FIANNA FÁIL government of Jack LYNCH on 1 October 1971 to ban the broadcasting of interviews with members of the Provisional IRA. The legislation allowed for the banning of 'any matter that could be calculated to promote the aims or activities of any organizations who engage in, promote, encourage or advocate the attaining of any political objective by violent means'. The decision was prompted by the appearance of a number of prominent Provisionals on the RTÉ current affairs programme *Seven Days* the previous week, which Lynch described as 'one of the worst examples of the propagandizing of the activities of illegal military organizations'. Section 31 stayed in force for almost three decades, through many changes of government, until it was lifted following the IRA ceasefire in 1994.

See also OXYGEN OF PUBLICITY.

Sedulius Scottus (*fl.*9th century). One of the best known of the Irish *docti*, the Irish scholars who brought their learning to the Europe of the Dark Ages. His name indicates his origin (Latin *Scottus*, 'Irish'), but little is known about his early life. He arrived at Liège *c.*848 and became, like his fellow-countryman John Scottus ERIU-GENA, a member of the court of CHARLES THE BALD (823–77), the grandson of Charlemagne. He was granted a 'grace-and-favour' house with a garden in Liège, and as a scholar-courtier was noted for the wit and elegance of his verse. In one eight-line *jeu-d'esprit* he thanks a friend called Robert for a gift of wine, putting the donor's second-declension Latin name *Robertus* into each of its grammatical cases. His prose works include a handbook for his royal master, *On Christian Rulers*. His temperament was epicurean rather than ascetic, but there is no indication that he was anything other than celibate. Nothing more is heard of Sedulius after 860.

> *Aut lego aut scribo, doceo scrutorve sophiam.*
> *Obsecro celsisthronum nocte dieque meum.*
> *Vescor, poto libens, rithmizans invoco ...*
> *Dormisco stertens ...*
> (I read or write or study wisdom. I plague heaven night and day. I eat and drink [too much]. I beat out my rhymes, snore as I sleep ...)
> 'Aut Lego aut Scribo' (c.850)

Seeding. *See* SESSION.

Segotia. A Dublin slang word of uncertain derivation, meaning a 'dear friend'. It is usually heard in the vocative phrase 'Me old segotia.'

Semi-states. Enterprises founded by the state, mainly in the early decades after independence (*see* LEMASS, SEÁN) to provide services (e.g. the Electricity Supply Board, AER LINGUS) or to exploit domestic resources (e.g. BORD NA MÓNA, Comhlacht Siúcra Éireann/the Irish Sugar Board). The minister for finance was normally the sole shareholder in these state companies. The recessions of the 1970s and 1980s and European Union competition legislation severely affected the semi-states, with some, such as Irish Shipping, collapsing, others being sold to the private sector, and still others being forced to adopt drastic rationalization plans in order to survive.

Semtex. A type of plastic explosive originally manufactured near the village of Semtin in the Czech Republic. It is easy to mould, undetectable and safe to handle. It was very popular with terrorists, especially during the 1980s, being particularly suitable for letter bombs. It was first used in Belfast in 1981, but it was the importation of 10 tons from LIBYA in 1984–5 that made its use by the Provisional IRA during the Northern Troubles so widespread. In 1991 the Czech government announced an end to its manufacture, but it was estimated that stocks worldwide could last for several decades.

Senan (d.*c.*540). A 6th-century saint born in Kilrush, Co. Clare, of rich parents. According to the legend, Senan had the religious life suggested to him when the waters of the Shannon estuary near his birthplace parted to allow him to walk across. He received his monastic training at Kilmanagh, near Callan in Co. Kilkenny, and established his first monastery at Enniscorthy in Co. Wexford, before making a pilgrimage to Rome. On his way home he visited St David at Menevia (now St David's), Pembrokeshire. His great foundation was on Scattery Island (Irish *Inis Chathaigh*, 'battle island' or 'Cathach's island') about 3 km (2 miles) south of Kilrush. It was destroyed by VIKINGS in the 10th century but continued as a significant ecclesiastic precinct until the Reformation, and there are the remains of six medieval churches and a round tower. Pebbles from Scattery were believed to protect mariners from shipwreck, and new boats from the area were initiated by sailing DEISEAL round the island.

Send war in our time. The cry from John MITCHEL in his 1861 anti-British polemic *The Last Conquest of Ireland (Perhaps)*. Implicit in his thinking was the principle dear to later

Republicans, stated as 'England's difficulty – Ireland's opportunity'.

Sensation. The quality that 19th-century theatre audiences craved according to the greatest of 'sensation' suppliers, Dion BOUCICAULT. He is supposed to have said in an interview: 'Sensation is what the public wants; you cannot give them too much of it.' Boucicault did at least some of his plays less than justice by this observation, but he could not resist the capacity that modern science – with mechanical, chemical and lighting effects – had given to stage machinery. In his many plays train wrecks, sailing ships, horse races and transparent mobile ghostly presences were commonplace, and scene-changing done mechanically and in view of the audience anticipated the revolving stages of later theatre.

Septic. A piece of Cork juvenile slang meaning 'conceited' or 'affected'.

Serious. A term of criticism or incredulity, used predominantly in the HIBERNO-ENGLISH of counties Cavan and Monaghan, as in 'He's serious!' about an excessively macho man or 'She's serious!' about an excessively talkative woman.

Servant boy. Servant boys and servant girls were the young people who went into service, agricultural or domestic.
See also SERVICE, TO BE IN.

Servant of the Queen, A. The somewhat surprising title of Maud GONNE's autobiography (1938). Any thoughts that this fierce Republican had gone soft are dispelled in her own foreword, 'I Saw the Queen', in which she describes a trip to Mayo, where (in Ballina) she was hailed as a heroine. On the way back to Dublin, she looks out of the train window …

> Then I saw a tall, beautiful woman with dark hair blown on the wind and I knew it was Cathleen ni Houlihan [CATHLEEN NÍ HOULIHAN, a personification of Ireland]. She was crossing the bog toward the hills, springing from stone to stone over the treacherous surface, and the little white stones shone, marking a path behind her, then faded into the darkness. I heard a voice say: 'You are one of the little stones on which the feet of the Queen have rested on her way to Freedom.'

Service, to be in. Up to the early decades of the 20th century, young men and women (known respectively as 'servant boys' and 'servant girls') from poor families went 'into service' with more prosperous farmers or shopkeepers in the towns, either at the HIRING FAIRS or through personal contacts. The term of contract was a year, and all those in service were obliged to work a TILLY at the end of that period. There are many stories of exploitation, of hunger and cold, of back-breaking work and even downright cruelty, but no doubt there were as many others who found fair and generous employers. PEIG Sayers was in service in Dingle as a teenager.

Session. An impromptu concert of traditional music, thought to have taken its name from the 'jam sessions' of jazz, in which a collection of musicians playing different instruments took part. Much of the music is likely to be lively dance music played by the whole group, but there may also be slow airs and solo pieces. Sessions now usually take place in pubs, but may also occur in halls, at private parties or at music festivals. The essence of a session is its apparent spontaneity: it may not start until late in the night when players and audience alike are 'well-oiled', and at *fleadhs* (*see* FLEADH CHEOIL) and summer schools sessions may well be totally spontaneous and non-commercial. However, pub owners elsewhere sometimes pay 'house' musicians to play on certain nights, thereby 'seeding' a session. One of the great advantages of the session is that young or learning musicians may find themselves playing with masters; there is, however, a pecking-order among musicians, with more senior or celebrated musicians exercising more control on the repertoire or pace of the session. Sessions are one of the joys of Irish life and a great attraction for tourists.
See also CEOL AGUS CRAIC.

Setanta. The given name of CÚCHULAINN before he becomes the 'hound of Culann'.

Set dances. Dances consisting of a number of varied movements and performed by four couples, now regarded as 'traditional' but deriving from French cotillions and quadrilles (the term 'set dance' comes from a 'set' of quadrilles) brought from England to Ireland by British soldiers and other travellers. Sets were adapted by the 18th-century DANCING MASTERS, who taught them to their pupils using the dance tunes and steps already popular in a particular area, such as HORNPIPES, JIGS, POLKAS and REELS: hence the survival of local 'jig', 'reel' or 'polka' sets. Among the popular sets are the quadrille or 'plain' sets of Clare, the 'Lancer' quadrilles, also danced in Clare and thought to have been originally devised for a Lancer regiment, and the polka sets of SLIABH LUACHRA. CÉILÍ or specialist set-dancing bands provide music for these dances.

Frowned upon by the GAELIC LEAGUE, who promoted STEP DANCES or CÉILÍ DANCES in its place, set dancing went into decline in many areas in the first half of the 20th century, although it continued to be popular in areas like Sliabh Luachra and west Clare where there was a strong dance-music tradition. Since the traditional revival of the 1960s there has been a parallel revival in the fortunes of set dancing. Summer schools and *fleadhs* (*see* FLEADH CHEOIL) now provide tuition for pupils and opportunities for CÉILÍS, and thousands of people attend weekly classes in their local area. The revival of recent decades has also been due to the commitment of modern-day dancing masters such as Timmy 'the Brit' McCarthy, Pat Murphy and Connie Ryan, who not only taught at home and abroad but researched and revived old and forgotten local sets.

Settle or **settle bed.** A wooden structure, common in rural houses until the modernization of the mid-20th century, that could be used as a seat by day and at night converted into a bed for visitors or a family member. Settle beds can be seen in BUNRATTY FOLK PARK and Muckross Traditional Farms in Killarney, Co. Kerry.

Sevendable. An Ulster word meaning 'excellent' or 'strong', often used to describe a severe hiding, as in, 'He gave him a sevendable thrashing.' It is pronounced with the stress on the second syllable.

'Seven Drunken Nights'. An English-language version of a traditional Irish ballad, which, with vocals by gravel-voiced Ronnie Drew, became a British chart hit for The DUBLINERS in 1967. It takes the form of dialogue between a cuckolded husband and his wife, with an accompanying commentary by the husband:

> Oh, as I went home on Monday night as drunk as drunk could be,
> I saw a horse outside the door where my old horse should be.
> Well, I called me wife and I said to her, 'Will you kindly tell to me
> Who owns that horse outside the door where my old horse should be?'
> 'Ah, you're drunk, you're drunk you silly old fool,
> Still you cannot see
> That's a lovely sow that me mother sent to me.'
> Well, it's many a day I've travelled a hundred miles or more,
> But a saddle on a sow sure I never saw before.

The release claimed to have sold 40,000 copies within two days. The singer Joe Heaney (*see* Ó HÉANAIGH, SEOSAMH), who had earlier recorded the song in Irish, is said to have given the group only five of the seven verses, but it was still banned for indecency by RTÉ (the seven-verse Irish version went unbanned). It could, however, be heard by Irish people on British radio and on the pirate Radio Caroline. The final verse goes:

> As I went home on Sunday night as drunk as drunk could be,
> I saw a thing in her thing where my old thing should be.
> Well, I called me wife and I said to her, 'Will you kindly tell to me

Who owns that thing in your thing where my old
thing should be?'

Ah, you're drunk, you're drunk you silly old fool,
Still you cannot see
That's a lovely tin whistle that me mother sent
to me.

Well, it's many a day I've travelled a hundred
miles or more
But hair on a tin whistle sure I never saw before.

Seventy-seven. The pejorative nickname of
Richard MULCAHY, the most demonized of
CIVIL WAR leaders, for his part, as Free State
minister for defence, in prosecuting the war,
during which 77 ANTI-TREATYITES were executed while in custody. Mulcahy was also nicknamed 'Dirty Dick'.

Shackleton, Abraham. *See* ANNALS OF BALLI-
TORE, THE.

Shackleton, Ernest [Henry] (1874–1922). Arctic
explorer. He was born on 14 February 1874 in
Kilkea Castle, Co. Kildare, of an Anglo-Irish
family, and educated at Dulwich College, after
which he entered the merchant navy. He was
a lieutenant on Captain Scott's first expedition
to Antarctica (1901–4), and in 1908 set out in
the *Nimrod* from New Zealand on his own
polar expedition, during which he and his
party reached by sledge to within 123 km (77
miles) of the South Pole, returning safely home
the following year. He was knighted, and his
book *Heart of the Antarctic* (1909) describes
his adventures. On 7 August 1914 Shackleton
embarked on the Imperial Trans-Antarctic Expedition, his most celebrated journey. In
October 1915 his ship the *Endurance* was destroyed by ice; some of the party remained on
Elephant Island, where they had eventually
taken refuge, while Shackleton and five others,
including Irishman Tom Crean (*see* SOUTH
POLE, THE), set off by small boat on an epic
journey to South Georgia, nearly 1300 km (800
miles) away. Shackleton eventually managed to
return to rescue the men on Elephant Island on
30 August 1916. This expedition is described
in his last book, *South*, published in 1919. In
September 1921 Shackleton set out on board
the *Quest* on a third expedition, but died
suddenly in South Georgia in January 1922,
following a heart attack. He is buried on that
island.

Shadow of a Gunman, The. The first, shortest
– and weakest – of Sean O'CASEY's Dublin
trilogy of plays, all of which are set in the inner
city and have eloquent and grittily humorous
working-class people as characters. Set in May
1920 during the ANGLO-IRISH WAR, the play's
main character, Donal Davoren, is a posturing
poetaster who allows himself to be taken for an
IRA gunman on the run, thereby winning the
admiration of Minnie Powell, a naïve young
woman who lives in the same house. She is shot
trying to escape from the AUXIES, having removed a cache of bombs left in Davoren's room
by a friend of his roommate Seumas Shields,
a pedlar. Though O'Casey calls the play 'a
tragedy in two acts' there is much humour in
the mournful rant of Shields and in the wording
of a petition got up by another tenant to protest
against the behaviour of a slum family:

> While leaving it entirely in the hands of the
> gentlemen of The Republican Army, the
> defendant, that is to say, James Gallogher of
> fifty-five St. Teresa Street, ventures to say that
> he thinks he has made out a Primmy Fashy Case
> against Mrs. Dwyer and all her heirs, male and
> female as aforesaid mentioned in the above
> written schedule.

Shaggy cloak. A type of mantle worn by the
native Irish until the decline of the Gaelic order
in the 17th century. It was so called because
the pile of the woollen cloth was curled up or
brushed to give a shaggy effect. The style of dress
that included the shaggy cloak was described
by English engraver John Derrick, who visited
Ireland in 1581. His book *The Image of Ireland*
(1581) contains a woodcut of an Irish outlaw or
wood-kerne (*see* RUG-HEADED KERNS) wearing
the Irish cloak: 'And with the mantle commonly/
The Irish karne do go.' The Anglo-Norman and
later English settlers were forbidden to wear the
cloak, and in the reign of Henry VIII the Tudor
administration tried to get rid of it altogether.

Subsequently the shaggy cloak was associated with the Elizabethan rebellions, particularly in Ulster, where the Irish were least affected by English custom and law: 'A fit house for an outlaw, a meet bed for a rebel, and an apt cloak for a thief,' wrote the poet Edmund SPENSER of these cloaks in *A VIEW OF THE PRESENT STATE OF IRELAND* (1596). Many people, whether of high or low birth, favoured a modest dark mantle, but the more dashing wore cloaks of red, green or yellow, some with contrasting fringes. Cloaks were also exported: in 1502, 2320 cloaks were exported to Bristol alone.

Shaky Bridge. The name by which Daly's Bridge, a swaying footbridge in Cork city, is known. A picturesque suspension bridge across the north channel of the River Lee, it connects Sunday's Well with the MARDYKE and Western Road. It was constructed in 1926 and has a 46-m (150-ft) span.

Sham. A Cork slang word for a person of either sex, perhaps deriving from the SHELTA word *sam* ('boy'). It is used in conversation: 'See you later, sham.'

Sham Fight. *See* SCARVA.

Shamrock¹ (Irish *seamróg*). A trifoliate plant (i.e. with the leaf divided into three) of uncertain botanical identity, used as a symbol of Ireland since the 17th century. It has been variously identified as lesser yellow trefoil, wood sorrel (Irish *seamsóg*), red clover, white clover and black medick. With its three-part leaf on one stem, it was legendarily used by St PATRICK to explain the doctrine of the Blessed Trinity.

The shamrock achieved musical immortality via the pen of Andrew Cherry (1762–1812), the Limerick-born actor and playwright who became manager of the Theatre Royal, Drury Lane, in 1802. His song 'The Green Little Shamrock', which is still sometimes heard, gives an interesting account of its origins:

> There's a dear little plant that grows in our isle;
> 'Twas St Patrick himself sure that set it;
> And the sun in its labour with pleasure did smile
> And the dew from his eye often wet it.

It thrives through the bog, through the brake and the mireland
And he called it the dear little shamrock of Ireland.

Shamrock². The pen name used by Richard D'Alton Williams (1822–62), the NATION poet and member of the political movement YOUNG IRELAND. He was born in Dublin on 8 October 1822, the natural son of Count D'Alton, and qualified as a doctor in Edinburgh in 1850. He had begun to write verse in 1842, and lives in memory for a near proverb from one of his poems, 'The Dying Girl':

> From a Munster vale they brought her,
> From the pure and pleasant air;
> An Ormond peasant's daughter,
> With blue eyes and golden hair.
> They brought her to the city
> And she faded slowly there –
> Consumption has no pity
> For blue eyes and golden hair.
> 'The Dying Girl' (1842)

In 1848 he edited the *Irish Tribune*, a paper brought out to replace the suppressed UNITED IRISHMAN that had been founded by his political master John MITCHEL. He was arrested that year and successfully defended by Samuel FERGUSON against a charge of treason-felony. He emigrated to Alabama in 1851, and served as professor of belles-lettres in the Jesuit College at Springhill, Mobile, until 1856, when he married and moved to Louisiana to practise medicine. He died (like his dying girl) of tuberculosis, in Thibodaux, Louisiana, in 1862.

Sham Squire, the. The nickname of Francis Higgins (1764–1802). He was born in Dublin of poor parents, but by posing as a gentleman he married a woman of good fortune, and went on to become wealthy by operating gaming houses. Strongly pro-government and virulently opposed to the UNITED IRISHMEN, he inveighed against them in the *FREEMAN'S JOURNAL*, his own newspaper. He was a government informer, and is thought to have received a reward of £1000 (then a substantial sum) for betraying the whereabouts of Lord Edward FITZGERALD.

Shanahan, Bishop. *See* HOLY GHOST FATHERS.

Shanavest. *See* CARAVATS AND SHANAVESTS.

'Shandon, The Bells of'. *See* 'BELLS OF SHAN-DON, THE'.

Shandrydan. An old carriage or chaise, the worse for wear, a term current at the beginning of the 20th century. Shan is from the Irish *sean* ('old'), but the derivation of the second part of the word is obscure.

Shane, Elizabeth. The pseudonym of the poet Gertrude Hind (1877–1951), a rector's daughter who spent much of her life in west Donegal. She published several books of poetry set around the Rosses and Gweedore, and her best-known poem is 'Wee Hughie':

> He's gone to school, Wee Hughie,
> An him not four,
> Sure I saw the fright was in him
> When he left the door,
> But he took a hand of Denny
> An a hand of Dan,
> Wi Joe's owld coat upon him –
> Och, the poor wee man!

Shane Bwee (Irish *Seán Buí*, 'Yellow John'). A term of contempt used in John O'Cunningham's 'The Wild Geese' (1732) for the followers of William III (KING BILLY), though he had been dead for 30 years. *Buí* was pressed into service as 'orange', *flannbuí* ('blood yellow') the correct term, having little currency:

> They'll accomplish whate'er may in man be.
> Just heaven! They will bring
> Desolation and woe
> On the hosts of the tyrannous Shane Bwee!

Shane the Proud. *See* O'NEILL, SHANE.

Shankill Butchers, the. A gang led by Lenny Murphy, a renegade member of the UVF, which was responsible for the deaths of 19 Catholics in the mid-1970s. The killings were done in the name of LOYALISM, but there were such suggestions of torture that even members of the

UVF were offended by their grisliness. In 1979, 11 members of the gang were given life sentences, but Murphy, one of the greatest mass murderers in British history, was released in 1982. He was shot on 16 November that year by three Provisional IRA members outside his girlfriend's house in Forth River Park, Glencairn. It was believed that the UVF either collaborated in the hit or gave their assent. A chilling film, *Resurrection Man* (1997), based on the novel of the same name (1994) by Eoin McNamee and starring Stuart Townsend and James Nesbitt, was based on Murphy's horrific exploits.

Shankill Road. A thoroughfare in Belfast, the Loyalist equivalent of the FALLS ROAD, and having as much metaphorical significance. Its TROUBLES history was generally less violent than that of the Falls, as the inhabitants did not usually engage with the security forces. By a certain grim irony it was the scene of the first killing of an RUC man, when Constable Victor Arbuckle was shot during a riot on 12 October 1969. The street gave its name to the notorious SHANKILL BUTCHERS, and was the scene on the afternoon of Saturday 23 October 1993 of a bomb that exploded prematurely and without warning in Frizzell's fish shop, resulting in the deaths of ten people. Among the dead was Thomas Begley, one of the perpetrators, and when Gerry ADAMS was seen to carry the coffin at his funeral on 26 October it caused a setback to the peace talks between Adams and John HUME. Adams later admitted, when pressed by newsmen, that the bombing could not be excused. In the week that followed the UFF (*see* UDA/UFF) and UVF killed 11 people, 7 in the Halloween TRICK OR TREAT KILLINGS in the Rising Sun bar at Greysteel, Co. Derry, on 30 October. The area between the Falls and Shankill has been the scene of much slum clearance, with a considerable loss of the old sense of community on both sides of the sectarian divide.

Shanley, Eleanor. *See* DÉ DANANN.

Shannon. Ireland's longest river, with a length

of 386 km (240 miles). It rises in the Shannon Pot, a deep pool in the karst country of the Cuilceach Mountains of west Co. Cavan, and enters the sea at Limerick. The Shannon includes three large lakes, Lough Allen (Co. Leitrim), Lough Ree (where the three counties of Longford, Westmeath and Roscommon meet), and Lough Derg (Clare and Tipperary), all of which are navigable and popular among users of pleasure craft. Shannon Airport, much used for transatlantic flights, is located near the new town of Shannon in Co. Clare, 20 km (12 miles) from Limerick city.

Shannon, Sharon (b.1968). An ACCORDION player from east Co. Clare, and one of the most popular traditional musicians of her generation. Her first solo album was released in 1990. She has performed with traditional musicians from all over the world, and her style and repertoire are influenced by Cajun and French Canadian music.

Shannon Callows. The low-lying land bordering the River SHANNON that is liable to be submerged when the river is high. There are large areas of callows, especially in the flatter parts of counties Galway, Offaly and Westmeath. The term is thought to derive from the Irish *caladh*, 'riverside meadow'.

Shannon–Erne Waterway. A canal for leisure craft linking the rivers Shannon and Erne in the border counties of Cavan, Fermanagh and Leitrim. It was developed from the Ballinamore and Ballyconnell Canal.

Shannon Pot. *See* SHANNON.

Shanty Irish. The lowest class of Irish immigrant as observed by America WASPS (White Anglo-Saxon Protestants), appalled as much by their capacity to survive as by the primitive nature of their makeshift dwellings. The word 'shanty' is likely to have originated from the Irish *sean-tí*, 'old house', though an alternative suggestion is the Canadian-French word *chantier*, 'log-hut'. *See also* DRAFT RIOTS; FIVE POINTS, THE; 'I'M RISING IN THE WORLD'.

Shan Van Vocht. The phonetic rendering of *sean-bhean bhocht* (*see* POOR OLD WOMAN, THE), and the title of a Nationalist magazine edited by Alice MILLIGAN and Ethna CARBERY. It ran from January 1896 to April 1899, with contributions from Seumas MACMANUS, F.J. BIGGER and the editors.

Shanwick. A joint (Shannon and Prestwick) air-control authority for the North Atlantic, with a base in Shannon, Co. Clare.

Shape. A HIBERNO-ENGLISH term meaning to put on an act, throw a tanturm or behave in a conceited or affected way. In his 1983 song 'LISDOONVARNA', as well as 'Arab sheiks, Hindu Sikhs, Jesus freaks,' Christy Moore describes 'RTÉ makin' tapes, takin' breaks, throwin' shapes.' In Cork schoolboy slang, 'shaping' means swanking or showing off. A person who throws shapes might be called a 'shaper'.

Shape-shifting. The process by which heroes in Celtic mythology take the form of one or more animals.

Shaughraun, The (Irish *seachrán*, 'roving'). The third of Dion BOUCICAULT's romantic Irish melodramas. It had its first performance at Wallack's Theatre, New York, in 1875 when its author and star was 55, and opened at Drury Lane in London later the same year. *The Shaughraun* was notable in that the part of the irresistible STAGE-IRISH card (always played by the author), previously a subsidiary character in Boucicault's plays, now became the chief character – 'Conn the Shaughraun, the soul of every fair, the life of every funeral, the first fiddle at all weddings and patterns'. The plot rather daringly has a FENIAN as one of its dramatis personae, and one of the villains is a police spy. Conn's nickname arose partly from his journey to Australia to rescue 'the young masther', Robert Ffolliot, and it is he rather than Robert who is shot 'while trying to escape'. The chief comedy of the play is concentrated on Conn's wake in Act III, when his comments about the mourners' praise of him and his pantomimic capers are in notable contrast to the KEEN of the wailing women. (Boucicault trained his troupe in the authentic musical cadence of the requiem.) The free pardon for the Fenian that assists the happy ending had reverberations outside the theatre.

> Biddy: His name will be the pride of the O'Kellys for evermore.
>
> Conn (aside): I was a big blackguard when I was alive.
>
> Biddy: Noble and beautiful!
>
> Conn (aside): Ah! Go on out o' that!
>
> Biddy (taking up her jug): Oh, he was sweet and sthrong – Who the devil's been at my jug of punch?

See also ARRAH-NA-POGUE; COLLEEN BAWN, THE.

Shaw, George Bernard. *See* GBS.

Shawlie.
A term originally denoting the large embracing garment worn by Dublin fisher-women and then by extension to any older women workers who wore it. The shawl was the universal outer garb of poorer women of all ages throughout Ireland up until the out-break of the Second World War, as common among mill girls in Belfast as with Connemara farm girls. The word 'shawlie' had connotations of age and class:

> I hated the very shape of a shawl; it meant an immediate descent in the social scale from the 'hatties' to the 'shawlies' – the poorest of the poor.
>
> FRANK O'CONNOR: *An Only Child* (1958)

Shebeen
(Irish *síbín*, 'little mug', 'weak beer', 'illicit ale-house'). A word, originating in the 18th century, for a small unlicensed liquor store in Ireland. The root word *séibe* (of which *síbín* is the diminutive) meant a standard mea-sure, the capacity of a mug of fixed size. The term shebeen was later used of similar estab-lishments in Scotland and in South Africa. Now it is applied loosely to any small, not especi-ally salubrious, public house:

> Well, first we reconnoithered round o'
> O'Sullivan's Shebeen,
> It used to be 'The Shop House' but we call it,
> 'The Canteen':

> But there we saw a notice which the bravest heart
> unnerved
> 'All liquor must be settled for before the dhrink
> is served.'
>
> PERCY FRENCH (1854–1920): 'Shlathery's Mounted Fut' (1889)

Shed a tear for Parnell, to.
A phrase used euphe-mistically by Irish males to signal a visit to the lavatory to urinate.

Sheegogue.
A type of large barrel made of ropes of straw (SÚGÁN) and used for holding grain after threshing. The derivation of the term is uncertain.

Sheehan, Canon [Patrick Augustine]
(1852–1913). Novelist, best known for MY NEW CURATE (1900). Patrick Augustine Sheehan was born in Mallow, Co. Cork, on 17 March 1852 and educated at Maynooth. He became parish priest of Doneraile, Co. Cork, in 1894 and canon in 1903, staying there for the rest of his life. He began writing novels (of which he composed ten in all) as a counter to certain trends he observed in the church. His early novels bore too obviously the reek of the pulpit, but later ones had more congenial subjects, mediated through realistic characters in real situations. Among these are *Miriam Lucas* (1912), about the travails of a Catholic heiress involved in labour strikes in Dublin and journalism in Am-erican slums; *Glenanaar* (1905), which fea-tures agrarian crimes; *The Graves of Kilmorna* (1915), involving Fenianism and the Land War; and *Luke Delmege* (1901), about an in-tellectual priest learning humility in the context of a rural parish. Sheehan died in Doneraile on 5 October 1913.

Sheehy, Nicholas
(1726–66). A Catholic priest executed in Clonmel at a time of bitter agrar-ian conflict and protest against TITHES. He had been involved in anti-tithe protests and, despite being acquitted when indicted for these offences in Dublin, he was convicted and sentenced in Clonmel, along with three other local Catholics, although the evidence against them was flimsy. The execution of Sheehy and

the other Catholics is seen as evidence of the continuing judicial repression of Catholics at a time when the severity of the POPERY LAWS appeared to have diminished.

Sheehy-Skeffington, Hanna (1877–1946). Feminist, Republican and labour activist. She was born on 24 May 1877, christened Johanna Sheehy and reared in the family home in Loughmore, Co. Tipperary. Her father David (1843–1932) was an Irish Party MP for south Galway and an IRB member, and her uncle, Father Eugene Sheehy (1841–1917), was a land agitator who became known as the LAND LEAGUE PRIEST. Hanna was educated at the Dominican convent in Eccles Street, Dublin, and the ROYAL UNIVERSITY OF IRELAND, where she became interested in the rights of women. She married the Cavan-born academic Francis (Frank) Skeffington (1878–1916) in 1903 and the couple combined their surnames, both becoming known as Sheehy-Skeffington. They lived in Rathmines in Dublin, where they held a famous 'at home' on Wednesday evenings. Hanna taught and Francis worked as registrar of University College Dublin and later as a journalist. In 1908 she and Margaret Cousins founded the Irish Women's Franchise League to campaign for female suffrage (it was later amalgamated into the Irish Women's Suffrage Federation in 1911).

In 1912 Frank and Hanna Sheehy-Skeffington founded the IRISH CITIZEN, a newspaper that was feminist, pacifist and Nationalist, and supported the ITGWU in the 1913 LOCKOUT. Hanna edited the paper herself during the period when Frank was imprisoned for anti-conscription agitation after the outbreak of the First World War, and again after his death during the 1916 EASTER RISING. (Frank was shot without trial by a mentally unstable British officer, Captain Bowen-Colthurst, after being arrested while he tried to stop the looting of Dublin's shops.) In 1918 Hanna had a meeting with US President Woodrow Wilson, the first SINN FÉIN member to do so, and she served as a judge in the DÁIL COURTS in Dublin.

Although a pacifist, she supported the Anglo-Irish War of 1919–21. During the CIVIL WAR she became involved, along with Maud GONNE and Charlotte DESPARD, with the Women's Prisoners Defence League.

Sheehy-Skeffington became an executive member of the new FIANNA FÁIL party in 1926, but resigned quickly when she realized that the party was neither feminist nor progressive. She remained a Republican and was for a period editor of AN PHOBLACHT. With Maud Gonne and Kathleen CLARKE, she campaigned against de Valera's CONSTITUTION OF 1937. Born a Catholic, she died an 'unrepentant pagan', refusing the rites of the church. Her sister Mary was married to Thomas KETTLE, and another sister, Kathleen, married Conor O'Brien, father of Conor CRUISE O'BRIEN.

'Sheep and Lambs'. See TYNAN, KATHARINE.

'She is far from the land'. See CURRAN, SARAH.

Shelta. The language of TRAVELLERS, also called cant or gammon, or, by the travellers themselves, minker's torri.

Sheppard, Oliver (1865–1941). Sculptor. He was born in Cookstown, Co. Tyrone, the son of a sculptor. The family moved to Dublin when he was still a baby. He studied at the Metropolitan School of Art in Dublin, and in London and Paris. After teaching for some years in England, he returned to Dublin in 1902, taught modelling in the Metropolitan School and was professor of sculpture at the Royal Hibernian Academy (RHA). Sheppard's most famous piece is *The Death of Cuchulainn* (1911–12); James Sleator, president of the RHA, was the model for the head. The sculpture was later chosen as a memorial of the 1916 EASTER RISING, and may still be seen in the GPO in Dublin. Sheppard died in Dublin on 14 September 1941.

Shergar. A famous thoroughbred horse, winner of the Irish and British Derby (the latter by a record length), who was kidnapped from the Aga Khan's Ballymany Stud in Co. Kildare on 8 February 1983 and never seen again. Rumour and legends abounded in relation to the fate of Shergar, but it is thought that the gang – presumed to have been terrorists, and with whom all contact ceased after four days – simply killed the horse when he proved too difficult for them to manage.

Sheridan, Margaret Burke (1889–1958). Opera singer. She was born in Castlebar, Co. Mayo, on 15 September 1889, the youngest of five children. Her mother died in 1893 and her father took the rest of the family to America, leaving her at home. When he died in 1901 she became a permanent boarder with the Dominican sisters in Eccles Street, Dublin, and it was they who discovered the beauty of her lyric soprano voice. Dr Vincent O'Brien, her singing teacher, who had also taught John McCORMACK and James JOYCE, managed to send her to study for two years to the Royal Academy of Music. It was Marconi, the inventor of the wireless telegraph, who brought her to Italy in 1917. The following year she made her début as Mimi in *La Bohème*. Her most famous role was as Madame Butterfly in the Puccini opera of that name. Puccini himself came to see her and decided to coach her personally for the leading role in his opera *Manon Lescaut*. When he died in 1924 she was the leading performer in many concerts held in his memory throughout Italy. She also appeared frequently in Covent Garden in London, partnering the conductor Toscanini. In 1936, after an unhappy love affair, she decided to retire, abandoning the stage at the height of her powers, and in 1939 she returned to Ireland. Until her death from cancer on 16 April 1958 she lived partly in America and partly in Ireland.

Sheridan, Philip Henry (1831–88). US Civil War general. He was born in Co. Cavan but taken to live in America as a child. Educated at West Point Military Academy (1848–53), he distinguished himself as a cavalry commander in the American Civil War, winning the last great battle of the war at Five Forks on 1 April 1865. After the war he was appointed military governor in Texas and Louisiana, and campaigned against the Native Americans on the western frontier. He succeeded General Sherman as commander-in-chief of the US army in 1884, and died in Massachusetts.

Sheridan, Richard Brinsley (1751–1816). Dramatist and politician. He was born in Dublin and educated at Harrow. He married Elizabeth Ann Linley in 1773 and she, a professional singer, could have supported him while he read law at the Middle Temple, but he was unhappy about this arrangement and began to write plays. *The Rivals* (1775), set in Bath (to which his family had moved), showed him a born dramatist, with a fine line in comic invention and the ability to create such memorable characters as Bob Acres, Mrs Malaprop and Sir Lucius O'Trigger, an authentic Hibernian. It was followed by *St Patrick's Day* (1775), a brisk farce, blazoning the origin of its deviser. *The SCHOOL FOR SCANDAL* (1777), his masterpiece, was staged in what was soon to be his own house, the Theatre Royal in Drury Lane. *The Critic* (1779), his last original play, was a hilarious satire on the kind of theatre in which elaborate staging was used to cover up inferior material. Sheridan's long career in Parliament was marked by rigorous honesty and brilliance of oratory, two rare qualities in the politics of the time. His finances never recovered from the burning of his theatre (*see* HIS OWN FIRESIDE), and he died in extreme destitution. Ironically his funeral was magnificent, with four peers acting as pall-bearers.

She Stoops to Conquer. A comedy (subtitled 'The Mistakes of a Night') by Oliver GOLDSMITH, first performed, to great acclaim, at Covent Garden in London in 1773. The plot is based on a practical joke from Goldsmith's own experience that is played on two young men, Marlow and his friend Hastings. They are led to believe that the home of Kate Hardcastle – whom Marlow's father wishes him to marry although Marlow himself has not met her – is an inn, and that Kate is a servant and Mr

Hardcastle the landlord. As it happens, Marlow courts and falls in love with Kate; she accepts his attentions with a good grace and earns his devotion. Hastings in turn falls in love with Kate's cousin, Constance Neville. The series of mistaken identities reveals itself after the arrival of Marlow's father, Sir Charles, with both young couples happily and acceptably in love at the end of the play.

> ... the Mistakes of the Night shall be crowned with a merry tomorrow; so boy, take her; and as you have been mistaken in the mistress, my wish is, that you may never be mistaken in the wife.

Sheugh or **schuch.** An ULSTER-SCOTS word meaning 'ditch', 'water-filled drain'. In spite of its onomatopoeic suggestion of unpleasantness, it carries no especial distaste for Ulster people, who use it is for any easily crossable drain, even extending it meiotically to the North Channel between Co. Antrim and Scotland.

Shiels, George (1886–1949). Playwright. Shiels was born in Ballymoney, Co. Antrim, in 1886 and emigrated to Canada in 1906 to work as an engineer on the railroad, returning home crippled after an accident in 1913. His early plays were written for the ULT, under the pen name George Morshiel, but the many kitchen comedies for which he was famous between 1922 and 1948 were as popular and as lucrative for the ABBEY THEATRE box-office as anything by Sean O'Casey. In 30 plays, including *Paul Twining* (1922), *Professor Tim* (1924), *The New Gossoon* (1936), *The PASSING DAY* (1936) and *The Caretakers* (1948), he dealt with small-town and rural characters, fly men, sharp practice, lost wills, family dissension and generation clash. They are mostly naturalistic and tersely eloquent, portraying Ulster life in a comic vein that grew darker as the author grew older. They remained the staple until the 1960s of many amateur companies, who found them both stageable and inoffensive for their mildly puritanical audiences.

Shillelagh. A placename in Co. Wicklow, the site of oak forests (*Síol Éalaigh*, although this might mean 'the descendants of Éláthach', he being a warrior from the 9th century). It may have given its name to the stout cudgel, hewn from oak or (more usually) from the harder blackthorn, traditionally used as a weapon in FACTION FIGHTING (*see KING OF FRIDAY'S MEN, THE*). However, the name of the cudgel is more likely to derive from a combination of *saill* ('willow') and *éille*, the genitive of *iall*, meaning 'thong' or 'strap' (also 'shoelaces'). In Irish-America the shillelagh became a stock-Irish or STAGE-IRISH accoutrement. Blackthorn shillelaghs are now sold commercially as souvenirs.

> Who has e'er the luck to see Donnybrook fair?
> An Irishman all in his glory is there,
> With his sprig of shillelagh and shamrock so green,
> His clothes spick and span new without even a speck
> And a neat Barcelona tied round his neat neck
> He goes to the tent and he spends half-a-crown,
> He meets with a friend and for love knocks him down
> With his sprig of shillelagh and shamrock so green
>
> EDWARD LYSAGHT (1763–1810): 'The Sprig of Shillelagh', in *Poems* (1811)

Shinners. A nickname, usually derogatory, applied to members of SINN FÉIN by political opponents, by the security forces and by the British administration at the time of the 1916 EASTER RISING and the ANGLO-IRISH WAR of 1919–21. The name is also used as a general term for Catholics in Northern Ireland. Since the recent election of a number of Sinn Féin TDs to the Dáil, the term has again come to be used in the Republic.
See also MÉ FÉINER.

Shin shin (Irish *sin sin*). A HIBERNO-ENGLISH phrase meaning 'That's that'. 'Well, sin sin', might be used to end a conversation or draw a line under a topic.

Shinty. A Scottish game like HURLING, played with a team of 12 and a curved stick called a CAMÁN. It is said to be the fastest ball game in the world.

Shirley, James. *See* ST PATRICK FOR IRELAND.

'Shlattery's Mounted Fut'. The title of a comic song by Percy FRENCH. It was written in 1889, and gave an eerily satirical prophecy of the rise of such local militias as the UVF.

> An' back to the mountains went the squadrons
>   and platoons,
> Four-an'-twenty fightin' min an' a couple o'
>   sthout gossoons.
> The band was playin' cautiously their patriotic
>   tunes;
> To sing the fame if rather lame, o' Shlathery's
>   Light Dhragoons.

Shoneen. A HIBERNO-ENGLISH term of abuse (from the Irish *seoinín*) for a flunkey, someone who apes those he considers his betters (in this case the British). *Seon* is a Gaelicization of John, in this case meaning John Bull, the archetypal Englishman. In the late 1960s, Seán Ó RIADA fulminated against 'shoneenism' in his talks on RTÉ radio, but since then the term has not been heard on the airwaves (nor indeed in the conversation) of a modernized outward-looking Ireland.
See also MORAN, D[ANIEL] P[ATRICK].

Shook¹. 'Startled', 'surprised' (the word is a solecistic HIBERNO-ENGLISH version of 'shaken'). Someone who is looking pale or ill might be described as 'shook', 'a bit shook' or 'shook-looking'.

Shook² or **Mr Shook.** *See* STEPHENS, JAMES KENNETH.

Shooler. A wanderer, TRAVELLER or beggar, from the Irish *siúlóir*, 'walker'.

Shoot-to-kill. *See* STALKER, JOHN.

Shop bread. White or 'loaf' bread, as opposed to CAKE bread.

Shorten the road, to. A HIBERNO-ENGLISH phrase meaning to make a long journey on foot appear shorter by telling a story or singing a song or just by having company.

Showbands. The main feature of Irish social life for young people in the 1960s was going to dances in halls with a capacity of 2000–4000 (the Majestic in Mallow and the Lilac in Inniskeen – both Co. Cork – were typical of these monster halls) where music was provided by showbands playing pop music, often cover versions of the hits of the day by international singers, or country-music bands. A typical line-up in a showband would include vocals, a fair bit of wind (such as trumpet, saxophone, clarinet), drums, guitars, piano and sometimes double bass. Showbands began to emerge in 1956–7 and were firmly on the scene by 1960–1. The most celebrated bands included The Royal (from Waterford), fronted by Brendan Bowyer, Brendan O'Brien and the Dixies (from Cork) and Joe Dolan and the Drifters. Bands also played for the immigrant community in Britain, in halls like the GALTYMORE in Cricklewood. The showband boom peaked in 1966, and was in decline by the end of the 1960s.

In one of the most notorious incidents of the Troubles, three members of the Miami Showband were murdered by members of the UVF near Newry on 31 July 1975.
See also 'BALLROOM OF ROMANCE, THE'.

Shrone. *See* CITY, THE.

Shrovetide. The period before Lent when weddings were traditionally celebrated, Shrove Tuesday itself being the most auspicious day of all. Marriage in Lent was forbidden by church law, so people thought it best to get married before Lent, the long winter evenings having afforded opportunity for courting and MATCHMAKING.
See also SALT MONDAY; SKELLIGS LIST, THE.

'Shule Aroon' (Irish *Siúil, a rúin*, 'hurry, my love'). A MACARONIC 18th-century military ballad, sung by a soldier's lass who wishes him back with her. In some versions the original Irish is almost buried:

> I wish I were on yonder hill,
> 'Tis there I'd sit and cry my fill,
> That every tear should turn a mill,
> Gotheen mavourneen slaun.
>
> (*Go dtéidh tú mo mhúirnín slán*, 'May you be safe, my
> darling.)

The chorus holds the title:

Siúil, siúil, siúil, a rúin;
Siúil go socair agus siúil go ciuin.
Siúil go dtí an doras agus ealaí liom.
Is go dtéidh tú a mhúirnín slán
(Hurry, hurry, hurry, my love;
Hasten but quietly;
Come to the door and we'll fly together
And may you be safe, my darling.)

Siamsa Tíre ('national entertainment'). The national folk theatre, drawing on traditional music, dance and song, established by Father Pat Ahern in Tralee, Co. Kerry, in 1968 as Siamsa na Ríochta ('entertainment of the KINGDOM') and known as Siamsa Tíre since 1972. Chief executive Martin Whelan (1949–2002) developed the company from a voluntary community-based group to a professional performing company with its own theatre in Tralee (opened in 1991), a five-person core group of full-time performers, a staff of 22 and a turnover in 2001 of £2 million. The company has earned critical plaudits both at home and on its frequent foreign tours for shows based on Irish mythology, such as *The Children of Lir* and *Oisín in Tír na nÓg*.

Síbhín. An Irish word for 'chive', 'leek', pronounced 'saiveen'. The word is still used by older people in HIBERNO-ENGLISH.

Sick, on the. *See* ON THE SICK.

Sidhe or **Sí** (Irish, 'fairy folk'). The inhabitants of the fairy OTHERWORLD, who in Irish folklore have frequent congress with mortal man. They were also called the Good or Gentle Folk, although they were believed to be capable of mischief or even malice, and were treated with a wary respect. Food was left outside the door for them at night, and in the west of Ireland the first run of POTEEN was sacrificed to appease them. It was believed that the Sidhe were the descendants of the TUATHA DÉ DANAAN, the tribe of Danu, who had fled to the raths (RING FORTS) when they were defeated by the FOMORIANS. Alternatively they were believed to be fallen angels, banished from heaven at the time of the Fall of man.

The Celtic imagination envisaged a very fluid boundary between this world and the world of the dead or the supernatural. At certain times of the year (*see* SAMHAIN) this boundary dissolved completely and ghosts, spirits and fairies were free to walk among men. Many rural areas contain large numbers of ring forts, and these were believed to be sacred to the Sidhe. They were sometimes called 'fairy forts', and a blackthorn tree on or near the fort would be called the 'fairy tree'. Accounts are legion in folklore of unscrupulous, impious or greedy farmers who levelled ring forts or merely uprooted a sacred tree and who did not live to see the morning. One farmer got a horrible skin disease; another had his head turned backwards on his shoulders. Occasionally, even in the 21st century, one hears in the media an account of a local person protesting at the destruction of a place sacred to the Sidhe in order to build a road or lay a water pipe.
See also AIRY FIT; CHANGELING.

Sidney, Sir Henry (1529–86). Lord deputy. He was appointed by Elizabeth I and served for three periods between 1565 and 1578. A strong promoter of what is popularly called the TUDOR RECONQUEST, he established 'presidencies' in Connacht and Ulster, and defeated Shane O'NEILL. During his third period as lord deputy his major initiative was 'composition', by which payments to maintain local armies and government troops were commuted into one tax. He succeeded in pushing through composition in Connacht and Munster but it – and the lord deputy – was roundly rejected by the OLD ENGLISH of the Pale.

Siege of Derry. *See* DERRY, SIEGE OF.

'Siege of Ennis, The'. *See* CÉILÍ DANCES.

Sí gaoithe (Irish, 'fairy wind'). A wind thought to blow up out of nowhere into a whirlwind, even on a fine still summer's day. It would then subside just as suddenly. People were afraid that they would be carried away by the fairies when they found themselves caught outside in this wind, but an antidote did exist (as always): a person caught in the *sí gaoithe* should throw something, even a blade of grass, into the path of the wind.

Sigerson, Dora (1866–1918). Poet. She was born in Dublin, the eldest child of George SIGER-SON, and moved to England in 1896 on her marriage to Clement King Shorter (1857–1926), pioneer of the English pictorial press, editor of the *Illustrated London News* and founder of the *Tatler* (1903). She was a friend of Alice Furlong and Katharine TYNAN, and produced much more verse than either, publishing 13 volumes of mainly ballad poetry. She was deeply affected by the outcome of the EASTER RISING, as her volume *Sixteen Dead Men* (1919) makes clear.

> Sixteen dead men! Where do they go?
> *'To join their regiment, where Sarsfield leads;*
> *Wolfe Tone and Emmet, too, well they do know.*
> *There shall they bivouac, telling great deeds.'*

Sigerson, George (1836–1925). Physician and anthologist. He was born near Strabane, Co. Tyrone, and educated in Letterkenny and at Queen's College, Cork, graduating in medicine with a special qualification in self-taught Irish. He specialized in neurological problems and was appointed professor of zoology at what became University College Dublin. His main work was *Bards of the Gael and Gall* (1897), which, together with his foundation in 1892 of the National Literary Society, played an important part in the success of both the IRISH LITERARY REVIVAL and the language revival. He was the father of the poet Dora SIGERSON.

Sigerson Cup. The GAA football competition for third-level colleges, named after George SIGERSON, who donated his salary from his post at University College Dublin (UCD) so that a trophy could be purchased for the competition. The inaugural winners of the competition, in 1911, were UCD.

Sign. A word used negatively in HIBERNO-ENGLISH phrases, mainly in Ulster, to mean 'a bit': 'He needn't be one sign ashamed.'

Signor Balfo. The name used by Michael William Balfe (1808–70), the Irish singer, violinist and composer, for his stage appearances in Paris in 1827. He was born in Dublin on 15 May 1808 in Pitt Street, which was later called Balfe Street in his honour, and is now demolished. He began to compose at the age of seven and was performing professionally two years later. In 1823 he went to London and then studied (1825–6) under Rossini, who engaged him to sing Figaro in a new production of *The Barber of Seville* and retained him in the company until 1830. Returning to London Balfe began a busy career as a writer of opera, composing 29 pieces, of which *The Bohemian Girl*, written for the Drury Lane season of 1843, is still known, if only because of its songs, 'I Dreamt I Dwelt in Marble Halls' and 'The Heart Bowed Down' (the libretto was by Alfred Bunn). Balfe died in his home, Rowney Abbey, in Hertfordshire on 20 October 1870, and is commemorated by a plaque in Westminster Abbey.

Signor Ochelly. The Italianate form of the name of Michael Kelly (1764–1826), tenor, composer and friend of Mozart and Haydn. He was born in Dublin in December 1764, the son of the master of ceremonies of the CASTLE, and appeared when quite young in SMOCK ALLEY. By 1783 he was principal tenor at the Vienna Opera, and on 1 May 1786 appeared as the first Basilio in *Le nozze di Figaro*, in which role he ignored the composer's instructions, as he recalls in his *Reminiscences* (1826): 'It certainly was not in nature that I should stutter all through the part and when I came to the *sestetto*, speak plain, and after that piece of music was over return to stuttering.' In London from 1787 he appeared with great success in concerts and opera, becoming musical director of Drury Lane in 1797. He wrote music for around 60 theatrical pieces, including an opera *The Gypsy Prince* (1800) with Thomas MOORE. A music shop that Kelly opened in 1802 led to bankruptcy. He died, after years of suffering from gout, on 9 October 1826.

Silenced priest. A Catholic priest from whom the permission to preach has been withdrawn by his superiors because he is suspected of unorthodox views on doctrine or morality. There is a portrait of such a priest in Shaw's play JOHN BULL'S OTHER ISLAND.

Silence, exile and cunning. The means devised by Stephen DEDALUS to protect himself and his art, as elaborated to his friend Cranly in A PORTRAIT OF THE ARTIST AS A YOUNG MAN (1916):

> I will not serve that in which I no longer believe, whether it call itself my home, my fatherland, or my church. And I will try to express myself in some mode of life or art as freely as I can and as wholly as I can, using for my defence the only arms I allow myself to use, silence, exile, and cunning.

Silken Thomas. The nickname of Thomas Fitzgerald (1513–37), Lord Offaly and 10th Earl of Kildare and instigator of the Kildare Rebellion. He was appointed deputy governor of Ireland by his father, the 9th Earl, Gearóid Óg, in February 1534 when the former was summoned to Dublin. Tradition has it that Thomas heard in June of that year that his father had been killed in the Tower, but it is more likely that Gearóid sent him a message to trigger a show of force against the Tudor administration. Fitzgerald summoned the Council of State for Ireland to a meeting in St Mary's Abbey in Dublin on 11 June and formally renounced his allegiance to England. (The nickname 'Silken Thomas' is attributed to the fact that the 140 horsemen accompanying him on his ride to Dublin wore helmets with silken fringes.) The following month he unsuccessfully attacked Dublin, killed Archbishop John Alen, the lord chancellor and an enemy of the Fitzgeralds, and sought help from the pope and Catholic rulers, Henry VIII's Parliament having passed the Act of Supremacy in 1534.

Thereafter Fitzgerald fought from bases in Maynooth and surrounding areas in Co. Kildare against English forces led by Sir William Skeffington. (Meanwhile his father was imprisoned in the Tower, where he died in September 1534.) In March 1535 Skeffington captured

Fitzgerald's castle in Maynooth, applying the MAYNOOTH PARDON to some of the garrison. On 25 August 1535 Fitzgerald surrendered unconditionally to Sir Leonard GREY, who had arrived in Ireland as marshal in July and who was a brother-in-law to his father. Grey gave him a guarantee that his life would be spared, but he was imprisoned in the Tower and with his five uncles he was hanged, drawn and quartered at Tyburn on 3 February 1537. In all 75 were executed for treason in connection with the rebellion, a small number by the standards of the time.

The Kildare Rebellion brought to an end the enormous political power hitherto wielded by the Fitzgeralds (see for example GREAT EARL, THE), and caused a radical change in the governance of Ireland, which was henceforth ruled directly from London with an English governor and garrison.

Silk of the kine. A personification of Ireland, from the Irish *síoda na mbó*. The song that includes this phrase, 'A Dhroimeann Donn Dílis' ('Oh faithful white-backed brown cow'), collected in Hardiman's *Irish Minstrelsy* (1831), although of uncertain date, is certainly Jacobite in sentiment:

> A dhroimeann donn dílis,
> A shíoda na mbó,
> Cá ngabhann tú san oíce
> Is cá mbíonn tú sa ló?
> Ó bímse sna coillte
> 's mo bhuachaill am' chomhair
> Is d'fhág sé siúd mise
> Ag sileadh na ndeor.
> (Oh faithful brown cow
> Oh silk of the kine,
> Where do you wander at night?
> Where do you go during the day?
> I stay in the woods
> Where my herdsman looked after me,
> But now he has left me,
> I shed bitter tears.)

In 'The Little Black Rose' Aubrey DE VERE refers to this symbol of Ireland:

> The Silk of Kine shall rest at last;
> What drove her forth but the dragon-fly?

In the golden vale she shall feed full fast,
With her mild gold horn and her slow, dark eye.

Silver Tongue and Smile of Witchery. A part of an obituary diatribe against Daniel O'CONNELL by John MITCHEL in his *Jail Journal*; Mitchel felt O'Connell had betrayed YOUNG IRELAND:

Poor Old Dan! Wonderful, mighty, jovial and mean old man! With silver tongue and smile of witchery and heart of melting ruth! Lying tongue, smile of treachery, heart of unfathomable fraud! What a royal yet vulgar soul! With the keen eye and potent swoop of a generous eagle of Cairn Tual – with the base servility of a hound and the cold cruelty of a spider!

Simnel, Lambert (*c.*1475–1535). Yorkist pretender to the English throne during the WARS OF THE ROSES. Simnel was claimed by Yorkists to be Edward, Earl of Warwick, rival claimant to Henry VII, although the real Warwick, a prisoner of Henry, was put on display in London. Simnel landed in Dublin on 5 May 1487 with an army of 2000 men raised by Yorkist sympathizers in England, and was crowned Edward VI in Christ Church Cathedral on 24 May. Géaróid Mór Fitzgerald, 8th Earl of Kildare (*see* FIT TO RULE ALL IRELAND; GREAT EARL, THE), acted as his lord lieutenant in Ireland. (The town of WATERFORD opposed Simnel; *see* KILLING THE MESSENGER.) On 4 June Simnel sailed to England with a Yorkist army, but was defeated at Stoke Field, Nottinghamshire, on 16 June. He was captured and put to work in the kitchen of Henry's palace as a scullion.

Simon Pure. The real man, the authentic article. The expression comes from the play *A Bold Stroke for a Wife* (1718) by the Irish dramatist Susannah CENTILIVRE. In the play the Quaker character Simon Pure announces in the last act that he is the 'real Simon Pure' and not Captain Feignwell who has been using his name to woo Miss Lovely.

Simpson, Alan. *See* PIKE THEATRE; ROSE TATTOO AFFAIR, THE.

Sinclair, Betty (1910–81). Trade unionist and CIVIL RIGHTS activist. She was born in Belfast to a Protestant working-class family and began to work as a linen reeler as soon as she left school. A full-time Communist Party worker from the 1940s, she became secretary to the Belfast Trades Council in 1947. She was elected chair of the Northern Ireland Civil Rights Association in 1968 but resigned from the executive in 1970 in protest at the influence of the more militant (and Republican) PEOPLE'S DEMOCRACY.

Sin é. The Irish phrase (pronounced 'shin ay') for 'that's it' or 'that's that'. Sin É is the name of a fashionable Irish bar in New York.

Sinell (*fl.*6th century). One of FINNIAN OF CLONARD'S TWELVE APOSTLES OF IRELAND. Following his master's admonition to found his own abbey, he chose Cleenish, a tiny island in Upper Lough Erne, Co. Fermanagh, not far from that of his brother apostle MOLAISE OF DEVENISH. His foundation was noted for the severity of its rule, and it was there that COLUMBAN, the great missionary to Europe, spent his years as a novice. Cleenish was affiliated to COMGALL's abbey at BANGOR, where Columban completed his studies. It is believed that Sinell succeeded Comgall as abbot of Bangor. His feast day is 12 November.

Singer, Dr Paul. A notorious 1950s fraudster. Singer was born in what is now the Czech Republic in 1911 and worked in London in the family finance firm. After its collapse he moved to Dublin in February 1954 and set up a bogus philately investment business using as his base a local auctioneering firm, Shanahan's. He promised riches to people with 'small capital which you want to invest with absolute security but with an unusually large return'. For five years, until May 1959, he paid investors generous dividends, funded by the investments of others, not by sales of stamps. When the enterprise collapsed after publicity about the theft of a valuable stamp collection from Singer's offices, he owed £1.8 million to about 9000 investors. Singer, who had a lavish lifestyle in Ireland and had banked large sums of money abroad, was charged with fraud, but after several years of trials and appeals he was acquitted. He left the country in 1963. Austin CLARKE's poem 'Over Wales' describes a plane journey:

... Passengers read the news:
Singer, the Common Market – turn the pages –
Hire purchase. Shipping. Ford strike for better
    wages.

In *Later Poems* (1961)

Singing Priest, the. Dublin priest Michael Cleary (d.1993). He was relaxed, informal, accessible, and he always had the popular appeal of the 'singing priest' who had as a younger man performed in fund-raisers for good causes. However, like Bishop Éamonn Casey (*see FOR-BIDDEN FRUIT*), he conformed totally with hardline church teaching on sex, abortion and divorce, and expounded his views on these subjects in his weekly column in the *Sunday Independent*. He died of cancer on New Year's Eve 1993. In early 1995, Phyllis Hamilton, who had been his housekeeper, revealed that she, Michael Cleary and their son Ross had lived together as a family in Harold's Cross since Ross's birth in 1976. They had given their first child up for adoption. Many people simply refused to believe Phyllis Hamilton's story, but it was corroborated, controversially, by consultant psychiatrist Ivor Brown, who knew them both well, and later by DNA testing. What shocked the public most was not that Cleary had not lived a celibate life but his hypocrisy in railing against the sins of the flesh. 1995 was an *annus horribilis* for the Catholic Church in Ireland: there was the fallout from the BRENDAN SMYTH AFFAIR of December 1994 and Smyth's conviction, plus other cases of clerical abuse, not to mention BISHOP BRENDAN's statement on priestly celibacy.

Singing pubs. *See* BALLAD GROUPS.

Single. The way to ask for a bag of chips in a chip shop is to say 'a single'. More than one single can also be bought. Three singles means three bags of chips separately wrapped. *See also* ONE AND ONE.

Single-Speech Hamilton. The nickname of William Gerard Hamilton (1729–96), chancellor of the exchequer, who allegedly made only one speech – his maiden speech – in the Westminster House of Commons, on 13 November 1755, astounding his audience with his eloquence. Hamilton was born in London, the son of a prosperous Scottish barrister, and became MP for Petersfield, Hampshire. In 1761 he was appointed chief secretary to the then lord lieutenant of Ireland, Lord Halifax, sitting in the Irish House of Commons as MP for Killybegs, Co. Donegal. He became chancellor of the Irish exchequer in 1763 and later held other positions in the Irish administration. He died in London in 1796.

Single transferable vote. The Republic of Ireland has a complex proportional representation (PR) system of voting based on the single transferable vote and multi-seat (three, four or five) constituencies, unlike, for instance, the UK system of first-past-the-post single-seat constituencies. The voter casts his or her vote in order of preference for candidates from one or more parties, and transfers are of crucial importance in determining the outcome. Thus a candidate with a relatively small number of first preferences may be elected with either the surplus from a party colleague or lower preferences from a party colleague who is eliminated on second or subsequent counts.

Election counts in Ireland are therefore long and often nail-biting, and the role of TALLY-MEN in estimating the distribution of lower preferences is vital. Although FIANNA FÁIL was in government for most of the period from 1932 to 1973 it became clear to the party that achieving an overall majority of DÁIL seats would become increasingly difficult because of the subtleties of PR, where a small decrease in the number of votes won countrywide could mean a significant reduction in the number of seats.

A Fianna Fáil minister for local government, Kevin BOLAND, tried on two occasions, 1959 and 1968, to abolish multi-seat constituencies by putting a referendum to that effect before the Irish people, but on both occasions the proposal was rejected. Meanwhile it was expected that the party in office would redraw electoral boundaries for its own advantage. During the long period Kevin Boland was minister for local government, his periodical redrawing of constituency boundaries was known as 'Boland's Gerrymander'. The coalition government of 1973–7, not to be outdone, also changed the constituency boundaries. In this case, Labour's Jimmy Tully being minister for local government, it was known colloquially as the 'Tullymander'.

Singlings. The first, lethal run of POTEEN, usually put through the process again to produce DOUBLE. It was potent and used medicinally as an antiseptic and cure for sprains:

'I've seen men drink the singlings – the first run. They did it out of greed not ignorance. Damn good stillers some of them in their day – '

'Dead?'

'Oh, as doornails.'

SAM HANNA BELL (1909–90): 'The Way to Catch the Mountain Dew', in *Erin's Orange Lily* (1956)

Sinn Féin (Irish, 'ourselves'). The radical Nationalist movement founded by Arthur GRIFFITH and Bulmer HOBSON in 1905. Its main aim was dual monarchy under the British crown with an emphasis on the development of Irish economic independence. Its weapon was to be passive resistance and it advocated that Irish MPs should abandon Westminster and form their own national assembly in Dublin. The Irish should gradually withdraw support from what were seen as British institutions, beginning with the courts. Griffith had been very interested in the success that the Hungarians had in achieving an element of political autonomy in the Austrian empire after 1848, and felt that a similar scheme might work in Ireland.

The name Sinn Féin was gradually taken over by the IRISH VOLUNTEERS and in the 1918 election they won enough seats to put Griffith's idea of an Irish assembly into practice. The

perhaps inevitable result was the ANGLO-IRISH WAR of 1919–21. During the CIVIL WAR, and thereafter, Sinn Féin remained fastened to the IRA (*see* DE VALERA, ÉAMON), and the continuing policy of the armed struggle made a mockery of what Griffith stood for.

Despite a long period of marginalization following the creation of FIANNA FÁIL in 1926, Sinn Féin returned to prominence with the onset of the TROUBLES in NORTHERN IRELAND as the political wing of the Provisional IRA. It has two ministers in the Northern Ireland Assembly set up by the GOOD FRIDAY AGREEMENT, and won six seats in the DÁIL election of 2002.

The truth is, however, that what brought the last insurrection to a successful issue was that, unlike all other Irish movements of the kind, it was based on, or at least allied to, the passive resistance movement of Arthur Griffith.

ROBERT LYND (1879–1949): 'Arthur Griffith: the Patriot', in *Both Sides of the Road* (1934)

See also ADAMS, GERRY; ARMALITE AND THE BALLOT BOX, THE; LABOUR PARTY.

SIPTU. *See* ITGWU.

Sirr, Henry Charles (1764–1841). Town major (chief of police) in Dublin (1796–1808). He was born in Dublin Castle on 25 November 1764, the son of the serving town major, Joseph Sirr. He served in the army (1778–91) and was a wine trader in Dublin until he became acting town major. In 1798 his position as town major was confirmed and he too was given a residence in Dublin Castle. He prevented the rebellions of the UNITED IRISHMEN (1798) and of Robert EMMET (1803) from having any success by moving early and decisively to arrest the ringleaders, notably Lord Edward FITZGERALD on 19 May 1798 and Emmet himself in July 1803. He also interviewed Sarah CURRAN, Emmet's sweetheart, and interrogated Anne DEVLIN in prison. From 1808, when the police force in Dublin was reorganized, until his retirement in 1826, he served as an assistant magistrate, retaining his Dublin Castle residence. He died on 7 January 1841, having amassed a valuable collection of Irish antiquities. Sirr is a hated figure in Nationalist history, on a par with informers and spies.

Sisters of Mercy. *See* MACAULEY, CATHERINE.

Sitric Silkbeard (*c*.969–1042). Norse ruler in Dublin (989–1036). It was a turbulent period in the city's history, during which it was sacked by Mael Seachnaill (Malachy) II in 995. Sitric and his allies were defeated in two major battles, Glen Máma near Saggart, outside Dublin (999), and CLONTARF (1014). During Sitric's reign coins were minted in Dublin for the first time in Ireland (995). Sitric became a Christian and founded Christ Church in about 1030.

Sive. A tragic folk drama (1959) by Kerry dramatist John B. KEANE about an orphaned teenage schoolgirl called Sive, who is prevented from marrying the young man she loves by her avaricious uncle Mike Glavin and her aunt Mena. They intend instead to make a match for her with Seán Dóta, 'an old dotard' in Keane's words, using the services of a corrupt matchmaker, Thomasheen Seán Rua. The play culminates in the death of Sive, when she dashes from the house in a fog to escape Thomasheen and drowns in a bog hole. A sung chorus is supplied by two travellers, Pats Bocock and his son Parthalawn, who accompanies his father on the BODHRÁN:

> Oh, come all good men and true,
> A sad tale I'll tell to you
> All of a maiden fair, who died this day.
> Oh, they murdered lovely Sive,
> She would not be a bride,
> And laid her dead to bury in the clay.

Ernest BLYTHE and Tomás MacAnna of the ABBEY THEATRE rejected the play, and it had its first production by an amateur company, the Listowel Drama Group, which triumphed at the Amateur Drama Festival in Athlone in 1959. Originally a three-act play, *Sive* was rewritten for the Abbey in two acts for a 1985 production.

Six Counties, the. The term used in deprecation for NORTHERN IRELAND and its constituent counties, by those (Nationalists and Repub-

licans) who disapprove of its separate existence.

See also FATDAD.

Six Gifts of Womanhood. The qualities prized by the ancient Celts: beauty, chastity, sweet speech, needlework, voice and wisdom. They are possessed to perfection by EMER, the wife of CÚCHULAINN.

Six-Pack. A paramilitary punishment shooting in which the ankles and elbows are injured as well as the more usual KNEECAPPING.

16th-century Irish diet. Don Francisco de Cuellar, captain of the *San Pedro*, an Armada galleon, and a survivor of shipwreck on the Sligo coast, describes the diet of his temporary hosts:

> They do not eat oftener than once a day, and this at night; and that which they usually eat is butter with oaten-bread. They drink sour milk, for they have no other drink; they don't drink water though it is the best in the world. On feast days they eat some flesh half-cooked, without bread or salt. They clothe themselves, according to their habit, with tight trousers and short loose coats of very coarse goat's hair. They cover themselves with blankets, and wear their hair down to their eyes.

See also GLIB; DRESS CODE; IRISH MANTLE.

Sizar. An undergraduate of Trinity College Dublin (TCD) who receives a grant from the college authorities to help with his expenses. Formerly sizars had to perform menial duties to indicate that they received their 'sizings' (allowances of food) free.

> O, she's too rich for a Poddle swaddy
> With her tortoise comb and mantle fine,
> A Hellfire buck would fit her better,
> Driking brandy and claret wine.
> I'm just a decent College sizar,
> Poor as a sod of smouldery coal;
> And how would I dress the Spanish Lady
> And she so neat about the sole?
> ANON.: 'The Spanish Lady' (18th century)

Skeffington, Frank. *See* SHEEHY-SKEFFINGTON, HANNA.

Skellig Rocks. Two barren rocky islands off Ballinskelligs in the Iveragh Peninsula in Co. Kerry. They comprise the Great Skellig, on which the monastery of SCEILIG MHICHÍL was built, and the Little Skellig. The Skelligs were typically the last part of Ireland seen by sorrowing emigrants on their way west by boat to the United States.

Skelligs List, the. A broadsheet in verse lampooning those who should have married during SHROVETIDE but didn't do so, so called because it was believed that the monks in the monastery on SCEILIG MHICHÍL kept a different calendar from the rest of Christendom and could marry people when Lent forbade marriage on the mainland. Pages with these verses were slipped under the doors of the relevant parties on Ash Wednesday:

> There's Mary the Bridge
> And Johnny her boy friend,
> They are walking out now
> For twenty-one springs!
> There's no ditch nor no dyke
> That they haven't rolled in –
> She must know by now
> The nature of things!

Skelly. An Ulster word, still current, used as both a verb and (in the form 'skelly-eyed') as an adjective, meaning 'squint', as in 'He was that skelly-eyed you wouldn't know whether he was looking at you or the boy beside you.'

Skelp. *See* SCEILP.

Skerries goat. 'Goat' is the nickname for an inhabitant of Skerries, a small seaside town in north Co. Dublin. The legend runs that inhabitants of Skerries killed and ate St Patrick's goat while the saint ministered elsewhere.

Skibbereen. *See* 'REVENGE FOR SKIBBEREEN'.

Skibbereen Eagle, The. A local newspaper, published in the small west Cork town of Skibbereen, reputed to have once told Lord Palmerston that it had 'got its eye both upon him and on the Emperor of Russia'.

Skillingers, the. The nickname of the 6th (Inniskilling) Dragoons, also known as the SKINS. In 1922 they was amalgamated with the 5th Dragoon Guards to form the 5th Royal Inniskilling Dragoon Guards. These were joined with the 4th/7th Dragoon Guards in 1992 to form the Royal Dragoon Guards.

Skins, the. The nickname of the Royal Inniskilling Fusiliers but also applied to the Inniskilling Dragoons (*see* SKILLINGERS, THE). The alleged origin of the name was an incident after the Battle of Maida on the toe of Italy on 6 July 1806 when the soldiers of the regiment were given permission to bathe in the sea and were then called to arms at the approach of what was thought wrongly to be French cavalry. With no time to dress the soldiers seized their muskets and prepared to repel the enemy in the nude. A more likely source is the difficulty of saying their regimental name in full, 'Skins' being a convenient abbreviation. In 1968 they were amalgamated with the Royal Ulster Rifles and Royal Irish Fusiliers to form the Royal Irish Rangers.

Skin-the-Goat. The nickname of James Fitzharris, who drove the decoy cab after the PHOENIX PARK MURDERS carried out by the INVINCIBLES. He was unlikely to have been privy to the assailants' intentions, but was not released on parole until 1902.

> With a big sharp knife may they take his life,
> While his vessel is still afloat,
> And pick his bones as clean as stones,
> Is the prayer of poor Skin the Goat.
>> ANON.: 'Skin the Goat's Curse on Carey' (late 19th century). Carey was the leader of the Invincibles who turned queen's evidence on his colleagues.

Skite. A HIBERNO-ENGLISH word for an expedition, particularly one undertaken for fun. 'We're going on a skite' might indicate that a drinking session is envisaged.
See also BATTER, TO BE ON THE.

Skrake or **screagh** or **skraik.** An Ulster word for 'screech', most commonly used in the expression 'the skrake o'dawn', i.e. cockcrow, as in 'He's been up since the skrake.'

Skrine, [Agnes] Nesta. *See* O'NEILL, MOIRA.

Sky farmer. A farmer who owns a virtual farm only, who having lost his land maintains a cow by grazing her along the roadside verges.

Slachtmhar (Irish, 'neat'). A word used in HIBERNO-ENGLISH to mean 'carefully dressed', 'tidy' (of a person); 'in good condition', 'finished' (of a room of building). There is also a noun, *slacht*: 'Put a bit of *slacht* on the house before the priest comes.'

Slag. A common verb in HIBERNO-ENGLISH, meaning to 'tease' or to 'ridicule', kindly or unkindly. 'Only slagging' is a disclaimer heard frequently in Irish conversation. To 'slag off' is also used. To slag can also mean to criticize severely. When Brian TREVASKIS criticized the Bishop of Galway on the *The* LATE LATE SHOW in March 1966, presenter Gay BYRNE was attacked by a member of the audience for having a guest on the show for the purpose of 'slagging the clergy'.

Sláinte. *See* TOASTS.

Slán. The Irish word for 'goodbye', often used by those with CÚPLA FOCAL. The word *slán* literally means 'safe' or 'whole'.

Slán abhaile. An Irish phrase meaning 'safe home', often used by a compère at the end of an evening's entertainment.
See also GOODNIGHT, GOD BLESS AND SAFE HOME.

'Slasher' O'Reilly. *See* FINEA, BRIDGE OF.

Slates, to be away for. A slang expression for being in a good position, for example after winning money, getting a new job or coming into an inheritance.

Sleán. A specially-designed spade for cutting TURF, pronounced 'shlawn'.

Sleeveen. A HIBERNO-ENGLISH word for a sly, untrustworthy individual, and sometimes used as a more general term of abuse. Disgraced Dublin West Fianna Fáil TD Liam Lawlor called the lawyers of the Flood Tribunal (*see* TRIBUNALS) 'sleeveens' in Dáil Éireann on 7 February 2002; he was released from Mountjoy Prison, where he was serving a one-month sentence for failing to cooperate with the tribunal, in order to speak during the debate on an all-party Dáil motion calling for his resignation. The word derives from the Irish *slíbín*, meaning 'sly person'.

'Sliabh Geal gCua na Féile'. A heartfelt exile's lament written in 1912 by Pádraig Ó Miléadha (1877–1947), a DÉISE (Waterford Gaeltacht) poet who was then living in Wales:

A Shliabh Geal gCua na féile is fada uait i gcéin mé
Am shuí cois cuain im aonair go tréith-lag fé bhrón
An tuile buí ar thaobh díom
'Dir mé is tír mo chléibhe …
(O noble Sliabh Geal gCua you are far from me now
As I sit by the shore alone bowed down by grief
The frothy tide by my side
Flows between me and the country of my heart …)

Sliabh Luachra. An area in east Kerry–northwest Cork, roughly bounded by the towns or villages of Castleisland, Killarney, Gneeveguilla and KNOCKNAGREE and famous for its living and unbroken tradition of music, especially polkas and KERRY SLIDES played on the fiddle or accordion. Historically it is also famous as the birthplace of two of the great Kerry poets, Aogán Ó RATHAILE and Eoghan Rua ó Súilleabháin (*see* EOGHAN AN BHÉIL BHINN), of the lexicographer Pádraig Ó Duinnín (*see* DINNEEN'S DICTIONARY) and of the SEANCHAÍ Éamon Kelly. Among the most illustrious musicians of the past century were fiddlers Pádraig O'KEEFFE, Denis Murphy (DENIS THE WEAVER) and his sister Julia Clifford, and accordion player Johnny O'LEARY.

Slide. *See* KERRY SLIDE.

Slievenamon. A mountain in the GOLDEN VALE in Co. Tipperary, the name of which means 'the mountain of the women' and which in folklore has always been associated with the OTHER-WORLD. It is 721 m (2364 ft) high and provides views over five counties. One of the many stories about the mountain tells how three hags visited a young bride one night, under the pretext of teaching her to spin – fairies were supposed to be skilful spinners. The terrified young woman got rid of them by pretending that Slievenamon was on fire: the hags rushed away, concerned for the safety of their children on the mountain. The story is also told how all the fairest women raced to the top to claim the hand of the warrior FIONN MAC CUMHAIL. Fionn secretly liked GRÁINNE, the daughter of the High King of Ireland, so he advised her how to win the race. Although it looks like a solitary height, Slievenamon is surrounded by a series of lower heathery humps. Some of these, like the main summit, are crowned by ancient burial cairns. The highest cairn is said to mark the entrance to the mysterious Celtic underworld.

'Slievenamon'. A popular song of lost love by Charles KICKHAM. It is usually played to waltz tempo and, although melancholy, can be sung rousingly (like 'The FIELDS OF ATHENRY'). It is the anthem of the Co. Tipperary hurling team.

> Alone, all alone, on a wave-wash'd strand,
> All alone in a crowded hall.
> The hall it is gay, and the waves they are grand
> But my heart is not there at all.
> It flies far away, by night and by day
> To the time and the joys that are gone!
> And I never can forget the sweet maiden I met
> In the valley near Slievenamon.

Slightly constitutional party, a. The description of FIANNA FÁIL by Seán LEMASS in March 1928. The party had entered the DÁIL for the first time the previous year, having until then been an ABSTENTIONIST party opposed to the TREATY.

Slí Mór. See ESKER RIADA.

Sling calf. An aborted calf. Brucellosis in cows causes spontaneous abortion so a farmer be-

set with the ill-luck of having cows losing their calves might attempt to get rid of his own misfortune by dumping a sling calf on a neighbour's farm.

See also EGGS; PISHOGUES; SPANCEL.

Sliogeadal. An Irish word for 'quagmire', 'quicksand'. The Sliogeadal is also the name of a beautiful and remote mountainous pass through which runs a little-used road between Shrone and Clydagh in the SLIABH LUACHRA area of east Kerry.

Sliotar. A small round hard ball used for playing hurling. It is pronounced 'slithar'. Such is its potential force and velocity in a championship match that most players now wear protective helmets and visors. The young SETANTA (Cúchulainn) killed the hound of Culann the blacksmith by hitting a *sliotar* with great force down the animal's throat.

Slipe. A kind of litter, triangular in shape, and used for the transport of stones, peat or brushwood on terrain where a wheeled cart would be impractical.

Sloane, Sir Hans (1660–1753). Physician and naturalist. He was born in Killyleagh, Co. Down, on 16 April 1660 and graduated in medicine in 1683 after studies in Paris and Montpellier. He was physician to the governor of Jamaica (1687–9) and while there collected 800 new botanical specimens (cataloguing them in Latin in 1696). Returning to London he became secretary to the Royal Society (1693–1713) and later president (1727–40). His name lives on in the salubrious Kensingston/Chelsea environs of Sloane Square and Hans Crescent, land that he judiciously purchased. His collections of specimens and library of 58,000 volumes formed the nucleus of the British Museum, which was opened to the public in 1759. He died in London on 11 January 1753.

Slob or **slab** (Irish *slaba*). Reclaimed land, which at certain stages of its evolution is largely mud; hence the metaphorical use of the word for a person of slovenly habits and appearance.

Slog. A Cork verb meaning 'steal', but viewed as a misdemeanour rather than a crime: 'He caught me slogging apples.'
See also FECK³.

Slow air. A solo performance of a meditative tune on a traditional instrument, which has been compared to SEAN-NÓS singing. The plangent quality of the UILLEANN PIPES makes them particularly suitable, as the recordings of Séamus ENNIS or Willie CLANCY testify, but master fiddlers such as DENIS THE WEAVER exercised their own *draíocht* ('magic') in this kind of music.

Slow, Lazy and Never Comfortable. Sean O'FAO-LAIN's interpretation of the acronym SL&NC – Sligo, Leitrim and Northern Counties (Railway) – in *An Irish Journey* (1941).

Smerwick Harbour. A bay on the northwestern coast of the Dingle Peninsula. In 1579 a force of 80 Spaniards landed here with a papal nuncio in support of the DESMOND REBELLION, and established a strongpoint within the ancient Dún an Óir (Irish 'golden fort'), known by them as Fort-del-Oro. The following year they were reinforced by 600 Italian soldiers, but on 10 November the fort was captured and its garrison (apart from the officers) massacred by an English force under Lord Deputy Grey and Admiral Winter; Sir Walter RALEIGH and Edmund SPENSER are said to have been on the English side during this episode. The affair features in Charles Kingsley's Don-bashing adventure, *Westward Ho!* (1855), in which the author smugly writes:

> Many years passed before a Spaniard set foot again in Ireland.

Smile like moonlight on a gravestone. The description by Kevin O'HIGGINS of Lord BAL-FOUR, who presided at the Imperial Conference of 1926, at which O'Higgins led the Irish delegation.

Smith, Erasmus. *See* ERASMUS SMITH SCHOOLS; ERASMUS SMITH TRUST.

Smithereens. A noun always used in the plural to mean 'fragments' or 'tiny parts' and believed to derive from Irish *smiodar*, meaning 'fragment' (plus the diminutive suffix *-ín*). The word is in common use in HIBERNO-ENGLISH, and is also used widely in British English: 'She dropped the plate and it broke in smithereens.' Smithereens is also used rhetorically to mean wholesale destruction: in a Dáil debate on 3 April 2003 Joe Higgins TD claimed (with regard to the US war in Afghanistan): 'This is what complicity with the American war machine means in reality. They are assisting war planes to break children to smithereens.'

Smithson, Annie M[ary] P[atricia] (1873–1948). Romantic and patriotic novelist. She was born in Sandymount, Dublin, and trained as a nurse. On her mother's remarriage she became a Catholic and a fervent Nationalist, and was an activist in CUMANN NA MBAN during the CIVIL WAR. Her 19 novels, which reflect elements of her own life, are full of ladylike, ultimately patriotic (that is to say Republican) and feminist young women who often succeed in converting their heroic lovers to Catholicism. *The Walk of a Queen* (1922) and *The Laughter of Sorrow* (1925) both contain some descriptions of ordinary Dublin life during the TROUBLES. Her work was once extremely popular, in spite of its decorousness and total lack of irony, but recent attempts to revive interest in it have failed.

Smithson, Harriet (1800–54). Actress. The daughter of a theatre manager, she was born in Ennis, Co. Clare, and had her first role in Crow Lane Theatre in Dublin in 1815. She played in other Irish theatres and in Drury Lane in London but it was not until 1828, when she appeared on the Paris stage in Shakespearean roles, that she received great acclaim. The French composer Hector Berlioz fell in love with her and composed his *Symphonie Fantastique* (1830) in her honour. She refused to marry him at this juncture, but in the summer of 1833, ill and in debt, she relented and they were married in October of that year.

> Miss Smithson was married last week, in Paris, to Derlioz [sic], the musical composer. We trust this

marriage will insure the happiness of an amiable young woman, as well as secure us against her reappearance on the English boards.

The Court Journal (London), October 1833

Madame Berlioz, as she was now called, made only one further appearance on the stage in Paris, in an unsuccessful attempt to raise money to pay her own debts. In 1840 the couple separated, although Berlioz contributed to her support. Smithson died in Montmartre on 3 March 1854.

Smock Alley. A theatre in Essex Street West in Dublin, established in 1662, the first theatre to be opened in Ireland after the Restoration. Built by Edinburgh-born John Ogilby (1600–76) and Thomas Stanley, the holders of the master of revels licence for Ireland, it was the home of the THEATRE ROYAL until 1759. The theatre was dominated by actor-managers, including Thomas Sheridan the Younger (the father of Richard Brinsley SHERIDAN) from 1745. It offered as many as 50 plays a year in repertory: Shakespeare was popular (Peg WOFFINGTON played Cordelia in *King Lear* in 1742), but the repertory also included works by Irish dramatists (who often acted as well) such as Charles MACKLIN, Arthur Murphy and John O'KEEFFE. The theatre was dependent on the custom of the CASTLE set, so it set a very conservative course politically, which was not always palatable to its plebeian audience; riots and disturbances were frequent for political or personal reasons. An act of Parliament of 1786 that prohibited unlicensed theatres sounded the death knell for Smock Alley, and the building was demolished in 1813 to make room for the Catholic church of SS Michael and John.

Smurfit, Michael (b.1936). Businessman. He was born in Lancashire on 7 August 1936, the son of John Jefferson Smurfit, founder of the Smurfit (originally Jefferson Smurfit) group, and was educated at Clongowes. He became chairman and CEO of the Smurfit Group PLC, and endowed the Michael Smurfit Graduate School of Business at University College Dublin, which runs a popular MBA course.

Smut. A HIBERNO-ENGLISH term of uncertain derivation, meaning a 'pout' or 'sulky' expression.

Smyllie, Robert Maire. *See* NICHEVO.

Smyth, Brendan. *See* BRENDAN SMYTH AFFAIR.

Smyth, Patrick G. *See* LOUGH GILL.

Sned. A verb meaning to cut the leaves and root off a vegetable, especially a turnip.

Snig. A verb meaning to cut or prune with a knife.
See also SNED.

Sniper at work. A sign mocked up to look like a triangular road warning notice, showing a masked gunman and the legend as above, seen in several places in south Armagh during Northern Ireland's TROUBLES.
See also BANDIT COUNTRY.

Snuff at a wake, like. A phrase indicating profusion, as in 'In Houlihan's last night he was throwing money round him like snuff at a wake.' At 20th-century wakes quantities of cigarettes and snuff for the older women replaced the clay pipes and tobacco that were essentials at earlier functions. Nowadays wakes are marked by a continuous catering of tea, whiskey, sandwiches, biscuits and cake, giving rise to a linked phrase, 'like biscuits at a wake'.

Social Democratic and Labour Party. *See* SDLP.

Social Justice. An anti-Semitic periodical (1936) published by Charles Coughlin, a Catholic priest from Detroit. He was born of Irish ancestry in Hamilton, Ontario, Canada, on 25 October 1891, and became a remarkable performer on radio in the late 1920s, commenting upon all aspects of American life. When F.D. Roosevelt (FDR) became US president in 1932 he supported his New Deal policies, but soon joined with those who called them the 'Jew Deal'. He publicly supported Mussolini and Hitler, making a scandalously approving broadcast after *Kristallnacht* in November 1938 and printing the forged, fictitious and grossly anti-Semitic *Protocols of the Elders of Zion* (1905) in *Social Justice*. Throughout his career he was supported by his bishop Michael Gallagher, but when in 1942 FDR threatened to jail him for sedition, Gallagher's replacement silenced him. Coughlin died in Royal Oak on 27 October 1979.

Society for the Preservation of the Irish Language. *See* SPIL.

Society of Friends. The formal name for the Quakers. The Society of Friends was introduced to Ireland at the time of the English Civil War, and established on an organized basis by George Fox (1624–91), the society's founder, who visited from England, and William Edmundson (1627–72), who was Westmorland-born but who settled as a merchant in Antrim and was the recognized head of the Quakers in Ireland. By the beginning of the 18th century they had gained a measure of legal acceptance, although, like Catholics and Dissenters, their refusal to pay TITHES laid them open to seizure of their goods and even imprisonment. Despite their relatively small numbers, Quakers became prominent in the commercial life of the country, in shipping, manufacturing and shopkeeping: among the best known families were the Jacobs, founders of Jacobs Biscuits in Dublin, and the Bewleys, tea and coffee merchants and proprietors of the famous Oriental cafés in Dublin. During the GREAT FAMINE Quakers from Ireland and England contributed greatly to relief works.

Sodom and Begorrah. The anonymous witty description of the theatre in Dublin in the 1940s. It was the heyday of the GATE THEATRE's provision of modern and classical plays, produced and acted by the Mac Liammóir–Edwards partnership (*see* BOYS, THE²) whose sexual relationship was known but, considering the mores of the time, generously tolerated, while the ABBEY THEATRE in its post-Yeatsian years seemed to stage too many realistic peasant plays.

Soft day. When the weather in Ireland is discussed with a passer-by, a 'soft day' or a 'grand soft day' means a day on which 'there is no cold' but on which there is often a light mist or drizzle or the threat of rain, as described by Winifred M. LETTS in her poem 'A Soft Day':

> A soft day, thank God!
> A wind from the south
> With a honeyed mouth;
> A scent of drenching leaves ...

Soften [someone's] cough, to. A phrase applied to something that punctures someone's pride, or brings someone back to reality or back down to earth, as in 'That will soften his cough for him.'

Soggarth Aroon. An anglicization of *sagart a rún* ('darling priest'), a term of endearment. It was the title of a poem (1831) by John BANIM, whose popularity lasted into the 20th century, and was put in the mouth of Joxer DALY by Sean O'CASEY in *JUNO AND THE PAYCOCK*. The poem certainly contributed to the phrase's universal use:

> Who on the winter's night,
> Soggarth Aroon,
> When the cawld blast did bite,
> Soggarth Aroon,
> Came to my cabin door
> And on my earthen-flure
> Knelt by me rich and poor,
> Soggarth Aroon?

Soldiers of Destiny. A mistranslation of the name of the political party FIANNA FÁIL, normally now used in a bathetic or mildly derogatory manner.

Soldiers of the Rearguard. A nickname for soldiers of the OLD IRA, veterans of the Anglo-Irish War of 1919–21, recruited for service during the EMERGENCY into the 26th Battalion of the Irish army.

'Soldier's Song, A'. The national anthem of the Irish state, in its English and Irish versions (for the latter *see* 'AMHRÁN NA BHFIANN'). It is a marching song by Peadar KEARNEY, with music picked out on his melodeon by his friend

Patrick Heeney (1881–1911). It was sung as early as 1907, but first published by Bulmer HOBSON in *Irish Freedom* in 1912:

Soldiers are we,
Whose lives are pledged to Ireland.
Some have come,
From a land beyond the sea,
Sworn to be free
No more our ancient sireland
Shall shelter the despot or the slave ...

The song was officially adopted as Ireland's national anthem in 1926, after a competition adjudicated by Lennox ROBINSON, James STEPHENS and W.B. YEATS had not produced another song worthy of the 50-guinea prize. At the Dublin horse show in August of that year the tricolour flew over the governor-general's box while 'A Soldier's Song' was played. Kearney received a royalty of £1000 for the song in 1933.

As the national anthem is likely to be sung in Irish, for many years even people who knew the words gave little thought to their meaning, but in recent decades the Northern TROUBLES and REVISIONIST historiography have encouraged Irish people to distance themselves from the violence attending the birth of their state. This has led to suggestions that 'A Soldier's Song' should be abandoned in favour of something more peaceful in flavour. The 'LONDONDERRY AIR' ('Danny Boy') seems the most popular alternative.

Solemn League and Covenant. *See* ULSTER COVENANT.

Soloheadbeg. A quarry 4 km (2.5 miles) from Tipperary town, scene of an attack on 21 January 1919 on two popular local RIC constables, McDonnell and O'Connell, that is generally regarded as the beginning of the ANGLO-IRISH WAR. They were accompanying 76 kg (168 lb) of gelignite from the military magazine in the town to the quarry. The IRA had imprecise intelligence of the operation, and members of the South Tipperary Brigade led by Seán Treacy (*see* 'TIPPERARY SO FAR AWAY') and Dan BREEN lay in wait for three days until

the party was sighted. Treacy shot both the constables with his rifle before they had time to unsling their own weapons, and a hail of revolver bullets made sure that they were dead. The county council workers who had driven the cart were unharmed and one recognized Breen, because his mask slipped, as he jumped over the gate behind which he had been concealed. The government issued a wanted poster offering £1000 reward and describing him as having a 'sulky bulldog appearance'. The attack on fellow Irishmen was almost universally condemned at the time, Dr Harty, the Archbishop of Cashel, declaring it morally wrong.

Solomons, Estella (1882–1968). Artist. She was born in Dublin to a Jewish family and studied under William ORPEN at the Metropolitan School of Art in Dublin and with Walter Osborne in the RHA Schools. In the early 1900s she went to Paris to study life drawing, and in 1911 visited the Netherlands on a painting trip with her cousin, Louis Jacobs. At home she embraced Republicanism and feminism, becoming a member of CUMANN NA MBAN and participating in the 1916 EASTER RISING. She married the writer James Starkey (whose pseudonym was Seumas O'SULLIVAN). Her artistic reputation is based on her atmospheric landscapes in muted colours and her portraits of many of the leading literary and political figures of her day, including Frank Aiken, Pádraic Colum, Alice Milligan, An t-Ath Pádraig Ó Duinnín and Jack B. Yeats (now in the NILAND GALLERY).

Some Experiences of an Irish RM. The first volume (1899) of a series of comic stories by SOMERVILLE AND ROSS, originally intended as hunting sketches, but blossoming into useful social documents of turn-of-the-century Irish rural life. Published as *Some Experiences of an Irish RM* (1899), *Further Experiences of an Irish RM* (1908) and *In Mr Knox's Country* (1908), they recount the misadventures of the naïve Major Yeates RM ('resident magistrate'), his friendly Anglo-Irish adversary Flurry Knox, Slipper the wily drunken horse-dealer, the housekeeper Mrs Cadogan and many other characters both peasant and half-mounted (*see* HALF-MOUNTED GENTLEMEN). The stories were disowned as STAGE-IRISH by SINN FÉIN and as unpoetic by members of the IRISH LITERARY REVIVAL, but, in their precise and sympathetic observation of Irish life as it was lived – with decaying 'gintry', Nationalist petite bourgeoisie and clear-eyed surviving peasantry – they give a remarkably true picture of post-Parnellite Ireland. Edith Somerville was firmly Nationalist, but it was Violet Martin (of Catholic ancestry and Unionist inclination) whose dark imagination supplied the Gothic elements in some otherwise light-hearted stories.

Somerville and Ross. Edith Œnone Somerville (1858–1949) and Martin Ross (pseudonym of Violet Martin, 1862–1915), novelists and short-story writers. Edith, the elder, was born in Corfu but spent much of her life in Drishane, the family home in Castletownshend, Co. Cork. She was educated mainly by governesses and early showed an artistic ability equal to her horse-womanship. She formed a literary partnership with her cousin Violet, one of the Martins of Ross, a family numbered among the tribes of Galway (*see* CITY OF THE TRIBES), whom she first met in 1886. Together the pair wrote 16 books, including five novels (notably *The REAL CHARLOTTE*) and three collections of comic stories in the Irish RM series (*see SOME EXPERIENCES OF AN IRISH RM*), before Violet's sudden death in 1915.

Their collaboration was non-specific in its details but a reasonable division was that Edith supplied the humour and equine details, and Violet the darker elements, the Gothic atmosphere and the consciousness of the irreversible decay of the BIG HOUSE. Her own home of Ross, near Moycullen, Co. Galway, had had to be closed, and her brother had become an entertainer to pay off estate debts. Edith and Violet were both suffragists and became respectively president and vice-president of the Munster Women's Franchise League in 1913, but Edith was much more aware of the justice of Nationalist claims (and wrote letters to the newspapers appealing for clemency for the leaders of the 1916 Easter Rising), while Violet, of Catholic ancestry, remained a WYNDHAMite Unionist.

Edith continued to write after the death of Violet, whom she loved beyond the usual affection of cousins, and insisted on both their names appearing on the published books, claiming Ross's collaboration from beyond the grave. The chief book of this ghostly partnership was *The Big House at Inver* (1925), about the decline of the Ascendancy Prendevilles, who in their deterioration abandon the social codes of their class and 'go native'. The germ of the book lay in a visit that Violet paid to such a crumbling house in 1912. Edith died in Castletownshend and she and Violet are buried together in the local churchyard.

Somme, Battle of the. A First World War battle that began on 1 July 1916, lasted until 18 November and involved large numbers of the 'volunteers' with which KITCHENER had supplemented his greatly depleted armies. It has assumed a special place in Unionist iconography because of the involvement of the 36th (Ulster) Division on the Ancre salient, where 5000 men were lost in the first two days, some of them wearing, by special permission, Orange collarettes over their uniforms. This 'blood sacrifice' was held to be a proof of Ulster's unwavering loyalty to the Union, in noted contrast to the action of the 'back-stabbers' who two months earlier had occupied the GPO in the EASTER RISING. There is no doubt that the men fought gallantly, like so many others in those wasteful months, including the Irish Division who arrived in September 1916 and who like the Ulstermen stayed for the remainder of the war. Of the 50,000 Irishmen who were killed in the war, half at least were Catholic and presumed Nationalist.

See also OBSERVE THE SONS OF ULSTER MARCHING TOWARDS THE SOMME; UVF.

Sonsie or **sonsy.** An epithet implying all kinds of physical health and beauty, together with a pleasant and fortunate disposition, as in 'a fine sonsie girl'. The word is also used in Scots.

Sons of Usna. In Irish mythology, NAOISE, AINLÉ and ARDÁN, the three sons of Usna and Ebhla, the daughter of the druid CATHBAD and the granddaughter of AONGHUS ÓG, the love god. They figure in the story of DEIRDRE, the eldest as her lover, and the others as companions and bodyguards during their sojourn in ALBA. They are tricked into returning to Ireland and are killed on the orders of CON-CHOBHAR.

Soolock (Irish *súlach*, 'dirty liquid'). A word current in HIBERNO-ENGLISH, meaning 'dirty running water', 'bile', 'farmyard effluent'.

Sorra. A HIBERNO-ENGLISH version of the word 'sorrow', often used in mild imprecations:

> Over here in England I'm helpin' wi' the hay
> An' I wisht I was in Ireland the livelong day;
> Weary on the English hay, an' sorra take the
>   wheat!
> Och Corrymeela an' the blue sky over it.
>   MOIRA O'NEILL (Nesta Skrine, 1865–1955):
>   'Corrymeela', in *Songs of the Glens of Antrim* (1901)

Souperism. The practice by which indigent or starving Catholics were encouraged to convert to Protestantism in exchange for food (soup), particularly during the GREAT FAMINE of 1845–9. 'Taking the soup' was the colloquial contemporary term for changing religion, and those who did so were known as 'soupers', 'jumpers' or 'perverts'. It is now thought unlikely that there is any truth in allegations of widespread pressure to convert.
See also MISSIONARY SETTLEMENT, THE; SE-COND REFORMATION.

Soupers. *See* SOUPERISM.

South, Seán. *See* 'SEÁN SOUTH FROM GARRY-OWEN'.

South Dublin Union. *See* SPIKE, THE[1].

South/North. *See* NORTH/SOUTH.

South Pole, The. The name of a pub in An-nascaul, near Dingle in Co. Kerry, originally owned by Tom Crean (d.1938), who accompanied Ernest SHACKLETON on his Antarctic expedition in 1914. Crean was a valuable colleague in adversity, known for his great strength and endurance.

South Wall. *See* GREAT SOUTH WALL, THE.

Spadar. An Irish word literally meaning 'wet, heavy turf', and used in HIBERNO-ENGLISH to denote a useless, cloddish person.

Spalpeen (Irish *spailpín*). A HIBERNO-ENGLISH word for an itinerant or migratory (usually penniless) labourer; also a common workman. Spalpeens, carrying their spades or scythes, hired themselves out at HIRING FAIRS or informally. The title of the traditional song '*An Spailpín Fánach*' means 'the wandering workman'.

Spancel. A rope to tie the hind legs of a cow together so that she would not kick while she was being milked; thus also the verb 'to spancel'. In a self-sufficient society the spancel would often be made from the tail-hair of cattle, so spancels were an ideal means of working PISHOGUES: a 'foreign' spancel (from another farm) on which a spell had been worked would be left near the herd. When it was used on a cow, her milk would dry up or her cream would not churn. Burning the spancel robbed the pishogue of its power. The origin of the word is uncertain but it may derive from the Dutch *spansel*.

'Spancil Hill'. An anonymous emigrant ballad that takes its name from a location near Feakle in east Clare. It is extremely popular and evocative of Irish nostalgia for the homeland felt even by people living in Ireland. Because of its length it qualifies in spirit if not technically as a COME-ALL-YE.

> Last night as I lay dreaming of pleasant days gone
>   by
> My mind being bent on rambling, to Ireland I
>   did fly,
> I stepped aboard a vision and I followed with a
>   will
> Till next I came to anchor at

The cross of Spancil Hill

...

I paid a flying visit to my first and only love,
She's as fair as any lily, as gentle as a dove.
She threw her arms around me saying, 'Johnny, I
   love you still!'
She's Matt the farmer's daughter
And the pride of Spancil Hill.

I dreamt I held and kissed her as in the days of
   yore,
She said, 'John, you're only joking, like many's
   the time before!'
But the cock he crew in the morning, he crew
   both loud and shrill,
I awoke in California, many miles from Spancil
   Hill!

On a famous occasion in 1994 Shane MC-
GOWAN and Christy MOORE sang 'Spancil Hill'
together on *The* LATE LATE SHOW.

Spanish Civil War (1936–9). The war between
the Nationalists under General Franco and the
democratically elected Popular Front (Republican) government. It divided Irish opinion,
with the Catholic Church and much of the press
and public opinion on Franco's side, especially
after news emerged of alleged brutality by Republican forces against priests and nuns. However, the FIANNA FÁIL government of Éamon
DE VALERA maintained a neutral stance. Eoin
O'DUFFY's Irish Brigade went to Spain to fight on
Franco's side, but saw little action (*see* ANGELS
OF MONASTEREVIN), while 150–200 Irishmen,
mainly Republicans, formed the Connolly Column of the International Brigade, under Frank
RYAN. They were involved in serious fighting,
and incurred many casualties.

Spark. A tiny amount of light, a HIBERNO-
ENGLISH word normally used figuratively and
in the negative: 'He hasn't a spark of sense', or,
simply, 'He hasn't a spark.'

Special Branch. An armed unit of the GARDA
SÍOCHÁNA, colloquially known 'the branch'.
It was de facto established in 1925, after the
assimilation of the DMP into the national police
force, to fight political crime and activities
perceived as being subversive of the state, then

and since mainly by Republican opponents of the
status quo. Members are recruited from within the ranks of uniformed gardai or plain-clothes
detectives. Among the activities for which they
are criticized by Republicans are surveillance
at Republican funerals, fund-raisers and other
commemorations and alleged harassment of
sympathizers. The RUC, now PSNI, also has
a 'special branch', the activities of which are
still greatly resented by Republican activists in
Northern Ireland.

Special category. A status granted to members of
paramilitary organizations by William WHITE-
LAW, secretary of state for Northern Ireland, in
June 1972 after a hunger strike in Belfast prison.
They were not required to work, could wear
their own clothes and had extra visiting privileges. Merlyn Rees, secretary of state (1974–6),
began to phase out the status from 1 March
1976, giving rise eventually to the BLANKET
PROTEST, the DIRTY PROTEST and the H-BLOCK
HUNGER STRIKES.

Special Criminal Court. A non-jury court established in the Republic on 30 May 1972 under
the terms of the Offences Against the State Act,
and for many years seen as an important element in the armoury of the state in the fight
against Republican terrorism. It follows the
procedures of the central criminal court, decisions being made by three judges. The court was
reviewed as part of the GOOD FRIDAY AGREE-
MENT, but retained by the reviewing committee.
Since the subsidence of the recent Troubles in
Northern Ireland it is more likely to be used to
try serious criminals – such as those charged
with the murder of Veronica GUERIN – than to
try subversives. The state's justification for this
is that jury members in such cases would be at
risk of intimidation.

Special men. The name applied to Irish prisoners in English jails in the 1880s. They had
been found guilty under the TREASON-FELONY
ACT of 1848 and were invariably harshly treated
by the warders. At one period O'DONOVAN
ROSSA was kept for 35 days with his hands
manacled behind his back, except at meals

when they were manacled at the front, because he had thrown the contents of his chamber pot at the prison governor. During this period he managed to read by turning the pages of his books with his teeth. Others treated with similar harshness included Thomas CLARKE.

Special position of the Catholic Church. *See* ARTICLE 44.

Special Powers Act. A set of draconian measures passed in 1922 as a means of dealing with the threat of civil war in the new state of Northern Ireland but retained long after the threat was over, and made permanent in 1933. It was the STORMONT government's main means of denying Catholics their civil rights, giving wide powers of arrest and detention to the RUC, and arrogating to the Northern Ireland minister for home affairs the right to ban marches and intern without trial. The act was devised mainly by Sir [Richard] Dawson Bates (1876–1949), who was home affairs minister from 1921 until 1943, and was regarded with envy by the apartheid leaders of South Africa. Bates had been a tireless lieutenant to James CRAIG and had been the organizer of the ULSTER COVENANT of 1912. Craig probably deplored Bates's ultra-extremism, but with a characteristic mixture of unease and inertia did little to curb it, while the latter maintained his hardline anti-Catholicism until the end. Throughout its period on the statute books the act proved impervious to legal challenge, and was not repealed until 1973, after Stormont fell.

Speech from the dock. *See* LET NO MAN WRITE MY EPITAPH.

Speed exhortations. HIBERNO-ENGLISH has typically exaggerated admonitions to show urgency: 'Don't be there till you're back again!'; 'If you fall don't wait to get up!'

Spenser, Edmund (*c.*1552–99). Poet and planter. He was born in London and educated at Cambridge. In 1580 he was appointed secretary to the Irish lord deputy, Lord Grey de Wilton, and was rewarded for his help in putting down the DESMOND REBELLION in 1586 with Kilcolman Castle and its estate of 3000 acres (1200 ha) near Doneraile in northeast Cork. While living there he completed the first three books of *The Faerie Queen* (1590), but it was in Book IV (1596) that he celebrates in elegant verse and with apparent affection the rivers of Ireland. His *A View of the Present State of Ireland* (1596) argued for the use of ruthless methods against the natives, not even stopping at extermination by starvation. He stayed in Kilcolman until 1598 when insurgents burned the castle. He died the following year in London.

> The pleasaunt Bandon crownd with many a
>   wood,
> The spreading Lee, that like an Island fayre
> Encloseth Corke with his devided flood.
>   *The Faerie Queen* (1596), IV, xi, 44

See also ANATOMIES OF DEATH.

Speranza. The pen name of Jane Francesca Wilde (1821–96), Nationalist poet. She was born Jane Francesca Elgee in Co. Wexford into a Protestant, Unionist family, and her father was a solicitor. She was converted to Nationalism by reading *The* NATION, and under the pen name Speranza ('hope') began to write for that paper at the height of the GREAT FAMINE. In 1848 *The Nation* carried a piece so inflammatory as to cause editor Charles Gavan DUFFY to be charged with sedition. Jane Elgee claimed authorship from the public gallery: 'I am the criminal who, as the author of the article that has just been read, should be in the dock. Any blame … belongs to me.' By this action she became a heroine among Nationalists. She married William WILDE in 1851 and had three children, Willie, Oscar (*see* WILDE, OSCAR) and Isola, who died tragically in 1867 at the age of nine. She became Dublin's best-known hostess, her salons in the Wildes' home at 1 Merrion Square attracting up to a hundred guests every week. However, she disapproved of the FENIANS: 'Heaven keep us from a Fenian republic!' she wrote. Jane Wilde moved to London after her husband's death, and to support herself published books of folklore and history during the 1880s. She died in London on 3 February 1896.

Spike, the[1]. The nickname for the South Dublin Union, a workhouse for paupers, unmarried mothers and abandoned babies. 'I'd rather die in the gutter than end my days in the Spike,' was a declaration commonly heard in Dublin. In 1667 Dublin Corporation laid foundations for a poorhouse in the site now occupied by St James's Hospital and in 1727 a foundling hospital was opened. This was closed and the buildings used as a workhouse – the South Dublin Union – from the early 19th century. Its infirmary gradually took on a wider role to cater not just for inmates but for the sick poor of south Dublin. During the 1916 EASTER RISING the South Dublin Union complex was occupied by rebels under the command of Éamonn CEANNT (the second-in-command was Cathal BRUGHA) and a nurse was accidentally killed during the fighting. After the foundation of the state and the closure of the workhouse the hospital developed as a municipal facility, its name changed to St Kevin's. The new St James's Hospital, comprising some of the original workhouse buildings and many modern additions, occupies a 60-acre (24-ha) site and is the largest hospital in the Republic of Ireland.

Spike, the[2]. A nickname for the Millennium Spire on Dublin's O'Connell Street. *See also* NELSON'S PILLAR.

SPIL. The Society for the Preservation of the Irish Language, one of the precursors of the GAELIC LEAGUE. Founded on 29 December 1876, its aims were to encourage the use of Irish and to promote a modern literature in the language. Its main committee members were David Comyn and P.W. JOYCE, and Archbishop MACHALE became its patron. Comyn left the society to found the GAELIC UNION after three years, bringing with him, significantly, Douglas HYDE.

Spin doctors. To an outsider, it might have seemed as if media experts, or spin doctors as they came to be called, were ruling Ireland in the 1980s and 1990s. Among the most celebrated were Fianna Fáil's P.J. MARA, Seán Duignan and Frank Dunlop, Labour's Fergus Finlay, and freelance media adviser Terry Prone. To spin doctors Ireland owes the improved media performance of politicians, but also the manipulation of all opinions, news and information for the benefit of the party involved.

'Spinning Wheel, The'. A love ballad by John Francis Waller (1809–94), made famous by Delia MURPHY.

> Slower – and slower – and slower the wheel
>   swings;
> Lower – and lower – lower the reel rings;
> Ere the reel and the wheel stopped their ringing
>   and moving,
> Through the grove the young lovers by moonlight
>   are roving.

Spit, the. A HIBERNO-ENGLISH colloquialism used to indicate resemblance, especially among family members: 'You're the spit of your father.' 'The dead spit' is used for emphasis.

Spoiled priest. An old term for a man who left the seminary before ordination, or (more loosely) who left the priesthood, thereby depriving his relatives and especially his mother of the honour of 'having a priest in the family'. It is difficult to exaggerate the anguish and shame this decision would bring on the ex-cleric's family, at a time of devotional fervour and a virtually all-powerful Catholic Church, especially in rural Ireland. The reforms of the Second Vatican Council and the gradual liberalization of 1960s society brought a more compassionate attitude to bear on priests and families alike, so that the term 'spoiled priest' is now rarely used.

Spoons. A percussion instrument in traditional music. Ordinary teaspoons or dessert spoons can be used to accompany traditional tunes on the fiddle or flute. The spoons are grasped between the fingers of one hand and tapped or banged on the back of the other hand or on the knee, leg or arm. In the hands of a skilful exponent, this unlikely percussion instrument can make quite a sound. The spoons are a relic of the days when Irish people had more music than instruments to play it.

Spreading the News. A short play by Lady GREGORY that with Yeats's *On Baile's Strand* opened the ABBEY THEATRE on 27 December 1904. It is a typically efficient Gregory comedy, dealing in a humorous way with the serious potential of rumour to make mischief in a small community. Jack Smith leaves his hayfork behind him at the fair of Cloon and his neighbour Bartley Fallon heads up the road after him to return it. The situation develops until Bartley is about to be arrested for murder by an officious magistrate, and he is saved only by Jack's reappearance. Lady Gregory first envisioned the play as a tragedy:

> I kept seeing as in a picture people by the roadside, and a girl passing to the market, gay and fearless. And then I saw her passing by the same place at evening, her head hanging, the heads of others turned from her, because of some sudden story that had arisen out of a chance word, and had snatched away her good name.

In fact her point is made very successfully in comedy, and the picture she paints of the lively community centred on Cloon is a necessary counterblast to the gloom of much of the Abbey's offerings. She makes good use of the KILTARTAN idiom she devised for her work (based upon the HIBERNO-ENGLISH spoken on her estate): 'Hadn't I enough care on me with that fork before this, running up and down with it like the swinging of a clock, and afeard to lay it down in any place!'

Spring, Dick (b.1950). Politician. He was born in Tralee, Co. Kerry, on 29 August 1950, son of Labour TD Dan Spring, to whose Dáil seat he succeeded in 1981, and educated at Trinity College Dublin and King's Inns. A versatile sportsman, he played both Gaelic football and hurling at county level, was thrice capped for the Irish rugby team in 1979 and famously played golf with US president Bill Clinton on the links at Ballybunion, Co. Kerry, during Clinton's second presidential visit in 1998. On his first day in the Dáil Spring was appointed a junior minister in the short-lived Fine Gael–Labour coalition (1981–2) led by Garret FITZGERALD and was catapulted into the leadership of his own party after the resignation of Michael O'Leary in 1982.

Spring is credited with reviving the fortunes of the Labour Party, which was associated with the successful candidature of Mary ROBINSON for the presidency in 1990 and achieved the impressive total of 33 Dáil seats in the 1992 general election. Spring served as tánaiste (deputy taoiseach) in the coalition government of 1982–7, and as minister for the environment (1982–3) and energy (1983–7). But it was as minister for foreign affairs in the 1992–4 Fianna Fáil–Labour coalition and in the RAINBOW COALITION coalition of 1994–7 that he is perceived as having made his greatest contribution, particularly in the protracted Anglo-Irish negotiations leading to the GOOD FRIDAY AGREEMENT of April 1998, during which his manifest political ability made him a popular ambassador for his country. US president Bill Clinton and he developed a cordial personal relationship, and Clinton's 1995 visit to Ireland was an important propaganda victory for the peacemakers (he made two further presidential visits, in 1998 and 2000).

The fortunes of the Labour Party declined catastrophically in the 1997 general election, and the poor showing of the party's candidate, Adi Roche, in that year's presidential election damaged Spring's credibility; shortly afterwards he resigned the leadership of the party, although he retained his Dáil seat. In the general election of 2002, to the dismay of his supporters and of many observers nationwide, he narrowly lost his North Kerry seat (which had come to be seen almost as a fiefdom of the Spring family) to Sinn Féin's Martin Ferris.

Squad, the. The nickname given to a hand-picked group of men chosen and trained by Michael COLLINS to assassinate undercover British agents in Dublin during the ANGLO-IRISH WAR of 1919–21; it was never intended as a bodyguard for Collins as was sometimes thought. In early 1919 Collins was made director of intelligence of the IRISH VOLUN-TEERS, and it was in the area of counter-intelligence that he made his greatest contribution to the war.

The establishment of the Squad was authorized by Richard MULCAHY, chief-of-staff of the Volunteers, and Cathal BRUGHA, minister for defence of the first Dáil. At first it comprised 7 men, but the numbers soon grew to 12; this gave rise to the ironic nickname 'the Twelve Apostles', which was used even after the group exceeded 12 in number. Most of the squad were friends and companions of Collins from his time in FRONGOCH; they were working men who were paid £4 10s a week to carry out assassinations on a full-time basis. Vinny Byrne, one of the squad, had a carpentry workshop near Dublin Castle which provided cover; Byrne appeared on Robert Kee's *Ireland: a Television History* in 1982 and spoke dispassionately about 'plugging' spies. 'Our chief function,' Bill Stapleton, another member, wrote in the *Capuchin Annual* of 1969, 'was the extermination of British spies and individuals.'

The Squad planned to assassinate the viceroy, Lord FRENCH, but never succeeded. They did, however, kill a number of important DMP (Dublin Metropolitan Police) detectives, for information on whose killing Dublin Castle offered substantial awards. Alan Bell, an elderly resident magistrate, was dragged from a tram in Ballsbridge and murdered in broad daylight in April 1920. On BLOODY SUNDAY 1920 eight different assassination teams from the Squad shot and killed 11 members of the CAIRO GANG in eight different locations at 9.00 a.m. precisely. The successes of this extremely efficient murder squad outraged Dublin Castle and the administration in London.

Squireen. A term of mild condescension formed by adding the HIBERNO-ENGLISH diminutive suffix '-een' to the English word 'squire'. It was applied to a growing class of small landowners who aped the manners of the gentry.

See also HALF-MOUNTED GENTLEMEN.

SSIA. Special savings incentive account, an investment scheme introduced by the FIANNA FÁIL government of 1997–2002 whereby the government would add 25% to the sums accrued over five years' regular savings in these special accounts, opened in 2001–2. It was estimated that one million Irish people took advantage of their government's generosity, in a scheme initiated in the run-up to the general election of 2002 and due to mature in time for the next general election in 2006–7.

Stab City. *See* LIMERICK.

Stack, Tommy (b.1945). Jockey and racehorse trainer. He was born in Moyvane, Co. Kerry, on 15 November 1945, grew up on the family farm and was educated at Mungret College in Limerick. Having failed to gain a place on the army equitation team he went to work for an insurance company in Dublin. At the age of 20 he had his first win as an amateur jockey for the trainer Bobby Renton of Ripon. His greatest achievement as a jockey was to ride RED RUM to victory in the 1977 Aintree Grand National. Later that year Stack had a serious paddock accident and retired from riding; he became a successful trainer, winning the English One Thousand Guineas at Newmarket with Las Meninas.

Stafford, Earl of. *See* WENTWORTH, THOMAS.

Stag. An old word meaning 'informer':

> The two worst informers against a private [illicit] distiller, barring a stag, are a smoke by day and a fire by night.
>
> WILLIAM CARLETON: in *Irish Penny Journal*

Stage coaches. The main system of long-distance public transport in the 18th and early 19th century, being superseded in the 1840s by the railways. Unlike BIANS, which plied between provincial towns (especially in the south), stage coaches ran on routes to and from Dublin. The first regular service between the capital and Belfast ran twice weekly from 1788 in coaches taking 12 passengers inside and 8 on top, paying respectively 27s.6d. and 15s. (plus a tip for the coachman) for a journey that in 1838 took

12 hours. By then the need for armed guards had ceased.

Stage-Irish. Stereotypical characterization of the Irish was in the past common in plays, especially in the 18th and 19th centuries. One of the earliest examples is the fiery explosives expert Captain Macmorris in Shakespeare's *Henry V* (III.ii) with his reiterated cries about his nation: 'What ish my Nation?' (An extra piece of black humour emerged from this character in productions of the play at the height of the Northern Ireland Troubles, with such telling lines as 'I would have blowed up the town, so Chrish save me, la! in an hour.')

At first the Irish characters were portrayed as savages or enemies of Britain, but as the 18th century progressed they were rendered slightly more sympathetically, although still characterized – even by such Irish dramatists as FARQUHAR, MACKLIN and SHERIDAN – as cards, comic servants and officers in foreign armies, a fair representation of the shifts to which the Irish were driven at the time.

> As for the Captain O'Cutters, O'Blunders, and Denis Bulgrudderies of the English stage, they never had any existence except in the imagination of those who were as ignorant of the Irish people as they were of their language and feeling.
>
> WILLIAM CARLETON (1794–1869): *Traits and Stories of the Irish Peasantry* (1830)

In time the reputation of the Irish for hard drinking, outrageous BROGUES and opportunism was mitigated. They were still capable of bulls (*see* IRISH BULL) and blunders, and their patriotism was as great as ever (*see* BRAVE IRISHMAN, THE). Yet the reputation of the Irish for charm and wit grew steadily, and with such writers as O'KEEFFE and BOUCICAULT they became positively winning. The necessarily puritanical attitudes of early 20th-century Nationalists made them regard any exuberance of action or language as suspect, and even SYNGE and O'CASEY came in for their share of criticism. The depiction of stage-Irishry endured in Hollywood films such as *The QUIET MAN* (1952) and *RYAN'S DAUGHTER* (1970).

Contemporary Irish stand-up comics and television comedy shows also draw on stock figures, such as the drunken priest Father Jack in *FATHER TED* but, free from the taint of racism, they do not cause offence to Irish people. With the current popularity in Britain of such playwrights as Martin MCDONAGH it would seem that a new kind of stage-Irishness, characterized by extreme violence of action and a minimum of wit has replaced the older sentimental kind.

> *Subtleman:* And how do you intend to live?
> *Teague:* By eating, dear joy, fen I can get it; and by sleeping when I can get none: 'tish the fashion in Ireland.
>
> GEORGE FARQUHAR (1667–1707): *The Twin-rivals* (1702)

See also IRISH JOKE.

Staigue Fort. An early Iron Age stone fort situated near Caherdaniel on the Iveragh peninsula of Co. Kerry. Similar in style to DÚN AENGHUS on Inis Mór in the Aran Islands and the Grianán of Aileach (*see* AILEACH) in Co. Donegal, it is one of the largest and finest of such forts in Ireland. A wall 4 m (13 ft) thick and up to 5.5 m (18 ft) high encloses an area 27.5 m (90 ft) in diameter, and the whole fort is surrounded by a large bank and ditch.

Stailc. The Irish word for an industrial strike, but used earlier for the jibbing of a horse or a fit of sulks in a child, often in the HIBERNO-ENGLISH form 'sthalk'.

Stalker, John (b.1939). Policeman. The former deputy chief constable of Greater Manchester, Stalker headed an inquiry into allegations of an official 'shoot-to-kill' policy by the police in Northern Ireland (centring on the deaths of six men killed by the RUC in a five-week period in 1982). The inquiry, which began in 1986, was abandoned in May 1986 after Stalker was accused of corruption and disciplinary offences, of which he was later cleared. In 1988 he published a book, entitled *Stalker*, about his experiences.

Stand. A location for business, especially retail: 'That's a fine stand you have there.'

Stand and Give Challenge. See MACMANUS, FRANCIS.

Stand idly by, we cannot. Frequently misquoted as 'We cannot stand idly by', the phrase 'The government of Ireland can no longer stand by' occurred in an address broadcast by the taoiseach, Jack LYNCH, on RTÉ television on the evening of 13 August 1969. The previous day, the traditional APPRENTICE BOYS march in Derry had predictably ended in sustained violence, culminating in the Battle of the BOGSIDE. Northern Nationalists, including MP Bernadette DEVLIN, fearing continued violence against Catholics, appealed to the Dublin government for help. At an emergency cabinet meeting, Republican hardliners like Neil BLANEY and Kevin BOLAND influenced Lynch's speech, to the consternation of Lynch's usual adviser on Northern Ireland, civil servant T.K. WHITAKER, who always advocated a conciliatory approach but who was on holiday at the time. What Lynch said was, 'The government of Ireland can no longer stand by and see innocent people injured and perhaps worse.' He added that the Irish government had asked its British counterpart to apply to the United Nations for a peacekeeping force to be sent to Northern Ireland, and said that the Irish army had been instructed to set up field hospitals near the Border in Co. Donegal to cater for casualties in Derry. The speech angered the British government, who at this period insisted that 'outsiders' in the Republic could have no role in internal British (Northern Ireland) affairs; the speech also outraged all Unionists, and created unrealistic hopes of intervention by the Republic among Northern Nationalists. Lynch backtracked in a more conciliatory speech in Tralee the following month, but there is no doubt that the events of August 1969, in which Lynch failed to control the more hawkish members of his cabinet, paved the way for the ARMS CRISIS of the following year and for the undermining of Lynch as taoiseach in the last year of his leadership by Fianna Fáil TDs such as Síle de Valera and Bill Loughnane playing the Republican card.

Stanford, Charles Villers (1852–1924). Composer. He was born in Dublin on 30 September 1852 and educated at Cambridge University and at Leipzig and Berlin. A prolific composer, he wrote operas, choral works, symphonies, chamber music and church music, but he is best remembered in Ireland for his six *Irish Rhapsodies*, which are based on native melodies. He also composed many settings for Irish poems: these are published in the collections *An Irish Idyll* (1901), *Cushendall* (1910) and *Songs from Leinster* (1914). Stanford was professor of composition at the Royal College of Music and professor of music at Cambridge University from the 1880s until his death, and proved himself to be a gifted teacher, numbering Ralph Vaughan Williams and Gustav Holst among his pupils. He died in London on 29 March 1924.

Stardust, the. A ballroom in Artane in north Dublin, scene of a fire on 14 February 1981 at a St Valentine's Day disco, in which 48 young people died. It was alleged that exits were locked or obstructed, preventing the escape to safety of all the many hundreds of dancers present, and the findings of the Barrington Compensation Tribunal of 1985 did not satisfy the families of the victims.

Starry Plough, the. The flag of the IRISH CITIZEN ARMY, first used by its strike force during the 1913 LOCKOUT and later in the 1916 EASTER RISING. The flag displayed the stars of the Plough constellation imposed on a representation of an actual ploughshare, with a sword at its front. The plough was coloured yellow with seven silver stars against a brown background. It gave Sean O'Casey, the historian of the ICA, the idea for the title of his finest play, *The PLOUGH AND THE STARS. The Plough and the Stars* has also been at different times the name of several Republican publications, in particular the monthly journal of the IRSP (*see* INLA).
See also TRICOLOUR.

Starve with cold. A common Ulster expression

in which the physical feelings of extreme cold are equated with those of extreme hunger, as in 'The poor wee things; when they came in from the snow they were starving wi' cold.'

Statement of Intent. The announcement made by W.B. YEATS, Lady GREGORY and Edward MARTYN after their decision to found an Irish National Theatre (*see* IRISH LITERARY THEATRE):

> We propose to have performed in Dublin, in the spring of every year certain Celtic and Irish plays, which will be written with a high ambition, and so build up a Celtic and Irish school of dramatic literature. We hope to find in Ireland an uncorrupted and imaginative audience trained to listen by its passion for oratory, and believe that our desire to bring upon the stage the deeper thoughts and emotions of Ireland will ensure for us a tolerant welcome, and that freedom to experiment which is not found in theatres of England, and without which no new movement in art or literature can succeed. We will show that Ireland is not the home of buffoonery and easy sentiment, as it has been represented, but the home of an ancient idealism. We are confident of the support of all Irish people, who are weary of misrepresentation, in carrying out a work that is outside all the political questions that divide.

Staters. Members of the FREE STATE army in the CIVIL WAR; a term of abuse from the point of view of Republicans.
See also IRREGULARS.

Stations. A feature of religious and social life in rural Ireland since the 18th century, in which Mass was said in each house in the station district in rotation (your turn might come every five or six years, depending on the number of houses in your district). It was an occasion of festivity as well as devotion: all the public areas of the house would be cleaned and painted; the parish priest would come, hear confessions, say Mass and collect his dues (for the stations were partly a fund-raising exercise); a sit-down meal would be provided to all comers throughout the day, and at nightfall a tierce (half barrel) of porter would be brought out and the musi-

cians would strike up for the dance. There was normally a spring station and an autumn station, times when the work of the farm would not be too onerous, and the stations provided a great opportunity for informal socializing for families living in isolated areas.

Stations of the Cross. A popular Catholic devotion, particularly in Lent, in which the faithful stop and pray ('do the stations') before 14 statues or plaques with images commemorating different stages of the Passion of Christ. The devotion originated with the Franciscan order in the 15th century.

Statue, the. The focal point of the city of Cork, comparable to An LÁR (and formerly NELSON'S PILLAR) in Dublin; it is the bronze statue of Father Theobald Mathew, the APOSTLE OF TEMPERANCE, by John Henry Foley (1817–74), which was erected by the citizens of Cork. It was unveiled in 1864 and stands at the northern end of Patrick Street, near St Patrick's Bridge. All city bus services radiate from 'the Statue', as did the trams they replaced, which ran from December 1898 to September 1931. A ribald anonymous ballad, 'The Boys of Fair Hill', opens with the lines:

> The smell on Patrick's Bridge is wicked
> How does Father Mathew stick it?

Statute of Kilkenny. *See* KILKENNY, STATUTE OF.

Staving. Very drunk.

Steam of his piss, the. Of someone who is very parsimonious it is said that 'he wouldn't give you the steam of his piss'.

Steele, Sir Richard (1672–1729). Essayist and playwright. He was born in Dublin in March 1672 and educated at Charterhouse, where he met his future colleague Joseph Addison (1672–1719), and at Merton College, Oxford, leaving without a degree to join the Life Guards and later the Coldstreams. A duel fought with another Irishman called Kelly, in which his opponent nearly died, had a profound effect upon his life, and he became a kind of public moralist, determined to make society more refined and to counter the coarseness of Restoration plays. The first aim he achieved by writing with Addison entertaining essays in the *Tatler* (1709–11) and the *Spectator* (1711–12) that tacitly approved good behaviour and contained subtle admonitions to moral improvement. He became for a while the licensee of Drury Lane, and his only successful play, *The Conscious Lovers* (1722), established a taste for sentimental drama. As with many of his class and insecure position, his fortunes depended on the approval of the government in power, and, though knighted by George I, he was never free from money worries. Financial troubles required that he leave London for Wales in 1724, and he died in Carmarthen on 1 September 1729.

> I am, dear Prue, a little in Drink but at all times
> Yr faithfull Husband
>   Letter to his wife (1708)

Steeplechasing (also called national hunt). A horse race with fences, now over a prepared course. It had its origin in Irish hunting, and is said to have been invented in north Co. Cork in 1752, when Edmund Blake challenged his friend Cornelius O'Callaghan to race from where they sat on their hunters at St John's Church in Buttevant to St Mary's in DONERAILE, the steeple of which they could see in the distance. The race lasted for more than 6 km (4 miles) – over ditches, a river and other obstacles – from church to church, steeple to steeple; hence such races became known as 'steeplechasing'. A cask of wine was the wager, suggested by O'Callaghan when he accepted Blake's challenge. It is not known who won the bet. Irish horses (such as ARKLE and ISTA-BRAQ), trainers and riders have since excelled at steeplechasing on Irish and British courses, especially in such races as the Hennessy Gold Cup (the Curragh), the Aintree Grand National and the Cheltenham Gold Cup.

Stelfox, Dawson (b.1958). Mountaineer, the first Irishman to stand on top of Mount Everest. He was born in Belfast on 24 March 1958 and

educated at INST and Queen's University Belfast, qualifying as an architect. He has climbed extensively in many countries, and is one of three Irishmen qualified to act as a professional mountain guide around the world. He was the leader of an Irish expedition that left for Everest on 17 March 1993, and was the only member to reach the summit, which he did via the North Ridge on 27 May.

Step dance. A type of dance nowadays executed mainly for competition by male or female dancers, solo or in groups. Step dances are mostly to traditional reel, jig or hornpipe tunes. An Coimisíun le Rincí Gaelacha (the Irish Dances Commission), which was established in 1929, now dominates step-dance teaching and competitions on a worldwide basis (Irish step dancing is especially popular and well organized in the USA), although there are other dance bodies. The All-Ireland Championships, organized by An Coimisíun le Rincí Gaelacha since 1933, last for six days, with 110 hours of dancing. The World Championship, held in Ireland, can attract up to 2000 dancers.
See also CÉILÍ DANCES; DANCE COSTUMES; DANCING MASTERS; RIVERDANCE; SET DANCES.

Stephen D. A play by Hugh LEONARD, quarried out of Joyce's STEPHEN HERO and A PORTRAIT OF THE ARTIST AS A YOUNG MAN, which introduced the wayward character of Stephen DEDALUS to a wider audience. It was first staged as part of the Dublin Theatre Festival in 1962, with Norman Rodway in the chief part.

Stephen Dedalus. *See* DEDALUS, STEPHEN.

Stephen Hero. An earlier and much longer version of James JOYCE's A PORTRAIT OF THE ARTIST AS A YOUNG MAN. It was written 1904–7. Much of it was destroyed, but a surviving portion, corresponding to the last section of *A Portrait*, was published in 1944.

Stephens, James (1880–1950). Poet, novelist and short-story writer. He was born in Dublin, although other details of his early life are obscure. His novels include *The Charwoman's*

Daughter (1912), *The Crock of Gold* (1912) and *Etched in Moonlight* (1928), in all of which knowingness, verbal pyrotechnics, quirky humour, patriotism and fantasy are headily mixed. *The Insurrection in Dublin* (1916) is an eye-witness account of the EASTER RISING. Always a brilliant talker and possessing a distinctive voice, Stephens recorded many talks for the BBC on poets, poetry and reminiscence, and his American tours were a great success. His poetry is as quirky as his prose, his versions of the Gaelic poets in *Reincarnations* (1918) being particularly effective. His poems 'The Snare', 'The Shell' and 'Danny Murphy' usually find their way into children's anthologies.

Stephens, James Kenneth (1824–1901). FENIAN and founder of the IRB. He was born in Kilkenny and trained as an engineer. He was a supporter of YOUNG IRELAND and acted as aide-de-camp to Smith O'Brien in the Ballingarry Rising of 1848 (*see* WIDOW MCCORMICK'S CABBAGE PATCH). Reported dead, he escaped arrest and fled to Paris, where he met John O'Mahony (who was to become the founder of the American Fenians) and was strongly influenced by French radicalism. In 1856 he returned to Ireland, and for the next two years travelled all over the country with the aim of establishing a secret organization, earning the nickname 'the Wandering Hawk', the Irish form of which, *An Seabhach Siúlach*, was anglicized to form his nickname 'Shook' or 'Mr Shook'.

On the receipt of a small financial contribution from the Irish-Americans, Stephens founded the Irish Republican Brotherhood (originally called the Irish Revolutionary Brotherhood) on 17 March 1858. He became 'head centre' of what by then had become known as the Fenians, and *de facto* leader of separatist Irish opinion, and in 1863, along with Jeremiah O'DONOVAN ROSSA and John O'LEARY, established an influential newspaper, *The Irish People*, which was suppressed in 1865. Stephens was arrested, but later escaped from Richmond Prison.

Stephens's relationship with John O'Mahony

and the American Fenians deteriorated, and in 1866, while he was on a visit to New York, he was deposed as head centre of the Fenians because of his postponement of the rising he had promised for that year. He lived in Paris until 1885, and thereafter in Switzerland until, after the intercession of PARNELL, he was eventually permitted to return to Ireland in 1891. His only public appearance thereafter was at the centenary celebrations of the Rebellion of 1798, organized by the Supreme Council of the IRB.

Stephen's Green Club. A gentlemen's club on the north side of St Stephen's Green in Dublin, which opened in 1837.

Stepmother's breath. A politically incorrect term for a cold, biting gust of wind.

Sterne, Laurence (1713–68). Novelist. He was born in Clonmel, Co. Tipperary, of an Irish mother and an English soldier father and spent much of his early childhood with Irish relatives. He was educated at Cambridge and took holy orders in 1738, acquiring a living in Sutton-on-the-Forest, Yorkshire. He is best known for *The Life and Opinions of Tristram Shandy*, which appeared in successive volumes (1759–67) and, despite some negative reactions from critics such as Dr Johnson, became immediately popular. *The Sermons of Yorick* (Yorick being a character in *Tristram Shandy*), published 1760–9, were also extremely popular. Sterne, who had suffered from tuberculosis since he was a young man, made several trips to France and Italy (1762–6), on which he based *A Sentimental Journey* (1768). He died – of pleurisy and in debt – in London. Sterne's novels show elements of subversive comic genius influenced by Swift (*see* DEAN, THE), and his style is seen as a forerunner of the stream-of-consciousness practised by James JOYCE.

> Writing, when properly managed (as you may be sure I think mine is) is but a different name for conversation.
>
> *Tristram Shandy*, book 2, chapter 11

Steward of Christendom, The. A one-man play

(1995) by the Dublin-born novelist and play-wright Sebastian Barry (b.1955), in which a former head of the DMP (Dublin Metropolitan Police) remembers his life as he lies in a lunatic asylum. When it was first staged with Donal MCCANN as the policeman it was regarded as one of the most significant Irish productions of the 1990s.

Stewart, Charles. *See* I'LL PUT YOU ALL ON BOARD AGAIN!

Stickies, the[1]. The name by which the Official IRA came to be known after the split that generated the Provisional IRA (*see* IRA). At the ARMY CONVENTION in 1969 a militarist wing anxious to use the erupting violence to begin a final ARMED STRUGGLE and adamant about a policy of ABSTENTIONISM broke away to form the Provisional IRA, which rapidly became the dominant group. The Officials – more concerned eventually to engage in radical but constitutional politics – suspended military operations in May 1972 after concluding that such events as the murder of Senator Jack Barnhill, the ALDERSHOT BOMB that killed civilians in England and the murder of Catholic Ranger William BEST while home on leave in Derry weakened rather than generated support for a continued armed struggle. The origin of the nickname is not clear; one suggestion is that the Officials' Easter lilies, worn in commemoration of the 1916 EASTER RISING, are adhesive rather than fastened by pins.
See also WORKERS' PARTY.

Stickies, the[2]. The nickname of the Royal Irish Rifles (later the Royal Ulster Rifles), supposed to be an allusion to a parade of rifle-green uniformed soldiers looking like a row of factory chimneys or stacks – the nickname may originally have been 'Stackies'. They have been part of the Royal Irish Rangers since 1968.

Stick of the meat, the. The rafter in the kitchen from which flitches of cured bacon would be hung until needed for the table.

Stiletto in the Ghetto. A nickname for the Millennium Spire, which stands on the site of NELSON'S PILLAR.

Stirabout. A common HIBERNO-ENGLISH word for oatmeal porridge, the name taken from the action required to make it.

Stocious. One of many words for 'intoxicated', used throughout Ireland.

Stoker, Abraham (Bram). *See* UNDEAD, THE.

Stolen child. *See* CHANGELING.

Stoop Down Low Party. *See* SDLP.

Stop-the-clock. A pessimistic person, always expecting the worst, deriving from the custom of stopping the clock in the house at the hour of death and restarting it only after the funeral of the deceased.

Stormont. The suburb of Belfast where the NORTHERN IRELAND Parliament Buildings were opened on 16 November 1932. Its mile-long approach drive is dominated at its end by a belligerent statue of Sir Edward CARSON. It houses the Northern Ireland Assembly (set up by the GOOD FRIDAY AGREEMENT), when it is not in suspension. The term was used as shorthand for the government and parliament of Northern Ireland before its suspension on 24 March 1972.

Strabane. A market town in Co. Tyrone about 8.5 km (14 miles) south of Derry, where the River Foyle becomes the Mourne. It was the birthplace of Brian O'Nolan (*see* O'BRIEN, FLANN) on 5 October 1911, and it was in Strabane that John Dunlap, the man who printed the American Declaration of Independence, learned his trade (the elegant bow-fronted façade that once belonged to the printer's works may still be seen). The hymnodist Cecil Frances ALEXANDER lived in Milltown House from 1833 to 1850.

Straight and Narrow Path, The. A satirical novel (1958) by the English-born writer Honor TRACY, the epigraph of which was taken from a sermon that urged the congregation to 'stay on the straight and narrow path between good and evil'.

Strand. A word commonly used for 'beach' and as a translation for the Irish *trá* or *tráigh*. In the DINGLE PENINSULA *Tráigh an Fhíona* is 'wine strand'.

Strap. A vigorous and well-built young woman might be described as 'a fine strap of a girl'. The Irish word *strapaire* can also be applied to men: in Máire MHAC AN TSAOI's poem, 'Jack', the young man from west Kerry, is described as '*strapaire fionn sé troithe ar aoirde*' ('a fair well-built young man of six feet').

Strawboys. Uninvited but usually welcome guests, who came in disguise to a wedding or house party wearing a headpiece and cape fashioned from ropes of straw. They were called 'soppers' in Co. Limerick. A captain gave orders to a company of perhaps ten young men, identifying them by numbers in order to retain anonymity. When the strawboys came in they would wish a health to the bride and groom, and the captain would ask for a drink for him and his men. They would then dance a set, or two of them would dance a hornpipe on a flag or on a door taken off its hinges for the purpose. Women of the party were very keen to dance with the strawboys in order to have the fun of trying to identify them. Finally one of the strawboys might sing a song or play a tune on an instrument. The strawboys left the gathering, still anonymous, when this was done. It was said that strawboys did not so much fear being identified as being set alight by a mischievous or drunken guest with a lighted splinter. At SHROVETIDE strawboys were kept busy going from wedding to wedding. The phrase 'to go strawing' was also used.
See also GO BOYS.

Strawkawling (Irish *strácáil*, 'to drag along'). A HIBERNO-ENGLISH term for 'struggling on', 'muddling through'. The term might be used in reply to a greeting, as in 'I'm strawkawling away.' There is also the Irish phrase *ag strácáil leis an saol*, 'striving', 'struggling with life'.

Streel or **streeler.** *See* STREELISH.

Streelish (Irish *sraoilleach*, 'slatternly'). An adjective used commonly in HIBERNO-ENGLISH to indicate a person (often a woman) who is untidy or unkempt in appearance. Such a person is also called a 'streel' (Irish *sraoille*) or less commonly a 'streeler' or 'streeleen'. The word is, however, not always gender-specific: in J.M. Synge's *The Playboy of the Western World* (1907), Old Mahon describes Christy as 'an ugly young streeler with a murderous gob on him'.

Streepach (Irish *stríopach* or *striapach*). A HIBERNO-ENGLISH word, literally meaning 'whore' or 'woman of doubtful virtue'. The word is also used as a general term of abuse or exasperation.

Street. In northern parts of the country the yard or drive around a house is called a street: thus, 'front street' and 'back street'. The phrase 'the dogs on the street', which connotes those who are the last to know ('The dogs on the street know that politician is taking bribes'), derives from this.

Stripping. The last drop of milk in a hand-milked cow; it was called the 'stripping' because of the action of the hands at the end of milking. This was the richest of all the milk, and was often kept for COLOURING the tea.

Stroaker, the. *See* GREATRAKES, VALENTINE.

Stroke¹. The word used in HIBERNO-ENGLISH for an action, often illicit or of doubtful legality or morality, that will benefit the doer. Politicians 'pull strokes' by opening new roads or hospitals in an election year, by forging dubious alliances or by organizing referendums to distract the electorate from other issues. Many people would see Irish politics mainly as the art of pulling strokes, and cognoscenti regard Charles HAUGHEY as being the finest stroke-puller of all. The phrase may also be used humorously or ironically: when Brendan BEHAN faints during his Confirmation ceremony, thereby missing the Bishop's PLEDGE, his father is pleased:

He said this was a master stroke, and showed real presence of mind.

'The Confirmation Suit', in *Brendan Behan's Island* (1962)

Stroke². An appetite, a term usually heard in combination with the adjective 'great', as in: 'She has a great stroke.'

Stroke City. A solution to the problem of the naming of Ulster's second city devised by radio personality Gerry Anderson, as recorded in his book of memoirs *Surviving in Stroke City* (1999): 'I ... took to naming the city Derry Stroke Londonderry until ultimately settling for the more natural user-friendly "Stroke City".'

Strokestown Park. A Palladian mansion in Strokestown, Co. Roscommon, designed by Richard CASTLE; it was the family home of the Packenham Mahon family until 1979. It was built by Thomas Mahon MP (1701–82) on lands that had been granted to his grandfather, Nicholas, for his support of the crown in what has become known as the TUDOR RECONQUEST. In 1979 it was sold to a local company, the Westward Group, who refurbished it and opened it to the public in 1987. The house retains virtually all of its original furnishings. The Famine Museum, situated in the stable ward, displays original documents and letters relating to the years of the famine on the Strokestown Park Estate, when Major Denis Mahon owned the property. The museum is twinned with a historic site at Grosse Ile in Quebec, where large numbers of Irish emigrants came ashore during the Famine. The park also includes an extensive walled pleasure garden, which was restored and opened to the public in 1997; this has the longest herbaceous border in Ireland.

Strongbow. The nickname of Richard fitz Gilbert, alias Richard de Clare (d.1176), chief of the Anglo-Norman invaders of Ireland. Sometime Earl of Pembroke, he led an army of Welsh adventurers (with the watchful approval of HENRY II) to re-establish the deposed king of Leinster, Dermot MACMURROUGH (Diarmait Mac Murchada). Strongbow arrived in August 1170 and soon and bloodily took Waterford with the aid of Raymond le Gros (*see* CREEKE OF BAGGANBUN, THE). Strongbow and McMurrough's daughter Aoife were married, as part of the deal, and having successfully taken and held Dublin against Rory O'Connor (Ruadrí Ua Conchobair) (*see* LAST HIGH KING, THE) was declared heir to the kingdom of Leinster. (The marriage became the subject of a huge imaginative painting by Daniel MACLISE.) When Dermot died in 1171 Strongbow succeeded him – not without opposition from the English king. Accommodation with Henry was finally reached, and he was restored to his English and Welsh titles. He died in 1176 and is buried in CHRIST CHURCH CATHEDRAL in Dublin.

Strumpet City. The first novel (1969) in a Dublin trilogy by James PLUNKETT, set in Dublin in the period 1907–14 and having as its main theme the effect on workers and their families of the industrial unrest that culminated in the 1913 LOCKOUT. The workers at Morgan's foundry, including the foreman Bob Fitzpatrick, strike in support of their demand for overtime payments, supported by coal-carters and transport workers, led by James LARKIN. The poverty and hunger among the strikers' families is vividly described. When the strike is broken, Fitzpatrick, in order to feed his children, enlists in the British army to fight in the First World War.

Stuart, Francis. *See* BLACK LIST SECTION H.

Stump (Irish *stumpa*). A stubborn or obdurate person. The word is most commonly used in HIBERNO-ENGLISH in expressions such as 'stump of a fool' and 'ignorant stump'.

Suarach. The Irish word for 'mean', 'despicable', and also for 'runt'. The word is in use in HIBERNO-ENGLISH, particularly in the west of Ireland.

Substitution of service. A 19th-century means of serving a process by posting it on a church or other public place instead of by delivering it personally.

Sucky. A word for a suckling calf; also a pet name for a cow.

Súgán. An Irish word for rope made by hand from straw and used to tie haycocks and make the seats of chairs. *Súgán* chairs were part of the furnishings of every rural kitchen.

Sugar Island. An area in Newry, Co. Down, so called because in the 18th century the town was a port (on a canal from Carlingford Lough) for produce including West Indian sugar.

Suibhne Geilt. A king who in the Christianized myth is cursed by St RONAN after he goes mad at the Battle of Moira, Co. Down. Suibhne (anglicized as Sweeney) throws a spear at the saint while he is measuring out the bounds of a new church. The saint imposes upon him many characteristics of a bird, so, although he retains human form, he perches on the branches of trees and utters birdlike cries. Suibhne lives naked or scantily clothed in the wilderness for many years, lamenting his fate but celebrating also the beauty of nature and carrying on a dialogue with a Scottish madman he meets on the way. Eventually, after travelling throughout Ireland, he arrives in the monastic settlement of St Moling (Mullins in Co. Carlow) where he ends his life, and is buried in the graveyard there. Sweeney is the archetypal wild man, a visionary divested of the trappings of society. Suibhne Geilt could be translated into English as 'Sweeney Astray', the title Seamus HEANEY used for his 1983 version of *Buile Shuibhne*, the 12th-century account of the tale. Other writers who have used the story include Flann O'BRIEN in *AT SWIM-TWO-BIRDS* (1939) and Joseph O'Connor in *The Salesman* (1997).

Suir. A river in Munster, one of the THREE SISTERS. The Suir, which is 160 km (99 miles) long, rises on SLIEVENAMON in Co. Tipperary and flows south by Thurles and Cahir, then east by Clonmel and Carrick-on-Suir, before joining the BARROW to form Waterford Harbour. As the poet Edmund SPENSER put it in *The Faerie Queen* (1590):

> ... the gentle Shure that making way
> By sweet Clonmell, adornes rich Waterford.
>   IV, xi, 43

Suitable places, ready students. *See* AACHEN.

Sullivan, Anne. *See* MIRACLE WORKER, THE.

Sullivan, Barry. *See* 2500 RICHARD IIIS.

Sullivan, John L[aurence]. *See* BOSTON STRONG BOY, THE.

Sunday schools. Established in Ireland, particularly in the province of Ulster, in the first half of the 19th century by benevolent Anglican-controlled organizations such as the Hibernian Sunday School Society (established 1809), the Sunday schools provided the poorer classes with scripture lessons but also with social outings, picnics, parades and opportunities for basic education. They were, however, essentially a means of proselytizing, an element of what is known as the SECOND REFORMATION.

Sunningdale Agreement. *See* WHITELAW, WILLIAM.

Sunningdale for slow learners. *See* MALLON, SEAMUS.

Surrender and Regrant (1541–3). An important and far-reaching Tudor instrument of policy, by which legal control was exercised over hitherto recalcitrant Gaelic rulers: the kingdom of Ireland was established (1541); the Gaelic lord in question then *surrendered* his lands and recognized the king, renouncing his Gaelic title and promising to promote English law and custom; the lord received in turn an English title and a charter (or *grant*) of the lands of his clan. Lands granted by the crown could be confiscated for treason. For some Gaelic lords the attraction of the policy was that it gave them, in theory, control of the lands of the whole clan and the chance of applying the English system of primogeniture instead of Gaelic succession. The greatest propaganda success of this initial phase of Surrender and Regrant was the elevation of The

O'Neill to Earl of Tyrone in London with much public ceremony in 1542. Although apparently a conciliatory policy, it was in reality an instrument of the TUDOR RECONQUEST, and attempts by English lord deputies to impose it provoked some of the major conflicts of the period.

Sutherland, Peter (b.1946). Lawyer. He was born in Dublin on 25 April 1946 and educated at Gonzaga, University College Dublin and the King's Inns, where he was called to the Bar. He practised at the Bar (1979–81) and served as Irish attorney-general (1981–4). From 1985 to 1989 he was Ireland's commissioner in Europe, his main portfolio being competition policy. He was director-general of GATT (General Agreement on Tariffs and Trade; 1993–5) and has been director-general of the World Trade Organization (WTO) since January 1995.

SVP. *See* ST VINCENT DE PAUL, SOCIETY OF.

Swaddler. A Dublin word for 'Protestant', or more precisely 'Methodist', in use from the mid-18th century. The term was supposed to have come from the reaction of a Catholic priest hearing a Methodist preach to the text: 'And she brought forth her first-born son, and wrapped him in swaddling clothes and laid him in a manger.' (Luke 2:7).

> Last week I saw a marching band,
> Small Protestants in grey clothes, well-fed pairs
> Led by a Bible teacher …
> Suddenly Catholic joylets
> Darted from alleys, raggedy cherubs that dared
>   them:
> 'Luk, feckin' bastards, swaddlers, feckin'
>   bastards!'
>   AUSTIN CLARKE (1896–1974): 'Street Game', in
>   *Flight to Africa* (1963)

Swallow. A HIBERNO-ENGLISH word denoting the capacity to consume liquid, particularly but not exclusively alcohol, normally used with 'great': 'He has a great swallow.'

Swan, Charlie (b.1968). National-hunt jockey. He was born in Co. Tipperary and is best known for having ridden the celebrated steeplechaser ISTABRAQ to victory in three Champion Hurdles in Cheltenham, beginning in 1998. Twice leading jockey at the Cheltenham Festival, he has ridden more national-hunt winners in Ireland than any other jockey, although victory in both the Cheltenham Gold Cup and the Grand National eluded him. He retired from racing in 2003 in order to concentrate on training horses.

Swanskin. The fine, nappy commercial flannel, distinguished from the coarse heavy homemade kind.

Swarry. An anglicization of the French *soirée*, meaning 'party', 'evening gathering'. Like the concept, the word now seems dated.

Swastika Laundry. A Dublin laundry with the swastika as its trademark. The vans tended to produce a certain cognitive dissonance in British visitors seeking peace and unrationed meat during the Second World War.

Sweaters. *See* PINKINDINDIES.

Sweeney, Mad. *See* SUIBHNE GEILT.

Sweeny, Manus (d.1798). A priest educated in the COLLÈGE DES IRLANDAIS in Paris who acted as interpreter for the French forces under General Hoch who landed at Killala, Co. Mayo, in 1798. He was hanged in Newport, Co. Mayo, for his part in the rebellion.

Sweep, the. *See* IRISH HOSPITALS SWEEPSTAKES.

Sweetie. A book (1999) by the journalist Kevin O'Connor detailing the long-running (27-year) affair (and many expensive dinners in Dublin's Le Coq Hardi restaurant) between Charles J. HAUGHEY and journalist Terry Keane. Before the book was published, in a pre-emptive bid to show that the affair was based on real and mutual love, Keane appeared on the *The LATE LATE SHOW* on 14 May 1999 and revealed all. Although the affair had been common knowledge in political and media circles in Dublin for many years and had been the subject of frequent *SCRAP SATURDAY* sketches, and although Keane had been wont to refer in code ('Sweetie') to her lover in her *Sunday Independent* 'Keane Edge' column, confirmation of the affair caused the embattled Haughey to sink even further in public estimation. After Keane left the *Sunday Independent* she wrote a series of articles about the affair for *The Sunday Times*.

'Sweet Kingswilliamstown'. A ballad about a SLIABH LUACHRA village, Ballydesmond, Co. Cork, which was formerly called Kingwilliamstown. It was built as a model village in 1832 during the reign of William IV (1765–1837). Just over a century later, in 1938, the inhabitants decided to change its name to Ballydesmond, chosen because of the area's association with Gerald, 14th Earl of Desmond (1533–83) who is said to have taken refuge in a hut in the nearby townland of Meneganine during the DESMOND REBELLION of 1579–83. The ballad was written by a local man, Danny Buckley (d.1918), who survived the sinking of the *Titanic* only to be killed in France on the last day of the First World War in November 1918:

My bonny barque bounced light and free
Across the surging foam,
Which bears me far from Innisfail,
To seek a foreign home.
A lonely exile driven neath
Misfortune's coldest frown,
From my loved home and cherished friends
In dear Kingwilliamstown.

(INNISFAIL is a poetic name for Ireland.)

Sweetness and light. The superior stance of the bees (the ancient authors) over the spiders (the moderns) in the preface to *The Battle of the Books* (1704) by Jonathan Swift (*see* DEAN, THE):

Instead of dirt and poison we have chosen to fill our hives with honey and wax; thus furnishing mankind with the two noblest of things, which are sweetness and light.

Swift, Carolyn. *See* PIKE THEATRE; ROSE TATTOO AFFAIR, THE.

Swift, Jonathan. *See* DEAN, THE.

Swim-two-birds (Middle Irish, *Snamh Dá Én*). A site on the right bank of the Shannon opposite CLONMACNOISE, where SUIBHNE GEILT rested. Swim-two-birds is mentioned in the *BOOK OF ARMAGH*:

Venit ergo Patricius sanctus per alveum flumnis Sinnae per Vadum Duorum Avium (Snám Dá Én) in Campum Ai.
(So St Patrick came along the basin of the River Shannon through the Ford of Two Birds to the plain of Ai.)

It supplied Flann O'BRIEN with the title of his first novel, *AT SWIM-TWO-BIRDS*.

Swiss Cottage. A cottage *orné* on the banks of the River Suir about a mile from Cahir in Co. Tipperary, built in the early 1800s as a summer refuge by the Butler family (*see* CAHIR CASTLE), who had their townhouse in the town's square. The design was by the famous Regency architect, John Nash. The cottage features a graceful spiral staircase and exquisitely decorated rooms. The wallpaper in the salon manufactured by the Dufour factory was one of the first commercially produced Parisian wallpapers. The cottage has been restored and is now a tourist attraction.

Synge, J[ohn] M[illington] (1871–1909). Dramatist and poet. He was born of evangelical Dublin parents on 16 April 1871 but rejected all religion while still a young man. Instead he pursued a kind of extreme life, as if forewarned of its relative shortness. Though often ill as a child Synge became a great walker and cyclist, acquiring an intimate knowledge of the rainy glens of Co. Wicklow. While taking a leisurely pass degree at Trinity College Dublin he learned Irish, which proved useful when, after a period of fashionable dilettantism in Paris he elected (whether because of prompting by YEATS or otherwise) to spend five summers (1898–1902) in the ARAN ISLANDS, especially Inis Meáin. The immediate result was the matchless prose work *The ARAN ISLANDS* (1907) and the acquisition of both the raw material and the appropriate linguistic register for his plays.

As well being the most significant dramatist

of the IRISH LITERARY REVIVAL, Synge is also the author of sharply satiric and violent verse, mitigated by a few love lyrics written for Mollie ALLGOOD (1887–1952), who played PEGEEN MIKE in his finest play *The PLAYBOY OF THE WESTERN WORLD* (1907). A collection of travel sketches, written mainly for the *Manchester Guardian* with appropriate illustrations by Jack B. YEATS, the poet's brother, was published as *In Wicklow and West Kerry*, two years after his death from Hodgkin's disease. Yeats dubbed him 'that rooted man' in the poem 'The Municipal Gallery Revisited' (1937), adding to his earlier view: 'that slow man, that meditative man' ('Coole Park, 1929').

Lord, confound this surly sister,
Blight her brow with blotch and blister,

Cramp her larynx, lung, and liver,
In her guts a galling give her.
Let her live to earn her dinners
In Mountjoy with seedy sinners:
Lord, this judgement quickly bring
And I'm your servant, J.M. Synge
 'The Curse' ('To a sister of the author's who disapproved of *The Playboy*')

See also CHINK IN THE FLOOR; *DEIRDRE OF THE SORROWS*; *IN THE SHADOW OF THE GLEN*; *RIDERS TO THE SEA*; *TINKER'S WEDDING, THE*; *WELL OF THE SAINTS, THE*.

Synge's Chair. A hollow cliffside rock in Inis Meáin in the ARAN ISLANDS, where the playwright J.M. SYNGE is reputed to have sat to look at the sea.

Synod of Whitby. *See* WHITBY, SYNOD OF.

T

Taaffe, Pat. *See* ARKLE.

Tablet, The. A Roman Catholic periodical founded in 1840 by an English convert, Frederick
Lucas (1812–55), who as MP for Co. Meath
was a prominent member of the POPE'S BRASS
BAND. The journal, whose offices Lucas moved
to Dublin in 1850, has always maintained
its independence, not necessarily reflecting
the views of the institutional church. Lucas
himself successfully appealed to Rome against
Cardinal CULLEN's ban on clerical involvement
in politics.

The *Tablet*'s most charismatic editor in mod-
ern times was Douglas Woodruff (1897–1978).
In 'Talking at Random', a weekly causerie, he
suggested that *Gloriana* (1955), the opera about
Elizabeth I commissioned from Sir Benjamin
Britten for coronation year, should be called
Orgy and Bess; he also memorably referred
to the contraception controversy surrounding
Pope Paul VI's encyclical *Humanae Vitae* as
the 'Grim Pill's Progress'.

Tabula tantum (Latin, 'the width of a table').
The riposte made by the *doctus* John Scottus
ERIUGENA (*c*.810–77) to the gibe of the Holy
Roman Emperor CHARLES THE BALD (823–
77): '*Quid distat inter Scottum et sotum?*'
('What is the difference between an Irishman
and a drunkard?').

Taca. An organization (*taca* is the Irish word
for 'support') established in 1966, at the end of
the LEMASS era, to formalize business support
for FIANNA FÁIL under the chairmanship of
Desmond MacGreevy (1924–2002), and associated primarily with Charles HAUGHEY and
Donogh O'Malley. For a donation of £100
a year, 500 selected businesspeople were invited to a dinner in a Dublin hotel where they
might rub shoulders with cabinet ministers.
While there was no overt selling of favours, it
was understood that ministers would look
favourably on the interests of the businessmen
involved. At the first Taca dinner, enthusiastically organized by Haughey, all the cabinet
attended and Haughey allocated one minister
per table. Kevin BOLAND, at the time minister
for local government, noticed that everyone at
his table was connected with the construction
industry.

When the existence of Taca became known
in early 1967, there was public disquiet at the
too-close identification of Fianna Fáil with
business interests, especially with builders and
property developers, but Taca was robustly
defended by Haughey, by Donogh O'Malley
and even by Jack LYNCH himself. It was in
relation to Taca that George Colley made his
'LOW STANDARDS IN HIGH PLACES' speech in
May 1967. Eventually, at the end of 1968, the
compositon of Taca was changed when it was
announced that anyone could join, but since

that defeated the purpose of the scheme, it quietly faded away.

Taca is of particular interest, given the later history of Charles Haughey, and because it was the first time in the history of the state that a political party systematically sought donations from businesspeople.

Tack. A word meaning 'very little', 'none': 'She didn't take a tack of notice of me.'

Tadhg an dá thaobh (Irish, 'Tadhg of both sides'; Tadhg is the Irish version of Timothy). Someone who tries to satisfy both sides, a double dealer, a position frequently assumed by leaders of Gaelic Ireland and the OLD ENGLISH until the end of the TUDOR RECONQUEST.

Taibhdhearc, An. A small Irish-language theatre in Galway, founded in 1927 by Séamus Ó Béirne of Oranmore and Liam Ó Briain, professor of French at University College Galway. The latter managed to obtain a small grant from the government and to persuade Micheál Mac Liammóir to play the lead in his own play *Diarmaid and Gráinne* for its opening production. Siobhán MCKENNA, the distinguished Irish actress, began her career there. The name of the theatre, which has as its elements the Irish words for spirit and vision, is pronounced 'tive-yark'. The premises were modernized in 1988.

Taig. *See* TEAGUE.

Tailor and Ansty, The. A book (1942) by Eric CROSS, in which he recreates the conversation and SEANCHAS of the Tailor Buckley, along with the bawdily anarchic interruptions of Ansty, his wife. Tim Buckley (1863–1945, born in Kilgarvan, Co. Kerry) and his wife Anastasia (1872–1947) lived near GOUGANE BARRA in west Cork. In his introduction to the second edition (1948), Frank O'CONNOR describes the effect of the banning of *The Tailor and Ansty* by the Irish Censorship Board in 1942 for 'being in its general tendency indecent', and the reaction of the couple to three visiting priests who terrorized the Tailor into burning a copy of the book in his own fire. Once it

became available again (it was banned for ten years) it became a classic of folkloric literature. The Tailor's motto '*Glac bog an saol agus glacfaidh an saol bog thú*' ('take life easy and life will be easy on you') enabled him to weather the agitation, but it certainly shortened Ansty's life. Her death is the subject of one of Sean O'FAOLAIN's tenderest stories, 'The Silence of the Valley' (1947).

Éamon KELLY and his actress wife Maura O'Sullivan played Tim Buckley and Ansty for the ABBEY THEATRE, a production adapted successfully for RTÉ television. In 1978 *Seanchas an Táilliúra* ('the tailor's stories'), edited by Aindrias Ó Muimhneacháin, was published; the *seanchas* in this book was collected by Seán Ó Cróinín of the IRISH FOLKLORE COMMISSION in 1942.

> One clear star above the mountain wall gleamed.
> Seeing it her eyebrow floated upward softly for sheer joy
>   'Yes,' she said quietly, 'it will be another grand day – tomorrow.'
>   And her eyebrows sank, very slowly, like a falling curtain.
>   'The Silence of the Valley'

Tailors' Hall. A handsome and historic building in Back Lane, near CHRIST CHURCH CATHEDRAL in Dublin. It has been the national headquarters of An TAISCE since 1985. It is the last surviving guildhall and thought to be the oldest surviving large house in Dublin. The tailors came to the site in 1706, and in 1798 it was commandeered as an army barracks; in 1820 it was turned into a debtors' court. In 1792 a series of meetings organized by the CATHOLIC COMMITTEE was held in Tailors' Hall, and it came to be known as the 'Back Lane Parliament'. An upstairs hall is now named in honour of Wolfe TONE, secretary of the Catholic Committee. The Society of UNITED IRISHMEN also held meetings there until 1792. The attic floor has deep window recesses, and legend has it that Lord Edward FITZGERALD hid in these attics when attempting to escape arrest in 1798.

Tailteann Games. *See* AONACH TAILTEANN.

Tailtu. In Irish mythology, a FIRBOLG princess who becomes foster-mother to LUGH and gives her name to Tailtinn (Teltown), between NAVAN FORT and KELLS. She wears herself out clearing the forests and levelling plains and is buried in the necropolis in Teltown. Mourning games were held at the beginning of August each year on the orders of her foster-child. The event, *Óenach Tailten* (*see* AONACH TAILTEANN), was later incorporated in the festival of LUGH-NASA.

Táin Bó Cuailnge (*The Cattle Raid of Cooley*). The epic account of the struggle between MEDB of Connacht and CONCHOBHAR for possession of the Donn Cuailnge (the BROWN BULL OF CUAILNGE or Cooley). This epic, like Homer's *Iliad*, with which it may reasonably be compared, is concerned with warriors, weapons and the involvement of deities in mortal affairs. It also gives a picture of Ireland many hundred of years before the birth of Christ. Part of the Red Branch or ULSTER CYCLE, it is preserved in the 11th-century *Lebor na hUidre* (*The* BOOK OF THE DUN COW). Finnbhenach ('the white-horned bull') refuses to become part of a woman's herd and joins that of Medb's husband, AILILL, thus making his herd greater than that of his wife. She musters an army to carry off the Donn Cuailnge from the Cooley peninsula in Co. Louth. The Ulster territory is defended by CÚCHULAINN, who is the only one of the RED BRANCH KNIGHTS unaffected by the curse of MACHA. The epic ends with a battle between the two bulls which the Donn wins, carrying the carcase of Finnbhenach on his horns in rampage through the centre of Ireland until he too drops dead.

> Finnbennach refusing to be led by a woman, had gone over to the king's herd. Medb couldn't find in her herd the equal of this bull, and her spirits dropped as though she hadn't a single penny.
> Medb had the messenger Mac Roth called, and she told him to find where the match of the bull might be found, in any province in Ireland.

> 'I know where to find such a bull and better,' Mac Roth said: 'in the province of Ulster, in the territory of Cuailnge, in Dáire mac Fiachna's house. Donn Cuailnge is the bull's name, the Brown Bull of Cuailnge.'
> *Táin Bó Cuailnge*, translated by Thomas Kinsella (1969)

Taisce, An. An organization (pronounced 'on tashka') established in 1948 and committed to preserving the natural and built heritage of Ireland (*taisce* means 'treasure'). An Taisce has suffered from the mistaken perception that it is an organization of middle-class urban (read Dublin) meddlers: its interventions in the planning process in rural areas of natural beauty are often met with resentment. Despite gallant efforts it did not succeed in preventing the destruction of large areas of Georgian Dublin in the name of 1960s progress, nor in arresting the spread of the BUNGALOW BLIGHT all over rural Ireland.
See also TAILORS' HALL.

Taj Mahaughey. *See* CHAS MAHAL.

Take-a-hand. *See* HAND, TAKE A.

Take the Floor. A 1950s RTÉ radio programme presented by Din Joe which featured CÉILÍ music and STEP DANCING (on air) by the Rory O'Connor troupe of dancers. (Rory O'Connor himself, the foremost dancer of his age, was reputed to have danced for Hitler during the Berlin Olympics of 1936.) SEANCHAÍ Éamon KELLY provided stories on the show. By the mid-1950s RURAL ELECTRIFICATION meant that many people for the first time had plug-in radios, and the programme had a huge following in rural Ireland.

Taking the boat. The term used colloquially for emigration to Britain in the 1950s and 1960s. The boat was usually the night mail from Dún Laoghaire to Holyhead, with a rail connection to London's Euston Station. This was also used as a cattle boat, and in the 1950s the human cargo was treated little better than the animals.

Talbot, Matt (1856–1925). A Dubliner of extra-ordinary sanctity, who worked first for the Dublin Ports and Docks Board and then for the last 25 years of his life in the timber yard owned by the Martins on the North Wall. When he collapsed and died he was found to have been wearing penitential chains under his clothing. His coffin is on display in Our Lady of Lourdes Church in Seán McDermott Street in the south inner city, and a bridge (completed in 1978) over the River Liffey in Dublin, south of Butt Bridge and the Custom House, is called Matt Talbot Bridge. He was declared 'Venerable' by the Vatican in October 1976, and the process for his canonization continues.

Talbot, Richard (d.1449). Archbishop of Dublin, commemorated in St Patrick's Cathedral in that city. He served as chancellor (1423–6, 1427–31), and was a participant in the Talbot–Ormond feud, siding with his brother John Talbot (1387–1453) against James, 4th Earl of Ormond.

Tallon iron. An Italian iron, used by women for smoothing fluting or the seams of starched caps until the beginning of the 20th century.

Tally. Fun, CRAIC, particularly of an innocent non-alcoholic family kind. The derivation of this common HIBERNO-ENGLISH word is uncertain.

Tallymen. An institution at all Irish elections. Proportional representation (see SINGLE TRANSFERABLE VOTE) is a complex voting system: transfers among party members and between parties are often of vital importance, and counts tend to be protracted because of multi-seat (three-, four- or even five-seat) constituencies. Tallymen are party members who watch closely as each ballot box is emptied and the votes counted, and then without computers or calculators (and often on the back of cigarette packets) calculate the first, second, third and fourth preference votes to form a picture of the candidates' relative positions. Tallying is part-skill, part-art, and is based on years of experience. Media commentators quote tally-men in electoral commentaries, sometimes relying on their figures even when they contradict computer predictions or more official estimates. And they are seldom wrong.

Tallysticks. Sticks that were used to record dues; for instance, when a labourer worked for a farmer in return for a smallholding, the number of days he worked (usually about 80 per year were required) was recorded by cutting grooves in a tallystick or *bata scóir*. In NATIONAL SCHOOLS tallysticks were used as instruments of chastisement for children who used Irish, English being the only permitted language.

Tallywomen. Daughters of tenants who were used as sexual companions by landlords in a kind of *droit de seigneur*. Some were treated badly; others received gifts and comforts and were established by the landlord with a suitable tenant farmer and perhaps a baby (the landlord's) when the master tired of them.
See also KING OF FRIDAY'S MEN, THE.

Tame as domestic cats. The condition of the seditious Irish promised by John FITZGIBBON, Earl of Clare, while lord chancellor of Ireland (1789–1801). He was execrated particularly because his father had been a convert from Catholicism, and he was thought to have connived with CASTLEREAGH to foment the REBELLION OF 1798 as a means of securing the Act of UNION – this in spite of his initiative in rooting out sedition from among the Trinity College undergraduates during his much publicized visit to the college in February 1798. The Dublin mob – with clear memory and mordant humour – threw mud and dirt during his funeral procession from his home in Ely Place to St Peter's in Aungier Street, and at least one dead cat hit the coffin.

Tánaiste (Irish, 'heir presumptive'). Deputy to the TAOISEACH and second-in-command in the Irish government, according to the CONSTITUTION OF 1937. In recent years, the tánaiste has tended to be the leader of the 'junior' coalition partner. The name derives from the *tanist*, the designated successor to the *taoiseach* in Gaelic society. The English administration in the 16th and 17th centuries used the term *tanistry* to mean the Gaelic system of succession, which they regarded as inimical to the stability (i.e. conquest) of the country (*see* TUDOR RECONQUEST). The 'Case of Tanistry' in 1608 officially abolished tanistry, facilitating the acquisition of the lands of the northern chieftains and the ULSTER PLANTATION.

Tandy, [James] Napper (1740–1803). Radical activist. He was born in Dublin and worked variously as a fishmonger and rent collector. He was commander of artillery in the Dublin VOLUNTEERS and leader of a radical movement that campaigned for parliamentary reform. In 1791 he became secretary of the Society of UNITED IRISHMEN, though he remained at odds with Wolfe TONE about tactics. He fled to America in 1793 because his association with the DEFENDERS rendered him liable to a capital charge.

In 1798 Tandy was part of the group led by Tone in Paris that hoped to launch a French invasion of Ireland. As General Tandy he sailed from Dunkirk in the corvette *Anacreon* on 4 September; it was intended as a supply ship for an Ireland already in revolt, but they were unaware that Humbert had been defeated at Ballinamuck (*see* REBELLION OF 1798). The *Anacreon* landed at Rutland Island off Burtonport in west Donegal to find that the local population had fled. The ship's company dined ashore and then a drunken Tandy had to be carried back on board. En route back to the Continent they avoided capture by a British ship off the Orkneys, Tandy sitting drinking brandy on deck with cannon balls in his pocket so that he might drown more quickly if he had to leap overboard.

Tandy was arrested in Hamburg (in spite of its Hanseatic neutrality) and sentenced to death at Lifford in Co. Donegal. His sentence was finally commuted and at Napoleon's insistence he was released to France during the brief Peace of Amiens in 1802. He died at Bordeaux on 24 August 1803. Tandy remains a figure of comic relief in a broader tragedy, and he is remembered in one of Ireland's most potent patriotic ballads, 'The WEARING OF THE GREEN' (*c.*1830).

Tanist. *See* TÁNAISTE.

Tanistry, Case of. *See* TÁNAISTE.

Tans, Black and. *See* BLACK AND TANS.

Tan War. A synonym of the ANGLO-IRISH WAR of 1919–21. Use of this phrase – which refers to the hated BLACK AND TANS – is an indication of the Republican politics of the speaker: the war is seen as having achieved only a partial or flawed political freedom and thence cannot be rightly called a 'War of Independence'. The term is cognate with the use of SIX COUNTIES and TWENTY-SIX COUNTIES. At the time, the conflict of 1919–21 was known to ordinary people simply as the TROUBLES.

Taoiseach (Irish, 'leader', 'head'). The formal name for the Irish prime minister (pronounced 'tee-shock'), a term chosen by Éamon de Valera and included in the CONSTITUTION OF 1937. (The head of government from the foundation of the FREE STATE had been called 'President of the Executive Council'.)

> The President shall on the nomination of Dáil Éireann appoint the Taoiseach, that is the Head of Government or Prime Minister.
>
> *Bunreacht na hÉireann*, 13.1.1

See also TÁNAISTE.

Taoscán. A HIBERNO-ENGLISH word for a measure or glassful, as in 'She poured me out a fine taoscán.' It comes from the Irish verb *taoscadh*, meaning 'to pour', 'to drain'.

Tara. The Hill of Tara (*Temair* or *Teamhair* in Irish), near Navan in Co. Meath, was traditionally associated with the HIGH KINGS of Ireland, being the site of the LIA FÁIL, the inauguration stone or pillar. The prehistoric remains at the site include a Neolithic passage tomb, a fort, and several barrows and fortifications. Tara is associated with the legendary kings of Ireland such as CORMAC MAC ART, and in the early Christian period with the clash of pagan and Christian, the former exemplified by the fire of Loégaire, king of Tara, and his druids on the Hill of Tara, the latter by the Paschal fire lit by St Patrick at Easter 433 on the nearby Hill of Slane. It is thought that the fertility rite or *feis* relating to KINGSHIP was celebrated there until the 6th century.

The kingship of Tara remained the highest aspiration for the chieftains of Leinster, Ulster and the UÍ NÉILL throughout the early Christian period, although it is unlikely that there existed an accepted 'high king' in the modern sense until the early 11th century (*see* BRIAN BORU). Even then the control of Tara, although now of less strategic importance than, for instance, the town of Dublin, remained an important, though largely symbolic aspiration.

Tara retained a symbolic importance into recent centuries. Daniel O'CONNELL held a MONSTER MEETING there on 15 August 1843, said to have been attended by a million people. In the early 20th century it again assumed symbolic importance in a clash between representatives of the CELTIC REVIVAL and British Israelites (*see* ARK OF THE COVENANT).

> The harp that once through Tara's halls
> The soul of music shed,
> Now hangs as mute on Tara's walls
> As if that soul were fled.
>
> THOMAS MOORE: 'The Harp that Once through Tara's Halls', in *Irish Melodies* (1807)

Tara Brooch. The most magnificent of the extant 8th-century ring-brooches, unique in that it is decorated back and front. It is made of silver, heavily gilt with inset panels of gold filigree and glass and amber studs, accompanied by a chain of silver mesh attached to the ring by a hinge in which are inset two minute human faces of cast violet glass. The brooch was found on the Irish seashore near Drogheda; the TARA connection is purely fanciful.

Taranagers. A mild expletive, a corruption of '[Christ's] tears and aches'. Like its associated 'tare-an-ouns' ('[Christ's] tears and wounds') it

was once common, but its use had largely died out by the beginning of the 20th century.

> On Egypt's banks, contagious to the Nile
> The Ould Pharaoh's daughter, she went to bathe in style.
> She took her dip and she came unto the land,
> And to dry her royal pelt she ran along the strand.
> A bulrush tripped her whereupon she saw
> A smiling baby in a wad of straw;
> She took him up and says she in accents mild
> 'Oh! taranagers, girls, now, which of yis owns the child?'
>
> ZOZIMUS (?1794–1846): 'The Finding of Moses' (*c*.1830)

Tarbh Bán (Irish, 'white bull'). The jocular nickname of the bovine artificial insemination service in some GAELTACHT areas, arising from the fact that the officials invariably arrived in white cars.

Tare-an-ouns. *See* TARANAGERS.

Tarry-boy. A word for a Lothario, or 'womanizer'.

Tarry Flynn. The only novel (1948) of Patrick KAVANAGH, which describes the toil, frustrations and moments of Joycean epiphany of a young Monaghan small farmer as he writes his poetry, sows his potatoes and longs for a suitable wife. Set during the bleak years of the 1930s, it was banned for indecency.

> He loved virtuous girls. And that was one of the things he admired the Catholic religion for – because it kept girls virtuous until such time as he'd meet them.

Tart with the Cart. *See* DISH WITH THE FISH.

Tassel. A slang term for 'penis'. 'Four little children and not one tassel in my house,' a man is quoted as saying plaintively in Alice Taylor's *Quench the Lamp* (1990).

Tasty. Neat and painstaking, sometimes connoting a houseproud woman. A house that is newly done up might be 'tasty'.

Tate, Nahum (1652–1715). Playwright and 'improver' of Shakespeare. He was born in Dublin, the son of a Co. Cavan Presbyterian minister, a refugee from the Ulster REBELLION OF 1641. His own plays proving unpopular, he gave some of Shakespeare's tragedies happy endings: in *The History of King Lear* (1681) Cordelia marries Edgar, and Regan's and Goneril's thirds are restored to the rightful king. He wrote the libretto for Henry Purcell's *Dido and Aeneas* (1689), and the often parodied carol 'While Shepherds Watched Their Flocks by Night'. He was appointed poet laureate in 1692.

Táthaire. An Irish word for 'compressed', 'welded', applied in HIBERNO-ENGLISH to a ne'er-do-well or impertinent boy.

Tatie-howkers or **tatty-hokers.** The nickname applied to the Donegal seasonal migrant workers who travelled to Scotland for potato-picking. The word was used both in Ulster and in Scotland, not usually in disparagement. In both places 'taties' (or 'tatties') was a common corruption of 'potato', and the gerund 'hoking' is still used for vigorous digging and metaphorical searching, the equivalent of the English word 'rooting'. The tatie-howkers were treated with a mixture of affection and disdain by the native Scots, and a number moved to Scotland permanently. The following is a parody of a Scots piper's march:

Wha saw the tatie-howkers,
Wha saw them gang awa,
Wha saw the tatie-howkers,
Sailing doon the Broomielaw?
Some of them wore bits and stockings,
Some of them wore nane ata,
Some of them wore bits and stockings
Sailing doon the Broomielaw.
(The Broomielaw is a dockside area in Glasgow, on the north bank of the Clyde.)

Taw Shays. A nickname for students of Irish with limited capacity, from the phrase *tá sé* ('it is'), which occurs in descriptions of people, things and the weather, as in '*Tá sé fuar*' ('It is cold').

Taylor, Alice. See TO SCHOOL THROUGH THE FIELDS.

Taylor, Jeremy (1613–67). A Church of Ireland bishop and theologian. He was born in Cambridge and educated at Cambridge University. Associated with the high-church movement of Archbishop of William Laud, he was made Bishop of Down and Connor in 1661, after the Restoration. His flock, which was composed mainly of Scottish Presbyterian settlers and their descendants, proved unwilling to conform to high-church practice and Taylor, frustrated, unsuccessfully sought an alternative ecclesiastical post in England. He was best known for his theological works such as *A Dissuasive from Popery* (1664).

Tay-Pay. The popular name of the politician and journalist Thomas Power O'Connor (1848–1929), from a pronunciation of his initials with an over-heavy BROGUE. A strong Parnellite, he was elected Nationalist MP for Galway in 1880 and for Scotland Division, Liverpool, in 1885, which he continued to represent – latterly as Father of the House – until his death on 18 November 1929. O'Connor founded the liberal and popular evening paper the *Star* in 1887, but he relinquished interest in 1890, preferring the more literary *T.P.'s Weekly* (costing only a penny) that he started in 1902 and ran until 1916, when he became Britain's first film censor.

TCD. Trinity College Dublin, the sole college of the University of Dublin. It is situated in the centre of Dublin, on COLLEGE GREEN. It was built on the site of ALL HALLOWS PRIORY, which was suppressed on 16 September 1538 and mostly lay idle for the next 50 years, in the ownership of the mayor and citizens of Dublin. In December 1591 Elizabeth I ordered the lord deputy to establish a college, and early in 1592 the city assembly agreed that the site of All Hallows be used for this purpose. Elizabeth issued a charter for the university in March 1592, and the foundation stone was laid in the same month. The buildings were in use by early 1594. Although the college was not avowedly sectarian, its early provosts were Puritans, and from the beginning it catered largely for the Protestant New English (*see under* OLD ENGLISH), with only Provost William Bedell (*see* BEDELL'S BIBLE) promoting the use of Irish. After the Restoration TCD settled with some distinction into its role of being a Protestant university for a Protestant ASCENDANCY. The 18th-century Irish Parliament, which sat a stone's throw away across College Green, generously supported the college's construction programme, which produced a set of fine Georgian buildings, beginning with the famous library in 1712. A brief flirtation with French-style radicalism occurred among some of the student body in the late 18th century, centred on the Debating Club founded by Edmund BURKE in 1747. Wolfe TONE was auditor in 1795, and the lord chancellor, John FITZGIBBON, had several students, including Robert EMMET, expelled in 1798 for being UNITED IRISHMEN.

After 1922 Trinity initially accommodated itself uneasily to the independent Irish state, an unease accentuated by the fact that, until 1970, Catholics were forbidden by their own church to attend. The college first received state financial support in the 1950s, and gradually came to be seen as simply another Irish university, with the same entry procedures as the NATIONAL UNIVERSITY colleges and the Dublin Institute of Technology. Trinity used to attract many Protestant students from Northern Ireland, but they are now more likely to go to English or Scottish universities. Although still a smaller university than University College Dublin, TCD has achieved significant development in recent decades, its ambitious building projects including the Berkeley Library and a new arts block and, more recently, the O'Reilly Institute (Computer Science).

TD. The commonly used abbreviation for *Teachta Dála*, meaning 'delegate to the DÁIL' and pronounced 'tochta dolla'. A TD is the Irish equivalent of an MP in the Westminster Parliament.

Tea. A drink that has been very popular among the Irish since the middle of the 19th century.

There is a rueful proverb on the subject: 'Dead from tea and dead from the lack of it' (*Marbh le tea agus marbh gan é*).

Buck Mulligan, hewing thick slices from the loaf, said in an old woman's wheedling voice:
– When I makes tea I makes tea, as old Mother Grogan said. And when I makes water I makes water.
– By Jove, it is tea, Haines said.
Buck Mulligan went on hewing and wheedling:
– *So I do, Mrs Cahill,* says she. *Begob. Ma'am,* says Mrs Cahill, *God send you don't make them in the same pot.*
JAMES JOYCE: *Ulysses* (1922)

See also LADY MORGAN MAKIN' TAY.

Teach Airneáil. *See* AIRNEÁN.

Teague or **Taig** or **Teigue.** HIBERNO-ENGLISH versions of the Irish forename Tadhg, which was taken as the Irish version of 'Timothy'. Such biblical names as Luke, Matthew, Bartholomew and Timothy were popular in the 18th and 19th century and Tadhg in its Teague form became the standard name for an Irish 'rude mechanical' in English drama (*see* STAGE-IRISH; 'TISH THE FASHION OF IRELAND). The form Taig – sometimes Teig – became a common term of disparagement of Catholics by their adversaries at the time of the first HOME RULE Bill (1886), and has continued in use in mob shouts and graffiti, of which the mildest is 'Taigs Out!' By a very Irish irony the surname of the chairman of the SHANKILL Defence Association, John McKeague (1930–82), in its Irish form, Mac Thaidhg, means literally 'son of Taig'.

Teaspach. An Irish word for 'ardour', 'exuberance', 'liveliness', 'high spirits'. It is used in the HIBERNO-ENGLISH of Munster (with a heavy emphasis on the second syllable) to signify any of these qualities, in humans or in animals. It is sometimes pejorative but only slightly so. A horse might be 'full of *teaspach*' after a feed of oats, or it might be said of a lively youth sent to work a long day in the fields,

'That will knock the *teaspach* out of him.' The Irish word derives from *teas*, meaning 'hot'.

Teebane Cross. The scene on the Omagh–Cookstown road of a Provisional IRA attack on a party of eight Protestant workmen who had been working at the security base in Omagh. On 17 January 1992 a 680-kg (1500-lb) bomb blew their minibus apart, killing all of them. It was the sort of soft-target attack that had the effect of turning public opinion against the IRA.

Teflon Taoiseach. A nickname of TAOISEACH Bertie AHERN, because of his apparent ability to repel any contamination from the FIANNA FÁIL scandals of the 1990s.
See also BERTIE BOWL.

Teigue. *See* TEAGUE.

Teilifís na Gaeilge. *See* TG4.

Temple Bar. An area of Dublin city centre bounded by Dame Street, the south LIFFEY Quays and Winetavern Street that was the beneficiary of an extensive urban renewal programme in the 1990s funded by the exchequer and the European Union. The area, which its creators conceived of as 'Dublin's Cultural Quarter', now includes many restaurants and pubs, some residential units and novel cultural facilities such as the Irish Film Centre (IFC) and The Ark, a performance centre for children. Much of the credit for the development, both mercantile and cultural, must go to a company called Temple Bar Properties Ltd, established in 1991 under the terms of the Temple Bar Area Renewal and Development Act of the same year. The proliferation of super-pubs and the arrival of coachloads of tourists interested only in sampling CEOL AGUS CRAIC has for many people been the downside of the development of Temple Bar.

Temple of Liberty, the. An amenity, built at Toomebridge, Co. Antrim, by John Cary (1800–91) in 1860. All that now remains is a roadside well and pump, known as the Fountain of Liberty. The essayist Robert LYND visited the

place in 1904 before the ruins were demolished and cleared, as he records in the essay 'Hibernia Rediviva', in *Irish and English* (1908):

> Once a man lived in this part of the country who believed that all men should have liberty to express their opinions without being knocked on the head for it. Consequently he bequeathed to his countrymen this now shattered building, whose title in full is the Temple of Liberty, Learning and Select Amusement. ... Old and highly coloured frescoes, misrepresenting all the known gods from Aphrodite to Robert Burns, are falling in flakes from the panels of the damp walls.

Temporary little arrangement. The comment made by Taoiseach Albert REYNOLDS about the FIANNA FÁIL–Progressive Democrat (*see* PEE DEES) coalition government of 1992 in which Des O'Malley of the Pee Dees was tánaiste (deputy premier). Coalitions have never really been to Fianna Fáil's taste. A conflict of evidence between Reynolds and O'Malley before the BEEF TRIBUNAL led to the end of the coalition (12 January 1993).
See also CORE VALUE.

Tenant League. A precursor of the more radical LAND LEAGUE. The Tenant League was founded in Dublin in August 1850 by Charles Gavan DUFFY and Frederick Lucas with the aim of achieving TENANT RIGHT for all tenants by parliamentary means. Originally conceived as an all-Ireland organization, the appeal of the league in the north narrowed when it attracted the support of Nationalist Catholic clergymen such as Thomas (later Archbishop) CROKE. In the general election of July 1852 more than 40 members of the Tenant League, including Duffy and Lucas, were returned (because of the extension of the franchise in 1850 to occupiers of land valued at £12) and in September of that year these MPs formed the Independent Irish Party. The party's fortunes declined, however, when leading members William Keogh and John Sadleir (*see* POPE'S BRASS BAND, THE) defected, and Lucas became involved in a public dispute with Cardinal Paul CULLEN. After Lucas's death and the emigration of Duffy to Australia in 1855 both the League and the party declined. They had disappeared by 1860.

Tenant Right. One of the THREE FS. Tenant right was normally understood to be that of free sale, that is the right of a departing tenant to dispose of his interest in the tenancy, thereby recouping any investment he might have made, and also profiting from any difference that might exist between the market value of the rent and the sum he was paying. It was one of the main aims of the TENANT LEAGUE of the 1850s. The LAND ACT of 1870 conceded tenant right in areas where the custom already prevailed, while that of 1881 conceded it generally.

Ten Commandments. The marks left on the body after a two-handed attack by fingernails: 'She put her ten commandments on his face.'

Tène, La. *See* LA TÈNE.

Tent. A now obsolete word for the amount of ink taken up at a time by a pen dipped in a bottle, perhaps aphaeretic for 'content'. By the end of the 19th century there was nearly universal literacy in Irish homes and the ink-bottle and a penholder with a steel nib were important items in many Irish kitchens. The universal ballpoint has, of course, made the penholder as obsolete as its original 'tent'.

Termon. A defined area around a church or monastery that provided legal protection or sanctuary. The word is a version of the Irish *tearmann*, itself derived from the Latin *terminus* ('limit'), and survives in Irish placenames such as Termonfeckin, Co. Louth ('Termon of St Feichín').

Termonfeckin. *See* TERMON.

Terry Alts. An agrarian SECRET SOCIETY, active in the 1830s in Co. Tipperary and in the west of Ireland. It was one of many such groups active in the early 19th century and probably connected with the WHITEBOYS. Like Threshers, CARDERS, Whitefeet and MOLLY MAGUIRES, their make-up and aims are difficult to determine, since their common characteristic was an almost theatrical secrecy. Their activities usually coincided with agricultural slumps and their adversaries were not so much the landlords as the growing class of tenant farmers, who were if anything more oppressive on their COTTIERS and the agricultural labourers than the older 'enemies'.

Tertiaries. *See* THIRD ORDER.

TG4. The Irish-language television station, originally called Teilifís na Gaeilge ('Irish-language television'). It made its first broadcast on 31 October 1996, and was established to cater for a countrywide Irish-speaking audience, not just for the GAELTACHT areas. Although the channel is publicly funded, the programming is not at all conservative or worthy: all Irish-language programmes are subtitled, and the channel broadcasts films and advertisements in English. Despite some controversial programming decisions, the channel is generally accounted to be a success, and it is popular also among non-Irish speakers. TG4 has its headquarters in Indreabhán in the Connemara Gaeltacht, and its policy of commissioning independent productions, for instance travel programmes, has given rise to an amount of creative native entrepreneurship in Co. Galway and surrounding areas.
See also RAIDIÓ NA GAELTACHTA; *ROS NA RÚN*.

Thanks a million, big fella. The words of thanks popularly believed to have been said by Charles HAUGHEY to Ben Dunne (*see* BEN DUNNE KIDNAPPING), after the latter had handed him three bank drafts to the value of £210,000 sterling on a visit to his home in Kinsealy in November 1991. (In fact Haughey said, 'Thanks, big fella.') *Thanks a Million, Big Fella* is also the title of a 1997 book by journalist Sam Smyth detailing Haughey's financial dealings with Dunne. It emerged from the McCRACKEN TRIBUNAL that Ben Dunne had given Haughey a total of at least £1.3 million in the early 1990s.

Thatch. A method of roofing once common-place in Ireland, the materials being cheap and available locally. Thatch could be of reed (in Munster) oat-straw (in the Midlands and east) or of rye, flax or heather (in the north). In other areas, for instance in Co. Clare, thatch was composed of sod cut from a field or bog. When the house was built the rafters were put on and crossed by runners called *tábháns*. Then big scraws (rolls of turf) were laid over the runners by a local man skilled in the matter. These were a couple of feet wide, two inches thick and rolled on like modern Astroturf. The scraw had to be tough and elastic so it could not be cut from any old bog. The thatch was secured by scallops (Irish *scolb*), i.e. rods pointed at both ends, or by sticks of BOG DEAL. A well-known proverb asserted '*Ní hé lá na gaoithe lá na scolb*' ('A windy day is not the best day to thatch'). Small pieces of waste bog-deal (called *smutáns*) were used for kindling.

That play of mine. See CATHLEEN NÍ HOULI-HAN.

That rooted man. See SYNGE, J[OHN] M[ILLING-TON].

Theatre Royal. Historically the title granted to the theatre whose manager held the royal patent of master of the revels, and applied at different times to such Dublin theatres as Werburgh Street, SMOCK ALLEY and CROW STREET THEATRE. In modern times it was the name of three large theatres in Hawkins Street, the first having burnt down in 1880 and the last one rebuilt in 1935 and closing in 1962. The theatre was known for its pantomimes, cine-variety and a spectacular dance troupe known as the Royalettes.

'There Is an Isle'. The anthem of St Mary's Island Parish in Limerick (the island is formed by a loop of the River Shannon in Limerick city) and by extension the whole of Limerick. It is particularly significant in the context of Thomond Rugby Club.

There is an isle, a bonny isle,

Stands proudly from the sea,
And dearer far than all this world
Is that fair isle to me.
It is not that alone it stands
Where all around is fresh and fair,
But because it is my native land
And my home, my home is there.
　ANON.

There is an Isle is the title of a memoir (1998) by Criostóir Ó Floinn (b.1927), which contains a rebuttal of the portrayal of Limerick in Frank McCourt's ANGELA'S ASHES. *See also* ALONE IT STANDS.

There's one fair county in Ireland. The opening line of the song 'The Boys from the County Armagh', sung as an anthem in the context of GAA football matches. Armagh won the senior football championship, defeating favourites Kerry, for the first time ever in 2002. Record crowds thronged the recently reconstructed stadium at CROKE PARK and the rest of Dublin, and it was said that 31 of the 32 counties (and half of Kerry too) supported the orange-jerseyed Armagh players, led to victory by the gifted and indefatigable Kieran McGeeney. No sooner was the game over than football folklore preserved for posterity the tough motivational speech of manager Joe McKernan in the half-time dressing room ('Do you want the runners-up medals, boys?') and the tearful rendition of the anthem (which concludes with 'Sure my heart is at home in old Ireland, / In the county of Armagh') by the whole arms-linked team in the dressing room after the match. There was a particular political resonance to Armagh's victory because of the tension between the British Army and the GAA in the south of that county: David TRIMBLE, Northern first minister, declined to attend the match, pleading a prior engagement.

These Islands. A cumbersome but neutral term to replace the once acceptable BRITISH ISLES. That term is seen as politically inflammatory as well as historically inaccurate. *See also* HIBERNIAN ARCHIPELAGO; MAINLAND, THE.

They haven't gone away, you know. A remark, about the Provisional IRA, quiescent since its 1994 ceasefire, made by Gerry ADAMS at a rally in Belfast on 13 August 1995. Adams's words proved to be sadly prophetic: at 7 p.m. on 9 February 1996 the Provisional IRA ended its first ceasefire by exploding a massive bomb at CANARY WHARF in London's Docklands, killing two people.

Thingmote or **thingmount.** A venue for public meetings, sporting tournaments and passing laws in Dublin, taking its name from the Old Norse words for people's assembly (*thing*) and mound (*mote*). Until the end of the 17th century, a Norse thingmote survived in the centre of Dublin, bounded by COLLEGE GREEN, Suffolk Street and Church Lane, in the area known as HOGGEN GREEN. The conical mound was 12 m (40 ft) high and 73 m (240 ft) in circumference. At Christmas 1172, HENRY II held a feast for Gaelic chieftains on the thingmote, in an attempt to win their approval for the arrival of the Anglo-Normans. Sir William Davis, city recorder and chief justice, had the thingmote removed in order to develop property on the site in the late 17th century.

Think long. An Ulster phrase meaning 'to pine' or 'to be homesick' as in 'Whenever I hear somebody singing "Danny Boy" I think long.'

Third order. An informal name for the Tertiaries, a lay confraternity for men associated with the Franciscan order. Members were buried in a brown robe like that of the Franciscan friars. In past decades TOSF (Third Order of St Francis) frequently appeared after the name of the deceased in newspaper death notices.

Thirteen. An Irish shilling, which before 1825 was worth 13 pence. The nickname endured long after the Irish coin was standardized with the English one.

Thirty-one. A card game much played in the southwest of Ireland, particularly in Co. Kerry. It involves winning six tricks in a round of games, the best trick in each game (the five of trumps or the ace of hearts) earning an extra point. A person who reneges (does not follow suit) for strategic reasons is heartily despised. It has been said that men whom the CIVIL WAR had failed to divide fell out over a game of thirty-one.

> A month or so before he took to bed,
> We quarrelled at a game of cards,
> He led the Five,
> I reneged the Ace of Hearts
> But – as I am an honourable man –
> I did so only in devilment …
> But McCormack would not be pacified.
> Rising from his table and turning away,
> He said, 'Rules are rules and the man
> Who cheats on one will cheat on all.'
> We haven't spoken since that day.
> PADDY KENNELLY (b.1945): 'Kevin Flynn', in *A Place too Small for Secrets* (2002)

Thirty-two Counties, the. The whole of the island of Ireland, comprising the SIX COUNTIES of Northern Ireland and the TWENTY-SIX COUNTIES of the Republic. The term is mostly used by Republicans who do not accept the 1921 PARTITION, and provides a title for a popular Republican song, beginning:

> Here's to Donegal and her people brave and tall,
> Here's to Antrim, to Leitrim and to Derry,
> Here's to Cavan and to Louth, here's to Carlow in
>   the South,
> Here's to Longford, to Waterford and Kerry.

The song proceeds to enumerate and celebrate the remaining 22 counties.

The Thirty-two County Sovereignty Committee is a Republican organization critical of the GOOD FRIDAY AGREEMENT of 1998, and the revisions subsequently made to the constitution of the Republic. It is sometimes abbreviated to 32CSC, and is said to have links with the REAL IRA, although both bodies deny this.

Thom, Alexander (1801–79). Printer and publisher who carried out a number of government contracts. In 1844 he acquired *Wilson's Dublin Directory*, which had first appeared in 1752, and published it as *Thom's Irish Almanac and Official Directory*. Although the ownership of the title and the title itself have varied, the directory has continued to be published since 1844.

Thomond (Irish *Tuadh Mumhan*, 'north Munster'). An ancient kingdom of northern Munster, covering what is now Co. Clare, two-thirds of Co. Tipperary, most of Co. Limerick and the very north of Kerry. Up to the 12th century, the rulers of Thomond (the Dál gCais) and neighbouring DESMOND ('south Munster') took it in turns to be kings of Munster. The O'Briens became kings of Thomond in the 13th century, at a time when the kingdom was being encroached upon in the east by the Anglo-Norman Butlers, whose territory became known as OR-MOND ('east Munster'). The O'Briens' kingdom of Thomond was gradually reduced to what is now Co. Clare, and in 1543, having submitted to the English crown, the O'Briens became Earls of Thomond. Thomond still has its own identity, and Thomond Park in Limerick is home to Munster's rugby union team.

Thompson, Sam (1916–65). Playwright and actor. He was born in Belfast on 21 May 1916 and apprenticed as a painter in the ISLAND. Encouraged by Sam Hanna BELL he wrote such radio features as *Brush in Hand* (1956), *Tommy Baxter: Shop Steward* (1957) and *The General Foreman* (1958). His play *Over the Bridge* (1957), about a failed attempt by a well-meaning shop steward to oppose sectarianism in the shipyard, was cancelled by the ULSTER GROUP THEATRE and, after a successful suit for breach of contract, was produced with great success by James Ellis (who had resigned as artistic director from the Group when the play was withdrawn) in the Empire Theatre on 26 January 1960. *The Evangelist* (1963) was a tour de force for the actor Ray McAnally (1926–89) as the Pastor Earls of the title, while the teleplay *Cemented with Love* (a traditional Orange ARCH and BANNER motto) described with only minimal exaggeration the chicanery that characterized elections in Northern Ireland. Thompson had a real but limited talent, his 1960s success as much a function of the

relative peacefulness of the period as of his tackling hitherto unmentionable subjects. His premature death from heart failure in Belfast on 15 February 1965 was regarded as a serious loss to Irish drama.

> *Davy*: There's nothing civilized about a mob, Warren, be it Protestant or Catholic. They can store their bigotry for a long time. Then they spew it out in violence.
>
> *Over the Bridge* (1957)

Thompson, William (*c*.1785–1833). Political economist. He was born in Cork city, the son of a wealthy merchant, and as a young man inherited his father's business and an estate of 1500 acres (600 ha) at Cloonkeen, Rosscarbery, overlooking Glandore harbour. His experience as a landlord of the poverty of his tenants led him to question the established economic order, and he was the first political thinker to promote the redistribution of wealth – in his 1824 publication *An Enquiry into the Principles of the Distribution of Wealth Most Conducive to Human Happiness*. The title of an 1825 publication written with the collaboration of his friend Anna Wheeler, *Appeal of One Half of the Human Race, Women, Against the Pretentions of the Other Half, Men, to Retain Them in Political and Thence in Civil and Domestic Slavery*, is self-explanatory. Thompson was a friend of the English social reformer Jeremy Bentham (1748–1832) and supported the cooperative community ideal of Robert Owen (1771–1858). He died in his Cloonkeen home on 28 March 1833 and left most of his estate to the poor, to be distributed according to the principles of the cooperative movement, but after years of legal wrangling and litigation by a nephew his will was overturned by the courts. Thompson was an atheist and a Republican, and one of the founding fathers of socialism.

Thompson in Tír na nÓg. A frequently revived satire on Irish and Orange Ulster attitudes by Gerald MacNamara, the pseudonym of the Belfast dramatist Harry C. Morrow (1866–1938), staged in the Opera House, Belfast, on

9 December 1912, at the height of the UVF anti-HOME RULE agitation. The hero, Andy Thompson, is taking part at the SCARVA Sham Fight when his old gun bursts. He gets 'blew up' and when he awakes he finds himself in TÍR NA NÓG (the Celtic Otherworld) still wearing his Orange sash and obligatory bowler hat. He meets the Celtic immortals who dwell there, including such heroic stalwarts as CÚCHULAINN, Grania (GRÁINNE), Finn (FIONN MAC CUMHAIL) and Maev (MEDB), and they are unimpressed to meet a contemporary Irishman who knows no Irish heroes but KING BILLY. They are also appalled that the Irish have lost their Gaelic tongue and speak a barbarous language that their druid tells them is English. The wily Grania is sent to discover what kind of creature Thompson is:

> *Grania:* And you know not if your army was victorious or not?
> *Thompson:* Sure I told you I was on King William's side. Of course we won the day.
> *Grania:* Why do you say 'of course'? The fortunes of war are so uncertain.
> *Thompson:* Sure it wasn't a real fight. It was a sham fight.
> *Grania:* A make-believe?
> *Thompson:* Aye the very thing.
> *Grania:* But have you been in a real fight?
> *Thompson:* O aye, I was in a scrap in Portadown last Sunday.
> *Grania:* And whom were you fighting in Portadown?
> *Thompson:* The Hibernians.
> *Grania:* The Hibernians! But are not all the people in Eirinn Hibernians?

The play ends with the disposal of Thompson and the immortals' relief at the restoration of Gaelic. It was originally commissioned by the GAELIC LEAGUE as a three-act play, but with typical humourlessness they rejected it because 'it held up the Gaelic heroes to ridicule'. Morrow rewrote it as a one-act play and offered it to the ULT, whose most popular play it became. The geniality of the piece and, most of all, the continuing relevance of its jokes to the situation in Northern Ireland, have ensured its continuing popularity.

Thom's Directory. *See* THOM, ALEXANDER.

Thomson, George. *See* FICHE BLIAN AG FÁS.

Thoor Ballylee. W.B. YEATS's name for the tower of Ballylee Castle, near Gort, Co. Galway, which he had converted along with the adjoining cottages as living quarters. 'Thoor' was his phonetic rendering of the Irish word *túr* ('tower'). He used the place mainly during the summer months of the 1920s, abandoning it in 1929. His poetry collection *The Tower* (1928) was written there. Thoor Ballylee was rescued from dereliction as a Yeats museum in 1965, as part of the celebration of the centenary of the poet's birth. A tablet attached to the front celebrates his sojourn there:

> I, the poet William Yeats,
> With old mill boards and sea-green slates
> And smithy work from Gort forge,
> Restored this tower for my wife George;
> And may these characters remain
> When all is ruin once again.

Thoroughbred County. A nickname for Co. Kildare, because of its association with horse training and stud farms, a branding recently adopted, along with a horse, as the county's official logo. The CURRAGH of Kildare also has a popular racecourse.

Thraneen or **thrawneen** (Irish *tráithnín*). A blade of hay or straw. The word is often used disparagingly in HIBERNO-ENGLISH, as in 'Sure that's not worth a thraneen.' In *Ralph Rashleigh* (1845), a 'convict novel' by the Australian James Tucker, is the line 'I'll not charge you a traneen for all you'll ate of the besht of good living.' Like most words originating from the diminutive Irish suffix *-ín*, it has less currency in Ulster than in other parts of Ireland.

Three Candles Press. A printing and publishing company, properly called At the Sign of the Three Candles Press, and located at 6 Fleet Street in Dublin (1926–89). It was founded by Colm Ó Lochlainn (1892–1972), a bookbinder and leather-worker, in 1926, and in its heyday it employed 40 people, including lithographic artists Michael Ó Briain and Karl Uhlemann. The company was famous for the quality of its print and design. The name derives from the Irish proverb of the three candles that light up every darkness: truth, nature and knowledge.

Three Cs. *See* O'BRIEN, WILLIAM.

Three Fs. The conveniently alliterative demands made by tenant farmers after the GREAT FAMINE: fair rent, fixity of tenure and free sale. The third F was also known as TENANT RIGHT, and also as 'the Ulster custom', because of the practice in the northern province. There was no general consensus as to the meaning of tenant right, but it implied a departing tenant's right to dispose of his interest in the property to the highest bidder with the landlord's approval. This usually included compensation for any improvements that the outgoing tenant had made. All three Fs were granted in law by W.E. Gladstone's second LAND ACT of 1881: the fairness of the rent was to be determined by arbitration, tenure was secure while rent was paid, and the right was granted to the tenant to sell his right of occupancy at the best market price.

Three Great Saints of Ireland, the. The encomiastic title applied to PATRICK, BRIGID and COLUM CILLE.
See also IN BURGO DUNO TUMULO.

Three Jacks, the. The nickname of the triumvirate of powerful politicians in late-18th-century Dublin: John BERESFORD, John FITZ-GIBBON and John FOSTER.

Three Sisters, the. The collective name given to three rivers of southern Ireland, the SUIR, the BARROW and the NORE. The Nore joins the Barrow just north of New Ross, while the Suir and the Barrow join at Waterford Harbour.

Three spaces of time. Three-quarters (nine months) of the year, the duration of a pregnancy. The expression is a direct translation of the Irish *trí ráithe*.

Three-years-old and **Four-years-old.** The names

of two rival factions (*see* FACTION FIGHTING) in Limerick, Cork and Tipperary in the early 19th century.

Threshold. A literary journal associated with the Lyric Theatre in Belfast. It was begun in 1957 by Mary O'Malley, the theatre's founder, and had a series of guest editors including John BOYD, Seamus DEANE, Seamus HEANEY, Brian FRIEL and John MONTAGUE. It was the longest-lasting Ulster journal, with a notable list of contributors, including most modern Irish poets. Its last appearance was in the 1990s.

Throughother. A term for 'confused' or 'mixed up', deriving from the Irish *TRÍNA CHÉILE*.

Thump. A potato dish consisting of potatoes boiled in their skins and mixed with scallions boiled in milk. It is so called because the potatoes were mashed or 'thumped'.
See also CHAMP; POUNDIES.

Thunder and Lightning Hurling Final. The ALL-IRELAND hurling final at CROKE PARK between Kilkenny and Cork played on the day the Second World War was declared, 3 September 1939. A thrilling game, it was remembered as the 'thunder and lighting final' because it ended with a heavy thunderstorm and lashing rain. Kilkenny held out to win by a single point. Jack LYNCH was captain of the Cork team that day.

Thundering disgrace, a. A comment made about President Cearbhall Ó Dálaigh (1911–78) by Paddy Donegan, minister for defence, at an army function in Mullingar, Co. Westmeath on 18 October 1976: 'In my opinion he is a thundering disgrace. The fact is that the army must stand behind the state.' Ó Dalaigh, a former Supreme Court judge and an able and liberal lawyer, was the successful FIANNA FÁIL nominee for the presidency in 1974 when the 1973–77 FINE GAEL–LABOUR PARTY coalition was in power. When Ó Dalaigh referred the Emergency Powers Bill, a response to IRA terrorism, to the Supreme Court for a ruling on its constitutionality, Donegan and other coalition ministers were outraged, seeing the actions of the president as being soft on terrorism. Don Lavery, a journalist from the local *Westmeath Examiner*, was present at the function and alerted the national media. Donegan's subsequent apology – he seemed genuinely surprised at all the fuss – did not prevent a constitutional crisis and Ó Dálaigh's resignation in order to 'assert publicly my personal integrity and independence as President of Ireland and to protect the dignity and independence of the presidency as an institution'. He was succeeded as president by another Fianna Fáil nominee, Patrick HILLERY.

Thurot, Commodore François (1727–60). French naval commander. He was born in Nuits in Côte-d'Or and spent his early years on a privateer. He was imprisoned for a year in Dover until a successful escape involving the seizure of a boat. In 1748 he managed to gather enough money to equip a merchant ship. The next seven years were spent partly in England, but mostly in smuggling and piracy. At the outbreak of the Seven Years' War in 1755 he was given command of a squadron with which he harried the east coast of England. In 1759 he attempted to sail into Lough Foyle with 1200 soldiers, but was beaten off by the usual high gales. He then steered his three ships into Belfast Lough on 21 February 1760 and occupied the town of Carrickfergus. The castle was captured and held until reinforcements arrived on 27 February led by Lord CHARLEMONT. The resourceful Thurot again put to sea with his three ships, but was killed in an engagement with British frigates off the Isle of Man on the 28th.

Thy Tears Might Cease. A semi-autobiographical novel (1963) by Michael FARRELL, describing the career of Martin Matthew Reilly in early-20th-century Ireland. His Catholic education makes him bitterly anticlerical, and the EASTER RISING kills his residual Redmondism (*see* REDMOND, JOHN [EDWARD]). Reilly happily joins the IRA but, emerging from imprisonment in Mountjoy, regards with little enthusiasm the contours of the emerging Free State.

The novel's high point is the description of idyllic pre-school childhood.

Tibb's Eve. The fictitious feast of St Tibb (or Tib), regarded as the eve of Doomsday. In colloquial use it denotes a day that will never come, as in the expression 'You'll be standing there till Tibb's Eve!'

Tigeen. *See* TRAVELLERS.

Tiger Bay. Originally an area in dockland Cardiff; the name has been applied to a Loyalist enclave in North Belfast.

Tilly (Irish *tuilleadh*, 'addition', 'increase'). Originally a HIBERNO-ENGLISH word for a small extra helping of milk. It dates from the days before bottled milk, when the vendors used pint and quart measures to pour into buyers' jugs. The tilly (close in pronunciation to the Irish *tuilleadh*, 'till-you') had its own little measure. The word became applied to any little token of goodwill. The word also connotes the extra two weeks all servants and labourers hired on a yearly wage had to work for nothing.

> He [Stephen Dedalus] watched her pour into the measure and hence into the jug rich white milk ... She poured again a measureful and a tilly ... She praised the goodness of the milk pouring it out.
> JAMES JOYCE (1882–1941): *Ulysses* (1922)

Tilly lamp. An elaborate paraffin lamp with a globe and incandescent mantle that was used for domestic light in rural areas of Ireland from the 1920s on.
See also RUSH LIGHT; BOG DEAL SPLINTERS; RURAL ELECTRIFICATION.

'Tim Finnegan's Wake'. An Irish-American ballad that (without the apostrophe) gave James Joyce the title for his final prose work, FINNEGANS WAKE. The ballad describes how Tim, a bricklayer who 'to rise in the world carried a hod', is killed in a fall from a ladder. The wake was as riotous as convention demanded:

> Then Mickey Maloney raised his head,
> When a noggin of whiskey flew at him.
> It missed and falling on the bed
> The liquor scattered over Tim;
> Bedad he revives! See how he rises

And Timothy rising from the bed
Says 'Whirl your liquor round like blazes,
Thanam o'n dhoul, do you think I'm dead?'

('Thanam o'n dhoul' hides the Irish phrase *ANAM 'ON DIABHAL*, 'Your soul to the devil!')

Tim Healy Pass. A high and beautiful pass (330 m / 1084 ft) over the Caha Mountains on the road from Adrigole, near Bantry, Co. Cork, to Lauragh, Co. Kerry. The summit marks the spot where Cork and Kerry meet on the Beara peninsula. The pass, completed in 1931, was named in honour of Tim HEALY, a native of Bantry, who was then governal-general of the Irish Free State.

Tinkers. *See* TRAVELLERS.

Tinker's wedding. Any lavish and expensive celebration might be described as being 'like a tinker's wedding'. TRAVELLERS are famous for having lengthy and lavish celebrations of weddings and funerals, probably because the gathering together of scattered travelling families is so infrequent.

Tinker's Wedding, The. A play by J.M. SYNGE, set like IN THE SHADOW OF THE GLEN in Co. Wicklow. It was written in 1902 but not staged during the author's lifetime. It is a rather raw comedy, generated by Synge's admiration of the free thought and language of TRAVELLERS. Sarah Casey decides to marry her partner, Michael, and strikes a bargain with the local priest that he will marry them for ten shillings and a new can. He refuses to go through with the ceremony when it is discovered that Mary Byrne, Michael's mother, has sold the can for drink. They bundle him into a sack and keep him prisoner until he agrees to keep his promise. When released he regains the upper hand by calling down a curse upon the three of them couched in impressive Latin. The final stage direction reads:

They rush out leaving the Priest master of the situation.

The play is slight compared with Synge's other work, with few memorable lines, and reveals his instinctive rejection of all forms of clericalism. Yeats decided that it would be injudicious to stage the play in Dublin since it would certainly have caused wide offence. Its first production was at His Majesty's Theatre, London, on 11 November 1909 by the Afternoon Theatre Company. Yeats found the production disgraceful and left after the first act.

Tintawn. A brand of buff-coloured sisal carpeting that took its name from the Irish *tinteán*, meaning 'fire', 'hearth' or, by extension, 'home'. It was manufactured by Curragh Carpets (now Curragh Tintawn Carpets) in Newbridge, Co. Kildare.

Tintown. *See* CURRAGH, THE.

Tin whistle. *See* WHISTLE.

Tiocfaidh ár lá (Irish, 'Our day will come'). The chief slogan of the Provisional IRA, expressed in Irish in the usual mixture of respect and political expediency, and often shouted from the dock. It is pronounced 'chucky ar law', which has caused the Provisionals to be known in Republican enclaves as 'Chuckies'. In the series of high-level Republican meetings that preceded the IRA ceasefire of 31 August 1994 the chief participants were seen to be extremely well-dressed, giving rise to a journalist's gibe: '*Tiocfaidh Armani!*' And similarly, when Sinn Fein was perceived to be attempting to appeal to a more middle-class electorate in November 2003, a journalistic wag referred to the phenomenon of the '*Tiochfaidh ar la-de-da* vote'.

Tipperary. The sixth largest county in Ireland (4255 sq km / 1643 sq miles) and the only one to have two administrative units, illogically called North Riding and South Riding after the Yorkshire model (illogical because a riding is literally a *thriding*, Old English for 'third part'). Because of 'It's a long way to Tipperary', a British army marching song in the First World War (but said to predate that war), Tipperary is one of the most internationally recognizable of Irish placenames, hence its choice as a brand name for cheese and for a bottled water that rivals BALLYGOWAN for sales.

'Tipperary So Far Away'. The title of a ballad about the Republican hero Sean Treacy (1895–1920) who was killed in Dublin during the Anglo-Irish War. Treacy was a leading GAELIC LEAGUE organizer in south Tipperary, and a member of the IRISH VOLUNTEERS. With Dan BREEN he led the SOLOHEADBEG ambush that began the War of Independence. He and Breen were also involved in an attempt to assassinate the viceroy, Lord FRENCH, in Dublin in December 1919. Treacy was killed in a gun battle in Talbot Street, Dublin, on 14 October 1920. The ballad begins, inaccurately: 'The moon shone down on O'Connell Street / Where a dying rebel lay,' and concludes 'in Tipperary so far away'. US President Ronald Reagan quoted a line from the ballad when he visited his supposed ancestral home at Ballyporeen, Co. Tipperary, on 3 June 1984.

Tír na mBan (Irish, 'the land of women'). In Irish mythology, a territory (pronounced 'cheer na man') full of the beautiful and desirable women of the OTHERWORLD, who are able to fulfil all earthly desires. It is usually visited by voyagers in IMMRAM tales, but, with typical human perversity, the lucky visitors eventually grow tired of all the entertainment provided and begin to long for home.
See also MAEL DÚIN.

Tír na nÓg (Irish, 'the land of youth'). In Irish mythology, the strongest and most desirable of the many manifestations of the Celtic OTHERWORLD. It is the Irish equivalent of Elysium or Valhalla, where gods and fortunate mortals remain eternally young and live in perfect amity. It has passed into HIBERNO-ENGLISH idiom (pronounced 'cheer na nogue') as a metaphor for childhood, interpreted as 'the land of the young'.
See also THOMPSON IN TÍR NA NÓG.

Tirry, William. An Augustinian priest executed in Clonmel on 2 May 1654. He was one of the 17 Irish martyrs beatified in 1992. In 1656 the Augustinians were given a college in Rome, San Matteo, in order to educate priests to return to the ministry in Ireland. The Irish Augustinians still have a church in Rome, St Patrick's in Via Boncompagni.

Tír Tairnigiri (Irish, 'the land of promise'). In Irish mythology, a paradisaical island, the home of MANANNÁN MAC LIR and his daughter Niamh (*see* OISÍN). It is pronounced 'cheer tarna geary'.

'Tis all over. The last recorded words of Lord CASTLEREAGH, who committed suicide on 18 August 1822 by cutting his throat. The testimony was given by Dr Bankhead at the inquest, the following day:

> I stepped into his dressing-room, and saw him standing with his front towards the window, which was opposite to the door at which I entered. His face was directed towards the ceiling. Without turning his head, on the instant he heard my step, he exclaimed: 'Bankhead, let me fall on your arm – 'tis all over!' I caught him in my arms as he was falling, and perceived that he had a knife in his right hand, very firmly clenched, all over bloody. I did not see him use it; he must have used it before I came into the room.

'Tish the fashion of Ireland. An early example of STAGE-IRISH charm from George Farquhar's *The Twin-rivals* (1702). The hero Hermes Woudbe's comic servant, significantly named TEAGUE, plays a vital part in outwitting miscreants in a plot to deprive his master of his rightful inheritance and the hand of his fiancée, Constance. First he has to pretend that he is possessed of great simplicity, as in this encounter with the villain Subtleman:

> *Subtleman:* And how do you intend to live?
> *Teague:* By eating, dear joy, fen I can get it; and by sleeping when I get none: 'tish the fashion of Ireland.

Titanic. A White Star liner, launched in Belfast in 1912 by HARLAND AND WOLFF. Regarded as virtually unsinkable, she hit a huge iceberg off Newfoundland at 11.40 p.m. on 14 April and sank at 2.20 a.m., resulting in the deaths of 1515 of her complement of 2021. The story has continued to fascinate and has been the subject of at least six films, including the very successful *A Night to Remember* (1958) and *Titanic* (1997). The sinking had a serious psychological effect on Belfast as a buoyant manufacturing city.

> You feeling-hearted Christians, oh listen to my tale;
> The gallant ship Titanic for New York land did sail.
> She was lovely, and the largest boat that ever yet was seen
> But she lies with fifteen hundred souls beneath the Atlantic Sea.
>
> 'The Titanic', in *Songs of Belfast* (1978), ed. David Hammond

See also 'CONVERGENCE OF THE TWAIN, THE'; 'SWEET KINGSWILLIAMSTOWN'; *UNSINKABLE MOLLY BROWN, THE*.

Tithe. An exaction for the support of the Church of Ireland levied on the population at large and defined as 'the tenth part of the increase, yearly arising and renewing from the profits of the lands, the stock upon lands, and the personal industry of the inhabitants'. Presbyterians and Catholics alike bitterly resented the imposition, which in the late 18th and early 19th centuries intensified support for agrarian SECRET SOCIETIES and in the 1830s led to what is known as the TITHE WAR. Liability was assessed by tithe-proctors, who were often Catholics, and who aroused great enmity. Although the burden of tithes was made less contentious by the reforms of the 1830s, it was not until the DISESTABLISHMENT OF THE CHURCH OF IRELAND in 1869 that the problem was entirely solved.

Tithe War. A conflict relating to the payment of TITHES that peaked in the period 1830–8. The first incident of the war occurred in Graiguenamanagh, Co. Kilkenny, and involved a local priest whose cattle were to be seized. Father Doyle organized resistance among local people, with the blessing of the bishop, and there were many other such instances involving Catholic clergy. The conflict involved robberies, burnings, riots, attacks on houses, cattle-maiming, assaults and killings. In January 1831, 12 people were killed in Newtownbarry, Co.

Wexford; in an incident in Doon, Co. Tipperary, in 1834, 19 civilians were killed by the military. Counties Kilkenny, Tipperary, Cork and Waterford were worst affected, as well as some areas in the Midlands. Successive administrations made various attempts to solve the problem by shifting the burden of tithe-payment from tenants-at-will. Finally in 1838 the Tithe Rent Charge Act, brought before government by Thomas DRUMMOND, made the head landlord liable for payment of tithes, of which he could then add a proportion as a charge on the rent paid by the tenant. The office of tithe-proctor (*see* TITHE) was abolished.

Titmarsh, Michael Angelo. The pen name used by William Makepeace Thackeray (1811–63) for, among other works, *The Irish Sketchbook* (1843), though in a dedicatory epistle he reveals his true name for the first time in his literary career, laying 'aside the travelling-title of Mr Titmarsh' and acknowledging 'these favours in my own name'. The tribute was to the Irish novelist Charles LEVER (1806–72), 'a good Irishman ... from whom I have received a hundred acts of kindness and cordiality', in whose house he finished the book. Thackeray's first Irish journey (begun in 1840 with a contract from Chapman and Hall) had to be aborted when his unstable Irish wife, Isabella Creagh Shawe of Doneraile, Co. Cork, attempted suicide. The book is marred by caricature, not so much in the accounts of the characters met on the journeys as in some of the illustrations accompanying the text. One shows:

> Lord Mayor Mr O'Connell. I saw him in full council, in a brilliant robe of crimson velvet, ornamented with white satin bows, and sable collar, in an enormous cocked-hat, like a slice of an eclipsed moon – in the following costume, in fact –

There follows a sketch showing the clothes only slightly caricatured but the face of O'CONNELL is that of a predatory toad. Unlike most of the travellers of the time, Thackeray's view of the country is satirical, but he is too good a writer not to let the uncomfortable truth of the poverty and sectarianism of pre-Famine Ireland peep through the persiflage:

> To have 'an opinion about Ireland' one must begin by getting the truth; and where is that to be had in the country? Or rather there are two truths, the Catholic truth and the Protestant truth. The two parties do not see things with the same eyes.

Toasts. *Sláinte* ('health') is the most common Irish toast, and the word has passed into general use in Ireland and among the Irish abroad. More imaginative toasts in Irish are characteristically tongue-in-cheek:

> The health of the salmon: a sound heart, a wet mouth and death in Ireland.
> (*Sláinte an bhradáin: croí folláin, gob fliuch agus bás in Éirinn.*)
> May you have health and companionship,
> May you never be in need
> And may hair grow on your body
> As long as the whiskers of a goat.
> (*Sláinte chughat is cabhair*
> *is dealbh do deo ní rabhair*
> *Is go bhfásfaidh clúmh ar do chabhail*
> *Chomh fada le meigeal ghabhair.*)

See also ORANGE TOAST.

Tóchar Phádraic. An ancient pilgrim path (TOGHER) from Ballintubber to Croagh Patrick (*see* REEK, THE) in Co. Mayo.

To every cow her calf. The legendary judgement of Diarmait Mac Cerbaill, the high king of Ireland, in the matter of FINNIAN OF MOVILLE's psalter. A character as significant as COLUM CILLE inevitably gathered about him many stories, most of them fanciful. This tale recounts the surreptitious copying by the saint of the scriptural text that was the property of Finnian of Moville. Finnian claimed exclusive rights and asked the high king to arbitrate. The judgement was probably the earliest statement about copyright in literary history. As recorded in modern Irish in *Beatha Colaim Cille* (1532), the biography of the saint written under the direction of Maghnus Ó Domhnaill (d.1536), the lord of Donegal, it read; '*Le gach boin a boinín, le gach leabhar a leabhrán*' ('To every cow its calf; to every book its version'). The legend continues that Colum Cille's rage

was such that he resolved vengeance on Diarmait, and when the son of the king of Connacht (who was under the saint's protection) was executed for an accidental killing, war was inevitable. Colum Cille's next move was to incite hostilities between the Ulster UÍ NÉILL and the king with resultant losses to Diarmait of 3000 of his soldiers at the Battle of CÚL DREIMHNE.

Tóg go bog é (Irish, 'take it soft'). An exhortation to calm down. The phrase is an example of a CÚPLA FOCAL known to almost all Irish people, even those who claim to know no Irish.

Togher. An Iron Age roadway (from the Irish *tóchar*) made of logs or stones and enabling travel through wet or boggy areas. One of the most celebrated toghers, which dendrochronology shows to date from exactly 148 BC, was excavated in Corlea bog in Co. Longford in 1975. Of the 3 km (2 miles) of oak track exposed, 40 m (44 yds) were transported to Co. Clare and laid in the outdoor archaeological museum at CRAGGAUNOWEN.

See also TÓCHAR PHÁDRAIC.

Tóibín, Colm (b.1955). Novelist, journalist and critic. He was born in Enniscorthy, Co. Wexford, and educated at University College Dublin. *The South* (1990), his prize-winning first novel about an Irish artist's love affair in and with Spain, was followed by *The HEATHER BLAZING* (1993). *The Story of the Night* (1996) describes in a deliberately unstructured way the life of a gay, HIV-positive Argentine with an English mother during the Falklands War. Tóibín's latest novel is *The Master* (2004). His non-fiction includes *Homage to Barcelona* (1989), *Walking along the Border* (1987), a remarkable look at Ulster, and *Lady Gregory's Toothbrush* (2002).

Tóibín, Nioclás (1928–94). Singer. Regarded as one of the greatest of all SEAN-NÓS singers, Nioclás Tóibín was born in Ring, in the Co. Waterford Gaeltacht (*see* DÉISE, THE) and learned traditional songs from his parents. He was All-Ireland champion in the Oireachtas *sean-nós* competition (now Corn Uí Riada) for an unprecedented three consecutive years (1961–3). Tóibín, who was admired for the purity of his tone and the depth of feeling he conveyed, had a repertoire of more than 300 traditional songs, some of them, like 'The CON-NORYS' local to his area, others like 'RÓISÍN DUBH' ('Dark Róisín') in the category of *amh-ráin mhóra* ('great' songs) that are to be found countrywide. A compilation of Nioclás Tóibín's performances from the archives of RTÉ was released as *Rinn na Gael*; it includes a heartbreakingly beautiful rendition of 'Róisín Dubh'.

Tolka Row. A popular RTÉ television drama series which was first broadcast in 1963. Set in working-class Dublin and scripted by Maura Laverty (*see* FULL AND PLENTY), it was the home station's first attempt at realistic warts-and-all programming, a precursor of the modern soap opera. James Bartley and Laurie Morton were among the stars.

Tom and Jerry. A comic pair invented by Pierce Egan (1772–1849) – not the cat and mouse of the Hanna-Barbera cartoons (though there may have been some unconscious sugges-tion when it came to naming the characters). Though his birthplace is usually given as Lon-don, Egan was almost certainly born in Ireland. His collection of sketches, *Life in London, or The Day and Night Scenes of Jerry Hawthorn Esq. And his Elegant Friend, Corinthian Tom*, was published by George Cruikshank (1792–1878) and his brother Robert in 1821. It gave a graphic slangy picture of the life of the men about town of the time. The same year Egan published *Real Life in Ireland, or the Day and Night Scenes, roving rambles, sprees, blunders, bodderation and blarney of Brian Boru, Esq. And his elegant friend, Sir Shawn O'Dogherty … by a Real Paddy*. Brian and Shawn became the Tom and Jerry of Dublin. The stuff was the STAGE-IRISH that its English audience demand-ed, but the paddiness was authentic.

Tom Billy (1875–1943). Tom Billy Murphy was a blind fiddler who travelled throughout

SLIABH LUACHRA on a self-piloting donkey in order to teach music, specializing in fiddle and tin whistle. He would stay in a particular house for a week or more, teaching the young people during the day and entertaining the adults by night. He is said to have known more than 100 reels and was also famous for slow airs. There are no recordings of his work.

Tomelty, Joseph (1911–95). Actor, playwright and novelist. He was born in Portaferry, Co. Down, and left school at 12 to become a house painter in Belfast. His first play, *Barnum Was Right* (1940), a broad comedy, was originally a radio play, and he was to write much for that medium, especially a Belfast series, *The* MCCOOEYS (1948–54). Apart from his best-known drama ALL SOULS NIGHT he wrote 12 other plays, including *The End House* (1944) about the sectarian strife of the 1930s, and *Is the Priest at Home?* (1954), a sympathetic account of Ulster clerical life. *All Souls Night* is set in the region of Strangford Lough, near Tomelty's birthplace, also the scene of his first novel *Red Is the Port Light* (1948), about pas-sion, madness and the rip-tides of the lough. *The Apprentice* (1953), also set in the Belfast of the 1930s, draws heavily on his experiences as a decorator. His appearance in George Shiels's play *The* PASSING DAY, one of three put on in the Belfast Opera House to celebrate the Festi-val of Britain in 1951, won him a film contract and a busy career as a character actor. This ended tragically with a serious car crash during the making of the film *Bhowani Junction* in 1954. He never fully recovered from his in-juries and his careers as writer and actor were effectively finished. He died in Belfast on 7 June 1995.

Tomhaisín. A small measure, for instance of whiskey; also a paper cone to hold a measure of snuff. The word derives from *tomhas*, the Irish word for 'measurement', followed by the diminutive *-ín*. The word is used in HIBERNO-ENGLISH: 'He poured me out a *tomhaisín*.'

Tone, Matilda (1769–1849). The wife of Wolfe TONE. She was born Matilda Witherington, and married Tone when she was only 16 after he met her gaze from an upper window of her father's draper's premises in Grafton Street, Dublin. They had one son, William Theobald Wolfe Tone (b. 1791), and Matilda would help him to prepare for publication Wolfe Tone's *Journals*, published as *The Autobiography of Wolfe Tone* in Washington in 1826. She died in the USA and was buried in Washington, but her body was later re-interred in the Green-Wood cemetery in Brooklyn, New York. In 1996 Irish President Mary ROBINSON unveiled a restored memorial over her grave.

Tone, (Theobald) Wolfe (1763–98). Patriot. He was born at 44 Stafford Street (now Wolfe Tone Street), Dublin, on 20 June 1763, the son of a Protestant coachmaker, educated at Trinity College Dublin and the King's Inns, and called to the Bar in 1789. He first championed the cause of Catholics with *An Argument on Behalf of the Catholics of Ireland* (1791), and in the same year co-founded in Belfast and Dublin, along with Thomas Russell (*see* MAN FROM GOD KNOWS WHERE, THE) and Napper TANDY, the Society of UNITED IRISHMEN, influenced by the radicalism and secularism of the French Revolution. His political thinking – separatist and non-sectarian – is most famously expressed in one of the holy texts of Republicanism, contained in his own posthumously published autobiography:

> To subvert the tyranny of our execrable government, to break the connection with England, the never-failing source of all our political evils and to assert the independence of my country – these were my objects. To unite the whole people of Ireland, to abolish the memory of all past dissensions and to substitute the common name of Irishman in place of the denominations of Protestant, Catholic and Dissenter – these were my means.
>
> *The Autobiography of Wolfe Tone*, 1826

In July 1792 Tone became secretary to the CATHOLIC COMMITTEE and was a delegate to London on behalf of the CATHOLIC CONVENTION, but he soon despaired of the willingness of the government to grant any substantial measure of CATHOLIC EMANCIPATION. In 1795 he was investigated, after having associated with William JACKSON, a Republican sent by the French government to Ireland to investigate the possibility of an invasion of England, and agreed to emigrate to America, having signed a confession of treason.

Tone arrived in Paris via Philadelphia in February of the following year, travelling under the name 'Citizen Smith', and approached the Committee of Public Safety to persuade them to mount an expedition to Ireland. His mission was successful: the expedition of December 1796 that scattered in the storms of BANTRY BAY had General Hoche as leader and Tone himself as adjutant-general. After he received news of the REBELLION OF 1798, he persuaded the French to launch another expedition, this time under the command of General Hardy (Hoche had died the year before), which sailed on 12 October 1798. Tone was captured aboard the *Hoche* during an action against the English fleet in Lough Swilly on 16 October, tried and sentenced to death on 10 November ('a fig for disembowelling if they hang me first' he wrote in his journal). He had pleaded guilty to treason: 'I mean not to give this court any useless trouble and wish to spare them the idle task of examining witnesses. I admit the facts alleged.' On the morning appointed for his execution, while legal challenges by his counsel John Philpot CURRAN were still being prepared, he cut his throat with a penknife, cutting his windpipe instead of his jugular ('I find I am but a poor anatomist') and died on 19 November 1798.

For his courage, personal charm and wit, and for his formulation and expression of the doctrine of Republicanism, Tone is one of Nationalist Ireland's great heroes, and his grave at BODENSTOWN CHURCHYARD, Co. Kildare, is a place of pilgrimage.

See also TONE, MATILDA; TONEHENGE; WOLF TONES, THE.

Tonehenge. A monument to Wolfe Tone (1967)

at the northeastern corner of ST STEPHEN'S GREEN in Dublin by sculptor Edward Delaney (b.1930). It is nicknamed 'Tonehenge' because the statue of Tone is surrounded by granite standing stones.

Tonna, Charlotte Elizabeth (1790–1846). Poet and novelist, who used the pen name Charlotte Elizabeth in all her published work. She was born in Norwich and came to live in Kilkenny with her husband, a Captain Phelan. They were soon divorced and she married Lewis Tonna, going to live with him in Ulster. She wrote many religious tracts as 'Charlotte Elizabeth' and at least 30 novels, mainly on the social problems afflicting the England of the time. Firmly anti-Catholic, regarding 'Popery as the curse of Ireland', it was almost inevitable that she should turn her art to the great victory of Irish Protestantism, the Siege of DERRY, which she celebrated in two ballads, 'The MAIDEN CITY' (a sobriquet by which the city was subsequently known) and 'No Surrender' (the cry of defiance of the defenders). One of her novels, *Derry – A Tale of the Revolution of 1688* (1839) weaves a romantic and partisan tale around the city's 17th-century history:

> The few seconds that elapsed before that cloud of smoke rolled away, leaving the *Mountjoy* once more fully visible – those few seconds seemed long indeed to the breathless gazers. They passed, and the gallant ship reappeared, not lying in stranded helplessness upon the bank, but, majestically floating in deep water, she ploughed the dancing tide onward towards the town.
>
> 'That broadside saved her!' shouted Walker. 'She has bounded from the shore – she has passed the boom! Derry and Victory!'

Tooth in it, not to put a. *See* NOT TO PUT A TOOTH IN IT.

Top of the morning to you, the. A HIBERNO-ENGLISH forenoon greeting, well-intentioned and conversational in the 19th century but now either comic or mocking. It successfully crossed the Atlantic where its suggestion of the best time of day for agricultural work would have been meaningless in the Irish ghettos. It became a harmless stage and film label for the Oirish looking back to the old country. The likely modern response would be: 'And the rest of the day to yourself.'

> O Ireland, isn't it grand you look –
> Like a bride in her rich adornin'!
> With all the pent-up love of my heart,
> I bid you the top of the mornin'!
>
> JOHN LOCKE (1817–89): 'Dawn on the Irish Coast', in *Irish Literature*, V (1904)

Torc. A gold collar or armband worn by Celtic nobles. Often elaborately decorated with precious stones, they represented the most perfect form of early Irish art. The most recent Irish find was in November 2001 on the beach of Dooyork, Geesala, Co. Mayo; three torcs were discovered by two local brothers. Subsequent excavations revealed amber beads. Torcs and beads were both dated as from 3000 BC, suggesting that torcs were worn in Ireland long before the arrival of the Celts.

Torc Waterfall. An 18-m (60-ft) waterfall on Torc Mountain, 5 km (3 miles) south of Killarney, Co. Kerry. It is the 'wild cataract' of Tennyson's poem, and a popular tourist attraction. In 1848 Tennyson paid a visit to Killarney while he was staying for a month with Aubrey DE VERE at de Vere's home, Curragh Chase in Co. Limerick. He wrote the lyric 'The Splendour Falls' (published in the 1850 edition of *The Princess*, and in the third edition of *The Rose*, 1853), when he heard a bugle blown beneath the mountain known as the Eagle's Nest, and 'eight distinct echoes'. The 'castle walls' must be those of ROSS CASTLE, which is in reality several miles away, even as the crow flies.

> The splendour falls on castle walls
> And snowy summits old in story;
> The long light shakes across the lakes,
> And the wild cataract leaps in glory.
> Blow, bugle, blow, set the wild echoes flying,
> Blow, bugle; answer, echoes, dying, dying, dying.

Torna. The pseudonym of Tadhg Ó Donnchadha (1874–1949), Irish-language poet, editor and scholar. He was born in Carrignavar near Cork city and educated at the North Monastery in Cork and St Patrick's College in Dublin. While a teacher in Dublin he joined the GAELIC LEAGUE and became acquainted with the figures of the IRISH LITERARY REVIVAL, translating into Irish some of the work of Yeats and George Moore and publishing a collection of his own poetry, *Leoithne Andeas* ('south winds') (1905). He was professor of Irish at University College Cork (1916–44), and prepared editions of several great Gaelic poets, among them Aogán Ó RATHAILE (with Pádraig Ó Duinnín; *see* DINNEEN'S DICTIONARY).

Torrent of dark, muddled stuff. The description of the Irish language that poured from the lips of Douglas HYDE by George Moore in *Hail and Farewell I: Ave* (1911):

> … and then a torrent of dark muddied stuff flowed from him, much like the porter that used to come up from Carnacun to be drunk by the peasants on Midsummer nights when a bonfire was lighted. It seemed to me a language suitable for the celebration of some Celtic rite, but too remote for modern use. It had never been spoken by ladies in silken gowns with fans in their hands.

Tory (Irish *toraí*, 'pursuer', 'bandit'). The name applied in the 17th century to Irish Catholic outlaws and bandits who harassed the English in Ireland. In the reign of Charles II (1660–85) the name came to be used as an abusive term for the supporters of the crown and its prerogatives at the time of the struggle over the Exclusion Bills. As supporters of the Church of England, Tories opposed nonconformist and Catholic alike, and it is from this conservatism that the modern political term originates. In Ireland the word, first used around the 1650s, was used as the equivalent of RAPPAREE. *See also* 'PEELER AND THE GOAT, THE'.

Tory Island. An island some 10 km (6 miles) off the northwest coast of Donegal. There are two main settlements, East Town and West Town. In Irish mythology Tory Island was the home of the FOMORIANS. Their king, BALOR OF THE EVIL EYE, gave his name to Dún Bhalair (Irish,

'Balar's fort'), a promontory fort at the east end of the island. Later, in the 6th century, COLUM CILLE founded a monastery here; there are a few scant remains. There being no rats on the island, visitors are advised to take Tory clay back to the mainland and to spread it around the house to guard against rat infestation. Tory Island is separated from the mainland by Tory Sound – and by frequent storms, hence its fuller Irish name Toraigh na dTonn ('Tory of the breakers'). In 1974 a storm cut off the island for more than eight weeks, and almost led to a permanent evacuation. However, the fortunes of the Irish-speaking islanders have since revived, and the people survive on tourism, lobsters and – surprisingly – painting: the Tory School of naïve art has developed an international audience since the 1960s. One of the painters, Patsy Dan Rodgers, has the title 'King of Tory Island', a role that involves attracting visitors and generally promoting the place.

To School through the Fields. The first volume (1988) in a series of autobiographical books by Alice Taylor, who was born in the Newmarket area of north Co. Cork in 1938 and who after her marriage presided over the post office in the village of Inishannon near Bandon. *To School through the Fields* is a rose-tinted account of a traditional rural Irish childhood in pre-electrification days, more 'prosperous and happy' than 'poor but happy'. The book was enormously successful, sales helped by the winning personality of the author and her popularity as a guest of Gay Byrne on *The LATE LATE SHOW*. Taylor produced several similar volumes of autobiography: *Quench the Lamp* (1990), *The Village* (1992) and *The Woman of the House* (1997). She has also published poetry and a novel.

Toss. To 'knock down' or 'demolish'. This verb, heard in the northern half of the country, might be applied to a person, a tree or a building.

Tosser. 'I haven't a tosser' means 'I haven't a penny'.

Tóstal, An. The National Tourism Festival, a national festival of culture (the Irish word *tóstal* means 'pageant', 'display', 'parade'), which ran 5–26 April 1953 with the support of the FIANNA FÁIL government. Perhaps because it was so ambitious the project in general was not a success, and it survived only in Drumshanbo, Co. Leitrim, because of the enthusiasm of the local organizer Joe Mooney (*see* JOE MOONEY SUMMER SCHOOL). The successful and long-running Dublin Theatre Festival developed out of it.

Tottenham in his boots. A toast popular with the PATRIOTS because of a parliamentary victory in 1731. Colonel Charles Tottenham (1685–1758), the member for New Ross, Co. Wexford, arrived in Dublin in time for a crucial vote on the national debt, still wearing a large pair of riding-boots.

> He had ridden all through the night, nearly sixty Irish miles [76.4 miles / 122 km], to cast his votes for the patriots. For many a long year after that 'Tottenham in his Boots' was a standing toast in patriot circles.
>
> MAURICE CRAIG (b.1919): *Dublin 1660–1860* (1952)

Tough as *táithéalann*, as (Irish, *Chomh righin le táithéalann*). A simile referring to *táithéalann* (wild honeysuckle, more commonly called woodbine in Ireland), which is hard to break and does not snap cleanly.

Tourism. Pre-Famine Ireland attracted tourists in very small numbers, although tours of the country (with attendant publications) by such as Arthur YOUNG and Anna Maria Hall were popular. Access to the interior was improved by the Bianconi cars (known as BIANS), by the construction of canals and especially by the development of a railway network in the mid-19th century, which meant that resorts such as KILLARNEY and SALTHILL could be reached in comfort. The visit of Queen Victoria to Killarney in 1858 and of Edward VII to Connemara for fishing in 1903 did much to popularize these unspoilt and picturesque areas. Thomas Cook offered the first package tour to Killarney and Glengarriff in 1895, and many American tourists still visit the southwest on such tours.

After the establishment of the Free State and Northern Ireland, both governments established tourist boards to exploit the country's landscape. In 1948 and 1955 respectively the Northern Ireland Tourist Board (NITB) and BORD FÁILTE (Fáilte Ireland since 2001), were put in place. For the Republic the period since the 1960s has seen enormous expansion in tourist numbers and income, so that tourism is now the leading indigenous industry; however, tourism in Northern Ireland suffered greatly during the Troubles. Since the beginning of the peace process the sister organizations have cooperated in campaigns to promote Ireland as a tourist destination, emphasizing relaxation, fresh air and the cultural commodities of *CEOL AGUS CRAIC*. An all-Ireland body, Tourism Ireland, was established under the framework of the GOOD FRIDAY AGREEMENT of 1998 to promote increased tourism to the island of Ireland. It is jointly funded by the two governments. The perception of Dublin as a centre of entertainment (a perception that accompanied the rise of the CELTIC TIGER) has also attracted large numbers of young short-break tourists from Britain and Europe.

Tourism Ireland. *See* TOURISM.

Tout. The most usual colloquial term for 'informer' used during the Northern Ireland TROUBLES. It features regularly in graffiti.

Towards. A HIBERNO-ENGLISH expression meaning 'while' or 'whereas', and often used to introduce a statement: 'Towards when *I* go to Cork, I take the train.'

Tower house. A fortified defensive dwelling, of the type built between 1400 and 1650 by Anglo-Irish settlers or gentry, mainly in or near towns or in areas owned by marcher lords such as the Burkes of Clanrickard. Usually square and of four storeys, they were surrounded by BAWNS[3]. It is estimated that up to 3000 tower houses were built, but those that survive are mostly in ruins. Yeats's THOOR BALLYLEE is such a tower house.

Town it climbs the mountain, the. The town of Cahirciveen, on the western side of the Ring of KERRY in the IVERAGH PENINSULA. 'The Boys from Barr na Sráide' (literally the 'top of the street' or 'top of the town') is the title of a poem by Sigerson Clifford (1913–85), who was born in Co. Cork but spent his childhood in Cahirciveen. It was published in *Ballads of a Bogman* (1955).

> O the town it climbs the mountain and looks
> upon the sea,
> And sleeping time or waking 'tis there I long to be,
> To walk again that kindly street, the place I grew
> a man
> And the boys of Barr na Sráide went hunting for
> the wran.

See also 'GHOST TRAIN FOR CROKE PARK, THE'.

Townland. The smallest local unit in the country, containing anything from two or three to dozens of houses. It is estimated that in the whole of Ireland there are about 51,000 townlands. They take their original Irish names from geographical or farming features, from early settlements or churches, or from mythology.

Town politically reliable, a. The description of Portadown, Co. Armagh, by the novelist Anthony Powell (1905–2000) in his memoirs *To Keep the Ball Rolling* (1976–82):

> The Battalion was first stationed at Portadown, a
> town politically reliable, if scenically unromantic.

Portadown is now notorious for the semipermanent DRUMCREE STAND-OFFS.

Townsend, John Sealy Edward (1868–1957). Physicist. He was born in Galway and educated at Trinity College Dublin. He was the first to calculate (in 1897) the electrical charge of one ion of gas. His publications include *Theory of Ionisation of Gases by Collision* (1910) and *Electricity in Gases* (1915).

Town with the hole in the middle, the. A fanciful description of Banbridge, Co. Down, because the level of the carriageway of the main street

was lowered in the mid-19th century and the sides joined by a bridge. It was the birthplace of Captain Francis Crozier (1796–1848), who was Sir John Franklin's second-in-command on his final, fatal voyage to find the Northwest Passage.

Tracy, Honor (1913–89). English novelist and journalist who made Ireland her home. She was born in Bury St Edmunds and educated at the Sorbonne. She settled in Ireland after a wartime career in the Women's Auxiliary Air Force (WAAF) and worked in the offices of *The* BELL, where she continued the work of therapeutic criticism of Irish mores begun by her mentor Sean O'FAOLAIN, with whom she had an affair. Her book of satirical reportage, *Mind You I've Said Nothing* (1956), caused controversy and litigation. She wrote several stylish comedies of Irish rural life and much about Spain.

See also STRAIGHT AND NARROW PATH, THE.

Traditional music. Irish music, both instrumental and vocal, that is regarded as being old, of the people and part of a living tradition. Not all of it is transmitted aurally, as there are also written sources, but the emphasis in learning and playing is still on the acquisition of tunes from listening to other players or singers.

See also COMHALTAS CEOLTÓIRÍ ÉIREANN; Ó RIADA, SEÁN; *SEAN-NÓS*; STEP DANCE.

Tragedies of Kerry. An account (1924) by Dorothy MACARDLE (1899–1958) of CIVIL WAR atrocities that took place in Kerry, told with a strong Republican bias. It includes an account of the BALLYSEEDY MASSACRE and the COUNTESS BRIDGE KILLINGS.

Traitors' Gate. The derisive nickname given by Nationalists to the triumphal arch on the north-west corner of ST STEPHEN'S GREEN commemorating the soldiers of the Royal Dublin Fusiliers who died in the Boer War (1899–1902). The original Traitors' Gate is in the Tower of London.

Traits and Stories of the Irish Peasantry. The title of a collection of prose pieces (1830) by William CARLETON, including two novellas ('Denis O'Shaughnessy' and 'The Poor Scholar'), short stories based on folklore, and accounts of the traditions of the peasants. *Traits and Stories* contains passages of vivid HIBERNO-ENGLISH dialogue, but also mockery and criticism of the peasantry.

Trake or **traich.** A still-current Ulster word, deriving from 'trek', used both as noun and verb to indicate the undertaking of a long, weary journey:

> You know, Frank, I've been thinking. When you are lifting the praties from that lough field it'll be a long traich up to Rathard. Would it no be better to clear one of the cottages on top o'the hill for a pratie house?
>
> SAM HANNA BELL (1909–80): *December Bride* (1951)

Tralee. The county town and administrative centre of Co. Kerry, situated on Tralee Bay, at the entrance to the DINGLE PENINSULA. It is also known as a tourist centre and has hosted the ROSE OF TRALEE contest since the 1950s. Originally the seat of the Fitzgeralds, Earls of DESMOND, the town was granted to an Elizabethan soldier, Edward Denny, in 1583, after the failure of the second DESMOND REBELLION, and the town's main street is Denny Street. The IRA was active in the town and its hinterland during the Anglo-Irish War of 1919–21, and the townspeople were subjected to martial law and reprisals, especially during the period November–December 1920. Tralee is the home of SIAMSA TÍRE and of the KERRY GROUP.

Tramore. A celebrated resort 16 km (10 miles) south of Waterford city. It boasts one of the longest stretches of beach in the country, and is also famous for its race meetings.
See also METAL MAN.

Translations. A play by Brian FRIEL, with which FIELD DAY was launched on 23 September 1980 in Derry Guildhall, with Ray McAnally, Liam Neeson and Stephen Rea among the cast. Set in Friel's Everyvillage, Ballybeg, in 1833, it describes the arrival of a detachment of Royal Engineers to map the place for the ORDNANCE SURVEY, and primarily concerns the effect of their presence on the two sons of Big Hugh, who runs the local HEDGE SCHOOL. Owen, the younger son, is happy to help the cartographic survey with translations of placenames, while Manus, the elder son, sees the survey as a symbol of colonization and the obliteration of Irish culture. Irish is taken as the only language spoken by the natives (though heard by the audience as English), and one of the highlights of the play is the love dialogue between Lieutenant Yolland and Máire Catach with neither understanding the words that the other is saying, yet fully aware of their deeper import. In this scene and in others the play's title is seen as multivalent.

> *Hugh:* Yes, it is a rich language, Lieutenant, full of the mythologies of fantasy and hope and self-deception – a syntax opulent with tomorrows. It is our response to mud cabins and a diet of potatoes; it is our only method of replying to … inevitabilities.

Transportation. A means of judicial punishment utilized from the mid-17th to the mid-19th century. Transportation from Ireland began in the Cromwellian period. In the 1650s thousands of prisoners of war, priests, homeless people and other undesirables were dispatched to the West Indies. For more than a hundred years, until the American Revolution of 1776, individuals reprieved from sentence of death or convicted of non-capital offences were shipped to the Caribbean and North America, where they worked as convict labourers for periods of 7 or 14 years or for life. Thereafter new penal colonies were founded in BOTANY BAY and VAN DIEMEN'S LAND (Tasmania) in Australia. About 40,000 convicts were transported to Australia between 1788 and 1868 (when transportation was abolished), many of them common criminals, but people convicted of agrarian or political offences (*see* SECRET SOCIETIES; WHITEBOYS) were also transported.
See also NORFOLK ISLAND.

Travel. A term once used in Ulster to describe

journeys on foot in contradistinction to riding or using other forms of transport.

Travellers. Up to the 1960s all travellers in Ireland were called 'tinkers'. Twenty years earlier, before aluminium and stainless steel receptacles had become available, they genuinely did earn their living as itinerant tinsmiths (the literal meaning of 'tinker'). Now the word 'tinker' is considered politically incorrect. The term 'itinerant' was also used by some people in the interim, but it quickly fell out of favour. Some people in the settled community simply call all travellers by the offensive name 'knackers', which has come to mean those who buy and sell door-to-door or from caravans or the boots of cars.

There are several travellers' rights and welfare groups to protect the interests of members of the community. The issues are complex, involving health, education (it was estimated in 2002 that 95% of travellers are illiterate), property and social welfare. Although the term 'travelling community' is widely used, in reality the travelling population is not homogeneous: some travellers want to settle down in houses (among the 'settled community') and send their children to school; others want decent halting sites but want to retain the option of being itinerant; others seem to want to set up camp wherever the spirit moves them. Those who wish to stay on the roads are helped to obtain caravans, and throughout the country local authorities are encouraged to provide intermediate sites with living accommodation and space for collections of scrap for those who feel they might eventually become part of the settled community. The accommodation units are known to the people as 'tigeens', from the Irish *tigín*, 'little house'. Because of the influx of refugees and asylum-seekers into Ireland in the latter half of the 1990s, the focus of racial prejudice has moved away from travellers. There is a body of travellers that moves between Ireland and the UK, using price differentials between the two countries to generate profit: local authorities in the United Kingdom also provide halting sites for Irish travellers.

> We are freeborn men of the travelling people;
> Got no fixed abode, with nomads we are
>   numbered …
>   EWEN MACCOLL (1915–89): 'The Travelling People'

Travelling teachers. The Irish-speaking teachers who travelled about the country to teach adults in the early days of the GAELIC LEAGUE. Known in Irish as *múinteoirí taistil*, they were assigned special areas and taught several classes in each, travelling from one venue (usually the local national school) to the next, usually by bicycle.

> 'We will wile away the time with fiddle, dance and
>   song;
> The way,' they say, 'is rough and the school is too
>   far to reach.'
> But wait – a stir at the door and in through the
>   jostling throng
> Comes the man skin-drenched from his wheel,
>   who said he would come to teach.
>   ALICE MILLIGAN (1866–1953): 'The Man on the
>   Wheel', in *We Sang for Ireland* (1950)

Treacy, Philip (b.1968). Milliner. He was born in Ahascragh, Co. Galway, and studied at the National College of Art and Design in Dublin and the Royal College in London. He is known for his exotic and elaborate confections, worn on catwalks all over the world by supermodels, and has worked with all the leading *haute couture* designers.

> I'm a great champion of the hat and England is
> the home of the hat. I sometimes have to remind
> myself that I am actually Irish … I've had a great
> time in [England] and I've had nothing but good
> spirit towards me. I just happen to be Irish …

Treacy, Sean. *See* 'TIPPERARY SO FAR AWAY'.

Treason-Felony Act. A measure rushed through Parliament in 1848 to allow the authorities to arrest members of YOUNG IRELAND. Those at risk of the law were persons 'who by open and advised speaking, compassed the intimidation of the crown or parliament'. The penalty for those found guilty was transportation for terms ranging from 14 years to life. The bill received the royal assent on 22 April and on 26 May John MITCHEL became the first Young Irelander to be found guilty under its terms. *See also* SPECIAL MEN.

Treaty, the. The Anglo-Irish Treaty of 6 December 1921, ending the ANGLO-IRISH WAR that had begun in 1919. The agreement was the result of negotiations begun in London on 11 October 1921 between a British team led by LLOYD GEORGE and an Irish delegation with plenipotentiary powers, led by Arthur GRIFFITH and Michael COLLINS. On the evening of 5 December Lloyd George issued an ultimatum to Griffith, threatening a resumption of war within three days if the Treaty was not agreed. After much discussion the delegates signed an agreement which made Ireland a FREE STATE within the Commonwealth; it also stipulated an OATH OF ALLEGIANCE to the crown for members of Parliament, and made permanent the GOVERNMENT OF IRELAND ACT of 1920 that established the statelet of NORTHERN IRELAND (*see also* PARTITION). The Treaty put a definite end to the Anglo-Irish War, but marked the beginning of a period of unrest and conflict leading to the CIVIL WAR. At a cabinet meeting on 8 December, the agreement was ratified by four votes to three, DE VALERA being the most significant dissenter. The oath of allegiance was at this stage seen by Republicans as the most unacceptable element in the Treaty.

Treaty of Limerick. *See* LIMERICK, TREATY OF.

Treaty ports. The ports retained for strategic reasons (harbour defences and aviation) by Britain by the terms of an annex to the TREATY of 1921. The ports concerned were Berehaven and Cobh in Co. Cork, Lough Swilly in Co. Donegal, and Belfast Lough. Oil-storage facilities were retained in Haulbowline, Co. Cork, and Rathmullen, Co. Donegal. The Free State government attempted to regain control of these ports in 1927 and 1932, but their proposals were rejected by the British administration. By 1938, however, they were considered by the chiefs of staff to be a liability,

given DE VALERA's refusal to sign a defence agreement with Britain, and were returned unconditionally in July of that year. *See also* 'NATION ONCE AGAIN, A'.

Treenahayla. *See* TRÍNA CHÉILE.

Trench, Richard Chenevix (1807–86). Church of Ireland Archbishop of Dublin (1864–84). He was born in Dublin on 5 September 1807, the son of the the writer Melasina Trench (1768–1827), whose letters and journals he edited in *Remains* (1862). As Archbishop of Dublin he fought against the DISESTABLISHMENT OF THE CHURCH OF IRELAND. He published collections of poems and devotional works, and his distinction as a philologist is reflected in his *Study of Words* (1851).

Trench, William Steuart (1808–72). Agronomist and writer. He was born in Queen's County (Co. Laois) and educated at Trinity College Dublin. He worked as land agent on the Shirley estate in Co. Monaghan (1843–5) and on the Lansdowne estate in Kenmare, Co. Kerry, from 1859. His book *Realities of Irish Life* (1868) drew on his experiences as a land agent and was a great popular sucess. Other works included *Ierne: a Tale* (1871) and *Sketches of Life and Character in Ireland* (1872).

Treoir. A traditional music magazine (*treoir* means 'direction') published since 1968 by COMHALTAS CEOLTÓIRÍ ÉIREANN.

Trevaskis, Brian. A radical student from Trinity College Dublin who became infamous for his attack on Bishop Michael Browne of Galway on *The* LATE LATE SHOW in March 1966, the month after the BISHOP AND THE NIGHTIE affair. Trevaskis called Bishop Browne a 'moron' for squandering money on building new churches instead of addressing social problems. The following week the presenter Gay BYRNE invited Trevaskis on the show again to apologize to Bishop Browne, but he compounded the insult by inquiring whether the bishop knew the meaning of the word 'Christianity'. On episodes such as this was founded

The Late Late Show's reputation for being iconoclastic.

Trevelyan, Charles (1807–86). Public administrator. As assistant secretary to the treasury, he was responsible for relief measures during the GREAT FAMINE of 1845–9. A firm believer in free trade, he defended the export of grain (*see* TREVELYAN'S CORN) and controlled the distribution of public funds through public works. In 1848, despite an outbreak of cholera, he suspended treasury grants to Irish Poor Law districts. Trevelyan later summed up the situation in 1848 in the anonymously published *The Irish Crisis*:

> The deep and inveterate root of social evil has been laid bare by a direct stroke of an all-wise and all-merciful providence.

Trevelyan was also responsible for recommending major reforms in the recruitment and organization of the British civil service. He served in India, as governor of Madras, and published books on India and on Hinduism.
See also BLACK '47.

Trevelyan's corn. In Irish Nationalist history one of the greatest wrongs ever perpetrated against the Irish people by a British administration was the export of grain at the height of the GREAT FAMINE. For this allegedly genocidal decision Charles TREVELYAN is held largely responsible. Trevelyan deployed troops 'to be directed on particular ports at short notice' to ensure the continued export of grain in the face of public disorder.
See also 'FIELDS OF ATHENRY, THE'.

Trevor, William (b.1928). Short-story writer, novelist and playwright. He was born William Trevor Cox in Mitchelstown, Co. Cork, and educated at St Columba's College in Dublin. He went to live in England in 1954 and published a series of upsettingly comic novels, filled with eccentrics whose bizarre speech matched their personalities. The Irish writer began to surface in the novel *Mrs Eckdorf in O'Neill's Hotel* (1969), in which his descriptions of a seedy Dublin have an even greater authenticity than his London scenes. His various collections of short stories, including *The Day We Got Drunk on Cake* (1967), *The Ballroom of Romance* (1972), *Angels at the Ritz* (1975), all have their complement of insightful evocations of Irish life, often from the viewpoint of a reticent child narrator, in the small towns of the south and west. Trevor has continued to publish fiction of distinction at regular intervals, including the novels *Felicia's Journey* (1994), *Death in Summer* (1998) and *The Story of Lucy Gault* (2002), which won the Irish fiction prize sponsored by the KERRY GROUP at LISTOWEL WRITERS WEEK in 2003.
See also 'BALLROOM OF ROMANCE, THE'.

Triads. Frequently used in proverbs, lore and set expressions in Irish and HIBERNO-ENGLISH:

> The three things that can't be hidden: love, thirst, itching. (*Trí rudaí nach féidir a cheilt: grá, tart, tochas.*)
>
> The three worst things to have in a house: a dissatisfied woman, a leaking roof, a smoking chimney. (*Trí rudaí is measa sa tigh: bean mhíshásta, díon ag ligint braon anuas, simní plúchta.*)
>
> The three things impossible to understand: a woman's mind, the work of bees, the ebb and flow of the tide. (*Trí rudaí nach bhfuil aon tuiscint orthu: intleacht na mban; obair na mbeach; teacht agus imeacht na taoide.*)
>
> The three sharpest things on earth: a hen's eye after a grain; a blacksmith's eye after a nail; and an old crone's eye after her son's wife. (*Na trí rudaí is géire ar bith: súil circe i ndiaidh gráinne; súil gabha i ndiaidh táirne; agus súil caillí i ndiaidh bean a mhic.*)
>
> The three great lies of Irish life: the cheque is in the post; just one for the road; of course I'll still love you tomorrow.

Tribe. A term that has traditionally been cognate with the unit of population or community known as *tuath*, but the term is now rejected by historians of early and medieval Ireland on the grounds that it is too general and that it carries an association of blood-kinship with the chieftain that did not in fact exist. The word *fine* in the name of the political party

FINE GAEL, usually translated as 'tribe', more exactly means an extended family or kinship group.

Tribunals. In the aftermath of the McCRACKEN TRIBUNAL of 1997 two further judicial tribunals were set up under high-court judges to investigate allegations of political corruption. One such tribunal, under Mr Justice Michael Moriarty, was to investigate the ANSBACHER DEPOSITS and related payments to politicians, while the other, under Mr Justice Fergus Flood, was set up in November 1997 to investigate corruption in relation to the planning process in north Co. Dublin; this corruption included allegations of payments to politicians. An interim report in September 2002 confirmed the existence of such corruption. The tribunal continues to sit.

Trick or Treat Killings. The grisly nickname given to the Hallowe'en shootings in the Rising Sun bar in Greysteel, Co. Derry, on Saturday, 30 October 1993. The seven dead included two women and an 81-year-old man; six were Catholics and one a Protestant; 13 people were injured. The attack, claimed as a reprisal for the SHANKILL ROAD bombing of the previous Saturday, was carried out by the Ulster Freedom Fighters (*see* UDA/UFF). The nickname came from the cry of one of the killers, who coolly reloaded before completing his task.

Tricolour. In the CONSTITUTION OF 1937 the 'tricolour of green, white and orange' (often called gold) was declared the Irish national flag. Association of the tricolour with Nationalist aspirations dates from 1848, when Thomas Francis Meagher (MEAGHER OF THE SWORD) brought home to Ireland a gift of the flag from the citizens of France. He presented it to the Irish Confederation in Dublin and John MITCHEL declared: 'I hope to see that flag one day waving as our national banner.' The tricolour is associated in particular with the 1916 EASTER RISING, when it was raised over the GPO. *See also* STARRY PLOUGH, THE.

Triduum. A Catholic devotion lasting three days,

much practised in Ireland up till the end of the 1960s.

Trimble, [William] David (b.1944). Politician and barrister. He was educated at Queen's University Belfast and lectured in the law department (1968–90) there, becoming assistant dean of the faculty. In the 1970s he was deputy leader of the Vanguard Unionists, a party founded in 1973 out of disenchantment with the policies of the proximate Unionist leaders. The party had largely disintegrated by 1977, and the following year Trimble joined the UUP (Ulster Unionist Party) and won the Upper Bann seat in a by-election in 1990. Regarded as a stern right-winger, he was involved in the first serious DRUMCREE STAND-OFF on 11 July 1995; in his euphoria at a resolution favourable to the marchers he was caught on camera tripping hand in hand with his DUP rival Ian PAISLEY as they proceeded along the Garvaghy Road. In August that year he was confirmed as leader of the party.

Trimble brought fresh energy to the UUP, making it the dominant Unionist party at the NORTHERN IRELAND FORUM elections in May 1996. He was back at Drumcree in July, publicly supporting the Orange marchers against the RUC. He continued in a seeming stance of uncompromising hardline politics, but eventually supported the GOOD FRIDAY AGREEMENT on 10 April 1998. He became first minister, but continued to insist that SINN FÉIN could not be part of the executive without DECOMMISSIONING. In December 1998 he and John HUME of the SDLP were awarded the Nobel Peace Prize. Since then he has been under constant attritional attack by anti-agreement Unionists in his own party led by Jeffrey Donaldson and from without by the DUP. The convenient weapon is the lack of significant moves on decommissioning by the Provisional IRA and the suggestion that they are in constant breach of the ceasefire.

Trim Castle. An Anglo-Norman castle in Co. Meath, one of the finest in the country, built by Hugh de Lacey, a rival of STRONGBOW.

HENRY II granted the Irish kingdom of Midhe (Meath) to de Lacey in 1172, and the castle was built in three phases over a 50-year period, beginning in 1176. The castle is strategically situated, overlooking a ford on the River Boyne on the site of an earlier monastic foundation. Three out of the original four towers and the original keep survive.

'Trimmin's on the Rosary, The'. A poem as by John A. O'Brien (pen name of P.J. Hartigan, an Australian priest), recalling in exile the extra prayers that inevitably followed the saying of the family ROSARY at home in Ireland. They seemed to give great solace to the mothers who insisted they be said, but were a cause of great impatience to the younger members of the family. Hartigan, who was born in Yass, New South Wales, was parish priest of Narrandera. Following publication of his book, *Around the Boree Log* (1921), he became known as 'the poet laureate of the Irish settlers in Australia'.

> ... They were long, long prayers in truth
> And we used to call them 'Trimmin's' in my
>   disrespectful youth.
> She would pray for kith and kin, and all the
>   friends she'd ever known,
> Yes, and everyone of us could boast a 'trimmin'
>   all his own.
> She would pray for all our little needs, and every
>   shade of care
> That might darken o'er the Sugarloaf, she'd meet
>   it with a prayer.
> She would pray for this one's 'sore complaint' or
>   that one's 'hurted hand'
> Or that someone else might make a deal and get
>   'that bit of land'.

Trimmlin' the chairs. A folk practice at rural funerals. When the coffin was ready to leave the death house it was placed on four chairs before being placed on the shoulders of the bearers for the first LIFT. The chairs were then knocked down to dismiss the spirit of the dead from the WAKE house. (The word *trimmlin'* is a dialect form of 'trembling'.) The practice ceased about the middle of the 20th century:

... as the coffin was lifted I saw an old man knock over one of the chairs with a dunch of his knee. It looked like clumsy old age. Then he pushed over the second chair.

'What's the idea in knocking the people's furniture about?'

'He's "trimmlin" the chairs: that's to say he's making sure that the spirit of the departed hasn't gone to roost while the corpse is on its way to the churchyard.'

> SAM HANNA BELL (1909–80): 'To Crack by the Hearth', in *Erin's Orange Lily* (1956)

Trína chéile. An Irish term for 'mixed up', 'in disorder'. The HIBERNO-ENGLISH version, 'treenahayla', gives the pronounciation of the Irish. 'THROUGHOTHER', the literal translation of the Irish *trína chéile*, is used commonly to describe untidiness in a room or mild dysfunction in a personality.

Trinity College. *See* TCD.

Tripe. A Cork delicacy, traditionally sold from stalls in the ENGLISH MARKET. Tripe is sheep's stomach, and provides a cheap and nutritious family meal when cooked in milk with onions and butter.

Tripes out of, to cut the. To scold severely.

Trócaire (Irish, 'mercy', 'compassion'). The official overseas development agency of the Catholic Church in Ireland. It was established in 1973 by the Irish Bishops' Conference, with a mandate to support long-term development projects and respond to humanitarian crises, and also to campaign for global change. Trócaire is administered from MAYNOOTH. Among the organization's successful initiatives are the Lenten fast (proceeds to development work) and Lenten collection boxes, more than one million of which are distributed to all primary-school pupils. In 2001, £9.7 million was collected in Trócaire Lenten boxes.

Trollope, Anthony (1815–82). English novelist and Post Office official. He lived in various Irish towns – Banagher (1841), Clonmel (1844–45), Mallow (1845–51), Belfast (1853–4) and Dublin (1854–9) – using his position to confirm the efficiency of the new idea of the pillar box for posting. At the same time he indulged his love of hunting, cured his asthma and found the peace and energy to begin writing.

> On the 15th September 1841, I landed in Dublin, without an acquaintance in the country, and with only two or three letters of introduction from a brother clerk in the Post Office. I had learned to think that Ireland was a land of fun and whiskey, in which irregularity was the rule of life, and where broken heads were looked upon as honourable badges. I was to live in a place called Banagher, on the Shannon, which I had heard of because of its once having being conquered, though it had heretofore conquered everything, including the devil.
>
> *An Autobiography* (1883)

Of Trollope's 47 novels, 4, including the unfinished *The Landleaguers* (1883), were set in Ireland. There are no Irish tinges in his great Barsetshire sequence, but Phineas FINN, based on several successful Irish Catholic politicians, lends his name to the second and fourth of the Palliser novels and is a character in all but the first and third. Trollope was a Unionist but understood the Catholic Irish better than any of his peers, and his novels *The Macdermots of Ballycloran* (1847), *The Kellys and the O'Kellys* (1848) and *Castle Richmond* (1860) are good sources for the nature of Irish life in the mid-19th century, the last full of searing descriptions of the GREAT FAMINE. His Irish diagnoses tend to be flawed; his last novel, *The Landleaguers*, written a quarter of a century after he left Ireland, is totally unsympathetic to the motives of the LAND LEAGUE:

> The Laague, then, isn't such an old friend of mine. I niver heerd of the Laague, not till nigh three years ago. What with Faynians, and Moonlighters, and Home-Rulers, and now thim Laaguers, they don't lave a por boy any pace.

Troops Out Movement. A group, based in London, that at the height of the Northern Ireland TROUBLES campaigned for the immediate withdrawal of British troops. It was active from 1970 and drew its support from left-wing activists, members of trade unions and a small number of Labour MPs. The peace process has made its purpose superfluous.

Troubles. A characteristic understated term used to describe various periods of unrest in Irish history. In the 20th century the name became particularly associated with the ANGLO-IRISH WAR of 1919–21 and the CIVIL WAR that followed. (The events of 1919 form the backdrop for J.G. Farrell's novel *Troubles* (1970).) More recently the term 'the Troubles' has denoted the period of violence that began in Northern Ireland in the late 1960s. (One of the most useful histories of the period, published in 2000, was David McKittrick's and David McVea's *Making Sense of the Troubles*, and a series of programmes by Thames Television had *Troubles* as its general title.)

The province had been relatively peaceful since the end of the Second World War. The IRA BORDER CAMPAIGN (1956–62) had had little effect, and it was not until the CIVIL RIGHTS MOVEMENT took to the streets in 1968 that politics became heated. The partisan response of the RUC to various peaceful protest marches, together with the Protestant backlash in which Ian PAISLEY played a significant part, made sectarian violence commonplace. Continuous rioting, notably in the Bogside in Derry (*see* FREE DERRY; BOGSIDE, BATTLE OF THE) and Nationalist areas of Belfast (*see* NO-GO AREAS; ANDERSONSTOWN; ARDOYNE; BOMBAY STREET; MURPH, THE) led to the British army being called out in August 1969, first in Derry and then two days later in Belfast, as a short-term measure. They were to stay for more than 30 years, and became involved in BLOODY SUNDAY 1972, one of the blackest days of the recent Troubles.

In 1970 the IRA began a campaign against the security forces and commercial targets, committed to an ARMED STRUGGLE to recover a united Ireland lost in 1921 (see TREATY, THE). This in turn generated Loyalist violence from the UDA/UFF and the UVF. The result was a direct death toll by 1998 of 3289, and a total of injured people of 42,216. Direct rule by Westminister imposed in March 1972 was intended to end with the establishment of a POWER-SHARING EXECUTIVE under the Sunningdale Agreement (*see* WHITELAW, WILLIAM), but it collapsed after pressure from the UWC strike. Other initiatives failed until talks in the 1990s, at first secret, led to a 'peace process' that led to the politicization of paramilitaries and eventually to the GOOD FRIDAY AGREEMENT and a wary peace.

Troy, John Thomas (1739–1823). Catholic prelate. He was born in Porterstown, Castleknock, Co. Dublin, on 10 May 1739. Ordained as a Dominican priest in San Clemente, Rome, in 1762 he became prior of the establishment ten years later, but was recalled to Ireland in 1774 as Bishop of Ossory. From his arrival in Ireland he advocated an expedient obedience to the government, determined to set the church on a sound footing and hoping for a gradual removal of penal disadvantage (*see* POPERY LAWS). He publicly condemned all anti-government agitation, denouncing the WHITEBOYS, and later, as Archbishop of Dublin (1786–1823), condemning the activities of the UNITED IRISHMEN in the 1790s as 'the French disease'. He accepted Pitt's promise of CATHOLIC EMANCIPATION after the Act of UNION and the often demeaning conditions imposed by the government in the matter of clerical appointments (supporting the government's right of veto; *see* VETO CONTROVERSY). He also concurred with the Irish Parliament's establishment of St Patrick's Seminary, MAYNOOTH, in 1795. Under his supervision appropriate places of worship began to be built in Dublin, and in 1815 he laid the foundation stone of the Pro-Cathedral (then known as St Mary's Metropolitan Chapel) in Marlborough Street. When he died on 11 May 1823 there was barely enough money to pay for his funeral.

Truce, the. The truce, commencing on 11 July 1921, that brought the ANGLO-IRISH WAR to an end. It was agreed, as a preliminary to discussions, between Éamon DE VALERA and General Sir Nevil MACREADY. Although some unofficial and reprisal activities continued on the part of the IRA, in general an uneasy peace prevailed while the discussions culminating in the Anglo-Irish TREATY of 6 December 1921 were under way.

Trucileers. A disparaging nickname for young men who joined the IRA after the TRUCE of July 1921 had removed the risk of fighting.

Trucker. A term for a man who acted as go-between for jobbers buying cattle from farmers at the FAIRS.

True-Born Irishman, The. A good-natured satirical play (1762) by Charles MACKLIN, intended as a vehicle for his own talents. Its subtitle 'The Fine Irish Lady' describes the wife of Murrough O'Donerty, who, returning from the coronation of George III in 1760, has decided that with her fine new English accent she should be known as Diggerty. The play attacks provincial snobbery, the general self-seeking dysfunction of the Irish Parliament, and ABSENTEE LANDLORDS. It was successfully adapted by Brian FRIEL as *The London Vertigo* (1991), Mrs Diggerty's diagnosed complaint.

Tuaiplis. An Irish word for a blunder or bungle, a false move in a game. In HIBERNO-ENGLISH the word is often used in a more general sense, to mean a misfortune not of one's own making: 'That's an awful *tuaiplis*!'

Tuarastal. An Irish word, also used in HIBERNO-ENGLISH, for a wage, salary or stipend.

Tuath. Originally construed as synonymous with TRIBE, the old Irish word *tuath* is now understood as a community of people led by a king. Because *tuatha* ranged greatly in size, it is impossible to estimate their number. The word *tuath* survives in placenames such as Tuath Ó Siosta (Tuosist in Co. Kerry).
See also TUATHA DÉ DANAAN.

Tuatha Dé Danaan (Old Irish, 'the people of the goddess DANA[1]). The old gods of Ireland, who, coming on the fifth wave of colonists (*see BOOK OF INVASIONS*), enslave the native menial FIRBOLG and carry on murderous wars of attrition with the FOMORIANS, who are the quintessence of evil. They are typical offsprings of their mother Dana, with all the mortal failings, especially lust and envy. The Christian scribes who recorded their deeds, hitherto preserved only in oral memory, denied them deity (there was only one true God) but allowed them heroic deeds and some residual magic. They are defeated by the last wave of invaders, the MILESIANS, and go underground. There they lived as the SIDHE, becoming *Na Daoine Beaga* ('wee folk'), the fairies of later folklore, whose possible malevolence had to be placated in anticipation.

See also AONGHUS ÓG; BANBA; BOANN; DAGDA, THE; ÉIRE; FODLA; LUGH; MÓRRIGÁN; NUADA.

Tubaiste. An Irish word for 'misfortune', 'disaster', also used in HIBERNO-ENGLISH: 'That's an awful *tubaiste*.' An adjective, *tubaisteach*, is also used.

Tuberculosis. A major cause of death in Ireland in the 19th and early 20th century, especially in the 20–34 age group; it was sometimes known as the 'Irish disease'. Although the TB Prevention Act of 1908 empowered local authorities to develop clinics and sanatoria for the treatment of the disease, progress was hampered by lack of funds, by rural poverty and by overcrowding, poor nutrition and poor sanitation in city tenements. In the first INTERPARTY GOVERNMENT (1948–51), the minister for health Noël BROWNE (members of whose own family had suffered from the disease) had the political will to tackle the problem, building emergency sanatoria throughout the country. Shortly afterwards streptomycin, an antibiotic treatment for tuberculosis, began to be made available. In 1957 the number of fatalities from TB was reduced to 694 and, by using a combination of three antibiotics, the disease was virtually eradicated by the 1960s.

Tubridy, Michael. *See* CEOLTÓIRÍ CHUALANN; CHIEFTAINS, THE.

Tucks. Plenty of something, as in 'tucks of food', 'tucks of time'.

Tudor Reconquest. A term used to denote the expansion and consolidation of English power in Ireland during the reigns of the Tudor monarchs of the 16th century, involving efforts to pacify, fortify and plant areas of Ireland outside the PALE. This generally only occurred after serious or extended conflicts – the rebellion of SILKEN THOMAS, Earl of Kildare, the DESMOND REBELLIONS, and the NINE YEARS' WAR – although a parallel policy of control through conciliation existed in the 1540s (*see* SURRENDER AND REGRANT). The Reconquest is regarded as having begun in 1534 with the rebellion of Silken Thomas, which coincided with the passing of the Act of Supremacy by Henry VIII in London. England's schism with Rome meant that the country lacked allies during this period, and Gaelic and OLD ENGLISH leaders alike were thus able to appeal for help on religious grounds to the Catholic powers, France and Spain. This in turn made the English administration of lord deputies such as GREY and PERROT more paranoid and more militaristic. At a time of significant population increase and the beginnings of a colonial sensibility, Ireland was perceived by the younger sons of English gentry as providing rich pickings in terms of lands and status, if only the country could be pacified.

See also LAOIS AND OFFALY, PLANTATION OF; MUNSTER PLANTATION.

Tuke, James Hack (1819–96). Philanthropist. Tuke was an English Quaker who carried on a family tradition of philanthropy and banking; his grandfather William Tuke (1732–1822) had been a pioneer in the treatment of the insane. James was active in the distribution of relief in 1847, probably the worst year of the GREAT FAMINE, and again in January 1880 after another potato failure in September 1879, when the parish priest of Carna, Co. Galway, warned of famine deaths. With 30 years of experience behind him he not only organized efficient relief, but also – confronted with people who begged him 'Send us anywhere, Your Honour, to get us out of our misery' –

began an assisted emigration scheme. During 1882–4 he raised enough money to find passages for 9500 people from the worst-hit areas of the west. His book *Irish Distresses and its Remedies* (1880) played a significant part in the setting-up of such initiatives as the CONGESTED DISTRICTS BOARD.

Tulc. An Irish word for 'flood', 'gush', also used for a fit or spasm of laughter or (less commonly) of grief. It is often used in the plural in HIBERNO-ENGLISH, as in 'She was in *tulcs* of laughter' or 'She was in the *tulcs*.'

Tulla Céilí Band. A band that originated in the Tulla area of east Clare in 1945–6 and continued until the 1980s. It was one of the most famous of all CÉILÍ BANDS, playing not only in Ireland but for emigrants in England and America from the late 1950s.

Tullaghogue Stone. A prehistoric standing stone near Cookstown, Co. Tyrone, where each O'Neill chieftain was inaugurated. The rite required that the heads of the O'Cahan and the O'Hagan clans officiate, the first throwing a shoe over the new chief's head while the other presented a rod of office. The Tullaghogue Stone was destroyed by Lord Deputy MOUNTJOY in 1602 as he moved against Hugh O'NEILL, Earl of Tyrone, after the Battle of KINSALE. Mountjoy's act of destruction was symbolic, his intention being to signal the end of Gaelic Ireland.

See also DUNGANNON.

Tullamore Dew. A WHISKEY manufactured in Tullamore distillery in Co. Offaly. The distillery, the only Catholic one in Ireland, was founded in 1829 by Michael Molloy, who was succeeded by his nephew, Bernard Daly, in 1857. In 1862 at the age of 14 Daniel E. Williams, a local farmer's son, came to work in the distillery, by then known as B. Daly Distillery. Over the next 40 years, D.E. Williams, who became general manager and eventually owner of most of the company, developed the distillery and also built a bonded warehouse and bottling plant. He gave his initials to the company's signature brand, Tullamore Dew, which adopted the slogan 'Give every man his dew'.

Irish whiskey production suffered from Prohibition in the USA, and when Prohibition was lifted in 1933 Scottish distillers were in a better position to satisfy the demand that immediately resulted. The Second World War, however, was a boom period for Irish whiskey owing to the shortage of Scotch, and Tullamore distillery used turf to fuel the stills. So great a demand was there for the product that even the best customers were limited to 12 bottles each. Tullamore produced the first ever blended Irish whiskey after the Second World War; up until then all Irish whiskeys were pure pot still. The Williams family ceased production of Tullamore Dew in Tullamore in 1954 and the brand was bought by Irish Distillers. The liqueur IRISH MIST, which contains Tullamore Dew, was acquired in 1985 by a soft-drinks company. There is now a heritage centre in the Tullamore Dew distillery.

Tullymander. *See* SINGLE TRANSFERABLE VOTE.

Tumbling paddy. A horse-drawn wooden rake used to turn hay a few days after it had been cut. It was one of the few mechanical aids available in the yearly battle to save fodder.

Tundish. A word the *Oxford English Dictionary* dismisses as 'local' but defines as a shallow dish with a tube that acts like a funnel for fitting into a cask. Shakespeare saw its bawdy potential when in *Measure for Measure* he has Lucio give the reason for Claudio's imprisonment for lechery as 'for filling a bottle with a tundish' (III.i. 422). Its best-known Irish use is in Joyce's *A PORTRAIT OF THE ARTIST AS A YOUNG MAN*, when Stephen has an aesthetic discussion with the dean of studies at the Royal University about the nature of learning:

– To return to the lamp, he said, the feeding of it is also a nice problem. You must choose the pure oil and you must be careful when you pour it not to overflow it, not to pour in more than the funnel can hold.

– What funnel? asked Stephen.

– The funnel through which you pour the oil into your lamp.

– That? said Stephen. Is that called a funnel? Is it not a tundish? –

– What is a tundish?

– That. The … the funnel.

– Is that called a tundish in Ireland? asked the dean. I never heard the word in my life.

– It is called a tundish in Lower Drumcondra, said Stephen laughing, where they speak the best English.

Tunnel tigers. The nickname for the Irish workers – mainly from west Donegal and North Mayo – who dug the tunnels for the hydro-electric schemes in postwar Scotland, and later worked on the Jubilee tube line in London and the Channel Tunnel. Most recently they have been engaged in building a tunnel under the Liffey, and will no doubt be hired for Dublin's projected metro.

Tuppenny rush. The special children's matinées put on up to the end of the 1940s at reduced prices (the balcony seats cost threepence) with, usually an 'appropriate' programme of cartoons, cops-and-robbers and cowboy films. The last item of the programme was a serial (known in Ulster as the 'continues' from the flashed legend 'continued next week') with the hero or heroine left in a cliff-hanging situation each time. The serials had such titles as *The Masked Rider* and *The Clutching Hand*. Those seated in the balcony were accused of spitting down on the groundlings. Matinées were held on Sunday afternoons in Éire but on Saturdays in the puritan North.

Turbary. The right to cut TURF on the land of another farmer. Turbary was allocated by the LAND COMMISSION.

Turf. Peat, cut and saved on the BOG[1] and burned for fuel. If turf is dry it burns very fast, and even a domestic fire has to be constantly stoked. If turf is wet – as in 1947, when, notoriously, a very wet summer was followed by a very cold winter – it is reluctant to burn at all. Turf was the staple fuel in rural Ireland, for cooking as well as for heat, until RURAL

ELECTRIFICATION in the 1950s and the modernization of the 1960s. It was also brought on barges to Dublin along the Royal Canal from the bogs of the Midlands. During the EMERGENCY of 1939–45, turf was the only fuel widely available in Ireland – even the trains ran, very slowly, on turf. BORD NA MÓNA is Ireland's national turf exploitation body.

Turf as it stands, wood as it falls. When building a fire it is advisable to set the sods of turf upright as turf burns better in this position. The opposite is the case with wood.

Turgesius (d.845). VIKING invader. His native name was Thorgestr, and he was known to the Irish as Turgéis. In 837 he appeared with a large fleet in Dublin Bay and at the mouth of the Boyne, assuming command of all Irish Vikings. The Irish river system, highly susceptible to longship navigation, enabled him to penetrate deep into the country. In 841 he sailed up the Bann to Lough Neagh and laid waste to Armagh; by 844 he was on the Shannon, devastating most of the Midland foundations and desecrating the altar of CLONMACNOISE by making love to his wife Ota there before declaring her high priestess. He was drowned in Lough Owel, Co. Westmeath, by Máel-Shechlainn I (d.862). The event and the men were celebrated in Tom MOORE's 'Let Erin Remember':

Malachy wore the collar of gold
Which he won from the proud invader.

Túr Gloine, An (Irish, 'the glass tower'). A studio (pronounced 'tour glun-ya') at 24 Upper Pembroke Street, Dublin, dedicated to the production of stained glass, established in 1903 by Sarah PURSER and Edward MARTYN. Among its more significant artists were Evie HONE (1894–1955) and Michael Healy (1873–1941). The studio closed in 1944, a year after Purser's death.
See also MESPIL HOUSE.

Turlough. A lake (from the Irish *tur*, 'dry') that is dry or marshy in the summer and re-appears in the winter. The feature is common in limestone areas such as the BURREN in Co. Clare, where the water drains through the porous stone.

Turlough Park. *See* MUSEUM OF COUNTRY LIFE.

Turoe Stone. A carved stone with decorations in the LA TÈNE style. Dating from between the 3rd and the 1st century BC, it stands in a field near Loughrea, in Co. Galway. It is thought to have been associated with Iron Age religious practices. The name is a phonetic version of the Irish *Cloch an tuair rua*, 'stone of the red pasture'.

'Twas Only an Irishman's Dream'. The title of a song written in 1916 by John J. O'Brien, Al Dubin and Ronnie Cormack, which crystallizes the safe sentimentality of Irish-Americans, usually of first or second generation, as they contemplate a kind of dream Ireland to which they are not required to return:

> Sure, the shamrocks were growing on Broadway,
>> Every girl was an Irish colleen,
> And the town of New York was the county of Cork,
>> All the buildings were painted green.
> Sure, the Hudson looked just like the Shannon,
>> Oh, how good and real it did seem.
> I could hear mother singin',
>> The sweet Shandon bells ringin',
> *'Twas only an Irishman's dream.*

Tweed. *See* BREADEEN.

Twelfth of August. The day of the annual celebration by the APPRENTICE BOYS of the relief of the Siege of DERRY on 31 July 1689 (the calendar having been changed in 1752). The marchers wear Derry crimson collarettes, carry banners and are accompanied by bands as on the Orangemen's day, TWELFTH OF JULY. The most significant part of the day's ceremonies is the circuit of Derry's Walls, and until accommodation was made with the Bogside Residents' Association (BRA) this important element was often problematical. The walls overlook the Bogside on the west and frequently in the past the residents were subject to mockery and insult by the marchers. Now

agreed procedures are worked out in advance of the day between the representatives of the BRA and the ruling committee of the Apprentice Boys.

Twelfth of July. The day of the annual commemoration of the defeat of the supporters of JAMES II at the Battle of the BOYNE on 1 July 1690 (old style) by members of the ORANGE ORDER. Marches are held to different venues, known as FIELDS, where members are addressed by speakers who remind them of their Orange principles. Each Loyal Orange Lodge (LOL) holds a short parade in its own area before boarding coaches for more central venues. The largest parade is that in Belfast to the field at Edenderry, south of the city. Each lodge is accompanied by gaudily decorated BANNERS depicting significant events in the Protestant past. Of these one of the most common is that of the victorious William III (KING BILLY) crossing the Boyne on a white horse. *See also* ARCH.

Twelve Apostles, the. *See* SQUAD, THE.

Twelve Apostles of Ireland, the. The second rank of Irish monastic founders who received their training at CLONARD under St FINNIAN OF CLONARD. They are: CANICE, CIARÁN OF CLONMACNOISE, CIARÁN OF SAIGHIR, BRENDAN OF BIRR, BRENDAN THE VOYAGER, COLMÁN OF TERRYGLASS, COLUM CILLE, MOLAISE OF DEVENISH, MOBHI, NINIDH, RUADHAN and SINELL.

Twenty-six Counties, the. A term used to distinguish the Republic of Ireland from the whole of Ireland (the THIRTY-TWO COUNTIES) and Northern Ireland (the SIX COUNTIES), emphasizing the inadequacy of the claim of those 26 counties to be called 'Ireland'. The term has fallen into disuse and now seems dated, but the semantics of northern Republicanism still dictate that it and its corollary 'the Six Counties' be used by the movement's spokesmen and supporters at all times.

Twig. A term used in Ulster to mean 'appearance' or 'state of mind': 'I was not in good twig at the time.'

Twisted. Very drunk.

Twisting of the Rope, The. *See* CASADH AN TSÚGÁIN.

Twopenny ticket. A cheap matinée cinema ticket for children.
See also TUPPENNY RUSH.

2 RN. The name (call sign) by which the Irish radio service was originally known. 2 RN began broadcasting on 1 January 1926 from a studio in Little Denmark Street in the centre of Dublin; Séamus Clandillon was the first director. The station, which changed its name to Raidió Éireann in the 1930s, moved to the third floor of the GPO in Henry Street (it was part of the Department of Posts and Telegraphs), from where Teilifís Éireann was launched in 1961. The services were combined as Raidió Teilifís Éireann (RTÉ) in 1966, and moved to a modern facility in MONTROSE, Donnybrook, in 1972.

2500 Richard IIIs. The probably true claim of the stocky, pock-marked tragedian, Barry Sullivan, as to the number of times he played Richard III in Shakespeare's play. Sullivan was born in London of Irish parents in 1821 and was a professional actor from 1837, beginning his career with Charles Kean (1811–68) in Cork. Though an impressive Benedick to the Beatrice of Helen Faucit (1817–98) in *Much Ado about Nothing* at the opening of the Shakespeare Memorial Theatre in Stratford-upon Avon on 23 April 1879 (he also played Hamlet that same season), he rarely took romantic parts after the slimness of his figure and notable agility deserted him in middle age. He remained very popular in Ireland and the USA, and is remembered by a memorial statue beside his grave at GLASNEVIN CEMETERY. Perhaps conscious of his limitations when compared with his idol William Macready (1793–1873), he was rarely seen in England and did not risk appearing in Dublin until 1870, when he was rapturously received. He remained the most popular actor of his day, and captivated that often cranky critic GBS so much that in his view he was 'Hyperion to a satyr' compared with all the opposition. His last appearance was in Liverpool in 1887, again as Richard III. He died in Dublin in 1891.

Tynan, Katharine (1861–1931). Poet and novelist. She was born in Clondalkin in Dublin to a Nationalist family, and educated by the Dominicans in Drogheda. An enthusiastic constitutional Nationalist and feminist, she was mistress of a literary salon where she met W.B. Yeats, who became a lifelong friend. *Louise de la Vallière* (1885) was the first of many collections of verse, but she is remembered mainly for anthology pieces such as 'The Witch', 'Any Woman', a proud statement of quiet feminism, and 'Sheep and Lambs' (also known as 'All in the April Evening'), popular among parents and teachers because of its gentle piety, and frequently sung chorally in church. Her husband, the barrister H.A. Hinkson, was appointed RM (resident magistrate) for Mayo in 1915, but she left Ireland for good on his death in 1919, finding no common cause with Republicanism, and travelled extensively in Europe. In all she wrote 105 novels, including historical romances, 12 collections of short stories, 18 verse collections and 5 volumes of reminiscences, as well as numerous articles on social questions and the health and working conditions of women and children.

> All in the April evening,
> April airs were abroad,
> The sheep with their little lambs
> Passed me by on the road.
> The sheep with their little lambs
> Passed me by on the road;
> All in the April evening
> I thought on the Lamb of God.
>> KATHARINE TYNAN (1861–1931): 'All in the April Evening'

Tyndall, John (1820–93). Physicist. He was born in Leighlinbridge in Co. Carlow to a Protestant family of modest status, and at the age of 19 joined the ORDNANCE SURVEY in Carlow. Later he moved to England and began to work as a teacher of mathematics. Always an experimentalist, he established the first school laboratory in Britain, in Queenswood College. He received a PhD in diamagnetism from Marburg College in Germany in 1849 and in 1860 collaborated with T.H. Huxley on *The Glaciers of the Alps*. Tyndall was an atheist, and also a Unionist, because he feared Catholic domination if Home Rule was granted to Ireland. His 'Belfast [presidential] Address' to the British Association in 1874 drew the ire of several churches, who condemned him as materialistic. In the 1870s he researched improvements in sterilization and in 1877 he invented a method called 'tyndallization' that involved intermittent heating. He is now best known for having discovered the so-called 'Tyndall effect', the scattering of light by particles of matter that causes the sky to appear blue. The Rio Tyndall in Patagonia is named after him, as are glaciers in Alaska. John Tyndall died from accidental poisoning by chloral and is buried in his home town of Leighlinbridge.

Typhoid Mary. The nickname of the Irish-American cook Mary Mallon (*c.*1870–1938), the first identified carrier of typhoid fever in the United States. Her case first arose in 1903 when an epidemic of typhoid spead over Oyster Bay and nearby towns on Long Island. The sources were traced by Dr Soper of the New York Department of Health to households where Mary had been working. When he attempted to examine her she attacked him with a rolling-pin and escaped. She was eventually committed to an isolation centre and released only in 1910 on condition that she never worked with food again. But she resumed her occupation, and in 1914 a further epidemic broke out in New Jersey and at a Manhattan maternity hospital, both places where Mary had worked. Altogether 51 cases of typhoid, including three deaths, were attributed to her, although she herself was immune to the typhoid bacillus. Her nickname

became a metaphor for pollution and for the evil a single person can inflict on society.

Tyrconnell, Richard Talbot, 1st Earl of (1630–91). Soldier and politician. He was born in Malahide, Co. Dublin, the younger son of a Catholic OLD ENGLISH family. After the CONFEDERATE WAR, in which he narrowly escaped death, he became an ally of the Duke of York (later JAMES II) and spied for his brother Charles in England during the Protectorate. He became a well-known courtier at the Restoration, outdoing the others in rake-hellery. With the accession of James II in 1685, his power base was enlarged and in 1687, by then Earl of Tyrconnell, he was made lord deputy of Ireland with control of the army, which he immediately began to make Catholic. He applied the same techniques to the civil administration, removing Protestants from office where necessary.

With the Revolution of 1688, Talbot, now titular Duke of Tyrconnell, considered treating with William III (*see* KING BILLY), before deciding to hold Ireland for James. His role at the Battle of the BOYNE was controversial, since he appeared lethargic and indecisive. He returned to Ireland as Stuart lord lieutenant in 1691, having accompanied James to France in 1690. After the Jacobite defeat at AUGHRIM on 12 July 1691, he fell back on Limerick to prepare for a siege but died of apoplexy on 14 July. His wife Frances (d.1731), who was a sister of Sarah, Duchess of Marlborough, was, after a period of outlawry, secured in her part of the estate in 1702.

Talbot was immortalized in 'LILLIBULÉRO', the anti-Catholic squib written by Thomas, 1st Marquess of Wharton (1648–1714) in 1687. It is notable that the Irish phrase, *go leor* ('enough', 'plenty'; *see* GALORE) was current.

> Now that Tyrconnel is come ashore,
> Lillibuléro, bullen a la,
> And we shall have Commissions *go leor*
> Lillibuléro, bullen a la.

U

Ua Floinn, Riobard. The Irish form of his own name devised by Robert LYND, who learned Irish well enough to teach it. The 'Ua' was an alternative older form of Ó, and Lynd probably had links with the name Flynn. Lynd used the Irish form for his pamphlet *The Orangemen and the Nation* (1907):

> England's game has always been to whisper one suspicion in the ear of the Protestant and another suspicion in the ear of the Catholic, until the two of them become irritated with each other, almost to the point of murder.

Ualach. An Irish word for 'burden', 'load', 'responsibility', commonly used in HIBERNO-ENG-LISH in rural areas: 'That's no *ualach*' or 'That's a terrible *ualach*.'

UCC. University College Cork (*see* NATIONAL UNIVERSITY).

UCD. University College Dublin (*see* NATIONAL UNIVERSITY).

UCG. University College Galway (*see* NATIONAL UNIVERSITY).

UDA/UFF (Ulster Defence Association/Ulster Freedom Fighters). The largest Protestant paramilitary organization in Northern Ireland. The UDA dates from August 1971, and its numbers grew steadily to 40,000 during 1972. In its early years the UDA was associated with the Ulster Vanguard movement, and saw itself as a reactive force, protective of Protestant privileges. It organized mass protests about the dissolution of the STORMONT Parliament in 1972, and gathered under its umbrella a number of local defence associations in such Protestant areas as Lisburn, Newtownabbey and Dundonald. The UFF gradually evolved as its armed force, assassinating known Republicans but also randomly selected Catholics. The UFF was proscribed on 10 August 1992 by Sir Patrick Mayhew, secretary of state (1992–7). The UDA/UFF finds itself in opposition to the UVF (Ulster Volunteer Force), both territorially and ideologically, and at times this opposition has risen to the level of feud, with killings on both sides. It has resisted any domination by more conventional political parties like the DUP (Democratic Unionist Party), and since the GOOD FRIDAY AGREEMENT has declared itself inactive. This was a necessary condition for the release of UDA/UFF prisoners. Its political wing, the UDP (Ulster Democratic Party) failed to win seats in the Northern Ireland Assembly and suffered defections to splinter groups. The UDA is one of several organizations held responsible for continuing sectarian trouble along the various Belfast peace lines.
See also MAD DOG.

UDP (Ulster Democratic Party). The political wing of the UDA/UFF, founded as the Ulster Loyalist Democratic Party (ULDP) in June 1981. It is led by Gary McMichael, whose father, a UDA leader, was killed in Lisburn by an IRA car bomb on 22 December 1987. The UDP was especially prominent during the negotiations relating to the Irish peace process, and most politically minded members of the UDA/UFF were active during the Northern Ireland Assembly elections in 1998. Its failure to win any seats was a serious setback.

UDR (Ulster Defence Regiment). A force, with both full-time and part-time members, that replaced the discredited B-SPECIALS on 1 April 1970. It was intended to supplement the security activities of the British army and RUC. Its numbers varied from 6000 to 9000, with a generally high turnover. The government had hoped for a cross-community force, but the UDR soon became almost entirely Protestant. Many Protestants joined the force to protect their community from IRA attacks, and its personnel were regarded from the beginning as legitimate targets by Republican paramilitaries.

The charge by Nationalists that it was simply an alternative force of B-Specials, largely manned by Loyalist extremists, had sufficient substance to lead eventually to its merging on 23 July 1992 with the regular Royal Irish Rangers as a new force known as the Royal Irish Regiment. In spite of its unpopularity, and the proven involvement of some of its members in sectarian attacks, even its critics admitted that its discipline and professionalism increased.

UFF. *See* UDA/UFF.

Uilleann pipes. A form of bagpipes, also known as the Irish pipes. As the name (*uilleann* is Irish for 'elbow') suggests, they are pipes in which air is introduced into the bellows by means of the elbow. They are a version of an instrument that is found in many parts of the world, closest to home the Scottish bagpipes and the Galician *gaita*. It is believed that they were used for playing traditional music from the late 18th century. Traditional groups like PLANXTY[2] did much to popularize the uilleann pipes in the 1970s.

Uí Néill. The rulers of the northern half of Ireland between the 7th century and the 11th centuries (*see* LETH CUINN AND LETH MOGA). They saw themselves as descendants of the semi-legendary kings, NIALL OF THE NINE HOSTAGES and CONN OF THE HUNDRED BATTLES. Two of Niall's supposed sons, Eógan and Conall, were thought to have conquered Donegal (giving their names respectively to its two parts, INISHOWEN and Tír Chonaill), and their descendants, known as the Cenél Neógain and the Cenél Conaill, formed the dynasties that are known to modern historians as the northern Uí Néill. From them the great O'Neill lords of Ulster claimed descent (*see*, for example, O'NEILL, HUGH, 2ND EARL OF TYRONE; O'NEILL, OWEN RUA; O'NEILL, SHANE).
See also AILEACH; *ANNALS OF ULSTER*; CÚL DREIMHNE, BATTLE OF.

'Úirchill an Chreagáin' ('The Churchyard of Creagán'). *See* MAC CUMHAIDH, ART.

Uisce beatha. *See* USGUEBAUGH.

Uisce faoi thalamh (Irish, 'subterannean water'). A conspiracy, intrigue or secret goings-on.

Ulaid. A dynastic group, which gave its name to the northern province of Ulster and had EMAIN MACHA as its centre of power. Their conflicts with the Connachta of CONNACHT form the background of the epic *TÁIN BÓ CUAILNGE*. In the middle of the 5th century they were driven out of Emain Macha by the UÍ NÉILL, and thereafter kept east of the River BANN. A sub-group from the Antrim Glens, the DÁL RIATA, leapt the narrow sea to colonize western Scotland.

Ullagone (Irish, *olagón*). A HIBERNO-ENGLISH word for 'lament', 'dirge', 'wailing aloud'. The gerund 'ullagoning' is also used: a person considered to be crying excessively might be admonished, 'Stop your ullagoning!'

Ullamh. An Irish word meaning 'prepared'. *Ullamh*, which is pronounced 'ulloo' in Ulster and 'ullav' elsewhere, is to be found on the badges and belts of Irish boy scouts; *Bí ullamh* is therefore the Irish equivalent of Baden-Powell's 'Be prepared!'

Ullans. *See* ULSTER-SCOTS.

Ulster. The northern province of Ireland, administratively divided in the 17th century into nine counties: Antrim, Armagh, Cavan, Donegal, Down, Fermanagh, Londonderry, Monaghan and Tyrone. Since the GOVERNMENT OF IRELAND ACT (1920) Cavan, Donegal and Monaghan were taken as part of the FREE STATE, while the remaining six formed the new political unit of NORTHERN IRELAND. The term Ulster is strictly applicable only to the full nine counties (as Nationalists will tirelessly point out), but for the convenience of newspaper headlines and Protestant rhetoric, it is regularly taken as referring to the SIX COUNTIES of Northern Ireland.

Ulster was one of the ancient kingdoms of Ireland (*see* FIVE FIFTHS, THE). The ancient ULAID rulers of Ulster, with their seat at EMAIN MACHA, were pushed to the east of the River Bann by the UÍ NÉILL in the 5th century; one group, the DÁL RIATA, sailed northeast to colonize Scotland. Although there was a medieval Anglo-Norman earldom of Ulster, originating in the early 13th century, its power had fizzled out by 1461 when England annexed the province. Despite this nominal annexation, Ulster continued to be dominated by the O'Neill Earls of Tyrone and the O'Donnell Earls of Tyrconnell, and remained one of the most Gaelic areas of Ireland prior to the FLIGHT OF THE EARLS in 1607. After this it was subjected to plantation by English and Scottish settlers (*see* ULSTER PLANTATION).

Ulster Covenant. The 'Solemn League and Covenant' that 474,414 people signed at the City Hall in Belfast on Ulster Day, Saturday 28 September 1912, to show their opposition to any suggestion of HOME RULE. The text, devised by Edward CARSON and James CRAIG, was deliberately emotional and apocalyptic, borrowing the title of an agreement made in 1643 between Scots Presbyterians and English parliamentary opponents of Charles I:

> Being convinced in our consciences that Home Rule would be disastrous to the well-being of

Ulster as well as the whole of Ireland, subversive of our civil and religious freedom, destructive of our citizenship and perilous to the unity of the Empire, we, whose names are underwritten, men of Ulster, loyal subjects of His Gracious Majesty King George V … do hereby pledge ourselves in Solemn Covenant throughout this our time of calamity to stand by one another in defending for ourselves and our children our cherished position of equal citizenship in the United Kingdom, and in using all means which may be found necessary to defeat the conspiracy to set up a Home Rule Parliament in Ireland.

Ulster custom. *See* THREE FS.

Ulster Cycle. A group of heroic tales of Irish mythology, also known as the Red Branch Cycle (*see* RED BRANCH KNIGHTS), comparable in its cast of characters, high deeds and political and historical detail to Homer's *Iliad*. Transmitted orally for nearly 1000 years, the tales preserve details of the early life of Celtic Ireland. The main texts are to be found in the 12th-century *Lebor na hUidre* (*BOOK OF THE DUN COW*) and *Lebor Laigenach* (*BOOK OF LEINSTER*). The chief epic is that of the *TÁIN BÓ CUAILNGE*, which tells of the wars between the ULAID (which gives the cycle its title) and the Connachta of CONNACHT. Other tales in the cycle include 'BRICRIU's Feast' and 'The Fate of the Children of Usna' (the story of DEIRDRE and her lover Naoise). Versions of the tales by P.W. JOYCE, Standish O'GRADY, Lady GREGORY and others gave great stimulus to the IRISH LITERARY REVIVAL.

Ulster Defence Association. *See* UDA/UFF.

Ulster Defence Regiment. *See* UDR.

Ulster Democratic Party. *See* UDP.

Ulster Freedom Fighters. *See* UDA/UFF.

Ulster fry. A lethal combination of fried sausages, bacon, eggs – a version of the 'full English' – with the necessary extras of fried soda bread and potato cake, the latter known regionally as 'fadge' or 'slim'. Known not entirely jocularly as a 'heart attack on a plate', it is the second 'B' always served in an Ulster B and B.

Ulster Group Theatre. A company that presented plays in Belfast between 1941 and 1960. It began at a period when amateur theatre was enjoying a golden age, and it was no surprise that the better companies with talented actors should attempt to reach a standard of at least semi-professionalism. The Ulster Group Theatre emerged out of some of the better companies in the city – the Ulster Theatre, led by Gerald Morrow and Nita Hardie, the Jewish Institute Dramatic Society under Harold Goldblatt, and the NIP (Northern Irish Players). Most of the productions were staged in the Ulster Minor Hall.

Many of the actors who played with the Ulster Group Theatre were to achieve wider fame. They included Stephen Boyd, Colin Blakely, J.G. Devlin, James Ellis, Harold Goldblatt, Denys Hawthorne, Allan McClelland, Patrick MAGEE, Joseph TOMELTY and Harry Towb. The playwrights most closely associated with the Group were George SHIELS (a stalwart of the ULT), St John ERVINE and Tomelty, though it also provided opportunities for other writers who had dramatic ambitions.

One of these writers was – or should have been – Sam THOMPSON; his play *Over the Bridge* (1957), about sectarian violence in the ISLAND, was accepted by the board but withdrawn from production when the author refused to delete or alter certain passages in the script. The board announced that they were 'determined not to mount any play which would offend or affront the religious or political beliefs or sensibilities of the man in the street of any denomination or class in the community and which would give rise to sectarian or political controversy of an extreme nature'. As the playwright Stewart Parker put it in his introduction to the printed playscript (1970), it was a 'staggering repudiation of drama as a serious art form'. It spelled the end of the Group; there were many resignations, led by that of the artistic director, James Ellis, and a successful suit for breach of contract effectively finished the

enterprise. *Over the Bridge* was produced with great success by Ellis in the Empire Theatre in 1960.

Ulster King of Arms. Formerly the chief heraldic officer for Ireland and registrar of the ORDER OF ST PATRICK, created by Edward VI in 1553. The Ulster king's bureau was maintained in Dublin Castle until 1943, when DE VALERA established a state genealogical office that was initiated by the chief herald of Ireland, Edward MacLysaght (1887–1986), and served the same heraldic purposes, checking pedigrees and establishing entitlements to arms. At that date the Ulster King of Arms was incorporated into the College of Arms in London; its jurisdiction since then has been confined to Northern Ireland.

Ulster Liberal Party. A small party in the old STORMONT Parliament, a relict of the old Irish Liberal grouping that was destroyed by the early HOME RULE agitation. Its most effective period was 1958–69, and Sheelagh Murnaghan (1924–93) sat as an MP for QUB (Queens University Belfast) from 1961 to 1969. She and the chairman, the Rev. Albert McElroy, a Non-Subscribing Presbyterian minister, were very vocal about the abuses of the time. Liberal support, which in the 1960s comprised 4% of the electorate, gradually disappeared with the growth of the ALLIANCE PARTY in the early 1970s.

Ulster Literary Theatre. *See* ULT.

Ulster Plantation. The colonization in the early 17th century of the ULSTER counties of Armagh, Cavan, Donegal, Fermanagh, Londonderry (earlier called Coleraine) and Tyrone, escheated to the crown following the FLIGHT OF THE EARLS in 1607. A kind of informal plantation of parts of Antrim and Down had been taking place from the mid-16th century. The purpose was to impose segregation and 'civility'. The land was divided into lots varying from 1000 to 3000 acres (400 to 1200 ha) and assigned to 'undertakers' – people who subscribed to the Oath of Supremacy, which guaranteed their religious orthodoxy. Though they were forbidden to permit any Irish tenants on their lands, they found that they could not work the huge tracts granted without native help. The intention of erasing a Gaelic Ulster from the blackboard and drawing a British one was partially successful. Towns were built, forests cleared and mires drained, but the dispossessed Irish remained as a menacing problem. By 1612 the injunction about Irish tenants was a dead letter, but the true colonists, mainly Scots from Galloway, as opposed to those after quick profits, found it advisable to build fortified enclosures called bawns (*see* BAWN[3]). Their fear of the woodkernes, their generic term for the unruly bands of Irish guerrillas who still supported the old chieftains, was not baseless, as the REBELLION OF 1641 was to prove.

See also HONOURABLE, THE IRISH SOCIETY, THE; PLANTATION.

Ulster-Scots (also called **Ullans**). A regional variation of the lowland Scots dialect, Lallans, which was brought to northeast Ireland by 17th-century settlers and colonists (*see* ULSTER PLANTATION). The greatest concentration of these settlers was in Antrim, north Derry, east Donegal and northwest Tyrone, and residual elements of their dialect survive, mitigated somewhat by the intrusion of HIBERNO-ENGLISH. Ulster-Scots has since the 1990s acquired a politico/cultural element, its advocates suggesting, with more energy than conviction, that it deserves its place alongside Irish as a living language. Its detractors insist it is merely a dialect, used by an elderly and therefore diminishing population. Thanks to the efforts of the Ulster-Scots Language Society (1992) many public institutions give their titles in English, Irish and Ullans.

Ulster Unionist Party. *See* UUP.

Ulster Will Fight. The recurring Unionist warcry originating with Lord Randolph CHURCHILL (1849–94) in an anti-HOME RULE speech made on landing at Larne on 22 February 1886: 'Ulster at the supreme moment will resort to the supreme arbitrament of force. Ulster will fight and Ulster will be right.'

Ulster Workers Council. *See* UWC.

ULT (Ulster Literary Theatre). A theatre founded by Bulmer HOBSON and David Parkhill in 1902, which became a Belfast version of Dublin's ABBEY THEATRE, home of the Irish National Theatre Society. The pair of northern cultural Nationalist activists had gone to visit the members of the National Theatre Society in 1902 to get permission to put on some of their plays in Belfast. As Hobson recalled in a letter to Sam Hanna BELL, everybody was most cordial except Yeats, who was 'haughty and aloof'. They wanted to put on Yeats's *Cathleen Ní Houlihan* and James Cousins's *The Racing Lug*:

> But Yeats refused permission. When Máire [Quin] reported this to Maud Gonne, Maud said, 'Don't mind Willie. He wrote that play for me and gave it to me. It is mine and you can put it on whenever you want to.'

Sam Hanna Bell later wrote:

> One evening in the autumn of 1902, two young men were travelling homeward on the Belfast-bound train from Dublin. They had just parted from the most remarkable group of men and women in that Ireland of the new century and had achieved more than partial success in the errand that had taken them to the capital. But idealists are inclined to chafe under anything less than complete success. Young Mr Bulmer Hobson and young Mr David Parkhill from Belfast were, above all else, idealists. It is not recorded at what point on that historic journey Hobson struck the arm of his seat and exclaimed, 'Damn Yeats, we'll write our own plays!' What can be said is that that blow laid the foundation of the Ulster Literary Theatre.
>
> SAM HANNA BELL: *The Theatre in Ulster* (1972)

The playwrights of the ULT began a tradition of specifically Ulster plays, often kitchen comedies, with effective work by Rutherford Mayne (*see* DRONE, THE), Lynn DOYLE, Gerald MacNamara and George SHIELS. Most of the ULT dramatists also wrote for the Abbey. The company had no permanent base and staged its plays mainly in the Grand Opera House in Belfast. It was wound up in 1934.

See also THOMPSON IN TÍR NA NÓG.

Ultach. The Irish word for 'Ulsterman'. It was used as a pen name by the academic and writer, J[ames] J[oseph] Campbell (1909–69), for a series of articles written originally for the *Capuchin Annual* and published in booklet form as *Orange Terror*. Campbell was born in Belfast and educated at St Malachy's College and Queen's University Belfast. He returned to St Malachy's as classics master in 1931, and after lecturing in education at St Mary's and St Joseph's College of Education (1950–69) became head of the Institute of Education at Queen's, chairman of convocation and a member of senate. He served on many committees, notably the CAMERON COMMISSION on the local disturbances in 1969. Though remaining a constitutional Nationalist, Campbell continued to write and broadcast in a splendidly ironical way about the invidious position of Catholics in the province.

Ultan (d.686). The brother of Saints FURSA and FOILLÁN. He accompanied them from Ireland to BURGH CASTLE in East Anglia, where they founded Cnobheresburg monastery. He became abbot of Lagny in France on Fursa's death and also of PÉRONNE when Foillán was murdered. His feast day is 2 May.

Ultimi habitatores mundi. *See* COLUMBAN.

Ultramontanism. The ecclesiastical opinion in the Roman Catholic Church, from the word *ultramontane*, meaning 'beyond the mountains' (i.e. the Alps), favouring papal over national or diocesan authority. The term was associated in Ireland mainly with Cardinal Paul CULLEN (1803–78) who played a significant part in the First Vatican Council (1869–70). In spite of opposition from Archbishop John MACHALE (1791–1881) and others, he succeeded in establishing papal infallibility as an article of belief: when the pope speaks *ex cathedra* and defines a doctrine concerning faith or morals, the doctrine is to be held by the whole church.

Ulysses. A novel (1922) by James JOYCE, which details the events of a single day, 16 June 1904 (the day that Joyce met his future wife Nora BARNACLE), as experienced by three Dubliners. As the title suggests, there are obvious Homeric parallels, both in parodic equivalents of the events in the *Odyssey* and in the protagonists – Stephen DEDALUS being Telemachus, the son in search of a father, while Leopold Bloom, who sells advertising space in a newspaper, is the returning Odysseus, and his wife Molly is the ironically patient, if hardly chaste, Penelope. Bloom's single day of roaming about Dublin mirrors Odysseus's years of wandering. Stephen is the same autobiographical figure as in A PORTRAIT OF THE ARTIST AS A YOUNG MAN, but the other two protagonists are richly original creations. The city of Dublin is precisely rendered, and the erotic unpunctuated musings of the unfaithful Penelope – Joyce's version of stream-of-consciousness technique – that gave the book its initial scandalous reputation, now seem not only innocuous but apposite.

The novel was first published by Sylvia Beach in 1922 in Paris, because the printing of some excerpts in the American *Little Review* from 1918 had led to obscenity prosecutions. Copies of the Paris edition were burned in New York and seized by customs officers at Folkestone. It was not until the United States District Court found the book not obscene in 1933 that an American edition followed in 1934 and a British one in 1936. Fashionable Ireland has long ago gathered the erring book (never banned there) to its bosom, and among the many people who celebrate BLOOMSDAY each 16 June are some who have actually read it.

> ... and I thought well as well him as another and then I asked him with my eyes to ask again yes and then he asked me would I yes to say yes my mountain flower and first I put my arms round him yes and drew him down to me so he could feel my breasts all perfume yes and his heart was going like mad and yes I said yes I will Yes.

Uncle Arthur. *See* GUINNESS.

Uncle Tim's Cabin. The name applied to the residence of the Irish governor-general (*see* ÁRAS AN UACHTARÁIN) in PHOENIX PARK by its first incumbent, Tim HEALY.

Uncrowned King, the. In full 'the uncrowned king of Ireland', a sobriquet applied to Charles Stewart PARNELL. The phrase was coined by Tim HEALY, one of Parnell's most ardent supporters before the party split over the O'Shea case (*see* O'SHEA WHO MUST BE OBEYED). Parnell died only four months after marrying Kitty O'Shea in 1891.

> Mr Casey, freeing his arms from his holders, suddenly bowed his head on his hands with a sob of pain.
>
> – Poor Parnell! he cried loudly. My dead king! He sobbed loudly and bitterly.
>
> Stephen, raising his terrorstricken face, saw that his father's eyes were full of tears.
>
> JAMES JOYCE: *A Portrait of the Artist as a Young Man* (1916)

The death of Parnell also haunts James Joyce's short story 'IVY DAY AT THE COMMITTEE ROOM' (in *DUBLINERS*, 1914).

Undead, The. The author's original title of the most successful of all Gothic romances, *Dracula* (1897), written by the Dubliner Bram Stoker (1847–1912). The theme of the vampire (which gave its name to the Amazonian bat) was not a new one. Byron had mentioned one in *The Giaour* (1813):

> But first, on earth as Vampire sent,
> Thy corse shall from its tomb be rent:
> Then ghastly haunt thy native place
> And suck the blood of all they race.

The melodramas *The Vampire: or the Bride of the Isles* (1820) by James Robertson Planché and *Varney the Vampire* (1847) by James Malcolm Rymer were part of the repertoire of the theatrical stock companies, the former leading to the invention of the 'vampire trap' for ghostly effects.

Stoker's predatory Transylvanian count was based partly upon the story of the 15th-century Wallachian tyrant Vlad Dracul, known as 'The Impaler', and partly on the superior tale 'Carmilla' (*see* IN A GLASS DARKLY) by Stoker's kinsman Sheridan LE FANU. *Dracula* belongs to a kind of writing (often quite pedestrian) that transcends literature because of its creation of a mythic archetype. Like Sherlock Holmes, the figure of Dracula has shaken itself free of its origins. This is partly due to the popularity of the *Dracula* story in the cinema, with more than 160 films (second only to Holmes with over 220), and also to the story's barely hidden but oddly respectable sexuality and the ever-present fear of transmitted disease. The Gothic elements of howling wolves, frightened coach drivers, craggy castles, garlic flowers and stakes through the heart also contribute, and occasionally Stoker can cause a frisson even in a generation that has supp'd deep with horrors:

> … my very feelings changed to repulsion and terror when I saw the whole man slowly emerge from the window and begin to crawl down the castle wall over that dreadful abyss, *face down*, with his cloak spreading out round him like great wings … I saw the fingers and toes grasp the corners of the stones, worn clear of mortar by the stress of years, and by thus using every projection and inequality move downwards with considerable speed, just as a lizard moves along a wall.

Stoker was born in Fairview, Dublin, on 8 November 1847 and educated at Trinity College Dublin, where he was a noted athlete, overcoming childhood illness. Like his father he joined the civil service, his first publication being *Duties of the Clerks of Petty Sessions* (1878); it was still in use when the Free State was established. He became fascinated with the theatre, acting as (unpaid) critic for the *Dublin Evening Mail* and becoming the manager of Sir Henry Irving (1838–1905) from 1878 until the great star's death. (The character of Dracula owed something to the appearance, temperament and relentless demands made upon Stoker by his master.) His first novel, *The Snake's Pass* (1891), set in Co. Mayo, is about gold, GOMBEENISM and gallantry, and is the only one of his books set in Ireland. Some of his short stories, notably 'The Judge's House' and 'The Squaw', are more chilling than the often ponderous *Dracula* and still deserve their places in any spooky anthology. Other full-length Gothic efforts are *The Jewel of the Seven Stars* (1903) and *The Lair of the White Worm* (1909), which has been filmed several times, the word 'worm' having its medieval connotation of 'serpent'. Stoker died in 1912, having published *Personal Reminiscences of Henry Irving* (1906).

Underboard. The position of the corpse between death and burial, from the practice at wakes of placing a board across the breast of the departed, with a Bible or prayerbook and a plate of snuff laid on it (*see* SNUFF AT A WAKE, LIKE).

Under the clock. Formerly a popular rendez-vous in Dublin, especially for first dates, in front of Clery's in O'Connell Street, the façade of which carries a clock.

Underworld. *See* OTHERWORLD.

Unfortunate Fursey, The. *See* WALL, MERVYN.

Uniformity, Acts of. Two acts (1560, 1666) that were intended to standardize Christian worship in Ireland. The first required all clergy to use the English Prayer Book of 1559; there were fixed punishments for dereliction, rising to unfrocking and life imprisonment. The act also stated that laity were to be fined for not attending Anglican churches. The second act, in 1666, applied to Ireland the revised Prayer Book introduced into the English church in 1662. The acts were of their nature hard to enforce and served mainly as a means of keeping Nonconformists out of the church. They did little more than provide an opportunity for public expressions of loyalty.

Union, Act of. The measure that abolished the Irish Parliament (*see* GRATTAN'S PARLIAMENT) on 1 January 1801. It was the response of the British prime minister, William Pitt, to a number of factors, notably the REGENCY CRISIS,

the REBELLION OF 1798 and the perceived reluctance of the Protestant-dominated Dublin government to deal with Catholic demands and maintain fiscal rectitude. The implied suggestion of the granting of full CATHOLIC EMANCIPATION following the successful passing of the bill gained the prospect of Union wide support among Catholics, and government patronage organized by CORNWALLIS and CASTLEREAGH, seen by many as an unabashed form of bribery, helped to remove opposition within the Irish Parliament itself. As it turned out, George III found that any alleviation of Catholic penalties (*see* POPERY LAWS) went against his coronation oath and he would not agree to any measures that would ameliorate their political position. As a consequence, both Pitt and Castlereagh resigned from office.

In actual practice the 'Union' of Britain and Ireland remained ineffective. The country continued to be run from Dublin Castle (*see* CASTLE, THE) under the direction of the lord lieutenant and chief secretary. Provision was made for 100 MPs, 28 peers and 4 bishops to represent Ireland in the Westminster Parliament, but even the name the 'United Kingdom of Great Britain and Ireland' indicated the anomaly. The prosperity of the country seemed to disappear with its aristocracy, many of whom found life in Britain more congenial, and Dublin, its glory days over, became a dusty provincial capital, while in contrast Belfast, trustworthy because Unionist and Protestant, was favoured. The dereliction was anticipated by PLEASANT NED Lysaght (1763–1810), one of the anti-Union MONKS OF THE SCREW, in his poem 'A Prospect' (1800):

Thro' Capel-street soon as you rurally range,
You'll scarce recognize it the same street;
Choice turnips shall grow in your Royal Exchange
And fine cabbages down along Dame-street.
...
Our Custom House quay, full of weeds, of rare
  sport,
But the Ministers, minions, kind elves, sir!
Will give free leave all our goods to export
When we've got none at home for ourselves, sir!

Once it was realized that Catholics were no better off, emancipation and repeal of the Union became the main preoccupation of all Nationalist leaders from Daniel O'CONNELL to John REDMOND. The Union was dissolved in January 1922 with the acceptance by the Dáil of the terms of the Anglo-Irish TREATY setting up the Free State.

Unionism. A political movement that is anxious to maintain the terms of the Act of UNION. Irish Unionists, nearly all Protestant, wish to maintain the separation of NORTHERN IRELAND from the Republic of Ireland, and to remain part of the United Kingdom. As a political entity Unionism was created out of the Liberal Party by Joseph Chamberlain (1836–1914) and the Marquess of Hartington (1833–1908) in 1886 when Gladstone (*see* GOM) introduced his first HOME RULE Bill for Ireland. They led 78 Liberals into alliance with the Conservatives to defeat the bill. From that date the Conservatives were also known as Unionists, and the party was officially named the Conservative and Unionist Party from 1909. In modern Northern Ireland over the last 30 years there have been several Unionist parties, including the DUP and UUP.

United Irish League. An agrarian grassroots organization founded in 1898 by William O'BRIEN to campaign for redistribution of large farms in the west of Ireland among small farmers. It adopted a militant position in Connacht in its early years, but soon fell under the control of the IRISH PARTY (John REDMOND was president from 1900), which needed the support of large ranchers as well as small farmers, and this diluted its effectiveness. Support for the organization declined, and by 1914 it had ceased to exist.

United Irishman, The. A Republican newspaper of extreme views published 1847–8 by John MITCHEL after he broke with *The Nation*. It advocated armed insurrection and agrarian revolution, and carried instructions on street fighting. The paper was suppressed in 1848 and Mitchel was transported.

Arthur GRIFFITH also used the title for his weekly paper, which first appeared in March 1899 and which included contributions by YEATS and Æ. In 1906 Griffith changed the name of the paper to *SINN FÉIN*.

United Irishmen, Society of. An organization influenced by the radicalism of the American and French Revolutions, founded in Belfast and Dublin at the end of 1791 by Wolfe TONE, Thomas Russell (the MAN FROM GOD KNOWS WHERE) and Napper TANDY. The society aimed to unite Irishmen of all denominations, to achieve parliamentary reform and to end English influence over Irish affairs. Originally functioning as a debating and propaganda society, promoting its ideas through the medium of newspapers such as the *NORTHERN STAR*, the United Irishmen became an increasingly militant organization after the Dublin branch was suppressed in May 1794, at the time of the arrest of William JACKSON.

The Society of United Irishmen reconstituted itself as a secret oath-bound society dedicated to the founding of a republic by means of armed insurrection, and during 1795 and 1796 recruited members in Ulster and in Dublin and surrounding areas. Wolfe Tone's success in attracting French support after his visit to France in 1796 (*see* BANTRY BAY) boosted the organization's support, and by early 1798 it claimed 280,000 members and was closely allied with the DEFENDERS. But a campaign of repression by General LAKE in Ulster and Leinster from 1797 weakened the United Irishmen, and between March and May 1798 all the leading members of the Leinster Directory, including Lord Edward FITZGERALD and the Sheares brothers, were arrested in Dublin by Major SIRR. Whether the June rising in Wexford was fomented by the United Irishmen or was a spontaneous Defender-led rebellion is still a matter of debate (*see* REBELLION OF 1798).

After the suppression of the rebellion the society reformed, but it effectively disappeared after the failure of Robert EMMET's rebellion of 1803. However, the Republican creed of the

United Irishmen and the ideas and personality of Tone had a strong influence on later generations of patriots, particularly Republican separatists, an influence still to be seen today in Northern Republicanism.

See also TAILORS' HALL.

United Nations. Ireland became a member of the UN on 14 December 1955, with the stated policy of independence from association 'with particular blocs or groups' as far as possible, while simultaneously aligning itself with countries that were dedicated to preserving freedom from communism. Frederick H. Boland was the country's first ambassador to the UN during the session of 1956. Irish troops served with distinction as part of UN peacekeeping forces in the Congo, Cyprus, Israel and the Lebanon in the 1960s and 1970s.

Unity by consent. Speaking at the SINN FÉIN *ard fheis* (party conference) in March 1998 Gerry ADAMS of Sinn Féin made the following conciliatory remarks about unity by consent to Ulster Unionists:

> We want to make peace with you, we want to end centuries-old conflict, we want to be reconciled with you, this is your country every bit as much as it is ours, and we want to share it with you on a democratic and equal basis.

University College (Cork, Dublin, Galway). *See* NATIONAL UNIVERSITY.

Uno duce, una voce. An off-the-record comment by P.J. MARA, Charles HAUGHEY's media adviser, in 1984, when the publication of the New Ireland Forum report was causing dissension within Fianna Fáil, and Des O'Malley (*see* CONDUCT UNBECOMING; PEE DEES; REYNOLDS, ALBERT; TEMPORARY LITTLE ARRANGEMENT) had been expelled from the parliamentary party. What Mara said was, 'Uno duce, una voce. In other words, we are having no more nibbling at my leader's bum.' The comment, recalling the dictum of Italian Fascist leader, Benito Mussolini (*un duce, una voce*, 'one leader, once voice'), was unfortunate because it confirmed among his opponents Haughey's reputation for not tolerating dissent.

Unsinkable Molly Brown, The. A Broadway musical (1960) by Meredith Wilson (1902–84), later a film (1964), based loosely on the actual career of the Irish-American Molly Tobin. She was born in Denver, Colorado in 1867, and by 1890 had become very rich because of gold shares. Her great claim to fame was her surviving the sinking of the TITANIC in April 1912. Being not far removed from the SHANTY IRISH, her attempts to break into Denver's Waspish society had been unsuccessful, despite her wealth, but after her 'unsinkability' was established she was fêted everywhere. This satisfied her social ambitions but ruined her marriage. She died of a stroke in New York in 1932, and there is a museum devoted to her in Denver.

Untilled Field, The. A collection of stories by George MOORE, written in 1902 as models for new writers in Irish, as his contribution to the work of the GAELIC LEAGUE. They were translated into Irish by TORNA (Tadhg Ó Donnchadha) and published as '*An tÚr-Ghort, Sgéalta*, le Seórsa Ó Mordha', the translation of the English title followed by the Irish words for 'stories' and the author's name. Some of the stories were turned back into English by T.W. ROLLESTON, and Moore announced that they had been improved by 'their bath in Gaelic'. (He privately admitted that he was intrigued to see his name in Irish on the cover.) In fact the Gaelic League did not even display the book in their window, because the material was regarded as irreligious and anticlerical. Some stories mentioned illegitimate births and the country way of dealing with the problem:

> And when the signs of her weakness began to show, the widow Sheridan took the halter off the cow and tied Margaret (she that was playing Good Deeds in the play, yer honour) to the wall and she was in the stable till the child was born.
> 'A Playhouse in the Waste'

Equally reprehensible in the eyes of the League was the portrayal of the avaricious Father

Maguire, not to mention the unworldly Father McTurnan who, worried by rural depopulation, avers that priests should marry and have children.

The hope of providing appropriate textbooks for the youth of Ireland proved evanescent – Joseph Hone, one of Moore's early biographers, wrote in 1939:

> The Gaelic League as a literary force was spent, and under its influence the schools for which *The Untilled Field* was written were soon to have the worst text-books in the world.

Susan Mitchell, sometime secretary to the master, wrote even more emphatically (sideswiping at the *Simple Lessons in Irish*, devised for the Gaelic League by An tAthair Eoghan Ó GRAMHNA):

> The Gaelic League never seemed to cotton on to Moore and we doubt if *The Untilled Field* as a text-book ever enjoyed the popularity accorded to the manual that instructed our young Gaelic enthusiasm to 'Put the butter on the floor' or recorded the unnatural thirst of 'Art' who went so often to the well.
>
> *George Moore – Irish Men of Today* (1916)

Moore's stories represent a significant contribution to Irish literature, especially in their influence on Joyce and other masters of the form like Frank O'Connor and Sean O'Faolain. With characteristic, if impish, arrogance, Moore himself made even greater claims for *The Untilled Field*. Writing in the foreword to the uniform edition (1914), he notes a different influence:

> How Synge who had never before shown any sense of form should suddenly become possessed of an exquisite construction ... how Synge had sprung at once out of pure boarding-school English into a beautiful style ... Tricks of speech a parrot can learn, but it is impossible to learn through a crack [see CHINK IN THE FLOOR] how character acts and reacts upon character. The history of *The Playboy* was wrapped in unsearchable mystery until I began to read *The Untilled Field* for this edition ... I had come upon the source of Synge's inspiration. *The Untilled Field* was a landmark in Anglo-Irish literature, a

new departure, and Synge could not have passed it by without looking at it.

See also GRUEL SPOONED UP OFF A DIRTY FLOOR.

Up here you want it, down below for dancing. A humorous HIBERNO-ENGLISH usage in Munster, highlighting the intelligence (or low cunning) either of the speaker or of his interlocutor. It is sometimes abbreviated to 'Up here you want it.' The phrase is usually accompanied by a gesture indicating the head, meaning intelligence. The idea is to admire the cleverness or CUTEness of someone else or to boast of your own, meaning that while you need good legs for dancing, a clever move is proof of a good head. In other words, 'Well done!'

Upon your soul. An interjection or intensifier in HIBERNO-ENGLISH. 'Upon your soul!' might be a response to surprising news, while 'I did, upon your soul' means 'I did indeed.' The phrase is likely to have derived from the Irish phrase *Ar m'anam*, meaning 'On my soul', which has the force of an oath.

Urbs Intacta Manet. *See* WATERFORD.

Urination Once Again. An irreverent nickname for the 1966 statue (with fountain) of Thomas DAVIS by Edward Delaney in College Green, Dublin, deriving from Davis's famous patriotic poem 'A NATION ONCE AGAIN'.

Urney time. An advertising catchphrase for Urney chocolate ('Any time is Urney time'), originally produced as a cottage industry in the village of Urney, Co. Tyrone.

Usguebaugh. An old HIBERNO-ENGLISH term for whiskey, from the Irish *uisce beatha*, 'water of life'.
See also 'AQUA VITAE'; ISKY BIAHA.

Usna. The husband of Ebhla, the daughter of the druid CATHBAD and granddaughter of AONGHUS ÓG, the love god. Their three sons, NAOISE, AINLÉ and ARDÁN, figure in the story of DEIRDRE, the eldest as her lover and the others as companions and bodyguards during their sojourn in ALBA. They are tricked into returning to Ireland and killed on the order of CONCHOBHAR.

U2. A rock group, founded in 1976 by four teenagers in Mount Temple comprehensive school, on the northside of Dublin: Paul Hewson (Bono, b.1960), vocals; David Evans (the Edge, b.1961), guitar; Adam Clayton (b.1960), bass; and Larry Mullen (b.1960), drums. The first name of the band was Feedback, which changed to U2 in 1978. The band still has the same line-up. Under the managership of Paul McGuinness they have released a number of hugely successful albums, notably *Unforgettable Fire* (1984) and *The Joshua Tree* (1987), and have appeared in sell-out concerts in the largest stadia in the world. They are regularly voted the most popular and most influential rock band in the word, and have brought rock fans as tourists to Dublin for the first time. Members of the band, especially Bono, have also campaigned on humanitarian issues, such as the relief of Third World debt.

UUP. The Ulster Unionist Party, once known as the Official Unionist Party to distinguish it from other Unionist parties. It provided the government of NORTHERN IRELAND from 1921 (*see* GOVERNMENT OF IRELAND ACT) to 1972, when direct rule from London was imposed. In 21st-century politics, under the leadership of David TRIMBLE, it remains a supporter of the GOOD FRIDAY AGREEMENT, in sharp distinction to the Democratic Unionist Party (*see* DUP). In the Legislative Assembly elections held on 6 November 2003 the party was beaten into second place by the DUP by 30 seats to 27.
See also STORMONT; UNIONISM.

UVF (Ulster Volunteer Force). A Unionist–Protestant force established in January 1913 to fight HOME RULE. They formed the majority of the 36th (Ulster) Division in the British army during the First World War (*see* CARSON'S ARMY; SOMME, BATTLE OF THE).

The name was revived in 1966 for a paramilitary organization formed specifically in opposition to the perceived liberal tendencies of the government of Terence O'NEILL; two Catholics were killed that May. As the Northern Ireland TROUBLES intensified, the UVF, numbering about 1500 by the time of the fall of STORMONT in 1972, pursued its policy of indiscriminate assassination of Catholics, often using the cover name Protestant Action Force. It declared a ceasefire in 1994, but it is believed that a hardcore remains intermittently active around Portadown, where they are said to have taken part in the DRUMCREE STAND-OFFS.

UWC (Ulster Workers Council). The body that organized the Loyalist strike in May 1974 that brought down the POWER-SHARING EXECUTIVE set up by the Sunningdale Agreement (*see* WHITELAW, WILLIAM). Power supplies were cut and there was much intimidation by Protestant paramilitaries. The chief of the coordinating committee was the Vanguard member Glenn Barr; other members included Harry West of the UUP, Ian PAISLEY of the DUP and William Craig of Vanguard (a Unionist party of the 1970s). After 14 days the Unionist members resigned from the power-sharing executive and both it and the strike were over. Significant in the success of the strike was the government's perceived inertia and the army's apparent inability to operate the power stations. Merlyn Rees, the secretary of state (1974–6), was severely criticized by Nationalists for his caution. Two other UWC strikes were held, in 1977 and 1981, but the crucial element of participation by the power workers was missing, and both strikes petered out quickly.

V

Valentia. An island (Irish, *Oileán Dairbhre*, 'oak island') off the IVERAGH PENINSULA in south Co. Kerry. It can now be reached by bridge from Portmagee, although local people and tourists alike often prefer to make the short ferry trip from Knightstown, the main village, to Reenard Point near Cahirciveen. Knightstown takes its name from the owner of most of the island, the Knight of Kerry, an improving landlord who opened a slate quarry in 1816 that gave employment to 400 people (slates from Valentia were used to roof the House of Commons and other public buildings in Britain); he also started a weaving industry on the island. The fine gardens at his residence, Glanleam House, are open to the public. Valentia was chosen as the receiving point for the first transatlantic cable, from New York, in 1858.

Valley of Knockanure. The scene of an incident in north Kerry during the Anglo-Irish War. At Gortagleanna Bridge, on 12 May 1921, Walsh, Lyons and Dalton, three members of the North Kerry FLYING COLUMN, were surprised by a lorryload of BLACK AND TANS. All were killed, supposedly while evading arrest. A Celtic cross marks where they died, and their names are still revered in memory and in 'The Valley of Knockanure', a ballad by Bryan MacMahon (*see* MASTER, THE):

You may sing and speak about Easter Week or the
heroes of 'Ninety-eight;
Of the Fenian men who roamed the glen in victory
or defeat.
Their names are placed on History's page, their
memory will endure;
Not a song is sung for our darling sons in the
Valley of Knockanure.

Valley of the Squinting Windows, The. The first novel (1918) of Brinsley MacNamara (pseudonym of John Weldon, 1890–1963). It caused a sensational book-burning in the town of Delvin in Co. Westmeath, where the author's father was a schoolteacher. The novel tells of the hopes of Nan Brennan, a woman with a past, that her legitimate son John will become a priest, but the boy is led astray by his dissipated half-brother Ulick Shannon. The new teacher, Rebecca Kerr, with whom John is in love, is hunted from the village of Garradrimna after her affair with Shannon becomes known, and in revenge John kills him. The book was attacked for the grim picture it painted of Irish rural life. Since then the title has become proverbial.

Van Diemen's Land. The former name for Tasmania, given in 1642 by its Dutch discoverer Abel Jans Tasman (1603–*c*.1659) in honour of his patron, the Dutch governor-general of Batavia. It became a British settlement in 1803 and its name was changed to Tasmania in 1853, to obliterate memories of its associations with convicts, transportation having ceased at the time. Among many temporary residents were John MITCHEL, MEAGHER OF THE SWORD and Smith O'BRIEN.

> Poor Thomas Brown from Nenagh town, Jack Murphy and poor Joe
> Were three determined poachers as the country well does know.
> By the keeper of the land, my boys, one night they were trepanned
> And for fourteen years transported unto Van Diemen's Land.
> 'Van Diemen's Land', in *Irish Street Ballads* (1939)

Vanithee. *See* BEAN A' TÍ.

Van the Man. The nickname of the rock singer Van Morrison (b.1945). George Ivan Morrison was born in Belfast on 31 August 1945 to a musical family. He taught himself the guitar and saxophone while still a boy, and in 1957 joined a skiffle group called Deannie Sands and the Javelins, later playing with a SHOW-BAND, The Monarchs, and a band called Them (1964–7). His music gradually absorbed some of the influences of jazz, soul and rhythm and blues, and he spent a period in the later 1960s working in Boston, where he was influenced by the producer Bert Berns. Among his most successful singles are 'Brown-Eyed Girl' and 'Dark Side of the Road'. He has released many albums, including *Astral Weeks* (1968), *Moondance* (1974), *Enlightenment* (1990) and *Too Long in Exile* (1993). In the 1970s Morrison returned to live in Europe, at first in England, then for long periods in Ireland, where he recorded with The CHIEFTAINS and where he still performs regularly. His song 'Days Like This' became associated with the Northern peace process and the visit of US President Bill Clinton. He is regarded as one of the most influential songwriters of his generation.

Vardy. A verb, usually in the imperative mood, meaning 'look at'. It is one of several words from the glossary of Polari, the secret vocabulary devised by actors in self-protection in the 18th century. It is still in use in the gay community in Dublin and other Irish cities.

Varina. The Latinate nickname bestowed by Swift (*see* DEAN, THE) – as was his wont with his women – upon Jane Waring, the daughter of the Archdeacon of Dromore to whom he proposed marriage, largely out of boredom, in 1696. He was then 29 and undoubtedly attracted to her sexually, as he admits in a letter:

> ... a violent desire is little better than a distemper, and therefore men are not to blame in looking after a cure. I find myself hugely infected with this malady.

In time he was glad to distance himself from her, effectively driving her away by a distinctly cold letter written in 1700:

> I shall be blessed to have you in my arms, without regarding whether your person be beautiful, or your fortune large. Cleanliness in the first, and competence in the other, is all I look for.

Vatican Councils. The name of two Catholic ecumenical councils, both of which had significance for Ireland. In fact Vatican Council documents refer to the whole church, but for political reasons they are not always immediately put into practice. Many of the strictures promulgated by the Council of Trent (1545–63), including those about Catholic education, could not be carried out in Ireland until the second half of the 19th century.

The First Vatican Council met in Rome under Pope Pius IX (1792–1878) in 1869 and was concerned mainly with papal infallibility. Archbishop CULLEN had a large part in devising the formula that was finally carried. Though it was a victory for ULTRAMONTANISM, it met with minority opposition in Ireland, notably from Archbishop MACHALE.

The decrees of the Second Vatican Council (1962–5), under Pope John XXIII (1881–1963), were intended to modernize doctrine, organization and discipline, and to suggest a new role for the laity. The decrees were accepted by the Irish hierarchy, even if their implementation was not entirely heartfelt. Their attitude was best epitomized by the remark of Archbishop MCQUAID on his return from the final session of the Council: 'No change will worry the tranquillity of your Christian lives.' The gradual decline in traditional Irish Catholicism, with its drop in church attendance and personal disregard of some doctrines, had its beginnings about that time, but the Second Vatican Council's part in those changes may have been largely coincidental.

Vee, the. A V-shaped gap and noted beauty spot in the Knockmealdown Mountains on the border of south Tipperary and Waterford. From it can be gained a spectacular view of the GOLDEN VALE, spreading across Tipperary, Waterford, Kilkenny and part of Cork.

Veins of nicety, done up to the. Done up with great care and taste; the expression may be applied both to a house and to a woman. The phrase, with its fastidious-sounding and artificial arrangement of words, is satirical in intent.

Vessel. A HIBERNO-ENGLISH word for the womb of a cow or other animal. The Irish word *soitheach* means both vessel and womb, and it is likely that the usage derives from this.

Veto Controversy (1782–1829). A controversy over the right of the British government to reject the appointment of Catholic bishops to which it had 'any proper objection', with a view to ensuring the loyalty of the Irish Catholic hierarchy and thereby making CATHOLIC EMANCIPATION more acceptable to the government and to Protestants. The veto in question was first proposed as part of a Catholic-relief measure in 1782. The veto clause appeared again as part of Henry GRATTAN's Catholic Relief Bills of 1808 and 1813. At a meeting in Maynooth in 1799 the four archbishops and six bishops (*see* TROY, JOHN THOMAS) favoured the veto as a means of quickly achieving emancipation, but when after the Act of UNION it became clear that emancipation would not be forthcoming, ordinary Catholic lay and clerical opinion, led by Daniel O'CONNELL, moved away from it. In 1814 Monsignor Quarantotti, secretary of the Congregation for the Propagation of the Faith, issued a statement

in its favour, and a pro-veto group of loyalist Catholics seceded from the CATHOLIC COMMITTEE in 1815. The controversy hardened Catholic opinion against state control and divided Catholics from Loyalists, whether Catholics or liberal Protestants. Catholic Emancipation was granted without a veto in 1829.

Victoria, Queen. *See* DARLING LITTLE QUEEN, THE.

Victoria Cross. The premier British award for bravery in the presence of the enemy, instituted by Queen Victoria at the end of the Crimean War in 1856. The Victoria Cross is inscribed simply 'For Valour'. The bronze Maltese crosses are made from the metal of Russian guns captured at Sebastopol in 1855. A number of Irishmen were recipients.

Victoria Fountain. A wrought-iron fountain commemorating Queen Victoria's visit to Dún Laoghaire in 1901. The original fountain was destroyed as an anti-British gesture in 1981 and a replica completed in 2003 by the same Glasgow firm that made the original fountain.

Vienna. The capital city of Austria. It was settled by the Celts, became a military centre under the Caesars and was the home of the later Holy Roman emperors. Duke Henry founded the *Schottenkloster* ('Irish monastery') of Our Lady *c*.1156 and from it a daughter house was established at Kiev, the capital of modern Ukraine, but it was abandoned in 1241 because of the Mongol invasion. The present Schottenkirche is in the centre of the city on the Schottengasse, and the abbey has the full title *Abtei Unserer Lieben-Frau zu den Schotten* ('Irish abbey of Our Lady'). The Schottenkloster and the Schottenkirche were Benedictine monasteries that once had a predominance of Irish monks. They originated in Ratisbon, where MARIANUS SCOTTUS (OF RATISBON) built the Weih-Sankt-Peter in 1076.

View of the Present State of Ireland, A. A polemic (1596) by Edmund SPENSER in the form of a dialogue between proponents respectively of a harsh or a more lenient English policy in Ireland. It is savagely critical of the traitorous and barbarous Irish and of the OLD ENGLISH who had adopted their language and customs, promoting instead the 'civilizing' values of the TUDOR RECONQUEST and PLANTATION. It includes harrowing descriptions of the sufferings of the native people of Munster from war and famine during the DESMOND REBELLIONS (*see* ANATOMIES OF DEATH), although it does not take issue with the government policy that caused these misfortunes. The *View* was an influential piece of propaganda, shaping colonial opinion of Ireland.

Vignoles, Charles Blacker (1793–1875). Engineer. He was born in Co. Wexford, educated at Sandhurst Military Academy and served in Europe and Canada. From 1816 he worked as an engineer on railways and canals, and in 1832 became engineer-in-chief of the first Irish railway line, from WESTLAND ROW STATION in Dublin to Kingstown (Dún Laoghaire), which opened in 1834. He had a considerable reputation and was appointed first professor of civil engineering at University College London in 1841. He died at his home in Hampshire on 17 November 1875.

Vikings. The Scandinavian adventurers, from Norway and Denmark, known to themselves as Ostmen and to the Irish as *Lochlannaigh* ('lakelanders'), who were involved in Irish affairs for some 400 years (795–*c*.1200). Most of the early marauders lived up to their names (*viking* is Old English for 'pirate'); they were fierce and cruel warriors, amphibious as no other peoples in Europe, and with the ultimate weapon of the clinker-built warship they menaced the known world. (They did not fear death since the souls of heroes slain in battle were carried immediately to Valhalla, the celestial hall where they would spend an eternity of joy and feasting.)

Different groups of Vikings had different geographical foci. The Swedes tended to look east, and eventually penetrated the Russian plains, founding the cities of Novgorod and Kiev. The Danes concentrated on the North Sea, conquering most of eastern England and settling in limited numbers in southeast Ireland. It was the Norwegian warriors who were the fiercest, most affected by overpopulation at home and most conscious of the culture of booty. They, taking the 'outer line', did most harm to Ireland, sacking the monasteries (the only settlements that these instinctive town-builders could see), robbing them of the gold and bejewelled chalices, monstrances and lay ornaments that were the country's pride. The Vikings also took people, who could be sold as slaves or held hostage for ransom.

The Irish predilection for building their holy structures on islands or sea capes made the pirates' task easier. IONA was attacked in 795, 802 and 806. Even the inland foundations were not safe; the shallow-draught ships could penetrate far up the Shannon beyond CLONMACNOISE, row up the lower Bann and anchor in Lough Neagh. The Slaney, Barrow, Nore, Suir and Blackwater rivers were all navigable, and Lough Foyle, Belfast Lough, the bays of Dublin and Galway and the harbours of Wexford, Waterford and Cork made landings and settlement comparatively easy. There was never a country more amenable to Viking invasion than Ireland.

In time the Irish learned to distinguish the Norwegians from the Danes. The former were *Fionnghaill* ('fair-haired foreigners') and greatly feared; the latter were *Dúghaill* ('dark-haired foreigners'), and they came in the 10th century to exploit the Norse settlements at DUBLIN. The names of the other main towns, Wexford and Waterford, are both Norse in origin. Cork and Limerick owe their existence and their mercantile prosperity to the trading instincts of the Ostmen, which was even greater than their propensity for raiding. In time they were successfully assimilated into the country, as earlier invaders had been.

Since tonight the wind is high,
The sea's white mane a fury

I need not fear the hordes of Hell
Coursing the Irish Channel.

> Written in the margin of the 9th-century St Gall
> manuscript, translated from the Irish by Frank
> O'Connor

See also BRIAN BORU; CLONTARF, BATTLE OF;
ROUND TOWERS; TURGESIUS.

Vincents. The nickname for members of the
charitable Society of ST VINCENT DE PAUL. It is
also the popular name for St Vincent's Hospital, a foundation of the Irish Sisters of Charity, originally located in St Stephen's Green
in Dublin and now a major acute hospital on
Merrion Road to the south of the city centre.

Vinegar Hill[1]. A low hill outside the town of
Enniscorthy in Co. Wexford, remembered as
the location of the last stand of the Wexford
rebels (*see* REBELLION OF 1798). Early in the
morning of 24 June General LAKE raked the
rebel camp with artillery fire, and after several hours routed the rebels, who were armed
mostly with pikes and had no chance to fight
at close quarters. Owing to the late arrival
of General Needham (thereafter known as
'the late General Needham'), whose troops had
been intended to close the gap on the south
side of the hill, many of the pikemen escaped
and retreated to Wexford – it is estimated that
there were about 500 casualties on the field of
battle, from a force of 20,000 rebels, although
there is a popular perception that thousands
were massacred:

> Until, on Vinegar Hill, the fatal conclave,
> Terraced thousands died, shaking scythes at
>   cannon.
> The hillside blushed, soaked in our broken wave.
> They buried us without shroud or coffin
> And in August the barley grew up out of the
>   grave.
>
> SEAMUS HEANEY (b.1939): 'Requiem for the
> Croppies', in *Door into the Dark* (1969)

When General Lake's cavalry took control of
the hill, they killed mainly the camp followers – women and children, the old and the
wounded. After Vinegar Hill, the rebel army
divided into two: Father John MURPHY led one

group to Co. Kilkenny, while the second group
marched through Wicklow to north Dublin,
but neither group succeeded in attracting
support. The rebellion in Wexford effectively
ended with Vinegar Hill.

> On Vinegar Hill, o'er the pleasant Slaney
> Our heroes vainly stood back to back ...
>
> P[ATRICK] J[OSEPH] MCCALL (1861–1919):
> 'Boolavogue', in *Songs of Erinn* (1899)

Vinegar Hill[2]. The name given to an Irish
rebellion in 1804 in the Australian penal colony of Parramatta, near Sydney. Some 500
participants in the REBELLION OF 1798 who had
been spared the gallows were transported to
BOTANY BAY, including Co. Wicklow leader
Joseph Holt and a number of Catholic priests
accused of sedition. The colony was nervous
of these 'political' prisoners, and from 1800
the authorities dealt severely with any hint of
conspiracy (on information supplied by informers) by administering brutal floggings of
up to 500 lashes and sending ringleaders to
NORFOLK ISLAND (Holt himself included, although there was no evidence that he was involved in any such conspiracy).

On Sunday 4 March 1804 about 250 Irish
convicts, led by Philip Cunningham and William Johnston, finally rebelled in the remote
settlement of Castle Hill and marched in the
dusk on Parramatta. An Irish informer named
Keogh had already brought news of the rebellion to Parramatta and Sydney. Governor King
dispatched some 60 soldiers from barracks in
Sydney and the CROPPIES made their stand the
next morning on a knoll that later became
known as 'Vinegar Hill', in homage to the
Wexford battle site of 1798 – 'Vinegar Hill' was
also their rallying cry. The demoralized and
badly led rebels scattered and were captured
by the Redcoats over the next few days. Eight
of the ringleaders were hanged in chains, their
rotting bodies left on view for months *pour
encourager les autres*. The rest were brutally
flogged or sent to work in chain gangs.

Although Britain continued to send political
prisoners to New South Wales in the coming

decades, many of them WHITEBOYS or other agrarian rebels, they were widely dispersed in the colony, which itself was expanding westward, and never again presented a danger of rebellion.

Viney, Michael. *See* 'ANOTHER LIFE'.

Virgil. *See* FERGAL.

Virginia. A pretty town in Co. Cavan which stands on the north shore of the beautiful Lough Ramor (its original name before the PLANTATION OF ULSTER). It was part of the territory of the O'Reillys but was granted to Captain John Ridgeway in 1611, who eccentrically named it after the new English colony of Virginia in North America, a tribute to the most celebrated characteristic of Elizabeth I. Cuilcagh House near the town was the home of the Rev. Thomas Sheridan (1687–1738), a close friend of Jonathan Swift (*see* DEAN, THE) and grandfather of Richard Brinsley SHERIDAN, the dramatist. St KILIAN was born at Mullagh, two miles to the southeast. The town is very conscious of the beauty of its location and has become one of the 'must-visit' Irish tourist destinations because of the neatness of its layout and the profusion of flower-baskets. It was the winner of the government-sponsored 'Tidy Town' competition in 1965.

Vita Sancti Columbae (Latin, 'the life of St Columba', i.e. Colum Cille). One of the earliest pieces of Irish hagiography, written by Adamnán (*c*.625–704), the ninth abbot of IONA and as such an appropriate biographer of his kinsman COLUM CILLE, the founder of the monastery. Adamnán was born near Raphoe in what is now Co. Donegal. Little is known of his early life, but he seems to have joined the community of Iona in 652 and become abbot in 679, serving until his death in 704. In 686 he visited the kingdom of Northumbria and obtained from King Ailfrid, a former pupil, the release of 60 Irish captives, and got to know the monks of Jarrow and Wearmouth. The period was one of considerable monastic

turmoil, with the Celtic foundations refusing to follow Roman practices as ordained at the Synod of WHITBY. Adamnán made it his mission to bring about reconciliation between the two traditions, but did not succeed with his own monks. He did, however, found several 'Roman' houses, one sited near his birthplace. In 697 at the Synod of Birr he sponsored the *Cáin Adamnáin*, sometimes known as the *Lex Innocentium* ('law of the innocent'), a codex that protected the rights of secular priests, those in holy orders, women and children, especially in time of war.

Adamnán's chief work, *Vita Sancti Columbae*, was written during the decade beginning 688, and his other book, *De Locis Sanctis* ('on the holy places'), was based upon the reports of a Bishop Arculf, who claimed to have been shipwrecked in Palestine. The *Fís Adamnáin* ('vision of Adamnán') unreliably attributed to him is to be found in the 11th-century BOOK OF THE DUN COW. Its vision of heaven and hell, along with the ecstasies of FURSA, provided the main inspiration for Dante's *Divine Comedy* (1307–21). As St Eunan, titular saint of the diocese of Raphoe, he has a feast day on 23 September.

Volta Theatre. The first 'cinematograph' to be opened in Dublin, by the unlikely entrepreneur James JOYCE. He had seen how popular cinemas were in Trieste, and on a visit home in 1909, prompted by his sister Eva, he thought that he might at last find a good source of income in a city without a picture-house. With promises of finance from four Trieste businessmen he rented premises at 45 Mary Street, off Dublin's principal thoroughfare, Sackville Street (now O'Connell Street). He had little interest in the project, however, and was happy to let one of his Triestine backers, Francesco Novak, manage the theatre. Novak proved an unfortunate choice, knowing little of the temper of Dublin audiences and showing too many Italian films. The cinema was sold in July 1910 to the Provincial Theatre Company, an English firm, and Joyce, who had returned to Trieste in January, lost less money than he might have.

Volunteer Earl, the. *See* CHARLEMONT, JAMES CAULFEILD, 1ST EARL OF.

Volunteers, the. The part-time force organized during the middle years of the American War of Independence, intended to defend from invasion an Ireland with a significantly depleted garrison of regular troops. Volunteering began in 1778, with numbers rising from an estimated 40,000 in September 1779 to over 60,000 in 1782, the year after the American war ended. The need was perceived as real; memories of Commodore THUROT's capture of Carrickfergus in 1760 were still fresh.

The Volunteers were essentially middle-class and mostly Protestant (though there were Catholic members, mainly in Munster). The nature of individual corps was largely determined by the local squire, some intensely loyal, others rather more radical; they were led by such PATRIOTS as Henry GRATTAN, Henry FLOOD, the Duke of Leinster, the Earl Bishop Frederick Augustus HERVEY and his adversary Lord CHARLEMONT.

Gradually it dawned on some of the more acute members that the movement had real political power, and this became clear to the Parliament at Westminster when the Volunteers held a convention at Dungannon, Co. Tyrone, on 15 February 1782. The campaign begun then led to the concession in July of the measure of legislative independence that is known to history as GRATTAN'S PARLIAMENT. This achieved, Charlemont, fearing government suppression, did his best to de-radicalize the movement, and was largely successful.

After the fall of the Bastille and the tide of revolutionary ideas that swept the country, there were attempts by the UNITED IRISHMEN to widen the membership of the Volunteers and make it a mass movement. Repressive government legislation, notably in the form of the Gunpowder Act, prohibiting the import of arms, and the Convention Act, forbidding assembly, both passed in 1793, effectively ended the Volunteers, and the establishment of the yeomanry (*see* YEOS) removed any need for its existence as a defensive force.

See also FREE TRADE OR THIS; IRISH VOLUNTEERS; NATIONAL VOLUNTEERS.

Waddell, Helen [Jane] (1889–1965). Medievalist. She was born in Tokyo, the daughter of a Presbyterian minister, and educated at Victoria College and at Queen's University, both in Belfast. Intended for an academic career, she spent seven years tending an ungrateful invalid stepmother before going to Oxford. *The Wandering Scholars* (1927) is a history of the medieval *vagantes* and an anthology, with translations, of the often ribald poetry ascribed to them, some of which, otherwise known as the *Carmina Burana*, she included in a later collection, *Medieval Latin Lyrics* (1929). *Peter Abélard* (1933) is a novel about the great French nominalist philosopher (1079–1142) and his tragic love affair with his pupil Héloïse (1098–1164). Like her brother Rutherford Mayne (*see* DRONE, THE), she was a ULT playwright, contributing the rather esoteric *The Spoiled Buddha* in 1915.

Waddell, Samuel John. *See* DRONE, THE.

Wadding, Luke (1588–1657). Franciscan scholar. He was born in Waterford on 16 October 1588, and after study in Lisbon and Coimbra joined the Franciscan order. He was president of the Irish college at Salamanca in 1617 and theologian to the Spanish embassy in Rome in 1618. While there he was active in the promotion of the doctrine of the Immaculate Conception, which, however, did not become part of Cath-

olic teaching until 1854 by decree of Pope Pius IX (1792–1878). Wadding founded the Irish Franciscan College of St Isidore in Rome (*see* PONTIFICAL IRISH COLLEGE) and encouraged similar foundations at Leuven (Louvain) and Prague. His monumental work, *Annales Minorum*, the history of his order in eight volumes, was begun in 1625 and not completed until 1654. In 1639 he published his 12-volume edition of the work of his great Franciscan predecessor Duns Scotus (*c.*1265–1308) whom he claimed as Irish. Though he remained in Rome for the rest of his life he maintained a keen interest in Irish affairs, especially during the period of the CONFEDERATE WAR, persuading Pope Innocent X to send arms and money with Owen Rua O'NEILL in 1642 and to appoint Giovanni Battista Rinuccini as nuncio in 1645. One of his apparently insignificant achievements that was to have worldwide consequences was his insertion of the feast day of ST PATRICK (17 March) into the liturgical calendar. Wadding died on 18 November 1657, having refused all ecclesiastical honours.

Wag-at-the-wall. A wall clock with a visible pendulum and weights.

> The ould wag-at-the-wall was goin' 'tack-tack, tack-tack', very slow an' steady.
>   LYNN DOYLE (1873–1961): *Ballygullion* (1908)

Wain. *See* WEAN.

Waiting for Godot. The best-known play of Samuel BECKETT, first performed in French as *En Attendant Godot* (1952). It has been described as the play where nothing happens – twice. Two tramps, Vladimir and Estragon, wait on a country road for the coming of the mysterious Godot and pass the time with casual conversation and serious clowning, which owes much to French circuses and the films of Laurel and Hardy. They are visited by the loud Pozzo and his roped slave Lucky. In the second act the setting is the same but there are signs of deterioration: Pozzo is dumb and Lucky blind and the single leaf has fallen off the tree. The boy who told them of Godot's coming returns with the same message and, in spite of a voiced determination to move, the last stage direction indicates their philosophical stasis: '*They do not move.*'
See also PIKE THEATRE.

Wake. *See* WAKES.

Wake amusements. Relics of pagan practices were to be seen in the wake amusements that survived until well into the 20th century. Drinking, smoking, taking snuff and courting were practised universally, and the more formal games included athletic contests and feats of skill for the young men. *Irish Wake Amusements* (1967) is a comprehensive account of these customs by folklorist Seán Ó SÚILLEABHÁIN.

Wakes. The custom of watching or 'waking' with the corpse and relatives of the dead person was part of the grieving ritual in traditional Irish society. There was a tradition that the body should never be left alone for the night (or even two nights) that it remained in the house before being removed to the church. Unless the death in question was particularly tragic or untimely, there was no sense of wakes being tragic affairs. Porter aplenty was served to men in bowls, snuff was provided and clay pipes were passed around for everyone to share. WAKE AMUSEMENTS were devised to pass the time, especially among younger people. Keening (*see* KEEN) was part of the wake, as it was of the funeral.

Walk. The word deliberately used (in preference to 'march') for ORANGE ORDER parades to emphasize their peaceful aspect. There are many such walks during what has come to be called 'the marching season', the most important being those held on TWELFTH OF JULY and TWELFTH OF AUGUST each year.

Walker, George (*c.*1646–90). Protestant leader. Little is known about his early life, but he is believed to have been born in England and educated at Trinity College Dublin. In 1674 he was appointed rector of Donoughmore, where he formed the anti-Jacobite Charlemont Regiment and marched them to Derry in 1688. Early in 1689 he was chosen as joint-governor of the besieged city (*see* DERRY, SIEGE OF). When the siege was lifted he was sent to London to meet William and Mary, and he returned bringing unfulfilled promises of compensation and the gift of the bishopric for himself. His *True Account of the Siege of Londonderry* (1689), which gives marvellously graphic details of the privations of the citizenry, was severely criticized for ignoring the Presbyterian contribution to the defence. He was killed at the Battle of the BOYNE.

> He falls – the veteran hero falls, renowned along
>   the Rhine
> And he, whose name, while Derry's walls endure,
>   shall brightly shine.
> O! would to heav'n that churchman bold, his
>   arms with triumph blest,
> The soldier spirit had controll'd that fir'd his
>   pious breast.
>   WILLIAM BLACKER (1777–1858): 'The Battle of the
>   Boyne' (?1848)

Walking Gallows. The nickname of Edward Hepenstall, an exceptionally tall and strong officer of the Wicklow Militia during the REBELLION OF 1798, who, according to one account, practised the technique of half-hanging victims by the neck over his shoulder.

Walking Sunday. Originally the day before a fair, when farmers from afar would have to begin to walk their animals to the venue. The term subsequently came to mean a viewing day, the first day of the fair or sporting event, on which large crowds come to see the exhibits or sample the activities.

Walking the land. A pre-nuptial activity, by which the father and brothers of the party MARRYING IN to the farm (and bringing a dowry) would inspect the land, livestock and equipment to ascertain that the dowry suggested was worth paying. The term 'seeing the land' was also used.

Wall, Mervyn (1908–97). The pseudonym of Eugene Welpy, a novelist and short-story writer who spent his whole working career as a civil servant. *The Unfortunate Fursey* (1946), about a possessed lay-brother, is an affectionate parody of the received view of Irish monasticism and an effective attack on the contemporary church. It and its sequel *The Return of Fursey* (1948) became a cult. *Leaves for the Burning* (1953) and *No Trophies Raise* (1956) are darker, sourer accounts of Ireland seen as a 'grocer's republic', in which public piety and the right connections are essential for success. Wall also wrote two ABBEY THEATRE plays.

Wall-falling. A colloquial expression, current in Dublin, meaning 'very tired'. It is often used of children, particularly of a child who refuses to go to bed despite being exhausted.

'Walls of Limerick, The'. *See* CÉILÍ DANCES.

Walsh, Louis [Joseph]. *See* POPE IN KILLYBUCK, THE.

Walsh, Maurice (1879–1964). Writer of romances and historical fiction. He was born near Listowel in Co. Kerry, and he joined the customs service in 1901. Much of his professional life was spent in the Scottish Highlands, which provided him with themes and settings for such popular romances as *The Key above the Door* (1926) and *While Rivers Run* (1928). His story 'The QUIET MAN' from *Green Rushes* (1935) became one of John Ford's most famous films, and another novel, *Trouble in the Glen* (1950), was filmed with Orson Welles in 1954. *Blackcock's Feather* (1932) and *Son of the Swordmaker* (1938) are historical romances.

Waltons. A music and instrument shop, a Dublin institution since the 1920s. It was based for many years in North Great Frederick Street, and once had its own music-publishing and recording business. The founder, Martin Walton (b.1901), himself a talented fiddler, was associated with the Republican side during the CIVIL WAR and was interned with Peadar KEARNEY. He published songs by Kearney and many others, including Delia MURPHY and Leo MAGUIRE, and Leo ROWSOME's tutor for uilleann pipes in 1932; he also developed an export business for emigrants. Walton's Glenside record label released recordings by Joe Lynch, Leo Maguire, Delia Murphy, Noel PURCELL and the Glenside Céilí Band. Walton's shop in South Great George's Street continues to sell music and instruments.

Wan and wan. *See* ONE AND ONE.

Wanderley Wagon. A popular puppet show created by Eugene and Mai Lambert and their family. It was broadcast on RTÉ television from 1968 to 1982.

Warbeck, Perkin (d.1499). Yorkist pretender. Warbeck, a commoner from Flanders, claimed to be Richard IV, Duke of York, the dead brother of Edward V. He arrived in Cork in 1491 and attracted considerable support not only in that city and throughout Ireland but from Charles VII of France, James IV of Scotland and other European kings, thereby becoming a real threat to Henry VII. In 1495 Warbeck returned to Ireland to join a rebellion led by the Earl of Desmond, but the rebel forces failed to take WATERFORD. After another abortive visit to Ireland in 1497 he returned to England, but was captured. Along with the former mayor of Cork, John Water, he was hanged in 1499; Perkin Warbeck's execution marked the formal end of the WARS OF THE ROSES.
See also REBEL COUNTY, THE; YORK, RICHARD PLANTAGENET, DUKE OF.

War in Partry. *See* LAVELLE, PATRICK.

War of Independence. A term sometimes applied to the ANGLO-IRISH WAR of 1919–21, but not used by those who believe that full independence was not achieved by that conflict. In such cases the term TAN WAR is often preferred.

War of the Brown Bull. The name by which the mythological war for supremacy between Connacht and Ulster was known (*see TÁIN BÓ CUAILNGE*).

War of the Three Kings. A name sometimes given to the WILLIAMITE WAR, as it involved Louis XIV, William III (KING BILLY) and JAMES II. To the Irish it was *Cogadh an Dá Rí* ('the war of the two kings'), referring to William and James's battles in Ireland.

Warrenpoint. A town in Co. Down that was the scene of two explosions on 27 August 1979 in which 18 British soldiers were killed. It was the incident that inflicted the most serious loss of life on the British army during the whole of the Northern Ireland TROUBLES. Coming only a few hours after the explosion that killed Lord MOUNTBATTEN at Mullaghmore in Co. Sligo, it was regarded in Republican circles as a really spectacular 'spectacular'.

Wars of the Roses. The name by which the series of 15th-century civil wars (*c.*1455–87) between the houses of Lancaster and York is known. OLD ENGLISH families in Ireland aligned themselves with one or other side, notably the Fitzgerald Earls of Desmond and Kildare (who were Yorkists) and the Earl of Ormond (a Lancastrian). The popularity of the Yorkist cause in Ireland was evidenced by support for the invasion of England by Richard Plantagenet, Duke of YORK, in 1460, and in 1487 for the invasion led by Lambert SIMNEL; the pretender Perkin WARBECK also received much Irish support in his campaign to usurp the authority of Henry VII in the 1490s.
See also ARISTOCRATIC HOME RULE.

Watchpot. A person who used to visit houses about mealtimes in the hope of being asked to partake.

Waterford. A city of about 50,000 inhabitants, the capital of the county of the same name, situated on a fine natural harbour on the southeast coast. It was founded around 914 and because of its situation developed quickly into a significant urban centre (*see* REGINALD'S TOWER). In 1170 the city fell to STRONGBOW's Anglo-Norman army, and Strongbow married Aoife, daughter of Dermot MACMURROUGH there. HENRY II, who visited Ireland in 1170, retained Waterford and Dublin for the crown.

Waterford became a thriving port, importing wine from France and exporting wool and hides and seeing off the mercantile threat of New Ross, a competing port on the same estuary. The city remained loyal to the crown when the Pretender Perkin WARBECK mounted an attack, earning the motto '*Urbs Intacta Manet*' (Latin, 'the city remains intact'). The Catholic merchants of the city survived the Reformation, but many were expelled when the Cromwellian army under General Ireton took the city. In the 18th century, Waterford, like Dublin, experienced an architectural flowering; Waterford-born John Roberts designed City Hall and both Protestant and Catholic cathedrals. Waterford was a leader in urban and cultural regeneration in the closing years of the 20th century.

Waterford election of 1826. *See* BERESFORD, JOHN.

Waterford glass. A world-famous hand-blown lead crystal manufactured in the city of WATERFORD. The enterprise was established by local Quaker brothers, George and William Penrose, in 1783. Their glass won several gold medals at the great London Exhibition of 1851, and the brand was revived in 1950 by Joseph McGrath (1887–1966), a former CUMANN NA NGHAEDHEAL minister (*see* ARMY MUTINY), as a symbol of craftsmanship and beauty.

The most popular and bestselling stemware pattern in the world is Waterford's Lismore range, introduced to the market in October 1952. It was created by Mirek Havel, who emigrated from Czechoslovakia in 1947 and became chief designer at the factory. In 1967

Jacqueline Kennedy toured the factory while staying nearby, and ordered Waterford glass chandeliers for the Kennedy Centre in New York. This association cemented the product's popularity among Irish-Americans, who account for a large proportion of sales both in Ireland and the USA.

Wattle and daub. Woven branches (wattle) plastered with clay (daub), the material from which basic rural habitations were constructed until the 19th century.

> I will arise and go now and go to Innisfree
> And a small cabin build there of clay and wattles made …
>
> W.B. YEATS: 'The Lake Isle of Innisfree', in *The Rose* (1893)

'Waves of Tory, The'. *See* CÉILÍ DANCES.

Waxies Dargle. A gathering of cobblers (waxies) at Irishtown/Ringsend in Dublin. The banks of the River Dargle in Wicklow were a well-known place of resort in the 19th century.

> Oh says my old one to your old one
> Will you come to the Waxies Dargle?
> Says your old one to my old one
> Sure I haven't got a farthing.
>
> ANON: 'The Waxies Dargle'

Wayne, Mad Anthony (1745–96). The hero of the capture of Stony Point during the American War of Independence. The son of Irish parents, he was born in Paoli, Pennsylvania, and like many other Irish-Americans joined the FRIENDLY SONS OF ST PATRICK. Commissioned general early in the Revolutionary War, on 15 July 1779 he captured in a daring night raid the British-held garrison of Stony Point on the Hudson. His force of 1300 men crossed a swamp, used axes to break through the stockade and with fixed bayonets soon took the fort. When asked earlier by Washington if he could storm the fort, he had replied, 'I'll storm hell, sir, if you'll make the plans!' Washington replied with typical dryness, 'Better try Stony Point first, General.' After the war he defeated a combined force of Native Americans led by the Shawnee chief Blue Jacket at Fallen Tim-

bers, Ohio, on 20 August 1794, and a year later concluded a treaty with the eastern tribes of the Northwest Territory by which they ceded most of their land to the whites.

> Urging the vanguard on prone doth the leader fall,
> Smitten, sudden and sore by a foeman's musket-ball;
> Waver the changing lines; swiftly they spring to his side,
> Madcap Anthony Wayne, the patriot army's pride!
> *Forward, my braves*! he cries, and the heroes hearten again;
> *Bear me into the fort, I'll die at the head of my men!*
>
> CLINTON SCOLLARD (1860–1932): 'Wayne at Stony Point'

Way with horses, a. The sharp put-down by Louis MacNeice of the BIG HOUSE culture of the ASCENDANCY, sceptical of Yeats's adulation of them. In *The Poetry of W.B. Yeats* (1967) he wrote:

> In most cases these houses maintained no culture worth speaking of – nothing but an obsolete bravado, an insidious bonhomie and a way with horses.

Wean. A Scots word for 'child', used widely in Ulster. The spelling 'wain' is also used, but is less common. A popular saying to indicate urgency is 'Here it is nine o'clock and not a wean washed in the house!'

'Wearing of the Green, The.' The title of an anonymous early 19th-century ballad about the REBELLION OF 1798. Dion Boucicault used it in his play ARRAH-NA-POGUE.

> O Paddy dear, and did ye hear the news that's going 'round?
> The shamrock is by law forbid to grow on Irish ground!
> No more St Patrick's Day we'll keep, his colour can't be seen,
> For there's a cruel law against the Wearing of the Green.
> I met with Napper Tandy and I shook him by the hand

And I asked him 'How is old Ireland and how
  does she stand?'
'Tis the most distressful country that you have
  ever seen
For they're hanging men and women for the
  wearing of the green.

Wear one – just in Casey. The slogan appearing
on T-shirts for sale in Dublin after Bishop Eamonn Casey had admitted that he had fathered
a son (*see FORBIDDEN FRUIT*).

We cannot stand idly by. *See* STAND IDLY BY,
WE CANNOT.

Wee City, the. A nickname applied to Derry
because of the overuse of the epithet 'wee',
applied with indiscriminate affection to everything from cinema tickets to supermarket loyalty cards.

'Wee Hughie'. *See* SHANE, ELIZABETH.

Wee Joe. A universally used nickname of
Joseph Devlin, who was the leading Ulster
Nationalist from 1902 until his death. Born
in Hamill Street in working-class Belfast on
13 February 1871 he worked as a barman before becoming a self-educated journalist with
the *IRISH NEWS* and later Belfast correspondent of the *FREEMAN'S JOURNAL*. Though of
small stature, his talent for fiery oratory caused
him to be dubbed the DUODECIMO DEMOS-
THENES by Tim HEALY. He became strongly
identified with the Catholics of West Belfast,
so much so that he was able to hold his parliamentary seat in 1918 against DE VALERA. He
had been elected unopposed for North Kilkenny in 1902 and defeated the sitting Unionist
in the Falls in 1906. Devlin's presidency of an
Irish AOH from 1905 gave him an unrivalled
political machine, but though a founder of the
IRISH VOLUNTEERS he had no sympathy with
the EASTER RISING or the postwar SINN FÉIN.
  Like many other Nationalists in the new
state of Northern Ireland, Devlin felt betrayed
by the Free State government in Dublin, and
though elected to the Belfast Parliament and
for the House of Commons at Westminster he
found, as he had anticipated, that he could
make little impression on the entrenched

Unionist position. Instead he concentrated upon his constituency and did what he could to
improve the lives of his beloved Belfast poor.
He regularly financed holidays for children
and established a holiday home for their sorely
tried mothers. When he died unmarried on
18 February 1934 his funeral was huge, and
even though he had used his oratorical gifts
to castigate them, Unionist government representatives joined all other Irish political parties
to follow his coffin.

Wee North. A description, mostly affectionate,
of the province of Ulster because of the conversational prevalence of the word 'wee'.
See also WEE CITY, THE.

Weeny. A word associated with the Scots
word 'wee' (current throughout Ireland but
especially in Ulster) meaning 'tiny':

In a shady nook one moonlit night,
      A leprahaun I spied
In scarlet coat and cap of green,
      A cruiskeen by his side.
'Twas tick, tack, tick, his hammer went
      Upon his weeny shoe,
And I laughed to think of a purse of gold,
      But the fairy was laughing too.
      ROBERT DWYER JOYCE (1830–83): 'The
      Leprahaun' (1861)

Weld, Dermot. *See* BREEDERS' CUP.

Weldon, John. *See* VALLEY OF THE SQUINTING
WINDOWS, THE.

Well. *See* WELLS.

Well-got. A HIBERNO-ENGLISH adjective or adverbial phrase meaning 'prosperous', 'of a
good family' (for example, when talking about
a prospective spouse).

Well-heeled articulate women. The disparaging
description by George Colley TD, minister for
finance (1970–3), of working women agitating
for the reform of discriminatory tax laws.

Wellington, Arthur Wellesley, 1st Duke of (1769–
1852). Irish-born soldier and statesman. The
third son of the Earl of Mornington, an Irish
peer, he is supposed to have decried his Dublin

birth with the words 'Because a man is born in a stable that does not make him a horse.' (An alternative attribution makes it a gibe of Daniel O'CONNELL's in the Commons when the 'Iron Duke' made to speak as an authority on Irish affairs.) The family name was originally Wesley. Nearly all of Wellesley's time was spent away from Ireland, winning victory after victory in the Peninsular War and finally defeating Napoleon at Waterloo after 'hard pounding' (he had been made Duke of Wellington in 1814). He was an all but absentee chief secretary for Ireland (1807–9) but managed in the little time he was in the country to reorganize the Dublin police. Wellington, though he had supported the Catholic Relief Bill of 1793 as MP for Trim, Co. Meath (1790–5), resisted full emancipation during his premiership (1828–30) until his fear of civil unrest made him acquiesce in 1829.

Wellington's eldest brother Richard (1760–1842), lord lieutenant of Ireland from 1821, took a more liberal view of CATHOLIC EMANCIPATION than his younger sibling. He resigned the lord lieutenancy when his brother became prime minister, but by the time he reassumed the post in 1833 had seen Wellington settle the issue in the Catholics' favour.

See also DRAGGING DOWN SOME NOBLE STAG.

Well lit. A synonym of NICELY.

Well of Knowledge, the. A store of wisdom located variously at the source of the Boyne or the Shannon. The knowledge comes from nine hazel trees whose nuts drop into the well. The well chases the goddess BOANN to form the River Boyne (or Shannon), bringing the magical salmon FINTAN with it.

Well of the Saints, The. A play by J.M. SYNGE, first produced by the Irish National Theatre Society in the ABBEY THEATRE on 4 February 1905 to a less than enthusiastic reaction. Since the staging of IN THE SHADOW OF THE GLEN the Nationalist press had treated all Synge's work with suspicion. Accusations that his work was un-Irish or a slur on the decent people of the country were common, and they were to reach their climax with the response to *The* PLAYBOY OF THE WESTERN WORLD. Though relatively inoffensive, the theme of this, Synge's first full-length drama to be staged, was wry and disturbing, and did not have the positive and patriotic elements that Arthur GRIFFITH felt Irish literature required.

Martin and Mary Doul, an elderly blind pair of beggars – the name Doul is a phonetic rendering of the Irish *dall* ('blind') – live with the twin illusions that they are handsome and that the visible world is full of wonders. When their sight is miraculously restored by a travelling 'saint', they find to their dismay that both beliefs are vain. They realize that they are old and ugly, and they are mocked by the people who once acquiesced in the deception. When in the third act the effect of the miracle begins to wear off, Martin dashes the can of holy water from the saint's hands rather than risk another miracle. The two are stoned out of the village, but they prefer their happy darkness and uncertain future to the facts of sighted life.

Well on. A synonym of NICELY.

Wells. The wells and the water taken from them were central to Irish rural society before running water and internal sanitation became a feature of everyday life. Usually all the families of a village or townland shared a well, and its maintenance would require cooperation, even among families who might otherwise be at enmity. The women of the locality might meet and gossip at the well, as at the well at Bun an Bhaile on the Great Blasket. There are some thinkers who attach great symbolism to wells, regarding their depths as the interface between the material and supernatural world. On May morning, BEALTAINE, there was a rush to go to the well because it was believed that the first bucket of spring water drawn from the well on that morning would bring good luck to the drawer.

See also HOLY WELLS.

Well steamed. A synonym of NICELY.

Well wear. A congratulatory remark in HIBERNO-ENGLISH on seeing someone, particularly a child, wearing new clothes or footwear. It was the custom in rural areas to give the child a penny or other small coin to mark the occasion. The incantation 'Health to wear, strength to tear and money to buy another pair' was also used.

Welpy, Eugene. *See* WALL, MERVYN.

Wentworth, Thomas (1593–1641). Earl of Strafford (1640), lord deputy to Charles I (1632–40) and lord lieutenant (1640–1), nicknamed 'Black Tom Tyrant' because of his authoritarianism. Wentworth's aim in Ireland was to increase the power and prosperity of the king and the Anglican church, at the expense of all sectors of society, especially the OLD ENGLISH landowners, the New English administration and the Catholic Church. He extracted a new subsidy for the king by misleadingly suggesting to the Old English that the GRACES that had been agreed during the previous decade would now be ratified; he installed high-church Anglican bishops in an effort to expunge Calvinism; and in 1635, by means of packed local juries, he asserted ancient crown titles over large Old English estates in Connacht and Munster with a view to appropriating these lands and planting them. (The vast estate of the Burke Earls of Clanrickard was one such, but King Charles eventually exempted it from seizure.)

After war broke out in Scotland in 1639, Wentworth, at the prompting of Scottish Royalists, imposed the BLACK OATH on all Scots settlers in Ulster, by which they abjured the National Covenant. The king appointed him his chief adviser, but the English Parliament – alarmed by his activities, especially the raising of a Royalist army in Ireland to fight against the Scots – attainted him. By then he had alienated all sectors of Irish society, and Old and New English alike supported the bill of attainder. Charles, deprived of all support, was obliged to consent to Wentworth's execution, on 12 May 1641.

West Briton. A person, who, living in Ireland, professed loyalty to the British crown and aped British manners. The disparaging term was invented by D[avid] P[atrick] MORAN, who used

it and the analogous term SHONEEN regularly in the Nationalist paper, the *Leader*, which he founded in 1900. The phrase was eagerly adopted by SINN FÉIN and the GAA and is still occasionally heard, usually to mean individuals who, titled or otherwise, are members of what was known as the ASCENDANCY and who appear to Irish people to speak with an English accent. It may also be used of Irish people who, perhaps living in Britain, appear to have entirely abandoned their own linguistic heritage of HIBERNO-ENGLISH.
See also ANGLO-IRISH; JACKEEN.

West Clare Railway. A narrow-gauge railway of great renown which ran for 86 km (54 miles) from Ennis to Kilkee in Co. Clare. It was locally nicknamed Kate Mac, for reasons that are not altogether clear. The first sod in the construction of the railway was turned by Charles Stewart PARNELL at Miltown Malbay on 26 June 1885; the West Clare branch of CIÉ, as it was by then known, was closed by CIÉ chairman Todd ANDREWS on 31 January 1961. The decision was inevitable – the line was losing £23,000 per annum, the stock needed replacement, the gauge was not compatible with anything else – but the railway's demise was a source of great regret not only to the people of west Clare but to tourists and all those who appreciated the beauty of the scenery along the line.
See also 'ARE YE RIGHT THERE, MICHAEL?'

Westland Row Station. A station in Dublin, now a DART station and officially named, like the adjacent street, after Patrick PEARSE. The station is notable as it was from here that the first railway in Ireland ran, its other terminus being a station near the west pier of Kingstown (Dún Laoghaire). The line was opened on 18 December 1834, and on that celebratory day 5000 passengers travelled to Kingstown in 19 trains. The *Dublin Penny Journal* reported at the time:

> Hurried forward by the agency of steam, the astonished passenger glides, like Asmodeus, over the summits of the streets and houses of our city

– presently is transported through green fields and tufts of trees – then skims across the surface of the sea.

Extension of the line to a new terminus in Kingstown took a further three years and involved the destruction of the MARTELLO TOWER there.

Westlife. A successful 'boy band' that originated in the Sligo area – hence Westlife (although Nicky Byrne and Bryan McFadden are from Dublin). Directed by pop manager Louis Walsh since 1998, the band consisted of five members – Shane Filan (b.1979), Kian Egan (b.1980), Mark Feehily (b.1981), Nicky Byrne (b.1978) and lead singer Bryan McFadden (b.1980); McFadden announced in March 2004 that he was leaving the band. The band was groomed for international recording and concert success with a series of easy-listening cover versions and ballads, beginning with 'Swear It Again' in April 1999. Westlife was the successor to Walsh's original boy band, BOYZONE.

Westport House. A mansion (the seat of Lord Altamont) in a spectacular setting overlooking Clew Bay, within a few miles of the pretty tourist town of Westport, Co. Mayo. Designed by Palladian architect Richard CASTLE in 1731, the house acquired new north and south wings in 1816 and 1819 respectively. It is now a tourist attraction, with a theme park and a zoo in the grounds.

Westropp, Thomas Johnson (1860–1922). Antiquarian. He was born in Attyflynn, Co. Limerick, and trained as an engineer. He surveyed the archaeological remains of Co. Clare and between 1910 and 1913 published a large body of work on the traditions and folklore of counties Clare and Limerick in *Folk-Lore*, the journal of the English Folklore Society. In 1916 he was elected president of the Royal Society of Antiquaries of Ireland. Westropp's contribution to the collection of folklore, ethnographic and antiquarian in tendency, has been obscured by the achievement of personalities such as James Hamilton DELARGY and

Seán Ó SÚILLEABHÁIN and by the very different methodology employed by the IRISH FOLKLORE COMMISSION established in 1935.

Wet week. A phrase used variously in HIBERNO-ENGLISH to indicate a period of time. 'As long as a wet week' conveys a slow, tedious experience. 'She's not here a wet week' suggests a person's relative newness in a job.

Wet winter. The beginning of a partially accurate prophecy for the year 1798:

> A wet winter, a dry spring,
> A bloody summer, and no king.

The 'bloody summer' refers to the REBELLION OF 1798; the 'no king' to the vain hope of its success in setting up an independent republic.

Wexford. *See* BULLRING, THE.

Wexford Bard, the. The sobriquet of the ballad writer Michael O'Brien, who sold his ballad sheets for a penny at fairs, races and sporting events in Wexford around the turn of the last century. Among his songs, 'Ballyshannon Lane' and 'The Alfred D. Snow' are still in the repertoire of ballad and traditional singers.

Wexford Carols. A collection of carols, some composed by the Counter-Reformation Bishop of Ferns, Luke WADDING (*c.*1628–91), and published in Ghent as *A Small Garland of Pious and Godly Songs* in 1634; others are by a Father William Devereux. The carols were then published in a combined volume, *A New Garland Containing Songs for Christmas*, in the 1730s. These carols formed part of the musical tradition of some parishes in Co. Wexford, and two are still sung in Kilmore church at Christmas by a choir of six men. The one most commonly referred to as 'The Wexford Carol' begins:

> Good people all, this Christmas-time
> Consider well and bear in mind
> What our good God for us has done
> In sending His beloved Son.

Wexford Opera Festival. An annual festival held in Wexford in October–November, founded by Dr Tom Walsh in 1951 and featuring leading performers in lesser-known operas, as well as concerts, recitals and exhibitions.

Wexford Rebellion. *See* REBELLION OF 1798.

Whack. An old term for food and sustenance as part of a wage, as in 'He gets 2s 6d a day and his whack.'

Whaling. *See* MULLET PENINSULA, THE.

Whatever look I gave. A HIBERNO-ENGLISH conversational filler to indicate surprise or to add to the anticipation of the listener, as in 'Whatever look I gave, there was the book on top of the television.'

Whatever you're having yourself. A phrase added to the end of a list, usually dismissively or negatively, with the meaning of 'and so on', such as 'murder, rape, pillage and whatever you're having yourself'. The phrase derives from an invitation to a companion to have a drink or to a waiter or barman to have a drink on the speaker, as in: 'A gin and tonic, a double Powers … and whatever you're having yourself.'

What's on you? (Irish *Cad tá ort?*). A common usage in HIBERNO-ENGLISH, especially in the west of Ireland, instead of 'What's the matter with you?'

Wheen. A Scots word meaning 'few' or 'a small amount', still in common use in Ulster, as in 'Don't cry; she'll be back in a wheen of days!'

Whelan, Bill. *See* RIVERDANCE.

'When Irish Eyes Are Smiling'. One of the best known of Irish-American songs, first aired in New York in 1913 in the musical play *The Isle o' Dreams*. The music was by Ernest Ball (1878–1927) and Chauncey Olcott (*see* 'MY WILD IRISH ROSE') with words by George Graff (1887–1973). Though at best sham-Irish, like 'Mother MACHREE' by the same composers, it was happily accepted in its doubtful homeland. Even now it is hard to imagine a barroom singsong without one or other of these unforgettable ditties.

> When Irish eyes are smiling sure it's like a morn in spring.

> In the lilt of Irish laughter you can hear the angels sing.
> When Irish hearts are happy all the world seems bright and gay,
> And when Irish eyes are smiling sure they'd steal your heart away.

When We Were Boys. A popular FENIAN novel (1890) by William O'BRIEN, the Nationalist politician, which is both a defence of the revolutionary movement and a portrait of the author's elder brother Jim.

Where Finbarr taught, let Munster learn. The motto and title of the anthem of University College Cork, now a constituent college of the NATIONAL UNIVERSITY and formerly one of the QUEEN'S COLLEGES. The reference is to St FINDBAR, patron saint of Cork.

Whiddy Island Disaster. On 9 January 1979 the French oil-tanker *Betelgeuse* caught fire and exploded at the Gulf Oil terminal on Whiddy Island in Bantry Bay, Co. Cork. Casualties included 7 local Gulf Oil workers and 43 members of the ship's crew. An inquiry opened in Bantry in May 1979 and concluded in December of that year. Its report, published in May 1980, found Gulf Oil and Total, the owners of the *Betelgeuse*, responsible for the tragic accident. The incident put an end to the use of Bantry Bay as an oil terminal.

Whin. An Ulster word for the prolific prickly shrub with bright yellow flowers known botanically as *Ulex*. The usual terms, 'gorse' or 'furze', are virtually unknown in Ulster.

> I think it will be winter when I die
> For no one from the North could die in spring –
> And all the heather will be dead and grey
> And the bog-cotton will have blown away
> And there will be no yellow on the whin.
>> HELEN WADDELL (1889–1965): 'I Shall Not Go to Heaven' (1925)

Whiskey. Regarded by some as the national drink (*see* GUINNESS), Irish whiskey (*uisce beatha*, the 'water of life') is certainly of far greater antiquity. It is thought that whiskey is an Irish invention: Celtic monks are reputed to have adapted the distillation process from

Arabic perfume-makers. The difference between Irish whiskey and Scotch is that Irish whiskey is distilled three times, Scottish whisky twice. *See also* PADDY[2]; POWERS; TULLAMORE DEW.

Whist (Irish *éisteacht*, 'listen'). A HIBERNO-ENGLISH command to be quiet and listen: 'Will you whist!' or 'Hold your whist!' It is sometimes pronounced 'fhuist' in the southwest. The word and its associated expressions are also heard in Scotland, sometimes in the form 'wheesht'.

Whistle. The penny or, as it is usually known, the tin whistle. It is now normally made of brass or, as the name would indicate, of tin, and is the most readily and cheaply available of all instruments on which it is possible to play a traditional Irish tune. Whistle kits, including a book of techniques and basic tunes, can be bought for a few pounds in almost every tourist outlet in Ireland. The whistle is seen as a beginner's instrument, and is also favoured for school bands, but in the right hands it can produce a virtuoso performance. Most tunes for the flute and UILLEANN PIPES can be played on a tin whistle.

Whitaker, T[homas] K[enneth] (b.1916). Public servant. He was born in Rostrevor, Co. Down, on 8 December 1916; the family moved to Drogheda when he was six. After attending the Christian Brothers school in Drogheda he joined the civil service in 1934, taking a degree in economics from London University, and rose to the position of secretary of the Department of Finance in 1956. He served as a governor of the Central Bank (1969–76) and after his retirement from the civil service he served as a company director, a senator and chancellor of the NATIONAL UNIVERSITY.
See also WHITAKER PLAN, THE; LEMASS, SEÁN.

Whitaker Plan, the. In 1958, the First Programme for Economic Expansion was formulated by T. K. WHITAKER, secretary of the Department of Finance, at the behest of minister for finance Dr James Ryan and Seán LEMASS, minister for industry and commerce. It was adopted

by government in November 1958 and strongly supported by Lemass when he succeeded DE VALERA as taoiseach in 1959. This was a key initiative in the development of the Irish economy, which up to this point had been protectionist, isolationist and stagnant.

Whitby, Synod of (664). A council held under the auspices of Oswy, king of Northumbria, at Whitby Abbey on the Yorkshire coast to reconcile the difference between the practices of the Celtic and Roman churches. The most obvious point at issue was the *computus*, the calculation of the date of Easter: BEDE records that at one point the king had finished the Lenten fast and was celebrating Easter while his wife Eanflaed, who was a Kentish princess and followed the Roman dating, was keeping Palm Sunday. This was just the thing likely to confuse and scandalize new converts. The struggle went deeper than debates about dates and monastic tonsures (another point of divergence); it was about central authority and local autonomy.

FINAN, the successor of AIDAN as abbot of LINDISFARNE, had stood out against the persuasions of Rónán, a southern Irish monk who had accepted the Roman system. COLMÁN OF LINDISFARNE, who replaced Finan on his death in 661, took an even harder line. The Roman faction inevitably won the day since COLUM CILLE, taken as the Celtic church's founder, had not the universal authority of St Peter. Colmán refused to accept the Synod's findings and led his monks with some English adherents to Ireland via IONA. Most of the Irish houses had conformed by 630, but it was not until the last quarter of the 8th century that all the Celtic foundations were in communion with Rome, IONA and the Ulster houses being the most resistant to change.

Whitby prevented a serious schism, but the influence of a strong lay ruler was significant, and a clash between the authority of Rome and that of equally pious and adamant local clerics remained a possibility until it became a reality in the 16th century, with the advent of the Reformation.

White, Terence de Vere (1912–94). Novelist and literary editor. He was born in Dublin and educated at Trinity College Dublin while working as an apprentice solicitor. He set up his own law firm, retiring from it to become literary editor of the *Irish Times* (1961–77) and to devote more time to writing. His autobiography, *The Fretful Midge* (1959), has all the charm and style of his novels, notable among which are *Lucifer Falling* (1966), about the clash between cultured academics and the new breed, *Tara* (1967), about the final days of a one-shot Irish man of letters, and *The Lambert Mile* (1969), about an Anglo-Irish enclave persisting in south Dublin. *The Distance and the Dark* (1973) mixes social comedy and the Northern TROUBLES as a BIG HOUSE landlord discovers that a member of the FCA local defence force (*see* FREE CLOTHES ASSOCIATION) is also a member of Gallowglass, a virulent splinter group of the IRA, and can find no one to bring him to justice. White wrote biographies of Isaac BUTT (1946), Kevin O'HIGGINS (1948), Oscar Wilde's parents, Sir William WILDE and SPERANZA (1967), and Thomas MOORE (1977), several travel books, a history of the Royal Dublin Society (1955) and *The Anglo-Irish* (1972).

Whiteboys. An agrarian SECRET SOCIETY active 1761–5 and 1769–75, so called because of the practice of wearing white shirts over ordinary clothes. Their main grievances were the recurring ones of enclosures, use of tillage land for stock grazing and the paying of TITHES. Legislation against the offences of burnings, killing and maiming of cattle and the occasional deaths of farmers or 'traitors' made all Whiteboy activities capital offences. The name was used generically for such protest movements right up until the Great Famine.

White horses. The sign that potatoes are coming to the boil, from the patches of froth that form near the top of the pot.

White Lady, the. The ghostly apparition of a bride said to walk the ramparts of CHARLESFORT in Kinsale. Shortly after the fort was constructed,

Colonel Warender was appointed governor. His daughter Wilful married Sir Trevor Ashhurst, an officer in the fort. On the evening of her wedding day, the bride walked on the battlements of the fort with her groom. She admired flowers growing on the rocks below and Sir Trevor offered to swap places with the soldier on guard if the soldier would fetch the flowers for his bride. Sir Trevor fell asleep on guard duty and was shot by Colonel Warender in a case of mistaken identity. Wilful flung herself over the battlements in despair, still wearing her wedding dress.

Whitelaw, William (1918–99). The first secretary of state for Northern Ireland (1972–3). Popularly known as 'Willie' and a brilliant negotiator, he came within a hair's-breadth of reaching a working peace in Ulster with the Sunningdale Agreement (named after Sunningdale in Berkshire, the venue for the talks). The agreement set up a POWER-SHARING EXECUTIVE, led by the Unionist Brian FAULKNER and Gerry FITT of the SDLP, on 1 January 1974. It lasted only five months, having been brought down by the UWC strike. Whitelaw, who had ended NO-GO AREAS and brought a semblance of order to the province, regarded the agreement as his greatest political achievement. He was called back to Britain by PM Edward Heath to help settle the miners' strike in November 1973, and it is generally felt that if he had been allowed to continue in the post he might have obviated the pointlessly destructive UWC strike. He died – having been elevated to the peerage as Viscount Penrith – on 13 June 1999.

White martyrdom (Irish *bán-martra*). The renunciation by the early Irish monks of everything they loved for God. The most cruel relinquishing possible was that of their homeland, practised by the *PEREGRINI*. An implied distinction was that made with 'red' martyrdom, where blood was spilled and death suffered, a fate almost unknown in the christianizing of Ireland. The biblical text associated with white martyrdom was Genesis 12:1:

Now the Lord said unto Abram, 'Get thee out

of thy country, and from thy kindred, and from thy father's house, unto a land which I shall shew thee.'

'Green' martyrdom was a colourful description of the penance involving fasting and hard labour, characteristic of most early foundations.

Whittret or whittrick. The Scots word for a 'weasel', applied in Ireland to the stoat – inaccurately, as there are no weasels in Ireland. The name may come from 'white throat', and the usual 'weasel-like' characteristics of savagery and treachery are associated with the word, as in 'He came at me like a whittret!' Ulster children who are imprecise about the name of the carnivore are appalled at a joke by their elders about the weasel being weasely recognized while the other is stoatly different.

'Who Fears to Speak of Ninety-Eight'. *See* INGRAM, JOHN KELLS.

Whole-duck. A term for mallard, as opposed to the half-duck, teal or widgeon.

Whole of Derry, the. A comic exaggeration to describe a large crowd. Its use is confined to the northwest of Ireland, as the complete phrase indicates: 'The whole of Derry and the half of Strabane.' Strabane is a market town about 20 km (12 miles) from the city.

Wide Street Commissioners. The Commissioners for Making Wide and Convenient Streets, to give them their full title, were an *ad hoc* body established in Dublin by Parliament in 1757. Their first task was to make a wide and convenient street from Essex Bridge (opposite Capel Street) to Dublin Castle. They had considerable powers of commandeering (and compensation) and often began demolition before the tardy owners had left. They made a significant contribution to the elegance of Georgian Dublin and, under the leadership of the dynamic John BERESFORD (1750–1805), they were responsible for shifting the north–south axis from Essex Bridge to the new Carlisle Bridge (now O'Connell Bridge), providing a memorable pedestrian sequence from ST STEPHEN'S GREEN along

Sackville Street (now O'CONNELL STREET) mall to the ROTUNDA.

Widgery Report. The findings of the enquiry led by John Passmore, Lord Widgery (1911–91), about the killing of (finally) 14 people by the Parachute and Royal Anglian regiments in Derry on BLOODY SUNDAY, 30 January 1972. Published in April 1972 it found that there would have been no deaths if the illegal march had not taken place, that the army should have kept to its usual 'low-key' response but that they would not have responded had they not been fired on first. The Nationalist population rejected the report as a cover-up and Jack LYNCH, then in his first period as taoiseach (1966–73), called for an international examination of the activities of the British army. It was the first of many calls for an inquiry, but the request had to wait for 26 years before the setting up of the Saville Tribunal. Nationalist attitudes were summed up by the Nationalist leader Eddie MCATEER in *The Irish Times* on 20 April 1972:

> This is a political judgement by a British officer and a British judge upon his darling British Army. I suppose we are lucky he didn't also find that the thirteen committed suicide.

Widow McCormick's Cabbage Patch. The mock description of the YOUNG IRELAND rebellion of Smith O'Brien (1803–64) in 1848. Born in Co. Clare, O'Brien served as Tory MP for Ennis in 1825 and for Limerick in 1835, but by 1844 had become a fervent advocate of the repeal of the Act of UNION. With Charles Gavan DUFFY he founded the IRISH CONFEDERATION in 1847, and, fired with the revolutionary enthusiasm of the revolt against Louis Philippe in Paris in 1848, decided on a YOUNG IRELAND rising at what was then the height of the GREAT FAMINE, even though the effective leaders like John MITCHEL had been arrested.

MEAGHER OF THE SWORD and John Blake DILLON tried to stir up disaffection in Dublin, but the government's spy network was highly effective, and habeas corpus was suspended on

25 July. Dillon held a rally at Killenaule, Co. Tipperary, on 28 July, but it was dispersed without bloodshed. O'Brien reluctantly assumed command – he had always regarded himself as a 'Middle-Aged Irelander' – and on 29 July he led a band of 100 followers to surround the Widow McCormick's farmhouse at Ballingarry, 11 km (7 miles) from Killenaule, where 46 RIC officers had barricaded themselves. Two of his men were killed in the battle of the cabbage patch and he was arrested, convicted of high treason and had his death sentence commuted to TRANSPORTATION to Van Diemen's Land for life. He returned to Ireland under the general amnesty in 1856 and took no further part in politics.

Widow McGrath's Tavern. A public house on Sir John Rogerson's Quay in Dublin, where Major SIRR arrested 11 leaders of the UNITED IRISHMEN in April 1798.

Wife-swapping sodomites. The term of abuse for supporters of DIVORCE and for reporters perceived as belonging to the same liberal coterie, coined by Úna Bean Mhic Mhathúna, an anti-divorce activist at the end of the divorce referendum campaign of 1996: 'Go away, ye wife-swapping sodomites!'

Wigs on the Green. A phrase meaning 'trouble anticipated', as in the phrase 'There'll be wigs on the green.' It comes, probably, from the 18th-century practice of removing wigs before a duel. Dublin's ST STEPHEN'S GREEN was the 'green' used in the phrase, being a favourite place for 'satisfactions'.

'Wild Colonial Boy, The'. The title of a ballad about a 19th-century Australian Robin Hood figure, thought to be a mythical amalgam of outlaw Jack DONAHUE and another bushranger, Jack Dowling.

There was a wild colonial boy,
Jack Duggan was his name.
He was born and bred in Ireland
In a town called Castlemaine.
He was his father's only son,
His mother's pride and joy,
And dearly did his parents love

This wild colonial boy.
At the early age of sixteen years
He left his native home,
And to Australia's sunny shores
He was inclined to roam.
He robbed the wealthy squireen,
All arms he did destroy,
And a terror to Australia was
This wild colonial boy.
    ANON.

Wilde, Oscar [Fingal O'Flahertie Wills] (1854–1900). Playwright and wit. He was born in Dublin, the son of the surgeon Sir William WILDE and the poet SPERANZA, and educated at Portora Royal School, Enniskillen, Co. Fermanagh, and at Trinity College Dublin (TCD) and Magdalen College, Oxford. His mentor at TCD was MAHAFFY, and at Oxford, where he won the Newdigate Prize for poetry, Walter Pater (1839–94), the apostle of aestheticism. Though instinctually Irish, he reinvented himself by fin-de-siècle posturing, which caused him to be parodied by W.S. Gilbert in *Patience* (1881). His wit was dazzling and he worked very hard at journalism, editing *The Women's World* (1887–9) and keeping his wife and two sons in comfort in a show house in Chelsea.

Wilde was an active homosexual from 1886, and his relationship with Lord Alfred Douglas, the spoiled son of the erratic Marquess of Queensbury, led to a charge of gross indecency and a sentence of two years' hard labour in Reading jail. Released in 1897 but broken in health, he lived in Italy and France, using the name 'Sebastian Melmoth' (a combination of the saintly martyr and the hero of Charles MATURIN's Gothic novel *Melmoth the Wanderer*). He was ultimately deserted by 'Bosie', as he called Douglas, but supported by Robbie Ross, one of his first lovers, and died in Paris of meningitis. He was buried in Père Lachaise, commemorated by a monument by Jacob Epstein, since defaced.

At the time of the ill-advised action urged on him by the defendant's son, Wilde had reached the pinnacle of dramatic success with four brilliant and ultimately serious comedies of class,

Lady Windermere's Fan (1891), *A Woman of No Importance* (1893), *An Ideal Husband* (1895) and *The Importance of Being Earnest* (1895), which are constantly revived. His lush play *Salomé* (1894), first written in French, no longer shocks and *The Happy Prince* (1888), a collection of stories told to his own children, is now a classic. Other essential Wildeana are *The Picture of Dorian Gray* (1890), a wittily decadent horror story, *De Profundis* (1905), his prison apologia, and *The Ballad of Reading Gaol* (1898).

Wilde's Irishness consists of more than the mere panoply of his Hibernian forenames; his father and mother were strongly patriotic, and he himself sang his children to sleep with the same Irish lullabies that his parents had used with him. His clandestine Irishness may have been the cleverest part of his love/hate relationship with the aesthetic and fashionable establishment of the country of his adoption.

Wilde, Sir William [Robert Wills] (1815–76).

Surgeon, antiquarian, husband of SPERANZA and father of Oscar WILDE. He was born near Castlerea, Co. Roscommon, and educated at the Royal College of Surgeons. He later specialized in ENT (ear, nose and throat) in London, Berlin and Vienna, financed by the proceeds of a book describing his travels in Madeira and Tenerife. He set up practice in Dublin in 1841, becoming the leading surgeon in his field and official ophthalmologist to the CASTLE. He was knighted in 1864, but a libel case brought by a former patient (and mistress), which she won with a farthing damages, all but ruined his career. He was the first to suggest Ménière's syndrome as the cause of Swift's apparent madness (*see* DEAN, THE).

Wilde's interest in Irish antiquities, as evidenced in such volumes as *The Beauties of the Boyne and the Blackwater* (1849) and *Lough Corrib and Lough Mask* (1867), was recognized by the award of the Royal Irish Academy medal in 1873. This antiquarian work was completed by his wife, whom he had married in 1851.

Wild Geese, the.

The term applied to Irishmen who served in foreign armies in the 17th and 18th centuries. Around 50,000 left for France, Spain, Austria (and even Sweden and the New World) in the years 1691–1791. Such service was illegal, but with the loss of the Irish aristocracy and the severity of the POPERY LAWS many young Catholic males found it an attractive career, even though it implied exile. Initially it was aristocratic Irish leaders with their men who sought service with the armies of France and Spain, but later their numbers included priests and students, seeking the education denied them at home, and exiled merchants who moved to continental ports, whence they continued to carry on a surreptitious business with home.

The phrase first occurs in a poem by Conchur Ó Briain (1650–1720): '*Atáid na Géanna Fiaine go buartha is iad ag gluaiseacht go tláth*' ('The Wild Geese are mournful as they travel on weak wings'). Sir Arthur Conan Doyle (*see* 'SAID THE KING TO THE COLONEL'), ever conscious of his Irish blood, expressed the case more graphically:

> Just two hundred Irish lads are shouting on the
>   wall;
> Four hundred more are lying, who can hear no
>   slogan call.
> But what's the odds of that,
> For it's all the same to Pat
> If he pays his debt in Dublin or Cremona.
>   *Songs of Action* (1928)

Some optimistic Irishmen kept hoping that they would return. In fact a band of them did in 1745 with the YOUNG PRETENDER, but the despairing Irish hoped for continental armies:

> The Wild Geese shall return and we'll welcome
>   them home,
> So active, so armed and so flighty;
> A flock was ne'er known to this island to come
> Since the years of Prince Fionn the mighty.
>   JOHN O'CUNNINGHAM: 'The Wild Geese' (1732).
>   The reference is to FIONN MAC CUMHAIL.

See also AMERICAN WILD GEESE.

Wild Rose of Lough Gill. *See* LOUGH GILL.

William III. *See* KING BILLY.

Williamite. *See* KING BILLY.

Williamite War. The war between the supporters of William III (KING BILLY) and the Jacobites – the supporters of the deposed JAMES II. Also known as the War of the Three Kings (Louis XIV of France being the third), it was a part of the warfare carried on by Louis from 1689 against the Grand Alliance of Spain, Britain, Holland, Bavaria, Austria and Pope Innocent XI, an alliance formed with the aim of preventing further territorial expansion by France.

After William had taken the English throne, James fled to France and was quickly accepted as a useful ally by Louis. To the Irish the struggle became *Cogadh an Dá Rí* ('the War of the Two Kings'), as William and James settled in Ireland the succession to the British throne. At the Battle of the BOYNE on 1 July 1690 the Williamite forces outnumbered and had much greater firepower than the Jacobite force of French and Irish troops, and James, to his ever-lasting shame among the long-memoried Irish, left the field early (*see* SÉAMAS AN CHACA). One reason for the relative lack of aggressiveness on the part of the French troops was their commander Lauzun's promise to Mary of Modena, James's wife, that at all costs the king's life would be preserved. It was he who gave orders for cavalry protection for the king and advised his early withdrawal. Like the Siege of DERRY the previous year, the battle achieved iconic status among Protestants, and the ORANGE ORDER celebrate it vociferously each 12 July (new calendar). The battle was seen in Europe as a defeat for Louis and, ironically for a Protestant victory, a *Te Deum* was sung in the Stephansdom in Vienna; contrary to popular belief this was not authorized by the new pope, Alexander XVIII, though he too was as antagonistic to Louis as his predecessor.

The decisive battle of the war was actually fought not at the Boyne but at AUGHRIM, on 12 July 1691. The Irish Jacobites under Patrick SARSFIELD ended the war with the later-repudiated Treaty of LIMERICK on 3 October.

William of Malmesbury. *See* MALMESBURY.

Williams, Richard D'Alton. *See* SHAMROCK².

Willie Clancy Summer School. A week-long school offering tuition in traditional instruments and set dancing and with concomitant *CEOL AGUS CRAIC*. It has been held annually in Miltown Malbay in Co. Clare, Willie CLANCY's birthplace, since shortly after his death in 1973. The 'Willie Week', as it has been called, is one of the best-established and most popular of these schools, attracting scores of teachers, musicians, dancers and listeners from all over Ireland and abroad. The opening event is a memorial lecture in honour of Breandán BREATHNACH.

Willie Week. *See* WILLIE CLANCY SUMMER SCHOOL.

Wilson, R.A. *See* MAGLONE, BARNEY.

WIMPEY. A comic acronymic based on the name of one of Britain's largest construction firms. Standing for, 'We imploy [sic] more Paddies every year', it is a terse piece of Irish social history. It underlines the steady drain by emigration of young Irishmen for a quarter of a century after 1945, glad to be able to find work on roads and building sites.
See also NAVVIES.

Win. To save or harvest hay, turf or any crop, a term used in Ulster. Given the tendency of Irish summer weather to be wet, winning turf or hay is at times a feat of epic proportions.

Winchester Three, the. In 1988 three young Irish people, Martina Shanahan, Finbar Cullen and John McCann, were sentenced at Winchester Crown Court to 25 years' imprisonment on charges of conspiracy to murder Tom King, then secretary of state for Northern Ireland. They were freed on appeal in 1990.
See also BIRMINGHAM SIX, THE; GUILDFORD FOUR, THE.

Windgall. A word denoting redness of the skin from wind and cold.
See also IRE.

Windows of wonder. *See* MASTER, THE.

Winkers. A horse's blinkers.

Wirrasthrue. (Irish, *A Mhuire, 's trua!*, 'O Mary! What a pity.') A pious exclamation signifying 'alas!' Its use is now entirely jocose, often as a mocking epithet. Even 100 years ago it was not taken seriously, as Joyce indicates in *Stephen Hero* (1944):

> – Doesn't he look like a wirrasthrue Jaysus? said Stephen pointing to the Tsar's photograph …
> Cranly looked in the direction of McCann and replied, nodding his head:
> – Wirrasthrue Jaysus and hairy Jaysus.

Wisha. An introductory exclamation or linking word in HIBERNO-ENGLISH, deriving from the Irish *más ea* ('if it be so') and existing also in the forms (closer to the original) of 'musha', 'mossa' and 'mush': 'Wisha, what would you do that for?' The tautological 'Wisha now' or 'Wisha then' are also used.

Within Our Province. *See* BELL, SAM HANNA.

Without My Cloak (1931). The title of a novel by Kate O'BRIEN that chronicles the life of three generations of the Considines, a bourgeois family of merchant origin living in Mellick (Limerick), but centring on Denis, the sensitive son. It is one of the few Irish novels of its era to recreate a world based in neither the BIG HOUSE nor the peasant's cabin.

Wobblies. *See* JONES, MOTHER.

Woeful. A word not signifying grief but rather used as an intensifier.
See also BRUTAL; ODIOUS.

Woffington, the. The by-name of the actress Peg Woffington (*c.*1718–60). She was born in George's Court, a slum area of Dame Street in Dublin; she, her mother and her sister were left almost destitute on the death of her father. When she was 12 her beauty attracted the attention of a Madame Violante, an acrobatic performer from Europe, and she had her first acting part in a pirated production of John Gay's *The Beggar's Opera*. Thereafter she acted in comedy in the THEATRE ROYAL, also providing song-and-dance routines during intervals. When she was 19 a lucky break had her playing Ophelia in SMOCK ALLEY's 1737 production of *Hamlet* to great acclaim, and from then on she toured London and Paris, adding 'breeches' parts to her repertoire. In 1740 she made her début at Convent Garden, under manager John Rich, and became the toast of London. She switched her allegiance to Drury Lane Theatre the following year, and there she met the most famous actor of the day, David Garrick. They lived together for several years, although they never married: Garrick was notoriously mean, criticizing Peg for making tea (an expensive commodity at the time) so strong that it was 'as red as blood'; in contrast, Peg was extravagantly generous.

Disputes with rival actresses caused the Woffington to leave Drury Lane, but when she returned to Covent Garden she found a rival worthy of her mettle: George Anne Bellamy (*see* APOLOGY). An incident where she threatened Bellamy with a knife caused her to leave London and return to work in Smock Alley Theatre in Dublin, now under the management of Thomas Sheridan the Younger (the father of Richard Brinsley SHERIDAN). Together they had some great successes, but the hoi polloi of Dublin objected to her conversion to Protestantism and her friendliness with members of the British administration – the 'Castle' set – and stormed the theatre one evening, wrecking the building. In May 1757 she was taken ill of a stroke while playing Rosalind in *As You Like It* at a benefit performance in Covent Garden. She died three years later and was buried near her home in Teddington, outside London.

Wogan, Terry (b.1938). Broadcaster. He was born Michael Terence on 3 August 1938 in Limerick and educated there and at Belvedere College, Dublin. He worked for some time in a bank before joining RTÉ as an announcer in 1963, and by 1967 he was established as a highly popular Irish voice on BBC radio and television. 'Jobbing broadcaster', his self-description in his *Who's Who* entry, is a good example of his precise use of words and a sincere, if whimsical, self-appraisal of his worth. Though a genial, witty and superbly competent presenter of such television programmes as the *Eurovision Song Contest* (since 1972), *Come Dancing* (1973–9), *Blankety-Blank* (1979–83) and *Auntie's Bloomers* (since 1991), and the host of a thrice-weekly chat show (1985–92), he seems most himself on his Radio 2 morning programme, where he makes no attempt to conceal his wide reading and irrepressibly literate wit. His invention and development of the Togs (tough old geezers), his supposedly typical audience, caught the imagination of his senior listenership and reaches daily new heights of surrealism. Apart from such active pastimes as swimming, tennis and golf, he lists among his recreations reading and writing, the latter proven by nearly a half-dozen publications culminating in the Woganesque autobiography *Is It Me?* (2000), a title with several layers of meaning but originating in the customary beginning of a typical Tog letter of complaint. He was made an honorary OBE in 1997, his Irish citizenship precluding the unalloyed honour.

Wojus. Dublin slang for WOEFUL, probably deriving from a combination of 'woeful' and 'odious'.

Wolfe Tones, The. A ballad group formed in Dublin in 1963 that continues to attract large audiences in Ireland and abroad, despite a split and the loss of one of the founding members, Derek Warfield, in 2002. The group originally comprised brothers Brian (tin whistle) and Derek Warfield (mandolin) and Noel Nagle (tin whistle), neighbours from the Dublin suburb of Inchicore. The following year vocalist Brian Byrne (the group's enduring attraction) joined the trio after they met him at the FLEADH CHEOIL in Elphin, Co. Roscommon.

As indicated by their choice of name, the music of The Wolfe Tones has a strong Republican emphasis which, if anything, became more pronounced after the outbreak of the recent Northern TROUBLES – 'a strong sense of national pride and identity,' as Brian Warfield

puts it. Like The DUBLINERS and The CLANCY BROTHERS, The Wolfe Tones helped to create and profited from the great revival of interest in traditional Irish music in the 1960s, and after a spell playing the Irish circuit in Britain they returned to Ireland in 1965 to fame and fortune. They perform a mixture of folk/traditional material like 'The Spanish Lady' and newly-penned songs of protest or political comment like 'The Helicopter Song', written by Brian Byrne to mark the escape of three Republican prisoners from Mountjoy, and 'Joe McDonnell', a lament for one of the 1981 H-BLOCK HUNGER STRIKERS. With an emphasis on rousing patriotic ballads rather than musicianship or quality they still play the Republican card north and south of the border and among the Irish in the UK and USA.

Women and Childers Party. A nickname of the ANTI-TREATYITE group in the Dáil, which included all the women deputies (*see* CLARKE, KATHLEEN; PEARSE, MARGARET[1]; MACSWINEY, MARY) and Erskine CHILDERS.

Women's Christmas. The Feast of the Epiphany, 6 January, which marks the end of the Christmas period. It is also called Small or Little Christmas.
See also BETWEEN THE TWO CHRISTMASES; BIG CHRISTMAS.

Women's education. Until the establishment of the NATIONAL SCHOOLS system in 1831, with its uniform curriculum and the opportunity for bright pupils to become monitors and assistant teachers, very little opportunity existed for the systematic education of women. Compulsory education, introduced in 1892, also made a contribution. In the same year, the QUEEN'S COLLEGES in Belfast, Cork and Galway began to admit women to all courses (the Dublin universities did not admit women until 1910), as a result of pressure exerted by a small number of feminists. Since the introduction of FREE EDUCATION in 1967 brought about the participation of the majority of young people in second- and third-level education, the number of women matriculating and graduating has risen steadily, so that women now outnumber men in third-level education. This trend has, however, not been reflected in the number of women holding senior academic positions, and there has not yet been a woman provost or president of an Irish university.

Women's Prisoners Defence League. *See* GONNE, MAUD.

Women's suffrage. The campaign for the vote for women began in Ireland with the establishment of the Dublin Women's Suffrage Society in 1875, which developed into the Irishwomen's Suffrage and Local Government Association. Under the reforming Local Government Act of 1898 women were granted the vote in local elections. In 1911 Louie BENNETT and Helen Chenevix established the umbrella organization, the Irish Women's Suffrage Federation. At the end of the First World War, the Representation of the People Act of 1918 gave the vote to women over 30. Constance Markievicz (*see* REBEL COUNTESS, THE) was the first women elected to the Westminster Parliament in the general election of 1918, but as a member of the secessionist SINN FÉIN party she refused to take her seat. Women under 30 were granted the vote in the Free State in 1923, five years before their sisters in Britain.

Wood as it falls. *See* TURF AS IT STANDS, WOOD AS IT FALLS.

Woodenbridge. The venue in Co. Wicklow of a speech by John REDMOND on 20 September 1914, in which he called on the IRISH VOLUNTEERS to assist the British war effort 'for the freedom of small nations' by enlisting in the army. The majority, who supported Redmond, became known as NATIONAL VOLUNTEERS; those who opposed him retained the name IRISH VOLUNTEERS. It was this latter, IRB-dominated group that orchestrated the EASTER RISING of 1916.

Wood, Keith (b.1972). Rugby union player for GARRYOWEN, Harlequins, Ireland and the British and Irish Lions. Wood was born in Limer-

ick of rugby-playing stock, his father Gordon having made 29 international appearances for Ireland in the 1950 and 1960s. Wood junior made his international debut for Ireland against Australia in 1994. Genial, popular and courageous, he would mature into one of the finest hookers of his generation. He toured twice with the British and Irish Lions, in 1997 and 2001, playing with particular distinction in the 1997 series against South Africa and helping the Lions to a 2–1 series victory. Wood was increasingly dogged by injury in the later years of his career. His last appearance in an Ireland shirt was in Ireland's defeat by France in the 2003 World Cup quarter-final. He played a total of 58 times for his country (a record 33 times as captain), and scored 15 tries – a national record for a forward. Wood's trademark was his barnstorming, territory-gaining runs that often startled opponents with their pace and suddenness. His baldness led to his being affectionately nicknamed 'Uncle Fester' after the character from the Addams Family.

Wood of the Whispering, The. *See* MOLLOY, M[ICHAEL] J[OSEPH].

Wood Quay. A quay on the south side of the River Liffey in Dublin between the Grattan and Father Mathew Bridges. In 841 a Viking LONGPHORT was established in this tidal part of the Liffey. Over the next 400 years residents constructed numerous banks of earth, wooden fences and stone walls, reclaiming about 80 m (87 yds) of land from the water. From the early 14th until the end of the 17th century Wood Quay was a centre of water-born commerce in Dublin. An early 17th-century map shows Wood Quay as a street with one row of houses backing on to the river, and a second row facing the river. As there were no gaps between the houses, access to the Liffey appears to have been through the houses. In about 1687 when the opening span in Essex Bridge (now named Grattan Bridge and usually called Capel Street Bridge because it joins Capel Street and Parliament Street), which is downriver from Wood Quay, was closed, there was an end to the importance of Wood Quay as a centre of maritime trade.

Between 1977 and 1994, on either side of Wood Quay, new civic offices for Dublin Corporation were commissioned and constructed, the buildings to the south of the site designed by Sam Stephenson, those to the north by Scott, Tallon and Walker. Many residents objected to the appearance of the offices, likening them to 'concrete bunkers', and for several years demonstrations were held on Wood Quay by historians and other public (and private) figures protesting at the destruction in the building process of valuable archaeological evidence – an excavation in the years 1973–81 had revealed some of this material. This cause célèbre prompted the following ballad of Wood Quay by Paddy Healy, which can be sung to the tune of 'The SASH MY FATHER WORE':

> It was old but it was beautiful
> And its structure was of wood,
> It was stratified by the Liffeyside
> Where the Viking fortress stood.
> These men of old were brave and bold
> And they shared our forefathers' blood,
> But we will fight for the Wood Quay site
> And the banks of Viking mud.

Workers' Party. A party of the left that began life as the political wing of the Official IRA (see STICKIES, THE[1]) in January 1977. It successively called itself Sinn Féin the Workers' Party (1977–1983) and The Workers' Party (1983–92). In March 1992 six of the party's seven TDs broke away and called themselves New Agenda, an avowedly interim appellation. From the end of the following month the party was known as Democratic Left, maintaining a Dáil presence of four exceptionally able and committed TDs until in 1999 it amalgamated with the Labour Party. Former Democratic Left TD Pat Rabbitte succeeded Ruairí Quinn as leader of the Labour Party in 2002. The remaining Workers' Party stalwart, Tomás MAC GIOLLA, lost his Dáil seat in the general election of 1992. The Democratic Left, led by Proinsias DE ROSSA, took part in the RAINBOW COALITION (1994–7).

Workers Union of Ireland. *See* ITGWU.

Workhouse. The poorhouse or union, so called because assistance for able-bodied men was dependent on their participating in public works or famine schemes. Workhouses were designed to a uniform plan by the English architect George Wilkinson, and their atmosphere, furnishings and food, as well as the necessary segregation of men from their wives and families, were calculated to deter all but the most needy. Until recent times, these workhouses, gaunt Victorian buildings of evil repute, survived in many Irish towns as homes for the elderly poor, and it was a common fear among older people that circumstances would lead to the indignity of their ending their life in one of them. 'All that's between me and the workhouse' was a common expression to indicate a paucity of resources, temporary or otherwise, until the mid-20th century.
See also GREAT FAMINE, THE.

World and his mother, the (Irish *an domhan and a mháthair/a bhean*). A very big crowd, everyone. Sometimes 'wife' is substituted for 'mother'.

Worm Ditch. *See* BLACK PIG'S DYKE.

Would God that this were for Ireland! The traditional dying words of Patrick SARSFIELD, Earl of Lucan, as he lay dying on Landen Field (1693):

> Farewell, O Patrick Sarsfield, May luck be in your path!
> Your camp is broken up; your work is marred for years,
> But you go to kindle into flame the King of France's wrath
> Though you leave sad Erin in tears.
> Och; ochone.
>> ANON.: 'Och; Ochone' (*c.*1700)

Wran. The HIBERNO-ENGLISH word for a wren. On St Stephen's Day (26 December) it was customary for a party of youths ('wrenboys') to catch and kill a wren and to place it in a branch or a small bush, which they carried from house to house. They then sang or played an instrument and collected money 'to bury the wran'. The activity was known as 'doing the wran' or 'going on the wran'.

> The wran, the wran, the king of all birds,
> St Stephen's Day was caught in the furze.
> Although he was little his family was great
> So rise up, landlady, and give us a trate.
> Up with the kettle and down with the pan
> And give us a penny to bury the wran.

The Wran – as this ritual is called – has survived in places such as Dingle, Co. Kerry, although real birds are no longer used. Like other traditional practices such as those of BIDDY BOYS and STRAWBOYS, the Wran has enjoyed a revival in recent years, in the form of a family festival in urban centres on St Stephen's Day.

Wreck. The liquor of the third-run (and therefore strongest and purest) POTEEN.
See also DOUBLE; SINGLINGS.

Wrenboys. *See* WRAN.

Wrens. The name given to the encampment of women, some of them with children, who lived on the outskirts of the CURRAGH military camp in Co. Kildare in the 1850s and 1860s. A journalist from the *Pall Mall Gazette* in London visited the Curragh in September 1867 and saw the wrens' encampment. He described ten 'nests' in all, accommodating 60 women aged between 17 and 25, some of whom had been there for almost ten years. The nests were constructed of sods in a clump of furze, with an earthen floor and a box and shelf for furniture. The women slept in the straw. They were all Irish and came from different parts of the country. Some had come to follow a lover or the father of their children, but the majority had come to make their living. They lived, gave birth and died in their 'nests'. The publicity caused by the appearance of the article in *Pall Mall Gazette* led to the passing of legislation allowing the military authorities to regulate the use of the Curragh. In 1868–9 a hospital was built in Kildare for the treatment of women with venereal diseases.

Wright, Billy. *See* KING RAT.

WUI. *See* ITGWU.

Würzburg. A city in Bavaria associated with the Irish saint, KILIAN, who evangelized the Thuringians and the Franconians in the second half of the 7th century. His remains are enshrined in the crypt of the cathedral, which became a place of pilgrimage for medieval Irish travellers. CLEMENT SCOTTUS died there in the 9th century, and it was there that MARIANUS SCOTTUS (OF COLOGNE) was ordained priest in 1059 prior to his immediate immurement. A scholar, clearly of Irish origin, but known only as David Scottus ('David the Irishman') was master of the cathedral school under Emperor Henry V (1081–1125) and accompanied his master on his Italian expedition to write a history of it. In the 11th century there was a considerable Irish community, and in 1138–9 the *Schottenkloster* ('Irish monastery') was built, remaining in Irish Benedictine hands until 1497.

WYBMADIITY? An acronym to be found occasionally in Irish pubs. When innocents ask what it signifies they hear: 'Will you buy me a drink if I tell you?'

Wyndham, George (1863–1913). Chief secretary (1900–5). A Conservative, Wyndham, who had Irish connections, was a proponent of the 'Constructive Unionism' policy of Prime Minister Balfour (*see* KILLING HOME RULE WITH KINDNESS). His LAND ACT of 1903 extended the policy of enabling tenants to purchase their holdings, and incorporated many of the recommendations of the Land Conference of 1903, which brought together landlords and tenants. The Wyndham Act and the devolution crisis of 1904–5, during which Wyndham was forced to repudiate plans for a form of moderate self-government drawn up by his under-secretary, Anthony McDonnell, earned the hostility of northern Unionists, who eventually forced his resignation in 1905, his health impaired. He was a classical, Shakespearean and literary scholar and published several books relating to these interests, including *Ronsard and La Pléiade* (1906).

XYZ

X Case (1992). The name given to a legal and constitutional crisis that arose in early 1992 as a result of the constitutional ban on abortion introduced after a referendum in 1983 (*see* ABORTION REFERENDUMS). 'X' was the tag used to protect the identity of the 14-year-old girl at the centre of the controversy. The Dublin girl had become pregnant after being sexually abused by a neighbour, and her parents decided that she should have an abortion in the UK. Because of the criminal case pending they consulted with the gardai about the possible loss of DNA evidence. As a result of this inquiry the attorney-general obtained an injunction preventing the girl from travelling to England; a High Court judge upheld the injunction, considering that the threat to the unborn baby from the abortion was more real and serious than any threat to the mother, who by this time claimed to be suicidal. In the end the Supreme Court overturned this decision, the girl went to England to have an abortion (but had a miscarriage) and the abuser was sentenced to three years' imprisonment. The politicians – and pro-life campaigners – who had not heeded warnings from legal experts looked very silly indeed. Subsequent abortion referendums (1992 and 2002), which were attempts to 'row back' the Supreme Court judgement of 1992, merely added to the confusion.

XMG. The abbreviation used by British soldiers serving in Northern Ireland during the Troubles for the Republican stronghold of Crossmaglen, in the so-called BANDIT COUNTRY of south Armagh.

Ya-boy-ya or **ye-boy-ye.** A male-to-male expression of admiration or congratulations, or an exhortation, for instance to a racehorse or greyhound: 'Come on, ya-boy-ya!'

Yahoos. The degraded humanoid creatures in the land of the Houyhnhms (Swift's rendering of a horse's whinny) visited by Lemuel Gulliver in the last of his travels (*see* GULLIVER'S TRAVELS). Gulliver's realization that he is in fact of the same species makes him recoil from his family on his return home, replicating the instinctive misanthropy of his creator (the DEAN).

> I began last week to permit my wife to sit at dinner with me, at the farthest end of a long table; and to answer (but with the utmost brevity) the few questions I asked her. Yet the smell of a Yahoo continuing very offensive, I always keep my nose well stopped with rue, lavender, or tobacco leaves.
> *Gulliver's Travels* (1726)

Yahoo was the title of a play about Swift written by Lord Longford (1902–61) in 1933.

'Yankee Doodle Dandy'. The best-known song of the Irish-American vaudeville star, composer and writer George Michael Cohan (1878–1942). It comes from his Broadway show

Little Johnny Jones (1904), and also provided the title of the biopic about him (1942) starring James Cagney.

> I'm a Yankee Doodle dandy,
> A Yankee Doodle, do or die;
> A real live nephew of my Uncle Sam's
> Born on the Fourth of July.

Cohan was born on 3 July 1878 in Providence, Rhode Island, to Jerry Cohan, who had changed his Irish father's name from Keohane. In his brash opportunistic way George insisted that he had been born on 'the fourth of July' as more appropriate to the red-blooded American patriot he imagined himself to be. He developed a characteristically energetic style of tap-dancing (brilliantly impersonated by Cagney in the film), and, as he toured from an early age with father, mother and sister as the Four Cohans, learned vaudeville from the inside. The act always ended with the stocky George M. (as he was known) stepping to the footlights and saying, 'My father thanks you, my mother thanks you, my sister thanks you and I thank you!'

Other Broadway show standards from his active pen were: 'Mary's a Grand Old Name' (1906), 'Give My Regards to Broadway' (1907), 'Little Nelly Kelly' (1922) and the martial 'Over There' (1917), which saw service in two wars and contributed to the Congressional Medal of Honour awarded by Roosevelt (whom he had played in the musical *I'd Rather be Right* in 1937). His life and songs were the basis of the successful Broadway musical *George M!* (1968). He died on 5 November 1942. Friends said of his often abrasive character, 'He'd liked to have been as nice as the character played by Cagney.'

See also HARRIGAN, NED.

Yanks. The name given to family members, relatives or neighbours who had emigrated to the United States, when they came home on holidays: 'The Yanks are coming on holidays this summer.' 'Returned Yanks', who spent a period of years in the United States but then came home to live, were a fairly common feature of rural Ireland up to the 1960s.

See also DAGENHAM YANKS.

Yawl. The traditional working boat of Achill Island off the Co. Mayo coast. The yawl, a small sailing boat, was to Achill what the GALWAY HOOKER was to the ARAN ISLANDS, transporting goods and turf to and from the island for more than a century. In recent years there have been attempts to revive the craft of yawl-building, which had fallen into disuse.

Year of the French, The. A novel (1979) by the American scholar Thomas Flanagan (1923–2002) that has as its backdrop and theme the French invasion of Co. Mayo during the REBELLION OF 1798. It is based on an eye-witness account by Bishop Joseph Stock published in 1800 and called *A narrative of what passed at Killala in the County of Mayo, and the parts adjacent, during the French invasion in the summer of 1798.* Flanagan's main narrator is the Rev. Arthur Vincent Broome and his title mimics Stock's: *An impartial narrative of what passed at Killala in the summer of 1798.* After the temporary success at the RACES OF CASTLEBAR, the novel, which is conducted in different first-person voices, focuses largely on defeat and despair. The hero is Owen McCarthy, a Gaelic schoolteacher and poet, a reluctant rebel who is hanged after the rising. *The Year of the French* was adapted for television by Eugene MCCABE and dramatized on RTÉ in 1987.

Yeats, Jack B[utler] (1871–1957). Artist and writer. The younger brother of the poet W.B. YEATS, he was born in London on 29 August 1871 and like his brother spent much of his growing years in Sligo with his Pollexfen grandparents. After some time at London art schools he became a professional illustrator in 1890, drawing comic strips (including the earliest one of Sherlock Holmes), later contributing to *Punch*, using the pseudonym W. Bird. (He signed his work 'Jack B. Yeats' to prevent confusion with his artist father John Butler YEATS.) He accompanied J.M. SYNGE on his tour of the west coast of Ireland in 1905, illustrating the articles commissioned by the *Manchester Guardian*.

Sympathetic to the Republican cause, Yeats captured the atmosphere of the Anglo-Irish War and the Civil War with paintings by which he is best known, such as *Communicating with the Prisoners* and *The Funeral of Harry Boland* (*see* BOLAND, HARRY). As his reputation as a leading Irish artist became established his painting became more and more impressionistic, as if to match the avant-garde writing of such plays as *La La Noo* (1942) and *In Sand* (1949), fictionalized reminiscences, *Sailing, Sailing Swiftly* (1933), *Ah Well* (1942) and *The Careless Flower* (1947). He died in Dublin on 28 March 1957, recognized as a supreme Irish artist and a writer of remarkable imagination.

Yeats, John Butler (1839–1922). Portrait painter. He was born on 16 March 1839, the son of the rector of Tullylish, Co. Down, and educated in the Isle of Man and at Trinity College Dublin. He was called to the Bar in 1866, the year after the birth of his poet son W.B. YEATS, but did not practice. He went to London in 1867 to become a painter and established a reputation as a portraitist, but made little money. This impecuniousness dogged him for most of his life, and meant that the five children of his marriage to Susan Pollexfen advantageously spent much of their childhoods with their maternal grandparents in Sligo. Yeats painted the leading figures of the Ireland of the turn of the century, including those of the IRISH LITERARY REVIVAL. He went to New York in 1908 for a short holiday and stayed there till he died on 2 February 1922, leaving behind him the reputation of being the most brilliant conversationalist in a famously garrulous city.

Yeats, Lily (Susan) (1866–1949) and **Yeats, Lolly** (Elizabeth) (1868–1940). The younger sisters of W.B. and Jack B. Yeats. They were obliged by their father's improvidence and their mother's mental instability to earn their living instead of being in a position to find suitable

husbands. In the late 1880s and early 1890s Lily trained in embroidery in London with William Morris, and became an instructor. Lolly taught art and published two watercolour manuals. In 1902 the whole family moved back to Ireland and took a house in Dundrum, a Dublin suburb.

First the sisters established an arts-and-crafts cooperative, the Dun Emer Guild, with their friend, Evelyn Gleeson, that as the Dun Emer Press published books 1902–8, but it was their Cuala Industries, established in 1908 and especially its publishing arm, the CUALA PRESS, that earned them fame. While Lily embroidered, Lolly designed, typeset and produced beautiful books by modern Irish and international authors, including Yeats himself, Lady Gregory, Ezra Pound, Shaw, Synge, Gogarty and Elizabeth Bowen. There were tensions between the sisters and relations were poor between Yeats and his sister Lolly especially. The Yeats sisters were largely apolitical, although, like Yeats, they supported the TREATY. Lolly worked in the Cuala Press until her death of a heart attack in 1940; Lily survived her sister by nine years, despite having had poor health.

Yeats, W[illiam] B[utler] (1865–1939). Poet and playwright. He was born in Dublin on 13 June 1865, the eldest child of the impecunious portrait painter John Butler YEATS (1839–1922). Much of his boyhood was spent with his mother's family, the Pollexfens, who owned mills and a shipping company in Sligo, and it was to there he returned aesthetically when his early fin-de-siècle poetry dissatisfied him. The result was a focusing on Irish mythology and the rich folklore of the region. His collection of essays *The CELTIC TWILIGHT* (1893) became a kind of manifesto for the IRISH LITERARY REVIVAL, and his poetry collection *The Wind among the Reeds* (1899) – containing such poems as 'The Hosting of the Sidhe', 'The Host of the Air', 'The Song of the Wandering Aengus' and 'The Fiddler of Dooney' – shows a vigour and the confident discovery of a theme that had been missing in earlier work.

Yeats's sense of Irishness had been honed by his passionate, romantic obsession with Maud GONNE, the daughter of an English army officer, who had become an ardent Nationalist. It was for her that he wrote CATHLEEN NÍ HOULIHAN in 1902, by which time he was deeply immersed in the business of creating a national theatre. Though he complained later, 'All things tempt me from this craft of verse', he hugely enjoyed running the ABBEY THEATRE and writing plays for it, though they had not the dramatic excellence of the works of Lady GREGORY, SYNGE or O'CASEY.

As the century proceeded and Yeats grew in confidence, his verse began to show an originality and a strength that depended upon nothing but his own genius, now sharpened by experience and the consideration of many philosophies. He had been supported morally and financially by Lady Gregory, finding in her house at COOLE PARK the necessary leisure and cosseting that he felt he required as a gifted mage. He celebrated the woman and the place in many poems, notably in the collections *The Wild Swans at Coole* (1919), *The Winding Stair* (1933) and *New Poems* (1938). His successful marriage in 1917 to Georgie Hyde-Lees (1892–1968), a woman half his age, gave order to what had always been a restless and often worrisome life. The horrors of the First World War and the TROUBLES at home were survived, but the poet's imagination grew darker, as such poems as 'The Second Coming' from *Michael Robartes and the Dancer* (1921) make clear:

> Things fall apart; the centre cannot hold;
> Mere anarchy is loosed upon the world,
> The blood-dimmed tide is loosed, and everywhere
> The ceremony of innocence is drowned;
> The best lack all conviction, while the worst
> Are full of passionate intensity.

Yet in his home at THOOR BALLYLEE (and his house in Merrion Square in Dublin) he felt himself to be rootedly Irish at last. He won the Nobel Prize in 1923, characteristically asking how much it was worth.

Appointed a senator in the Free State in 1922

he took his duties seriously, playing his part in debates on the new coinage and the divorce legislation. He left Ireland in the early 1930s to seek better health by the Mediterranean but continued to write powerful and challenging poetry right up to his death in Roquebrunne in France on 28 January 1939. The Second World War delayed until 1948 the fulfilment of his wishes about his final resting-place, as anticipated in his epitaph in *Last Poems* (1939), by which time he was celebrated even by late detractors as a great Irishman and a towering literary figure:

> Under bare Ben Bulben's head
> In Drumcliff churchyard Yeats is laid
> …
> No marble, no conventional phrase,
> On limestone quarried near the spot
> By his command these words are cut:
> *Cast a cold eye*
> *On life, on death.*
> *Horseman, pass by.*

Ye-boy-ye. *See* YA-BOY-YA.

Yellowbellies. The Wexford hurling team, so called because their strip is purple and gold. Under the management of Liam Griffin, the Wexford hurling team won the ALL-IRELAND final of 1996 after a gap of 28 years.

'Yellow Bittern, The'. *See* 'BONNÁN BUÍ, AN'.

Yellow Ford, Battle of the (14 August 1598). The greatest Irish victory of the NINE YEARS' WAR, and one of the greatest defeats ever suffered by an English army on Irish soil. The army of Henry BAGENAL, the English marshal, comprising 4000 foot and 300 horse (a considerable force for the time), was on a mission to relieve Blackwater Fort, when it was decimated at the Yellow Ford on the River Blackwater north of Armagh town by the forces of Hugh O'NEILL, Earl of Tyrone, in boggy terrain very suitable to the tactics of the Ulstermen. (The Yellow Ford was apparently so called because of the sandy river bed, and at a crucial juncture a huge artillery piece belonging to the English got stuck in the mud.)

O'Neill had constructed an elaborate defensive system, but contrary to the usual reputation of the Irish for conducting skirmishes or a kind of guerrilla warfare, in this battle they charged in 'compact order'. According to a contemporary report by Fynes MORYSON in *An Itinerary* (1617), O'Neill 'pricked forward with rage of envy and settled rancour against the marshal, assailed the English and, turning his full force against the marshal's person, had the success to kill him'. As well as Bagenal, 18 captains were killed, and many hundreds of men were butchered on the battlefield after the battle was won. Estimates of English casualties began at 2500, but were later revised down to 600. Moryson admitted that 1500 were killed, and it is indisputable that of the 4300 troops who set out, only 1500 made it back.

O'Neill was at the height of his power after this battle, and the rebellion against the English spread to the colonized areas of Munster, but the Ulster rebels failed to press home their advantage. After the Battle of the Yellow Ford the saying 'Better hang at home than die like a dog in Ireland' became current in Chester, the main port of embarkation for troops bound for Ireland, where desertion was commonplace.

Yellowpack. A derogatory noun or adjective, deriving from the packaging of a line of 'own-brand' cut-price groceries introduced by the grocery chain Quinnsworth in the 1980s. As well as meaning inferior goods, the term is used for the rank-and-file of a workforce, in which the individuals are indistinguishable from one another.

Yelvertonian tears. *See* YELVERTON'S ACT.

Yelverton's Act (1782). An act introduced in the Irish Parliament by Barry Yelverton (1736–1805), a PATRIOT, which mitigated the power of POYNING'S LAW, and whereby legislation passed by both houses of the Dublin Parliament could become law, as long as the royal assent was granted. Henry FLOOD attacked the act as an inadequate measure, as royal assent could be withheld by the English privy council, although in practice this rarely happened.

Yelverton subsequently became attorney-general (1782) and presided over the trial in September 1797 of the United Irishman William Orr, a Co. Antrim farmer (1766–97) who was charged with administering the United Irish oath to two soldiers; Yelverton's tears before passing the death sentence prompted William DRENNAN, Orr's laureate, to remark, 'I hate those Yelvertonian tears.' Yelverton supported the Act of UNION.

Yeomanry. *See* YEOS.

Yeos. The dismissive plural used by those who felt the scourge of the Yeomanry, the sectarian and undisciplined force that was set up in 1796 by the Earl of Camden, the lord lieutenant, because of the unsettled state of the country. The revolution in France and the activities of the UNITED IRISHMEN and the DEFENDERS had created a great deal of unrest, and the usual military garrisons had been depleted by the foreign wars. The Militia, originating in 1793, was suspect because most of the rank and file were Catholic, and it was believed that the force was heavily infiltrated by subversives. Camden freely admitted that he was arming Protestants against Catholics, and this description proved all too accurate in General LAKE's harrying of Catholic areas in the years just before the REBELLION OF 1798 and more so in the bloody aftermath:

> Then the Yeos at Tullow took Father Murphy
> And burned his body upon the rack
>> P. J. MCCALL (1861–1919): 'Boolavogue', in *Songs of Erinn* (1899)

Yer man. An often ironic means of referring to a significant male person, not present or, at least, not in earshot, whose name need not be uttered, as in 'And who should I see but yer man walking in the procession!' The expression YER WAN will pass for the feminine form.

Yerra (Irish *dhera*, 'indeed'). An introductory phrase or interjection common in contemporary HIBERNO-ENGLISH. 'Yerra' can act as an intensifier meaning 'indeed', but its use is more commonly deprecatory or ironic, as in 'Yerra, would you look at your man.'

See also ARRAH.

Yer wan. A slightly derogatory term for a woman, often used in narrative, as in 'Yer wan said', 'Yer wan did'. The phrase 'Who's yer wan?' may be used to indicate surprise or scorn, for instance at someone's mannerisms or appearance.

See also YER MAN.

Yes, aye or no. A phrase used negatively in HIBERNO-ENGLISH to indicate lack of response, as in 'She didn't say yes, aye or no!'

Yes and no. This linguistic characteristic of speakers of HIBERNO-ENGLISH is rooted in the Irish language, which has no separate words for the English 'yes' and 'no'. Positive and negative responses are indicated by the repetition of the verb. Thus the answer to the question *An raibh tú ansin?* ('Were you there?') is either *Bhí (mé)* ('(I) was'] or *Ní raibh (mé)* ('(I) was not'). This feature, carried over into HIBERNO-ENGLISH, made the use of 'yes' and 'no' much rarer than in standard English, as in 'Are you in this town this day?' 'I am!' The following excerpt from a letter written by the poet Gerard Manley HOPKINS to his father in July 1884 gives an interested stranger's reaction:

> Everyone in the country parts and most markedly the smallest children, if asked a question answer it by repeating without 'yes' or 'no'. 'Were you at school on Friday?' 'I was, sir'; 'You would be afraid to go where the bull is?' 'I would not.' The effect is very pretty and pointed.

Yoke. A word, often used malevolently, for a (recalcitrant) piece of machinery. It is used with less passion for any unspecified (or unspecifiable) object: 'Where did you get that yoke?' (applied to cars, scooters, tools, eggbeaters and devices for getting stones out of horse's hooves). It also serves for something the correct name of which momentarily escapes the speaker: 'Give us that yoke with the blade sticking out of it.'

Yola. A dialect of English, the oldest in Ireland, formerly spoken in the Wexford baronies of Forth and Bargy that lie between Wexford Harbour and Bannow Bay in the southeast of the county. It was one of the earliest parts of the country to be colonized by the Anglo-Normans, and the inhabitants stayed exclusive, marrying only with their own kind and remaining unaffected by the re-Gaelicization of the county in the 14th and 15th centuries. They were steadfastly Catholic and Royalist, and lost much of their estates to the Cromwellians in the 1650s. The peasantry, though of pure English stock, played a significant part in the REBELLION OF 1798. In this old song the word 'yola' has its root meaning 'old':

> Haraw ee bee, dhree yola mydes
> Fo naar had looke var to be brides
> Vo no own caars fadere betides
>   Dhree yola mydens.
> (Here we are, three old maids,
> Who never had luck to be brides.
> For whom no one cares whate'er betides
> Three old maidens.)
>   ANON. (18th century)

York, Richard Plantagenet, Duke of (1411–60). A descendant of Edward III and leader of the Yorkist side in the WARS OF THE ROSES. York was Henry VI's lieutenant in France before serving as lord lieutenant of Ireland from 1447 until his death. He made two personal visits to Ireland (1449–50 and 1459–60), which are famous for his success in bringing about the submission of Gaelic chieftains in Leinster and Ulster and for the strength of support he garnered for his Yorkist cause. He took refuge in Ireland in October 1459, and, despite his attainder for treason in England, the Irish Parliament in Drogheda defied the crown to protect him by a declaration of 1460. The invasion of England by the Yorkists in the summer of 1460 was planned in Ireland. York returned to England, where he was killed in the Battle of Wakefield in December 1460. Yorkist sympathy in Ireland remained strong, however (*see* SIMNEL, LAMBERT; WARBECK, PERKIN).

Youghal (Irish *eochaill*, 'yew wood'). A market town, resort and fishing port on the south coast of Co. Cork, associated with Sir Walter RALEIGH, who was given the town as part of his prodigious grant during the MUNSTER PLANTATION in 1588. Most of the local stories about his association with the town are myths: he spent very little time in Youghal, did not plant the first Irish potatoes in the garden of Myrtle Grove (known also as Raleigh's House), nor sit smoking his pipes of Virginia tobacco there. In 1602 he sold his landed interests to the notorious Richard BOYLE, Earl of Cork, who developed the town. It took the side of Parliament during the Cromwellian campaign in 1649 and was used as winter quarters by the lord protector. It became Nantucket for the John Huston film *Moby Dick* (1954–5).

> By Raleigh 'twas planted at Youghall so gay
> And Munster potatoes are famed to this day;
> Ballinamora ora
> A laughing red apple for me.
>
> In *The Popular Songs of Ireland* (1839), ed. Thomas
> Crofton Croker

Young, Arthur (1741–1820). An English agronomist and travel writer, best known for his *A Tour of Ireland* (1780). He was born in London and his early publications included novels and agricultural works. He first arrived in Ireland in June 1776 and his observations of agrarian and social realities during this and a subsequent lengthy visit formed the basis of his *Tour*. His sympathy for peasants and condemnation of ABSENTEE LANDLORDS, corrupt middlemen and religious intolerance did not endear him to the ASCENDANCY, but writers such as Maria EDGEWORTH admired his writing, and for future generations of Nationalist writers he was a source for accounts of the social history of Ireland in the 18th century. During his second visit Young worked for a time as a landlord's agent in Co. Cork, seeing at first hand the abuses of the agrarian system. He returned to London in 1779. A later work, his celebrated *Travels in France*, appeared in 1792.

Young Catullus. The nickname mischievously applied to Tom MOORE by Byron in his satire *English Bards and Scotch Reviewers* (1809), in a reference to Moore's second book *The Poetical Works of Thomas Little* (1801):

> Who in soft guise, surrounded by a choir
> Of virgins melting, not to Vesta's fire,
> With sparkling eyes, and cheeks by passion
>   flush'd,
> Strikes his wild lyre, whilst listening dames are
>   hush'd?
> 'Tis Little! young Catullus of his day.

Though Moore later challenged Byron to a duel (*see* MOST LICENTIOUS OF MODERN VERSIFIERS, THE) they became fast friends. The reference was to Gaius Valerius Catullus (*c*.84–*c*.54 BC), the Roman poet, whose amorous poetry was regarded as better 'left in the decent obscurity of a learned language', to use the phrase of Edward Gibbon (1737–94).

Young Ireland. A political movement of the 1840s, founded by Thomas DAVIS (1814–45), Charles Gavan DUFFY, and John Blake DILLON. Its title and to some extent ideology were influenced by the Risorgimento movement of Giuseppe Mazzini (1805–72) and his underground journal *Young Italy*, but Irish conditions were different.

At first the members of Young Ireland allied themselves strongly with Daniel O'CONNELL's movement for the repeal of the Act of UNION, even to the extent of acquiescing in his backing down over Clontarf (*see* MONSTER MEETINGS). However, the strongest influence in Young Ireland was that of Davis, who as a Protestant favoured a non-sectarian approach, and he found O'Connell's pragmatism, unswerving constitutionalism, Whig alliances and perceived susceptibility to Church pressure intolerable. It was he who contributed most of the ideas of cultural Nationalism, promotion of a national literature and the revival of the Irish language.

Davis's death of scarlet fever in 1845, the depredations of the GREAT FAMINE, the abject failure of the Smith O'Brien insurrection of

1848 (*see* WIDOW MCCORMICK'S CABBAGE PATCH), the arrest and transportation of John MITCHEL and MEAGHER OF THE SWORD, and the imprisonment and death of James Fintan LALOR spelled the end of the movement. The linking of the essentially romantic Trinity College graduates who founded *The* NATION, conservative Protestants like Smith O'Brien and radicals like Mitchel and Lalor made Young Ireland an inherently unstable entity. The members finally parted with O'Connell in 1846 over the question of the absolute renouncing of force. They took the side of the militant Meagher and felt impelled to join with Continental radicals in making 1848 the 'year of the revolutions', with disastrous results. The condition of the famine-riven country made most political activity pointless, and the deaths of both Davis and O'Connell (1847) removed the best minds from the scene.

Young Pretender. The name by which Prince Charles Edward Stuart (1720–88) was known to his British enemies (from the French verb *prétendre*, 'to claim by right'). He was Bonnie Prince Charlie or the Young Chevalier to his faithful and betrayed Jacobites, and on the death of his father, the OLD PRETENDER (1688–1766), he took to calling himself, logically, Charles III of Great Britain. When he landed at Moidart on the west coast of Scotland to launch the disastrous '45 Rebellion, four of his companions, the so-called 'seven men of Moidart', were Irish: John Richard MacDonnell from Co. Antrim; George Kelly, a Church of Ireland clergyman; Tom Sheridan, the prince's tutor; and John William O'Sullivan from Co. Kerry, who served as quartermaster and adjutant general of the prince's army. There were also 400 WILD GEESE in the victorious army at Prestonpans (21 September 1745).

Young Roscius. The nickname given to the boy actor William Henry Betty (or Batty), inspired by that of the great Roman actor Quintus Roscius (120–62 BC). Betty was born in Dromore, Co. Down in 1791; although some reference books give his birthplace as Shrewsbury, his debut at the age of 10 was made in Belfast so the Ulster birthplace is the more likely. In the 1804–5 season he essayed with great success the main classical roles in Covent Garden and Drury Lane. The House of Commons adjourned on a motion of Pitt the Younger, then prime minister, so that the members could see Betty as Hamlet. London was in the grip of Bettymania and his meretricious father made a lot of money. The bubble soon burst; Betty's popularity waned as he ceased to be a child prodigy. In 1808 at the age of 17 he went up to Cambridge, left to try the stage again in 1811 but with no success. The rest of his long life (he died in 1874) was passed in obscurity.

Your Choice and Mine. A popular weekly opera programme presented by Tommy O'Brien on RTÉ radio for 40 years. O'Brien was born in Clonmel and worked as a journalist and later editor on the local paper, the *Nationalist*. Operatic music became a great interest, and during his holidays he visited Covent Garden and La Scala and assembled a collection of thousands of records. His homely, chatty style of broadcasting endeared him to generations of listeners.

Your eye! An expression of disbelief, often used with a negative meaning, as in 'You did in your eye!' The negative intensifier 'I did in my eye!' is also used.
See also ARSE, TO DO IN ONE'S.

YY. The pseudonym used for his weekly essays in the *New Statesman* by the Belfast Nationalist, Robert LYND. Asked once to explain the significance of the usage he replied, perhaps jocosely, 'too wise'.

Zozimus. The nickname of the maker of street ballads, Michael Moran, who was born, probably in 1794, in Faddle Alley, off Drucker's Lane, in Lower Clanbrassil Street, in the Dublin LIBERTIES:

> I live in Faddle Alley
> Off Blackpitts, near the Coombe
> With my poor wife Sally
> In a narrow dirty room.

He went blind at the age of two weeks and made his living by performing comic and topical ballads (his own and those of others), which he rapped rather than sang since he had no ear for music. He acquired his nickname from the frequent recitation of the poem 'St Mary of Egypt', written by Dr Coyle, Bishop of Raphoe, about the conversion of a 5th-century harlot by Bishop Zozimus. His ballads were sharp and popular, as for example 'The Dan Van Vought' about O'CONNELL's imprisonment in and release from the Richmond Bridewell in 1844:

'You put me in the cage
The people to enrage
But I'm once more on the stage,'
Says the Dan van Vought

('Dan van Vought' is a variant on *An tSeanbhean Bhocht*, often anglicized as Shan Van Vocht; *see* POOR OLD WOMAN, THE.) 'The Finding of Moses' is still performed at Irish social gatherings (*see* TARANAGERS), and also still popular is 'St Patrick Was a Gentleman':

Saint Patrick was a gentleman; he came of decent
people.
In Dublin town he built a church and upon it put
a steeple.
His father was a Callaghan; his mother was a
Brady;
His aunt was an O'Shaughnessy and his uncle was
a Grady.

He died on 3 April 1846, at Eastertide, and was buried in GLASNEVIN CEMETERY, Dublin, where a monument was unveiled on 6 April 1988.

REFERENCE